a Wolters Kluwer business

Financial Instruments

by Rosemarie Sangiuolo and Leslie F. Seidman, CPA

Highlights

CCH's *Financial Instruments* is a comprehensive reference manual on accounting for financial instruments, including loans, securities, securitizations, and derivatives. It integrates and analyzes all of the existing accounting literature on this topic into one volume, including guidance issued by the Financial Accounting Standards Board (FASB), the FASB's Emerging Issues Task Force (EITF) and Derivatives Implementation Group (DIG), as well as accounting guidance issued by the American Institute of Certified Public Accountants (AICPA).

Author's Observation

A recurring theme in accounting standard-setting has been the need to simplify and improve the accounting model for financial instruments. The FASB has consistently expressed the view that fair value is the most relevant measurement attribute for all financial instruments. In 2007, through the issuance of FASB Statement No. 157, *Fair Value Measurement*, the FASB accomplished the important goal of simplifying the application of the fair value measurement objective in GAAP by addressing conceptual and practical issues relating to fair value measurement. FAS-157 provides a single definition of fair value and a framework for measuring fair value for financial instruments already required to be measured at fair value under existing accounting pronouncements.

Although FAS-157 will foster consistency in fair value measurements already required by GAAP, certain other issues must be resolved before the use of a fair value measurement attribute can be expanded further. The FASB's research project on financial instruments, conducted jointly with the International Accounting Standards Board (IASB), is addressing those issues, which include defining which instruments should be measured at fair value, how changes in fair value should be presented in the financial statements, and whether to continue to permit hedge accounting for forecasted transactions. Some of those individual issues are being tackled through current projects. For example, through its project on Financial Statement Presentation, the FASB will address how information about financial instruments measured at fair value should be reported in financial statements. Completion of these projects will assist in moving the FASB and IASB closer to the long-term objectives of requiring that all financial instruments be measured at fair value and simplifying or possibly eliminating the need for special hedge accounting requirements for transactions involving financial instruments.

A related development in 2007 is the issuance of FASB Statement No. 159, *The Fair Value Option for Financial Assets and Financial Liabilities,* which provides an election for fair value measurement of a wide range of financial instruments. FAS-159 is an important milestone because it is expected to expand the use of fair value measurements and bring the FASB closer to achieving its longer term objective of entities reporting all financial instruments at fair value. In addition, the availability of the fair value option in FAS-159 on an instrument-by-instrument basis is expected to reduce the need for fair value hedge accounting because it achieves an offsetting accounting effect for the changes in the fair values of related financial assets and financial liabilities without having to apply the hedge accounting provisions of FAS-133. An instrument-by-instrument election also accomplishes further convergence with International Accounting Standards, which contain a fair-value election for certain financial instruments.

Another high-profile issue in recent years has been the quality of financial reporting and investor confidence in published financial information. A development on this front occurred in January 2007 when the Center for Audit Quality was established by the AICPA and public company auditing firms to create a public policy and information forum to help serve investors, public company auditors, and the financial markets. The organization is autonomous and has an objective of making the audit process more reliable for investors at a time of growing market globalization and complexity and to foster confidence in the capital markets.

Another initiative aimed at improving the quality of financial reporting—the FASB's codification and retrieval project—is well under way. That project has an objective of simplifying, integrating, and organizing accounting guidance in a topical format. Detailed information about the FASB's codification project and all of the FASB's technical activities is updated regularly on its website (http://www.fasb.org).

2008 Edition

This edition covers various new accounting standards in the area of financial instruments, including:

- FASB Statement No. 157, "Fair Value Measurements"

- FASB Statement No. 159, "The Fair Value Option for Financial Assets and Financial Liabilities"

- Numerous FASB Staff Positions (FSPs), including FSP EITF 00-19-2, "Accounting for Registration Payment Arrangements," FSP FIN 39-1, "Amendment of FASB Interpretation No. 39," and FSP FIN 46(R)-7, "Application of FASB Interpretation No. 46(R) to Investment Companies"

- Several EITF Issues, including EITF 06-6, "Debtor's Accounting for a Modification (or Exchange) of Convertible Debt Instruments," and EITF 06-7, "Issuer's Accounting for a Previously Bifurcated Conversion Option in a Convertible Debt Instrument When the Conversion Option No Longer Meets the Bifurcation Criteria in FASB Statement No. 133"

- Various EITF D-Topics, including EITF Topic D-109, "Determining the Nature of a Host Contract Related to a Hybrid Financial Instrument Issued in the Form of a Share under FASB Statement No. 133"

- Various revised DIG Issues, including DIG Issue B40, "Embedded Derivatives: Application of Paragraph 13(b) to Securitized Interests in Prepayable Financial Assets," and DIG Issue G26, "Cash Flow Hedges: Hedging Interest Cash Flows on Variable-Rate Assets and Liabilities That Are Not Based on a Benchmark Interest Rate"

Numerous other accounting developments are reflected in this edition.

Accounting Research Manager™

Accounting Research Manager is the most comprehensive, up-to-date, and objective online database of financial reporting literature. It includes all authoritative and proposed accounting, auditing, and SEC literature, plus independent, expert-written interpretive guidance.

Our Weekly Summary e-mail newsletter highlights the key developments of the week, giving you the assurance that you have the most current information. It provides links to new FASB, AICPA, SEC, PCAOB, EITF, and IASB authoritative and proposal-stage literature, plus insightful guidance from financial reporting experts.

Our outstanding team of content experts takes pride in updating the system on a daily basis, so you stay as current as possible. You'll learn of newly released literature and deliberations of current financial reporting projects as soon as they occur! Plus, you benefit from their easy-to-understand technical translations.

With **Accounting Research Manager**, you maximize the efficiency of your research time, while enhancing your results. Learn more about our content, our experts, and how you can request a FREE trial by visiting us at **http://www.accountingresearchmanager.com.**

CCH Learning Center

CCH's goal is to provide you with the clearest, most concise, and up-to-date accounting and auditing information to help further your professional development, as well as a convenient method to help you satisfy your continuing professional education requirements. The CCH Learning Center* offers a complete line of self-study courses covering complex and constantly evolving accounting and auditing issues. We are continually adding new courses to the library to help you stay current on all the latest developments. The CCH Learning Center courses are available 24 hours a day, seven days a week. You'll get immediate exam results and certification. To view our complete accounting and auditing course catalog, go to: **http://cch.learningcenter.com.**

---

* CCH is registered with the National Association of State Boards of Accountancy (NASBA) as a sponsor of continuing professional education on the National Registry of CPE Sponsors. State boards of accountancy have final authority on the acceptance of individual courses for CPE credit. Complaints regarding registered sponsors may be addressed to the National Registry of CPE Sponsors, 150 Fourth Avenue North, Nashville, TN 37219-2417. Telephone: 615-880-4200.

* CCH is registered with the National Association of State Boards of Accountancy as a Quality Assurance Service (QAS) sponsor of continuing professional education. Participating state boards of accountancy have final authority on the acceptance of individual courses for CPE credit. Complaints regarding QAS program sponsors may be addressed to NASBA, 150 Fourth Avenue North, Suite 700, Nashville, TN 37219-2417. Telephone: 615-880-4200.

11/07

2008

Financial Instruments

A Comprehensive Guide to Accounting and Reporting

ROSEMARIE SANGIUOLO
LESLIE F. SEIDMAN, CPA

.CCH
a Wolters Kluwer business

This publication is designed to provide accurate and authoritative information in regard to the subject matter covered. It is sold with the understanding that the publisher is not engaged in rendering legal, accounting, or other professional services. If legal advice or other professional assistance is required, the services of a competent professional person should be sought.

—From a *Declaration of Principles* jointly adopted by a Committee of the American Bar Association and a Committee of Publishers and Associations

ISBN: 978-0-8080-9127-1

©2007 CCH. All Rights Reserved.
4025 W. Peterson Ave.
1 800 248 3248
Chicago, IL 60646-6085
http://CCHGroup.com

Portions of this work were published in a previous edition.

Excerpts from FASB documents are copyrighted by the Financial Accounting Standards Board, 401 Merritt, P.O. Box 5116, Norwalk, CT 06856-5116, U.S.A. Portions are reprinted with permission. Complete copies of these are available from the FASB.

Printed in the United States of America

Contents

Preface   v
About the Authors   xi

PART I: FINANCIAL ASSETS

Chapter 1:   Cash and Cash Equivalents   1.01
Chapter 2:   Investments in Debt and Equity Securities   2.01
Chapter 3:   Loans and the Allowance for Credit Losses   3.01
Chapter 4:   Servicing of Financial Assets   4.01
Chapter 5:   Transfers of Financial Assets   5.01
Chapter 6:   Securitizations   6.01
Chapter 7:   Calculating Yields on Debt Investments   7.01

PART II: FINANCIAL LIABILITIES

Chapter 8:   Debt Financing   8.01
Chapter 9:   Securities Lending Arrangements and
             Other Pledges of Collateral   9.01
Chapter 10: Convertible Debt and Similar Instruments   10.01
Chapter 11: Extinguishments of Debt   11.01

PART III: DERIVATIVES AND HEDGING ACTIVITIES

Chapter 12: Introduction to Derivatives Accounting   12.01
Chapter 13: Embedded Derivatives   13.01
Chapter 14: Hedge Accounting   14.01
Chapter 15: Disclosures about Derivatives   15.01

PART IV: EQUITY INSTRUMENTS

Chapter 16: Issuer's Accounting for Equity Instruments
             and Related Contracts   16.01

PART V: PERVASIVE ISSUES

Chapter 17: Offsetting Assets and Liabilities in the
             Balance Sheet   17.01
Chapter 18: Fair Value Measurements, Fair Value
             Disclosures, and Other Financial
             Instrument Disclosures   18.01
Chapter 19: The Fair Value Option for Financial Instruments   19.01

Glossary   GL.01
Cross-References to Authoritative Pronouncements   CR.01
Index   IND.01

Preface

Accounting for financial instruments has undergone monumental changes in recent years. Previously, most financial instruments such as loans, securities, and derivatives were carried at historical cost (which was sometimes nothing) in the balance sheet and for many years that model seemed adequate. But changes in regulation and increasing volatility in the capital markets inspired innovations in the nature of financial instruments and new ways to bundle them, unbundle them, and modify them. Accounting for these newfangled instruments and nontraditional activities has been controversial. Several well-publicized accounting debacles, including gains-trading of securities, unforeseen losses on derivatives, upfront gain recognition on securitizations of subprime loans, inadequately documented loan loss reserves, and, most recently, off-balance-sheet financing, motivated the recent and ongoing changes in the accounting model.

The Financial Accounting Standards Board (FASB)—the primary accounting standard-setter in the United States—has been attempting to comprehensively address accounting for financial instruments for over 20 years. However, as each recent financial reporting crisis arose, it demanded immediate attention, and, therefore, solutions were developed separately in sequence. The current state of affairs is a "multi-attribute model" that is instrument-specific and characterized by detailed rules and numerous interpretations of those rules. The trend in these recent standards is a broader use of market-based measures and a more "legalistic" determination of when risks have been transferred from one party to another. Exceptions abound, however, and there is currently no driving principle behind the accounting for all financial instruments.

Accountants and others (including bankers, analysts, and lawyers) who deal with the accounting for financial instruments in their professions face a difficult task because the available guidance is fragmented and spread over hundreds of pieces of literature—and new rules continue to emerge, practically every month. To determine the proper accounting for a particular type of instrument, a practitioner must navigate a disjointed matrix of standards and interpretations issued by numerous standard-setters, including the FASB, the Emerging Issues Task Force (EITF), and other FASB implementation groups as well as the American Institute of Certified Public Accountants (AICPA) and its subcommittees. Depending on the circumstances, guidance issued by the Securities and Exchange Commission, and other regulators may come into play. Simply identifying all of the relevant literature is a daunting task. For example, over 50 pieces of literature address accounting for securities. Deciphering the complex rules (and the terms of the instruments themselves) is challenging for the most experienced accountants.

In acknowledgment of the increasing complexity and fragmentation of many areas of the accounting literature, in 2005, the FASB began a major project to codify U.S. GAAP literature with the goal of creating a single authoritative source of U.S. GAAP. The codification will organize existing FASB, AICPA, and SEC accounting literature by topic and will provide a consistent structure for presenting guidance in each topic. Creation of the codification and the related retrieval system will substantially change the way financial reporting standards are accessed. The codification and retrieval project is well under way, with a draft expected to be publicly available late in 2007. Upon completion of an extended verification process, designed to ensure that the codification accurately reflects existing U.S. GAAP, the codification will become the single authoritative source of U.S. GAAP and will supersede all existing standards.

In addition, in an effort to improve the GAAP hierarchy and the quality of the standard-setting process, in April 2005, the FASB issued an Exposure Draft (ED), "The Hierarchy of Generally Accepted Accounting Principles." The ED proposes moving the GAAP hierarchy from AICPA SAS-69, *The Meaning of Present Fairly in Conformity with Generally Accepted Accounting Principles in the Independent Auditor's Report*, to the FASB literature. In addition, the ED proposes the expansion of the sources of Category A to include accounting principles that are issued after being subject to the FASB's due process—namely FASB Staff Positions (FSPs) and Statement 133 Implementation Issues (DIG Issues). The FASB has considered comments by respondents and supported the issuance of a final statement concurrently with similar documents being issued by the AICPA and PCAOB (Public Company Accounting Oversight Board). While the timing of the issuance of those documents is uncertain, the documents will have uniform effective dates.

As a longer-term objective, in connection with the release of the final codification, the FASB is pursuing the creation of a flattened GAAP hierarchy comprising only two levels—authoritative and nonauthoritative—to further simplify U.S. GAAP.

PURPOSE OF THIS BOOK

Financial Instruments is written for practicing accountants and other professionals who need to understand the accounting for financial instruments. This book pulls together all of the existing accounting literature on financial instruments into one volume, organizes it logically, and describes the requirements as simply as possible. Given the complexity of the subject matter, there are limits on how "simple" one can make this material. However, this comprehensive, topic-based approach will save practitioners time and effort in researching accounting issues and provide a comfort level knowing that they have considered all of the relevant guidance. The text includes visual aids whenever possible; obsefrvations, such as differences between instrument types; practice pointers; and examples to help readers understand the requirements. The book also includes a cross-reference to the original pronouncements and cites the chapter(s) in which they are discussed, a glossary of terms that includes references to the applicable chapter(s), and a detailed index.

WHAT THIS BOOK COVERS

Financial Instruments is a comprehensive reference manual of generally accepted accounting principles (GAAP) in the United States about financial instruments.[1] It includes guidance issued by the Financial Accounting Standards Board, and the FASB's Emerging Issues Task Force and Derivatives Implementation Group. It also includes accounting guidance issued by the American Institute of Certified Public Accountants (AICPA), including standards issued by the Accounting Standards Executive Committee (AcSEC), and the audit and accounting guides issued by various committees of the AICPA. It covers accounting requirements for public and private companies and touches on unique aspects of reporting financial instruments by nonprofit organizations. Over 400 pieces of authoritative literature are referenced in this book.

Financial Instruments does not cover certain transactions that are technically financial instruments, but that are accounted for under specialized accounting models, including stock compensation and other forms of employee benefits (from the issuer's perspective), most leasing transactions, and insurance contracts. This book does not address the equity method of accounting (for investments that convey significant influence over the investee), consolidation of operating entities (for investments that convey control over the investee), or business combinations. CCH's *GAAP Guide Level A* addresses all of those subjects in detail. However, this book does address consolidation of special-purpose entities that are used to securitize financial assets. This book does not discuss in detail the specialized accounting models used by pension plans, brokers and dealers in securities, and investment companies whereby substantially all of their assets (and certain liabilities) are carried at fair value.

This book refers to positions of the SEC staff (and other guidance published by the SEC) when it interprets or elaborates on a financial reporting requirement established by the FASB or AICPA. This book does not represent a comprehensive guide to SEC reporting requirements, even for financial instruments. This book refers to some guidance that does not represent GAAP, including auditing

---

[1] A financial instrument is cash, an ownership interest in another entity (such as common stock), or a contract that conveys an obligation and a corresponding right to require delivery of (or exchange) a financial instrument(s). The right may be contingent (such as an option) or unconditional (such as a loan). A financial instrument is ultimately convertible to cash (or stock) and does not involve the delivery of goods or services. (FAS-107, par. 3)

standards published by the AICPA, rulings of the Internal Revenue Service, and regulatory principles developed by the federal banking agencies and the National Association of Insurance Commissioners. Those references are intended merely to provide context and depth to the discussion of the topic being discussed. This book contains cross-references to the source documents so that readers can carefully review the full text and other relevant material.

HOW THIS BOOK IS ORGANIZED

Financial Instruments is organized into five parts:

- Part I: Financial Assets, including cash, securities, loans, and servicing rights
- Part II: Financial Liabilities, including debt, securities lending arrangements, and convertible debt
- Part III: Derivative Instruments, including hedging activities
- Part IV: Equity Instruments, including various forms of stock and contracts indexed to a company's own stock
- Part V: Pervasive Issues, such as fair value offsetting and fair value measurement and disclosures

Within each part, the chapters are organized by instrument type in the order in which they typically appear in a company's balance sheet. Each chapter integrates all of the available guidance for that type of instrument and alerts the reader to potential changes in accounting (such as an outstanding FASB Exposure Draft or an EITF Issue under discussion). Each chapter covers the relevant accounting questions for that type of instrument, including:

- When and how to initially recognize the instrument in the balance sheet.
- How to present the instrument in the financial statements.
- How to measure the instrument in subsequent periods (e.g., cost or fair value).
- How to recognize income or expense.
- When and how to recognize impairment.
- When to remove the instrument from the balance sheet (and whether to recognize a gain or loss).
- What to disclose in the footnotes.

Each chapter also highlights any interesting aspects of regulatory reporting for certain institutions and areas of audit risk that stem from the financial reporting requirements. Certain positions of the

Securities and Exchange Commission (and its staff) are included when they relate directly to information that must be included in the audited financial statements of a public company.

To facilitate additional research, *Financial Instruments* includes references to pertinent paragraphs of the original pronouncements. Readers who are familiar with a specific pronouncement can locate that pronouncement in the cross-reference section (CR.01) and then refer to the chapter(s) in which it is discussed. The glossary and index can also be used to locate guidance on specific instruments and accounting topics.

This edition reflects authoritative guidance that pertains to financial instruments through the standard number or date indicated below:

- FASB Statement No. 159, "The Fair Value Option for Financial Assets and Financial Liabilities"

- FASB Interpretation No. 46(R), "Accounting for Variable Interest Entities" (Revised December 2003)

- FASB Technical Bulletin No. 01-1, "Effective Date for Certain Financial Institutions of Certain Provisions of Statement 140 Related to the Isolation of Transferred Financial Assets"

- Derivatives Implementation Guidance that has been cleared by the FASB through June 2007

- FASB Staff Positions issued through June 2007

- FASB Staff Implementation Guide, "A Guide to Implementation of Statement 140 on Accounting for Transfers and Servicing of Financial Assets and Extinguishments of Liabilities"

- Consensuses of the Emerging Issues Task Force reached through March 2007

- AICPA Statement of Position No. 03-3, "Accounting for Certain Loans or Debt Securities Acquired in a Transfer"

- AICPA Practice Bulletin 15, "Accounting by the Issuer of Surplus Notes"

- AICPA Audit and Accounting Guides, 2005 editions (or the latest edition available)

- Statement on Auditing Standards No. 101, "Auditing Fair Value Measurements and Disclosures"

Establishing a "cut-off" for this book was difficult, given the dynamic nature of this subject and the lead-time necessary to publish a book of this length. Readers should understand that the accounting standard-setters continuously address new issues and interpret and amend existing standards. There are inevitable time delays between the promulgation of new standards and their inclusion in this or future editions of this book. Readers may find the following websites useful to monitor accounting developments:

- FASB website: www.fasb.org (includes FASB, EITF, and DIG)

- AICPA website: www.aicpa.org (includes proposed Statements of Positions, Practice Bulletins, and Audit and Accounting Guides)

- U.S. Securities and Exchange Commission website: www.sec. gov (includes guidance from the Office of the Chief Accountant and the Division of Corporation Finance)

The author and publisher welcome your suggestions to improve future editions of this book. Please send your comments to Amy Havlan, Developmental Editor, at amy.havlan@wolterskluwer.com.

ACKNOWLEDGMENTS

The authors thank Anita Rosepka, Executive Editor; Amy Havlan, Developmental Editor; Curt Berkowitz, Senior Manuscript Editor; and the staff at CCH Tax and Accounting for their guidance and efforts in bringing this manual to press. Thanks are also due to James Green for his helpful review and comments on the manuscript of this edition.

About the Authors

Rosemarie Sangiuolo is an independent consultant with background in the financial services industry and accounting standard-setting. She specializes in accounting and reporting for financial instruments. She is currently a member of the project team working on the FASB's codification and retrieval project. Previously, Ms. Sangiuolo was a project manager at the Financial Accounting Standards Board, where she focused primarily on standard-setting efforts associated with derivatives and hedging, asset transfers, and securitization transactions. In that capacity, she contributed to numerous accounting pronouncements issued by the FASB, the Emerging Issues Task Force, and the Derivatives Implementation Group. Prior to joining the FASB, Ms. Sangiuolo was a Vice President at J.P. Morgan & Co., where she dealt with accounting policy, regulatory, and financial reporting issues relevant to the financial services industry.

Ms. Sangiuolo graduated summa cum laude from Fordham University with a major in economics and received her M.B.A. from New York University's Stern School of Business.

Leslie F. Seidman is a certified public accountant with extensive experience in the financial services industry and in accounting standard-setting. With an English major from Colgate University and a Masters Degree in accounting from New York University Stern School of Business, Ms. Seidman has a unique combination of writing ability and accounting knowledge.

Ms. Seidman started her career as an auditor for Ernst & Young LLP before joining J.P. Morgan, where she was a Vice President of accounting policy for many years. Ms. Seidman was selected for an industry fellowship at the Financial Accounting Standards Board, where she later served as assistant director of implementation and practice issues. Subsequently, Ms. Seidman had her own financial reporting consulting firm, serving financial institutions, accounting firms, and other organizations. She has authored, reviewed, and edited hundreds of accounting pronouncements of the FASB and AICPA, and contributed to several books and other publications.

Ms. Seidman is a member of the AICPA and the Institute of Management Accountants, where she served on the Financial Reporting Committee.

Subsequent to writing this book, Ms. Seidman was appointed to a three-year term as a member of the Financial Accounting Standards Board. She was reappointed to a five-year term in March 2006.

PART I:
FINANCIAL ASSETS

CHAPTER 1
CASH AND CASH EQUIVALENTS

CONTENTS

Overview	1.02
Background	1.02
Components of Cash	1.03
Cash Equivalents	1.03
Cash Reserve Accounts	1.04
Accounting for Cash and Cash Equivalents	1.04
Recognizing Cash	1.04
Cash Received as Collateral	1.05
Measurement of Cash and Cash Equivalents	1.05
Foreign Currency	1.05
Cash Equivalents That Are Securities	1.05
Balance Sheet Presentation	1.06
Current and Noncurrent Assets	1.06
Reciprocal Balances	1.07
Cash Flow Statement Presentation	1.07
Reporting Cash Equivalents	1.08
Gross and Net Cash Flows	1.08
Classification of Cash Receipts and Payments	1.09
Exhibit 1-1: Summary of Gross versus Net Reporting on Cash Flow Statement	1.10
Foreign Currency Cash Flows	1.13
Exhibit 1-2: Common Classifications of Cash Flows from Financial Instruments	1.13
Disclosures	1.14
Cash Equivalents	1.14
Deposits in Excess of Insured Limits	1.14
Restricted Cash	1.14
Auditing Considerations	1.15
Illustrations	1.16

Illustration 1-1: Disclosure of Securities Reported as
Cash Equivalents   1.16

Illustration 1-2: Disclosure of Compensating Balances   1.17

OVERVIEW

Cash is the most basic form of financial instrument. Accounting for cash is straightforward. Certain short-term, highly liquid debt investments are considered cash equivalents and may be included along with cash in the balance sheet. There are very few measurement issues with cash, although certain cash equivalents that are securities may be carried at fair value and foreign currency balances must be adjusted to reflect current exchange rates. There are a few balance sheet presentation issues with cash. Cash that is restricted from use must be reported separately from unrestricted cash and be excluded from current assets in a classified balance sheet.

Most types of companies report cash flows in a statement of cash flows. There are several "elections" in preparing the statement of cash flows, but as a general rule, cash receipts and payments must be classified as investing, financing, or operating. Generally, cash inflows and outflows must be presented separately (gross), but there are several exceptions that allow net reporting of cash flows. For example, changes in cash equivalents may be reported net in the cash flow statement. In addition, companies are allowed to present cash flows from certain short-term, high turnover financial instruments on a net basis. The exceptions are broader for financial institutions.

Ordinarily, amounts on deposit with financial institutions may not be offset against liabilities to those same institutions. However, certain financial institutions may offset reciprocal balances with other financial institutions in certain circumstances.

BACKGROUND

FAS-95, as amended by FAS-102, FAS-104, and other literature, provides guidance on the definition of cash equivalents and cash flow reporting. FAS-95 requires that cash receipts and payments be classified in a cash flow statement according to whether they stem from operating, investing, or financing activities and definitions of each category are provided.

    ☛ **PRACTICE POINTER:** CCH's *GAAP Guide Level A*, Chapter 5, "Cash Flow Statement," provides a comprehensive discussion of the requirements of FAS-95, as amended, including how to prepare a cash flow statement using the *direct method* and the *indirect method.* This chapter focuses on the unique aspects of reporting cash flows from financial instruments.

ARB-43, Chapter 3A, provides guidance on classifying cash balances as current or noncurrent, depending on whether use of the cash is restricted in any way.

Components of Cash

Cash includes currency on hand in U.S. dollars and foreign currency. Cash also includes amounts on deposit with banks and other financial institutions that may be withdrawn at any time without prior notice or penalty. This includes demand deposits and other similar arrangements. (FAS-95, fn.1) Financial institutions call these amounts "Due from banks."

Cash Equivalents

Cash equivalents are short-term, highly liquid investments that are both:

- Readily convertible to known amounts of cash and
- So near their maturity that they present insignificant risk of changes in value because of changes in interest rates.

Investments with original maturities of three months or less qualify under that definition. (FAS-95, par. 8)

> ☛ **PRACTICE POINTER:** Original maturity means original maturity *to the entity holding the investment.* For example, both a three-month U.S. Treasury bill and a three-year Treasury note purchased three months from maturity qualify as cash equivalents. However, a Treasury note purchased three years ago does not become a cash equivalent when its remaining maturity is three months. (FAS-95, fn. 2)

Examples of items commonly considered cash equivalents are:

- Treasury bills,
- Commercial paper,
- Money market funds, and
- Federal funds sold (for an enterprise with banking operations).

OBSERVATION: Some investments that qualify as cash equivalents are securities. Accounting for securities is addressed in Chapter 2, "Investments in Debt and Equity Securities." Cash equivalents that are securities must be measured and disclosed in accordance with FAS-115.

SEC REGISTRANT ALERT: With respect to auction rate securities held, the SEC staff believes that the classification of such securities as cash equivalents on the balance sheet is inappropriate. Auction rate securities are long-term bonds tied to short-term interest rates that reset through a "dutch auction" process. Investors consider these securities to be highly liquid due to the interest rate reset feature, which can result in the interest rate resetting every three months or more frequently. Auction rate securities generally do not meet the definition of cash equivalents in FAS-95, however, because of their long-term contractual maturity dates and the lack of a guarantee that the holder can liquidate the securities. Registrants should account for auction rate securities held in accordance with FAS-115. If a classified balance sheet is presented, registrants must classify all securities as either current or noncurrent in accordance with ARB-43. Registrants should refer to FAS-95 for the proper classification of these securities in the cash flow statement. (Current Accounting and Disclosure Issues in the Division of Corporate Finance of the SEC, March 4, 2005)

Cash Reserve Accounts

In certain securitization transactions, the seller of assets maintains a cash reserve account (usually a "hold back" of cash as a credit enhancement for the investors in the certificates issued). Cash reserve accounts are a form of beneficial interest in the assets transferred. Accounting for cash reserve accounts is addressed in Chapter 6, "Securitizations."

ACCOUNTING FOR CASH AND CASH EQUIVALENTS

Recognizing Cash

Cash should be recorded as an asset when it is received. If cash is received in connection with a trust department or other similar activities, an obligation to return the cash should also be recorded. (AICPA Audit and Accounting Guide, *Depository and Lending Institutions: Banks and Savings Institutions, Credit Unions, Finance Companies and Mortgage Companies,* par. 20.16)

A depository institution should record checks that are deposited by customers as assets and liabilities when they are deposited, even if they are in the process of collection and not currently available for withdrawal (deposit float). (SOP 01-6, par. 10(c))

In some instances, transactions involving cash equivalents that are securities are recorded on the trade date. Trade date accounting is discussed in Chapter 2, "Investments in Debt and Equity Securities."

Cash Received as Collateral

Cash "collateral" is sometimes exchanged in securities lending transactions. For example, if a bank lends a security to a broker who needs it temporarily to cover a short position, the bank might receive cash as collateral in case the broker fails to return the security. Cash collateral should be recorded as an asset by the party receiving it, together with a liability for the obligation to return it to the payer. The payer should record a receivable. (FAS-140, fn. 4 and par. 241)

Measurement of Cash and Cash Equivalents

The carrying amount of items classified as cash and cash equivalents generally approximates market value, because the period to maturity is very short. However, if the cash or cash equivalent is (1) denominated in a foreign currency or (2) is in the form of a security, certain adjustments must be made at each reporting period.

Foreign Currency

At each balance sheet date, cash on hand that is denominated in a foreign currency should be adjusted to reflect the exchange rate that exists at the balance sheet date. The difference should be recognized in income for the period. (FAS-52, par. 16(b)) For accounting purposes, the currency is considered a foreign currency if it does not represent the *functional currency* of the reporting entity. The functional currency of an entity is the currency in which the entity transacts most of its business.

> ☞ **PRACTICE POINTER:** See CCH's *GAAP Guide Level A*, Chapter 18, "Foreign Operations and Exchange," for additional information about foreign currency accounting.

Cash Equivalents That Are Securities

Cash equivalents that are securities must be accounted for under FAS-115. Chapter 2, "Investments in Debt and Equity Securities," discusses accounting for securities in detail. Briefly, securities must be classified as held-to-maturity, available-for-sale, or trading, depending on the investor's intent and ability to hold the securities. If the entity does not intend to hold a cash equivalent security to maturity, the security must be carried at fair value in the financial statements.

> **OBSERVATION:** Cash equivalents that are securities must meet the same stringent "held-to-maturity" standards as other forms of securities. However, the exception in paragraph 11(a) of FAS-115 may be particularly relevant for cash equivalents. If a sale of a security occurs near enough to its maturity date that changes in the market price would not significantly affect the fair value of the security (for example, within three months), the sale may be considered a maturity. By definition, a cash equivalent should meet that condition, so a sale would not "taint" the accounting for other held-to-maturity securities.

> ☛ **PRACTICE POINTER:** The "benefit" of classifying an investment as a cash equivalent is that cash flows from purchases, sales, and maturities are not required to be presented separately on the statement of cash flows.

Balance Sheet Presentation

The balance sheets of most companies show separate classifications of *current assets* and *current liabilities* (so-called "classified" balance sheets) to facilitate the calculation of *working capital*. Enterprises in several specialized industries (including broker-dealers and finance, real estate, and stock life insurance enterprises) prepare unclassified balance sheets, because the current/noncurrent distinction is not particularly relevant.

Current and Noncurrent Assets

For entities that prepare a classified balance sheet, cash and cash equivalents are generally presented as current assets. However, cash that is designated for a specific use should not be included with cash that is available for operations. In the following circumstances, cash should be reported as a noncurrent asset:

- Cash and claims to cash that are restricted as to withdrawal or use for other than current operations,
- Cash that is designated for expenditure in the acquisition or construction of noncurrent assets, or
- Cash that is segregated for the liquidation of long-term debts. (ARB-43, Ch. 3A, par. 6)

> ☛ **PRACTICE POINTER:** Funds that are to be used in the near future to pay off long-term debts, payments to sinking funds, or

for similar purposes should be excluded from current assets even when they are not actually set aside in special accounts. However, funds that will pay off maturing debt that has properly been recorded as a current liability may be classified as current assets. (ARB-43, Ch. 3A, par. 6, fn. 2) Chapter 8, "Debt Financing," addresses the classification of debt instruments.

Reciprocal Balances

Generally, amounts on deposit at a bank are considered *cash*, not a receivable. (FIN-39, fn. 2) Accordingly, when a company has cash on deposit with a bank and also owes the same bank money (in the form of a loan), the cash and debt may *not* be offset.

Exception for financial institutions Entities that accept deposits (banks and other financial institutions) should offset reciprocal balances, that is, balances due to and due from a single depository institution if they will be offset in the process of collection or payment. Similarly, overdrafts may be offset against other accounts at the same depository institution. Otherwise, overdrafts should be reclassified as liabilities. (SOP 01-6, par. 14(b))

> **OBSERVATION:** The ability to net reciprocal balances at banks and other financial institutions is a specific exception in FIN-39, paragraph 7. It is not appropriate for other types of companies to net "reciprocal balances" by analogy.

Cash Flow Statement Presentation

A statement of cash flows is required as part of a full set of financial statements for all business enterprises and not-for-profit organizations other than certain employee benefit plans and highly liquid investment companies that meet specified conditions. FAS-95, as amended, paragraphs 131 through 149, includes a series of comprehensive examples illustrating how to prepare a statement of cash flows using the direct method and the indirect method, as well as the required disclosures. This section focuses on reporting the cash flow effects of transactions involving financial instruments.

> **SEC REGISTRANT ALERT:** The SEC staff believes that a cash flow statement using the direct method provides more useful information than the indirect method. Registrants using the indirect method should ensure that the cash flow statement and related disclosures in the financial statement footnotes and MD&A are meaningful and useful to financial statement users. (Current Accounting and Disclosure Issues in the Division of Corporate Finance of the SEC, March 4, 2005)

Reporting Cash Equivalents

FAS-95 allows companies to elect to report the net amount of receipts and payments from cash equivalents in a statement of cash flows. (FAS-95, par. 9) A company should establish a policy concerning which short-term, highly liquid investments that satisfy the definition in FAS-95 are treated as cash equivalents, if any. Any change to that policy is a change in accounting principle. The financial statements of earlier years presented should be restated for comparative purposes. (FAS-95, par. 10)

> **OBSERVATION:** The rationale for this exemption is that purchases and sales of cash equivalents are part of the enterprise's cash management activities rather than part of its operating, investing, and financing activities.

> ☛ **PRACTICE POINTER:** As noted previously, cash equivalents that are securities are subject to the measurement and disclosure provisions of FAS-115. Technically, a company is allowed to classify a cash equivalent security as held-to-maturity, available-for-sale, or trading. However, given the very short maturities of cash equivalents and the specific exception in FAS-115, paragraph 11(a) allowing sales of instruments with near maturities and negligible market risk, it would seem simplest to classify cash equivalent securities as held-to-maturity, and avoid the need to record any unrealized changes in fair value.

Gross and Net Cash Flows

As a rule, FAS-95 requires that cash receipts and cash payments during a period be reported separately, that is, as gross amounts. In addition to cash equivalents, the following types of transactions are allowed to be presented net:

- Assets and liabilities whose turnover is quick, amounts are large, and original maturities are three months or less (or payable on demand) including cash receipts and payments relating to:
  - Investments (other than cash equivalents),
  - Loans receivable, and
  - Debt. (FAS-95, par. 13)
- Demand deposits of a bank and customer accounts payable of a broker-dealer, where the enterprise is substantively holding or disbursing cash on behalf of its customers. (FAS-95, par. 12)
- For banks, savings institutions, and credit unions:
  - Deposits placed with other financial institutions and withdrawals of deposits,

— Time deposits accepted and repayments of deposits, and

— Loans made to customers and principal collections of loans.

If the bank or other institution is a subsidiary of a consolidated enterprise that is not itself a bank, savings institution, or credit union, the net amounts for deposit or lending activities should be reported *separately*, not combined with other gross amounts of cash receipts and cash payments reported by the consolidated enterprise. (FAS-104, par. 7(a))

> **OBSERVATION:** Each of these exceptions is an accounting policy choice to be made by the company-the company may choose to report the cash flows from these transactions on a gross or net basis. Companies engaged in similar activities could report the cash flow effects very differently. In some cases, disclosure of the company's policy is explicitly required, but in other cases, that policy may not be disclosed if it is not deemed a "significant" accounting policy by the company. Exhibit 1-1 summarizes the choices that may be made with respect to gross versus net reporting of cash flows.

Classification of Cash Receipts and Payments

FAS-95 requires that cash receipts and cash payments be classified in one of three categories in the statement of cash flows: investing, financing, or operating. Cash flows from various activities involving financial instruments should be classified as follows:

Investing

- Making and collecting loans held for investment
- Selling loans made by the company (FAS-95, par. 16)
- Purchases, sales, and maturities of held-to-maturity and available-for-sale securities (FAS-115, par. 18)

Investing activities *exclude* acquiring and disposing of loans or other debt or equity instruments that are acquired specifically for resale. (FAS-102, par. 10(b))

Financing

- Issuing equity and providing owners with a return on, and a return of, their investment (including paying dividends)
- Borrowing money and repaying amounts borrowed, or otherwise settling the obligation

EXHIBIT 1-1
SUMMARY OF GROSS VERSUS NET REPORTING
ON CASH FLOW STATEMENT

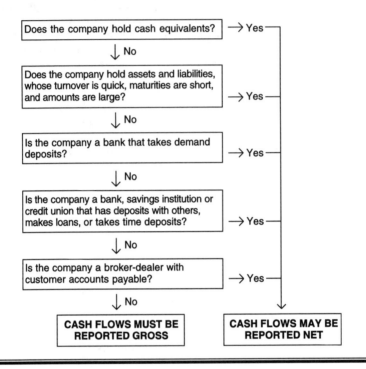

- Paying debt issue costs (EITF 95-13)
- Obtaining and paying for other resources obtained from creditors on long-term credit (FAS-95, par. 18)
- For a nonprofit organization, receiving resources that by donor stipulation must be used for long-term purposes (FAS-117, par. 30(c))

Operating

- Purchases and sales of securities and other assets (other than those classified as trading under FAS-115 and for which the fair value option has been elected as discussed below) that are acquired specifically for resale and are carried at market value in a trading account (FAS-102, par. 8, as amended by FAS-145)
- Cash flows from producing and delivering goods and providing services (including sales of the related accounts receivable and payable)

- Interest income and expense (including "dividends" that are accounted for as interest expense under FAS-150)
- Dividend income on stocks held (but *not* dividends paid to owners)
- Taxes, fines, and penalties (FAS-95, pars. 22 and 23), including deductions from the exercise of certain employee stock options (EITF 00-15)
- All other transactions and events that are not defined as investing or financing activities (FAS-95, par. 21)

> **OBSERVATION:** The classification of cash flows is important to financial statement analysts who often value companies using projections of operating cash flow.

> ☛ **PRACTICE POINTER:** Examples of activities that must be classified as operating include the following:
>
> - Purchases and sales of mortgage loans held for sale under FAS-65 and trading account activities at broker-dealers and other diversified financial institutions.
>
> - Cash flows from trading securities, even if they are not specifically held for resale. FAS-115 Q&A, paragraph 35, indicates that securities may be classified as trading at acquisition, even if the company does not plan to sell them in the near term.
>
> - Significant noncash interest income (for example, arising from loans with negative amortization features resulting in the addition of interest income to the princpal balance of an outstanding loan before the cash is received). (FSP SOP 94-6-1)

> **SEC REGISTRANT ALERT:** In December 2005, as part of the National Conference on Current SEC and PCAOB Developments, the SEC staff disseminated views on the appropriate classification of cash flows arising from loans held for resale and interests that continue to be held in securitizations in the statement of cash flows. Refer to the SEC Registrant Alert in Chapter 3, "Loans and the Allowance for Credit Losses," for the SEC staff's views related to cash flows on loans that were originated or purchased specifically for resale and are held for short periods of time and to the SEC Registrant Alert in Chapter 6, "Securitizations," for the SEC staff's views related to cash flows on interests that continue to be held in securitized loans.

Cash flows from trading activities and from financial assets and financial liabilities for which the fair value option is elected Cash receipts and cash payments resulting from purchases and sales of securities classified as trading securities under FAS-115 and for financial assets and financial liabilities for which the fair value option has been elected must be classified in the cash flow statement based on the nature and purpose for which they were acquired. (FAS-159, par. A42)

Instruments with significant prepayment risk   FAS-140, paragraph 14, requires that certain instruments with significant prepayment risk be subsequently measured like securities under FAS-115. Examples include interest-only (I/O) strips and prepayable instruments purchased at a significant premium above the amount at which the instrument can be prepaid. However, FAS-140 Q&A, paragraph 105 states that other provisions of FAS-115 that do not relate to measurement (such as disclosure) need not be applied. Thus, cash flows from instruments that are accounted for like securities under FAS-115 should be classified under FAS-95 according to their nature.

> ☞ **PRACTICE POINTER:**   Such investments would generally be considered investing activities, unless they are acquired specifically for resale and carried in a trading account at market value.

Cash flows from derivatives   Generally, each cash receipt or payment should be classified according to its nature without regard to whether it stems from an item intended as a hedge of another item. For example:

- The purchase or sale of a futures contract is generally an investing activity even though the contract is intended as a hedge of a firm commitment to purchase inventory.
- The proceeds of a borrowing are a financing cash inflow even though the debt is intended as an economic hedge of an investment.

However, cash flows from derivative instruments that are accounted for as fair value hedges or cash flow hedges under FAS-133 may be classified in the same category as the cash flows from the items being hedged provided that the derivative instrument does not include an other-than-insignificant financing element at inception other than a financing element inherently included in an at-the-market derivative instrument with no prepayments and that the accounting policy is disclosed. If, for any reason, hedge accounting for an instrument that hedges an asset, liability, firm commitment, or forecasted transaction is discontinued, any subsequent cash flows from the derivative should not be matched with the cash flows of the hedged item; rather, they should be classified according to their nature. (FAS-95, fn. 4) Chapter 14, "Hedge Accounting," provides additional information.

If a derivative instrument includes an upfront cash flow that does not merely represent points on an at-the-money forward, the premium on an at-the-money or out-of-the-money option contract, or a similar arrangement, the "borrower" must classify all cash flows on the derivative as cash flows from financing activities. (FAS-133, par. 45A)

Foreign Currency Cash Flows

Foreign currency cash flows are reported in the statement of cash flows at the reporting currency equivalent using the exchange rates in effect at the time of the cash flows. An appropriately weighted-average exchange rate for the period may be used. (FAS-95, par. 25)

The effect of exchange rate changes on cash balances held in foreign currencies should be reported separately as part of the reconciliation of the change in cash and cash equivalents during the period. (FAS-95, par. 25)

Exchange rate changes do not give rise to cash flows of themselves. Therefore, exchange gains and losses that are included in net income that do not have any cash flow effect for the period (for example, from remeasuring a receivable that is denominated in a foreign currency into the reporting currency), are *not* included in the cash flows from operating activities. Companies that use the indirect method of reporting cash flow from operating activities should present such transaction gains and losses as a reconciling item between net income and net cash from operating activities. (FAS-95, par. 32)

EXHIBIT 1-2
COMMON CLASSIFICATIONS OF CASH FLOWS FROM FINANCIAL INSTRUMENTS

Investing

Inflows	*Outflows*
Sales and maturities of held-to-maturity[1] and available-for-sale securities	Purchases of held-to-maturity and available-for-sale securities
Sales and repayments of loans held for investment	Originations and purchases of loans held for investment
Repayments of reverse repurchase agreements	Issuance of reverse repurchase agreements
Sales of servicing rights	Purchases of servicing rights

Financing

Inflows	*Outflows*
Issuance of stock	Repurchase of (treasury) stock and payment of dividends
Acceptance of deposits (for a depository institution)	Withdrawal of deposits (for a depository institution)
Issuance of debt: CDs, short-term borrowings, long-term debt	Repayment of debt and debt issue costs
Issuance of repurchase agreements	Repayment of repurchase agreements

Operating

Inflows	*Outflows*
Sales of and collections on customer trade receivables and notes	Payments on payables to suppliers for goods and services
Sales and maturities of loans held for resale	Originations and purchases of loans held for resale
Net decrease in accounts receivable	Net increase in accounts receivable
Incurrence of trading related liabilities	Repayment of trading related liabilities
Net increase in accounts payable	Net decrease in accounts payable
Interest and dividend receipts	Interest payments

---

[1] Sales of held-to-maturity securities should be rare. (FAS-115, par. 15) See Chapter 2, "Investments in Debt and Equity Securities."

DISCLOSURES

Cash Equivalents

An enterprise should disclose its policy for determining which items are treated as cash equivalents in the statement of cash flows. (FAS-95, par. 10)

Securities that are considered cash equivalents are subject to the disclosure requirements of FAS-115, such as disclosure of amortized cost and fair value by major security types. Companies should provide a note explaining what portion of each category of securities (held-to-maturity, available-for-sale, or trading) is reported as cash equivalents in the statement of financial position and the statement of cash flows. (FAS-115 Q&A, par. 51)

Deposits in Excess of Insured Limits

Cash on deposit with banks and other depository institutions in excess of federally insured limits should be appropriately disclosed if it represents a significant concentration of credit risk. (AICPA TPA 2110.06) Concentrations of credit risk are discussed in Chapter 18, "Fair Value Measurements, Fair Value Disclosures, and Other Financial Instrument Disclosures."

Restricted Cash

For finance companies, banks and savings institutions, mortgage banks and credit unions, restrictions on the use or availability of certain cash balances, such as deposits with a Federal Reserve

Bank, Federal Home Loan Bank, or correspondent financial institution to meet reserve requirements or deposits under formal *compensating balance* agreements, should be disclosed in the notes to the financial statements. (SOP 01-6, par. 14(a))

> **SEC REGISTRANT ALERT:** Legally restricted deposits held as compensating balances against short-term borrowing arrangements must be segregated and appropriately described on the balance sheet of an SEC registrant. The amount and terms of any compensating balances that are maintained to assure future credit availability or that are not subject to legal agreements should be disclosed in the footnotes. (SEC Regulation S-X, section 210.5-02)

> ☛ **PRACTICE POINTER:** All companies should consider the disclosure requirements of FAS-5, paragraph 18, which includes disclosure of (1) assets pledged as security on a loan (which could include cash or cash equivalents) and (2) obligations to reduce debt, maintain working capital, or restrict dividends.

AUDITING CONSIDERATIONS

Accounting for cash and cash equivalents is fairly straightforward. The primary areas of financial reporting that could contribute to audit risk include:

- Formal and informal restrictions on the use of cash must be identified and reflected in the classification of cash as a current or noncurrent asset.
- Several aspects of cash flow reporting are elective. They include:

  — Preparing the cash flow statement using the direct or indirect method.
  — Reporting short-term, liquid securities as cash equivalents.
  — Reporting other short-term, high turnover, large items on a net basis.
  — Specific exceptions for customer activities at banks and broker dealers.
  — Reporting the cash flows on derivatives that are used as hedges.

  In each of these cases, the company should have a policy about how the election was made, the policy should be disclosed if material, and the policy should be applied consistently for all similar items.

- Cash flows must be properly classified as operating, financing, and investing in the statement of cash flows according to their nature and any specific rules.

ILLUSTRATIONS

Illustration 1-1: Disclosure of Securities Reported as Cash Equivalents

The following information is an excerpt from the 2005 Annual Report of the Coca-Cola Company and Subsidiaries as filed in its 10-K.

Note 1—Significant Accounting Policies

Marketable securities that are highly liquid and have maturities of three months or less at the date of purchase are classified as cash equivalents. [FAS-95, par. 10]

Note 7—Short-Term Borrowings and Credit Arrangements

...Some of the financial arrangements require compensating balances, none of which is presently significant to our Company. [Voluntary disclosure in the spirit of FAS-5 and SEC Regulation S-X, section 210.5-02]

Note 10—Financial Instruments

[Note: Information unrelated to cash equivalents has been omitted.]

On December 31, 2005, these investments were included in the following captions (in millions): [Note: The company also provided data for 2004, which has been omitted for brevity.]

December 31, 2005	Available-for-Sale Securities	Held-to-Maturity Securities
Cash and cash equivalents	$ —	$346
Current marketable securities	64	2
Cost method investments, principally bottling companies	239	—
Other assets	13	8
	$316	$348

[FAS-115, par. 117]

Illustration 1-2: Disclosure of Compensating Balances

The following information is an excerpt from the 2002 Annual Report of Payless Shoesource, Inc.

Notes Payable

The Company has entered into $9.5 million of demand notes payable to efficiently finance its Central American subsidiaries. The Company maintains cash balances of $9.5 million in certificates of deposit as compensating balances to collateralize the notes payable. The notes payable accrue interest at 10%. The certificates of deposit earn interest at 9.65% and are included in other current assets in the accompanying balance sheet. [FAS-5, par. 18 and SEC Regulation S-X, section 210.5-02]

CHAPTER 2
INVESTMENTS IN DEBT AND EQUITY SECURITIES

CONTENTS

Overview	2.03
Background	2.03
Definition of a Security	2.04
Debt Securities	2.05
Equity Securities	2.06
Exhibit 2-1: Deciding Which Literature Applies to Equity Securities	2.08
Other Instruments That Must Be Accounted for Like Securities	2.10
Accounting for Securities by For-Profit Enterprises	2.11
Trade Date Accounting	2.11
Exhibit 2-2: FAS-133 and Trade Date Accounting	2.12
Initial Measurement of Securities Transactions	2.13
Fair Value Option for Certain Hybrid Financial Instruments	2.13
Classification and Subsequent Measurement of Securities under FAS-115	2.13
Exhibit 2-3: Classification under FAS-115	2.14
Held-to-Maturity Debt Securities	2.14
Trading Securities	2.19
Available-for-Sale Securities	2.20
Fair Value Option for Debt Securities Classified as Available for Sale and Held to Maturity	2.22
Transfers between Categories	2.23
Determining Fair Value	2.25
Sales and Other Transfers of Securities	2.27
Sale of Held-to-Maturity Securities	2.27
Sale of Trading Securities	2.28
Sale of Available-for-Sale Securities	2.28
Short Sales of Securities	2.29

Dividend and Interest Income   2.29

  Dividends   2.29

  Interest Income   2.30

Financial Statement Presentation   2.30

  Current and Noncurrent Assets   2.30

  Reporting Cash Flows   2.30

Presentation of Available-for-Sale and Trading
Securities Subsequently Measured at Fair Value   2.31

Disclosure   2.31

  *Exhibit 2-4: Summary of Disclosure Requirements
  under FAS-115*   2.32

Accounting for Equity Method Investments and
Nonmarketable Equity Securities   2.35

Accounting for Securities Held by
Not-for-Profit Organizations   2.37

  Accounting for Debt Securities and Marketable
  Equity Securities   2.37

  Measurement   2.37

  Gains and Losses on Securities   2.37

  Dividend, Interest, and Other Investment Income   2.37

  Accounting for Other Financial Investments   2.38

  *Exhibit 2-5: Summary of Accounting for Other
  Investments Held by Not-for-Profit Organizations*   2.38

Impairment of Investment Securities   2.39

  Determining Whether an Investment is Impaired   2.39

  Evaluating Whether an Impairment is
  Other-Than-Temporary   2.40

  Recognizing an Impairment Loss if the Impairment
  is Other-Than-Temporary   2.43

  Disclosure Requirements of FSP FAS 115-1 and FAS 124-1   2.43

  *Exhibit 2-6: Summary of Disclosure Requirements
  under FSP FAS 115-1 and FAS 124-1*   2.44

Miscellaneous Topics Relating to Securities   2.45

  Applicability of Investment Company Accounting   2.45

  Changes in Marketability, Level of Influence, or Form   2.47

  Nonmarketable Equity Security Becomes Marketable   2.47

  Change from Equity Method to FAS-115   2.47

  Exchange of Cost Method Investments
  in a Business Combination   2.47

  Conversion of a Loan into a Debt Security
  in a Debt Restructuring   2.47

  Receipt of Stock as Part of a Demutualization   2.48

Contracts to Purchase Securities That Are Not Derivatives	2.48
Exhibit 2-7: Application of EITF Issue 96-11	2.48
Accounting When Investor Holds an Equity Method Investment and Other Forms of Securities	2.49
Accounting for Structured Notes Acquired for a Specific Investment Strategy	2.50
Equity Instruments Received as Consideration for Goods and Services	2.51
Regulatory Considerations	2.51
Auditing Considerations	2.52
Illustrations	2.54
Illustration 2-1: Accounting for a Securities Portfolio	2.54
Illustration 2-2: Disclosures Required by FAS-115	2.58

OVERVIEW

Accounting for securities varies, depending on several factors: the type and marketability of the security, management's intended holding period for the security, the nature of the transaction, and the type of entity holding the security. The major accounting issue for securities is how they are measured in the financial statements.

If an investor has the intent and ability to hold a debt security to maturity, the security is classified as "held-to-maturity" and carried at amortized cost. All other debt securities and investments in marketable equity securities that do not convey significant influence or control over the investee must be carried at fair value. Investments in securities that are bought to generate profits on short-term price changes are called "trading." Investments in securities that an investor intends to hold for indefinite periods of time are called "available-for-sale." Changes in fair value are recorded either in other comprehensive income if classified as available-for-sale, or in income if classified as trading. There are restrictions against certain transfers between the classifications of securities. Nonmarketable equity securities are generally carried at cost.

Impairment is recognized in earnings when a decline in value is other than temporary, and the current fair value becomes the new cost basis for the security. Numerous disclosures are required about securities, including the net carrying amounts, fair values, and maturities. Not-for profit organizations follow different rules.

BACKGROUND

Accounting for investments in securities is covered primarily by FAS-115, APB-18, ARB-51, and FIN-46(R). Accounting for securities held by not-for-profit organizations is covered by FAS-124. FAS-115 addresses the accounting for debt securities and investments in certain equity securities where the investor does not have significant influence or control over the investee company (so-called "passive" investments). When an investor has significant influence or control over another entity, the investor does not account for the securities as financial instruments—rather, the investor applies a specialized accounting model to reflect his level of participation in the operating and financial decisions of the company. APB-18 discusses the "cost method" of accounting and the "equity method" of accounting for equity securities. ARB-51, as amended by FAS-94, discusses consolidation of majority-owned subsidiaries. FIN-46(R) addresses consolidation of thinly capitalized entities, also known as "variable interest entities."

Exhibit 2-1 provides an overview of the applicable literature to decide whether an investment in stock should be accounted for under the cost method, the equity method, or consolidation. Consolidation and the equity method are robust accounting topics that are covered in depth in CCH's *GAAP Guide Level A*, Chapters 7 and 14, respectively.

Definition of a Security

Whether a financial instrument is a security or not is important, because investments are accounted for differently, depending in part on their legal form. FAS-115, paragraph 137, modeled its definition of a security after the Uniform Commercial Code definition, which subsequently changed. For accounting purposes, a security is:

> A share, participation, or other interest in property or in an enterprise of the issuer or an obligation of the issuer that (a) either is represented by an instrument issued in bearer or registered form or, if not represented by an instrument, is registered in books maintained to record transfers by or on behalf of the issuer, (b) is of a type commonly dealt in on securities exchanges or markets or, when represented by an instrument, is commonly recognized in any area in which it is issued or dealt in as a medium for investment, and (c) either is one of a class or series or by its terms is divisible into a class or series of shares, participations, interests, or obligations.

Each type of instrument must be tested against the accounting definition to determine whether it is a security. The FASB resolved the question for a few common instruments:

- Accounts receivable, leases, and loans, including conforming mortgage loans and insured loans, do not meet the definition of a security unless legally they have been converted into securities (in a securitization or through a debt restructuring). (FAS-115, par. 137, FTB 94-1, par. 3, and FAS-115 Q&A, pars. 1 and 2)

- Most options to buy and sell securities are derivatives that should be accounted for under FAS-133, not as securities. (FAS-115 Q&A, par. 3) Whether an instrument is considered a derivative for accounting purposes is discussed in detail in Chapter 12, "Introduction to Derivatives."
- Some securities have embedded derivatives that must be accounted for separately under FAS-133, paragraphs 12 through 16. For example, investments in convertible debt securities that involve publicly traded stocks are considered to represent a debt instrument (the host contract) and an embedded equity derivative (an option). (FAS-133, par. 199) If an embedded derivative is separated from a host contract that is a security, the remaining security-host component is accounted for as a security that does not contain an embedded derivative. (FAS-115, par. 4, as amended by FAS-133) Embedded derivatives are discussed in detail in Chapter 13, "Embedded Derivatives."

In addition, the SEC staff believes that *beneficial interests* that are in the form of certificates generally meet the definition of a security. (December 10, 1997, speech by Robert Uhl, then a Professional Accounting Fellow at the SEC)

> ☛ **PRACTICE POINTER:** It is not advisable to generalize about whether certain types of instruments are securities. For example, most Certificates of Deposit (CDs) would not meet the definition, but a negotiable jumbo CD might. If questions arise about whether a particular instrument is a security, it may be necessary to engage legal counsel.

> **OBSERVATION:** Investment bankers and issuers have some latitude about how a particular financial instrument is structured. Under current GAAP, securities and nonsecurities, such as loans, are accounted for differently—cost accounting is popular and fair value accounting is unpopular. Practitioners should be cognizant of "accounting arbitrage," that is, the ability to select between different accounting models that exist between securities and other forms of investment and ensure that the instruments are properly categorized for accounting purposes.

Debt Securities

A debt security is a security that represents a creditor relationship (that is, one party owes another party a specified or determinable amount of money). The following types of instruments are considered debt securities (FAS-115, par. 137):

- U.S. Treasury bonds, notes, and bills and government agency securities
- Municipal bonds
- Corporate bonds and commercial paper
- Convertible debt
- Securitized debt instruments, including collateralized mortgage obligations (CMOs) and real estate mortgage investment conduits (REMICs)
- *Interest-only* and *principal-only* strips
- Preferred stock that is mandatorily redeemable by the issuer or that is redeemable at the option of the investor
- Securitized financial assets issued in equity form that nonetheless represent a creditor relationship (see EITF 99-20)

Similar instruments issued by foreign entities are also debt securities.

Applicability of FAS-115   All debt securities are accounted for under FAS-115. The marketability of a debt security is not relevant to the accounting.

> ☛ **PRACTICE POINTER:**   After the securitization of a mortgage loan held for sale, any retained mortgage-backed security must be classified in accordance with FAS-115.

Equity Securities

An equity security is a security representing an ownership interest in an enterprise or the right to acquire or dispose of an ownership interest in an entity at a fixed or determinable cost. Examples of equity securities include:

- Common, preferred, and other capital stock.
- Warrants and options that do not meet the definition of a derivative (see Chapter 12, "Introduction to Derivatives").

Investments in convertible debt and preferred stock that is either mandatorily redeemable by the issuer or redeemable at the option of the investor are considered debt securities for accounting purposes, *not* equity securities.

> ☛ **PRACTICE POINTER:**   Chapter 16, "Issuer's Accounting for Equity Instruments and Related Contracts," addresses the characteristics of equity securities from the issuer's perspective.

The accounting for equity securities generally depends on whether the security has a readily determinable fair value, that is, whether it is marketable. Equity securities are considered marketable in the following circumstances (FAS-115, par. 3):

- A U.S. equity security: Bid/asked quotations or sales prices are currently available on a securities exchange registered with the Securities and Exchange Commission or in the over-the-counter (OTC) market, provided that the quotations or prices are reported by NASDAQ or by the National Quotation Bureau (so-called "pink, yellow, and blue sheets").
- An equity security traded only in a foreign market: The foreign market has a breadth and scope comparable to one of the U.S. markets described above.
- A mutual fund share: The fund determines and publishes fair value per share data and those amounts are the basis for current transactions. An investment in a mutual fund that invests only in debt securities is an equity security. (EITF 86-40)

Restricted stock   Restricted stock is considered not marketable if governmental or contractual restrictions limit the sale of the stock for one year or more from the date of acquisition. (FAS-115, par. 3) A security that can be expected to qualify for sale within one year, for example, under Rule 144 or similar rules of the SEC, is not considered restricted. Side agreements between the investor and another party, such as a pledge of the security as collateral in a lending agreement, do not qualify as "contractual restrictions." (FAS-115 Q&A, par. 8)

☞ **PRACTICE POINTER:**   Stock of the Federal Reserve Bank or Federal Home Loan Bank held by member banks is considered restricted stock. (SOP 01-6, par. 8(i))

Applicability of FAS-115   If an equity security has a readily determinable fair value, it must be accounted for under FAS-115. If an equity security does not have a readily determinable fair value, it must be accounted for using the cost method under APB-18, except if they are measured at fair value under the fair value option in FAS-159 (see Chapter 19, "The Fair Value Option for Financial Instruments") or if such investments are held by insurance enterprises (see below).

☞ **PRACTICE POINTER:**   If a nonmarketable equity security is convertible into a marketable equity security, or vice versa, the investor should evaluate the marketability of the security that he or she *currently holds*. For example, a nonmarketable preferred stock that is convertible into marketable common stock is considered *nonmarketable*, and therefore is outside the scope of FAS-115. It is not appropriate to "look through" the current investment to the nature of the potential or underlying asset. If the convertible instrument is a *debt* security, the security must be accounted for under FAS-115, regardless of its marketability. (FAS-115 Q&A, par. 9)

Such instruments may contain embedded derivatives that require separate accounting. See Chapter 13, "Embedded Derivatives."

Insurance company exception Investments in nonmarketable equity securities that are held by a for-profit insurance enterprise are reported at fair value. Changes in fair value are reported as unrealized gains and losses, net of applicable income taxes, in other comprehensive income. (FAS-60, par. 46, as amended)

> **OBSERVATION:** It is unclear why insurance companies are required to carry nonmarketable equity securities at fair value, but not other types of entities investing in private equities.

EXHIBIT 2-1
DECIDING WHICH LITERATURE APPLIES
TO EQUITY SECURITIES

Level and Type of Ownership	Relevant GAAP	General Principle, if Fair Value Election is Not Made
Stock of a corporation held in its own treasury*	ARB-43, Ch. 1A, as amended by FAS-135	Report as treasury stock, not as an asset. (Also see EITF Issue 98-2.)
< 20 percent ownership of voting common stock leads to the presumption that the investor does not have significant influence, absent evidence to the contrary	APB-18, par. 20 FAS-159	Cost method applies. If marketable, apply FAS-115.
≥ 20 percent investment in voting common stock, absent evidence to the contrary, leads to the presumption that the investor has significant influence	APB-18, par. 20 FAS-159	Equity method applies.
Exception: Control does not rest with majority owner	APB-18 footnote 4 (as amended by FAS-94 and FAS-144) FAS-159	Cost method applies. If marketable, apply FAS-115.
Presumptions in APB-18 stand until overcome by evidence to the contrary*	FIN-35	Examples of "evidence to the contrary" include inability to obtain information, side agreements, and exclusive control by majority owner.
Corporate joint ventures	FAS-94, par. 15(e), EITF 00-1 FAS-159	Equity method applies.

Level and Type of Ownership	Relevant GAAP	General Principle, if Fair Value Election is Not Made
Real estate investment trust's (REIT's) investment in a service corporation*	If not a VIE under FIN-46(R), EITF 95-6	Provides examples of factors that suggest the ability to influence or control notwithstanding the ownership level.
Partnership interests and ventures	AIN-APB 18, 2, SOP 78-9 (by analogy), EITF 00-1 FAS-159	Equity method would generally be appropriate.
Limited partnership interests	EITF D-46 FAS-159	SEC registrants must account for investments > 3 to 5 percent under the equity method, even if they do not have significant influence.
> 50 percent ownership of outstanding voting shares	ARB-51, pars. 2 and 3 (as amended by FAS-94)	Consolidation applies.
Exception: Control does not rest with majority owner	ARB-51, pars. 2 and 3 (as amended by FAS-94 and FAS-144) FAS-159	Cost method applies (APB-18 has the same exceptions). If marketable, apply FAS-115.
Effect of veto rights held by minority shareholders*	EITF 96-16	Certain types of veto rights can overturn consolidation presumption for majority owner.
Consolidation of qualifying special-purpose entities (QSPE)*	FAS-140, par. 46, FIN-46(R), par. 4(d)	Transferor, affiliates, and others generally do not consolidate a QSPE. If not consolidated, investors accounts for investments according to their form (for example, securities, loans, and derivatives). Chapter 6, "Securitizations," provides additional information about QSPEs.
Consolidation of variable interest entities (VIEs)*	FIN-46(R)	Primary beneficiary of entity should consolidate the assets and liabilities of the entity. Chapter 6, "Securitizations," provides additional information about VIEs used to securitize financial assets.

*Fair value election not available.

> **OBSERVATION:**   Under current GAAP, there are "special" mod-
> els for investments in securities that afford the investor significant
> influence (the equity method) or control (consolidation). However,
> the form of the investment—common stock—is indisputably a fi-
> nancial instrument. The FASB consistently has excluded equity
> method and consolidated investments from standards that account
> for financial instruments at fair value.

Other Instruments That Must Be Accounted for Like Securities

FAS-133 provides a scope exception for interest-only and principal-only
strips with specific characteristics. A security that qualifies for the scope
exception should be accounted for like a debt security, as discussed in
this section. An interest-only strip or principal-only strip is outside the
scope of FAS-133 if it meets both of the following conditions:

- It represents only the rights to receive only a specified proportion of the contractual interest or principal cash flows of a specific debt instrument, and
- It does not incorporate any terms that are *not* present in the
  original debt instrument.

Except for instruments that are within the scope of FAS-133, interest-
only strips, loans, other receivables, or interests that continue to be
held in securitizations that can contractually be prepaid or otherwise
settled in such a way that the holder would not recover substantially
all of its recorded investment must be subsequently measured like
investments in debt securities under FAS-115—*whether or not they are
actually securities.* (FAS-140, par. 14) All of the measurement provisions
of FAS-115, including impairment and transfers, and the related interpretive guidance apply to instruments with these characteristics.
(FAS-140 Q&A, par. 110) However, the disclosure requirements of
FAS-115 must only be applied to instruments that are actually securities. (FAS-140 Q&A, par. 105)

> ☞ **PRACTICE POINTER:**   This provision applies primarily to pre-
> payable debt instruments purchased at a significant premium
> over the amount at which they can be prepaid and prepayable
> instruments with no "principal" balance, such as interest-only
> strips. FAS-115 requires that instruments with significant prepay-
> ment risk be carried at fair value, not amortized cost. (See restric-
> tions under "Held-to-Maturity Securities" section.)

All other instruments that have contractual terms that allow the
instrument to be prepaid or otherwise settled in such a way that the
holder would not recover substantially all of its recorded investment
must be evaluated in accordance with FAS-133 to determine if they
are freestanding instruments or hybrid instruments containing an
embedded derivative that must be accounted for separately.

☛ **PRACTICE POINTER:** Chapter 12, "Introduction to Derivatives," discusses the types of instruments discussed above
would be considered derivatives in their own right; Chapter 13,
"Embedded Derivatives," discusses which of these instruments
contain embedded derivatives that require separate accounting.

ACCOUNTING FOR SECURITIES BY FOR-PROFIT ENTERPRISES

Trade Date Accounting

Under trade date accounting, purchases of securities are recognized
in the balance sheet at the trade date, not the date the security is
actually received and paid for.

Security	XXX,XXX	
Trade date payable		XXX,XXX

Gains and losses on sales or disposals of securities also are recognized in the statement of operations on the trade date.

Trade date receivable	XXX,XXX	
Security		XXX,XXX
Gain (or loss) on sale		X,XXX

The following GAAP requires trade date accounting for regular-way
securities transactions:

- FAS-35, *Defined Benefit Pension Plans*
- SOP 01-6, *Accounting by Certain Entities (Including Entities With Trade Receivables) That Lend to or Finance the Activities of Others*
- AICPA Audit and Accounting Guide, *Brokers and Dealers in Securities*
- AICPA Audit and Accounting Guide, *Employee Benefit Plans*
- AICPA Audit and Accounting Guide, *Investment Companies*
- AICPA Audit and Accounting Guide, *Property and Liability Insurance Companies*
- AICPA Audit and Accounting Guide, *Life and Health Insurance Entities*

Under FAS-133, a commitment to buy or sell a security in the future
meets the definition of a derivative (a forward contract) if the underlying security is readily convertible to cash or the contract can be net
settled, generally for cash. However, paragraphs 10(a) and 59(a) of
FAS-133, as amended, provide a scope exception for (1) securities
trades that are required to be recognized on the trade date under
other GAAP and (2) securities trades with the following characteristics:

- The transaction is "regular-way." That is, it requires delivery of an existing security within the time generally established by regulations or conventions in the marketplace or exchange in which the transaction is being executed and the transaction cannot be net settled, either through the provisions of the contract or through a market mechanism.

- Forward purchases or sales of "to-be-announced" or "when-issued" securities when (1) there is no other way to purchase the security, (2) delivery will occur within the shortest possible period for that security, and (3) it is probable throughout the life of the transaction that delivery will occur (that is, the transaction will not be settled net). (FAS-133, par. 59(a))

If the transaction meets these conditions, it is *not* subject to derivative accounting and other GAAP applies.

Certain contracts to purchase securities are accounted for under EITF Issue 96-11 (discussed later in the "Miscellaneous Securities Issues" section). All other purchases and sales of securities should be accounted for under FAS-140. Under FAS-140, a sale (or purchase) of a financial asset is recorded only when certain conditions are met (see Chapter 5, "Transfers of Financial Assets," for a detailed discussion of these conditions).

EXHIBIT 2-2
FAS-133 AND TRADE DATE ACCOUNTING

	Regular-Way Transactions	When-Issueds, TBAs, and Other Transactions That Are beyond Regular-Way
Qualifications for scope exception under FAS-133	Specific GAAP requires trade date accounting *OR*	Specific GAAP requires trade date accounting *OR*
	—Settles according to normal market conventions *AND*	—No other way to purchase or sell that security,
	—Cannot be net settled (¶10(a))	—The terms indicate the earliest possible delivery date *AND*
		—It is probable that delivery will occur (¶59(a))
Transaction does not meet FAS-133 definition	Apply EITF 96-11 to certain purchases and FAS-140 to all other transactions	Apply EITF 96-11 to certain purchases and FAS-140 to all other transactions

OBSERVATION: Trade date accounting only applies to certain *securities* transactions. Trade date accounting practices may not be extended to originations of loans, issuances of debt, or subsequent transactions involving those instruments.

Initial Measurement of Securities Transactions

A purchased security should be recorded at its cost, which is the fair value of the consideration given. The amount recorded for a purchased *debt* security includes the amount paid to the seller plus any fees paid or less any fees received. (FAS-91, par. 15) There is no general guidance on the accounting for transaction costs, such as broker commissions, involving purchases of equity securities. Many companies include any directly related fees and commissions in the cost basis of the equity security.

Fair Value Option for Certain Hybrid Financial Instruments

Certain investments that are hybrid financial instruments are eligible to be initially and subsequently measured at fair value, with changes in fair value recognized currently in earnings. Such hybrid instruments must have an identified embedded derivative that is required to be bifurcated under FAS-133. However, such an election has important scope limitations. Investments accounted for under the equity method and equity investments and minority interests in consolidated subsidiaries are not eligible for the fair value option. Also, if an entity identifies an embedded derivative but determines that it is not required to be bifurcated under FAS-133, the hybrid financial instrument is *not* eligible for the fair value option. The fair value option is discussed in greater detail in Chapter 13, "Embedded Derivatives."

Classification and Subsequent Measurement of Securities under FAS-115

FAS-115 requires that, at acquisition, an enterprise classify debt and marketable equity securities into one of three categories:

1. Held-to-maturity (HTM)
2. Trading
3. Available-for-sale (AFS)

At each reporting date, the appropriateness of the classification must be reassessed. (FAS-115, par. 6) However, the focus of this reassessment is on the investor's current ability to hold the securities, not its intent. That is, the restrictions on held-to-maturity securities and the limitations on transfers between the categories discussed below still apply. (FAS-115, par. 7, FAS-115 Q&A, par. 11).

> ☛ **PRACTICE POINTER:** Classification decisions should be made at acquisition and, preferably, formally documented. It is not appropriate to use "hindsight" to classify securities transactions, perhaps by considering changes in value after acquisition.

An entity decides how to classify securities based on its intended holding period for each individual security, using the framework in FAS-115. In establishing its intent, an entity should consider relevant trends and experience, such as previous sales and transfers of securities.

EXHIBIT 2-3
CLASSIFICATION UNDER FAS-115

Classification	Ongoing Measurement Attribute	Eligible Securities
Held-to-maturity	Amortized cost	Debt securities only
Trading securities	Fair value, with changes in fair value recorded in earnings	Debt securities or marketable equity securities
Available-for-sale	Fair value, with changes in fair value recorded in other comprehensive income	Debt securities or marketable equity securities

Held-to-Maturity Debt Securities

Held-to-maturity debt securities are measured at amortized cost, meaning that the amount paid is adjusted for the amortization of any premium or discount over time. Equity securities are not eligible for the held-to-maturity category because they have no maturity date or redemption amount. To qualify for the held-to-maturity category, the investor must have the positive intent and ability to hold the debt security in question to maturity. (FAS-115, par. 7) Changes in an investor's intent or ability to hold a held-to-maturity security can call into question the investor's intent to hold other debt securities to maturity in the future. That is, if an investor subsequently sells or transfers a held-to-maturity security for a reason other than one of the specific exceptions discussed below, any remaining held-to-maturity securities may need to be reclassified to another category. A pattern of sales or transfers of held-to-maturity securities is inconsistent with an expressed current intent to hold similar debt securities to maturity. (FAS-115, par. 59)

Acceptable reasons to sell or transfer held-to-maturity securities A sale or transfer of a held-to-maturity debt security will not call into question the investor's original classification if it occurs for one of the following reasons:

- Evidence of a significant deterioration in the issuer's creditworthiness. (FAS-115, par. 8(a)) A downgrading of an issuer's published credit rating is an example of such evidence (FAS-115 Q&A, par. 23), but an enterprise need not wait for an actual downgrading in the issuer's published credit rating or inclusion on a "credit watch" list. (FAS-115, par. 72)

- A change in tax law that eliminates or reduces the tax-exempt status of interest on the debt security (but not changes that affect the investor's marginal tax rate). (FAS-115, par. 8(b)) Securities that may need to be sold to implement tax-planning strategies should be classified as available-for-sale, not held-to-maturity. (FAS-115, par. 71)

- A major business combination or a major disposition (such as the sale of a component of an entity) that *necessitates* the sale or transfer of securities to maintain the investor's existing interest rate risk or credit policy. (FAS-115, par. 8(c), as amended by FAS-144) Sales of securities to fund an acquisition do not meet this condition. (FAS-115 Q&A, par. 24) *Necessary* sales or transfers should occur concurrent with or shortly after the business combination or disposition, not before. (FAS-115, par. 74 and FAS-115 Q&A, pars. 26 and 27)

- A change in statutory or regulatory requirements that modifies either what constitutes a permissible investment or the maximum level of investment in certain types of securities for all entities affected by the requirements (FAS-115, par. 8(d)) such that the investor must sell the security. (FAS-115 Q&A, par. 28) A regulator's overall divestiture authority does not automatically preclude an institution from concluding it has the intent and ability to hold any security to maturity; the specific facts and circumstances must be evaluated. (EITF D-39)

- A significant increase in the industry's capital requirements that causes the entity to downsize by selling held-to-maturity securities. (FAS-115, par. 8(e)) A sale of held-to-maturity securities to realize gains to replenish regulatory capital that had been reduced by a provision for loan losses does not meet this condition. (FAS-115, par. 76)

- A significant increase in the risk weighted capital requirements for debt securities. (FAS-115, par. 8(f))
- Other events that are isolated, nonrecurring, and unusual and that could not have been reasonably anticipated by the investor. FAS-115 provides an example of an "extremely remote disaster scenario, such as a run on a bank or insurance company." Very few events would meet this condition. (FAS-115 Q&A, par. 32) An unsolicited tender offer for the securities does not meet this condition. (FAS-115 Q&A, par. 29)

☞ **PRACTICE POINTER:** Several of the acceptable reasons to sell held-to-maturity securities involve regulations affecting the type of security held. Note that only some *changes* in those regulations justify sales of securities. Investors are expected to understand all of the relevant regulations before they initially classify securities.

In addition, for practical reasons, paragraph 11 of FAS-115 allows the following types of transactions to be considered *de facto* maturities, not sales:

- The sale of a security that occurs close enough to its maturity date (or call date if exercise of the call is probable) such that changes in market interest rates would not have a significant effect on the security's fair value.
- The sale of a security that occurs after the enterprise has already collected a substantial portion (at least 85 percent) of the principal outstanding at acquisition due either to prepayments on the debt security or to scheduled payments on a debt security payable in equal installments (of both principal and interest) over its term (for example, certain level-payment mortgage-backed securities). For variable-rate securities, the payments should be equal absent a change in interest rates. (FAS-115 Q&A, par. 33)

In addition, the following implementation guidance allows certain transactions involving held-to-maturity securities without causing a *taint* of remaining securities:

- Transactions involving held-to-maturity securities *that are not accounted for as sales under FAS-140*. Examples include pledges of held-to-maturity securities as collateral and repurchase agreements that are accounted for as secured borrowings, provided that the entity intends and expects to be able to repay the borrowing and recover access to its collateral. (FAS-115 Q&A 16 and 17; FAS-140 Q&A, par. 53)
- Certain exchanges involving held-to-maturity securities *that are not accounted for as sales under FAS-140*. Examples include

desecuritization of held-to-maturity securities into loans (that is, the process by which securities are transformed into their under- lying loans or financial assets), provided that the assets received are held to maturity. (EITF D-51) Most bond swaps and wash sales *would be* accounted for as sales under FAS-140, and there- fore would *not* meet this condition (except when there is a con- current contract to repurchase the transferred asset from the buyer). (FAS-140, par. 99)

- The issuer's exercise of a call option on callable debt. (FAS-115, par. 77)

> **OBSERVATION:** These specific "acceptable reasons" or excep-
> tions are the *only* circumstances that will not jeopardize the
> accounting for held-to-maturity securities. It is not appropriate
> to analogize to these exceptions in other seemingly similar
> circumstances. (FAS-115 Q&A, par. 31)

Restrictions against held-to-maturity classification   An entity may not classify a security as held-to-maturity if the investor intends to hold the security for only an indefinite period of time. A debt security should *not* be classified as held-to-maturity if the investor anticipates that the security might be sold (or tendered in an exchange), for example, in response to the following events or circumstances (FAS-115, par. 9 unless noted):

- Liquidity needs
- Changes in funding sources and terms
- Changes in market interest rates and related changes in the security's prepayment risk
- Changes in the availability of and the yield on alternative invest- ments
- Changes in foreign currency risk
- Exercise of a conversion feature on convertible debt, even if the components are accounted for separately under FAS-133 (FAS- 115 Q&A, par. 18)
- Exercise of a put option on a debt security (FAS-115 Q&A, par. 20)

Even if the investor does not anticipate that a security might be sold, a security may not be classified as held-to-maturity in the following circumstances:

- The security is designated as a hedged item under FAS-133 and the designated risk is either interest rate risk or the risk of changes in the overall fair value of the security. (However, it is acceptable to designate foreign currency risk, credit risk, or, in a fair value hedge, the price risk from a prepayment option.) (FAS-133, pars. 21(d) and 29(e))

- The debt security has contractual terms that allow it to be prepaid or otherwise settled in such a way that the holder would not recover substantially all of its recorded investment. (FAS-115, par. 7, as amended by FAS-140, par. 362) The *likelihood* of prepayment or other form of settlement is irrelevant. (FAS-140 Q&A, par. 106)

This restriction does not apply to potential losses from noncontractual events, such as losses from changes in foreign currency exchange rates or borrower default. (FAS-140 Q&A, par. 111)

> ☛ **PRACTICE POINTER:** A prepayable debt security that is purchased late enough in its life such that the investor would recover substantially all of its recorded investment if the instrument were prepaid could be classified as held-to-maturity. (FAS-140 Q&A, par. 108)

Consequences of unacceptable sales or transfers   A sale or transfer of a held-to-maturity security for any reason other than those specifically mentioned in paragraphs 8 and 11 of FAS-115 and related interpretive guidance (listed under "acceptable reasons" above) calls into question whether any remaining held-to-maturity securities should continue to be classified in that category. Any remaining held-to-maturity securities should be reclassified to the available-for-sale category when the sale or transfer represents a material contradiction with the entity's stated intent or when a pattern of such sales has occurred. The reclassification would be recorded in the period in which the sale or transfer occurred and accounted for as a transfer of securities. (FAS-115 Q&A, par. 12) This "taint" applies not just to the type of security that was sold or transferred, but to *all remaining securities* that are classified as "held-to-maturity." (FAS-115 Q&A, par. 13)

> ☛ **PRACTICE POINTER:**   The FASB did not specify how long a held-to-maturity securities portfolio would be "tainted." (FAS-115 Q&A, par. 14) However, the SEC staff has imposed a two-year ban against the use of the held-to-maturity category for registrants that have sold or transferred securities from the held-to-maturity category for "unacceptable" reasons. (December 11, 1996, speech by Armando Pimentel, then a Professional Accounting Fellow at the SEC)

> ☛ **PRACTICE POINTER:** The SEC has strictly interpreted and enforced the held-to-maturity requirements in practice. A mere lack of intent to sell is not adequate support for the held-to-maturity

category. The investor must plan to hold the securities to maturity, even if favorable market opportunities subsequently arise.

Trading Securities

The trading securities category includes securities that are bought and held principally for the purpose of selling them in the short term. Trading generally reflects active and frequent buying and selling, and trading securities are generally used with the objective of generating profits on short-term differences in price. (FAS-115, par. 12(a)) "Short-term," in this context, is intended to be measured in hours and days, rather than in months or years. However, an entity is not precluded from classifying as trading a security it plans to hold for a longer period, as long as that designation occurs *at acquisition.* (FAS-115 Q&A, pars. 34 and 35)

Trading securities are carried at fair value in the balance sheet. (FAS-115, par. 12) Unrealized holding gains and losses are recognized in earnings currently. (FAS-115, par. 13) This measurement scheme is also called "mark-to-market" or "fair value accounting."

Required classification as trading   Certain types of transactions are required to be classified as trading activities.

- *Certain mortgage banking activities.* After the securitization of a mortgage loan held for sale, a mortgage banking enterprise must classify as trading any retained mortgage-backed securities that it commits to sell before or during the securitization process. (FAS-65, par. 6, as amended by FAS-134, par. 3)

- *Certain structured notes.* Structured notes that, by their terms, suggest that it is reasonably possible that the investor could lose all or substantially all of its original investment (other than through default) should first be evaluated under FAS-133 to determine whether they contain embedded derivatives that must be accounted for separately. (Embedded derivatives are discussed in detail in Chapter 13, "Embedded Derivatives.") If the instrument does not have an embedded derivative or the embedded derivative is not required to be accounted for separately under FAS-133, then the structured note should be marked to market with all changes in fair value reported in earnings (EITF 96-12).

☛ **PRACTICE POINTER:**   A structured note with the potential for significant loss would most likely contain an embedded derivative under FAS-133.

Elective use of trading category Companies may elect to classify securities that they plan to hold for longer periods of time as trading. For example, a company might desire symmetry in the accounting for a deferred compensation obligation that is adjusted to fair value and the securities being held to fund the obligation. Plan D of EITF Issue 97-14 discusses this transaction. However, the decision to classify a security as trading must occur *at acquisition*; securities may not subsequently be transferred into the trading category for this reason. (FAS-115 Q&A, pars. 34 and 35)

Hedges of trading securities FAS-133 does not permit hedge accounting for items that are (or will be) carried at fair value with changes in fair value recognized currently in earnings, including existing and forecasted purchases or sales of trading securities. (FAS-133, pars. 21(c) and 29(d)) Hedge accounting was not perceived as necessary, because the changes in fair value of both the security and the derivative are recognized in earnings in the same period. Entities should describe their objectives in holding derivatives that are economic (but not accounting) hedges of trading securities.

Available-for-Sale Securities

Available-for-sale is the "default" category for securities. It includes securities held for indefinite periods of time that are not classified either as trading securities or as held-to-maturity securities. Available-for-sale securities are carried at fair value in the balance sheet. (FAS-115, par. 12) Unrealized holding gains and losses are excluded from earnings and recognized in a separate component of other comprehensive income (OCI), net of the related tax effects, until realized. (FAS-115, par. 13) However, if an available-for-sale security is designated as being the hedged item in a fair value hedge, all or a portion of the unrealized holding gain and loss is recognized in earnings during the period of the hedge (to match the treatment of the derivative—see Chapter 14, "Hedge Accounting"). (FAS-133, par. 534(b)(2))

> **OBSERVATION:** Available-for-sale securities may be sold for any reason and may be hedged as permitted by FAS-133. Temporary changes in value are reported in the balance sheet (other comprehensive income), not the income statement. As a result, many financial institutions no longer attempt to classify debt securities as held-to-maturity so that they have the flexibility to respond to changes in market conditions and other developments without an accounting "taint" or penalty.

> ☛ **PRACTICE POINTER:** It is permissible to segregate a debt securities portfolio into a portion that is available to be sold and a

portion that is not available for sale. The securities unavailable for sale may be classified as held-to-maturity only if the entity has the positive intent and ability to hold those individual securities to maturity. (FAS-115, par. 10)

Foreign currency considerations for available-for-sale securities FAS-52 (foreign currency translation) generally requires that transaction gains and losses on foreign-currency-denominated monetary assets and liabilities be reported in earnings. FAS-115 requires that changes in the fair value of available-for-sale securities be reported in a separate component of other comprehensive income until realized. In the case of foreign-currency-denominated available-for-sale securities, the change in fair value expressed in an entity's functional currency is the total of (1) the change in market price of the security as expressed in the local currency due to factors such as changes in interest rates and credit risk and (2) the change in the exchange rate between the local currency and the entity's functional currency.

EITF Issue 96-15 requires that the entire change in the fair value of foreign-currency-denominated available-for-sale securities be reported in other comprehensive income (*not* divided between foreign currency transaction gains and losses and other market changes). However, in a fair value hedge of an available-for-sale security, the adjustment of the hedged item's carrying amount should be recognized in earnings rather than in other comprehensive income in order to offset the gain or loss on the hedging instrument. Thus, only the changes in the available-for-sale security's fair value attributable to unhedged risks are reported in other comprehensive income.

FAS-133 permits the use of fair value hedge accounting for the foreign currency risk from *equity* securities classified as available-for-sale only if the following two conditions are met:

1. The security is not traded on an exchange (or other established marketplace) on which trades are denominated in the investor's functional currency and
2. Dividends or other cash flows to investors are all denominated in the same foreign currency as the currency expected to be received upon sale of the security. (FAS-133, par. 38)

Refer to Chapter 14, "Hedge Accounting," for additional information.

Deferred tax and available-for-sale securities FAS-109, *Income Taxes*, paragraph 36, provides guidance on reporting the tax effects of unrealized holding gains and losses reported in other comprehensive income. The FASB staff addressed the following implementation questions about deferred taxes:

*   If an entity establishes a deferred tax asset that relates only to an unrealized loss on an available-for-sale security, and the entity

concludes in the current year that it is more likely than not that the asset will not be realized, the offsetting entry to the valuation allowance is reported in the FAS-115 component of other comprehensive income. (FAS-115 Q&A, par. 54) If the entity determines in a subsequent year that the asset will likely not be realized, the offsetting entry should be included in income from continuing operations, not other comprehensive income. (FAS-115 Q&A, par. 56)

- An entity might have deferred tax assets that relate both to other deductible temporary differences in a previous year (say pension expense) and an unrealized loss on an available-for-sale security in the current year. If the entity concludes that the asset is not realizable, a valuation allowance must be established. The offset should be included in other comprehensive income only to the extent that the valuation allowance is related directly to the unrealized loss on the available-for-sale securities that arose in the current year. The remainder should be included in income from continuing operations. (FAS-115 Q&A, par. 55)

EITF Topic D-41 discusses certain tax consequences associated with initially adopting FAS-115, primarily by insurance companies.

Fair Value Option for Debt Securities Classified as Available for Sale and Held to Maturity

> **AUTHOR'S NOTE:** In February 2007, the FASB issued FASB Statement No. 159, *The Fair Value Option for Financial Assets and Financial Liabilities.* FAS-159 provides companies with an option to report certain financial assets and liabilities at fair value with subsequent changes in value reported currently in earnings. The specific provisions of FAS-159 applicable to investments in debt and equity securities are covered in this Chapter. Chapter 19, "The Fair Value Option for Financial Instruments," provides general guidance on the fair value option in FAS-159. FAS-159 is effective for calendar-year-end companies as of January 1, 2008. Early adoption is permitted as of the beginning of a fiscal year that begins on or before November 15, 2007, provided the entity also elects to apply FAS-157.

Available-for-sale and held-to-maturity securities held at the effective date of FAS-159 (January 1, 2008, for calendar-year-end companies) are eligible for the fair value option at that date. If the fair value option is elected for any available-for-sale or held-to-maturity security, that security must be reported as a trading security under FAS-115. However, the accounting for a transfer to the trading category under paragraph FAS-115, par. 15(b) does not apply. Electing the fair value option for an existing held-to-maturity security will not call into question the intent of an entity to hold other debt securities to maturity in the future. (FAS-159, pars. 28–29)

If the fair value option is elected for any of those securities at the effective date, cumulative unrealized gains and losses at that date shall be included in the cumulative-effect adjustment. The amount of unrealized gains and losses reclassified from accumulated other comprehensive income (for available-for-sale securities) and the amount of unrealized gains and losses previously unrecognized (for held-to-maturity securities) must be separately disclosed.

> ☞ **PRACTICE POINTER:** If FAS-157 (fair value measurement) is adopted concurrently, any change in the measurement of the fair value of available-for-sale securities at the effective date due to application of the guidance in FAS-157 must be included in the cumulative-effect adjustment if the fair value option is elected.

Transfers between Categories

FAS-115, paragraph 15, states that transfers from the held-to-maturity category should be rare, except for transfers that occur for one of the specific "acceptable" reasons in paragraphs 8 and 11 and other authoritative implementation guidance. Transfers to and from the trading category should be rare. Transfers should be recorded at fair value. The unrealized holding gain or loss at the date of transfer should be treated as follows:

- *From trading*   Do *not* reverse any unrealized gain or loss out of earnings.
- *To trading*   Recognize any unrealized gain or loss in earnings (that has not previously been recognized, for example, as part of hedge accounting). The gain or loss should be classified in a manner consistent with the classification of realized gains and losses for the category *from which* the security is being transferred, not the category into which the security is being transferred. (FAS-115 Q&A, par. 44)
- *From HTM to AFS*   Record any unrealized gain or loss in other comprehensive income. The security's amortized cost basis carries over to the available-for-sale category for the following purposes: (1) the subsequent amortization of the historical premium or discount, (2) the comparisons of fair value and amortized cost for the purpose of determining unrealized holding gains and losses, and (3) the required disclosures of amortized cost. (FAS-115 Q&A, par. 43)
- *From AFS to HTM*   The difference between the par value of the security and its fair value at the date of transfer remains in other

comprehensive income, but is amortized as a yield adjustment, generally over the remaining life of the debt security. (FAS-115 Q&A, par. 45) Chapter 7, "Calculating Yields on Debt Investments," addresses the effective yield method. That fair value amount, adjusted for subsequent amortization, becomes the security's amortized cost basis for disclosure purposes. (FAS-115 Q&A, par. 43)

☛ **PRACTICE POINTER:** When an investor decides to sell an available-for-sale security, it should not first transfer the security into the trading category prior to the sale. Similarly, if an investor decides to sell a held-to-maturity security (even for an "acceptable" reason), it should not first transfer it into the available-for-sale category. (FAS-115 Q&A, par. 36)

OBSERVATION: The restrictions against transfers are to prevent "cherry-picking" of gains and losses in earnings. Very few transactions would qualify as an acceptable reason to transfer securities into or out of trading. One transaction that the FASB staff has reportedly accepted is a transfer between a broker-dealer subsidiary and a bank subsidiary of the same financial institution, where the broker-dealer buys and sells securities on behalf of the bank.

SEC REGISTRANT ALERT: FAS-115 indicates that transfers into and from the trading account should be "rare." The SEC staff reminds registrants that there is a very high threshold for such transfers to be permissible and observes that the following reasons for transferring securities into and out of the trading account are inconsistent with the notion that such transfers should be rare: (1) changes in investment strategies, (2) achieving accounting results that more closely match economic hedging activities, and (3) repositioning a portfolio due to anticipated changes in the economic outlook. (Speech by John M. James, Professional Accounting Fellow, Office of the Chief Accountant of the SEC, at the December 2004 AICPA National Conference on SEC and PCAOB Developments)

Reclassification of prepayable loan accounted for like a security A loan that when initially acquired or retained was required to be accounted for like a security because it had substantial prepayment risk (under FAS-140, par. 14) may be reclassified from trading or available-for-sale to held for investment (and carried at cost) later in its life if:

- It would no longer be possible for the holder not to recover substantially all of its recorded investment upon contractual prepayment or settlement and

- The conditions for amortized cost accounting are met (for example, paragraph 6 of FAS-65 and paragraph 8(a) of SOP 01-6).

Any unrealized holding gain or loss arising under the available-for-sale classification that exists at the date of the reclassification would continue to be reported in other comprehensive income, but should be amortized over the remaining life of the loan as an adjustment of yield. (The loan would not be classified as held-to-maturity because, under FAS-115, only debt *securities* may be classified as held-to-maturity.) (FAS-140 Q&A, par. 109) If the loan had been classified as trading, any unrealized trading gain or loss would not be reversed.

Determining Fair Value

AUTHOR'S NOTE: In September 2006, the FASB issued FASB Statement No. 157, *Fair Value Measurements*. FAS-157 provides a single definition of the term *fair value*, establishes a framework for measuring fair value where required by existing GAAP, and expands disclosures about fair value measurements. Specific fair value measurement guidance applicable to investments in debt and equity securities is covered in this Chapter. Chapter 18, "Fair Value Measurements, Fair Value Disclosures, and Other Financial Instrument Disclosures," provides the detailed provisions of FAS-157 and specific fair value measurement guidance applicable to all financial instruments required to be measured at fair value under GAAP. The 2008 edition of *CCH Financial Instruments* has been updated to incorporate the provisions of FAS-157. FAS-157 is effective for calendar-year-end companies as of January 1, 2008. Unless a company chooses to early adopt, prior GAAP is applicable for financial statements issued for 2007.

As this book went to press, the FASB was addressing a possible delay of FAS-157's effective date. The FASB agreed to consider delaying the effective date for nonfinancial instruments and for certain types of entities, including private companies and "smaller" public companies (not yet defined). Readers should monitor the FASB's further deliberations regarding the nature of any delay of FAS-157's effective date. Also, readers should refer to the 2007 edition for GAAP related to the fair value measurement of financial instruments applicable before the effective date of FAS-157.

FAS-157 defines fair value is the price that would be received to sell an asset or paid to transfer a liability in an orderly transaction between market participants at the measurement date. FAS-157 established a single framework for determining fair value that is applicable for existing accounting pronouncements that require or permit fair value measurements, including available-for-sale and trading investment securities under FAS-115. The fair value measurement model in FAS-157 applies for both initial measurement and subsequent measurement.

Note: FAS-157 preserves existing practicability exceptions to fair value measurement in GAAP; however, there is no fair value "practicability" exception in FAS-115 for the securities that are within its scope.

> ☞ **PRACTICE POINTER:**   For debt securities that do not trade regularly or that trade only in principal-to-principal markets, a reasonable estimate of fair value can be made using a variety of pricing techniques, including, but not limited to, discounted cash flow analysis, matrix pricing, option-adjusted spread models, and fundamental analysis. (FAS-115, par. 111)

Fair value of restricted securities   The fair value measurement of a restricted security includes consideration of whether the restriction would be factored in by market participants in pricing the asset. The fair value of a restricted security would be based on the quoted price for an otherwise identical unrestricted security of the same issuer that trades in a public market, adjusted to reflect the effect of the restriction. The adjustment would reflect the amount market participants would demand because of the risk relating to the inability to access a public market for the security for the specified period.

For example, a restriction that limits the sale of the security to qualifying investors under Rule 144 of the SEC would be based on the quoted price for an otherwise identical unrestricted security of the same issuer that trades in a public market, adjusted for the effect of the restriction. The adjustment would reflect the amount market participants would demand because of the incremental risk imposed by the restriction. The amount of the adjustment may depend on the following:

- The nature and duration of the restriction
- The extent to which buyers are limited by the restriction (for example, there might be a large number of qualifying investors)
- Other factors specific to both the security and the issuer (qualitative and quantitative). (FAS-157, par. A29)

Fair value of mortgage-backed securities for mortgage bankers FAS-65 provides specific guidance for determining the fair value of mortgage-backed securities held as part of mortgage banking activities.

- Mortgage-backed securities covered by investor commitments should be based on the fair values of the securities, not the loans.
- Fair value for mortgage-backed securities that have not yet been committed to be sold and are collateralized by a mortgage banking enterprise's own loans should ordinarily be based on the fair value of the securities or published mortgage-backed securities yields. However, if the trust holding the loans may be readily

terminated and the loans sold directly, then fair value for the securities should be based on the fair value of the loans or the securities, depending on the mortgage banking enterprise's sales intent. (FAS-65, par. 9, as amended by FAS-115)

> **SEC REGISTRANT ALERT:** The SEC provides some guidance on valuing equity securities, particularly during an initial public offering (IPO). A valuation generally should include, among other things, discussion of the company's performance, reconciliation of differences between the determination of the equity instrument's fair value and the IPO price, discussion of valuations of the company performed by underwriters who have been approached about an IPO, and discussion of transactions with independent third parties. Refer to the Division of Corporate Finance Accounting Guidance, Current Accounting and Disclosure Issues, Section II-H, for additional information.

Sales and Other Transfers of Securities

FAS-140 addresses when a transfer of a security (or other financial asset) should be accounted for as a sale versus a secured borrowing. The term "transfers" includes:

- Sales
- Securitizations
- Repurchase agreements
- Securities borrowing and lending
- Pledges of collateral

Generally, a transaction that purports to be a sale and where the seller has *no* continuing involvement with the transferred security is accounted for as a sale. Continuing involvement includes recourse, servicing, and commitments or options to repurchase the transferred assets. Chapter 5, "Transfers of Financial Assets," discusses the conditions that must be met to account for a transfer of financial assets as a sale or a secured borrowing. Chapter 6, "Securitizations," addresses the transformation of financial assets into securities. Chapter 9, "Securities Lending Arrangements and Other Pledges of Collateral," addresses repurchase agreements and other similar transactions.

Sale of Held-to-Maturity Securities

When a held-to-maturity security is appropriately accounted for as sold, a debit to cash (or trade date receivable) is recorded for the sales proceeds, and a credit is recorded to remove the security at its carrying amount (amortized cost, adjusted for any other-than-temporary impairment that has been recognized). A gain or loss would be recognized in earnings for the difference between the selling price and the carrying amount of the security. If the security is sold for an unacceptable reason, the classification of any remaining held-to-maturity securities is called into question (see section "Consequences of Unacceptable Sales or Transfers"). Certain disclosures also must be made (see "Disclosure" section).

Sale of Trading Securities

When a trading security is appropriately accounted for as sold, a debit to cash (or trade date receivable) is recorded for the sales proceeds, and a credit is recorded to remove the security at its fair value (or sales price). Because trading securities are carried at fair value, the sale of a trading security may not give rise to a gain or loss. However, a gain or loss would be recognized for any change in value since the last mark to market (for example, if fair value changes are recorded at the end of each day). If the enterprise is not taxed on a mark-to-market basis, the deferred tax accounts would be adjusted. (FAS-115 Q&A, par. 40)

Sale of Available-for-Sale Securities

When an available-for-sale security is appropriately accounted for as sold, a debit to cash (or trade date receivable) is recorded for the sales proceeds, and a credit is recorded to remove the security at its fair value (or sales price). The amount recorded in other comprehensive income, representing the unrealized gain or loss at the date of sale, is reversed into earnings, and the deferred tax accounts are adjusted. This procedure would be adjusted for enterprises that have not yet recorded the security's change in value up to the point of sale (perhaps because they only record changes in fair value quarterly) or when a write-down for other-than-temporary impairment has been recognized. (FAS-115 Q&A, par. 39)

Realized gains and losses on securities may not be deferred to future periods, either directly or indirectly. (FAS-60, par. 50, as amended by FAS-97, par. 28)

> ☛ **PRACTICE POINTER:** FAS-130 (reporting comprehensive income) requires that when a gain or loss on an available-for-sale security is realized and included in net income of the current period and that gain or loss had also been included in other comprehensive income as an unrealized holding gain or loss in the period in which it arose, a reclassification adjustment must be recorded to avoid counting the same gain or loss twice. (FAS-130, par. 18)

Short Sales of Securities

A short sale is the commitment to sell a security that that the company does not currently own. The short seller often borrows the security from a broker (for a fee) to make delivery on the sale transaction and then buys the security in the marketplace at a future date to return it to the broker. Short sales are *obligations,* not investments, but they are often considered part of a company's securities portfolio. Short sales are generally marked to fair value in accordance with audit and accounting guides published by the AICPA for certain industries. (FAS-115 Q&A, par. 7) SOP 01-6 states that obligations incurred in short sales should be reported as liabilities and carried at fair value in the balance sheet. Such liabilities are generally called "securities sold, not yet purchased." Changes in fair value are recognized in earnings currently and in the same caption as gains and losses on securities. Interest on the short positions should be accrued periodically and reported as interest expense. (SOP 01-6, par. 10(b))

Dividend and Interest Income

Dividend and interest income, including amortization of any premium and discount arising at acquisition, for all three categories of investments in securities is generally included in earnings.

Dividends

Cash dividends on "cost method investments" are accounted for as income by the investor. There is no general guidance on which date should be used to accrue dividends, but the holder of the security at the date of record (usually several days after the dividend declaration date) is entitled to the dividend. The quoted price of the security generally includes the dividend from the date of declaration up until the ex-dividend date; after that date, the price of the security falls because subsequent owners of the stock will not receive that dividend.

Dividends-in-kind (distribution of assets other than stock) are recorded at fair value and are reported as income. (APB-29, par. 23 and EITF 01-2)

Stock dividends and stock splits are *not* recorded as income by the investor. The cost basis of shares previously held should be allocated equitably to the total shares held after the stock dividend or split up. The adjusted basis should be used to calculate realized and unrealized gains and losses. (ARB-43, Chapter 7, par. 9)

Interest Income

Interest income is generally calculated the same way for all three categories of securities, even though the accounting methods differ. That is, interest income for a fixed-rate instrument is calculated using the amortized cost of the security and the market yield at acquisition, *not* its current fair value and current market yield. The methods used for recognizing and measuring the amount of interest income are discussed in Chapter 7, "Calculating Yields on Debt Investments," including the calculation of effective interest on debt securities (FAS-91), accounting for interest income on purchased securities with credit concerns (AICPA SOP 03-3), structured notes (EITF 96-12), and beneficial interests in securitized financial instruments (EITF 99-20).

Financial Statement Presentation

Current and Noncurrent Assets

An enterprise that presents a classified statement of financial position should report individual held-to-maturity securities, available-for-sale securities, and trading securities as either current or noncurrent, as appropriate, under the provisions of ARB-43, Chapter 3A (current assets and current liabilities). (FAS-115, par. 17, as amended by FAS-135, par. 4(t)) Classification under ARB-43 is based on management's intended holding period and the realizability of the asset, *not* the stated maturity of a debt security.

> ☛ **PRACTICE POINTER:** Most trading securities are classified as current assets, due to their short intended holding period. However, if a trading security was intended to be held for more than one year, perhaps to fund a deferred compensation arrangement, it would appropriately be classified as noncurrent.

The balances in the three categories of investments may be presented either on the face of the statement of financial position or in the notes. (FAS-115, par. 117)

Reporting Cash Flows

Cash flows from purchases, sales, and maturities of securities should be classified *separately* as follows (FAS-115, par. 18):

- Held-to-maturity securities: Investing activities
- Available-for-sale: Investing activities
- Trading: Based on the nature and purpose for which the securities were acquired

Cash receipts from returns on investments, that is, interest and dividends, are considered cash flows from *operating activities*. (FAS-95, par. 22(b))

> ☞ **PRACTICE POINTER:** Companies are permitted to report activity for cash equivalents as a net change. If a company classifies certain debt securities as cash equivalents in accordance with FAS-95, they should also apply the accounting and disclosure requirements of FAS-115 and explain in the notes what portion of each category of securities is reported in the balance sheet and the statement of cash flows. (FAS-115 Q&A, par. 51)

> **OBSERVATION:** Unrealized gains and losses on trading securities can create a reconciling item for companies that prepare their cash flow statements using the indirect method. That is, changes in fair value do not generate current cash flows, but they affect net income. If material, companies should disclose the effect of "mark-to-market accounting" as a reconciling item on the cash flow statement. (FAS-95, pars. 28 and 29)

Presentation of Available-for-Sale and Trading Securities Subsequently Measured at Fair Value

Companies must report investments in available-for-sale securities and trading securities separately from similar assets that are subsequently measured using another measurement attribute on the face of the statement of financial position. The following alternatives are available:

- Present two separate line items to display the fair value and non-fair-value carrying amounts for investments in debt and equity securities
- Present amounts that aggregate those fair value and non-fair-value amounts in the same line item and parenthetically disclose the amount of fair value included in the aggregate amount (on the face of the entity's statement of financial position). (FAS-115, par. 17, as amended by FAS-159)

Disclosure

FAS-115 requires that the following information be presented in all complete sets of financial statements. When more than one category is affected, the disclosure must be made separately for each category. Interim reports (such as 10-Qs) that include summarized financial information need not include the disclosures. (FAS-115 Q&A, par. 52)

EXHIBIT 2-4
SUMMARY OF DISCLOSURE REQUIREMENTS UNDER FAS-115

Disclosure Requirement	HTM	AFS	Trading	Frequency	Notes
Aggregate fair value of securities	X	X		For each balance sheet	By major security type[1] (FAS-115, par. 19)
Gross unrealized gains and gross unrealized losses	X	X		For each balance sheet	(FAS-115, par. 19)
Net carrying amount	X			For each balance sheet	(FAS-115, par.19)
Gross gains and losses in OCI for any derivatives that hedged the forecasted acquisition of securities	X			For each balance sheet	(FAS-115, par.19)
Contractual maturities	X	X		Most recent balance sheet	Maturity information may be combined in appropriate groupings[2] (FAS-115, par. 20)

[1] For financial institutions, "major security type" must include at a minimum, the following categories: Equity securities, debt securities issued by the U.S. Treasury and other U.S. government corporations and agencies, debt securities issued by states of the United States and political subdivisions of the states, debt securities issued by foreign governments, corporate debt securities, mortgage-backed securities, other debt securities.

[2] Financial institutions must disclose the fair value and the net carrying amount (if different from fair value) of debt securities based on at least four maturity groupings: (a) within 1 year, (b) after 1 year through 5 years, (c) after 5 years through 10 years, and (d) after 10 years. Securities not due at a single maturity date, such as mortgage-backed securities, may be disclosed as a separate group rather than divided among several maturity groupings. However, if the securities are divided, the method also must be disclosed. (FAS-115, par. 20)

Disclosure Requirement	HTM	AFS	Trading	Frequency	Notes
How the cost of a security sold or the amount reclassified out of OCI into earnings was determined	X[3]	X[3]	X	Each statement of operations	For example, fication (FAS-115, par. 21(b)
Proceeds from sales of securities and the gross realized gains and gross realized losses that have been included in earnings as a result of those sales		X		Each statement of operations	(FAS-115, par. 21(a))
Sales or transfers from HTM: • The net carrying amount of the sold or transferred security, • The related realized or unrealized gain or loss, and the net gain or loss in OCI for any derivative that hedged the forecasted acquisition of the security, • The reason for the sale or transfer the security	X			Each statement of operations	Does not apply if the sale or transfer was for "acceptable" reasons. (FAS-115, par. 22) Transfers out of HTM should be rare. (FAS-115, par. 15)

---

[3] Could include amounts deferred from cash flow hedges.

Disclosure Requirement	HTM	AFS	Trading	Frequency	Notes
The amount of the net unrealized holding gain or loss that has been included in OCI and the amount of gains and losses reclassified out of OCI for the period (and method)		X		Each statement of operations	(FAS-115, par. 21(d))
Gross gains and gross losses included in earnings from transfers of securities from AFS to trading		X	X	Each statement of operations	(FAS-115, par. 21(c)) Transfers in and out of trading should be rare. (FAS-115, par. 15)
The portion of trading gains and losses for the period that relates to trading securities still held at the reporting date			X	Each statement of operations	In other words, the unrealized portion. (FAS-115, par. 21(e))

☛ **PRACTICE POINTER:** The term "net carrying amount" includes any adjustment resulting from the application of fair value hedge accounting. Hedge accounting is discussed in Chapter 14, "Hedge Accounting."

FAS-140 requires additional disclosures for interests that continue to be held in securitized financial assets and for securities that have been pledged as collateral. See Chapter 6, "Securitizations," and Chapter 9, "Securities Lending Arrangements and Other Pledges of Collateral," for more information.

SEC REGISTRANT ALERT: In addition to the explicit requirements of FAS-115, the Division of Corporate Finance of the Securities and Exchange Commission expects the following disclosures regarding the investment portfolio in filings made by public financial institutions (banks and thrifts, finance and insurance companies):

- The fair value of the portfolio should be disclosed on the face of the balance sheet. If the portfolio's fair value is less than its cost, the Management's Discussion and Analysis section of the annual report (MD&A) should comment on the significance of the unrealized loss relative to net worth and regulatory capital requirements.

- Proceeds from sales and maturities of debt securities should be reported separately in the cash flow statement or in the notes.

- MD&A should analyze and quantify the likely effects on current and future earnings, investment yields and on liquidity and capital resources of:

  — Material unrealized losses in the portfolio;

  — Material sales of securities at gains; and

  — Material shifts in average maturity.

- If the portfolio consists of securities that are not actively traded, MD&A should disclose the nature of the securities and their proportion to the portfolio, the source of fair value information, and any material risks associated with the investment relative to earnings and liquidity.

(SEC Division of Corporate Finance: Frequently Requested Accounting and Financial Reporting Interpretations and Guidance, Section I.E.)

SEC registrants that are bank holding companies must also provide certain disclosures about securities as part of the 1934 Act Industry Guide 3. The SEC is revising Guide 3 to reflect subsequent developments in accounting standards. The timetable is uncertain.

Chapter 18, "Fair Value Measurements, Fair Value Disclosures, and Other Financial Instrument Disclosures," outlines additional disclosures applicable for investments measured at fair value.

ACCOUNTING FOR EQUITY METHOD INVESTMENTS AND NONMARKETABLE EQUITY SECURITIES

Investments in securities accounted for under the equity method are addressed by APB-18. Accounting for such investments is not within the scope of this Chapter. However, companies may elect to measure investments in equity securities that are otherwise required to be accounted for under the equity method at fair value under election provided by FAS-159.

AUTHOR'S NOTE: In February 2007, the FASB issued FASB Statement No. 159, *The Fair Value Option for Financial Assets* *and Financial Liabilities.* FAS-159 provides companies with an option to report certain financial assets and liabilities at fair value with subsequent changes in value reported in earnings. The specific provisions of FAS-159 as they apply to Investments are covered in this Chapter. Chapter 19, "The Fair Value Option for Financial Instruments," provides general guidance on the fair value option in FAS-159. FAS-159 is effective for calendar-year-end companies as of January 1, 2008. Early adoption is permitted as of the beginning of a fiscal year that begins on or before November 15, 2007, provided the entity also elects to apply FAS-157.

If the fair value option is applied to an investment that otherwise would be accounted for under the equity method, the election should be applied to all of the investor's financial interests in the same entity that are eligible for the fair value option.

Chapter 19, "The Fair Value Option for Financial Instruments," provides detailed guidance on the application of that Statement to eligible items, including incremental disclosure requirements.

Passive investments in nonmarketable equity securities are accounted for under the cost method (except for investments held by insurance enterprises subject to FAS-60 and by not-for-profit organizations). (APB-18, par. 17) Under the cost method, the investor:

- Records its stock investment at cost.

- Recognizes as income dividends received that are distributed from net accumulated earnings of the investee since the date of acquisition by the investor.

- Records any dividends received in excess of earnings subsequent to the date of investment as a reduction of the cost of the investment (a return of investment). (APB-18, par. 6(a))

- Recognizes other-than-temporary impairment as a reduction of the cost basis of the investment, with a loss recognized in earnings. (AICPA Guide, *Auditing Derivatives Instruments, Hedging Activities, and Investments in Securities*, par. 3.40 and FAS-60, par. 51, as amended by FAS-115, par. 127(d))

> **OBSERVATION:** The term "cost method" in APB-18 means, "not accounted for under the equity method." However, if an equity security is within the scope of FAS-115, it is carried at fair value, not carried at cost. In the post-FAS-115 era, only nonmarketable equity securities are actually carried at cost.

> ☛ **PRACTICE POINTER:** Beneficial interests of a securitization trust that are in the form of equity and that do not meet the definition of a debt security are accounted for under APB-18 when they are nonmarketable. (EITF 99-20)

ACCOUNTING FOR SECURITIES HELD BY NOT-FOR-PROFIT ORGANIZATIONS

FAS-124 provides accounting guidance for certain types of securities held by not-for-profit organizations. FAS-124 applies to the same securities as FAS-115, and uses the same definitions of "security" and "readily determinable fair value." However, the accounting requirements are different for business and not-for-profit organizations.

Accounting for Debt Securities and Marketable Equity Securities

Measurement

Report all investments in equity securities with readily determinable fair values and all investments in debt securities at fair value in the statement of financial position. (FAS-124, par. 7)

The fair value measurement guidance discussed in the section title "Accounting for Investments Held by Not-for-Profit Organizations" and in Chapter 18, "Fair Value Measurements, Fair Value Disclosures, and Other Financial Instrument Disclosures," is applicable to investments in securities by not-for-profit organizations.

Gains and Losses on Securities

Report as unrestricted net assets unless their use is temporarily or permanently restricted by explicit donor stipulations or by law. (FAS-124, par. 8) EITF Topic D-49 provides interpretive guidance on the effect of legal restrictions on the appreciation on certain investments in a donor-restricted endowment fund.

Dividend, Interest, and Other Investment Income

Report as increases in unrestricted net assets unless the use of the assets received is limited by donor-imposed restrictions. Donor-restricted investment income is reported as an increase in temporarily restricted net assets or permanently restricted net assets, depending on the type of restriction. (FAS-124, par. 9) Paragraphs 11 through 13 of FAS-124 provide additional information on donor-restricted endowment funds. Paragraphs 14 through 16 require certain disclosures about securities.

> **OBSERVATION:** FAS-124 does not include a held-to-maturity or available-for-sale category. However, not-for-profit organizations are allowed to identify securities as available-for-sale and held-to-maturity and exclude the unrealized gains and losses on

those securities from an operating measure within the statement of activities. (FAS-124, par. 49)

Accounting for Other Financial Investments

Other investments held by not-for-profit organizations include, among others, mortgage notes, venture capital funds, partnership interests, and equity securities that do not have readily determinable values. Appendix A of Chapter 8 of the AICPA Audit and Accounting Guide, *Not-for-Profit Organizations*, provides guidance on the accounting for other investments. Exhibit 2-5 summarizes that guidance.

EXHIBIT 2-5
SUMMARY OF ACCOUNTING FOR OTHER INVESTMENTS
HELD BY NOT-FOR-PROFIT ORGANIZATIONS

Type of Organization	Initial Measure If Purchased	Initial Measure If Donated	Subsequent Measurement*	Other
Colleges and Universities	Cost	Fair value at date of gift	Cost or fair value	Total performance of other investments must be disclosed
Voluntary health and welfare organizations	Cost	Fair value at date of gift	Lower of cost or market (aggregate portfolio) or fair value	—
Other	Cost	Fair value at date of gift	Fair value or lower of cost or fair value (aggregate portfolio)	Recoveries on securities carried at the lower of cost or fair value should not exceed the original cost of the securities

*The same measurement attribute should be used for all other investments.

IMPAIRMENT OF INVESTMENT SECURITIES

FAS-115 and FSP FAS 115-1 and FAS 124-1, "The Meaning of Other-Than-Temporary Impairment and Its Application to Certain Investments," address the recognition of impairment on investment securities. FSP FAS 115-1 and FAS 124-1 provides guidance for debt and equity securities subject to FAS-115, debt and equity securities held by not-for-profit organizations that are subject to FAS-124 (and that are held by an investor that reports a "performance indicator"), and investments accounted for under the cost method on the determination as to when an investment is impaired, whether the impairment is other-than-temporary, and the measurement of an impairment loss.

> ☞ **PRACTICE POINTER:** FSP FAS 115-1 and FAS 124-1 was issued in November 2005 and is effective for reporting periods beginning after December 15, 2005, with earlier application permitted. The FSP replaces EITF Issue 03-1, "The Meaning of Other-Than-Temporary Impairment and Its Application to Certain Investments." The FSP carries forward some of the provisions of EITF 03-1. The effective date of the recognition and measurement provisions of EITF 03-1 had been delayed by FSP EITF 03-1-1, "Effective Date of Paragraphs 10–20 of EITF Issue No. 03-1, 'The Meaning of Other-Than-Temporary Impairment and Its Application to Certain Investments'."

Determining Whether an Investment is Impaired

An investment is impaired if the fair value of the investment is less than its cost basis. (Cost includes adjustments made for accretion, amortization, previous other-than-temporary impairments, and hedging.) Impairment must be evaluated at the individual security level (that is, the level and method of aggregation used to measure realized and unrealized gains and losses of securities). The term *individual security level* takes into account situations in which an investor aggregates equity securities with the same CUSIP number purchased in separate trade lots for the purposes of measuring realized and unrealized gains and losses. Securities may not be combined with guarantees, credit enhancements, or other contracts for the purposes of determining whether impairment exists.

> ☞ **PRACTICE POINTER:** It is not appropriate to record a general reserve for unidentified impairment in a portfolio of securities. (FAS-115 Q&A, par. 48)

An investor must assess whether an investment is impaired in each reporting period or, for cost-method investments, each time the investor estimates the fair value of the investment (e.g., for FAS-107 disclosures).

For reporting periods in which the fair value of a cost-method investment is not estimated, the investor must determine whether an "impairment indicator" is present. If an impairment indicator is present, the fair value of the investment must be estimated in order to test impairment of the investment. Examples of impairment indicators are:

- A significant deterioration in the earnings performance, credit rating, asset quality, or business prospects of the investee
- A significant adverse change in the regulatory, economic, or technological environment of the investee
- A significant adverse change in the general market condition of either the geographic area or the industry in which the investee operates
- A bona fide offer to purchase (whether solicited or unsolicited), an offer by the investee to sell, or a completed auction process for the same or similar security for an amount less than the cost of the investment
- Factors that raise significant concerns about the investee's ability to continue as a going concern, such as negative cash flows from operations, working capital deficiencies, or noncompliance with statutory capital requirements or debt covenants

If the fair value of an investment is less than its cost, an investment is considered impaired and the investor must evaluate whether the impairment is other-than-temporary.

Evaluating Whether an Impairment is Other-Than-Temporary

FAS-115 sets forth a general rule that an other-than-temporary impairment has occurred if the value of a security has declined and it is probable that the investor will be unable to collect all amounts due according to the contractual terms of a debt security not impaired at acquisition. (FAS-115, par. 16) The following conditions would generally indicate that an other-than-temporary impairment has occurred:

- The value of the security has declined and it is probable that the investor will be unable to collect all the amounts due according to the contractual terms of the debt security not impaired at acquisition. (FAS-115, par. 16)
- Market interest rates have increased or foreign exchange rates have changed since the acquisition and the security will be disposed of before it matures or the investment is not realizable. (FAS-115 Q&A, par. 46)
- For certain purchased or retained beneficial interests in securitized assets, it is probable, based on a holder's best estimate of

cash flows and discount rates that a market participant would use in determining the current fair value of the beneficial interests, that the holder of the beneficial interest will be unable to collect all remaining estimated cash flows. (EITF Issue 99-20) The accounting for yields on these beneficial interests is discussed in detail in Chapter 7, "Calculating Yields on Debt Investments."

- If a decision is made to sell a specific security at a loss shortly after the balance-sheet date and the investor does not expect the fair value of the security to recover prior to the expected time of sale, the security shall be deemed other-than-temporarily impaired in the period in which the decision to sell is made. However, if the impairment is deemed other-than-temporary, the investor shall recognize an impairment loss even if a decision to sell has *not* been made. (FSP FAS 115-1 and FAS 124-1 and FAS-115 Q&A, par. 47)

SAS-92 and SEC Staff SAB Topic 5M (SAB-59) provide additional guidance for assessing whether a decline in value is other-than-temporary.

☛ **PRACTICE POINTER:** FSP FAS 115-1 and FAS 124-1 and SAB Topic 5M (as modified by SAB-103) emphasize that *other-than-temporary* does not mean permanent. (See the "Audit Considerations" section of this chapter for more details.)

SEC REGISTRANT ALERT: The SEC staff has provided the following reminders, consistent with the guidance in SEC SAB Topic 5M, to registrants regarding the evaluation of whether an impairment is other-than-temporary:

- Once a security is in an unrealized loss position, registrants must consider all available evidence relating to the realizable value of the security and assess whether the decline in value is other-than-temporary. The assessment of the net realizable value should begin with the contemporaneous market price. Objective evidence (e.g., earnings trends, dividend payments, and asset quality) is required to support a realizable value in excess of the contemporaneous market price.

- The impairment analysis must be more robust and exhaustive as the length of time in which a recovery needs to occur becomes shorter and the magnitude of the decline becomes more significant.

- Registrants should not infer that securities with declines of less than one year are not other-than-temporarily impaired or that declines of greater than one year are automatically impaired. An other-than-temporary decline could occur within a very short time frame and/or a decline in excess of a year might still be temporary.

- An investor's intent to hold an equity security indefinitely would not, by itself, permit an investor to avoid recognizing an other-than-temporary impairment.

- A market price recovery that cannot reasonably be expected to occur within an acceptable forecast period should not be included in the assessment of recoverability.

- Facts and circumstances surrounding the sale of a security at a loss for which an entity previously asserted its intent to hold until recovery should be considered in determining whether the hold to recovery assertion remains valid for other securities in the portfolio (that is, the assertion is not automatically invalidated).

- Registrants should apply a systematic methodology for identifying and evaluating market declines below cost that includes the documentation of all factors considered.

(Speech by John M. James, then a Professional Accounting Fellow, Office of the Chief Accountant of the SEC, at the December 2004 AICPA National Conference on SEC and PCAOB Developments and Current Accounting and Disclosure Issues in the Division of Corporate Finance of the SEC, March 4, 2005)

In addition, the SEC has taken action in situations when other than temporary declines in value were not reported in an appropriate and timely manner. The SEC observes that a registrant's assessment of the realizable value of a marketable security should begin with its contemporaneous market price because that price reflects the market's most recent evaluation of the total mix of available information. Objective evidence is required to support a realizable value in excess of a contemporaneous market price, including the company's financial performance, the near term prospects of the company, the financial condition and prospects of the company's region and industry, and the investment intent. (SEC Current Accounting and Disclosure Issues, November 2006)

If an investment previously tested for impairment was deemed *not* other-than-temporarily impaired, the investor shall continue to evaluate whether the investment is impaired in each subsequent reporting period until either the investment experiences a recovery of fair value up to (or beyond) its cost or the investor recognizes an other-than-temporary impairment loss.

Recognizing an Impairment Loss If the Impairment is Other-Than-Temporary

When an other-than-temporary impairment is deemed to exist at the balance sheet date:

- The investor must recognize in earnings an impairment loss equal to the difference between the investment's cost and its fair value at the balance sheet date of the reporting period for which the assessment is made.
- The investment is written down to its fair value and fair value becomes the new cost basis for the investment. The new cost basis of the investment should not be adjusted for subsequent recoveries in fair value.
- Subsequent increases and decreases in the fair value of available-for-sale securities are included in other comprehensive income by comparing the security's *new* cost basis with its current fair value (unless the decrease is further other-than-temporary impairment). (FAS-115 Q&A, par. 49)
- Recoveries in fair value are not recorded in earnings until the security is sold. (FAS-115 Q&A, par. 49)

> **OBSERVATION:** "Impairment" of a trading security is recognized on an ongoing basis as it is marked to market.

Disclosure Requirements of FSP FAS 115-1 and FAS 124-1

Exhibit 2-6 summarizes the disclosure requirements of FSP FAS 115-1 and FAS 124-1 by type of investment covered by the scope of the guidance.

> ☞ **PRACTICE POINTER:** If the value of an investor's securities declines after the balance sheet date because of a downturn in the stock market, the effect should be disclosed, if material, as a Type II subsequent event. (AU Section 560 on subsequent events and EITF Topic D-11)

EXHIBIT 2-6
SUMMARY OF DISCLOSURE REQUIREMENTS UNDER FSP FAS 115-1 AND FAS 124-1

Required Disclosure	Frequency	Comments
Debt and equity securities subject to FAS- 115 (AFS and HTM) and debt and equity securities subject to (FAS-124 including those that fall within the scope of ETIF 99-20)		
For investments with unrealized losses for which OTT impairments have *not* been recognized: 1. Aggregate amount of unrealized losses 2. Aggregate related fair value	In annual financial statements, for each statement of financial position presented	Segregated by investments in continuous unrealized loss position for (1) less than 12 months and (2) 12 months or longer*
Information considered in determining that the impairments are not OTT, including: 1. Nature of the investment(s) 2. Cause(s) of the impairment(s) 3. Number of investments in an unrealized loss position 4. Severity and duration of the impairment(s) 5. Other evidence	For most recent statement of financial position presented	Aggregation by investment category permitted. Individually significant unrealized losses should not be aggregated.
Cost method investments		
Aggregate carrying amount of: 1. Cost method investments 2. Subset not evaluated for impairment Disclosure of the fact that fair value is not estimated if there are no changes in circumstances having a significant ad-verse effect on the investment's fair value and (1) it is not practicable to estimate fair value (under FAS-107) or (2) the investor is exempt from estimating fair value (under FAS-126).	In annual financial statements, for each statement of financial position presented.	Certain of these disclosures may not be applicable in all periods or for all investments.

* The determination of this timeframe is based on the balance sheet date of the reporting period in which the impairment is identified. If interim financial information is not prepared, the timeframe would be based on the annual balance sheet date of the period during which the impairment was identified.

SEC REGISTRANT ALERT: The SEC staff expects registrants to document the factors considered in reaching conclusions regarding other-than-temporary impairments. In addition, the SEC staff expects disclosures in the MD&A related to other-than-temporary impairments that may be incremental to existing requirements, including the following:

- The amount of the charge
- Specific discussion of the reasons for and timing of the charge
- Identification of the segment to which the charge relates if it is not included in the segment's profit or loss measure under FAS-131
- Risks and uncertainties about future declines
- Estimated effects that material declines would have on the registrant's liquidity

(December 11, 2003, speech by D. Douglas Alkema, then a Professional Accounting Fellow, Office of the Chief Accountant of the SEC, at the AICPA National Conference on Current SEC Developments)

MISCELLANEOUS TOPICS RELATING TO SECURITIES

Applicability of Investment Company Accounting

The AICPA Audit and Accounting Guide, *Investment Companies,* sets forth specialized accounting and reporting principles for entities that are within its scope. Investment companies (such as mutual funds) mark to market all of their investments through earnings. Investment companies do not generally apply the equity method of accounting or consolidation, even if they hold significant positions in equity securities. Some industrial and financial entities hold numerous investments in stocks (and bonds).

OBSERVATION: Some companies prefer to use investment company accounting for investments in nonmarketable stocks that would normally qualify for either the equity method or consolidation. Even though they must apply mark-to-market accounting, there are no ready markets for such investments, so often, the cost of the investment serves as a "proxy" for market value (unless there is clear impairment). Meanwhile, the investor does not recognize any share of investee losses that would be required under the equity method or consolidation. The AICPA is seeking to close this "loophole" and narrow the scope of the Investment Company Guide.

The AICPA Audit and Accounting Guide, Audits of Investment Companies, provides ambiguous guidance on when "investment company accounting" must be followed by an entity (or a subsidiary of an entity) that is not a registered investment company. Other than a separate account of an insurance company, an investment company must be a separate legal entity to be within the scope of the Guide. Accordingly, specialized accounting principles in the Guide should be applied to an investment made after March 27, 2002, only if the investment is held by an investment company that is a separate legal entity. (EITF D-74)

In June 2007, AICPA SOP 07-1, *Clarification of the Scope of the Audit and Accounting Guide "Investment Companies" and Accounting by Parent Companies and Equity Method Investors for Investments in Investment Companies,"* was issued. The SOP provides that the specialized accounting guidance in the Guide ("investment company accounting") should be applied by an entity for the purpose of separate company financial statements only if the entity meets the detailed definition of an *investment company* in the SOP or if it is an entity regulated by the Investment Company Act of 1940 or similar requirement such that it is required to report investments at fair value for regulatory reporting purposes. Also, in instances where an investment company that is within the scope of the Guide is a subsidiary of another entity or an investment of an investor that applies the equity method of accounting, the SOP provides guidance for determining when the specialized accounting guidance in the Guide may be retained in the financial statements of the parent company or the equity method investor.

> **AUTHOR'S NOTE:** As this book went to press, the FASB was drafting a proposal that would delay the effective date of AICPA SOP 07-1 indefinitely in response to a number of implementation issues identified in practice. In connection with the decision to propose such a delay of the SOP's effective date, the FASB would plan to address specific implementation issues. Readers should monitor the FASB's further deliberations of these issues. Until any revised guidance is effective, entities should continue to follow the existing guidance in the AICPA Audit and Accounting Guide, *Investment Companies,* and its current accounting policies for determining whether the Guide applies to investees of the entity or to companies that are controlled by the entity.

> ☞ **PRACTICE POINTER:** Certain entities, including hedge funds and venture capital subsidiaries of corporations, may be required to apply FIN-46(R) to determine whether their investees should be consolidated, if they are not included in the scope of the AICPA Audit and Accounting Guide, Investment Companies, as clarified by AICPA SOP 07-1. Refer to Chapter 6, "Securitizations," for additional information about consolidation of variable interest entities.

Changes in Marketability, Level of Influence, or Form

Nonmarketable Equity Security Becomes Marketable

If a nonmarketable security becomes marketable, the cost basis of the nonmarketable security (reduced by any other-than-temporary impairment that has been recognized) should become the basis of the security to be accounted for under FAS-115. To the extent that a change in marketability provides evidence that an other-than-temporary impairment has occurred, a write-down should be recorded prior to applying FAS-115, and the loss should be classified in a manner consistent with other write-downs of similar investments. (FAS-115 Q&A., par. 37)

Change from Equity Method to FAS-115

If a marketable equity security should no longer be accounted for under the equity method (for example, due to a decrease in the level of ownership), the earnings or losses that relate to the stock retained should remain as a part of the carrying amount of the investment and the investment account should not be adjusted retroactively. The security's initial basis under FAS-115 would be the previous carrying amount of the investment. Refer to paragraphs 6 and 19 of APB-18 for additional information. (FAS-115 Q&A, par. 38)

Exchange of Cost Method Investments in a Business Combination

If an investor holds a passive ("cost method") investment in the stock of a company that either is acquired by or acquires another company, the exchange of the old stock for the new stock should be accounted for at fair value. The fair value of the new stock would become the new cost basis for the security and any gain or loss would be recorded in earnings. (If the "old" security had been accounted for as available for sale under FAS-115, any amount reported in other comprehensive income would be reversed.) (EITF 91-5)

Conversion of a Loan into a Debt Security in a Debt Restructuring

In a debt restructuring, the creditor may receive a debt security issued by the original debtor with a fair value that differs from the creditor's basis in the loan at the date of the debt restructuring. The initial cost basis of the security received should be the security's fair value at the date of the restructuring. Any excess of the fair value of the security received over the net carrying amount of the loan (that is, net of any allowance on the loan) should be recorded as a recovery on the loan. Any excess of the net carrying amount of the loan over the fair value of the security received should be recorded as a charge-off to the allowance for credit losses. Subsequent to the restructuring, the security should be accounted for under FAS-115.

A security received in a restructuring in settlement of only the past-due interest on a loan should be measured at the security's fair value at the date of the restructuring and accounted for in a manner consistent with the entity's policy for recognizing cash received for past-due interest. Subsequent to the restructuring, the security should be accounted for under FAS-115. (EITF 94-8)

Receipt of Stock as Part of a Demutualization

Several mutual insurance companies have undergone demutualization transactions and converted to stock enterprises. In order to effect a demutualization, a company may issue consideration, often in the form of stock, to existing participating policyholders in exchange for their current membership interests. Stock received from a demutualization should be accounted for at fair value with a gain recognized in income from continuing operations. (EITF 99-4)

Contracts to Purchase Securities That Are Not Derivatives

Most options and forward contracts to buy FAS-115 securities will meet the definition of a derivative and be accounted for under FAS-133 (or qualify for the regular-way securities exception). However, if a contract to buy securities does not meet the definition of a derivative, perhaps because the contract requires physical delivery of a security that is not marketable, and the contract has no intrinsic value, the contract is accounted for under EITF Issue 96-11. Contracts accounted for under EITF Issue 96-11 are not eligible for hedge accounting.

Under EITF Issue 96-11, the investor must, at inception, designate the contract as held-to-maturity, available-for-sale, or trading. The contract is accounted for in a manner consistent with those categories. Exhibit 2-7 summarizes the guidance in Issue 96-11.

EXHIBIT 2-7
APPLICATION OF EITF ISSUE 96-11

Category	HTM	AFS	Trading
Changes in value	Not recognized except other-than-temporary	Recognized in OCI except other-than-temporary	Recognized in earnings

Category	HTM	AFS	Trading
	impairment (in earnings)	impairment (in earnings)	
Initial carrying amount if purchased with forward contract	Forward contract price at settlement date	Fair value at settlement date	Fair value at settlement date
Initial carrying amount if purchased with option contract	Option strike price plus any remaining premium	Strike price plus fair value of option	Fair value at settlement date
Option expires worthless, security purchased in market	Market price plus any remaining premium	Market price plus any remaining premium	Fair value at settlement date

☛ **PRACTICE POINTER:**   Only contracts to acquire debt securities may be classified as held-to-maturity. Failure to take delivery of the debt security under a forward contract or to purchase the same security in the market if an option expires worthless will "taint" any remaining held-to-maturity debt securities held by the investor.

Accounting When Investor Holds an Equity Method Investment and Other Forms of Securities

When an investor holds common stock that is accounted for under the equity method and other forms of investment of the same issuer, such as debt securities, preferred stock or loans, questions arise about how the APB-18 equity method loss pick-up interacts with FAS-115 (securities) and FAS-114 (loans) when the carrying amount of the common stock has been reduced to zero. EITF Issue 98-13 provides extensive guidance on the interaction of these standards. Briefly, when the adjusted cost basis of another investment is positive:

- Equity method losses should continue to be recognized to the extent of and as an adjustment to the adjusted cost basis of the other investment(s).
- If there is more than one form of "other investment," losses should be applied first against the most senior claims (that is, highest priority in liquidation).
- Other applicable literature, such as FAS-115 and FAS-114, should then be applied to the adjusted cost basis for the other investment. For example, the unrealized gain or loss on an available-for-sale debt security would be calculated by comparing the fair value of the security with the adjusted cost basis of the security (that is, net of any write-down for equity method losses).
- An investor should *not* recognize equity method losses based solely on the percentage of investee common stock held by the investor. Equity method losses should be based either on (a) the ownership level of the particular investee security or loan/ad-

vance held by the investor to which the equity method losses are being applied or (b) the change in the investor's claim on the investee's total book value. (EITF 99-10)

- If an investor that has suspended equity method loss recognition in accordance with both paragraph 19(i) of APB-18 and EITF Issue 98-13 makes an additional investment, the investor should recognize some or all previously suspended losses if the additional investment represents, in substance, the funding of prior losses. Whether the investment represents the funding of prior losses depends on the facts and circumstances. (EITF 02-18)

> **OBSERVATION:** This "layering" of the equity method and other standards applies only when the equity method investment has persistent losses. If the equity method investment is profitable, the other forms of investment are not considered in applying the equity method.

Accounting for Structured Notes Acquired for a Specific Investment Strategy

EITF Issue 98-15 addresses a scenario where an investor simultaneously purchased two securities with opposite interest rate reset provisions. The goal was apparently to time the recognition of a loss by selling one security and recognize an above-market yield for the remaining life of the other security. In the scenario described, the investor should account for the two structured note securities as a unit until one of the securities is sold, at which time, the previous carrying amount should be allocated between the security sold and the security retained, based on the relative fair values of the notes at the date of sale.

The EITF identified several indicators that suggest that two securities should be viewed as a unit:

- The fair values of the securities will move in opposite directions based on changes in interest rates on a specified date.
- The securities are issued in contemplation of one another and at the same time.
- The securities are issued by the same counterparty and/or the same issuer.
- The securities were purchased by the investor to achieve a desired accounting result, and the individual transactions would serve no valid business purpose.

All of these indicators are not required to exist in order for the securities to be accounted for as a unit. Judgment is required in reaching a determination.

A related issue is addressed in Chapter 12, "Introduction to Derivatives Accounting." The section entitled "Structuring to Avoid FAS-133" discusses situations in which two separate transactions involving the same parties have the same net effect as a derivative. That section discusses indicators that should be considered to determine whether transactions should be accounted for as a unit rather than separately.

Equity Instruments Received as Consideration for Goods and Services

Companies sometimes sell goods or services in exchange for stock or other equity instruments issued by the purchaser of the goods or services. EITF Issues 00-8 and 00-18 address the measurement of the equity instruments for the purpose of recognizing revenue and the recipient's accounting for the equity instruments after the measurement date. EITF Issue 00-18 remains an open issue on the EITF agenda. Among other items, the EITF is considering whether there should be symmetry between the accounting by the issuer and the recipient of the equity instruments. That issue is on hold pending further progress in phase two of the FASB's project on share-based payments, which will consider transactions with nonemployees. Readers should monitor further developments.

> ☞ **PRACTICE POINTER:** The issuer's accounting (i.e., the purchaser of services or grantor of equity) is addressed in FAS-123(R), Share-Based Payments and several EITF Issues, including Issue 96-18, Issue 01-1, and Issue 02-8. CCH'S *GAAP Guide Level A*, Chapter 43, "Stock-Based Payments," and CCH'S *GAAP Guide Levels B, C, and D*, Chapter 38, "Stock-Based Payments," provide additional information.

> **SEC REGISTRANT ALERT:** FAS-123(R) does not change the accounting guidance for share-based payment transactions with nonemployees in FAS-123 as originally issued and in EITF 96-18. The SEC staff, however, believes entities should apply FAS-123(R) by analogy to share-based payment transactions with nonemployees unless the accounting is addressed more clearly in other authoritative literature or the application of FAS-123(R) would be inconsistent with the terms of the instrument issued to a nonemployee in a share-based payment transaction. (SEC SAB 107 (Topic 14))

REGULATORY CONSIDERATIONS

For regulatory accounting purposes (that is, call reports or other filings with financial institution regulators), banks, credit unions, thrifts, and savings institutions apply GAAP; however, unrealized gains and losses from available-for-sale debt securities and some equity securities are excluded from the calculation of regulatory capital. (FFIEC Call Report Instructions, Schedule RC-R)

For statutory accounting purposes, insurance companies follow statutory accounting principles of the National Association of Insurance Commissioners (NAIC), which differ from the requirements of FAS-115 in several respects (for example, the carrying amount in the balance sheet, impairment recognition, determination of fair value, and yield calculations). Relevant pronouncements include SSAP 26 (bonds), SSAP 30 (common stock), SSAP 32 (preferred stock), and SSAP 43 (loan-backed securities). Practitioners should be aware of the numerous differences between GAAP and SAP in the preparation and review of insurance company financial statements.

AUDITING CONSIDERATIONS

The primary audit guidance for securities is provided in SAS-92, *Auditing Derivative Instruments, Hedging Activities, and Investments in Securities*. This guidance is expanded and analyzed in a new AICPA Audit Guide, *Auditing Derivative Instruments, Hedging Activities, and Investments in Securities*. There are several aspects of accounting for securities that are judgmental and contribute to audit risk. The highlights include:

1. Management's intent and ability to hold securities significantly affect the appropriate accounting for securities. SAS-92 indicates that an auditor should consider whether management's activities corroborate or conflict with its stated intent. An auditor should assess whether management's activities, contractual agreements, and the entity's financial position provide evidence of its ability to hold securities. (SAS-92, par. 57(d)) In addition to performing other auditing procedures, the auditor ordinarily should obtain written representations from management confirming its intent and ability to hold a debt security to its maturity. (SAS-92, par. 58)

2. Judgment is required to determine the fair value of certain securities. SAS-92 identifies sources of fair value information for securities, the hierarchy of such sources, procedures the auditor should perform when quoted market prices are not available, the auditor's responsibility for understanding the method used to develop fair value estimates, and the auditor's responsibility for evaluating the reasonableness and appropriateness of models used for valuation. Some highlights include:

   a. Quoted market prices obtained from financial publications or from national exchanges and NASDAQ are generally considered to provide sufficient evidence of the fair value of investments. (SAS-92, par. 36)

   b. For securities that do not trade regularly, the auditor should consider obtaining estimates of fair value from broker-dealers or other third-party sources to corroborate management's estimate. In some situations, the auditor may determine that it is necessary to obtain fair value estimates from more than one pricing source. (SAS-92, par. 38) The auditor should consider the auditing guidance on using the work of a specialist (AU 336) and processing transactions by service organizations (AU 324), as applicable. (SAS-92, par. 39)

   c. If the security is valued by the entity using a valuation model, the auditor does not function as an appraiser and should not substitute his or her judgment for that of the entity's management. Rather, the auditor should assess the reasonableness and appropriateness of the model, including the supportability of the market variables and assumptions being used. (SAS-92, par. 40)

d. In some circumstances, auditing procedures require verifying the existence and testing the measurement of investments in securities where a readily determinable fair value does not exist (for example, an investment in a hedge fund that owns interests without readily determinable fair values). A confirmation of the existence of the investment received from a third party would constitute adequate audit evidence only if provided on a detailed, security-by-security basis. However, third-party confirmation of fair values, even on a security-by-security basis, does not constitute adequate audit evidence with respect to testing the valuation of investments in such securities. The auditor should consider the guidance in AU Section 328, which discusses, among other things, testing fair value measurements and evaluating conformity of fair value measurements and disclosures with GAAP. (AU 332, Interpretation 1)

3. Judgment is required to identify other-than-temporary impairment losses. An auditor should evaluate management's conclusions about the existence of other-than-temporary impairment of a security. In evaluating management's conclusions, the auditor should obtain evidence about conditions that tend to corroborate or conflict with such conclusions, including the following factors (SAS-92, par. 47):

a. Fair value is significantly below cost and:

(1) The decline is attributable to adverse conditions related to the specific security or to specific conditions in an industry or in a geographic area.

(2) The decline in fair value has existed for an extended period of time.

(3) Management does not possess both the intent and the ability to hold the investment for a period of time sufficient to allow for any anticipated recovery in fair value.

b. A debt security has been downgraded by a rating agency.

c. The financial condition of the issuer has deteriorated.

d. Dividends have been reduced or eliminated, or scheduled interest payments on debt securities have not been made.

e. The entity recorded losses from the security subsequent to the end of the reporting period.

SAS-101, *Auditing Fair Value Measurements and Disclosures*, also provides general information about auditing fair value estimates (although it does not address specific instruments, such as SAS-92 on securities and derivatives).

ILLUSTRATIONS

Illustration 2-1: Accounting for a Securities Portfolio

Remsen Company maintains a portfolio of stock and bond investments. During 20X1 and 20X2, Remsen engaged in the following transactions:

Date	Investment Type	Transaction	Cost	Fair Value 12/31/X1	Fair Value 12/31/X2	Selling Price
1/02/X1	City of New York munic-ipal bond, 6.5% tax-exempt coupon, par value $1,000,000, 5 year re-maining life Market yield 5%	Purchase	$1,065,000	$1,064,000	$1,055,000	n.a
3/31/X1	Warehouse Corp. com-mon stock (a 3% interest)	Purchase	$3,000,000	$2,950,000	$2,700,000	n.a.
11/1/X1	Striker Corp. common stock (a 1% interest)	Purchase	$250,000	$260,000	—	n.a.
1/15/X2	Striker Corp. common stock	Sale				$274,000

Remsen would account for its portfolio as follows (taxes are ignored for simplicity).

Initial Classification:

- Remsen classifies the New York City municipal bond, which is tax-exempt, as held-to-maturity because it has the positive intent and ability to hold the security to maturity. The bond will be carried at amortized cost (see table below).

- Remsen plans to hold the Warehouse Co. common stock for long-term appreciation and income. The stock is restricted from sale, but the restriction expires on 12/31/X1. At 3%, Remsen's ownership level does not provide significant influence over the management of Warehouse Co. Remsen classifies the stock as available for sale, because it has an indefinite holding period for the security. The Warehouse Co. stock will be carried at fair value with changes in fair value recognized in a separate component of other comprehensive income.

- Remsen plans to hold the Striker Corp. common stock for a short period of time. Remsen hopes to realize a gain from a rapid increase in the value of the stock. The stock is publicly traded. Remsen's ownership of 1% of the voting stock does not provide significant influence over the management of Warehouse Co. Remsen classifies the Striker stock as trading. The stock will be marked to market through earnings.

Impairment Review:

- At 12/31/X1, the cost of the Warehouse Co. stock exceeds its fair value by $50,000. Remsen Co. believes the stock is not impaired because the financial condition of the issuer is still strong, there has been a general downturn in the market, and Remsen plans to hold the security for the forseeable future. The unrealized holding loss is reported in other comprehensive income.

Other comprehensive income—FAS-115	$50,000	
Valuation account on AFS security		$50,000

- On 12/31/X2, a major rating agency downgraded the outstanding debentures of Warehouse Co. from AA to single-B. Warehouse Co. lost a major contract with a large manufacturer and announced that it would not pay a dividend in 20X2. Remsen concludes that the stock has suffered an other-than-temporary impairment the difference between the cost basis of the stock and the current fair value ($300,000). Remsen plans to sell the stock early in 20X3. The loss is recorded as a write-down of the cost basis of the stock, and the previous entry to other comprehensive income is reversed:

Other-than-temporary impairment loss on AFS security	$300,000	
Valuation account on AFS security	$50,000	
AFS security		$300,000
Other comprehensive income		$50,000

Interest Income:

Remsen bought the New York City municipal bond at a premium. The premium is amortized over the life of the bond as a reduction of interest income. Interest income would be recognized as follows:

	A Reported interest income (original market yield $\times$ D)	B Cash received (coupon)	C Premium amortization (A–B)	D Amortized cost at endof period (D+C)
				1,064,942
Year 1	53,247	65,000	-11,753	1,053,189
Year 2	52,659	65,000	-12,341	1,040,849
Year 3	52,042	65,000	-12,958	1,027,891
Year 4	51,395	65,000	-13,605	1,014,286
Year 5	50,714	65,000	-14,286	1,000,000

The entry in Year 1 would be:

Cash	$65,000	
Interest income (premium amortization)	$11,753	
HTM security		$11,753
Interest income		$65,000

The entry in Year 2 would be:

Cash	$65,000	
Interest income (premium amortization)	$12,341	
HTM security		$12,341
Interest income		$65,000

The premium would continue to be amortized using this schedule until the bond is actually sold (see below).Chapter 7, "Calculating Yields on Bond Investments," provides detailed information about recognizing yields on securities and other forms of investment.

Dividend Income:

- On November 30, 20X1, Warehouse Co.declares a dividend of $0.03 per share. Remsen holds 100,000 shares ($3,000). Dividends are recognized in income (not as a reduction of the investment).

Cash (or receivable)	$3,000	
Dividend income		$3,000

On November 30, 20X2, Warehouse announces that it will not pay a dividend in 20X2.

- No dividends are declared or paid on Striker Corp. common stock during Remsen's holding period.

Transfer of HTM Securities:

- On December 31, 20X2, the Internal Revenue Service announced that effective January 1, 20X3, interest on New York City municipal bonds will no longer be tax-exempt for certain types of taxpayers, and Remsen is adversely affected by the change. Remsen no longer has the intent to hold the bonds to maturity. Under paragraph 8(b) of FAS-115, Remsen is allowed to sell or transfer the bonds without undermining its original decision. Remsen decides to transfer the bonds to available for sale and sell them in 20X3.The amortized cost of the bonds is $1,040,849 and the fair value is $1,055,000. The difference is recorded as an increase to other comprehensive income.

Available-for-sale security	$1,040,849	
Valuation account for AFS securities	$14,151	
HTM security		$1,040,849
Other comprehensive income— FAS-115		$14,151

Sale of Trading Securities:

On January 15, 20X2, Remsen commits to sell the Striker Corp. shares. The transaction will settle on January 18, 20X2. The securities were last marked to market on December 31, 20X1.

January 15, 20X2

Trade date receivable	$274,000	
Trading securities		$260,000
Gain on trading securities		$14,000

January 18, 20X2

Cash	$274,000	
Trade date receivable		$274,000

Accounting for Remsen's portfolio

Balance Sheet	20X1	20X2
Current assets		
Trading securities (at fair value)	$260,000	—
Available-for-sale securities (at fair value)	—	$3,755,000
Noncurrent assets		
Held-to-maturity debt securities (at amortized cost)	1,053,189	—
Available-for-sale securities (at fair value)	2,950,000	—
Stockholders' equity		
Other comprehensive income:		
Unrealized holding loss (gain) on AFS securities[1]	50,000	(14,151)
Income Statement		
Interest income	53,247	52,659
Dividend income	3,000	—
Other income: Gains on trading securities	10,000	14,000
Other-than-temporary impairment loss	—	(300,000)
Cash Flow Statement		
Operating activities		
Purchase/sale of trading security	(250,000)	274,000
Interest income (cash)	65,000	65,000
Dividend income	3,000	—
Investing activities		
Purchase of securities	(4,065,000)	—

---

[1] The deferred tax consequences of these amounts would be recognized in accordance with FAS-109, par. 36.

Illustration 2-2: Disclosures Required by FAS-115

The following disclosure is adapted from the 2001 Annual Report of Ford Motor Company. Ford Motor Company provides the disclosures for prior years, as required, and breaks out certain information by sector. Some of that information has been omitted here for brevity.

Note 4. Marketable and Other Securities Trading securities are recorded at fair value with unrealized gains and losses included in income. Available-for-sale securities are recorded at fair value with net unrealized gains and losses reported, net of tax, in other comprehensive income. Held-to-maturity securities are recorded at amortized cost. Equity securities that do not have readily determinable fair values are recorded at cost. Realized gains and losses are accounted for using the specific identification method. [FAS-115, par. 21(b)]

The fair value of substantially all securities is determined by quoted market prices. The estimated fair value of securities for which there are no quoted market prices is based on similar types of securities that are traded in the market. Equity securities that do not have readily determinable fair values are recorded at cost. Book value approximates fair value for all securities.

Expected maturities of debt securities may differ from contractual maturities because borrowers may have the right to call or prepay obligations with or without penalty.

Investments in securities held by the Financial Services Sector at December 31, 2001, were as follows (in millions):

	Amortized Cost	Unrealized Gains	Unrealized Losses	Book/ Fair Value
Trading	$95	—	—	$95
Available-for-sale				
U.S. government and agency	78	2	1	79
Government — non-U.S.	18	1	—	19
Corporate debt	163	6	1	168
Mortgage-backed	207	4	2	209
Equity	29	27	4	52
Total AFS securities	495	40	8	527
Held-to-maturity Securities				
U.S. government	6	—	—	6
Total	$596	$40	$8	$628

Note: Comparable data for Ford's Automotive Sector has not been presented here.

The amortized cost and fair value of investments in available-for-sale securities and held-to-maturity securities by contractual maturity for Automotive and Financial Service sectors were as follows (in millions):

Contractual	Available-for-Sale		Held-to-Maturity	
Maturity	Amortized Cost	Fair Value	Amortized Cost	Fair Value
1 year	$22	$22	$—	$—
2–5 years	1,284	1,302	1	1
6–10 years	289	292	3	3
11 years and later	221	223	2	2
Mortgage-backed securities	207	209	—	—
Equity securities	29	52	—	—
Total	$2,052	$2,100	$6	$6

[FAS-115, par. 20]

The proceeds and gains/(losses) from available-for-sale securities were as follows (in millions):

	Proceeds	Gains/(Losses)
Automotive	$12,395	$47
Financial Services	745	11

[FAS-115, par. 21]

Ford Motor Company discloses the amount of the net unrealized holding gain or loss that has been included in other comprehensive income as a separate line on the Consolidated Statement of Shareholders' Equity. [FAS-115, par. 21(d)]

CHAPTER 3
LOANS AND THE ALLOWANCE FOR CREDIT LOSSES

CONTENTS

Overview	3.03
Background	3.04
Definition of a Loan	3.05
ADC Loans	3.05
Accounting for Loans	3.06
Initial Measurement of Loan Transactions	3.06
Loans Measured at Fair Value under the Fair Value Option Election	3.06
Originated Loans	3.07
Purchased Loans	3.08
Lending Fees and Costs	3.08
Exhibit 3-1: Elements of Recorded Investment (Amortized Cost) in a Loan	3.09
Servicing Rights	3.09
Pledges of Collateral	3.09
Loans That Must Be Accounted for Like Securities	3.09
Loans with Embedded Derivatives and the Fair Value Option for Certain Hybrid Financial Instruments	3.10
Classification and Subsequent Measurement of Loans	3.10
Loans Held for Investment	3.11
Nonmortgage Loans Held for Sale	3.11
Exhibit 3-2: Differences in Accounting and Terminology for Loans and Securities	3.12
Impairment of Loans	3.12
Relationship between FAS-5 and FAS-114	3.13
Impairment of Loans under FAS-114	3.13
Exhibit 3-3: Summary of Literature on Impairment of Debt Investments	3.14

Exhibit 3-4: *Application of FAS-114 and FAS-5 to a Loan Portfolio* 3.16

Exhibit 3-5: *Measurement Methods under FAS-114* 3.18

Guidance Applicable to All Three Methods 3.19

Impairment of Loans under FAS-5 .... 3.22

Eligibility of Loans Evaluated under FAS-114 for Accrual under FAS-5 .... 3.24

Troubled Debt Restructurings 3.25

Exhibit 3-6: *Creditor's Accounting for a Troubled Debt Restructuring* 3.27

Implementation Issues for TDRs 3.29

Credit Losses on Off-Balance-Sheet Commitments 3.30

Charge-Offs of Loans 3.31

SEC Staff Accounting Bulletin No. 102, Selected Loan Loss Allowance Methodology and Documentation Issues 3.32

Exhibit 3-7: *Reporting Credit-Related Losses* 3.32

Deferred Tax Consequences 3.34

Income Recognition after Impairment Recognition (Nonaccrual Loans) 3.34

Sales and Other Transfers of Loans 3.34

Decision to Sell a Loan Held for Investment 3.35

Sale of Bad-Debt Recovery Rights (EITF 86-8) 3.36

Presentation in the Statement of Cash Flows 3.36

Exception for Certain Financial Institutions 3.37

Mortgage Banking Model under FAS-65 .... 3.37

Mortgage Loans Held for Sale (FAS-65) 3.38

Exhibit 3-8: *Transfers between Loan Categories* 3.40

Disclosures 3.41

Important Notice: FASB Project on Loan Disclosures 3.41

Accounting Policies and Other Disclosures about Loans 3.41

Exhibit 3-9: *General Disclosures about Loans* 3.42

Quantitative Disclosures about Impaired Loans 3.43

Recorded Investment 3.43

Exhibit 3-10: *Disclosures about the Recorded Investment in an Impaired Loan* 3.44

Other Quantitative Disclosures about Impaired Loans 3.45

Off-Balance-Sheet Credit Risk 3.47

Miscellaneous Issues Involving Loans 3.47

Foreign Debt-Equity Swaps 3.47

Recording Interest on LDC Loans   3.48

Mortgage Loan Payment Modifications (EITF 84-19)   3.48

Accounting When Investor Holds Equity Method
and Other Forms of Investments   3.48

Government Guarantee of Foreign Loans with
Credit Risk and Transfer Risk (EITF Topic D-4)   3.48

Certain Collateralized Loans (Other Than TDRs)   3.49

Regulatory Considerations   3.49

Audit Considerations   3.51

Classification of Loans   3.51

Ceasing Recognition of Interest Income   3.52

Recognition of Impairment   3.52

Measuring Impairment   3.52

Differences between GAAP and Regulatory
Accounting Principles   3.53

Illustrations   3.53

Illustration 3-1: Loan Impairment under FAS-114   3.53

*Illustration 3-2: How to Apply FAS-5 and
FAS-114 to a Loan Portfolio*   3.55

Illustration 3-3: Disclosure under FAS-118   3.56

OVERVIEW

Accounting for loans depends on several factors: (1) the type of entity making the loan, (2) the intended holding period for the loan, (3) the nature of the return, and (4) whether it is probable that all amounts due according to the contractual terms of the arrangement will be collected. If the lender has the intent and ability to hold a loan for the foreseeable future or until maturity, the loan is considered "held for investment" and carried at amortized cost. Loans "held for sale," including loans held for indefinite periods of time and loans held specifically for sale, are carried at the lower of cost or market value. Loans with significant prepayment risk must be accounted for like available-for-sale or trading securities under FAS-115. Other loans with unusual payment terms contain embedded derivatives that must be split out and accounted for separately under FAS-133. Loans with returns that are integrally linked to the return on a real estate project must be accounted for as real estate investments, not loans. Special rules apply to certain mortgage banking activities.

Impairment is recognized on a loan or group of loans when it is probable that the lender will be unable to collect all contractual payments as scheduled. For individual loans that have been identified as impaired, impairment is measured by discounting the expected future cash flows using the original effective rate on the loan. As a practical expedient, impairment may be measured at the observable market price of the loan (or the fair value of collateral, less costs to sell, if the loan is collateral dependent). An allowance is recorded to reduce the carrying amount of the loan, with a corresponding charge to bad-debt expense. For loans that have not been individually identified as impaired and smaller-balance homogeneous loans that are collectively evaluated for impairment, a loss should be recognized if it is probable that a group of similar loans includes some losses at the balance sheet date, even though the loss cannot be identified to a specific loan. Determining when a loan is impaired and measuring the amount of loss require a great deal of professional judgment. The methodology used to identify impairment and estimate loan losses must be systematic, well documented, and consistently applied.

Troubled debt restructurings are generally considered impaired loans by the creditor. The accounting depends on the nature of the restructuring: receipt of assets, modification of terms, or a combination of types.

Numerous disclosures are required about impaired loans and loans on nonaccrual status.

BACKGROUND

SOP 01-6 sets forth the basic accounting for loans held as assets—that guidance applies to any institution that lends, unless other specific literature applies. FAS-114 addresses loan impairment for loans individually identified as impaired and certain types of troubled debt restructurings; FAS-5 addresses impairment of other loans and receivables. FAS-15, as amended by FAS-114, addresses the accounting for troubled debt restructurings. FAS-65 contains a special model for certain mortgage banking activities.

The primary focus of this chapter is subsequent measurement of loans. Other accounting issues relating to loans are addressed in the following chapters:

- Chapter 4, "Servicing of Financial Assets"
- Chapter 5, "Transfers of Financial Assets"
- Chapter 6, "Securitizations"
- Chapter 7, "Calculating Yields on Debt Investments"
- Chapter 9, "Securities Lending Arrangements and Other Pledges of Collateral"
- Chapter 18, "Fair Value and Other Disclosures about Financial Instruments" (including disclosures about concentrations of credit risk)
- Chapter 19, "The Fair Value Option for Financial Instruments"

The debtor's accounting for loans is addressed in Chapter 8, "Debt Financing."

Definition of a Loan

A loan is a contractual right to receive money on demand or on a fixed or determinable date that is recognized as an asset in the lender's (creditor's) statement of financial position. Examples include accounts receivable (with terms exceeding beyond one year), credit card receivables, and notes receivable. (FAS-114, par. 4) A loan that has been transformed into a security (through the process of securitization) is accounted for as a security, not a loan. Accounting for securities is discussed in Chapter 2, "Investments in Debt and Equity Securities."

> ☛ **PRACTICE POINTER:** Commitments to lend are not recognized as loans in the balance sheet of the lender unless and until the borrower exercises the commitment and the lender disburses funds. Loan commitments and other forms of "potential loans," such as guarantees, are discussed later in this chapter.

ADC Loans

The AICPA's Notice to Practitioners on acquisition, development, and construction (ADC) arrangements requires that certain ADC arrangements be accounted for as investments in real estate (in conformity with FAS-66 and FAS-67) or real estate joint ventures (in conformity with SOP 78-9) rather than as loans.[1] ADC arrangements should be

- Accounted for as real estate if the lender expects to receive more than 50 percent of expected residual profit.
- Accounted for as a loan if the lender expects to receive less than 50 percent of expected residual profit and at least one of the following conditions is met:
  — The borrower has an equity interest in the project that is not funded by the lender.
  — The lender has recourse to other assets of the borrower.
  — The borrower has provided a substantive credit enhancement from a creditworthy third party that is in effect for the entire term of the loan, including a take-out commitment for the full amount of the loan.

---

[1] The Notice appears as Exhibit I in AICPA Practice Bulletin 1, *Purpose and Scope of AcSEC Practice Bulletins and Procedures for Their Issuance.*

— Noncancelable sales contracts or lease commitments from creditworthy third parties are in effect and will provide sufficient net cash flow on completion of the project to service the loan, including principal and interest.

— The borrower has provided a qualifying personal guarantee.

Otherwise, the arrangement should be accounted for as a real estate investment.

Loans that are accounted for as real estate investments or joint ventures should not be reported or accounted for as loans and are usually classified in other assets or other real estate owned.

ACCOUNTING FOR LOANS

Initial Measurement of Loan Transactions

Loans Measured at Fair Value under the Fair Value Option Election

AUTHOR'S NOTE: In February 2007, the FASB issued FASB Statement No. 159, *The Fair Value Option for Financial Assets and Financial Liabilities.* FAS-159 provides companies with an option to report certain financial assets and liabilities at fair value with subsequent changes in value reported in earnings. The specific provisions of FAS-159 applicable to loans are covered in this Chapter. Chapter 19, "The Fair Value Option for Financial Instruments," provides generalized guidance on the fair value option in FAS-159. FAS-159 is effective for calendar-year-end companies as of January 1, 2008. Early adoption is permitted as of the beginning of a fiscal year that begins on or before November 15, 2007, provided the entity also elects to apply FAS-157.

In addition, in September 2006, the FASB issued FASB Statement No. 157, *Fair Value Measurements.* FAS-157 provides a single definition of the term *fair value,* establishes a framework for measuring fair value where required by existing GAAP, and expands disclosures about fair value measurements. Specific fair value measurement guidance applicable to loans is covered in this Chapter. Chapter 18, "Fair Value Measurements, Fair Value Disclosures, and Other Financial Instrument Disclosures," provides the detailed provisions of FAS-157. The 2008 edition of CCH *Financial Instruments* has been updated to incorporate the provisions of FAS-157. FAS-157 is effective for calendar-year-end companies as of January 1, 2008. Unless a company chooses to early adopt, prior GAAP is applicable for financial statements issued for 2007.

As this book went to press, the FASB was addressing a possible delay of FAS-157's effective date. The FASB agreed to consider delaying the effective date for nonfinancial instruments and for certain types of entities, including private companies and "smaller" public companies (not yet defined). Readers should monitor the FASB's further deliberations regarding the nature of any delay of FAS-157's effective date. Also, readers should refer to the 2007 edition for GAAP related to the fair value measurement of financial instruments applicable before the effective date of FAS-157.

Companies may elect to measure loans at fair value under the fair value option election provided by FAS-159. That election can be made only at initial recognition of the loan or in response to certain specified events and is irrevocable. The election is generally permitted on an instrument-by-instrument basis. One restriction, however, relates to multiple advances are made to a borrower under a single contract. In such a lending arrangement, the fair value option must be applied to the entire balance and not to each advance individually, on the basis that each advance loses its identity and becomes part of the larger loan balance.

If the fair value option is elected, a loan is initially and subsequently measured at fair value and with subsequent changes in fair value recognized in earnings. Origination fees and costs must be expensed as incurred. FAS-91 does not apply to loans measured at fair value with changes in value reported in earnings. Chapter 19 provides detailed guidance on the application of that Statement to eligible items, including incremental disclosure requirements.

FAS-157 is the primary guidance for fair value measurement under GAAP. Fair value is the price that would be received to sell an asset or paid to transfer a liability in an orderly transaction between market participants at the measurement date. The objective of a fair value measurement under FAS-157 is to determine the price that would be received to sell the asset or paid to transfer the liability at the measurement date (an exit price) using assumptions that market participants would use. The fair value measurement model in FAS-157 applies for both initial measurement and subsequent measurement of loans that are required to be measured at fair value and loans for which the fair value option is elected.

Chapter 18, "Fair Value Measurements, Fair Value Disclosures, and Other Financial Instrument Disclosures," provides specific fair value measurement guidance applicable to all financial instruments required to be measured at fair value under GAAP.

> ☛ **PRACTICE POINTER:** The fair value option election in FAS-159 triggers significant new disclosure requirements for affected items and does not eliminate other incremental disclosure requirements. In addition, in FAS-157 establishes disclosure requirements related to fair value measurements.

Originated Loans

Loans that are originated by the lender are recorded in the balance sheet when cash is disbursed, that is, the "settlement date." Originated loans are recorded by the lender at the amount of the initial investment (cash loaned), adjusted for certain amounts, including qualifying loan origination fees and costs. If the loan results from a loan commitment being exercised, any unamortized net commitment fees are rolled into the loan balance and amortized as an adjustment of yield in accordance with FAS-91, paragraph 8. Chapter 7, "Calculating Yields on Debt Investments," addresses the accounting for loan origination fees and costs and loan commitments in more detail. Chapter 7 also addresses certain situations where interest must be imputed on a loan, which can give rise to a premium or discount that must be amortized over the life of a loan.

Purchased Loans

Loans purchased from another entity should be recorded when the investor obtains control of the loan at fair value (usually the amount paid). (FAS-140, par. 9) Loans acquired through transactions that are considered purchases under FAS-140, loan participations, and purchase business combinations are considered purchased loans. Purchase premiums and discounts generally should be amortized over the life of the loan as a yield adjustment. (FAS-91, par. 15) SOP 03-3 addresses accounting for loans or debt securities purchased at a discount that is attributable in part to credit concerns. EITF Issue 99-20 addresses the method of interest income recognition for certain beneficial interests that are purchased or retained after a securitization of financial assets. Yields on purchased and retained beneficial interests in a special-purpose entity and loans purchased at a discount that is related in part to credit concerns are discussed in Chapter 7, "Calculating Yields on Debt Investments."

> **OBSERVATION:** There is no "trade date accounting" exception for loans, even when they are purchased.

Lending Fees and Costs

Certain types of loan origination fees and costs are required to be deferred as part of the recorded investment in the loan and amortized over the life of the loan as a yield adjustment. Methods for recognizing deferred fees and direct loan origination costs as an adjustment of yield are discussed in Chapter 7, "Calculating Yields on Debt Investments." All other lending-related costs should be expensed as incurred. (FAS-91, par. 7) Transaction costs on purchased loans are considered part of the cost of the loan. However, other types of fees and costs, including due diligence reviews, should not be included in the cost basis of the loan.

Exhibit 3-1 summarizes the elements of the recorded investment in a loan. Note that the term "recorded investment" does not include any related allowance for credit losses.

EXHIBIT 3-1
ELEMENTS OF RECORDED INVESTMENT
(AMORTIZED COST) IN A LOAN

Loan principal amount
−Any direct write-downs (charge-offs) ⎫ See Chapter 7, "Calculating
+Purchase premium   ⎬ Yields on Debt Investments"
+Net deferred loan origination costs ⎮
−Purchase discount   ⎮
−Net deferred loan origination fees ⎭
+Accrued interest receivable

+/- Deferred gains and losses from ⎫ See Chapter 14, "Hedge
    fair value hedges   ⎭ Accounting"

Servicing Rights

Servicing a loan or other receivable involves activities such as collecting cash payments and remitting amounts to taxing authorities, insurers, and guarantors. Servicing is inherent in all financial assets. Accounting for servicing assets and liabilities and transfers of servicing rights is addressed in Chapter 4, "Servicing of Financial Assets."

Pledges of Collateral

Lenders often receive a security interest in certain assets of the debtor as collateral on a loan. Generally, lenders do not recognize collateral received in their balance sheets unless the borrower defaults on the loan. Chapter 9, "Securities Lending Arrangements and Other Pledges of Collateral," discusses accounting for pledges of collateral and the required disclosures in detail.

Loans That Must Be Accounted for Like Securities

Except for instruments that are within the scope of FAS-133, interest-only strips, loans, other receivables, or interests that continue to be held in securitizations that can contractually be prepaid or otherwise settled in such a way that the holder would not recover substantially all of its recorded investment must be subsequently measured like investments in debt securities under FAS-115—*whether or not they are actually securities.* (FAS-140, par. 14) All of the measurement provisions of FAS-115, including impairment and transfers, and the related interpretive guidance apply to instruments with those characteristics. (FAS-140 Q&A, par. 110) However, the disclosure requirements of FAS-115 only apply to instruments that are actually securities.

(FAS-140 Q&A, par. 105) The disclosure requirements of this chapter apply to all loans.

Loans with Embedded Derivatives and the Fair Value Option for Certain Hybrid Financial Instruments

Some loans are hybrid instruments that have embedded derivatives that are required to be bifurcated under FAS-133. One example is a loan that gives the borrower the option to repay the loan in U.S. dollars or a fixed amount of another currency, which would be considered to represent a loan (the host contract) and an identified embedded foreign currency option. If an embedded derivative is separated from a host contract that is a loan, the remaining loan-host component is accounted for as a loan that does not contain an embedded derivative. (FAS-133, par. 16)

Certain loans that are hybrid financial instruments are eligible to be initially and subsequently measured at fair value, with changes in fair value recognized currently in earnings. Such loans must have an identified embedded derivative that is required to be bifurcated under FAS-133. However, such an election has important scope limitations (e.g., it does not apply to lease contracts). Also, if an entity identifies an embedded derivative but determines that it is not required to be bifurcated under FAS-133, the hybrid financial instrument is *not* eligible for the fair value option. In some cases, an entity may not elect fair value measurement because bifurcation of the instrument permits the embedded derivative to be designated as a hedging instrument. If the embedded derivative cannot be identified, the hybrid instrument must be measured at fair value under the practicability exception in FAS-133. Embedded derivatives and the fair value option are discussed in greater detail in Chapter 13, "Embedded Derivatives."

Classification and Subsequent Measurement of Loans

For loans measured at fair value under the fair value option election provided in FAS-159, subsequent changes in fair value are recognized in earnings. Origination fees and costs must be expensed as incurred. (FAS-159, par. A41) "The subsequent measurement of a loan." The subsequent measurement of a loan for which the fair value option is not elected depends on the lender's intent and ability to hold the loan for the foreseeable future or until maturity.

Loans Held for Investment[2]

Loans and trade receivables that management has the intent and ability to hold for the foreseeable future, or until maturity or payoff, should be reported in the balance sheet at the amortized cost of the loan, adjusted for any charge-offs and the allowance for loan losses (or the allowance for doubtful accounts). (SOP 01-6, par. 8(a))

Desecuritization of held-to-maturity securities Desecuritization means contractually changing a security into a loan or other form of receivable. EITF Topic D-51 addresses accounting for the desecuritization of a debt security that was classified as held-to-maturity under FAS-115 in a transaction that is not accounted for as a sale under FAS-140. In order for a desecuritization transaction to be consistent with an entity's stated intent to hold to maturity other debt securities under FAS-115, the entity must likewise hold the financial assets received or retained (i.e., loans) *to maturity.*

> **OBSERVATION:** This consensus prevents a company from circumventing the "held-to-maturity" security rules by selling a loan after it has been desecuritized under the less stringent "held-for-investment" loan standard. Refer to Exhibit 3-2 for an overview of the differences in accounting for loans and securities.

Nonmortgage Loans Held for Sale

Nonmortgage loans and trade receivables held for sale should be reported at the lower of cost or market value (LOCOM). (SOP 01-6, par. 8(b)) LOCOM may be determined either in the aggregate for loans held for sale or on an individual loan basis. (SOP 01-6, par. 13(a)(2)) Mortgage loans held in connection with mortgage banking activities are covered as a special model later in this chapter.

> ☛ **PRACTICE POINTER:** The method used to determine LOCOM is an accounting policy decision that should be documented and applied consistently. When LOCOM is determined in the aggregate, any appreciated loans provide a buffer before an overall loss is recognized on the group of loans. When LOCOM is determined on an individual loan basis, a loss is recognized on every "underwater" loan. No gains are recognized on appreciated loans until the loans are sold.

---

[2] SOP 01-6 uses the term "loans not held for sale" rather than the term "loans held for investment."

EXHIBIT 3-2
DIFFERENCES IN ACCOUNTING AND TERMINOLOGY FOR
LOANS AND SECURITIES

Classification	Loans	Securities	Subsequent Measurement	Comments
Held for investment	Intent and ability to hold to maturity or *the foreseeable future*	Not applicable	Carried at amortized cost	
Held to maturity	Not applicable	Intent and ability to hold *to maturity*	Carried at amortized cost	Cost accounting requirements are stricter for securities
Held for sale	All other loans	Not applicable	LOCOM through earnings	Individual or aggregate basis
Available for sale	See comment	Securities held for indefinite periods of time	Fair value with changes through equity	Loans with significant prepayment risk classified as AFS or Trading[1]
Trading	See comment	Securities held for short-term appreciation	Mark to market through earnings	

Presentation of loan categories Loans (and receivables) held for investment and held for sale must be presented separately in the balance sheet. (SOP 01-6, par. 13(e))

Impairment of Loans

FAS-5 establishes the basic principle that a loss contingency should be recognized only if past and current events indicate that it is *probable* that an asset has been impaired or that a loss has been incurred as of the balance sheet date. For a loan, a loss should be recognized when it is probable that all amounts due will not be collected according to the terms of the arrangement (both the amount and timing of payments). There will not always be a single, distinct event that can be identified as the cause of an impairment. Instead, there may be a series of events that have occurred resulting in the impairment of an individual loan or a pool of loans. This basic guidance applies to all loans that are accounted for under FAS-5 or FAS-114. Loans that are carried at LOCOM or fair value are subject to other literature, as indicated in Exhibit 3-3.

> **OBSERVATION:** The allowance for loan losses should reflect loss accruals for probable incurred losses based on past events and current economic conditions. Losses should not be accrued for possible or even probable future losses.

Relationship between FAS-5 and FAS-114

FAS-5 provides the basic guidance for recognition of impairment losses for all receivables (except those receivables specifically addressed by other accounting literature, such as loans held for sale, debt securities, or loans accounted for like securities).

FAS-114 provides more specific guidance on measurement and disclosure for a subset of the population of loans:

- Loans that are identified for evaluation and that are individually deemed to be impaired.
- Loans that are restructured in a troubled debt restructuring involving a modification of terms (unless they meet one of the FAS-114 scope exceptions). FAS-114 amended this section of FAS-15.

Exhibit 3-4 depicts the relationship between FAS-5 and FAS-114.

Impairment of Loans under FAS-114

FAS-114 addresses how to measure a loss contingency for loans that have individually been identified as impaired. FAS-114 also applies to loans restructured in a troubled debt restructuring that involve a modification of terms. A creditor's accounting for troubled debt restructurings is discussed later in this chapter.

> **OBSERVATION:** The scope of FAS-114 is difficult to understand. FAS-114 only applies if a lender has selected (identified) the loan for individual impairment review. If the loan is considered impaired, the loss is measured under FAS-114. If the loan is not individually considered impaired, it could then be evaluated

EXHIBIT 3-3
SUMMARY OF LITERATURE ON IMPAIRMENT
OF DEBT INVESTMENTS

Type of Loan or Receivable	FAS-114 Best Estimate	FAS-5 Estimate	Other GAAP
Loans individually identified for review, including troubled debt restructurings			
Impairment identified	✓		
Impairment not identified		✓	
Large groups of smaller-balance loans evaluated collectively for impairment:		✓*	
— Residential mortgages			
— Commercial mortgages			
— Consumer loans			
— Credit card receivables			
— Trade receivables			
— Other			
Other groups of loans that contain unidentified impairment		✓	
Loans measured at LOCOM			✓ (FAS-65 and SOP 01-6)
Loans with significant prepayment risk that are accounted for at fair value in accordance with FAS-140, par. 14			✓ (FAS-115)
Securities			✓ (FAS-115)
Purchased and retained interests in an SPE			✓ (EITF 99-20)
Purchased loans with concerns about collectibility	✓		✓ (SOP 03-3 and PB-6)***
Lease receivables			✓ (FAS-13)

Type of Loan or Receivable	FAS-114 Best Estimate	FAS-5 Estimate	Other GAAP
Standby letters of credit, guarantees, recourse arrangements		✓**	✓ (FIN-45)

---

* Loss estimates are based on groups of loans with similar risk characteristics

** Recorded as a separate liability, not as part of the allowance for credit losses. FAS-133 and SOP 01-6 apply in some cases.

*** SOP 03-3 supersedes PB-6 for transactions entered into after the SOP's initial application (that is, loans acquired in fiscal years beginning after December 15, 2004). For loans acquired in fiscal years beginning on or before December 15, 2004, PB-6, as amended by SOP 03-3, continues to apply.

---

under FAS-5 in connection with a group of similar loans. It is incorrect to say that FAS-114 applies to "large loans" and FAS-5 applies to "smaller-balance homogeneous loans."

Identifying loans for evaluation FAS-114 does not specify how a creditor should identify loans that are to be individually evaluated for collectibility under FAS-114. However, the following sources of information are useful in identifying loans for evaluation (EITF D-80, Q. 4):

- A specific materiality criterion (for example, all loans greater than $1,000,000)
- Regulatory reports of examination
- Internally generated listings such as "watch lists," past due reports, overdraft listings, and listings of loans to insiders
- Management reports of total loan amounts by borrower
- Historical loss experience by type of loan
- Loan files lacking current financial data related to borrowers and guarantors
- Loan documentation and compliance exception reports
- Borrowers experiencing problems such as operating losses, marginal working capital, inadequate cash flow, or business interruptions
- Loans secured by collateral that is not readily marketable or that is susceptible to deterioration in realizable value
- Loans to borrowers in industries or countries experiencing economic instability

EXHIBIT 3-4
APPLICATION OF FAS-114 AND FAS-5 TO A LOAN PORTFOLIO

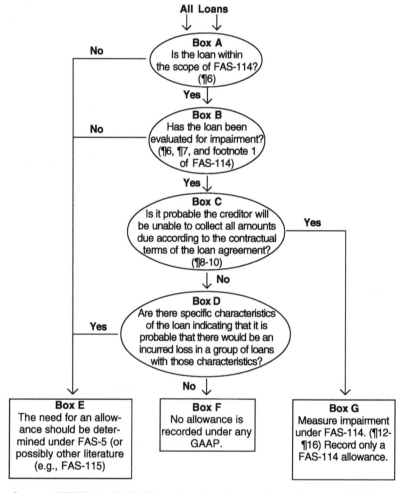

Source: EITF Topic D-80. Reproduced with permission from the FASB.

> **OBSERVATION:** The process of identifying loans for evaluation—that is, deciding which loans to review individually—is subjective and requires a great deal of judgment. A company's procedure has the effect of determining which loans are in the scope of FAS-114 (loans selected that are impaired) and which loans are in the scope of FAS-5 (loans selected that are not individually impaired and loans not selected). Companies should develop a written policy to document this process and apply it consistently.

Determining whether an identified loan is impaired A loan is impaired when, based on current information and events, it is probable that a creditor will be unable to collect all amounts due according to the contractual terms of that loan agreement. (FAS-114, par. 8) Existing "environmental" factors (e.g., existing industry, geographical, economic, and political factors) should be considered when assessing a loan that has been identified for evaluation. (EITF D-80, Q. 7)

> ☞ **PRACTICE POINTER:** A loan would be considered impaired if it is probable that contractual interest payments, principal payments, or both will not be collected as scheduled in the loan agreement. An insignificant delay or shortfall in amount of payments does not meet this condition.

FAS-114 does not specify *how* a creditor should determine that it would be unable to collect all amounts due according to the contractual terms. A creditor should follow its normal loan review process in making that judgment. (FAS-114, par. 8) Identified loans may not be grouped for the purpose of determining whether all of the contractual cash flows are collectible. (EITF D-80, Q. 13)

> **OBSERVATION:** Determining when a loan is impaired is one of the most subjective judgments in accounting. The concept in GAAP is that impairment should be recognized when it is probable that a loss has been incurred based on past events and conditions existing at the balance sheet date. Losses should not be recognized too soon—(for example, anticipating possible or even probable future losses) or too late—(e.g., waiting for a confirming event to occur, such as a bankruptcy, in a period after the loss was probable).

Subsequent events and loan losses Information sometimes becomes available after the balance sheet date but before the financial statements are issued for the period indicating that a loan or group of loans is impaired. If the subsequent event provides evidence of a condition that *existed at the balance sheet date*, for example, a bankruptcy, the impairment should be recognized as of the balance sheet date (a

Type I subsequent event under AU 560). If the subsequent event is a consequence of an event that occurred *after the balance sheet date,* for example, a devastating fire, any impairment on the loan should be reported in the next accounting period; the financial statements about to be issued should not be adjusted (a Type II subsequent event under AU 560). However, disclosure may be required if the loss is material.

Troubled debt restructurings Usually, a loan whose terms are modified in a troubled debt restructuring already will have been identified as impaired before the formal restructuring takes place. However, if a loan was previously evaluated for impairment as part of a group of small balance loans, the creditor should apply FAS-114 to that loan when it is restructured. (FAS-114, par. 9) A creditor's accounting for troubled debt restructurings is discussed later in this chapter.

Measuring impairment under FAS-114 There are three different measurement approaches under FAS-114. The methods are required in certain situations, but may be elected in others. Exhibit 3-5 outlines the parameters for using the three methods.

EXHIBIT 3-5
MEASUREMENT METHODS UNDER FAS-114

Method	Applicability	Comments
Present value of expected future cash flows discounted at the loan's effective Interest rate	Generally required, except as noted below.	Using the effective rate "isolates" the change in value due to credit and does not reflect other changes such as the general level of interest rates.
Observable market price of loan	May be used as a practical expedient.	It is not acceptable to substitute the *fair* value of the loan, that is, by discounting the expected cash flows at a market rate of interest.
Fair value of collateral less costs to sell	May be used as a practical expedient when the loan is collateral dependent. *Must* be used when foreclosure is probable.	A loan is collateral dependent if repayment of the loan is expected to be provided solely by the underlying collateral.

Guidance Applicable to All Three Methods

Recording impairment—If the present value of expected future cash flows (or, alternatively, the observable market price of the loan or the fair value of the collateral) is less than the recorded investment in the loan (including accrued interest, net deferred loan fees or costs, unamortized premium or discount, and any adjustment from fair value hedge accounting), a creditor should recognize impairment by creating a valuation allowance with a corresponding charge to bad-debt expense or by adjusting an existing valuation allowance for the impaired loan with a corresponding charge or credit to bad-debt expense. (FAS-114, par. 13, as amended by FAS-118, and DIG F-4)

Costs to sell—Under all three methods, a creditor should consider estimated costs to sell, on a discounted basis, in the measure of impairment only if those costs are expected to reduce the cash flows available to repay or otherwise satisfy the loan. (FAS-114, par. 13)

> ☛ **PRACTICE POINTER:** If repayment or satisfaction of a loan were dependent only on the operation, rather than the sale, of the collateral, the measure of impairment would not incorporate estimated costs to sell the collateral. (FAS-114, par. 46)

Grouping loans under FAS-114—Some impaired loans have risk characteristics that are unique to an individual borrower, and the creditor should measure impairment on a loan-by-loan basis. However, when impaired loans have risk characteristics in common with other impaired loans, a creditor may aggregate those loans and use historical statistics, such as the average recovery period and average amount recovered, along with a composite effective interest rate to measure impairment of those loans. (FAS-114, par. 12, as amended by FAS-118) Common risk characteristics could include the loan type, term, geographic location, past-due status, and risk classification.

> ☛ **PRACTICE POINTER:** A creditor may select the measurement method on a loan-by-loan basis. However, the method chosen for an individual loan should be applied consistently and a change in method should be justified by a change in circumstances. (EITF D-80, Q. 25)

Recognizing changes in expected future cash flows—Subsequent to the initial measurement of impairment, if there is a significant change (increase or decrease) in the amount or timing of an impaired loan's expected future cash flows, or if actual cash flows are significantly different from the cash flows previously projected, a creditor should remeasure impairment using the same method and adjust the valuation allowance. A recovery may be reflected in the net carrying amount of the loan, but not beyond the recorded investment in the loan. (FAS-114, par. 16)

FAS-114, as amended by FAS-118, does not address how to classify changes in cash flow estimates or the passage of time in the income statement.

> ☞ **PRACTICE POINTER:** Companies generally report these changes either as an adjustment of bad-debt expense, or they distinguish between the passage of time (accretion of a discount, which is reported as interest income) and an adjustment of bad-debt expense. Both methods are permissible and must be disclosed.

Implementation guidance for present value method   The present value amount should be based on an estimate of the expected future cash flows of the impaired loan, discounted at the loan's effective interest rate.

The estimates of expected future cash flows should be the creditor's best estimate based on reasonable and supportable assumptions and projections. All available evidence should be considered in developing the estimate of expected future cash flows. The weight given to the evidence should be commensurate with the extent to which it can be verified objectively. If a creditor estimates a range for either the amount or timing of possible cash flows, the likelihood of the possible outcomes must be considered in determining the best estimate of expected future cash flows. (FAS-114, par. 15)

The expected future cash flows should be discounted using the effective interest rate of the loan. The effective interest rate is the rate of return implicit in the loan (that is, the contractual interest rate adjusted for any net deferred loan fees or costs, premium, or discount existing at the origination or acquisition of the loan and any subsequent adjustments relating to fair value hedge accounting under FAS-133). (DIG F-4) The effective interest rate for a loan restructured in a troubled debt restructuring is based on the *original* contractual rate, not the rate specified in the restructuring agreement. (FAS-114, par. 14) The effective rate for a purchased loan is the rate that equates the investor's estimate of the loan's future cash flows with the purchase price of the loan. (FAS-114, fn. 3)

If the loan's stated interest rate varies based on subsequent changes in an independent factor, such as an index or rate (for example, the prime rate, the London interbank offered rate (LIBOR), or the U.S.

Treasury bill weekly average), that loan's effective interest rate may be calculated based on:

- The factor as it changes over the life of the loan; or
- The rate may be fixed at the rate in effect on the date the loan meets the impairment condition.

The creditor's chosen method should be applied consistently for all loans whose contractual interest rate varies based on subsequent changes in an independent factor. Projections of changes in the factor should not be made for purposes of determining the effective interest rate or estimating expected future cash flows. (FAS-114, par. 14, as amended by FAS-118)

> **OBSERVATION:** The probability-weighted approach described in CON-7 may be used to determine the best estimate of expected future cash flows under FAS-114. However, it would not be appropriate to use a current market rate to discount the cash flows, as would normally be the case under CON-7. Under FAS-114, lenders are required to use the loan's effective rate to discount the revised set of cash flows. CON-7 describes this exercise as a "catch-up approach" rather than a "fresh start" measurement.

Implementation guidance for the observable market price method FAS-114 permits use of an observable market price to measure impairment of a loan as a practical expedient. That method involves a fair value measurement, and as such is subject to the guidance in FAS-157. Chapter 18, "Fair Value Measurements, Fair Value Disclosures, and Other Financial Instrument Disclosures," provides the detailed requirements of FAS-157.

Implementation guidance for fair value of collateral method For loans that are collateral dependent, companies may elect to use the fair value of the collateral to measure impairment as a practical expedient. That method must be used when foreclosure is probable. The fair value of the collateral involves a fair value measurement, and as such is subject to the guidance in FAS-157. Chapter 18, "Fair Value Measurements, Fair Value Disclosures, and Other Financial Instrument Disclosures," provides the detailed requirements of FAS-157. A loan for which foreclosure is probable should continue to be accounted for as a loan until foreclosure actually occurs and the creditor becomes the owner of the underlying collateral. (FAS-114, par. 71)

Foreclosed and repossessed assets should be classified separately in the balance sheet (or included in other assets with footnote disclosure). However, assets that will be used by the entity in its operations, such as inventory, should not be classified separately. (SOP 01-6, par. 13(f))

Impairment of Loans under FAS-5

FAS-5 addresses the impairment of receivables, except when other specific GAAP applies, such as FAS-65 or SOP 01-6 (for loans held for sale), FAS-114, or FAS-115 (for securities and receivables accounted for like securities). FAS-5 requires recognition of a loss when:

1. Information available prior to issuance of the financial statements indicates that it is probable that an asset has been impaired at the date of the financial statements, *and*
2. The amount of the loss can be reasonably estimated.

Losses from uncollectible receivables should be accrued when both of these conditions are met.

> **SEC REGISTRANT ALERT:** EITF Topic D-86 provides guidance about when financial statements are considered to have been "issued." Generally, the SEC staff believes that financial statements are considered issued when they are distributed for general use and reliance, in a format that complies with GAAP (and for annual statements, they include an audit report that states that the auditors have complied with generally accepted auditing standards). The issuance of an earnings release does not constitute the issuance of financial statements because it is not in a format that complies with GAAP and GAAS.

Condition 1 is met if, based on current information and events, it is probable that the enterprise will be unable to collect all contractual principal and interest due according to the contractual terms of the receivable. An insignificant delay or shortfall in amount of payments does not meet this condition. (FAS-5, par. 23, as amended by FAS-114)

Condition 2 depends on several factors including the experience of the creditor, information about the borrower's ability to pay, and assessment of the receivables in light of the current economic environment. When a creditor has no experience of its own, it may refer to the experience of other enterprises in the same business. FAS-5 requires a reasonable basis for quantifying the amount of loss. (FAS-5, par. 23)

> **OBSERVATION:** When a lender lacks experience with a particular type of loan or receivable, it may use industry data to develop impairment estimates. However, the data must be based on loans that are comparable to the creditor's own portfolio to provide the basis for a reasonable estimate.

Grouping loans under FAS-5 Under FAS-5, the impairment recognition conditions may be considered in relation to individual receivables or in relation to groups of similar types of receivables. If the conditions are met, accrual should be made even though the particular receivables that are uncollectible may not be identifiable. (FAS-5, par. 22)

> **OBSERVATION:** Loans may not be grouped for recognition purposes under FAS-114, that is, determining whether a loan is impaired. However, once individual loans have been identified as impaired, they may be grouped for measurement purposes.

Measuring impairment under FAS-5 FAS-5 does not specify a method or methods for measuring the amount of loss. A creditor could assess a group of loans using its historical loss experience in collecting loans in similar situations, such as the typical recovery rate, including the amount and timing. However, the use of historical statistics alone would be inappropriate if the nature of the loans or current environmental conditions differ from those on which the statistics were based. For example, fully collateralized loans should be excluded from the pool, because no loss is expected. Other loans should be divided or stratified into groups of loans with similar risk characteristics. (EITF D-80, Illustration)

Use of historical loss rates When loans are evaluated as a group, impairment is generally measured using the historical loss rate for similar loans over a period of time as a starting point. That historical rate should be reviewed and adjusted for the following factors:

- Trends in loan volume, delinquencies and restructurings
- Levels of and trends in recovery rates for prior charge-offs
- Trends in volume and terms of loans
- Effects of any changes in lending policies, procedures and practices, including the experience and competence of lending officers and management
- National and local economic trends and conditions
- Concentrations of loans in certain industry sectors, geographic locations, and types of borrowers (AICPA Audit and Accounting Guide, Depository and Lending Institutions: Banks and Savings Institutions, Credit Unions, Finance Companies and Mortgage Companies, par. 9.13)

Support for estimates under FAS-5 Any allowance recorded under FAS-5 must be reasonably estimable and supported by an analysis of all available and relevant information about circumstances that exist at the balance sheet date. The allowance for credit losses should be based on observable data, and changes in the allowance should be directionally consistent with changes in the observable data.

If the reasonable estimate of the loss is a range, and some amount within the range appears to be a better estimate than any other amount within the range, that amount should be accrued. If no amount within the range is a better estimate than any other amount, however, the *minimum* amount in the range should be accrued. (FIN-14, par. 3)

> **OBSERVATION:** On the contrary, FAS-114 requires that the single best estimate be used, and does not permit an entity to default to the minimum in a range.

Legal costs   Some companies expense legal costs associated with loss contingencies as incurred, but others include the expected amount of legal fees in the measurement of the loss contingency. Companies are required to disclose their accounting policy for legal costs, if material, and apply that policy consistently. (EITF D-77)

> **OBSERVATION:** Loss amounts calculated under FAS-5 require a great deal of judgment. Both the determination of when a loss should be recognized and the selection of a method to measure the loss are very subjective. The approach for determining the allowance should be well documented and applied consistently from period to period (with documented adjustments for changes in facts and circumstances).

Eligibility of Loans Evaluated under FAS-114 for Accrual under FAS-5

An individual loan specifically identified for evaluation that is *not* considered impaired under FAS-114 may be included in the assessment of the allowance for loan losses under FAS-5 *only if* specific characteristics of the loan indicate that it is probable that there would be an incurred loss in a group of loans with similar characteristics.

- Characteristics or risk factors must be specifically identified to support an accrual for losses that have been incurred but that have not yet reached the point where it is probable that amounts will not be collected on a specific individual loan.
- A creditor should consider all factors and information obtained in the evaluation of the loan's collectibility. For example, a fully collateralized loan should not be included with a group of uncollateralized loans. (EITF D-80, Q. 11)

If a creditor concludes that an individual loan specifically identified for evaluation *is* impaired, the allowance provided for a specific loan under FAS-114 may *not* be supplemented by an additional allowance under FAS-5. The FAS-114 allowance should be the sole measure of impairment for that loan, even if that amount is zero. The measure of impairment could be zero in the following circumstances:

- The lender has used the cost-recovery method or a cash-basis method of recognizing interest income, and the recorded investment in the loan is less than the present value of expected future cash flows.
- The fair value of the collateral on a collateral-dependent loan or the observable market price of a loan might be greater than the recorded investment in the loan.
- The recorded investment of an impaired loan might have been written down (charged-off) to a level that is less than the measure of impairment under FAS-114.

In such cases, no allowance is required under FAS-114, but the loan is still considered impaired. (EITF D-80, Q. 12 and 13)

> **OBSERVATION:**   "Double counting" by applying FAS-114 and then applying FAS-5 to measure the same loss is not in accordance with GAAP. Exhibit 3-4 explains the relationship between the two statements.

Troubled Debt Restructurings

A restructuring of debt is considered a troubled debt restructuring (TDR) if the debtor is experiencing financial difficulties and the creditor grants a concession to the debtor that it would not otherwise consider. In a TDR, a debtor can obtain funds from other sources only at interest rates so high that it cannot afford to pay them, if at all. (FAS-15, par. 7)

Under FAS-15, TDRs generally fall into one or a combination of the following categories:

- The debtor transfers assets (such as receivables from third parties, real estate, or other assets) to satisfy fully or partially a debt (including a transfer resulting from foreclosure or repossession).
- The debtor issues or grants an equity interest to satisfy fully or partially a debt (except as part of convertible debt).
- The creditor agrees to modify the terms of a debt, on an absolute or contingent basis, including one more of the following concessions
  — Reduction of the stated interest rate to a below-market rate.
  — Extension of the maturity date or dates.
  — Forgiveness of a portion of the face amount of the debt.
  — Forgiveness of accrued interest.

> **OBSERVATION:** In a TDR, the creditor's objective is to make the best of a difficult situation. That is, the creditor expects to obtain more cash or other value from the debtor by granting the concession than by not granting it. The term troubled debt restructuring is used even when the debt is fully satisfied and no longer outstanding as a result of the negotiations.

The following transactions are not considered TDRs for accounting purposes even if the debtor is experiencing some financial difficulties (FAS-15, par. 7, except as noted):

- From the creditor's perspective, the fair value of assets accepted by the creditor in satisfaction of the debt at least equals the creditor's recorded investment in the receivable.

- The creditor reduces the interest rate on a loan to reflect a decrease in market interest rates or a decrease in risk in order to maintain a relationship with a debtor that can readily obtain funds from other sources at market rates for nontroubled debtors.

- The debtor issues new marketable debt bearing a market interest rate for nontroubled debt with similar terms in exchange for its old debt.

- A restructuring in connection with bankruptcy proceedings that results in a general restatement of the debtor's liabilities, for example, $.50 on the dollar. (FTB 81-6)

> ☛ **PRACTICE POINTER:** EITF Issue 02-4 provides additional information about when a restructuring is considered a TDR from the debtor's perspective. Refer to Chapter 11, "Extinguishments of Debt," for additional information.

This chapter addresses the *creditor's* accounting for a troubled debt restructuring. Chapter 7, "Calculating Yields on Debt Investments," addresses the creditor's accounting for modifications (including refinancings and restructurings) of debt in nontroubled situations. Chapter 11, "Extinguishments of Debt," addresses the debtor's accounting. The creditor's accounting for a TDR depends on the type of restructuring. Exhibit 3-6 summarizes the creditor's accounting for various types of TDR's under FAS-15, as amended by FAS-114 and FAS-144.[3]

---

[3] In August 2001, the FASB issued Statement No. 144, *Accounting for the Impairment or Disposal of Long-Lived Assets*, which supersedes Statement No. 121, *Accounting for the Impairment of Long-Lived Assets and for Long-Lived Assets to Be Disposed Of*. FAS-144 carries forward several amendments of FAS-15 regarding assets held for sale.

EXHIBIT 3-6
CREDITOR'S ACCOUNTING FOR A TROUBLED DEBT RESTRUCTURING*

Type of TDR	Accounting Method	Loss Calculation	Loss Recognition
Receipt of assets (including equity of the debtor) (FAS-15, par. 28, as amended by FAS-144; FSP FAS 144-1)	Record assets received at fair value. Record long-lived assets held for sale at fair value less costs to sell. Subsequently, account for assets received as if they had been acquired for cash.	(1) Recorded investment in loan less (2) fair value of assets received (less costs to sell, if applicable).	Record loss in income to the extent it is not offset against allowance for uncollectible amounts. Loss recognition is required for any subsequent write-down to fair value less cost to sell under FAS-144. A gain is recognized for any subsequent increase in fair value less cost to sell, but *only* to the extent of the cumulative loss recognized for a write-down of the asset to its fair value less cost to sell. (FSP FAS 144-1) Any gain or loss on the subsequent sale of assets is reported separately. (FAS-15, par. 29)

Type of TDR	Accounting Method	Loss Calculation	Loss Recognition
Modification of terms only; also applies to substitution of debtors when the new debtor is a related party or agent of the old debtor (FAS-15, par. 42)	Apply FAS-114 to identify and measure impairment.	(1) Recorded investment in loan less (2) measure of impairment under FAS-114. Any fees re-ceived should re-duce the recorded investment in the loan.(FAS-91, par. 14)	Record loss in income to cre-ate or adjust the allowance for uncollect-ible amounts to the appropriate level.
Combination: par-tial satisfaction with new assets and modification of remaining re-ceivable** (FAS-15, par. 33, as amended by FAS-114 and FAS-144)	Record assets received at fair value less costs to sell, if applicable; apply FAS-114 to the remain-ing receivable.	(1) Recorded investment in loan less (2) fair value of assets received ceived (less costs to sell) less (3) measure of im-pairment under FAS-114 for re-maining balance. The original effec-tive rate should be used if the mea-sure is based on discounted cash flows. Adjust recorded invest-ment in the loan for any fees received. (FAS-91, par. 14)	Record loss in income to cre-ate or adjust the allowance for uncollect-ible amounts to the appropriate level. Any gain or loss on the subsequent sale of assets is reported separately. (FAS-15, par. 39)
Insubstance fore-closure (creditor receives debtor's assets in place of some or all of re-ceivable) or sub-stitution of debtors involving an un-related third party	Account for as receipt of assets or a combination (partial satis-faction and modification). (FAS-15, par. 34 and 42, as amended by FAS-114)	See applicable guidance above.	See applicable guidance above.

---

*   This Exhibit assumes that the TDR occurred in fiscal years beginning after December 15, 1994. If the restructuring took place before then, the creditor is allowed to apply the original guidance In FAS-15, paragraph 30, only if the loan is *not* considered impaired according to the terms of the restructuring agreement. (FAS-114, par. 27)

** This accounting applies even if the stated terms of the remaining receivable, for example, the interest rate and the maturity date, are not changed in connection with the receipt of assets.

Implementation Issues for TDRs

Legal fees—Legal fees and other direct costs, including direct loan origination costs, incurred by a creditor as part of a troubled debt restructuring should be expensed as incurred. (FAS-15, par. 38, as amended)

Valuation of repossessed real estate—Assume that a seller of real estate finances the buyer's purchase of the property, and profit is being recognized under the full accrual method under FAS-66 (Sales of Real Estate). If the borrower subsequently defaults on the loan and the seller forecloses on the property, the seller-creditor should record the foreclosed property at fair value under FAS-15. However, if the original real estate sale had instead qualified for either the installment or cost recovery method under FAS-66, the repossessed property would be recorded at the lower of the net amount of the loan or the fair value of the property. For this purpose, the net amount of the loan includes the principal and interest receivable that is appropriate to accrue, less any deferred profit on the sale of the property and any related allowance. (EITF 89-14)

Use of zero-coupon bonds in a TDR—In connection with a TDR, a debtor sells the collateral on the loan, which has a fair value less than the creditor's net investment in the related loan, and invests the proceeds in a series of zero-coupon bonds that are received and held by the creditor as collateral for the newly restructured loan. The bonds will mature at a value equal to each year's debt service requirement under the newly restructured terms. The creditor should recognize a loss equal to the amount by which the net investment in the loan exceeds the fair value of the zero-coupon bonds, less costs to sell. (EITF 87-18) The creditor should apply FAS-140 to determine the appropriate accounting for the bonds held as collateral. Refer to Chapter 9, "Securities Lending Arrangements and Other Pledges of Collateral," for additional information.

Substituted debtors in a TDR—In connection with a troubled debt restructuring, a debtor, with the creditor's approval, sells the collateral (real estate) on a contract for deed for a purchase price, the present value of which is less than the creditor's net investment in the related loan. The creditor does not release its lien on the property. The seller-debtor provides 100 percent financing for the third-party purchaser, with payment terms identical to the seller-debtor's obligation under the restructured terms. The third-party purchaser must make the monthly payments directly to the creditor and not to the seller-debtor. The creditor should recognize a loss for the amount by which the net investment in the loan exceeds the fair value of the payments to be received from the purchaser. (EITF 87-19)

Conversion of loan into security—In a debt restructuring, the creditor may receive a debt security issued by the original debtor with a fair value that differs from the creditor's basis in the loan at the date of the debt restructuring. The accounting should be as follows:

- The initial cost basis of the debt security should be its fair value at the date of the restructuring.
- Any excess of the fair value of the security received over the net carrying amount of the loan should be recorded as a recovery on the loan.
- Any shortfall between the fair value of the security received and the net carrying amount of the loan should be recorded as a charge-off to the allowance for credit losses.
- A security received in a restructuring in settlement of a claim for only the past-due interest on a loan should be accounted for in a manner consistent with the entity's policy for recognizing cash received for past-due interest.
- Subsequent to the restructuring, the security should be accounted for according to the provisions of FAS-115. (EITF 94-8)

Credit Losses on Off-Balance-Sheet Commitments

Off-balance-sheet commitments, such as loan commitments, standby letters of credit, and financial guarantees that have not been drawn down, and other similar instruments present the creditor with credit risk. Losses on off-balance-sheet commitments should be recognized and measured in accordance with FAS-5—that is, when it is probable that a loss has occurred at the balance sheet date and the amount of loss is reasonably estimable.

> **AUTHOR'S NOTE:** The term "off-balance-sheet" is no longer technically correct for a financial guarantee or a standby letter of credit that is subject to FIN-45. FIN-45 requires that a liability be recorded for the "stand-ready" portion of a guarantee at the inception of the arrangement. The contingent obligation to provide funding is still subject to FAS-5 and would remain "off-balance-sheet" until payment is

probable and estimable. This chapter should be read in that context. Refer to Chapter 8, "Debt Financing," for additional information.

☛ **PRACTICE POINTER:** If a company makes a commitment to lend, and the potential "borrower" begins to experience financial difficulties, the lender should accrue a loss in accordance with FAS-5—when it is probable and reasonably estimable. The lender should not wait until the borrower exercises the commitment to record a probable loss.

An accrual for credit loss on an off-balance-sheet financial instrument should be recorded as a separate liability, not as part of the allowance for loan losses. Credit losses for off-balance-sheet financial instruments should be deducted from the liability for credit losses in the period in which the liability is settled. (SOP 01-6, par. 8(e))

Chapter 7, "Calculating Yields on Debt Investments," addresses the accounting for fees received from writing credit-related commitments.

☛ **PRACTICE POINTER:** Certain types of credit-related commitments are considered derivatives for accounting purposes. Derivative instruments are carried at fair value on the balance sheet and therefore are not considered "off-balance-sheet commitments." Any credit-related concerns are included in the determination of fair value. Chapter 12, "Introduction to Derivatives," describes the characteristics of contracts that must be accounted for as derivatives.

SEC REGISTRANT ALERT: The allowance for loan losses should not include amounts provided for losses on off-balance-sheet items, for example, credit derivatives used as economic hedges of loans. Loss provisions not related to interest income should be recorded in other appropriate categories of income or expense. Direct transfers of amounts between the allowance for loan losses and other credit loss allowances are not appropriate, except for a circumstance in which an off-balance-sheet loan commitment becomes an outstanding loan. (March and December 2005 Current Accounting and Disclosure Issues in the Division of Corporation Finance, SEC)

Charge-Offs of Loans

A loan should be charged off, that is, written down, in the period in which the loan is deemed uncollectible. Credit losses from charge-offs of loans and trade receivables, which may be for all or part of a particular loan or trade receivable, should be deducted from the allowance for loan losses. Recoveries of loans and trade receivables previously charged off should be recorded when received. (SOP 01-6, par. 8(d)) Practices differ in the way recoveries are recorded—some industries typically credit recoveries directly to earnings while financial institutions typically credit the allowance for loan losses for recoveries. (SOP 01-6, fn. 9)

> **OBSERVATION:** AcSEC decided not to prescribe a single method for recording recoveries because the combination of this practice and the convention of frequent evaluation of the allowance for loan losses results in the same credit to earnings in an indirect manner.

SEC Staff Accounting Bulletin No. 102, Selected Loan Loss Allowance Methodology and Documentation Issues

In recent years, the SEC has challenged the accounting for loan loss allowances that did not appear to respond to improvements or deteriorations in market conditions. The SEC identified changes in loan loss reserves as a way that companies can "manage earnings." SAB 102 makes it absolutely clear that the SEC expects lenders to follow a rigorous, methodical approach to estimating loan losses, and to adjust the allowance to respond to changes in overall market conditions and specific factors that affect the entity's portfolio.

EXHIBIT 3-7
REPORTING CREDIT-RELATED LOSSES

	Reported In:	
Nature of Credit Losses	**Balance Sheet**	**Income Statement**
Impairment of loans and receivable	Allowance for loan losses	Provision for bad-debt expense
Charge-offs for uncollectible amounts	Loan balance reduction	Provision for bad-debt expense (or against a previously recognized allowance)
Probable losses on off-balance sheet commitments	Other liabilities	Provision for bad-debtexpense*

*There is no clear guidance on how to classify losses on off-balance-sheet commitments. Note that fees received for various types of commitments are classified as other income or interest income, depending on facts and circumstances. See Chapter 7, "Calculating Yields on Debt Investments."

> **OBSERVATION:** In many cases, the SEC maintained that loan loss allowances were too big, not too small. This debunked the long-held belief of some bankers and accountants that a loan loss

allowance can never be too big (that is, it is safe to err on the side of conservatism). The SEC views over-reserving as a form of "saving for a rainy day," which is not in accordance with GAAP.

SAB-102 sets forth the SEC's expectations for developing and documenting a methodology for identifying impaired loans, measuring impairment on individual loans, and estimating loan losses on groups of loans. The SAB does not set new accounting standards, but it prescribes numerous documentation requirements that affect whether certain accounting requirements are properly applied. The SAB is very detailed—registrants engaged in lending activities should carefully review the entire SAB and make sure they are in compliance with all of the requirements (available on the SEC's website, www.sec.gov/interps/account/sab102.htm).

The SAB applies to all SEC registrants, not just banks. The SAB is generally consistent with the Policy Statement on the allowance for loan and lease losses (ALLL) published by the FFIEC on July 6, 2001 (see the section on "Regulatory Considerations" later in this chapter).

A lender must include the following key elements to substantiate a systematic methodology for loan loss accounting:

- Conduct a detailed review of the entire loan portfolio regularly.
- Identify loans to be evaluated individually under FAS-114 and segment the remaining portfolio into groups that have similar risk characteristics for evaluation under FAS-5.
- Consider all current relevant factors that affect collectibility, including the risks of certain types of lending, collateral values, and existing environmental factors.
- Base the estimate on reliable, current data and document the rationale followed and the conclusions reached for each loan or group of loans including the period over which the loss occurred, the rationale behind any groupings and details about a loan-grading system, if applicable.
- Documentation should address both (1) loans identified and measured under FAS-114, including why one of the three acceptable measurement techniques was selected, and (2) loans reviewed and measured under FAS-5, including the rationale for grouping loans, determining a loss rate, the effect of qualitative factors, and support for the best estimate within a range.
- Adjustments of the initial estimate of the allowance (for example, by credit committee reviews) must be substantiated, documented, and reviewed by management and made available to the independent accountants.
- Documentation should include a trail that would allow an examiner to relate the findings of the loan review process with

the amount, if any, recorded as an allowance or charge-off in the financial statements.

Deferred Tax Consequences

The allowance for loan losses (and other loss contingencies) can give rise to a temporary difference, depending on how an entity deducts loan losses for tax purposes. For larger institutions that are covered under Internal Revenue Code Section 166, there is no bad-debt reserve for tax purposes and, therefore, the entire allowance for credit losses in the financial statements is a temporary difference. In those cases, the allowance for loan losses generally gives rise to a deferred tax asset (expense is recognized for book before it is deducted on the tax return). FAS-109 addresses the deferred tax consequences of temporary differences.

Income Recognition after Impairment Recognition (Nonaccrual Loans)

Generally, interest income should not be accrued if collectibility of principal or interest is doubtful. FAS-118 requires disclosure of how an entity recognizes interest on impaired loans (for example, the *cost-recovery method* or the cash-basis method). Several industries have developed practices for putting loans on nonaccrual status; often these practices are based on regulatory guidelines.

Deferred net fees or costs should not be amortized when a loan is on nonaccrual status. (FAS-91, par. 17)

> ☞ **PRACTICE POINTER:** The federal banking agencies have adopted guidelines that banks generally should not accrue interest on any asset (1) that is maintained on a cash basis because of deterioration of the borrower's financial condition, (2) for which full payment of principal and interest is not expected, or (3) upon which principal or interest has been in default for a period of 90 days or more unless the asset is both well secured and in the process of collection. (FFIEC, Call Report Instructions, Glossary) The National Credit Union Association also has developed guidelines for nonaccrual loans.

Sales and Other Transfers of Loans

FAS-140 addresses when a transfer of a loan (or any other financial asset) should be accounted for as a sale versus a borrowing. The term "transfer" includes the following types of transactions that commonly involve loans (and receivables):

- Sales
- Participations

- Securitizations
- Factoring arrangements

Generally, a transaction that purports to be a sale and where the seller has *no* continuing involvement with the transferred security is accounted for as a sale. Continuing involvement includes recourse, servicing, commitments or options to repurchase, and pledges of collateral. The "Background" section of this chapter provides cross-references to chapters that address various types of transfers of financial assets and transfers of servicing rights.

Decision to Sell a Loan Held for Investment

Once a decision has been made to sell mortgage or nonmortgage loans or trade receivables not previously classified as held for sale, the loans should be transferred into the held-for-sale category and carried at the lower of cost or market value. At the time of the transfer, any amount by which cost exceeds market value should be accounted for as a valuation allowance. (SOP 01-6, par. 8(c))

> **OBSERVATION:** This accounting differs from the accounting for securities under FAS-115. Under FAS-115, when a decision is made to sell a security, the security is not transferred into a different category. However, if the entity does not expect the fair value of the security to recover prior to the expected time of sale, the security is written down to its fair value (through a charge-off, not an allowance). (FAS-115 Q&A, par. 48)

> ☞ **PRACTICE POINTER:** FAS-65 provides specific guidance for mortgages held for sale that are transferred into the held for investment category. See the section on mortgage banking activities later in this chapter.

> **SEC REGISTRANT ALERT:** Loans are recognized as *not* held for sale when management has the intent and ability to hold the loan for the foreseeable future. Once a decision has been made to sell a loan not previously classified as held for sale, the loan should be transferred into the held-for-sale classification and reported at LOCOM. Continuing to report such loans on an adjusted cost basis is inappropriate because it may delay recognition of losses due to declines in fair values. The SEC staff indicated that a positive intent to sell is not required for loans to be classified as held for sale.
>
> (March 2005 Current Accounting and Disclosure Issues in the Division of Corporation Finance, SEC, and December 2005 Presentation, *Current Developments in the Division of Corporation Finance*, at the National Conference on Current SEC and PCAOB Developments)

Sale of Bad-Debt Recovery Rights (EITF 86-8)

A lender may sell without recourse its right to future recoveries from loans that it has charged off. The buyer is entitled to recoveries equal to the purchase price plus a market rate of interest on the unrecovered purchase price. The EITF concluded that the transaction is a secured borrowing, and no gain should be recognized at the date of the transaction. The EITF did not address whether the proceeds should be considered in determining the loan loss allowance.

> **OBSERVATION:** This transaction is not analyzed under FAS-140 because, after the charge-off, the loan is unrecognized. FAS-140 only addresses transfers of recognized financial assets.

Presentation in the Statement of Cash Flows

Cash outflows from making loans and inflows from collecting principal on loans are generally reported gross as investing activities. (FAS-95, par. 15) Cash receipts resulting from sales of loans that were not specifically acquired for resale should be classified as investing cash inflows regardless of a change in the purpose for holding those loans. (FAS-102, par. 9) However, the following types of transactions are reported as operating activities:

- Receipts from collection or sale of accounts and notes receivable from customers arising from sales of goods or services. (FAS-95, par. 22)
- Acquiring and disposing of loans that are acquired specifically for resale, and that are carried at LOCOM (or market value in connection with specialized industry practice). (FAS-102, par. 10(b))
- Interest earned on loans. (FAS-95, par. 22(b))

> **SEC REGISTRANT ALERT:** A registrant that decides to sell a loan not previously classified as held for sale should follow the required classification in FAS-102 for cash flows related to loans held for resale and held for short periods of time. Cash flows related to such loans should be classified as operating.
>
> Additionally, registrants should follow the required classification in FAS-102 for cash flows related to loans that were originated or purchased specifically for resale and are held for short periods of time. The classification of cash flows is affected by whether the loan resulted from the sale of goods or services or whether it was initially classified as held for sale or later transferred to the held-for-sale category.

The guidance from the SEC staff states that the following be classified as operating:

- Cash flows from the sale of short- and long-term notes receivables arising from the sales of goods or services
- Cash flows resulting from the acquisitions and sales of loans that are acquired for resale and carried at LOCOM

The guidance states that the following should be classified as investing:

- For manufacturing companies, only loans that do not result from inventory sales to the company's customers that are acquired with the intention of holding for the foreseeable future
- For finance companies, all loans that are acquired with the intention of holding for the foreseeable future

No cash inflows or outflows should be reported for the exchange of loans or trade receivables for interests that continue to be held in securitized loans, but the exchange may need to be disclosed as a noncash investing activity.

(March 2005 Current Accounting and Disclosure Issues in the Division of Corporation Finance, SEC, and December 2005 Presentation, *Current Developments in the Division of Corporation Finance*, at the National Conference on Current SEC and PCAOB Developments)

Exception for Certain Financial Institutions

Banks, savings institutions, and credit unions are allowed to report net amounts of cash receipts and cash payments for loans made to customers and principal collections of loans. (FAS-104, par. 7(a)) Refer to Chapter 1, "Cash and Cash Equivalents," for additional information.

Mortgage Banking Model under FAS-65

FAS-65 provides a special model for entities involved in mortgage banking activities. Mortgage banking activities consist primarily of two separate but related activities:

1. Origination or acquisition of mortgage loans and the sale of the loans to permanent investors and
2. Subsequent long-term servicing of the loans.

This chapter addresses the accounting for the loans before they are sold. The "Background" section of this chapter provides cross-references to related accounting topics.

☛ **PRACTICE POINTER:** FAS-65 applies to all entities engaged in "mortgage banking activities," not just entities calling themselves mortgage banks. (EITF D-2)

Mortgage Loans Held for Sale (FAS-65)

Mortgage loans held for sale include all mortgages that do not qualify as held for investment, not just mortgages for which the entity has the positive intent to sell. Mortgage loans held for sale are reported at the lower of cost or market value (LOCOM), determined as of the balance sheet date. The amount by which cost exceeds market value should be accounted for as a valuation allowance. Changes in the valuation allowance should be included in the determination of net income of the period in which the change occurs. (FAS-65, par. 4)

☛ **PRACTICE POINTER:** Mortgage bankers must account for commitments to originate mortgages that will be held for sale as derivatives under FAS-133, but commitments to originate mortgages that will be held for investment are excluded. (A potential borrower does not have to account for a loan commitment as a derivative.) Commitments to buy and sell existing loans must be evaluated under the definition of a derivative to determine whether FAS-133 applies. (FAS-133, pars. 6(c) and 10(i), as amended, and DIG C-13)

Components of the cost basis Capitalized mortgage servicing rights associated with the purchase or origination of mortgage loans are *not* included in the cost of mortgage loans for the purpose of determining the lower of cost or market value. (FAS-65, par. 10, as amended by FAS-140)

The loan's "cost" basis used in lower-of-cost-or-market accounting should reflect the effect of any adjustments of its carrying amount made as part of fair value hedge accounting under FAS-133. (FAS-133, par. 529(a))

Determining fair value for mortgage loans The fair value of mortgage loans should be determined by type of loan.

1. Fair value must be determined separately for residential (one- to four-family dwellings) and commercial mortgage loans.
2. Lower of cost or fair value may be calculated either on an individual loan basis or in the aggregate for each type of loan.
3. Fair value for loans subject to investor purchase commitments (committed loans) and loans held on a speculative basis (uncommitted loans) should be determined separately as follows:

    a. *Committed Loans:*   Mortgage loans covered by investor commitments should be based on the fair values of the loans.

    b. *Uncommitted Loans:* Fair value for uncommitted loans should be based on the market in which the mortgage banking enterprise normally operates. That determination would include consideration of the following:

        (1)   Market prices and yields sought by the mortgage banking enterprise's normal market outlets;

        (2)   Quoted Government National Mortgage Association (GNMA) security prices or other public market quotations for long-term mortgage loan rates; and

        (3)   Federal Home Loan Mortgage Corporation (FHLMC) and Federal National Mortgage Association (FNMA) current delivery prices. (FAS-65, par. 9, as amended by FAS-133, par. 529(b) and FAS-159, Par. E10)

Transactions with affiliates When a mortgage banking entity decides to sell a mortgage loan to an *affiliate*, the carrying amount of the mortgages should be adjusted to the lower of cost or market value. The decision date should be determined based on, at a minimum, formal approval by an authorized representative of the purchaser, issuance of a commitment to purchase the loans, and acceptance of the commitment by the selling enterprise. The amount of any adjustment should be charged to income. (FAS-65, par. 12)

If a particular class of mortgage loans or all loans are originated exclusively for an affiliate, the originator is acting as an agent of the affiliated enterprise, and the loan transfers should be accounted for at the originator's acquisition cost. Such an agency relationship, however, would not exist in the case of "right of first refusal" contracts or similar types of agreements or commitments if the originator retains all the risks associated with ownership of the loans. (FAS-65, par. 13)

Transfers between categories Mortgage loans transferred from held for sale to held for investment should be transferred at the lower of cost or market value on the transfer date. (FAS-65, par. 6) Any difference between the carrying amount of the loan and its outstanding principal balance should be recognized as an adjustment to yield using the interest method. (FAS-91, par. 27(a))

Mortgage loans held for investment should be transferred into the held-for-sale category and carried at the lower of cost or market value when a decision is made to sell the loan. At the time of the transfer, any amount by which cost exceeds market value should be accounted for as a valuation allowance. (SOP 01-6, par. 8(c)).

EXHIBIT 3-8
TRANSFERS BETWEEN LOAN CATEGORIES

Transfer

From	To	Accounting Treatment
Held for investment	Held for sale	• Transfer when decision to sell is made • Record a valuation allowance for any excess of cost over market • Carry at LOCOM until sold
Held for sale	Held for investment	• Transfer at the lower of cost or market • Amortize any difference between the carrying amount and par as a yield adjustment

---

SEC REGISTRANT ALERT: The SEC staff provided views on the classification of loans held for sale and of cash flows related to such loans in the Statement of Cash Flows. Refer to the SEC Registrant Alerts in sections *Sales and Other Transfers of Loans* and *Presentation in the Statement of Cash Flows* in this chapter for further details.

Securitization of mortgages held for sale   After the securitization of a mortgage loan held for sale, any retained mortgage-backed securities (MBS) should be classified and accounted for under FAS-115 as follows (FAS-134, par. 3):

- MBS committed to be sold before or during the securitization process: Required to be classified as trading
- Uncommitted MBS: Classify as either held-to-matority (HTM), available-for-sale (AFS), or trading in accordance with FAS-115

Chapter 6, "Securitizations," discusses other aspects of securitizations, including the interplay with FAS-133 (derivatives) and consolidation of special-purpose entities used to effect a securitization.

Balance sheet classification   Mortgage banking enterprises using either a classified or unclassified balance sheet must distinguish between (a) mortgage loans held for sale and (b) mortgage loans held for long-term investment. (FAS-65, par. 28)

DISCLOSURES

IMPORTANT NOTICE
FASB PROJECT ON LOAN DISCLOSURES

In January 2007, the FASB began a project on disclosures related to the allowance for credit losses associated with financing receivables (loans and finance leases subject to FAS-13). The project was added to address the perceived need for improved disclosures related to the determination of the allowance for credit losses due to the diversity in practice related to the application of FAS-5 and FAS-114. The project will reconsider existing disclosure requirements for credit quality of financing receivables and the allowance and develop new disclosures related to the allowance for credit losses including information about credit quality, credit risk exposures, and potentially more transparency related to an entity's accounting policies. An Exposure Draft is expected to be issued as early as the third quarter of 2007. Readers should monitor developments in this project.

Numerous disclosures are required about loans and other receivables. Disclosures about accounting policies, certain types of transactions, and impaired loans are discussed below. Other disclosures involving loans are discussed in the chapters cross-referenced in the "Background" section of this chapter.

For loans measured at fair value under the fair value option, FAS-159 requires specific disclosures as outlined in Chapter 19, "The Fair Value Option for Financial Instruments." One objective is to provide information about nonperforming loans that would have been disclosed if the fair value option was not elected. In addition, FAS-157 requires disclosures about fair value measurements that are incremental to other existing disclosure requirements. Chapter 18, "Fair Value Measurements, Fair Value Disclosures, and Other Financial Instrument Disclosures" outlines those disclosure requirements.

Accounting Policies and Other Disclosures about Loans

Exhibit 3-9 provides a summary of the required disclosures about significant accounting policies for loans and about certain transactions involving loans.

EXHIBIT 3-9
GENERAL DISCLOSURES ABOUT LOANS

Disclosure	Applicable GAAP
The basis of accounting (cost or LOCOM) for loans and trade receivable	SOP 01-6, par. 13(a)(1); FAS-65, par. 29
Method for determining LOCOM for loans and receivables held for sale (aggregate or individual)	SOP 01-6, par. 13(a)(2), FAS-65, par. 29
Description of the method(s) used to determine and significant factors affecting:	SOP 01-6, par. 13(b)
• Allowance for loan losses • Allowance for doubtful accounts • Liability for off-balance-sheet credit losses and • Related provisions	
Policy for placing loans and receivables on non-accrual status, recording any payments received, and resuming accrual of interest*	SOP 01-6, par. 13(c)(1); also FAS-118, par. 6(i)(b)
Policy for charging off uncollectible loans and receivables	SOP 01-6, par. 13(c)(2)
Policy for determining past due or delinquent status	SOP 01-6, par. 13(c)(3)
Related party loans—amounts due, terms, manner of settlement	FAS-57, par. 2(d)

* Includes acquired loans in the scope of SOP 03-3, if impaired.

☛ **PRACTICE POINTER:** Paragraph 13 of SOP 01-6 applies to entities that engage in lending activities, including mortgage bankers. Many of the disclosures above would relate primarily to the held for investment portfolio of a mortgage banker.

SEC REGISTRANT ALERT: Because the determination of the allowance for loan losses must be based on past events and current economic conditions, disclosures that explain the allowance in terms of potential, possible, or future losses rather than probable losses suggest a lack of compliance with GAAP and are inappropriate. (March 2005 Current Accounting and Disclosure Issues in the Division of Corporation Finance, SEC)

SEC REGISTRANT ALERT: The SEC staff has provided specific views on the following disclosure issues related to loans: allowances for loan losses, disclosures related to loans/receivables held for sale, and disclosures about residential loan products. Because the determination of the allowance for loan losses must be based on past events and current economic conditions, disclosures that explain the allowance in terms of potential, possible, or future losses rather than on probable losses suggest a lack of compliance with GAAP and are inappropriate.

A registrant that intends to sell loans and receivables should consider the need for a clarifying disclosure that identifies the amount of loans/receivables held for sale; explains how it determines which loans/receivables are initially accounted for as held for sale or are later transferred to the held-for-sale classification; describes the method it uses to determine the LOCOM amount for loans/receivables held for sale; and reconciles the changes in loans/receivables held-for-sale balances to amounts presented in the cash flow statement.

Lenders that offer residential loan products with features that increase credit risk exposure (for example, option adjustable-rate mortgages) should provide detailed disclosures in the MD&A to provide a complete picture of the lender's credit risk. The SEC specifies the following disclosures that should be considered:

- Disaggregated information about residential mortgage loans with features that may result in higher credit risk

- A description of risk mitigation activities used to reduce exposure to credit risk related to residential mortgage loans

- Trends related to such loans that are reasonably likely to have a material affect on net interest income after the provision for loan loss

The SEC staff provides some examples for each general disclosure.

(March and December 2005 Current Accounting and Disclosure Issues in the Division of Corporation Finance, SEC)

Quantitative Disclosures about Impaired Loans

Recorded Investment

FAS-118 requires that certain disclosures be made about the recorded investment in a loan that is considered impaired, including certain troubled debt restructurings. Exhibit 3-10 summarizes the required disclosures.

EXHIBIT 3-10
DISCLOSURES ABOUT THE RECORDED INVESTMENT
IN AN IMPAIRED LOAN

Description of Loans	Required Disclosures about the Recorded Investment in Loans That Meet the Definition of an Impaired Loan		
	(A) The Total Recorded Investment in the Impaired Loans*	**(B)** The Amount of the Recorded Investment in (A) for Which There Is a Related Allowance For Credit Losses*	**(C)** The Amount of the Recorded Investment in (A) for Which There Is No Related Allowance for Credit Losses*
1. Loans that meet the definition of an impaired loan and that have not been charged off fully	Included. The amount disclosed in (A) must equal the sum of (B) and (C).	Included if there is a related allowance for credit losses.	Included if there is no related allowance for credit losses.
2. Loans that meet the definition of an impaired loan and that have been charged off fully	Excluded. The recorded investment and allowance for credit losses are equal to zero.		
3. Loans restructured in a troubled debt restructuring	May be excluded in years after the restructuring if (a) the new interest rate is ≥ the market rate for a new receivable with comparable risk and (b) the loan is not impaired based on the terms specified by the restructuring agreement. Otherwise, refer to items 1 and 2 above.		
4. Large groups of smaller-balance homogeneous loans that are collectively evaluated for impairment and other loans that are excluded from the scope of this section	Excluded unless restructured in a troubled debt restructuring (refer to item 3 above).		

Adapted from FAS-118, par. 6(i).

---

* Includes acquired loans in the scope of SOP 03-3, if impaired.

Other Quantitative Disclosures about Impaired Loans

For each period for which the results of operations are presented, the following should be disclosed (FAS-118, par. 6(i)):

- The average recorded investment in impaired loans for the period.
- The amount of interest income recognized on impaired loans during the period (with separate disclosure of the amount recognized on a cash basis, unless not practical).
- The following information about the total allowance for credit losses determined under FAS-114 and FAS-5

    — The beginning and ending balance of the allowance.

    — Additions charged to income from operations'.

    — Direct write-downs charged against the allowance.

    — Recoveries of amounts previously charged off.

- For TDRs, all disclosures applicable to impaired loans, plus the amount of any commitments to lend additional funds to borrowers whose debt has been restructured in a TDR. (FAS-15, par. 40(b))

    SEC REGISTRANT ALERT: SEC registrants that are bank holding companies (or engaged in similar activities) must also provide numerous disclosures about loans and the allowance for loan losses as part of the 1934 Act Industry Guide 3. The SEC is currently revising Guide 3 to reflect subsequent developments in accounting standards. The timetable is uncertain.

Loan splitting When a loan is restructured in a TDR into two (or more) loan agreements, the restructured loans should be considered *separately* when assessing the applicability of the disclosures in paragraphs 20(a) and 20(c) of FAS-114, as amended by FAS-118, in years after the restructuring because they are legally distinct from the original loan. The creditor would continue to base its *measure* of loan impairment on the contractual terms specified by the original loan agreement in accordance with paragraphs 11 through 16 of FAS-114, as amended. (EITF 96-22)

    SEC REGISTRANT ALERT: If impaired loans are restructured into multiple loans through troubled debt restructurings or another form of restructuring that does not involve concessions, the SEC staff believes that registrants should present clearly the resulting impact of the multiple loan structures on the loan portfolio and the allowance for loan losses. This discussion could include the following, if applicable, for each reported period:

- The aggregate balance of restructured loans and the volume of the restructuring activity.

- The nature of any concessions on restructured loans and the reasons for renegotiating loans into multiple loan structures.

- The impact of loan restructurings on trends in the past-due, nonaccrual, and impaired loan disclosures.

- The impact of loan restructurings on the allowance for loan losses on current period earnings.

SEC Division of Corporation Finance, Current Accounting and Disclosure Issues, Section II.L provides additional information.

Nonaccrual and past due loans   The recorded investment of loans (and trade receivables) that are on nonaccrual status or are past due 90 days and still are accruing interest should be disclosed as of each balance sheet date. For trade receivables that do not accrue interest until a specific period of time has elapsed, the receivable is considered "nonaccrual" when accrual is suspended after the receivable becomes past due. (SOP 01-6, par. 13(g))

Certain loans acquired in a transfer   In addition to certain disclosures for impaired loans required by paragraphs 20(a) and 20(b) of FAS-114, as amended by FAS-118, entities that have acquired loans that are within the scope of SOP 03-3 should disclose the following:

- The outstanding balance and carrying amount at the beginning and end of the period

- The amount of accretable yield at the beginning and end of the period, with a reconciliation for additions, accretion, loan disposals, and reclassifications to or from nonaccretable difference during the period

- For loans acquired during the period, the contractually required payments receivable, cash flows expected to be collected, and fair value at the acquisition date

- For loans on nonaccrual status, the carrying amount at acquisition (if acquired during the reporting period) and carrying amount at the end of the period

- The amount of any an impairment loss (expense recognized under paragraph 8(a) of SOP 03-3)

- Any reductions of the allowance established after acquisition of the loan due to an increase in the present value of cash flows expected to be collected (recognized under paragraph 8(b) of SOP 03-3)

- The allowance for uncollectible accounts at the beginning and end of the period (SOP 03-3)

Off-Balance-Sheet Credit Risk

Finance companies, banks and savings institutions, mortgage banks, and credit unions that hold financial instruments with off-balance-sheet credit risk should disclose the following information:

- The face or contract amount.
- The nature and terms, including, at a minimum, a discussion of the credit and market risk of those instruments, cash requirements of those instruments and accounting policy.
- The entity's policy for requiring collateral or other security to support financial instruments subject to credit risk, information about the entity's access to that collateral or other security, and the nature and a brief description of the collateral or other security supporting those financial instruments.

Examples of activities and financial instruments with off-balance-sheet credit risk include loan commitments, letters of credit, financial guarantees, recourse obligations, and note issuance facilities. (SOP 01-6, par. 14(m))

> ☛ **PRACTICE POINTER:** Although this requirement of SOP 01-6 is limited to certain types of financial institutions, FIN-45 requires similar disclosures for any type of entity that guarantees the indebtedness of another party, directly or indirectly. Refer to Chapter 8, "Debt Financing," for additional information.

Miscellaneous Issues Involving Loans

Foreign Debt-Equity Swaps

AICPA Practice Bulletin 4 addresses the accounting for exchanges of loans to debtors in financially troubled countries for equity investments in companies in the same countries. Typically, investors in U.S. dollar-denominated debt of a particular country convert that debt into equity investments in the same country, based on the official exchange rate at the time of the transaction. (A discount from the official exchange rate is often charged on the transaction.) Debt/equity swaps should be accounted for at fair value at the date on which both parties agree to the transaction. Any loss resulting from the exchange should be charged to the allowance for loan losses, including any discount from the official exchange rate that is charged as a transaction fee. (Other transaction costs should be charged to expense as incurred.) Gains or recoveries resulting from the exchange should not be recognized until the equity investment is realized in unrestricted cash or cash equivalents. PB-4 provides guidance on determining fair values of debt/equity swap transactions.

Recording Interest on LDC Loans

AICPA Practice Bulletin 5 addresses how to record receipt of interest payments on nonaccrual loans to borrowers in financially troubled countries (also called "LDC loans," with LDC standing for less developed countries) when the debtor resumes payment of principal and interest. When a country becomes current as to principal and interest, and assuming the allowance for loan losses is adequate, the creditor may recognize interest receipts as income.

Mortgage Loan Payment Modifications (EITF 84-19)

EITF Issue 84-19 discusses a loan modification whereby the borrower agrees to increase his mortgage payments for a specified period, at the conclusion of which the lender forgives a portion of the remaining principal on the loan. The borrower may terminate the arrangement at any time but receives no principal reduction if he makes less than 12 consecutive increased payments. Assuming it is probable that the borrower will continue to make the increased payments for the specified period, the EITF concluded that the expense relating to the partial forgiveness should be accrued over the period of increased payments.

Accounting When Investor Holds Equity Method and Other Forms of Investments

EITF Issues 98-13, 99-10, and 02-18 address loss recognition under the equity method when the investor holds voting common stock and other forms of investment in the same issuer, including loans. Chapter 2, "Investments in Debt and Equity Securities," provides an overview of the order in which APB-18, FAS-115, and FAS-114 are to be applied in that situation (refer to the section on "Miscellaneous Issues Involving Securities").

Government Guarantee of Foreign Loans with Credit Risk and Transfer Risk (EITF Topic D-4)

EITF Topic D-4 addresses a situation in which the Argentine government had control over the currency transfer process as private-sector Argentine borrowers remitted payments on their loans to U.S. lenders. Instead of remitting currency, the Argentine government gave U.S. lenders dollar-denominated 10-year notes backed by the Argentine government. A majority of the AICPA Banking Committee believed that the transaction did not warrant accounting recognition but that the Argentine government notes should be assessed for collectibility.

Certain Collateralized Loans (Other Than TDRs)

Loans that are acquired primarily for the rewards of ownership of the underlying collateral (for example, using the collateral in operations or significantly improving the collateral for resale) should be accounted for as loans until the creditor is in possession of the collateral. Income should not be accrued on such loans. (SOP 03-3, pars. B22 and B35)

REGULATORY CONSIDERATIONS

The following guidance issued by the federal banking agencies may be relevant to the accounting for loans under GAAP:

- Interagency Guidance on Credit Card Account Management and Loss Allowance Practices (January 8, 2003), which addresses loan loss methodologies and accounting for recoveries.
- Policy Statement on Allowance for Loan and Lease Losses Methodologies and Documentation for Banks and Savings Institutions (July 6, 2001), which is consistent with SAB-102. It also includes numerous illustrations of implementation practices that institutions may find useful for enhancing their own allowance processes. Also see the May 28, 2002, Policy Statement of the NCUA. (National Credit Union Administration).
- Joint Interagency Letter to Financial Institutions (March 10, 1999), which discusses bank allowance policy issues. (Included as part of EITF Topic D-80.)
- The Uniform Retail Credit Classification and Account Management Policy (February 10, 1999), which describes how institutions are to review and classify retail credit loans and residential mortgage loans, including when to recognize charge-offs. These guidelines should be incorporated into a lender's "normal loan review procedures" under FAS-114.
- The Interagency Guidelines on Subprime Lending (March 1, 1999), which includes, among other things, a discussion of how default risk may be measured.
- Joint Interagency Letter to Financial Institutions (March 1, 2004), which identifies the current sources of GAAP and supervisory guidance related to the allowance for loan losses applicable for financial institutions.
- Interagency advisory on accounting and reporting for commitments to originate and sell mortgage loans (May 2005). The advisory provides accounting and regulatory reporting guidance for derivative loan commitments (that is, commitments to originate mortgage loans that will be held for resale)

and forward sales commitments (that is, commitments to sell mortgage loans) that meet the definition of a derivative. The advisory discusses characteristics that should be considered in determining whether mandatory delivery contracts and best efforts contracts are derivatives. In addition, it addresses guidance that should be considered in determining fair values of such instruments and illustrates one approach that may be used to value commitments to originate mortgage loans that will be held for resale.

- Interagency guidance on nontraditional mortgage product risks (September 2006), addressing products such as interest-only loans and "payment option" adjustable rate mortgages, where a borrower has several payment options including a potential for negative amortization. The guidance was developed to clarify how institutions can offer nontraditional mortgage products in a safe and sound manner, and in a way that clearly discloses the risks that borrowers may assume. Among other things, the guidance addresses underwriting criteria and risk management practices to assist institutions in managing the heightened risks associated with offering such products.

- Final guidance issued by the FFIEC (December 2006) addressing concentrations in commercial real estate lending and sound risk management practices. The purpose of the guidance is to reinforce sound risk management practices for institutions with high and increasing concentrations of commercial real estate loans on their balance sheets. The guidance identifies institutions with commercial real estate loan concentrations that are subject to cyclical commercial real estate markets and provide guidance on risk management practices and capital considerations appropriate for the risks arising from those concentrations.

- Proposed guidance issued by the FFIEC (March 2005) that would replace the current categories for classification of commercial credit exposures (special mention, substandard, doubtful) with a framework that would focus on (1) borrower creditworthiness and (2) estimated loss severity related to nonaccrual loans or loans that have been partially or fully charged-off in an event of borrower default. (Readers should monitor developments on this proposed FFIEC guidance.)

Refer to the individual regulators' websites for additional information. In addition, http://www.fdic.gov/regulations/resources/call/crinst/601rc-r.pdf provides complete instructions about what portions of the allowance for loan losses may be included in regulatory capital.

Statutory accounting principles for insurance companies differ from GAAP in some respects, including the accounting for impaired loans. For example, when impairment is recognized on a mortgage loan, it is measured using the collateral value less costs to sell, not using the FAS-114 present value method. In addition, loan origination fees and costs are not accounted for under FAS-91 (SSAP No. 37) and cash flows are not reported under FAS-95 (SSAP No. 69). Practitioners should be alert to differences between SAP and GAAP.

AUDIT CONSIDERATIONS

There are several areas of accounting for loans that are subjective and pose significant audit risk. They include the classification of loans, when to cease recognition of interest income, and recognition and measurement of impairment. The allowance for credit losses is an estimate that involves substantial judgment. Reported earnings are directly affected by the process management uses to identify and measure impaired loans. Audit risk is heightened by the fact that the relevant accounting standards rely on the company's "normal loan review process." Clearly, a strong internal control environment is a critical factor in accurate reporting of loans and the allowance for credit losses.

The primary auditing standard affecting the measurement of loans is AU 342, *Auditing Accounting Estimates*. Chapter 9 of the AICPA Audit and Accounting Guide, *Depository and Lending Institutions: Banks and Savings Institutions, Credit Unions, Finance Companies, and Mortgage Companies*, provides detailed guidance about audit procedures to be performed, including procedures that relate to documentary evidence supporting the loan loss allowance (especially, paragraphs 9.43–9.88). The auditor must obtain an understanding of how management developed the estimate, and must apply that understanding to the review and testing of the estimation process and its results. Auditors should be skeptical of an allowance that remains a constant percentage of the loan portfolio through volatile economic times.

The AICPA Practice Aid, *Auditing Estimates and Other Soft Accounting Information*, provides additional guidance on auditing estimates such as loss allowances.

The key areas of risk that relate to financial reporting of loans are highlighted below. Well-documented policies and procedures that are applied consistently can significantly reduce the risk of material misstatement of loans and help a reporting entity withstand second-guessing by regulators and others.

Classification of Loans

Management's intent and ability to hold loans significantly affects the proper accounting. Sections of SAS-92, which address classification of securities under FAS-115, may be helpful to auditors by analogy (for example, paragraphs 57 and 58). Certain types of real estate loans should not be accounted for as loans.

Ceasing Recognition of Interest Income

Current GAAP does not specify when accrual of interest on a loan or receivable should be discontinued (or when it should be resumed). Lenders in regulated industries may need to comply with regulatory guidelines for nonaccrual loans.

Recognition of Impairment

The accounting standards do not specify how to determine whether it is probable that all amounts due will be collected as scheduled or how to identify individual loans for impairment review. Management should follow its normal loan review procedures.

Impairment of receivables should be recognized when, based on all available information, it is probable that a loss has been incurred based on past events and conditions existing at the date of the financial statements. It is usually difficult, even with hindsight, to identify any single event that made a particular loan uncollectible. AU 560, *Subsequent Events*, provides additional information that is relevant to deciding when a loss should be recorded.

Measuring Impairment

For impaired loans that are measured using the present value method under FAS-114, the lender's best estimate of cash flows is affected by a variety of factors, including the entity's interpretation of how existing environmental factors affect projections about future cash flows.

For collateral dependent loans, appraisals may be required to determine the fair value of the collateral (when it is used to measure impairment). Auditors should refer to AU 336, *Using the Work of a Specialist*.

Only loans with similar risk characteristics may be measured in groups (under FAS-114 and FAS-5). The term "similar risk characteristics" is not well defined in GAAP.

For impaired loans and receivables measured collectively, historical loss data may be used as a starting point but should be adjusted based on changes in economic conditions, the make-up of the current loan portfolio, and any other factors that suggest that the historical data may not be relevant.

"Topside adjustments" made by senior management must be subject to and result from the same disciplined and well documented measurement process that was used to develop the estimate of loan losses. SAS-61, *Communication with Audit Committees*, as amended, provides guidance about discussing certain significant estimates with audit committees.

Differences between GAAP and Regulatory Accounting Principles

In recent years, the banking agencies have clarified their rules so it is clear that regulatory accounting principles (RAP) must follow GAAP for loan loss allowances. However, GAAP/RAP differences could still exist in other industries, including insurance, due to differing objectives, the use of different approaches and the subjectivity inherent in estimating the amount of loss. Auditors should be skeptical of GAAP/RAP differences and assure that they are justified based on the particular facts and circumstances. (EITF 85-44)

ILLUSTRATIONS

Illustration 3-1: Loan Impairment under FAS-114

The following example illustrates how to measure impairment using two of the acceptable methods under FAS-114.

Assumptions:

- Castle Enterprises has a loan outstanding to Bygones, Inc. Castle identifies the loan for review this period. Bygones is experiencing major financial difficulties and missed its last few interest payments. Castle concludes that it is probable that it will not collect all principal and interest as scheduled from Bygones. Thus, the loan is considered impaired.
- Castle's recorded investment in the loan is $10,500 (including a net deferred loan fee of $1,000 and accrued interest of $1,500).
- The stated interest rate on the loan is 8.125%, and the effective interest rate of the loan is 8%, or 4% semiannually (including the effect of the net deferred loan fee).

Case 1:

- Castle Enterprises agrees to a troubled debt restructuring whereby the new loan terms require semiannual interest payments of 2% on a reduced principal amount of $7,500, due at the end of three years.
- Castle expects to collect the revised cash flows from Bygones according to the restructured terms.

Case 2:

- Assume instead that the loan is collateral dependent and that foreclosure is probable. The fair value of the collateral is $11,000 and the expected costs to sell the collateral are $1,250.

Accounting under Case 1

Calculation of loan impairment:

Recorded investment in loan	$10,500
Less PV of expected future cash flows	6,714†
Impairment loss to be recognized	$ 3,786

†Present value of expected future cash flows:

Semi-Annual Period	Expected Cash Flow	PV Factor	Present Value at 4%**
6/30/X1	150	.96154	144
12/31/X1	150	.92456	139
6/30/X2	150	.88900	133
12/31/X2	150	.85480	128
6/30/X3	150	.82193	123
12/31/X3	7,650	.79031	6,045
PV of expected cash flows			$6,714*

* $2 difference due to rounding.
** The original effective rate on the loan (8% annually or 4% semiannually) is used to discount the expected cash flows.

Note: The exact same method would be used to discount management's best estimate of the expected future cash flows on an impaired loan whose terms were not actually restructured.

Journal entry

Provision for loan losses	$ 3,786	
Allowance for loan losses		$ 3,786

To record impairment on loan to Bygones Inc. using the discounted cash flow method under FAS-114. The loan would be reported at a net amount of $6.714 on the balance sheet ($10.500 – $3.786).

If Castle subsequently determines that the loan to Bygones is uncollectible, the loan would be charged off. Assume for simplicity that the recorded investment is still $10,500. (Depending on the Castle's policy for nonaccrual loans, Castle could have been accruing interest and amortizing the deferred net fees.)

Journal entry

Provision for loan losses	$6,714	
Allowance for loan losses	3,786	
Loan		$10,500

To write off the loan to Bygones, Inc. Any recovery subsequently received would be recorded under Castle's accounting policy, which could be either (1) as a reduction of the provision for loan losses in the period that cash or other assets are received or (2) as a credit to the allowance for loan losses (which would then be adjusted to the appropriate level for the current portfolio, through earnings).

Accounting under Case 2

Calculation of loan impairment:

Recorded investment in loan	$10,500
Less: Fair value of collateral minus	
estimated costs to sell	9,750
Impairment loss to be recognized	$ 750

Journal entry

Provision for loan losses	$ 750	
Allowance for loan losses		$ 750

To record impairment on loan to Bygones, Inc. using the fair value of collateral method under FAS-114. The loan would be reported at a net amount of $9,750 on the balance sheet ($10,500 – $750). Note that the valuation allowance would be adjusted for changes in the value of the collateral and estimated selling costs until the foreclosure actually occurs. However, the net carrying amount of the loan should not exceed the recorded investment.

Illustration 3-2: How to Apply FAS-5 and FAS-114 to a Loan Portfolio

The purpose of this example is to show how a lender applies GAAP to the individual loans or groups of loans in its loan portfolio.

Assume Charter Bank Corp. has 9 loans to businesses in a geographic region that suffered a major economic downturn (for example, a devastating flood has closed many businesses and caused others to relocate). Some of the loans are collateralized and some are not. Charter Bank identifies all 9 loans for review under its normal loan review procedures. The following chart shows how Charter Bank would apply FAS-114, FAS-5, or both to the loans comprising its portfolio. The amount reported as an allowance for these loans would be the sum of the measures calculated in the two right-hand columns.

Loan #	Collection Status	Impaired?	Collateral and Other Information	Impairment Measured Under	
				FAS-114 (Method #) ‡	FAS-5
1	Delinquent	Yes	Collateral dependent, foreclosure probable, collateral insufficient	2	N/A
2	Delinquent	Yes	No collateral	1	N/A
3	Delinquent	Yes	Observable market price available	3	N/A
4	Delinquent	Yes	Fully collater-alized	N/A	N/A
5	Terms modified	Yes	No collateral	1	N/A
6	Restructur-ing in process	Yes	Working out new terms	1	N/A
7	Performing	No*	No collateral	N/A	Evaluate
8	Performing	No*	No collateral	N/A	as a group
9	Performing	No*	No collateral	N/A	for uniden-tified im-pairment

‡ FAS 114 methods:
  1. Present value of expected cash flows, discounted at original effective rate
  2. Fair value of collateral less costs to sell
  3. Observable market price

* The loan is not considered individually impaired because the entity could not conclude that it was probable that it would be unable to collect all cash flows as scheduled on that specific loan. However, the bank would include the loan with a group of other "unimpaired" loans to borrowers in that economic region, and determine whether there is an incurred but not yet identified loss in the group.

Illustration 3-3: Disclosure under FAS-118

The following information is excerpted from Bank of America Corporation's 2001 Annual Report. It illustrates the quantitative disclosures required by FAS-118 for impaired loans. Note 1 of Bank of America's financial statements includes a qualitative discussion of the company's significant accounting policies relating to loans, the allowance for credit losses, nonperforming loans and loans held for sale, and foreclosed properties.

Note 6—Loans and Leases

The following table presents the recorded investment in specific loans that were considered individually impaired in accordance with FAS-114 at December 31, 2001 and 2000:

(in millions)	2001	2000
Commercial—Domestic	3,138	2,891
Commercial—Foreign	501	521
Commercial real estate—Domestic	240	412
Commercial real estate—Foreign	—	2
Total Impaired Loans	$3,879	$3,826

The average recorded investment in certain impaired loans for the years ended December 31, 2001, 2000 and 1999 was approximately $3.7 billion, $3.0 billion and $2.0 billion, respectively. At December 31, 2001 and 2000, the recorded investment in impaired loans requiring an allowance for credit losses was $3.1 billion and $2.1 billion, and the related allowance for credit losses was $763 million and $640 million, respectively. For the years ended December 31, 2001, 2000 and 1999, interest income recognized on impaired loans totaled $195 million, $174 million and $84 million, respectively, all of which was recognized on a cash basis. [FAS-118, par. 6(i)]

[Other disclosures about nonperforming loans and foreclosed assets have been omitted for brevity.]

Note 7—Allowance for Credit Losses

The table below summarizes the changes in the allowance for credit losses on loans and leases for 2001, 2000, and 1999:

(in millions)	2001	2000	1999
Balance, January 1	$6,838	$6,828	$7,122
Loans and leases charged off (1)	(4,844)	(2,995)	(2,582)
Recoveries of loans and leases previously charged off	600	595	582
Net charge offs	(4,244)	(2,400)	(2,000)
Provision for credit losses (2)	4,287	2,535	1,820
Other, net	(6)	(125)	(114)
Balance, December 31	$6,875	$6,838	$6,828

(1) Includes $635 million related to the exit of the subprime real estate lending business in 2001.

(2) Includes $395 million related to the exit of the subprime real estate lending business in 2001.

[FAS-118, par. 6(i)]

CHAPTER 4
SERVICING OF FINANCIAL ASSETS

CONTENTS

Overview   4.02

Background   4.03

  Definition of Servicing   4.03

Accounting for Servicing Rights   4.04

  Recognition of Servicing Assets and Servicing Liabilities   4.04

    Exhibit 4-1: Illustration of Servicing Assets and Liabilities   4.05

    Exception for Certain Held-to-Maturity Securities   4.05

    Revolving-Period Securitizations   4.06

    Implementation Guidance about Adequate
Compensation   4.06

  Initial Measurement   4.06

    Recording I-O Strips   4.07

  Subsequent Measurement   4.07

    Servicing Assets and Servicing Liabilities   4.07

    Identifying Classes for Purposes of Subsequent
Measurement   4.07

    Transfers Between Classes   4.08

    Impairment Evaluation of Servicing Assets in Classes
Using the Amortization Method   4.08

    Hedging Servicing Assets—Interaction with FAS-133   4.10

    *Exhibit 4-2: Comparison of Subsequent Measurement Methods
for Servicing Assets and Servicing Liabilities*   4.12

    I-O Strips   4.12

    *Exhibit 4-3: Key Differences between I-O and Servicing
Accounting*   4.13

    Determining Fair Value of Servicing Rights   4.14

  Sales and Other Transfers of Servicing Rights   4.16

    Sale of Servicing Rights for Participation in Income Stream   4.17

    Sale of Servicing Rights with a Subservicing Agreement   4.17

    *Exhibit 4-4: Interpretation of "Substantially All Risks and
Rewards"*   4.18

    Subcontracting Servicing Obligation to Others   4.18

Balance Sheet Presentation   4.19

Income Statement Presentation   4.19

Cash Flow Statement Presentation   4.20

Miscellaneous Issues Involving Servicing Rights   4.20

    Costs of Issuing Certain Government National Mortgage
      Association (GNMA) Securities   4.20

    Accounting for a Purchased Servicing Right When Loans
      Are Refinanced   4.21

    Transfers of Servicing Assets for No Cash Consideration   4.21

Disclosures for Servicing Assets and Servicing Liabilities   4.21

Regulatory Considerations   4.23

Audit Considerations   4.23

Illustrations   4.25

    *Illustration 4-1: Recording and Amortizing a Servicing Asset
      Obtained*   4.25

    Illustration 4-2: Sale of Receivables with Servicing Obtained   4.26

OVERVIEW

All financial assets require some level of servicing—for example, collecting cash from borrowers, disbursing cash to investors, guarantors, taxing authorities, insurers, and the like. Servicers are usually compensated for their efforts, sometimes explicitly and sometimes implicitly, as part of the interest rate on the asset. Contractual rights to service financial assets, such as mortgages, student loans, and credit card receivables, are often bought and sold by market participants. Servicing rights can represent assets or liabilities, depending on the level of compensation involved in the contract relative to the average market cost of servicing. Reporting servicing assets and liabilities separate from the assets being serviced leads to an accurate calculation of the gain or loss on sale of the servicing right, the assets being serviced, or both (at different times).

FAS-140 (as amended by FAS-156) is the primary guidance for accounting for servicing assets and liabilities. Under that guidance, separately recognized servicing assets and servicing liabilities are required to be initially measured at fair value. For each class of separately recognized servicing assets and servicing liabilities, an entity is permitted to elect subsequent measurement based on either the fair value method or the amortization method. Under the fair value method, changes in fair value in the servicing asset or servicing liability are recognized in current earnings. Under the amortization method, servicing assets and liabilities are subsequently measured by (a) amortization in proportion to and over the period of estimated net servicing income or loss and (b) assessment for asset impairment or increased obligation based on fair value.

Sales of servicing rights should be accounted for as sold if substantially all of the risks and rewards of ownership have passed to the buyer and certain other criteria are met. Numerous disclosures must be provided about servicing rights.

BACKGROUND

FAS-156, the primary accounting literature for servicing rights, amends the provisions of FAS-140 relating to accounting for servicing rights. FAS-156 establishes when a servicing right must be recognized, establishes that servicing rights must be initially measured at fair value, and provides an election for subsequent measurement of servicing rights. FAS-140 provides guidance on recognition of impairment for those servicing rights not subsequently measured at fair value. FAS-156 applies to all rights to service financial assets, not just to mortgage servicing rights. FAS-140 Q&A addresses numerous implementation questions about servicing rights. Sales of servicing rights and subservicing arrangements are addressed by various EITF Issues and certain literature from the AICPA. (Transfers of servicing rights are not within the scope of FAS-140 because they are not themselves financial instruments.)

Note: The conditions of a qualifying special-purpose entity (QSPE), including what types of servicing activities are permissible, are discussed in Chapter 6, "Securitizations."

Definition of Servicing

Servicing involves the collection of payments from debtors and payment of collected funds to investors and others (such as guarantors, insurers, and taxing authorities). A servicer also maintains payment records and pursues defaults. Servicing of mortgage loans, credit card receivables, and other financial assets commonly includes, but is not limited to:

- Collecting principal, interest, and escrow payments from borrowers;
- Paying taxes and insurance from escrowed funds;
- Monitoring delinquencies;
- Executing foreclosure if necessary;
- Temporarily investing funds pending distribution;
- Remitting fees to guarantors, trustees, and others providing services; and

- Accounting for and remitting principal and interest payments to the holders of beneficial interests in the financial assets. (FAS-140, par. 61)

The right to perform servicing is potentially lucrative because the servicer usually receives a fee, but also because the servicer is entitled to the "float" (earnings on funds collected that have not yet passed on to the investors in the loans and others). In addition, depending on the terms of the contract, the servicer may be entitled to other income stemming from the assets, such as delinquency and prepayment fees.

ACCOUNTING FOR SERVICING RIGHTS

Recognition of Servicing Assets and Servicing Liabilities

All financial assets require some level of servicing. For accounting purposes, an entity recognizes servicing rights as a distinct asset or liability each time it undertakes an obligation to service a financial asset by entering into a servicing contract in connection with any of the following situations:

- A transfer of the servicer's financial assets that meets the requirements for sale accounting
- A transfer of the servicer's financial assets to a qualifying SPE in a guaranteed mortgage securitization in which the transferor retains all of the resulting securities and classifies them as either AFS securities or trading securities in accordance with FAS-115
- An acquisition or assumption of an obligation to service a financial asset that does not relate to financial assets of the servicer or its consolidated affiliates

A servicer of financial assets commonly receives the *benefits of servicing*—revenues from contractually specified servicing fees, a portion of the interest from the financial assets, late charges, and other ancillary sources, including "float," all of which it is entitled to receive only if it performs the servicing and incurs the costs of servicing the assets. *Adequate compensation* is a benchmark of the amount a market participant would require to service the assets, including a normal profit margin. Usually, the benefits of servicing are expected to more than adequately compensate the servicer for performing the servicing, and the contract results in a servicing asset. However, if the benefits of servicing are not expected to adequately compensate the servicer for performing the servicing, the contract results in a servicing liability.

A servicing asset may become a servicing liability, or vice versa, if circumstances change.

A servicer would account for its servicing contract that qualifies for separate recognition as a servicing asset or a servicing liability initially measured at fair value regardless of whether explicit consideration was exchanged.

A servicer that transfers or securitizes financial assets in a transaction that does not meet the requirements for sale accounting and is, therefore, accounted for as a secured borrowing may not recognize a servicing asset or servicing liability. However, an exception is permitted for servicing assets and servicing liabilities created in a guaranteed mortgage securitization in which a transferor retains all of the resulting securities and classifies them as either AFS securities or trading securities under FAS-115. In that case, even though the transaction does not qualify for sale accounting, the transferor must separately recognize a servicing asset or servicing liability.

> ☞ **PRACTICE POINTER:** If an entity sells only part of a financial asset but continues to service the entire asset, a servicing asset or liability should be recorded for the portion of the asset it sold. (FAS-140 Q&A, par. 96)

EXHIBIT 4-1
ILLUSTRATION OF SERVICING ASSETS AND LIABILITIES

Scenario	A Benefits of Servicing*	B Adequate Compensation	Treatment of Servicing Right
1	125 b.p.	100 b.p.	A > B Servicing asset
2	100 b.p.	100 b.p.	A = B No servicing asset or liability
3	75 b.p.	100 b.p.	A < B Servicing liability

* Includes contractually specified servicing fees plus, depending on the contract terms, ancillary revenues such as late charges and float.

Exception for Certain Held-to-Maturity Securities

If all of the following conditions are met, the inherent servicing asset or liability need not be accounted for separately and may be reported together with the asset being serviced:

- The assets are transferred to a qualifying special-purpose entity (QSPE) in a *guaranteed mortgage securitization* (Chapter 6, "Securitizations," addresses QSPEs.)
- The transferor retains all of the resulting securities, and
- Classifies them as debt securities held-to-maturity in accordance with FAS-115. (FAS-140, par. 13)

☛ **PRACTICE POINTER:** An entity can elect to report a servicing asset or liability separate from held-to-maturity mortgage-backed securities, even when the conditions of the exception are met.

Revolving-Period Securitizations

In a revolving-period securitization (for example, home equity loans or credit card receivables), recognition of servicing assets or liabilities is limited to the servicing of receivables that exist and have actually been transferred into the securitization trust. As new receivables are sold, rights to servicing them become assets and liabilities that should be recognized. (FAS-140, par. 78)

Implementation Guidance about Adequate Compensation

Adequate compensation varies depending on the type of asset being serviced. For example, the level of effort required to service a home equity loan likely would be different from the amount of effort required to service a credit card receivable or a small business administration (SBA) loan. (FAS-140 Q&A, par. 88) Adequate compensation does *not* vary according to the costs of a specific servicer. (FAS-140 Q&A, par. 78)

An agreement that specifies the amount of servicing fees that would be paid to a replacement servicer does not affect the determination of adequate compensation, which is a market-based number. However, the replacement fee does affect the amount of *contractually specified servicing fees* and therefore the identification of any interest-only strip. (FAS-140 Q&A, par. 89)

Initial Measurement

Each separately recognized servicing asset or servicing liability must be measured at fair value, if practicable. Fair value is presumptively the price paid or received if the servicing asset or servicing liability is purchased or assumed. If it is not practicable to initially measure a servicing asset or servicing liability at fair value, a servicing asset should be recorded at zero. In the case of a servicing liability, a transferor should not recognize a gain on the transaction giving rise to the servicing liability. Refer to the section "Determining Fair Value of Servicing Rights" below for further information.

OBSERVATION: The fair value "practicability" exception only applies to servicing rights that arise in transactions where the servicer used to own the assets being serviced and those assets were transferred in a transaction that qualifies as a sale under FAS-140. Outright acquisitions or assumptions of servicing must be accounted for at fair value.

Recording I-O Strips

Rights to future interest income from the serviced assets that exceed contractually specified servicing fees should be accounted for separately as financial assets. Effectively they are interest-only strips (I-Os) that should be accounted for as investments with significant prepayment risk in accordance with FAS-140, paragraph 14. (FAS-140, par. 63(c))

> ☛ **PRACTICE POINTER:** Whether a right to future interest income should be accounted for as an interest-only strip, a servicing asset, or a combination of the two, depends on whether a servicer would continue to receive that amount (that is, the value of the right to future interest income) if a substitute servicer began servicing the assets. Any portion of the right to future interest income from the serviced assets that would continue to be received even if the servicing were shifted to another servicer should be reported separately as a financial asset in accordance with FAS-140, paragraph 14. (FAS-140 Q&A, par. 93)

Subsequent Measurement

Servicing Assets and Servicing Liabilities

Servicing assets and servicing liabilities must be separated into classes for subsequent measurement purposes. Entities may elect to subsequently measure *each* class of servicing assets and servicing liabilities using one of the following methods:

- *Fair value method* Measure servicing assets and servicing liabilities at fair value at each reporting date with changes in value recognized in current earnings
- *Amortization method* Amortize servicing assets or servicing liabilities as follows:
  - For servicing assets, amortize the excess of servicing revenues over servicing costs in proportion to and over the period of estimated net servicing income
  - For servicing liabilities, amortize the excess of servicing costs over servicing revenues over the period of the estimated net servicing loss

Identifying Classes for Purposes of Subsequent Measurement

Classes of servicing assets and servicing liabilities must be defined for the subsequent measurement election based on one or both of the following:

- The availability of market inputs used in determining the fair value of the servicing assets and servicing liabilities
- An entity's method for managing the risks of its servicing assets or servicing liabilities

The subsequent measurement election must be made separately for each class of servicing assets or servicing liabilities (that is, different elections can be made for different classes).

An election to measure a class using the fair value measurement method is irrevocable. Such an election can be made at the beginning of any fiscal year.

Transfers Between Classes

An entity can transfer servicing assets or servicing liabilities from a class measured under the amortization method to a class measured under the fair value method at the beginning of any fiscal year. However, once a servicing asset or servicing liability is reported in a class for which an entity elects the fair value measurement method, that servicing asset or servicing liability cannot be transferred to a class for which the entity has elected the amortization method.

Impairment Evaluation of Servicing Assets in Classes Using the Amortization Method

For any class of servicing assets and servicing liabilities for which the amortization method is elected for subsequent measurement purposes, an entity must stratify that class to determine whether impairment has occurred.

> ☞ **PRACTICE POINTER:** The identification of classes for subsequent measurement purposes is *not* analogous to the guidance for stratifying servicing assets and servicing liabilities for measurement of impairment. The identification of classes for subsequent measurement purposes is based on the availability of market inputs used to determine the fair value of the servicing assets and servicing liabilities and/or an entity's method for managing the risks of its servicing assets or servicing liabilities. Stratification of servicing assets must be based on the predominant risk characteristics of the underlying financial assets. A servicer may, but is not required to, consider the major asset type of the underlying financial asset when identifying its classes.

> ☞ **PRACTICE POINTER:** Classes of servicing assets and servicing liabilities that are subsequently measured at fair value will not be separately assessed for impairment because all changes in fair value are reported in current earnings.

Servicing assets should subsequently be evaluated for impairment and measured as follows:

- Stratify (group) servicing assets within a class based on one or more of the predominant risk characteristics of the underlying financial assets. Those characteristics may include:
  - Financial asset type, such as conventional, government guaranteed and insured mortgages, and sub-prime loans
  - Size, such as jumbo or conforming
  - Interest rate, such as adjustable rate or fixed rate
  - Date of origination
  - Term
  - Geographic location (FAS-140, par. 63(f))

  The criteria used to stratify each class of servicing assets subsequently measured using the amortization method should be applied consistently unless significant changes in facts and circumstances indicate that the significant risk characteristics and resulting strata have changed. (Such a change should be accounted for as a change in accounting estimate under FAS-154.) (FAS-140 Q&A, par. 100)

  ☞ **PRACTICE POINTER:** An entity that has recognized a servicing asset relating to loan products whose terms may give rise to a concentration of credit risk is required, when determining impairment, to consider whether the predominant risk characteristics of the specific product type result in a separate stratum. Examples of features that may increase credit risk are terms that permit principal payment deferral or payments smaller than interest accruals, a high loan-to-value ratio, multiple loans on the same collateral that, when combined, result in a high loan-to-value ratio, option adjustable-rate mortgages, an initial interest rate that is below the market interest rate for the initial period of the loan term that may increase significantly when that period ends, and interest-only loans. (FSP SOP 94-6-1)

  SEC REGISTRANT ALERT: In the past, the SEC staff has said that stratifications based on loan type, interest rate risk, or both are reasonable ways to stratify a portfolio of servicing rights. Registrants should be able to demonstrate that their servicing rights have been stratified using "predominant" risk characteristics. (September 7, 1995, speech by Russell B. Mallett III, then a Professional Accounting Fellow at the SEC)

- Carry each stratum within a class at the lower of the amortized carrying amount or fair value within a class (a form of LOCOM). Recognize declines in value (impairment) through a valuation allowance for each individual stratum. The fair value of servicing assets that have not been recognized should not be used in the evaluation of impairment. (FAS-140, par. 63(f)(2))

☛ **PRACTICE POINTER:** Adjustments for fair value hedge accounting under FAS-133 should be included as a component of the amortized cost of servicing rights for the purposes of measuring impairment. (DIG Issue F-1)

- Recoveries in fair value may be recognized, but not above the carrying amount for each stratum. (FAS-140, par. 63(f)(2))

For servicing assets and liabilities subsequently measured using the amortization method, if subsequent events have increased the fair value of the liability above the carrying amount, for example, because of significant changes in the amount or timing of actual or expected future cash flows from the cash flows previously projected, the servicer should revise its earlier estimates and recognize the increased obligation as a loss in earnings. (FAS-140, par. 63(g)) Recoveries (that is, reductions) in the value of a servicing obligation may be recognized, but not below the amortized measurement of the initially recognized servicing liability. (FAS-140 Q&A, par. 101)

OBSERVATION: Even if the servicer expects to incur a loss on the contract (that is, its own costs of servicing will exceed the servicing fee), the entity should *not* accrue a loss under so-called loss contract accounting. A servicer can avoid these future losses by selling the servicing contract to a more efficient servicer. (FAS-140 Q&A, par. 94)

Hedging Servicing Assets—Interaction with FAS-133

Servicers of financial assets sometimes seek to hedge certain risks, including interest rate risk and the risk that the underlying assets will prepay FAS-156 enables servicers to elect subsequent measurement of servicing assets and servicing liabilities at fair value and to report changes in value in earnings. Subsequent measurement of servicing assets and servicing liabilities at fair value obviates the need for entities that use derivatives to manage risks inherent in servicing assets and servicing liabilities to qualify for special hedge accounting under FAS-133 and to apply complex hedge accounting procedures. Such entities can achieve natural income statement offset by measuring servicing assets and servicing liabilities and related derivatives, which must be measured at fair value under FAS-133.

☛ **PRACTICE POINTER:** For entities that use financial instruments, other than derivatives, that are *not* measured at fair value and whose change in value is measured in earnings, as hedges of risks inherent in serving assets and servicing liabilities, subsequent measurement at fair value would result in greater income statement volatility because of the differing measurement attributes of the hedging instrument and the servicing asset or servicing liability. For example, entities that use AFS securities to offset the effect of recognizing impairment or an increased obligation associated with servicing assets and servicing liabilities would now have a mismatch between the measurement of the hedged servicing assets and servicing liabilities (measured at fair value through earnings) and the AFS securities (measured at fair value through other comprehensive income). For this reason, FAS-156, upon its adoption, permits a one-time option to reclassify AFS securities to trading securities, only if those securities are used to offset the income statement effects of changes in fair value of servicing assets and servicing liabilities that will be subsequently measured using the fair value measurement method.

Entities that use derivatives to hedge servicing assets that will be subsequently measured using the amortization method and that wish to apply special hedge accounting to such relationships (usually to offset possible impairment adjustments) must apply the hedge accounting criteria and procedures specified in FAS-133.

In order to qualify as a portfolio of similar assets that may be designated as a hedged item in a fair value hedge under FAS-133, servicing assets must be grouped using risk strata that meet certain criteria:

- The individual assets in a pool of similar assets must share the risk exposure for which they are designated as being hedged.
- The change in fair value attributable to the hedged risk for each individual item in the hedged portfolio must be expected to respond in a generally proportionate manner to the overall change in fair value of the aggregate portfolio attributable to the hedged risk. (FAS-133, par. 21(a)(1))

These criteria are much more stringent than the requirements of FAS-140, par. 63(f). Upon adopting FAS-133, mortgage bankers and other servicers of financial assets were permitted to restratify their servicing rights in a manner that would enable individual strata to comply with the FAS-133 definition of "a portfolio of similar assets." (DIG Issue F-1) FAS-140 also allows changes in stratification in certain circumstances. (FAS-140 Q&A, par. 100) See Chapter 14, "Hedge Accounting," for more information about fair value hedge accounting.

☛ **PRACTICE POINTER:** Servicers have some latitude in determining how to stratify their servicing rights under FAS-140. Servicers are allowed to stratify differently for impairment purposes under FAS-140 and hedging purposes under FAS-133. (FAS-140 Q&A, par. 99) However, it could be quite onerous to maintain accurate records when different approaches are used. For example,

consider the administrative burden of recording hedge accounting adjustments to servicing rights stratified first by interest rate
characteristics for hedging purposes under FAS-133 and then by
date of origination for impairment purposes under FAS-140.

EXHIBIT 4-2
**COMPARISON OF SUBSEQUENT MEASUREMENT METHODS FOR
SERVICING ASSETS AND SERVICING LIABILITIES**

	Fair Value Method	Amortization Method
Balance sheet carry-ing amount	Fair value as of the reporting date	Initial fair value, adjusted for accumulated amortization, impairments, and any addi-tional liability
Income recognition method	Income and fair value adjustments recognized in earnings currently	Recognize servicing income in proportion to and over the period of estimated net servic-ing income
Recognition of impairment (servicing assets) or an increased obliga-tion (servicing liabil-ities)	Any impairment or increased obligation recognized in earnings currently through fair value adjustments	Impairment must be measured for each class of servicing assets by stratifying servicing assets within a class. Initial im-pairment recognized by estab-lishing a valuation allowance for the amount by which the carry-ing amount of an individual stratum exceeds its fair value. Subsequent impairments recognized by adjusting the valuation allowance with any change recognized in earnings. Increased obligation recog-nized as a loss in earnings.
Restrictions	Decision to subse-quently measure a class of servicing assets and liabilities at fair value is *irrevocable* either at ini-tial application of FAS-156 or as of the beginning of any subsequent fiscal year.	Transfers *from* a class subse-quently measured at fair value to a class subsequently measured using the amortiza-tion method not permitted. However, transfers to a class subsequently measured at fair value permitted as of the beginning of any fiscal year.

I-O Strips

An interest-only (I-O) strip is considered an instrument with significant
prepayment risk under FAS-140, paragraph 14. An I-O strip must be

evaluated under FAS-133 to determine if it must be accounted for as a derivative. FAS-133, paragraph 14, provides a scope exception for an I-O strip if it represents the right to receive only a specified proportion of the contractual interest cash flows of a specific debt instrument and if it does not incorporate any terms not present in the original debt instrument. An allocation of a portion of the interest cash flows to provide adequate compensation to a servicer would also qualify for this scope exception; however, an allocation of a portion of the interest cash flows to provide for servicing in excess of adequate compensation (or for any other purpose) would not meet the narrow scope exception.

An I-O strip, unless it is subject to the requirements of FAS-133, should be accounted for like an available-for-sale or trading security under FAS-115. That is, it should be subsequently measured at fair value, with changes in fair value recognized in other comprehensive income or earnings, as appropriate. Chapter 2, "Investments in Debt and Equity Securities," discusses the accounting for securities in more detail.

Interest income and impairment on an I-O strip should be recognized under EITF Issue 99-20. See Chapter 7, "Calculating Yields on Debt Investments."

EXHIBIT 4-3
KEY DIFFERENCES BETWEEN I-O AND SERVICING ACCOUNTING

Accounting Issue	I-O Strip	Servicing Rights
Subsequent measurement	Fair value (either AFS or trading, or possibly a derivative)	For each class, entities can elect either the fair value method (subsequent measurement based on current fair value) or the amortization method (subsequent method based on lower of amortized cost or fair value)
Income recognition	If AFS, effective yield under EITF 99-20; otherwise mark to market (MTM)	Classes using the fair value method recognize income and fair value adjustments through current earnings; classes using the amortization method recognize income/expense as servicing is performed; amortization offsets
Impairment	If AFS, individual assessment with direct write-down; if trading, MTM	Classes using the fair value method currently recognize impairment through fair value adjustments; classes using the amortization method assess impairment by stratum and utilize valuation allowances

Accounting Issue	I-O Strip	Servicing Rights
Transfers	FAS-140 (control-based)	EITF and AICPA literature ("all-or-nothing" risks and rewards analysis)

> **OBSERVATION:** To the degree that servicers elect to apply the fair value method for subsequent measurement of servicing assets and servicing liabilities, the issuance of FAS-156 bridges the gap between the differing accounting models for servicing rights and I-O strips under previous GAAP. However, because servicers can still elect the amortization method for subsequent measurement of servicing assets and servicing liabilities, there remains some opportunity to engineer structured transactions to create a desired level of servicing rights versus I-O strips.

Determining Fair Value of Servicing Rights

> **AUTHOR'S NOTE:** In September 2006, the FASB issued FASB Statement No. 157, *Fair Value Measurements*. FAS-157 provides a single definition of the term *fair value*, establishes a framework for measuring fair value where required by existing GAAP, and expands disclosures about fair value measurements. Specific fair value measurement guidance applicable to servicing assets and liabilities is covered in this Chapter. Chapter 18, "Fair Value Measurements, Fair Value Disclosures, and Other Financial Instruments Disclosures," provides the detailed provisions of FAS-157 and specific fair value measurement guidance applicable to all financial instruments required to be measured at fair value under GAAP. The 2008 edition of CCH *Financial Instruments* has been updated to incorporate the provisions of FAS-157. FAS-157 is effective for calendar-year-end companies as of January 1, 2008. Unless a company chooses to early adopt, prior GAAP is applicable for financial statements issued for 2007.
>
> As this book went to press, the FASB was addressing a possible delay of FAS-157's effective date. The FASB agreed to consider delaying the effective date for nonfinancial instruments and for certain types of entities, including private companies and "smaller" public companies (not yet defined). Readers should monitor the FASB's further deliberations regarding the nature of any delay of FAS-157's effective date. Also, readers should refer to the 2007 edition for GAAP related to the fair value measurement of financial instruments applicable before the effective date of FAS-157.

FAS-157 is the primary guidance for fair value measurement under GAAP. Fair value is the price that would be received to sell an asset or paid to transfer a liability in an orderly transaction between market participants at the measurement date. The objective of a fair value measurement under FAS-157 is to determine the price that would be received to sell the asset or paid to transfer the liability at the measurement date (an exit price) using assumptions that market participants would use. The fair value measurement model in FAS-157 applies for both initial measurement and subsequent measurement of servicing assets and liabilities.

Chapter 18, "Fair Value Measurements, Fair Value Disclosures, and Other Financial Instrument Disclosures," provides specific fair value measurement guidance applicable to all financial instruments required to be measured at fair value under GAAP.

Benefits of servicing   Some elements of the benefits of servicing are dependent on the outcome of future transactions. In such cases, the fair value estimate should include the value of the right to benefit from the cash flows of future transactions (such as the collecting late charges), *not* the value of the cash flows expected to be collected from those future transactions. (FAS-140 Q&A, par. 86)

Adequate compensation   When market data is not available about adequate compensation, it is not acceptable for the servicer to substitute its *own expected costs* plus a profit margin to estimate the fair value of a servicing asset or liability. (FAS-140 Q&A, par. 79) It is permissible to estimate adequate compensation using a cash flow model, provided that *market-based* assumptions are used. (FAS-140 Q&A, par. 80)

Not practicable to determine fair value   When an entity transfers assets in a transaction accounted for as a sale under FAS-140 but continues to hold the servicing rights related to some or all of the assets sold, if it is not practicable to initially measure a servicing asset or servicing liability at fair value, the transferor must initially recognize the servicing asset or servicing liability using the following procedures and include it in a class of servicing assets and servicing liabilities that is subsequently measured using the amortization method:

- A servicing asset should be recorded at zero.
- A servicing liability should be recorded at the greater of:
  — The amount that results in no gain or loss on the transaction—that is, the sum of the excess, if any, of:
    (1) The fair value of assets obtained less the fair value of other liabilities incurred over
    (2) The sum of the carrying values of the assets transferred or
  — The amount that would be recognized under FAS-5, as interpreted by FIN-14.

For a loss to be accrued under FAS-5, it must be probable that a liability has been incurred (or an asset impaired) and the amount must be reasonably estimable. (FAS-140, par. 71)

In situations where it is not practicable to determine the fair value of a servicing right, the transferor should not automatically assume that an asset exists (that is, not automatically assume that the answer is zero). The transferor must evaluate whether a liability has been incurred as a result of its obligations under the servicing agreement. (FAS-140 Q&A, par. 102)

If, subsequently, it becomes practicable to determine the fair value of a servicing asset or liability:

- Servicing assets should not be remeasured;
- Servicing liabilities should be remeasured, but not to an amount less than the amortized measurement of its initially recognized amount; and
- Servicing assets and servicing liabilities subsequently measured using the amortization method should be evaluated for impairment or increased obligation based on fair value at each reporting date. (FAS-140 Q&A, par. 71)

"Practicable" is not defined in FAS-140. However, paragraph 298 of FAS-140 explains that to conclude that it is not practicable to determine fair value, the estimate must not be sufficiently reliable to justify recognition of a gain following a sale of assets. FAS-140 Q&A, paragraph 69 states that in a vast majority of circumstances, it should be practicable to estimate fair values.

Sales and Other Transfers of Servicing Rights

Servicing rights are not financial instruments. Accordingly, the accounting for transfers of servicing rights is not within the scope of FAS-140. The accounting for sales of mortgage servicing rights is addressed by a series of EITF Issues and certain literature of the AICPA. Although some of this guidance addresses sales of *mortgage* servicing rights, it all should be applied by analogy to any sale of servicing rights. (SOP 01-6, par. 8(g))

EITF Issue 95-5 provides that sales of rights to service mortgage loans should be recognized when the following conditions have been met:

- Title has passed,
- Substantially all risks and rewards of ownership have irrevocably passed to the buyer, and
- Any protection provisions retained by the seller are minor and can be reasonably estimated.

If a sale is recognized and minor protection provisions exist, a liability should be accrued for the estimated obligation associated with those provisions. The seller retains only minor protection provisions if:

- The obligation associated with those provisions is estimated to be no more than 10 percent of the sales price and
- Risk of prepayment is retained for no longer than 120 days.

A temporary subservicing agreement in which the subservicing will be performed by the seller for a short period of time would not necessarily preclude recognizing a sale at the closing date. (EITF 95-5)

The following criteria should also be considered when evaluating whether a transfer of servicing rights qualifies as a sale (SOP 01-6, par. 8(g));

- The seller should receive written approval from the investor, if required.
- The buyer should be a currently approved seller/servicer and not be at risk of losing approved status.
- If the seller finances a portion of the sales price, an adequate nonrefundable down payment should be received and the note receivable from the buyer should provide full recourse.
- The seller should be adequately compensated for any agreement to temporarily service the transferred assets.

Sale of Servicing Rights for Participation in Income Stream

EITF Issue 85-13 addresses the sale of servicing rights in exchange for a participation in the future interest stream of the loans. In the fact pattern discussed, the servicer does not own the loans being serviced. The Task Force concluded that a gain should be recognized at the sale date. In measuring the gain, the seller of mortgage servicing rights should consider all available information, including the amount of gain that would be recognized if the servicing rights were to be sold outright for a fixed cash price.

Sale of Servicing Rights with a Subservicing Agreement

A sale of mortgage servicing rights with a subservicing agreement should be treated as a sale with gain deferred if substantially all the risks and rewards inherent in owning the mortgage servicing rights have been effectively transferred to the buyer. (EITF 90-21) A loss should be recognized currently if the transferor determines that prepayments of the underlying mortgage loans may result in performing the future servicing at a loss. (EITF 87-34) The risks and rewards associated with a seller performing purely administrative functions under a subservicing agreement would not necessarily preclude sale treatment. Exhibit 4-4 outlines some indicators that risks and rewards have not been transferred to the buyer. If substantially all risks and rewards of ownership have not been transferred to the buyer, the transaction should be accounted for as a financing. (EITF 90-21)

> **OBSERVATION:** EITF Issue 90-21 does not specify the amortization period for the gain. In the discussion of EITF Issue 87-34, several Task Force members suggested that the transferor should amortize the gain on the sale over the estimated lives of the underlying loans.

EXHIBIT 4-4
INTERPRETATION OF "SUBSTANTIALLY ALL RISKS AND REWARDS"

Automatic financing treatment if seller/subservicer performs one or more of the following:	Rebuttable presumption that financing treatment is appropriate if one or more of the following is present (this list is not meant to be all-inclusive):
Directly or indirectly guarantees a yield to the buyer, including guarantee of prepayment speeds or default rates	Seller/subservicer directly or indirectly provides financing or guarantees the buyer's financing (e.g., nonrecourse financing)
Commits to advance servicing fees on a nonrecoverable basis to the buyer prior to receipt of the loan payment from the mortgagor	Subservicing agreement unduly limits the buyer's ability to exercise ownership control over the servicing rights or results in the seller's retaining some of the risks and rewards of ownership
Indemnifies the buyer for damages due to causes other than failure to perform its duties under the terms of the subservicing agreement	The buyer is a special-purpose entity without substantive capital at risk
Absorbs losses on mortgage loan foreclosures not covered by guarantors, if any, including absorption of foreclosure costs and costs of managing foreclosed property	
Retains title to the servicing rights (EITF 90-21)	

Subcontracting Servicing Obligation to Others

There is no specific literature that addresses the accounting by an entity that subcontracts its obligation to service certain financial assets with another servicer. However, FAS-140 Q&A, paragraph 97, states that the subcontracting arrangement should be accounted for separate from the initial recording of the servicing right as an asset or liability, even if the arrangements are entered into contemporaneously (in other words, the two transactions should not necessarily be netted or offset). Generally, an obligation should not be removed from the books and records unless the agreement is terminated or the service provider is relieved of its obligations under the contract.

> **SEC REGISTRANT ALERT:** A transaction that, in substance, transfers only a portion of the servicing revenues does not result in transfer of substantially all of the risks and rewards of ownership. Those transactions should be accounted for in accordance with EITF Issue 88-18, "Sales of Future Revenues." (EITF 90-21)

Balance Sheet Presentation

A servicer that recognizes a servicing asset or liability should account for the contract to service financial assets separately from those assets (if they are also held by the servicer). Servicing assets should be reported separately from servicing liabilities in the statement of financial position. (FAS-140, par. 63(a))

Income Statement Presentation

The following aspects of servicing affect the income statement (I-Os are discussed separately in Chapter 2, "Investments in Debt and Equity Securities," and in Chapter 7, "Calculating Yields on Debt Investments"):

- Recognition of servicing fees and ancillary revenues, such as float, as revenue as it is earned.
- Recognition of the costs of servicing as they are incurred.
- Amortization of servicing assets and liabilities.
- Impairment or increased obligations of servicing rights.
- Gain or loss on sale of servicing.

There are no specific GAAP requirements for the classification of these items in the income statement. Material items should be separately disclosed.

> **REGULATORY ALERT:** The Call Report instructions for banks and other financial institutions specify how certain elements of servicing should be classified under regulatory accounting principles (RAP). For example, amortization of servicing assets should be netted against servicing revenue and reported as "Net servicing

fees." Regulated financial institutions should be mindful of any specific classification requirements for RAP.

Cash Flow Statement Presentation

The various cash flows arising from servicing rights should be reported in the Statement of Cash Flows in accordance with FAS-95. For example:

- Servicing fees and expenses should be reported as operating cash flows. (FAS-95, par. 21)
- Interest income (float) should be reported as operating cash flows. (FAS-95, par. 22(b))
- Purchases and sales of servicing rights are generally reported as investing cash flows. (AICPA Audit and Accounting Guide, *Depository and Lending Institutions: Banks and Savings Institutions, Credit Unions, Finance Companies and Mortgage Companies,* par. 6.20)

For companies using the indirect method of preparing the Cash Flow Statement, the amortization, impairment and recovery in value of servicing rights will be reconciling items between net income and operating cash flows.

Miscellaneous Issues Involving Servicing Rights

Costs of Issuing Certain Government National Mortgage Association (GNMA) Securities

A mortgage banking enterprise that issues GNMA securities may pay investors using different methods, including the *internal reserve method.* For issuers electing the internal reserve method, one month's interest cost, which is required to be paid to a trustee, should be capitalized and amortized. The aggregate amount capitalized, including amounts capitalized as a servicing asset, should not exceed the present value of net future servicing income. The rate used to determine the present value should be an appropriate long-term interest rate. For this purpose, estimates of future servicing revenue should include expected late charges and other ancillary revenue. Estimates of expected future servicing costs should include direct costs associated with performing the servicing function and appropriate allocations of other costs. Estimated future servicing costs may be determined on an incremental cost basis. The amount capitalized should be amortized in proportion to, and over the period of, estimated net servicing income—the excess of servicing revenues over servicing costs. (FAS-65, par. 15)

OBSERVATION: The method of calculating the "cap" for capitalized assets described above may *not* be used to determine the fair value of servicing assets generally. FAS-140 Q&A is clear that a servicer should NOT use its own cost structure in lieu of adequate compensation (paragraph 83), and that the benefits of servicing should include the *right* to ancillary revenue, not the expected amounts (paragraph 85).

Accounting for a Purchased Servicing Right When Loans Are Refinanced

When an entity is servicing a mortgage loan that is refinanced (resulting in prepayment of the old loan and origination of a new loan), the servicer should not consider the estimated future net servicing income (that is, servicing revenue in excess of servicing costs) from the *new* loan in determining how to amortize any capitalized cost related to acquiring the mortgage servicing right for the old loan. However, if the servicer did not anticipate the prepayment in its original cash flow estimates, an adjustment to the *cost* of a mortgage servicing right that is subsequently measured using the amortization method. If the servicing right is subsequently measured using the fair value measurement method, the entity would recognize any adjustment as a result of the refinancing transaction directly in earnings. (FTB 87-3)

Transfers of Servicing Assets for No Cash Consideration

Occasionally, servicing assets are transferred in exchange for no cash compensation. The substance of such transactions should be carefully scrutinized. The rights may be transferred (1) as consideration for goods and services received previously or (2) as a capital contribution, in which case the transaction should be accounted for the same as if cash had been transferred. However, if no consideration can be identified, it is possible that the recipient has overvalued the asset. Such transactions should be evaluated for changes in terms, restrictions on sale, and other factors that would adversely affect the value of the contract. (FAS-140 Q&A, par. 98)

DISCLOSURES FOR SERVICING ASSETS AND SERVICING LIABILITIES

The following disclosures are required for all servicing assets and liabilities:

- Management's basis for determining its classes of servicing assets and servicing liabilities

- A description of the risks inherent in servicing assets and servicing liabilities and the instruments used to mitigate the income statement effect of changes in fair value
- The amount of contractually specified servicing fees, late fees, and ancillary fees earned for each period for which results of operations are presented, including a description of where each amount is reported in the statement of income
- A description of the valuation techniques or other methods used to estimate the fair value of servicing assets and servicing liabilities. If a valuation model is used, the description should include the methodology and model validation procedures as well as quantitative and qualitative information about the assumptions used in the valuation model (for example, discount rates and prepayment speeds)

The following disclosures are encouraged:

- Quantitative information about the instruments used to manage the risks inherent in servicing assets and servicing liabilities, including the fair value of those instruments at the beginning and end of the period, and
- A description of the valuation techniques as well as quantitative and qualitative information about the assumptions used to estimate the fair value of those instruments.

Incremental disclosures required for servicing assets and servicing liabilities subsequently measured using the fair value method are as follows: for each class, the activity in the balance of servicing assets and the activity in the balance of servicing liabilities (including a description of where changes in fair value are reported in the statement of income for each period for which results of operations are presented), including the beginning and ending balances, additions, disposals, changes in fair value during the period, and other changes that affect the balance and a description of those changes.

Incremental disclosures required for servicing assets and liabilities subsequently measured using the amortization method are as follows:

- For each class, the activity in the balance of servicing assets and the activity in the balance of servicing liabilities (including a description of where changes in the carrying amount are reported in the statement of income for each period for which results of operations are presented), including the following:
  — The beginning and ending balances
  — Additions

— Disposals

— Amortization

— Application of valuation allowance to adjust carrying value of servicing assets

— Other-than-temporary impairments

— Other changes that affect the balance and a description of those changes

- For each class, the fair value of recognized servicing assets and servicing liabilities at the beginning and end of the period, if it is practicable to estimate the value

- The risk characteristics of the underlying financial assets used to stratify recognized servicing assets for purposes of measuring impairment

- The activity by class in any valuation allowance for impairment of recognized servicing assets—including beginning and ending balances, aggregate additions charged and recoveries credited to operations, and aggregate write-downs charged against the allowance—for each period for which results of operations are presented

REGULATORY CONSIDERATIONS

The federal banking agencies limit the aggregate amount of servicing assets, which includes mortgage-servicing assets, that may be included in regulatory capital. (Call Report Instructions, Schedule RC-M) In addition, the Call Report instructions specify how certain elements of servicing should be reported in the income statement for RAP.

On February 25, 2003, the federal banking agencies issued an advisory on mortgage banking activities. The advisory addresses methods used to determine the fair value of servicing rights and to manage risks.

For statutory accounting purposes, insurance companies generally follow GAAP for recognized servicing rights. However, servicing rights are considered nonadmitted assets for statutory purposes. (SSAP 33, Securitizations) (If an asset is considered nonadmitted, it should be reported as a nonadmitted asset and charged against surplus, because insurance regulators have determined that it is not readily available to fulfill policyholder obligations.)

AUDIT CONSIDERATIONS

There is no specific auditing standard that addresses audit issues for servicing rights. Several aspects of accounting for servicing rights are judgmental and contribute to audit risk. The key areas of financial reporting of servicing rights that affect audit risk include:

- *Determining fair value* If quoted prices are not available, fair value must be estimated. Fair value estimates of servicing rights are driven by several factors, including assumptions about interest rates, default, prepayment, and volatility. The auditor should assess the reasonableness of the assumptions used and test the accuracy of the model. AU 342, *Auditing Accounting Estimates*, provides general guidance on auditing significant accounting estimates. The guidance in SAS-92 and the Audit Guide, *Auditing Derivative Instruments, Hedging Activities, and Investments in Securities*, may provide useful guidance by analogy, especially with respect to valuation. AU 336, *Using the Work of a Specialist*, provides guidance on using a specialist, such as a broker, to assist in auditing fair value information.

> **OBSERVATION:** Auditors sometimes provide valuation services to clients, including advising on the methodologies and assumptions for estimating the fair value of servicing rights. Auditors should take care to avoid independence issues when they provide valuation services in connection with an audit. (In 1999, the Independence Standards Board (ISB) recognized this concern, and issued an interpretation, "FAS-133 Assistance," that discusses the types of services that would raise concerns about independence. Auditors may find that guidance helpful by analogy.)

- *Determining that it is not practicable to estimate fair value* The "alternative procedures" described in FAS-140, paragraph 71 serve to reduce the amount of gain on sale that is recognized at the date of sale. Because many entities dislike the volatility of "gain on sale" accounting, auditors should be very skeptical of assertions that it is not practicable to estimate the fair value of servicing rights. This subject is discussed more broadly in Chapter 6, "Securitizations."
- *Stratifying servicing rights for impairment purposes* Impairment is measured in the aggregate by stratifying assets within a class subsequently measured using the amortization method. The strata are determined by predominant risk characteristics, which is a loosely defined term in FAS-140. The opportunity exists to mask losses by identifying strata that contain naturally offsetting characteristics (whereas, if a different risk characteristic had been used, such as interest rate risk, all of the assets would have responded in a similar fashion). Auditors should ensure that management's identification of predominant risk characteristics is appropriate and consistently applied.

- *Risks and rewards of sales* The standard for sales of servicing rights is a subjective assessment of whether substantially all of the risks and rewards of ownership have been transferred. Auditors should review all of the relevant facts and circumstances to confirm the appropriateness of management's assessment.

ILLUSTRATIONS

Illustration 4-1: Recording and Amortizing a Servicing Asset Obtained

On January 1, 20X1, Car Loan Finance Co. sold interest-bearing receivables to an investor with a principal amount of $500,000. The receivables pay $100,000 in principal at the end of each year through December 31, 20X5. CLF obtains the right to service the sold receivables and is entitled to a servicing fee of 100 basis points times the outstanding principal balance at the beginning of each year. The market rate for servicing receivables of this type (adequate compensation) is 50 basis points per year. The servicing right is an asset because the benefits of servicing exceed adequate compensation. Assume the following for purposes of this illustration:

- The servicing asset obtained upon sale of the receivables is recorded on 1/1/20X1 at its fair value of $6,427,
- The entity elects to subsequently measure the servicing asset based on the amortization method,
- The servicing asset does not become impaired, and
- All cash flow predictions turn out to e accurate and therefore represent the actual amounts earned/expensed.

Table 4-1
Recording and Amortizing a Servicing Asset

Year Ended	A Net Servicing Cash Flows (1)	B Amortization of Servicing Asset (2)	C Net Income from Servicing (3)	D Balance Servicing Asset (4)
1/01X1				$6,427
12/31/X1	$2,500	$2,142	$358	4,284
12/31X2	2,000	1,714	286	2,570
12/31/X3	1,500	1,285	215	1,285
12/31/X4	1,000	857	143	428
12/31/X5	500	428	72	0
Total	$7,500	$6,427	$1,073	

Notes:

1. Projected by servicer, using market data for adequate compensation, and a declining principal balance.
2. Net servicing income for the period / total net servicing income × initial fair value of servicing asset.
3. Column (A) minus column (B).
4. Fair value calculated as present value of net servicing cash flows (Column A) discounted at a market rate of 7%.

Journal entries

January 1, 20X1

Cash	$493,573	
Servicing asset	6,427	
Receivables		$500,000

To record the sale of receivables and recognize a servicing asset.

December 31

	20X1	**20X2**	**20X3**	**20X4**	**20X5**
Cash	2,500	2,000	1,500	1,000	500
Servicing asset	2,142	1,714	1,285	857	428
Net servicing income	358	286	215	143	72

To record the amortization of the servicing asset and other servicing revenues and expenses. Note that the servicing revenues, expenses, and amortization would all be recorded separately. They are shown net here for simplicity.

Illustration 4-2: Sale of Receivables with Servicing Obtained

Student Loan Corp. sells loans with a carrying amount of $725,000. SLC will pass through all of the interest to the investor except 200 basis points. The servicer is entitled to 100 b.p.4 as compensation for servicing; the remaining 100 b.p. is considered an I-O strip. (The I-O strip in this case clearly would not be considered a derivative under FAS-133.) At the date of the sale, the fair value of the loans is $728000. Under Case 1, the fair value of the servicing is estimated at $32,000 and the fair value of the I-O strip is estimated at $40,000. Under Case 2, the fair value of the servicing right is not practicable to estimate and the fair value of the I-O strip is estimated at $40,000.

Table 4-2
Case 1: Allocation of Carrying Amounts Based on
Relative Fair Values

Computation of net proceeds

	Fair Value of Proceeds	Fair Value of Interests That Continue to Be Held
Cash proceeds	728,000	
Servicing asset	32,000	
I-O strip		40,000
Net proceeds	760,000	

Allocation of previous carrying amount between loans sold and interests retained [FAS-140, par. 10(b)]

	Fair Value	% of Total Fair Value	Allocated Carrying Amount
Loans sold	760,000	.95	688,750
I-O strip	40,000	.05	36,250
	800,000	100%	725,000

Gain on sale calculation

Net proceeds	760,000
Carrying amount of loans sold	(688,750)
Gain on sale	71,250

Journal entries

Cash	728,000	
Servicing asset	32,000	
Loans		688,750
Gain on sale		71,250

To record the transfer of receivables and recognize the I-O strip and servicing asset obtained. Subsequently, the servicing asset would be measured at either fair value with changes in value recognized in earnings or amortized and tested for impairment, based on the election made under FAS-140, as amended by FAS-156.

I-O strip	36,250	
Loans		36,250

To reclassify the I-O strip that continues to be held by the transferor. The I-O strip would be measured under FAS-115 like an available-for-sale or trading security. Because the I-O strip is recorded at an allocated amount less than its fair value, it may be necessary to record an adjustment the first time the I-O strip is marked to market.

> **AUTHOR'S NOTE:**   FAS-156, which amends FAS-140, changes the computation of gains and losses for transfers qualifying for sale treatment under FAS-140 by requiring that servicing assets be considered part of the proceeds received by the transferor rather than as a retained interest. Prior to the issuance of FAS-156, separately recognized servicing assets were included as part of retained interests (now referred to as "interests that continue to be held by the transferor").

Table 4-3
Case 2: Fair Value of Servicing Not Practicable to Determine

Computation of net proceeds

	Fair Value of Proceeds	Fair Value of Interests That Continue to Be Held
Cash proceeds	728,000	
Servicing asset	0	
I-O strip		40,000
Net proceeds	728,000	

Allocation of previous carrying amount between loans sold and interests retained [FAS-140, par. 10(b)]

	Fair Value	% of Total Fair Value	Allocated Carrying Amount
Loans sold	728,000	.948	687,300
I-O strip	40,000	.052	37,700
	768,000	100%	725,000

Gain on sale calculation

Net proceeds	728,000
Carrying amount of loans sold	(687,300)
Gain on sale	40,700

Journal entries

Cash	728,000	
Loans		687,300
Gain on sale		40,700

To record sale of the loans and the resulting gain.

I-O strip	37,700	
Loans		37,700

To reclassify the I-O strip that continues to be held by the transferor. The I-O strip would be measured under FAS-115 like an available-for-sale or trading security. Because the I-O strip is recorded at an allocated amount less than its fair value, it may be necessary to record an adjustment the first time the I-O strip is marked to market.

CHAPTER 5
TRANSFERS OF FINANCIAL ASSETS

CONTENTS

Overview	5.02
Background	5.03
Exhibit 5-1: *Terminology for Transfers of Financial Assets*	5.03
Exhibit 5-2: *Transactions Excluded from the Scope of FAS-140*	5.05
Organization of Chapters 5 and 6	5.06
Exhibit 5-3: *Applying the Guidance in Chapters 5 and 6*	5.07
Accounting for Transfers of Financial Assets	5.08
Criteria for Sale Accounting	5.08
Important Notice: FASB Project to Amend FAS-140	5.09
Recording a Transfer	5.09
Transfers Recorded as Sales—Transferor's Accounting	5.09
Exhibit 5-4: *Steps upon Completion of a Transfer*	5.10
Classification in Financial Statements	5.11
New Interests and Interests That Continue to Be Held	5.11
Transfers Accounted for as Sales—Transferee's Accounting	5.12
Transfers Recorded as Borrowings	5.12
Classification in Financial Statements	5.13
Changes in Control	5.13
Changes That Cause a Loss of Control	5.14
Implementation Guidance	5.14
General	5.14
Paragraph 9(a): Isolation	5.15
Paragraph 9(b): Transferee Can Pledge or Exchange	5.17
Paragraph 9(c): Transferor Does Not Effectively Control	5.18
Interests That Continue to Be Held by a Transferor	5.22
Exhibit 5-5: *Summary of Effect of Rights to Reacquire Transferred Assets*	5.22
Exhibit 5-6: *Treatment of New Interests and Interests That Continue to Be Held by the Transferor*	5.25
Fair Value Measurement	5.27
Transfers Accounted for as Borrowings	5.29

Exhibit 5-7: *Accounting for Elements of a Transfer in a Borrowing*   5.30

Deferred Tax Consequences   5.31

Disclosures   5.31

    Not Practicable to Estimate Fair Value   5.31

    Other Disclosures   5.31

Regulatory Considerations   5.32

Audit Considerations   5.32

    Achieving Isolation   5.32

    Fair Value Estimates   5.33

Illustrations   5.34

Illustration 5-1: *Transfer of Assets Accounted for as a Sale*   5.34

Illustration 5-2: *Transfer of Assets Accounted for as a Secured Borrowing*   5.36

OVERVIEW

Transfers of financial assets include many types of common transactions-sales, exchanges, securitizations, and pledges of collateral. Accounting for transferred financial assets is straightforward when the transferor has no continuing involvement with the transferred asset or with the transferee. Transfers of financial assets in which the transferor retains an interest in the transferred assets or is involved with the transferee raise questions about whether the transfer should be accounted for as a sale or a secured borrowing. Off-balance-sheet accounting and the related issue of gain or loss recognition are crucial accounting considerations for many companies, particularly those concerned about capital requirements, debt ratios, and the pattern of earnings.

Accounting for transfers of financial assets is different from transfers of other types of assets because the cash flows of a financial asset can be divided and controlled simultaneously by different parties. Under the "financial-components approach," an entity recognizes a sale when it has surrendered control over a financial asset (or parts of it) and it receives consideration that does not merely represent an interest in the transferred asset. Several criteria must be met to conclude that control has been surrendered, and a lawyer's letter is generally required to substantiate one of them. The transferring entity continues to report any interests that continue to be held at their allocated carrying amounts and records any new interests it receives or obligations it incurs at fair value, if practicable. Subsequently, those interests are accounted for under applicable GAAP, depending on the instrument type. When control has not been surrendered, the transaction is accounted for by both parties as a secured borrowing.

The sale criteria discussed in this chapter generally apply to transfers of financial assets that involve special-purpose entities, including securitizations. Chapter 6, "Securitizations," discusses the specific application of these conditions to securitizations, as well as when consolidation of a special-purpose entity is required.

BACKGROUND

FAS-140 is the primary GAAP for transfers of financial assets. A lengthy FASB Staff Implementation Guide on FAS-140 and several EITF Issues address numerous implementation questions.

> **AUTHOR'S NOTE:** FAS-140 superseded FAS-125 and other previous implementation guidance, but certain transactions were grandfathered. This chapter addresses the *current* requirements of FAS-140. In addition, this chapter and Chapter 6, "Securitizations," reflect the requirements of FAS-156, which changes the computation of gains and losses for transfers qualifying for sale treatment under FAS-140. Refer to the 2006 edition of CCH's *Financial Instruments* for guidance prior to the issuance of FAS-156.

FAS-140 uses terminology that may not be familiar to some accountants and market participants. Exhibit 5-1 provides a translation between FAS-140 and common usage.

EXHIBIT 5-1
TERMINOLOGY FOR TRANSFERS OF FINANCIAL ASSETS

FAS-140	Common Usage	
	Sale	Borrowing
"Transferor"	Seller of asset	Borrower of cash; collateral provider
"Transferee"	Buyer of asset	Lender of cash

FAS-140 has a wide-ranging effect on financial institutions and the treasury function at other types of companies. For example, the following types of transactions are all considered *transfers* of financial assets:

- Sales of receivables with recourse
- Securitizations
- Loan participations

- Factoring arrangements
- Secured borrowings
- Bond swaps
- Repurchase agreements
- Dollar rolls
- Securities lending transactions

FAS-140 addresses transfers of financial assets that are recognized in the balance sheet. FAS-140 applies to transfers involving the following instruments:

- Receivables and loans
- Investments in debt and equity securities
- Most equity-method investments
- Minimum lease payments relating to sales-type and direct financing leases and guaranteed residual values (FAS-140, par. 89)
- Derivatives, including derivatives accounted for under FAS-133 that are not financial instruments (EITF 99-8) (Note: Derivatives that could become liabilities would be subject to the extinguishment of liabilities provisions of FAS-140, rather than the transfer of assets provisions. (FAS-140 Q&A, par. 15) See Chapter 11, "Extinguishments of Debt.")
- Beneficial interests in securitization trusts that hold nonfinancial assets (unless the interests are held by a related party or the holder must consolidate the trust) (FAS-140 Q&A, par. 7)

Accounting questions arise when the transferor continues to hold one or more forms of continuing involvement with the transferred financial asset. Common examples of continuing involvement include:

- Continuing to service a financial asset that has been transferred.
- Providing recourse to the buyer of the transferred asset (perhaps in the form of a put option).
- Sharing in the revenues from the transferred asset (e.g., retaining an interest-only strip or residual interest).
- Providing collateral to a lender.
- Converting the interest rate or currency on the transferred asset.
- Continuing to hold an option to repurchase the transferred asset.

Exhibit 5-2 sets forth numerous transactions that are *not* accounted for under FAS-140, some of which involve financial assets, for the reason(s) indicated.

EXHIBIT 5-2
TRANSACTIONS EXCLUDED FROM THE SCOPE OF FAS-140

Transaction Type Transfer of . . .	Reason for Exclusion	Applicable GAAP, if Any
Real estate and equity method investments that are in substance real estate	Not a financial asset	FAS-66, EITF Issue 98-8
Equipment under lease	Not a financial asset	FAS-66, FIN-43
Future revenues (e.g., as royalties, income from a business line)	Not a recognized financial asset (such as an accounts receivable)	EITF Issue 88-18
Servicing rights	Not a financial asset (FAS-140, par. 4)	See Chapter 4
Securitized stranded costs by utility companies	Not a financial asset (FAS-140 Q&A, par. 6)	EITF Issue 88-18
Judgment from litigation (unless it represents a contract for fixed payments)	Not a financial asset (FAS-140 Q&A, pars. 8 and 9)	—
Minimum lease payments on an operating lease	Not recognized in the balance sheet (FAS-140 Q&A, par. 1)	FAS-13, as amended
Unguaranteed residual values on a lease	Not a financial asset	FAS-13, as amended, and FTB 86-2
Leveraged leases, money-over-money and wrap lease transactions	Specific scop exception	FAS-13, as amended, and FTB 88-1
Bad debt recovery rights	Not recognized in the balance sheet (previously written off)	See Chapter 3
Stock of consolidated subsidiary	Special model for controlled entity (FAS-140 Q&A, par. 10, 11, and 12)	See Chapter 16

Transaction Type Transfer of...	Reason for Exclusion	Applicable GAAP, if Any
A company's own equity	Equity, not an asset to the company (FAS-140 Q&A, par. 4)	See Chapter 16
Loan syndication	Not a transfer (each lender funds its own loan; the lead lender is acting as servicer) (FAS-140, par. 103)	See Chapter 3
Origination, settle-ment, or restructuring of receivables	Not a transfer (FAS-140 Q&A, par. 3)	See Chapter 3 (re-structuring) and Chapter 6 (origination fees)
Charitable contributions	Not a transfer (FAS-140 par. 4)	FAS-116, FAS-136

FAS-140 covers several topics in addition to transfers of financial assets. Those other subjects are addressed in the following chapters of this book:

Subject	Cross Reference
Investments with significant prepayment risk	Chapter 2, "Investments in Debt and Equity Securities" and Chapter 13, "Embedded Derivatives"
Servicing rights	Chapter 4, "Servicing of Financial Assets"
Securitizations involving QSPEs and other entities	Chapter 6, "Securitizations"
Repurchase agreements, securi-ties lending transactions, accounting for pledges of collateral	Chapter 9, "Securities Lending Arrangements and Other Pledges of Collateral"
Extinguishments of liabilities	Chapter 11, "Extinguishments of Debt"

ORGANIZATION OF CHAPTERS 5 AND 6

The two broad categories of transfers of financial assets under FAS-140 are:

1. Transfers to "operating" companies whose activities are not severely restricted (including nonqualifying special-purpose entities) *and*

2. Transfers to "qualifying special-purpose entities" (QSPEs), which are commonly used to securitize financial assets.

While the same basic sale criteria apply to both categories of transactions, the criteria are modified somewhat when the transferee is a QSPE. In addition, the definition of a QSPE is complex and has been heavily interpreted. To enhance the reader's ability to retrieve information about securitization accounting, the guidance on transfers of financial assets has been divided into the following chapters in this book:

Chapter 5: Criteria for determining when a transfer of financial assets to an operating entity (or a nonqualifying SPE) should be accounted for as a sale or a borrowing

---

EXHIBIT 5-3
APPLYING THE GUIDANCE IN CHAPTERS 5 AND 6

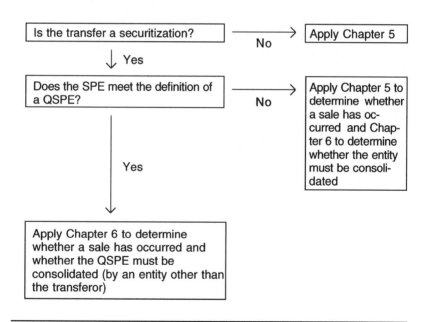

Chapter 6: Application of the sale criteria in transfers involving QSPEs and a discussion of consolidation of both QSPEs and nonqualifying special-purpose entities

These chapters are very interrelated and a practitioner encountering securitizations should read both chapters thoroughly.

ACCOUNTING FOR TRANSFERS OF FINANCIAL ASSETS

Criteria for Sale Accounting

A transfer of financial assets (or a portion of a financial asset) should be accounted for as a sale only if, and to the extent that, the transferor:

- Surrenders control over those financial assets *and*
- Receives cash or other *proceeds* in exchange.

Beneficial interests in the retained assets are not considered proceeds. (FAS-140, par. 9)

The transferor has surrendered control over transferred assets only if *all* of the following conditions of FAS-140 are met:

- Isolation: The transferred assets have been isolated from the transferor—put presumptively beyond the reach of the transferor and its creditors, even in bankruptcy or other receivership. (paragraph 9(a))
- Transferee can pledge or exchange: Each transferee has the right to pledge or exchange the assets it received, and no condition both (1) constrains the transferee from taking advantage of its right to pledge or exchange and (2) provides more than a trivial benefit to the transferor. (paragraph 9(b))
- Transferor does not effectively control: The transferor does not maintain effective control over the transferred assets through either (1) an agreement that both entitles and obligates the transferor to repurchase or redeem them before their maturity or (2) the ability to unilaterally cause the holder to return specific assets, other than through a *cleanup call*. (paragraph 9(c))

If *all* of these conditions are met, the transfer should be accounted for as a sale. If one or more of the conditions is not met, the transfer should be accounted for as a secured borrowing. A transaction can be partially a sale and partially a borrowing or neither a sale nor a borrowing to the extent that only beneficial interests in the transferred assets are received.

> **AUTHOR'S NOTE:** Each of these conditions has been heavily interpreted. The section below titled "Implementation Guidance" is integral to the appropriate accounting for transfers of financial assets.

IMPORTANT NOTICE
FASB PROJECT TO AMEND FAS-140

In its current project to amend FAS-140, the FASB's objectives are to address practice issues related to the permitted activities of a qualifying SPE, application of the isolation criterion for sale accounting, and various other issues that arose during redeliberaitons of the August 2005 FASB Exposure Draft, "Accounting for Transfers and Servicing of Financial Assets and Extinguishments of Liabilities." The FASB began redeliberations of in the second quarter of 2006 and is expected to issue another Exposure Draft with proposed amendments to FAS-140 as early as the fourth quarter of 2007. Readers should be alert to developments on this important project.

Recording a Transfer

Regardless of whether a transfer is accounted for as a sale or a borrowing, the transferor should continue to report any interest it continues to hold in the transferred assets, such as securities backed by the transferred assets, cash reserve accounts, and undivided interests. (FAS-140, par. 10 (a) and 58) (Note: Servicing assets and servicing liabilities are considered part of net proceeds in a sale, not a retained interest.)

> ☞ **PRACTICE POINTER:**   FAS-156, issued in March 2006, changes the computation of gains and losses for transfers qualifying for sale treatment under FAS-140. FAS-156 requires that servicing assets be considered part of the proceeds received by the transferor rather than as an interest that continues to be held by interest of the transferor. Prior to the issuance of FAS-156, separately recognized servicing assets were included as part of the interest continued to be held by the transferor.

Transfers Recorded as Sales—Transferor's Accounting

If the transfer qualifies as a sale (or a partial sale), the transferor (seller) should:

- Allocate the previous carrying amount between the assets sold, if any, and the interests that continue to be held by the transferor, if any, based on their relative fair values at the date of transfer. (FAS-140, par. 10(b))
- Remove all assets (or parts of assets) sold from the balance sheet (*derecognize* them). (FAS-140, par. 11(a))
- Recognize all assets obtained and liabilities incurred in consideration as proceeds of the sale at their fair values unless it is not

practicable to do so. (FAS-140, par. 11(b) and 11(c)) Examples of "new" assets and liabilities that are included in net proceeds include cash, put or call options held or written (for example, recourse or guarantee obligations), interest rate swaps, and servicing assets and servicing liabilities.

- Recognize in earnings any gain or loss on the sale as the difference between the net proceeds and the carrying amount attributed to the assets sold. (FAS-140, par. 11(d))

> **OBSERVATION:** The term "previous carrying amount" is not defined in FAS-140. However, based on definitions in other GAAP, including FAS-15 and FAS-114, the carrying amount should include any unamortized premium or discount, deferred fees and costs, accrued interest, deferred fair value hedge gains and losses, and any allowance for doubtful accounts or direct write-downs. (FSP FAS 140-1)

> **OBSERVATION:** FAS-140 focuses on the *initial* recognition and measurement of assets and liabilities that result from transfers of financial assets. FAS-140 addresses *subsequent* measurement of only servicing rights and beneficial interests with significant prepayment risk. Other GAAP addresses subsequent measurement of other new interests and interests that continue to be held by the transferor.
>
> Exhibit 5-4 summarizes the steps by a transferor upon completion of a transfer.

EXHIBIT 5-4
STEPS UPON COMPLETION OF A TRANSFER

Treatment of . . .	Has a Sale Occurred?	
	No	**Yes**
Proceeds:	Report as borrowing	Record net of liabilities at fair value, if practicable
Transferred asset:	Continue to report	Allocate carrying amount based on relative fair value; derecognize portion sold
Gain/loss calculation:	Not applicable	Net proceeds minus allocated carrying amount of assets sold

Classification in Financial Statements

FAS-140 does not specifically address the classification of gains and losses on sales of financial assets in the income statement. However, given the nature of the transaction, such gains and losses should be included as part of operating income (expense). SOP 01-6 requires that the aggregate amount of gains or losses on sales of loans or trade receivables be presented separately in the financial statements or in the notes to the financial statements. (SOP 01-6, par. 13(d))

Proceeds from sales of financial assets should be classified as follows in the Cash Flow Statement:

- Sales of customer trade receivables and notes—operating (FAS-95, par. 22(a))
- Sales of certain loans or other debt or equity instruments that are acquired specifically for resale—operating (FAS-102, par. 10(e))
- Sales of other loans and investments in equity securities of another entity—investing (FAS-95, par. 16)

> **SEC REGISTRANT ALERT:** The SEC staff expressed the following views on the classification of cash flows related to interests that continue to be held by the transferor in securitized loans:
>
> - Principal payments received on an interest that continues to be held should be recognized only when the interest is accounted for in the same way as trading securities instead of in the same way as available-for-sale or held-to-maturity securities.
> - Loans that are acquired for sale in a securitization that involves the receipt of subordinate interests that continue to be held by a transferor that are accounted for in the same way as available-for-sale securities may result in *negative operating cash flows* because the loan acquisitions are operating cash outflows, the cash proceeds from sale are operating cash inflows, and the cash flows from the interest received as a result of the securitization are investing cash flows.
>
> (December 2005 Presentation, *Current Developments in the Division of Corporation Finance*, at the National Conference on Current SEC and PCAOB Developments)

New Interests and Interests That Continue to Be Held

New assets obtained, liabilities incurred, and interests that continue to be held by the transferor should be recognized *separately* upon completion of a transfer of financial assets.

Any asset obtained (including separately recognized servicing assets) that is not an interest in the transferred asset is part of the proceeds from the sale (it is "new"). Any liability incurred, even if it is related to the transferred assets (including separately recognized servicing liabilities), is a reduction of the proceeds. Any derivative financial instrument entered into concurrently with a transfer of financial assets is either an asset obtained or a liability incurred and part of the proceeds received in the transfer. (FAS-140, par. 56) If a transferor cannot determine whether an asset is an interest that continues to be held or proceeds from the sale, the asset should be treated as proceeds, and measured at fair value, if practicable. (FAS-140, par. 58)

Transfers Accounted for as Sales—Transferee's Accounting

Upon completion of a transfer, the transferee (buyer) should recognize all assets obtained and any liabilities incurred and initially measure them at fair value (in total, presumptively the price paid). (FAS-140, par. 11)

Transfers Recorded as Borrowings

If the transfer does not qualify as a sale, both the transferor and transferee should account for the transfer as a secured borrowing. The transferor (borrower) should not recognize a gain or loss for the difference between the fair value of the transferred asset and the amount of proceeds. (FAS-140, par. 12)

> **OBSERVATION:** Paragraphs 10(b) and 58 of FAS-140 require that the transferor allocate the carrying amount of the transferred assets between the portion sold, if any, and the interests that continue to be held by the transferor, if any, *regardless* of whether the transaction is accounted for as a sale or as a borrowing.

Accounting for pledges of collateral in a secured borrowing is discussed in detail in Chapter 9, "Securities Lending Arrangements and Other Pledges of Collateral."

> **OBSERVATION:** Accounting under FAS-140 is intended to be symmetrical—if the transferor concludes that it has surrendered control, the transferee must be in control and the transfer should be accounted for as a sale and purchase, respectively. Likewise, if the transferor has not surrendered control, both parties should account for the transfer as a secured borrowing. However, FAS-140 does not require a party to "check on" the accounting by the other party.

Classification in Financial Statements

When a transaction is accounted for as a secured borrowing, the difference between the amount of proceeds loaned (borrowed) and the amount due (owed) should be classified as interest income (expense). (FAS-140, par. 93)

Proceeds from transfers of financial assets that are accounted for as secured borrowings should be classified as cash flows from investing or financing activities in the Cash Flow Statement, for the lender and borrower, respectively. (FAS-95, pars. 15-20, as amended)

Changes in Control

After a transfer has been accounted for as a sale, a change in circumstances could occur that indicates that the transferor has regained control of the transferred assets. Examples could include:

- A change in law, so that the assets are no longer isolated.
- The transferor has a contingent right to reacquire assets and the contingency is resolved (such as a call option on defaulted loans or a removal of accounts provision that becomes exercisable).

The transferor should account for such a change as a purchase of the assets from the former transferee(s) in exchange for liabilities assumed. The transferor should initially measure those assets and liabilities at fair value on the date of the change, even if the transferred asset has not physically been returned. (FAS-140, pars. 55 and 88) The initial fair value measure should incorporate any concerns about the collectibility of the asset. That is, a separate allowance for credit losses should not be established. (EITF 02-9)

The transferor should not recognize a gain or loss with respect to any interests that continue to be held by the transferor, because those portions were never sold. A gain or loss may be recognized only with respect to beneficial interests that are "re-purchased" from third parties (that is, the portion of the transferred assets that were sold) and only if the contingent right held by the transferor is not at-the-money, resulting in the fair value of those beneficial interests being greater or less than related obligations to the transferee. (EITF 02-9)

> ☞ **PRACTICE POINTER:** The above guidance is limited to contingent rights that are not being accounted for as derivatives under FAS-133. An option that is being accounted for as a derivative would not result in an earnings impact upon the "re-recognition" of third-party beneficial interests because all changes in fair value would already have been recognized in earnings.

The re-recognized assets should be accounted for under applicable literature, depending on their form. (EITF 02-9) Refer to Chapter 6, "Securitizations," for a discussion of changes in the qualifying status of a QSPE.

The former transferee would derecognize the assets on that date, as if it had sold the assets in exchange for a receivable from the transferor. (FAS-140, par. 55)

> ☞ **PRACTICE POINTER:**   A change in market prices does not give rise to a change in control. For example, if the transferor originally concluded that a freestanding call was sufficiently out-of-the-money that it was judged not to constrain the transferee, a subsequent increase in price that moves the call into-the-money would not cause a transferor to resume control of the assets. (FAS-140, par. 55)
>
> **SEC REGISTRANT ALERT:**   If a transferor regains control of an asset that was previously accounted for as having been sold (for example, in the case of a call option that becomes exercisable upon the event of borrower default), the original balance sheet classification of the asset when originally transferred should be maintained when control over that asset is re-recognized by the transferor. For example, if the asset subject to the call or repurchased by the transferor is a loan, the balance-sheet classification by the transferor upon re-recognition should be Loans (not Other Assets). (March 2005 Current Accounting and Disclosure Issues in the Division of Corporation Finance, SEC)

Changes That Cause a Loss of Control

FAS-140 does not explicitly address accounting for a transfer that was initially recorded as a secured borrowing because one of the conditions of paragraph 9 is not met, but subsequently, circumstances change and all of the criteria are met. It seems logical that the transaction would be accounted for as a sale on the day that all of the criteria of paragraph 9 are met, because the transferor no longer controls the asset. This view is supported by paragraph 55 of FAS-140 and an example in Question 49 of the FAS-140 Implementation Guide (the first example of a removal of accounts provision).

Implementation Guidance

General

Each contractual provision must be evaluated individually under the sale criteria and also in the context of other contractual provisions.

For example, a right held by the transferor to reacquire the transferred assets might not constrain the transferee or give the transferor effective control, but perhaps could cause a lawyer to conclude that the assets are not isolated from the transferor in certain jurisdictions. On the flipside, an individual right looked at in isolation might satisfy all three criteria, but the combination of rights and relationships among the parties involved might indicate that the transferor has maintained effective control over the transferred assets.

Paragraph 9(a): Isolation

Determining whether transferred assets are put beyond the reach of the transferor, its affiliates, and agents depends on all available facts and circumstances. Derecognition of transferred assets is appropriate only if the available evidence provides reasonable assurance that the transferred assets would be beyond the reach of the powers of a bankruptcy trustee or other receiver for the transferor or any consolidated affiliate of the transferor. (FAS-140, par. 27) The likelihood of a bankruptcy occurring is irrelevant—the standard is a worse-case scenario assessment. (FAS-140 Q&A, par. 18)

Some of the key factors to consider in assessing whether assets have been isolated include:

- Whether the contract or circumstances permit the transferor to revoke the transfer,
- The kind of bankruptcy or other receivership into which the transferor might be placed,
- Whether a transfer of financial assets would likely be deemed a true sale at law, and
- Whether the transferor is affiliated with the transferee, and other factors pertinent under applicable law. (FAS-140, par. 27)

> **OBSERVATION:** FAS-140 is often described as "legalistic." If the assets are not legally isolated, a sale cannot be recorded. Other GAAP (for example, FAS-66 on sales of real estate and EITF Issue 95-5 on sales of mortgage servicing rights) is based on an overall assessment of whether the "risks and rewards of ownership" of an asset have been transferred.

> ☛ **PRACTICE POINTER:** The AICPA issued an auditing interpretation to assist auditors in evaluating whether the available evidence provides reasonable assurance that the transferred assets would be beyond the reach of the powers of a bankruptcy trustee or other receiver. See the section "Auditing Considerations" later in this chapter.

Entities subject to FDIC receivership Assets transferred by an entity subject to possible receivership by the FDIC are isolated from the transferor if the FDIC or another creditor either cannot require return of the assets or can only require return in receivership, after a default, and in exchange for payment of, at a minimum, principal and interest earned (at the contractual yield) to the date investors are paid. (FTB 01-1, Appendix B, Q.1) Entities subject to the U.S. Bankruptcy Code may not apply this guidance by analogy. (FTB 01-1, Appendix B, Q.2)

> ☛ **PRACTICE POINTER:** In July 2000, the FDIC adopted a new Policy Statement, "Treatment by the Federal Deposit Insurance Corporation as Conservator or Receiver of Financial Assets Transferred by an Insured Depository Institution in Connection with a Securitization or Participation," which modifies the FDIC's receivership powers so that, subject to certain conditions, it shall not recover, reclaim, or recharacterize as property of the institution or the receivership any financial assets transferred by an insured depository institution that meet all conditions for sale accounting treatment under GAAP, other than the "legal isolation" condition in connection with a securitization or participation. The new Policy Statement should enable companies and their legal advisors to conclude that transfers within the scope of the rule would be isolated if the bank (transferor) were to go into receivership.

Entities subject to receivership under jurisdictions other than the FDIC or the U.S. Bankruptcy Code For entities that are subject to other possible bankruptcy, conservatorship, or other receivership procedures in the United States or other jurisdictions, judgments about whether transferred assets have been isolated need to be made in relation to the powers of bankruptcy courts or trustees, conservators, or receivers in those jurisdictions. (FAS-140, par. 84)

Sales between related parties A transfer from one subsidiary (the transferor) to another subsidiary (the transferee) of a common parent may be accounted for as a sale in the transferor subsidiary's separate company financial statements if:

- All of the conditions in paragraph 9 are met *and*
- The transferee's assets and liabilities are not consolidated into the separate-company financial statements of the transferor.

This would also be the case if the transferee were an equity method investee of the transferor. (FAS-140 Q&A, par. 20)

Paragraph 9(b): Transferee Can Pledge or Exchange

When a transferee has the ability to obtain all or most of the cash inflows from the transferred asset, either by exchanging the asset or by pledging it as collateral, there is evidence that the transferor no longer controls the asset. (FAS-140 Q&A, par. 22) Any condition that constrains the transferee from enjoying those rights must also provide more than a trivial benefit to the transferor to preclude sale accounting:

- Constraints imposed by the transferor presumptively provide more than a trivial benefit to the transferor.
- Constraints imposed by others depend on the facts and circumstances.

Some examples of constraints that would preclude sale accounting include:

- A provision that prohibits the transferee from selling or pledging a transferred loan (including some loan participations, see FAS-140, par. 106).
- Transferor-imposed contractual constraints that narrowly limit timing or terms, for example, allowing a transferee to pledge only on the day assets are obtained or only on terms agreed upon with the transferor. (FAS-140, par. 29)
- A free-standing call option written by the transferee and held by the transferor on transferred assets that are not readily obtainable in the marketplace, unless it is so far out-of-the money that it is probable that the transferor will not exercise it. (FAS-140, par. 32)
- A put option written by the transferor to the transferee on transferred assets that are not readily obtainable in the marketplace that is so deep-in-the-money when it is written that it is probable that the transferee will exercise it. (FAS-140, par. 32)

Some examples of constraints that would *not* of themselves typically preclude sale accounting include (FAS-140, pars. 30–32):

- A transferor's right of first refusal on an offer from a third party to purchase the transferred asset.
- A requirement to obtain the transferor's permission to sell or pledge that will not be unreasonably withheld.
- A prohibition on sale to the transferor's competitor if other potential willing buyers exist.
- A regulatory limitation such as on the number or nature of eligible transferees (as in the case of securities issued under Secu-

rities Act Rule 144A or privately placed debt), provided that a sufficient number of qualified buyers exists. (FAS-140, par. 30)

- Illiquidity (for example, the absence of an active market).
- A constraint about which the transferor is unaware.
- A freestanding right to reacquire transferred assets that are readily available in the marketplace.
- A put option on marketable securities (however, a put option may interfere with isolation (paragraph 9(a)). (EITF 85-40)
- A transfer to an SPE (*not* a QSPE) that is significantly limited in its ability to pledge or exchange the transferred assets, *but* where the transferor has no continuing involvement of any kind and therefore does not benefit from the constraints. (FAS-140 Q&A, par. 22A)

> **OBSERVATION:** It is important to evaluate the overall effect of related rights and obligations to determine whether a transferee is constrained or a transferor has maintained effective control. For example, if the transferor or its affiliate is the servicer for the transferred asset and is empowered to put the asset up for sale, and has the right of first refusal, that combination would place the transferor in a position to unilaterally cause the return of a specific transferred asset and thus maintain the transferor's effective control of the transferred asset. (FAS-140, fn. 15)

> ☛ **PRACTICE POINTER:** EITF Issue 03-15, "Interpretation of Constraining Conditions of a Transferee in a CBO Structure," involves the EITF's preliminary discussion of the specific application of paragraph 9(b) of FAS-140. It addresses a collateralized bond obligation (CBO) structure—a securitization of high-yield debt, bank loan participations, or other similar financial assets involving a vehicle that is not a QSPE (at all times, it has the discretion to hold or sell defaulted assets)—that permits the SPE to sell up to between 20 percent and 30 percent annually of the aggregate principal balance of collateral during the reinvestment period (the "free trade basket"). At issue is whether the "free trade basket" violates paragraph 9(b) of FAS-140 and precludes sale treatment by the transferor. EITF Issue 03-15 is "on hold" until the project to amend FAS-140, which is currently underway, is finalized.

Paragraph 9(c): Transferor Does Not Effectively Control

Paragraph 9(c) has two parts:

1. Agreements to repurchase or redeem transferred assets (two-way forward contracts) and

2. Rights to cause the return of specific transferred assets to the transferor (call options that require physical settlement).

These two criteria were included to remove ambiguity about the effect that the financial components approach might otherwise have on certain types of transactions. For example, paragraph 9(c)(1) was included primarily to ensure that traditional repurchase agreements would continue to be accounted for as borrowings, not as sales. Paragraph 9(c)(2) clarifies when a call option on specific transferred assets represents a form of effective control. This condition was designed in part to address accounting for removal of accounts provisions (ROAPs), which are common in securitizations of receivables. See Chapter 6, "Securitizations."

Paragraph 9(c)(1): Commitments to repurchase or redeem transferred assets If the transferor commits to repurchase or redeem transferred assets from the transferee, the transferor is deemed to have maintained effective control only if all of the following conditions are met:

- The assets to be repurchased or redeemed are the same or *substantially the same* as those transferred.
- The transferor is able to repurchase or redeem them on substantially the agreed terms, even in the event of default by the transferee, by maintaining at all times during the contract term cash or other collateral sufficient to fund substantially all of the cost of purchasing replacement assets from others. (FAS-140, par. 49)
- The agreement is to repurchase or redeem them before maturity, at a fixed or determinable price.
- The agreement is entered into concurrently with the transfer. (FAS-140, pars. 47-49)

If all of these criteria are met, the transaction should be accounted for as a secured borrowing. If all of these criteria are *not* met, the arrangement should be evaluated as a call option under paragraph 9(c)(2). (FAS-140 Q&A, par. 49)

Paragraph 9(c)(1) primarily affects repurchase agreements, dollar-rolls, and securities lending transactions. The applicability of the sale criteria and the related implementation guidance on transfers involving securities under agreements to repurchase them are discussed in detail in Chapter 9, "Securities Lending Arrangements and Other Pledges of Collateral."

☛ **PRACTICE POINTER:**   "Wash sales" and bond swaps generally are accounted for as sales under FAS-140 because, at the time of the sale, there is no concurrent agreement to repurchase the same or substantially the same asset. (FAS-140, par. 99)

Paragraph 9(c)(2): Ability to unilaterally cause the return of specific transferred assets   A right to reacquire transferred assets results in the transferor's maintaining effective control over the transferred assets when it has the *unilateral ability* to cause the return of specific transferred assets at a fixed or determinable price (unless that price is so far out of the money or for other reasons, it is probable when the option is written that the transferor will not exercise it). (FAS-140, par. 52) Sometimes these rights are referred to as "call options;" however the name applied to a contractual provision, if any, is inconsequential.

A unilateral ability must be in contractual form and legally enforceable. A noncontractual understanding between the parties involved does not meet this condition. (FAS-140 Q&A, par. 52)

Partial sales   Sometimes, the transferor maintains effective control over a portion of the transferred assets. For example:

- The transferor has a call on the remaining balance of amortizing assets at a specified point in time.
- The transferor has a call on any loans that remain from a portfolio of prepayable loans after a threshold has been met.
- The transferor has a call on a few individual loans in a transfer of a portfolio of loans.

Assuming that the other sale criteria are met, such transfers should be accounted for partially as a sale and partially as a borrowing. Where individual assets are subject to a call, sale accounting is precluded only for those assets. (FAS-140 Q&A, par. 50) When an allocation must be made of a group of transferred assets, the portion of the transferred assets to be derecognized and retained should be based on the relative fair values of:

- Cash flows expected to have been distributed to investors before the option becomes exercisable and
- The balance of future cash flows expected to remain when the option becomes exercisable. (FAS-140 Q&A, par. 49, fn.†)

Removal of accounts provisions (ROAPs) are discussed in Chapter 6, "Securitizations," because they are more commonly found in securitizations. However, the analysis would be the same if a ROAP were to exist in a different type of transfer of assets.

Examples Some examples of provisions that would preclude sale accounting under paragraph 9(c)(2) include:

- A call option held by the lead bank (the transferor) in a loan participation that allows the participating banks to resell, but reserves the right to call the loan at any time from whoever holds it. (FAS-140 Q&A, pars. 49 and 51)
- A fixed-price call option held by the transferor that has been attached (stapled) to the transferred asset (an *attached call*). (FAS-140, par. 52)
- The transferor has a call exercisable when assets decline to a specified low level, but the transferor is *not* the servicer. (A clean-up call can only be held by the servicer.) Control is maintained over the amount of assets estimated to be called at that time, *not* all of them. (FAS-140 Q&A, pars. 49 and 55)

Examples of provisions that do not (of themselves) preclude sale accounting under paragraph 9(c)(2):

- A recourse obligation (the transferor can not cause the borrower to default on its obligations).
- A right to call specific transferred assets by paying their then-current fair value. However, if the transferor also holds the residual interest, it does maintain effective control, because the transferor can pay any price it chooses and recover any excess paid over fair value through its residual interest. (FAS-140, par. 53)
- A callable instrument, such as a callable bond where the *issuer* holds the right to call the instrument (not the transferor). (FAS-140 Q&A, par. 49)
- A clean-up call that is held by the transferor-servicer, even if the servicing is contracted out to a third party (but not if the servicing right is *sold*). (FAS-140 Q&A, par. 56)

Exhibit 5-5 provides a summary of the effect of several common rights and obligations to reacquire transferred assets.

Interplay with FAS-133 If the transaction must be accounted for as a *sale*, the terms of the agreement that both entitles and obligates the transferor to repurchase or redeem the transferred assets or a right to do so should be analyzed to determine whether it meets the definition of a derivative under FAS-133. (If the transaction were accounted for as a borrowing, the agreement would typically be an impediment to sales accounting and be excluded from the scope of FAS-133 using the exception in paragraph 10(f) of FAS-133.) (EITF Topic D-65)

Interests That Continue to Be Held by a Transferor

Note receivable from investor as proceeds   A note receivable that is a general obligation of the third-party investor would represent proceeds from a sale. However, a note receivable that is solely collateralized by the transferred assets without recourse to the third-party investor represents a beneficial interest in the transferred assets that would preclude sale accounting to the extent of the beneficial interest that continues to be held by the transferor. (FAS-140 Q&A, par. 21)

Allocating the previous carrying amount   Allocating the previous carrying amount of an asset can give rise to a discount or premium. On a debt instrument, that difference should be amortized in the same manner that interest is recognized on that type of asset. (FAS-140 Q&A, par. 64) Chapter 7, "Calculating Yields on Debt Investments," discusses accounting for premiums and discounts in detail.

EXHIBIT 5-5
SUMMARY OF EFFECT OF RIGHTS TO REACQUIRE
TRANSFERRED ASSETS

Transferor holds . . .	Effect on Accounting[†]
Unconditional Attached Call [¶364]*	
– On all transferred assets	No sale [¶9(c)(2)]
– On a portion of the assets and:	
- Can choose assets	No sale on covered assets [¶9(c)(2); ¶52; ¶86(a)]
- Cannot choose assets	Sale of part of the asset(s) [¶9(c)(2); ¶52; ¶87(a)]

Unconditional Embedded Call [¶364]*	
– In assets (embedded by issuer)	Does not preclude sale [¶50]

Unconditional Freestanding Call [¶364] (fixed-price)*	
– On assets readily obtainable	Does not preclude sale [¶9(b); ¶9(c)(2); ¶32]
– On assets not readily obtainable	No sale [¶9(b); ¶32]

ROAPs*	
– Unconditional	Analyze as if it were either an attached or freestanding unconditional call.
– Conditional‡	Re-analyze as an unconditional call when the condition is resolved.

Exceptions	
Cleanup call	Does not preclude sale [¶9(c)(2); ¶364]
Fair value call (no residual interest)	Does not preclude sale unless it constrains the transferee. [¶9(c)(2); ¶52; ¶53]
Conditional call	Does not preclude sale. Re-analyze provision when condition resolved.

Other Rights to Reclaim Assets	
Forward purchase agreement:	
–With collateral maintenance, etc	No sale [¶9(c)(1); ¶47–49]
–Without collateral maintenance	Analyze as either an attached or freestanding call. [¶9(c)(2)]
Auction where transferor holds residual	Analyze as either an attached or freestanding call. [¶9(c)(2); ¶53]
Right of first refusal§	Reanalyze as an unconditional call when the condition is resolved. [¶30]

† All rights require physical settlement (not net cash settlement) and involve a fixed exercise price unless otherwise noted.

* Unless the call is so far out of the money or for other reasons it is probable when the option is written that the transferor will not exercise it.

‡ Conditional ROAPs are rights to reclaim assets that the transferor does not have the unilateral right to exercise.

§ Unless the transferor can trigger activation of the right (see FAS-140, fn. 15). In that case, the right should be analyzed as an in-substance call option.

Source: Adapted from FAS-140 Q&A, par. 49.

Interests that continue to be held by the transferor with magnified risks Many forms of interests that continue to be held by the transferor concentrate the risks previously existing in an asset or group of assets. For example, if the transferor continues to hold an interest-only strip, it now has an instrument with significant *prepayment risk*—that is, it can contractually be settled in such a way that the transferor would not recover substantially all of its recorded investment (in this case, the allocated carrying amount). (FAS-140, par. 14) Similarly, a transferor may continue to hold a subordinated residual interest in the cash flows of the transferred assets and thereby maintain the same level of *credit risk*, even though the assets have been sold. The accounting for the interest that continues to be held by the transferor—including subsequent measurement, impairment, and income recognition—depends on the form of the interest and the source of the supporting cash flows. Exhibit 5-7 summarizes the literature that applies to various forms of new interests and interests that continue to be held by a transferor and provides cross-references to other chapters in this book.

Credit enhancements and recourse Credit enhancements are designed to reduce the investors' risk that the transferred assets would default. Some credit enhancements are interests that continue to be held by a transferor (assets) that bear significant amounts of credit risk—for example, subordinated residual interests and cash reserve accounts. Other credit enhancements are liabilities, such as guarantees and credit derivatives. The initial accounting for recourse and other forms of credit enhancements depends on whether the transferor might have to make a cash payment to the transferee and the specific terms of the arrangement (such as whether the agreement meets the definition of a derivative or whether the arrangement is in the form of a security).

Recourse embedded in an interest that continues to be held by a transferor A transferor might continue to hold a beneficial interest in the transferred assets that is subordinate to the claims of other investors—that is, the transferor is paid only after other investors in the transferred assets are paid. Effectively, the transferor has kept much of the credit risk of the transferred assets. If the transferor has *no liability beyond the amount of the subordinated interests that continue to be held:*

- A separate liability should *not* be recorded.
- The interest that continues to be held should be recorded at its allocated previous carrying amount.
- Credit losses from the underlying assets would affect the measurement of the interest that continues to be held. See Exhibit 5-6. (FAS-140 Q&A, pars. 67 and 68)
- The fair value of the interest that continues to be held (for the purpose of allocating the previous carrying amount) must consider the timing of cash flows (including any restrictions on use), credit uncertainties, and other assumptions that market participants would use to value the asset. (FAS-140 Q&A, par. 76)

Separate recourse obligations If the transferor commits to reimburse the transferee for a failure of debtors to pay when due (up to a certain amount), and the transferor would need to fund those amounts from its own resources (above and beyond any cash flows generated by its interest that continues to be held):

EXHIBIT 5-6
TREATMENT OF NEW INTERESTS AND INTERESTS THAT CONTINUE TO BE HELD BY THE TRANSFEROR

Instrument Type	Could Be Proceeds? (Initially Measure at Fair Value, if Practicable)	Could Be Interest That Continues to Be Held? (Initially Measure At Allocated Amount Based On Relative Fair Value#)	Subsequent Measurement if Recognized Separately After the Transfer	Applicable GAAP	Discussed in Chapter
Beneficial interests with embedded derivatives	No*	✔**	FAS-159 fair value election is available for the hybrid instrument. Prior to effective date of FAS-159, hybrids may be measured at fair value in its entirety under the FAS-133 fair value election (if applicable); If not, derivative and host accounted for separately.	FAS-133, several DIG issues, FAS-159	13, 19
Instruments with significant prepayment risk and some credit risk; I/Os (no embedded derivative)†	No*	✔	At fair value like (or as) an AFS or trading security	FAS-140, par. 14, FAS-115, par. 7 (as amended), EITF 99-20	2, 6
Servicing assets	✔	No	Entities can elect fair value method or amortization method	FAS-140, par. 63 b, d, e, and f	4
Servicing liabilities	✔	No	Entities can elect fair value method or amortization method	FAS-140, par. 63 b, d, e, and g	4

Instrument Type	Could Be Proceeds? (Initially Measure at Fair Value, if Practicable)	Could Be Interest That Continues to Be Held? (Initially Measure At Allocated Amount Based On Relative Fair Value#)	Subsequent Measurement if Recognized Separately After the Transfer	Applicable GAAP	Discussed in Chapter
Loan or note receivable from transferee	No*	✔	At amortized cost. Also, FAS-159 fair value election for the loan or note receivable is available.	FAS-114, or FAS-5 as appropriate, FAS-159	3, 19
Marketable equity securities	No*	✔	At fair value as an AFS or trading security	FAS-115	2
Nonmarketable equity securities	No*	✔	At cost, adjusted for impairment. Also, FAS-159 fair value election is available for the loan or note receivable.	APB-18, FAS-159	2, 19
Debt securities	No*	✔	At cost or fair value, as applicable	FAS-115, FAS-65 (as amended), EITF Issue 99-20	2
Derivatives (including credit derivatives)	✔	No	At fair value	FAS-133	12–15
Liabilities incurred (recourse, guarantees, etc.)	✔	No	Estimated probable loss. Also, FAS-159 fair value election is available for liabilities incurred.	FAS-5, FIN-45, FAS-159	3, 8, 19

* Would only represent proceeds if the instrument derives its cash flows from a source other than the transferred assets. For example, the transferee could give the transferor marketable securities of another issuer as proceeds in a transfer. Similarly, a transferee could give the transferor servicing rights relating to different assets as proceeds in a transfer.

** The derivative component would always be considered "new."

† Instruments with embedded derivatives are discussed in Chapter 13, "Embedded Derivatives."

Readers should be alert to developments in the FASB's project to amend FAS-140, in which the FASB has tentatively decided to change the initial measurement attribute for interests that continue to be held by a transferor to be held to fair value, rather than based on allocated carrying amounts based on relative fair value.

(Adapted from FAS-140 Q&A, par. 58)

- A separate liability should be recorded at fair value. (FAS-140 Q&A, pars. 67 and 68 and FIN-45)
- Subsequent measurement depends on the specific terms of the arrangement:
  - A traditional recourse obligation (guarantee) is accounted for under FAS-5 as a loss contingency. EITF Issue 92-2 says that if the obligation is discounted, subsequent accruals should be at the rate inherent in determining the initial obligation.
  - A credit derivative is accounted for at fair value under FAS-133. Chapter 12, "Introduction to Derivatives," provides guidance on identifying credit derivatives.

> **OBSERVATION:** Carrying over a previous loan loss allowance relating to the transferred assets is not in accordance with GAAP. The recourse obligation should reflect all probable credit losses over the life of the receivables, not only the ones recognized and measured under FAS-5 or FAS-114 prior to the transfer date. (EITF Issue 92-2)

Fair Value Measurement

> **AUTHOR'S NOTE:** In September 2006, the FASB issued FASB Statement No. 157, *Fair Value Measurements*. FAS-157 provides a single definition of the term *fair value*, establishes a framework for measuring fair value where required by existing GAAP, and expands disclosures about fair value measurements. Specific fair value measurement guidance applicable to investments in debt and equity securities is covered in this Chapter. Chapter 18, "Fair Value Measurements, Fair Value Disclosures, and Other Financial Instruments Disclosures," provides the detailed provisions of FAS-157 and specific fair value measurement guidance applicable to all financial instruments required to be measured at fair value under GAAP. The 2008 edition of CCH's *Financial Instruments* has been updated to incorporate the provisions of FAS-157. FAS-157 is effective for calendar-year-end companies as of January 1, 2008. Unless a company chooses to early adopt, prior GAAP is applicable for financial statements issued for 2007.
>
> As this book went to press, the FASB was addressing a possible delay of FAS-157's effective date. The FASB agreed to consider delaying the effective date for nonfinancial instruments and for certain types of entities, including private companies and "smaller" public companies (not yet defined). Readers should monitor the FASB's further deliberations regarding the nature of any delay of FAS-157's effective date. Also, readers should refer to the 2007 edition for GAAP related to the fair value measurement of financial instruments applicable before the effective date of FAS-157.

Fair value is the price that would be received to sell an asset or paid to transfer a liability in an orderly transaction between market participants at the measurement date. FAS-157 establishes a single definition and framework for determining fair value and is applicable for existing accounting pronouncements that require or permit fair value measurements (with several specific scope exceptions). The fair value measurement model in FAS-157 applies for both initial measurement and subsequent measurement of assets and liabilities required to be measured at fair value.

> **OBSERVATION:** FAS-157 is now the primary guidance for measuring fair value. The guidance in FAS-140, paragraphs 68–70 has been superseded.

The objective of a fair value measurement under FAS-157 is to determine the price that would be received to sell the asset or paid to transfer the liability at the measurement date (an exit price) using assumptions that market participants would use. FAS-157 provides a framework for determining fair value consistently, including a fair value hierarchy for prioritizing inputs when valuation techniques are used for estimating fair value.

Chapter 18, "Fair Value Measurements, Fair Value Disclosures, and Other Financial Instrument Disclosures," provides specific fair value measurement guidance applicable to all financial instruments required to be measured at fair value under GAAP.

Not practicable to determine fair value FAS-140 includes "an alternative measure" if it is not practicable for the transferor to determine the fair value of an asset or liability in certain circumstances. (FAS-140, par. 71) In this context, it is not practicable to determine fair value if the estimate is not sufficiently *reliable* to justify recognition of a gain following a sale of assets. (FAS-140, par. 268 and FAS-140 Q&A, par. 69)

> ☛ **PRACTICE POINTER:** FAS-157 does not eliminate the practicability exception that permits use of a transaction price (an entry price) to measure fair value at initial recognition of financial assets and liabilities under FAS-140, rather than an exit price, which is required by FAS-157. In addition, FAS-157 does not eliminate practicability exceptions in FAS-140 and EITF Issue 85-40, "Comprehensive Review of Sales of Marketable Securities with Put Arrangements," which provide exemptions to the requirement to measure fair value if it is not practicable to do so.

> **OBSERVATION:** FAS-107 (fair value disclosures) includes a different "description" of *not practicable*. In FAS-107, *not practicable* means the estimate cannot be made without incurring excessive costs. (FAS-107, par. 15)

If it is not practicable for the transferor to determine the fair value of an asset or liability, the entity must use the following alternative procedures:

1. An asset should be recorded at zero.
2. A liability should be recorded at the greater of:

    a. The amount that results in no gain or loss on the transaction (that is, the excess, if any, of:

        (1) The fair value of assets obtained less the fair value of other liabilities incurred over

        (2) The sum of the allocated carrying values of the assets transferred) *or*

    b. The amount that would be recognized under FAS-5, as interpreted by FIN-14. For a loss to be accrued under FAS-5, it must be probable that a liability has been incurred (or an asset impaired) and the amount must be reasonably estimable. (FAS-140, par. 71)

If it later becomes practicable to determine the fair value of an asset or liability, the asset or liability (or the resulting gain or loss) would generally not be remeasured with two exceptions:

1. Other GAAP requires that the instrument be measured at fair value (or another amount) and that GAAP does not include a practicability exception (e.g., FAS-115 and FAS-133).

2. Servicing liabilities would be remeasured, but not less than the amortized measurement of its initially recognized amount. (FAS-140 Q&A, par. 71)

> **OBSERVATION:** This practicability exception only applies to *initial* measurement by the transferor after a transfer is complete. (FAS-140, par. 299) *Subsequent* measurement of each component depends on the form of the instrument and certain other factors (such as the nature of the entity, the form of the instrument, and the entity's intended holding period). Neither FAS-115 (securities) nor FAS-133 (derivatives) includes a practicability exception. It would be unusual for an entity to claim that it is impracticable to determine the fair value of an instrument for *initial* measurement purposes under FAS-140, but then somehow be able to determine the fair value for *subsequent* measurement purposes, if required under other GAAP. FAS-140 Q&A, paragraph 69, states that in a vast majority of circumstances, it should be practicable to estimate fair values.

Transfers Accounted for as Borrowings

When a transfer is accounted for as a secured borrowing, the transferred assets remain on the books of the transferor, and the cash proceeds are recorded as a borrowing. The other elements of the transaction do not receive separate accounting because to do so would result in counting the same exposure twice. Exhibit 5-7 summarizes the treatment of various elements of accounting for a transfer of loans as a borrowing.

EXHIBIT 5-7
**ACCOUNTING FOR ELEMENTS OF A TRANSFER
IN A BORROWING***

Element of Transaction	Recognized Separately?	Rationale
Transferred (pledged) assets	Yes	Assets remain on balance sheet along with borrowing Refer to Chapter 9 for collateral accounting
Residual interests	No	The transferred loan remains on the balance sheet
Servicing	No	Servicing fee included in interest rate on loans
Interest-only strip	No	Entire coupon is accrued on the loan
Recourse	No	Maximum credit loss already recorded on the balance sheet (the loans themselves)
Interest rate swap	No	Recognized on an accrual basis as the difference between the loans (asset) and borrowing (liability)
Call (and put) options, forward repurchase contracts	No	The assets subject to the option are already on the balance sheet

* This Exhibit assumes that neiter the transferred assets nor the secured borrowing contain embedded derivatives that require separate accounting.

OBSERVATION: While some of those elements are "already recorded," in many cases, the subsequent measurement of them would be different if they were accounted for separately. For example, a servicing asset would be measured at either fair value or the lower of cost or market (depending on the election made for subsequent measurement), an interest rate swap would be measured at fair value, and most options and forwards would be measured at fair value.

Deep-in-the-money puts In a transfer of marketable securities subject to a put option that must be accounted for as a borrowing (for example, because the security is not readily obtainable and the put is deep in the money), the transferor should amortize the difference between the original "sales price" and the put price over the period to the first put date. (EITF 85-40)

Mortgage-backed bonds Finance companies, banks and savings institutions, mortgage banks and credit unions should classify transfers of mortgages accounted for as secured borrowings separately from advances, other notes payable, and subordinated debt. (SOP 01-6, par. 14(i))

Deferred Tax Consequences

Deferred taxes should be provided for any temporary differences that arise between the accounting for a transfer for book purposes (GAAP) and tax purposes. It is common for entities to seek sale treatment for book purposes and debt treatment for tax purposes. FAS-109 provides guidance about deferred tax accounting.

DISCLOSURES

FAS-140 requires that certain disclosures be made by entities that transfer financial assets during the period.

Not Practicable to Estimate Fair Value

If it is not practicable to estimate the fair value of certain assets obtained or liabilities incurred in transfers of financial assets during the period, the transferor must provide a description of those items and the reasons why it is not practicable to estimate their fair value. (FAS-140, par. 17(d))

Other Disclosures

Other disclosures required by FAS-140 are addressed in the chapters indicated below.

- Securitized financial assets accounted for as sales, and interests that continue to be held by a transferor are discussed in Chapter 6, "Securitizations."
- Disclosures about servicing rights are discussed in Chapter 4, "Servicing of Financial Assets."
- Disclosures about collateral are discussed in Chapter 9, "Securities Lending Arrangements and Other Pledges of Collateral."
- Fair value disclosures are discussed in Chapter 18, "Fair Value Measurements, Fair Value Disclosures, and Other Financial Instrument Disclosures."

Interests that continue to be held by a transferor may be subject to other disclosure requirements, depending on their form. For example, securities are subject to the requirements of FAS-115. In addition, the nature and amount of any direct or indirect guarantees written as part of a transfer of financial assets must be disclosed in accordance with the requirements of FIN-45. Refer to Chapter 8, "Debt Financing," for additional information.

REGULATORY CONSIDERATIONS

Banks, thrifts, and credit unions follow GAAP in the preparation of their Call Reports. However, there are regulatory capital implications for certain types of continuing involvement, including recourse. Chapter 6, "Securitizations," discusses recent changes in capital requirements for certain financial institutions.

For statutory accounting purposes, insurance companies must apply SSAP No. 91, *Accounting for Transfers and Servicing of Financial Assets and Extinguishments of Liabilities,* which supersedes SSAP No. 18, *Transfers and Servicing of Financial Assets and Extinguishments of Liabilities;* SSAP No. 33, *Securitization;* and SSAP No. 45, *Repurchase Agreements, Reverse Repurchase Agreements and Dollar Repurchase Agreements.* SSAP No. 91 is modeled on the guidance in FAS-140 and has an effective date of January 1, 2005.

AUDIT CONSIDERATIONS

There are numerous aspects of the accounting for transfers of financial assets that introduce significant audit risk. Paramount among them is the fact that differences in terms, relationships among the parties, applicable laws and regulations, and the nature of the assets involved can significantly affect the accounting. Auditors can reduce this risk by carefully reviewing all of the terms and surrounding conditions of material transactions. The points below are central to most transfers of financial assets involving operating entities. Audit issues relating to securitizations are discussed in Chapter 6, "Securitizations."

Achieving Isolation

Paragraph 9(a) is the crux of FAS-140—a sale should be recognized only if there is reasonable assurance that the transferred assets *would* be beyond the reach of a bankruptcy trustee or other receiver for the transferor or any other consolidated affiliate of the transferor (FAS-140, par. 27). Determining whether isolation has been achieved is primarily a legal judgment. Therefore, unless the transfer is routine with no continuing involvement, the auditor typically will not be able to evaluate management's assertion that transferred assets are appropriately isolated in the absence of a legal letter prepared by an experienced attorney.

The Audit Issues Task Force of the AICPA has issued guidance about evaluating legal interpretations in support of management's assertion that the isolation criterion has been met (AU 336, *Using the Work of a Specialist*). The interpretation includes numerous examples of language that provides support for, or undermines, a conclusion that the assets have been isolated for entities subject to U.S. bankruptcy law and receivership by the FDIC.

In evaluating whether transferred assets are isolated beyond the reach of the transferor (and the transferor's creditors, even in bankruptcy), a legal specialist should consider the following factors: (1) the structure of the transfer, (2) the nature of any continuing involvement, (3) the type of insolvency or other receivership proceedings applicable to the transferor, and (4) other applicable legal factors.

The legal letter must not (1) restrict the auditor's ability to rely on the letter, (2) disclaim an opinion, (3) restrict its scope to facts and circumstances not applicable to the particular transfer, or (4) express its conclusions using conditional language (e.g., "In our opinion, the transfer *should* be considered a sale..." or "...In our opinion, it is probable that..."). In a two-step transfer, the lawyer's letter should address both transfers.

The auditor should evaluate the need for periodic updates of a legal letter to confirm that there have been no changes in relevant law or regulations that may affect previous or future transfers (see paragraph 55 of FAS-140).

Fair Value Estimates

Determining the fair value of components of financial instruments and proceeds received in a transfer is a critical part of the application of FAS-140. Components of financial instruments and residual interests frequently do not have quoted market prices and fair values must be determined by the entity using internally or externally developed valuation models. As described in SAS-92, auditors should obtain evidence supporting the fair value recorded or disclosed by their clients by performing procedures such as:

- Assessing the reasonableness and appropriateness of the model,
- Independently verifying the underlying assumptions through reference to external sources,
- Independently recalculating the fair value, and
- Comparing the fair value and assumptions used with recent transactions.

Similar procedures should be used to audit fair value disclosures and the sensitivity analysis for residual interests in a securitization.

Auditors should consider the guidance in ISB Interpretation 99-1, FAS-133 Assistance, which, among other things, addresses certain independence issues with respect to valuation services. For fair value estimates obtained from third-party sources, auditors should consider the applicability of the guidance in AU 336, *Using the Work of a Specialist*, or AU 324, *Reports on the Processing of Transactions by Service Organizations*. In addition, when the determination of fair value requires the use of estimates, auditors should consider the guidance in AU Section 342, *Auditing Accounting Estimates*, and AU Section 328, *Auditing Fair Value Measurements*.

ILLUSTRATIONS

Illustration 5-1: Transfer of Assets Accounted for as a Sale

Triumph Company sells a portfolio of loans with a par value of $10,000,000 and a carrying amount of $10,100,000 (including accrued interest, net deferred loan fees, and an allowance for loan losses) to Regency Bank for $10,050,000. Triumph agrees to repurchase any loans that default from Regency for a defined period of time and up to a maximum dollar amount (representing a limited recourse obligation). Triumph will service the loans. It will receive more than adequate compensation for the servicing. Triumph also agrees to convert the interest rate on the loans from their contractual floating rate to a fixed rate of interest that reflects current market terms (this provision meets the definition of a derivative, and thus would be considered "proceeds," not an interest that continues to be held by a transferor).

Evaluating the sale criteria

9(a): Legal counsel for Triumph writes a reasoned legal letter that concludes that the assets would be isolated from Triumph in the event that Triumph were to go bankrupt (even though the likelihood of bankruptcy is remote). Therefore, this condition is met.

9(b): There are no constraints on Regency. Therefore, this condition is met.

9(c): Triumph has agreed to repurchase any loans that default. This condition is met because Triumph cannot unilaterally control the return of any specific assets.

Evaluating proceeds (including "new" assets and liabilities incurred) and interests that continue to be held by a transferor

A sale may only be recognized to the extent that consideration other than an interest that continues to be held by the transferor in the transferred asset is received (that is, net proceeds). Any interests that continue to be held by a transferor remain on the books at their allocated carrying amounts. (FAS-140, pars. 10 and 11)

Computation of net proceeds

	Fair Value of Proceeds
Cash proceeds	10,050,000
Interest rate swap	250,000
Servicing asset	300,000
Recourse obligation	(400,000)
Net proceeds	10,600,000

Gain on sale calculation

Net proceeds	10,200,000
Carrying amount of loans sold	(10,100,000)
Gain on sale	100,000

Journal entry

Cash	10,050,000	
Interest rate swap	250,000	
Servicing asset	300,000	
Loans		10,100,000
Recourse obligation		400,000
Gain on sale		100,000

To record the sale of loans, new assets obtained and liabilities incurred, and the gain and loss on sale. [FAS-140, par. 11] Chapter 12, "Introduction to Derivatives," addresses the subsequent accounting for the interest rate swap. Chapter 4, "Servicing of Financial Assets," addresses the subsequent measurement of the servicing asset.

If it were not practicable to determine the fair value of the recourse obligation, the calculations would be revised as follows:

Computation of net proceeds

	Fair Value of Proceeds
Cash proceeds	10,050,000
Interest rate swap	250,000
Servicing asset	300,000
Recourse obligation	—
Net proceeds	10,600,000

Journal entry

Cash	10,050,000	
Interest rate swap	250,000	*At fair value*
Servicing asset	300,000	*At fair value*
Loans	10,100,000	*At carrying amount*
Recourse obligation	500,000	*At the amount that results in no gain*
Gain on sale	0	

To record the sale of loans, new assets obtained and liabilities incurred, and the gain and loss on sale. [FAS-140, par. 11] Chapter 12, "Introduction to Derivatives," addresses the subsequent accounting for the interest rate swap. Chapter 4, "Servicing of Financial Assets," addresses the subsequent measurement of the servicing asset.

> **OBSERVATION:** FAS-156 amended FAS-140 and requires that servicing assets be considered part of the proceeds received by the transferor rather than as an interest that continues to be held by the transferor. In this illustration, the gain on sale and the amount of the recourse obligation was determined based on the original carrying amount of the loans. However, if the transferor continued to hold an interest in the transferred loans, an allocation of the previous carrying amount of the loans would be required and the loans sold, the gain on sale, and the amount of the recourse obligation would be determined based on the allocated carrying amount.

> ☛ **PRACTICE POINTER:** Illustration 4-2 of Chapter 4, "Servicing of Financial Assets," illustrates the accounting for a transfer of loans where it is not practicable to determine the fair value of a servicing asset. Illustration 6-1 in Chapter 6, "Securitizations," illustrates a transfer of loans where the transferor continues to hold a subordinated interest in the transferred assets, requiring an allocation of the previous carrying amount of the loans.

Illustration 5-2: Transfer of Assets Accounted for as a Secured Borrowing

Assume the same facts as above, except that Triumph's legal counsel was unable to conclude that the assets would be isolated in the event of a bankruptcy. Also assume that Regency Bank is not constrained from pledging or exchanging the transferred assets, and, in fact, sells the loans shortly after receiving them.

Transferor's accounting

Elements of Transfer	Proceeds	Comments
Cash	$10,050,000	Recorded as a borrowing
Interest rate swap	N/A	Interest expense is recorded on the borrowing using the fixed rate promised to the transferee. Interest on the loans pledged as collateral continues to be accrued at the floating rate of interest.
Recourse obligation	N/A	Impairment would be recognized on loans remaining on balance sheet
Servicing asset	N/A	Servicing is not recognized as a separate asset when the transaction is recorded as a borrowing

Cash	$10,050,000	
Secured borrowing		$10,050,000

To record the transfer as a secured borrowing. (FAS-140, par. 12)

Loans pledged as collateral	$10,100,000	
Loans		$10,100,000

To reclassify loans that are pledged as collateral in a secured borrowing. [FAS-140, par. 15] See Chapter 9, "Securities Lending Arrangements and Other Pledges of Collateral."

Transferee's accounting

Regency Bank also accounts for the transaction as a secured loan. Regency would accrue interest income at the fixed rate of interest promised by Triumph. Regency Bank would not record the loans as its own assets unless and until Triumph defaults under the terms of the contract. When Regency Bank sells the collateral, assume that that transfer also must be accounted for as a secured borrowing under FAS-140.

Journal entries

Secured loan	$10,050,000	
Cash		$10,050,000

To record the transfer as a secured loan. The loans pledged as collateral should not be recorded on Regency's balance sheet. [FAS-140, pars. 12 and 15]

When Regency sells the "collateral":

Cash	$10,050,000	
Obligation to return collateral		$10,050,000

The loan to Regency and the obligation to return the collateral to Regency should only be offset if all of the criteria of FIN-39 are met.

When the loans mature:

Obligation to return collateral	$10,000,000	
Secured loan		$10,000,000

To remove the secured loan and the obligation to return collateral to Regency.

CHAPTER 6
SECURITIZATIONS

CONTENTS

Overview	6.03
Background	6.03
Common Features of Securitizations	6.04
Significance of Qualifying Special-Purpose Entities	6.06
Exhibit 6-1: Diagram of Typical Securitization Involving QSPE	6.06
Accounting for Securitizations	6.07
Attributes of a Qualifying Special-Purpose Entity (QSPE)	6.07
Attribute 1: The SPE Is Demonstrably Distinct from the Transferor	6.07
Attribute 2: Prescribed and Limited Activities	6.08
Attribute 3: Limits on Holdings of a QSPE	6.09
Attribute 4: Limited and Automatic Sales	6.12
Exhibit 6-2: Analysis of Sales by an SPE	6.13
Exhibit 6-3: Summary of Terms That Would Disqualify an SPE	6.14
Applying the Sale Criteria in Transfers Involving QSPEs	6.14
Paragraph 9: Consideration Other Than Beneficial Interests in the Transferred Assets	6.15
Paragraph 9(a): Isolation	6.15
Paragraph 9(b): Conditions That Constrain the Transferee	6.17
Paragraph 9(c)(2): Maintaining Effective Control	6.17
Exhibit 6-4: Analysis of Removal of Accounts Provisions	6.19
Exhibit 6-5: Effect of Rights to Reacquire Assets in a Securitization Involving a QSPE	6.19
Accounting for a Transfer of Assets in a Securitization	6.21
Subsequent Measurement of Beneficial Interests Issued in a Securitization	6.22
Classification in Financial Statements	6.23
Unique Aspects of Accounting for Transfers Involving QSPEs	6.23

Exhibit 6-6: Summary of Accounting for Securitizations — 6.27

Change in Status of a QSPE — 6.28

Consolidation of Securitization Entities — 6.28

Consolidation of QSPEs — 6.29

Transition Issues — 6.30

Consolidation of Adequately Capitalized Entities That Issue Voting Equity — 6.30

Consolidation of Variable Interest Entities — 6.31

Exhibit 6-7: Entities Excluded from FIN-46(R) — 6.34

Exemption for *Di Minimus* Involvement — 6.35

Identifying Variable Interests — 6.35

Exhibit 6-8: Examples of Variable Interests in an Entity — 6.39

General Principle — 6.40

Assessing Expected Losses and Residual Returns — 6.40

Exhibit 6-9: Consolidating a Variable Interest Entity (FIN-46(R)) — 6.42

Timing of Assessments — 6.44

Consolidating a Variable Interest Entity — 6.45

Deconsolidating a Variable Interest Entity — 6.46

Disclosures — 6.46

Securitizations of Financial Assets — 6.47

Guarantees Written — 6.48

Disclosures about Variable Interest Entities — 6.48

Exhibit 6.10: Required Disclosures under FIN-46(R) — 6.49

Public Company Disclosures about Asset-Backed Security Transactions — 6.50

Regulatory Considerations — 6.52

Audit Considerations — 6.54

Identification of SPEs — 6.55

Consolidation of SPEs — 6.55

Illustrations — 6.56

Illustration 6-1: Securitization of Financial Assets Involving a QSPE — 6.56

OVERVIEW

Securitization is the process of transforming assets such as loans and receivables into securities. Special-purpose entities (SPEs) are often used as to effect a securitization—the transferor transfers assets into an SPE (often accompanied by a credit enhancement and derivatives to modify the cash flows), which then issues beneficial interests in that pool of assets to investors. To determine whether the original assets have been "sold" (that is, removed from the balance sheet), the transferor applies the sale criteria of FAS-140 somewhat differently, depending on whether the special-purpose entity has certain qualifying characteristics—which would make it a qualifying special-purpose entity (QSPE). QSPE status is desirable because transferors and, generally, most other investors, do not consolidate the assets and liabilities of a QSPE. Transfers involving nonqualifying special-purpose entities and other legal structures could require consolidation by the party that is the primary beneficiary of the arrangement—that is, all of the assets and liabilities of the SPE would be recorded on the balance sheet of that party. Therefore, consolidation of a securitization entity thwarts a goal of off-balance-sheet financing.

The following chart illustrates the differences between sale accounting, partial sale-partial borrowing accounting (say 50%), and consolidation accounting for a transferor (assume that the SPE is not qualifying). Assume the entity securitized $1,000 of loans for $1,100.

	Sale Accounting	Partial Sale	Consolidation
Cash	$1,100	$1,100	$1,100
Transferred assets balance	0	$500	$1,000
Debt	0	**$550**	**$1,100**
Gain on sale	$100	$50	0

Under sale accounting, the assets are removed from the balance sheet and a gain or loss is recorded. Under the partial sale scenario, some of the assets are removed from the balance sheet, some debt is recorded, and a proportionate gain or loss is recognized. In the consolidation scenario, the assets remain on the balance sheet, all of the debt issued to outsiders is recorded on the balance sheet, and no gain or loss is recognized. Clearly, the need to consolidate an SPE vastly changes the reported assets and liabilities (and income statement) of a transferor (or other party that is the primary beneficiary).

BACKGROUND

FAS-140 addresses when a transfer of financial assets should be accounted for as a sale or a borrowing, including securitization transactions involving SPEs. FAS-140 also addresses consolidation of a QSPE by a transferor. A FASB Staff Implementation Guide on FAS-140 addresses numerous implementation issues. Subsequent accounting for components that continue to be held by a transferor, purchased, or incurred after a securitization is addressed by several accounting standards, depending on the type of asset or obligation. Consolidation of QSPEs by entities other than the transferor and consolidation of other types of securitization entities by any party involved in the transaction is addressed in FIN-46(R) and ARB-51, as amended by FAS-94 and FAS-144.

This chapter addresses securitization of recognized financial assets, which includes minimum lease payments on sales-type and direct-financing lease receivables and guaranteed residual values of leases. Specialized accounting literature addresses accounting for other types of transactions involving leases and other nonfinancial assets such as real estate. Such transactions are outside the scope of this book.

> ☛ **PRACTICE POINTER:** As discussed in Chapter 5, "Transfers of Financial Assets," FAS-140 superseded FAS-125 and other previous implementation guidance, but certain transactions were grandfathered. This chapter addresses the *current* requirements of FAS-140.

Common Features of Securitizations

Securitizations are often achieved using a special-purpose entity (SPE), also called a special-purpose vehicle (SPV). An SPE is an entity such as a trust, corporation, or limited liability company that is created by the transferor or sponsor to carry out a specific activity or transaction. Loans, receivables, and even securities are transferred into the SPE, and usually some form of credit enhancement is provided for the benefit of investors. (For simplicity, this section will refer to the transferred assets as "loans.") Sometimes derivatives are included in the securitization pool to modify the interest rate characteristics (for example, fixed to floating), currency, maturity, and other characteristics of the loans. The SPE then issues beneficial interests in those assets, often in the form of certificates or securities, and the proceeds are used to pay the transferor for the transferred assets.

Companies engage in securitizations for a variety of reasons. If the transferor intends to *sell* most of the beneficial interests (securities), the motivations for a securitization can include:

- Asset-backed securities may be more appealing to investors than the loans themselves, because pools of assets can be diversified and the operational requirements of holding many small loans can be reduced.
- Asset-backed finance can provide a lower cost of funds than other funding alternatives.

- Appropriately recognizing the transaction as a sale and not consolidating the entity avoids adding debt to the balance sheet of a company.

If the seller of assets seeks to *retain* most of the assets in their new form, the motivations can include:

- Securities often bear a lower capital charge than loans.
- Liquid securities are easier to use as collateral in other transactions.
- The accounting model for securities is different from the loan model (primarily impairment recognition and carrying amounts).

There are two broad categories of securitizations (FAS-140, par. 74):

1. In a "pass-through" and "pay-through" securitization, receivables are transferred to the SPE at the inception of the securitization, and no further transfers are made. All cash collections are paid to the holders of beneficial interests in the SPE.
2. In a "revolving-period" securitization, receivables are transferred at inception and also periodically thereafter for a defined period, referred to as the revolving period. During the revolving period, the SPE uses most of the cash collections to purchase additional receivables from the transferor on prearranged terms (a forward contract).

Securitizations are often discussed in the context of off-balance-sheet finance. There are two key accounting questions relating to securitizations that determine whether securitized assets are removed from (or stay off of) the balance sheet:

1. Does the transfer of assets to an SPE qualify as a sale?
2. Must the transferor, sponsor, or investor in the beneficial interests of the SPE consolidate the assets and liabilities of the SPE (thereby putting them (back) on the balance sheet)?

Determining whether the transferor should account for a securitization of loans as a sale or a borrowing depends on whether the SPE meets certain qualifying criteria, which are discussed in detail, later in this chapter:

- Securitizations involving a "nonqualifying" SPE or other legal entity are treated like any other transfer of financial assets and the SPE is considered the transferee. The sale-versus-financing question is answered by applying the guidance in Chapter 5, "Transfers of Financial Assets." Consolidation of a nonqualifying SPE is discussed later in this chapter.

- Securitizations involving a qualifying SPE are accounted for using a modified set of criteria that reflect the unique features of those transactions. Consolidation of a QSPE is discussed later in this chapter.

Significance of Qualifying Special-Purpose Entities

The FASB coined the term "QSPE" to describe a unique legal entity that is used as a "vessel" to transform one form of financial assets into another (for example, fixed-rate prepayable loans into floating-rate securities). The powers and activities of a QSPE are carefully constructed to distinguish this unique "repackaging" function from other transactions involving operating entities.

QSPEs are significant for accounting purposes because in a properly designed transaction, the transferor does not consolidate the assets and liabilities of the QSPE into its own balance sheet. Instead, the transferor accounts for any interests it retains, according to their form. In FIN-46(R), the FASB broadened this consolidation exemption to other parties involved with a QSPE, unless they have certain rights that indicate control over the entity. Thus, QSPEs play a critical role in many securitization transactions where the goal is (1) to remove certain assets from the balance sheet, (2) to account for any retained financial instruments according to their new form, or (3) both. The QSPE rules are exceedingly detailed and form driven—only a very narrow set of transactions is allowed this "no consolidation" safe haven.

EXHIBIT 6-1
DIAGRAM OF TYPICAL SECURITIZATION INVOLVING QSPE

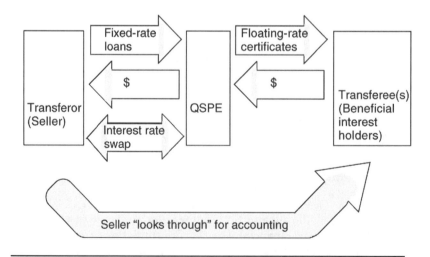

ACCOUNTING FOR SECURITIZATIONS

The first step in accounting for a transfer of assets that is a securitization is determining whether the transferee is a qualifying SPE.

Attributes of a Qualifying Special-Purpose Entity (QSPE)

A qualifying special-purpose entity (QSPE) is a trust or other legal vehicle that exhibits four essential attributes (FAS-140, par. 35):

1. It is legally distinct from the transferor.
2. Its activities are prescribed and significantly limited.
3. It holds only passive financial instruments and any new instruments are directly related to the assets transferred.
4. Sales of assets may only occur automatically and in response to certain specified events and circumstances.

If an SPE does not possess *all* of these qualities, it is not "qualifying." (Transfers to nonqualifying SPEs are covered by Chapter 5, "Transfers of Financial Assets.") Each of these attributes is discussed more fully below.

Attribute 1: The SPE Is Demonstrably Distinct from the Transferor

A qualifying SPE is demonstrably distinct from the transferor only if:

- It cannot be unilaterally dissolved by any transferor, its affiliates, or its agents and
- Either
  - At least 10 percent of the fair value of its beneficial interests is held by entities other than any transferor, its *affiliates*, and its agents (hereafter referred to as third parties) *or*
  - The transfer is a *guaranteed mortgage securitization.*

> **OBSERVATION:** The amount held by third parties must be at least 10% *throughout the life of the QSPE*—otherwise the SPE would no longer be qualifying (except for guaranteed mortgage securitizations).

Examples of the ability to unilaterally dissolve an SPE include the transferor or its affiliate:

- Holding sufficient amounts of beneficial interests to demand that the trustee dissolve the SPE,

- Having the right to call all the assets transferred to the SPE, and
- Having a right to call or a prepayment privilege on the beneficial interests held by other parties. (FAS-140, par. 36)

Attribute 2: Prescribed and Limited Activities

The activities of a QSPE must be significantly limited. This term is not defined in FAS-140 but, in context, it means only those actions that are necessary to collect cash flows relating to the transferred assets and disburse them to beneficial interest holders. All of the permitted activities of a QSPE must be specified in the legal documents that (1) established the SPE or (2) created the beneficial interests in the transferred assets that it holds. The permitted activities may be changed only with the approval of the holders of at least a majority of the beneficial interests held by third parties. (FAS-140, par. 35(b))

> ☞ **PRACTICE POINTER:** The activities of many kinds of entities are not *limited,* even if they are narrow in focus. For example, any bank, insurance company, pension plan, or investment company has powers that are not sufficiently limited for it to be a QSPE. (FAS-140, par. 37)

Examples of activities that are permitted by a QSPE include:

- A QSPE may be a conduit for more than one transferor (a "condominium structure"), provided that each individual unit or silo meets all of the conditions of a QSPE. The individual silos may hold different kinds of financial assets. (FAS-140 Q&A, par. 36)
- A servicer may exercise discretion to work out a loan, initiate foreclosure, and dispose of foreclosed assets that it temporarily holds, provided that discretion is included in the prescribed and limited powers of the SPE and that the activities do not violate other constraints on a QSPE. (FAS-140 Q&A, pars. 25, 25A, 28B, and 28C)
- A QSPE may assume an obligation of the transferor (that is, become the new obligor), provided that the legal documents that established the SPE specifically encompass that activity. This can be accomplished by the creditor accepting a beneficial interest in the SPE in exchange for the loan previously held. Whether the transferor's debt is extinguished depends on the facts and circumstances. (FAS-140 Q&A, par. 34 and FAS-140, par. 35)

Examples of activities that are not permitted by a QSPE include:

- A servicer may not initiate new lending to the borrower through the SPE as a result of the workout. Examples of activities that are not considered new lending are:

— Payments made by a servicer after a debtor fails to pay them (for example, property taxes and insurance).

— Advances of funds by servicers to facilitate timely payments to the beneficial interest holders, after which the servicer has a priority right to recoup its advances from future cash inflows.

— Extension of further credit by a transferor in a credit card securitization or revolving-period securitization and the subsequent transfer of the resulting loan by the transferor to a QSPE. (FAS-140 Q&A, par. 28B)

• A servicer may not subcontract for another entity to perform activities on behalf of a SPE that otherwise would not be permitted activities of a QSPE. (FAS-140 Q&A, par. 24A)

☞ **PRACTICE POINTER:** As part of its project to amend FAS-140, the FASB will address whether certain activities of a servicer are permissible under paragraph 35(b) of FAS-140. Specifically, the FASB will address the extent of servicer discretion consistent with the permitted activities of a QSPE with respect to certain activities (e.g., the substitution of collateral for a loan held by a QSPE, activities in connection with a sale of real estate temporarily held by a QSPE). Readers should monitor developments on this project.

Attribute 3: Limits on Holdings of a QSPE

A QSPE may hold *only:*

• *Financial* assets transferred to it that are *passive* in nature.

• *Passive* derivative financial instruments that *pertain to* beneficial interests issued or sold to third parties.

• Financial assets (for example, guarantees or rights to collateral) that would reimburse it if others were to fail to adequately service financial assets transferred to it, or to timely pay obligations due to it that it entered into when it was established, when assets were transferred to it, or when beneficial interests (other than derivative financial instruments) were issued by the SPE.

• Servicing rights related to financial assets that it holds (and those servicing activities must be limited as discussed in Attribute 2).

• Temporarily, nonfinancial assets obtained in connection with the collection of financial assets that it holds, such as through foreclosure of a mortgage loan.

• Cash collected from assets that it holds and investments purchased with that cash pending distribution to holders of beneficial interests that are appropriate for that purpose (that is, money-market or other relatively risk-free instruments without options and with maturities no later than the expected distribution date). (FAS-140, par. 35(c))

- The residual value of a sales-type or a direct financing lease only to the extent that it is guaranteed at the inception of the lease either by the lessee or by a third party financially capable of discharging the obligations that may arise from the guarantee. (FAS-140, par. 41)

A derivative financial instrument *pertains to* beneficial interests issued only if:

- The derivative is entered into (1) when the beneficial interests are issued to third parties or (2) when a passive derivative financial instrument needs to be replaced, such as in the case of a default of the counterparty. (FAS-140, par. 40(a))
- The notional amount does not initially exceed the amount of beneficial interests held by third parties and is not expected to exceed them in the future. (FAS-140, par. 40(b))
- The characteristics of the derivative relate to and counteract a risk associated with the beneficial interests issued to third parties or the related transferred assets. For example, an interest rate swap that provides the cash flows to convert a fixed-rate coupon on the transferred assets to a variable-rate beneficial interest would meet this condition. (FAS-140, par. 40(c))

The criteria in paragraphs 40(b) and 40(c) of FAS-140 must be met when beneficial interests are initially issued by a QSPE or when a passive derivative financial instrument needs to be replaced upon the occurrence of a specified event outside the transferor's control. The assessment of whether the criteria in paragraphs 40(b) and 40(c) are met is based on expectations at inception, such as the anticipated level of beneficial interests held by third parties over the life of the QSPE. For example, a transferor may obtain derivatives with a particular notional amount to mitigate risks for the term of the underlying financial assets based on anticipated future payment scenarios. Subsequent unexpected events (for example, an unexpected prepayment of the QSPE's assets that causes the notional amount of the derivatives it held to exceed the amount of beneficial interests held by third parties) and events that are outside of the control of the transferor that affect whether a derivative meets the criteria in paragraphs 40(b) and 40(c) would *not* result in a QSPE becoming nonqualifying. Similarly, purchases of beneficial interests by a transferor (or its affiliates or agents) from third parties in connection with treasury or market-making activities, which may cause the notional amount of passive derivatives held by an SPE to exceed the amount of beneficial interests held by third parties, should *not* be considered when assessing whether the criteria in paragraphs 40(b) and 40(c) are met if such interests are held temporarily and classified as trading securities. Further, any measure taken to "rebalance" the derivatives with the amount of beneficial interests held by third parties must be taken in accordance with the governing documents of the QSPE. (FSP FAS 140-2)

> **OBSERVATION:** The restrictions on the types of derivatives that a QSPE can hold are intended to uphold the limited purpose of a QSPE (that is, to transform assets from one form to another). The derivative must serve as a bridge between the characteristics of the transferred assets and the beneficial interests held by outsiders, subject to certain limitations.

> ☞ **PRACTICE POINTER:** As discussed in the Important Notice in Chapter 5, "Transfers of Financial Assets," one objective of the FASB's current project to amend FAS-140 is to resolve various practice issues related to the permitted activities of a qualifying SPE. The FASB is currently studying an approach that would eliminate the qualifying SPE concept from FAS-140. The FASB began is expected to issue another Exposure Draft with proposed amendments to FAS-140 as early as the fourth quarter of 2007. Readers should be alert to developments on this important project.

Examples of assets that may *not* be held by a QSPE are:

- Real estate or investments that are in-substance real estate (except temporarily, after a foreclosure).
- An investment accounted for by the equity method if the SPE or any related entity has significant influence over the investee. However, certain limited partnership interests that must be accounted for by the equity method even when the investor does not have significant influence could be considered passive investments. (FAS-140 Q&A, par. 30 and FAS-140, par. 39)
- A derivative entered into *after* a QSPE is established unless (1) it coincides with the issuance of beneficial interests to third parties or (2) replaces an existing derivative under circumstances that are outside the control of the transferor and that were specified upfront in the legal documents that established the QSPE. (FAS-140 Q&A, par. 27)
- A derivative instrument (such as a written option) that gives it the power to sell assets with the primary objective of realizing a gain, maximizing a return, or any other violation of Attribute 4. (FAS-140 Q&A, pars. 26 and 28)

☞ **PRACTICE POINTER:** A QSPE may hold caps and floors and European-style options.

Attribute 4: Limited and Automatic Sales

A QSPE can sell or otherwise dispose of financial assets (other than cash) only in *automatic* response to one of the following conditions:

- Occurrence of an event or circumstance that:
  - Is specified in the legal documents that established the SPE or created the beneficial interests in the transferred assets that it holds,
  - Is outside the control of the transferor, its affiliates, or its agents, *and*
  - Causes or is expected to cause the fair value of those financial assets to *decline* by a specified degree below the fair value of those assets when the SPE obtained them (not for gains or to maximize return).
- Exercise by a third-party beneficial interest holder (BIH) of a right to put that holder's beneficial interest back to the SPE.
- Exercise by the transferor of a call option or removal of accounts provision (ROAP) specified in the legal documents that established the SPE, transferred assets to the SPE, or created the beneficial interests in the transferred assets that it holds (the terms of the provision may affect whether a transfer should be accounted for as a sale or a borrowing).
- Termination of the SPE or maturity of the beneficial interests in those financial assets on a fixed or determinable date that is specified at inception. (FAS-140, par. 5(d))

☞ **PRACTICE POINTER:** Some servicing agreements include "specific-decision" rules that involve estimation of the value of an asset and input of subjective assumptions, such as estimating future vacancy and rental rates, the projected timing and sale price of foreclosed property, and the terms of a workout arrangement still to be negotiated. A specific-decision rule is *not* automatic if it requires the involvement of highly experienced personnel or it contains provisions that permit other beneficial interest holders (BIHs) to review and challenge the inputs to the formula. (FAS-140 Q&A, par. 25B)

Examples of powers to sell or otherwise dispose of assets that are permitted by a QSPE include:

- A servicer may dispose of a defaulted loan if that power and the requisite conditions are specified in the servicing agreement and the servicer has no choice in the matter. (FAS-140 Q&A, par. 25A).
- A servicer or other BIH in a QSPE may retain the right (an option) to purchase defaulted loans (that is, through physical settlement in some cases for a fixed amount and in other cases at fair value).
  — If the party holding the default call option is the transferor (or its affiliates or its agents), the option is a default removal-of-accounts provision (ROAP) or other physically settled contingent call option that is specifically permitted by paragraph 35(d)(3) of FAS-140.
  — If a third party holds the default call option, that right is a beneficial interest. Paragraph 44(a) of FAS-140 permits a qualifying SPE to dispose of assets in response to a third-party BIH exercising its right to put its beneficial interest back to the qualifying SPE in exchange for a full or partial distribution of the assets held by the qualifying SPE. (FAS-140 Q&A, par. 28A)

Examples of powers to sell or otherwise dispose of assets that would disqualify a QSPE include:

- A QSPE may not have the power to decide which loans to sell in response to adverse changes in an industry for which a concentration of loans exists (FAS-140 Q&A, par. 25) (Also causes a problem with pars. 9(c)(2), 54, and 86(a).)
- A QSPE may not have a servicing agreement that requires the servicer to either dispose of or hold (work out or foreclose) defaulted nonrecourse loans using a computation that is designed to maximize the return on the defaulted loan (that provision would violate paragraph 35(d)(1) of FAS-140). (FAS-140 Q&A, par. 28D)

EXHIBIT 6-2
ANALYSIS OF SALES BY AN SPE

PERMISSIBLE SALES BY A QSPE *Automatic sale in response to...*	POWERS TO SELL THAT WOULD DISQUALIFY AN SPE
• Failure of a servicer to perform	• Ability to *choose* to either sell or hold transferred assets in response to an event or condition outside the control of the transferor
• Default by or downgrade of the obligor below a specified level	• Ability to *choose* which assets to sell on predetermined termination dates
• Decline in fair value of transferred assets below a specified level	• Ability to sell transferred assets that have appreciated

- Involuntary insolvency of the transferor
- Exercise of a put by a third-party BIH
- Termination of the structure or maturity of the beneficial interests, provided a date(s) is specified at inception
- Ability to sell assets in a manner that maximizes return
- Ability to sell transferred assets in response to the violation of a nonsubstantive contractual provision

(FAS-140, pars. 42, 43, and 44)

EXHIBIT 6-3
SUMMARY OF TERMS THAT WOULD DISQUALIFY AN SPE

- Transferor holds a call option on beneficial interests and could unilaterally dissolve the SPE
- Unrelated parties do not hold at least a 10% interest in the beneficial interests of an otherwise qualifying SPE throughout the life of the arrangement
- The SPE has the power to engage in frequent and active buying and selling of assets
- Servicer has discretion to sell assets in a manner that maximizes gains or that requires professional judgment
- Transferor has the power—directly or indirectly—to "trigger" a sale of specific assets
- Assets held are not recognized financial assets (e.g., operating leases, nonfinancial assets), or assets that are not passive in nature, such as voting equity shares
- The notional amount of any derivatives exceeds the beneficial interests held by outsiders or the derivative is entered into after the SPE is established or beneficial interests are issued (except when an original derivative must be replaced)
- A derivative held by the SPE is not passive (for example, a decision must be made about whether to exercise an option)
- A derivative does not "pertain" to the transferred assets
- SPE can reinvest cash collections in assets that require sale before maturity of beneficial interests

---

Applying the Sale Criteria in Transfers Involving QSPEs

All of the criteria in paragraph 9 of FAS-140, as described in Chapter 5, "Transfers of Financial Assets," also apply to transfers involving QSPEs. The application of them differs in some respects because of the nature of a securitization transaction involving a QSPE. This section discusses certain unique features of applying the sale criteria in a securitization involving a QSPE.

Paragraph 9: Consideration Other Than Beneficial Interests in the Transferred Assets

It is very common in a securitization for a transferor to continue to hold beneficial interests in the transferred assets. Sometimes the transferor retains only a residual interest in some of the cash flows. In other cases, the transferor might continue to hold virtually all of the beneficial interests, such as in a guaranteed mortgage securitization. A sale can only be recorded if control is surrendered and *only to the extent that* consideration other than beneficial interests in the transferred assets is received in exchange.

> ☛ **PRACTICE POINTER:**   If the transferor continues to hold beneficial interests in 80 percent of the transferred assets, a sale should be recognized *to the extent* that consideration other than beneficial interests in the transferred assets is received in exchange (assuming the criteria of paragraph 9 are met). In this case, 20 percent would be considered sold.

Desecuritizations of financial assets   An exchange of securities or beneficial interests in a securitized pool of financial assets in which the transferor receives only the financial assets backing those securities or interests should not be accounted for as a sale. (EITF Topic D-51) Chapter 2, "Investments in Debt and Equity Securities," discusses this issue in more detail.

Paragraph 9(a): Isolation

The same standard applies to transfers involving QSPEs—the transferred assets must be beyond the reach of the transferor, its affiliates and its creditors. A securitization carried out in one transfer or a series of transfers may or may not isolate the transferred assets beyond the reach of the transferor and its creditors. Whether it does depends on the structure of the securitization transaction taken as a whole, considering such factors as the type and extent of further involvement in arrangements to protect investors from credit and interest rate risks, the availability of other assets, and the powers of bankruptcy courts or other receivers. (FAS-140, par. 80)

> ☛ **PRACTICE POINTER:**   In its August 2005 Exposure Draft to amend FAS-140, the FASB proposes that any arrangements, such as transferor guarantees and derivative transactions with beneficial interest holders would be evaluated as if they were provided directly to the QSPE for the purposes of determining whether transferred assets are isolated under paragraph 9(a) of FAS-140. Readers should refer to the Important Notice in

Chapter 5, "Transfers of Financial Assets," for a summary of major changes proposed by the Exposure Draft. Readers should be alert to developments on this important project. The FASB is currently redeliberating these issues and a second Exposure Draft outlining proposed amendments to FAS-140 is expected to be issued in the fourth quarter of 2007. Readers should be alert to developments on this important project.

Taken as a whole, the following "two-step" securitizations generally would be judged under present U.S. law as having isolated the assets beyond the reach of the transferor and its creditors, even in bankruptcy or other receivership (FAS-140, par. 84):

- The first transfer is to a special-purpose corporation that is designed such that the likelihood that the transferor or its creditors could reclaim the assets it is remote. This transfer is designed to be judged a true sale at law.

- The second transfer is from the special-purpose corporation to a bankruptcy remote trust or other legal vehicle with certain enhancements to investors. This second transfer might *not* be judged to be a true sale at law.

This structure works because FAS-140 allows these two transfers to be looked at together.

> **OBSERVATION:** In a two-step transfer involving a QSPE, the QSPE is the *second* SPE—that is, the entity that issues beneficial interests to investors.

Equitable right of redemption Under the "equitable right of redemption" available to secured debtors, after default, under U.S. law, a transferor may be able to require the return of transferred assets, but only in exchange for payment of principal and interest earned (at the contractual yield) to the date investors are paid. In such circumstances, the assets are considered not isolated, even if the likelihood of exercising that power is remote. Thus, "single-step" securitizations previously used by financial institutions subject to receivership by the FDIC and sometimes used by other entities will usually not satisfy paragraph 9(a). (FTB 01-1, Appendix B, Q.3)

Refer to *Securitization of Financial Assets* (Aspen Publishers, Inc., 2nd edition 2000, J. Kravitt, ed.) for additional information.

> ☛ **PRACTICE POINTER:** FTB 01-1 provided an additional transition period for application of FAS-140 paragraphs 9(a), 27, 28, and 80 through 84 for banks and other financial institutions subject to possible receivership under the FDIC (and for other affected entities that had previously considered their transfers of financial assets in "single-step" securitizations to have isolated those assets in similar circumstances), to transfers of financial assets occurring after December 31, 2001. The additional transition period ended June 30, 2006.

Paragraph 9(b): Conditions That Constrain the Transferee

In a securitization involving a QSPE, the transferee-buyer is considered the beneficial interest holder (BIH), not the QSPE. We *look through* the QSPE to determine whether each holder of a beneficial interest may pledge or exchange its beneficial interests and no condition both (1) constrains the BIHs from enjoying those rights and (2) provides more than a trivial benefit to the transferor.

- The lack of a market for the beneficial interests is not considered a constraint. (FAS-140, par. 30)
- A restriction under Rule 144A on the beneficial interests does not represent a constraint, provided that there is a large number of eligible investors. (FAS-140 Q&A, par. 24)

☛ **PRACTICE POINTER:** In a securitization involving a nonqualifying SPE, the transferee, not the BIHs, is considered the SPE.

Paragraph 9(c)(2): Maintaining Effective Control

If the transferee is a QSPE, it is by definition constrained from choosing to exchange or pledge the transferred assets. Accordingly, any call option held by the transferor (or an affiliate) is effectively *attached* to the transferred assets and could—depending on the price and other terms of the call—maintain the transferor's effective control over transferred assets through the ability to unilaterally cause the transferee to return specific assets.

Some examples of rights and relationships that maintain effective control and preclude sale accounting include:

- A transferor-servicer has the right to call the assets in the pool when it amortizes to 20 percent of its value (determined at the date of transfer) and the right is not a clean-up call. Control is maintained over 20 percent of the assets, *not* all of them. (FAS-140 Q&A, par. 49)
- A transferor's unilateral ability to cause a QSPE to return to the transferor or otherwise dispose of *specific* transferred assets at will or, for example, in response to its decision to exit a market or a particular activity. (FAS-140, par. 51)
- An embedded call that allows a transferor to buy back the beneficial interests of a QSPE at a fixed price (unless it is a cleanup call and the transferor or its affiliate is the servicer). (FAS-140, par. 52)
- The transferor holds *both* a call option on the beneficial interests held by third parties and the residual interest. This condition affects the transferor's ability to participate in an auction of the transferred assets upon termination of an SPE. (FAS-140 Q&A, par. 49 and FAS-140, par. 53)

A transferor that has a right to reacquire transferred assets from a QSPE does *not* maintain effective control (that is, sale accounting would not be precluded) if:

- The assets would be *randomly selected* and the amount of the assets reacquired is sufficiently limited. (FAS-140, par. 87(a))
- The right is conditional and could be invoked only after an event occurs that is outside the control of the transferor, such as a specified failure of the servicer or a right that must be triggered by a third-party BIH. (FAS-140, pars. 42(a), 44, and 54) However, after such a condition occurs, the transferor has effective control and must record the assets as a purchase, even if the right has not yet been exercised. (FAS-140, par. 55)
- In a turbo structure, the terms of the call options embedded in third-party beneficial interests mirror the options embedded in the transferred assets. (FAS-140 Q&A, par. 49)
- The right is a clean-up call held by the servicer. (FAS-140, par. 9(c)(2))

> **OBSERVATION:** There is overlap between (1) the definition of a QSPE (paragraph 36) and (2) the sale criterion that the transferor may not retain effective control over the transferred assets (paragraphs 9 (c)(2), and 50–54 of FAS-140). If the trans-feror holds a call option that allows it to call enough beneficial interests to unilaterally dissolve the SPE, the SPE is not *qualifying* and the transaction should be evaluated under Chapter 5, "Transfers of Financial Assets." If the transferor holds a smaller call option that allows it to call only some of the beneficial interests, the call does not "taint" the QSPE, but could affect sale accounting for some or all of the assets (depending on whether the call is random or on specific assets).

Removal of accounts provisions (ROAPs)   Removal of accounts provision (ROAP) is common in a revolving-period securitization of receivables, such as credit cards. A ROAP allows the transferor to remove receivables from the securitization trust under specified circumstances. Some of the common business reasons include sale of a business unit that includes the transferred receivables and loss of an affinity relationship ("private-label" credit cards) that involves the transferred receivables. Whether a ROAP precludes sale accounting for the transferor depends on whether paragraph 9(c)(2) has been met: (a) whether the transferor has the unilateral right to remove receivables and (b) whether the ROAP involves specific receivables or randomly selected receivables. Paragraphs 85 through 88 of FAS-140 address ROAPs in detail. Exhibit 6-4 summarizes those provisions.

When a ROAP does not preclude sale accounting, the receivables subject to the ROAP should be recognized in the balance sheet of the transferor as soon as an event or circumstance has occurred such that the transferor has the right to reclaim the assets (for example, receivables have defaulted or a private-label relationship has been terminated), even if the transferor has not yet exercised its rights. (FAS-140, par. 88) The assets should be recognized at fair value, along with an obligation to pass through cash flows to the trust. A gain or loss may be recognized only with respect to the portion of the reacquired asset that had been accounted for as sold (but not for any interest that the transferor continued to hold), assuming the ROAP had not been accounted for as a derivative and the ROAP was not at the money. (EITF 02-9) Refer to Chapter 5, "Transfers of Financial Assets," for a broader discussion of changes in control.

EXHIBIT 6-4
ANALYSIS OF REMOVAL OF ACCOUNTS PROVISIONS

ROAPs that Preclude Sale Accounting	ROAPs that Do Not Preclude Sale Accounting
A ROAP that allows the transferor to specify the assets that may be removed (for all assets that might be specified)	A ROAP for random removal of excess assets from the pool, if the ROAP is sufficiently limited so that the transferor cannot effectively remove specific transferred assets
A ROAP conditioned on a *transferor's decision* to exit some portion of its business (for all assets that might be affected)	A ROAP for defaulted receivables
A ROAP that allows the transferor to remove receivables if it *decides* to terminate an affinity relationship	A ROAP conditioned on a third-party cancellation, or expiration without renewal, of an affinity or private-label arrangement
(FAS-140, pars. 86 and 87)	

EXHIBIT 6-5
EFFECT OF RIGHTS TO REACQUIRE ASSETS IN A
SECURITIZATION INVOLVING A QSPE

Transferor holds . . .	Effect on Accounting[†]
Unconditional Attached Call [¶364] OR Unconditional Freestanding Call [¶51] OR Unconditional Call Embedded in Beneficial Interests by QSPE [¶51]*	
– On all transferred assets	No sale [¶9(c)(2)]
– On a portion of the assets and:	
• Can choose assets	No sale on covered assets [¶9(c)(2); ¶52; ¶86(a)]
• Cannot choose assets	Sale of part of the asset(s) [¶9(c)(2); ¶52; ¶87(a)]

ROAPs*	
– Unconditional	Analyze as if it were an attached unconditional call.
– Conditional‡	Re-analyze as an unconditional call when the condition is resolved.
Exceptions	
Cleanup call held by servicer	Does not preclude sale [¶9(c)(2); ¶364]
Fair value call (no residual interest)	Does not preclude sale unless it constrains the transferee. [¶9(c)(2); ¶52; ¶53]
Conditional call	Does not preclude sale. Reanalyze provision when condition resolved.
Other Rights to Reclaim Assets	
Forward purchase agreement:	
– With collateral maintenance, etc	No sale [¶9(c)(1); ¶47–49]
– Without collateral maintenance	Analyze as an attached or freestanding call. [¶9(c)(2)]
Auction where transferor holds residual	Analyze as either an attached or freestanding call. [¶9(c)(2); ¶53]
Right of first refusal§	Re-analyze as an unconditional call when the condition is resolved. [¶30]

1. Note: The only part of this Exhibit that is unique to QSPEs is the first category—Unconditional Attached, Freestanding, and Embedded Calls. The effect of all other rights is identical to those described in Exhibit 5-6 in Chapter 5. The Exhibit is reproduced here for easy reference in a QSPE securitization transaction.

† All rights require physical settlement (not net cash settlement) and involve a fixed exercise price unless otherwise noted.

* Unless the call is so far out of the money or for other reasons it is probable when the option is written that the transferor will not exercise it.

‡ Conditional ROAPs are rights to reclaim assets that the transferor does not have the unilateral right to exercise.

§ Unless the transferor can trigger activation of the right (see FAS-140, fn. 15). In that case, the right should be analyzed as an in-substance call option.

Source: Adapted from FAS-140 Q&A, par. 49.

Accounting for a Transfer of Assets in a Securitization

The same basic steps discussed in Chapter 5, "Transfers of Financial Assets," are followed to record a securitization involving a QSPE as a sale or as a secured borrowing. If the criteria of paragraph 9 (as modified for transactions involving QSPEs) are met, the transfer of financial assets is recorded as a sale. In summary, the transferor should:

- Recognize any proceeds, derivatives, servicing assets and servicing liabilities, and other liabilities incurred at fair value, if practicable.
- Allocate the previous carrying amount of the transferred assets between the portion sold and the portion(s) that continue to be held by the transferor based on their relative fair values at the date of transfer.
- Recognize gain or loss for the difference between the net proceeds (including new interests) and the allocated basis of the amount sold.
- Adjust the accounting for any interests that continue to be held by the transferor that have changed in character, such as servicing rights now accounted for separately, interests that continue to be held by the transferor that are in the form of a security, interest-only strips, etc. (FAS-140, pars. 10 and 11)

> ☛ **PRACTICE POINTER:** FAS-156, issued in March 2006, changes the computation of gains and losses for transfers qualifying for sale treatment under FAS-140. FAS-156 requires that servicing assets be considered part of the proceeds received by the transferor rather than as an interest that continues to be held by the transferor. Prior to the issuance of FAS-156, separately recognized servicing assets were included as part of interests that continue to be held by the transferor.

The transferee should recognize all assets obtained and any liabilities incurred and initially measure them at fair value. (FAS-140, par. 11)

As discussed in the section, "Fair Value Measurement," in Chapter 5, "Transfers of Financial Assets," FAS-157 provides the primary guidance for measuring fair value under GAAP. Fair value is the price that would be received to sell an asset or paid to transfer a liability in an orderly transaction between market participants at the measurement date. With respect to interests that continue to be held by a transferor in securitization transactions, the timing and amount of future cash flows for interests that continue to be held in securitizations are often uncertain, especially for subordinated interests. As a result, estimates of future cash flows used for fair value measurement depend heavily on assumptions about default and prepayment of all of the asses securitized, because of the implicit credit or prepayment risk arising from the subordination. (FAS 140, par. 17(i), footnote 9a, as amended by FAS-157)

Refer to Chapter 18, "Fair Value Measurements, Fair Value Disclosures, and Other Financial Instrument Disclosures," for specific fair value measurement guidance applicable to all financial instruments required to be measured at fair value under GAAP.

> **AUTHOR'S NOTE:** The 2008 edition of CCH *Financial Instruments* has been updated to incorporate the provisions of FAS-157. FAS-157 is effective for calendar-year-end companies as of January 1, 2008. Unless a company chooses to early adopt, prior GAAP is applicable for financial statements issued for 2007.
> As this book went to press, the FASB was addressing a possible delay of FAS-157's effective date. The FASB agreed to consider delaying the effective date for nonfinancial instruments and for certain types of entities, including private companies and "smaller" public companies (not yet defined). Readers should monitor the FASB's further deliberations regarding the nature of any delay of FAS-157's effective date. Also, readers should refer to the 2007 edition for GAAP related to the fair value measurement of financial instruments applicable before the effective date of FAS-157.

If the criteria for a sale are not met, both parties should account for the transaction as a secured borrowing. Note that certain elements of a securitization that is accounted for as a secured borrowing do not receive separate accounting recognition if they would resulting in double counting, as discussed in Chapter 5, "Transfers of Financial Assets."

> **OBSERVATION:** Adding receivables to a QSPE, in itself, is neither a sale nor a secured borrowing, because that transfer only increases the transferor's beneficial interest in the QSPE's assets. A sale or secured borrowing does not occur until the transferor receives consideration other than beneficial interests in the transferred assets. (FAS-140, par. 79)

Subsequent Measurement of Beneficial Interests Issued in a Securitization

Subsequent measurement of new interests and interests that continue to be held by the transferor depends primarily on the form of the interest (for example, derivatives, securities, servicing rights, recourse obligations). A common issue arising in securitizations is the accounting for interests that continue to be held by the transferor that have significant prepayment risk, credit risk, or both. Instruments with significant prepayment risk are addressed in Chapter 2, "Investments in Debt and Equity Securities." Yield calculations on interests that continue to be held by a transferor are discussed in Chapter 7, "Calculating Yields on Debt Investments."

Another common issue related to the evaluation of beneficial interests, including residual interests, is the identification of embedded derivative features. Both interests purchased by third parties in securitization transactions and interests that continue to be held by transferors must be evaluated under FAS-133 to determine whether they are hybrid instruments that have embedded derivatives requiring bifurcation or whether they are freestanding derivatives. Refer to Chapter 13, "Embedded Derivatives," for further discussion of embedded derivatives in beneficial interests issued in securitization transactions.

> ☞ **PRACTICE POINTER:** After the effective date of FAS-155, an investor in a beneficial interest issued in a securitization transaction must evaluate its interest held to determine whether it contains an embedded derivative feature. If the investor identifies an embedded derivative feature and the hybrid financial instrument is eligible (as discussed in Chapter 13, "Embedded Derivatives"), the investor can elect fair value measurement for the interest. In some cases, fair value measurement will not be elected because bifurcation of the instrument permits the embedded derivative to be designated as a hedging instrument. If the investor cannot identify the embedded derivative, it must measure the hybrid instrument at fair value under the practicability exception in FAS-133.
>
> Also refer to Exhibit 5-6 in Chapter 5, "Transfers of Financial Assets," for a summary of the accounting literature that applies to new interests and interests that continue to be held by the transferor that are recognized separately after a transfer of financial assets.

Classification in Financial Statements

The guidance provided in Chapter 5, "Transfers of Financial Assets," about classification of the income statement effects of transfers of assets and cash flows from transfers of assets is equally applicable to securitization transactions.

Unique Aspects of Accounting for Transfers Involving QSPEs

The principles underlying the accounting for transfers are the same, whether or not a QSPE is involved. However, the customized nature of a securitization involving a QSPE raises issues about identifying and valuing the components and the interaction with securities accounting.

Calculating the gain or loss on sale   All of the guidance in Chapter 5, "Transfers of Financial Assets," concerning the determination of fair values applies in a securitization of financial assets. Determining the fair value of certain interests that continue to be held in a securitization can be very difficult, especially residual interests that concentrate the credit risk, interest rate risk, or both. The fair value estimates bear directly on the gain or loss calculation. If the amount of the gain recognized, after allocation, on a securitization with a subordinated interest that continues to be held by the transferor is greater than the gain would have been had the entire asset been sold, the transferor needs to be able to identify why that can occur. Otherwise, it is likely that the impact of subordination has not been adequately considered in the determination of the fair value of the subordinated interest that continues to be held by the transferor. (FAS-140, par. 59)

> **OBSERVATION:** This requirement is intended to be a "high hurdle." Determining the fair value of residual interests has been a significant practice issue.

Assumptions involved in valuing subordinated interests that continue to be held by a transferor The timing and amount of future cash flows for many types of interests that continue to be held by a transferor in a securitization are uncertain, especially if those interests are subordinate to more senior beneficial interests. In a subordinated (residual) interest, the credit and prepayment risk from all of the securitized assets has been concentrated or magnified, making the assumptions about default and prepayment particularly important. (FAS-140, fn. 21)

> **SEC REGISTRANT ALERT:** The SEC staff has been concerned with the application of GAAP to a sale or securitization of financial assets and to assets that are retained or received or liabilities that are incurred. In EITF Topic D-69, the SEC staff reminded registrants of the following guidelines:
>
> - Recognition of gains or losses on the sale of financial assets is not elective.
>
> - In estimating the fair value of new interests and interests that continue to be held by a transferor, the assumptions used in those valuations must be consistent with market conditions.
>
> - Assumptions and methodologies used in estimating the fair value of similar instruments should be consistent.
>
> - Significant assumptions used in estimating the fair value of new interests and interests that continue to be held by a transferor at the balance sheet date should be disclosed. Significant assumptions generally include quantitative amounts or rates of default, prepayment, and interest.

> **OBSERVATION:** This guidance was issued in response to several subprime lenders announcing in the late 1990s that they were "abandoning" gain-on-sale accounting, as well as concerns about the assumptions being used to value various components. Some securitizers dislike the volatility in income that arises from recognizing gains and losses upfront (at the time of sale) rather than over the life of the transferred assets. GAAP does not allow "rigging" the fair value assumptions so that no gain or loss results.
>   A legitimate alternative is to structure a transaction as a financing that must be accounted for as a secured borrowing (or as a sale to an entity that must be consolidated). An undesirable consequence of those alternatives is that the balance sheet of the transferor is "grossed up" for both the transferred assets and the borrowing.

Valuing cash reserve accounts The proceeds that are put in a cash reserve account (as a form of credit enhancement) are considered interests that continue to be held by a transferor, not new interests. (FAS-140 Q&A, par. 74) Cash reserve accounts can be difficult to value (for the purpose of allocating the previous carrying amount), because the likelihood of default or prepayment must be assessed and any restrictions on the timing of cash flows must be considered. FAS-140 Q&A, paragraph 77, includes a detailed illustration of how to value a cash reserve account using the expected present value technique.

Accrued interest receivable   In credit card and other types of securitizations, an institution transfers a pool of receivables and the right to future collections of principal, finance charges, and fees on the receivables to the trust. The seller continuously replaces receivables that have been repaid or written off with new receivables. Often, the seller retains a subordinated interest in the right to receive accrued fee and finance charges (accrued interest receivable or AIR) on the investors' portion of the transferred assets. In a transfer that is accounted for as a sale, the seller's right to AIR is a form of interest that continues to be held by a transferor that should be considered one of the components of the sale transaction, included in the initial allocation of the previous carrying amount, and subsequently accounted for as a subordinated receivable (not a loan). The AIR is not required to be subsequently measured like an investment in debt securities classified as available for sale or trading under FAS-115 and FAS-140, because the AIR cannot be *contractually* prepaid or settled in such a way that the owner would not recover substantially all of its recorded investment. FAS-5 provides guidance on accounting for loss contingencies, including the collectibility of receivables. (FSP FAS 140-1)

Identifying new interests in a commingled QSPE   In some securitization transactions, more than one transferor contributes assets to the QSPE. In such cases, a transferor should treat the beneficial interests as "new" assets to the extent that the source of the cash flows to be received are assets transferred by another entity. Any derivatives, guarantees or other contracts entered into by the QSPE should also be considered new. However, any beneficial interests whose cash flows are derived from assets transferred by the transferor should be considered interests that continue to be held by the transferor. (FAS-140 Q&A, par. 60)

Accounting for the transferred assets when a sale has not occurred Mortgage-backed securities that continue to be held by the transferor in a guaranteed mortgage securitization in which the SPE meets all conditions for being a qualifying SPE are classified in the financial statements of the transferor as *securities* that are subsequently measured under FAS-115. (FAS-140, fn.17) This is true whether the transaction is accounted for as a borrowing, as a partial sale, or as neither a sale nor a borrowing (because only beneficial interests in the transferred assets are received). Chapter 2, "Investments in Debt and Equity Securities," discusses certain circumstances where mortgage bankers must classify retained mortgage-backed securities as trading in accordance with FAS-65, as amended by FAS-134.

FAS-140 does not specifically state that changes in legal form may be recognized in securitizations of nonmortgage financial assets involving QSPEs that must be accounted for as a secured borrowing, or as neither a sale nor a borrowing (because only beneficial interests in the transferred assets have been received). Presumably, the same principle that applies to mortgage securitizations would apply in other securitizations involving bona fide QSPEs (meaning that unrelated parties hold at least 10 percent of the beneficial interests). Literature indicating securities accounting includes paragraphs 10 and 58 of FAS-140, paragraph 58 of the FAS-140 Q&A, and FTB 94-1.

> ☛ **PRACTICE POINTER:** In a transaction accounted for as a secured borrowing, the securitized loans would be subject to the collateral accounting requirements of paragraph 15 of FAS-140. Refer to Chapter 9, "Securities Lending Arrangements and Other Pledges of Assets."

Securitization of existing securities If a FAS-115 security is "repackaged" in a securitization, and the new securities convey rights to the same cash flows, the security may *not* be reclassified from available for sale to trading as a result of the securitization. (FAS-140 Q&A, par. 61) See Chapter 2, "Investments in Debt and Equity Securities," for a discussion of restrictions on transfers under FAS-115.

If an available-for-sale security is securitized, any amount that had been recorded in other comprehensive income should not be released into earnings until it is realized. To the extent that net proceeds are received in the transfer, a prorated amount would be recognized in earnings. The remaining gain or loss would not be considered realized until the SPE sells the assets to third parties. (FAS-140 Q&A, pars. 62 and 63)

Revolving-period securitizations There are a few ways in which the dynamic nature of a revolving-period structure affects the accounting for a securitization:

- The fair value of an interest that continues to be held by a transferor should not include the estimated cash flows relating to receivables that do not yet exist but that will be originated and transferred during the revolving period. (FAS-140 Q&A, par. 66)
- The fair value of an interest that continues to be held by a transferor should reflect the effect of disproportionate distributions of cash to investors (such as *turbo settlement provisions*). (FAS-140 Q&A, par. 123)

Securitizations   **6.27**

EXHIBIT 6-6
SUMMARY OF ACCOUNTING FOR SECURITIZATIONS

	FAS-140 Accounting Treatment	
Components:	**Sale**	**Borrowing**
Transferred Assets	Remove from balance sheet	Remain on balance sheet
Proceeds (Cash or Marketable Securities)	Record at fair value	Record as assets along with an obligation to return them
Other Proceeds, including servicing assets and liabilities, derivatives, recourse, etc.	Record at fair value; subsequently account for based on their form	N/A (inconsistent with borrowing accounting)
Interests that continue to be held by a transferor, including I/Os, residuals	Record at allocated carrying amount; subsequently account for based on their form	N/A (redundant with assets that remain on balance sheet)
Journal Entry	DR Proceeds (such as cash)	DR Proceeds (such as cash)
	DR Other proceeds	CR Borrowing
	DR Servicing asset CR Transferred asset	If loans are securitized:
	CR Other liabilities (for example, recourse obligation)	
	DR/CR Gain or loss on sale	DR Securities* CR Transferred asset

*Could require presentation separate from other securities in accordance with FAS-140, par.15. Refer to Chapter 9, "Securities Lending Arrangements and Other Pledges of Collateral."

- The value of the servicing rights, if obtained or incurred, should reflect only cash flows from existing receivables (new servicing rights are recorded as new receivables are transferred). (FAS-140, par. 78)
- The value of the contract to sell additional receivables into the trust is usually zero upfront if it is on market terms. Unless the assets being transferred are readily convertible to cash, the forward would not generally be considered a derivative and subsequent changes in value would not be recognized.
- Transaction costs relating to the sale of receivables may be recognized over the initial and reinvestment periods in a rational and

systematic way (because in a revolver, some of the costs benefit future periods and thus qualify as an asset). (EITF 88-22)

Change in Status of a QSPE

The BIHs other than the transferor, its affiliates, or its agents may have the ability to change the powers of a qualifying SPE. If the powers of a previously qualifying SPE are changed so that the SPE is no longer qualifying, the sale criteria must be reviewed at the time of the change. However, in applying paragraph 9(b)—transferee's right to sell or pledge—the SPE would be considered the transferee, *not* the BIHs. If any of the criteria are no longer met, the transferred assets are deemed back under the control of the transferor. (FAS-140, par. 38) In such cases, the transferor must recognize any remaining transferred assets along with an obligation to pass through those cash flows to the BIH at their fair value as of the date of the change.

The fair value of the re-recognized assets should be determined based on the fair value of the assumed liabilities because all of the cash flows must be passed through to the BIH. Other instruments held in the SPE that could affect the fair value of the assets and liabilities should be considered (for example, cash collections that have been temporarily reinvested in money market instruments). (EITF 02-9)

See the "Changes in Control" section in Chapter 5, "Transfers of Financial Assets," for more information.

> ☛ **PRACTICE POINTER:** A change in the qualifying status of an SPE is an event that triggers an assessment of whether any involved party should consolidate the assets and liabilities of the trust. The transferor should apply paragraph 55 of FAS-140 *first*, and then apply the relevant accounting literature (most likely, FIN-46(R)) to determine whether the entire SPE should be consolidated. Other entities that are not the transferor should reassess their consolidation decisions under the applicable literature (most likely, FIN-46(R)). Consolidation of securitization entities is discussed in the following section.

CONSOLIDATION OF SECURITIZATION ENTITIES

When a securitization involves a separate legal entity—often called a special purpose entity—the transferor, sponsor, and other investors in the SPE must consider whether they are in control of the *entity* by virtue of their investment or through other means. In other words, in some situations, it is possible that a transferor has surrendered control over the *transferred asset(s)*, but must continue to recognize those assets (and perhaps others) because the assets and liabilities of the securitization *entity* must be consolidated.

The new consolidation rules differ depending on whether the entity involved is a QSPE or another type of entity. The remainder of the guidance in this chapter is divided into three categories:

1. Consolidation of QSPEs
2. Consolidation of adequately capitalized entities that issue voting interests
3. Consolidation of variable interest entities

> **AUTHOR'S NOTE:** The phrase "variable interest entity" is an accounting term that does not fit neatly into the vernacular for securitization transactions. In other words, not all SPEs will be considered variable interest entities under FIN-46(R), and conversely, some entities historically considered as stock companies could be considered as variable interest entities (even if they have nothing to do with a securitization). This book continues to use the term "SPE" to describe a subset of securitization vehicles, but readers should be aware that FIN-46(R) is much broader and could apply to entities that issue common stock if certain tests are not met.

Exhibit 6-9 provides a flowchart for determining which literature applies in securitization transactions involving various types of entities.

Consolidation of QSPEs

The transferor and its affiliates should *not* consolidate the assets and liabilities of a QSPE. (FAS-140, par. 46) All other parties (including third-party investors in the beneficial interests of an SPE, unrelated servicers, and sponsors) also should not consolidate a QSPE unless they have the unilateral right to liquidate the entity or to change its governing documents such that it no longer qualifies. (FIN-46(R), par. 4(d))

> **OBSERVATION:** FIN-46(R) broadened the "consolidation safe-haven" that was previously limited to transferors and their affiliates.

> ☛ **PRACTICE POINTER:** The "majority-ownership" approach to consolidation does not apply in a transaction involving a QSPE. The transferor can own up to 90 percent of the beneficial interests and still not have to consolidate the QSPE. (Unless the transaction is a guaranteed mortgage securitization, an unrelated third party must own at least 10 percent of the beneficial interests, or the SPE will not be qualifying.) (FAS-140 Q&A, par. 40)

Transition Issues

Paragraph 25 of FAS-140 permits an SPE that qualified under FAS-125 (and the related implementation guidance), but fails to meet one or more conditions for being a qualifying SPE under FAS-140 to continue to be considered a QSPE if it:

- Maintains its qualifying status under previous accounting standards
- Does not issue new beneficial interests after March 31, 2001 (the effective date), and
- Does not receive assets it was not committed to receive before March 31, 2001 (the effective date).

Otherwise, a formerly qualifying SPE and assets transferred to it would be subject to FIN-46(R), and to all of the provisions of FAS-140. (FAS-140 Q&A, par. 37)

> ☛ **PRACTICE POINTER:** FTB 01-1 extended the effective date of FAS-140 relating to the isolation of certain voluntary transfers of financial assets under prior contractual arrangements (as opposed to committed transfers, which are eligible for permanent grandfathering under paragraph 25 of FAS-140). The additional transition period was granted to permit the necessary changes in structure (primarily involving existing master trusts) and ends three months after the earliest date at which sufficient approvals to permit the necessary changes can be obtained from BIHs, but not later than June 30, 2006.

Consolidation of Adequately Capitalized Entities That Issue Voting Equity

ARB-51, as amended by FAS-94, FAS-144, and other literature, applies to entities that issue equity instruments with voting rights. Generally, the party that holds the majority of the voting equity should consolidate the entity. FIN-46(R) introduces new tests that restrict the application of ARB-51 to entities that are adequately capitalized and whose voting interests convey meaningful decision-making rights. *These restrictions are not limited to special-purpose entities.* Reporting entities must review the level of capitalization in all of the entities with which they have significant financial relationships (the "investee") unless it is clear that their interest would not be a significant variable interest and the reporting entity (or its related parties or defacto agents) was not involved in the formation of the entity. (FIN-46(R), par. 6)

If the investee entity issues equity with voting interests, both of the following conditions must be met to apply ARB-51:

- As a group, the equity holders must have meaningful, proportionate, decision-making powers, and their investment must have significant potential for both losses and gains based on the performance of the entity ("substantive equity"). The owners must provide the equity using their own resources (not financed or contributed by the organizers of the entity).

- The amount of substantive equity must be adequate to finance the activities of the entity without support from other parties. The total amount of substantive equity must exceed the expected losses of the entity. The calculation of expected losses is described later in this chapter under "Consolidation of Variable Interest Entities."

If the entity does *not* issue equity with voting rights or it fails either of the above characteristics, the entity must be analyzed under FIN-46(R). (FIN-46(R), par. 5)

> **OBSERVATION:** The discussion of ARB-51 above explains in simple terms the types of entities that are subject to the traditional consolidation model. In practice, however, in order to determine whether consolidation is required, all entities that are not qualifying special-purpose entities must be analyzed under the provisions of FIN-46(R) to determine whether the entity is a variable interest entity. The "substantive equity" requirements apply to all types of entities, including equity-method investees, joint ventures, partnerships, research and development arrangements, and start-up companies. Investors, guarantors, and others with significant involvement with another company must determine that those other companies have adequate, substantive capital. Otherwise, FIN-46(R) applies, and consolidation could be required, depending on the nature and extent of the company's involvement.

CCH's *GAAP Guide Level A,* Chapter 7, "Consolidated Financial Statements," discusses the application of ARB-51 and FIN-46(R) in more detail.

Consolidation of Variable Interest Entities

If an entity is not a QSPE or an adequately capitalized voting interest entity, as described in the previous two sections, the entity must be analyzed further under FIN-46(R). The FASB invented the term *variable interest entity* or "VIE" to describe a default category of legal structures or entities (not just groups of assets) that lack the attributes of an adequately capitalized stock entity.

☞ **PRACTICE POINTER:** FIN-46(R) was issued as a replacement of FIN-46 in 2003. In 2006, additional guidance for the application of FIN-46(R) was issued in the form of FSP FIN-46(R)-6, "Determining the Variability to Be Considered in Applying FASB Interpretation No. 46(R)." The FSP was issued to resolve major implementation issues—specifically, the identification of certain arrangements (for example, certain types of derivative instruments) as variable interests in a variable interest entity (VIE). It allows the design of the entity to be used as the basis for determining the variability to consider in applying FIN-46(R).

Variable interest entities are entities that meet one of the following characteristics:

1. The equity investment at risk is not sufficient to permit the entity to operate without additional financial support. The equity investment at risk includes equity investments that participate significantly in the entity but excludes such investments issued in exchange for subordinated interests in other VIEs or amounts financed for or provided to the equity investor by the entity or third parties involved with the entity.

   ☞ **PRACTICE POINTER:** Less than 10 percent equity risk is presumed to be inadequate (but more than 10 percent is not presumed to be adequate). This presumption may be overcome if it can be determined that the entity's equity risk equals or exceeds that of other comparable entities that operate without additional subordinated financial support or the entity has demonstrated that it can finance its activities without additional subordinated financial support. If those qualitative assessments are inconclusive, then the presumption may be overcome if the amount of the equity invested exceeds the expected losses of the entity based on reasonable quantitative evidence. Some entities that engage in risky activities may need more than 10 percent equity to satisfy this requirement. (FIN-46(R), pars. 9 and 10)

2. The holders of the equity investment at risk lack one of the following characteristics of a controlling financial interest:

   a. Rights to make decisions regarding the entity's activities that significantly impact the success of the entity. When assessing whether it lacks this characteristic, an equity investor with disproportionate or nonsubstantive voting interests must also consider its obligation to absorb expected losses and its rights to receive residual returns and whether substantially all of the entity's activities are conducted on behalf of that investor.

    b.   The obligation to absorb the entity's expected losses, which are not mitigated by a form of credit protection or guarantee issued by the entity or a third party involved with the entity. (Note that the term *expected losses* means possible negative variances in the fair value of the net assets excluding variable interests—it does not mean that the entity is expected to incur operating losses.)

    c.   The right to receive the entity's expected residual returns, which are not effectively capped by other arrangements.

(FIN-46(R), par. 5, and FSP FIN 46(R)-2)

> **SEC REGISTRANT ALERT:** If a registrant concludes that it has disproportionately few voting rights as compared to the economic gains and losses allocated to it under the arrangement, the registrant must assess whether substantially all of the entity's activities are conducted on behalf of the registrant. All facts and circumstances, qualitative and quantitative, should be considered in performing the assessment. (December 2003, speech by Eric Schuppenhauer, then a Professional Accounting Fellow, Office of the Chief Accountant of the SEC, at the AICPA Conference on Current SEC Developments)

> ☛ **PRACTICE POINTER:** In situations where decision-making abilities are shared by the equity investors and other parties, the ability of the equity investors to make decisions that affect the success of the entity and the extent to which those investors absorb expected losses and receive expected residual returns should be evaluated when determining whether a controlling financial interest exists. In a typical franchise arrangement, generally, a franchisor's ability to enforce business standards does not override the franchisee's decision-making ability and therefore does not automatically cause a franchise to be a variable interest entity. Situations in which decision-making ability is shared should be carefully evaluated. (FSP FIN 46(R)-3)

Certain types of entities are not required to apply FIN-46(R). Such entities should be accounted for under other applicable literature, as described in Exhibit 6-7.

EXHIBIT 6-7
ENTITIES EXCLUDED FROM FIN-46(R)

Type of Entity	Applicable Literature
Not-for-profit organizations, unless they are related parties of another entity or they are being used to circumvent FIN-46	SOP 94-3, AICPA Audit and Accounting Guide, *Health Care Organizations*, etc.
Employee benefit plans, by the employer	FAS-87, FAS-106, FAS-112
QSPEs	FAS-140, FIN-46(R)
Investments of 1940 Act investment companies	SEC Regulation S-X Rule 6-03(c)(1)*
Separate accounts of insurance companies (as defined by the AICPA Audit and Accounting Guide, *Investment Companies*)	AICPA Audit and Accounting Guide, *Investment Companies*
"Virtual" SPEs, that is, groups of assets and liabilities that are not separate legal entities (unless they are part of a bigger VIE)	Various, depending on asset and liability types
Entities created before December 31, 2003, for which the holder of an interest in the entity, after making exhaustive efforts, is unable to obtain information necessary to apply key provisions of FIN-46(R)—determining whether the entity is a VIE, determining whether the entity is the PB, or performing consolidation accounting if required.	Various, depending on the legal structure of the entity
Entities deemed to be a business, as defined, unless specified conditions are met.	Various, depending on the legal structure of the business
Governmental organizations and financing entities established by governmental organizations unless used to circumvent FIN-46(R)	GASB pronouncements

* FSP FIN-46(R)-7, issued in May 2007, was intended to revise this guidance to provide a scope exception to FIN 46(R) for an entity that is within the scope of the AICPA Audit and Accounting Guide, *Investment Companies*, as revised by AICPA SOP 07-1. However, the FASB has proposed an indefinite delay of the effective date of AICPA SOP 07-1. Therefore, the effect of FSP FIN 46(R)-7 is also delayed indefinitely as it relates to those entities. See Chapter 2,"Investments in Debt and Equity Securities," for further discussion of the FASB's proposal to delay the effective date of AICPA SOP 07-1.

Source: FIN-46(R), par. 4

SEC REGISTRANT ALERT: The SEC staff expects that the scope exception provided for situations in which the investor in an entity cannot obtain the information needed to apply FIN-46 (R) will be used infrequently. The SEC staff is expected to evaluate the use of the exception on a case-by-case basis and, as part of that evaluation, will consider whether registrants operating in the same industry with similar types of arrangements were able to obtain the necessary information to apply the guidance. The "information scope out" is applicable only for entities created prior to December 31, 2003. It is not applicable, however, to entities that existed before December 31, 2003, that were reconfigured or reconstructed after that date. The SEC staff expects that all information necessary to make a FIN-46(R) assessment (and, if required, consolidate a VIE) is available for entities created after December 31, 2003. Companies that avail themselves of the "information scope out" for entities created prior to December 31, 2003, should be prepared to support how they have satisfied the exhaustive efforts criterion for its use.

☛ **PRACTICE POINTER:** Use of the scope exception for lack of information generally is inappropriate if the reporting entity participated in its formation. The reporting entity must continue to make an exhaustive effort to obtain the necessary information to apply FIN-46(R) for as long as the reporting entity holds an interest in the entity (that is, the ability to obtain the necessary information is not a one-time assessment). FIN-46(R) requires specific disclosures if the scope exception is used.

Exemption for Di Minimus Involvement

A reporting entity is not required to determine whether an entity with which it is involved is a variable interest entity if it is clear that the nature of the involvement would not be a significant variable interest and the reporting entity (or its related parties and *de facto* agents) was not involved in forming the entity. (FIN-46(R), par. 6)

Identifying Variable Interests

The term *variable interests* includes contractual forms of involvement that subject the holder to changes in the net assets of the entity excluding variable interests. (FIN-46(R), par. 2(c)) Variable interests need not have both upside and downside potential (like a typical equity investment or a residual interest). Rather, some forms of variable interests are contingent liabilities that only expose the writer to potential losses. Other forms of involvement, such as investment management contracts, generate fees (not gains or losses *per se*). While the term is broad, it is important to note that only contracts that convey involvement in the entity as a whole or at least a majority of the assets held count toward the quantitative tests in FIN-46(R). For example, a guarantee that relates only to a small amount of specific assets held by an entity is *not* considered a variable interest under

FIN-46(R) and therefore should be accounted for under other applicable literature. (FIN-46(R), par. 12)

To identify variable interests, a determination of which assets, liabilities, or contracts create or receive the entity's variability must be made. The entity's variable interests are the contracts that absorb or receive the variability. Typically, the entity's assets and operations (which are *not* variable interests) create its variability, which is absorbed by liabilities and equity interests (which *are* variable interests). Certain contracts, such as derivatives and other arrangements, can be either assets or liabilities (either recorded or unrecorded) and, therefore, may appear to both create and absorb variability. Referring to an item as an asset, liability, equity, or as a contractual arrangement does not determine whether the item is a variable interest. The *role* of the item, which often depends on the design of the entity, should be the key factor in the determination of whether an interest should be treated as creating or absorbing variability. (FIN-46(R), par. B4 and FSP FIN 46(R)-6)

To determine which interests in the entity are designed to absorb the variability created by its assets or operations, the reporting enterprise must first determine the variability to consider based on the following steps:

Step 1: *Analyze the nature of the risks in the entity* Those risks include, but are not limited to, credit risk, interest rate risk, prepayment risk, foreign currency risk, commodity price risk, equity price risk, and operations risk. The risks in the entity create the variability that is passed to its interest holders.

Step 2: *Determine the purpose of the entity and determine the variability that the entity is designed to create and pass along to its interest holders* The facts and circumstances to be considered in determining the purpose of the entity include, but are not limited to

a. The activities of the entity.

b. The terms of the contracts into which the entity has entered, including an analysis of the original formation documents, governing documents, marketing materials, and other contractual arrangements into which the entity has entered.

c. The nature of the entity's interests issued, including consideration of whether the terms of the interests transfer all or a portion of the risk or return of certain assets or operations of the entity to the interest holders.

d. The negotiation or marketing of the entity's interests to potential investors.

e. The parties that significantly affected the entity's design or redesign.

In addition, the following are considered strong indicators of variability that the entity is designed to create and pass on to interest holders:

- Substantive subordination of an interest that absorbs the variability (subordination is substantive if the interest can be considered equity-at-risk under paragraph 5 of FIN-46(R))
- Variations in cash proceeds received upon anticipated sales of fixed-rate investments in an actively managed portfolio or in a static pool that, by design, will be required to be sold prior to maturity to satisfy obligations of the entity, which are the result of interest rate fluctuations
- A derivative instrument that is strongly indicated as creating variability if:
  — Its underlying is an observable market rate, price, index of prices or rates, or other market observable variable
  — The derivative counterparty is senior in priority relative to other interest holders in the entity

After determining the variability to consider, the reporting enterprise can then determine which interests are designed to absorb that variability. The existence of certain derivative instruments, such as total return swaps or written options, that have the characteristics of the items under the third bullet item above and that transfer substantially all of the risk or return related to a majority of the assets or operations of the entity require further analysis of the design of the entity to determine whether that instrument should be considered as creating variability or a variable interest. (FSP FIN 46(R)-6)

> **AUTHOR'S NOTE:** FSP FIN 46(R)-6 provides numerous examples to illustrate how to apply the guidance, including whether arrangements (such as derivative instruments or guarantees of value) create variability (and therefore *are not* variable interests) or absorb variability (and therefore *are* variable interests).

In identifying variable interests, a reporting entity must consider both explicit and implicit interests. An implicit variable interest exists if there is an agreement between the reporting entity and the VIE or potential VIE that may cause the reporting entity to absorb or receive variability indirectly from the entity, for example, an implicit agreement that protects holders of other interests in the entity from suffering losses. The determination of whether an implicit variable interest exists is a matter of judgment that depends on the relevant facts and circumstances. Examples of those facts and circumstances include whether there is an economic incentive for the reporting entity to act as a guarantor or to provide funds, whether the reporting entity has done so in similar circumstances in the past, and whether acting as a guarantor or providing funds would be considered a conflict of interest or illegal. The existence of implicit variable interests must be considered in determining whether a potential VIE should be considered a VIE, in calculating expected losses and expected residual returns, and determining which party is the primary beneficiary of the VIE. (FSP FIN 46(R)-5)

> **SEC REGISTRANT ALERT:**   The SEC staff has stressed the importance of identifying implicit variable interests and has emphasized that implicit interests can result from both noncontractual interests and contractual agreements with unrelated variable interest holders. With respect to contractual arrangements, the SEC staff highlights that a registrant can absorb a majority of expected losses through implicit interests without having direct contractual interest in the variable interest entity (VIE). Examples of activities that should be evaluated based on the substance of the arrangement include loans to other investors in the VIE, equity investments between investors, puts and calls between the registrant and other investors or noninvestors, service arrangements between the registrant and investors and noninvestors, and derivatives such as total return swaps. When considering whether a contractual interest with a variable interest holder is an implicit variable interest in the entity, the SEC staff has stated that registrants should consider the following factors with respect to the arrangement:
>
> - Whether it was entered into in contemplation of the entity's formation
>
> - Whether it was entered into contemporaneously with the issuance of a variable interest
>
> - Whether it was transacted with a variable interest holder instead of with the entity
>
> - Whether it references specific assets of the VIE
>
> (Speeches by Jane D. Poulin, Associate Chief Accountant, Office of the Chief Accountant of the SEC, at the December 2004 AICPA National Conference on SEC and PCAOB Developments and by Mark Northan, Professional Accounting Fellow, Office of the Chief Accountant of the SEC, at the December 2005 AICPA National Conference on SEC and PCAOB Developments)

> **OBSERVATION:**   The identification of implicit variable interests theoretically can cause an entity to be a VIE under FIN-46 (R). Most frequently, however, this issue arises when a reporting entity has an implicit interest in a VIE and a related party holds a variable interest in the same VIE. In that case, the implicit interest should be considered in determining the primary beneficiary of the VIE. Considerable judgment must be applied in calculating expected losses and expected residual returns attributable to implicit interests in a VIE for the purpose of identifying the primary beneficiary. Although the FASB believes that the requirement to consider implicit interests in

a VIE or potential VIE was implied in FIN-46(R) and should not require a change in practice, effective date and transition guidance was provided in the FSP.

Exhibit 6-8 analyzes several types of contracts that are commonly found in a securitization.

EXHIBIT 6-8
EXAMPLES OF VARIABLE INTERESTS IN AN ENTITY

Instruments that typically would be considered variable interests:

- Equity investments whose risks and rewards are not limited contractually
- Subordinated beneficial interests or debt instruments
- Guarantees of the assets or liabilities of a variable interest entity for a commensurate fee
- A contract to buy assets or equity securities from a VIE, unless the contract is short or the volatility of the related asset is low.
- Derivatives that reduce the VIE's exposure to risks that cause variability, *but* derivatives based on market interest rates or currency rates with no leverage features probably would not convey the majority of the expected losses or residual returns
- Total return swaps
- Fees paid to a decision-maker, *unless* specific characteristics in paragraph B19 of FIN-46(R) are met that indicate that there is an employer–employee relationship between the VIE and the decision-maker
- Service contracts (other than with a decision-maker), *unless* specific characteristics in paragraph B22 of FIN-46(R) are met that indicate that there is an employer-employee relationship between the VIE and the hired service provider
- Residual value guarantees of leased assets and options to acquire leased assets at the end of a lease term at specified prices

Instruments that typically would *not* be considered variable interests:

- Equity investments that do not participate significantly in GAAP profits and losses of the entity
- Senior debt instruments with fixed interest rates (unless the subordinated interests are not large enough to absorb the entity's expected losses or there are embedded derivatives that expose the instrument to losses)
- Guarantees of specific assets that represent a minority of the entity's assets (unless the holder also has a nontrivial variable interest in the entity as a whole)
- Fixed and unconditional liabilities to a VIE
- Leases with a VIE that do not have residual value guarantees
- Operating leases in which the VIE is the lessor that exclude features such as a residual value guarantee and an option to purchase the leased assets at specified prices

- Embedded derivatives within another instrument that are clearly and closely related economically to its asset or liability host contract

☛ **PRACTICE POINTER:** A variable interest in specified assets of a VIE is only considered a variable interest in the entity if the fair value of the specified assets is more than half of the total fair value of the assets of the VIE. (FIN-46(R), par. 12)

Source: FIN-46(R), pars. B7 through B26.

General Principle

A party that is exposed to the majority of the expected losses, residual returns, or both, of a variable interest entity through its variable interests is the Primary Beneficiary of the entity and must consolidate the VIE. For purposes of determining whether it is the Primary Beneficiary, the reporting entity must include any variable interests held by related parties and *de facto* agents along with its own variable interests. (FIN-46 (R), par. 16) If no party (or group of related parties) holds the majority of the variable interests, no one would consolidate the entity. If one party holds the majority of the residual rewards, and a different party holds the majority of the expected losses, the party with the majority of the expected losses should consolidate the entity. (FIN-46(R), par. 14)

Assessing Expected Losses and Residual Returns

Expected losses and residual returns are calculated by projecting the returns of the VIE under various scenarios and weighting those possible outcomes according to their probability of occurrence. The calculation of expected losses and expected residual returns are based on the techniques in FASB Concepts Statement No. 7, *Using Cash Flow Information and Present Value in Accounting Measurements.* The calculations required by FIN-46(R) focus on determining the single probability-weighted expected outcome (that is, an estimate of cash flows) arising from the entity that variable interest holders either absorb (expected losses) or receive (expected residual returns). FIN-46(R) requires that only those cash flows that arise from interests that are not variable interests in the entity be used in the calculation of expected cash flows. The single expected outcome (estimate of cash flows) arising from the calculation is used as a basis for comparing each possible cash flow scenario that reflects different possible outcomes, resulting in the derivation of expected losses and expected residual returns.

- Expected losses represent the negative *differences* between the possible outcomes and the single expected outcome (i.e., the single probability-weighted expected outcome). Even an entity that has been and is expected to continue to be profitable will calculate some expected losses for the points in the range of possible outcomes that are less than the single expected outcome.

- Expected residual returns represent the positive *differences* between possible outcomes and the single expected outcome.

☞ **PRACTICE POINTER:** The expected loss test is also used to determine whether a voting interest entity is adequately capitalized. That is, the total amount of substantive equity must be greater than the expected losses of the entity, as calculated above.

To identify the Primary Beneficiary, the entity must calculate the expected losses and residual returns for (1) the entity as a whole, (2) its own variable interests (along with any interests held by related parties and *de facto* agents), and (3) possibly other variable-interest holders, if the reporting entity has the majority of the residual returns, and another party has the majority of the expected losses.

OBSERVATION: These numerical tests represent the crux of FIN-46. The present value techniques in CON-7 require complex and subjective estimates of future cash flows, including the effect of changes in interest rates, credit quality, and other factors. Appendix A of FIN-46(R) includes a numerical example, but the fact pattern is not realistic (e.g., there is no discussion of servicing rights, guarantees, swaps, or various tranches of beneficial interests). This aspect of FIN-46(R) is challenging to apply in practice.

OBSERVATION: To summarize, consolidation of an entity is generally *not* appropriate when: (1) the entity is an adequately capitalized voting interests entity, and the reporting entity holds less than half of the voting equity; (2) the entity is a QSPE under paragraph 25 or 35 of FAS-140; or (3) the entity is a VIE, but the reporting entity holds less than the majority of the variable interests (calculated as described above).

SEC REGISTRANT ALERT: The SEC staff considers all of the factors in paragraph 17 of FIN-46(R)—which specifies how to determine which of the related parties is the primary beneficiary—to be relevant in making that determination, along with all other factors that may be relevant in making the assessment. All relevant factors should be viewed in their entirety, and the facts and circumstances of the situation should be considered to determine whether one factor or another is more important. (Speech by Jane D. Poulin, Associate Chief Accountant, Office of the Chief Accountant of the SEC, at the December 2004 AICPA National Conference on SEC and PCAOB Developments)

Silos If an entity is deemed to be a variable interest entity, it is possible that there are "mini-VIEs" within the larger VIE. If a reporting entity has variable interests in specified assets of a VIE (including any credit enhancements) that are essentially the only source of repayment for specific liabilities of the VIE, it should treat that "silo" or unit as a separate VIE. Similar arrangements that are not part of a broader

VIE should not be considered VIEs. The expected loss and residual rewards tests should be applied only to the components of the silo to identify its Primary Beneficiary. If someone must consolidate the silo, the silo's assets and liabilities should not be included in the tests performed by variable interest holders in the broader VIE. However, if no party is required to consolidate the silo, all of the assets and liabilities of the broader VIE, including the silo, should be considered in the tests of the broader VIE. (FIN-46(R), par. 13)

EXHIBIT 6-9
CONSOLIDATING A VARIABLE INTEREST ENTITY (FIN-46(R))

[Numbers in brackets refer to paragraph numbers in FIN-46(R)]

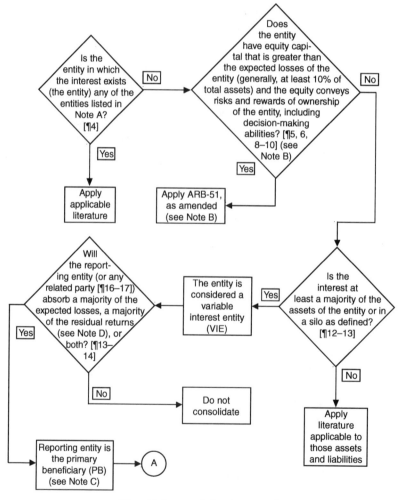

(See Notes on following page)

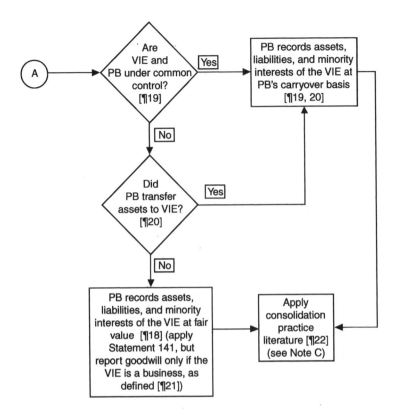

Note A: A qualifying special-purpose entity (QSPE) as defined in FAS-140 (QSPEs are not consolidated by the transferor or by any other party unless that other party has the unilateral ability to change the entity or liquidate its assets), a not-for-profit entity, a pension plan, a 1940 Act investment company (unless the reporting entity is also a 1940 Act investment company), a separate account of an insurance company, an entity deemed to be a business, as defined, an entity created before December 31, 2003, for which the entity holding the interest cannot obtain the information necessary to apply FIN-46 (R), or a governmental organization.

Note B: Reconsider if: governing documents change, equity is returned to investors, the entity's expected losses change because of a change in activities, or the entity receives an additional equity investment at risk. [¶7]

Note C: Reconsider if: governing documents of the entity are changed to reallocate expected losses or expected residual returns between the PB and unrelated parties PB; sells variable interest to unrelated parties; new interests are issued to parties other than the PB and its related parties; or new entity acquires variable interests [¶15]

Note D: If another party has the majority of the expected losses, that party must consolidate.

Timing of Assessments

The determination of whether an entity is a variable interest entity is made when the reporting entity becomes involved with another entity. It is reassessed only upon the occurrence of triggering events, including:

- The entity's governing documents or the contractual arrangements among the parties change such that it changes the characteristics or adequacy of the equity investment at risk.
- Some or all of the equity investment is returned to investors, and other interests become exposed to expected losses.
- The activities of the entity change or the entity acquires additional assets beyond those anticipated that increase the entity's expected losses. (FIN-46(R), par. 7)
- The entity receives an additional equity investment at risk or curtails or modifies its activities such that its expected losses are decreased.

> **OBSERVATION:** The reporting entity would likely know if the first two triggers occurred. The last item—the entity acquires additional risky assets—could occur without the timely knowledge of the investors (for example, in an equity-method investee).

The determination of whether the reporting entity (together with any related parties) is the Primary Beneficiary should be reassessed only upon the occurrence of triggering events, including:

- The entity's governing documents or the contractual arrangements among the parties change such that there is a reallocation of the obligation to absorb expected losses and the right to receive residual returns between the existing Primary Beneficiary and other unrelated parties,
- The Primary Beneficiary sells some or all of its variable interests to unrelated parties or if the VIE issues new interests to parties other than the Primary Beneficiary or its related parties, and
- A party other than the Primary Beneficiary acquires additional variable interests. (FIN-46(R), par. 15)

> ☛ **PRACTICE POINTER:** A troubled debt restructuring as defined in FAS-15 is not a reconsideration event for determining whether the entity is a VIE or whether an entity is a Primary Beneficiary of a VIE under FIN-46(R). (FIN-46(R), pars. 7 and 15)

> ☛ **PRACTICE POINTER:** If, as a result of new authoritative literature, a reporting entity becomes the Primary Beneficiary of a VIE and, consequently, must consolidate the VIE, the effects of a pre-existing fair value or cash flow hedging relationship that would

otherwise be discontinued should be preserved. The reporting entity must designate a "surrogate" hedged item or forecasted transaction (as appropriate) for purposes of reflecting the ongoing effect of the previous hedge accounting for that pre-existing hedging relationship. A new hedging relationship designated subsequent to consolidation of the VIE must comply with all required hedge criteria in FAS-133. Hedge criteria are discussed further in Chapter 14, "Hedge Accounting." (DIG Issue E-22)

☛ **PRACTICE POINTER:**   FIN-46(R) applies to a nontransferor's investment in a QSPE that becomes nonqualifying. Such a change would warrant an assessment of whether the entity is a variable interest entity and whether the reporting entity is the Primary Beneficiary. EITF Issue 02-9 addresses the transferor's accounting for a QSPE that becomes nonqualifying under paragraph 55 of FAS-140 (see the discussion earlier in this chapter).

Consolidating a Variable Interest Entity

Generally, the assets, liabilities, and noncontrolling (minority) interests of a VIE should be recorded at fair value by the Primary Beneficiary at the date the entity becomes the Primary Beneficiary.

A gain or loss could arise from the difference between the net amount added to the balance sheet and the amount of any previously recognized interest(s) in the newly consolidated entity. In such cases, any gains should first be allocated and reported as a *pro rata* adjustment of the carrying amounts of certain assets (see paragraphs 44 and 45 of FAS-141). Under FAS-141, any remaining amount would be recognized as an extraordinary gain. Any loss should be reported by the Primary Beneficiary as goodwill, if the VIE is a business (as defined in Appendix C of FIN-46(R)), or an extraordinary loss if the entity is not a business. (FIN-46(R), par. 21)

However, the carryover basis (with no gain or loss recognition) should be used in the following specific cases (FIN-46(R), pars. 18–20):

- Primary beneficiaries and VIEs under common control.
- The primary beneficiary transferred assets and liabilities to the VIE shortly before consolidating them.

☛ **PRACTICE POINTER:**   Based on discussions with the FASB staff, if the circumstances leading to consolidation occur long after the assets and liabilities were transferred, the transaction should be recorded at fair value.

After the initial measurement of the assets, liabilities, and minority interests, the general consolidation principles of ARB-51, as amended, apply, including elimination of intercompany balances, transactions, and fees.

☛ **PRACTICE POINTER:** If consolidation is required, the transferred assets would be recorded in their form prior to the securitization. The consolidation procedures in ARB-51, paragraph 6, eliminate for accounting purposes the securities that were issued as beneficial interests in the transferred assets. In addition, AICPA TPA 1400.29 indicates that it is inappropriate for a reporting entity that is the primary beneficiary of a VIE to issue combined financial statements in place of consolidated financial statements.

Deconsolidating a Variable Interest Entity

An entity will need to be deconsolidated in certain situations, such as:

- At transition, for entities that previously had been considered SPEs that are not considered VIEs (perhaps because they are not separate entities).
- At transition, for nontransferors that previously consolidated QSPEs.
- When the legal documents of an entity are changed so that a nonqualifying SPE becomes a QSPE (or an adequately capitalized voting equity entity and the reporting entity does not hold the majority of the voting equity).
- When a Primary Beneficiary sells some of its variable interests so that it no longer holds the majority.
- At transition, for an entity that previously consolidated an SPE that is considered a VIE but for which it is not considered the Primary Beneficiary.

☛ **PRACTICE POINTER:** Certain trust preferred structures involving SPEs must be deconsolidated as a result of initial application of FIN-46(R). Refer to Chapter 16, "Issuer's Accounting for Equity Instruments and Related Contracts," for further discussion.

FIN-46(R) does not provide any guidance on how to deconsolidate a former VIE.

DISCLOSURES

FAS-140 requires that certain disclosures be made by entities that transfer financial assets during the period. The disclosures required for securitizations are extremely detailed—quite a price to pay for off-balance-sheet accounting. FIN-46(R) requires disclosures about significant variable interests in variable interest entities.

Securitizations of Financial Assets

For financial assets securitized during any period presented that are accounted for as a sale, all of the following disclosures must be provided *for each major asset type* (e.g., mortgage loans, credit card receivables, and automobile loans):

- Accounting policies for initially measuring the interests that continue to be held by the transferor, if any, and servicing assets or servicing liabilities, if any, including the methodology and key assumptions used in determining their fair value.
- A description of the transferor's continuing involvement with the transferred assets.
- The gain or loss from sale of financial assets in securitizations (SOP 01-6, paragraph 13(d), requires that the amount of gains or losses on sales of loans or trade receivables be presented separately, either in the income statement or in the notes to the financial statements).
- Cash flows between the securitization SPE and the transferor, unless reported separately elsewhere in the financial statements or notes including:
  - Proceeds from new securitizations,
  - Proceeds from collections reinvested in revolving-period securitizations,
  - Purchases of delinquent or foreclosed loans,
  - Servicing fees, *and*
  - Cash flows received on interests that continue to be held by the transferor. (FAS-140, par. 17(h))

If the entity has interests that continue to be held by the transferor in securitized financial assets that if has securitized or servicing assets or servicing liabilities relating to assets that it has securitized at the date of the latest statement of financial position presented, all of the following disclosures must be provided *for each major asset type:*

- Accounting policies for *subsequently* measuring those interests that continue to be held by a transferor, including the methodology and key assumptions used in determining their fair value (including certain quantitative information about discount rates, expected prepayments, and anticipated credit losses).
- A sensitivity analysis or stress test showing the hypothetical effect on the fair value of those interests (including any servicing assets or servicing liabilities) of two or more unfavorable variations from the expected levels for each key assumption that is reported (holding each of the others constant). For example, the effect of a 10% and a 20% increase in the assumed discount rate.

- For the off-balance-sheet securitized assets and any other recognized financial assets that it manages together with them (except if servicing is the only form of continuing involvement):
    — The total principal amount outstanding, the portion that has been derecognized, and the portion that continues to be recognized in each category reported in the statement of financial position, at the end of the period.
    — Delinquencies at the end of the period.
    — Credit losses, net of recoveries, during the period.
- Disclosure of average balances during the period is encouraged, but not required.

(FAS-140, par. 17(i))

> ☛ **PRACTICE POINTER:** These disclosures apply to securitizations involving QSPEs and nonqualifying SPEs. They must be presented in the audited footnotes to the financial statements.

Guarantees Written

Entities that have written guarantees, including *indirect guarantees,* as part of a securitization transaction should disclose information about the nature and amount of those arrangements in accordance with FIN-45. Refer to Chapter 8, "Debt Financing," for additional information.

Disclosures about Variable Interest Entities

In addition to any disclosures required by other standards, including FAS-140 for securitizations, FIN-45 for guarantees, and SEC FR-67 for off-balance-sheet financing activities, entities must report the following information about their involvement with variable interest entities. (FIN-46(R), pars. 23–26)

The disclosures must be included inthe same note as any disclosures about securitizations required by FAS-140. Information about similar entities may be grouped (unless it obscures material information).

> ☛ **PRACTICE POINTER:** If the reporting entity is the Primary Beneficiary and consolidates the VIE, it would *not also* disclose a guarantee under FIN-45, the securitization disclosures required by FAS-140 for sale transactions, or the SEC FR-67 disclosures about off-balance-sheet financing activities.

EXHIBIT 6-10
REQUIRED DISCLOSURES UNDER FIN-46(R)

FIN-46(R) Disclosure Required	Primary Beneficiary	Others Involved with VIE (not PB)	Entities Subject to Paragraph 4(g) Scope Exception
Nature, purpose, size, and activities of VIE	✓	✓	✓ (Disclose size of VIE, if available.)
Nature of involvement with VIE and when it began		✓	✓ (Not required to disclose when involvement began.)
Carrying amount and classification of consolidated assets that are collateral for the VIEs obligations	✓		
Lack of recourse if creditors of a consolidated VIE do not have recourse to the general credit of the PB	✓		
Maximum exposure to loss as a result of involvement with VIE		✓	✓
The number of entities to which FIN-46(R) is not being applied and the reason why the necessary information is not available.			✓
Amount of income, expense, purchases, sales, or other measure of activity between the reporting entity and the entities for all periods presented.			✓ (Information for prior periods not required in the first set of financial statements issued if not practicable.)

*Unless the Primary Beneficiary also holds a majority voting interest.

**Includes situations in which the reporting entity holds a significant *implicit* interest in a VIE.

SEC REGISTRANT ALERT: The SEC's Financial Reporting Release No. 67 (FR-67), "Disclosure in Management's Discussion and Analysis about Off-Balance-Sheet Arrangements and Aggregate Contractual Obligations," requires disclosure of all material off-balance-sheet transactions, arrangements, and obligations (including certain contingent obligations) in a separate caption of MD&A in all quarterly and annual reports filed with the SEC. Among other things, these disclosure requirements apply to all material variable interests in unconsolidated entities, regardless of whether those entities are deemed VIEs under FIN-46(R), and to retained or contingent interests in assets transferred to an unconsolidated entity that serve as credit, liquidity, or market risk support to the entity for those assets. Refer to Chapter 18, "Fair Value Measurements, Fair Value Disclosures, and Other Financial Instrument Disclosures" for a more detailed discussion of these disclosure requirements.

Public Company Disclosures about Asset-Backed Security Transactions

In December 2004, the SEC issued Regulation AB, which codifies and formalizes registration requirements, prospectus disclosure requirements, ongoing reporting requirements for asset-backed securities registered with the SEC, and communications with investors during the offering process. Regulation AB is a principles-based set of disclosures, the primary objective of which is to increase the transparency surrounding the registration process and reporting process. The following general categories are included in the disclosure requirements:

- Transaction summary and risk factors
- Disclosures regarding the roles of the various parties involved in a securities offering—originators, sponsors, depositors, issuers, servicers, and trustees.
- Static pool data to provide information on the quality of pool selection and asset performance.
- Description of the pool assets and composition and significant obligors of pool assets
- Transaction structure
- Credit enhancement and other support
- Certain derivative instruments
- Compliance with servicing criteria
- Additional disclosures: tax matters, legal proceedings pending, affiliations, certain relationships, and related transactions, need for minimum ratings, pool performance data

A significant change to current practice brought about by Regulation AB is the new requirement to provide static pool disclosures, if applicable and material, related to the asset-backed security transaction. A summary of required static pool disclosures for amortizing asset pools and revolving master trusts follows:

- *Amortizing asset pools* The final rule requires static pool information regarding delinquencies, cumulative losses and prepayments for prior securitized pools of the sponsor for that asset type. (If the sponsor has less than three years of experience securitizing assets of the type to be included in the pool, the static pool information should be provided by vintage origination years regarding originations or purchases by the sponsor, as applicable, for that asset type. A vintage origination year represents assets originated during the same year.) In addition, provide summary information for the original characteristics of the prior securitized pools or vintage origination years.

  The static pool data must be provided for five years or as long as the sponsor has been securitizing assets of the same asset type or, in the case of vintage origination years, originating or making purchases of assets of the same asset type. Delinquency, cumulative loss and prepayment data for each prior securitized pool or vintage origination year, should be presented in periodic increments (e.g., monthly or quarterly), over the life of the prior securitized pool or vintage origination year. The most recent periodic increment for the data must be as of a date no later than 135 days of the date of first use of the prospectus.

- *Revolving asset master trusts* The final rule requires data on delinquencies, cumulative losses, prepayments, payment rate, yield, standardized credit scores in separate increments (at a minimum in 12-month increments through the first five years of the account's life based on the date of origination of the pool assets). If the information required above is not material, but alternative static pool information would provide material disclosure, that alternative information should be provided.

Regulation AB is effective for any registered offering of asset-backed securities issued after December 31, 2005. Transactions with an initial offering date before December 31, 2005, are grandfathered such that compliance with the new rules is not required. Specific transition rules for asset-backed securities shelf registrations are also specified in the final rule. The new disclosure requirements of Regulation AB are extensive and detailed and practitioners should carefully review the final rule. The full text of the final rule can be found on the SEC's website at www.sec.gov/rules/final/33-8518.htm.

REGULATORY CONSIDERATIONS

Banks, thrifts, and credit unions follow GAAP in the preparation of their Call Reports. However, there are regulatory capital implications for certain types of continuing involvement. On November 29, 2001, the federal banking agencies issued a revised rule on the regulatory capital treatment of recourse obligations, residual interests, and direct credit substitutes that expose banks, bank holding companies, and thrifts (collectively, banking organizations) to credit risk ("securitization capital rule"). The rule treats recourse obligations and direct credit substitutes more consistently than the agencies' previous risk-based capital standards, and introduces a credit ratings-based approach to assigning risk weights within a securitization. The rule also imposes a "dollar-for-dollar" capital charge on residual interests and a concentration limit on credit-enhancing interest-only strips, a subset of residual interests. In May 2002, the agencies released several questions and answers that had been raised about the rule. In addition, in March 2005, the federal banking agencies issued supplemental guidance that explains the qualifying criteria for using an internal risk-rating system for assigning risk-based capital on exposures to credit enhancements issued by banks in connection with asset-backed commercial paper programs. The guidance clarifies the required conditions for using the risk-rating system approach defined in the Securitization Capital Rule and provides standards to determine whether a banks' internal system is reasonable in comparison to the rating agencies' methodology for assigning credit ratings. The supplemental guidance can be found at http://www.fdic.gov/news/news/financial/2005/fil2605.html.

In May 2002, the federal banking agencies issued interagency guidance on implicit recourse in asset securitizations. Implicit recourse exists when an institution supports a securitization after the point of sale, even though it is not required to do so contractually. Examples could include:

- Selling assets to the securitization trust at an amount less than the contractual terms of the arrangement (typically par value).
- Purchasing assets from the trust at an amount greater than fair value.
- Exchanging performing assets for nonperforming assets.
- Funding credit enhancements beyond contractual requirements.

If the regulator concludes that an organization is providing implicit recourse, additional capital requirements could apply.

In July 2004, the federal banking agencies issued further guidance on the capital treatment of asset-backed commercial paper programs. The final rule establishes the following requirements:

- Assets consolidated under FIN-46(R) related to asset-backed commercial paper programs and any related minority interests are permanently excluded from risk-weighted assets and Tier 1 capital for the calculation of risk-based capital ratios by banking organizations. Sponsoring banking organizations, however, must continue to include in risk-based capital calculations any other exposures they have to these programs (e.g., credit enhancements).

- Banking organizations are required to hold risk-based capital against "eligible" liquidity facilities provided to asset-backed commercial paper programs with an original maturity of one year or less (as defined by the rule). Previously, no risk-based capital was required for such facilities. Specifically, risk-based capital on "eligible" facilities will be assessed using a conversion factor of 10% of the facility amount if the facility has an original maturity of one year or less, and using a conversion factor of 50% if the maturity is greater than one year. In order to be considered "eligible," the liquidity provider must have no obligation to fund against assets that are 90 days or more past due, in default, or below investment grade, unless the liquidity provider can access credit enhancements that exceed the amount of such assets. As of September 30, 2005, liquidity facilities that are not "eligible" (because they provide credit protection to investors by permitting the purchase of non-investment grade securities) will be treated more punitively: risk-based capital will be assessed based on 100% of the facility amount.

OBSERVATION: The final rule does not modify the risk-based capital treatment of certain types of securitizations of revolving retail credit facilities that incorporate early amortization features, as originally proposed.

In December 2006, a final statement on complex structured financing transactions was issued as supervisory guidance by the Board of Governors of the Federal Reserve, the Office of the Comptroller of the Currency, the Federal Deposit Insurance Corporation, the Office of Thrift Supervision, and as a policy statement by the SEC. The final Statement applies to financial institutions that are engaged in complex structured finance transactions that may create heightened levels of legal or reputational risks. Using a principles-based approach, the Statement highlights the characteristics of a noncomplex transaction to guide institutions in considering whether a particular type of transaction should be considered a complex structured finance transaction. The Statement outlines characteristics of transactions that may warrant additional scrutiny by an institution. The guidance describes the types of risk management principles that can assist financial institutions in identifying the risks presented by types of complex structured finance activities and in evaluating, managing, and addressing those risks through the financial institution's internal control framework. The Statement provides the following guidance:

- If a financial institution determines that its participation in the transaction would create significant legal or reputational risk, the institution should take appropriate steps to manage and address the risks, including modifying the transaction.
- Institutions should maintain effective controls to determine whether ambiguities in laws or accounting principles applicable to complex structured finance activities may create significant risks and to manage and address any such risks.
- A financial institution should decline to participate in a complex structured finance transaction if the transaction presents unacceptable risks to the institution or would result in a violation of applicable laws, regulations, or accounting principles.

The guidance is effective as of January 11, 2007. Full text of the final Statement can be found at http://www.federalreserve.gov/board-docs/press/bcreg/2007/20070105.

For statutory accounting purposes, insurance companies must apply SSAP No. 91, *Accounting for Transfers and Servicing of Financial Assets and Extinguishments of Liabilities*, which superseded SSAP No. 18, *Transfers and Servicing of Financial Assets and Extinguishments of Liabilities*; SSAP No. 33, *Securitization*; and SSAP No. 45, *Repurchase Agreements, Reverse Repurchase Agreements and Dollar Repurchase Agreements*. SSAP No. 91 is modeled on the guidance in FAS-140 and has an effective date of January 1, 2005.

AUDIT CONSIDERATIONS

The high level of audit risk associated with accounting for securitizations has received a great deal of press in recent years. Securitization transactions present unique and significant reporting risks, relating to the magnitude of most transactions, the desire for a specific accounting treatment (usually, off-balance-sheet treatment), the use of thinly capitalized legal entities, and the customized, nonstandard nature of most deals. The accounting rules are fragmented and complex—securitization transactions and questions about consolidating SPEs challenge the most experienced accountants. Auditors of public companies should encourage clients to "preclear" material transactions with the SEC staff to avoid second-guessing and possible restatement of the financial statements.

The key areas of audit risk involving securitizations are improper identification of a QSPE and application of the wrong sale criteria, and improper application of the consolidation policy standards and guidance to legal entities used to effect a securitization. All of the audit considerations discussed in Chapter 5, "Transfers of Financial Assets," are equally applicable to other aspects of a securitization transaction, including legal isolation of transferred assets and valuation of residual interests.

Identification of SPEs

Accounting for securitizations (and other transfers) depends, in part, on the nature of the transferee. Auditors should review the internal control environment to ensure that the personnel responsible for recording and reporting on transactions on behalf of an entity have adequate information to determine the nature of the counterparty to the transaction. The controller's area must be able to determine whether the counterparty is an SPE set up by the reporting entity or its affiliate, examine any intercorporate relationships that might be relevant, and have knowledge of any side agreements that convey significant rights or obligations that would significantly affect the accounting conclusion.

In order to evaluate whether the provisions of FAS-140 have been applied properly in a transfer of financial assets, the auditor must determine whether or not the counterparty to a transfer is a QSPE. Auditors should review the documentation of each material transaction, as well as any side agreements or other relevant information, to determine whether the SPE meets the qualifying conditions of FAS-140. Seemingly minor differences in deal structure can have a major effect on the accounting, so auditors should not simply accept assertions that two deals are "basically the same" or that any changes in an existing SPE were "minor." Auditors should perform tests to ensure that each of the sale criteria has been properly applied. Chapter 5, "Transfers of Financial Assets," discusses the need to use a legal specialist in evaluating whether transferred assets have been isolated from the transferor.

Consolidation of SPEs

To evaluate whether management's conclusion about off-balance-sheet treatment is appropriate under GAAP, auditors should ensure that they understand the ownership structure of the transferee (SPE) and all significant transactions and agreements between the reporting entity and the SPE. Transferors should not consolidate their investments in QSPEs. Other parties involved with a QSPE also should not consolidate the entity unless they have the unilateral right to dissolve the entity or to change it so it is no longer qualifying. In all other scenarios, the transferor and other involved parties should apply FIN-46(R).

A high degree of professional judgment is required to assess whether a reporting entity should consolidate a securitization entity. The new, unfamiliar "expected loss test" of FIN-46(R) is pivotal in determining whether ARB-51 or FIN-46(R) applies. Auditors should stay alert to any implementation guidance issued by the FASB on how this test should be applied. Auditors should be aware that certain nonequity forms of involvement, such as guarantees and asset management contracts, can trigger consolidation if those arrangements convey the majority of the expected losses or expected residual returns (generally in the form of fees or variability in earnings). To properly assess the relative magnitude of its variable interests, the reporting entity must have knowledge about the rights and obligations of others involved in the transaction. Auditors should review clients' processes for identifying and evaluating such information. Certain events trigger a reconsideration of the initial consolidation decision—auditors should review the client's procedures for determining whether such events have occurred and their effect on the original consolidation decision.

The AICPA Practice Alert 2005-1, *Auditing Procedures With Respect to Variable Interest Entities,* provides guidance to auditors on planning and performing auditing procedures with respect to variable interest entities (VIEs). The Practice Alert outlines detailed steps for performing such procedures, including procedures for determining whether an entity has properly identified the complete population of variable interests in VIEs, considering whether the entity has properly determined whether it is the primary beneficiary in a VIE, determining whether an entity has properly consolidated VIEs for which it is the primary beneficiary, determining whether an entity has properly accounted for its interests in VIEs for which it is not the primary beneficiary, and evaluating the adequacy of disclosures. The full text of the Practice Alert may be downloaded from the AICPA website at www.aicpa.org/download/auditstd/.

ILLUSTRATIONS

Illustration 6-1: Securitization of Financial Assets Involving a QSPE

Premier Finance Co. decides to securitize a group of prepayable loans with a net carrying amount of $50,000,000 from its consumer finance portfolio. Premier concludes that investors desire a high credit rating, more predictable maturities, and a variable interest rate, rather than the terms present in the loans. Premier designs a two-step transfer—first to a special-purpose corporation to achieve a true sale at law, and then to a bankruptcy-remote SPE. The sole function of the (second) SPE is to collect the cash flows on the loans, modify the payment terms, and make payments to the beneficial interest holders in the loans. Premier will be the servicer of the loans, and will receive more than adequate compensation. The SPE will enter into an interest rate swap with Premier to convert the interest rate on the loans to a floating rate. Premier retains a subordinated residual interest in the SPE, which will absorb prepayment risk and credit risk on the transferred loans. Premier plans to sell the remaining beneficial interests in the second SPE to third parties. The SPE will not be permitted to sell loans, except to the transferor (as servicer) when a loan defaults. The life of the SPE is limited—the SPE will terminate when the beneficial interests mature.

Step 1—Assessing the QSPE Criteria for the Second SPE

Distinct standing—Met. Third parties hold more than 10% of beneficial interests.

Limited activities—Met. All of the permitted activities are narrow and directly related to the transferred assets and beneficial interests.

Passive holdings—Met, as long as the notional amount of the interest rate swap does not exceed the amount of beneficial interests actually held by third parties at inception and is not expected to exceed them subsequently.

Automatic, restricted sales—Met. The only sales permitted are in response to a default of the transferred assets.

Conclusion: The SPE would be considered a QSPE. Therefore, paragraph 9(b) of FAS-140 should be applied using the rights of the beneficial interest holders and Premier should not consolidate the assets and liabilities of the SPE. If the entity were not considered a QSPE, paragraph 9(b) would be applied using the rights of the SPE (not the beneficial interest holders) and the need to consolidate would be evaluated under applicable consolidation literature.

Step 2—Assessing the Sale Criteria

9(a): Legal counsel for Premier writes a reasoned legal letter that concludes that, taken together, the two-step transfer would isolate the assets from Triumph in the event that Triumph were to go bankrupt (even though the likelihood of bankruptcy is remote). Therefore, this condition is met.

9(b): There are no constraints on the third party beneficial interest holders. Therefore, this condition is met.

9(c): Regency will function only as the servicer of the loans. Regency cannot unilaterally control the return of any specific assets.

Conclusion: The sale criteria are met.

Step 3—Account for the transfer as a sale

Computation of net proceeds

	Fair Value of Proceeds	Fair Value of Interests That Continue to Be Held
Cash proceeds	51,000,000	
Interest rate swap	400,000	
Servicing asset	700,000	
Residual interest		2,000,000
Net proceeds	52,100,000	

Allocation of previous carrying amount between loans sold and interests that continue to be held by the transferor. [FAS-140, par. 10(b)]

	Fair Value	Percentage of Total Fair Value	Allocated Carrying Amount
Loans sold	52,100,000	.963	48,150,000
Residual interest	2,000,000	.037	1,850,000
	54,100,000	100%	50,000,000

Gain on sale calculation

Net proceeds	52,100,000
Carrying amount of loans sold	(48,150,000)
Gain on sale	3,950,000

Journal entries

Cash	51,000,000		
Interest rate swap	400,000		*At fair value*
Servicing asset	700,000		*At fair value*
Loans		48,150,000	*At allocated carrying amount*
Gain on sale		3,950,000	

To record the sale of loans, new assets obtained, and the gain on sale. [FAS-140, par. 11] Chapter 12, "Introduction to Derivatives," addresses the subsequent accounting for the interest rate swap. Chapter 4, "Servicing of Financial Assets," addresses the subsequent measurement of the servicing asset.

Residual interest	1,850,000		*At allocated carrying amount*
Loans		1,850,000	*Reclassification of remaining loan balance*

To reclassify the residual interest that continues to be held by the transferor. Chapter 2, "Investments in Debt and Equity Securities," addresses the subsequent accounting for the residual interest (assuming it does not contain an embedded derivative). The residual must be accounted for like an available-for-sale or trading security because it bears significant prepayment risk. [FAS-115, par. 7] Chapter 4, "Servicing of Financial Assets," addresses the subsequent accounting for servicing rights.

CHAPTER 7
CALCULATING YIELDS ON
DEBT INVESTMENTS

CONTENTS

Overview	7.03
Background	7.04
Applicability of Concepts Statement 7	7.04
Terminology to Describe Cost Basis of Investments	7.05
Imputing Interest on Receivables and Payables	7.07
Imputing Interest	7.08
Selecting a Discount Rate	7.08
Premiums and Discounts	7.09
Exhibit 7-1: Par Value, Premiums and Discounts	7.09
Amortizing Premiums and Discounts	7.09
Notes with Bundled Rights and Privileges	7.10
Notes Exchanged for Goods or Services	7.10
Notes with Embedded Derivatives That Must Be Accounted for Separately under FAS-133	7.11
Notes Measured at Fair Value under the Fair Value Option	7.11
Yields on Debt Investments	7.12
Fees and Costs from Lending and Investing Activities	7.12
Loan Origination Fees and Costs	7.14
Exhibit 7-2: Treatment of Internal Costs from Lending Activities	7.16
Fees and Costs on Purchased Loans	7.18
Fees and Costs on Refinancings and Restructurings (Other Than a Troubled Debt Restructuring)	7.19
Fees and Costs in a Troubled Debt Restructuring	7.20
Other Types of Fees, Including Commitments	7.20
Application of the Interest Method under FAS-91	7.25
Aggregation of Loans	7.25
Exhibit 7-3: Components of Net Investment (Amortized Cost) in a Loan	7.26

The Effective Interest Rate	7.26
Variable Interest Rates	7.27
Anticipating Prepayments in the Effective Yield Calculation	7.28
Loans with Uncertain Payment Terms	7.30
Exhibit 7-4: Amortization Methods for Common Loan Types	7.31
Nonaccrual Loans	7.32
Balance Sheet Presentation	7.32
Income Statement Presentation	7.32
Cash Flow Statement Presentation	7.32
Special Application of the Interest Method for Certain Investments	7.33
Structured Notes (EITF 96-12)	7.33
Beneficial Interests in a Securitization Trust (EITF 99-20)	7.36
Exhibit 7-5: Recognizing Interest and Impairment on Beneficial Interests in Securitized Assets	7.39
Instruments Purchased at a Discount Due to Credit Quality (SOP 03-3)	7.41
Exhibit 7-6: Depiction of Recognizable Cash Flows under SOP 03-3	7.43
Exhibit 7-7: Accounting for Changes in Expected Cash Flows under SOP 03-3	7.44
Investment Income for Not-for-Profit Organizations	7.46
Exhibit 7-8: Methods of Reporting Changes in Estimated Cash Flows on Investments	7.47
Mortgage Banking Activities	7.49
Disclosures	7.49
Imputed Interest	7.49
Entities Engaged in Lending Activities	7.49
Anticipating Prepayments	7.50
Credit Card Purchases and Originations	7.50
Loans and Securities Purchased at a Credit-Related Discount (SOP 03-3)	7.50
Exhibit 7-9: Disclosures Required by SOP 03-3	7.51
Investments in Beneficial Interests in Securitized Assets with Unrealized Losses (FSP FAS 115-1 and FAS 124-1)	7.52
Audit Considerations	7.53
Illustrations	7.53

Illustration 7-1: *Amortization Based on Contractual Payment Terms* 7.54

Illustration 7-2: *Amortization Based on Estimated Prepayment Patterns Adjusted for Change in Estimate* 7.55

Illustration 7-3: *Application of Increasing-Rate Provisions with No Prepayment Penalty* 7.56

Illustration 7-4: *Application of Variable-Rate Provisions Based on Factor at Inception* 7.58

Illustration 7-5: *Recognizing Yields and Impairment on Subordinated Beneficial Interests in Securitized Financial Assets* 7.59

Illustration 7-6: *Application of SOP 03-3 to an Acquisition of Loans Purchased at a Discount Due to Credit Concerns* 7.62

OVERVIEW

Interest should be recognized on a debt instrument using the effective yield method (also called the *interest method*). The objective of the interest method is to report interest income or expense in a manner that reflects a constant effective yield on the recorded amount of the receivable or payable (that is, the principal amount adjusted by unamortized premium or discount and certain other items). This general principle applies to both assets and liabilities that are not being marked to market through earnings. Specific issues relating to liabilities are discussed in Chapter 8, "Debt Financing."

Certain types of loan origination fees and costs are deferred by the lender and amortized as an adjustment of the yield of the instrument. Generally, origination fees and costs are netted and amortized over the contractual life of the instrument; prepayments may be anticipated in certain circumstances. Other types of lending fees are generally recognized when they are earned and other types of costs are generally recognized as expenses as they are incurred.

There are special ways of applying the interest method for investments purchased at a discount that is related to credit concerns, structured notes, and beneficial interests in a special-purpose entity. Some debt instruments with unusual rates or payment terms contain embedded derivatives that must be accounted for separately.

Certain conditions must be met to treat a loan refinancing or a modification of terms as a new loan. The requirements are different for the lender and the borrower. When the revised loan is not considered new, many of the related fees and costs are treated as a prospective yield adjustment, rather than as current income or expense.

BACKGROUND

The primary accounting literature applicable to recognizing interest on debt instruments is APB-21 and FAS-91. APB-21 applies to both receivables and payables and establishes the general principle that interest should be recognized using an effective rate of interest, not the nominal or stated rate. FAS-91 (and the related Q&A) addresses how to factor in nonrefundable fees and costs relating to originations and purchases of loans and debt securities held as *assets*, as well as the treatment of callable and prepayable instruments. SOP 03-3 addresses accounting for loans or debt securities purchased at a discount that is attributable in part to credit concerns. A few EITF Issues address unusual yields on investments in debt instruments, including EITF Issue 96-12 and EITF Issue 99-20. CON-7 discusses the objective of present value measurements and methods to estimate cash flows.

This chapter discusses the effective yield method and issues relating to debt instruments held as investments (assets to the reporting entity). Chapter 8, "Debt Financing," addresses issues relating to the calculation of interest expense on debt financing (liabilities to the reporting entity).

Applicability of Concepts Statement 7

In February 2000, the FASB issued Concepts Statement No. 7, *Using Cash Flow Information and Present Value in Accounting Measurements*. FAS-157, *Fair Value Measurements*, issued in September 2006, establishes fair value measurement guidance applicable to existing pronouncements that require such a measure and incorporates guidance from CON-7 related to the use of present value techniques to measure fair value. By incorporation into FAS-157, the guidance is now Level A GAAP, and is applicable to all fair value measurements determined based on present value techniques. CON-7 provides a framework for using future cash flows as the basis for accounting measurements at initial recognition, and for the interest method of amortization. CON-7 establishes principles that govern the use of present value, especially when the amount of future cash flows, their timing, or both, are uncertain. Present value techniques are used often to estimate the fair value of a financial instrument, to impute an interest rate, and to amortize a premium or discount on a note.

Those techniques include the discount rate adjustment technique and the expected present value technique. The measurement for receivables and payables under APB-21 using a present value technique is a fair value measurement under FAS-157. The discount rate for contractual cash flows described in APB-21 (rate that is commensurate with the risk) is consistent with the discount rate used in the traditional approach (the discount rate adjusted technique) in CON-7.

Terminology to Describe Cost Basis of Investments

A variety of terms are used to describe the cost basis of an investment in a debt instrument. The following chart summarizes the common elements of the cost basis of an investment, and how they are reflected in various terms. Note that there is overlap among some commonly used terms. The primary distinguishing factor is whether the allowance for doubtful accounts is included in the measure.

Terminology to Describe Cost Basis of Investments

Terminology	GAAP Reference	Amount Due at Maturity	Unamortized Premium Discount	Accrued Interest	Deferred Fees and Costs	FV Hedge Gains and Losses	Direct Write Downs	Allowance for Doubtful Accounts
Amortized cost	Conceptually defined in EITF 96-12. Also used in FAS-115†. Narrowly defined in SOP 03-3.	✓	✓	✓*	✓	✓	✓	
Recorded Investment	FAS-15, par. 28 and FAS-114, fn2; DIG F-4	✓	✓	✓	✓	✓	✓	
Net carrying amount‡	FAS-114, fn2	✓	✓	✓	✓	✓*	✓	✓
Net investment in original loan Standard	FAS-91, fn5	✓	✓	✓	✓	✓*		

* Not stated explicitly in the Standard, but within the spirit of the Standard.

† EITF 99-20 uses a variation of amortized cost called the reference amount, which equals the initial investment (or allocated carrying amount) less cash received to date, plus yield accreted to date, less any other-than-temporary impairment recognized to date.

‡ FAS-15, footnote 7, uses the term "carrying amount" with the same meaning as "net carrying amount."

IMPUTING INTEREST ON RECEIVABLES AND PAYABLES

Receivables and payables represent contractual rights to receive money and contractual obligations to pay money on fixed or determinable dates, whether or not there is any stated provision for interest. Receivables and payables include loans, notes, long-term trade receivables, capital leases, and debt securities. APB-21 is the primary source of guidance on when interest must be imputed on receivables and payables. APB-21 is not intended to apply in the following circumstances:

- Trade receivables and payables that are due within one year
- Security deposits or downpayments
- Customary lending and deposit-taking activities of banks (covered by FAS-91)
- Transactions where interest rates are affected by tax attributes or legal restrictions
- Related-party transactions

Often, a receivable or payable (for simplicity, a note) will bear a stated rate of interest called the coupon, which reflects the general level of interest in the marketplace for a note of that term, the creditworthiness of the borrower (the "credit spread"), and other factors at the time the arrangement is made. In that case, the present value of the contractual cash flows will equal the par value or principal amount of the note at inception.

Interest must be imputed on a note when:

- There is no stated interest rate.
- The stated interest rate is not reasonable, that is, the rate does not reflect the general level of interest rates, the creditworthiness of that particular borrower, or the amount of time until payments are due.
- The face amount of the note differs materially from the fair value of the goods or services received in exchange.

In those cases, the par value of the note does not represent the present value of the contractual cash flows. To determine the present value, an appropriate interest rate must be identified (or imputed). (APB-21, par. 12)

Imputing Interest

Imputing interest means identifying the interest rate that equates the contractual cash flows with the present value of the note. The note is recorded on the balance sheet at its present value, and any difference between the par value and discounted value is recognized as an adjustment of interest income or expense. When notes are traded in the open market, the market rate of interest and market value of the note provide evidence of the present value of the note. (APB-21, par. 9)

Selecting a Discount Rate

The objective in selecting a discount rate is to approximate the rate that an independent borrower and lender would negotiate in a similar transaction under comparable terms and conditions, with the option to pay the cash price upon purchase or to give a note for the amount of the purchase that bears the prevailing rate of interest to maturity. (APB-21, par. 13)

> ☛ **PRACTICE POINTER:** Prevailing rates for similar instruments of issuers with similar credit ratings often will help determine the appropriate interest rate for determining the present value of a specific note at its date of issuance.

The selection of a rate may be affected by many considerations. For example, the choice of a rate may be influenced by:

- Prevailing market rates for the source of credit that would provide a market for sale or assignment of the note;
- The prime rate for notes that are discounted with banks, giving due weight to the credit standing of the issuer;
- Published market rates for similar quality bonds;
- Current rates for debentures with substantially identical terms and risks that are traded in open markets; *and*
- The current rate charged by investors for first or second mortgage loans on similar property. (APB-21, par. 14)

Premiums and Discounts

When the stated (contractual) interest rate on a note equals the rate that a current lender would charge for an instrument with the same credit quality, maturity and timing of cash flows, the note would be issued or purchased at par value.

When the stated (contractual) interest rate on a note is less than the rate that a current lender would charge for an instrument with the same credit quality, maturity and cash flows, the note would be issued or purchased at a discount, that is, an amount lower than par value. Investors are not willing to pay the face amount, because they could earn more on an alternative investment. The amount of proceeds is adjusted so that the investment bears a market rate of return.

When the stated (contractual) interest rate on a note is higher than the current market rate for a comparable instrument issued by that debtor, the note would be issued or purchased at a premium, that is, an amount higher than par value. Investors are willing to pay more than the face amount of the note, because the contractual cash flows are more than those of alternative market investments. The amount of proceeds is adjusted so that the investment yields a current market return.

EXHIBIT 7-1
PAR VALUE, PREMIUMS AND DISCOUNTS

Assumes a $100,000, 4-year note with semi-annual interest payments.

		Contractual Rate		
		7%	8%	10%
Market Rate	7%	**100,000**	103,437	110,311
	8%	96,634	**100,000**	106,733
	10%	90,305	93,537	**100,000**

Amortizing Premiums and Discounts

The difference between the par value and present value of the note is amortized over the life of the note, so that the sum of any stated interest plus the amortization (which could be positive or negative) results in a level effective rate of interest on the outstanding balance at the beginning of any period. The effective rate should represent the market rate of interest that existed at the inception (or subsequent purchase) of the note. Unless the note has an explicit variable rate, the initial effective rate should not be adjusted for subsequent changes in market rates. (APB-21, par. 12) (Variable rates are discussed later in this chapter.)

A note amortization table is typically set up as follows:

Dates	Cash Interest	Market Yield	Premium or Discount Amortization	Balance Unamortized Premium or Discount	Cost Basis of Note
	Coupon times principal amount	Carrying amount times market rate at inception	Cash interest minus market rate	Initially, difference between par value and present value. Subsequently adjusted for this period's amortization	Par value plus unamortized premium or discount
Starting date					xx,xxx,xxx
Year 1	xx,xxx	xx,xxx	x,xxx	xxx,xxx	x,xxx,xxx
Year 2	xx,xxx	xx,xxx	xxx	xx,xxx	xxx,xxx
Year 3	xx,xxx	xx,xxx	xxx	0	0

Illustration 7-1 at the end of this chapter includes a numerical example of the amortization of a discount under the interest method.

Notes with Bundled Rights and Privileges

If cash and some other rights or privileges are exchanged for a note, the value of the rights or privileges must generally be carved out and recorded separately. The premium or discount created by the allocation of the note's carrying amount should be amortized over the life of the note as a yield adjustment. (APB-21, par. 11) One notable exception is the accounting for convertible debt when the conversion feature is not separable and does not meet the definition of a derivative under FAS-133. Convertible debt is discussed in Chapter 10, "Convertible Debt and Similar Instruments."

Notes Exchanged for Goods or Services

When interest must be imputed on a note that is received in exchange for goods or services, the note, the sales price, and the cost of the property, goods, or services exchanged for the note should be recorded at the fair value of the property, goods, or services or at an amount that reasonably approximates the fair value of the note, whichever is the more clearly determinable. (APB-21, par. 12)

> ☛ **PRACTICE POINTER:** Transactions in which captive finance companies offer favorable financing to increase sales of related companies must be accounted for under APB-21. (SOP 01-6, par. 12)

Notes with Embedded Derivatives That Must Be Accounted for Separately under FAS-133

Under FAS-133, certain hybrid instruments that contain multiple risk characteristics must be split apart and accounted for separately. For example, a debt instrument with a return that is linked to changes in an equity index is considered a debt instrument and an embedded equity derivative. When a derivative is required to be separated or bifurcated from the host contract, the amount allocated to the host instrument often will differ from the face value of the instrument. Any premium or discount resulting from the allocation process should be amortized in accordance with FAS-91 or APB-21, as appropriate. FAS-133 also provides a fair value measurement election, subject to certain scope limitations, for certain debt instruments that are hybrid financial instruments with an identified embedded derivative that is required to be bifurcated. Such instruments are eligible to be initially and subsequently measured at fair value, with changes in fair value recognized currently in earnings. Chapter 13, "Embedded Derivatives," discusses how to identify embedded derivatives, the fair value election, and other related issues in detail.

> ☛ **PRACTICE POINTER:** All of the preceding guidance applies to debt instruments that are both assets and liabilities. The remainder of this chapter addresses investments in debt instruments (assets to the reporting entity). Chapter 8, "Debt Financing," provides additional guidance on the income statement effects of debt instruments that are recognized as liabilities by the reporting entity.

Notes Measured at Fair Value under the Fair Value Option

Companies may elect to measure notes at fair value under the fair value option provided by FAS-159. The fair value option is discussed in detail in Chapter 19, "The Fair Value Option for Financial Instruments." If the fair value option is elected, a note is initially measured at fair value and subsequent changes in fair value are recognized in earnings. The guidance related to amortization of premium or discount under APB-21 does not apply to items for which the fair value option has been elected. In addition, FAS-159 does not specify a method to be used for recognizing and measuring the amount of dividend income, interest income, and interest expense for items for which the fair value option has been elected; however, FAS-159 requires disclosure of a description of how interest and dividends are measured and where they are reported in the income statement for each period for which an income statement is presented.

FAS-157 is the primary guidance for fair value measurement under GAAP. Fair value is the price that would be received to sell an asset or paid to transfer a liability in an orderly transaction between market participants at the measurement date. Chapter 18, "Fair Value Measurements, Fair Value Disclosures, and Other Financial Instrument Disclosures," provides specific fair value measurement guidance applicable to all financial instruments required to be measured at fair value under GAAP.

> **AUTHOR'S NOTE:** The 2008 edition of CCH's *Financial Instruments* has been updated to incorporate the provisions of FAS-157. FAS-157 is effective for calendar-year-end companies as of January 1, 2008. Unless a company chooses to early adopt, prior GAAP is applicable for financial statements issued for 2007.
>
> As this book went to press, the FASB was addressing a possible delay of FAS-157's effective date. The FASB agreed to consider delaying the effective date for nonfinancial instruments and for certain types of entities, including private companies and "smaller" public companies (not yet defined). Readers should monitor the FASB's further deliberations regarding the nature of any delay of FAS-157's effective date. Also, readers should refer to the 2007 edition for GAAP related to the fair value measurement of financial instruments applicable before the effective date of FAS-157.

YIELDS ON DEBT INVESTMENTS

Fees and Costs from Lending and Investing Activities

Interest income is imputed on loans and other investments in debt securities. For certain types of lending activities, the fees charged and related transaction costs can be significant. FAS-91 addresses how those fees and costs are factored into the yield calculation.

FAS-91 addresses the treatment of nonrefundable fees and costs associated with:

- Lending transactions, such as making loans, extending lines of credit, and issuing credit cards
- Making commitments to lend
- Refinancing and restructuring outstanding loans

- Syndicating loans (coordinating multiple lenders for a large loan)
- Purchasing debt instruments
- Direct finance leasing transactions

FAS-91 also addresses the accounting for:

- Premiums and discounts
- Variable interest rates
- Prepayment rights and penalties

All of these items affect the effective yield calculation in certain circumstances.

> **OBSERVATION:** It is important to properly identify a fee or cost as an origination, commitment, or service fee, because they are classified differently in the income statement and potentially recognized over different periods of time.

FAS-91 does *not* address the accounting for:

- Yields on instruments that are carried at fair value with changes in fair value recorded in earnings, including those for which the fair value option in FAS-159 is elected.
- Nonaccrual loans or securities.

> ☞ **PRACTICE POINTER:** FAS-91 applies to available-for-sale securities, which are carried at fair value; however, changes in fair value are recognized in other comprehensive income, not earnings.

> ☞ **PRACTICE POINTER:** The interest method is required even if there are no significant origination fees or costs associated with a transaction. This basic principle was established in APB-12 and it remains in effect. Alternative methods, such as the rule of 78's, sum-of-the-years'-digits, and straight-line, may be used only if the results do not differ materially from those obtained by using the interest method, even if interest is collectible on a loan using one of those methods. (FAS-91 Q&A, par. 46 and EITF D-10)

> **OBSERVATION:** FAS-91 applies to all entities engaged in lending, certain leasing activities, and investing in debt instruments, such as loans, notes, and bonds. FAS-65 provides a few exceptions for mortgage bankers (discussed later in this chapter). All other industries must apply FAS-91 for GAAP reporting purposes, as long as the loan or other investment is performing and not specifically excluded above.

Loan Origination Fees and Costs

FAS-91 requires that certain nonrefundable loan origination fees and costs be recorded as an adjustment of the carrying amount of the loan and amortized over the life of the loan as an adjustment to interest income (a yield adjustment). Specifically, deferring loan origination fees and costs has the following effect on yields:

- *Deferring fees received* Enhances yield over life of loan
- *Deferring costs paid* Reduces yield over life of loan

Only one entity originates a loan, even if there are subsequent investors in the loan. Origination means the entity that underwrites the loan-evaluates the creditworthiness of the borrower, prepares the loan documentation, and disburses cash to the borrower. Purchases of loans and other investments are *not* considered loan originations-fees and costs on purchased loans are accounted for differently, as discussed below.

> ☞ **PRACTICE POINTER:** SEC Staff Accounting Bulletin 101, *Revenue Recognition*, and the related "Frequently Asked Questions," address the accounting for *refundable* fees. The primary issue involves when the fee has been earned.

Loan origination fees that should be deferred and recognized as an enhancement of the loan's yield Loan origination fees are fees charged to the borrower in connection with the process of originating, refinancing, or restructuring a loan or lease. The following fees are considered loan origination fees (FAS-91, par. 36 and FAS-91 Q&A, par. 20):

- Fees to reimburse the lender for origination activities, including application fees, management, arrangement, and placement fees.
- Fees that are charged to the borrower as "prepaid" interest or to reduce the loan's nominal interest rate, such as points and interest "buy-downs" (explicit yield adjustments).
- Fees that are, in substance, implicit yield adjustments because a loan is granted at off-market terms (for example, certain syndication fees).
- Underwriting fees charged to the borrower that relate directly to making the loan (for example, fees that are paid to the lender as compensation for granting a complex loan or agreeing to lend quickly).
- Loan syndication and participation fees to the extent they are associated with the portion of the loan retained by the lender. (FAS-91 Q&A, par. 35)

Loan origination costs that should be deferred and recognized as a reduction of the loan's yield   FAS-91 permits deferral of only two categories of loan origination costs:

- Incremental direct costs incurred in transactions with independent third parties for that loan, so called "external costs." (FAS-91, par. 6(a))
- Certain internal costs directly related to specified loan origination activities performed by the lender for that loan. (FAS-91, par. 6(b))

> ☛ **PRACTICE POINTER:**   FAS-91 identifies the only circumstances where lending fees and costs should be offset and deferred. The accounting is required, not elective. Previous practices of netting anticipated bad debt expense against unearned fee revenue are not acceptable. (EITF D-8)

External loan origination costs   External loan origination costs must have both of the following characteristics:

- The costs result directly from and are essential to the lending transaction; and
- The costs would *not* have been incurred by the lender had *that* lending transaction not occurred. (FAS-91, par. 8)

"Independent third parties" generally possess the following characteristics (FAS-91 Q&A, par. 9):

- They are not employees of the lender.
- They are not receiving employee benefits from the lender.
- The party also provides similar services to other entities unrelated to the lender.
- The party is not under the control or significant influence of the lender.

A nominal passive investment from the standpoint of both the lender and the provider of service probably would not affect the provider's independence. (FAS-91 Q&A, par. 10)

> ☛ **PRACTICE POINTER:**   Costs incurred with third parties that are not considered "independent" may be treated as internal costs, as long as they represent origination costs, as defined below. (FAS-91 Q&A, par. 11)

☛ **PRACTICE POINTER:** FAS-91 does not apply to costs that are incurred by a lender in transactions with independent third parties *if* the lender bills those costs directly to the borrower. However, costs that are not billed directly to the borrower, but instead, are expected to be recovered through the interest rate charged to the borrower, are within the scope of FAS-91. (FAS-91 Q&A, par. 5)

☛ **PRACTICE POINTER:** Fees paid to a service bureau for loan processing are not eligible for deferral because the services are not related to loan origination, that is, the services are performed *after* the loan has been made. (FAS-91 Q&A, par. 17)

Internal loan origination costs Certain internal costs, such as employees' salaries and benefits, directly related to specified loan origination activities performed by the lender for that loan should be deferred and amortized as a reduction of the yield on the loan. Exhibit 7-2 evaluates various activities and outlines the types of internal costs that should be deferred and the types of internal costs that should be expensed as incurred.

EXHIBIT 7-2
TREATMENT OF INTERNAL COSTS FROM LENDING ACTIVITIES

Costs From Loan Origination Activities That Should Be Deferred	Costs That Should Be Expensed As Incurred
Source: FAS-91, par. 6, FAS-91 Q&A, par. 20	FAS-91, par. 7, FAS-91 Q&A, pars. 13-15 and 39
Evaluating the prospective borrower's financial condition	Advertising, soliciting potential borrowers
Initial credit analysis and investigation	Supervision and administration
Appraisals	Establishing and monitoring credit policies
Evaluating and recording guarantees, collateral, and other security arrangements	Servicing existing loans
Negotiating loan terms, including discussing alternative borrowing arrangements with borrowers	Unsuccessful loan origination efforts and idle time

Costs From Loan Origination Activities That Should Be Deferred	Costs That Should Be Expensed As Incurred
Preparing and processing loan documents	Administrative costs, rent, depreciation, and all other occupancy and equipment costs (including data processing equipment and software dedicated to originating loans)
Quality control review performed during the underwriting period internally	Investment advisory costs, whether paid to third parties or incurred
Loan evaluation and approval committees (all activities involved in origination decisions)	
Closing the transaction	

Calculating internal costs Only that portion of the employees' total compensation (including bonuses) and payroll-related fringe benefits directly related to time spent performing those activities *for that loan* and other costs related to those activities that would not have been incurred but *for that loan* should be deferred. (FAS-91, par. 6 and FAS-91 Q&A, par. 18) Examples of such costs include:

- The portion of executive compensation, such as salaries of members of a loan approval committee, attributable to review of successful loans prior to funding. (FAS-91 Q&A, par. 24)
- For an employee paid commissions only for successful loan production, the portion relating to loan *origination* activities. (FAS-91 Q&A, par. 19)
- Reimbursement of travel costs, itemized telephone calls, and reimbursement for mileage and tolls to personnel involved in a successful loan origination. (FAS-91 Q&A, par. 12)
- Fringe benefits, including payroll taxes, insurance, retirement plans, stock compensation plans, and overtime meal allowances. (FAS-91 Q&A, par. 16)

Standard costing methods may be used to calculate direct loan origination costs, provided that the costs of originating loans are similar. (FAS-91 Q&A, par. 21) A successful-efforts-based system should be developed at the functional level (e.g., application, verification, underwriting, appraisal, closing) and may be based on the percentage of successful and unsuccessful efforts determined for each function, adjusted for idle time and time spent on activities for which the related costs cannot be deferred. (FAS-91 Q&A, par. 22)

☞ **PRACTICE POINTER:** Idle time represents the time that a lender's employees are not actively involved in performing origination activities for specific loans. Idle time can be measured through the establishment of standard costs, time studies, ratios of productive and nonproductive time, and other methods. (FAS-91 Q&A, par. 23)

Costs on pending loans Origination costs on a loan in process may be deferred until the loan is either closed or considered an unsuccessful effort. If a loan in process is determined to be unsuccessful after the balance sheet date but before the financial statements are issued, costs that have been deferred through the balance sheet date should be charged to expense in the period ending with the balance sheet date. (FAS-91 Q&A, par. 30)

Fees and Costs on Purchased Loans

Purchased loans are recorded at the amount paid to the seller, plus any transaction fees paid or less any fees received. The initial investment frequently differs from the related loan's principal amount at the date of purchase. This premium or discount should be recognized as an adjustment of yield over the life of the loan. All costs incurred in connection with acquiring loans or committing to purchase loans should be charged to expense as incurred. (FAS-91, par. 15) This includes loans acquired through a loan participation. (FAS-91 Q&A, par. 35) Loans purchased at a discount, that is due in part to credit concerns, are accounted for under SOP 03-3, not FAS-91. SOP 03-3 is discussed later in this chapter.

> **OBSERVATION:** A purchased loan has already been originated by another party. Therefore, the purchaser is not allowed to defer any costs as "origination" fees or costs, including the cost of due diligence reviews.

Loans purchased as a group A purchaser may allocate the initial investment to the individual loans or may account for the initial investment in the aggregate. The cash flows provided by the underlying loan contracts should be used to apply the interest method, except when prepayments are anticipated, as allowed by paragraph 19 of FAS-91. If prepayments are not anticipated and prepayments occur or some of the purchased loans are sold, a proportionate amount of the related deferred fees and purchase premium or discount should be recognized in income so that the effective interest rate on the remaining portion of loans continues unchanged. (FAS-91, par. 16) (As discussed later in this chapter, EITF Issue 88-20 provides guidance for credit card receivables purchased as a group.)

Fees and Costs on Refinancings and Restructurings (Other Than a Troubled Debt Restructuring)

When the terms of a loan are contractually revised in a nontroubled situation, the lender must determine whether the revised agreement should be accounted for as a new loan (an origination) or a continuation of the old loan.

> ☞ **PRACTICE POINTER:** A concession made to reflect a general decline in market interest rates or a decrease in risk so as to maintain a relationship with a debtor that can readily obtain funds from other sources at current market rates is generally *not* a troubled debt restructuring. (FAS-15, par. 7)

Tests for a new loan   A loan with revised terms should be considered a "new loan" if both of the following conditions are met:

- The terms of the new loan are at least as favorable to the lender as the terms for comparable loans to other customers with similar collection risks who are not refinancing or restructuring a loan with the lender. This condition would be met if the new loan's effective yield were at least equal to the effective yield for such loans.
- The modifications of the terms of a loan are more than minor. (FAS-91, pars. 12-13) The term "minor" is defined below.

The accounting for any unamortized fees and costs and any new fees and costs would be:

- *If "new loan" conditions are met:*   Write off any unamortized fees and costs to interest income when the new loan is granted. (FAS-91, par. 12) Defer any fees received to modify an existing loan, net of any direct loan origination costs and recognize over the remaining life of the loan as an adjustment of yield. (FAS-91 Q&A, par. 6)
- *If "new loan" conditions are not met:*   Carry forward any unamortized fees and costs as a part of the net investment in the new loan. The new loan balance would consist of the remaining net investment in the original loan, any additional amounts loaned, any fees received, and direct loan origination costs associated with the refinancing or restructuring. (FAS-91, par. 13)

Definition of *minor*   A modification of a loan should be considered more than *minor* under paragraph 13 of FAS-91 if the present value of the cash flows under the terms of the new debt instrument is at least

10 percent different from the present value of the remaining cash flows under the terms of the original instrument. If the difference between the present value of the cash flows under the terms of the new debt instrument and the present value of the remaining cash flows under the terms of the original debt instrument is less than *10 percent*, a creditor should evaluate whether the modification is more than *minor* based on the specific facts and circumstances (and other relevant considerations) surrounding the modification. The 10 percent test should be performed using the computational guidance in EITF Issue 96-19. (EITF 01-07) Chapter 11, "Extinguishments of Debt," discusses the provisions of EITF Issue 96-19 in detail.

> ☞ **PRACTICE POINTER:** The definition of *minor* is only relevant to the creditor's accounting for a loan refinancing or restructuring when the terms of the new loan are at least as favorable to the lender as the terms for comparable loans to other customers with similar collection risks who are not refinancing or restructuring.

Blended-rate loans Blended-rate loans involve lending new funds at market interest rates combined with existing loans at rates currently lower than market rates. The combined loan yields an interest rate between the existing loan rate and the market rate. This arrangement is a refinancing, but it does not meet the "new loan" yield test, that is, the blended rate is below the market rate of loans with similar collection risks made to the lender's other customers. Thus, the unamortized net fees and costs on the existing loan as well as the net fees and costs relating to the refinancing should carry over to the new loan. (FAS-91 Q&A, par. 38)

Fees and Costs in a Troubled Debt Restructuring

Fees received by the lender in connection with a modification of terms of a troubled debt restructuring as defined in FAS-15 should be applied as a reduction of the recorded investment in the loan. All related costs, including direct loan origination costs, should be charged to expense as incurred. (FAS-91, par. 14) Chapter 3, "Loans and the Allowance for Credit Losses," discusses the creditor's accounting for a troubled debt restructuring in detail.

Other Types of Fees, Including Commitments

Loan commitments Fees received for a commitment to originate or purchase a loan or group of loans are generally netted against any direct loan origination costs (FAS-91, par. 9), deferred, and:

- If the commitment is exercised, recognized over the life of the loan as an adjustment of yield, and
- If the commitment expires unexercised, recognized in income upon expiration of the commitment. (FAS-91, par. 8)

Lines of credit and credit cards are viewed as forms of loan commitments under FAS-91.

- *Exercise of commitment is remote*   If, based on the entity's experience with similar arrangements, it is remote that the commitment will be exercised, a net commitment fee should be recognized over the commitment period on a straight-line basis as service fee income. If the commitment is subsequently exercised during the commitment period, the remaining unamortized commitment fee at the time of exercise should be recognized over the life of the loan as an adjustment of yield. (FAS-91, par. 8(a)) Any *net cost* should be charged to expense immediately. (FAS-91 Q&A, par. 26)
- *Commitment fees determined retrospectively*   If the amount of the commitment fee is determined retrospectively as a percentage of the line of credit available but unused in a previous period, the commitment fee should be recognized as service fee income as of the determination date if:
  — That percentage is nominal in relation to the stated interest rate on any related borrowing, and
  — That borrowing will bear a market interest rate at the date the loan is made. (FAS-91, par. 8(b))
- *Lines of credit*   Qualifying origination costs should be deferred and amortized based on the terms of the line of credit or commitment facility.
  — Revolving line of credit: Straight-line basis over the period that the revolving line of credit is active.
  — Revolver with option to convert to a term loan: Straight-line basis over the combined life of the revolving line of credit and term loan.
  — Not a revolving line of credit: Straight-line basis over the commitment period. (FAS-91 Q&A, par. 27)
- *Credit facilities with multiple, unscheduled drawdowns with varying maturities*   The commitment fee should be deferred until the facility is exercised and a drawdown is made. Given the multiple, unscheduled drawdowns intended under the facility, a *pro rata* portion of the commitment fee (equal to the percentage of the loan drawn down to the total facility) should be recognized over the life of the applicable drawdown as an adjustment of its yield. (FAS-91 Q&A, par. 28, including a detailed example)

☛ **PRACTICE POINTER:** Some lenders offer "multi-option facilities," which contain several credit structures that borrowers
may use in any combination. Lenders may receive a variety of
fees in connection with that type of facility. Generally, all fees
received must be deferred. However, the fees must be allocated to
each product in the facility because the amortization of certain
fees must be reported as service fee income while the amortization of other fees must be reported as interest income. (FAS-91
Q&A, par. 29)

Credit card fees and costs   Various types of entities issue credit
cards, debit cards, bank charge cards, and other similar cards (collectively, credit cards) with a variety of terms. Fees charged in connection with credit card issuances are viewed as loan commitment fees
and certain costs associated with issuing a credit card are viewed as
origination costs.

Credit card originations   EITF Issue 92-5 concludes that credit card
origination costs that qualify for deferral under FAS-91 should be
netted against the related credit card fee, if any, and the net amount
should be amortized on a straight-line basis over the "privilege period" as an adjustment of interest income. "Privilege period" means:

- *If a significant fee is charged*   The period that the fee entitles the
  cardholder to use the credit card.
- *If no significant fee is charged*   One year.

Individual credit card originations and purchases   Amounts paid to a
third party to acquire individual credit card accounts should be
treated as originations, that is, deferred and netted against the related
credit card fee, if any, and the net amount should be amortized on a
straight-line basis over the privilege period. (EITF 93-1)

Fees paid for solicitations of new customers   When a lender pays a fixed
fee to an independent third party to solicit new cardholders, none of
the fee is eligible for deferral, because the lender would have incurred
all of the solicitation costs regardless of the number of credit cards
issued. Accordingly, the entire fee should be charged to expense.
(FAS-91 Q&A, par. 32)

Renewal fees   Periodic renewal fees for the continued extension of
credit card privileges generally cover many services to cardholders.
Renewal fees should be deferred and recognized on a straight-line
basis over the period the fee entitles the cardholder to use the card as
service fee income. (FAS-91, par. 10)

Purchases of credit card portfolios   EITF Issue 88-20, as amended by
FAS-140, requires that when an enterprise purchases a credit card
portfolio including the cardholder relationships, the credit card

receivables should be recorded at their fair values. The difference between the amount paid and the fair value of the credit card loans at the date of purchase (the premium) should be attributed to the cardholder relationships acquired. The amount relating to the cardholder relationships represents an identifiable intangible asset that should be amortized over the period estimated to be benefited in accordance with FAS-142, paragraph 12. Any difference between the fair value and principal balances of the loans should be amortized over the life of the loans in accordance with FAS-91.

Loan commitments that must be accounted for as derivatives   Loan commitments that relate to the origination of mortgage loans that will be held for resale, as discussed in paragraph 21 of FAS-65 (as amended), must be accounted for as derivative instruments in accordance with FAS-133 by the lender (but not the borrower). In addition, commitments to buy and sell existing loans must be evaluated under FAS-133. However, loan commitments that relate to the origination of mortgage loans that will be held for investment and all other commitments to originate loans should be accounted for as described in this section, even if they technically meet the definition of a derivative. (FAS-149, pars. 6(c) and 10(i), and DIG C-13)

> **OBSERVATION:** After the issuance of FAS-133, the FASB learned that many types of loan commitments would meet the definition of a derivative under FAS-133, either because the loan commitments are transferable (and therefore can be "net settled") or because the underlying loans were readily convertible to cash (such as in the case of a conforming mortgage loan). DIG Issue C-13 creates a scope exception for most loan commitments involving originated (new) loans, except for the creditor when the loan is considered held for resale under the specialized mortgage banking model.

Standby commitments to purchase loans   A standby commitment is, in substance, a written put option that will be exercised only if the value of the loans is less than or equal to the strike price. If a standby commitment meets the definition of a derivative, it must be accounted for under FAS-133. Standby commitments that are not derivatives should be accounted for as follows.

> If the settlement date is (a) within a reasonable period of time (for example, a normal loan commitment period) *and* (b) the entity has the intent and ability to accept delivery without selling assets, loans purchased under standby commitments should be recorded at cost on the settlement date, net of the standby commitment fee received, in accordance with FAS-91, paragraph 8.

Otherwise, the standby commitment fee should be recorded as a liability and accounted for at the greater of the initial standby commitment fee or the fair value of the written put option. Unrealized gains (that is, recoveries of unrealized losses) or losses should be credited or charged to current operations. (SOP 01-6, par. 8(f))

> **OBSERVATION:** If a standby commitment does not meet the definition of a derivative under FAS-133 but must be accounted for "like" a derivative (a written put option), the commitment may not be designated as a hedge.

Loan syndication fees When a company seeks to borrow a large amount of money, lenders sometimes share the risk by forming a syndicate. One lender typically manages the transaction with the borrower (the syndicator), but each member of the syndicate funds its respective portion of the loan. Typically, the lead syndicator receives a fee from the borrower and passes through some or all of that fee to the other lenders.

The institution managing a loan syndication (the syndicator) should recognize loan syndication fees as follows:

- *If a portion of the loan is retained* Defer a portion of the syndication fee to produce a yield on the portion of the loan retained that is not less than the average yield on the loans held by the other syndication participants (including the fees passed through by the syndicator). Any excess should be recognized as revenue when the syndication is complete.
- *No loan retained* Recognize as revenue when the syndication is complete. (FAS-91, par. 11)

Delinquency fees Delinquency fees should be recognized in income when chargeable, assuming collectibility is reasonably assured. (SOP 01-6, par. 8(j))

Prepayment fees Prepayment penalties should not be recognized in income until loans or trade receivables are prepaid, except that the existence of prepayment penalties could affect the application of paragraph 18(a) of FAS-91, which is discussed later in this chapter. (SOP 01-6, par. 8(k))

Rebates Rebates represent refunds of finance charges on installment loans or trade receivables that occur when payments are made early. The possibility that rebates may be calculated using on a method different from the interest method should not affect the accrual of interest income on installment loans or trade receivables, except that the possibility of rebates could affect the application of paragraph 18(a) of FAS-91. Differences between rebate calculations and accrual of interest income merely adjust original estimates of interest income and should be recognized in income when loans or trade receivables are prepaid or renewed. (SOP 01-6, par. 8(l))

Factoring commissions Factoring usually involves selling accounts receivable to a transferee (the factor) that assumes the full risk of collection, without recourse to the transferor in the event of a loss. The accounting for factoring commissions by the factor depends on whether the transfer is accounted for as a purchase/sale or a secured borrowing under FAS-140. (Chapter 5, "Transfers of Financial Assets," discusses the conditions necessary for a sale or financing in detail.) If the transaction is accounted for as a purchase of receivables by the factor, the purchase discount (factoring commission) should be accounted for under either FAS-91 or SOP 03-3, as appropriate, depending on whether the discount is attributable in part to concerns about credit quality. If the transaction is accounted for as a secured loan, factoring commissions should be recognized over the period of the loan contract under FAS-91, beginning when the entity funds a customer's credit and ending when the customer's account is settled. (SOP 01-6, par. 8(m))

Application of the Interest Method under FAS-91

The objective of the interest method is to arrive at periodic interest income that represents a constant effective yield on the net investment in the receivable (that is, the principal amount of the receivable adjusted by unamortized fees or costs and purchase premium or discount). Certain gains and losses on fair value hedges are also included in the carrying amount of a loan or debt security. Hedge accounting is discussed in Chapter 14, "Hedge Accounting."

As discussed in the previous section, when an entity originates a loan, certain fees and costs are required to be deferred and amortized as an adjustment of the yield of the loan under FAS-91. Loan origination fees and direct loan origination costs for a given loan should be offset and only the net amount should be deferred and amortized. (FAS-91, par. 5) All other lending-related costs should be expensed as incurred. (FAS-91, par. 7)

Aggregation of Loans

Loans may be aggregated if the enterprise holds a large number of similar loans for which prepayments are probable and the timing and amount of prepayments can be reasonably estimated (FAS-91, par. 19) or if the resulting recognition does not differ materially from the amount that would have been recognized on an individual loan-by-loan basis. (FAS-91, par. 4)

Subsequent sale of aggregated loan   If loans are aggregated and a loan in the pool is subsequently sold, the deferred net fees and costs should be allocated either on a *pro rata* basis (based on the ratio of the outstanding principal balances of the loans sold) or, if detailed records are available, on a specific identification basis to calculate the gain or loss. (FAS-91 Q&A, par. 49)

> ☞ **PRACTICE POINTER:**   Recognizing net fees over the estimated average life of a group of dissimilar loans is not in accordance with GAAP.

EXHIBIT 7-3
COMPONENTS OF NET INVESTMENT (AMORTIZED COST) IN A LOAN

Loan principal amount

+ Purchase premium

+ Net deferred loan origination costs

− Purchase discount

− Net deferred loan origination fees

+ Accrued interest

+/− Deferred gains and losses from fair value hedges (See Chapter 14, "Hedge Accounting")

> **REGULATORY ALERT:**   Insurance companies do not apply FAS-91 in some cases under statutory accounting principles. For example, nonrefundable origination fees (other than points) are recognized in income when they are received, and origination costs are expensed as incurred. (SSAP 37, *Mortgage Loans*) Practitioners should be alert to differences between SAP and GAAP for insurance companies.

The Effective Interest Rate

The effective interest rate is the rate that equates the present value of the future cash inflows to the initial net cash outflow, including any deferred fees and costs. This rate is also called the internal rate of return. Theoretically, the effective rate should represent the market rate for that loan at its inception; however, because certain origination costs and fees may be deferred, the effective rate sometimes differs from the market rate (that is, a purchaser would not incur *origination* costs).

Once the effective interest rate is determined, any deferred origination fees and costs, or purchase premium or discount must be amortized over the life of the loan (or a shorter period, if prepayments may be estimated—see below). The amount of amortization for the period equals the difference between:

- Interest income determined using the interest method *and*
- The stated interest on the loan.

Illustration 7-1 provides an example of this calculation.

Variable Interest Rates

When the stated interest rate is not constant throughout the term of the loan, the interest method should be applied as follows (FAS-91, par. 18):

Increasing-rate loans If the loan's stated interest rate increases during the term of the loan (so that interest accrued under the interest method in early periods would exceed interest at the stated rate), interest income should not be recognized to the extent that the net investment in the loan would increase to an amount greater than the amount at which the borrower could settle the obligation. Prepayment penalties should be included in determining the settlement amount only if the penalties are imposed throughout the loan term. (FAS-91, par. 18(a)) Refer to Illustration 7-3.

The recorded net investment in the loan can exceed the amount at which the borrower can settle the loan only if the excess results from a purchase premium (for a purchased loan) or loan costs that qualify for deferral in excess of loan fees (originated loans). (FAS-91 Q&A, par. 41)

> ☞ **PRACTICE POINTER:** If a teaser-rate loan is purchased at a discount during the period that the interest-rate is below market, the investor should amortize the discount over the life of the loan. However, because the discount should be amortized in a manner that creates a level yield, the majority of the discount will be amortized in the first year. (FAS-91 Q&A, par. 53)

Decreasing-rate loans If the loan's stated interest rate decreases during the term of the loan, the stated periodic interest received early in the term of the loan would exceed the periodic interest income that is calculated under the interest method. In that circumstance, the excess should be deferred and recognized in those future periods when the constant effective yield under the interest method exceeds the stated interest rate. (FAS-91, par. 18(b))

Variable-rate loans If the loan's stated interest rate varies or adjusts based on future changes in an independent factor, such as an index or rate (for example, the prime rate, the London Interbank Offered Rate (LIBOR), or the U.S. Treasury bill weekly average rate), the calculation of the constant effective yield necessary to recognize fees and costs should be based either on:

- The factor (the index or rate) that is in effect at the inception of the loan or
- On the factor as it changes over the life of the loan. (FAS-91, par. 18(c))

The lender must select either method a. or b. above for a given loan and apply the method consistently over the life of the loan. (FAS-91 Q&A, par. 45) An example of the first method is provided in Illustration 7-4. If the lender selects the second method, and the factor changes, the calculation of the constant effective yield should be made from the time of the change (not the inception of the loan). (FAS-91 Q&A, par. 47)

If a variable-rate loan has an initial rate that differs from the rate its base factor would produce, the constraints in paragraphs 18(a) and 18(b) of FAS-91 apply, including the treatment of prepayment penalties. (FAS-91 Q&A, par. 40)

Sum-of-the-years'-digits When interest is collected on a loan by the sum-of-the-years'-digits method, any interest collected in the early years of the loan that exceeds the amount computed using the interest method must be deferred and recognized in later periods. (FAS-91 Q&A, par. 46 and EITF D-10)

> ☞ **PRACTICE POINTER:** Teaser-rate adjustable rate loans are subject to the constraints in paragraphs 18 (a) and (c) during the discount period. After the discount period, only paragraph 18(c) applies. (FAS-91 Q&A, par. 42)

Anticipating Prepayments in the Effective Yield Calculation

Ordinarily, the contractual cash flows specified by the loan agreement should be used to apply the interest method, and prepayments of principal should not be anticipated to shorten the term of the loan. However, prepayments may be anticipated if:

- The lender holds a large number of similar loans for which prepayments are probable and
- The timing and amount of prepayments can be reasonably estimated. (FAS-91, par. 19)

Prepayments may *not* be anticipated if:

- A loan-by-loan approach is used to defer fees and costs. (FAS-91 Q&A, par. 48)
- An investor holds an individual callable loan or bond purchased at a premium or a discount. (FAS-91 Q&A, par. 50)
- A lender originates a single callable loan. (FAS-91 Q&A, par. 58)

> ☞ **PRACTICE POINTER:** To estimate future prepayments, the lender should consider historical internal prepayment data and external information, including current and forecasted interest rates and economic conditions and published mortality and pre-payment tables for similar loans. (FAS-91 Q&A, par. 52)

Grouping loans to anticipate prepayments The following factors should be considered in identifying a large group of similar loans (FAS-91 Q&A, par. 52):

- Loan type and size
- Nature and location of collateral
- Coupon interest rate
- Maturity
- Period of origination
- Prepayment history of the loans (if seasoned)
- Level of net fees or costs
- Prepayment penalties
- Interest rate type (fixed or variable)
- Expected prepayment performance in varying interest rate scenarios

Changes in estimated cash flows If the enterprise anticipates pre-payments in applying the interest method and a difference arises between the prepayments anticipated and actual prepayments received, the enterprise must recalculate the effective yield to reflect actual payments to date and anticipated future payments. The net investment in the loans is then adjusted to the amount that would have existed had the new effective yield been applied since the ac-quisition of the loans. The offsetting entry is a charge or credit to interest income. (FAS-91, par. 19)

> **OBSERVATION:** This calculation is called the *retrospective method* of adjusting cash flow estimates.

☞ **PRACTICE POINTER:** Periodic changes in *estimated* cash flows also should be accounted for using the retrospective method. (FAS-91 Q&A, par. 52)

Loans with Uncertain Payment Terms

FAS-91 provides special guidance for loans with uncertain payment terms.

Demand loans For a loan that has no scheduled payment terms and is payable at the lender's demand, any deferred net fees or costs may be recognized as an adjustment of yield on a straight-line basis over a period that reflects:

- The understanding between the borrower and lender or
- If no understanding exists, the lender's estimate of the period of time over which the loan will remain outstanding.

Any unamortized amount should be recognized when the loan is paid off. (FAS-91, par. 20(a))

☞ **PRACTICE POINTER:** Estimates should be monitored regularly and revised as appropriate. However, if a loan remains outstanding beyond the anticipated payment date (and all the net fees and costs have been fully amortized), no adjustment is necessary. (FAS-91 Q&A, par. 55)

Construction loans and permanent financing When a lender has made both a construction loan and a commitment for the permanent financing that the lender believes has more than a remote probability of being exercised, the net amount of fees received and costs that meet the criteria for deferral should be amortized as an adjustment of yield over the combined life of the construction and permanent loans. If the commitment to provide permanent financing expires unused, any unamortized fees and costs should be recognized as income at that time. (FAS-91 Q&A, par. 44)

Revolving lines of credit For a loan that allows the borrower to make multiple borrowings up to a specified amount, to repay portions of previous borrowings, and then reborrow under the same contract (or similar loan arrangements), any deferred net fees or costs should be recognized in income on a straight-line basis over the period the revolving line of credit is active, assuming that borrowings are outstanding for the maximum term provided in the loan contract. If the borrower pays all borrowings and cannot reborrow under the contract, any unamortized net fees or costs should be recognized in income upon payment. When the loan agreement provides a schedule for payment and no additional borrowings are allowed under the agreement, any net unamortized fees or costs should be recognized using the interest method. (FAS-91, par. 20(b))

> ☛ **PRACTICE POINTER:** If the borrower continues to have a contractual right to borrow under the revolving line of credit, net fees and costs associated with revolving lines of credit should be amortized over the term of the revolver even if the revolver is unused for a period of time. (FAS-91 Q&A, par. 56)

EXHIBIT 7-4
AMORTIZATION METHODS FOR COMMON LOAN TYPES

Loan Type	Amortization Method
Negative amortization loans	Interest
Biweekly mortgages	Interest
Line of credit loans or arrangements with similar characteristics	Straight-line
Overdraft protection loans	Straight-line
Home equity loans	Generally the interest method, but the straight-line method may be used if the arrangement has the characteristics of a revolving line of credit
Acquisition, development, and construction arrangements accounted for as loans prior to completion of funding	
a. Single project	Interest*
b. Multiple projects	Generally the interest method, with partial drawdowns but the straight-line method and payments may be used if the arrangement has the characteristics of a revolving line of credit

* For loan contracts in which the timing and amount of payments are not specified, estimates must be made to apply the interest method.

Source: FAS-91 Q&A, par. 44. Reproduced with permission from the FASB.

Nonaccrual Loans

Deferred net fees or costs should not be amortized during periods in which interest income on a loan is not being recognized because of concerns about the realization of loan principal or interest. (FAS-91, par. 17)

Generally, interest income should not be accrued if collectibility is doubtful. FAS-118 requires disclosure of how an entity recognizes interest on impaired loans (for example, the cost-recovery method or the cash-basis method). Several industries have developed practices for putting loans on nonaccrual status; often these practices are based on regulatory guidelines. Loan impairment is discussed in Chapter 3, "Loans and the Allowance for Credit Losses."

Balance Sheet Presentation

Yield-related items on assets should be presented on the balance sheet as follows:

- Unamortized origination and certain commitment fees and costs of completed loans and commitments to lend should be netted and reported along with the related loans. (FAS-91 Q&A, par. 59)
- Unamortized purchase (or imputed) premiums and discounts should be netted and reported along with the related loans. (APB-21, par. 16 and FAS-91, par. 21)
- Commitment fees that meet the criteria of paragraph 8(a) of FAS-91 should be classified as deferred income in the financial statements. (FAS-91 Q&A, par. 59)

Income Statement Presentation

Loan origination, commitment, and other fees and costs recognized as an adjustment of yield should be reported as part of interest income. Amortization of other fees, such as commitment fees that are being amortized on a straight-line basis over the commitment period or included in income when the commitment expires, should be reported as service fee income. (FAS-91, par. 22)

> **OBSERVATION:** FAS-91 does not specify how non-yield-related syndication fees should be classified in the income statement.

Cash Flow Statement Presentation

Cash receipts from returns on loans, other debt instruments of other entities, and equity securities—interest and dividends—are reported as operating cash flows. (FAS-95, par. 22)

Special Application of the Interest Method for Certain Investments

Generally, the interest method must be applied to recognize interest income on debt instruments. However, several models have been developed to deal with changes in estimated cash flows for instruments with nontraditional interest rates, prepayment features, structured transactions, and concerns about credit risk. The scope of each of these special models is precise—as a rule, they should not be applied by analogy in other situations. Exhibit 7-6 summarizes the applicable GAAP for various instruments.

> ☛ **PRACTICE POINTER:** Entities may elect to apply the fair value option in FAS-159 to eligible instruments that may otherwise be subject to the guidance discussed in the sections below. In that case, the instrument would be measured initially and subsequently at fair value with changes in fair value recognized in current earnings and the guidance discussed in the sections below would not be applicable. Refer to Chapter 19, "The Fair Value Option for Financial Instruments," for scope and other guidance related to the fair value option in FAS-159.

Structured Notes (EITF 96-12)

EITF Issue 96-12 addresses accounting for structured notes (that is, securities with uncertain principal amounts, interest amounts, or both) that have one or more of the following characteristics:

- The principal is at risk (for other than failure of the borrower to pay the contractual amounts due).
- The interest rate or return on investment is variable (other than due to credit rating changes of the borrower) because there is either (a) no stated coupon rate or (b) the change in return on investment is not a constant percentage of, or in the same direction as, changes in market-based interest rates or (c) a portion of the potential yield is based on the occurrence of future events.
- The maturity of the bond is based on a specific index or on the occurrence of specific events outside the control of the parties to the transaction, other than the passage of time or normal covenant violations.

EITF Issue 96-12 only applies to *securities* with one or more of these characteristics that are classified as available-for-sale or held-to-maturity debt securities in accordance with FAS-115. However, structured note securities that, by their terms, suggest that it is reasonably possible that the investor could lose all or substantially all of its original investment amount (for other than failure of the borrower to pay the contractual amounts due) should be marked to market with all changes in fair value reported in earnings.

There is currently some overlap between the scope of EITF Issue 96-12, EITF Issue 99-20, and FAS-133. Regarding the overlap with FAS-133, a security with the characteristics described above would nonetheless be accounted for under FAS-133 if it contains an embedded derivative that is *not* clearly and closely related to the host contract (even if the embedded derivative is not accounted for separately and the entire instrument is marked to market). Chapter 13, "Embedded Derivatives," addresses embedded derivatives in detail. However, the FASB allowed companies to grandfather hybrid instruments that were entered into before either January 1, 1998, or January 1, 1999, as elected by the entity (see paragraph 50 of FAS-133, as amended). Accordingly, some structured notes that technically contain embedded derivatives may continue to be accounted for under EITF Issue 96-12.

In terms of the overlap with EITF Issue 99-20, a security with the characteristics described above would be accounted for under EITF Issue 99-20 if it is a beneficial interest in a special-purpose entity that could contractually be prepaid in such a way that the investor would not recover substantially all of its initial investment (and the instrument does not contain an embedded derivative that should be accounted for separately under FAS-133).

EITF Issue 96-12 does not apply to loans, traditional convertible bonds, multicurrency debt securities, debt securities participating directly in the results of an issuer's operations (for example, participating mortgages or similar instruments), or reverse mortgages.

The following types of securities would typically be considered structured notes that should be accounted for under EITF Issue 96-12 (that is, the embedded derivative is considered clearly and closely related to the host contract and should *not* be accounted for separately under FAS-133, plus any grandfathered structured notes that otherwise would be accounted for under FAS-133):

- Inverse floater (a bond with a coupon rate of interest that varies inversely with changes in specified interest rates or indexes (for example, LIBOR) or a leveraged inverse floater (the specified index is multiplied by a number greater than 1) *that contractually limits the amount of principal that can be lost* to the amount of the initial cash investment. (Note: Many inverse floaters do not contain this type of limit and would therefore contain an embedded derivative.)

- Delevered floater (a bond with a coupon rate of interest that lags overall movements in specified interest rate levels or indices).

- Range floater (a bond with a coupon that depends on the number of days that a reference rate stays within a preestablished collar; otherwise, the bond pays either zero percent interest or a below-market rate).

- Ratchet floater (a bond that pays a floating rate of interest and has an adjustable cap, adjustable floor, or both that move in sync with each new reset rate).

- Fixed-to-floating note (a bond that pays a varying coupon, for example, the first-year coupon is fixed, second- and third-year coupons are based on LIBOR, Treasury bills, or prime rate).
- Indexed amortizing note (a bond that repays principal based on a predetermined amortization schedule or target value), provided that the investor's recorded investment is not at risk, and the contractual yield could not rise to a level that is both double the initial rate on the instrument and twice the current market rate for a similar instrument.
- Step-up bond (a bond that provides an introductory above-market yield and steps up to a new coupon, which will be below then-current market rates or, alternatively, the bond may be called in lieu of the step-up in the coupon rate).
- Credit-sensitive bond (a bond that has a coupon rate of interest that resets based on changes in the issuer's credit rating).
- Inflation bond (a bond with a contractual principal amount that is indexed to the inflation rate but cannot decrease below par).

☛ **PRACTICE POINTER:** Refer to FAS-133, Appendix B, Section 2, for a detailed analysis of these and other instruments for the presence of embedded derivatives that must be accounted for separately under FAS-133.

Recognizing yields on structured notes The retrospective interest method should be used to recognize income on structured note securities that are within the scope of EITF Issue 96-12. Under the retrospective interest method, the income recognized for a reporting period is measured as the difference between the amortized cost of the security at the end of the period and the amortized cost at the beginning of the period, plus any cash received during the period. The amortized cost would be calculated as the present value of estimated future cash flows using an effective yield, which is the yield that equates all past actual and current estimated future cash flow streams to the initial investment. If the effective yield were negative (that is, the sum of the newly estimated undiscounted cash flows is less than the security's amortized cost), the amortized cost would be calculated using a zero percent effective yield.

All estimates of future cash flows should be based on quoted forward market rates or prices in active markets, when available; otherwise, they should be based on current "spot" rates or prices as of the reporting date.

If other-than-temporary impairment is recognized, the investor should subsequently factor collectibility into its determination of estimated future cash flows.

☛ **PRACTICE POINTER:** Exhibit B of EITF Issue 96-12 provides a numerical example of the retrospective method for a note whose principal amount is dependent on changes in the S&P 500 Index. That note would be considered to contain an embedded derivative that requires separate accounting under FAS-133; however, the calculations in the example are equally applicable to other types of structured notes.

Beneficial Interests in a Securitization Trust (EITF 99-20)

There is a special model of interest income recognition for certain beneficial interests that are retained or purchased after a securitization of financial assets. The EITF Issue 99-20 model applies to beneficial interests that are retained by the transferor after a securitization that was accounted for as a sale under FAS-140 or that are purchased by investors if the interests:

- Are considered debt securities for accounting purposes or must be accounted for like securities under FAS-115 (regardless of whether they are classified as available-for-sale or trading) and

- Can contractually be prepaid or otherwise settled in such a way that the holder would not recover substantially all of its recorded investment.

EITF Issue 99-20 does *not* apply to:

- High-quality debt instruments with traditional interest rates, including variable rates (FAS-91);

- Loans or securities purchased with credit concerns (SOP 03-3);

- Beneficial interests measured at fair value under the fair value option in FAS-159;

- Hybrid instruments measured at fair value under FAS-133, paragraph 16, when the investor does not report interest income separately (although this section would apply to the host contract portion of a hybrid instrument that has been bifurcated if it otherwise meets the scope of EITF Issue 99-20);

- Beneficial interests that are considered equity for accounting purposes (apply FAS-115, APB-18 or EITF Issue 96-12, as applicable); or

- Beneficial interests that result in consolidation by the holder of the beneficial interests (the underlying assets and liabilities would be recorded).

> **OBSERVATION:** In terms of credit risk, the scope of EITF Issue 99-20 covers the area between FAS-91 (high quality instruments where the payments are expected to be collected) and SOP 03-3 (purchased instruments where it is likely that all of the contractual

payments will not be collected). Said another way, EITF Issue 99-20 addresses retained and purchased instruments with prepayment risk and some concern about the collectibility of cash flows.

SEC REGISTRANT ALERT: The SEC staff believes that only beneficial interests with a credit rating of "AA" or better should be considered to be of "high credit quality" for the purposes of assessing whether a beneficial interest is subject to the scope of EITF 99-20. (December 11, 2003, speech by John M. James, Professional Accounting Fellow, Office of the Chief Accountant of the SEC, at the AICPA National Conference on Current SEC Developments)

☛ **PRACTICE POINTER:**   EITF Issue 99-20 superseded EITF Issues 89-4 and 93-18.

Recognizing yields on beneficial interests   EITF Issue 99-20 requires accretion of the difference between:

- Initial estimate of undiscounted cash flows attributable to the beneficial interest and
- Initial cash investment (if purchased) or the allocated carrying amount (if retained after a transfer under FAS-140).

This difference is called the "accretable yield." Initially, the amount of accretable yield is not recorded on the balance sheet—over time, the accretable yield is recognized using the interest method.

Changes in cash flow estimates   The holder of a beneficial interest should continue to update the estimate of the timing and amount of cash flows over the life of the beneficial interest, using information and events that a market participant would use in determining the current fair value of the beneficial interest.

Favorable changes in estimated cash flows   A favorable change means that the present value of the newly estimated cash flows is greater than the present value of the original (or most recently updated) cash flow estimates for the beneficial interest. (Both sets of cash flows are discounted using the rate currently being used to accrete the beneficial interest.) The investor should recalculate the amount of accretable yield as the excess of estimated cash flows over the beneficial interest's reference amount (the reference amount is equal to (1) the initial investment less (2) cash received to date less (3) other-than-temporary impairments recognized to date plus (4) the yield accreted to date). The adjustment should be accounted for *prospectively*—that is, the amount of periodic accretion is recognized as a yield adjustment over the remaining life of the beneficial interest.

Adverse changes in estimated cash flows   An adverse change means that the present value of the revised estimated cash flows is lower than the present value of the original (or most recently updated) cash flow estimates for the beneficial interest. The accounting for an adverse change depends on whether an other-than-temporary impairment has occurred.

- *Fair value less than carrying amount*   If the fair value of the beneficial interest is less than its carrying amount and the holder determines there has been an adverse change in cash flows, an other-than-temporary impairment has occurred. The beneficial interest would be written down to its fair value, with a charge to income. (FAS-115, par. 16) The yield would be adjusted prospectively to reflect the new market rate.

- *Fair value greater than or equal to carrying amount*   Impairment has not occurred and the change in yield is recognized prospectively, as a yield adjustment over the remaining life of the beneficial interest.

Variable-rate instruments   The yield would normally be revised to reflect changes in the referenced interest rate as they occur. However, it may be necessary to recognize other-than-temporary impairment if the rate is calculated using leverage or an inverse factor, or if the credit quality of the issuer declines.

Fair value not estimable   When it is not practicable for a transferor to estimate the fair value of the beneficial interest at the initial transfer date, interest income should not be recognized using the interest method. For such beneficial interests (that is, those beneficial interests that continue to be held by the transferor that are recorded at $0 pursuant to FAS-140, par. 71), the transferor should use the cash basis for recognizing interest income because the beneficial interest will have an allocated carrying amount of zero.

> **OBSERVATION:**   The EITF Issue 99-20 model is different from the FAS-91 model in several respects: (1) the investor is allowed to anticipate prepayments, even for a single instrument, (2) most changes in estimate are recorded prospectively (unless impairment is recognized), rather than by adjusting the carrying amount, and (3) for interests that continue to be held by a transferor, the initial discount rate may differ from a market rate because the recorded amount is an allocation of cost rather than fair value. It is very important to understand the scope of the various pieces of literature so that the investment is accounted for properly.

Exhibit 7-5 highlights the application of the consensuses under different scenarios.

EXHIBIT 7-5
RECOGNIZING INTEREST AND IMPAIRMENT ON BENEFICIAL INTERESTS IN SECURITIZED ASSETS

Is Fair Value of the Beneficial Interest Greater Than or Equal to the Carrying Amount?	Has a Change in Estimated Cash Flows Occurred from the Last Revised Estimate (Considering Both Timing and Amount)?	Is an Other-Than-Temporary Impairment Recognized?	Is the Yield Revised for the Change?	Should the Original or Last Revised Estimated Cash Flows Be Used for Future Impairment Purposes?
Yes.	Yes, decrease (adverse change).	No.	Yes. The change in yield is recognized prospectively.	Last revised.
Yes.	No.	No.	N/A.	If the estimated cash flows have been previously revised, use the last revised cash flows. Otherwise, use the original cash flows.
Yes.	Yes, increase (favorable change).	No.	Yes. The change in yield is recognized prospectively.	Last revised.
No.	Yes, decrease (adverse change)	Yes.[1]	Yes. The yield is changed to the market rate.[1]	Last revised.
No.	No.	Generally, no.[2]	If an other-than-temporary impairment is recognized, the yield is	If the estimated cash flows have been previously revised, use the last revised cash

Is Fair Value of the Beneficial Interest Greater Than or Equal to the Carrying Amount?	Has a Change in Estimated Cash Flows Occurred from the Last Revised Estimate (Considering Both Timing and Amount)?	Is an Other-Than-Temporary Impairment Recognized?	Is the Yield Revised for the Change?	Should the Original or Last Revised Estimated Cash Flows Be Used for Future Impairment Purposes?
			changed to the market rate.	flows. Otherwise, use the original cash flows.
			If an other-than-temporary impairment is not recognized, the yield is not changed.	
No.	Yes, increase (favorable change).	Generally, no.[2]	If an other-than-temporary impairment is recognized, the yield is changed to the market rate.	Last revised.
			If an other-than-temporary impairment is not recognized, the change in yield is recog-nized is recognized prospectively.	

[1] See discussion of variable rates above.

[2] FSP FAS 115-1 and FAS 124-1, SAB-59, SAS-92, and FAS-115 Q&A provide additional information.

Adapted from EITF Issue 99-20, Exhibit 99-20A

Instruments Purchased at a Discount Due to Credit Quality (SOP 03-3)

Sometimes a loan or security is purchased at a discount and the discount is due at least partly to concerns about the collectibility of the contractual cash flows. The method of amortizing the discount depends on whether it is probable that the investor will collect all of the contractual cash flows receivable on the loan or security.

> ☛ **PRACTICE POINTER:** SOP 03-3 supersedes AICPA Practice Bulletin 6 (which became outdated with the issuance of FAS-114 and FAS-115) for transactions entered into after the SOP's initial application date (that is, for loans acquired in fiscal years beginning after December 15, 2004). For loans acquired in fiscal years beginning on or before December 15, 2004, PB-6, as amended by SOP 03-3, continues to apply.

SOP 03-3 applies to the following transactions when it is probable at acquisition that all of the contractual cash flows receivable will *not* be collected:

- Individual purchases of loans or securities
- Purchases of pools or groups of loans or securities
- Repurchases of loans previously sold in a transfer accounted for as a sale under FAS-140 that are subject to a recourse provision (AICPA TPA 2130.18)
- Loans and securities purchased in a business combination
- Loans and securities transferred to a newly created subsidiary if the transferee has written down the loan to fair value with the intent of transferring the stock of the subsidiary as a dividend to the shareholders of the parent company (see EITF 87-17 for more information)
- Contributions or transfers of loans or securities that satisfy a prior promise to give

The determination of whether a loan is subject to the scope of SOP 03-3 may be based on policies set for different types of loan products to indicate whether evidence of credit quality deterioration exists and when such loan products should be reviewed for application of SOP 03-3. AICPA TPA 2130.12 discusses considerations for various types of loan products. SOP 03-3 should not be applied if the amount of delayed payments or shortfalls regarding contractually required payments is insignificant. That assessment should be guided by an accounting policy applied consistently by the investor. (AICPA TPA 2130.11)

> ☛ **PRACTICE POINTER:** In a transfer of a pool or group of loans, each loan within the pool must be evaluated individually to determine whether it is subject to the SOP because the investor will be unable to collect all contractual cash flows receivable.

SOP 03-3 does *not* apply to:

- Originated loans (covered by FAS-91)

- Purchases of loans or securities where all contractual cash flows are expected to occur, even if they are purchased at a discount (covered by FAS-91)

- Loans or debt securities acquired shortly after origination for which there has been no evidence of deterioration of credit quality from the date of origination (covered by FAS-91)

- Loans and securities carried at fair value with changes in value recognized currently in earnings (including loans accounted for as trading securities under paragraph 14 of FAS-140)

- Mortgage loans classified as held for sale under FAS-65

- Leases as defined in FAS-13

- Loans acquired in a business combination accounted for at historical cost

- Loans held by liquidating banks (see EITF 88-25 for more information)

- Revolving credit agreements (for example, consumer revolving arrangements, such as credit cards and home equity loans, and commercial revolving loans, if the revolving privileges exist at the acquisition date) (AICPA TPA 2130.16)

- Loans that are retained interests (accounted for under EITF 99-20)

- Loans that are derivative instruments in their entirety (accounted for under FAS-133)

☞ **PRACTICE POINTER:**   SOP 03-3 can be applied, for example, to purchases of subprime loans or junk bonds purchased at a discount due to poor credit quality (unless they are held for trading or meet one of the other scope exceptions).

☞ **PRACTICE POINTER:**   SOP 03-3 is applicable to nonaccrual loans that meet its scope criteria. Specific disclosures are required for such loans. Refer to Exhibit 7-9 for disclosures required by SOP 03-3. (AICPA TPA 2130.13–2130.14)

Initial measurement and valuation allowances   SOP 03-3 requires that loans or securities acquired in a transfer (including individual loans, groups or pools of loans, and loans acquired in a purchased business combination) be recorded at their fair value. A valuation allowance may not be established for such loans at acquisition and may not be "carried over" to reflect losses incurred by the transferor. A valuation allowance may be recorded for purchased loans only when losses have been incurred by the investor after acquisition.

A loan previously transferred in a sale under FAS-140 that is repurchased at a price that is more than its fair value should be recorded at fair value and a loss should be recognized for the difference between the price paid and the fair value (if not already recognized as part of the original transfer). A loan that is repurchased at a price that is less than its fair value should be recorded at the purchase price and the excess of expected cash flows over the initial investment should be recorded as yield under SOP 03-3. (AICPA TPA 2130.19–2130.20)

Recognizing interest income   The difference between the fair value of purchased loans and the undiscounted cash flows expected to be collected at acquisition is considered the "accretable yield." The cash flows not expected to be collected are considered the "nonaccretable difference." Cash flows expected at acquisition include all cash flows directly related to the acquired loan, including those expected from collateral, late fees, and other fees. (AICPA TPA 2130.34–2130.35)

Initially, the amount of accretable yield is not recorded on the balance sheet-over time, the accretable yield is recognized in interest income using the interest method. Interest income is recognized using the rate that equates the cash flows expected to be collected with the amount paid (the fair value at inception). The nonaccretable difference is not recognized unless there is a favorable change in estimate and more cash flows are expected to be collected than initially projected.

> **OBSERVATION:**   The SOP 03-3 model differs from traditional loan accounting, because credit risk is recognized over the life of the loan. That is, by using the *expected* cash flows rather than contractual cash flows, the yield is adjusted to reflect the implicit credit losses. With a purchased loan, the investor pays only for the cash flows he or she *expects* to collect; he or she does not pay for the cash flows that are considered uncollectible. Therefore, the model is designed to reflect the accrual of cash flows that are considered collectible. Of course, if the original cash flow estimates turn out to be uncollectible, an impairment charge would be recognized. This model may be applied only to purchased loans and securities specifically within its scope.

> ☞ **PRACTICE POINTER:**   SOP 03-3 does not specify how prepayments must be considered. However, it does require that expected prepayments not affect the nonaccretable difference through consistent treatment for the determination of expected cash flows and projections of contractual cash flows. (SOP 03-3, par. 9)

EXHIBIT 7-6
DEPICTION OF RECOGNIZABLE CASH FLOWS UNDER SOP 03-3

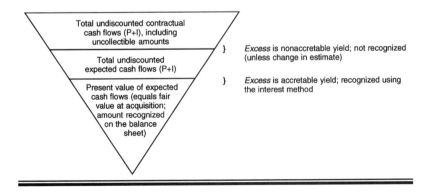

Changes in cash flow estimates The investor should update its estimate of expected future cash flows over the life of the investment. Cash flows should be reassessed at least quarterly, at the end of each reporting period, by entities that issue GAAP financial statements. (AICPA TPA 2130.28) The accounting for a change in expected cash flows depends on whether the purchased asset is a loan or a security (including loans accounted for like securities under FAS-140), as depicted in Exhibit 7-7.

EXHIBIT 7-7
ACCOUNTING FOR CHANGES IN EXPECTED CASH FLOWS
UNDER SOP 03-3

Investment Type	Decrease in Estimated Cash Flows	Significant Increase in Estimated Cash Flows	Comments
Security* (SOP 03-3, par. 7)	If fair value is less than carrying amount, record an OTT impairment, if required under FAS-115.	Recalculate the amount of accretable yield as the excess of (1) revised expected future cash flows over (2) the amortized cost of the security. The adjustment is a reclassification between accretable yield and nonaccretable difference. Recognize the adjusted accretable yield prospectively over the remaining life of the loan.	Amortized cost means the sum of (a) the initial investment *less* (b) cash *less* (c) write-downs *plus* (d) yield accreted to date.
Loan (SOP 03-3, par. 8)	If probable that all *expected* cash flows will not be collected as due, recognize impairment under FAS-114 or FAS-5, as appropriate.	First, reduce any valuation allowance recorded since acquisition, then recalculate the amount of accretable yield for the loan as the excess of (1) revised expected future cash flows over (2) the net carrying amount of the loan. The adjustment is a	The resulting yield becomes the new effective interest rate.

Investment Type	Decrease in Estimated Cash Flows	Significant Increase in Estimated Cash Flows	Comments
		reclassification between accretable yield and nonccretable difference. Recognize the adjusted accretable yield prospectively over the remaining life of the loan.	
Refinanced or restructured loan or security originally purchased at a credit-related discount (other than TDRs) (SOP 03-3, par. 10)	Apply guidance above for securities or loans, as appropriate.	Apply guidance above for securities or loans, as appropriate.	Loans restructured in a TDR are not subject to SOP 03-3. A creditor accounts for a TDR under FAS-114 or FAS-115, as appropriate.
Variable rate loans (SOP 03-3, par. 11)	Decreases directly attributable to a change in the index rate should be recognized prospectively as a yield reduction. Apply guidance above for securities and loans for other decreases in expected cash flows.	Apply guidance above for securities or loans, as appropriate.	At acquisition, the index rate in effect should be used to estimate expected cash flows and the effective interest rate.

---

* Includes instruments measured like debt securities, such as certain receivables subject to paragraph 14 of FAS-140 that can contractually be prepaid or otherwise settled such that the holder would not recover substantially all of its recorded investment.

OBSERVATION: The provisions in Exhibit 7-7 are designed to discourage gamesmanship in reviewing the cash flow estimates. Generally, an adverse change in cash flows may be recognized only when the normal "impairment" threshold is met. A favorable change in cash flows must be recognized prospectively. The restructuring provisions preclude an investor from recognizing an immediate gain by renegotiating a loan when a borrower experiences a significant improvement in creditworthiness.

Application to groups of loans Investors may aggregate loans that have common risk characteristics and use a composite interest rate. Once grouped, the excess of contractual payments receivable over the investor's initial investment (whether accretable yield or nonaccretable difference) for a specific loan or a group of loans may not be used to "offset" changes in cash flows from a different loan or a group of loans. (SOP 03-3, par. 12)

> ☛ **PRACTICE POINTER:** Each loan within the pool must individually meet the scope criteria of SOP 03-3. Aggregated loans must have been acquired in the same fiscal quarter.

Once assembled, loans should remain in the pool and may be removed only if the investor sells, forecloses, or otherwise receives assets in satisfaction of the loan or if the loan is written off. A loan should not be removed at its initial fair value unless it is very shortly after its acquisition and the creation of the pool. (AICPA TPA 2130.33) Generally, a loan must be removed at its carrying amount. The removal of the loan should not change the effective yield for the remaining pool. The carrying amount of the loan should be allocated on specific cash flow data, if available, for the loan being removed. If the cash flows in the pool were estimated such that there is no specific information on the carrying amount of the loan being removed, the investor should employ a pro-rata allocation of the carrying amount to the loan. (SOP 03-3, par. 13 and AICPA TPA 2130.32)

> ☛ **PRACTICE POINTER:** AICPA TPAs 2130.36–2130.37 illustrate the effect on the accounting for a pool of loans if one loan is written off and removed from the pool (1) if the investor does not change its estimate of cash flows expected to be collected and (2) if the investor decreases the estimate of expected cash flows.

Investment Income for Not-for-Profit Organizations

FAS-117 permits nonprofit organizations to report investment revenues net of related expenses, such as custodial fees, and investment advisory fees, provided that the amount of expenses is separately disclosed. (FAS-117, par. 24)

Interest and dividends that are donor restricted for long-term purposes are not part of operating cash receipts in the Statement of Cash Flows. (FAS-117, par. 30(e))

EXHIBIT 7-8
METHODS OF REPORTING CHANGES IN ESTIMATED CASH FLOWS ON INVESTMENTS

Applicable Literature	Instruments Covered	Purchased, Originated, or Retained	Estimated or Contractual Cash Flows	Method of Reflecting Changes in Cash Flows	Cash Flow Estimates Reflect Credit Concerns?	Comments
FAS-91	Individual loans or debt securities not marked to market through earnings	Purchased or originated	Contractual to maturity of loan	Retrospective	No	Impairment addressed separately under applicable GAAP
FAS-91	Large group of homogeneous loans	Purchased or originated	Estimated, including anticipated prepayments	Retrospective	No	Does not apply to single Instruments
EITF Issue 96-12	Structured notes	Purchased	Estimated	Retrospective	No, except when impairment has been recognized	Yield that equates all past actual and current estimated cash flows to the initial investment

Applicable Literature	Instruments Covered	Purchased, Originated, or Retained	Estimated or Contractual Cash Flows	Method of Reflecting Changes in Cash Flows	Cash Flow Estimates Reflect Credit Concerns?	Comments
EITF Issue 99-20	Beneficial interests in an SPE that have significant prepayment risk	Purchased[†] or retained	Estimated (collectible)	Prospective, if favorable or if unfavorable, but OTT impairment is not recognized; write-down if OTT impairment.	Yes	Impairment is recognized under FAS-115.
SOP 03-3	Loans or securities purchased at a discount due to credit concerns	Purchased	Expected (collectible)	Prospective if increase. For variable rate loans, decreases attributable only to changes in the index rate are recognized prospectively. Otherwise, decrease is recognized only if OTT impairment.	Yes	Impairment is recognized under FAS-114 or FAS-115, as appropriate.

[†] Certificates issued by an SPE that are purchased at a discount due to credit quality are subject to the provisions of SOP 03-3.

Mortgage Banking Activities

Fees and costs associated with originating or acquiring mortgage loans held for investment are accounted for as described for other loans in this chapter. (FAS-91, par. 27(e)) However, FAS-65, as amended, provides a few exceptions to the general model for entities engaged in certain mortgage banking activities.

- *Fees for services rendered* Fees representing reimbursement for the costs of specific services performed by third parties with respect to originating a loan, such as appraisal fees, should be recognized as revenue when the services have been performed. (FAS-65, par. 22)

- *Loans held for resale* Loan origination fees and direct loan origination costs should be deferred until the related loan is sold. (FAS-65, par. 21, as amended by FAS-91, par. 27(c)) Purchase discounts should not be amortized as interest revenue during the period that the loans are held for sale. (FAS-65, par. 5)

- *Commitment fees relating to loans held for sale* Loan commitments that relate to the origination of mortgage loans that will be held for resale, as discussed in paragraph 21 of FAS-65 (as amended), must be accounted for as derivative instruments in accordance with FAS-133. (FAS-133, par. 6(c), as amended)

- *Placement fees on loans held for sale* Fees for arranging a commitment directly between a permanent investor and a borrower should be recognized as revenue when all significant services have been performed. (FAS-65, par. 24)

- *Expired commitments and prepayments of loans* If a loan commitment expires without the loan being made or if a loan is repaid before the estimated repayment date, any related unrecognized fees should be recognized as revenue or expense at that time. (FAS-65, par. 27)

   ☛ **PRACTICE POINTER:** Presumably, if the loan commitment had been accounted for as a derivative in accordance with DIG Issue C-13, the fair value of an expired commitment would have dissipated to zero.

Disclosures

Imputed Interest

APB-21 requires a description of a note for which interest has been imputed, including the effective interest rate and the face amount of the note. (APB-21, par. 16)

Entities Engaged in Lending Activities

All entities engaged in lending activities should disclose the method for recognizing interest income on loan and trade receivables, including a statement about the entity's policy for treatment of related fees and costs and the method of amortizing net deferred fees or costs. (SOP 01-6, par. 13(a)(4))

Entities must also disclose the classification and method of accounting for instruments with significant prepayment risk that are accounted for in accordance with paragraph 14 of FAS-140; that is, interest-only strips, loans, other receivables, or retained interests in securitizations that can be contractually prepaid or otherwise settled in a way that the holder would not recover substantially all of its recorded investment. (SOP 01-6, par. 13(a)(3))

Anticipating Prepayments

Enterprises that anticipate prepayments must disclose that policy and the significant assumptions underlying the prepayment estimates. (FAS-91, par. 19) Disclosures such as unamortized net fees and costs may be included in the footnotes to the financial statements if the lender believes that such information is useful to the users of financial statements. (FAS-91 Q&A, par. 59)

Credit Card Purchases and Originations

For both purchased and originated credit cards, an entity should disclose its accounting policy for credit card fees and costs, the net amount capitalized at the balance sheet date, and the amortization period(s). (EITF 92-5)

> **SEC REGISTRANT ALERT:** SEC registrants that are bank holding companies must also provide certain disclosures about yields as part of the 1934 Act Industry Guide 3. For example, the SEC requests that average yield information about investments available for sale, be computed using the historical cost balances, with footnote disclosure that the yield information does not give effect to changes in fair value that are reflected as a component of other comprehensive income. How- ever, for computation of ratios, such as return on assets and return on equity, the calculations should be based on recorded assets and liabilities, giving effect changes in market value of available-for-sale securities. The SEC is currently revising Guide 3 to reflect subsequent developments in accounting standards. The timetable is uncertain.

Loans and Securities Purchased at a Credit-Related Discount (SOP 03-3)

In addition to disclosures required by other GAAP (including FAS-5, FAS-114, FAS-115, and FAS-118), an investor must disclose the following information:[1]

---

[1] Quantitative disclosures must be made separately for loans accounted for as debt securities and those that are not accounted for as debt securities.

EXHIBIT 7-9
DISCLOSURES REQUIRED BY SOP 03-3

Required Disclosure	Loans	Debt Securities
How prepayments are considered in the determination of contractual cash flows and cash flows expected to be collected	✓	✓
If the relevant condition is met (see columns to the right), incorporate loans in the scope of SOP 03-3 into the following FAS-114 disclosures for impaired loans: • Total recorded investment in impaired loans at the end of each period for which a statement of financial position is presented. • Amount for which there is a related allowance and the amount of the allowance • Amount for which there is no related allowance • Policy for recognizing interest income on impaired loans (FAS-114, pars. 20(a) and 20(b), as amended by FAS-118)	✓ Disclosure required if, based on available information it is probable that the investor is unable to collect cash flows expected at acquisition plus any additional cash flows from a revised estimate. (SOP 03-3, par. 8 (a) and FAS-5, par. 8(A)	✓ Disclosure required only if an OTT impairment has occurred, (e.g., if based on available information), it is probable that the investor is unable to collect cash flows expected at acquisition plus any additional cash flows from a revised estimate. (SOP 03-3, par. 7(a) and FAS-115, par. 16)
Outstanding balance and related carrying amount at the beginning and end of the period	✓	✓
Amounts of accretable yield at the beginning and end of the period, reconciled for additions, accretion, disposals, and reclassifications from nonaccretable difference during the period	✓	✓
For loans acquired during the period, the contractually required payments receivable, cash flows expected to be collected, and fair value at acquisition	✓	✓
	✓	✓

Required Disclosure	Loans	Debt Securities
For loans where the income recognition model of SOP 03-3 is not applied (for loans placed on nonaccrual status) the carrying amount at acquisition for loans acquired during the period and the carrying amount of all loans at the end of the period		
The amount of any expense recognized under par. 8(a) and any reductions of allowance permitted by par. 8(b)(1) for each period an income statement is presented	✓	
The amount of the allowance for uncollectible accounts at the beginning and end of the period	✓	

☞ **PRACTICE POINTER:** Although not required, investors should consider whether to disclose the amount of the nonaccretable difference so that readers understand the amount that the investor expects will not be collected. (AICPA TPA 2130.23)

Investments in Beneficial Interests in Securitized Assets with Unrealized Losses (FSP FAS 115-1 and FAS 124-1)

An investor must provide the following disclosures for unrealized losses that have not been recognized as other than temporary under EITF Issue 99-20:

- For each statement of financial position presented, the aggregate amount of unrealized losses and aggregate related fair value for investments in an unrealized loss position for which other-than-temporary impairments have *not* been recognized. The disclosure must be made separately for investments in a continuous unrealized loss position for (a) less than 12 months and (b) 12 months or longer.
- For the most recent statement of financial position presented, a narrative explanation of the quantitative disclosures provided as well as a discussion of information considered in determining that the impairments are not other-than temporary, including:
  — Nature of the investment(s)
  — Cause(s) of the impairment(s)
  — Number of investments in an unrealized loss position
  — Severity and duration of the impairment(s)
  — Other evidence (analyst reports, sector credit ratings, security's fair value volatility)

AUDIT CONSIDERATIONS

Several areas of the accounting for yields involve judgment and contribute to audit risk. There is no specific auditing standard that addresses the audit issues relating to recognition of yields on debt instruments. However, the key areas of concern are as follows:

- *Categorizing fees and costs* The accounting for lending-related fees and costs depends on several factors, including the following:
  - Whether the fees or costs are associated with origination activities or purchase transactions,
  - Whether the costs were incurred internally or paid to independent third parties, *and*
  - Refundability of fees.

  Auditors should review management's classification of loan fees and costs to ensure that they are properly categorized and accounted for.

- *Distinguishing between originated and purchased loans* The accounting for fees and costs, yields, and impairment differs depending on whether a loan was purchased or originated. FAS-140 should be applied to determine whether a transfer (i.e., purchase or sale) has occurred. Auditors should evaluate the substance of transactions to corroborate management's classification of a transaction as a purchase or an origination. Situations involving agents and other intermediaries should be carefully reviewed for their substance.

- *Estimating future cash flows* Auditors should review management's approach to estimating future cash flows for the purpose of anticipating prepayments and reflecting changes in cash flows for loans where collectibility is considered. Auditors should review the assumptions and market data being used for reasonableness in the circumstances. Auditors should ensure that management is appropriately applying the guidelines to group loans with similar characteristics (for prepayment estimates).

- *Identifying embedded derivatives* Debt instruments with unusual interest rates or contingent payment features often will contain embedded derivatives that must be accounted for separately under FAS-133. The key risk is that management will fail to identify a hybrid instrument with an embedded derivative. Auditors should be knowledgeable about the characteristics of a debt instrument that signal an embedded derivative and when they must be bifurcated. Embedded derivatives are discussed in Chapter 13, "Embedded Derivatives."

ILLUSTRATIONS

Illustrations 7-1 through 7-4 are adapted from examples in Appendix B of FAS-91. Those illustrations assume that principal and interest payments are made on the last day of the year.

Illustration 7-1: Amortization Based on Contractual Payment Terms

On January 1, 20X7, Company A originates a ten-year $100,000 loan with a 10 percent stated interest rate. The contract specifies equal annual payments of $16,275 through December 31, 20Y6. The contract also specifies that no penalty will be charged for prepayments of the loan. Company A charges a 3 percent ($3,000) nonrefundable fee to the borrower and incurs $1,000 in direct loan origination costs (attorney fees, appraisal, title insurance, wages and payroll-related fringe benefits of employees performing origination activities, outside broker's fee). The carrying amount of the loan is computed as follows:

Loan principal	$100,000
Origination fees	(3,000)
Direct loan origination costs	1,000
Carrying amount of loan	$ 98,000

Company A accounts for this loan using contractual payments to apply the interest method of amortization. In calculating the effective rate to apply the interest method, the discount rate necessary to equate ten annual payments of $16,275 to the initial carrying amount of $98,000 is approximately 10.4736 percent. The amortization if no prepayment occurs is shown in Table 7-1.

Table 7-1
Amortization Based on Contractual Payment Terms

Year	(1) Cash (Out) Inflow	(2) Stated Interest	(3) Amortization	(4) Interest Income	(5) Remaining Principal	(6) Unamortized Net Fees	(7) Carrying Amount
	$(98,000)				$100,000		$98,000
1	16,275	$10,000	$264	$10,264	93,725	$1,736	91,989
2	16,275	9,373	262	9,635	86,823	1,474	85,349
3	16,275	8,682	257	8,939	79,230	1,217	78,013
4	16,275	7,923	248	8,171	70,878	969	69,909
5	16,275	7,088	234	7,322	61,691	735	60,956
6	16,275	6,169	215	6,384	51,585	520	51,065
7	16,275	5,159	189	5,348	40,469	331	40,138
8	16,275	4,047	157	4,204	28,241	174	28,067
9	16,275	2,824	116	2,940	14,790	58	14,732
10	16,275	1,485[a]	58	1,543	0	0	0
	Total amortization	$2,000					

Computations:

Column (1)—Contractual payments

Column (2)—Column (5) for prior year × the loan's stated interest rate (10%)

Column (3)—Column (4)–Column (2)

Column (4)—Column (7) for prior year × the effective interest rate (10.4736%)[b]

Column (5)—Column (5) for prior year–(Column (1)–Column (2))

Column (6)—Initial net fees – amortization to date

Column (7)—Column (5) – Column (6)

---

[a] $6 rounding adjustment.
[b] The effective interest rate is the discount rate that equates the present value of the future cash inflows to the initial net cash outflow of $98,000.

Illustration 7-2: Amortization Based on Estimated Prepayment Patterns Adjusted for Change in Estimate

On January 1, 20X7, Company D originates 1,000 ten-year $10,000 loans with 10 percent stated interest rates. Each contract specifies equal annual payments through December 31, 20Y6. The contracts also specify that no penalty will be charged for prepayments. Company D charges each borrower a 3 percent ($300) fee and incurs $100 in direct origination costs for each loan.

Company D chooses to account for this portfolio of loans using anticipated prepayment patterns to apply the interest method of amortization. Company D estimates a constant prepayment rate of 6 percent per year, which is consistent with Company D's prior experience with similar loans and Company D's expectation of ongoing experience.

Table 7-2 illustrates the adjustment required by paragraph 19 of FAS-91 when an enterprise's actual prepayment experience differs from the amounts anticipated (or when an estimate is revised). The loans have actually prepaid at a rate of 6 percent in years 1 and 2 and 20 percent in year 3, and based on the new information at the end of year 3, Company D revises its estimate of prepayment experience to anticipate that 10 percent of the loans will prepay in year 4 and 6 percent of the loans will prepay in remaining years. The carrying amount of the loans at the end of year 3 is adjusted to the amount that would have existed had the new effective yield been applied since January 1, 20X7. Included in amortization in year 3 is an adjustment for the difference in the prior effective yield and the new effective yield applied to amounts outstanding in years 1 and 2. Amortization in years 4–10 assumes the new estimates of prepayment experience occur as anticipated.

Table 7-2
Amortization Based on Estimated Prepayment Patterns Adjusted for a Change in Estimate

Year	(1) Cash (Out) Inflow	(2) Stated Interest	(3) Amortization	(4) Interest Income	(5) Remaining Principal	(6) Unamortized Net Fees	(7) Carrying Amount
	$(9,800,000)				$10,000,000		$9,800,000
1	2,227,454	$1,000,000	$35,141	$1,035,141	8,772,546	$164,859	8,607,687
2	2,049,623	877,255	31,946	909,201	7,600,178	132,913	7,467,265
3	2,944,644	760,018	41,951	801,969	5,415,552	90,962	5,324,590
4	1,653,939	541,555	23,294	564,849	4,303,168	67,668	4,235,500
5	1,246,229	430,317	18,998	449,315	3,487,256	48,670	3,438,586
6	1,129,164	348,726	16,050	364,776	2,706,818	32,620	2,674,198
7	1,016,331	270,682	13,005	283,687	1,961,169	19,615	1,941,554
8	906,285	196,117	9,849	205,966	1,251,001	9,766	1,241,235
9	795,875	125,100	6,574	131,674	580,226	3,192	577,034
10	638,249	58,023	3,192	61,215	0	0	0
	Total amortization		$200,000				

Computations:

Column (1) —Contractual payments + prepayments

Column (2)—Column (5) for prior year × the loan's stated interest rate (10%)

Column (3)—Column (4) – Column (2)

Column (4)—Column (7) for the prior year × the effective rate (10.5627% for years 1 and 2, and 10.6083% for years 3–10, + an adjustment of $8,876 in year 3 representing the cumulative effect[c] applicable to years 1 and 2 of changing the estimated effective rate)

Column (5)—Column (5) for prior year – (Column (1) – Column (2))

Column (6)—Initial net fees – amortization to date

Column (7)—Column (5) – Column (6)

---

[c] An adjustment would also be required if the level of prepayments realized was less than anticipated.

Illustration 7-3: Application of Increasing-Rate Provisions with No Prepayment Penalty

Company F grants a ten-year $100,000 loan. The contract provides for 8 percent interest in year 1 and 10 percent interest in years 2–10. Company F receives net fees of $1,000 related to this loan. The contract specifies that no penalty will be charged for prepayment of principal.

The discount factor that equates the present value of the cash inflows in Column 1 with the initial cash outflow of $99,000 is 9.8085 percent. In year 1, recognition of interest income on the investment of $99,000 at a rate of 9.8085 percent would cause the investment to be $93,807, or $710 greater than the amount at which the borrower could settle the obligation. Because the condition set forth in paragraph 18(a) is not met, recognition of an amount greater than the net fee is not permitted.

Table 7-3: Application of Increasing-Rate Provisions With No Prepayment Penalty

Year	(1) Cash (Out) Inflow	(2) Stated Interest	(3) Amortization	(4) Interest Income	(5) Remaining Principal	(6) Unamortized Net Fees	(7) Carrying Amount
	$(99,000)				$100,000		$99,000
1	14,903	$8,000	$1,000	$9,000	93,097	$0	93,097
2	16,165	9,310	0	9,310	86,242	0	86,242
3	16,165	8,624	0	8,624	78,701	0	78,701
4	16,165	7,870	0	7,870	70,406	0	70,406
5	16,165	7,041	0	7,041	61,282	0	61,282
6	16,165	6,128	0	6,128	51,245	0	51,245
7	16,165	5,124	0	5,124	40,204	0	40,204
8	16,165	4,021	0	4,021	28,060	0	28,060
9	16,165	2,806	0	2,806	14,701	0	14,701
10	16,165	1,464[f]	0	1,464	0	0	0
Total amortization			$1,000				

Computations:

Column (1)—Contractual payments

Column (2)—Column (5) for prior year × the loan's stated interest rate (8% in year 1, 10% in years 2–10)

Column (3)—Column (4) – Column (2)

Column (4)—Column (7) for the prior year × the effective interest rate (9.8085%) as limited by paragraph 18(a)

Column (5)—Column (5) for prior year – (Column (1) – Column (2))

Column (6)—Initial net fees – amortization to date

Column (7)—Column (5) – Column (6)

---

[f] $6 rounding adjustment.

Illustration 7-4: Application of Variable-Rate Provisions Based on Factor at Inception

Company H grants a ten-year variable rate mortgage. The loan's interest rate and payment are adjusted annually based on the weekly Treasury bill index plus 1 percent. At the date the loan is granted, this index is 7 percent and does not change until the end of year 3. The first year loan interest rate is 8 percent (equal to the Treasury bill index plus 1 percent). Company H receives net fees of $3,000. At the end of year 3 the index changes to 9 percent and does not change again. Therefore, the loan's stated interest rate is 8 percent for years 1–3 and 10 percent for years 4–10. Company H chooses to determine the amortization based on the index at the date the loan is granted and to ignore subsequent changes in the factor.

Table 7-4
Application of Variable-Rate Provisions Based on Factor at Inception

Year	(1) Cash (Out) Inflow	(2) Stated Interest	(3) Amortization	(4) Interest Income	(5) Remaining Principal	(6) Unamortized Net Fees	(7) Carrying Amount
	$(97,000)			$100,000		$97,000	
1	14,903	$8,000	$420	$8,420	93,097	$2,580	90,517
2	14,903	7,448	410	7,858	85,642	2,170	83,472
3	14,903	6,851	395	7,246	77,590	1,775	75,815
4	15,937	7,759	375	8,134	69,412	1,400	68,012
5	15,937	6,941	347	7,288	60,416	1,053	59,363
6	15,937	6,042	314	6,356	50,521	739	49,782
7	15,937	5,052	272	5,324	39,636	467	39,169
8	15,937	3,964	221	4,185	27,663	246	27,417
9	15,937	2,766	160	2,926	14,492	86	14,406
10	15,937	1,445[i]	86	1,531	0	0	0
	Total amortization		$3,000				

Computations:

Column (1)—Contractual payments

Column (2)—Column (5) for prior year × the loan's stated interest rate (8% in years 1–3, and 10% in years 4–10)

Column (3)—Calculated as if the index did not change—that is, the amount that would have been recognized for an 8%, 10-year $100,000 mortgage with no prepayments and a $3,000 net fee

Column (4)—Column (2) + Column (3)
Column (5)—Column (5) for prior year – (Column (1) – Column (2))
Column (6)—Initial net fees – amortization to date
Column (7)—Column (5) – Column (6)

---

[i] $4 rounding adjustment.

Illustration 7-5: Recognizing Yields and Impairment on Subordinated Beneficial Interests in Securitized Financial Assets

> **AUTHOR'S NOTE:** This illustration presents the accounting for changes in estimated cash flows under EITF Issue 99-20. The accounting for beneficial interests is complex, and this illustration only focuses on the yield calculations (and impairment recognition) in the year following a securitization Accounting for the beneficial interest under FAS-115 is outside. the scope of this example. The data used in this illustration are same as those used in Exhibit B of EITF Issue 99-20, which provides a great deal of additional information, including amortization tables in subsequent years, journal entries, FAS-115 accounting, and balance sheet presentation.

On December 31, 20X0, Bellwether Finance securitizes loans with a par value of $500 and a net carrying amount of $505 in a transaction involving a QSPE that qualifies to be accounted for as a partial sale under FAS-140. In exchange, Bellwether receives:

- Net cash proceeds of $300 from the sale of the QSPE's Senior Beneficial Interests to unrelated parties
- The QSPE's Subordinated Beneficial Interest, which is in the form of a debt security.

The expected cash flows (undiscounted) associated with the subordinated interest are as follows:

Year 1	$31
Year 2	27
Year 3	56
Year 4	104
Year 5	86
	$304

The market rate of interest for the retained interest is 10% at the time of the securitization, resulting in a fair value of $217. The allocated carrying amount of the interest continued to be held by the transferor (based on the relative fair values of the portions sold and retained) is $212. The rate that equates the undiscounted cash flows of $304 above with the initial carrying amount of $212 is 10.77%; that rate is the effective rate on the beneficial interest.The "accretable yield" is $92 [$304 – $212]. Assume the following information applicable to Year 1:

Original effective yield	10.77%
Beginning balance	$212
Interest income ($212 x 10.77%):	23
Cash received	(31)
Amortized cost before any impairment:	$204

At December 31, 20X1, Bellwether must update its estimates of the expected cash flows, using information that market participants would use to estimate fair value. Four different scenarios are presented below.

Scenario	Change in Estimated Cash Flows Due to Credit and/or Prepayment	Market Interest Rate for Beneficial Interest
1	Decrease	Increases to 12%
2	Decrease	Decreases to 8%
3	Increase	Increases to 12%
4	Increase	Decreases to 8%

All scenarios ignore income taxes.

The table below shows the present value of the original and revised cash flow estimates at December 31, 20X1, under each scenario, using the original effective rate of 10.77%. These calculations are used to determine whether there has been a reduction in estimated cash flows, as defined in EITF Issue 99-20. The table also shows the fair value of the retained beneficial interest at December 31, 20X1, under each scenario, using the current market rate as the discount rate. Fair value information is necessary to measure impairment, if indicated, and to report the security under FAS-115 (assuming that a market quote is unavailable).

Table 7-5A
Present Value and Fair Value of Revised Cash Flow Estimates

	End of Year 1 Fair Value	PV of Original Cash Flows at Original Rate	PV of Revised Cash Flows at Original Rate	Is PV Old > PV New?
Scenario 1				
Rate	12.00%	10.77%	10.77%	
Year 2	22.38	26.59	22.38	

	End of Year 1 Fair Value	PV of Original Cash Flows at Original Rate	PV of Revised Cash Flows at Original Rate	Is PV Old > PV New?
Year 3	63.40	56.17	63.40	
Year 4	98.48	104.45	98.48	
Year 5	77.04	85.79	77.04	
	189.58	203.62	195.50	Yes
Scenario 2				
Rate	8.00%	10.77%	10.77%	
Year 2	22.38	26.59	22.38	
Year 3	63.40	56.17	63.40	
Year 4	98.48	104.45	98.48	
Year 5	77.04	85.79	77.04	
	209.88	203.62	195.50	Yes
Scenario 3				
Rate	12.00%	10.77%	10.77%	
Year 2	28.69	26.59	28.69	
Year 3	49.01	56.17	49.01	
Year 4	108.88	104.45	108.88	
Year 5	93.29	85.79	93.29	
	201.47	203.62	207.92	No
Scenario 4				
Rate	8.00%	10.77%	10.77%	
Year 2	28.69	26.59	28.69	
Year 3	49.01	56.17	49.01	
Year 4	108.88	104.45	108.88	
Year 5	93.29	85.79	93.29	
	223.59	203.62	207.92	No

Table 7-5B shows how the amounts calculated above are used to determine whether the change in cash flows will be accounted for prospectively as a yield adjustment in future periods, or as a "catch-up" adjustment, with current recognition of impairment and a revised yield in future periods. Note that the change in cash flows is accounted for as a "catch-up" adjustment only in Scenario 1 because there has been both a decrease in expected cash flows and a decline in fair value below the amortized cost of the beneficial interest. In Scenarios 2, 3, and 4, the yield is adjusted prospectively, and the carrying amount does not change.

Table 7-5B
Recording Changes in Estimated Cash Flows

		Scenarios			
		1	2	3	4
1	12/31/X1 PV of revised cash flows discounted at 10.77% (from Table 7-5A)	196	196	208	208
2	Is the change in cash flows adverse or positive? (See Table 7-5A above)	Adverse	Adverse	Positive	Positive
3	12/31/X1 FV of revised cash flows discounted at market yield (See Table 7-5A)	190	210	201	224
4	Is FV < amortized cost?	Yes	No	Yes	No
5	If yes, and change in cash flow is adverse, recognize impairment (FV - $204)	(14)	–	–	–
6	Carrying amount at 12/31/X1	190	204	204	204
7	Rate that equates line 6 with revised cash flows (See Table 7-5A)	12.00%	9.17%	11.59%	11.59%
8	Interest income in Year 20X2 (line 6 x line 7)	23	19	24	24

This entire analysis would be performed at each reporting period until the beneficial interests mature or are sold, using updated estimates of cash flows and the current market yield for the beneficial interest. However, instead of using the rate of 10.77%, the effective rate in line 7 would be used to determine whether there has been a reduction in estimated cash flows.

ILLUSTRATION 7-6:   APPLICATION OF SOP 03-3 TO AN ACQUISITION OF LOANS PURCHASED AT A DISCOUNT DUE TO CREDIT CONCERNS

AUTHOR'S NOTE: This illustration presents the fundamental concepts of AICPA Statement of Position (SOP) 03-3. The transaction presented and data used in this example are the same as those used in the illustrations contained in Appendix A of SOP 03-3. However, Appendix A of SOP 03-3 contains significant additional computational detail, additional scenarios, and implications when the loan is accounted for as a debt security in certain scenarios.

Company A acquires a loan with a principal balance of $5,046,686 and accrued delinquent interest of $500,000 at a discount due to concerns about the debtor's credit quality that have occurred since the loan's origination. Company A pays $4,000,000 for the loan on December 31, 20X0. No fees were paid or received as part of the acquisition. The contractual interest rate is 12% per year. In addition to the delinquent interest, annual payments of $1,400,000 are due in each of the five remaining years to maturity. Company A determines it is probable that it will be unable to collect all amounts due according to the loan's contractual terms. Rather, Company A expects to collect only $1,165,134 per year for five years. For purposes of this illustration, it is assumed that the investor can reasonably estimate cash flows expected to be collected. In Company A's balance sheet, the loan will initially be displayed at its net carrying amount ($4,000,000 at December 31, 20X0). This Illustration assumes that the loan is not accounted for as a debt security. (**Note:** SOP 03-3 does not address whether the investor should or should not accrue income. The illustration presents the write-off of the uncollectible investment in the loan receivable at the end of the loan's term.)

Three scenarios are presented within this Illustration:

1. In Scenario A, Company A receives all the cash flows that it expected to collect.
2. In Scenario B, at December 31, 20X2, Company A determines it is probable that cash flows expected to be collected will be $250,000 more in 20X3 than previously expected but the company does not change i ts expectations of cash flows in years 20X4 and 20X5.
3. In Scenario C, at December 31, 20X2, Company A determines it is probable that cash flows expected to be collected will be $100,000 less in each of the remaining three years than expected at acquisition.

The initial calculation of nonaccretable difference and accretable yield associated with the acquired loan are presented below.

Initial Calculation of Nonaccretable Difference

Contractually required payments receivable (including delinquent interest)	$7,500,000
Less: Cash flows expected to be collected	(5,825,670)
Nonaccretable difference	$1,674,330

Initial Calculation of Accretable Yield

Cash flows expected to be collected	$5,825,670
Less: Initial investment	(4,000,000)
Accretable yield	$1,825,670

Table 7-6A
Loan Activity under Scenario A
(Actual Cash Flows Equal Cash Flows Expected for Years 20X1–20X5)

The table below illustrates activity for the acquired loan throughout its remaining term to maturity. In Scenario A, Company A received all of the cash flows it expected to collect. For years 20X1 through 20X5, the yield recognized is 14% (the discount rate that, at acquisition, equates all cash flows expected to be collected with the purchase price of the loan). The amount of the uncollectible investment in the loans receivable that is written off at the end of the loan's term is equal to the initial calculation of nonaccretable difference: $1,674,330.

	A Contractually Required Payments Receivable	B Cash Expected to Be Collected	C Nonaccretable Difference	D Accretable Yield	E Loans Receivable
			A - B		B - D
Acquisition	$7,500,000	$5,825,670	$1,674,330	$1,825,670	$4,000,000
20X1 collections	(1,165,134)	(1,165,134)		(560,000)	(605,134)
Balance	6,334,866	4,660,536	1,674,330	1,265,670	3,394,866
20X2 collections	(1,165,134)	(1,165,134)		(475,281)	(689,853)
Balance	5,169,732	3,495,402	1,674,330	790,389	2,705,013
20X3 collections	(1,165,134)	(1,165,134)		(378,702)	(786,432)
Balance	4,004,598	2,330,268	1,674,330	411,687	1,918,581
20X4 collections	(1,165,134)	(1,165,134)		(268,601)	(896,533)
Balance	2,839,464	1,165,134	1,674,330	143,086	1,022,048
20X5 collections	(1,165,134)	(1,165,134)		(143,086)	(1,022,048)
Balance	1,674,330	$ —	$ —	$ —	$ —
Disposition[2]	(1,674,330)				
	$ —				

In Scenario B, at December 20X2, Company A expects an increase in cash flows previously expected. Therefore, it must recalculate the amount of accretable yield for the loan, as follows:

Scenario B Recalculation of Accretable Yield

Remaining cash flows expected to be collected, December 31, 20X2		$3,745,402[1]
Less the sum of:		
Initial investment	$4,000,000	
Less: Cash collected to date	(2,330,268)[2]	
Less: Write-downs and allowance	—	
Plus: Yield accreted to date	1,035,281[3]	
		2,705,013

Remaining accretable yield as recalculated	1,040,389
Less: Unadjusted balance at December 31, 20X2	(790,389)[4]
Adjustment needed	$ 250,000

[1] The balance of cash flows expected to be collected after 20X2 collections plus $250,000.
[2] The sum of $1,165,134 collected in 20X1 and 20X2.
[3] Yield of $560,000 for 20X1 and $475,281 for 20X2 based on a 14% effective rate.
[4] Balance of accretable yield, based on expected cash flows at acquisition, after 20X2 collections.

Table 7-6B
Loan Activity under Scenario B
(Increase in Cash Flows of $250,000 Expected for Year 20X3)

The table below illustrates the impact of a $250,000 increase in year 20X3 on cash flows expected to be collected on accretable yield and nonaccretable difference. The $250,000 increase is required to be treated as a reclassification of nonaccretable difference to accretable yield. As a result, the yield recognized is 14% for years 20X1 and 20X2 and 18.9603% for years 20X3 through 20X5. The amount of the uncollectible investment in the loans receivable that is written off at the end of the loan's term is $1,424,330, which is determined as the original nonaccretable difference of $1,674,330 minus the adjustment of $250,000 reclassified from nonaccretable difference to accretable yield.

	A Contractually Required Payments Receivable	B Cash Expected to Be Collected	C Nonaccretable Difference	D Accretable Yield	E Loans Receivable
			A - B	B - D	
Acquisition	$7,500,000	$5,825,670	$1,674,330	$1,825,670	$4,000,000
20X1 collections	(1,165,134)	(1,165,134)		(560,000)	(605,134)
Balance	6,334,866	4,660,536	1,674,330	1,265,670	3,394,866
20X2 collections	(1,165,134)	(1,165,134)		(475,281)	(689,853)
Balance	5,169,732	3,495,402	1,674,330	790,389	2,705,013
Increase in cash flows expected		250,000	(250,000)	250,000	
20X3 collections	(1,415,134)	(1,415,134)		(512,878)	(902,256)
Balance	3,754,598	2,330,268	1,424,330	527,511	1,802,757
20X4 collections	(1,165,134)	(1,165,134)		(341,808)	(823,326)
Balance	2,589,464	1,165,134	1,424,330	185,703	979,431
20X5 collections	(1,165,134)	(1,165,134)		(185,703)	(979,431)
Balance	1,424,330	$ —	1,424,330	$ —	$ —
Disposition	(1,424,330)		(1,424,330)		
	$ —		$ —		

In Scenario C, at December 20X2, Company A expects a reduction of cash flows expected to be collected of $100,000 for the final three years of the loan's term. Because it is probable that Company A will be unable to collect all cash flows expected at acquisition, the loan is considered impaired. The calculation of the loan impairment and reduction of accretable yield as a result of the decrease in cash flows expected to be collected is presented below.

Measurement of Impairment

Recorded loan receivable prior to change in estimate	$2,705,013
Less: Present value of remaining cash flows expected to be collected (using the effective interest rate of 14%)	(2,472,850)
Measured impairment at December 31, 20X2	$232,163

Scenario C Recalculation of Accretable Yield

Remaining cash flows expected to be collected, December 31, 20X2		$3,195,402[1]
Less the sum of:		
Initial investment	$4,000,000	
Less: Cash collected to date	(2,330,268)[2]	
Less: Write-downs and allowance	(232,163)	
Plus: Yield accreted to date	1,035,281[3]	
		2,472,850
Remaining accretable yield as recalculated		722,552
Less: Unadjusted balance at December 31, 20X2		(790,389)[4]
Adjustment needed to accretable yield		$(67,837)

---

[1] The balance of cash flows expected to be collected after 20X2 collections minus $300,000.
[2] The sum of $1,165,134 collected in 20X1 and 20X2.
[3] Yield of $560,000 for 20X1 and $475,281 for 20X2 based on a 14% effective rate.
[4] Balance of accretable yield, based on expected cash flows at acquisition, after 20X2 collection

Table 7-6C Loan Activity under Scenario C
(Decrease in Cash Flows of $100,000 Expected for Years 20X3–20X5)

The table below illustrates the impact of a $300,000 decrease in cash flows expected to be collected on the amount of accretable yield and nonaccretable difference. The $300,000 decrease in cash flows expected to be collected represents a loss of $232,163 (carrying amount that will not be recovered) and forgone interest income in future years of $67,837. Under Scenario C, the amount of the uncollectible investment in the loans receivable that is written off at the end of the loan's term is $1,974,330, which is determined as the original nonaccretable difference of $1,674,330 plus the reduction in cash flows of $300,000.

	A Contractually Required Payments Receivable	B Cash Expected to Be Collected	C Nonaccretable Difference	D Accretable Yield	E Loans Receivable
			A - B		B - D
Acquisition	$7,500,000	$5,825,670	$1,674,330	$1,825,670	$4,000,000
20X1 collections	(1,165,134)	(1,165,134)		(560,000)	(605,134)
Balance	6,334,866	4,660,536	1,674,330	1,265,670	3,394,866
20X2 collections	(1,165,134)	(1,165,134)		(475,281)	(689,853)
Impairment		(300,000)	300,000	(67,837)	(232,163)
Balance	5,169,732	3,195,402	1,974,330	722,552	2,472,850
20X3 collections	(1,065,134)	(1,065,134)		(346,199)	(718,935)
Balance	4,104,598	2,130,268	1,974,330	376,353	1,753,915
20X4 collections	(1,065,134)	(1,065,134)		(245,548)	(819,586)
Balance	3,039,464	1,065,134	1,974,330	130,805	934,329
20X5 collections	(1,065,134)	(1,065,134)		(130,805)	(934,329)
Balance	1,974,330	$ —	1,974,330	$	$
Disposition	(1,974,330)		(1,974,330)		
	$ —		$ —		

Table 7-6D
Financial Statement Impact of Scenarios A through C

The table below summarizes the balance sheet and income statement impact of the acquired loan and the cash flows expected to be collected under Scenarios A, B, and C. In Scenario A, cash collected and interest income recognized are $1,825,670, as expected at acquisition. In Scenario B, cash collected and interest income recognized are $2,075,670, reflecting an increase in cash flows of $250,000. The increase is recognized as an adjustment of yield on a prospective basis. In Scenario C, cash collected is $1,525,670, reflecting a decrease in cash flows of $300,000. Upon determination that the loan is impaired, a loss of $232,163 is recorded in the current period as an allowance for loan losses. Interest income in Scenario C is $1,757,833; interest of $67,837 expected to be earned was not realized.

	Loans Receivable	Allowance	Net Loans Receivable	Bad Debt Expense	Cash	Interest Income
SCENARIO A						
Acquisition	$4,000,000		$4,000,000		$ (4,000,000)	
20X1 collections	(605,134)		(605,134)		1,165,134	$560,000
Balance	3,394,866		3,394,866			
20X2 collections	(689,853)		(689,853)		1,165,134	475,281
Balance	2,705,013		2,705,013			
20X3 collections	(786,432)		(786,432)		1,165,134	378,702

7.68 Calculating Yields on Debt Investments

	Loans Receivable	Allowance	Net Loans Receivable	Bad Debt Expense	Cash	Interest Income
Balance	1,918,581		1,918,581			
20X4 collections	(896,533)		(896,533)		1,165,134	268,601
Balance	1,022,048		1,022,048			
20X5 collections	(1,022,048)		(1,022,048)		1,165,134	143,086
Balance	$ –		$ –		$ 1,825,670	$1,825,670
SCENARIO B						
Acquisition	$4,000,000		$4,000,000		$(4,000,000)	
20X1 collections	(605,134)		(605,134)		1,165,134	$560,000
Balance	3,394,866		3,394,866			
20X2 collections	(689,853)		(689,853)		1,165,134	475,281
Balance	2,705,013		2,705,013			
20X3 collections	(902,256)		(902,256)		1,415,134*	512,878
Balance	1,802,757		1,802,757			
20X4 collections	(823,326)		(823,326)		1,165,134	341,808
Balance	979,431		979,431			
20X5 collections	(979,431)		(979,431)		1,165,134	185,703
Balance	$ –		$ –		$ 2,075,670	$2,075,670
SCENARIO C						
Acquisition	$4,000,000		$4,000,000		$(4,000,000)	
20X1 collections	(605,134)		(605,134)		1,165,134	$ 560,000
Balance	3,394,866		3,394,866			
20X2 collections	(689,853)		(689,853)		1,165,134	475,281
Impairment		$(232,163)	(232,163)	$ 232,163		
Balance	2,705,013	(232,163)	2,472,850			
20X3 collections	(718,935)		(718,935)		1,065,134	346,199
Balance	1,986,078	(232,163)	1,753,915			
20X4 collections	(819,586)		(819,586)		1,065,134#	245,548
Balance	1,166,492	(232,163)	934,329			
20X5 collections	(934,329)		(934,329)		1,065,134#	130,805
Balance	232,163	(232,163)	$ –	$232,163	$1,525,670	$1,757,833
Disposition	(232,163)	232,163				
	$ –	$ –				

*Reflects receipt of $250,000 increase in cash flows expected to be collected.

#Reflects decrease of $300,000 in cash flows expected to be collected.

PART II:
FINANCIAL LIABILITIES

CHAPTER 8
DEBT FINANCING

CONTENTS

Overview	8.03
Background	8.04
Definition of a Liability	8.04
Off-Balance-Sheet Finance	8.05
Distinguishing between Debt and Equity	8.05
Hedging Activities	8.06
Debt with Embedded Derivatives	8.06
Accounting for Debt Instruments	8.07
Recognition and Initial Measurement	8.07
Debt Instruments Subject to Registration Payment Arrangements	8.07
Fair Value Option for Certain Debt Instruments	8.08
Subsequent Measurement of Debt	8.09
Balance Sheet Classification	8.11
Current Liabilities	8.11
Exhibit 8-1: Financial Ratios Involving Current Assets and Current Liabilities	8.13
Short-Term Debt Expected to Be Refinanced	8.13
Exhibit 8-2: Classifying Short-Term Debt	8.16
Exhibit 8-3: Limitations on Amounts Excludable from Current Liabilities	8.18
Callable Long-Term Debt	8.19
Exhibit 8-4: Classification of Long-Term Debt	8.20
Classification of Subsidiary Debt in Consolidated Balance Sheet	8.21
Income Statement Recognition	8.22
Capitalization of Interest Costs	8.22
Debt Issue Costs	8.23
Special Application of the Interest Method for Certain Liabilities	8.23
Extinguishments of Debt	8.26

Modification or Exchange of Debt Instruments
  with Different Terms (EITF 96-19)   8.26

Changes in Line-of-Credit or Revolving Debt
  Agreements (EITF 98-14)   8.27

  *Exhibit 8-5: Accounting for Changes in a
  Line-of-Credit or Revolving Debt Agreements*   8.28

Reporting Cash Flows   8.28

Accounting for Guarantees   8.29

  Exhibit 8-6: Scope Exceptions to FIN-45   8.30

  Initial Recognition   8.31

  Subsequent Measurement   8.32

  Interplay with FAS-140   8.33

Disclosures   8.34

  Short-Term Debt   8.34

  Long-Term Debt   8.34

    Maturities   8.34

    Restrictive Covenants and Violations of Covenants   8.35

    Participating Mortgages   8.35

    Noncash Financing Activities   8.35

  Disclosures Applicable to Certain Financial Institutions   8.35

    Terms of Debt   8.36

    Deposit Liabilities   8.36

    Categories of Borrowings   8.36

    Secured Borrowings   8.37

  Interest Costs   8.37

  Available Sources of Credit   8.37

  Guarantees   8.37

  Certain Public Company Disclosures in Management's
    Discussion and Analysis (MD&A)   8.39

  Related Topics   8.40

Audit Considerations   8.40

Illustrations   8.41

  Illustration 8-1: Disclosures of Long-Term Debt—General   8.42

  *Illustration 8-2: Disclosures of Future Payments of
  Long-Term Debt*   8.42

  *Illustration 8-3: Classification of a Short-Term Obligation
  Expected to Be Refinanced*   8.43

  *Illustration 8-4: Modification of Revolving Credit
  Arrangement*   8.44

Illustration 8-5: Disclosure of Callable Long-Term Debt   8.45

Illustration 8-6: Disclosure of Long-Term Debt Classified
as Current Because of Violations That Existed at the
Balance Sheet Date Absent a Waiver   8.45

Illustration 8-7: Disclosure of a Long-Term Debt
Agreement with a Lock-Box Arrangement   8.46

Illustration 8-8: Disclosure of Interest Elements of Debt   8.46

Illustration 8-9: Recording a Guarantee as Part of
a Transfer of Assets   8.46

OVERVIEW

Debt financing can take many forms. Debt can be interest bearing or noninterest bearing, subordinated or senior, secured or unsecured. It can be obtained from banks, finance companies, customers or suppliers, public offerings, private placements, by mortgaging property, or from numerous other domestic and foreign sources.

The issuer's accounting for debt instruments is fairly straightforward. When debt is issued, the debtor/issuer generally records its obligation at the amount of proceeds received. Subsequent changes in the fair value of the instrument, if any, are not recognized but are disclosed in the financial statements. Interest is accrued using the effective yield method. (Accounting for convertible debt is addressed in Chapter 10, "Convertible Debt and Similar Instruments.")

A significant accounting issue related to debt is how it should be classified in a company's balance sheet. Generally, debt that has a remaining maturity date that is less than one year from the balance sheet date is classified as current. Debt that has a remaining maturity date extending beyond one year from the balance sheet date is generally classified as noncurrent.

Generally, interest expense is recognized using the effective yield method. There are special models for recognizing interest on certain liabilities, including indexed debt instruments and participating mortgages. Debt issue costs are generally deferred and amortized over the life of the debt. Gains and losses are recognized for debt extinguishments and significant modifications when certain criteria are met. Accounting for significant modifications of debt and extinguishments of debt are addressed in Chapter 11, "Extinguishments of Debt." When a modification is not significant, the change in terms is generally recognized as a yield adjustment. Accounting for changes in the terms of lines of credit and revolving debt agreements depends on whether the debtor's borrowing capacity has increased or decreased. Numerous disclosures are required about debt financing.

Financial guarantees should initially be recorded at fair value, even if no explicit compensation is received, the likelihood of having to pay is remote, or both.

BACKGROUND

Chapter 3A of ARB-43 and FAS-6 are the primary accounting literature applicable to debt instruments from the debtor's perspective. Chapter 3A of ARB-43 provides the underlying principles relating to the classification of obligations in a company's classified balance sheet. FAS-6 amended Chapter 3A of ARB-43 to provide specific guidance relating to when *short-term obligations* expected to be refinanced on a long-term basis should be excluded from classification as *current liabilities*. FAS-78 amended Chapter 3A of ARB-43 to provide guidance relating to when certain *long-term obligations* should be classified as current liabilities. FIN-8, FTB 79-3, and numerous EITF Issues provide guidance on applying those general principles to various fact-specific scenarios.

APB-21 establishes the general principle that interest should be recognized on debt instruments using an effective rate of interest. The first section of Chapter 7, "Calculating Yields on Debt Investments," discusses the application of APB-21 to debt instruments—both assets and liabilities. Unusual yields on debt instruments are addressed by FAS-133 (if the debt contains an embedded derivative) and a few EITF Issues. FAS-34 addresses capitalization of interest costs.

Extinguishments of debt, including the debtor's accounting for debt restructurings and exchanges, are discussed primarily in Chapter 11, "Extinguishments of Debt." However, some modifications of debt are that not significant, as defined in EITF Issue 96-19, are addressed in this chapter (because they are essentially treated as yield adjustments). EITF Issue 98-14 covers accounting for fees and costs in exchanges and modifications of lines of credit and revolving debt arrangements in cases where some amounts or no amounts have been drawn down.

FIN-45 addresses the accounting and disclosure of guarantees that are issued on a stand-alone basis or embedded in various forms of contracts. Accounting for guarantees undertaken in connection with a transfer of assets or an extinguishment of debt is addressed by FAS-140. Accounting for guarantees that meet the definition of a derivative are addressed by FAS-133. However, FIN-45 requires disclosures about some guarantees that are accounted for under FAS-140 and FAS-133.

Insurance companies follow a specialized accounting model for obligations under insurance contracts. Chapter 49, "Insurance," of CCH's *GAAP Guide Level A* provides guidance on the insurance accounting model.

Definition of a Liability

Liabilities are "probable future sacrifices of economic benefits arising from present obligations of a particular entity to transfer assets or provide services to other entities in the future as a result of past transactions or events." (CON-6, par. 35) A financial liability represents an agreement to pay a specified or determinable amount of money to another party. Financial liabilities, or debt instruments, such as corporate bonds, notes, loans, mortgages, and commercial paper, are the focus of this chapter. Other obligations generally considered to be akin to debt, such as obligations under capital leases and debt related to employee stock ownership plans (ESOPs), follow specialized accounting principles and are not included in this scope of this publication.

Off-Balance-Sheet Finance

FAS-140 addresses accounting for transfers of financial assets. As discussed in depth in Chapter 5, "Transfers of Financial Assets," specific criteria must be met in order to account for a transfer of financial assets as a sale (whereby the assets are taken "off-balance-sheet" and the proceeds are recorded as cash). Chapter 6, "Securitizations," provides additional guidance for transfers involving special-purpose entities. Certain transfers of financial assets that do not meet the sale criteria of FAS-140 must be accounted for as secured borrowings. (FAS-140, pars. 11 and 12) FAS-140 does not address the balance sheet classification or subsequent measurement of transfers that must be accounted for as secured borrowings. Chapter 9, "Securities Lending Arrangements and Other Pledges of Collateral," addresses repurchase agreements and similar transactions, as well as the accounting for pledges of collateral. This chapter applies to all other transfers of financial assets that are properly classified as secured borrowings.

In some situations, the sale of future revenues (such as expected royalty receipts) is accounted for as debt of the seller. EITF Issue 88-18 provides a list of factors that would create the presumption that proceeds from the sale of future revenues should be accounted for as debt, including the intent of the parties, continuing involvement of the seller, recourse for payments due, and limits on the investor's return. Refer to Chapter 4, "Balance Sheet Classification and Related Display Issues," of CCH's *GAAP Guide Levels B, C, and D* for additional information. The provisions of this chapter apply to a sale of future revenue that should be accounted for as debt.

Various other accounting standards and EITF Issues address other sale versus financing arrangements that involve transfers of nonfinancial assets. In some cases, a gain or loss on a sale must be deferred until certain conditions are met. In other cases, the transaction must be accounted for as a financing arrangement. Such transactions should be accounted for under applicable accounting standards.

Distinguishing between Debt and Equity

Certain financial instruments possess characteristics of both debt and equity. Some debt instruments are convertible into equity of the issuer. Accounting for those instruments is addressed in Chapter 10, "Convertible Debt and Similar Instruments." Chapter 16, "Issuer's Accounting for Equity Instruments and Related Contracts," provides guidance for instruments issued in the form of equity that, in substance, represent obligations of the issuer, such as mandatorily redeemable preferred stock. This chapter addresses accounting for nonconvertible instruments properly identified as debt of the issuer.

> ☛ **PRACTICE POINTER:** The FASB has on its agenda Phase 2 of the Liabilities and Equity project, a summary of which appears in the Important Notice in Chapter 16, "Issuer's Accounting for Equity Instruments and Related Contracts."

Hedging Activities

Companies often seek to convert the contractual interest rates on their debt instruments from a fixed rate to a floating rate, or from a floating rate to a fixed rate through the use of derivatives. Companies also use derivatives to hedge the effects of prepayment risk, changes in foreign currency exchange rates on foreign-currency-denominated debt instruments, and other risks. Chapter 14, "Hedge Accounting," provides additional information about the criteria that must be met and subsequent accounting for hedging transactions.

Debt with Embedded Derivatives

Some financial instruments (referred to as hybrid instruments) contain multiple risk characteristics that must be split apart and accounted for separately in accordance with FAS-133. For example, a debt instrument with a return that is linked to changes in an equity index is considered a debt instrument and an embedded equity derivative. In some situations, put and call options that can accelerate or extend the repayment of principal in a debt instrument may be considered embedded derivatives. FAS-133 also provides a fair value measurement election, subject to certain scope limitations, for certain debt instruments that are hybrid financial instruments with an identified embedded derivative that is required to be bifurcated. Such instruments are eligible to be initially and subsequently measured at fair value, with changes in fair value recognized currently in earnings. Embedded derivatives and the fair value election are discussed later in this chapter in the section "Subsequent Measurement of Debt" and in greater detail in Chapter 13, "Embedded Derivatives." This chapter addresses accounting for the remaining "debt host contract" after a derivative has been separated for accounting purposes under FAS-133.

ACCOUNTING FOR DEBT INSTRUMENTS

Recognition and Initial Measurement

In general, a debt instrument should be recorded as a liability in the borrower's balance sheet at the present value of the consideration received in the exchange. Ordinarily, the amount of proceeds received represents the present value of the debt instrument at its inception. However, in the following circumstances, interest should be imputed at an appropriate current rate to determine the present value of the debt:

- Noninterest-bearing payables and other forms of indebtedness.
- Debt with an unreasonable stated interest rate (for example, it does not reflect the general level of interest rates, the creditworthiness of the particular borrower, or the amount of time until payments are due).
- The face amount of the debt is different from the fair value of the goods or services received.

Imputing an appropriate interest rate results in a premium or discount on the debt that should be amortized over the life of the instrument.

☛ **PRACTICE POINTER:** The interest element is often ignored for trade payables that are due on customary terms that do not exceed one year. (APB-21, par. 3(a))

☛ **PRACTICE POINTER:** Debt assumed in a purchase business combination should be recorded at its fair value. Quoted market prices should be used if available. If a present value technique is used to estimate fair value, the estimated future cash flows should reflect all relevant provisions of the debt agreement (for example, the right of the issuer to prepay). (EITF 98-1)

Issues unique to recognizing interest expense on debt financings are discussed later in this chapter in the section "Income Statement Recognition."

Debt Instruments Subject to Registration Payment Arrangements

Companies may enter into registration payment arrangements as part of the issuance of a financial instrument, such as a warrant, preferred stock, or a debt instrument. Chapter 16, "Equity Instruments and Related Contracts," outlines the required accounting in FSP EITF 00-19-2 for registration payment arrangements that are issued concurrent with the issuance of various types of financial instruments (see the section entitled, "Equity Instruments Subject to Registration Payment Arrangements").

For a financial instrument involving a registration payment arrangement that meets specific characteristics, separate accounting for the contingent obligation under the registration payment arrangement and the financial instrument subject to the arrangement is required. The contingent obligation to make future payments or otherwise transfer consideration under a registration payment arrangement must be recognized and measured separately in accordance with FAS-5, *Accounting for Contingencies*, and FIN-14, *Reasonable Estimation of the Amount of a Loss*. If an entity would be required to deliver shares under a registration payment arrangement, the transfer of that consideration is probable, and the number of shares to be delivered can be reasonably estimated, the issuer's share price at the reporting date must be used to measure the contingent liability under FAS-5.

The debt instrument subject to the arrangement must be accounted for under relevant GAAP for that instrument. If the transfer of consideration under a registration payment arrangement is probable and reasonably estimable (under FAS-5 and FIN-14), the contingent liability must be included in the allocation of proceeds from the related financing transaction using the measurement guidance in FAS-5. The remaining proceeds must be allocated under other applicable GAAP for the instruments.

See Chapter 16, "Equity Instruments and Related Contracts," for incremental disclosure requirements applicable to an issuer's registration payment arrangements.

Fair Value Option for Certain Debt Instruments

AUTHOR'S NOTE: In February 2007, the FASB issued FASB Statement No. 159, *The Fair Value Option for Financial Assets and Financial Liabilities.* FAS-159 provides companies with an option to report certain financial assets and liabilities at fair value with subsequent changes in value reported in earnings. The specific provisions of FAS-159 applicable to debt instruments are covered in this Chapter. Chapter 19, "The Fair Value Option for Financial Instruments," provides generalized guidance on the fair value option in FAS-159. FAS-159 is effective for calendar-year-end companies as of January 1, 2008. Early adoption is permitted as of the beginning of a fiscal year that begins on or before November 15, 2007, provided the entity also elects to apply FAS-157.

In addition, in September 2006, the FASB issued FASB Statement No. 157, *Fair Value Measurements,* FAS-157 provides a single definition of the term *fair value,* establishes a framework for measuring fair value where permitted or required by existing GAAP, and expands disclosures about fair value measurements. Specific fair value measurement guidance applicable to debt instruments is covered in this Chapter. Chapter 18, "Fair Value Measurements, Fair Value Disclosures, and Other Financial Instrument Disclosures," provides the detailed provisions of FAS-157. The 2008 edition of CCH *Financial Instruments* has been updated to incorporate the provisions of FAS-157. FAS-157 is effective for calendar-year-end companies as of January 1, 2008. Unless a company chooses to early adopt, prior GAAP is applicable for financial statements issued for 2007.

As this book went to press, the FASB was addressing a possible delay of FAS-157's effective date. The FASB agreed to consider delaying the effective date for nonfinancial instruments and for certain types of entities, including private companies and "smaller" public companies (not yet defined). Readers should monitor the FASB's further deliberations regarding the nature of any delay of FAS-157's effective date. Also, readers should refer to the 2007 edition for GAAP related to the fair value measurement of financial instruments applicable before the effective date of FAS-157.

Companies may elect to measure certain debt instruments at fair value under the fair value option provided by FAS-159. If the fair value option is elected, a debt instrument is initially measured at fair value and subsequent changes in fair value are recognized in earnings. FAS-159 does not specify a method to be used for recognizing and measuring the amount of interest income and interest expense for items for which the fair value option has been elected; however, FAS-159 requires disclosure of a description of how interest and dividends are measured and where they are reported in the income statement for each period for which an income statement is presented.

FAS-157 is the primary guidance for fair value measurement under GAAP. Fair value is the price that would be received to sell an asset or paid to transfer a liability in an orderly transaction between market participants at the measurement date. For debt instruments, FAS-157 requires that an entity include changes in the issuer's credit spread in earnings. In addition, debt issue costs would be recognized immediately as an expense rather than deferred and amortized over the term of the debt. Chapter 18, "Fair Value Measurements, Fair Value Disclosures, and Other Financial Instrument Disclosures," provides specific fair value measurement guidance applicable to all financial instruments permitted or required to be measured at fair value under GAAP.

Subsequent Measurement of Debt

Ordinarily, the issuer of a debt instrument carries its obligation at the face amount, adjusted for any unamortized premium or discount and accrued interest. The issuer generally does not account for changes in the fair value of its own debt instrument. However, in certain cases, the carrying amount of a debt instrument does require adjustment to reflect changes in circumstances and certain hedging activities, as discussed below.

- *Foreign-Currency-Denominated Debt*—transaction gains and losses are recognized on debt that is denominated in a currency other than the *functional currency* of the reporting entity. Transaction gains and losses are measured using current (spot) rates at the balance sheet date and are generally reported in income currently. (FAS-52, par. 16) Foreign-currency-denominated debt may be designated as the hedging instrument in a hedge of the net investment in foreign operations under FAS-133. (This is a rare exception—nonderivatives are generally not allowed to be designated as a hedging instrument.) In such cases, the transaction gains and losses would be recognized in the Cumulative Translation Adjustment, a separate component of stockholders' equity. Refer to Chapter 14, "Hedge Accounting," for additional information.

- *Fair Value Hedges of Debt*—the carrying amount of debt that is designated as the hedged item in a fair value hedge under FAS-133 should be adjusted to reflect changes in fair value attributable to the risk being hedged. Refer to Chapter 14, "Hedge Accounting," for additional information.

- *Certain Hybrid Instruments*—certain debt instruments that are hybrid financial instruments are eligible to be initially and subsequently measured at fair value, with changes in fair value recognized currently in earnings. Such debt instruments must have an identified embedded derivative that is required to be bifurcated under FAS-133. There are important scope limitations of this election (for example, it does not apply to substantively extinguished debt whose accounting was grandfathered by FAS-140). In addition, if an entity identifies an embedded derivative but determines that it is not required to be bifurcated under FAS-133, the hybrid financial instrument is *not* eligible for the fair value election. In some cases, an entity may not elect fair value measurement because bifurcation of the instrument permits the embedded derivative to be designated as a hedging instrument. If a debt instrument has an embedded derivative that cannot be separated reliably, the entire instrument should be marked to market through earnings. (FAS-133, par. 16) Refer to Chapter 13, "Embedded Derivatives," for additional information.

- *Liabilities for Short Sales of Securities*—in accordance with certain industry practices, the obligation to purchase a security sold but not yet owned is generally marked to market. (FAS-115 Q&A, par. 7)

Substantial modification of the terms of outstanding debt obligations, including troubled debt restructurings, also can result in the remeasurement of a liability. Refer to Chapter 11, "Extinguishments of Debt." For debt instruments measured at fair value under the fair value option provided in FAS-159, subsequent changes in fair value are recognized in earnings.

Balance Sheet Classification

The following section applies only when an entity is preparing a classified balance sheet for financial accounting and reporting purposes. Companies in several specialized industries (including broker-dealers, banks, finance, real estate, and stock life insurance companies) prepare unclassified balance sheets because the current/noncurrent distinction is not particularly relevant.

> ☛ **PRACTICE POINTER:** As part of its short-term convergence project, the FASB considered various issues regarding balance-sheet classification. Rather than resolving those issues as part of the short-term convergence project, the FASB's tentative decisions will be considered as part of its project on financial performance reporting by business enterprises. Those tentative decisions include the following:
>
> - *Refinancings:* The FASB tentatively decided that a long-term financial liability due to be settled within 12 months of the balance sheet date should be classified as a current liability, unless an agreement to refinance the liability on a long-term basis is completed on or before the balance sheet date.
>
> - *Violation of debt covenants:* The FASB tentatively decided that a long-term financial liability payable on demand at the balance sheet date because the entity breached a loan covenant should be classified as current unless the lender has agreed on or before the balance sheet date to not demand payment as a consequence of the breach. In addition, the FASB decided that a loan agreement that has been breached but in which the lender effects a grace period during which the obligation is not callable for a period less than 12 months should be classified as a current liability *even if* the breach is expected to be rectified before expiration of the grace period or after the balance sheet date but before financial statements are issued.
>
> The timing of resolution of these items as part of the project on financial performance reporting by business enterprises is uncertain.

Current Liabilities

Current liabilities are defined in Chapter 3A of ARB-43 (par. 7) as "obligations whose liquidation is reasonably expected to require the use of existing resources properly classified as *current assets,* or the creation of other current liabilities." As a balance sheet category, the classification is intended to include obligations for items directly related to the *operating cycle.* Chapter 3A of ARB-43 (par. 7) and FAS-6 (par. 8), identify the following obligations relating to the operating cycle that should be classified as current liabilities:

- Payables incurred in the acquisition of materials and supplies to be used in the production of goods to be offered for sale or the performance of services
- Collections received in advance of the delivery of goods or the performance of services
- Accruals for salaries, rentals, royalties and taxes

> ☞ **PRACTICE POINTER:** Chapter 3A of ARB-43 discusses the concept of the operating cycle—the time it takes a company to purchase materials and/or services for cash, convert those items to inventory, sell that inventory for trade receivables, and collect upon those receivables as cash again. When a business has no clearly defined operating cycle, more than one operating cycle, or an operating cycle of less than one year, a one-year rule is used as the basis for classification of assets and liabilities. For simplicity, this chapter refers only to the one-year rule. However, for businesses whose operating cycle is longer than one year, the longer period should be used.

Other liabilities whose regular and ordinary liquidation is expected to occur within 12 months are considered short-term obligations, including:

- Short-term debts arising from acquisitions of capital assets
- Serial maturities of long-term obligations
- Sinking fund provisions

Short-term obligations generally should be classified as current liabilities. However, ARB-43 indicates that short-term obligations should be excluded from classification as current liabilities if they will *not* require the use of working capital, that is, they will be repaid using assets that have been properly classified as noncurrent or using long-term obligations incurred to provide increased amounts of working capital on a long-term basis. (ARB-43, Ch. 3A, par. 8, as amended)

Ratios involving current liabilities   Investors and potential investors frequently evaluate a company's balance sheet for certain relationships that help them assess prospective cash flows. Liquidity refers to a company's ability to meet its currently maturing obligations. Financial ratios that focus on the relationship between current assets and current liabilities help the user of financial statements assess a company's liquidity.

Although these ratios cannot predict the future performance of a company, they help highlight current and potential problems and strengths. Improperly excluding obligations from current liabilities can improve the appearance of a company's liquidity and distort ratios involving working capital.

EXHIBIT 8-1
FINANCIAL RATIOS INVOLVING CURRENT ASSETS
AND CURRENT LIABILITIES

Financial Ratio		Primary Use
Name	**Formula**	**Primary Use**
Working capital ratio (also known as Current ratio)	$\dfrac{\text{Current assets}}{\text{Current liabilities}}$	A broad indication of a company's liquidity
Quick ratio	$\dfrac{\text{Quick assets}}{\text{Current liabilities}}$	A more severe test of current liquidity. Quick assets include only cash, short-term investments held in lieu of cash, and accounts receivable presumed to be readily convertible into cash; it does not include inventory which may not be readily liquidated to cover current liabilities
Cash ratio	$\dfrac{\text{Cash}}{\text{Current liabilities}}$	The most demanding test of current liquidity

Short-Term Debt Expected to Be Refinanced

Some short-term debt obligations are expected to be refinanced on a long-term basis and therefore are not expected to require the use of working capital in the upcoming operating cycle. FAS-6 addresses when a short-term debt that is expected to be refinanced may be excluded from current liabilities.

☛ **PRACTICE POINTER:** Short-term payables arising in the normal course of business do not qualify for this exception. (FAS-6, par. 8)

Short-term debt, such as commercial paper, construction loans, and the currently maturing portion of long-term debt, may be refinanced on a long-term basis by:

- Replacing it with a long-term obligation.
- Replacing it with equity securities.
- Renewing, extending it, or replacing it with other short-term obligations for a period extending beyond one year. (FAS-6, par. 2)

Short-term debt that is expected to be refinanced on a long-term basis should be excluded from current liabilities only if the company has both the intent and the ability to consummate the refinancing. (FAS-6, par. 9) Intent and ability can be demonstrated by either one of the following conditions:

- The issuance, after the balance sheet date but before the issuance of the balance sheet, of a long-term obligation or equity securities for the purpose of refinancing the short-term obligation on a long-term basis, or

- Entering into a financing agreement, before the issuance of the balance sheet, that clearly permits the company to refinance the short-term obligation on a long-term basis. The terms of the financing agreement must be readily determinable. In addition, *all* of the following conditions must be met (FAS-6, par. 11):

  — The agreement must not expire or be cancelable by the lender (or the prospective lender or investor) within one year of the balance sheet date, except for *violation of a provision* with which compliance is objectively determinable or measurable.

  — Obligations incurred under the agreement must not be *callable* during the year following the balance sheet date, except for violation of a provision with which compliance is objectively determinable or measurable.

☞ **PRACTICE POINTER:** Financing agreements that contain *subjective acceleration clauses* would not meet these conditions because compliance with such clauses is not objectively determinable or measurable. Therefore, short-term debt expected to be refinanced on a long-term basis with a financing agreement that contains a provision such as a material adverse change clause is required to be classified as a current liability.

  — At the balance sheet date, and subsequent to the balance sheet date but before the issuance of the balance sheet, the company complies with all of the provisions of the agreement. If there is a violation of a provision either at the balance sheet date or before issuance of the balance sheet, it either must be cured or a waiver must be obtained before issuance of the balance sheet.

  — The lender (or the prospective lender or investor) under the agreement is expected to be financially capable of honoring the agreement.

☞ **PRACTICE POINTER:** If a foreign subsidiary negotiates a financing agreement, and intends to lend the proceeds to its parent company to liquidate parent company debt, the foreign subsidiary's refinancing agreement would not satisfy FAS-6 if local laws prohibit the transfer of funds outside the country. (FAS-6, par. 38)

OBSERVATION: The classification of short-term debt expected to be refinanced on a long-term basis is another example of intent-based accounting. Creditworthy companies with available lines of credit would appear to have some "flexibility" in classifying short-term obligations.

SEC REGISTRANT ALERT: Generally, the SEC staff believes that financial statements are "issued" as of the date they are widely distributed to all shareholders and other financial statement users or filed with the SEC. An earnings release does not constitute the issuance of financial statements. (EITF D-86)

Amount of short-term debt excluded from current liabilities

When all of the conditions for refinancing a short-term obligation on a long-term basis have been met, the amount of the debt obligation that may be excluded from current liabilities is subject to certain limitations set forth in FAS-6, paragraph 12. Exhibit 8-3 summarizes that guidance.

☛ **PRACTICE POINTER:**   If short-term debt is expected to be refinanced by the issuance of equity instruments, the obligation is excluded from current liabilities but is *not* included in stockholders' equity. (FAS-6, fn. 2)

Intent to seek new financing when another financing agreement exists

If a company intends to seek new financing rather than exercise its rights under an existing financing agreement (that meets the requirements of FAS-6), the company must intend to exercise the existing agreement as a fallback measure if the new financing is not obtained before the balance sheet is issued in order to properly exclude the short-term debt from current liabilities. The entity may lack the intent to exercise, for example, if the existing agreement contains unreasonable interest rates or collateral requirements. The following example illustrates this point.

Assume Company A has an existing line of credit that carries a 12 percent interest rate. Short-term debt is coming due within three months of Company A's balance sheet date. Interest rates have dropped to 7 percent and Company A, a creditworthy entity, intends to seek new financing for the purpose of refinancing the short-term debt on a long-term basis. Company A has sufficient working capital available to pay the short-term debt as it becomes due and would

EXHIBIT 8-2
CLASSIFYING SHORT-TERM DEBT

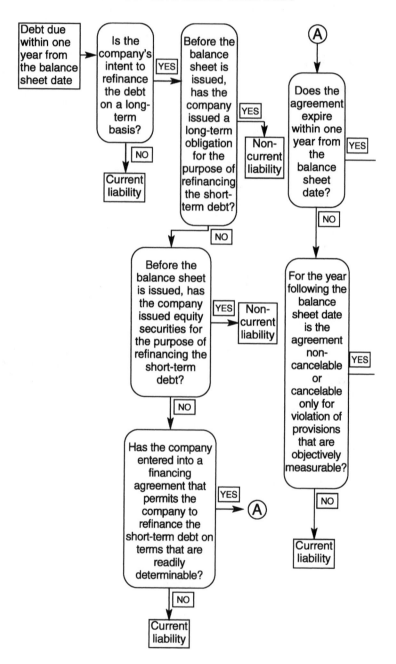

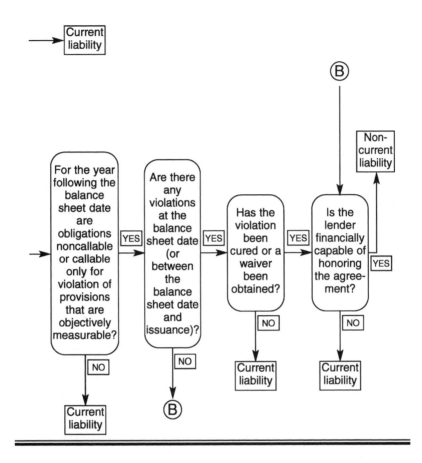

borrow under the line of credit only under dire circumstances. Because it would not be reasonable for Company A to borrow under the existing line of credit as the short-term debt becomes due, Company A could only exclude the short-term debt from current liabilities if, before issuance of the balance sheet, the new financing agreement is obtained and it meets the conditions of FAS-6.

Rollovers of short-term obligations The rollover of short-term debt after the balance sheet date but before the balance sheet is issued would not, by itself, change the classification of such obligations as current liabilities. To qualify for exclusion from current liabilities in the current period, additional conditions must be met:

**EXHIBIT 8-3
LIMITATIONS ON AMOUNTS EXCLUDABLE FROM
CURRENT LIABILITIES**

Form of Refinancing	Amount Excluded from Current Liabilities
Post-balance sheet issuance of a long obligation or equity securities	An amount not in excess of the term proceeds received
Existence of a financing agreement that meets the requirements of FAS-6	An amount not in excess of the amount available to reduce the obligation under the agreement
Existence of a financing agreement that meets the requirements of FAS-6, but the amounts available under the agreement fluctuate	A reasonable estimate of the minimum amount that will be available during the year. If no reasonable estimate can be made, the entire amount should be included in current liabilities

---

- If the replacement is made under the terms of a revolving credit agreement that provides for renewal or extension for an uninterrupted period extending greater than one year from the balance sheet date, the revolver must be a qualifying financing agreement.
- If the replacement is a rollover of commercial paper along with a long-term standby letter of credit, the standby letter of credit agreement must meet all of the requirements for a financing agreement. (FAS-6, par. 14)

Increasing-rate debt EITF Issue 86-15 addresses accounting for a debt instrument that matures three months from the date of issuance but can be extended at the option of the borrower for another three months at each maturity date until the final maturity five years from the original date of issuance. The debt instrument is considered to be a short-term obligation. The balance sheet classification of this instrument should be based on the borrower's anticipated source of repayment (that is, the use of current assets or a new short-term borrowing versus a long-term refinancing agreement that meets the requirements of FAS-6). Recognition of interest expense is discussed later in this chapter.

Short-term debt repaid prior to being replaced Short-term debt expected to be refinanced on a long-term basis may not be excluded from current liabilities if, after the balance sheet date, the company repays the short-term debt as it becomes due and subsequently (but also before issuance of the balance sheet) issues a long-term obligation or equity securities for the purpose of replacing the amounts used to repay the short-term debt. Since current assets were used before the funds were obtained from the long-term financing, the short-term debt is appropriately classified as a current liability. (FIN-8, par. 3)

Callable Long-Term Debt

The classification of long-term debt that is or may be *callable* at the balance sheet date by the creditor depends on facts and circumstances. Long-term debt that is due on demand at, or within one year of, the balance sheet date by its terms or because of a violation of an objectively determinable provision of the agreement existing at the balance sheet date is presumed to be a current liability. That presumption may be overcome if one of the following conditions is met (FAS-78, par. 5):

- The creditor has waived or subsequently lost the right to demand repayment for more than one year (or operating cycle, if longer) from the balance sheet date (for example, because the debtor cured the violation prior to the issuance of the financial statements).

- For long-term obligations containing a *grace period* within which the debtor may cure the violation, it is *probable* that the violation will be cured within that period, thus preventing the obligation from becoming callable.

> ☛ **PRACTICE POINTER:** A creditor may decide to waive its right to call a debt that is in violation of a covenant for a period greater than one year but retain future covenant requirements even though the debt agreement does not include an explicit grace period. Such a waiver should be evaluated in the same manner as a grace period. Similarly, a modification of debt that allows the debtor to comply with the revised covenants, but leaves in effect covenants affecting future periods, should be viewed as a grace period. (EITF 86-30)

Subjective acceleration clauses   Long-term debt that may be accelerated because of a violation of a subjectively determinable provision of the agreement is not technically callable at the balance sheet date and may be presumed to be a noncurrent liability if it is remote that acceleration of the due date will occur. (FTB 79-3, par. 3)

> **OBSERVATION:** Note that the literature makes a distinction between a "due on demand" provision (which makes the debt a current liability regardless of the probability of the debt being recalled) and a subjective acceleration clause (which considers the probability of the debt being accelerated for purposes of determining the proper balance sheet classification).

Exhibit 8-4 summarizes the effect of existing and potential covenant violations on the classification of long-term debt.

> **OBSERVATION:** Although short-term debt expected to be refinanced on a long-term basis must be presented as a current liability if the long-term refinancing agreement contains a subjective acceleration clause, long-term debt that contains a subjective acceleration clause is not necessarily presented as a current liability. This is viewed as an acceptably higher threshold for excluding a current obligation from classification as a current liability than for requiring a noncurrent liability to be classified as a current liability. (EITF D-23)

Lock-box arrangements   A revolving credit agreement (whose term extends greater than one year from the balance sheet date) that contains a lock-box arrangement, whereby remittances from the borrower's customers are automatically used to reduce amounts borrowed under the credit agreement, makes any borrowings under the agreement short-term obligations. In such arrangements, the borrowing is repaid with current assets. Short-term obligations may be excluded from classification as current liabilities only if an agreement other than the revolving credit agreement meets the conditions of FAS-6 for refinancing on a long-term basis. (EITF 95-22)

EXHIBIT 8-4
CLASSIFICATION OF LONG-TERM DEBT

Conditions Existing at the Balance Sheet Date	Presumed Balance Sheet Classification	Presumption Overcome If by the Date the Balance Sheet is Issued . . .
Long-term debt is due on demand or will be due on demand within 1 year of the balance sheet date	Current liability*	Creditor waives its right to demand repayment for greater than one year from the balance sheet date
Long-term debt is callable because of a covenant violation; no grace period	Current liability*	Creditor waives its rights for more than a year or debtor cures the violation
Long-term debt will become callable if a covenant violation is not cured within a specified grace period	Current liability*	Creditor waives its rights for more than a year *or* it is probable the debtor will cure the violation within the specified grace period
Long-term debt would have been callable absent a modification of a restrictive covenant; future covenants remain in effect	Noncurrent liability	It is probable that the debt or will not be able to comply with any applicable covenants over the next 12 months (EITF 86-30)

Conditions Existing at the Balance Sheet Date	Presumed Balance Sheet Classification	Presumption Overcome If by the Date the Balance Sheet is Issued ...
Long-term debt **not** in violation of any covenants at the balance sheet date but violations are probable within one year of the balance sheet date	Noncurrent liability	Not applicable. Disclosure of adverse consequences of failure to comply is required (EITF 86-30)
Long-term debt may be callable under a subjective acceleration clause	Noncurrent liability†	Recurring losses or liquidity problems make acceleration likely (FTB 79-3, par. 3)

---

* Short-term debt expected to be refinanced on a long-term basis should be excluded from classification as a current liability if the conditions of FAS-6 are met.

† If it is remote that the maturity of the debt would be accelerated.

☛ **PRACTICE POINTER:**   Some lock-box arrangements do not go into effect unless the lender exercises a subjective acceleration clause (a so-called "springing lock-box"). Long-term borrowings under such arrangements should be classified as noncurrent, because the customers' remittances do not automatically reduce the debt outstanding. The effect of the subjective acceleration clause should be evaluated under FTB 79-3.

Long-term debt with remarketing agreement   A provision in a debt instrument (whose term extends greater than one year from the balance sheet date) that permits the investor/creditor to redeem or put the bond to the issuer on short notice, makes the debt instrument a short-term obligation. A remarketing agreement supporting the debt instrument that states that an agent (investment banker) will make its *best efforts* to remarket the bond when redeemed would not meet the conditions of FAS-6 for having the ability to refinance the debt on a long-term basis. Thus, the debt instrument should be classified as a current liability. If, instead, the remarketing agreement is supported by a line-of-credit agreement that provides protection to the investor in the event that the redeemed debt cannot be remarketed, the debt instrument may be classified as a noncurrent liability if the line of credit meets the conditions of FAS-6. (EITF D-61)

Classification of Subsidiary Debt in Consolidated Balance Sheet

ARB-51, paragraph 4, provides that as long as the difference between a parent and subsidiary's fiscal year-ends is less than three months, the balance sheets may be consolidated. If a subsidiary balance sheet is dated October 31, 20X1, and the parent company's balance sheet is December 31, 20X1, a question arises as to how the debt of the subsidiary that is due November 15, 20X2 (noncurrent in its own balance sheet), should be classified in the consolidated balance sheet. The EITF was unable to reach a consensus on this issue.

> **SEC REGISTRANT ALERT:** In the example discussed above, the SEC staff would expect the debt of the subsidiary to be classified as current in the consolidated balance sheet. (EITF 88-15)

Income Statement Recognition

In general, interest expense should be recognized on debt instruments (and equity instruments that are considered debt for accounting purposes) using an effective rate of interest, not necessarily the nominal or stated rate, in accordance with APB-21. Refer to Chapter 7, "Calculating Yields on Debt Investments," for specific guidance related to imputing interest. Special models exist for certain types of liabilities whose interest rates or payment amounts are uncertain or contingent on changes in the price of a referenced asset or index. Those models are discussed in this section. The accounting for convertible debt by the issuer is discussed in Chapter 10, "Convertible Debt and Similar Instruments."

Capitalization of Interest Costs

FAS-34 establishes standards for capitalizing certain interest costs as part of the historical cost of an asset. Generally, interest on debt used to finance assets that require a period of time to get them ready for their intended use qualifies for capitalization. The amount of interest cost to be capitalized on qualifying assets is intended to be that portion of interest expense incurred during the acquisition period of the assets that theoretically could have been avoided if expenditures for the assets had not been made. (FAS-34, par. 12) See CCH's *GAAP Guide Level A*, Chapter 24, "Interest Costs Capitalized," for additional information, including the type of assets that qualify, the appropriate capitalization rate, and the capitalization period.

> ☛ **PRACTICE POINTER:** Amortization of adjustments to the carrying amount of a debt instrument from fair value hedge accounting should be considered in selecting the appropriate interest rate for capitalization of interest. (EITF 99-9) Chapter 14, "Hedge Accounting," provides additional information, including the treatment of hedge ineffectiveness and cash flow hedges of debt.

Debt Issue Costs

Debt issue costs generally are incurred in connection with the issuance of debt securities or other short- or long-term borrowings. APB-21 requires that debt issue costs be reported in the balance sheet as deferred charges (paragraph 16). Generally, debt issue costs are reported as an asset and amortized over the term of the debt. (EITF 95-13) For debt instruments measured at fair value under the fair value option election provided in FAS-159, debt issue costs would be recognized immediately as an expense. (FAS-159, par. A41)

Debtors also incur costs to establish line-of-credit or revolving-debt arrangements. Some or all of the costs are typically deferred and amortized over the term of the arrangement. (EITF 98-14)

Special Application of the Interest Method for Certain Liabilities

Increasing-rate debt EITF Issue 86-15 addresses a debt instrument that matures three months from the date of issuance but can be extended at the option of the borrower for another three months at each maturity date for a period of five years from its original issuance. The interest rate on the note increases a specified amount each time the note is renewed. Instruments that previously were accounted for under EITF Issue 86-15 would now likely be considered to have embedded derivatives under FAS-133, paragraph 61(g), because the interest rate does not reset to a market rate when the borrower elects to extend the term of the loan. Embedded derivatives are discussed in detail in Chapter 13, "Embedded Derivatives." However, increasing-rate debt would still be accounted for under EITF Issue 86-15 if:

- The rate contractually reset to a market rate each time the loan is renewed *or*
- The reporting entity elected the grandfathering provisions under paragraph 50 of FAS-133 (as amended), which permit entities to continue to apply previous accounting standards to contracts with embedded derivatives that were issued before January 1, 1998, or January 1, 1999, as elected by the entity.

If the instrument does not contain an embedded derivative, the borrower's periodic interest cost on increasing-rate debt should be determined using the interest method based on the *estimated* outstanding term of the debt. In estimating the term of the debt, the borrower would consider its plans, ability, and intent to service the debt. Debt issue costs should be amortized over the same period used in the interest cost determination.

> **SEC REGISTRANT ALERT:** SAB-77 requires that EITF Issue 86-15 be followed for bridge financing in a business combination that consists of increasing-rate date.

☛ **PRACTICE POINTER:** Interestingly, the Emerging Issues Task Force concluded that interest could be recognized over a period that differs from the presumed maturity of the debt for balance sheet classification purposes.

Indexed debt instruments   An indexed debt instrument has an interest rate or payment amount that is linked to the price of a specific commodity, index or other item. Many debt instruments that previously were accounted for under EITF Issue 86-28 are now considered to have embedded derivatives under FAS-133. Embedded derivatives are discussed in detail in Chapter 13, "Embedded Derivatives." An indexed debt instrument would still be accounted for under EITF Issue 86-28 if:

- The reporting entity elected to grandfather its hybrid instruments with embedded derivatives as permitted by FAS-133, paragraph 50 (discussed above) *or*

- The contingent payment feature does not meet the definition of a derivative (for example, it must be settled by delivery of an asset that is not readily convertible to cash).

The remainder of this section on indexed debt discusses circumstances where FAS-133 is not applicable.

If the investor's right to receive the contingent payment is separable, the issuer should allocate the proceeds between the debt instrument and the investor's stated right to receive the contingent payments. The premium or discount on the debt instrument resulting from the allocation should be accounted for using the interest method under APB-21.

Regardless of whether any portion of the proceeds is allocated to the contingent payment, as the applicable index value increases such that the issuer would be required to pay the investor a contingent payment at maturity, the issuer should recognize a liability for the amount that the contingent payment exceeds the amount, if any, originally attributed to the contingent payment feature. The liability for the contingent payment feature should be based on the applicable index value at the balance sheet date (the "spot rate") and should not anticipate any future changes in the index value. When no proceeds are originally allocated to the contingent payment, the additional liability resulting from the fluctuating index value should be accounted for as an adjustment of the carrying amount of the debt obligation.

> **OBSERVATION:** EITF Issue 86-28 is an intrinsic value model, not a fair value model. That is, the contingent payment is marked to the spot rate (if it would increase the liability), but other changes in value are not recorded, such as the effect of changes in interest rates (if the note bears a fixed rate of interest), credit risk, and liquidity risk. DIG Issue B-24 clarifies that the "fair value" excep-

tion in paragraph 12(b) of FAS-133 does *not* apply to indexed debt instruments because they are not carried at fair value.

Participating mortgages   A participating mortgage gives the lender the right to participate in appreciation in a mortgaged real estate project, the results of operations of a mortgaged real estate project, or both. SOP 97-1 addresses the borrower's accounting.

> **OBSERVATION:**   Even though a participating mortgage might appear to have an embedded derivative, paragraph 198 of FAS-133 specifically scopes them out (for both the borrower and the lender).

A borrower in a participating mortgage should recognize a liability for the fair value of the participation right at the inception of the loan, with a corresponding debit to debt discount.

Interest expense on a participating mortgage consists of the following elements, which should be accounted for as indicated in SOP 97-1, paragraphs 12-14:

* *Amounts designated as interest in the mortgage agreement*   Recognize as interest expense in the period it is incurred. If the stated rate varies based on changes in an independent factor, such as LIBOR, the calculation of interest should be based on the factor as it changes over the life of the loan.
* *Amounts related to the lender's participation in results of operations*   Amounts due to the lender's participation in the project's results of operations (as defined in the loan agreement) should be charged to interest expense in the borrower's corresponding financial reporting period, with a credit to the participation liability.
* *Amortization of debt discount related to the lender's participation in the market value appreciation of the project*   The discount should be amortized to interest expense by the interest method over the life of the loan using the effective interest rate.

In subsequent periods, the participation liability should be adjusted to its current fair value. The corresponding debit or credit should be to the debt discount account. The revised discount should be amortized prospectively, using the effective interest rate. (SOP 97-1, par. 15)

> ☛ **PRACTICE POINTER:**   All components of interest expense are eligible for capitalization under FAS-34. Once capitalized, the amounts should not be adjusted for the effects of reversals of amortization. (SOP 97-1, fn. 2)

> **OBSERVATION:**   The *lender's* accounting for participating mortgages is addressed by PB-1 on acquisition, development, or construction arrangements (ADC Loans). The PB-1 guidance

on income recognition is quite general. Practitioners may want to consider the requirements of FAS-5 on gain contingencies and SEC SAB-101 on revenue recognition to determine when to recognize their share of the appreciation on a property or their share of the results of a project. Chapter 3, "Loans and the Allowance for Credit Losses," discusses the lender's accounting for ADC arrangements in more detail.

Extinguishments of Debt

Gains and losses on extinguishments of debt are recognized only when certain criteria are met. Chapter 11, "Extinguishments of Debt," addresses debt extinguishments as well as the debtor's accounting for a troubled debt restructuring and significant modifications of debt.

Modification or Exchange of Debt Instruments with Different Terms (EITF 96-19)

From the perspective of the debtor, the major issue in a modification of the terms or exchange of an outstanding debt instrument is whether the modification of terms is significant enough to be considered an issuance of a new debt instrument and an extinguishment of the old instrument. The requirements of EITF Issue 96-19 are discussed in detail in Chapter 11, "Extinguishments of Debt." This chapter addresses modifications that are *not* considered extinguishments by the debtor-rather, they are essentially treated as yield adjustments.

> **OBSERVATION:** The debtor and the creditor apply different accounting requirements to determine the accounting for a modification of terms. The lender applies FAS-91 (paragraphs 12–13) and the debtor applies EITF Issue 96-19. It is entirely possible that the debtor and creditor would come to different conclusions about whether a modified debt instrument should be accounted for as a "new" loan.

New loan test When terms have been modified, but they do *not* result in at least a 10 percent change in the present value of the cash flows under the terms of the new debt instrument compared with the present value of the remaining cash flows under the terms of the original instrument (including any fees exchanged), then the debt has *not* been extinguished. The change in cash flows is recognized as a yield adjustment; that is, a new effective interest rate is determined based on the carrying amount of the original debt instrument and the revised cash flows. (Chapter 11 discusses the elements of this test in detail and the accounting when the change is 10 percent or greater.)

Fees paid by the debtor to the creditor or received by the debtor from the creditor (fees may be received by the debtor from the creditor to cancel a call option held by the debtor or to extend a no-call period) as part of the exchange or modification should be amortized, along with any existing unamortized premium or discount, as an adjustment of interest expense over the remaining term of the replacement or modified debt instrument using the interest method. Costs incurred with third parties directly related to the exchange or modification (such as legal fees) should be expensed as incurred.

Changes in Line-of-Credit or Revolving Debt Agreements (EITF 98-14)

Line-of-credit and revolving debt arrangements differ from traditional term debt because they permit the borrower/debtor to make multiple borrowings up to a specified maximum amount and to repay portions of prior borrowings at any time. EITF Issue 98-14 addresses the debtor's accounting for modifications to or exchanges of line-of-credit or revolving-debt arrangements resulting in either (1) a new line-of-credit or revolving-debt arrangement or (2) a traditional term-debt arrangement. In accounting for an exchange or modification of a line-of-credit or revolving debt arrangement, the *borrowing capacity* of the old arrangement is compared with the borrowing capacity of the new arrangement. A company's borrowing capacity is calculated as follows:

$$\text{Borrowing capacity} = \text{Remaining term of debt} \times \text{Maximum available credit under the line}$$

> **OBSERVATION:** The EITF invented the term "borrowing capacity" so that practitioners would have an objective way to evaluate changes in revolving credit arrangements.

The treatment of unamortized debt issuance costs and fees paid differs depending on whether the debtor's borrowing capacity has increased or decreased. Exhibit 8-5 summarizes the treatment of unamortized (and new) fees and costs relating to modifications of credit agreements in nontroubled situations.

> **OBSERVATION:** The creditor's accounting for a modification to an outstanding line-of-credit or revolving credit arrangement is not explicitly addressed in GAAP.

EXHIBIT 8-5
**ACCOUNTING FOR CHANGES IN LINE-OF-CREDIT OR REVOLVING
DEBT AGREEMENTS**

Change in Borrowing Capacity	Unamortized Deferred Costs	Fees Paid to Creditors and Other Third-Party Costs
Borrowing capacity of new is greater than or equal to borrowing capacity of old	Deferred and amortized over the term of the new arrangement	Deferred and amortized over the term of the new arrangement
Borrowing capacity of new less than borrowing capacity of old	Written-off currently into income (not an extra ordinary loss) in proportion to the decrease in borrowing capacity of the old arrangement. The remaining unamortized deferred costs should continue to be amortized over the term of the new arrangement	Deferred and amortized over the term of the new arrangement

Reporting Cash Flows

Proceeds received from issuing bonds, mortgages, and notes and from other short-term and long-term borrowings should be classified as cash inflows from financing activities. (FAS-95, par. 19) Funds used to repay amounts borrowed and other principal payments to creditors who have extended long-term credit should be classified as cash outflows from financing activities. (FAS-95, par. 19) Cash inflows from borrowings are generally reported *separately* from repayments of debt. (FAS-95, par. 31)

> ☞ **PRACTICE POINTER:** Chapter 1, "Cash and Cash Equivalents," discusses the circumstances in which companies are permitted to report *net* changes in certain debt instruments, including demand deposits and debt with an original maturity of three months or less.

Cash paid for interest is generally considered a cash outflow from *operating activities*. (FAS-95, par. 23(d)) However, interest appropriately capitalized in accordance with FAS-34 is considered a cash flow from investing activities. (FAS-95, fn. 7)

Cash payments for debt issue costs should be classified as cash flows from *financing* activities. (EITF 95-13)

The following are a few specific rules relating to cash flow reporting of debt:

- Seller-financed debt directly related to a purchase of property, plant, and equipment or other productive assets is a *financing* activity. However, advance payments, the down payment and other amounts paid at or around the time of purchase of such assets are considered cash outflows from *investing* activities. (FAS-95, footnotes 6 and 8)
- Changes in accounts and notes payable to suppliers made in connection with the purchase of materials for manufacture or goods for resale are considered cash flows from *operating* activities. (FAS-95, par. 23(a))

> **OBSERVATION:** Cash flow reporting of debt financing is a hodgepodge. For example, if some of the interest costs on a debt instrument are eligible for capitalization, the cash flows associated with that debt would be reported among all three cash flow categories as follows:
>
> - Inflow of proceeds (and outflow for repayment)—financing
> - Outflow for debt issue costs—financing
> - Outflow of interest (generally)—operating
> - Outflow of capitalized interest—investing

Accounting for Guarantees

Guarantees can take many forms. Essentially, a guarantee is a contractual arrangement whereby one party (the guarantor) agrees to pay another party (the beneficiary or guaranteed party) if certain events or conditions occur. There are two elements of a guarantee—first, the firm commitment to "stand-ready" to perform and, second, the contingent obligation to make a payment if the specified events or conditions occur. Two common forms of guarantees are (1) credit guarantees, where the guarantor agrees to compensate a third party if a debtor defaults on its obligation to that party, and (2) value guarantees, where the guarantor agrees to compensate (indemnify) the guaranteed party if the amount of that party's asset, liability, or equity instrument changes adversely. Guarantees can also be indirect, that is, not directly between the guarantor and the exposed party; for example, an arrangement could require a guarantor to transfer funds to a company that is indebted to a bank upon the occurrence of specified events. If those funds are available to the creditors of the debtor company, the guarantor has indirectly guaranteed the creditors of the debtor company.

> ☞ **PRACTICE POINTER:** Examples of guarantees include guarantees of debt, standby letters of credit, guarantees of the market price of a financial or nonfinancial asset, guarantees of collection of scheduled cash flows from assets held by special-purpose entities, and minimum revenue guarantees granted to a business or its owners for a specified period of time. (These examples do not constitute an all-inclusive list of arrangements covered by the scope of FIN-45.) Contracts that include material adverse change clauses, such as loan commitments or commercial letters of credit, are not considered guarantees because the lender can avoid making a payment if those conditions arise.

FIN-45 addresses the accounting and disclosure of guarantees that meet the conditions described above. Exhibit 8-6 summarizes certain contracts that are outside the scope of (1) the accounting provisions or (2) both the accounting and disclosure provisions of FIN-45, primarily because they are subject to other literature.

EXHIBIT 8-6
SCOPE EXCEPTIONS TO FIN-45

Contracts Excluded from All of FIN-45	Contracts Subject to Other GAAP and Disclosure under FIN-45
Loan commitments, commercial letters of credit, and guarantees of an entity's own performance	Guarantees in the form of derivatives (FAS-133). See Chapter 12, "Introduction to Derivatives."
Various forms of *assets* that are subordinated to the rights of other investors (e.g., credit enhancements in a securitization)	Product warranties (FTB 90-1)
Various forms of employee benefits, including stock compensation, and various forms of insurance and reinsurance contracts (see FAS-5, par.7 for specifics)	Contingent consideration in a business combination (FAS-141)
Residual value guarantees written by a lessee that accounts for the lease as a capital lease	A guarantee that would be considered equity (rather than a liability) under other GAAP, including EITF 00-19. See Chapter 16, "Issuers Accounting for Equity Instruments and Related Contracts"
Guarantees that impede sale accounting under other GAAP	Lessees that previously were primarily obligated, but become secondarily liable under a revised lease agreement (FAS-13)

Contracts Excluded from All of FIN-45	Contracts Subject to Other GAAP and Disclosure under FIN-45
Transactions that are accounted for as contingent rent or vendor rebates that are based on sales of the guaranteed party (FIN-45, pars. 4-7)	Guarantees between parents and subsidiaries, and guarantees of a parent or subsidiary's debt issued to third parties Indemnifications for intellectual property infringement (e.g. in a software licensing agreement) (FSP FIN 45-1)

Initial Recognition

FIN-45 requires that a liability be recorded when a guarantee is written, even if no explicit compensation is received and the likelihood of having to perform is remote. A guarantor should recognize a liability for the "stand-ready" obligation at the inception of the guarantee. (This liability essentially represents deferred revenue for agreeing to undertake the risk.) If a fee is (or will be) received in an arm's-length transaction, the stand-ready obligation should be recorded at the amount of the fee received by the guarantor as a practical expedient. In other circumstances, such as when no explicit fee is received, or in transactions that involve multiple elements, the stand-ready obligation should be recorded at fair value. In that case, guarantors should consider what premium would be received by the guarantor to issue the same guarantee in a stand-alone arms-length transaction with an unrelated party as a practical expedient. (FIN-45, par. 9)

> ☞ **PRACTICE POINTER:** When a guarantee is written as part of a broader transaction, ascribing a value to the guarantee obligation directly affects the gain or loss on the transaction. For example, if a seller of goods indemnifies a bank from loss on a customer's loan (financing the assets being purchased) for no explicit fee, the value of the guarantee liability reduces the profit on the sale.

> ☞ **PRACTICE POINTER:** Agreeing to guarantee a loan for no explicit fee is considered a contribution (expense) and a corresponding liability must be recognized at fair value. (FIN-45, par. 9(c))

The contingent obligation should be recognized and measured in accordance with FAS-5. That is, a liability should be recorded when it is *probable* that the company will have to assume responsibility under the guarantee and the amount of the loss is reasonably estimable. (FAS-5, par. 8) If a liability must be accrued for the contingent obligation at the inception of the arrangement (in other words, it is already probable that the guarantor will have to perform and that amount is estimable), the liability should be recorded at fair value, except in the unlikely event that the amount accruable under FAS-5 is higher. (FIN-45, par. 10)

Accounting for the debit When a liability is established for the stand-ready obligation, classification of the offsetting entry (the debit) depends on the circumstances (FIN-45, par. 11(a)):

- In a stand-alone guarantee issued for a premium, the debit would be to cash or a receivable.
- In a stand-alone guarantee issued to an unrelated party for no consideration, the debit would be to expense.
- In a guarantee provided as part of a sale of assets, the proceeds (cash or other assets) would be allocated between the portion attributable to the guarantee and the proceeds from sale of the assets, affecting the gain or loss.
- In a guarantee issued as part of an extinguishment of debt (for example, becoming secondarily liable for no explicit fee), the offsetting entry to recording a guarantee liability would be an adjustment of the gain or loss on extinguishment.
- In a guarantee issued in connection with the formation of a business or a venture accounted for under the equity method, the debit would be an increase to the carrying amount of the investment.
- In a residual value guarantee provided by a lessee-guarantor when entering into an operating lease, the debit would be to prepaid rent, which would be accounted for under paragraph 15 of FAS-13.

Subsequent Measurement

The stand-by obligation (the "imputed fee") should be recognized in earnings as the guarantor is released from risk. Depending on the nature of the guarantee, the liability should be reversed into earnings over the term of the guarantee in one of the following ways (FIN-45, par. 12):

- Only upon either expiration or settlement of the guarantee,
- Using a systematic and rational amortization method, *or*
- As the fair value of the guarantee changes.

> ☛ **PRACTICE POINTER:** A guarantor is not free to choose from the three methods when determining the appropriate method of subsequent measurement of the liability for its obligation under a guarantee. A guarantor may not subsequently measure its liability for its obligation under a guarantee at fair value unless such measurement is permitted under other GAAP, principally FAS-133 for guarantees accounted for as derivatives under that

Statement. Accordingly, guarantees that are excluded from the scope of FAS-133 are not eligible for subsequent measurement at fair value. Definition of a derivative and scope exceptions from the requirements of FAS-133 are discussed in Chapter 12, "Introduction to Derivatives." (FSP FIN 45-2)

☛ **PRACTICE POINTER:** Companies should document their accounting policies for subsequently measuring each type of guarantee that they issue. APB-22 provides guidance on disclosure of accounting policies.

Estimating fair value When a stand-alone guarantee is issued to an unrelated party for a fee, the liability should be recorded at the amount of the fee. In other more complex situations, such as transactions with several components, the amount of any fees received might not solely represent the fair value of the guarantee. In such cases, the fair value of the guarantee liability must be estimated. One way to estimate the fair value of an embedded or bundled guarantee is to look to the fee that the guarantor would require to issue the same or a similar guarantee in a stand-alone transaction with an unrelated party. If that type of information is not available, the expected present value measurement approach described in CON-7, which involves probability-weighted cash flows, may be used to estimate fair value. (FIN-45, par. 11(a))

☛ **PRACTICE POINTER:** In estimating the fair value of a guarantee, the entity should consider a range of possible payment amounts, the timing of those cash flows, and the time value of money weighted to reflect various probability levels. Fair value is *not* the same as "the single best estimate" notion under FAS-5.

Interplay with FAS-140

Guarantees often arise in conjunction with other transactions involving financial instruments, for example:

- As part of a transfer of financial assets, the seller agrees to indemnify the purchaser against credit losses (essentially, a guarantor).
- As part of an extinguishment of liabilities, the debtor may be released as the primary obligor, but remain secondarily liable (essentially, a guarantor).

Accounting for transfers of financial assets and extinguishments of debt are addressed by FAS-140, including recognition of any guarantees incurred at fair value, which directly affects any gain or loss on the transaction. However, FAS-140 includes a practicability exception in certain instances. Refer to Chapter 5, "Transfers of Financial Assets," and Chapter 6, "Securitizations," for additional information.

In addition to any disclosures required by FAS-140, the disclosures required by FIN-45, which are discussed later in this chapter, must be provided for guarantees that arise in transfers of assets that are accounted for as sales and in extinguishments of debt.

DISCLOSURES

Short-Term Debt

FAS-6 requires presentation in a classified balance sheet of a total for current liabilities. In addition, if short-term debt has been excluded from current liabilities in accordance with the conditions of FAS-6, the notes to the financial statements should include a general description of the financing agreement and the terms of any new obligation incurred or expected to be incurred or equity securities issued or expected to be issued as a result of the refinancing. (FAS-6, par. 15)

Long-Term Debt

Maturities

FAS-47 requires disclosure of the aggregate amount of maturities and sinking fund requirements for all long-term borrowings for each of the five years following the latest balance sheet date presented (paragraph 10(b)).

> ☛ **PRACTICE POINTER:** This disclosure applies to financial institutions, even if they present unclassified balance sheets. (SOP 01-6, fn. 30 to par. 14(g))
>
> **SEC REGISTRANT ALERT:** In January 2003, the SEC issued FR-67, "Disclosure in Management's Discussion and Analysis about Off-Balance Sheet Arrangements and Aggregate Contractual Obligations," which, among other things, requires registrants to disclose in a tabular format the amounts of payments due under various contractual obligations, for specified time periods (for example, less than one year, one to three years, three to five years, and more than five years). The table should be organized by category of contractual obligation, including long-term debt, capital and operating leases, purchase obligations, and other long-term liabilities that are recognized under GAAP, and the amounts should be aggregated within each category. FR-67 also requires robust disclosure about liquidity and off-balance-sheet arrangements. Those requirements are discussed in Chapter 6, "Securitizations." Refer to SEC Release Nos. 33-8182, 34-47264, and FR-67 for detailed information about this important rule.

Restrictive Covenants and Violations of Covenants

Restrictive covenants, such as obligations to reduce debts, maintain a minimum amount and ratios of working capital, and limitations on purchases of property, plant, and equipment should be disclosed. In addition, assets pledged or subject to lien should be disclosed. (FAS-5, par. 18)

If, at the balance sheet date, long-term debt is callable by the creditor because a provision of the agreement has been violated but the debt is presented in noncurrent liabilities because it is probable that the debtor will cure the violation within a specified grace period allowed by the creditor that extends beyond the date the financial statements are to be issued, the circumstances about the violation and potential cure should be disclosed in accordance with paragraph 7 of Chapter 3A of ARB-43, as amended by FAS-78.

> ☛ **PRACTICE POINTER:** This disclosure requirement also applies to institutions that prepare unclassified balance sheets, but include long-term liabilities in the disclosure of debt maturities. (FAS-78, par. 5)

If it is probable that a violation of a provision of the agreement will occur and will make the obligation callable within one year of the balance sheet date, the adverse consequences of the probable violation should be disclosed. (EITF 86-30)

Participating Mortgages

The borrower must disclose the aggregate amount of participating mortgages, with separate disclosure of the aggregate participation liabilities and related debt discounts. The borrower must also disclose the terms of the lender's participation rights. (SOP 97-1, par. 17)

Noncash Financing Activities

Disclosure should be made of all noncash financing activities such as conversions of debt to equity or the acquisition of assets by the assumption of directly related debt. (FAS-95, par. 32)

Disclosures Applicable to Certain Financial Institutions

In addition to disclosures required by other GAAP, banks, savings institutions, mortgage companies, credit unions, and finance companies must provide the following disclosures about liabilities in accordance with SOP 01-6.

Terms of Debt

Financial institutions should disclose the principal terms of their debt agreements, including but not limited to:

- The title or nature of the agreement.
- The interest rate, and whether it is fixed or floating.
- The payment terms and maturity date(s).
- Any collateral pledged.
- Conversion or redemption features.
- Whether it is senior or subordinated.
- Restrictive covenants (such as dividend restrictions), if any. (SOP 01-6, par. 14(h))

> ☞ **PRACTICE POINTER:** Companies in other industries generally provide this information as well, in some cases, in accordance with SEC regulations.

Deposit Liabilities

Disclosures about deposit liabilities should include the following:

- The aggregate amount of time deposits (including certificates of deposit) in denominations of $100,000 or more at the balance sheet date.
- Financial instruments that serve as collateral for deposits, that are otherwise not disclosed under FAS-140 (perhaps because they have not been transferred to the depository institution).
- The amount of any overdrafts of demand deposit accounts that have been reclassified as loans at the balance sheet date.
- Information about deposits that are received on terms that are not customary. (SOP 01-6, par 14(e))

Categories of Borrowings

Significant categories of borrowings should be presented as separate line items in the liability section of the balance sheet, or as a single line item with appropriate note disclosure of components. Alternatively, financial institutions may present debt based on its priority (that is, senior or subordinated) with separate disclosure of significant categories of borrowings in the footnotes. (SOP 01-6, par 14(f))

Secured Borrowings

If a transfer of mortgages must be accounted for as a secured borrowing under FAS-140, those liabilities should be classified as debt, separate from other debts of the institution. (SOP 01-6, par. 14(i))

Interest Costs

The following information about interest costs should be disclosed in the financial statements or related notes (FAS-34, par. 21):

- If no interest cost is capitalized during the period, the amount of interest cost incurred and charged to expense during the period.
- If some interest cost is capitalized during the period, the total amount of interest cost incurred for the period and the amount that has been capitalized.

Entities that prepare the Statement of Cash Flows using the indirect method should disclose the amount of interest paid (net of amounts capitalized) during the period. (FAS-95, par. 129)

Available Sources of Credit

Companies should disclose their available (unused) letters of credit. (FAS-5, par. 18)

> ☛ **PRACTICE POINTER:** Most companies interpret this requirement broadly and also disclose loan commitments obtained from financial institutions and available credit lines.

Guarantees

A guarantor must disclose the following information about each guarantee within the scope of FIN-45 (see Exhibit 8-6), or each group of similar guarantees, even if no fees were received, the likelihood of the guarantor's having to make any payments under the guarantee is remote, or both (FIN-45, par. 13):

- The nature of the guarantee, including the approximate term of the guarantee, how the guarantee arose, and the events or circumstances that would require the guarantor to perform under the guarantee.

- The maximum potential amount of future payments (undiscounted) that the guarantor could be required to make under the guarantee. If the terms of the guarantee are unlimited, or if the guarantor is unable to develop an estimate of the maximum potential amount of future payments under its guarantee, the relevant facts and circumstances should be disclosed.

- The current carrying amount of the liability for the guarantor's obligations under the guarantee (including the amount, if any, recognized as a contingent liability under paragraph 8 of FAS-5) regardless of whether the guarantee is freestanding or embedded in another contract.

- The nature and extent of any recourse provisions or collateral that would enable the guarantor to recover from third parties all or a portion of the amounts paid under the guarantee.

OBSERVATION: The disclosures required by FIN-45 are in addition to any disclosures that might be required under other GAAP, including FAS-5 (contingencies), FAS-57 (related parties), FAS-107 (fair value), and FAS-133 (guarantees that are in the form of a derivative). Public companies should also ensure compliance with FR-67 (off-balance-sheet financing).

☛ **PRACTICE POINTER:** FIN-45 also requires certain disclosures about product warranties. Because such arrangements are not financial instruments, they are not included in this book. Refer to paragraph 14 of FIN-45 for additional information.

SEC REGISTRANT ALERT: Regulation S-X, Rule 3-10 requires certain disclosures about guarantors and issuers when a registered security is guaranteed; generally, the issuer and guarantor must file financial statements as registrants. Recently, those requirements were modified for related party guarantors—for example, a parent company guarantee of subsidiary debt, a subsidiary guarantee of parent company debt, and a subsidiary guarantee of another subsidiary's debt.

In addition, if an investor's return is materially dependent upon a third-party credit enhancement (which differs from a guarantee in that the investor is not a direct party to the arrangement), the SEC staff requires disclosure of sufficient information about the third party to permit an investor to determine the ability of the third party to fund the credit enhancement. (SEC Division of Corporation Finance: Frequently Requested Accounting and Financial Reporting Interpretations and Guidance, Section III-E)

Certain Public Company Disclosures in Management's Discussion and Analysis (MD&A)

In December 2003, the SEC issued FR-72, *Interpretation: Commission Guidance Regarding Management's Discussion and Analysis of Financial Condition and Results of Operations.* The Interpretation does not establish new requirements; however, it reminds registrants of existing disclosure requirements related to MD&A in order to elicit more meaningful disclosures in several areas. The Interpretation indicates that a company should disclose historical financing arrangements and their importance to cash flows and should discuss and analyze the following:

- External debt financing
- Use of off-balance-sheet financing arrangements
- Issuance or purchase of derivative instruments linked to its stock
- Use of stock as a form of liquidity
- The potential impact of known or reasonably likely changes in credit ratings or ratings outlook

A company also should discuss the types of financing that are available (or of the types of financing that are desired but unavailable) and the impact of available financing on the company's cash position and liquidity. Furthermore, the company should consider whether discussion and analysis of material covenants related to its outstanding debt, guarantees, or other contingent obligations is required. A company that is or is reasonably likely to be in breach of such covenants must disclose the following information about that breach and analyze the impact on the company (if material):

- The steps that the company is taking to avoid the breach
- The steps that the company intends to take to cure, obtain a waiver of, or otherwise address the breach
- The impact of the breach (including the effects of any cross-default or cross-acceleration provisions) on the company's financial condition or operating performance
- Alternative sources of funding to pay off resulting obligations or replace funding

Further, if covenants limit a company's ability to undertake financing, the company is required to discuss the consequences of the limitation to the company's financial condition and operating performance, the alternate sources of funding and, if material, the consequences of accessing those alternate sources of funding.

This Interpretation was immediately applicable upon issuance (that is, no transition was provided). The entire reporting release is available on the SEC's website at http://www.sec.gov/rules/interp/ 33-8350.htm.

Related Topics

Numerous other disclosures are required about debt instruments, depending on the facts and circumstances. Refer to the following chapters for specific disclosure requirements.

Topic	*Addressed in*
Compensating balances	Chapter 1, "Cash and Cash Equivalents"
Imputed interest	Chapter 7, "Calculating Yields on Debt Investments"
Securities lending arrangements and collateral	Chapter 9, "Securities Lending Arrangements and Other Pledges of Collateral"
Extinguishments and substantive modifications of debt terms	Chapter 11, "Extinguishments of Debt"
Fair value disclosure	Chapter 18, "Fair Value Measurements, Fair Value Disclosures, and Other Financial Instrument Disclosures"

> **SEC REGISTRANT ALERT:** Regulation S-X requires voluminous disclosures about debt instruments; many of them overlap with, but are more detailed than, GAAP requirements. In addition, bank holding companies must disclose information about deposits and interest-bearing liabilities, interest rates and interest differentials, and short-term borrowings in accordance with SEC Industry Guide 3. The SEC is currently revising Guide 3 to reflect subsequent developments in accounting standards. The timetable is uncertain.

AUDIT CONSIDERATIONS

While accounting for debt is generally straightforward, there are several exceptions that involve subjective assessments. In some circumstances, classifying debt as current or noncurrent is based on the intent and ability of management to refinance, and the probability that violations will be cured or subjective acceleration clauses will be exercised. Given the significance of the current versus noncurrent designation, auditors should consider obtaining written representations from management about its intent and ability to refinance debt and about assessments of probability. Auditors should be particularly skeptical of arrangements that have the effect of reclassifying current liabilities to noncurrent.

Following are the key areas of audit risk related to the accounting for debt:

- All debt has been recorded (refer to Chapter 5, "Transfers of Financial Assets," and Chapter 6, "Securitizations," for specific issues related to off-balance-sheet financing).
- The debt has been properly described, valued, and classified, taking into account the nature and effect of any acceleration clauses, noncompliance with covenants, and other relevant factors on the appropriate accounting and disclosure.
- Interest has been properly imputed, if necessary, and premiums and discounts are properly measured and amortized (refer to Chapter 7, "Calculating Yields on Debt Investments").
- Debt retirements and modifications have been properly accounted for (refer to Chapter 11, "Extinguishments of Debt").

(Adapted from the AICPA Audit and Accounting Guide, *Depository and Lending Institutions, Banks and Savings Institutions, Credit Unions, Finance Companies and Mortgage Companies.*)

ILLUSTRATIONS

The following examples are provided for illustrative purposes only and are not intended to represent full and complete disclosures. Comparative information for prior years has been excluded for brevity.

Illustration 8-1: Disclosures of Long-Term Debt—General

Long-term debt consists of the following at December 31, 20X1:

Revolving credit facility, unsecured, weighted-average interest of 7.25%	$50
Commercial paper, weighted-average interest of 6.9%	40
5.75% Senior debentures, due 20Y8	110
7.10% Senior debenture, due 20X6	100
6.4% Senior Notes, due 20X9	85
6.25% Senior Notes, due 20Y1	75
Pollution control and industrial revenue bonds, 4.2% to 7.5%, due 20X3-20Z8	60
Total long-term debt	520
Less: current maturities	(15)
Long-term debt	$505

In October 20X0, the company entered into a five-year revolving credit agreement with a group of banks in an amount not to exceed $1,000. Borrowings under the credit agreement bear interest at prime plus an amount based on the financial condition of the company. The credit agreement contains customary financial covenants and restrictions on dividends and capital expenditures. At December 31, 20X1, the company was in compliance with all covenants.

At December 31, 20X1, all commercial paper outstanding was reported as long-term reflecting the company's intent and ability to refinance these borrowings on a long-term basis through the revolving credit facility.

Illustration 8-2: Disclosures of Future Payments of Long-Term Debt [FAS-47]

Aggregate maturities of long-term debt for each of the years subsequent to December 31, 20X1, are as follows:

20X2	$100
20X3	20
20X4	240
20X5	70
20X6	110
Thereafter	375
	$915

Illustration 8-3: Classification of a Short-Term Obligation Expected to Be Refinanced [FAS-6]

At December 31, 20X5, Ryan & Co. has a short-term obligation of $7,000,000 representing the portion of its 7% long-term debt maturing in February 20X6. Ryan & Co. intends to refinance the current maturity of long-term debt. In December 20X5, Ryan & Co. negotiates a financing agreement with a major bank for a maximum borrowing of $7,000,000 at any time through December 20X7 with the following terms:

- Borrowings are available at Ryan & Co.'s request for any purpose it deems appropriate.
- Amounts borrowed will be due in four years and the interest rate will be set at LIBOR.
- The agreement is cancelable by the lender only if Ryan & Co.:
  - Fails to maintain its current consolidated net worth and leverage ratio
  - Violates restrictions imposed by the bank on (1) the early retirement of other debt, (2) incurring additional debt, and (3) payment of common dividends.

Assume that the lender is expected to be capable of honoring the agreement, that there is no evidence of a violation of any provision, and that the terms of borrowings available under the agreement are readily determinable.

Ryan & Co.'s intention to refinance meets the conditions of FAS-6. Therefore, the current maturity of long-term debt would be excluded from current liabilities.

The liability section of Ryan & Co.'s balance sheet at December 31, 20X5, and the related footnote disclosures are presented below. Because the balance sheet is issued subsequent to the February 20X6 maturity of the long-term debt, the footnote describes the refinancing of that obligation.

	December 31, 20X5
Current Liabilities:	
Accounts payable and accruals	$10,000,000
Total Current Liabilities	$10,000,000
Long-Term Debt:	
7% debt due February 20X6 (Note 1)	7,000,000*
Other long-term debt	$25,000,000
Total Long-Term Debt	32,000,000
Total Liabilities	$42,000,000

---

* This debt may also be shown in a caption separate from both current liabilities and long-term debt, such as "Interim Debt," "Short-Term Debt Expected to Be Refinanced," or "Intermediate Debt."

Note 1—The Company has entered into a financing agreement with a commercial bank that permits the Company to borrow at any time through 20X7 up to $7,000,000 at the bank's prime rate of interest. The Company must pay an annual commitment fee of 1% of the unused portion of the commitment. Borrowings under the financing agreement mature four years after the date of the loan. Among other things, the agreement requires the company to maintain its current net worth and imposes certain limitations on additional borrowings, early retirement of other debts and the payment of common dividends during the term of the refinancing. In February 20X6, the Company borrowed $7,000,000 at 6.5% and liquidated the 7% long-term debt.

Illustration 8-4: Modification of Revolving Credit Arrangement [Adapted from EITF 98-14, Exhibit A]

Gilmore Corporation has a revolving credit arrangement with the Bank of Utica that has three years remaining and a commitment amount of $10,000,000. The borrowing capacity under this agreement is $30 million:

Remaining term (3 years) x Commitment amount
($10 million) = 30 million

Gilmore renegotiates the terms of its agreement with the Bank of Utica. Assume the following changes are made under four independent scenarios:

Scenario 1: The commitment amount is increased to $15 million, the term of the new arrangement remains at three years (new borrowing capacity is $45 million)

Scenario 2: The commitment amount is decreased to $2 million, the term of the new arrangement is 5.5 years (new borrowing capacity is $11 million)

Scenario 3: The original revolver is replaced with a three-year, $7.5 million term loan, with principal due at the end of three years (new borrowing capacity is $22.5 million)

Scenario 4: The original revolver is replaced with a three-year, $10 million term loan, with principal due at the end of three years (new borrowing capacity is $30 million).

All of the scenarios involve the following fees and costs:

- $150,000 of unamortized costs relating to the original arrangement remain on Gilmore's balance sheet;
- Gilmore pays a fee of $100,000 to the creditor for the current modification; and
- Gilmore incurs legal fees and other direct costs to third parties of $200,000 for the current modification.

Gilmore Corporation would account for the unamortized deferred costs relating to the old revolver and the fees and third-party costs incurred to establish the new revolver as follows under the four scenarios:

	Borrowing Capacity (in millions)		Unamortized Deferred Costs	Fees And Third Party Costs Incurred
	Old	New		
1	$30	$45	$150,000 is amortized over 3 years	$300,000 is deferred and amortized over 3 years
2	$30	$11	63% of the unamortized costs ($94,500) are written off; the remaining costs ($55,500) are amortized over 5.5 years	$300,000 is deferred and amortized over 5.5 years
3	$30	$22.5	25% of the unamortized costs ($37,500) are written off; the remaining costs ($112,500) are amortized over 3 years	$300,000 is deferred and amortized over 3 years
4	$30	$30	$150,000 is amortized over 3 years	$300,000 is deferred and amortized over 3 years

Illustration 8-5: Disclosure of Callable Long-Term Debt [Chapter 3A of ARB-43]

... Since June 30, 20X1, the Company has not complied with several covenants of its credit agreement. These covenant violations have not been cured or waived, and the lender has the right to demand payment of outstanding borrowings. Accordingly, amounts payable under the credit agreement as of December 31, 20X1, are classified as subject to acceleration in current liabilities in the accompanying financial statements. If the violations are not waived or the compliance covenants are not revised, the Company may be required to liquidate stores or inventories in order to pay the debt or to take other action.

Illustration 8-6 : Disclosure of Long-Term Debt Classified as Current Because of Violations That Existed at the Balance Sheet Date Absent a Waiver [EITF 86-30]

... The credit agreement, including certain of the financial and other covenants, has been amended at various times since their originations and waivers of compliance with certain financial covenants have been granted by the lender. At June 30, 20X0, absent the waivers obtained from the lenders, the Company would not have been in compliance with various financial covenants contained in the credit agreement. Accordingly, amounts due under the agreement have been classified as current in the fiscal 20X0 financial statements.

Illustration 8-7: Disclosure of a Long-Term Debt Agreement with a Lock-Box Arrangement [EITF 95-22]

The Company is required to maintain a lock-box arrangement with the bank whereby remittances from the Company's customers are used to reduce the outstanding revolver balance of $9,000,000. Accordingly, a portion of the revolver balance ($6,500,000) has been classified as current at December 31, 20X0, although such balance is not due until May 1, 20X2.

Illustration 8-8: Disclosure of Interest Elements of Debt [FAS-34 and FAS-95]

Interest incurred, capitalized, expensed and paid during the year ending December 31, 20X0, were:

Interest costs	$9,567,000
Interest capitalized	(3,153,000)
Interest expensed	$6,414,000
Interest paid	$7,664,000

Illustration 8-9: Recording a Guarantee as Part of a Transfer of Assets

Lewis Enterprises enters into a sale of loans with a carrying amount of $1,000 to Royal Finance Company for $1,100, but agrees to indemnify Royal for any defaults on those loans that occur within the first year. Assume the loans are of a high credit quality, and the likelihood of default is low. Royal Finance does not pay an explicit fee for the indemnification. Assuming that the transfer qualifies as a sale under FAS-140, Lewis would record the following journal entries:

Cash	$1,100	
Loans		$ 1,000
Guarantee liability		60
Gain on sale of loans		40

To record the sale of loans, and the establishment of a guarantee liability. Refer to Chapter 5, "Transfers of Financial Assets," for additional information about FAS-140.

A quoted market price does not exist for this type of guarantee. Lewis estimates the fair value of the guarantee based on the present value of the amount of fees that would currently be charged to guarantee loans of a similar credit quality for a similar period of time. Lewis has a documented accounting policy to recognize deferred revenue on guarantee liabilities ratably over the course of the guarantee period, unless it becomes likely that a payment will be required. If it becomes probable that a transferred loan will default, and the amount of the loss is estimable, Lewis would record an incremental liability for the amount of the likely payment under FAS-5. Assuming none of the loans defaults, Lewis would recognize the following entry, shown in total for simplicity, over the course of the ensuing year:

Guarantee liability	$60	
Other income		$60

To record the deferred revenue relating to the guarantee in earnings.

CHAPTER 9
SECURITIES LENDING
ARRANGEMENTS AND OTHER
PLEDGES OF COLLATERAL

CONTENTS

Overview	9.02
Background	9.03
Terminology—Types of Securities Lending Transactions	9.04
Repurchase Agreement (Repo)	9.04
Dollar Rolls	9.04
Federal Funds Purchased and Sold	9.05
Securities Lending Agreements	9.05
Sell-Buybacks	9.05
Terminology for Transaction Elements	9.05
Exhibit 9-1: *Accounting Terminology in Secured Borrowings*	9.06
Accounting for Collateral	9.06
Pledges of Collateral	9.06
Exhibit 9-2: *Distinguishing Collateral from Proceeds in a Secured Borrowing*	9.07
Cash Collateral	9.07
Noncash Collateral	9.08
Exhibit 9-3: *Accounting for Pledges of Noncash Collateral*	9.09
Interaction with FAS-115	9.10
Sales of Collateral Received (Short Sales)	9.10
Safekeeping and Custody Arrangements	9.10
Accounting for Securities Lending Arrangements	9.10
Applying the FAS-140 Sale Criteria	9.10
Transferee's Right to Pledge or Exchange	9.11
Effect of Agreement to Repurchase or Redeem Transferred Assets	9.11
Exhibit 9-4: *Accounting Treatment for Securities Lending Transactions*	9.12

Proceeds Other than Beneficial Interests in the
Transferred Assets 9.16

Securities Lending Transactions Accounted for as Sales 9.17

Securities Lending Transactions Accounted for as
Secured Borrowings 9.18

Securities Lending Involving Restricted-Use or
No Collateral 9.19

Deferred Tax Considerations 9.20

Interplay with FAS-115 9.20

Cash Flow Statement Presentation 9.20

Sales and Purchases 9.20

Secured Borrowings 9.21

Disclosure Requirements 9.21

Pledges of Financial Assets as Collateral 9.21

Financial Assets Otherwise Serving as Collateral 9.21

Securities Lending Transactions 9.22

Regulatory Considerations 9.22

Audit Considerations 9.22

Illustrations 9.23

Illustration 9-1: *Accounting for a Sell-Buyback as a Sale* 9.23

Illustration 9-2: *Accounting for a Securities Lending
Transaction Treated as a Secured Borrowing* 9.25

Illustration 9-3: *Securities Lending Transaction Involving
Securities Collateral* 9.27

OVERVIEW

Accounting for collateral in a transaction accounted for as a secured borrowing depends primarily on the extent of the secured party's rights to use the asset. A secured party generally should not record collateral received in a lending transaction as its own asset unless it is cash. However, if the borrower defaults under the terms of the agreement and is no longer entitled to retrieve it, the lender should record the collateral as its own asset. A borrower should continue to report an asset it pledges as collateral but, if the secured party has the right to freely use the collateral, the assets should be reclassified into a category that indicates their restricted status. Borrowers and lenders must disclose certain information about assets pledged and received as collateral.

Securities lending arrangements involve temporary exchanges of securities for cash, other securities, or guarantees with an obligation to return the same (or very similar) securities at a future date. Some securities lending transactions are driven by the need for cash, and the securities function as collateral for the lender. Some securities lending transactions are driven by the need for a specific security, and the cash or other securities exchanged function as collateral. Regardless of the participants' motivation, the economics of these arrangements are similar.

Accounting for securities lending arrangements depends on whether the transferor has surrendered control over the assets, using the same criteria discussed in Chapter 5, "Transfers of Financial Assets." At first glance, the transferor in most securities lending transactions appears to maintain effective control because he has committed to repurchase the security. However, several additional conditions must be evaluated to conclude definitively on the matter.

When a securities lending transaction meets all the conditions for sale accounting, the transferor derecognizes the transferred asset, recognizes the proceeds as its own asset, and records a gain or loss. The transferee records the purchase of the transferred asset at fair value. Accounting for the forward purchase contract depends on whether the contract meets the definition of a derivative. When a securities lending transaction must be accounted for as a secured borrowing, the proceeds are reported as a payable by the transferor and a receivable by the transferee. The difference between the selling price and the repurchase price is recognized as interest expense and interest income by the transferor and transferee, respectively. The security being loaned is considered a pledge of collateral.

Receivables and payables from securities lending arrangements should not be netted (offset) in the balance sheet unless the legal right of setoff exists. However, payables and receivables that represent repurchase agreements and reverse repurchase agreements may be offset if several specific conditions are met.

BACKGROUND

FAS-140 addresses the accounting for transfers of collateral in transactions accounted for as secured borrowings (paragraph 15). FAS-140 provides guidance on whether securities lending arrangements, including repurchase agreements, dollar rolls, and security sell/buy-back transactions, should be accounted for as secured borrowings or sales. Thus, the topics are interrelated when a securities lending arrangement is accounted for as a secured borrowing. The sale criteria in paragraph 9 of FAS-140, which were discussed in Chapter 5, "Transfers of Financial Assets," also apply to securities lending transactions. (This chapter assumes that the transferee in a securities lending transaction is an operating entity, *not* a qualifying special-purpose entity.) Because the transfer of securities is accompanied by an agreement to repurchase them, the criteria in paragraphs 47–49 of FAS-140 also apply.

The Implementation Guide on FAS-140 and a few EITF Issues address several aspects of accounting for collateral and securities lending transactions. FIN-41 provides an exception to the general off-setting rules for payables and receivables from repurchase agreements and reverse repurchase agreements that meet several specific criteria.

> ☛ **PRACTICE POINTER:** FAS-140 modified the collateral provisions of FAS-125. Overall, FAS-140 restored the collateral accounting model that existed prior to FAS-125 except that, now, some asset transfers that market participants consider "collateral" are considered "proceeds" for accounting purposes and must be recognized in the balance sheet.

Terminology—Types of Securities Lending Transactions

Repurchase Agreement (Repo)

An agreement whereby one party agrees to sell securities to another for cash, with a simultaneous agreement to repurchase the same or equivalent securities at a specific price at a later date. Many repurchase agreements are for short terms, often overnight. Some repurchase agreements do not have explicit settlement dates—that is, they remain outstanding until one of the parties terminates the arrangement (called "till further notice" or TFN). The repurchase price is generally equal to the original selling price plus interest, typically at current money market yields. Economically, the "seller" is borrowing cash. A reverse repurchase agreement ("reverse repo" or "resale") is the flipside of a repo—a reverse repo is the purchase of a security for cash, with a simultaneous agreement to resell the same or equivalent securities at a later date for a specified price. Economically, the "purchaser" is lending cash. There are several kinds of custodial arrangements relating to repo transactions, including tri-party repos, deliver-out repos, and hold-in-custody repos. These custody arrangements can be relevant in determining whether the transferor has surrendered control of the securities.

Dollar Rolls

Repurchase and reverse repurchase agreements that involve similar, but not the same, securities. Dollar rolls typically involve mortgage-backed securities.

> ☛ **PRACTICE POINTER:** Banks, broker-dealers, insurance companies, and other financial institutions use the term "repo" to refer to sales/repurchases and the term "reverse repo" to refer to purchases/resales. Investment companies (e.g., mutual funds) use the same terminology to refer to the opposite transactions.

Federal Funds Purchased and Sold

Funds that commercial banks borrow (purchase) or deposit (sell) from Federal Reserve Banks for a term of one day (although the transactions may be rolled over). In a collateralized transaction, the purchaser of federal funds places U.S. Treasury securities in an account for the seller until the funds are repaid. Collateralized federal funds transactions are essentially a specific form of repurchase (resale) agreements.

Securities Lending Agreements

A loan of specific securities to a party who agrees to return a like quantity of the same security. The securities borrower typically obtains full title to the securities so that they can be delivered to another party, such as to cover a short sale or a customer's failure to deliver securities sold. The lender typically receives collateral, including cash, other securities, or a bank letter of credit, to secure the return of their securities. The lender receives a fee that is negotiated at the time of the transaction, often called a rebate. The length of the transaction can be overnight, open (cancelable on demand), or for a specified term. Typically, each security loan is initially collateralized at a predetermined margin that exceeds the value of the securities loaned; the collateral is adjusted as the market value of the security rises and falls.

Sell-Buybacks

Two transactions entered into at the same time whereby (1) a security is sold and (2) the same security is purchased for settlement at a future date. The forward price is derived using an interest rate such as the repo rate. Historically, these transactions were documented separately and not linked legally. Increasingly, however, the contracts are executed under fully documented, legally enforceable agreements.

> ☞ **PRACTICE POINTER:** These descriptions are based on a July 1999 report of the Technical Committee of the International Organization of Securities Commissions (IOSCO), Committee on Payment and Settlement Systems, called, "Securities Lending Transactions: Market Development and Implications." The report provides an overview of securities lending markets, typical transaction terms and a robust discussion of legal and regulatory issues.

Terminology for Transaction Elements

Sometimes it is difficult to identify for accounting purposes which element of a secured borrowing is collateral and which element is proceeds (e.g., in certain securities lending transactions). The confusion is caused partly by differences between the terminology used by market participants and FAS-140. It is helpful to remember that a secured borrowing has only *one* pledge of collateral—the other upfront flow represents the exchange of proceeds from the lender to the borrower.

Exhibit 9-1 summarizes the accounting terminology for three common transactions, assuming they are accounted for as secured borrowings.

EXHIBIT 9-1
ACCOUNTING TERMINOLOGY IN SECURED BORROWINGS*

1. Repurchase agreement (or a bank loan secured by marketable securities)

	Bank	Broker/dealer (initiator)
Cash (proceeds)	Lender	Borrower
Security posted as collateral	Transferee (secured party)	Transferor

2. Securities Lending (e.g., equity securities for cash "collateral")

	Bank	Broker/dealer (initiator)
Cash (proceeds)	Borrower	Lender
Security lent (considered collateral)	Transferor	Transferee (secured party)

3. Borrow versus Pledge Securities Lending (e.g., equity securities for Treasury bills as "collateral")

	Bank	Broker/dealer (initiator)
T-bills (proceeds)	Borrower	Lender
Security lent (considered collateral)	Transferor	Transferee (secured party)

* If, instead, the transactions were accounted for as sales, the transferor would be the seller of the security (lent) and the transferee would be the purchaser of the security (lent).

ACCOUNTING FOR COLLATERAL

Pledges of Collateral

A borrower may grant a security interest in certain assets to a lender (the secured party) to serve as collateral for its obligation under a borrowing, or under other kinds of contracts that could become obligations, such as interest rate swaps. When the collateral is transferred to the secured party, the arrangement is commonly referred to as a pledge. Secured parties sometimes are permitted to sell or repledge collateral held under a pledge.

FAS-140, paragraph 15, addresses the accounting for pledges of financial assets as collateral in all transactions that are accounted for as secured borrowings, including standard bank loans, corporate debt, and many securities lending transactions. Whether a securities lending transaction should be accounted for as a secured borrowing is addressed later in this chapter.

> **OBSERVATION:**   Even though paragraph 15 does not restrict its scope to pledges of financial assets, paragraph 114 of FAS-140 Q&A clarifies that was the FASB's intent.

Generally, when a specific security is being loaned, and the transaction is accounted for as a secured borrowing, *it* represents the collateral in the transaction for accounting purposes, and paragraph 15 applies. The cash or "fungible" securities provided by the securities borrower represents the proceeds in the transaction for accounting purposes—paragraph 15 does not apply to that leg of the transaction.

Exhibit 9-2 illustrates the distinction between collateral and proceeds in a securities lending transaction that is accounted for as a secured borrowing.

EXHIBIT 9-2
DISTINGUISHING COLLATERAL FROM PROCEEDS IN A SECURED BORROWING

Cash Collateral

Cash "collateral" is not subject to paragraph 15 of FAS-140. Rather, all cash collateral should be recorded as an asset by the party receiving it, together with a liability for the obligation to return it to the payer.

(FAS-140, par. 241) The payer of cash collateral should derecognize the cash and record a receivable from the borrower. (FAS-140, fn. 4)

> **OBSERVATION:** Technically, cash "collateral" received is considered proceeds of either a sale or a borrowing, not collateral *per se*.

Noncash Collateral

The accounting for pledges of other financial assets as collateral under FAS-140, paragraph 15, depends on whether the secured party has the right to sell or repledge the collateral and on whether the debtor has defaulted.

- If the secured party (transferee) has the right by contract or custom to sell or repledge the collateral, then the debtor (transferor) should reclassify that asset and report it separately in its balance sheet (for example, as a security pledged to creditors) from other assets not so encumbered.

- If the secured party (transferee) sells collateral pledged to it, it should recognize the proceeds from the sale and its obligation to return the collateral. The sale of the collateral is a transfer subject to FAS-140.

- The debtor (transferor) should continue to carry the collateral as its asset, and the secured party (transferee) should not recognize the pledged asset, unless the debtor defaults under the contract.

- If the debtor (transferor) defaults under the terms of the secured contract and is no longer entitled to redeem the pledged asset, it should derecognize the pledged asset. The secured party (transferee) should recognize the collateral as its asset, initially measured at fair value or, if it has already sold the collateral, derecognize its obligation to return the collateral.

> ☞ **PRACTICE POINTER:** When an asset pledged as collateral is required to be reclassified as an encumbered asset, the transferor should continue to follow the same measurement principles as before the transfer. For example, securities reclassified from the available-for-sale category to securities pledged to creditors should continue to be measured at fair value, with changes in fair value reported in other comprehensive income, while debt securities reclassified from the held-to-maturity category to securities pledged to creditors should continue to be measured at amortized cost. (FAS-140 Q&A, par. 117)

> **REGULATORY ALERT:** Under statutory accounting principles, insurance companies need only *disclose* assets that the secured party has the right to sell or pledge. Under GAAP, they must be reclassified in the balance sheet. (SSAP No. 33)

> **OBSERVATION:** Under FAS-15 (troubled debt restructurings) and FAS-114 (loan impairment), a creditor does not recognize the debtor's assets in a repossession or in-substance foreclosure until it receives physical possession of them. However, in some cases, a loss is recognized at an earlier point based on the fair value of the collateral (adjusted for any costs to sell, if applicable). Refer to Chapter 3, "Loans and the Allowance for Credit Losses," for more information.

EXHIBIT 9-3
ACCOUNTING FOR PLEDGES OF NONCASH COLLATERAL*

		Transferor of Collateral/ Borrower of Cash	Secured Party/ Lender of Cash
Does the recipient have the right to sell or repledge the noncash collateral?	→ No →	Continue to report asset as its own, no reclass required	No entry
↓ Yes		Reclassify the asset to a separate category for encumbered assets	No entry
Has the recipient sold or pledged the collateral?	→ Yes →	No entry	Recognize proceeds and obligation to return collateral
↓ No		No entry	No entry
Has the debtor defaulted and can no longer redeem pledged asset?	→ Yes →	Remove asset from balance sheet	Recognize asset as its own (or if the asset has been sold, derecognize the obligation to return collateral)

↓ No

Continue to report as above.

---

* Note: For accounting purposes, cash collateral is considered "proceeds" under FAS-140, not a pledge of collateral. See Exhibit 9-2.

Interaction with FAS-115

A debt security classified as held-to-maturity under FAS-115 may be pledged as collateral provided that the transaction is not accounted for as a sale and the entity intends and expects to be able to satisfy the obligation and recover access to its collateral. (FAS-115 Q&A, par. 16)

A debt security or marketable equity security received by a transferor as proceeds in a securities lending transaction should be accounted for under FAS-115. Given the nature of a securities lending transaction, it seems inconsistent with FAS-115 to classify debt securities received as proceeds as held-to-maturity.

Sales of Collateral Received (Short Sales)

A bank or other financial institution that, as transferee, sells transferred collateral should subsequently measure that liability like a short sale. (FAS-140 Q&A, par. 118) SOP 01-6 states that obligations incurred in short sales should be reported as liabilities and carried at fair value in the statement of position. Changes in fair value are recognized in earnings currently and in the same caption as gains and losses on securities. Interest on short positions should be accrued periodically and reported as interest expense. (SOP 01-6, par. 10(b))

Safekeeping and Custody Arrangements

Financial assets transferred to another party simply for safekeeping or custody continue to be carried as assets by the transferor. The custodian does not control the assets but must follow the transferor's instructions. The only consideration exchanged in those transfers is, perhaps, payment of a fee by the transferor to the custodian for the custodial services. (FAS-140, par. 261)

ACCOUNTING FOR SECURITIES LENDING ARRANGEMENTS

Applying the FAS-140 Sale Criteria

Securities lending transactions involve transfers of financial assets and therefore they are subject to FAS-140. To be considered a sale, a securities lending transaction must meet all of the following conditions, (discussed in detail in Chapter 5, "Transfers of Financial Assets"):

- The transferred assets have been isolated from the transferor. (par. 9(a))

- The transferee has the right to pledge or exchange the assets it receives, without a constraint that benefits the transferor. (par. 9(b))

- The transferor does not maintain effective control over the transferred assets through either (1) an agreement that both entitles and obligates the transferor to repurchase or redeem them before their maturity or (2) the ability to unilaterally cause the holder to return specific assets, other than through a cleanup call. (par. 9(c))

- The transferor must receive proceeds other than a beneficial interest in the transferred assets that it is permitted by contract or custom to sell or repledge. (par. 9 and fn. 22)

Securities lending transactions include an agreement that both entitles and obligates the transferor to repurchase or redeem them before their maturity (paragraph 9(c)(1)). Therefore, they must be analyzed further under paragraphs 47–49 of FAS-140. Exhibit 9-4 provides a decision tree for applying FAS-140 to securities lending transactions.

> **OBSERVATION:** The accounting for a single transaction should be symmetrical between the transferor and the transferee. That is, after evaluating the facts and circumstances, both parties should reach the same conclusion as to whether the transaction must be accounted for as a secured borrowing or as a sale/purchase of the transferred asset.

Transferee's Right to Pledge or Exchange

If a transferor has transferred securities to an independent third-party custodian, or to a transferee, under conditions that preclude the transferee from selling or repledging the assets during the term of the repurchase agreement (as in most tri-party repurchase agreements), the transferor has not surrendered control over those assets. Such transfers should be accounted for as secured borrowings. (FAS-140, par. 101)

Effect of Agreement to Repurchase or Redeem Transferred Assets

When an entity transfers a security (or other financial asset) subject to an agreement that both entitles and obligates the transferor to repurchase or redeem transferred assets from the transferee, the transfer is to be accounted for as a secured borrowing if all of the following conditions are met:

- The assets to be repurchased or redeemed are the same or *substantially the same* as those transferred.

EXHIBIT 9-4
ACCOUNTING TREATMENT FOR SECURITIES LENDING TRANSACTIONS

Does the transfer- → No → Off-balance-sheet
or receive cash or transaction
securities that it is
free to sell or
repledge?

↓ Yes

Is the transferred → No → Secured borrowing
security isolated?
[par. 9(a)]

↓ Yes

Does transferee → No → Secured borrowing
have ability to
pledge or ex-
change transfer-
red security?
[par. 9(b)]

↓ Yes

Does transferor → Yes → Did transferor enter → Yes → Secured
have right and into agreements borrowing
obligation to re- concurrently, main-
purchase trans- tains adequate
ferred security? collateral, **and**
[par. 9(c)(1)] commit to repurchase before
maturity? [pars. 47–49]

                      ↓

↓ No   No
                      ↓

Does transferor → Yes → Is transferred se- → No → Secured
have ability to curity readily borrowing
unilaterally cause obtainable?
the holder to [FAS-140
return specific Q&A, par. 49]
assets [par. 9(c)(2)]

↓ No   ↓
                      Yes

Sale by transferor, purchase by transferee

- The transferee provides sufficient collateral so that the transferor is able to repurchase or redeem the transferred assets on substantially the agreed terms, even in the event of default by the transferee.
- The agreement is to repurchase or redeem them before maturity, at a fixed or determinable price.
- The agreement is entered into concurrently with the transfer. (FAS-140, par. 47)

Each of these conditions is described in detail below.

Substantially the same   To be substantially the same, the asset that was transferred and the asset that is to be repurchased or redeemed must have *all* of the following characteristics:

- The same primary obligor (except for debt guaranteed by a sovereign government, central bank, government-sponsored enterprise or agency thereof, in which case the guarantor and the terms of the guarantee must be the same)
- Identical form and type so as to provide the same risks and rights
- The same maturity (or in the case of mortgage-backed pass-through and pay-through securities, similar remaining weighted-average maturities that result in approximately the same market yield)
- Identical contractual interest rates
- Similar assets as collateral
- The same aggregate unpaid principal amount or principal amounts within accepted "good delivery" standards for the type of security involved (FAS-140, par. 48)

> **OBSERVATION:**   This definition is consistent with the definition of substantially the same in SOP 90-3.

> ☞ **PRACTICE POINTER:**   The Bond Market Association publication, *Uniform Practices for the Clearance and Settlement of Mortgage-Backed Securities and Other Related Securities*, includes parameters for what is considered acceptable delivery.

Dollar rolls   The criterion that is substantially the same is particularly important in dollar-roll transactions. For transfers of *existing* securities under a dollar-roll repurchase agreement, the transferee must be committed to return substantially the same securities to the transferor to satisfy the condition in paragraphs 47(a) and 48. The transferor is only required to obtain a commitment from the transferee to return substantially the same securities and is not required to determine that the transferee already holds the securities that it has committed to return. (FAS-140 Q&A, par. 44)

The following exchanges would *not* meet the substantially the same criterion (SOP 90-3, fns. 5–7):

- The exchange of pools of single-family loans, because the mortgages making up the pool do not have the same primary obligor.

- Government National Mortgage Association (GNMA) I securities for GNMA II securities; loans to foreign debtors that are otherwise the same except for different U.S. foreign tax credit benefits (because such differences in the tax receipts associated with the loans result in instruments that vary "in form and type"); commercial paper for redeemable preferred stock.

- The exchange of a fast-pay GNMA certificate (that is, a certificate with underlying mortgage loans that have a high prepayment record) for a slow-pay GNMA certificate, because differences in the expected remaining lives of the certificates result in different market yields.

> ☞ **PRACTICE POINTER:** Dollar-roll repurchase agreements for which the underlying securities being sold do not yet exist or are to be announced (e.g., TBA GNMA rolls and forward commitment dollar rolls) are outside the scope of FAS-140 because those transactions do not arise in connection with a transfer of *recognized* financial assets. FAS-133 applies if the forward commitment meets the definition of a derivative. Otherwise, EITF Issue 84-20 requires that forward commitment dollar rolls be marked to market. (FAS-140 Q&A, par. 42)

Sufficient collateral To satisfy the "sufficient collateral" requirement, the arrangement must provide—at all times during the contract term—that the collateral would be sufficient to fund substantially all of the cost of purchasing replacement assets from others in the event that the fair value of the collateral or transferred assets changes, even if the probability of ever holding inadequate collateral appears remote. (FAS-140, par. 49 and EITF D-65)

- A mechanism to ensure that adequate collateral is maintained must exist even in transactions that are substantially overcollateralized (for example, "deep discount" and "haircut" transactions). (FAS-140 Q&A, par. 45)
- An arrangement that provides as much as 98 percent collateralization (for entities agreeing to repurchase) or as little as 102

percent overcollateralization (for securities lenders), with margin calls as the market price of the security changes and powers to use that collateral quickly in the event of default, clearly meets that guideline. (FAS-140, par. 218)

The sufficient collateral requirement may be met through a margining provision, or any other arrangement that has the same effect. For example, a contractual provision that a repurchase agreement is immediately terminated should the value of the collateral become insufficient to fund substantially all of the cost of purchasing replacement assets would satisfy the requirement in FAS-140, paragraph 49. (FAS-140 Q&A, par. 45)

> ☛ **PRACTICE POINTER:** The sufficient collateral requirement applies regardless of the requirements or customs in any particular market. For example, in markets where it is not customary to provide or maintain collateral in connection with securities lending transactions, the sufficient collateral requirement would not be met and sale accounting would not be precluded. (FAS-140 Q&A, par. 48)

Repurchase before maturity A transferor's agreement to repurchase a transferred asset would not be considered a repurchase or redemption before maturity if, because of the timing of the redemption, the transferor would be unable to sell the asset again before its maturity (that is, the period until maturity is so short that the typical settlement is a net cash payment). (FAS-140 Q&A, par. 48)

Repurchase agreements evaluated as call options If all of the requirements of FAS-140, paragraphs 47–49 are not met, the repurchase agreement must be analyzed under the call option provisions of FAS-140, paragraphs 9(c)(2) and 50–54. Only in that situation, the effect of the repurchase agreement depends on whether the assets subject to the repurchase agreement are readily obtainable. If assets are readily obtainable, the repurchase agreement does not preclude sale accounting. If assets are not readily obtainable, the repurchase agreement precludes sale accounting. (FAS-140 Q&A, par. 49)

> ☛ **PRACTICE POINTER:** In the unlikely event that the transferee in a securities lending arrangement involved a qualifying special-purpose entity, the repurchase agreement would be evaluated like an attached call under paragraph 51 of FAS-140.

> **OBSERVATION:** The actual wording in FAS-140, paragraph 47, suggests that if one of the conditions therein is not met, the transaction must be accounted for as a sale. (It says, "... the transfer is to be accounted for as a secured borrowing... if and only if all of the following conditions are met. ...") Furthermore, paragraph 98 indicates that repos to maturity and repos with insufficient

collateral should be accounted for as sales. However, in the FAS-140 Q&A, paragraph 49, the FASB staff indicates that if one of the criteria in paragraphs 47–49 is not met, the forward contract should be evaluated as a call option under paragraph 9(c)(2). If the security is not readily obtainable, sale accounting would be precluded.

OBSERVATION: These conditions can be manipulated if a specific accounting result is desired. For example, an entity can essentially elect sale accounting for securities lending arrangements involving marketable securities by not maintaining sufficient collateral (assuming the other sale criteria are met). When dealing with very creditworthy counterparties, the business effect may be negligible, but the financial reporting would be significantly different. Keep in mind that both parties' accounting is affected by arrangements of this nature.

Proceeds Other than Beneficial Interests in the Transferred Assets

The transferor of securities being "loaned" accounts for cash received in the same way whether the transfer is accounted for as a sale or a secured borrowing. Cash received should be reported as the transferor's asset—along with any investments made with that cash, even if made by agents or in pools with other securities lenders—along with the obligation to return the cash. (FAS-140, par. 94)

If securities that may be sold or repledged are received, the transferor of the securities being "loaned" accounts for those securities in the same way as it would account for cash received. (FAS-140, par. 94)

Borrow-versus-pledge (security-for-security) transactions Sometimes the borrower of a desired security provides a different security as "collateral" in the transaction. (For ease of reference, the "collateral" is identified as the "fungible" security as opposed to the "desired" security). Applying FAS-140 to these transactions is confusing, because the terminology used by market participants is different from the accounting terminology. For example:

- *Market terminology* Bank lends broker-dealer a desired security to cover a short position, and receives fungible securities such as Treasury bills as "collateral." Broker-dealer is considered the securities borrower.

- *FAS-140 terminology* Bank is the transferor of the desired security; if accounted for as a secured borrowing, desired security is collateral and the fungible securities (T-bills) are proceeds. Broker-dealer is the transferee of desired securities and the lender of Treasury bills.

FAS-140, paragraph 94, requires that the lender of the desired security (the transferor) record the security received as economic collateral as "proceeds" in a borrowing (assuming that the transferor may sell or repledge the security), along with the obligation to return it. The borrower of the desired security would not record that security on its balance sheet. However, if it sells or pledges those securities, it would record the proceeds from that transaction and an obligation to return the securities.

Illustration 9-3 provides an example of a borrow-versus-pledge transaction.

> **OBSERVATION:** The security lender's (transferor's) balance sheet is grossed-up from security-for-security transactions when the transferor has the right to sell or repledge the fungible securities received as "collateral" (proceeds for accounting purposes). Securities lenders should consider this punitive effect relative to other forms of "collateral," such as letters of credit and securities that are restricted from use.

Securities Lending Transactions Accounted for as Sales

If all of the sale criteria are met and consideration other than beneficial interests in the transferred assets is received, the transaction should be accounted for as follows, regardless of the market terminology for a transaction:

- *By the transferor*   As a sale of securities for proceeds consisting of cash (or securities that the holder is permitted by contract or custom to sell or repledge) and a forward repurchase commitment. The seller should remove the transferred securities from its balance sheet and record any gain or loss on the transaction.
- *By the transferee*   As a purchase of securities in exchange for cash (or securities that the holder is permitted by contract or custom to sell or repledge) and a forward resale commitment. The purchaser should record the transferred securities on its balance sheet, initially at fair value, and record the payment for the purchased assets (including the value of the forward resale commitment). (FAS-140, par. 92)

> ☞ **PRACTICE POINTER:** If the forward commitment meets the definition of a derivative, *both parties* should account for it under FAS-133. Generally, the forward contract would be considered a derivative if it requires delivery of a security that is readily convertible to cash or the contract may be settled net for cash.

Classification of gains and losses   For securities lending transactions that are accounted for as sales, the seller should classify the gain or loss on sale in the same manner as other gains and losses on sales of securities.

If the forward purchase/resale agreement meets the definition of a derivative, both parties should account for the gains and losses in accordance with FAS-133. Chapter 12, "Introduction to Derivatives," provides additional information. The derivative could qualify as a cash flow hedge of the forecasted purchase/sale of the security, as discussed in Chapter 14, "Hedge Accounting," and DIG Issue G-2, if certain conditions are met. EITF Issue 96-11 applies to certain forward contracts to *purchase* debt securities and marketable equity securities that do not meet the definition of a derivative. Refer to Chapter 2, "Investments in Debt and Equity Securities," for additional information.

Illustration 9-1 demonstrates the accounting for a securities lending arrangement that is accounted for as a sale.

Securities Lending Transactions Accounted for as Secured Borrowings

If a transfer does not satisfy all the sale criteria, the transaction should be accounted for as follows:

- *By the transferor* Cash (or securities that the holder is permitted by contract or custom to sell or repledge) received is considered the amount borrowed, the securities "loaned" are considered pledged as collateral against the cash borrowed (and reclassified as encumbered, if necessary under FAS-140, par. 15), and any "rebate" paid to the transferee of securities is interest expense on the cash borrowed. (FAS-140, par. 93)

- *By the transferee* The cash (or securities that the holder is permitted by contract or custom to sell or repledge) posted as "collateral" is recorded as a loan, the securities borrowed are not recorded (except in the event of default; FAS-140, paragraph 15), and any rebate received is recognized as interest income. If the transferee sells the assets it has received, it should recognize the proceeds from that transaction along with an obligation to return the assets to the transferor. (FAS-140, par. 93)

> **OBSERVATION:** When a securities lending transaction is accounted for as a borrowing, the forward contract is not accounted for separately (as a derivative or otherwise) by either party if the result would be to count the same asset twice. (DIG Issue C-6)

> ☞ **PRACTICE POINTER:** Chapter 7, "Calculating Yields on Debt Investments," provides guidance on recognizing interest income and expense.

Measurement of securities lending receivables and payables Securities lending arrangements that are accounted for as secured borrowings are carried at amortized cost.

> **OBSERVATION:** Broker-dealers and others experience an accounting mismatch when repos are considered secured borrowings—their trading assets are carried at market value and

their funding (repos) is carried at cost. However, the accounting is symmetrical when a securities lending arrangement is accounted for as a sale and the forward contract is marked to market (either because it is a derivative under FAS-133 or in accordance with specialized industry practice).

Classification of securities lending receivables and payables Entities that prepare classified balance sheets should present receivables and payables from securities lending transactions as current or noncurrent assets and liabilities in accordance with ARB-43, Chapter 3A. However, many entities that engage in securities lending activities do not prepare classified balance sheets.

> ☛ **PRACTICE POINTER:** FAS-140 does not specify the terminology to be used to describe liabilities incurred by either the secured party or debtor in securities borrowing or resale transactions. However, those liabilities should be classified separately. (FAS-140 Q&A, par. 116)

Offsetting receivables and payables Receivables and payables from securities lending transactions should be offset in the statement of financial position only if the right of setoff exists and the criteria of FIN-39 are met. Securities-borrowed and securities-loaned transactions that do not have explicit settlement dates do not meet the requirement, in paragraph 5(c) of FIN-39, that the reporting party intends to set off. (AICPA Audit Guide, *Brokers and Dealers in Securities*, par. 7.33)

FIN-41 allows more liberal netting of certain repurchase and reverse repurchase agreements that are executed under a master netting agreement and that meet numerous other conditions. Chapter 17, "Offsetting Assets and Liabilities in the Balance Sheet," discusses the conditions for that exception in detail.

> ☛ **PRACTICE POINTER:** The exception in FIN-41 only applies to repurchase agreements that meet numerous specific conditions. GAAP does not permit applying FIN-41 by analogy to other arrangements, such as securities lending transactions, that may be similar economically, but that do not meet all of the necessary conditions.

Illustrations 9-2 and 9-3 set forth the accounting for securities lending transactions accounted for as borrowings.

Securities Lending Involving Restricted-Use or No Collateral

If the transferor receives a letter of credit or noncash assets that are restricted from use as "collateral," or if no collateral is received, the transaction should be accounted for as a loan of securities from the transferor to the transferee. (FAS-140, fn. 22) While it is not explicitly stated in FAS-140, it would appear inappropriate for the transferor to recognize a restricted-use asset or letter of credit commitment that it receives as "collateral" as its own asset, because it does not yet control the potential benefits associated with the contract. (CON-6, par. 26)

There is no specific GAAP on how to classify any fees paid or received in such arrangements. Companies should disclose their accounting policies for recognizing such fees, if material.

> **OBSERVATION:** FAS-140 does not explicitly address accounting for securities loans that involve nontransferable or otherwise restricted "collateral." Paragraph 257 suggests that "collateral" received should not be recognized when the transferor's rights to use it are limited. Such transactions are essentially off-balance-sheet transactions for the transferor (except for the recognition of fees).

Deferred Tax Considerations

Deferred taxes should be provided for any temporary differences that arise between accounting for a securities lending transaction for book purposes (GAAP) and tax purposes. FAS-109 provides guidance about deferred tax accounting.

Interplay with FAS-115

Debt securities classified as held-to-maturity securities under FAS-115 may be used in securities lending transactions only if the transactions are appropriately accounted for as secured borrowings and the entity intends and expects to be able to satisfy the obligation and recover access to its collateral. (FAS-115 Q&A, par. 17)

Cash Flow Statement Presentation

Under FAS-95, as amended, the presentation of cash flows from securities lending transactions differs significantly, depending on whether the transaction is accounted for as a secured borrowing or a sale.

Sales and Purchases

- Purchases and sales of held-to-maturity and available-for-sale securities are considered cash flows from *investing* activities.
- Purchases and sales of trading securities are considered cash flows from *operating* activities. (FAS-115, par. 18)

Secured Borrowings

- Issuance and repayment of repurchase agreements and dollar rolls (liabilities) are typically considered cash flows from *financing* activities.
- Issuance and repayment of reverse repurchase agreements (loans) are typically considered cash flows from *investing* activities.
- Interest on secured borrowings is considered an operating cash flow.

☛ **PRACTICE POINTER:** Depending on the nature of the activity, broker-dealers sometimes report changes in repurchase and reverse repurchase agreements as cash flows from *operating* activities. (AICPA Audit and Accounting Guide, *Brokers and Dealers in Securities*, Exhibit 4-7)

OBSERVATION: Transactions that are very similar economically can be reported differently for accounting purposes. Cash flow reporting follows the accounting treatment, not the motivation of the parties or the economics of the transactions. Users of cash flow statements must understand the accounting before any conclusions are drawn on the sources and uses of cash flows from securities lending transactions.

DISCLOSURE REQUIREMENTS

Pledges of Financial Assets as Collateral

An entity that has pledged any of its assets as collateral that are not reclassified and separately reported in the statement of financial position pursuant to FAS-140 paragraph 15(a) must disclose the carrying amount and classification of those assets as of the date of the latest statement of financial position presented. (FAS-140, par. 17(a)(2))

An entity that has accepted collateral that it is permitted by contract or custom to sell or repledge must disclose:

- The fair value as of the date of each statement of financial position presented of that collateral,
- The portion of that collateral that it has sold or repledged, *and*
- Information about the sources and uses of that collateral. (FAS-140, par. 17(a)(3))

Financial Assets Otherwise Serving as Collateral

FAS-140 only applies to collateral that has been transferred to the secured party (that is, pledges of financial assets). Not all collateral arrangements involve a transfer of the assets to the secured party. SOP 01-6, paragraphs 13(i) and 14(d), require disclosure of the carrying amounts of loans, trade receivables, securities, and other financial instruments that serve as collateral for borrowings, even if they are not actually transferred to the secured party.

Securities Lending Transactions

An entity that has entered into repurchase agreements or securities lending transactions must disclose its policy for requiring collateral or other security. (FAS-140, par. 17(a)(1))

> **SEC REGISTRANT ALERT:** SEC registrants are required to disclose supplemental information about repurchase agreements and reverse repurchase agreements pursuant to S-X Rule 4-08(m) and S-K Item 303.

REGULATORY CONSIDERATIONS

In 1998, the Federal Financial Institutions Examination Council (FFIEC) issued a revised policy statement that provides guidelines for insured depository institutions including guidelines for written repurchase agreements, policies and procedures, credit risk management and collateral management. The terms of various collateral arrangements could have a direct effect on whether securities lending transactions are accounted for as sales or secured borrowings.

In February 2006, the Federal Reserve Board issued a final rule on the risk-based capital treatment of securities-borrowing transactions in which cash collateral is posted by the borrower. The rule is applicable only for banks that have implemented the "market risk amendment" to the risk-based capital rules. Subject to meeting certain conditions, the final rule would permit such banks to include only the net exposure arising from the arrangement (that is, the cash collateral less the market value of the borrowed security) in their risk-based capital computation, rather than the gross exposure, resulting in a reduced capital charge for the arrangement.

AUDIT CONSIDERATIONS

Chapter 5, "Transfers of Financial Assets," discusses the key areas of financial reporting risk for transfers of assets in general. The primary accounting risk for securities lending transactions is ensuring that transactions are properly classified as sales and purchases (off-balance-sheet) or secured borrowings (on balance sheet). Some key factors to consider include:

- Affirming that the sale criteria of FAS-140 have been applied properly based on the specific terms and arrangements for each transaction.
- For transactions that are accounted for as secured borrowings, ensuring that the additional criteria of paragraphs 47–49 have been applied properly, including the need for sufficient collateral and, for dollar-roll transactions, the definition of substantially the same.

A June 1985 report of the Auditing Standards Board (ASB) entitled, "Report of the Special Task Force on Audits of Repurchase Securities Transactions," provides additional guidance with respect to reporting, auditing, and risk considerations.

ILLUSTRATIONS

Illustration 9-1: Accounting for a Sell-Buyback as a Sale

Assume a securities dealer needs to borrow $100 million in MFS Corp. bonds for one month. The bonds, which are publicly traded, currently have a fair value of $130 million. Fuji Bancorp sells bonds that had a carrying amount of $128 million to the dealer, and separately agrees to buy them back for $131 million in 30 days. No margining provisions are established for the transaction, so the repurchase commitment must be evaluated as a call option (under FAS-140, par. 9(c)(2)). Because the bonds are readily obtainable, and all of the other criteria of FAS-140 paragraph 9 are met, the arrangement must be accounted for as a sale under FAS-140. Assume (1) that the forward contract meets the definition of a derivative, (2) the value of the bonds increases to $132 million and (3) the forward contract changes in value by $1 million during the 30-day period. The dealer carries all of its securities and derivatives at market value in accordance with industry practice. Because of the short term of the transaction, Fuji Bancorp does not elect hedge accounting for the forward contract (even though it might qualify as a cash flow hedge under FAS-133 if certain conditions are met).

Accounting Terminology (in millions):

Transferor: Fuji Bancorp
Transferee: Dealer
Proceeds: $130 cash, forward (repurchase) contract (fair value $0)
Collateral: N/A

Journal Entries for Fuji Bancorp (Transferor)

At inception:

Cash	130	
Securities		128
Gain on sale of securities		2

To record the sale of securities. The forward contract has a fair value of zero, and therefore is not recorded at inception.

Money market instruments	130	
Cash		130

To record investment of proceeds. [par. 94]

At conclusion:

Cash	130.5	
Interest income		0.5
Money market instrument		130

To record results of investment.

Forward contract asset	1	
Gain on forward contract		1

To record the change in value of the forward contract over the 30-day period, in accordance with FAS-133. Chapter 12, "Introduction to Derivatives," discusses the accounting for derivatives.

Securities	132	
Cash		131
Forward contract asset		1

To record repurchase of security at its current fair value of $132 for the agreed-upon price of $131.

Journal entries for the dealer (Transferee)

At inception:

Securities	130	
Cash		130

To record purchase of securities.

Cash	0.6	
Interest income		0.6

To record interest income on the securities purchased.

Securities	2	
Trading gains		2

To record the change in value of the securities during the 30-day period. Chapter 2 discusses the accounting for trading securities.

Loss on forward contract	1	
Forward contract liability		1

To mark to market the forward contract under FAS-133. Chapter 12 "Introduction to Derivatives," discusses the accounting for derivatives.

Cash	131	
Forward contract liability	1	
Securities		132

To record the resale of the securities at the agreed-upon price of $131.

Illustration 9-2: Accounting for a Securities Lending Transaction Treated as a Secured Borrowing

Semper Securities needs to borrow $1,000 XYZ Co. bonds, because a customer failed to deliver the bonds, and Semper already sold them to another party. To make delivery on the sale, Semper borrows the bonds from Bounty Bank, in exchange for cash "collateral" of $1,020. Semper agrees to return the bonds in 35 days for $1,024, a price calculated using current interest rates. The bonds are not scheduled to mature for several years. Semper and Bounty agree to adjust the amount of cash collateral if the price of the bonds changes. (For simplicity, assume that the fair value of the security does not change during the 35-day term of the transaction.) The transfer of bonds must be accounted for as a secured borrowing, because the sale criteria of paragraph 9 of FAS-140 are not met. Specifically, Bounty simultaneously agreed to repurchase the bonds (paragraph 9(c)(1)), and all of the criteria of paragraphs 47–49 are met.

Accounting Terminology:

Transferor: Bounty Bank
Transferee: Semper Securities
Proceeds: $1,020 cash
Collateral: $1,000 XYZ Co. bonds

Journal Entries for Bounty Bank (Transferor)

At inception:

Cash	1,020	
Securities lent payable		1,020

To record the receipt of proceeds (cash "collateral") along with the obligation to return the cash [pars. 11(b), 94]

Securities pledged to creditors	1,000	
Securities		1,000

To reclassify loaned securities that the secured party has the right to sell or repledge. [par. 15(a)]

Money market instrument	1,020	
Cash		1,020

To record investment of cash collateral. [par. 94]

At conclusion:

Cash	1,025	
Interest income		5
Money market instrument		1,020

To record results of investment of proceeds at 5%.

Securities	1,000	
Securities pledged to creditors		1,000

To record return of security.

Securities lent payable	1,020	
Interest expense ("rebate")	4	
Cash		1,024

To record repayment of cash collateral plus interest.

Journal Entries for Semper Securities (Transferee)

At inception:

Securities borrowed receivable	1,020	
Cash		1,020

To record transfer of cash "collateral."

Cash	1,000	
Obligation to return borrowed securities		1,000

To record sale of borrowed securities to a third party and the resulting obligation to return securities that it no longer holds.

At conclusion:

Obligation to return borrowed securities	1,000	
Cash		1,000

To record the repurchase of securities borrowed.

Cash	1,024	
Securities borrowed receivable		1,020
Interest income ("rebate")		4

To record the receipt of cash collateral and rebate interest.

Illustration 9-3: Securities Lending Transaction Involving Securities Collateral

Assume the same facts and circumstances described in Illustration 9-2 except that, instead of cash, Semper posts marketable Treasury bills as "collateral" in the transaction. Bounty is permitted to sell or repledge the Treasury bills.

Accounting Terminology:

Transferor: Bounty Bank
Transferee: Semper Securities
Proceeds: $1,020 Treasury bills
Collateral: $1,000 XYZ Co. bonds

Journal Entries for Bounty Bank (Transferor)

At inception:

Securities (T-bills)	1,020	
Securities lent payable		1,020

To record the receipt of proceeds (T-bills received as "collateral") along with the obligation to return them. [pars. 11(b), 94]. The T-bills would be accounted for under FAS-115.

Securities pledged to creditors	1,000	
Securities (XYZ bonds)		1,000

To reclassify loaned securities that the secured party has the right to sell or repledge. [par. 15(a)]

Securities (T-bills, accrued interest)	5	
Interest income		5

To record interest earned on proceeds. [par. 94]

At conclusion:

Securities (XYZ bonds)	1,000	
Securities pledged to creditors		1,000

To record return of security.

Securities lent payable	1,020	
Interest expense ("rebate")	4	
Cash	1	
T-bill		1,025

To record return of T-bills plus interest.

CHAPTER 10
CONVERTIBLE DEBT AND SIMILAR INSTRUMENTS

CONTENTS

Overview	10.02
Background	10.03
Descriptions of Securities	10.04
Traditional Convertible Debt	10.04
Debt with Detachable Warrants	10.05
Debt with Beneficial Conversion Features	10.05
Accounting for Convertible Debt and Other Debt-Equity Hybrids	10.06
Navigating the Literature	10.06
Exhibit 10-1: Evaluating the Components of Convertible Debt	10.08
Traditional Convertible Debt	10.08
Accounting at Inception	10.08
Conversion According to the Original Terms	10.10
Conversion According to Revised Terms	10.11
Exhibit 10-2: Evaluating When an Induced Conversion of Debt Is an Extinguishment	10.13
Accounting for Modifications or Exchanges of Convertible Debt Instruments	10.14
Debt with Detachable Stock Purchase Warrants	10.15
Accounting at Inception	10.15
Exercise of Warrants	10.16
Reacquisition of Warrants	10.16
"Nontraditional" Convertible Debt	10.16
Exhibit 10-3: Accounting for Convertible Debt with Cash Settlement Options	10.18
EITF Issues Changed or Resolved by FAS-133	10.21
Debt with Beneficial Conversion Features (EITF 98-5 and EITF 00-27)	10.22
Accounting at Inception	10.23
Ongoing Accounting	10.23

Exhibit 10-4: Convertible Securities with
Nondetachable BCFs 10.25

Presentation of Cash Flows 10.26

Income Tax Consequences 10.26

Convertible Debt Instruments Subject to Registration
Payment Arrangements 10.27

Fair Value Option for Certain Convertible Debt
Instruments 10.28

Disclosures 10.29

Information about Securities 10.29

Convertible Securities with Contingent Features 10.29

Beneficial Conversion Features 10.30

Embedded Conversion Options No Longer
Requiring Bifurcation 10.30

Earnings per Share 10.30

Basic EPS 10.32

Diluted EPS 10.33

Exhibit 10-5: EPS Treatment of Nontraditional
Convertible Debt 10.35

Audit Considerations 10.36

Illustrations 10.36

Illustration 10-1: Debt with Detachable Stock Purchase
Warrants 10.36

Illustration 10-2: Traditional Convertible Debt 10.37

Illustration 10-3: Induced Conversion of Convertible
Debt 10.38

Illustration 10-4: Convertible Debt with Beneficial
Conversion Feature (Fixed Terms and a Two-Year
Lock-Up Period) 10.39

Illustration 10-5: Convertible Debt with Beneficial
Conversion Feature (Fixed Terms, Convertible upon the
Occurrence of an IPO) 10.39

Illustration 10-6: Computation of Basic EPS for Convertible
Preferred Securities 10.40

OVERVIEW

The issuer's accounting for convertible debt that is convertible into
the issuer's stock depends on (1) whether the conversion feature
would be considered an equity instrument of the issuer when evaluated on a stand-alone basis and (2) whether the conversion feature is

detachable, that is, exercisable without tendering the debt. Convertible debt that has a nondetachable conversion feature that is considered an equity instrument of the issuer (or a consolidated affiliate) is accounted for as straight debt with no accounting recognition of the embedded conversion feature. Debt with detachable warrants that are considered equity instruments are accounted for as two separate instruments—a debt instrument (usually involving a discount) and an equity instrument that isrecorded in contributed capital. Convertible debt that has a nondetachable or detachable conversion feature that is considered a derivative (not equity) must be accounted for as two separate instruments under FAS-133—a debt host and a derivative that must be marked to market—unless the components cannot be separated reliably (in which case the entire instrument is marked to market). Convertible debt with a nondetachable conversion feature that is beneficial to the investor upon issuance is accounted for under a special model that generally allocates the proceeds between a debt instrument and the conversion feature based on the intrinsic value of the conversion feature.

When convertible debt is converted into stock according to its original terms, no gain or loss is recognized. When convertible debt is converted according to terms that are subsequently modified to induce prompt conversion, the transaction is generally considered an extinguishment of debt unless certain criteria are met. If those criteria are met, expense is recognized for the incremental amount of value transferred to investors; however a gain is never recognized.

Convertible debt and other debt-equity hybrids give rise to a variety of issues in computing diluted earnings per share.

BACKGROUND

The accounting literature for convertible debt and other debt-equity hybrids is very complex due to recent developments in the accounting literature. APB-14 addresses "traditional" convertible debt and debt with detachable warrants, but only if the embedded conversion feature or warrants meet the definition of equity under EITF Issue 00-19. Chapter 16, "Issuer's Accounting for Equity Instruments and Related Contracts," discusses the requirements of EITF Issue 00-19 in detail. If a conversion feature or warrant does not meet the definition of equity under EITF Issue 00-19, it must be evaluated under FAS-133 to determine whether it is a freestanding or embedded derivative. Chapter 12, "Introduction to Derivatives," and Chapter 13, "Embedded Derivatives," provide detailed guidance about making those determinations. EITF Issues 98-5 and 00-27 address convertible debt with beneficial conversion features. Various practice issues in this area exist. EITF Issue 00-27 remains an open issue on the EITF's agenda; further discussion is on hold pending progress on phase two of the FASB's liabilities and equity project. APB-26 addresses extinguishments of debt, including most conversions of debt not in accordance with its original terms. FAS-84 addresses accounting for induced conversions that meet certain criteria. FAS-128 addresses earnings-per-share computations along with several EITF Issues.

> ☛ **PRACTICE POINTER:** FAS-133 nullified several EITF consensuses on nontraditional forms of convertible debt and other debt-equity hybrids. However, in transitioning to FAS-133, companies were allowed to elect to continue to account for all of their pre-1998 or pre-1999 embedded derivatives under previous GAAP. (FAS-133, par. 50) This chapter only addresses post-FAS-133 accounting—that is, instruments that were not grandfathered by FAS-133.

Convertible debt and similar instruments that are granted or issued in exchange for goods and services are accounted for under a specialized accounting model for stock compensation. Refer to FAS-123(R) and EITF Issue 01-1 for additional information.

Descriptions of Securities

Traditional Convertible Debt

"Traditional" convertible debt typically has the following characteristics:

- A debt security is convertible into the common stock of the issuer or an *affiliated* enterprise at a specified price at the option of the holder.
- The security is sold at a price or has a value at issuance not significantly in excess of the face amount.
- It bears an interest rate that is lower than the issuer could obtain for nonconvertible debt, because the investor has potential upside from the conversion feature and limited downside.
- If converted, the issuer must deliver shares of the reporting entity's stock (or the stock of a consolidated affiliate) to the investor (i.e., physical settlement).
- The initial conversion price of the security is greater than the market value of the common stock at time of issuance (that is, it is "out of the money").

- The conversion price does not decrease (except pursuant to anti-dilution provisions).
- The securities are callable at the option of the issuer.
- The securities are subordinated to nonconvertible debt. (APB-14, par. 3)

In "traditional" convertible debt, the conversion feature is nondetachable, meaning that the security will either be converted into common stock (if converted) or be redeemed for cash. The holder cannot exercise the option to convert, unless he foregoes the right to redemption, and vice versa. (APB-14, par. 7) This limitation is central to the current accounting for convertible debt. Debt with detachable conversion features (e.g., warrants) is discussed below.

Debt with Detachable Warrants

Unlike convertible debt, the components of debt with detachable warrants to purchase stock are separately exercisable. Usually, the combination is issued with the expectation that the debt will be repaid when it matures. Detachable warrants often trade separately from the debt instrument. Thus, the two elements of the security exist independently and are treated as separate instruments for accounting purposes. In this chapter, the term "debt with detachable warrants" assumes that the warrants are considered equity instruments of the issuer under EITF Issue 00-19.

Debt with Beneficial Conversion Features

As mentioned above, convertible debt is typically issued with a conversion price that is greater than the current market price of the shares at issuance. However, debt also may be issued with a conversion price that is less than the current market price of the stock, that is, the conversion feature is in-the-money or "beneficial" at inception. It is difficult to generalize about the terms of such instruments, but usually the conversion feature is nondetachable; the securities can be immediately convertible, "locked up" for a period of time, or convertible only upon the occurrence of a specified event; and the conversion price can either be fixed or variable. Often these instruments involve the stock of nonpublic companies. The components of debt with beneficial conversion features are evaluated separately for accounting purposes, but measured differently than debt with detachable warrants.

> ☛ **PRACTICE POINTER:** Convertible securities do not fall neatly into the categories described in this section. Securities not explicitly discussed in this section should be dealt with according to their substance.

ACCOUNTING FOR CONVERTIBLE DEBT AND OTHER DEBT-EQUITY HYBRIDS

Navigating the Literature

Convertible debt is a classic example of a hybrid instrument—the components include (1) a debt "host" and (2) an embedded written call option on the issuer's stock. The issuer's accounting depends on whether a freestanding (detachable) instrument with the same terms as the embedded written option qualifies for the scope exception in paragraph 11(a) of FAS-133 relating to equity instruments of the issuer. The option should be evaluated under EITF Issue 00-19 to determine whether it should be classified as an equity instrument or as an asset/liability. The embedded conversion feature in "traditional" convertible debt would be considered an equity instrument. Therefore, separate accounting is *not* required. (Chapter 16, "Issuer's Accounting for Equity Instruments and Related Contracts," discusses EITF Issue 00-19 in detail.) Note that FAS-150 only nullified the sections of EITF Issue 00-19 involving obligations to *repurchase* stock. Convertible debt typically involves a potential *transfer* of stock by the issuer, and thus is not affected.

Briefly, under EITF Issue 00-19, if the terms of the conversion allow for a cash settlement rather than delivery of the issuer's shares at the investor's option, the exception in paragraph 11(a) for the issuer does *not* apply because the contract would not be classified in stockholders' equity in the issuer's statement of financial position. In that case, the instrument must be evaluated under FAS-133, because an option based on the entity's stock price is not clearly and closely related to an interest-bearing debt instrument. Generally, an asset/liability under EITF Issue 00-19 will meet the definition of a derivative and therefore, the components of the hybrid must be accounted for separately under FAS-133 (unless it is not practicable to do so).

Similarly, if debt is indexed to *another* entity's publicly traded common stock, the issuer should separate the embedded derivative from the host contract and account for it in accordance with FAS-133 because the option would not be considered an equity instrument *of the issuer.*

As discussed more fully in Chapter 13, "Embedded Derivatives," when separate accounting is required, the derivative is initially recorded at its fair value and any remaining basis is ascribed to the host contract. The allocation is not based on the APB-14 "relative fair value" method.

Exhibit 10-1 summarizes how to determine which accounting literature applies to convertible debt and similar instruments for the issuer.

> ☞ **PRACTICE POINTER:** A working draft of a technical practice aid, "Convertible Debt, Convertible Preferred Shares, Warrants, and Other Equity-Related Financial Instruments," has been prepared by a special AICPA task force and the AICPA staff. The working draft is meant to be a tool to assist in navigating the relevant GAAP for these instruments in existence as of December 1, 2006. It includes detailed flowcharts and illustrations to assist in understanding the interrelationship between the various accounting pronouncements relevant to the analysis of these instruments. The working draft incorporates many sources of GAAP related to these instruments, including the following:
>
> - Accounting Principles Board (APB) Opinion No. 14, *Accounting for Convertible Debt and Debt Issued with Stock Purchase Warrants*
>
> - FASB Statement No. 133, *Accounting for Derivative Instruments and Hedging Activities*
>
> - FASB Statement No. 150, *Accounting for Certain Financial Instruments with Characteristics of Both Liabilities and Equity*
>
> - EITF Issue 98-5, "Accounting for Convertible Securities with Beneficial Conversion Features or Contingently Adjustable Conversion Ratios"
>
> - EITF Issue 00-19, "Accounting for Derivative Financial Instruments Indexed to and Potentially Settled in, a Company's Own Stock"
>
> - *EITF Abstracts*, Topic D-98, "Classification and Measurement of Redeemable Securities"
>
> - SEC Accounting Series Release (ASR) 268, *Redeemable Preferred Stocks*.
>
> The working draft is nonauthoritative provides no interpretive guidance; however, practitioners may find it a useful tool in navigating the literature in this area due to the complex nature of these instruments. A copy of the working draft can be obtained from the AICPA's website at www.aicpa.org.

EXHIBIT 10-1
EVALUATING THE COMPONENTS OF CONVERTIBLE DEBT

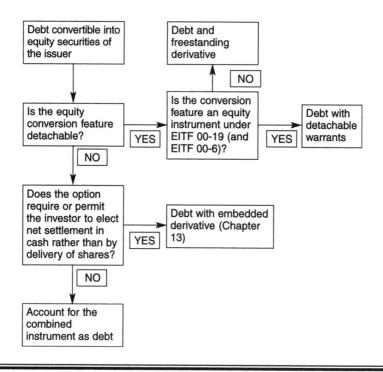

Traditional Convertible Debt

Accounting at Inception

Traditional convertible debt, with a nondetachable conversion feature, is recorded as a debt instrument in its entirety. The conversion feature is *not* ascribed a separate value in the financial statements. (APB-14, par. 12) Interest expense is recognized using the interest method, meaning that any premium or discount upon issuance is amortized over the life of the instrument. The effective rate will generally be less than the market rate for straight debt because the investor implicitly "pays for" the right to potential upside on the issuer's stock with limited downside risk.

> ☞ **PRACTICE POINTER:**   Inventive investment bankers have created various forms of zero-coupon convertible debt instruments with enough additional features such that the security is issued at par

with no stated rate of interest (for example, LYONS™ or "Liquid Yield Option Notes"). Such instruments should be carefully examined to determine whether they have embedded derivatives as defined in FAS-133. However, assuming they do not, such instruments have essentially no income statement effect (except amortization of issuance costs). In addition, when such a zero-coupon debt instrument is contingently convertible, there may be no effect on diluted earnings per share until the contingency has been met. Accounting for instruments such as these are likely to be affected in phase 2 of the FASB project on liabilities and equity.

☛ **PRACTICE POINTER:** When convertible debt is issued at a substantial premium, there is a presumption that such premium represents additional paid-in capital. (APB-14, par. 18)

OBSERVATION: In its day, the members of the Accounting Principles Board (and its constituents) were concerned that the values of components that were not separately exercisable could not be determined reliably. Clearly, the FASB has overcome that concern, because several recent standards require "split accounting" regardless of the separability of the components. In phase two of the liabilities and equity project, the FASB is exploring a model that would focus on the characteristics, rather than the form, of the instrument.

Debt convertible into the stock of a consolidated subsidiary The following forms of convertible debt should be accounted for as "traditional" convertible debt in the consolidated financial statements:

- Debt issued by a consolidated subsidiary that is convertible into that subsidiary's stock and
- Debt issued by a parent company that is convertible into the stock of a consolidated subsidiary.

That is, a nondetachable conversion feature should *not* be accounted for separately. (EITF 99-1)

However, a detachable warrant or option that is indexed to the stock of a consolidated subsidiary would not be considered an equity instrument by the parent-issuer because, under EITF Issue 00-19, the instrument *must* be indexed to the stock of the *reporting entity*. (EITF 00-6)

OBSERVATION: The accounting for debt convertible into subsidiary stock is inconsistent with the accounting for a freestanding (detachable) option on subsidiary stock. Conceptually, if a freestanding option is not an equity instrument (under EITF Issue 00-6), then it should not be an equity instrument when it is embedded in a debt instrument. However, APB-14 specifically applies to affiliated enterprises and, because of its place in the GAAP hierarchy, the EITF could not overturn that guidance. It is unclear why the EITF did not reach a conclusion on Issue 00-6 for the freestanding option that was consistent with APB-14 (that is,

they could have concluded that an option on the stock of a consolidated subsidiary is an equity instrument of the parent). Entities
can now select the desired accounting for such instruments by
structuring the instrument in the right form.

Participating mortgages   Accounting for debt convertible at the
option of the lender into equity ownership of the property should
be accounted for in accordance with APB-14. (SOP 97-1, fn. 1)

Conversion According to the Original Terms

Upon conversion of convertible debt according to its original terms,
the net carrying amount of the debt, including any unamortized
premium or discount, is credited to the equity accounts to reflect
the stock issued and no gain or loss is recognized. (AIN-APB 26, #1)

> ☛ **PRACTICE POINTER:**   The net carrying amount should also in-
> clude any interest accrued from the last interest payment date, if
> applicable, to the date of conversion. (EITF 85-17)

Some instruments are contingently convertible and involve call
options that provide an issuer the ability to call the debt at any
time to equity shares. The issuance of equity shares to settle a debt
instrument that became convertible upon the issuer's exercise of a call
option (pursuant to the instrument's original conversion terms)
should be accounted for as a conversion or debt extinguishment
based on whether the instrument contained a substantive conversion
feature as of the issuance date. If the conversion feature is substantive, the issuance of equity shares should be accounted for as a conversion, and no gain or loss should be recognized. If the conversion
feature is not substantive, the issuance of equity shares to settle the
debt instrument should be considered an extinguishment of debt, and
the fair value of the equity shares should be considered a component
of the reacquisition price of the debt.

A conversion feature (e.g., a market price trigger) is substantive if it
is at least reasonably possible of becoming exercisable in the future.
The following instruments are viewed as not having a substantive
conversion feature:

- Instruments that can become convertible *only* upon the issuer's
  exercise of its call option
- Instruments that involve a conversion price that is so high that
  conversion is not deemed at least reasonably possible at the issuance date, even if conversion is contingent only on the passage
  of time.

In addition, the following can be considered in determining whether a conversion feature is substantive:

- A comparison of the fair value of the conversion feature and the fair value of the entire convertible debt instrument
- A comparison of the effective annual interest rate of the debt instrument and the effective annual interest rate the issuer estimates it could obtain on a similar nonconvertible instrument
- A comparison of the fair value of the convertible debt instrument and the fair value of an identical instrument for which conversion is not contingent
- An assessment of the nature of the conditions under which the instrument may become convertible and the likelihood that the contingent event will occur. (EITF 05-1)

Conversion According to Revised Terms

Generally, a conversion of debt into equity according to terms that are *different* from the conversion privileges, if any, that are stated in the terms of the original debt agreement is considered an extinguishment of debt (unless it is a troubled debt restructuring subject to FAS-15 or it is an induced conversion that meets specific conditions discussed in the next section). (FTB 80-1, par. 4, as amended) Accounting for extinguishments of debt is addressed in Chapter 11, "Extinguishments of Debt."

Induced conversions Sometimes, the conversion privileges in a convertible debt instrument are changed or additional consideration is paid to the investors for the purpose of inducing prompt conversion of the debt to equity instruments.

The following means ("sweeteners") may be used to induce conversions:

- Reduce the original conversion price (resulting in the issuance of a greater number of shares).
- Issue warrants or other securities not provided for in the original conversion terms (effectively reducing the conversion price).
- Pay cash or other consideration to those investors who convert early.

The conversion of debt to equity (in a nontroubled situation) is *not* an extinguishment of the debt if:

- The conversion privileges were provided for in the terms of the debt at issuance, or
- The conversion privileges provided for in the terms of the debt at issuance were changed to induce conversion and:

— The changed conversion privileges were exercisable only for a limited period of time, and

— The conversion includes the issuance of all of the equity securities issuable pursuant to the *original* terms for each debt instrument that is converted. (FAS-84, par. 2)

This exception applies regardless of (1) whether the party that initiates the offer is the debtor or the debt holder or (2) whether the offer relates to all debt holders or only some debt holders. (EITF 02-15)

☛ **PRACTICE POINTER:** The term "limited period of time" is not defined in FAS-84. However, the examples in Appendix A of FAS-84 indicate that 30 days and 60 days both meet that condition.

☛ **PRACTICE POINTER:** If a debt instrument includes a provision that permits the debtor to change the terms of the debt to the benefit of the investors, the first condition above would not be met, even though the change is literally "provided for in the terms of the debt at issuance." (FAS-84, par. 29)

When an induced conversion meets these criteria, an expense is recognized for the *excess* of the fair value of all securities and other consideration issued over the fair value of securities issuable pursuant to the original conversion terms. That expense is *not* reported as an extraordinary item. (FAS-84, par. 3)

☛ **PRACTICE POINTER:** The fair value of the securities or other consideration should be measured at the earlier of the date the investors (1) enter into a binding agreement to do so or (2) actually convert the convertible debt into equity securities. An induced conversion may *not* be recognized before the debt holder has accepted the inducement offer. (FAS-84, pars. 4 and 30) Note that there could be more than one measurement date if investors convert (or accept the offer, if earlier) on different dates.

OBSERVATION: As discussed previously, gain or loss is generally not recognized on conversions of debt to equity according to the original terms. FAS-84 holds that basic concept intact and only requires loss recognition on the incremental consideration that is issued to induce the investors to convert. Gains, however, are not recognized when the fair value of the consideration issued is less than the fair value of the securities issuable pursuant to the original conversion terms.

Exhibit 10-2 summarizes when an induced conversion of debt is considered an extinguishment of debt

---

EXHIBIT 10-2
EVALUATING WHEN AN INDUCED CONVERSION OF DEBT
IS AN EXTINGUISHMENT*

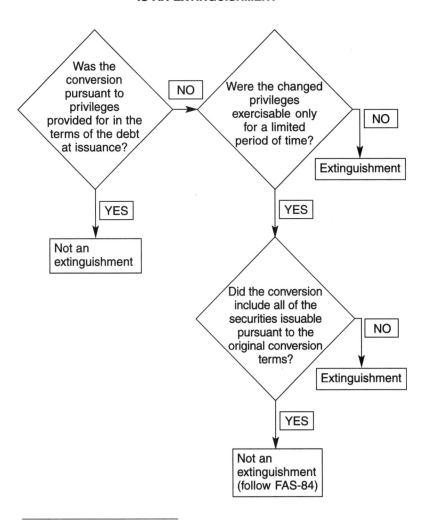

---

*Accounting for extinguishments of debt is addressed in Chapter 11, "Extinguishments of Debt."

Accounting for Modifications or Exchanges of Convertible Debt Instruments

When a debt instrument is modified to add a conversion option, eliminate a conversion option, or change the fair value of an existing conversion option, the effect of the modification on the embedded conversion option must be considered in the analysis of whether the instrument has been extinguished.

> ☞ **PRACTICE POINTER:** The guidance discussed in this section does not address modifications or exchanges of debt instruments in circumstances when the embedded conversion option bifurcated and accounted for separately under FAS-133.

The following steps must be used to determine whether the exchange of debt instruments or modification in the terms of an existing instrument must be accounted for as an extinguishment:

1. The issuer must evaluate whether the exchange or modification is an extinguishment using the cash flow test in EITF 96-19 *without* considering the change in the fair value of the embedded conversion option.

   Under EITF 96-19, an exchange of a debt instrument for a new debt instrument or modification of the terms of an existing debt instrument that results in the old debt instrument and new debt instrument having substantially different terms should be accounted for as an extinguishment. Exchanged or modified debt instruments are considered to be substantially different if the present value of the cash flows of the new debt instrument differs from the present value of the remaining cash flows of the old debt instrument by at least 10%. (Refer to Chapter 11, "Extinguishments of Debt," for further discussion of the guidance in EITF 96-19.)

2. If the cash flow test under EITF 96-19 indicates that a substantial modification or exchange has *not* occurred, the issuer must perform a separate test based on the change in fair value of the embedded conversion option.

   A modification or an exchange of debt instruments that adds a *substantive* conversion option or eliminates a substantive conversion option at the date of the modification or exchange would always be considered substantial, and debt extinguishment accounting would be required in those circumstances.

> ☞ **PRACTICE POINTER:** For purposes of evaluating whether an embedded conversion option was *substantive* on the date it was added to or eliminated from a debt instrument, the factors described in EITF 05-1 should be considered.

If the change in the fair value of the embedded conversion option is at least 10% of the carrying amount of the original debt instrument immediately prior to the modification or exchange, then a substantial modification or exchange has occurred and the issuer should apply extinguishment accounting. The change in the fair value of the option is determined as the difference between the fair value of the embedded conversion option immediately before and after the modification or exchange.

If a convertible debt instrument that is modified or exchanged is not required to be accounted for as an extinguishment pursuant to the guidance above, the modification or exchange is accounted for based on whether there is an increase or decrease in the fair value of the conversion option. The change in the fair value of the conversion option should be accounted for as follows:

- An *increase* in the fair value of the embedded conversion option should reduce the carrying amount of the debt instrument (increasing a debt discount or reducing a debt premium) with a corresponding increase in additional paid-in capital.

- A *decrease* in the fair value of an embedded conversion option resulting from a modification or an exchange should not be recognized. The issuer should not recognize a beneficial conversion feature or reassess an existing beneficial conversion feature upon a modification or exchange of convertible debt instruments in a transaction that is not accounted for as an extinguishment.

Debt with Detachable Stock Purchase Warrants

Accounting at Inception

The proceeds received from issuing debt with detachable stock purchase warrants should be allocated between the debt and warrants, based on the relative fair values of the two securities at time of issuance. The portion of the proceeds that is allocated to the warrants should be accounted for as additional paid-in capital. Any resulting discount or premium on the debt securities should be recognized using the interest method. (APB-14, par. 16)

> ☞ **PRACTICE POINTER:** The fair values of the components should generally be measured on the date when agreement as to terms has been reached and announced, even though the agreement is subject to certain further actions, such as directors' or stockholders' approval. (APB-14, par. 16, fn. 2)

If detachable warrants are issued in conjunction with debt as consideration in purchase transactions, the amounts attributable to each class of security issued should be determined separately, based on values at the time of issuance. The debt discount or premium is determined by comparing the value attributed to the debt securities with their face amounts. (APB-14, par. 17)

Exercise of Warrants

Debt that is tendered to exercise detachable warrants that were originally issued with that debt is considered a conversion pursuant to the terms of the debt, assuming that the debt is permitted to be tendered towards the exercise price of the warrants under the terms of the securities at issuance. Accordingly, no gain or loss would be recognized. (AIN-APB 26, #1)

Reacquisition of Warrants

If a company that previously recorded detachable stock warrants as a credit to contributed capital subsequently decides to reacquire the warrants for cash, the purchase price of the warrants should be deducted from either capital in excess of par value or retained earnings. (AICPA TPA 4130.03)

"Nontraditional" Convertible Debt

EITF Issue 90-19 addresses three "nontraditional" variations of convertible debt. All of the varieties involve the issuance of a debt instrument that is indexed to a fixed number of the issuer's common shares. However, the instruments contain different cash settlement requirements or options upon conversion, unlike traditional convertible debt, which requires settlement in shares upon conversion.

> ☛ **PRACTICE POINTER:**   After a consensus was reached in 1990, the FASB issued FAS-133 (derivatives) and FAS-128 (earnings per share). In addition, the EITF addressed the accounting for free-standing instruments indexed to a company's own stock (Issue 00-19). The guidance that appears below has been updated for the effects of that literature and is substantially different from the original consensus. If a company elected to grandfather its pre-1998 or pre-1999 instruments with embedded derivatives, as permitted by FAS-133, the company would continue to apply the accounting guidance in the original consensus.

The three scenarios contemplated are:

1. *Instrument A, Mandatory Cash Settlement*   Upon conversion, the issuer must satisfy the obligation entirely in cash based on the fair value of the fixed number of shares on the conversion date (conversion value).

2. *Instrument B, Optional Cash Settlement* Upon conversion, the issuer may elect to settle the entire obligation in either stock or cash equivalent to the conversion value.

3. *Instrument C, Part Mandatory, Part Optional Cash Settlement* Upon conversion, the issuer must settle the accreted value of the obligation (the amount accrued to the benefit of the holder exclusive of the conversion spread) in cash and may elect to settle the conversion spread (the excess conversion value over the accreted value) in either cash or stock.

In all cases, if the holder does not exercise the conversion option, the issuer must repay the accreted value of the debt in cash at maturity.

The accounting for the instruments primarily depends on whether the embedded conversion feature would be considered an equity instrument of the issuer if it were freestanding or detachable. The guidance in EITF Issue 00-19 is used to make that determination. (Chapter 16, "Issuer's Accounting for Equity Instruments and Related Contracts," discusses that guidance in detail.)

EITF 00-19 provides an exception for "conventional" convertible debt instruments such that, for the purposes of determining whether an embedded derivative indexed to the company's own stock would be classified as an equity instrument if freestanding, the embedded conversion option is not subject to specific conditions necessary for equity classification. As a result, conventional convertible debt instruments generally are not required to be bifurcated under FAS-133. An instrument can be considered a conventional convertible debt instrument if it provides the holder with an option to convert into a fixed number of shares or equivalent amount of cash (at the discretion of the issuer) and the ability to exercise the option is based on the passage of time or a contingent event. This would include instruments that contain "standard" antidilution provisions, which result in adjustments to the conversion ratio in the event of an equity restructuring transaction designed to maintain the value of the conversion option. (An equity restructuring is defined as a nonreciprocal transaction between an entity and its shareholders that causes the per-share fair value of the shares underlying the option or similar award, such as a stock dividend, a stock split, spinoff, rights offering, or recapitalization through a large, nonrecurring cash dividend, to change.)

☛ **PRACTICE POINTER:** Importantly, all of the supplemental equity conditions of EITF Issue 00-19 (paragraphs 12–32 involving feasibility of settling in shares) must be met when the hybrid is not "conventional" convertible debt in order for the embedded conversion feature to be considered an equity instrument of the issuer. (EITF 00-19, par. 4, as revised)

If the conversion feature is considered an equity instrument, the entire instrument should be accounted for on a combined basis as traditional convertible debt. If the conversion feature is not considered an equity instrument, the instrument must be evaluated under under FAS-133 to determine whether it contains an embedded derivative that must be accounted for separately. (Chapter 13, "Embedded Derivatives," discusses the mechanics of split accounting in detail.) Exhibit 10-3 summarizes the application of those basic principles to the three instruments. Earnings per share implications are discussed later in this chapter in the section "Disclosures."

EXHIBIT 10-3
ACCOUNTING FOR CONVERTIBLE DEBT WITH CASH SETTLEMENT OPTIONS

	Instrument A Requires Cash Settlement of Entire Obligation	Instrument B Issuer Choice to Settle Entire Obligation in Shares or Cash	Instrument C Must Satisfy Accreted Value in Cash; Issuer Choice to Settle Conversion Spread in Shares or Cash
Characterization for accounting purposes	Debt with embedded derivative	Traditional convertible debt	If conversion feature is equity under EITF 00-19, traditional convertible debt. If not, debt with embedded derivative
Split accounting?	Yes	No	Maybe
Accounting if bifurcation no longer required (EITF 06-7)	Reclassify the carrying amount of liability for the fair value of the conversion option to shareholders' equity. Continue to amortize any debt discount recognized upon bifurcation. Upon conversion, any unamortized discount recognized immediately as interest expense.	Same	Same, except that guidance for conversions in EITF 03-7 below should be applied, regardless of whether the embedded conversion option was previously reclassified to shareholders' equity.

	Instrument A Requires Cash Settlement of Entire Obligation	Instrument B Issuer Choice to Settle Entire Obligation in Shares or Cash	Instrument C Must Satisfy Accreted Value in Cash; Issuer Choice to Settle Conversion Spread in Shares or Cash
Extinguishment**	Gain or loss under APB-26	If settled in stock, no gain or loss. If settled in cash, gain or loss under APB-26	If conversion spread is settled in stock, shares transferred not considered in computing gain or loss on extinguish- ment of the debt component.* (EITF Issue 03-7)

*This does not apply when extinguishment accounting is required under EITF 05-1. In that case, the reacquisition price of the debt would include the cash payment for the accreted value of the debt and the fair value of the equity instruments issued to settle the conversion spread.

**If a convertible debt instrument is extinguished prior to its stated maturity and the carrying amount of the conversion option has been previously reclassified to share-holders' equity (because split accounting is no longer required as discussed in EITF 06-7), the portion of the reacquisition price equal to the fair value of the conversion option is allocated to equity and the remaining reacquisition price allocated to the extinguish-ment gain or loss.

Note: This Exhibit assumes that the entity has adopted FAS-133. Entities that elected to grandfather instruments with embedded derivatives would continue to apply the provisions of the original consensus on EITF Issue 90-19 for these instruments.

Embedded conversion options no longer requiring bifurcation   In some instances, an embedded conversion option that was required to be bifurcated upon issuance of convertible debt may cease to meet the bifurcation requirement under FAS-133.

In instances when an embedded conversion option that was initially bifurcated under FAS-133 is no longer required to be bifurcated, the issuer must reclassify the carrying amount of the derivative liability to shareholders' equity. At the date of conversion, the issuer should recognize any remaining unamortized discount immediately as interest expense. If the convertible debt is later extinguished, a portion of the reacquisition price equal to the fair value of the conversion option should be allocated to equity and the remaining reacquisition price is used to determine the amount of gain or loss upon extinguishment. (EITF 06-7)

Convertible preferred stock   Convertible preferred stock with a mandatory redemption date may qualify for the exception in 00-19 for "conventional" convertible debt if the economic characteristics of the instrument are more akin to debt than equity. Companies should consider the guidance in FAS-133 in assessing whether the instrument is more akin to debt or equity. If the preferred stock is more akin to equity than debt, the conversion feature would not require bifurcation.

> **SEC REGISTRANT ALERT:**   In assessing whether the instrument is more akin to equity or debt, the SEC staff believes the following factors should be included in the analysis: any redemption provisions in the instrument, the nature of the returns (stated or participating), whether the returns are mandatory or discretionary, whether there are any voting rights, whether there are any collateral requirements, whether the preferred stockholders participate in the residual, whether the preferred stockholders have preference liquidation, and whether the preferred stockholders have creditor rights. (Speech by Stephanie L. Hunsaker, Associate Chief Accountant, Division of Corporation Finance of the SEC, at the December 2006 AICPA National Conference on Current SEC and PCAOB Developments)

> **SEC REGISTRANT ALERT:**   In December 2005, the SEC reiterated the hierarchy of guidance required to be applied when analyzing the effect of embedded conversion features in convertible instruments. The SEC staff expressed concern over misapplication of guidance in this area and the lack of both analysis of certain embedded features and disclosure surrounding such features. Registrants should ensure they have appropriately applied FAS-133 and EITF Issue 00-19 and have analyzed all terms in convertible debt and convertible preferred stock. The SEC staff commented on the following specific features of these instruments that have caused practice problems:
>
> - A clause that provides that the number of shares issuable upon conversion is variable with no cap on the number of shares that will be issued upon conversion will cause the conversion feature to not be considered "conventional" and would not permit a registrant to assert that it will have sufficient authorized and unissued shares with which to settle the conversion option. Therefore, the conversion feature would not meet the conditions for equity classification and would be accounted for as a derivative liability. In addition, the variable share settlement clause may affect the classification of previously issued instruments or instruments issued in the future.
>
> - If an instrument is a conventional convertible instrument and the embedded feature would qualify for equity classification under EITF 00-19 and not be bifurcated under FAS-133, registrants should assess whether there is a beneficial conversion feature that must be accounted for under EITF 98-5 and EITF 00-27.

Registrants should provide robust disclosures about the features embedded in convertible instruments and the basis for the classification of such instruments should be provided (that is, an explicit statement in the disclosure of why or why not fair value accounting is applied).

(December 2005 Current Accounting and Disclosure Issues in the Division of Corporation Finance, SEC, and December 2005 Presentation, *Current Developments in the Division of Corporation Finance*, at the National Conference on Current SEC and PCAOB Developments)

EITF Issues Changed or Resolved by FAS-133

Numerous EITF Issues addressed the accounting for various "nontraditional" types of convertible debt. FAS-133 nullified many of those consensuses. Instruments that were not grandfathered as permitted by FAS-133 must be accounted for under the revised guidance.

The following table summarizes certain types of debt-equity hybrid instruments that are generally considered to have embedded derivatives under FAS-133:

EITF Issue	Instrument type	Components
85-9	Debt exchangeable into the stock of another entity	—Debt —Equity derivative*
85-29	Convertible bonds with a premium put (embedded feature that permits investors to: (1) to convert the debt to equity or (2) to cash-out at a multiple of the bond par value)	—Bond —Equity derivative
86-28	Equity-indexed note	—Debt —Equity derivative**
90-19	Convertible bond that must be settled entirely in cash upon conversion (Instrument A)	—Debt —Cash-settled written call option
90-19	Convertible bond where the issuer may elect to settle the conversion spread in either stock or cash (Instrument C)	—Debt —Written call option***

---

* It is possible that this feature would not meet the definition of a derivative if the terms *require* settlement in the stock of a private company (i.e., it cannot be net settled, as defined in FAS-133).

** It is possible that this feature would *not* meet the definition of a derivative if the terms *require* settlement in the stock of a private company. See Chapter 8, "Debt Financing," for accounting in that circumstance. If the note is tied to a stock market index (such as the S&P 500) and requires settlement in cash, it would always meet the definition of a derivative.

*** If the call option is considered equity under EITF Issue 00-19, including the supplemental conditions, the instrument should be accounted for as traditional convertible debt.

Debt with Beneficial Conversion Features
(EITF 98-5 and EITF 00-27)

Convertible debt securities and convertible preferred stock with a nondetachable conversion feature that is in the money at the *commitment date* (a beneficial conversion feature) are subject to a special accounting model. In addition to having an in-the-money conversion feature, such securities often have a variety of other characteristics, including the following:

- The securities may have a fixed conversion rate or be convertible at a fixed discount from the common stock's market price at the conversion date, whichever is lower.

- The conversion price may vary based on future events—for example, subsequent financing at a lower price than the original conversion price, the company's liquidation or a change of control, or an initial public offering (IPO) that has a lower price per share than the agreed-upon amount.

- The convertibles themselves may have warrants attached to them that are separately exercisable.

> **SEC REGISTRANT ALERT:** The SEC staff believes that convertible securities that are issued within a year of filing an initial registration statement with a conversion price below the initial offering price are presumed to have a beneficial conversion feature. The presumption can be overcome with evidence that the conversion price represented fair value at the commitment or issuance date. (December 7, 1999, speech by Pascal Desroches, then a Professional Accounting Fellow at the SEC)

This discussion assumes that the embedded conversion feature would be considered an equity instrument under EITF Issue 00-19. However, if the conversion feature would not be considered an equity instrument of the issuer (perhaps because it requires or permits cash settlement at the discretion of the holder), the contract must be evaluated under FAS-133 as an embedded derivative.

> ☞ **PRACTICE POINTER:** The model established in EITF Issue 98-5 gave rise to numerous practice issues. In Issue 00-27, the EITF modified some of the consensuses in Issue 98-5. Some significant practice issues remain unresolved as of the date this book went to publication. Accordingly, this chapter provides a discussion of the key aspects of the accounting for instruments with beneficial conversion features. Further discussion of EITF Issue 00-27 is on hold pending further progress on phase two of the FASB's liabilities and equity project. Readers should monitor the progress of the EITF on Issue 00-27 as the numerous implementation issues are addressed (or reconsidered).

Accounting at Inception

An embedded beneficial conversion feature (BCF) should be valued separately at the *commitment date*. The BCF should be measured at its intrinsic value, which means the difference between the conversion price and the *fair value* of the stock multiplied by the number of shares into which the security is convertible. The BCF should be recorded by allocating part of the proceeds equal to its intrinsic value to additional paid-in capital. If the conversion price changes in increments over time, intrinsic value should be measured using the terms most beneficial to the holder.

> ☛ **PRACTICE POINTER:** If the intrinsic value of the BCF exceeds the total amount of proceeds, the measurement of the BCF is limited to the proceeds allocated to the convertible instrument. *Issuance costs* paid to third parties should not be offset against the proceeds in calculating the intrinsic value of a conversion option. Any amounts paid to the *investor* when the transaction is consummated represent a reduction of proceeds (not issuance costs) and would affect the allocation of proceeds to BCF.

Variable prices and contingencies If a security (a) becomes convertible only upon the occurrence of a future event outside the control of the holder or (b) is convertible from inception, but contains conversion terms that change upon the occurrence of a future event, any contingent beneficial conversion feature should be *measured* at the commitment date, but not be recognized in additional paid-in capital until the triggering event occurs and the contingency is resolved. In such cases, intrinsic value should be measured using the most favorable conversion price that would be in effect at the conversion date, assuming no changes except for the passage of time.

If a security contains a contingent conversion feature that reduces the conversion price if, on specified dates prior to maturity, the fair value of the underlying stock declines to or below a specified price, a beneficial conversion amount should be recognized when the reset occurs.

Ongoing Accounting

Any recorded discount resulting from that allocation should be amortized to the stated redemption date as interest expense or dividends for convertible debt and convertible preferred securities, respectively, using the effective yield method. (For a perpetual preferred security, the discount should be amortized to the earliest redemption date.) However, if the security were convertible at issuance, the discount would be recognized upfront as interest expense or retained earnings, as appropriate. Changes in the fair value of the BCF are not recognized.

> ☛ **PRACTICE POINTER:** If a convertible security (containing a BCF) is issued with detachable warrants, first, the total proceeds

should be allocated between the warrants and convertible security using the relative fair value method described in APB-14. For this purpose, fair value should be measured on the commitment date as defined in EITF Issue 00-27 rather than the guidance in APB-14. Then, the accounting model described in this section should be applied to the proceeds allocated to the convertible securities (containing a BCF).

SEC REGISTRANT ALERT: Perpetual preferred stock that has no stated redemption date but that is required to be redeemed if a future event that is outside the control of the issuer occurs (such as a change in control) should be accounted for as temporary equity pursuant to SEC Accounting Series Release 268 (and the related SEC staff guidance).

If the amount allocated to the BCF requires adjustment because a contingency is resolved, the amount of the debt discount may also require adjustment. Any excess amortization should not be reversed. Any unamortized discount that exceeds the amount necessary for the total discount (amortized and unamortized) to be equal to the intrinsic value of the adjusted conversion option should be reversed through a debit to paid-in capital (as an adjustment to the intrinsic value measurement of the conversion option).

Conversion   When a security with a BCF is converted prior to the full amortization of the discount, all of the unamortized discount at the date of conversion should be immediately recognized as interest expense or as a dividend, as appropriate. If the amount of unamortized discount is recognized as an expense (because the convertible instrument was debt in form), the expense should *not* be classified as extraordinary.

OBSERVATION: This accounting differs from the treatment of unamortized premium or discount on traditional convertible debt, which is credited to capital.

Extinguishments   The Task Force may revisit its views on how much, if any, of the reacquisition price should be allocated to the BCF if convertible debt is extinguished (the current choices being the historical or current intrinsic value at the date of extinguishment). As of the date of this publication, the Task Force tentatively decided that when convertible debt is reacquired, an amount equal to the current intrinsic value of the BCF should be recorded as a reduction of paid-in capital, even if that amount exceeds the original intrinsic value of the option. The residual amount, if any, would be allocated to the convertible debt. A gain or loss would be recognized upon extinguishment of the debt.

Exhibit 10-4 summarizes accounting for convertible debt with various types of BCF and convertible perpetual preferred stock.

EXHIBIT 10-4
CONVERTIBLE SECURITIES WITH NONDETACHABLE BCFs

	Convertible Debt with BCF	Convertible Debt with BCF	Convertible Debt with Contingent BCF	Convertible Perpetual Preferred
Conversion price	Fixed	Variable	Variable*	Fixed or variable
Measurement date	— Commitment date —			
Valuation method	Intrinsic value	Intrinsic value using the terms terms most favorable to the investor		Same as similar form of convertible debt
Date BCF recorded	Commitment date	Commitment date	When contingency is resolved, recognize amount calculated at commitment date*	Same as similar form of convertible debt
Classification of BCF	Additional Paid in Capital (limited to proceeds attributable to debt or preferred stock).			
Discount from allocating proceeds to BCF (if not immediately convertible)	Amortize to stated redemption date		Amortize from date of recognition to stated redemption date	Analogous to a dividend; amortize discount to earliest conversion date.
Discount on debt if immediately convertible	Expense at inception.	Expense at inception.	Expense when contingency is resolved.	Charge to retained earnings at inception.
Conversion	Expense any unamortized discount (as ordinary income). Record conversion amount in equity.			Record any unamortized discount as a dividend (retained earnings). Record equity ssued at conversion amount.

	Convertible Debt with BCF	Convertible Debt with BCF	Convertible Debt with Contingent BCF	Convertible Perpetual Preferred
Extinguish-ment/re-demption	Allocate amount to BCF using current intrinsic value;[+][‡] recognize gain or loss on revised carrying amount of debt.			Allocate his-torical amount to BCF; any excess (shortfall) on revised carrying amount adjusts numerator in EPS.[‡]

---

[*] If the number of shares is not calculable until a contingent event occurs, the issuer should wait until that event occurs and calculate the incremental intrinsic value attributable to the change in terms (increased number of shares times the commitment date fair value). That incremental intrinsic value would be recognized when the contingent event occurs.

[+] Except when no amount was originally ascribed to a beneficial conversion feature.

[‡] Tentative conclusion that modifies an earlier consensus (from EITF Issue 98-5). Readers should monitor the discussions of the EITF on Issue 00-27.

Presentation of Cash Flows

The issuance of convertible debt results in a cash inflow from financing activities. While convertible debt is outstanding, the interest paid is a cash flow from operating activities. Converting debt to equity is a noncash transaction that requires separate disclosure under FAS-95. The disclosures must clearly relate the cash and non-cash aspects of transactions involving similar items. (FAS-95, par. 32)

> ☛ **PRACTICE POINTER:** Disclosure of noncash items may be included on the same page as the statement of cash flows or reported elsewhere in the financial statements, provided that they are clearly referenced to the statement of cash flows. (FAS-95, par. 74)
>
> **OBSERVATION:** Neither FAS-95 nor FAS-84 addresses the classification of a cash payment made to induce conversion of convertible debt.

Income Tax Consequences

Convertible debt and other hybrids involving the issuer's stock can give rise to a variety of book-tax differences for the issuer, including differences in the method of allocating proceeds between debt and conversion features and the treatment of conversions. FAS-109 provides guidance on accounting for income taxes.

Convertible Debt Instruments Subject to Registration Payment Arrangements

Companies may enter into registration payment arrangements as part of the issuance of a financial instrument, such as a warrant, preferred stock, or a debt instrument. Convertible debt instruments are also sometimes issued subject to registration payment arrangements. Chapter 16, "Equity Instruments and Related Contracts," outlines the required accounting in FSP EITF 00-19-2 for registration payment arrangements that are issued concurrent with the issuance of various types of financial instruments (see the section entitled, "Equity Instruments Subject to Registration Payment Arrangements").

> ☛ **PRACTICE POINTER:** Chapter 16 outlines the scope of FSP EITF 00-19-2. The scope does *not* include arrangements that require consideration in the form of an adjustment of the conversion ratio related to convertible debt or convertible preferred stock instruments.

A contingent obligation to make payments or transfer consideration under a registration payment arrangement must be recognized in accordance with FAS-5 and FIN-14. The convertible debt instrument subject to the arrangement must be accounted for under relevant GAAP for that instrument. If the transfer of consideration under a registration payment arrangement is probable and reasonably estimable (under FAS-5 and FIN-14), the contingent liability must be included in the allocation of proceeds from the related financing transaction using the measurement guidance in FAS-5. The remaining proceeds must be allocated under other applicable GAAP for the instruments.

In situations in which a company concurrently issues convertible debt and warrants subject to a registration payment arrangement, the effect of allocating the proceeds may affect the determination of whether a beneficial conversion feature exists under EITF 98-5 and EITF 00-27. For purposes of determining whether a convertible instrument contains a beneficial conversion feature, the conversion price must be adjusted to give effect to the amount of proceeds allocated to the convertible debt instrument.

Chapter 16, "Issuer's Accounting for Equity Instruments and Related Contracts," outlines incremental disclosure requirements applicable to an issuer's registration payment arrangements.

Fair Value Option for Certain Convertible Debt Instruments

AUTHOR'S NOTE: In February 2007, the FASB issued FASB Statement No. 159, *The Fair Value Option for Financial Assets and Financial Liabilities.* FAS-159 provides companies with an option to report certain financial assets and liabilities at fair value with subsequent changes in value reported in earnings. The specific provisions of FAS-159 applicable to convertible debt instruments are covered in this Chapter. Chapter 19, "The Fair Value Option for Financial Instruments," provides generalized guidance on the fair value option in FAS-159. FAS-159 is effective for calendar-year-end companies as of January 1, 2008. Early adoption is permitted as of the beginning of a fiscal year that begins on or before November 15, 2007, provided the entity also elects to apply FAS-157.

In addition, in September 2006, the FASB issued FASB Statement No. 157, *Fair Value Measurements.* FAS-157 provides a single definition of the term *fair value*, establishes a framework for measuring fair value where permitted or required by existing GAAP, and expands disclosures about fair value measurements. Specific fair value measurement guidance applicable to convertible debt instruments is covered in this Chapter. Chapter 18, "Fair Value Measurements, Fair Value Disclosures, and Other Financial Instrument Disclosures," provides the detailed provisions of FAS-157. FAS-157 is effective for calendar-year-end companies as of January 1, 2008. Unless a company chooses to early adopt, prior GAAP is applicable for financial statements issued for 2007.

As this book went to press, the FASB was addressing a possible delay of FAS-157's effective date. The FASB agreed to consider delaying the effective date for nonfinancial instruments and for certain types of entities, including private companies and "smaller" public companies (not yet defined). Readers should monitor the FASB's further deliberations regarding the nature of any delay of FAS-157's effective date. Also, readers should refer to the 2007 edition for GAAP related to the fair value measurement of financial instruments applicable before the effective date of FAS-157.

Issuers may elect to measure eligible convertible debt instruments at fair value under the fair value option provided by FAS-159. However, certain convertible debt instruments are not eligible for the election. FAS-159 provides that instruments that are, in whole or in part, classified by the issuer as a component of shareholder's equity are not eligible for the fair value option. Convertible debt securities with noncontingent beneficial conversion features are not eligible for this election, because the beneficial conversion feature is classified at the commitment date in additional paid-in-capital. (FAS-159, par. 8(f))

If the fair value option is elected for an eligible convertible debt instrument, it is initially measured at fair value and subsequent changes in fair value are recognized in earnings. FAS-159 does not specify a method to be used for recognizing and measuring the amount of interest income and interest expense for items for which the fair value option has been elected; however, FAS-159 requires disclosure of a description of how interest and dividends are measured and where they are reported in the income statement for each period for which an income statement is presented.

FAS-157 is the primary guidance for fair value measurement under GAAP. Fair value is the price that would be received to sell an asset or paid to transfer a liability in an orderly transaction between market participants at the measurement date. For an issuer of convertible debt for which the fair value option is elected, FAS-157 requires that the fair value of the liability must reflect nonperformance risk, including the effect of the issuer's own credit risk. In addition, debt issue costs would be recognized immediately as an expense rather than deferred and amortized over the term of the debt. (FAS-159, par. A41) Chapter 18, "Fair Value Measurements, Fair Value Disclosures, and Other Financial Instrument Disclosures," provides specific fair value measurement guidance applicable to all financial instruments required to be measured at fair value under GAAP.

DISCLOSURES

Information about Securities

Entities that issue convertible securities and other similar instruments must disclose the number of shares issued upon conversion, exercise, or satisfaction of required conditions during at least the most recent annual fiscal period and any subsequent interim period presented. (FAS-129, par. 5)

Entities that issue convertible securities and other similar instruments must explain the pertinent rights and privileges of the securities outstanding, including conversion or exercise prices or rates and pertinent dates, sinking fund requirements, unusual voting rights, and significant terms of contracts to issue additional shares. (FAS-129, par. 4)

Convertible Securities with Contingent Features

Significant terms of the conversion features of contingently convertible securities, including those with contingencies that have not been met, must be disclosed. Issuers of contingently convertible securities must disclose the conversion price and number of shares into which the security is potentially convertible. The following additional qualitative disclosures are required for contingently convertible securities:

- Events or changes in circumstances that would cause the contingency to be met
- Significant features necessary to understand the conversion rights and their timing

- Events or changes in circumstances and significant terms of such changes that could change the contingency, conversion price, or number of shares
- The manner of settlement upon conversion and any alternative settlement methods

In addition, the issuer should provide a discussion of whether shares that would be issued if the contingently convertible securities were converted in the calculation of diluted EPS (and reasons why or why not). A discussion of derivative transactions entered into in connection with contingently convertible securities would be useful in explaining the potential impact of the securities. (FSP FAS 129-1)

Beneficial Conversion Features

The issuer should disclose in the footnotes to its financial statements the terms of its convertible debt with beneficial conversion features, including the excess of the aggregate fair value of the instruments that the holder would receive at conversion over the proceeds received and the period over which the discount is being amortized. (EITF 98-5, as required by FAS-129)

Embedded Conversion Options No Longer Requiring Bifurcation

The following disclosures are required by an issuer for the period in which an embedded conversion option previously accounted for as a derivative under FAS-133 is no longer required to be bifurcated:

- A description of the changes causing the embedded conversion option to no longer require bifurcation under FAS-133
- The amount of the liability related to the conversion option reclassified to shareholders' equity. (EITF 06-7)

In addition, in circumstances where an embedded conversion option in a debt instrument no longer meets the bifurcation criteria in FAS-133, see above section, "'Nontraditional' Convertible Debt," for guidance on (1) reclassification of the carrying amount of the liability for the previously bifurcated conversion option and (2) the amortization of the debt discount that was recognized when the conversion option was bifurcated from the convertible debt.

Earnings per Share

Convertible debt and debt with detachable stock purchase warrants both can affect earnings per share when the effect would be dilutive. FAS-128 provides guidance on how to calculate basic and diluted earnings per share (EPS). Chapter 13 of CCH's *GAAP Guide Level A* and

Chapter 14 of CCH's *GAAP Practice Guide Levels B, C, and D,* both called, "Earnings per Share," include a comprehensive discussion of the guidelines for presenting EPS. The guidance in this section is limited to unique EPS issues involving the instruments discussed in this chapter.

In general, basic EPS is computed by dividing income available to common stockholders by the weighted-average number of common shares outstanding for the period.

- Preferred stock dividends should be deducted from net income (or added to the amount of a net loss) in computing income available to common stockholders.

- Shares contingently issuable are not included in basic earnings per share.

Diluted EPS reflects the potential dilution that could occur if securities or other contracts to issue common stock were exercised or converted into common stock or resulted in the issuance of common stock that then shared in the earnings of the entity. The computation of diluted EPS should not assume conversion, exercise, or contingent issuance of securities that would have an *antidilutive* effect on earnings per share.

> **SEC REGISTRANT ALERT:** Public companies should carefully review the SEC regulations and other guidance for presenting earnings per share. Numerous specific fact patterns are addressed that are outside the scope of this publication.
>
> At the December 2006 National Conference on Current SEC and PCAOB Developments, the SEC staff provided views on the computation of EPS when a company has a class of common stock that is convertible into another class of common stock. The computation of EPS in that situation is not directly addressed by FAS-128 or EITF 03-6 on participating securities. The SEC staff believes that a company with two classes of common stock must present both a basic and diluted EPS figure for each class regardless of conversion rights. Presentation of diluted EPS only for the class of common stock being converted into is not sufficient and inconsistent with the guidance in FAS-128 which requires presentation for basic and diluted EPS for each class of common stock. The SEC staff indicated that for the class being converted into, diluted EPS must be computed using the if-converted method if the result would be dilutive while for the convertible class, diluted EPS must be computed using the two-class method. Companies should also disclose an explanation of its computation of basic and diluted EPS. (Speech by Cathy J. Cole, Associate Chief Accountant, Office of the Chief Accountant, SEC at the December 2006 National Conference on Current SEC and PCAOB Developments)

> ☛ **PRACTICE POINTER:** The FASB currently has on its agenda a joint project with the IASB to address certain issues regarding the computation of EPS. As part of that project, certain decisions have

been reached specific to convertible securities. This project is expected to result in an amendment of FAS-128. A joint Exposure Draft is expected to be issued as early as the third quarter of 2007 (this is the third Exposure Draft to be issued by the FASB related to this project). A detailed summary of decisions on this project can be found on the FASB's website at http://www.fasb.org/project/short-term_intl_convergence.shtml.

In addition, the FASB staff has drafted a proposed FSP (FAS 128-a) to provide computational guidance addressing the application of the two-class method in computing diluted EPS when an entity has common stock, participating securities, and potential common stock. The proposed FSP sets forth three steps for computing diluted EPS under the two-class method and provides illustrations. It is expected that this guidance will be incorporated into FAS-128 through the joint project of the FASB and IASB to converge guidance related to the computation of EPS rather than through issuance of a final FSP.

Basic EPS

EITF Issue 03-6 requires participating convertible securities to be included in the computation of basic EPS using the two-class method. Under the two-class method, earnings for the period (after reduction for contractual preferred stock dividends) are allocated between the common shareholders and the other security holders based on their respective rights to receive dividends.

> ☛ **PRACTICE POINTER:** EITF Issue 03-6 clarifies the definition of a participating security and the application of the two-class method to such securities. Chapter 16, "Issuer's Accounting for Equity Instruments and Related Contracts," outlines the provisions of EITF Issue 03-6 in greater detail.

Undistributed earnings for the period must be allocated to a participating security based on the contractual participation rights of the security to share in those earnings on a pro forma basis *as if* all of the earnings for the period had been distributed. Undistributed earnings are allocated only if the terms of the participating security specify objectively determinable, nondiscretionary participation rights. In periods of net loss, an entity must allocate losses for purposes of computing basic EPS to participating securities if, based on their contractual terms, the securities had both the right to participate in the earnings of the issuer and the contractual obligation to share in the losses of the issuing entity on an objectively determinable basis. Such a determination must be made in each period. A contractual obligation to share in the losses of the issuing entity is present if *either* of the following conditions is present:

- The holder is obligated to fund the losses of the issuing entity through a transfer of additional assets to the issuer without any corresponding increase in the holder's investment interest, *or*
- The contractual principal or mandatory redemption amount of the participating security is reduced as a result of losses incurred by the issuing entity.

☞ **PRACTICE POINTER:** Although EITF Issue 03-6 indicates that a participation right may be in a form other than a dividend, a reduction of the conversion price or increase of the conversion ratio of a convertible security triggered by the declaration of dividends *does not* represent a participation right. However, such a feature should be evaluated under EITF Issue 98-5 and EITF Issue 00-27 to determine whether it is a beneficial conversion feature.

Diluted EPS

Convertible securities Convertible preferred stock and convertible debt that require settlement in shares, if converted, should be assumed to have been converted at the beginning of the period (or at time of issuance, if later). Shares assumed issued should be weighted for the period that the convertible securities were outstanding, and common shares actually issued should be weighted for the period the shares were outstanding. (FAS-128, par. 28) The resulting common shares should *not* be included in the denominator if the effect would be antidilutive. (FAS-128, par. 26)

In addition, the following adjustments should made to the numerator:

- Preferred dividends are added back on convertible preferred stock.
- Interest expense is added back for convertible debt (on a tax-effected basis).
- Income is adjusted for expenses based on net income (such as profit sharing) that would have been different without the interest expense (on a tax-effected basis).

☞ **PRACTICE POINTER:** This is called the "if-converted" method of computing diluted earnings per share under FAS-128.

OBSERVATION: Convertible debt is assumed to have been converted regardless of whether conversion is likely (that is, the embedded option could be "out-of-the-money"). However, if the effect of including convertible debt and the related adjustments to income is antidilutive, it would not ultimately be included in diluted earnings per share.

Contingently convertible instruments Certain instruments are contingently convertible into the issuer's shares upon meeting a market condition that is based in whole or in part on the issuer's share price (a "market price trigger"). Some such instruments have multiple contingencies and the instrument is convertible into shares upon meeting a market price trigger *or* a non-market-based contingency (but not both). These instruments should be included in diluted EPS, if dilutive, regardless of whether the market price trigger has been met. (EITF Issue 04-8)

Detachable warrants Warrants that require settlement in shares, if exercised, should be included in diluted earnings per share using the treasury stock method *only* when they are in-the-money (that is, the average market price during the period exceeds the strike price). Under the treasury stock method:

- Assume that the warrants were exercised; shares were issued and proceeds were received.
- The assumed proceeds are used to purchase common stock at the average market price during the period.
- The *incremental* number of shares (the difference between the number of shares assumed issued and the number of shares assumed purchased) should be included in the denominator of the diluted EPS computation.

If the warrants include cash settlement options, they should be included in diluted earnings per share as described in EITF Topic D-72. Refer to Chapter 16, "Issuer's Accounting for Equity Instruments and Related Contracts," for additional information.

Convertible debt with cash settlement features The effect of non-traditional convertible debt on diluted earnings per share depends on the terms of the debt. If the entire obligation may be settled in stock and the debt is accounted for like traditional convertible debt, the if-converted method should be used to calculate diluted earnings per share, as described above. If only the conversion feature may be settled in stock (not the whole instrument), the effect on diluted earnings per share should be computed using the guidance in EITF Topic D-72. Refer to Chapter 16, "Issuer's Accounting for Equity Instruments and Related Contracts," for additional information. If the instrument is viewed as debt with an embedded derivative, and cash settlement is required, no adjustment should be made to diluted earnings per share, because no part of the instrument is considered an equity instrument of the issuer. Exhibit 10-5 summarizes the effect on diluted earnings per share for the three forms of nontraditional debt profiled in EITF Issue 90-19.

EXHIBIT 10-5
EPS TREATMENT OF NONTRADITIONAL CONVERTIBLE DEBT

	Instrument A Requires Cash Settlement of Entire Obligation	Instrument B Issuer Choice to Settle Entire in Obligation Shares or Cash	Instrument C Must satisfy Accreted Value in Cash; Issuer Choice to Settle Conversion Spread in Shares or Cash
Basic accounting (see previous section for details)	Debt plus derivative	Convertible debt	Debt plus derivative OR convertible debt (if conversion feature is equity under 00-19)
If-converted method for DEPS?	No	Yes, if dilutive	No
Effect of cash-settled feature?	Not applicable	None	None
Effect of conver-sion spread?	Not applicable	None	Reflect in DEPS using EITF D-72

SEC REGISTRANT ALERT: To the extent that a market price contingency is included in the terms of Instrument C in EITF 90-19, the conversion spread is subject to EITF 04-8 and therefore must be included in an entity's diluted EPS in all periods in which it would be dilutive, regardless of whether the conversion contingency has been met. (Speech by Robert J. Comerford, Professional Accounting Fellow, Office of the Chief Accountant of the SEC, at the December 2004 AICPA National Conference on SEC and PCAOB Developments)

Induced conversion of preferred stock EITF Topics D-42 and D-53 provide guidance on the earnings per share implications for the redemption or induced conversion of preferred stock that is not man-datorily redeemable as defined in FAS-150. Briefly, the SEC staff believes that the excess of (1) fair value of the consideration trans-ferred to the holders of the preferred stock over (2) the carrying amount of the preferred stock in the registrant's balance sheet (reduced by the issuance costs of the preferred stock) should be subtracted from net earnings to arrive at net earnings available to common shareholders in the calculation of earnings per share. (Likewise, an excess of the carrying amount of preferred stock over the fair value of the consideration transferred to the holders of the preferred stock would be added to net earnings to arrive at net earnings available to common shareholders.)

AUDIT CONSIDERATIONS

There is no audit literature that specifically addresses issues relating to convertible debt and other forms of debt-equity hybrids. However, aspects of accounting for convertible debt, for example, determining whether a conversion feature or detachable warrant meets the definition of a derivative under FAS-133, are addressed by SAS-92 and the AICPA Audit Guide, *Auditing Derivative Instruments Heading Activities, and Investments in Securities.*

The key areas of audit risk relating to accounting for convertible debt and similar instruments are:

- Failure to properly characterize the conversion feature as an equity instrument or a liability (often, a derivative). Improper classification of the components has significant implications on stockholders' equity and reported income for the period.

- Failure to identify a beneficial conversion feature and apply the appropriate specialized accounting model in EITF Issues 98-5 and 00-27 (which continue to evolve).

- For hybrid instruments that require separate accounting, using inappropriate assumptions to estimate the fair value (or intrinsic value for a beneficial conversion feature) of the components for the purpose of allocating the proceeds between debt and an embedded derivative or a detachable warrant and for the ongoing accounting for a derivative. Auditors should take note that the definition of fair value in EITF Issue 98-5 (convertible debt with beneficial conversion features) prohibits adjustments to a quoted market price (if one is available). Estimating the fair value of an equity component can be especially difficult when the issuer is a private company.

- Failure to reflect convertible debt and other debt-equity hybrids properly in diluted earnings per share computations.

ILLUSTRATIONS

Illustration 10-1: Debt with Detachable Stock Purchase Warrants [APB-14]

Streamline Corporation, a private company, issued 100 $100 par value bonds with a 6% interest rate and a detachable warrant to purchase one share of

Streamline's common stock at a price of $4 per share. If exercised, the warrants must be settled by the delivery of one share of Streamline common stock. (That is, the warrants would be considered equity instruments of the issuer.) The bonds and warrants were issued for total proceeds of $9,900. At the time of issuance, the quoted market price of similar (nonconvertible) bonds was $97, and the fair value of the warrants was estimated to be $2 each. The transaction would be accounted for as follows:

Cash	$9,900	
Discount on bonds payable	300	
Bonds payable		$10,000
Paid-in capital (warrants)		200

The discount would be amortized to interest expense over the life of the debt using the interest method. Changes in the fair value of the warrants would not be recognized.

Subsequently, if all of the investors tendered their warrants for common stock, when the current market price of the stock is $7 per share, the following entry would be recorded:

Cash (100 warrants x $4)	$400	
Paid-in capital (stock warrants)	200	
Capital stock ($1 par value)		$100
Capital in excess of par (common stock)		500

Note that the current market value of the stock is irrelevant to the issuer's accounting for a conversion according to its terms—no gain or loss is recognized.

Illustration 10-2: Traditional Convertible Debt [APB-14]

Dorn Corporation issues a $100,000 7% convertible bond at par value that is due on December 31, 20X7. Each $1,000 bond is convertible into 20 shares of Dorn Corporation $1 par value common stock. Upon issuance, Dorn would record the transaction as follows:

Cash	$100,000	
Convertible bonds payable		$100,000

No portion of the proceeds would be allocated to the conversion feature. Interest expense would be accrued at 7%. (However, if the bond had been issued at a premium or discount, or if debt issue costs were incurred, the effective rate would reflect amortization of those items.)

On a stated conversion date, all of the bondholders elect to convert their bonds because the market value of the stock is far in excess of the conversion price of the bonds. Dorn would record the following journal entry:

Convertible bonds payable	$100,000	
Common stock ($1 par value)		$ 2,000
Capital in excess of par (common stock)		98,000

Note that no gain or loss is recognized upon conversion of convertible debt in accordance with its terms. The carrying amount of the payable would include any unamortized premium or discount and any interest accrued from the last payment date, if applicable, to the date of conversion.

Illustration 10-3: Induced Conversion of Convertible Debt [FAS-84]

Dorn Corporation has outstanding a $100,000 7% convertible bond, issued at par value and due on December 31, 20X7. Each $1,000 bond is convertible into 20 shares of Dorn Corporation $1 par value common stock. To induce bondholders to convert to its common stock, Dorn Corporation increases the conversion rate from 20 shares per $1,000 bond to 25 shares per $1,000 bond. This offer was made by Dorn Corporation for a limited period of 60 days commencing March 1, 20X2.

Assume for simplicity that all of the bondholders accepted the offer and tendered their bonds for conversion on April 1, 20X2, when the market price of Dorn's common stock was $60. Dorn Corporation would calculate the amount of incremental consideration as follows:

Incremental number of shares ((25-20) × 100 bondholders)	500
× Market price at April 1	$60
Incremental consideration	$30,000

Alternatively, Dorn could calculate the incremental consideration as the difference between (a) the fair value of the equity securities and/or other consideration required to be issued under the original terms of the conversion privilege and (b) the fair value of the equity securities and/or other consideration that is actually issued.

Market value of securities based on inducement	
(2,500 × $60)	$150,000
Market value of securities based on original terms	
(2,000 × $60)	(120,000)
Fair value of incremental consideration	$ 30,000

The journal entry to record the transaction is:

Convertible bonds payable	$100,000	
Debt conversion expense	30,000	
Common stock ($1 par value)		$ 2,500
Capital in excess of par (common stock)		127,500

The same accounting would apply if, instead of issuing an increased number of shares, a company reduced the conversion price per share.

Illustration 10-4: Convertible Debt with Beneficial Conversion Feature (Fixed Terms and a Two-Year Lock-Up Period) [EITFs 98-5 and 00-27]

Colwin Industries issued for $1,000,000 convertible debt at par value that is convertible any time after two years have passed into the issuer's common stock at $20 per share. The fair value of each share is $25 on the commitment date. Because the exercise price is lower than the current market value of the stock, it is "in-the-money" and is deemed to have a beneficial conversion feature. The accounting for such instruments is as follows:

1. Calculate the number of shares into which the debt will be converted at the conversion price: $1,000,000/$20 = 50,000 shares.
2. Calculate the intrinsic value of the beneficial conversion feature at the commitment date: fair value at the commitment date of $25 – $20 conversion price = $5 × 50,000 shares = $250,000.
3. The debt is recognized at $1,000,000. $250,000 of the debt proceeds are allocated to the beneficial conversion feature, which is credited to additional paid-in capital. The resulting $250,000 debt discount is amortized to interest expense over the period to the stated redemption date.

Illustration 10-5: Convertible Debt with Beneficial Conversion Feature (Fixed Terms, Convertible upon the Occurrence of an IPO)

Coltrane Corporation issued convertible debt for $1,000,000 at par value that is convertible, only upon the occurrence of an IPO, into the issuer's common stock at 80% of the fair value of a common share on the commitment date. The fair value of each share of Coltrane stock is $30 on the commitment date. Because the conversion price ($24) is lower than the current market value of the stock, the convertible debt has a beneficial conversion feature that is contingent upon the occurrence of a future event (the IPO). The accounting for such instruments is as follows:

1. Calculate the number of shares into which the debt will be converted at the conversion price: $1,000,000/$24 = 41,667 shares.
2. Calculate the intrinsic value of the beneficial conversion feature at the commitment date: Market value at the commitment date of $30 – $24 conversion price = $6 × 41,667 shares = $250,000.
3. The $1,000,000 debt is recognized at issuance, but the $250,000 beneficial conversion feature is not recognized unless and until the IPO occurs. Because the debt is immediately convertible upon the occurrence of an IPO, the total debt discount of $250,000 would be debited to interest expense at that time.

Illustration 10-6: Computation of Basic EPS for Convertible Preferred Securities [EITF 03-6]

Fortune Company has 5,000,000 shares of common stock and 1,000,000 shares of convertible preferred stock (issued at $100 par value per share) outstanding during 20X1. The Company had net income of $25,000,000 during 20X1. Each share of preferred stock is convertible into two shares of common stock. The terms of the preferred stock stipulate that it receives a cumulative annual dividend of 3% of the par value. The common shares receive a dividend of $2 per share for 20X1. After distributions to preferred and common shareholders, the preferred stock then participates in any additional dividends on a 1:1 basis.

Net income		$25,000,000
Less: Dividends on common stock	$10,000,000	
Dividends on cumulative preferred stock	3,000,000	
Distributed earnings for 20X1	$13,000,000	
Undistributed earnings for 20X1		$12,000,000

Allocation of undistributed earnings:

To common stock:
  5,000,000 shares/6,000,000 total shares = 0.83
  0.83 × $12,000,000 undistributed earnings = $10,000,000
  $10,000,000/5,000,000 shares = $2.00 per share

To preferred stock:
  1,000,000 shares/6,000,000 total shares = 0.17
  0.17 X $12,000,000 undistributed earnings = $2,000,000
  $2,000,000/1,000,000 shares = $2.00 per share

	Common Shares	Preferred Shares	Total
Distributed earnings	$10,000,000	$3,000,000	$13,000,000
Undistributed earnings	10,000,000	2,000,000	12,000,000
	$20,000,000	$5,000,000	$25,000,000

Basic EPS amounts:

	Common	Preferred
Distributed earnings	$2.00	$3.00
Undistributed earnings	2.00	2.00
Total	$4.00	$5.00

Although the presentation of basic and diluted EPS is not required for securities other than common stock, such a presentation is not precluded.

CHAPTER 11
EXTINGUISHMENTS OF DEBT

CONTENTS

Overview	11.02
Background	11.03
Accounting for Extinguishments and Modifications of Debt	11.03
Extinguishments of Debt	11.03
Criteria for Derecognition	11.03
Recognition of Extinguishments	11.04
Classification of Gain or Loss on Extinguishment	11.05
Accounting for Deferred Hedge Gains and Losses on Debt That Is Extinguished	11.05
Exhibit 11-1: *Accounting for Hedges of Debt That Is Extinguished*	11.06
Issues Involving Extinguishments	11.06
Extinguishment of Convertible Debt	11.07
In-Substance Defeasance	11.08
Nontroubled Exchanges and Modifications of Debt Instruments (EITF 96-19)	11.09
Criteria for Extinguishment Accounting	11.09
Accounting for Significant Exchanges and Modifications	11.11
Exhibit 11-2: Accounting for Exchanges and Modifications of Debt	11.11
Exhibit 11-3: *Identifying Agents and Principals*	11.12
Exhibit 11-4: *Transactions Involving Third-Party Intermediaries*	11.13
Troubled Debt Restructurings	11.15
Transfers of Assets in Full Settlement	11.16
Grant of Equity Interest in Full Settlement	11.17
Modification of Terms	11.18

Combination of Types	11.19
Exhibit 11-5: Debtor's Accounting for Troubled Debt Restructurings	11.20
Implementation Issues	11.20
Reporting Cash Flows	11.21
Disclosures	11.21
Guarantees	11.21
Troubled Debt Restructurings	11.22
In-Substance Defeasances (Grandfathered)	11.22
Audit Considerations	11.22
Illustrations	11.23
Illustration 11-1: Loss on Extinguishment of Debt	11.23
Illustration 11-2: Modification of Debt in a Nontroubled Situation	11.24
Illustration 11-3: Troubled Debt Restructuring—Modification of Terms	11.25
Illustration 11-4: Disclosure of Troubled Debt Restructuring—Combination of Types	11.26
Illustration 11-5: Disclosure of Troubled Debt Restructuring—Transfer of Assets in Full Settlement	11.26

OVERVIEW

A debtor generally decides to extinguish outstanding debt when there is a perceived economic advantage to be obtained. For example, a company may want to replace existing debt with debt that has a lower interest rate, or a company may have excess cash or other liquid assets that earn a rate of return that is less than the cash savings that could be achieved by extinguishing existing debt. In other situations, due to financial difficulties, the debtor may need to exchange or modify its outstanding debt to be able to service the debt.

Generally, a debt instrument is considered extinguished only if the debtor pays the creditor or is otherwise legally released of its obligations. A gain or loss is recognized in income in the period of the extinguishment. Not all reacquisitions of debt are accounted for as extinguishments. On the other hand, certain substantial modifications of debt instruments are accounted for like extinguishments even though the modified debt remains outstanding.

Gains and losses on extinguishments of debt are generally reported as a component of income from continuing operations.

BACKGROUND

FAS-140 is the primary literature that governs accounting for extinguishments of debt. APB-26 provides that the difference between the *reacquisition price* and the *net carrying amount* of debt is recognized as a gain or loss upon extinguishment of that debt. FAS-145 amended previous literature and generally precludes classifying gains and losses from extinguishments of debt as extraordinary items unless both of the conditions of APB-30 are met (i.e., the extinguishment is both unusual in nature and infrequent in occurrence).

Certain other transactions involving changes to outstanding debt instruments have specialized accounting models. The debtor's accounting for troubled debt restructurings is addressed in FAS-15. EITF Issue 96-19 covers accounting for exchanges and modifications of debt in nontroubled situations. If certain conditions are met, significant modifications of debt sometimes are reported like extinguishments of debt, even though the revised debt remains outstanding.

Convertible debt that is extinguished (that is, *not* converted according to its terms or in a qualifying induced conversion) is accounted for like any other extinguishment of debt. Conversions of debt according to their terms, including induced conversions of debt, are addressed in Chapter 10, "Convertible Debt and Similar Instruments."

> **AUTHOR'S NOTE:** Since the last edition of CCH's *Financial Instruments,* the FASB has eliminated its separate agenda project addressing the criteria for liability extinguishment. However, the FASB is continuing work related to the model for derecognition of liabilities as part of is longer-term project on Revenue Recognition.

ACCOUNTING FOR EXTINGUISHMENTS AND MODIFICATIONS OF DEBT

Extinguishments of Debt

Criteria for Derecognition

In accordance with FAS-140, a liability is considered extinguished and should be *derecognized* from a company's balance sheet only if:

- The debtor pays the creditor and is relieved of its obligations for the liability, or
- The debtor is legally released, judicially or by the creditor, from being the primary obligor under the liability. (FAS-140, par. 16)

The following transactions are ways in which the debtor may pay the creditor:

- Delivery of cash or other financial assets
- Issuance of equity securities (but not in accordance with the terms of convertible debt)
- Reacquisition of debt securities whether they are canceled or held as treasury bonds

☛ **PRACTICE POINTER:** An *in-substance defeasance* does not meet the requirements for extinguishment of debt under FAS-140. However, in-substance defeasances completed on or before December 31, 1996, were not required to be restated. Such "grandfathered" transactions are discussed later in this chapter.

☛ **PRACTICE POINTER:** If an old debt instrument is exchanged for a new debt instrument, EITF Issue 96-19 should be applied to determine whether the transaction should be recorded like an extinguishment (assuming the transaction does not represent a troubled debt restructuring). EITF Issue 96-19 is discussed later in this chapter.

Recognition of Extinguishments

Regardless of the means used by the debtor, all extinguishments should be accounted for in the same way. (APB-26, par. 19) Debt that has been extinguished is derecognized from the balance sheet at its *net carrying amount*. A gain or loss is recognized in income in the period of extinguishment for the difference between the *reacquisition price* and the net carrying amount.

Net carrying amount means the amount due at maturity, adjusted for unamortized premium, discount, debt issuance costs, and adjustments arising from fair value hedge accounting. (APB-26, par. 3 and EITF 00-9)

Reacquisition price means the amount paid on extinguishment, including any call premium and other miscellaneous costs of reacquisition. (APB-26, par. 3)

☛ **PRACTICE POINTER:** When debt (or redeemable or fixed-maturity preferred stock) is extinguished through the issuance of stock of the debtor, the reacquisition price is determined by the fair value of the stock issued or the fair value of the debt, whichever is more clearly evident. (FTB 80-1, par. 4, as amended) Conversion of debt according to its original terms is not considered an extinguishment. However, a conversion of debt is considered an extinguishment when the debtor issues stock to settle the obligation under terms that were not provided in the original debt instrument and the revised terms do not meet the conditions for an induced conversion under FAS-84. Refer to

Chapter 10, "Convertible Debt and Similar Instruments," for additional information.

☛ **PRACTICE POINTER:** Regulated entities should amortize the difference between the reacquisition price and the net carrying amount of extinguished debt as an adjustment of interest expense over the period during which it will be allowed for rate making purposes. (FAS-71, pars. 35–37)

Classification of Gain or Loss on Extinguishment

Gains and losses from extinguishments of debt should be classified in accordance with APB-30, as amended. To be classified as an extraordinary item, APB-30 requires that two conditions be met: the transaction must be both (1) unusual in nature and (2) infrequent in occurrence. Debt extinguishment transactions would seldom, if ever, meet both of these criteria, and thus would be reported as a component of income from continuing operations. (FAS-145, par. 7)

Extinguishments of participating mortgage loans If a participating mortgage loan is extinguished prior to its due date, the difference between the recorded amount of the debt (including the unamortized debt discount and the participation liability) and the amount exchanged to extinguish the debt is a debt extinguishment gain or loss that should be reported in accordance with APB-30. (SOP 97-1, par. 16) Chapter 8, "Debt Financing," addresses the accounting for participating mortgage loans in detail.

Accounting for Deferred Hedge Gains and Losses on Debt That Is Extinguished

Some companies use derivatives, such as interest rate swaps, to convert the interest rates on their debt instruments from fixed rate to floating, or from floating to fixed rate. Companies also use derivatives to hedge the effects of changes in foreign exchange rates on foreign-currency-denominated debt instruments and to hedge other risks. The accounting for hedging instruments when the related hedged debt instrument is extinguished depends on the type of hedge in place. The guidance provided in EITF Issue 00-9 is summarized in Exhibit 11-1.

EXHIBIT 11-1
ACCOUNTING FOR HEDGES OF DEBT THAT IS EXTINGUISHED

Type of Hedge	Accounting for Changes in Fair Value under FAS-133	Accounting upon Extinguishment of Debt
Fair value hedge (fixed-rate debt)	Recognized as adjustment of carrying amount of debt	Included in the calculation of gain/loss on extinguishment of debt—classify in accordance with APB-30.*
Cash flow hedge (floating rate debt)	Deferred in other comprehensive income; amortized as an adjustment of the yield on the hedged debt	Reclass from OCI recognized in income—*not* an extraordinary item
Cash flow hedge of forecasted transaction (rate lock on an anticipated issuance of debt)	Deferred in other comprehensive income; amortized as an adjustment of the yield on the hedged debt	Reclass from OCI recognized in income—*not* an extraordinary item

* Extinguishment gains and losses would generally *not* be classified as extraordinary items.

For additional guidance related to hedging activities associated with debt instruments, refer to Chapter 14, "Hedge Accounting."

Issues Involving Extinguishments

Extinguishments of related party debt Extinguishment transactions between related parties are generally considered capital transactions. For example, if a related party forgives a company's loan, the forgiveness should be recorded as a credit to equity, not a gain on extinguishment. (APB-26, par. 20, fn. 1 and AICPA Practice Alert 00-1, par. 27)

Becoming secondarily liable If the creditor legally releases a company as the primary obligor (debtor) under a debt instrument but makes the debtor secondarily liable for that instrument, the debt is considered extinguished by the original debtor but the original debtor has become a guarantor of the debt whether or not explicit consideration was paid for that guarantee. The debtor should record a guarantee obligation that should initially be measured at fair value with a corresponding reduction of the gain or increase of the loss on extinguishment of the debt. Subsequently, the guarantee should be accounted for and disclosed in accordance with FIN-45 and FAS-5. (FAS-140, par. 114) Refer to Chapter 8, "Debt Financing," for additional guidance related to written guarantees.

> ☞ **PRACTICE POINTER:** FIN-45, paragraph 9, provides guidance on estimating the fair value of a guarantee.

Sale of assets subject to liens   If a company sells assets and the purchaser assumes the related debt (such as a mortgage), the seller-debtor is effectively legally released of its obligations under the original debt, thus meeting the conditions of FAS-140 for extinguishment accounting. (FAS-140, par. 16, fn. 5) (The accounting for foreclosure on assets supporting nonrecourse debt is discussed later in this chapter in the section on troubled debt restructurings.)

Extinguishment of debt after the balance sheet date   Extinguishments of debt (including transactions that are accounted for like extinguishments) that occur after the balance sheet date but before issuance of the financial statements are Type 2 subsequent events. That is, the financial statements would not be adjusted to reflect the debt as extinguished at the balance sheet date. Disclosure of a planned extinguishment would be appropriate, if material. (SEC SAB Topic 5AA)

Extinguishment of Convertible Debt

Convertible debt instruments are debt instruments that are convertible into equity of the debtor/issuer at a specified price at the option of the investor. As discussed in depth in Chapter 10, "Convertible Debt and Similar Instruments," under current accounting rules, conversion of convertible debt in accordance with its original terms is *not* viewed as an extinguishment for accounting purposes, and a gain or loss is not recognized. (APB-14, par. 12)

However, if convertible debt is *extinguished* prior to conversion, it is accounted for in the same manner as any other extinguishment of debt. Accordingly, any gain or loss from the extinguishment of convertible debt should be recognized in the period of extinguishment. (APB-26, par. 21)

Induced conversions   A debtor who wishes to encourage the holders of its convertible debt to convert promptly may decide to favorably change the original conversion terms. Such changes may include (a) a reduction of the original conversion price to increase the number of shares of equity securities received by the bondholder, (b) the issuance of warrants or other securities, or (c) the payment of cash or some other type of consideration. (FAS-84, par. 2)

If an induced conversion meets the requirements of FAS-84, it is *not* accounted for as an extinguishment of debt. Briefly, the revised terms must be (a) exercisable only for a limited period of time and (b) include the issuance of all of the equity securities issuable pursuant to the original conversion privileges. (FAS-84, par. 2) An induced conversion that does not meet *both* of these conditions should be accounted for as an extinguishment of debt, because the conversion is not in accordance with the original terms and it does not meet the limited exception in FAS-84. (APB-26, par. 2, as amended)

Chapter 10, "Convertible Debt and Similar Instruments," discusses induced conversions in more detail.

Modifications and exchanges of convertible debt? The effect of modifying a debt instrument to add a conversion option, eliminate a conversion option, or change the fair value of an existing conversion option must be considered in the analysis of whether the debt has been extinguished. The issuer should evaluate whether the exchange or modification is an extinguishment using the cash flow test in EITF 96-19 *without* considering the change in the fair value of the embedded conversion option. If the cash flow test indicates that a substantial modification or exchange has *not* occurred, the issuer must perform a separate test based on the change in fair value of the embedded conversion option. Chapter 10, "Convertible Debt and Similar Instruments," discusses these tests and modifications and exchanges of convertible debt in more detail.

In-Substance Defeasance

In accordance with FAS-76, which was superseded by FAS-125 (and then, in turn by FAS-140), debt was accounted for as if extinguished when the debtor transferred essentially risk-free assets to an irrevocable trust and the cash flows from the trust assets approximated the scheduled debt service payments of the debt (an in-substance defeasance). In accordance with FAS-76, the debtor also derecognized the transferred assets. Under FAS-140, an in-substance defeasance does *not* meet the derecognition criteria for either the debt or the assets. (FAS-140, par. 311) FAS-140 was effective for extinguishments of debt occurring after December 31, 1996 (FAS-140 carried forward the effective date of FAS-125 for these transactions). Therefore, in-substance defeasances accomplished on or before December 31, 1996, were grandfathered and should continue to be reported as extinguishments.

Invasion of a grandfathered defeasance trust Generally, the invasion of a grandfathered defeasance trust will call into question the original accounting for the in-substance defeasance. EITF Issue 86-36 permitted a narrow exception for the reacquisition of outstanding debt (that had been extinguished through an in-substance defeasance) accomplished by the purchase of a proportional amount of the assets in the trust for purposes of taking advantage of the 1986 tax rate differential between capital gains and ordinary income, without calling into question the original accounting for the in-substance defeasance. The SEC staff would question a provision of a trust that permits the exchange of called or repurchased debt for the assets in a grandfathered defeasance trust in advance of their scheduled maturity, whether or not that provision is ever exercised. (January 12, 1993, speech by Jeffrey Swormstedt, then a Professional Accounting Fellow at the SEC)

Nontroubled Exchanges and Modifications of Debt Instruments (EITF 96-19)

Debtors and creditors sometimes agree to exchange or modify debt instruments, even in nontroubled situations. Modifications can be made to change the timing and amount of contractual cash flows, such as principal amounts, interest rates, and the maturity date. Changes can also be made to terms that would affect cash flows in the event of nonperformance or if options are exercised, such as recourse or nonrecourse features, the priority of the debt, the level of collateralization required, the nature of debt covenants and/or waivers, guarantors, or the terms of call and put options. Often, fees are exchanged to compensate the other party for making such changes.

Criteria for Extinguishment Accounting

The *exchange* of an outstanding debt instrument for a new debt instrument with the same lender/creditor results in an extinguishment of the old debt instrument if the debt instruments have *substantially different terms*. Similarly, a *modification* of the terms of an outstanding debt instrument should be accounted for like, and reported in the same manner as, an extinguishment if the old and new debt instruments have *substantially different terms*.

> **OBSERVATION:** The accounting for exchanges of debt with different terms and a modification of existing debt is the same because the debtor can achieve the same economic result in either transaction.

> ☛ **PRACTICE POINTER:** The contemporaneous exchange of cash between the same debtor and creditor in connection with the issuance of a new debt instrument and satisfaction of an existing debt instrument is, in substance, an exchange of debt instruments even though cash is used to pay off the old debt. Accordingly, under EITF Issue 96-19, the old debt would be considered extinguished only if the debt instruments have substantially different terms.

Definition of *substantially different* Exchanged or modified debt instruments are considered to be substantially different if the present value of the cash flows of the new debt differs from the present value of the remaining cash flows of the old debt by at least 10%. The following guidelines apply to performing the 10% test:

- The cash flows of the new debt instrument should include all contractual cash flows plus any fees or other amounts paid by the debtor less any amounts received by the debtor from the creditor. (The creditor might pay the debtor a fee to cancel a call option held or to extend a no-call period.)

- The effective interest rate (for accounting purposes) of the *old* debt instrument should be used to discount the remaining cash flows of both debt instruments.

- If either debt instrument bears a floating interest rate, the rate in effect at the date of the exchange/modification should be used to calculate the cash flows.

- If either debt instrument is callable or puttable, cash flows are analyzed twice—first assuming exercise and then assuming nonexercise of the call or put option. The analysis that results in the smaller change should be the basis for determining whether the 10% test is met.

- If either instrument contains contingent payment terms or an unusual interest rate, judgment should be used to estimate the cash flows.

- If the debt was exchanged or modified within one year of the current transaction but was not considered extinguished, the terms existing a year ago (not the most recent terms) should be used in the current 10% test.

☛ **PRACTICE POINTER:** These quantitative guidelines are also used by the lender to determine whether a modification of terms is "minor" in accordance with EITF Issue 01-07. However, the lender must also evaluate whether the new effective yield reflects current market conditions. Refer to Chapter 7, "Calculating Yields on Debt Investments," for additional information.

☛ **PRACTICE POINTER:** A loan subject to the scope of SOP 03-3 that is subsequently modified or restructured (other than through a troubled debt restructuring) continues to be accounted for by the creditor in accordance with SOP 03-3, rather than in accordance with FAS-91 and EITF 01-7. Under the provisions of SOP 03-3, the restructured loan should not be accounted for as a new loan and income arising from the restructuring should be recognized prospectively rather than currently in income.

Accounting for Significant Exchanges and Modifications

If the exchange or modification is significant, as defined, the old debt is considered extinguished and the new debt instrument is recognized initially at its fair value. The fair value of the new debt is considered the "reacquisition price" for the purpose of calculating the gain or loss on extinguishment. The effective interest rate of the new debt instrument is the rate that equates the contractual cash flows with the fair value (recorded amount) of the loan.

> **OBSERVATION:** The fair value of the new debt instrument is determined using current market rates, not the original effective rate of the old debt.

Exhibit 11-2 summarizes the appropriate accounting, depending on whether the terms of the new or modified instruments are considered to be substantially different. Chapter 8, "Debt Financing," discusses transactions that are *not* accounted for as extinguishments in more detail.

EXHIBIT 11-2
ACCOUNTING FOR EXCHANGES AND MODIFICATIONS OF DEBT

	Terms Are Substantially Different	Terms Are *Not* Substantially Different
Balance sheet recognition—initial recording of new debt	At its fair value	At the carrying amount of the old debt
Income statement recognition of exchange or modification	Gain or loss	Not applicable
Effective interest rate of new debt	Determined based on the fair value of the new debt	Determined prospectively based on the carrying amount of the old debt and the revised cash flows
Treatment of fees paid or received to/from lender	Included in the gain or loss on extinguishment of the old debt	Amortized as an adjustment of interest expense using the interest method
Treatment of debt issue costs (paid to third parties)	Amortized as an adjustment of interest expense on the new debt	Expensed as incurred

Transactions among debt holders   Transactions among debt holders (investors) (for example, a bond swap) that do not involve the debtor do not result in an exchange or modification of the original terms of the debt instrument. Therefore, there is no effect on the accounting by the debtor.

Transactions involving a third-party intermediary   The accounting for exchanges or modifications between a debtor and a creditor that are conducted through a third-party intermediary (such as an investment banker) depends on whether the third-party intermediary is acting as an agent of the debtor or as a principal. In general, an agency relationship exists when the third-party intermediary acts on behalf of the debtor and does not put its own funds at risk. Exhibit 11-3 identifies certain indicators of an agency relationship and a principal relationship.

When an intermediary is acting as an agent of the debtor, the intermediary is not viewed as a counterparty to the exchange or modification transaction. The accounting "looks through" the intermediary and views the agent's transactions as those of the debtor. When an intermediary is acting on his own behalf as a principal, the intermediary should be viewed as the counterparty to the transaction—a creditor or investor as the case may be. Exhibit 11-4 illustrates the significance of the intermediary's role in the accounting for transactions involving a company's debt.

EXHIBIT 11-3
IDENTIFYING AGENTS AND PRINCIPALS

Characteristics of Agents	Characteristics of Principals
The intermediary places or reacquires debt for the debtor without placing its own funds at risk.	The intermediary places or reacquires debt for the debtor with its own funds and is subject to the risk of loss of those funds.
The intermediary places or reacquires debt for the debtor with its own funds but is indemnified by the debtor.	
The intermediary places notes under a *best-efforts agreement*.	The intermediary places notes on a firmly committed basis, which requires the intermediary to hold any debt that it is unable to sell to others.
The debtor directs the intermediary and the intermediary cannot independently initiate an exchange or modification of the debt instrument.	The intermediary acquires debt from or exchanges debt with another debt holder in the market and is subject to loss as a result of the transaction.
The compensation derived by the intermediary is limited to a pre-established fee.	The intermediary derives gains based on the value of the security issued by the debtor.

EXHIBIT 11-4
TRANSACTIONS INVOLVING THIRD-PARTY INTERMEDIARIES

Transaction	Relationship	Accounting by the Debtor
Investment banker acquires old debt from investors in exchange for new debt	Agent	Extinguishment of the old debt if the terms of the new debt are substantially different
Investment banker acquires old debt from investors for cash and *contemporaneously* issues new debt instruments for cash	Agent	Extinguishment of the old debt if the terms of the new debt are substantially different
Investment banker acquires old debt from investors for cash and *subsequently* transfers a debt instrument with the same (or different) terms to the same (or different) investors	Agent	Extinguishment of the old debt
Investment banker acquires old debt from investors for cash and exchanges or modifies the debt with other investors	Principal	No impact on debtor's accounting

SEC REGISTRANT ALERT: In addressing the application of EITF Issue 96-19 to modified "remarketable put bond" transactions, the SEC staff illustrated that an investment bank may act as both a principal and an agent in a modification of remarketable put bonds. In the basic remarketable put bond transaction, an investment bank acts as a principal, acquiring the bond from the original investor for the par amount (through exercise of an in-the-money call option), resetting the interest rate as provided in the bond's original terms, and reselling the bond to a new investor at a premium. In those circumstances, the debtor does not recognize an extinguishment. The SEC staff discussed that recent transactions involve the investment bank increasing the remarketing put bond's principal amount and reducing its coupon to a market-based rate not contemplated in the original terms of the bond, and then reselling the bond to a new investor. When evaluated under EITF Issue 96-19, the SEC staff believes that the investment bank acts as principal in the modified transaction in acquiring the bond and modifying the terms of the replacement bond and then acts as agent in placing the modified bond with a new investor. The SEC staff believes the transaction must be viewed as the issuer's acquisition of its bonds, which must be accounted for as an extinguishment, and issuance of a new bond, which must be recognized at its fair value, with the difference recognized in the income statement as an extinguishment loss. (December 2003 speech by Robert J. Comerford, Professional Accounting Fellow, Office of the Chief Accountant of the SEC, at the AICPA Conference on Current SEC Developments)

Effect of a binding contract to reacquire debt   A binding contract entered into between a debtor and its debt holder(s) to redeem debt instruments for a specified amount at a future date (that is within one year of the date at which the contract becomes binding) does not automatically result in extinguishment accounting for the debt at the date the binding contract is entered into. The binding agreement represents a modificaton of the terms of the debt. Accordingly, extinguishment accounting would be appropriate only if the change is significant under EITF Issue 96-19—that is, the present value of the revised cash flows (in this case, the nearer maturity) is at least 10% different from the present value of the remaining cash flows of the debt under its original terms. An announcement by the debtor of its *intent* to call a debt instrument at the first call date does not represent an accounting event until a binding contract exists. Then, the change in terms would be evaluated under EITF Issue 96-19 as a modification of terms.

Modifications involving loan participations and loan syndications
A *loan participation* represents a debt instrument between the debtor and the lead bank. (The lead bank then sells undivided interests in the loan to other entities.) Therefore, any exchanges or modifications between the debtor and the lead bank should be evaluated in accordance with EITF Issue 96-19. Any exchanges or modifications *between* participating banks are akin to transfers among debt holders. Accordingly, the accounting by the debtor would not be affected.

A *loan syndication* represents a debt instrument between the debtor and each member of the syndication. Therefore, any exchanges or modifications between the debtor and any of the member creditors should be evaluated in accordance with EITF Issue 96-19. If an exchange or modification offer is made to all members of the syndicate but only some the creditors agree to the exchange or modification, then EITF Issue 96-19 applies only to those debt instruments held by the creditors who agree to the exchange or modification.

☛ **PRACTICE POINTER:** Modifications of line-of-credit and revolving debt arrangements are addressed in Chapter 8, "Debt Financing." The major accounting question is such cases is the treatment of deferred and new fees, rather than whether any amounts drawn down have been extinguished.

SEC REGISTRANT ALERT: The SEC staff's view on the accounting for modifications of convertible bonds is discussed in Chapter 10, "Convertible Debt and Similar Instruments." At issue is whether EITF 96-19 is applicable to modifications affecting an embedded conversion option.

Troubled Debt Restructurings

The two distinguishing characteristics of a troubled debt restructuring (TDR) are that the debtor is experiencing financial difficulties and the creditor grants a concession to the debtor that it would not otherwise consider. FAS-15 describes the following types of TDRs:

- *Transfer of assets*—transfer to the creditor of third-party receivables, real estate, or other assets to satisfy fully or partially a debt (including a transfer resulting from foreclosure or repossession).
- *Transfer of equity interests*—issuance or other granting of an equity interest to the creditor to satisfy fully or partially a debt (unless the equity interest is granted pursuant to existing terms for converting the debt into equity interests).
- *Modification of terms*—contractual changes in the terms of a debt, such as one or a combination of the following:
  — Reduction of the stated interest rate for the remaining life of the debt.
  — Extension of the maturity date(s) at a stated interest rate lower than the current market rate for debt with similar risk.
  — Reduction (forgiveness) of the face amount or maturity amount of the debt.
  — Reduction (forgiveness) of accrued interest.

OBSERVATION: The term troubled debt "restructuring" encompasses transactions where the debt is fully satisfied and no debt remains outstanding.

☞ **PRACTICE POINTER:** FAS-15 applies to TDRs of debtors involved in bankruptcy proceedings, except when the bankruptcy proceedings result in a general restatement of the debtor's liabilities, for example 50 cents on the dollar. ARB 43, Chapter 7A, and SOP 90-7 provide guidance for those situations. (FAS-15, par. 10, fn. 4 and FTB 81-6)

FAS-15 provides the following examples of situations that ordinarily would not be considered TDRs:

- The fair value of cash, other assets, or equity interests transferred is greater than or equal to the debtor's carrying amount of the debt.

- The creditor reduces the effective interest rate on the debt primarily to reflect a decrease in market interest rates or a decrease in risk so as to maintain a relationship with the debtor and the debtor could obtain financing from other sources at the same rate.
- The debtor issues new marketable debt with interest rates similar to debt issued by nontroubled debtors. (FAS-15, par. 7)

A debt restructuring (or exchange) that is not considered a TDR should be accounted for in accordance with EITF Issue 96-19 (discussed earlier in this chapter).

> ☛ **PRACTICE POINTER:** EITF Issue 02-4 provides interpretive guidance on how the debtor should distinguish between troubled and nontroubled debt restructurings involving a modification of terms or an exchange of debt instruments. This Issue is significant because the accounting models for troubled and nontroubled restructurings are vastly different. Practitioners encountering debt restructurings in practice should review the detailed guidance in Issue 02-4 to ensure that restructurings are properly categorized.

> ☛ **PRACTICE POINTER:** The tests for TDRs are not symmetrical between the debtor and the creditor when the debtor's carrying amount and the creditor's recorded investment differ (for example, if the creditor purchased the loan from the original lender). Therefore, a debtor may have a TDR while the creditor does not. (FTB 80-2) Refer to Chapter 3, "Loans and the Allowance for Credit Losses," for a discussion of the creditor's accounting for a TDR.

The accounting for a TDR by the debtor depends on whether there is a transfer of assets or equity interests in full settlement, a modification of terms, or a combination of those types of restructurings, including partial settlements.

Transfers of Assets in Full Settlement

FAS-15 requires a two-step approach to accounting for a TDR involving a transfer of assets:

1. A gain on debt restructuring is recognized for the excess of the *carrying amount* of the debt over the *fair value* of the assets transferred, *and*
2. A gain or loss on the transfer of assets is recognized for the difference between the fair value and the carrying amount of the assets transferred. (FAS-15, pars. 13–14)

Fair value of assets should be measured by their market value if an active market for them exists. If no active market for them exists, the selling prices of similar assets may be helpful in estimating the fair value of the assets transferred. If no market price is available, fair value may be estimated using a discounted cash flow analysis, using a rate commensurate with the risk involved. (FAS-15, par. 13)

☞ **PRACTICE POINTER:** For a full settlement, the fair value of the debt can be used to measure the gain on debt restructuring if it is more clearly evident than the fair value of the assets transferred. (FAS-15, par. 13, fn. 5)

Forfeiture of real estate subject to a nonrecourse loan The foreclosure or repossession of assets subject to a *nonrecourse loan* is considered a transfer of assets under FAS-15, paragraph 20. Any gain or loss on the asset transferred is measured separately from the extinguishment of debt, as shown in the following example:

In 20X1, Company A purchased land for $500 with a nonrecourse loan from Company B. In 20X3, the land had a fair value of $250 and the net balance due to Company B is $300. Company A defaults on the loan and transfers the land to Company B in full satisfaction of its debt. Company A recognizes a gain on the debt restructuring of $50 (the excess of the loan balance over the fair value of the assets transferred) and a loss on the transfer of the land of $250 (the difference between the fair value and the carrying amount of the land). (EITF 91-2)

☞ **PRACTICE POINTER:** Prior to the actual forfeiture of real estate under a nonrecourse loan, the assets subject to nonrecourse financing should be assessed for impairment in the same way as other assets—the amount of the loss should not be influenced by the ability to put the asset back to the creditor. Recognition of asset impairment and extinguishment of debt are two separate events; each should be recognized in the period in which it occurs. (FAS-144, par. B34)

Grant of Equity Interest in Full Settlement

A gain on debt restructuring is recognized for the excess of the carrying amount of the debt over the fair value of the equity interest granted. (FAS-15, par. 15)

☞ **PRACTICE POINTER:** For a full settlement, the fair value of the debt can be used to measure the gain on debt restructuring if it is more clearly evident than the fair value of the equity interest granted. (FAS-15, par. 15, fn. 8)

Modification of Terms

If the total future cash payments (undiscounted) specified by the new terms of the debt are greater than or equal to the carrying amount of the debt, the debtor accounts for the effects of the restructuring prospectively and does not change the carrying amount of the debt. That is, the effective interest rate of the restructured debt is recalculated as the discount rate that equates to the present value of the revised cash flows specified by the new agreement (excluding any contingent payments) with the carrying amount of the debt. Interest expense would be recognized in future periods using that revised rate. (FAS-15, par. 16)

If the total future cash payments (undiscounted) specified by the new terms of the debt are less than the net carrying amount of the debt, then a gain on debt restructuring is recognized for the excess of the carrying amount over the total (undiscounted) future cash payments. Thereafter, all cash payments under the terms of the debt should be accounted for as a reduction of the carrying amount of the debt and no interest expense should be recognized on the debt for the period between the restructuring and the maturity of the debt. (FAS-15, par. 17)

If the carrying amount of the payable includes several accounts (for example, face amount, accrued interest, and unamortized premium, discount, and issue costs) that are to be continued and possibly combined after the restructuring, the debtor may either (1) allocate the reduction in the carrying amount proportionately among the remaining accounts or (2) carry the amount designated as the face amount by the new terms in a separate account and adjust another account accordingly. (FAS-15, par. 17, fn. 11)

Estimating the cash flows—contingent payments   The terms of the restructured debt could include amounts payable only if certain specified events or circumstances transpire (including a variable interest rate—see below). In such cases, amounts contingently payable should be included in the "total future cash payments specified by the new terms" to the extent necessary to prevent recognizing a gain at the time of restructuring that may be offset by future interest expense. (FAS-15, par. 18)

Estimating the cash flows—variable interest rates   If a restructured payable bears a variable interest rate, such as the prime rate (plus a credit spread), estimates of maximum total future payments should be based on the interest rate in effect at the time of the restructuring. Changes in the interest rate after the restructuring should be accounted for as changes in estimate. However, the accounting for those fluctuations should not result in recognizing a gain on restructuring that may be offset by future cash payments (using the limits described in FAS-15, paragraphs 18 and 22). In such cases, future cash payments should reduce the carrying amount until the time that any gain recognized cannot be offset by future cash payments. (FAS-15, par. 23)

> **OBSERVATION:** The debtor's accounting for *modifications* does not use a fair value measurement (unlike transfers of assets and equity interests) or even reflect the time value of money. The rationale is that the terms are not negotiated using "market rates" and that it would be counterproductive to try to "impute" a market rate subsequent to the restructuring. That argument is not very compelling, because the creditor is required to discount the cash flows in a TDR (using the original effective rate) under FAS-114. Keep in mind that the debtor's accounting for a modification of terms in a *nontroubled* situation uses a fair value measurement when the modification is significant (under EITF 96-19). This aspect of FAS-15 seems very outdated compared with other literature addressing similar issues.

Combination of Types

A TDR may involve partial settlement of debt by the transfer of assets and/or the granting of an equity interest to the creditor with or without a modification of the terms of the remaining debt. For those restructurings, FAS-15, paragraph 19, sets forth the following procedures:

- Reduce the net carrying amount of the debt by the fair value of the assets transferred or equity interest granted (or by the amount of cash paid).

> **☞ PRACTICE POINTER:** For a partial settlement, the fair value of the assets transferred or equity interests granted should be used so that the fair value of the debt does not have to be allocated between the portion settled and the portion not settled. (FAS-15, par. 13, fn. 5)

- Recognize a gain or loss on transferred assets for the difference between their fair value and carrying amount.
- Account for the remaining carrying amount of the debt like a modification of terms *even if the stated terms of the remaining payable have not changed*:
  - If the total undiscounted cash payments specified by the new terms of the debt (including contingent payments) are *greater* than or equal to the remaining net carrying amount of the debt, account for the effect of the change prospectively as a yield adjustment.
  - If the total undiscounted future cash payments specified by the new terms of the debt (including contingent payments) are *less* than the remaining net carrying amount of the debt,

recognize a gain on restructuring for the excess of the remaining carrying amount over the total future cash payments. Future cash payments are recorded as a reduction of the payable, not as interest expense. (FAS-15, par. 19)

Exhibit 11-5 summarizes the debtor's accounting for TDRs, depending on the type of restructuring.

EXHIBIT 11-5
DEBTOR'S ACCOUNTING FOR TROUBLED DEBT RESTRUCTURINGS

Type of Restructuring	Accounting
Transfer of assets in full settlement	• Gain on restructuring = excess of carrying amount of debt over fair value of assets transferred.
	• Gain/loss on transfer of assets = difference between the fair value and the carrying value of the assets transferred.
Grant of equity interest in full settlement	Gain on restructuring = excess of carrying amount of debt over fair value of equity interest granted.
Modification of terms: —Total future cash flows ≥ carrying amount of debt	• No gain. Effective interest rate of debt is adjusted prospectively.
—Total future cash flows ≤ carrying amount of debt	• Gain on restructuring = excess of carrying amount of debt over total future cash flows. Future cash payments reduce the adjusted carrying amount; interest expense is not recognized.
Partial settlement	• Record the transfer of assets or equity.
	• Reduce payable for fair value of assets or equity.
	• Account for remaining payable as a modification of terms.

Implementation Issues

Measurement date of a TDR Troubled debt restructurings may occur before, at, or after the stated maturity of debt, and time may elapse between the agreement or court order and the actual transfer of assets or equity interest, the effective date of new terms, or the occurrence of another event that constitutes consummation of the restructuring. Amounts should be measured as of the consummation date in a TDR. (FAS-15, par. 6)

Income statement classification of a TDR   Gains on debt restructurings should be classified in accordance with APB-30. A gain, on restructuring a TDR would be classified as extraordinary only if it were unusual in nature and infrequent in occurrence. (FAS-145, par. 7 (b)) Similarly, gains and losses on assets transferred to settle a payable would only be considered extraordinary if the conditions of APB-30 are met. (FAS-15, par. 14)

Contingent payments   Contingent interest and principal payments should be recognized as a liability and interest expense in the period in which it becomes probable that the contingent payment will have to be paid and the amount of the contingent payment is reasonably estimated. However, if those amounts were included in "total future cash payments" and they prevented recognition of a gain at the time of restructuring, accrual or payment of those amounts should be deducted from the carrying amount of the restructured payable. (FAS-15, par. 22)

Direct costs   Legal fees and other direct costs of issuing equity interests should be recorded as a reduction of the fair value of the equity issued. All other direct costs of a TDR should reduce the gain, if any, on the debt restructuring or else be recognized as an expense in the period incurred. (FAS-15, par. 24)

Reporting Cash Flows

Cash used to repay amounts borrowed or otherwise extinguish outstanding debt should be classified as cash outflows from financing activities. (FAS-95, par. 20) If the indirect method is used to prepare the Statement of Cash Flows, gains and losses on extinguishments of debt should be reported as adjustments to net income to reconcile to net cash flows from operating activities. (FAS-95, par. 28)

DISCLOSURES

Guarantees

Disclosure requirements for guarantees assumed as part of a debt extinguishment are discussed in Chapter 8, "Debt Financing."

Troubled Debt Restructurings

The following information should be disclosed about troubled debt restructurings that have occurred during the period (FAS-15, par. 25, as amended):

- For each restructuring, a description of the principal changes in terms, the major features of settlement, or both.
- Aggregate gain on restructuring of debt.
- Aggregate net gain or loss on the transfers of assets.
- The per share amount of the aggregate gain on debt restructuring.

> ☛ **PRACTICE POINTER:** Separate restructurings of the same type of liabilities during the year may be grouped for disclosure purposes. (FAS-15, par. 25, fn.15)

In the periods after a troubled debt restructuring, the following should be disclosed:

- The extent to which amounts contingently payable are included in the carrying amount of the restructured debt.
- The total amounts that are contingently payable on restructured debt.
- When there is at least a reasonable possibility that a liability for contingent payments will be incurred, the conditions under which those amounts would become payable or would be forgiven. (FAS-15, par. 26)

In-Substance Defeasances (Grandfathered)

If debt was considered to be extinguished by an insubstance defeasance under the provisions of FAS-76, on or before December 31, 1996, disclose:

- A general description of the transaction *and*
- The amount of the debt that is considered extinguished at the end of the period as long as that debt remains outstanding. (FAS-140, par. 17(b))

AUDIT CONSIDERATIONS

There is no specific audit guidance related to debt extinguishments, modifications, and restructurings. The key areas of financial reporting risk are:

- That debt should be reported as extinguished only if the debtor is relieved of its obligation by paying the creditor or is legally released as obligor. To determine whether a debtor is legally released from an obligation, the auditor should consider using the work of a legal specialist.
- That a debt extinguishment be reported in the appropriate period and that any gain or loss be properly classified in accordance with APB-30. Generally, a debt extinguishment would *not* be considered an extraordinary item.
- If a debtor becomes secondarily liable, that a liability be recorded, initially at its fair value, even if no explicit compensation was involved. Recording a liability for a guarantee can directly affect the amount of gain or loss recognized upon extinguishment.
- That a debt restructuring be properly identified as a troubled or nontroubled situation, because the debtor's accounting for troubled and nontroubled restructurings is significantly different.
- In a troubled debt restructuring where equity securities of a private company are issued in full or partial settlement of a debt, that the fair value of those securities be estimated appropriately, because it bears directly on the gain calculation.
- In a nontroubled situation, that the significance of a modification of terms (or an exchange of debt instruments with different terms) be assessed in accordance with EITF Issue 96-19.
- That the role of an intermediary used to effect extinguishments, modifications, and exchanges of debt be properly characterized as an agent or a principal.
- For any grandfathered in-substance defeasances, that the auditor be aware that any transactions involving the debt or the assets held by the defeasance trust could call into question the original accounting for the transaction.

ILLUSTRATIONS

Illustration 11-1: Loss on Extinguishment of Debt [APB-26]

On December 31, 20X6, Colgate Industries decided to retire $500,000 of an original issue of $1,000,000 7% debentures, which are callable at $101 per bond. The company previously entered into an interest rate swap to effectively convert the fixed rate on the debentures to a floating rate. The hedge has been appropriately accounted for as a fair value hedge under FAS-133, with an adjustment (increase) of the carrying amount of the debt. (Chapter 14, "Hedge Accounting," discusses the details of fair value hedge accounting. Subsequent accounting for the swap is outside the scope of this example.) As of December 31, 20X6, the following amounts remain on Colgate Industries' balance sheet:

Unamortized debt issuance costs	$15,000
Unamortized debt discount	$10,000
Adjustment from fair value hedge	($12,000)

Based on the above information, and considering that only half of the debentures are being retired, the loss on reacquisition is computed as follows:

Reacquisition price:		
$500,000 x 101%		$505,000
Net carrying amount:		
Face value	($500,000)	
Debt discount	5,000	
Deferred hedging adjustment	(6,000)	
Debt issuance costs	7,500	(493,500)
Loss on extinguishment		$ 11,500

The journal entry to record the reacquisition of the bonds is as follows:

Bond payable	500,000	
Deferred hedging adjustment	6,000	
Loss on retirement of bonds payable	11,500	
Discount on bonds payable		5,000
Deferred legal and other expenses		7,500
Cash		505,000

The loss would be classified as a component of operating income, unless the transaction was considered both unusual and infrequent (APB-30), which would seldom be the case.

Illustration 11-2: Modification of Debt in a Nontroubled Situation [EITF 96-19]

On January 1, 20X1, Hefty Industries borrowed $1,000,000 from Commerce Bank, with a 5-year term and a fixed interest rate of 8%. Issue costs of $2,000 were deferred and are being amortized over the term of the debt. On January 1, 20X3, rates have dropped to 4%. Hefty, a creditworthy party, negotiates with Commerce to reduce the rate on its loan for the remaining term of 3 years to 4%. Hefty pays Commerce a fee of $1,000. Because this transaction is not a troubled debt restructuring, Hefty must apply the 10% significance test in EITF 96-19 to determine whether the original debt should be accounted for like an extinguishment.

Original effective rate	8.05%
Present value of revised cash flows (including fees) discounted at original rate of 8.05%	$896,722
Carrying amount of debt	$999,106
Difference	10.2%

Because the difference between the present value of the revised cash flows (using the original effective rate) differs from the carrying amount of the debt by more than 10%, Hefty would account for this transaction like an extinguishment of debt. The gain or loss is calculated as the difference between the carrying amount of the old debt and the fair value of the new debt, plus the amount of the fee paid to the lender. Because 4% is a market interest rate, the fair value of the debt equals its face value.

Loan payable (old, net of debt issue costs)	999,106	
Loss on extinguishment of debt	1,894	
Loan payable (new)		1,000,000
Cash (fee paid to lender)		1,000

The loss would generally be reported as a component of operating income.

Illustration 11-3:   Troubled Debt Restructuring—Modification of Terms [FAS-15]

On January 1, 20X1, Casualty Insurance Co. borrowed $1,000,000 from First County Bank, with a five-year term and a fixed interest rate of 8%. Issue costs of $2,000 were deferred and are being amortized over the term of the debt. During 20X2, Casualty Insurance experiences significant financial difficulties and approaches First County for a concession. The general level of interest rates remains at 8%. On 1/1/20X3, First County agrees to reduce the interest payments on Casualty's loan to $40,000 for each of the remaining three years, and to reduce the principal amount to $900,000, payable in three years. Because this transaction is a troubled debt restructuring, FAS-15 applies.

Undiscounted sum of revised cash flows	$1,020,000
Carrying amount of debt	$999,106

Because the sum of the revised cash flows exceeds the carrying amount of the debt, the change in terms is accounted for prospectively. No adjustment is made to the carrying amount of the debt. The rate that equates the revised cash flows with the carrying amount of the debt is 72%. Accordingly, interest expense will be recognized using the interest method at an effective rate of 72% for the remaining term of the debt.

**Illustration 11-4: Disclosure of Troubled Debt Restructuring—
Combination of Types [FAS-15]**

At December 31, 20X0, the Company had a 12% note payable to its primary
bank with an outstanding principal balance of $1,756,000, due in December
20X5. In September 20X1, the Company reached an agreement with the bank
to modify the terms of the note, due to cash flow problems experienced by the
Company. The bank has agreed to accept a cash payment of $250,000 and
installment payments on a note for a total of $900,000 at no interest, due in
December 20X5. As a result, the amount of the note to the bank was reduced
by $606,000 to reflect the revised terms, and a gain of $606,000 has been
included in the Statement of Operations for 20X0, representing $.27 per share.

**Illustration 11-5: Disclosure of Troubled Debt Restructuring—
Transfer of Assets in Full Settlement [FAS-15]**

At December 31, 20X0, the Company had an 11% note payable to its principal
vendor with an outstanding principal balance of $1,200,000, due in December
20X5. In September 20X1, the Company reached an agreement with the
vendor to transfer fixed assets in full settlement of the note. At the date of
transfer, the fair market value of the fixed assets transferred exceeded their
carrying amount by $179,000; an ordinary gain of $179,000 has been included
in the Statement of Operations in 20X1 relating to the transfer of fixed assets.
At the date of transfer, the carrying amount of the debt payable to the vendor
exceeded the fair market value of the fixed assets transferred by $611,000; a
gain of $611,000 has been included in the Statement of Operations in 20X1 for
the extinguishment of debt, representing $.16 per share.

PART III:
DERIVATIVES AND HEDGING ACTIVITIES

PART III
DERIVATIVES AND HEDGING ACTIVITIES

The accounting literature for derivatives and hedging activities is among the most complicated body of literature in U.S. GAAP. FASB Statement No. 133 (FAS-133), *Accounting for Derivatives and Hedging Activities,* issued in June 1998, represented a major change in the accounting of derivatives and hedging activities from prior practice by requiring fair value measurement of all derivatives. Since its issuance, FAS-133 has been both amended several times and heavily interpreted. The following Statements have amended FAS-133 since its issuance:

- FASB Statement No. 137, *Accounting for Derivative Instruments and Hedging Activities—Deferral of the Effective Date of FASB Statement No. 133*

- FASB Statement No. 138, *Accounting for Certain Derivative Instruments and Certain Hedging Activities*

- FASB Statement No. 149, *Amendment of Statement 133 on Derivative Instruments and Hedging Activities*

- FASB Statement No. 155, *Accounting for Certain Hybrid Financial Instruments—An Amendment of FASB Statements No. 133 and 140*

FAS-133, as amended and interpreted, is one of the lengthiest and most complex standards ever written. One reason for this is the complexity of the scope of the standard (i.e., determining whether a contract is a derivative under FAS-133). Because financial engineers can create derivative-like features in any kind of contract, the FASB had no choice but to attempt to describe the characteristics of instruments that were to be subject to fair value accounting rather than rely on the terms used by market participants. That approach led to the need for many scope exceptions so that long-standing accounting practices for some traditional financial contracts (such as insurance contracts, which are essentially options) were not overturned. A second reason for the complexity of FAS-133 is that hedge accounting methods were designed to accommodate certain long-standing hedge accounting practices. A third reason relates to the requirement that certain hybrid instruments that contain embedded derivatives be bifurcated, which is inherently difficult to apply in practice in many cases. In early 2006, the FASB issued FAS-155 to permit certain hybrid financial instruments requiring bifurcation to be measured at fair value in their entirety, thereby eliminating the need to perform complex bifurcation procedures. That fair value election is discussed in detail in Chapter 13, "Embedded Derivatives."

In addition to FAS-133 and its formal amendments, shortly after issuance of FAS-133, the FASB established a derivatives implementation group (DIG) to provide interpretive guidance. That guidance became authoritative once "cleared" by the FASB. The DIG, which is no longer active, published more than 160 interpretations of FAS-133. (The DIG interpretations are referred to in this book as "DIG Issues.") Many of the implementation issues addressed by the DIG evaluate lengthy fact patterns that are unlikely to be encountered by a wide range of companies. This book covers the "kernel" in each of the DIG Issues that clarifies or interprets a principle in FAS-133 that would have wide applicability. The entire body of DIG Issues is available on the FASB's website—www.fasb.org.

In addition, several EITFs have addressed issues related to the application of FAS-133, including several cases where a conflict of literature existed for a particular transaction. The FASB recently added to its agenda several projects to interpret FAS-133 that will likely to result in the issuance of FASB Staff Positions (FSPs). Readers should monitor the ongoing interpretations of FAS-133.

FAS-133, as amended, was effective for fiscal quarters beginning after June 15, 2000. Users of financial statements should be aware that FAS-133 grandfathered certain hybrid instruments that did not require bifurcation and that certain transition amounts might be recognized in earnings over long periods of time. Such amounts are required to be disclosed. (FAS-133, par. 53)

Section III comprises four chapters:

1. Chapter 12, "Introduction to Derivatives"
2. Chapter 13, "Embedded Derivatives"
3. Chapter 14, "Hedge Accounting"
4. Chapter 15, "Disclosures about Derivatives"

Each of these chapters discusses, where applicable, guidance under development related to derivatives activities and hedging activities.

IMPORTANT NOTICE
FASB PROJECT ON GAAP HIERARCHY

In an effort to improve the GAAP hierarchy and the quality of the standard-setting process, in April 2005, the FASB issued an Exposure Draft, "The Hierarchy of Generally Accepted Accounting Principles." The Exposure Draft would elevate DIG issues to Category A within the GAAP hierarchy, in accordance with the conclusion that Category A should be expanded to include accounting principles that are issued after being subject to the FASB's due process. DIG Issues become authoritative only after being "cleared" by the FASB. The FASB has indicated that it does not expect any changes in financial reporting to result from issuance of a final Statement.

CHAPTER 12
INTRODUCTION TO DERIVATIVES ACCOUNTING

CONTENTS

Overview	12.02
Background	12.03
Definition of a Derivative	12.03
Characteristics of a Derivative	12.03
Paragraph 6(a): The Payment Terms Are Determined by Reference to an Underlying	12.04
Paragraph 6(b): The Contract Requires No (or a Relatively Small) Initial Investment	12.06
Paragraph 6(c): The Contract May Be Net Settled	12.08
Exhibit 12-1: Indicators of a Market Mechanism	12.11
Structuring to Avoid FAS-133	12.14
Timing of Assessments	12.15
Exhibit 12-2: Evaluation of Common Contracts	12.16
Scope Exceptions	12.19
Outright Exceptions	12.19
Equity Contracts of the Issuer	12.19
Stock Compensation	12.20
Contracts Issued in Business Combinations	12.20
Certain Insurance Contracts	12.20
Certain Financial Guarantee Contracts	12.21
Derivatives That Serve as Impediments to Sale Accounting	12.22
Certain Loan Commitments	12.22
Interest-Only and Principal-Only Strips	12.23
Certain Contracts Held by Benefit Plans	12.24
Residual Value Guarantees	12.25
Investments in Life Insurance	12.25
Registration Payment Arrangements	12.25
Exceptions Granted to Simplify the Application of FAS-133	12.25

Certain Security Trades 12.25

Normal Purchases and Sales 12.26

Contracts Involving Physical and Other Variables 12.27

Exhibit 12-3: Applying the Nonfinancial Asset Exception 12.28

Accounting for Contracts that Meet a Scope Exception 12.28

Exhibit 12-4: Identifying Derivatives under FAS-133 12.29

Exhibit 12-5: Summary Analysis of Contract Types 12.30

Accounting for Derivatives 12.32

Balance Sheet Recognition 12.32

Determining Fair Value 12.33

Transfers and Extinguishments of Derivatives 12.34

Recognizing Changes in Value 12.34

Income Statement Classification 12.35

Cash Flow Statement Presentation 12.36

Derivatives with a Financing Element 12.36

Income Tax Considerations 12.36

Auditing Considerations 12.37

Properly Identifying All Derivatives 12.37

Discretionary Aspects of FAS-133 12.38

The Evolving Nature of Derivatives and Ongoing
Interpretations of FAS-133 12.38

Valuation 12.38

Regulatory Considerations 12.39

Illustrations 12.40

Illustration 12-1: Accounting for an Interest Rate Swap 12.40

Illustration 12-2: Accounting for an Option 12.41

OVERVIEW

For accounting purposes, there is no single type of contract that represents a "derivative." Rather, a derivative is any type of contract that has certain attributes that allow the holder to experience changes in the value of a referenced asset or other market variable with a smaller upfront investment (if any) than would be required to actually own that asset and experience similar gains and losses. The definition encompasses most contracts commonly thought of as derivatives, such as swaps, options, futures contracts, forward contracts, and warrants. However, there are numerous scope exceptions that preclude accounting for certain contracts as derivatives.

Contracts that do not meet the definition in their entirety (perhaps because they involve a significant upfront cash flow, such as a structured note) might contain embedded derivatives. Contracts that contain embedded derivatives must be evaluated to determine whether separate accounting of the host contract and the embedded derivative is required. A fair value election is permitted for certain hybrid financial instruments with embedded derivatives requiring bifurcation. Contracts containing embedded derivatives are discussed in Chapter 13, "Embedded Derivatives."

All derivatives must be reported in the balance sheet at fair value. Generally, gains and losses on derivatives should be reported in earnings as they occur. Derivatives that are used in hedging relationships that meet numerous conditions are carried at fair value, but the reporting of gains and losses is modified to match the income recognition pattern of the hedged item. Hedge accounting is discussed in Chapter 14, "Hedge Accounting."

BACKGROUND

FAS-133 provides a definition of a derivative for accounting purposes that is based on the attributes of a contract, not the "label" used by market participants. All contracts that have those attributes must be accounted for as derivatives under FAS-133 unless they qualify for a specific scope exception. A significant number of DIG Issues, and an EITF Issue, address the definition of a derivative and scope exceptions. FAS-133 addresses accounting for all derivatives, including those that are and are not designated as hedges."

DEFINITION OF A DERIVATIVE

Characteristics of a Derivative

For accounting purposes, FAS-133 defines a derivative as a financial instrument or other contract that has all of the following characteristics (par. 6):

- It has either (1) an underlying and a notional amount that together determine the amount of any payment or (2) a payment provision that is triggered by a change in an underlying.
- It requires no net initial investment or a smaller investment than would normally be required to have a similar response to market factors.
- It can be settled for a net change in value (net settled) in one of the following ways:

— The contract explicitly requires or permits net settlement of any change in value.

— It can be readily settled net by a means outside the contract (such as an exchange).

— It provides for delivery of an asset that is readily convertible to cash or another derivative.

☛ **PRACTICE POINTER:** A derivative can have more than one underlying and more than one notional amount. For simplicity, this chapter generally refers to contracts with one underlying and notional amount.

OBSERVATION: A derivative is not necessarily a *financial* instrument—for example, if it involves delivery of a nonfinancial asset such as a commodity.

Some common types of derivatives include futures contracts, swaps, forward contracts, forward rate agreements, options, caps and floors, collars, and warrants. However, contracts commonly known as derivatives are not automatically *accounted for* as derivatives under FAS-133. In contrast, many contracts that are not commonly thought of as derivatives *would be* accounted for as derivatives under FAS-133.

These three criteria and the related scope exceptions have yielded over 30 implementation issues to date (not including issues associated with embedded derivatives). This high level of interpretation is attributable to the newness of the attribute-based approach and the complexity of contracts in the marketplace today. Each of the conditions is discussed in more detail below.

Paragraph 6(a): The Payment Terms Are Determined by Reference to an Underlying

Underlying A derivative "derives" its value by reference to another item. An "underlying" is that "other item"—it can be any variable whose changes are observable or otherwise objectively verifiable. The following are common types of underlyings in a derivative contract (FAS-133, par. 57(a)):

- Interest rates
- Foreign exchange rates
- Prices of specific securities
- Stock market indexes (such the S&P 500, FTSE 100, and NIKKEI)
- Prices of specific commodities
- Indexes of prices (such as the Consumer Price Index)
- Credit ratings or indexes

- Insurance or catastrophe loss indexes

The occurrence or nonoccurrence of an event (such as a scheduled payment on a contract) can also be considered an underlying. (FAS-133, par. 7, as amended)

An underlying can have a fixed component and a variable component. For example, in products related to interest rates, it is common to see a variable such as the London Interbank Offered Rate (LIBOR) plus a fixed "credit spread," such as 50 basis points. LIBOR is considered the variable, but the credit spread should also be included in the calculation of the payment terms. (Also see DIG A-11, for certain commodity-based contracts that involve both a fixed and variable component.)

> ☞ **PRACTICE POINTER:** Certain types of underlyings are excluded from the scope of FAS-133. Scope exceptions are discussed in the next section.

Notional amount A notional amount is a *quantity* of the type of underlying or variable specified in the contract. Notional amounts include a stated number of the following:

- Dollars (or another currency)
- Shares of stock
- Bushels or pounds of a commodity
- Other units specified in the contract

The settlement amount of a derivative instrument with a notional amount is generally determined by multiplying that notional amount with the underlying. Sometimes, the amount may involve a formula with leverage factors or other constants. (FAS-133, par. 7) Some common combinations of notional amounts and underlyings are:

Interest rate swap	Number of dollars × Interest rate
Futures contract (on gold)	Number of troy ounces × Price of gold
Stock option	Number of shares × Price of stock
Currency option	Specified amount of currency × Exchange rate

Determinable notional amounts Some contracts do not appear to specify a fixed number of units, for example, a contract to provide all of a specific raw material needed by a manufacturer for a period of time (a requirements contract). If a contract contains explicit provisions that allow the parties to reliably determine an amount, then that contract has a notional amount. A notional amount would be deemed to exist in the following circumstances:

- Average historical usage or anticipated quantities are specified in the default provisions of a contract (this could lead to a notional amount that changes over time).
- A minimum amount is specified, and no other contractual provisions represent a better reliable estimate.
- If a maximum is specified, it should be used as an outer limit for the notional amount, if no other contractual provision represents a better estimate.

If a notional amount is *not* reliably determinable, the contract would not be considered a derivative. (DIG A-6)

☞ **PRACTICE POINTER:** Requirements contracts that are considered derivatives might qualify for the "normal purchases and sales" scope exception (FAS-133, par. 10(b)). Refer to the scope exception section.

Payment provisions   A payment provision requires payment of a fixed or determinable amount if the underlying behaves in a specified manner (for example, if the Dow Jones Industrial Average goes above a certain level, the counterparty owes $1 million).

Paragraph 6(b): The Contract Requires No (or a Relatively Small) Initial Investment

A distinguishing characteristic of a derivative is that the contract is leveraged—that is, the contract provides the potential for gains and losses from changes in the underlying *without having to make a cash investment equal to the effective notional amount* (or borrowing). FAS-133 did not use the word "leverage" for operational reasons, but that is the basic notion underlying the "no or smaller initial investment" condition.
   To illustrate the concept:

- An option to buy an exchange-traded equity security involves a cash payment for the premium that is much smaller than a cash investment in the same number of shares of stock. Yet the potential for gains is the same as if the investor had actually purchased the stock for cash.
- A futures contract to buy oil involves no upfront investment, yet the potential for gains and losses is the same as if the entity had purchased the same number of barrels of oil for cash.

Meaning of "small" initial investment   Some contracts involve upfront payments of cash that represent something besides time value or compensation for off-market terms. A question arises as to how much of a net investment is considered small enough that the contract is considered a derivative in its entirety rather than a loan or other instrument with an embedded derivative. Paragraph 8, as amended, indicates that if the initial net investment (after adjustment for the time value of money) is less, by more than a nominal amount, than the initial net investment that would be commensurate with an investment in the underlying (or a borrowing related to the underlying), the "small initial net investment" condition is met. That is, if the other characteristics are present, the contract would be considered a derivative in its entirety. The following diagram illustrates the significance of the amount of the initial net investment.

Amount of Initial Net Investment Relative to Commensurate Investment in Underlying

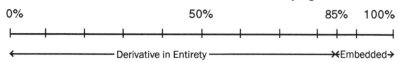

OBSERVATION: Although the phrase *more than a nominal amount* is not defined in FAS-133 or related literature, the qualitative guidance in paragraph 8 of the Statement and in DIG-A23 indicates that contracts that require a *very significant* net investment may satisfy the characteristic in paragraph 6(b). A very significant net investment would occur if the initial net investment in the contract is determined to be less than the net investment to acquire the asset or to incur the obligation related to the underlying by *more than a nominal amount*. An illustration in DIG A-23 indicates that a difference of 15 percent when comparing an initial net investment in a contract to the amount determined by applying the effective notional amount to the underlying is *more than a nominal amount*. DIG A-23 adds that the initial net investment for a contract could be less than the amount determined by applying the effective notional amount to the underlying by a percentage lower than 15 percent and still be considered to be "less, by more than a nominal amount" under paragraph 8 of FAS-133. Therefore, a contract with an initial net investment that is greater than 85 percent of the amount commensurate with a direct investment in the underlying can meet the definition of a derivative. The revised interpretation of paragraph 6(b) of FAS-133 is a reversal of the FASB's previous position on this issue, where "small" meant "very little." Now, if an entity exchanges *almost all* of the contract price, the transaction will be viewed as a derivative, but if it exchanges the entire contract amount, it will have a hybrid instrument that must be examined for embedded derivatives. Refer to Chapter 13, "Embedded Derivatives," for additional information.

The following types of upfront payments are considered to meet the "no or smaller initial investment" condition (FAS-133, pars. 8 and 57(b)):

- Premiums on options for time value.
- Premiums for off-market terms (e.g., a premium on a swap or forward contract with a price less than the current forward price).
- Mutual exchanges of liquid currencies or other assets at inception, in which case the net investment is the difference between the fair values of the assets exchanged.
- In a prepaid interest rate swap contract, an initial net investment that is less than the amount determined by applying the effective notional amount to the underlying by *more than a nominal amount*. (DIG A-23)

    ☛ **PRACTICE POINTER:**   As a result of the conclusion in DIG A-23 that prepaid interest rate swaps that meet the conditions described above do not meet the definition of a derivative in FAS-133, the number of situations affected by the paragraph 45A of FAS-133 (aided by FAS-149) is significantly reduced. Paragraph 45A requires that all cash flows arising from derivatives that contain other-than-insignificant financing elements must be reported as financing activities under FASB Statement No. 95, *Statement of Cash Flows.*

The following type of upfront payment does not meet the "no or smaller initial investment" condition and therefore would not be considered a derivative in its entirety:

- In a forward purchase contract (involving a commodity or marketable security), a prepayment of the entire purchase price of the contract at the current spot price. (The prepayment is considered a loan whose value fluctuates based on changes in the underlying asset.) (DIG A-1)
- In a prepaid interest rate swap contract, an initial net investment that is equal to the amount determined by applying the effective notional amount to the underlying, with no adjustment of the underlying. (DIG A-23)

    ☛ **PRACTICE POINTER:**   Interest-only strips and principal-only strips (I-Os and P-Os) are discussed as a scope exception later in this chapter.

Paragraph 6(c): The Contract May Be Net Settled

Net settlement means that the entity may settle the contract for only the changes in value that have accumulated since the inception of the contract, either through explicit contractual terms or other circumstances that leave the parties in essentially the same position as net settlement.

To illustrate, assume that on January 1, 20X1, Purchaser Company enters into a forward contract to buy an asset from Seller Company for $500 on March 31, 20X1. On March 31, the asset is worth $700.

Gross settlement: Purchaser gives Seller $500, and receives asset worth $700.

Net settlement: Seller gives Purchaser $200.

When the asset involved is readily convertible to cash (e.g., marketable securities or commodities), there is no substantive difference between gross settlement and net settlement.

A contract is deemed to be net settlement if it meets any one of the following three conditions:

1. The contract explicitly requires or permits net settlement (for the change in value), either in cash or any other asset(s). (FAS-133, pars. 9(a) and 57(c)(1)) Said differently, neither party is required to deliver an asset relating to the underlying with a value or principal amount equal to the notional amount of the contract. Net settlement provisions usually involve cash. However, under FAS-133, net settlement encompasses the transfer of any asset in exchange for only the change in value on the contract, even if those assets are not marketable.

Examples of contracts with net-settlement features include:

- A forward contract to purchase a commodity might state that the contract may be settled either by a physical exchange of the commodity against cash or by the party in a loss position paying the other party cash equal to the change in value.

- An interest rate swap that requires periodic settlement in cash for differences between the fixed and floating rate times the notional amount. The notional amount is not exchanged between the parties.

- An option on a basket of securities that, if exercised, requires the writer to pay the purchaser the difference between the strike price and the current market value of those securities times the stated number of shares (the notional amount). The actual shares in question are not delivered against cash.

- An option or warrant on a public or private stock that requires net settlement in shares of that company (a "cashless exercise"), even if the shares are restricted from sale for a period of time. Even though this contract literally requires delivery of "the underlying," the amount is based on the net change in value, not the notional amount. (DIG A-17) Issuers of such contracts should consider whether they qualify for the scope exception for contracts that are classified in stockholders' equity. (FAS-133, par. 11 (a)) Scope exceptions are discussed in the next section.

☞ **PRACTICE POINTER:**   A contract that provides for any gain (or loss) to be paid over a period of time meets the net settlement condition if the fair value of the cash flows to be received (or paid) by the holder under the payment terms are approximately equal to the amount that would have been received (or paid) if the gain (or loss) on the contract were settled immediately. The substance of other arrangements should be evaluated to determine whether they represent structured payouts in other forms. (DIG A-13 and B-2)

SEC REGISTRANT ALERT: In December 2005, the SEC reiterated certain guidance on the classification and measurement of freestanding stock purchase warrants in response to practice issues in this area. A stock purchase warrant that does not meet FAS-133's definition of a derivative must be evaluated under EITF 00-19 to determine whether the instrument should be accounted for as a liability or as an equity instrument. Refer to Chapter 16, "Issuer's Accounting for Equity Instruments and Related Contracts," for further discussion of application of the criteria in EITF 00-19 to stock purchase warrants.

(December 2005 Current Accounting and Disclosure Issues in the Division of Corporation Finance, SEC, and December 2005 Presentation, *Current Developments in the Division of Corporation Finance*, at the National Conference on Current SEC and PCAOB Developments)

Penalty clauses   Certain types of penalty clauses in contracts (that are invoked if a party defaults on the contract) constitute "net settlement" provisions.

- A *fixed* penalty for nonperformance is not a net settlement provision. (FAS-133, par. 57(c)(1))
- A *variable* penalty clause is considered a net settlement provision if it is based on changes in the price of the underlying. (FAS-133, par. 57(c)(1))
- If the contract contains both a fixed and a variable penalty clause, it is not considered a net settlement provision if the fixed component is significant enough to make default under the contract *remote* throughout the contract term. (DIG A-5)
- An "asymmetrical" default clause that requires the defaulting party to compensate the nondefaulting party for a loss, but does not allow the defaulting party to benefit from favorable price changes, is *not* considered a net settlement provision. (DIG A-8)

OBSERVATION: The logic behind these conclusions seems inconsistent. It seems as though the principle ought to be: If default is remote, a penalty clause is not a net settlement provision. (Other GAAP involving commitments allow a company to conclude that default is remote through means other than an explicit fixed penalty clause.) But that is not the case for contracts involving entirely variable penalty clauses. Companies should carefully review the penalty clauses of their contracts for "hidden" derivatives.

2. Net settlement could occur through a market mechanism outside the contract. (FAS-133, pars. 9(b) and 57(c)(2))   The terms of some contracts literally require gross settlement but the parties to the contract can "get out of the contract" for only the change in value of the contract through an organized exchange, a broker market, or a similar "market mechanism." A market mechanism that facilitates net settlement has four essential characteristics.

a. It is a means to settle a contract by enabling one party to readily liquidate its net position under the contract.

b. It results in one party to the contract becoming fully relieved of its rights and obligations under the contract.

c. Liquidation of the net position does not require significant transaction costs.

d. Liquidation of the net position under the contract occurs without significant negotiation and due diligence and occurs within a time frame that is customary for settlement of the type of contract. (DIG A-21)

Exhibit 12-1 identifies indicators of each of these characteristics. All of the indicators need not be present to conclude that a market mechanism exists for a specific contract.

EXHIBIT 12-1
INDICATORS OF A MARKET MECHANISM

Characteristic 1—Ease of Liquidation

• Access to potential counterparties is available regardless of the seller's size or market position.

• Risks assumed by a market maker can be transferred by a means other than repackaging the original contract into a different form.

Characteristic 2—Release from Contract

• There are multiple market participants willing and able to enter into a transaction at market prices to assume the seller's rights and obligations under a contract.

• There is sufficient liquidity in the market for the contract, as is indicated by the transaction volume as well as a relatively narrow observable bid/ask spread.

Characteristic 3—Transaction Costs

- Transaction costs are less than 10% of the fair value of the contract.

Characteristic 4—Evidence of "Market" Conditions

- Binding prices for the instrument are readily obtainable.
- Transfers of the instrument involve standardized documentation and settlement procedures, rather than contracts with entity-specific provisions.
- Individual contract sales do not require significant neotiation and unique structuring.
- The closing period is not extensive, as demonstrated by the need for legal consultation and document review.

Source: DIG A-21

The following situations are examples of market mechanisms:

- A mercantile exchange that trades futures contracts offers a ready opportunity to enter into an offsetting contract that can cancel the rights and obligations of another futures contract (because the counterparty legally is the futures exchange itself). (DIG A-15)
- Brokers and dealers who stand ready to buy and sell the contract in question (but not if they are only acting as agents, and the entity would not be relieved of his rights and obligations).

However, the ability to enter into a "mirror" or offsetting contract with the same counterparty does not satisfy the market mechanism condition if the original contract would remain in effect. In that case, the new offsetting contract does not *relieve* the original contract's set of legal rights and obligations. (DIG A-15)

Unit of measure   The market mechanism condition should be applied on an individual-contract basis and all of the terms should be considered. For example, if a company holds a portfolio of similar contracts, each one should be evaluated *individually*, even if the quantity of assets deliverable under the group of contracts is greater than the amount that could be rapidly absorbed by the market without significantly affecting the price. (DIG A-3) For another example, if a company holds a five-year contract that requires physical delivery of an asset, and a market only exists for contracts that are one year or less, the contract would not be considered a derivative for the first four years (see below for a discussion of changes in status). (DIG A-19)

Effect of an assignment clause   If a contract that would otherwise be considered to have a market mechanism contains an assignment clause that requires the other party's permission before the contract may be assigned, the likelihood that the party will withhold his consent must be evaluated. If it is remote that the counterparty would withhold permission to assign the contract, the provision does not overturn a conclusion that a contract may be net settled. If it is reasonably possible or probable that the other party will withhold its consent, the market mechanism condition would not be met. (DIG A-7)

3. The contract requires (1) delivery of an asset that puts the recipient in a position substantially the same as net settlement or (2) delivery of a derivative.   (FAS-133, pars. 9(c) and 57(c)(3))   To satisfy this condition, the asset must be readily convertible to cash and *not* involve significant conversion costs. An example of the first type of requirement is a forward contract that requires delivery of an exchange-traded commodity. An example of the second type of requirement is a swaption, which is an option on a swap, and an option on a futures contract.

"Readily convertible to cash" means assets that have:

a.   Interchangeable (fungible) units *and*

b.   Quoted prices available in an active market that can rapidly absorb the quantity in each contract held by the entity without significantly affecting the price.

c.   For contracts that involve multiple deliveries of the asset, these conditions should be applied separately to the expected quantity in each delivery, looking forward to the facts and circumstances in the period when delivery is scheduled to occur. (FAS-133, fn. 5 and DIG A-19)

> **OBSERVATION:**   When a contract requires delivery of an asset that is readily convertible to cash, the parties would generally be indifferent about whether they exchange cash or the assets stipulated in the contract. The FASB decided to treat such contracts the same as net settlement, primarily so that entities could not circumvent the standard by requiring delivery of a highly marketable asset (such as T-bills or a commodity).

Significant conversion costs   Conversion costs, including sales commissions and transportation costs, are considered "significant" when they are estimated to be 10 percent or more of the gross sales proceeds (based on the spot price at the inception of the contract) that would be received from the sale of those assets in the closest or most economical active market. The assessment of the significance of those conversion costs should be performed only at inception of the contract. (DIG A-10)

The following assets are generally considered readily convertible to cash:

- An actively traded security.
- An actively traded security (underlying a warrant) that, if exercised, would be restricted from sale (other than in connection with being pledged as collateral) for a period of 31 days or less (such as according to SEC Rule 144). (FAS-133, par. 57(c)(3))
- An actively traded commodity.
- A unit of foreign currency that is readily convertible into the functional currency of the reporting entity.
- A public security that is not very actively traded *if* the number of shares or other units of the security to be exchanged is small relative to the daily transaction volume. (FAS-133, par. 57(c)(3))

The following assets are generally *not* readily convertible to cash:

- Real estate
- Loans
- An agricultural product or mineral that does not have an active market
- Private securities
- A public security that is not very actively traded if the number of shares to be exchanged is large relative to the daily transaction volume (FAS-133, par. 57(c)(3))
- Public securities (underlying a warrant) that, if exercised would be contractually restricted from sale for more than 31 days (FAS-133, par. 57(c)(3))
- Currencies that are not readily exchangeable

> ☞ **PRACTICE POINTER:**   A contract that is a derivative solely because the asset to be delivered under the contract is readily convertible to cash might qualify for the regular-way securities trade exception under paragraph 10(a) if it is a marketable security or it might qualify for the normal purchases and sales exception under paragraph 10(b) if it is a nonfinancial asset.

Structuring to Avoid FAS-133

Sometimes two separate transactions involving the same parties have the same net effect as a derivative. For example, a simultaneous loan of cash at a floating rate and a borrowing of cash at a fixed rate with the same party has an economic effect similar to an interest rate swap (if the right of setoff exists). When two or more separate transactions have been entered into concurrently, the following indicators should be considered in the aggregate and, if present, the transactions should be accounted for as a unit, not separately:

- The transactions were entered into contemporaneously and in contemplation of one another.
- The transactions were executed with the same counterparty (or structured through an intermediary).
- The transactions relate to the same risk.
- There is no apparent economic need or substantive business purpose for structuring the transactions separately that could not also have been accomplished in a single transaction. (DIG K-1)

When these factors exist, the entity is presumed to be attempting to circumvent the provisions of FAS-133.

Timing of Assessments

The evaluation of whether a contract has a notional amount, a market mechanism exists, and whether items to be delivered under a contract are readily convertible to cash must be performed at inception and on an ongoing basis throughout a contract's life. If events occur subsequent to the inception or acquisition of a contract that cause the contract to meet the definition of a derivative instrument (for example, the underlying stock goes public), then that contract must be accounted for at that later date as a derivative under FAS-133. Similarly, if events occur subsequent to the inception or acquisition of a contract that would cause a contract that previously met the definition of a derivative to cease to meet the criteria (for example, a company becomes delisted from a national stock exchange and the contract requires physical settlement), then that contract cannot continue to be accounted for under FAS-133. However, changes in the significance of transaction costs do not affect the ongoing classification of a contract. (DIG A-18) Changes in the status of a contract should be accounted for as follows:

Contract ceases to be a derivative The carrying amount of that contract becomes its cost basis and the entity should follow applicable GAAP for that type of contract prospectively from the date that the contract ceased to be a derivative. The contract may no longer be designated as a hedging instrument.

Contract becomes a derivative The contract should be recorded at fair value at the date of change with the offset to earnings. The contract may prospectively be designated as a hedging instrument.

Exhibit 12-2 analyzes some common forms of derivatives to illustrate how the definition is applied.

EXHIBIT 12-2
EVALUATION OF COMMON CONTRACTS

Contract Type	Variable Times Notional?	No (Smaller) Initial Investment?	Permits/ Requires Net Settlement?	Conclusion
Interest rate swap	Met. Payment amount based on the difference between the contractual rate and the current rate × notional amount on the "receive leg" and the "pay leg"	Met. To get a "commensurate return," investor would need to INVEST the notional principal amount at the "receive leg" rate and LEND the principal amount at the "pay leg" rate. Generally no amounts are exchanged that relate to the principal amount	Met. The amount paid is the difference between the amounts due/owed, which is net settlement	Meets all three conditions: Derivative.
Futures contract (say on oil)	Met. Payment amount equals the difference between the contract price and the current price of oil × stated number of barrels	Met. (The margin amount is collateral, not a prepayment of the contract)	Met. Even if the contract explicitly requires delivery of oil, the contract meets the net settlement requirement because it may be closed out on an exchange	Meets all three conditions: Derivative.
Forward contract to buy or sell	Met. Value of contract depends on	Met. Generally no amount is	It depends. If the product is a traded	It depends. If the contract is a derivative, it

Contract Type	Variable Times Notional?	No (Smaller) Initial Investment?	Permits/ Requires Net Settlement?	Conclusion
an agricultural product	change in price of product times quantity	exchanged upfront	commodity, it would be readily convertible to cash. If the product is not exchange (or OTC) traded, and there is no way to net settle the contract, it would not meet the net settlement condition	could qualify for the normal purchases and sales exception (par. 10(b))
Interest rate or currency option (also caps and floors)	Met. Payment amount equals the difference between the rate stated in the contract (the "strike") and the current market rate × the notional amount IF and WHEN the contract is in-the-money (favorable to the holder)	Met. Although a premium might be paid, it is generally much less than the amount of cash that would have to be invested to yield the same potential return	Met. The amount paid to settle the contract is equal to the change in value of the option if it is in the money. If a broker market or exchange exists for the option, it automatically meets this condition	Meets all three conditions: Derivative.
Option on XYZ Co. common stock— stock is publicly traded (assume reporting entity is	Met. Value of contract arises from the difference between the price stated in the contract ("the strike") and the current market price × the	Met. Although a premium might be paid, it is generally much less than the amount of cash that would have	Met. Even if the contract requires settlement in shares (for cash), XYZ Co. stock would generally be considered readily	Meets all three conditions: Derivative.

Contract Type	Variable Times Notional?	No (Smaller) Initial Investment?	Permits/ Requires Net Settlement?	Conclusion
not XYZ Co.)	number of shares IF and WHEN the contract is in-the-money (favorable to the holder)	to be invested to yield the same potential return	convertible to cash	
Option on ABC Co. common stock— stock is NOT publicly traded (assume reporting is not ABC Co.)	Met. See above.	Met. See above.	It depends. If an option explicitly permits or requires net settlement in cash or shares, it meets the net settlement condition. If the option requires gross settlement in shares the option would not meet the net settlement	It depends. The decision will generally hinge on whether the option can be net settled
Currency swap	Met. Payment amount is based on the difference between the stated exchange rate and the current exchange rate × the notional amount on the "receive leg" and the "pay leg"	Met. Even if there is an exchange of currencies up front, the net amount is equal to the difference between the assets exchanged, not the notional principal amount	Met. The underlying currencies are readily convertible to cash (unless one of the currencies is blocked or not exchangeable)	Meets all three conditions: Derivative.

SCOPE EXCEPTIONS

Some contracts that literally meet the definition of a derivative are excluded from the scope of FAS-133. The scope exceptions fall into two broad categories:

1. Outright exceptions, because the contract is subject to another accounting model for one or both parties.
2. Exceptions granted to simplify the application of FAS-133.

If a contract qualifies for a scope exception in this section, it should not be accounted for as a derivative, and it should *not* be evaluated for embedded derivatives under Chapter 13, "Embedded Derivatives." (DIG B-18)

Outright Exceptions

The FASB granted scope exceptions for contracts in this category because they are already accounted for under a special accounting model that the FASB did not wish to overturn. Some of these exceptions only apply to one party; such limitations are noted below.

Equity Contracts of the Issuer

Contracts issued or held by the reporting entity that are both (1) indexed solely to its own stock and (2) classified in stockholders' equity in its statement of financial position should not be accounted for under FAS-133. (FAS-133, par. 11(a)) Other GAAP should be applied to determine whether the contract is appropriately classified in stockholders' equity. In addition, forward purchase contracts that require physical settlement involving the company's own shares that are accounted for under paragraphs 21 and 22 of FAS-150 are not subject to FAS-133. (FAS-133, par. 11(d), as amended by FAS-150) *These exceptions apply only to the issuer of the contract involving its own shares.* Chapter 16, "Issuer's Accounting for Equity Instruments and Related Contracts," provides additional information.

> ☞ **PRACTICE POINTER:** If a contract is not indexed *solely* to the entity's own stock, for example, it is indexed to the entity's stock and foreign exchange rates, the contract does not qualify for this exception. Furthermore, the contract may *not* be bifurcated into a component that meets the exception and a component that does not. (DIG C-8)

> ☞ **PRACTICE POINTER:** In February 2006, the FASB added to its agenda a project to clarify whether a conversion option that incorporates foreign currency risk qualifies for the scope exception in paragraph 11(a) of FAS-133, thereby precluding the need

to bifurcate the entity's convertible debt. Readers should monitor developments in this project.

Stock Compensation

Contracts issued by the entity that are deemed to be subject to FAS-123 (R) are exempt from FAS-133. However, in instances where contracts are issued to employees in exchange for employee service and the terms of a contract are modified when the holder is no longer an employee, the contract ceases to be subject to FAS 123(R). Following modification, the issuer must evaluate the terms of the contract to determine whether the contract is subject to FAS-133 or other GAAP. (That guidance applies to contracts issued in exchange for past or future employee service but not to contracts issued as consideration for goods or services.) Equity instruments granted to non-employees would no longer be subject to FAS-123(R) once performance has occurred. At that point, FAS-133 would apply (assuming the definition of a derivative has been met and the scope exception in paragraph 11(a) does not apply). (FAS 133, par. 11(b), DIG C-3, and FSP FAS 123(R)-1)

> ☞ **PRACTICE POINTER:** EITF Issue 96-18 discusses performance conditions in transactions involving the issuance of equity instruments to non-employees for goods and services and provides guidance for determining when performance is complete.

Contracts Issued in Business Combinations

Contracts issued by the entity as contingent consideration in a business combination that are addressed in FAS-141 are exempt from FAS-133. (FAS-133, par. 11(c)) *This exception only applies to the issuer of the contract.* In applying this paragraph, the issuer is considered to be the entity that is accounting for the combination using the purchase method.

Certain Insurance Contracts

A contract is not subject to FAS-133 if the holder will be compensated only if, as a result of an identifiable insurable event (other than a change in price), the holder incurs a liability or suffers a loss on a specific asset or liability. (Generally, insurance and reinsurance contracts of the type that are within the scope of FAS-60, FAS-97, and FAS-113, are not subject to the requirements of FAS-133 whether or not they are written by insurance enterprises.) (FAS-133, par. 10(c)) *This exception applies to both parties to the contract, and one would expect them to reach the same conclusion.*

Examples of contracts that meet the exclusion—for the issuer and the holder—are traditional life insurance contracts and traditional property and casualty contracts in which the identifiable insurable event is the death of the insured and a theft or fire, respectively.

Certain types of life insurance are indexed to the performance of a mutual fund or other assets. Such contracts are not subject to FAS-133 if they entitle the policyholder to be compensated *only* as a result of the death of the insured. (DIG B-10) For a property and casualty contract that provides for the payment of claims as a result of both an identifiable insurable event *and* changes in a variable to qualify for the insurance exclusion in paragraph 10(c)(2) of FAS-133, the payment must be limited to the amount of the policyholder's incurred loss and the insurable events must not be highly probable of occurring. (DIG B-26) Chapter 13, "Embedded Derivatives," discusses nontraditional insurance contracts in more detail.

> ☞ **PRACTICE POINTER:** Paragraph 10(c) is not a blanket exception for insurance companies—the terms of each contract must have the characteristics described above. In addition, "nontraditional" insurance products and investment contracts must be evaluated for embedded derivatives. Such contracts are discussed in Chapter 13, "Embedded Derivatives."

Certain Financial Guarantee Contracts

Financial guarantee contracts are not subject to FAS-133 if they meet all of the following three criteria:

1. Payments would be made only to reimburse the guaranteed party for failure of the debtor to satisfy its required payment obligations.

2. The amounts owed by the debtor are past due.

3. The guaranteed party is exposed to the risk of nonpayment throughout the term of the contract, either through direct legal ownership of the guaranteed obligation or through a back-to-back arrangement with another party that is required to maintain direct ownership of the guaranteed obligation. (FAS-133, par. 10(d), as amended)

This exception applies to both parties to the contract, and one would expect them to reach the same conclusion.

Some credit-related contracts would be considered derivatives, for example, a credit-indexed contract that requires a payment due to changes in the creditworthiness of a specified entity even if neither party incurs a loss from owning the underlying asset. (FAS-133, par. 59(b))

A provision limiting claims in the event the insured's credit losses exceed the credit losses in a referenced pool or index of consumer loans represents a type of deductible, rather than an embedded derivative. (DIG B-27)

Credit-related contracts that have *any* of the following attributes would not qualify for the financial guarantee exception:

- Payments are required based on *changes* in the creditworthiness of a referenced credit, rather than failure of that debtor to pay when due (i.e., default).

- The "guaranteed party" is not actually exposed to loss (i.e., he neither owns the referenced asset or is himself a guarantor of that asset) throughout the term of the contract.

- The compensation to be paid under the contract could exceed the amount of loss actually incurred by the guaranteed party.

☞ **PRACTICE POINTER:**   Refer to Chapter 8, "Debt Financing," for guidance on accounting for guarantees that are not considered derivatives.

Derivatives That Serve as Impediments to Sale Accounting

A derivative instrument that serves as an impediment to recognizing a related transaction as a sale by one party and a purchase by the counterparty is not subject to FAS-133. (FAS-133, par. 10(f)) *This exception applies to both parties, and one would expect them to reach the same conclusion.* For example, a call option that enables a transferor to repurchase a specific transferred asset that is not readily obtainable would preclude accounting for that transfer as a sale under FAS-140. (Under FAS-140, the asset would remain on the books of the transferor, along with a borrowing.) Such a call option would not be accounted for as a derivative under FAS-133, because to do so would result in double counting the transferred asset. However, if a transfer of assets that is required to be accounted for as a borrowing under FAS-140 involves a derivative, such as an interest rate swap, with an effective notional amount that exceeds the amount of the borrowing, the portion of the derivative in excess of the notional amount of the debt would not result in double counting, and should be accounted for separately as an embedded derivative. (DIG C-6) Refer to Chapter 13, "Embedded Derivatives," for additional information.

☞ **PRACTICE POINTER:**   On the contrary, if a transfer of assets qualifies as *a sale* under FAS-140 (or other applicable literature) and the entity retains certain rights and obligations relating to the asset, such as a commitment to repurchase the transferred asset (if it is readily available), or a commitment to modify the interest rate, those rights and privileges should be evaluated to determine whether they meet the definition of a derivative (both on a standalone basis and when they are embedded in another instrument).

Certain Loan Commitments

The following types of loan commitments are excluded from the scope of FAS-133:

- For the potential borrower/debtor, all loan commitments.

- For a lender that is not engaged in mortgage banking, all commitments to originate (new) loans.
- For a mortgage banker, all commitments to originate mortgage loans that will be classified as held for investment under FAS-65 (see Chapter 3, "Loans and the Allowance for Credit Losses"). (FAS-133, par. 10(i))

☛ **PRACTICE POINTER:**   A mortgage banker must account for all commitments to originate loans that will be held for sale as derivatives. Commitments to buy and sell *existing* loans (as opposed to new originations) must be evaluated under the definition of a derivative based on their terms. (DIG C-13)

☛ **PRACTICE POINTER:**   FAS-159, *The Fair Value Option for Financial Assets and Financial Liabilities,* issued in February 2007, provides companies with an option to report certain financial assets and liabilities at fair value with subsequent changes in value reported in earnings. The fair value option in FAS-159 is applicable to loan commitments that are not accounted for as derivatives under FAS-133. Chapter 19, "The Fair Value Option for Financial Instruments," outlines the scope and discusses the detailed provisions of FAS-159. FAS-159 is effective for calendar-year-end companies as of January 1, 2008.

Included in the scope of FAS-133 are loan commitments that relate to the origination of mortgage loans that will be held for sale, as discussed in paragraph 21 of FAS-65 (as amended). Those loan commitments must be accounted for as derivatives only by the issuer of the loan commitment (the potential lender under the arrangement) and measured at fair value.

SEC REGISTRANT ALERT: The SEC staff has clarified that the fair value measurement of a loan commitment issued may not incorporate expected future cash flows related to the associated servicing of the loan, once drawn, or any other internally-developed intangible asset, such as a customer relationship intangible asset. SEC registrants must apply this accounting for commitments entered subsequent to March 15, 2004, and should disclose the expected effect of the new guidance in any filings with the SEC prior to March 15, 2004. (SAB-105)

Interest-Only and Principal-Only Strips

Interest-only strips (I-Os) and principal-only strips (P-Os) are not subject to FAS-133 if they meet the following conditions:

- They represent the rights to receive only a specified proportion of the contractual interest or principal cash flows of a specific debt instrument and
- They do not incorporate any terms not present in the original debt instrument. That is, the cash flows from the original asset

simply "pass-through" to the holder(s) of the component(s). (FAS-133, par. 14)

☛ **PRACTICE POINTER:** A standard mortgage loan or a Treasury security that has been "cut up" into interest flows and principal flows meets the I-O/P-O exception (even if the mortgage was prepayable). However, an interest-only strip or principal-only strip bearing a guarantee by a government-sponsored enterprise or credit insurance by a third-party insurer would not qualify for the exception in paragraph 14 of FAS-133. An allocation of a portion of the interest or principal cash flows of a specific debt instrument to provide for a guarantee of payments excludes an interest-only strip and principal-only strip from the scope exception in paragraph 14.

Beneficial interests in a securitization trust A beneficial interest that does not qualify for the paragraph 14 scope exception may meet the definition of a derivative in its entirety or may have embedded derivatives that require separate accounting. Chapter 13, "Embedded Derivatives," discusses those situations in detail.

AUTHOR'S NOTE: FAS-155, issued in February 2006, clarified that the existing scope exception in paragraph 14 should be applied narrowly solely to simple separations of interest and principal cash flows of a debt instrument. Additionally, FAS-155 eliminated the interim exemption provided by DIG Issue D-1 that permitted beneficial interests in securitized financial assets to avoid bifurcation under FAS-133. Refer to the Important Notice and the related discussion under the *Beneficial Interests* section in Chapter 13, "Embedded Derivatives."

Certain Contracts Held by Benefit Plans

Insurance contracts and investment contracts that are accounted for under paragraph 4 of FAS-110 or paragraph 12 of FAS-35, as amended, are not subject to FAS-133. (FAS-133, par. 10(h), as amended) *This exception would apply only to the benefit plan, not to the counterparty to the contract.*

☛ **PRACTICE POINTER:** FSP AAG-1 and SOP 94-4-1, *Reporting of Fully Benefit-Responsive Investment Contracts Held by Certain Investment Companies Subject to the AICPA Investment Company Guide and Defined-Contribution Health and Welfare and Pension Plans,* eliminated the FAS-133 scope exception provided for fully benefit-responsive investment contracts reported at contract value in accordance with AIPCA SOP 94-4, *Reporting of Investment Contracts Held by Health and Welfare Benefit Plans and Defined-Contribution Pension Plans.* The FSP amends SOP 94-4 and requires that defined-contribution plans report all investments (including derivative contracts) at fair value. It concludes that contract value is the relevant measurement attribute for that portion of the net assets available for benefits of a defined-contribution plan attributable to fully benefit-responsive investment contracts as defined. In addition, the FSP establishes new financial statement presentation and disclosure guidance for fully benefit-responsive investment contracts.

Residual Value Guarantees

Residual value guarantees that are subject to the requirements of the lease accounting literature (including FAS-13) are not subject to FAS-133. (EITF 01-12)

Investments in Life Insurance

A policyholder's investment in a life insurance contract that is subject to FTB 85-4 or FSP FTB 85-4-1, *Accounting for Life Settlement Contracts by Third-Party Investors,* is not subject to FAS-133. (FAS-133, par. 10(g)) *This exception applies only to the holder of the contract.*

Registration Payment Arrangements

Registration payment arrangements issued in connection with certain financing transactions that are within the scope of FSP EITF 00-19-2 are not subject to FAS-133 for either the issuer of the arrangement or the counterparty. Those arrangements are subject to the accounting model in FAS-5 and related guidance in FSP EITF 00-19-2. The accounting for registration payment arrangements are discussed in Chapter 16, "Issuer's Accounting for Equity Instruments and Related Contracts."

Exceptions Granted to Simplify the Application of FAS-133

Each of the exceptions below would typically meet the definition of a derivative. However, the FASB granted an exception to ease implementation of the standard.

Certain Security Trades

(Applies to both parties to the contract, but they would not necessarily reach the same conclusion.) Securities trades that are required to be recognized on the trade date under other GAAP and securities trades with either of the following characteristics are not subject to FAS-133:

- The transaction is "regular-way," that is, it requires delivery of an existing security within the time generally established by regulations or conventions in the marketplace or exchange in which the transaction is being executed and the transaction cannot be net settled, either through the provisions of the contract or through a market mechanism.

- Purchases or sales of "when-issued" or other securities that do not yet exist when (1) there is no other way to purchase the security, (2) delivery will occur within the shortest possible period for that security, and (3) it is probable throughout the life of the transaction that delivery will occur (i.e., the transaction will not be settled net) and the rationale for that conclusion is documented. (FAS-133, pars. 10(a) and 59(a), as amended)

> ☛ **PRACTICE POINTER:** A pattern of net settlement would call into question the continued exclusion of "when-issued" or similar contracts. Chapter 2, "Investments in Debt and Equity Securities," provides guidance about trade date accounting.

Normal Purchases and Sales

(Available to both parties to the contract, but they would not necessarily reach the same conclusion.) Normal purchases and sales are forward contracts that provide for the purchase or sale of something that is readily convertible to cash (other than a financial instrument or derivative instrument) that will be delivered in quantities expected to be used or sold by the reporting entity over a reasonable period in the normal course of business. (FAS-133, par. 10(b))

Contracts that permit but do not require net settlement may qualify for the normal purchases and sales exception if it is probable at inception and throughout the term of the individual contract that the contract will not settle net and will result in physical delivery. However, longer-term contracts that require periodic net settlements do not qualify for this exception. Net settlement of individual contracts in a group of contracts designated as normal purchases and sales would call into question the classification of all such contracts as normal purchases or sales. Entities must document the basis for concluding that it is probable that the contract will result in physical delivery (for groups of similarly designated contracts or for each individual contract). (FAS-133, par. 10(b))

In determining whether a contract meets these conditions, an entity should consider all relevant factors, such as (1) the quantities provided under the contract and the entity's need for the related assets, (2) the locations to which delivery of the items will be made, (3) the period of time between entering into the contract and delivery, and (4) the entity's prior practices with regard to such contracts. (FAS-133, par. 58(b))

> ☞ **PRACTICE POINTER:** If a contract qualifies for the normal purchase and sale exception, it could be designated as the hedged item in a fair value hedge of a firm commitment or as a forecasted transaction in a cash flow hedge, depending on the facts and circumstances. (DIG E-17)

Some of the finer points of qualifying for the normal purchases and sales exception are:

- The normal purchases and sales exception is an election, not a requirement. However, once an entity documents compliance with the requirements of paragraph 10(b), which could be done at the inception of the contract or at a later date, the entity may not change its election at a later date and treat the contract as a derivative. (DIG C-12)

- The normal purchases and sales exception applies *only to forward contracts*, except as discussed in DIG Issue C-15 (see below). Forward contracts that contain optionality features would be eligible to qualify for the normal purchases and sales exception only if the optionality feature could not modify the *quantity* of the asset to be delivered under the contract. (If the optionality feature does affect the quantity, it would be eligible for the normal purchases and sales exception only after the optionality feature expires.) (DIG C-10, C-16)

- DIG Issue C-15 provides a narrow exception to allow certain capacity contracts involving electricity to qualify for the normal purchases and sales exception (even though they have optionality that affects the quantity of the contract). Readers who enter into electricity capacity contracts should carefully consider the detailed guidance of DIG C-15.

- A price adjustment feature would be considered *not* clearly and closely related to the asset being sold or purchased under the contract if the feature: (1) is unrelated to the asset being sold or purchased (with respect to the changes in its cost or fair value) or to an ingredient or direct factor in the production of the asset being delivered under the contract; (2) contains a leverage feature, *or* (3) is based on a foreign currency that is not one of the currencies listed in paragraph 15 of FAS-133, as amended by FAS-149. (DIG C-20, which replaces DIG C-11)

> **OBSERVATION:**   DIG Issue C-20 is significantly less stringent than the guidance it superseded in DIG Issue C-11. It generally provides that if there is a "valid" economic relationship between a price adjustment feature and the item being purchased or sold (or components thereof), the two can be considered clearly and closely related.

> ☞ **PRACTICE POINTER:**   GAAP does not permit an entity to separate a compound derivative into a portion that qualifies for the normal purchases and sales scope exception and a portion that must be accounted for as a derivative under FAS-133. (DIGB-18)

Contracts Involving Physical and Other Variables

Contracts that are based on one of the following types of underlyings are not subject to FAS-133 provided that the contract is *not* traded on an exchange. *(Applies to both parties to the contract if the stated conditions are met.)*

- A climatic, geological, or other physical variable, such as rainfall or the severity of an earthquake (so-called weather derivatives, unless they are exchange traded).
- The price or value of a nonfinancial asset (such as real estate or machinery) or liability that is not readily convertible to cash or does not require delivery of an asset that is readily convertible to cash. This exception applies only to nonfinancial assets that are *unique* and only if the nonfinancial asset is owned by the party that would not benefit under the contract from an increase in the price or value of the nonfinancial asset (if a call option, an increase in the price above the option's strike price). (See Exhibit 12-3 below.)
- Specified volumes of sales or service revenues of one of the parties to the contract, such as leases based on sales of the lessee or royalty agreements.

If a contract has more than one underlying and one, but not all, of them qualifies for one of these exceptions (e.g., it is indexed to real estate and the price of electricity), the contract is subject to FAS-133 if the contract as a whole behaves in a manner that is highly correlated with the behavior of a component that does not qualify for the exception (in this example, the price of electricity). (FAS-133, pars. 10(e) and 58(c))

If the contract also involves a financial variable, such as a contract that requires payment if aggregate property damage from a hurricane in Florida exceeds $50,000,000 during the year 20X1, the contract does not qualify for the scope exclusion in paragraph 10(e)(1) because of the presence of the financial variable (in this example, the "trigger" of $50,000,000). (DIG C-1)

EXHIBIT 12-3
APPLYING THE NONFINANCIAL ASSET EXCEPTION

To qualify for the exception under 10(e)(2):

Contract Type	Owner of "Unique" Item Must Be:	Nonowner Must Be:
Forward	Seller	Buyer
Option	Writer	Holder

Accounting for Contracts that Meet a Scope Exception

If a contract meets one of the scope exceptions in FAS-133, it should be accounted for under applicable GAAP for that contract type. The appropriate GAAP is specifically mentioned in FAS-133 for the first category of exceptions. The second category of exceptions is quite broad, but could include the following:

- Regular-way securities trades should be accounted for on the trade date as purchases and sales of securities as required by industry practices. (Refer to Chapter 2, "Investments in Debt and Equity Securities," for additional information.)
- A purchase order involving commodities (that qualifies for the normal purchases and sales exception) should be accounted for like any other purchase order held by the company.
- A weather derivative that is not exchange traded should be accounted for in accordance with EITF Issue 99-2.

The contract should *not* be analyzed for embedded derivatives under paragraph 12. (DIG B-18)

Exhibit 12-4 summarizes the process used to determine whether a freestanding contract is considered a derivative instrument.

EXHIBIT 12-4
IDENTIFYING DERIVATIVES UNDER FAS-133

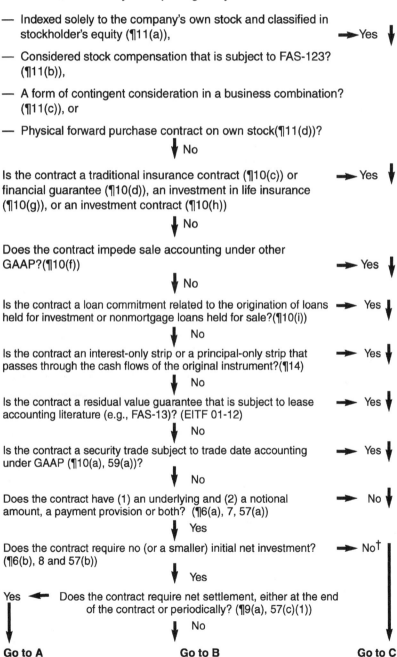

Is the contract *issued by* the reporting entity and:

— Indexed solely to the company's own stock and classified in stockholder's equity (¶11(a)), →Yes ↓

— Considered stock compensation that is subject to FAS-123? (¶11(b)),

— A form of contingent consideration in a business combination? (¶11(c)), or

— Physical forward purchase contract on own stock(¶11(d))?
↓ No

Is the contract a traditional insurance contract (¶10(c)) or financial guarantee (¶10(d)), an investment in life insurance (¶10(g)), or an investment contract (¶10(h)) → Yes ↓
↓ No

Does the contract impede sale accounting under other GAAP?(¶10(f)) → Yes ↓
↓ No

Is the contract a loan commitment related to the origination of loans held for investment or nonmortgage loans held for sale?(¶10(i)) → Yes ↓
↓ No

Is the contract an interest-only strip or a principal-only strip that passes through the cash flows of the original instrument?(¶14) → Yes ↓
↓ No

Is the contract a residual value guarantee that is subject to lease accounting literature (e.g., FAS-13)? (EITF 01-12) → Yes ↓
↓ No

Is the contract a security trade subject to trade date accounting under GAAP (¶10(a), 59(a))? → Yes ↓
↓ No

Does the contract have (1) an underlying and (2) a notional amount, a payment provision or both? (¶6(a), 7, 57(a)) → No ↓
↓ Yes

Does the contract require no (or a smaller) initial net investment? (¶6(b), 8 and 57(b)) → No† |
↓ Yes

Yes ← Does the contract require net settlement, either at the end of the contract or periodically? (¶9(a), 57(c)(1))
↓ No

Go to A　　　　　　**Go to B**　　　　　　**Go to C**

B

Does the contract permit net settlement or is there a market
mechanism to facilitate net settlement outside of the contract?

↓ Yes   ↓ No

Is the underlying a physical variable,   Does the contract require
the price of a unique nonfinancial   delivery of a derivative or
asset of the seller (or option writer)   an asset that is readily
or sales volumes or revenues of one   convertible to cash?
of the parties?(¶10(e))   (¶9(c), 57(c)(3))   No ↓

↓ Yes   ↓ No   ↓ Yes

Is the contract   Is the contract a regular-
exchange-traded?   way security trade or a
                                                qualifying when-issued?
↓   (¶10(a) and 59(a))   Yes ↓

No   Yes   Is it probable the   ↓ No
(Go to C) ➡   contract will result
                    in physical
                    delivery?(¶10(b))   Does the contract involve
                                                the purchase or sale of a
          ↓ No   Yes   nonfinancial asset in
                    ➡   quantities that will be used
                                                in the normal course of
                                                business? (¶10(b))
                                                                     Yes‡ ↓
          A   No   **C**
     Apply FAS-133   ⬅   **Do Not
                                                   Apply
                                                   FAS-133**

---

† Such contracts should be evaluated for embedded derivatives. See Chapter 13, "Embedded Derivatives."
‡ Entities meeting this condition may elect to apply FAS-133 to similar contracts as a policy
decision.

EXHIBIT 12-5
SUMMARY ANALYSIS OF CONTRACT TYPES

	Contract	Derivative?†, ‡	Underlying	Notional Amount
1	Equity security	No. Requires initial investment to purchase security	Not necessary to analyze	
2	Debt security or loan	No. Requires initial investment of face amount (or present value of future cash flows)	Not necessary to analyze	
3	Lease	No. Requires payments equal to the value of the right to use the property	Not necessary to analyze	

	Contract	Derivative?[†, ‡]	Underlying	Notional Amount
4	Option to buy or sell an exchange-traded security, including warrants	Yes, for investor No for issuer, if the option is considered equity	Price of security	Number of shares or bonds
5	Option to buy or sell a security not traded on an exchange	No, unless it can be net settled (broadly defined)	Price of security	Number of shares or bonds
6	Stock option (to employees or other service providers)	No for issuer; recipient should apply 4 and 5 above	Price of security	Number of shares
7	Futures contract	Yes, a market mechanism exists	Price of commodity, security, etc.	Specified quantity, face amount, etc.
8	Forward contract to buy an exchange-traded security	Yes, but could qualify as regular way trade	Price of security	Number of shares
9	Forward contract to buy or sell a security not traded on an exchange	No, unless it can be net settled (broadly defined)	Price of security	Number of shares or bonds
10	Contract to buy or sell exchange-traded commodities	Yes, unless normal purchase and sale conditions are met	Price of commodity	Number of bushels, barrels, etc.
11	Interest rate swap	Yes	Interest rate (index)	Specified currency amount
12	Currency swap	Yes (assuming both currencies are liquid)	Exchange rate	Specified currency amounts
13	Swaption	Yes (requires delivery of a derivative)	Value of swap	Notional amount of swap
14	Credit-indexed contract (not reimbursement of a specific default)	Yes	Credit index or rating	Specified payment amount (can be fixed or variable, depending on the degree of change)
15	Traditional insurance contract	No, if reimbursement for an insurable event		
16	Traditional financial guarantee	No, if reimbursement for a defaulted receivable		

Contract	Derivative?†, ‡	Underlying	Notional Amount
17 Synthetic guaranteed investment contract	No for holder Yes for issuer	Value of portfolio of assets and interest rates	Notional amount of contract (DIG A-16)
18 Loan commitment (on new loans)	No for holder No for lender, unless the mortgage will be classified as held for sale under FAS-65		
19 Weather derivative (such as a payment based on rainfall)	No, if not exchange traded (EITF 99-2)		
20 Option to buy or sell real estate (not cash settleable)	No, unless the owner of the property is the holder of the option or it is exchange traded	Price of real estate	A specified parcel of real estate
21 Purchase order to buy or sell machinery with a variable default clause	No, if the seller owns the machinery, delivery is probable and the contract is in the normal course of business		
22 Royalty agreement	No, based on sales of one of the parties		

---

† Some derivatives may qualify for scope exceptions in FAS-133, paragraph 10, depending on the facts and circumstances.

‡ This summary does not address embedded derivatives, which could exist in any contract with unusual or leveraged terms. Refer to Chapter 13, "Embedded Derivatives," for additional information.

Adapted from FASB Course on FAS-133.

ACCOUNTING FOR DERIVATIVES

Balance Sheet Recognition

FAS-133 requires that all derivative instruments, as defined, be reported in the balance sheet at fair value. Derivatives can be either assets or liabilities depending on the current rights or obligations under the contract. (FAS-133, par. 17)

> ☞ **PRACTICE POINTER:** Many types of derivatives, including forward contracts and swaps, have a fair value of zero at inception, if the terms reflect current market conditions. Those contracts will be recognized as assets or liabilities as their fair value changes. Options typically have a fair value at inception equal to the premium paid. The writer of the option has a liability, and the purchaser of the option has an asset.

> ☞ **PRACTICE POINTER:** Some derivatives have a forward price or strike price that equals the then current market price of the underlying. Such instruments are still derivatives, but generally they will have a fair value of zero.

Freestanding derivative assets and liabilities should be presented separately in the balance sheet unless the right of setoff exists. Refer to Chapter 17, "Offsetting Assets and Liabilities in the Balance Sheet," for a discussion of the necessary conditions.

> ☞ **PRACTICE POINTER:** Derivative contracts are often entered into subject to master netting agreements, which provide for net settlement of all contracts involving the same counterparties in the event of default or termination of a contract subject to the agreement. Such arrangements receive special accounting consideration, as discussed in Chapter 17.

Determining Fair Value

> **AUTHOR'S NOTE:** In September 2006, the FASB issued FASB Statement No. 157, *Fair Value Measurements*. FAS-157 provides a single definition of the term *fair value*, establishes a framework for measuring fair value where permitted or required by existing GAAP, and expands disclosures about fair value measurements. Specific fair value measurement guidance applicable to derivatives is covered in this Chapter. Chapter 18, "Fair Value Measurements, Fair Value Disclosures, and Other Financial Instrument Disclosures," provides the detailed provisions of FAS-157 and specific fair value measurement guidance applicable to all financial instruments required to be measured at fair value under GAAP. FAS-157 is effective for calendar-year-end companies as of January 1, 2008. Unless a company chooses to early adopt, prior GAAP is applicable for financial statements issued for 2007.
> As this book went to press, the FASB was addressing a possible delay of FAS-157's effective date. The FASB agreed to consider delaying the effective date for nonfinancial instruments and for certain types of entities, including private companies and "smaller" public companies (not yet defined). Readers should monitor the FASB's further deliberations regarding the nature of any delay of FAS-157's effective date. Also, readers should refer to the 2007 edition for GAAP related to the fair value measurement of financial instruments applicable before the effective date of FAS-157.

FAS-157 is the primary guidance for fair value measurement under GAAP. The fair value measurement model in FAS-157 applies for both initial measurement and subsequent measurement of derivatives subject to the scope of FAS-133.

Fair value is the price that would be received to sell an asset or paid to transfer a liability in an orderly transaction between market participants at the measurement date. The objective of a fair value measurement under FAS-157 is to determine the price that would be received to sell the asset or paid to transfer the liability at the measurement date (an exit price) using assumptions that market participants would use.

FAS-133 does not contain a "practicability exception" for freestanding derivatives. If quotes are not available, fair value must be estimated, regardless of the cost or lack of reliability. FAS-157 includes a fair value hierarchy for prioritizing inputs when valuation techniques are used for estimating fair value.

> ☛ **PRACTICE POINTER:** FAS-157 nullifies the guidance in footnote 3 of EITF 02-3, which precluded immediate recognition of an unrealized gain or loss if the fair value of an instrument was determined using significant unobservable inputs. The principles of fair value measurement under FAS-157 apply in all periods in which a derivative is measured at fair value, including at initial recognition. FAS-157 contains no "minimum reliability threshold" for fair value estimates at initial recognition of derivatives for which fair values are determined based on unobservable inputs. Instead, specific disclosures are required for assets and liabilities measured at fair value within Level 3 of the fair value hierarchy in order to highlight the subjective nature of the measurement.

Chapter 18, "Fair Value Measurements, Fair Value Disclosures, and Other Financial Instrument Disclosures," provides specific fair value measurement guidance applicable to all financial instruments required to be measured at fair value under GAAP.

Transfers and Extinguishments of Derivatives

Transfers of derivative instruments that represent assets are accounted for in accordance with (or by analogy to) FAS-140, regardless of whether the instrument is technically a financial asset. For example, a purchased commodity option that could require delivery of a nonfinancial asset is not considered a financial instrument. (EITF 99-8) Extinguishments of derivative liabilities are accounted for in accordance with FAS-140, paragraph 16. (FAS-140 Q&A, par. 16)

Recognizing Changes in Value

Changes in the fair value of a derivative (gains and losses) are recognized currently in earnings unless the derivative is designated as part of a qualifying hedging relationship. This is called "mark-to-market" accounting or "fair value accounting." The qualifications for and mechanics of hedge accounting are discussed in Chapter 14, "Hedge Accounting."

☞ **PRACTICE POINTER:** The fair value of a derivative can change significantly from period to period. Forward-based contracts that were assets in one period can become liabilities in the next period and vice versa. Changes in the fair value of derivatives can cause significant volatility in reported earnings.

Derivatives included in this category include:

- Derivatives held as part of a trading activity, for example at a large financial institution,
- Derivatives held in "separate accounts" of an insurance company,
- Derivatives being used as economic hedges of an asset or liability that is marked to market (according to applicable GAAP),
- Derivatives that do not qualify for hedge accounting treatment, and
- Derivatives held by companies who simply elect not to apply hedge accounting for some (or all) of their derivatives.

Income Statement Classification

There are no specific guidelines for classifying gains and losses on derivatives that are not designated in hedging relationships. If such amounts are material, the line-item classification should be disclosed as a significant accounting policy. Classification of gains and losses on derivatives designated in qualifying hedging relationships is discussed in Chapter 14, "Hedge Accounting."

☞ **PRACTICE POINTER:** EITF Issue 02-3 requires that gains and losses on derivative contracts (held for trading purposes) be presented net in the income statement, whether or not they are settled physically. EITF Issue 03-11 addresses physically settled derivative contracts not "held for trading purposes" and indicates that determining whether realized gains and losses on such contracts should be reported in the income statement on a gross or net basis is a matter of judgment that depends on the relevant facts and circumstances. An assessment of the facts and circumstances should involve (a) consideration of the context of the various activities of the entity (and not solely the terms of the contracts); (b) the economic substance of the transaction; (c) the guidance in APB-29 on nonmonetary exchanges; and (d) the gross vs. net reporting indicators in EITF Issue 99-19.

Entities that do not report earnings An entity that does not report earnings as a separate caption in a statement of financial performance (for example, a not-for-profit organization or a defined benefit pension plan) should recognize the gain or loss on a derivative instrument as a change in net assets in the period of change unless it qualifies for certain types of hedge accounting. (FAS-133, par. 43) Hedge accounting is discussed in Chapter 14, "Hedge Accounting."

Cash Flow Statement Presentation

Cash flows from derivative instruments that are not designated as part of a qualifying hedge relationship should be classified according to their nature. FAS-95 illustrates that the purchase or sale of a futures contract is an investing activity (paragraph 14, fn. 4). An exception applies for derivatives designated as part of a qualifying hedge relationship. Refer to Chapter 14, "Hedge Accounting," for additional information.

> **OBSERVATION:** The cash flows on derivatives likely will not coincide with changes in their values. Entities that prepare their Statement of Cash Flows using the indirect method should include gains and losses on derivatives as an adjustment to reconcile net income to net operating cash flow, if material.

Derivatives with a Financing Element

If a derivative instrument includes an upfront cash flow that does not merely represent points on an at-the-money forward, the premium on an at-the-money or out-of-the-money option contract, or a similar arrangement, then the "borrower" must classify all cash flows on the derivative as cash flows from financing activities. (FAS-133, par. 45A)

> ☛ **PRACTICE POINTER:** This provision applies to contracts that are derivatives in their entirety. In some cases, derivative-like contracts with upfront cash flows will be considered hybrids with embedded derivatives that require separate accounting. See Chapter 13, "Embedded Derivatives," for additional information.

Income Tax Considerations

Taxation of derivatives is an evolving, complex area that is outside the scope of this book. FAS-133 did not change the basic principles of accounting for income taxes. However, there may be differences in the way derivatives are accounted for under GAAP versus tax regulations, depending on the nature of the reporting entity, the type of derivative and how it is used. FAS-109 provides guidance on how to account for such differences.

> **AUTHOR'S NOTE:** The accounting for derivatives that are not part of a hedging relationship is quite straightforward (aside from valuation issues relating to derivatives that are not actively traded). The complexity in accounting for derivatives lies in (1) making sure all derivatives are properly identified and (2) the qualifications for and mechanics of hedge accounting. Many companies only use derivatives as part of a risk management (or hedging) program. Such companies are willing

to pay the price of hedge accounting because it better reflects the combined effect of their hedging strategies on net income—not just the changes in value of the derivative.

AUDITING CONSIDERATIONS

The primary audit guidance for derivatives is provided in SAS-92, "Auditing Derivative Instruments, Hedging Activities, and Investments in Securities." This guidance is expanded and analyzed in an AICPA Audit Guide, *Auditing Derivative Instruments, Hedging Activities, and Investments in Securities.* The complexity of both the derivative instruments themselves and the applicable accounting standards and interpretations contributes significantly to audit risk.

There are several aspects of accounting for derivatives that are error-prone, judgmental, or both. Independence Standards Board Interpretation 99-1, "FAS 133 Assistance," describes the nature of services that an auditor may perform in connection with the application of FAS-133 that would and would not impair his or her independence. Areas that could compromise independence include performing services that would also be subject to audit procedures such as compiling the inventory of derivatives, creating the initial journal entries to be recorded, initially determining whether specific derivatives meet the relevant criteria for hedge accounting, or making management decisions concerning the implementation of FAS-133. (ISB 99-1, par. 10) Valuation services are discussed separately below.

The key issues relating to scope and reporting all derivatives at fair value are highlighted below. (Issues relating to hedge accounting and disclosures are addressed separately in Chapters 14 and 15, respectively.)

Properly Identifying All Derivatives

Because some derivatives do not involve an upfront exchange of cash, it may be difficult to determine that all derivatives have been accounted for. In addition, the definition of a derivative in FAS-133 is extremely complex—it encompasses contracts that are not commonly thought of as derivatives, and it does not encompass some contracts that are commonly thought of as derivatives. The definition excludes several contracts that are economically similar to contracts that are derivatives. Some exceptions apply to the issuer, but not the holder, and vice versa. Generally, nonstandard or customized terms increase the risk that a contract will be characterized improperly.

Identifying *embedded* derivatives presents another significant audit risk. Contracts such as leases, loans, and insurance policies could unknowingly contain embedded derivatives. Failure to properly identify all derivatives is problematic because the default accounting is mark-to-market through earnings. A company that "discovers" a derivative cannot retroactively designate it as a hedging instrument. Therefore, the discovery must be recorded with a catch-up effect on earnings (if a change in value has occurred since inception of a contract).

In short, every company should cultivate "experts" on the definition of a derivative. All personnel involved in managing risk, drafting and negotiating contracts, and recording transactions for a company should be trained to identify provisions that signal FAS-133 accounting. Likewise, front-line personnel should be knowledgeable about the scope exceptions. Companies that lack this expertise on the front-line are exposed to significant financial reporting risk.

Discretionary Aspects of FAS-133

Management intent (and other elections) plays a key role in accounting for derivatives. For example:

- The normal purchases and sales scope exception for qualifying commodity (and other) contracts is elective and can be invoked after the inception of a contract. Because this exception has the effect of ignoring gains and losses on derivatives, auditors should carefully review management's documentation supporting the classification of such contracts, and test that physical settlement is actually occurring.
- Investors can elect to classify hybrid securities as trading and therefore not bifurcate any embedded derivatives (as permitted by FAS-115).
- Entities are allowed to elect to follow hedge accounting for some qualifying transactions but not others that have the exact same economic effect. (Chapter 14, "Hedge Accounting," addresses the extensive requirements for hedge accounting.)

All of these elections must be made in accordance with the applicable rules and, in some cases, consistently applied to similar transactions. However, they make the overall accounting model more complex and the task of identifying misstatements more difficult for the auditor.

The Evolving Nature of Derivatives and Ongoing Interpretations of FAS-133

Formal interpretations of FAS-133 may lag behind the development of new contract features or types of instruments. If companies miss developments in the accounting literature, some transactions will, in retrospect, have been accounted for incorrectly. If prospective transition is granted for an accounting change, a company could be following two different accounting methods for the same type of transaction, which adds complexity to an audit. Companies and their auditors must stay abreast of accounting developments for derivatives.

Valuation

Judgment is required to determine the fair value of certain derivatives, instruments with embedded derivatives, and the change in fair value of hedged items in a fair value hedge. FAS-133 provides some specific guidelines for determining fair value, and for measuring changes in fair value of certain hedged items. SAS-92 provides extensive guidance on auditing the valuation of derivatives (and securities). Chapter 2, "Investments in Debt and Equity Securities," highlights the key audit issues relating to fair value estimates.

Companies that engage in derivatives activities (broadly defined) must be in a position to value their open positions during the normal financial statement closing process, because the valuations affect the balance sheet and potentially the income statement in the current period. This more frequent reporting of derivatives greatly increases the need for good documentation of valuation methods, the assumptions that are being used, the sources of market information, and whether a transaction qualifies for hedge accounting (i.e., deferral of a gain or loss).

In auditing fair value estimates, auditors should consider the guidance in AU Section 328, *Auditing Fair Value Measurements and Disclosures*, AU Section 342, *Auditing Accounting Estimates*, and AU Section 336, *Using the Work of a Specialist*. Auditors should also consider the guidance in ISB Interpretation 99-1, "FAS 133 Assistance," which, among other things, describes the level of involvement that an auditor may have in assisting a client with valuation issues without compromising his or her independence. Generally, an auditor should not be responsible for selecting the appropriate assumptions, making the computations, or providing the client with a nonstandard model with which to value its derivatives. (ISB 99-1, par. 13)

REGULATORY CONSIDERATIONS

On December 29, 1998, the federal banking agencies issued a joint statement that banking organizations must adopt FAS-133 for regulatory reporting purposes when they adopt it for financial reporting purposes. That statement provides interim regulatory reporting and capital treatment guidance for institutions. Generally, banks should:

- Calculate risk-weighted assets for derivatives based on the credit equivalent amount of the derivative, not the on-balance-sheet fair value.

- For instruments with embedded derivatives, both the host financial instrument and the credit-equivalent amount of the derivative component should be included in risk-weighted assets.

The National Association of Insurance Commissioners (NAIC) recently adopted SSAP 86, *Accounting for Derivatives and Hedging Activities*. SSAP 86 requires statutory accounting that significantly differs from GAAP in several key respects. Most of the differences relate to hedge accounting, which is discussed in Chapter 14, "Hedge Accounting."

ILLUSTRATIONS

Illustration 12-1: Accounting for an Interest Rate Swap

On January 1, 20X1, Wharton Finance Corp. seeks to adjust its overall interest rate risk profile by entering into a 3-year receive-fixed, pay-LIBOR interest rate swap with a notional amount of $10,000,000. The fixed rate on the swap is 7%, which represents a market rate of interest. The floating rate of the swap resets December 31 of each year for the next year; payments are made on December 31. The swap does not qualify for hedge accounting because it is not specifically linked to an existing asset or liability held by the financial institution (rather, it is a "macro hedge"). Accordingly, the swap must be marked to market through earnings.

Assume the following information about the swap.

	Rate for Upcoming Year	Fair Value**	Change in Fair Value
01/01/X1	7%	$ —	$ —
12/31/X1	6%	180,000	180,000
12/31/X2	5%	190,000	10,000
12/31/X3	—	—	(190,000)

Wharton Finance would record the following annual journal entries (entries would be required at interim periods, but they are ignored for purposes of the illustration).

Inception

No journal entry is required, because the swap is entered into at market rates and the fair value is zero

December 31, 20X1

Interest rate swap asset	180,000	
Gain on swap		180,000

To mark to market the swap (two estimated payments of $100,000 discounted at 6%)

December 31, 20X2

Cash	100,000	
Gain on swap		100,000

To record the cash receipt on the swap. (The anticipated receipt could have been either reflected as part of the fair value of the swap or separately accrued. This entry looks through that interim step.)

** Calculated as the sum of the present value of expected future cash flows (after cash settlement)

| Interest rate swap asset | 10,000 | |
| Gain on swap | | 10,000 |

To mark to market the swap based on the remaining cash flows (one estimated payment of $200,000, discounted at 5%)

December 31, 20X3

| Cash | 200,000 | |
| Gain on swap | | 200,000 |

To record the cash receipt on the swap. (The anticipated receipt could have been either reflected as part of the fair value of the swap or separately accrued. This entry looks through that interim step.)

| Loss on swap | 190,000 | |
| Interest rate swap asset | | 190,000 |

To mark to market the swap.

Illustration 12-2: Accounting for an Option

On April 1, Agribusiness Company writes 6-month call options on 10,000 bushels of corn with a strike price of $2.30 per bushel for a premium of $2,200. The Company has written the options to provide limited protection against a decline in the value of its corn inventory, but the options do not qualify for hedge accounting. The price of corn and market value of the options are as follows on the following dates:

	Price of corn	Fair value of option	Change in Fair Value
April 1	$2.30	$2,200	—
June 30	$2.27	$500	$1,700
August 31	$2.55	$2,600	($2,100)

On September 1, prices are unchanged and Agribusiness enters into a closing transaction by buying September 30 calls for $2,600.

Agribusiness Co. would record the following journal entries.

April 1

| Cash | 2,200 | |
| Liability for written option | | 2,200 |

To record the written option.

June 30

Liability for written option	1,700	
Gain on options		1,700

To mark to market the written option

August 31

Loss on options	2,100	
Liability for written option		2,100

To mark to market the written option

September 1

Liability for written option	2,600	
Cash		2,600

To close out the transaction by purchasing a September 31 call option

> **OBSERVATION:**   Unlike previous GAAP, the premium on an option is not amortized over the life of the option. Furthermore, "covered call" strategies generally will not qualify for hedge accounting. Chapter 14, "Hedge Accounting," discusses strategies that qualify for hedge accounting in more detail.

CHAPTER 13
EMBEDDED DERIVATIVES

CONTENTS

Overview	13.02
Background	13.03
Meaning of the Term *Embedded*	13.03
Identifying Embedded Derivatives	13.04
Criteria for Separate Accounting	13.04
Exhibit 13-1: Determining When an Embedded Derivative Requires Split Accounting	13.06
Meeting the "Clearly and Closely Related" Condition	13.07
Timing of Assessment	13.07
Types of Host Contracts	13.07
Equity Instruments	13.08
Debt Instruments	13.09
Beneficial Interests	13.12
Exhibit 13-2: Embedded Puts and Calls in Debt Instruments	13.13
Leases	13.15
Contracts Denominated in a Foreign Currency	13.15
Exhibit 13-3: Evaluating Hybrid Debt Instruments for Embedded Derivatives	13.17
Insurance Products	13.18
Exhibit 13-4: Evaluating Insurance Contracts for Embedded Derivatives	13.20
Exhibit 13-5: Deferred Variable Annuity Contracts	13.23
Not-for-Profit Organization's Obligation Arising from a Split-Interest Agreement	13.26
Accounting for Embedded Derivatives	13.26
Bifurcation of Embedded Derivatives	13.26
Guidelines for Bifurcating Derivatives	13.28
Overall	13.28
Bifurcating Forward-Based Embedded Derivatives	13.28
Bifurcating Option-Based Embedded Derivatives	13.29
Combinations of Option Contracts	13.29

Exhibit 13-6: Combinations of Options with the Same Terms   13.30

The Host Contract   13.30

Balance Sheet Presentation of Embedded Derivatives   13.32

Elective Fair Value Measurement for Certain Hybrid
Financial Instruments   13:32

Fair Value Election for Hybrid Financial Instruments
under FAS-155   13:32

Fair Value Option for Hybrid Financial Instruments
under FAS-159   13:33

Fair Value Considerations for Hybrid Financial Instruments   13.34

Balance Sheet Presentation of Certain Hybrid Instruments   13.34

Audit Considerations   13.35

Regulatory Considerations   13.35

Illustrations   13.35

Illustration 13-1: Bifurcating an Equity-Linked Note   13.35

Illustration 13-2: The Negative Yield Test (paragraph 13(a))   13.38

*Illustration 13-3: Applying the Foreign Currency
Exception (paragraph 15)*   13.38

OVERVIEW

Certain financial instruments and other contracts have some or all of
their payment terms linked to market variables, such as equity indexes,
interest rates, and foreign exchange rates, in a way that suggests that a
derivative is embedded in the contract. If an instrument or contract
comprises dissimilar risks or has potential returns that are disproportionate with the level of investment, the contract is considered a
"hybrid instrument" and presumptively contains an embedded derivative. If the embedded derivative meets the FAS-133 definition of a
derivative and does not qualify for a scope exception, the derivative
must be bifurcated from the host contract and recognized at fair value,
unless it is not possible to do so reliably. Subsequently, the separated
derivative is accounted for under FAS-133 (including the hedge accounting provisions) and the host is accounted for under applicable
GAAP. If the components cannot be separated reliably, the entire contract must be marked to market and may not be designated in a hedging
relationship. Examples of hybrid instruments are inverse-floaters,
commodity-linked bonds, and equity-linked annuities.

> **AUTHOR'S NOTE:** While FAS-133 was being drafted, the FASB
> learned about certain transactions that were being developed to
> circumvent the new standard. Investment bankers, insurance

companies, and others were custom-designing contracts that appeared to be loans, bonds, and insurance contracts, but that had payment profiles similar to derivatives. Often, special-purpose entities were used to embed or combine a derivative with other traditional cash instruments—the beneficial interests sold to investors contained the desired derivative-like terms. The FASB added provisions to FAS-133 to ensure that the most egregious of these attempts were accounted for as derivatives—however, not every contract with embedded derivatives "trips the wire," so to speak. Readers must thoroughly understand the rules and carefully review their contracts for embedded derivatives. Companies should be very wary of novel contracts that purportedly "circumvent" FAS-133. If the FASB (or the SEC) learns of such a structure, it is within their purview to issue an interpretation to require FAS-133 accounting for existing and future structures.

BACKGROUND

Paragraphs 12–16 and 60–61 of FAS-133 address embedded derivatives. In addition, over 35 DIG Issues address embedded derivatives. FAS-133 overturned much of the accounting in numerous EITF Issues, including Issue 96-12 (for many but not all structured notes), Issue 86-28 (indexed debt), Issue 90-19 (nontraditional convertible debt), and others. However, the transition provisions of FAS-133 allowed entities to continue to apply previous GAAP to contracts with embedded derivatives (for simplicity, "hybrid" contracts or instruments) that were issued or substantively modified before December 31, 1997 or December 31, 1998, depending on when they adopted FAS-133 (paragraph 50). Entities that elected to continue previous accounting methods for these contracts had to do so on an all-or-nothing basis—they could not adopt FAS-133 for some but not all of those pre-1999 or pre-1998 contracts. This chapter addresses accounting under FAS-133 and does not address the legacy GAAP that might apply to grandfathered hybrid contracts.

Meaning of the Term *Embedded*

A derivative is *embedded* when provisions that meet the definition of a derivative are incorporated into a single contract by the issuer, and the derivative is not explicitly transferable independent of the host instrument. A hybrid instrument that hosts a derivative that is transferable or that has a derivative attached to it by another party results in the investor potentially having different counterparties for the derivative and the host contract. In such cases, the derivative should be evaluated as a freestanding (attached) contract under FAS-133 paragraphs 6, 9, and 57, by both the writer of the contract and the holder, not as an *embedded derivative*. (DIG B-3 and K-2)

☞ **PRACTICE POINTER:** After a transferable (or attached) derivative has been sold to another party, the transferor is no longer a party to the derivative. FAS-140 (and EITF Issue 99-8) applies to transfers of derivatives. Refer to Chapter 5, "Transfers of Financial Assets," for additional information.

IDENTIFYING EMBEDDED DERIVATIVES

Certain contracts that are not freestanding derivatives, such as bonds, insurance policies, and leases, may contain "embedded" derivative instruments—implicit or explicit terms that are based on an underlying and affect some or all of the cash flows or other exchanges required by the contract in a manner similar to a freestanding derivative. Contracts with these features are called "hybrid instruments." They are made up of a "host contract" and an embedded derivative. Examples include:

- Bonds with upside potential for changes in the price of a commodity.
- Equity-linked certificates of deposit.
- Common or preferred stock with cash-out options for fixed amounts.
- Annuity contracts that have both fixed and variable attributes.

Not all types of hybrid instruments that contain embedded derivatives require separate accounting. For example, the prepayment option in a mortgage does *not* require separate accounting. Embedded derivatives that meet the criteria in paragraphs 12–16 of FAS-133 require separate accounting.

Criteria for Separate Accounting

An embedded derivative must be separated (bifurcated) from the host contract and accounted for separately as a derivative instrument under FAS-133 only if all of the following criteria are met (paragraph 12, as amended):

- The economic characteristics and risks of the embedded derivative are not "clearly and closely related" to those of the host contract.
- The entire hybrid instrument is not marked to market through earnings under otherwise applicable GAAP. Mark to market means that *all* changes in fair value are recognized, including the effects of changes in interest rates, credit quality, and any other relevant factors. GAAP that requires some adjustments to the carrying amount of an instrument (such as changes in the spot rate of one component) but not all changes in value does not meet this condition. For example, indexed debt instruments do not meet this condition (DIG B-24), nor do equity-indexed annuities (DIG B-29).

- A separate instrument with the same terms as the embedded derivative instrument would meet the definition of a derivative as set forth in paragraphs 6–11 of FAS-133. (The initial net investment for the entire hybrid instrument should not be considered to be the initial net investment for the embedded derivative.) However, this criterion is not met if a separate instrument with the same terms as the embedded derivative would be classified in stockholders' equity if FAS-150 were ignored and other GAAP were applied (such as EITF Issue 00-19).

If an embedded derivative is considered *not* clearly and closely related to the host contract, the embedded derivative is required to be separated from the host contract and accounted for as a derivative instrument by both parties to the hybrid instrument, unless it either (1) fails to meet the definition of a derivative under FAS-133 or (2) qualifies for a scope exception under FAS-133. Exhibit 13-1 summarizes the basic criteria for split accounting.

☛ **PRACTICE POINTER:** The scope exception for equity instruments of the issuer (FAS-133, paragraph 11(a)) is often relevant for issuers of hybrid instruments that are combinations of debt instruments and equity derivatives. In evaluating whether an embedded equity derivative qualifies for the scope exception in paragraph 11(a), the issuer should apply EITF Issues 00-6 and 00-19, ignoring the effect that FAS-150 has on certain freestanding derivatives. (FAS-133, par. 12(c), as amended by FAS-150) Keep in mind that if the "unaltered" guidance in EITF Issue 00-19 would require that the component be classified in temporary equity, the component would still qualify for the scope exception under DIG Issue C-2.

SEC REGISTRANT ALERT: When a hybrid financial instrument that is not classified as an asset or liability under FAS-150 or other applicable GAAP contains an embedded derivative subject to EITF 00-19 and bifurcation of the embedded derivative is not required by FAS-133, registrants must consider the guidance in ASR-268 and EITF Topic D-98 to determine whether the hybrid instrument is its entirety is required to be classified and measured as temporary equity. The guidance in EITF Topic D-98 continues to apply to hybrid financial instruments classified in permanent or temporary equity. (EITF Topic D-98)

An embedded derivative that meets the definition of a derivative and does not qualify for a scope exception must be accounted for separately *unless* the entity cannot reliably identify or measure the embedded derivative, in which case the entire contract must be measured at fair value with changes in value recognized in earnings, or the hybrid instrument is eligible to be measured at fair value through earnings in its entirety and the entity elects such measurement. These circumstances are discussed later in this chapter.

EXHIBIT 13-1
DETERMINING WHEN AN EMBEDDED DERIVATIVE
REQUIRES SPLIT ACCOUNTING

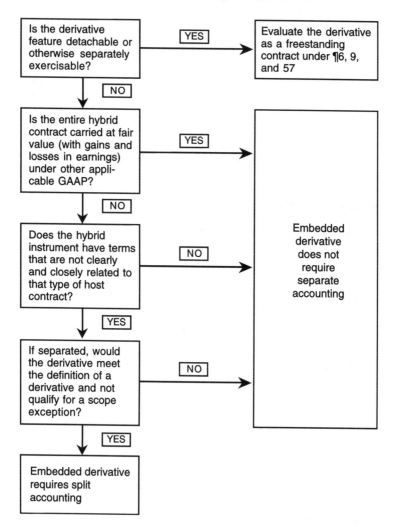

Note: This exhibit addresses only whether an identified embedded derivative requires separate accounting. If the entity cannot reliably identify (or measure) the embedded derivative, the entire contract must be measured at fair value through earnings. Also, if separate accounting is required, an entity may elect to measure the hybrid financial instrument at fair value through earnings if the instrument is eligible for such an election.

Meeting the "Clearly and Closely Related" Condition

"Clearly and closely related" refers to the similarity of the economic characteristics of the contract in question with the typical economic characteristics of that type of instrument. For example:

- A debt instrument typically has an interest rate based on general market conditions, the term of the borrowing, a credit spread relating to that specific borrower and, sometimes, inflation.
- The return on an equity instrument is typically tied to performance of the issuer of the shares.
- The return on a lease is typically tied to the value of the property, interest rates, and inflation.
- A cap or floor on the price of an asset in a purchase order is based on the price of the asset being sold. (DIG B-14)

In addition, the level of risk and reward provided by the contract should be commensurate with the amount invested in the contract. For example, if the terms of the contract are leveraged, an embedded derivative may need to be bifurcated even if the risk is of the same nature as the host contract.

> **OBSERVATION:** The "leverage" test for similar risks is not explicitly stated in FAS-133 (except as it relates to interest rates, which is discussed in the next section). However, a few DIG issues suggest that if the terms of the contract are leveraged, the portion in excess of the normal return on the host contract should be considered a derivative (for example, DIG B-4).

Timing of Assessment

Contracts should be assessed at the date that the hybrid instrument is acquired (or incurred) by the reporting entity. Thus, the acquirer of a hybrid instrument in the secondary market could reach a different conclusion than the issuer of the hybrid instrument if market conditions have changed since inception. (FAS-133, par. 13)

Types of Host Contracts

Several categories of host contracts have emerged for the purpose of evaluating whether the terms of a hybrid instrument are clearly and closely related to the host contract. However, any type of contract that is not a derivative in its entirety is subject to this section, even if it does not fall neatly into one of the categories below (unless it specifically qualifies for a scope exception).

The SEC staff has issued specific guidance related to the determination of the nature of a host contract for a hybrid financial instrument issued in the form of a share. For such instruments, the entity must determine whether the host contract is more akin to a debt instrument or an equity instrument based on all of the economic characteristics and risks of the host based on all of the stated and implied substantive terms and features of the entire hybrid instrument. In specific, the SEC staff indicated the following:

- The fact that a preferred stock contract without a mandatory redemption feature would be classified as temporary equity under EITF Topic D-98 does not indicate in and of itself that the nature of the host contract is equity.
- The guidance in DIG Issue C2, which extends the scope exception in paragraph 11(a) of FAS-133 to contracts classified in temporary equity, cannot be applied by analogy to conclude that the nature of a host contract is equity. (EITF D-109)

In addition, when a hybrid financial instrument that is not classified as an asset or liability under FAS-150 or other applicable GAAP contains an embedded derivative subject to EITF 00-19, registrants must consider the guidance in ASR-268 and EITF Topic D-98 to determine whether the host contract is required to be classified and measured as temporary equity when bifurcation of the embedded derivative is required by FAS-133. (EITF Topic D-98)

Equity Instruments

If the host contract represents a residual interest in an entity, then its economic characteristics and risks should be considered those of an equity instrument. For example:

- Common stock is an equity instrument.
- Cumulative participating perpetual preferred stock represents an equity instrument. (FAS-133, par. 61(l))
- Mandatorily redeemable preferred stock represents a *debt* instrument. (FAS-133, par. 61(l))

To be considered clearly and closely related to an equity instrument host, an embedded derivative would need to have equity characteristics related to the *same entity* as the host contract. (FAS-133, par. 60) For example, a right to convert perpetual preferred stock into the common stock of the same issuer would be considered clearly and closely related and would not require separate accounting under FAS-133.

The following features would *not* be considered clearly and closely related to an equity host (FAS-133, par. 61(e)):

- For the holder, a put option embedded in a publicly traded equity instrument that could force the issuer to reacquire that equity instrument for cash or other assets. The issuer also would generally be required to bifurcate such a put option unless the instrument qualifies for the paragraph 11(a) stockholders' equity exception.

- For the holder, a written call option embedded in a publicly traded equity instrument that allows the issuer to reacquire that equity instrument for cash or other assets. The issuer also would generally be required to bifurcate such a call option unless the instrument qualifies for the paragraph 11(a) stockholders' equity exception.

Debt Instruments

A debt host represents a form of creditor relationship where a stream of cash flows is agreed upon between the parties under preset terms and conditions or an instrument that must be redeemed by the issuer. Essentially, if the host contract does not embody a claim to the residual interest in an entity, the host contract should be considered a form of debt instrument. (FAS-133, par. 60) (Beneficial interests, leases, and certain forms of insurance are discussed separately below.)

The following underlyings are considered to have economic characteristics that are clearly and closely related to a debt host (FAS-133, par. 61):

- A stated interest rate or interest rate index.
- The rate of inflation in the economic environment and currency in which the instrument is denominated.
- The creditworthiness of the debtor (such as default or a change in debtor's credit rating). The creditworthiness of a party other than the debtor is *not* clearly and closely related to the debt host.

However, even if the economic characteristics are similar, the level of risk provided by the derivative relative to the typical return on an instrument of that type must be evaluated. Sometimes, a leverage factor (multiplier) will be involved in the formula for determining settlement. In other cases, the terms will be more subtle. FAS-133 provides a two-tiered test for how to identify disproportionate risk for debt instruments with embedded interest rate derivatives.

> ☞ **PRACTICE POINTER:** The tests below apply to any type of debt host, not just loans, notes, and debentures. For example, leases and investment contracts (which are discussed separately below) that have unusual interest rates would be subject to these tests.

The quantitative tests for interest rates An embedded derivative in which the underlying is an interest rate or interest rate index that alters net interest payments that otherwise would be paid or received on an interest-bearing host contract is not considered to be clearly and closely related to the host contract if either of the following conditions exists:

- *The negative yield test:* The terms of the hybrid instrument can *contractually* be settled in a such a way that the investor (creditor) could be forced to accept settlement at an amount that would not represent substantially all of its initial recorded investment. (FAS-133, par. 13 and DIG B-5) This is a worse-case scenario assessment—the likelihood of such a settlement is irrelevant—and the test should be based on the investor's (or creditor's) *undiscounted* net cash inflows over the life of the instrument. (FAS-133, par. 61(a))

- *The leveraged yield test:* The investor's initial rate of return could possibly increase to at least:

  — Twice its initial contractual level *and,* at the same time

  — Twice the current market return for a contract with the same terms as the host contract (using the effective notional amount) issued by a debtor with credit quality similar to the issuer's at inception. (FAS-133, par. 13)

☛ **PRACTICE POINTER:** Although the test is performed from the perspective of the investor, the presence of either of these conditions triggers embedded derivative accounting for *both* parties to the hybrid instrument.

☛ **PRACTICE POINTER:** The negative yield test is the exact same wording as paragraph 14 of FAS-140, which identifies certain instruments that may not be carried at cost. FAS-133 overrides FAS-140 when the embedded derivative meets the definition under FAS-133. However, FAS-140 would require that any remaining host contract (or the entire contract, if the embedded derivative does not meet the definition on a standalone basis) be carried at fair value, but would permit recognizing the gains and losses in either other comprehensive income (available-for-sale) or earnings (trading). Refer to Chapter 2, "Investments in Debt and Equity Securities," for additional information.

Clearly and closely related terms   The following features would generally *not* require separate accounting in a debt instrument (unless a form of leverage is present) (all paragraph references are to FAS-133):

- A variable interest rate such as LIBOR.
- Interest rate caps, floors, and collars that are at- or out-of-the money at issuance (or purchase) of the instrument. (par. 61(f))
- Call options or put options that are exercisable only in the event of default of the debtor. (par. 61(d))
- Call options or put options that accelerate the repayment of principal on an instrument that was issued or purchased close to par, and are not contingently exercisable. (DIG B-13)
- Options to roll over an account balance into a new investment with a guaranteed (favorable) rate. (DIG B-25)

The following characteristics are *not* considered clearly and closely related to a debt host and would require separate accounting under FAS-133 unless the derivative would not meet the definition on a standalone basis:

- A cap, floor, or collar that is in-the-money on the issuance (or purchase) date. (par. 61(f))
- A feature that significantly extends the remaining term to maturity, unless the interest rate is reset to a market rate and the instrument initially involved no significant discount. (par. 61 (g)) **Note:** It is inappropriate to apply this condition by analogy to other types of host contracts. (DIG B-17)
- Interest or principal payments that are linked to the price of specific marketable common stock or an index that is based on a portfolio of equity securities. (par. 61(h))
- Interest or principal payments that are linked to the price of a specific commodity that is readily convertible to cash or that aspect of the contract may be net settled. (par. 61(i))
- For the investor in convertible debt, a right to convert debt into the common stock of the issuer, unless the terms require delivery of common stock that is not publicly traded. For the issuer, the conversion feature would not require separate accounting if it is considered an equity instrument of the issuer under applicable GAAP. (par. 61(k)) Refer to Exhibit 10-1 in Chapter 10, "Convertible Debt and Similar Instruments," for additional information.
- Put and call options that require a cash settlement on the exercise date, even if they are indexed to interest rates, inflation, or credit risk. (par. 61(d))
- Put and call options that involve the repayment of principal and
  - The amount is indexed to a variable other than interest rates, the issuer's credit, or inflation *or*
  - The debt was issued at a premium or discount and the call is contingently exercisable (for example, a zero-coupon bond that is puttable at face value if interest rates increase more than a certain amount). (par. 61(d))
- A feature that introduces a credit risk exposure that is different from the credit risk arising from the obligor of the instrument, such that the value of the instrument is affected by the possible event of default or a change in creditworthiness of a third party. (par. 61(c) and DIG B-36)

A debt instrument with an embedded put option or call option (including a prepayment option) that would be settled through exercise of the option is deemed to meet the net settlement characteristic of a derivative because the debtor's exercise of the option is *not* considered delivery of an asset, despite the fact that, in some cases, the creditor tenders the instrument to the issuer upon exercise. Therefore, assuming that the option meets the other characteristics of the definition of a derivative, the option would require bifurcation. A debt instrument with an embedded call option (e.g., a loan with a prepayment option) would not require bifurcation, however, if the option could be exercised *only* by the issuer, because the investor would not have the unilateral ability to receive the high rate of return. (DIG B-38 and B-39)

☞ **PRACTICE POINTER:** The FASB's discussion leading up to the issuance of DIG Issue B-38 focused on loan prepayment options; however, the proposed guidance related to the net settlement characteristic is drafted broadly and impacts other types of instruments that are settled via exercise of the embedded option. DIG Issue B-39 preserves the treatment of common prepayment options in commercial loans as clearly and closely related to the debt host contract. While it mitigates the impact of DIG Issue B-38 in terms of the number of instruments potentially requiring bifurcation, it addresses only a subset of those options covered by the scope of DIG Issue B-38.

Exhibit 13-2 summarizes the effect of put and call options embedded in debt contracts (as set forth in DIG B-16).

☞ **PRACTICE POINTER:** The term "contingently exercisable" is not defined in FAS-133. However, the examples of contingently exercisable options in DIG B-16 include the following types of contingencies: (1) a 20 percent increase in the S&P 500, (2) a movement of LIBOR of at least 150 b.p., (3) a change in control, and (4) the issuer having an IPO. Note that contingencies based on changes in interest rates are considered contingently exercisable (even though the underlying is clearly and closely related to a debt instrument). However, options that are contingent on a default of the debtor would not require separate accounting (assuming no substantial premium or discount is involved).

☞ **PRACTICE POINTER:** Exhibit 13-2 only considers the effect of the put and call options. An instrument that does not require bifurcation of the put or call option still should be evaluated under the yield tests, in case other terms have derivative-like effects. (DIG B-16)

Beneficial Interests

A common issue regarding securitization transactions is the evaluation of whether beneficial interests that are purchased or held by a transferor incorporate embedded derivative features.

Both interests purchased by third parties in securitization transactions and interests that continue to be held by transferors must be evaluated under FAS-133 to determine whether they are freestanding derivative or hybrid instruments that have embedded derivatives requiring bifurcation. The evaluation must be based on an analysis of the contractual terms of the interest in securitized financial assets and on evidence that is sufficient for determining the existence of freestanding or embedded derivatives. The analysis of contractual terms may involve the following:

• An analysis of the contracts that govern the payoff structure and payoff priority of the interest;

EXHIBIT 13-2
EMBEDDED PUTS AND CALLS IN DEBT INSTRUMENTS

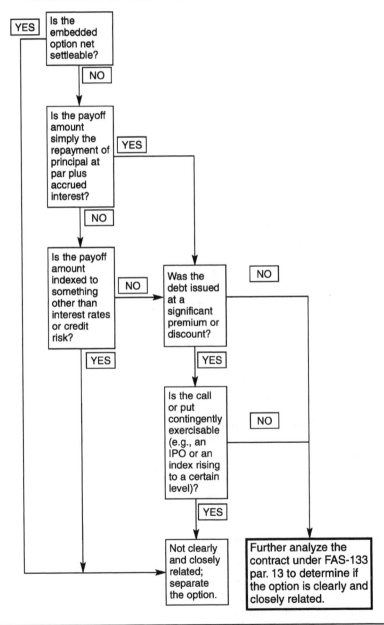

- An understanding of the nature and amount of assets, liabilities, and other financial instruments that make up the securitization transaction, which would provide an understanding of whether the combination of financial instruments held by the securitization entity provide the necessary cash flows to satisfy the requirements of the beneficial interests issued and represent the primary risks inherent in the beneficial interests issued; and
- In resecuritizations of tranches from previous transactions, an understanding of the securitizations that make up the overall transaction. (FAS-133, par. 14A and FAS-155, par. A19)

The following is additional implementation guidance on the analysis of beneficial interests:

- *Introduction of Credit Risk* The concentration of credit risk in subordinated beneficial interests in a securitization should not be considered an embedded credit derivative. However, a beneficial interest referenced to the credit risk of an external entity (that is, the referenced credit risk is not present in the financial instruments held by the securitization entity) would be considered a hybrid instrument with an embedded credit derivative.

- *Subordination* In securitizations involving payment of interest cash flows that could suffer a shortfall, because of adverse changes in interest rates, after payments are made to senior interest holders that may result in the inability of the subordinated interest holder to recover substantially all of its initial recorded investment, the subordinated (residual) beneficial interest would have an embedded interests rate derivative.

- *Interest Rate or Currency Conversion* Generally, in securitizations that involve the simple conversion of the interest rate or currency characteristics of a pool of financial instruments using an interest rate or cross-currency swap, in which the notional amount of the pool of financial instruments and the swap match, the resulting beneficial interests would not contain an embedded interest rate or currency derivatives. In that case, the financial instruments held by the securitization entity would provide the cash flows necessary to satisfy the requirements of the beneficial interests issued. (FAS 155, par. 4f)

Prepayment risk Certain securitized interests that contain only an embedded derivative tied to the prepayment risk of the underlying prepayable financial assets do not require bifurcation. DIG B-40 provides a scope exception from the criterion in paragraph 13(b) of FAS-133 related to interest rate derivatives for securitized interests that contain only an embedded derivative tied to the prepayment risk of the underlying prepayable financial assets and that meet the following criteria:

- The right to accelerate the settlement of the securitized interest cannot be controlled by the investor
- The securitized interest itself does not contain an embedded derivative for which bifurcation would be required (other than the embedded call options in the underlying financial assets). (DIG B-40)

Leases

A lease should be evaluated as a debt host under FAS-133, as described above. In addition, the following common provisions in leases do *not* require separate accounting under FAS-133 (par. 61(j)):

- Rental payments that are indexed to inflation (provided the payments are not leveraged).
- Contingent rentals based on sales of the lessee (assuming the contract is not exchange-traded).
- Contingent rentals based on a variable interest rate (provided the payments are not leveraged).

> ☞ **PRACTICE POINTER:** Although leases are identified as a debt host, they are considered a "nonfinancial contract" for the purpose of identifying foreign currency derivatives under paragraph 15. Refer to Illustration 13-3.

Contracts Denominated in a Foreign Currency

FAS-133, paragraph 15, provides that in any of the following circumstances, an embedded foreign currency derivative instrument should *not* be accounted for separately, provided that the other terms of the contract are clearly and closely related to the host contract (for example, the payment amount should not be leveraged). (DIG B-4)

Nonfinancial contracts The host contract is not a financial instrument (for example, a lease) and it requires payment(s) denominated in:

- The *functional currency* of any substantial party to that contract.
- The currency in which the price of the related good or service that is acquired or delivered is routinely denominated in international commerce (for example, the price of oil is routinely quoted in U.S. dollars in international transactions).
- The local currency of any substantial party to the contract.

- A currency used by a substantial party to the contract in a highly inflationary economy (pursuant to paragraph 11 of FAS-52). (FAS-133, par. 15, as amended)

An embedded foreign currency cap or floor must meet one of the above conditions and both of the following additional conditions to be considered clearly and closely related to its host contract:

- The embedded cap or floor (or combination thereof) does not contain leverage features *and*
- The embedded cap or floor (or combination thereof) does not represent a written or net written option. (A zero-cost collar would satisfy this requirement for both parties.) (DIG B-33)

☛ **PRACTICE POINTER:** This exception also applies to insurance contracts that involve (1) payment of losses in the functional currency of either of the two parties to the contract or (2) payment in the local currency of the country in which the loss is incurred, irrespective of the functional currencies of the parties to the transaction. (DIG B-28)

"Substantial party" All relevant facts and circumstances should be considered to identify the substantial parties to a contract, including whether the contracting party possesses the requisite knowledge, resources, and technology to fulfill the contract without relying on related parties. For example, a parent could be a substantial party to a contract entered into by its subsidiary if the parent will be providing the majority of resources required under the contract on behalf of the subsidiary, even though the subsidiary is the legal party to the contract. (DIG B-32) A guarantor would generally not be considered a substantial party to a contract but, in a related-party situation, all of the facts and circumstances should be considered. (DIG B-21)

"Routinely denominated in international commerce" Transactions for a certain product or service that are routinely structured around the world in one currency would qualify for the exception in paragraph 15(b). However, if similar transactions for a certain product or service are denominated in different currencies in different local or regional markets, the exception in paragraph 15(b) does not apply in any of those markets. (However, paragraph 15(a) could apply.) (DIG B-21)

Financial instruments Financial instruments that have their principal payments, interest payments, or both denominated in a foreign currency (including available-for-sale or trading securities and trade receivables and payables) do not contain embedded derivatives under FAS-133, provided the amounts are not leveraged. (FAS-133, par. 15 and DIG B-4) Foreign currency transaction gains or losses are recognized (using spot rates) in accordance with FAS-52 (and EITF Issue 96-15, for available-for-sale debt securities).

However, an instrument that provides the holder or the issuer with the *choice* of settling the principal, interest payments, or both in *either* a stipulated amount of U.S. dollars (assuming it is the functional currency) or a stipulated amount of a specified currency contains an embedded foreign currency option that is subject to FAS-133. (DIG C-9)

☛ **PRACTICE POINTER:** The assessment of whether a foreign currency qualifies for the exception in paragraph 15 is performed only at the inception of the contract.

Exhibit 13-3 summarizes the accounting for several common structured notes and other hybrid instruments with "debt hosts."

EXHIBIT 13-3
EVALUATING HYBRID DEBT INSTRUMENTS FOR EMBEDDED DERIVATIVES

Hybrid Instrument	Nature of Embedded Derivative	Separate Accounting Required?	Comments (FAS-133 ¶reference)
Inverse floater	Interest rate swap	Yes	Investor could lose a substantial amount of principal if rates increase ¶178–179
Range floater	Interest rate options	No	No potential for negative or leveraged yield ¶181
Ratchet floater	Changing interest rate caps and floors	No	No potential for negative or leveraged yield ¶182
Fixed-to-floating note	Changing interest rate swaps	No	No potential for negative or leveraged yield ¶183

Hybrid Instrument	Nature of Embedded Derivative	Separate Accounting Required?	Comments (FAS-133 ¶reference)
Equity-linked notes (not related to either party)	If a minimum principal amount is guaranteed, an equity option. If principal is at risk, an equity forward contract	Yes	Equity-based return is not clearly and closely related to the debt host ¶185, 186, 193
Disaster bond	Option linked to losses on a disaster	Yes, unless the option is considered insurance under ¶10(c)	Disaster experience is not clearly and closely related to the debt host ¶192
Dual currency bond	Foreign currency forwards	No, specific exception in ¶15	Instrument is subject to FAS-52 ¶194
Loan with option to repay in foreign currency	Foreign currency option	Yes (exception in ¶15 does *not* apply to options)	Foreign currency risk not clearly and closely related to debt host ¶195
Participating mortgage	Option on real estate	No	Embedded derivative excluded by ¶10(e)(2)
Convertible debt	Equity option	It depends	Refer to Exhibit 10-1 in Chapter 10
Volumetric production payments	Commodity forward	Yes, if the quantity is reliably determinable	FAS-19 applies if the quantity is not reliably determinable (DIG B-11)
Credit-linked note (tied to default of a third party)	Credit derivative	Yes	Credit of third party not related to interest rate or credit of issuer (DIG B-36)

Note: EITF Issue 96-12 covers structured notes that do not require separate accounting.

Insurance Products

Because FAS-133, as amended, carves out an exception for traditional insurance contracts (paragraph 10(c)), and, for the holder, investments in life insurance contracts (paragraph 10(g)), it is important to understand which contracts issued by insurance companies are accounted for as insurance contracts and which are accounted for as investment contracts under FAS-97 (typically because they lack significant mortality risk). Several common contracts are typically accounted for as follows (DIG B-25):

Contract type	*Classification*
Life insurance, payable upon death of insured	Insurance contract
Fixed or variable annuity contracts in the accumulation phase and period-certain annuities in the pay-out phase	Investment contracts
Fixed or variable annuities in the pay-out phase that provide for life-contingent payments	Insurance contracts
Payout phase period-certain plus life-contingent annuities	Insurance contracts unless: It is remote that life-contingent payments will be made; or The present value of the expected life-contingent payments is insignificant relative to the present value of all expected payments under the contract

The analysis for embedded derivatives under FAS-133 depends primarily on whether the instrument is accounted for as traditional insurance under other applicable GAAP. The effect of additional features depends on whether they are clearly and closely related to that type of host contract. Exhibit 13-4 provides a high-level summary of how insurance products are evaluated under FAS-133. Each major contract type is discussed in more detail later in this chapter.

☛ **PRACTICE POINTER:** In July 2003, the AICPA issued Statement of Position 03-1, *Accounting and Reporting by Insurance Enterprises for Certain Nontraditional Long-Duration Contracts and for Separate Accounts.* This SOP addresses insurance enterprises' accounting for certain nontraditional contract features that are not covered by other authoritative accounting literature, including FAS-133. Embedded derivatives within such nontraditional insurance contracts should be accounted for in accordance with FAS-133. Accounting for insurance contracts is outside the scope of this book.

The following types of contracts have been specifically addressed by the FASB or DIG.

EXHIBIT 13-4
EVALUATING INSURANCE CONTRACTS FOR EMBEDDED DERIVATIVES

Insurance Contract Building Blocks	Embedded Derivative?	Explanation
1. Life insurance policy	No	Specific scope excetion
Add-on: Early withdrawal feature and return is based on a market variable	Yes	Payout is not solely contingent on death of insured (DIG B-10)
2. Property and casualty policy	No	Specific scope exception
Add-on: Amount of the payment is tied to changes in the S&P 500 and could exceed insured's actual loss	Yes	Market variable not clearly and closely related to insured property (DIG B-26)
3. Variable annuity	No	Specific exception based on longstanding practice. Must meet a host of conditions (DIG B-7)
Add-on: Minimum guarantee of account balance or payments	Yes	Guaranteed floor amount not clearly and closely related to an equity-linked host (DIG B-8 and B-25)
4. Fixed-rate annuity	No	All terms clearly and closely related
Add-on: Fixed-rate annuity with potential upside based on a referenced equity index	Yes	Option on equity index not clearly and closely related to debt host (DIG B-29 and B-30)

Equity-indexed life insurance Equity-indexed life insurance contracts combine term life insurance coverage with an investment feature, similar to universal life contracts. Death benefit amounts are based upon the amount selected by the policyholder plus the account value. The policyholder's account value, maintained in the insurance company's general account (not a separate account), is based on the cumulative deposits credited with positive returns based on the S&P

500 Index or another equity index. The policy's cash surrender value is also linked to an equity index. The death benefit amount may also be linked to the cumulative return on the index.

If the holder can be compensated only in the event of the death of the insured, the entire contract is exempt from FAS-133 under paragraph 10(c). If the policyholder can obtain an equity-linked return by exercising the surrender option *prior to death*, the investment portion of the contract does not qualify for the insurance contract exemption. The host instrument (a universal life contract) is a debt instrument, and the embedded derivative is equity indexed. (DIG B-10)

Property and casualty insurance   A property and casualty insurance contract that provides for the payment of claims as a result of both an identifiable insurable event *and* changes in a variable would in its entirety qualify for the insurance exclusion in paragraph 10(c)(2) of FAS-133 provided that claims are paid only if an identifiable insurable event occurs (for example, theft or fire), the payment amount is limited to the amount of the policyholder's incurred insured loss, and the contract does not involve insurable events that are highly probable of occurring (such that the contract is essentially an indexed debt instrument). If there is an actuarially determined minimum amount of expected claim payments (and those cash flows are indexed to or altered by changes in a variable) that are the result of insurable events that are highly probable of occurring on a predictable basis, that "portion" of the contract does not qualify for the insurance exception. (For example, if an insured has received at least $2 million in claim payments from its insurance company for each of the previous five years related to specific types of insured events that occur each year, that minimum level of coverage would *not* qualify for the insurance exclusion.) (DIG B-26)

Variable annuity contracts   DIG Issue B-7 identifies a "traditional" variable annuity contract as a type of "host contract" that does *not* include derivatives that require separate accounting (including the minimum death benefit component during the accumulation period). The essential characteristic of a traditional variable annuity contract is that the policy holder bears the risks and rewards of the assets held on his behalf in the separate account of the insurance company.

A "traditional" variable annuity contract typically has the following characteristics:

- The variable annuity contract is established, approved, and regulated under special rules applicable to variable annuities (such as state insurance laws, securities laws, and tax laws).
- The policyholder's payments, after deduction of specified sales and administrative charges, are used to purchase units of a separate investment account (a "separate account"). The policy-

holder is not subject to insurer default risk to the extent of the assets held in the separate account.

- The policyholder directs the allocation of the account value among various investment options (typically various mutual funds) and the policyholder bears the investment risk. All investment returns are passed through to the policyholder (including dividends, interest, and gains/losses).

- The units may be surrendered for their current value in cash, although there is often a small surrender charge, or the units may be applied to purchase annuity income.

- The insurer guarantees mortality and maximum expense charges, and amounts are deducted periodically from the separate account to cover these charges.

- Deferred annuity contracts typically provide a death benefit during the accumulation period under which the policyholder may receive the greater of the sum of premiums paid or the value of total units to the credit of the account at time of the policyholder's death. (DIG B-7)

☞ **PRACTICE POINTER:** This guidance only applies to variable annuity contracts. GAAP does not permit analogizing to this guidance for other seemingly similar structures, such as beneficial interests in a special-purpose entity that might have many of the same attributes.

Nontraditional variable annuities Unlike a traditional variable annuity where the investment risk is borne entirely by the policy holder, in a nontraditional variable annuity, the insurance company bears some of the investment risk by guaranteeing a minimum account value at a specified date or over a specified period of time.

- DIG Issue B-8 covers minimum guarantees on variable annuity contracts that apply during the accumulation phase (prior to annuitization).

- DIG Issue B-25 covers minimum guarantees on *deferred variable annuity contracts* that apply after annuitization (during the payout phase).

Nontraditional variable annuities are considered to have embedded derivatives that are subject to FAS-133. The components would be analyzed as follows:

- The host contract would be a traditional variable annuity that does not contain an embedded derivative.

- The embedded derivative would be the nontraditional features (such as a guaranteed investment return through a minimum accumulation benefit or a guaranteed account value floor).

Separate accounting would be required only if the embedded derivative meets the definition of a derivative on a standalone basis. If the annuitant can only obtain the benefit of the guarantee by rolling his account balance over into a payout annuity contract, the minimum guarantee does not meet the definition of a derivative because it cannot be net settled.

The guidance in DIG Issues B-8 and B-25 is summarized in Exhibit 13-5.

Equity-indexed annuities An equity-indexed annuity (EIA) is a deferred fixed annuity contract with a guaranteed minimum interest rate plus a contingent return based on an equity index, such as the S&P 500. EIAs typically have minimal mortality risk and are therefore classified as investment contracts under FAS-97.

EXHIBIT 13-5
DEFERRED VARIABLE ANNUITY CONTRACTS

| Contract Feature | Separate Accounting For Embedded Derivative? | | Comments |
	Accumulation Phase	Payout Phase	
Guaranteed minimum account value *prior to* annuitization	Yes	Depends on terms (see below)	B-8: The guaranteed account value is not clearly and closely related to the variable annuity
Guaranteed minimum *interest rate* upon annuitization	No	No	Embedded derivative cannot be net settled; gain (from rate) must be rolled over into the payout annuity contract
Guaranteed minimum account value upon annuitization	No, unless the guaranteed amount may be withdrawn during the payout phase, or the payout phase is very short	No	Embedded derivative cannot be net settled; gain (from rate) must be rolled over into the payout annuity contract

	Separate Accounting For Embedded Derivative?		
Contract Feature	Accumulation Phase	Payout Phase	Comments
Guaranteed minimum payments on available payout annuity			
• Solely life contingent	No	No	Life Insurance exception in 10(c)* different from other guarantees because during the payout period, the embedded derivative is net settled against the payment that otherwise would be required
• Not solely life contingent	No	Yes, components are: • Variable annuity host • Guaranteed payment floor	

---

* DIG B-25 did not address whether a period-certain plus life-contingent annuity contract (e.g., the greater of Issue ten years or the annuitant's life) with similar features meets the insurance exception in its entirety.

There are two basic designs for EIA products:

1. Periodic ratchet—the customer receives the greater of the appreciation in the equity index during a series of one-year periods or the guaranteed minimum fixed rate of return over that period

2. Point-to-point—the customer receives the greater of the appreciation in the equity index during a specified period (for example, five or seven years) or the guaranteed minimum fixed rate of return over that period.

DIG Issues B-29 and B-30 address the accounting for equity-indexed annuities. An equity-indexed annuity represents a debt host and an embedded derivative (for the period-to-period design, an equity option and for the ratchet design, a series of forward-starting options) that must be accounted for separately under FAS-133. Under the ratchet design, the series of forward-starting options should be viewed as one compound derivative. DIG B-29 provides additional guidance on factors to consider in determining fair value for the options. The insurance company would ignore any minimum liability that exceeds the sum of the embedded derivative (at fair value) and the host debt instrument. (In other words, it no longer calculates a FAS-97 account value.)

Market value annuity contracts   A market value annuity contract (MVA) is typically accounted for as an investment contract under FAS-97, given its lack of significant mortality risk. An MVA provides for a return of principal plus a fixed rate of return if held to maturity, or alternatively, a "market adjusted value" if the surrender option is exercised by the contract holder prior to maturity. The market adjusted value is typically based on current interest crediting rates being offered for new MVA purchases.

Under FAS-133, MVAs are considered hybrid contracts with a debt host and a prepayment option. The prepayment option should be evaluated under DIG B-16, which is summarized in Exhibit 13-2. The prepayment option in an MVA typically would be considered clearly and closely related because:

- The underlying is interest rates.
- The prepayment option accelerates the repayment of principal.
- MVAs are not typically issued at a significant premium or discount.
- The put option is not contingently exercisable (it can be exercised at any time).
- The investor can elect to hold the contract to maturity and recover substantially all of its investment.
- There is no leverage present in the crediting rate. (DIG B-9)

Modified coinsurance arrangements   A modified coinsurance arrangement ("modco arrangement") is a reinsurance arrangement in which a ceding insurance company withholds funds, which creates a payable for the ceding insurance company and a receivable for the reinsurer (the reinsurer also recognizes a liability for insurance coverage assumed under the arrangement). The ceding insurance company's payable incorporates the return of the principal amount plus a return based on the ceding company's return on its investments (either general account assets or a specified portfolio of assets). DIG Issue B-36 addresses the evaluation of modco arrangements under FAS-133 and indicates that, for the arrangement described, the risk exposure of the ceding company's return based on its investments is not clearly and closely related to the risk exposure of the creditworthiness of the ceding company. Therefore, the ceding company's payable and the reinsurer's receivable both include an embedded derivative feature that is not clearly and closely related to the host contract (which can be a debt host or an insurance host contract).

Not-for-Profit Organization's Obligation Arising from a Split-Interest Agreement

A not-for-profit organization's liability for its obligation to the donor or the donor's beneficiary under an irrevocable split-interest agreement should be analyzed to determine whether it qualifies for the traditional insurance contract exception in paragraph 10(c). For example, if the obligation is solely life-contingent (that is, contingent upon the survival of an identified individual, in which case the payments are made only if the individual is alive when the payments are due), that obligation would qualify for the exception in paragraph 10 (c). If the not-for-profit organization's liability for its obligation under the split-interest agreement does not qualify for the exception in paragraph 10(c), the not-for-profit organization must determine whether that liability meets the definition of a derivative in its entirety under paragraph 6 or whether it contains an embedded derivative instrument that could warrant separate accounting under paragraph 12. The not-for-profit organization's liability for its obligation under a split-interest agreement would typically not meet the definition of a derivative instrument in its entirety because it would not meet the "no or smaller" initial investment criterion in paragraph 6(b). DIG B-35 provides numerous examples of the applicability of paragraph 12 to various split-interest agreements.

ACCOUNTING FOR EMBEDDED DERIVATIVES

Bifurcation of Embedded Derivatives

If an embedded derivative instrument is required to be separated from its host contract based on the guidance provided in this chapter, and the election for fair value measurement of the hybrid instrument (discussed later in this chapter) is not applied because the hybrid instrument is not eligible or the entity does not elect it, the following requirements apply:

- The derivative should be recorded at its fair value at inception and subsequently accounted for and disclosed under FAS-133, unless an entity cannot reliably identify and measure the embedded derivative. (FAS-133, pars. 12 and 16)

- The derivative is eligible to be designated as a hedging instrument in a qualifying hedge relationship.
- The fair value of the derivative should be deducted from the basis of the hybrid contract.
- The remaining carrying amount becomes the basis for the host contract which subsequently should be accounted for based on generally accepted accounting principles applicable to instruments of that type that do not contain embedded derivative instruments. (DIG B-6) For example:
    - An investor in a debt security should account for the "host" under FAS-115.
    - A bank should account for a loan under FAS-114.
    - A corporate issuer should account for a long-term debt like any other debt instrument issued at a premium or discount.
- If the host contract component of the hybrid instrument is reported at fair value with changes in fair value recognized in earnings or other comprehensive income (e.g., a debt security subject to FAS-115), then the sum of the fair values of the host contract component and the embedded derivative should not exceed the overall fair value of the hybrid instrument. (If the entire hybrid instrument were carried at fair value through earnings, the derivative would not be bifurcated as discussed in paragraph 12(b).) (DIG B-6)

SEC REGISTRANT ALERT: The SEC staff has addressed a specific bifurcation issue related to the issuance of a structured note that includes an embedded written option that is required to be bifurcated. If issued as freestanding, the fair value determined for the written option would support recognition of a dealer profit. (EITF Issue 02-3 permits recognition of a "dealer profit" at the inception of a contract only if the fair value is supported by a quoted market price or other observable market data. As part of its deliberations in the fair value measurement project, the FASB reconsidered this guidance and decided that the final standard on fair value measurements will *nullify* the guidance in footnote 3 of EITF 02-3. Refer to the section "Determining Fair Value" in Chapter 12, "Introduction to Derivatives," for a discussion of the requirements of EITF 02-3 in measuring the fair value of certain derivative instruments.) In instances where the derivative is embedded, however, the SEC staff believes that DIG Issue B-6 does not support recording a "day one" gain when bifurcating an embedded derivative from a host contract. Instead, any "day one" gain would be embedded in the host contract and amortized as a yield adjustment over the life of the host contract. (December 11, 2003, speech by John M. James, then a Professional Accounting Fellow, Office of the Chief Accountant of the SEC, at the AICPA National Conference on Current SEC Developments)

If an entity cannot reliably identify and measure an embedded derivative instrument that should be separated from the host contract, the entity must mark to market the entire contract through earnings. The combined instrument may *not* be designated as a hedging instrument. (FAS-133, par. 16)

> ☞ **PRACTICE POINTER:** It should be unusual that an entity cannot reliably separate an embedded derivative from a host contract. A company cannot simply *elect* to mark to market the entire contract.

Guidelines for Bifurcating Derivatives

> **AUTHOR'S NOTE:** FAS-133 contains almost no guidance about how to separate the components of a hybrid instrument. (A few DIG Issues provide some guidance in this area and they are discussed below.) The FASB's rationale in not providing guidance is that the parties who structure these transactions are sophisticated enough to put them together and price them—they should likewise be able to take them apart reliably. Subsequent investors would presumably have the requisite analytical abilities to (a) make the purchasing decision and (b) account for the components separately. (FAS-133, par. 301)

Overall

The only acceptable method of bifurcating a derivative is a method that records the derivative at its fair value at inception or, for the investor, upon acquisition, if later. Other methods, such as allocation based on relative fair values or the "with and without" method, are not acceptable substitutes. (DIG B-6) Embedded derivative features that would individually warrant separate accounting should be bundled together as a single, compound embedded derivative instrument. (Either all or a proportion of a compound embedded derivative may be designated as a hedging instrument, but not the individual components.) (DIG B-15)

Bifurcating Forward-Based Embedded Derivatives

Forward-based derivatives include forward contracts and swaps. The fair value of a forward-based embedded derivative (such as a swap or forward contract) should generally be equal to zero at the inception of the hybrid instrument or, for the investor, upon acquisition, if later. (DIG B-20 and B-23)

The embedded forward contract or swap should contain a notional amount and an underlying consistent with the terms of the hybrid instrument. That is, artificial terms should not be created to introduce leverage, hypothetical interest rate swaps, or some other risk exposure not already present in the hybrid instrument. Often, simply adjusting the stated forward price to be at-the-market will result in the embedded derivative having a fair value of zero at inception of the hybrid instrument. The effect of any off-market terms should be should be quantified and allocated to the *host contract* since it effectively represents a loan. (DIG B-20)

Bifurcating Option-Based Embedded Derivatives

Option-based derivatives include options (puts and calls), caps, floors, and collars. In separating an option-based embedded derivative from the host contract, either at inception or, for the investor, upon acquisition, if later, the strike price of the embedded option should be based on the terms stated in the contract. As a result, an embedded option may have a strike price at inception that does not equal the market price of the underlying asset. (DIG B-22) An embedded option whose strike price is the then-current market price of the underlying upon exercise would generally have a fair value of zero.

> **OBSERVATION:** If an embedded forward contract is issued with off-market terms, the initial fair value of the forward effectively represents part of the host loan, because a reverse cash flow will occur at maturity. However, if an option-based derivative is in the money at inception, that intrinsic value amount does not represent a lending activity since the option may never be exercised (that is, it may expire out-of-the-money due to a change in the underlying) and, therefore, a cash flow may not occur at or before maturity. These fundamental differences justify using the stated terms for options, but not for forward contracts.

Combinations of Option Contracts

In certain situations, separate options with mirror terms are required to be accounted for as a single forward contract under FAS-133. Whether two options should be accounted for separately or as a forward contract is significant, because there are differences in the way a forward contract and option should be bifurcated from a host contract, if embedded, and in the qualifications for hedge accounting. When a purchased option and written option that are entered into contemporaneously have the same terms (strike price, notional amount, and exercise date) and the same underlying, and neither of the two options is required to be exercised, they should be accounted for as summarized in Exhibit 13-6. (DIG K-3)

EXHIBIT 13-6
COMBINATIONS OF OPTIONS WITH THE SAME TERMS

First Option	Second Option	Counterparties*	Account for as ...
Embedded non-transferable purchased call (put) option	Embedded non-transferable written put (call) option	Same counter-party	Single forward contract
Freestanding purchased call (put) option	Freestanding or embedded non-transferable written put (call) option	Same or different counterparty	Two separate option contracts
Freestanding written call (put) option	Embedded non-transferable purchased put (call) option	Different counter-party	Two separate option contracts

*"Same counterparty" includes contracts entered into with a single party that are structured through an intermediary.

The Host Contract

The characteristics of a debt host contract generally should be based on the stated or implied substantive terms of the hybrid instrument. In the absence of stated or implied terms, an entity may make its own determination of whether to account for the debt host as a fixed-rate, floating-rate, or zero-coupon bond. Factors to consider include the features of the hybrid instrument, the issuer, and the market in which the instrument is issued, as well as other factors. (DIG B-19)

Interaction with FAS-115 When an embedded derivative is separated from a debt security, the host contract is subject to FAS-115. The entity should apply the classification criteria of FAS-115 considering all of the contractual terms of the combined contract, even if the derivative has been bifurcated. In other words, bifurcating a derivative that would have precluded classifying a security as held-to-maturity (such as a conversion option in convertible debt) does not "cure" or remove the contractual term that could affect the entity's intent. The fact remains that if the investor elects to convert the debt, the security would not be held to maturity.

FAS-115 requires that certain securities be classified as trading. In addition, FAS-115 permits entities to *elect to* classify securities as trading upon acquisition of the security (FAS-115 Q&A, par. 35). Derivatives embedded in trading securities should not be bifurcated under FAS-133, paragraph 12(b) and the entire hybrid security may not be designated in a hedging relationship. For securities electively classified as trading, entities may not subsequently "change their minds," and bifurcate a derivative at a later date if a hedging opportunity later emerges for two reasons: (1) the assessment of embedded derivatives should occur at acquisition (for the investor) and (2) transfers into and out of the trading category should be rare. Refer to Chapter 2, "Investments in Debt and Equity Securities," for additional information.

Fair value option for host contracts   FAS-159, discussed in the section below related to Hybrid Financial Instruments, provides a fair value option for host contracts after bifurcation of an embedded derivative. A host financial instrument that is in and of itself a financial instrument, upon separation of an embedded *nonfinancial* derivative instrument, is eligible for the fair value option, subject to the scope requirements discussed in Chapter 19, "The Fair Value Option for Financial Instruments."

> **AUTHOR'S NOTE:**   In February 2007, the FASB issued FASB Statement No. 159, *The Fair Value Option for Financial Assets and Financial Liabilities.* FAS-159 provides companies with an option to report certain financial assets and liabilities at fair value with subsequent changes in value reported in earnings. The specific provisions of FAS-159 applicable to hybrid instruments are covered in this Chapter. Chapter 19, "The Fair Value Option for Financial Instruments," provides generalized guidance on the fair value option in FAS-159.
>
> FAS-159 is effective for calendar-year-end companies as of January 1, 2008. Early adoption is permitted as of the beginning of a fiscal year that begins on or before November 15, 2007, provided the entity also elects to apply FAS-157, *Fair Value Measurements.*
>
> FAS-159 provides a fair value option that is broader than the current election provided in FAS-155. FAS-159 applies to many types of financial instruments, while FAS-155 applies only to hybrid financial instruments containing embedded derivatives that require bifurcation under FAS-133. Until the effective date of FAS-159 (January 1, 2008 for calendar-year-end companies), companies that wish to avail themselves of the fair value election for hybrid instruments that would otherwise require bifurcation can utilize the election under FAS-155. Once effective, it is expected that companies would apply the fair value option in FAS-159 to hybrid financial instruments. It is expected that the FASB will revisit the utility of FAS-155 after FAS-159 becomes fully effective. This edition of *Financial Instruments* presents the provisions of both FAS-159 and FAS-155 in the section below.

Balance Sheet Presentation of Embedded Derivatives

FAS-133 does not explicitly state whether embedded derivatives should be presented together with or separate from the host contract in the balance sheet. When both components are assets or both are liabilities, this is not a major issue. However, if, for example, a purchased option (an asset) that requires separate accounting is bifurcated from a liability, it is unclear whether the option should be separately displayed as an asset. When the fair value of the derivative is significant and the host contract is not carried at fair value, the difference in the balance sheet footings between net and gross presentation could be significant. (Note that the constraint in DIG Issue B-6 that the sum of the parts should equal the sum of the whole does not apply if the host contract is not measured at fair value under GAAP.)

> **REGULATORY ALERT:** The SEC staff has stated that although bifurcated for *measurement* purposes, embedded derivatives should be presented on a combined basis with the host contract in the balance sheet. (SEC Division of Corporate Finance, Current Accounting and Disclosure Issues, Topic II.D)

ELECTIVE FAIR VALUE MEASUREMENT FOR CERTAIN HYBRID FINANCIAL INSTRUMENTS

Fair Value Election for Hybrid Financial Instruments under FAS-155

Certain hybrid financial instruments that have an identified embedded derivative that is required to be bifurcated under FAS-133 are eligible to be initially and subsequently measured at fair value, with changes in fair value recognized currently in earnings. This election applies to hybrid *financial* instruments only; nonfinancial instruments are not eligible for the election. In addition, the following instruments are not eligible for this election:

- Employee benefits, including pensions, healthcare and life insurance, postemployment benefits, stock awards, and other forms of deferred compensation arrangements
- Substantively extinguished debt whose accounting was grandfathered by FAS-140
- Insurance contracts other than financial guarantees and investment contracts
- Lease contracts
- Warranty obligations and rights
- Unconditional purchase obligations

- Investments accounted for under the equity method
- Equity investments and minority interests in consolidated subsidiaries
- An entity's own equity instruments

The election may be made on an instrument-by-instrument basis. Once made, the fair value option for measurement of an individual instrument is irrevocable. The election is available upon acquisition or issuance of the hybrid financial instrument or, for a previously recognized financial instrument, upon the occurrence of a remeasurement event, which requires that a financial instrument be remeasured at fair value but does not require ongoing fair value measurement (for example, a business combination or significant debt modification under EITF Issue 96-19). The fair value election must be supported by concurrent documentation or a preexisting policy for automatic election. (FAS-133, par. 16, as amended by FAS-155)

☞ **PRACTICE POINTER:** The fair value election provided by FAS-133, as amended by FAS-155, does not provide wholesale permission to measure any hybrid financial instrument at fair value. As discussed above, FAS-155 specifies certain scope limitations for instruments eligible for this election. In addition, for those hybrid financial instruments within its scope, FAS-155 requires that an entity determine that the hybrid financial instrument contains an embedded derivative that must be bifurcated before it can be considered for fair value measurement. If an entity identifies an embedded derivative but determines that it is not required to be bifurcated under FAS-133, the hybrid financial instrument is *not* eligible for the fair value measurement election. If the entity cannot identify or measure the embedded derivative, the instrument falls under the existing FAS-133 practicability exception and must be measured at fair value in its entirety.

Fair Value Option for Hybrid Financial Instruments under FAS-159

Companies may elect to measure hybrid instruments at fair value under the fair value option provided by FAS-159. That election can be made only at initial recognition of the loan or in response to certain specified events and is irrevocable. The election is generally permitted on an instrument-by-instrument basis. If the fair value option is elected, a hybrid instrument is initially and subsequently measured at fair value and with subsequent changes in fair value recognized in earnings. Chapter 19 provides detailed guidance on the application of FAS-159 to eligible items, including incremental disclosure requirements.

☞ **PRACTICE POINTER:** FAS-159 simplifies the accounting for hybrid financial instruments by obviating the need to identify and separately account for embedded derivatives. Unlike the election under FAS-155, the fair value option under FAS-159 requires no specific criteria for its application. FAS-155 requires the company to both (1) identify the embedded instrument and (2) determine that the embedded derivative must be bifurcated under FAS-133.

FAS-157 is the primary guidance for fair value measurement under GAAP. Fair value is the price that would be received to sell an asset or paid to transfer a liability in an orderly transaction between market participants at the measurement date. The objective of a fair value measurement under FAS-157 is to determine the price that would be received to sell the asset or paid to transfer the liability at the measurement date (an exit price) using assumptions that market participants would use. The fair value measurement model in FAS-157 applies for both initial measurement and subsequent measurement of hybrid financial instruments for which the fair value option is elected.

Chapter 18, "Fair Value Measurements, Fair Value Disclosures, and Other Financial Instrument Disclosures," provides specific fair value measurement guidance applicable to all financial instruments required to be measured at fair value under GAAP.

☛ **PRACTICE POINTER:**   The fair value option in FAS-159 triggers significant new disclosure requirements for affected items, and does not eliminate other incremental disclosure requirements. In addition, in FAS-157 establishes disclosure requirements related to fair value measurements.

Fair Value Considerations for Hybrid Financial Instruments

In determining the fair value of hybrid instruments entered into subsequent to the adoption of FAS-155 for which the entity elects fair value measurement, entities should consider the fair value measurement guidance discussed in the Chapter 12, "Introduction to Derivatives," and Chapter 18, "Fair Value Measurements, Fair Value Disclosures, and Other Financial Instrument Disclosures."

Balance Sheet Presentation of Certain Hybrid Instruments

The following hybrid instruments have specific balance sheet presentation requirements:

- Hybrid financial instruments measured at fair value under the FAS-133 election
- Hybrid instruments measured at fair value under the FAS-133 practicability exception when an embedded derivative cannot be readily identified and measured

For those hybrid instruments, one of the following approaches must be used for reporting fair values *separately* from the carrying amounts of assets and liabilities subsequently measured using another measurement attribute on the face of the balance sheet:

- Display separate line items for the fair value and nonfair value carrying amounts
- Present an aggregated carrying amount and parenthetically disclose the fair value amount included in the aggregate balance

Additional disclosure requirements for certain hybrid instruments are discussed in Chapter 15, "Disclosures about Derivatives." (FAS-133, par. 44A)

AUDIT CONSIDERATIONS

Chapter 12, "Introduction to Derivatives," discusses the audit risk relating to properly identifying derivatives, including embedded derivatives. After an embedded derivative has been identified and separated for accounting purposes, the audit issues relating to the derivative are similar to those for freestanding derivatives.

Entities that wish to avoid FAS-133 accounting for derivatives sometimes pursue structured transactions that are designed to contain derivative-like characteristics that do not require separate accounting. Accounting firms are now precluded from writing "SAS-50" letters (referring to Statement on Auditing Standards No. 50, *Reports on the Application of Accounting Principles*) to intermediaries (such as investment bankers) on the application of accounting principles in situations that do not involve a specific transaction for a particular principal. Refer to SAS-97 for additional information.

REGULATORY CONSIDERATIONS

The NAIC recently adopted SSAP 86, *Accounting for Derivatives and Hedging Activities,* that addresses statutory accounting. SSAP 86 indicates that embedded derivatives would not be bifurcated from a host contract and accounted for separately, even if separate accounting is required for GAAP.

ILLUSTRATIONS

Illustration 13-1: Bifurcating an Equity-Linked Note

On January 1, 20X1, Propp Enterprises issues a two-year structured note with a principal amount of $1,000,000 indexed to the stock of an unrelated publicly traded entity (Alta Properties, Inc.). At maturity, the holder of the instrument will receive the principal amount plus any appreciation or minus any depreciation in the fair value of 10,000 shares of Alta Properties, with changes in fair value measured from the issuance date of the debt instrument. The note bears a floating rate of interest. The market price of Alta Properties shares is as follows: $100 per share at the issuance date; $90 at December 31, 20X1, and $125 on December 31, 20X2.

Identifying the embedded derivative The host contract is a debt instrument because the instrument has a stated maturity and because the holder has none of the rights of a shareholder, such as the ability to vote the shares and receive distributions to shareholders. The embedded derivative is an equity-based forward contract (it provides upside and downside potential) that has as its underlying the fair value of the stock of Alta Properties. The forward contract does not qualify for the exception in paragraph 11(a) because it is not indexed to Propp's own stock and it would not be considered an equity instrument of Propp Enterprises (the issuer of the hybrid). Assume that neither the issuer nor the investor elected to measure the hybrid financial instrument at fair value with changes in fair value recognized in earnings. Further assume that neither the issuer nor the investor designates the forward contract as a hedging instrument.

The forward-based derivative should initially be recorded at its fair value of $0. That is, all of the proceeds should be ascribed to the debt host contract. (DIG B-20 and B-23) Subsequently, the debt host is accounted for as debt by Propp Enterprises and as a debt security by the investors. The forward contract should be marked to market through earnings.

> ☛ **PRACTICE POINTER:**   The journal entries below treat the forward contract as a separate asset or liability to emphasize that the embedded derivative and host contract are measured separately. For financial reporting purposes, SEC registrants should combine the fair value of the derivative with the carrying amount of the host contract.

Issuer's Accounting

Propp would record the following journal entries (for brevity, the accrual of interest is not presented below):

At inception

Cash	$1,000,000	
Debt		$1,000,000

To record the issuance of the structured note; the derivative has a fair value of zero at inception, and as such, no separate journal entry is required.

December 31, 20X1

Forward contract asset	$100,000	
Gain on forward contract		$100,000

To mark to market the forward contract. [(90-100) x –$10,000].

December 31, 20X2

Loss on forward contract	$350,000	
Forward contract asset		$100,000
Forward contract liability		250,000

To mark to market the forward contract. [(125-90) x –$10,000]

Debt	$1,000,000	
Forward contract liability	250,000	
Cash		$1,250,000

To record settlement of the structured note with investors.

Investor's Accounting

If the investor classifies the security as a trading security under FAS-115, the derivative should not be bifurcated because the entire contract is marked to market under applicable GAAP. (FAS-133, par. 12(b)) Assume that the investors classify the security as available-for-sale under FAS-115. The investors would record the following journal entries (for simplicity, presented in total for all investors).

At inception

Debt security	$1,000,000	
Cash		$1,000,000

To record the purchase of the structured note; the derivative has a fair value of zero at inception, and as such, no separate journal entry is required.

December 31, 20X1

Loss on forward contract	$100,000	
Forward contract liability		$100,000

To mark to market the forward contract. [(90-100) x $10,000]

December 31, 20X2

Forward contract asset	250,000	
Forward contract liability	100,000	

Gain on forward contract
350,000
To mark to market the forward contract. [(125-90) x $10,000]

Cash   1,250,000

Forward contract asset
250,000

Debt security
1,000,000

To record settlement of the structured note.

Illustration 13-2: The Negative Yield Test (paragraph 13(a))

Copper Industries purchased a $10 million structured note with a 9% fixed coupon, and a term of five years from a AA-rated issuer at a time when the current market rate for five-year AA-rated debt is 7%. The terms of the note require that, at the beginning of the third year of its term, the principal on the note would be reduced to $7 million and the coupon would be reduced to zero for the remaining term to maturity if interest rates for AA-rated debt have increased to at least 8% by that date.

Applying paragraph 13(a)

If the rate for AA-rated debt were to increase to 8% over the next two years, the terms would be modified such that the investor could be forced to accept only $8.8 million ($1.8 million in interest payments for the first two years and $7 in principal), thus not recovering substantially all of its $10 million initial net investment. Thus, *both* the issuer and the investor must record an embedded derivative. Note that the test is performed on a worse-case basis, using undiscounted cash flows. (DIG B-5)

Illustration 13-3: Applying the Foreign Currency Exception (paragraph 15)

A U.S. parent company for which the U.S. dollar is both the functional currency and the reporting currency has a Venezuelan subsidiary. The subsidiary's functional currency is the Mexican peso (determined in accordance with FAS-52). However, assume that the economy in Mexico is highly inflationary, and therefore FAS-52 requires that the parent company's reporting currency (that is the U.S. dollar) be used as if it were the subsidiary's functional currency. The subsidiary enters into a lease with a British company for property in

Venezuela that requires the subsidiary to make lease payments in U.S. dollars. Further, assume that the British company's functional currency is the pound sterling. The Venezuelan subsidiary's local currency is the bolivar.

A lease denominated in any of the following currencies would qualify for the exception in paragraph 15, for both the lessee and the lessor (assuming they are the substantial parties to the contract):

(1)   The U.S. dollar

(2)   The Mexican peso

(3)   The Venezuelan bolivar, *or*

(4)   The pound sterling

If the lease were denominated in any other currency, the lease would contain an embedded foreign currency derivative that requires separate accounting. (FAS-133, paragraph 196 and DIG B-21)

CHAPTER 14
HEDGE ACCOUNTING

CONTENTS

Overview	14.04
Background	14.04
Description of Hedge Accounting	14.05
Different Types of Hedges	14.05
Exhibit 14-1: Characterization of Hedging Strategies under FAS-133	14.06
Exhibit 14-2: Summary of Derivatives and Hedge Accounting	14.08
Common Hedge Criteria	14.08
Documentation of the Hedging Relationship	14.09
Hedging Instruments	14.10
Hedged Items	14.13
Disqualified Hedged Items	14.14
Exhibit 14-3: Transactions That Do Not Qualify for Hedge Accounting	14.15
Unit of Measure Issues	14.17
Designating Part of a Derivative in a Hedging Relationship	14.17
Combining Derivatives	14.17
Hedges of Groups of Assets and Liabilities	14.18
Expectation of Offsetting Effects	14.18
Methods of Assessing Effectiveness	14.19
Data to Include in the Assessment	14.21
Consistency of Methods	14.22
Changes in Methods	14.22
Meaning of Highly Effective	14.22
Qualifying for Hedge Accounting versus Measuring Hedge Effectiveness	14.23
Fair Value Hedge Accounting	14.24
Common Fair Value Hedging Strategies	14.24
Documentation	14.24
Exhibit 14-4: Assessing and Measuring Effectiveness	14.25

Qualifications for Fair Value Hedge Accounting 14.26
Types of Hedged Items 14.26
Hedges of Discrete Risks 14.26
Hedging Groups of Assets or Liabilities 14.27
Hedging Parts of an Asset or Liability 14.28
Ongoing Expectation of Effectiveness 14.30
Methods of Assessing Effectiveness 14.30
Accounting for a Fair Value Hedge 14.31
Hedges of Interest Rate Risk (the Benchmark) 14.32
Accounting for Adjustments to the Hedged Item 14.34
The Shortcut Method for Fair Value Hedges 14.35
Required or Voluntary Termination of a Fair Value Hedge 14.39
Assessing Hedged Items for Impairment 14.40
Cash Flow Hedges 14.41
Common Cash Flow Hedging Strategies 14.41
Documentation 14.41
Qualifications for Cash Flow Hedge Accounting 14.43
Types of Hedged Items 14.43
Risks Being Hedged 14.43
Hedging Groups of Forecasted Transactions 14.46
Hedging Instruments 14.48
Ongoing Expectation of Effectiveness 14.49
Accounting for Cash Flow Hedges 14.53
Methods of Measuring Effectiveness 14.53
Exhibit 14-5: Methods of Measuring Effectiveness for Cash Flow Hedges 14.54
Reclassifying Amounts from OCI 14.55
Exhibit 14-6: Methods of Reclassifying Amounts Out of OCI into Earnings 14.56
Other Limitations on Amounts Deferred in OCI 14.56
The Shortcut Method for Cash Flow Hedges 14.57
Required or Voluntary Termination of a Cash Flow Hedge 14.60
Exhibit 14-7: Recap of Fair Value and Cash Flow Hedging Models 14.63
Foreign Currency Hedges 14.64
Highlights of FAS-52 14.65
Distinguishing between Foreign Currency Hedging Types 14.66

Common Foreign Currency Hedging Criteria 14.66
Exhibit 14-8: Foreign Currency Hedging Types 14.67
Exhibit 14-9: Intervening Subsidiary Rule 14.68
Foreign Currency Fair Value Hedges 14.68
Firm Commitments 14.68
Recognized Assets and Liabilities 14.69
Foreign Currency Cash Flow Hedges 14.70
Groups of Forecasted Transactions 14.71
Recognized Assets and Liabilities 14.71
Forecasted Purchases and Sales on Credit 14.71
Forecasted Intercompany Transactions 14.72
Exhibit 14-10: Simple Central Treasury Hedge 14.73
Hedge of the Net Investment in a Foreign Operation 14.75
Qualifying Hedging Instruments 14.76
Accounting for the Net Investment 14.77
After-Tax Hedging of Foreign Currency Risk 14.80
Entities That Do Not Report Earnings Separately 14.80
Not-for-Profit Health Care Organizations 14.81
Reporting Elements of Hedge Accounting 14.81
Balance Sheet Reporting 14.81
Classification of Derivatives 14.82
Income Statement Reporting 14.82
Extinguishments of Debt That Was Hedged 14.83
Capitalization of Interest Expense on Debt That
Was Hedged 14.83
Cash Flow Statement Presentation 14.84
Regulatory Considerations 14.84
Audit Considerations 14.85
Illustrations 14.87
Illustration 14-1: Firm Commitment—Comparison of Possible Designations 14.88
Illustration 14-2: Fair Value Hedge of Interest Rate Risk in Fixed-Rate Noncallable Debt 14.90
Illustration 14-3: Fair Value Hedge of Interest Rate Risk Using the Shortcut Method 14.91
Illustration 14-4: Fair Value Hedge of Equity Security Using a Net Written Option Collar 14.93
Illustration 14-5: Fair Value Hedge of Interest Rate Risk and Currency Risk on a Fixed-Rate Foreign-Currency-Denominated Loan (Fixed to Variable Scenario) 14.96

Illustration 14-6: Cash Flow Hedge of Interest Rate Risk Using the Interest Rate Swap Shortcut   14.98

Illustration 14-7: Cash Flow Hedge of Forecasted Issuance of Fixed-Rate Debt (Rate Lock)   14.100

Illustration 14-8: Cash Flow Hedge of Currency Risk in a Fixed-Rate Foreign-Currency-Denominated Loan   14.101

Illustration 14-9: Foreign Currency Hedge of a Forecasted Purchase on Credit   14.103

Illustration 14-10: Hedge of Forecasted Sale with a Purchased Put Option   14.105

Illustration 14-11: Central Treasury Hedge of Foreign Currency Forecasted Transactions   14.106

OVERVIEW

All derivatives must be carried at fair value in the balance sheet. However, for qualifying hedge transactions, gains and losses on derivatives may be deferred and recognized in earnings in a pattern that matches the hedged item. The mechanics of hedge accounting vary, depending on whether the risk being hedged is price risk, cash flow risk, or foreign currency risk. To qualify for hedge accounting, numerous criteria must be met, involving both the derivative and the hedged item. Hedge accounting is prohibited for several types of transactions. Hedging transactions must be designated and documented at the inception of the transaction and the entity must expect the derivative to be highly effective in offsetting the fluctuations in price or cash flow of the hedged item. Generally, ineffectiveness in a hedging relationship is recognized in earnings currently. Hedge accounting is elective for transactions that meet all of the necessary criteria.

BACKGROUND

FAS-133 is the primary source of literature for hedge accounting. There are over 80 DIG issues that address various aspects of hedge accounting, including methods of assessing and measuring effectiveness. FAS-133 nullified most of the previous GAAP that addressed hedge accounting. However, portions of FAS-52 were essentially carried forward into FAS-133. A few EITF Issues address classification of hedge gains and losses in certain circumstances.

Disclosures about derivatives and hedge accounting are discussed in Chapter 15, "Disclosures about Derivatives."

Description of Hedge Accounting

Hedge accounting is a special accounting practice that reflects an entity's intended strategy between two (or more) separate transactions with the same or different counterparties. Rather than applying the applicable GAAP to each component of the strategy, hedge accounting overrides GAAP for one or both components and allows the entity to recognize the gains or losses on the derivative in the same period as the income statement effect on the hedged item. Entities engaged in risk management strategies desire hedge accounting so that the income statement reflects the effect of their derivative transactions in the same period as the item being hedged. Because this accounting practice defers the recognition of gains and losses on derivatives, numerous conditions must be met both upfront and over the life of the hedging relationship; these are called hedge criteria. The criteria differ, depending on the nature of the risk being hedged.

☞ **PRACTICE POINTER:** There have been a number of recent practice issues surrounding the application of the shortcut method in FAS-133. In February 2006, the FASB began an effort to address specific practice issues related to the application of the shortcut method. In addition, in May 2007, the FASB decided to begin a broader project that will address the accounting for hedging activities in FAS-133. In that project, the FASB will consider a "fair value approach" that would focus on individually measuring the change in fair value of the derivative and the change in fair value of the hedged item (the hypothetical derivative for forecasted transactions). That approach could eliminate (1) the shortcut method, (2) the "critical terms match" approach, and (3) the assessment of effectiveness. Readers should monitor developments on these projects.

Different Types of Hedges

FAS-133 prescribes different methods of hedge accounting, depending on the type of risk being hedged. The FASB created three categories of hedging relationships. The categories share some common criteria, but each also has its own unique criteria and different mechanics for achieving matching in the income statement. The three categories are:

- *Fair Value Hedges* Hedges of changes in price or fair value of an existing asset, liability, or a *firm commitment* that has a fixed price. For example, the fair value of a fixed-rate bond changes as the general level of interest rates changes. That risk can be hedged with a receive-variable, pay-fixed interest swap. For another example, a firm commitment to buy grain at a fixed price becomes more or less valuable as the market price of grain rises and falls. That risk can be hedged with an option to sell grain.

Fair value hedges essentially convert a fixed price item to a floating rate (then current price) item—the combined position now has cash flow risk (see below).

- *Cash Flow Hedges*   Hedges of variable cash flows from an existing asset or liability, or from a transaction expected to occur in the future whose price has not yet been set (known as a forecasted transaction). For example, a floating-rate debt could require increased cash flows if interest rates rise. That risk can be hedged with a receive-floating, pay-fixed interest rate swap. For another example, a projected sale of a commodity whose terms have not yet been agreed upon could result in less cash if the market price of that commodity falls by the time a contract is struck. That risk can be hedged by selling a futures contract for settlement on approximately the same date as the commodity sale. Cash flow hedges essentially fix the cash flows for a transaction that previously had an uncertain amount of cash flow—the combined position now has price risk.

- *Hedge of a Net Investment in a Foreign Operation*   Hedges of the translation adjustment arising from remeasuring a company's net investment in the assets, liabilities, revenues, and expenses of a foreign subsidiary into the reporting currency of the investor under FAS-52. That risk can be hedged with a pay foreign currency, receive functional currency swap.

OBSERVATION: Fair value exposures and cash flow exposures are often mutually exclusive. By allowing hedges of both types of exposure, the FASB is permitting hedge accounting when a type of risk has been reduced for that one transaction. Under previous GAAP, an entity had to demonstrate enterprise-wide risk reduction, which was widely viewed as unoperational (in part, because reducing one type of risk increases another type of risk).

Exhibit 14-1 summarizes how several common hedging transactions would be characterized under FAS-133.

EXHIBIT 14-1
CHARACTERIZATION OF HEDGING STRATEGIES
UNDER FAS-133

Strategy	Hedge Type under FAS-133	Bottom-Line Effect on Income if Perfectly Effective
1. Swap interest rate from fixed to floating (same currency)	Fair value	Creates floating interest rate in interest income or expense

Strategy	Hedge Type under FAS-133	Bottom-Line Effect on Income if Perfectly Effective
2. Swap interest rate from floating to fixed (same currency)	Cash flow	Creates fixed interest rate in interest income or expense
3. Lock in fixed interest rate on anticipated debt-offering with a futures contract	Cash flow	When debt is issued, creates desired fixed rate
4. Lock in price of raw materials with a forward purchase contract (no purchase order exists). Assume same currency.	Cash flow	Cost of goods sold will reflect the locked in price of materials (ignoring any complications of inventory accounting).
5. Lock in minimum selling price of finished goods with an option (no sale contract with a customer exists). Assume same currency.	Cash flow	Sales revenue will reflect a minimum price of inventory, plus cost of option
6. Lock in US$ equivalent of a purchase of machinery from a foreign supplier (currency amount per contract)	Cash flow or fair value hedge	No effect until machine is depreciated, using the locked-in US$-equivalent cost as its basis
7. Monetizing a call option in a debt instrument (hedging an embedded option with an offsetting option)	Fair value	Creates effective interest rate for noncallable debt
8. Swap interest rate from fixed to floating and swap currency from foreign currency to functional currency (say US$)	Fair value	Creates floating US$ Interest rate in interest income or expense
9. Swap interest rate from floating to fixed and swap currency from foreign currency to functional currency (say US$)	Cash flow	Creates fixed US$ interest rate in interest income or expense
10. Lock in US$ equivalent of a forecasted sale of goods by a foreign subsidiary	Cash flow	Sales revenue will reflect the US$ equivalent of today's selling price of inventory

The mechanics of hedge accounting vary for these three major categories of hedges. To provide context for this long and detailed chapter, Exhibit 14-2 provides an overview of the way hedge accounting works for the three buckets. Then, each type of hedge is analyzed in detail, including the documentation requirements, the qualifications for hedging instruments and hedged items, and a detailed discussion of each type of hedge accounting.

EXHIBIT 14-2
SUMMARY OF DERIVATIVES AND HEDGE ACCOUNTING

	No Hedge Accounting	Qualifying Fair Value Hedges	Qualifying Cash Flow Hedges	Qualifying Hedges of Net Investment In Foreign Subsidiary
Derivative:				
Balance sheet	Fair value	Fair value	Fair value	Fair value
Treatment of gain or loss	Earnings	Earnings	First OCI (equity) to the extent effective, then earnings timed to match hedged item	CTA (equity), to the extent effective
Treatment of hedged item:				
Treatment of loss or gain	Not applicable	Earnings	Earnings (follow GAAP for hedged item)	CTA (equity)
Balance sheet	Not applicable	Adjust for changes in fair value of hedged risk(s)	Follow GAAP for hedged item	Translate into reporting currency under FAS-52
Bottom-line effect on income	Entire gain or loss on derivative	—Only ineffectiveness on derivative—		

Common Hedge Criteria

To qualify for hedge accounting, all hedges must meet all of the following threshold criteria:

- Derivatives used as hedges must be linked to a specific transaction that affects earnings and that relationship must be documented at inception.
- Throughout the term of the hedge, the entity must expect the hedging instrument to be highly effective in offsetting changes in the fair value or cash flow of the hedged item, using reasonable methods that are appropriate in the circumstances.
- Ineffectiveness from mismatches in terms and other factors must be recognized currently in earnings.

These key qualifying conditions are described below. Additional criteria that must be met for fair value hedges and cash flow hedges are discussed later in this chapter under those section headings.

Documentation of the Hedging Relationship

At the inception of every hedging transaction, the entity must document the following information (FAS-133, pars. 20(a) and 28(a)):

- Which instrument is the hedging instrument and which specific item it is hedging. Generally, long and short positions may not be hedged on a net basis. For example, an entity may not hedge its net interest rate gap position or net income for a period. It must dig deeper and identify specific transactions to hedge.
- The nature of the risk being hedged (e.g., overall changes in fair value, interest rate risk, or foreign currency risk).
- The entity's risk management objective or strategy (e.g., to convert a floating-rate instrument to a fixed rate, or to hedge corn inventory from declines in the price of corn).
- The method the entity will use to assess and measure effectiveness (prospectively and retrospectively).
- The method the entity will use to measure hedge ineffectiveness. (EITF D-102)

☛ **PRACTICE POINTER:** Documenting hedging relationships after the fact is not in accordance with GAAP and will disqualify a transaction for hedge accounting for the period prior to the designation.

SEC REGISTRANT ALERT: The SEC staff expects vigilant compliance with the documentation requirements of FAS-133, and the documentation should be contemporaneous with the designations of hedging relationships. For example, the SEC staff expects the documentation of the methods that will be used to measure ineffectiveness to be sufficiently detailed such that a third party could follow the documentation and compute the same amount. Refer to the Current Accounting and Disclosure portion of the SEC website for additional information. Reportedly, the SEC has required registrants to restate their financial statements for failure to comply with the documentation requirements of FAS-133. (December 7, 1999, speech by Pascal Desroches, then a Professional Accounting Fellow at the SEC.)

In addition, in the March 2005 update of Current Accounting and Disclosure Issues in the Division of Corporate Finance, the SEC staff reiterated that it will challenge the application of hedge accounting in situations where a registrant has not contemporaneously complied with FAS-133's documentation requirements upon designation of a hedge. The SEC staff stresses that, for hedges of forecasted transactions, the documentation must include the estimated date, nature, and hedged amount of the forecasted transaction. The methodology used to assess hedge effectiveness must be reasonable and must be documented at inception.

At the December 2006 National Conference on Current SEC and PCAOB Developments, the SEC staff again addressed hedge documentation. The SEC staff reiterated that if a company fails to document its approach for assessing hedge effectiveness, then the hedge documentation is insufficient and hedge accounting would be inappropriate. The SEC staff also cited a recent issue involving cash flow hedges where a group of individual transactions are part of one hedging relationship. In that case, the documentation must be sufficiently clear that the group of hedged items share the same risk exposure. If the transactions have different characteristics (e.g., a group of forecasted sales of commodities that have different delivery locations), additional analysis may need to be done to support the assertion that the group of hedged items share the same risk exposure. If there are changes in the composition of the group of transactions, the company may be required to update this analysis periodically throughout the life of the relationship. (Speech by Joseph D. McGrath, Professional Accounting Fellow, Office of the Chief Accountant, SEC at the December 2006 National Conference on Current SEC and PCAOB Developments)

Hedging Instruments

A contract that meets the definition of a derivative in FAS-133 and is accounted for separately may be designated as a hedging instrument if the transaction qualifies for hedge accounting. Cash instruments, such as debt instruments, equity securities, short sale liabilities, and other contracts that do not meet the definition of a derivative, may not be designated as the hedging instrument, except for two specific types of foreign currency hedges involving unrecognized firm commitments and the net investment in a foreign operation. (FAS-133, pars. 20 and 28) This general prohibition applies to the following hybrid instruments that are accounted for on a *combined basis*: hybrid financial instruments that the entity elects to initially and subsequently measure at fair value under the FAS-133 election (made on an instrument-by-instrument basis) and hybrid instruments that are measured at fair value under the FAS-133 practicability exception, which is applicable when an embedded derivative cannot be readily identified and measured. (FAS-133, par. 16) (Refer to Chapter 13, "Embedded Derivatives," for more information.)

To enhance readability, this chapter uses the term "derivative" instead of hedging instrument, except in narrow circumstances where other types of instruments may be designated as hedging instruments. Those circumstances are specifically noted later in this chapter in the section on "Foreign Currency Hedges."

Written options   When a company writes an option, it takes on a potential obligation and gives the counterparty a potential right if the option goes in the money. The option writer's potential for gain is limited to the amount of premium received, but his potential for loss is unlimited. The FASB views writing options primarily as a risk-taking activity and, as such, hedge accounting is allowed only in very narrow circumstances, as discussed below. A combination of a written option and a swap or forward contract (such as a swaption) should be considered a written option for purposes of applying the hedge accounting criteria. (FAS-133, par. 20(c)(1))

Qualifications for written options as hedges   A written option may be designated as a hedging instrument of a recognized asset or liability or an unrecognized firm commitment only if the combination of instruments has at least as much potential for gains as exposure to loss (the symmetrical gain and loss test). For example, the following strategies could, on a combined basis, provide symmetrical opportunities for gain and loss, depending on the facts and circumstances:

- A written option that hedges a callable debt.
- A collar (that is considered a net written option) that hedges an equity security. (DIG-F7)

However, a *covered call strategy* (that is, a call option written against an asset held) would generally not meet the symmetrical gain and loss test, because the asset alone has upside and downside potential, but in the combined scenario, it only has downside potential.

The symmetrical gain and loss test should be applied only at the inception of the hedging relationship. (DIG F-7) The time value of the written option may be excluded for the purpose of performing the symmetrical gain and loss test as long as that method is documented and consistent with the entity's risk management strategy. (FAS-133, par. 63(a) and DIG F-7)

Collars A combination of options (for example, a collar) in which the strike price and the notional amount of both the written option component and the purchased option component remain constant would be considered a net written option unless all of the following three conditions are met:

1. No net premium is received, either in cash or as a favorable term, either at inception or over the life of the contract.
2. Each option is based on the same underlying and has the same maturity date.
3. The notional amount of the written option component is nogreater than the notional amount of the purchased option component.

If the combination of options does not meet all of those conditions, it is subject to the symmetrical gain and loss test in paragraph 20(c) for fair value hedges and in paragraph 28(c) for cash flow hedges. For example, under this guidance, a combination of options having different underlying indices, such as a collar containing a written floor based on three-month Treasury rates and a purchased cap based on three-month LIBOR, must be considered a net written option even though those rates may be highly correlated. (DIG E-2)

If either the written option component or the purchased option component has a strike price or notional amount that could fluctuate over the life of the contract, these conditions must be applied on each date that either the strike prices or the notional amounts change. (DIG E-5)

If a collar is made up of a purchased option and a written option that have different notional amounts (but the notional amount of the written option is less than that of the purchased option), the hedged item may be specified as two different proportions of the same asset referenced in the collar, based on the upper and lower price ranges specified in the put and call options. That is, the quantities of the asset designated as being hedged may be different based on those price ranges in which the collar goes in the money. (DIG E-18)

☞ **PRACTICE POINTER:** The Chicago Board Options Exchange has an excellent interactive Learning Center on its website (www.cboe.com) that encourages scenario analysis with different strike prices, exercise dates, and other terms.

Limitations on intercompany derivatives Large organizations often centralize their hedging functions for a variety of reasons, including (a) one department (or subsidiary) has expertise in derivatives markets (including a subsidiary that might actually be a derivatives dealer) or (b) it is more efficient for the company to monitor its exposures globally and enter into as few derivative transactions as possible. To document this transfer of risk between entities, "internal" or intercompany derivatives are written between the central treasury department and the subsidiary seeking to hedge its exposure (and then the central treasury department would enter into an offsetting contract with a derivatives dealer). Internal derivatives do not qualify for hedge accounting in consolidation, except in narrow circumstances involving foreign currency hedges, and numerous criteria must be met. (The specific circumstances are discussed later in the "Foreign Currency Hedging" section of this chapter.) A parent company may enter into a derivative with a third party and designate it as a hedge of a subsidiary's risk in consolidation; however, in situations involving foreign currency hedges, certain additional conditions must be met. (DIG H-1)

To qualify for hedge accounting in the *separate company* financial statements of a hedging subsidiary, the subsidiary must be a party to the derivative, whether it is with a related party (e.g., a sister subsidiary or the parent company) or with a third party. (DIG E-3)

> **OBSERVATION:** This issue is highlighted for any large multinationals considering changing to U.S. GAAP. Prior to the adoption of FAS-133, this was a very contentious issue among U.S. corporations, who frequently hedged interest rate risk and foreign currency risk on a centralized basis. Now, only a very narrow subset of such transactions qualifies for hedge accounting.

Hedged Items

FAS-133 permits an entity to hedge specific assets, liabilities, contracts, and other transactions that affect (or will affect) earnings. An entity may hedge either (1) the entire change in fair value (or cash flow) arising from a hedged item or (2) changes in fair value or cash flow arising from some but not all of the risks inherent in a hedged item, subject to certain limitations. (FAS-133, pars. 20 and 28) FAS-133 uses the phrase, "change in fair value (or cash flow) *attributable to the risk being hedged*" in situations where only some designated risks have been hedged, as permitted. For example, a foreign-currency denominated bond would bear all of the following types of risk:

- Credit risk
- Interest rate risk (including prepayment risk)
- Foreign currency risk

An entity is permitted to hedge one or more of those risks, provided that the derivative (or combination of derivatives) would be highly effective in offsetting changes from those designated risks. Perhaps the most common example of this practice is swapping the interest rate on a debt instrument. In such cases, *only* interest rate risk is being hedged. The swap offers no protection against changes in credit risk, so changes in credit quality do not affect hedge accounting (except when default becomes possible). FAS-133 imposes certain limits on what qualifies as a discretely hedgeable risk—the limits on interest rate risk are discussed below. Other limitations are discussed in the fair value and cash flow hedge accounting sections.

> ☞ **PRACTICE POINTER:** This "bifurcation by risk" approach applies *only* to hedged items. A derivative (hedging instrument) may *not* be separated by risk, even if it is a compound derivative that has been bifurcated from a hybrid instrument. Designations of selected risks and the methods of assessing effectiveness must be meticulously documented, to avoid second-guessing by auditors and regulators.

> **OBSERVATION:** Although the bifurcation-by-risk approach seems unnecessarily complex at first glance, it was actually a concession by the FASB so that gains and losses from unhedged risks (such as credit) do not flow through earnings and make the intended hedge seem ineffective.

Hedges of interest rate risk FAS-133 introduces a new definition of interest rate risk that is critically important for hedgers to understand. If an entity seeks to hedge the interest rate risk of a hedged item, it must identify a *benchmark interest rate* inherent in (or explicitly stated in) that instrument. A benchmark interest rate is a widely quoted rate in an active market that is indicative of the overall level of interest rates attributable to high-credit-quality obligors in that market. Benchmark rates will be determined on a market-by-market basis. In the United States, Treasury rates and the LIBOR swap rate are currently the only acceptable benchmark rates. Any spread above the benchmark rate is considered a component of credit risk, not interest rate risk. (FAS-133, par. 540)

This narrow definition of interest rate risk significantly limits which hedging transactions will result in the desired level of offset in the income statement. Later in this chapter, "shortcut methods" of assessing the effectiveness of interest rate swaps in hedges of interest rate risk are described that mitigate those concerns for a narrow subset of transactions. Entities must understand that variable rates that are not linked to a benchmark rate can disqualify a transaction from the shortcuts and cause ineffectiveness to be recognized in earnings. That issue is highlighted again in the relevant sections.

Disqualified Hedged Items

The following items may *not* be designated as the hedged item in a fair value hedge or a cash flow hedge:

- An investment accounted for by the equity method in accordance APB-18.

- A minority interest in one or more consolidated subsidiaries.
- An equity investment in a consolidated subsidiary.
- A firm commitment or plan either to enter into a business combination or to acquire or dispose of a subsidiary, a minority interest, or an equity method investee.
- An equity instrument issued by the entity and classified in stockholders' equity in the statement of financial position. (FAS-133, par. 21(c) and FAS-133, par. 29(f))
- An existing or forecasted asset or liability that is (or will be) remeasured with the changes in fair value attributable to the hedged risk reported currently in earnings. (FAS-133, par. 21(c) and FAS-133, par. 29(d)) Remeasuring a foreign-currency-denominated asset or liability using the spot rate in accordance with FAS-52 does not meet this condition. (FAS-133, par. 36)

Other prohibitions that apply to fair value hedges or cash flow hedges are discussed later in this chapter in the applicable section; however, the prohibitions mentioned above apply across the board. Exhibit 14-3 summarizes some common economic hedging strategies that do not qualify for hedge accounting under FAS-133 (the reasons disqualifying some of these transactions are discussed in later sections).

> **OBSERVATION:** A prohibition against hedge accounting simply means that the entity may not defer gains and losses on the derivative. It does not mean that entities cannot engage in economic hedging strategies.

EXHIBIT 14-3
TRANSACTIONS THAT DO NOT QUALIFY FOR HEDGE ACCOUNTING

Strategy	Reason Does Not Qualify	Treatment of Derivative
1. Hedging net income (for example, for foreign currency exposure)	Derivative must be linked to specific transaction	Mark to market through earnings
2. Hedge of EPS (intended to hedge the number of shares or potential shares in the denominator)	Not a transaction that affects earnings (also, no antidilution in EPS)	Mark to market through earnings*
3. Use interest rate swap to open or close a gap identified by asset/liability management techniques	Derivative must be linked to specific transaction	Mark to market through earnings

Strategy	Reason Does Not Qualify	Treatment of Derivative
4. Covered calls (writing a call option against an asset held)	Combined position does not provide symmetrical risk/reward profile	Mark to market through earnings
5. Lock in price of commodity being purchased from foreign supplier (but not the functional currency cash flows)	Must hedge just foreign currency risk, or *both* price risk and foreign currency risk; may not hedge selected price risk of a nonfinancial item	Mark to market through earnings
6. Hedge of business combination, or divestiture, including currency risk	Specific exclusion	Mark to market through earnings*
7. Hedge of interest rate risk on a held-to-maturity security	Specific exclusion (conflicts with intent to hold to maturity)	Mark to market through debt earnings
8. Hedge of minority interest	Specific exclusion	Mark to market through earnings*
9. Hedge of equity method investment (including anticipated sale)	Specific exclusion	Mark to market through earnings

* EITF Issue 00-19 provides guidance for equity instruments used in these transactions (see Chapter 16, "Issuer's Accounting for Equity Instruments and Related Contracts").

☛ **PRACTICE POINTER:** FAS-159, *The Fair Value Option for Financial Assets and Financial Liabilities,* issued in February 2007, provides companies with an option to report certain financial assets and liabilities at fair value with subsequent changes in value reported in earnings. FAS-159 is applicable to many financial instruments. Chapter 19, "The Fair Value Option for Financial Instruments," outlines the scope and discusses the detailed provisions of FAS-159. FAS-159 is effective for calendar-year-end companies as of January 1, 2008.

FAS-159 provides entities with a means for mitigating volatility in reported earnings by enabling companies to report offsetting changes in fair value of related assets and liabilities in earnings. By electing the fair value option for related assets and liabilities, companies can recognize the effect of economic or "natural" fair value hedges in reported earnings, including situations in which hedge accounting is not permissible under FAS-133, such as when a nonderivative hedging instrument is used. In many situations, the fair value option will provide an alternative that avoids the application of complex hedge accounting rules in FAS-133.

FAS-159 does not provide an alternative to all hedging strategies currently accounted for under FAS-133, and companies may still wish to apply hedge accounting to achieve certain risk-management strategies. For example, FAS-133 (not the fair value option in FAS-159) would continue to be employed for hedges of fair value changes attributable to a specific risk, rather than the overall fair value changes of the hedged item. Similarly, FAS-133's cash flow hedge accounting provisions would continue to be applicable for cash flow hedges of forecasted transactions and for hedges of changes in future cash flows of existing instruments.

Unit of Measure Issues

Designating Part of a Derivative in a Hedging Relationship

Either all or a *proportion* of a derivative may be designated as the hedging instrument. The proportion must be expressed as a percentage of the *entire* derivative so that the profile of risk exposures in the hedging portion of the derivative is the same as that in the entire derivative. An entity may not separate a compound derivative into components representing different risks. For example, a $100 million swap with an embedded option may not be divided into a swap and an option; however, an entity could choose to designate only $50 million of the entire swap as a hedging instrument, provided the other hedge criteria are met. (Presumably, the hedged item would have an offsetting embedded option that was not accounted for separately.)

> ☞ **PRACTICE POINTER:** For simplicity, when this chapter refers to a derivative as a hedging instrument, it includes the use of only a proportion of a derivative. (FAS-133, par. 18)

> **OBSERVATION:** The restriction against separating derivatives into components is primarily to reduce complexity. Theoretically, it conflicts with other aspects of FAS-133 that allow/require split accounting for distinct risks.

Combining Derivatives

Two or more derivatives, or proportions thereof, may be designated together as a single hedging instrument. (FAS-133, par. 18) For example, an entity could designate a swap and an option together as a hedge of the interest rate risk in callable debt (assuming other hedge criteria are met).

> ☞ **PRACTICE POINTER:** Certain combinations of options are required to be accounted for as a single forward contract. Refer to Chapter 12, "Introduction to Derivatives," for additional information. (DIG K-3)

Hedges of Groups of Assets and Liabilities

Entities may hedge a group of similar existing assets or similar liabilities (or forecasted transactions) if they share the same risk exposure. An entity may not hedge the net effect of assets and liabilities or of forecasted purchases and sales in a single hedging designation. (FAS-133, pars. 21(a)(1) and 29(a)) Other specific limitations on portfolio hedges are discussed in the "Fair Value Hedge Accounting" section.

> **OBSERVATION:** The significance of this requirement is that hedge accounting is not permitted for macro hedges that seek toadjust an entity's overall risk position, such as in asset/liability management techniques used by financial institutions.

Expectation of Offsetting Effects

At inception and on an ongoing basis, the entity must expect that the derivative will be highly effective at offsetting the effects of changes in the hedged item attributable to the risk being hedged (e.g., changes in fair value or changes in cash flow). When the critical terms of the derivative and the entire hedged asset or liability or forecasted transaction are the same, including the underlying basis, the quantity or notional amounts, the presence or absence of optionality, and the payment and maturity dates, then the changes in fair value or cash flows attributable to the risk being hedged are likely to offset each other completely at inception and on an ongoing basis. (FAS-133, par. 65) In such cases, the entity should document the rationale behind their assessment that the hedge will be highly effective in offsetting changes in the hedged item and monitor the relationship for changes in circumstances, including deterioration in the credit quality of either counterparty.

> ☛ **PRACTICE POINTER:** Each hedge accounting section that follows discusses when it would be appropriate to assume no ineffectiveness. For example, certain "shortcuts" exist for interest rate swaps used to hedge interest rate risk in fair value and cash flow hedges.

In many cases, however, the critical terms of the derivative and hedged item do not match. The following types of differences may cause ineffectiveness in a hedging relationship:

- Differences between the basis of the derivative (its underlying) and the hedged item (e.g., cross-hedges involving different currencies or commodities).
- Differences in other key terms of the derivative and hedged item, including notional amounts or other quantities, maturities or delivery dates, and location.

- Adverse changes in the creditworthiness of the der¹ terparty or the counterparty to the hedged item tn₂. fault possible. (FAS-133, par. 66)

☞ **PRACTICE POINTER:** Frequently, a "hedge ratio" provides the best matching between the derivative results and changes in the value of the hedged item due to cross-hedging considerations, differences between expected cash flows on the derivative compared with cash flows relating to the hedged item, and tax effects.

When there are differences between the derivative and the hedged item (including when only selected risks have been hedged), an entity must assess hedge effectiveness from two different perspectives:

1. *Prospective considerations* Upon designation of a hedging relationship (and on an ongoing basis), the entity must be able to justify its *expectation* that the relationship *will be* highly effective over future periods in achieving offsetting changes in fair value or cash flows. This test allows a hedger to continue to apply hedge accounting.

2. *Retrospective evaluations* At least quarterly, but whenever earnings are reported, the hedging entity must determine whether the hedging relationship *has been* highly effective in achieving offsetting changes in fair value or cash flows through the date of the periodic assessment. This test determines whether a derivative gain or loss may be deferred in the current period. (FAS-133, pars. 20(b), 28(b), and 62 and DIG E-7)

☞ **PRACTICE POINTER:** The purpose of these assessments is to determine whether hedge accounting is appropriate. Methods to *measure* how much of the gain or loss on a derivative qualifies for deferral in a given period are discussed later in this section.

Methods of Assessing Effectiveness

FAS-133 permits some latitude in identifying appropriate methods for assessing effectiveness. Both forward-looking and backward-looking assessments can be based on quantitative techniques such as historical *correlation, regression analysis* and the *dollar-offset method*, or other relevant information.[1] Different methods may be used (consistently) for the prospective and retrospective assessments. Generally, the dollar-offset method provides a point-in-time assessment of

---

[1] Refer to an article titled, "Testing Hedge Effectiveness," by John M. Althoff and John D. Finnerly, published in the November 29, 2001, issue of *Institutional Investor Journals*, for a comprehensive discussion of the dollar offset method, regression analysis, and other methods used to assess hedge effectiveness.

the specific hedging relationship during the hedge period whereas the other methods evaluate the relationship between the variables underlying the hedge components over (longer) historical periods.

- The period of time over which correlation data should be assessed depends on the circumstances.

- Regression analyses (or other statistical analyses) should be updated periodically to determine whether the expectation of high effectiveness remains valid. If an entity elects at the inception of a hedging relationship to utilize the same regression analysis approach for both prospective considerations and retrospective evaluations of assessing effectiveness, then during the term of that hedging relationship those regression analysis calculations should generally incorporate the same number of data points. (DIG E-7)

- If the dollar-offset method is used for retrospective evaluations, the analysis for each hedging relationship may be performed on a period-by-period basis (limited to a period of 3 months) or on a cumulative basis. (DIG E-8)

> **OBSERVATION:** The application of a regression or other statistical analysis approach to assessing effectiveness is complex. Those methodologies require appropriate interpretation and understanding of the statistical inferences.

If the entity elects different methods for the prospective and retrospective assessments, it is possible that the retrospective method will not be considered highly effective while the prospective method still projects a highly effective hedge. In such cases, the entity may not switch methods midstream; the gain or loss on the derivative would not qualify for deferral that period. (DIG E-7) The entity may elect to remove the hedging designation for future periods.

> **SEC REGISTRANT ALERT:** The SEC staff believes that entities may not use an approach that employs a series of methods (e.g., a series of dollar-offset assessments or other statistical analyses using different hedging periods) in order to determine whether a hedge was highly effective on a retrospective basis because such an approach is inconsistent with FAS-133 and DIG E-7. In addition, the SEC staff believes that when using statistical techniques to assess hedge effectiveness, registrants must evaluate all relevant outputs to assess whether a hedge is expected to be highly effective, which may necessitate the use of specialists. (December 11, 2003, speech by John M. James, then a Professional Accounting Fellow, Office of the Chief Accountant of the SEC, at the AICPA National Conference on Current SEC Developments)

Data to Include in the Assessment

The data included in the assessment methodology must be reasonable in the circumstances and consistent with its strategy for that specific hedge. For example:

- A dynamic hedging strategy, such as *delta-neutral hedging* with options, should be assessed using a method that evaluates changes in the *fair value* of the options. (FAS-133, par. 86)
- The time value of money should be included if it is significant in the circumstances. For example, in a tailing strategy with futures contracts or other situations that involve periodic cash settlements, an entity adjusts the size or contract amount of futures contracts used in a hedge so that earnings (or expense) from reinvestment (or funding) of daily settlement gains (or losses) on the futures do not distort the results of the hedge. (FAS-133, par. 64)
- A static hedging strategy (buy-and-hold) could be assessed using either a method that evaluates only changes in spot prices (that is, intrinsic value) or a method that evaluates changes in the fair value of the derivative.

Excluding time value   When it would be consistent with its hedging strategy, an entity may exclude all or part of the derivative's time value from the assessment of hedge effectiveness as follows:

- For an option, one or more of the following components of the change in time value may be excluded from the assessment of effectiveness:
  — Theta: the portion of the change attributable to the passage of time.
  — Vega: the portion of the change attributable to volatility.
  — Rho: the portion of the change attributable to interest rates.
- For a forward or futures contract, the difference between the spot price and forward price may be excluded when effectiveness will be assessed based on changes in spot prices.

No other components may be excluded from the assessment of hedge effectiveness. (FAS-133, par. 63 and DIG E-19) DIG E-19 provides guidelines on the process for isolating changes attributable to one or more components of time value.

Amounts excluded from the effectiveness test are automatically included currently in earnings, together with any hedge imperfections that are required to be recognized for that type of hedge. (FAS-133, par. 63 and DIG E-19)

> ☛ **PRACTICE POINTER:**   For purchased options used in certain cash flow hedges and derivatives used in net investment

hedges, effectiveness may be assessed in such a way that the entire change in fair value may be deferred (in a cash flow hedge, until the forecasted transaction occurs). Those circumstances are discussed later in this chapter.

☞ **PRACTICE POINTER:**   In FAS-133, the term "ineffectiveness" does not include amounts that have been excluded from the effectiveness test. This is somewhat confusing, because, like ineffectiveness, these amounts are also recorded in earnings currently. Excluding a component from the effectiveness test may help to justify hedge accounting for the "effective" part of the derivative's change in value, but recognizing those excluded amounts in earnings may cause significant volatility.

Consistency of Methods

Generally, similar methods should be used for similar types of hedging strategies, including whether a time value component of fair value is excluded from the assessment. The use of different methods for similar hedges should be justified. An entity must apply its selected method consistently throughout the hedge period. (FAS-133, par. 62)

Changes in Methods

If the entity identifies an improved method, it must "true up" under the existing method, end the existing hedge designation, and designate a new hedging relationship that reflects the desired change. Keep in mind that changing methods for one hedge has implications for other similar hedges because the use of different methods for similar hedges must be justified. (FAS-133, par. 62)

☞ **PRACTICE POINTER:**   A change in the method of assessing effectiveness is *not* a change in accounting principle under FAS-154. (DIG E-9)

Meaning of Highly Effective

"Highly effective" is essentially the same as the notion of "high correlation" under FAS-80 (which was superseded by FAS-133). In practice, high correlation usually means that changes in fair value of the derivative have been within a range of 80–125% of the change in fair value of the hedged item (attributable to the hedged risk). (AICPA Audit Guide, "Auditing Derivative Instruments, Hedging Activities, and Investments in Securities," par. 3.35) Keep in mind that unlike previous GAAP, even if correlation is very high, every dollar of "ineffectiveness," as defined, must be recognized in earnings currently under FAS-133. For example, if the derivative changes by $100 and the hedged item changes by $85, the hedge will be highly effective (100/85=117%). However, $15 will have to be recognized in earnings in the current period. Therefore, entities seeking to avoid volatility in earnings will want to interpret "highly effective" more narrowly than 80–125% when the dollars involved are significant.

When an entity is assessing whether a hedging relationship is expected to be highly effective, the entity must consider all *possible* changes in fair value or cash flows of the derivative for the hedge period. For example, in situations where the hedged item has an embedded option, but the derivative does not, an entity would need to continuously demonstrate that the embedded option is expected to have a minimal effect on the change in fair value or cash flow of the hedged item (attributable to the risks being hedged) in order to conclude that the derivative is expected to be highly effective. (DIG E-11) An entity may consider the possible changes in the fair value of the derivative and the hedged item over a shorter period than the remaining life of the derivative in formulating its expectation that the hedging relationship will be highly effective in achieving offsetting changes in fair value (or cash flow) for the risk being hedged, if that method of assessing effectiveness is consistent with its documented risk management strategy. (DIG F-5)

Qualifying for Hedge Accounting versus Measuring Hedge Effectiveness

As discussed previously, hedging relationships must demonstrate a high degree of offset to qualify for hedge accounting—that is, to qualify for deferral and matching of some or all of the gain or loss on the derivative. However, when measuring the amount that qualifies for deferral, the amounts are calculated using the total change in value of the derivative (even if time value has been excluded for purposes of qualifying) and the change in fair value, or cash flow, or foreign currency translation risk, attributable to the risk being hedged, depending on the type of hedge. (That guidance is included in FAS-133, paragraph 22 for fair value hedges, paragraph 30 (and DIG Issues G-7 and G-20) for cash flow hedges, and paragraph 42 (and DIG Issue H-8) for net investment hedges, and certain exceptions apply. Each of those approaches is discussed later in this chapter.) For purposes of clarity, this book uses the term "effectiveness or ineffectiveness" to describe the qualifications for hedge accounting. This book uses the term "earnings effect" to describe any differences that do not qualify for deferral and must be recognized in earnings currently.

For example, assume that a farmer engages in a cross-hedge using a derivative based on the price of Columbian coffee to hedge its inventory of Brazilian coffee. Historically, the spot price of Columbian coffee has been very highly correlated with the price of Brazilian coffee, so the farmer concludes that the derivative qualifies for fair value hedge accounting. However, to *measure* the portion of the gain or loss on the derivative that qualifies for deferral, the farmer would compare:

- The actual change in fair value of the derivative (which would be based on a forward price).
- The actual change in fair value of the coffee inventory (which is based on spot prices for Brazilian coffee).

Paragraphs 72–103 of FAS-133 contain narrative examples of how to identify ineffectiveness in a hedging relationship and some examples of acceptable and unacceptable methods of assessing effectiveness. The key methods are discussed for each type of hedge in the following sections.

Exhibit 14-4 summarizes the process for assessing and measuring effectiveness.

FAIR VALUE HEDGE ACCOUNTING

An entity may designate a derivative as hedging the exposure to changes in the fair value of a recognized asset or liability or a firm commitment, subject to the limitations discussed below.

Common Fair Value Hedging Strategies

- Hedge of interest rate risk on a fixed rate bond (asset or liability)
- Hedge of interest rate risk on operating leases
- Hedge of interest rate risk on mortgage servicing rights
- Hedge of currency risk on a fixed-rate bond
- Hedge of price risk on an investment in an equity security
- Hedge of price risk (including currency risk) on inventory
- Hedge of price risk (including currency risk) on a firm commitment to buy or sell goods

Documentation

In a fair value hedge, the entity must document the following:

- Components involved in the hedging relationship, including specific identification of:
  — The derivative.
  — The hedged item and the specific risk(s) being hedged (including identification of the benchmark rate in a hedge of interest rate risk).
- How the entity will assess and measure the effectiveness and ineffectiveness of the derivative in providing offsetting gains and losses for changes in the fair value of the hedged item attributable to the risk being hedged. (FAS-133, par. 20(a) and EITF D-102)

- How the entity plans to recognize the asset or liability arising from a hedged firm commitment (such as an operating lease) in earnings. (FAS-133, par. 20(a))

EXHIBIT 14-4:
ASSESSING AND MEASURING EFFECTIVENESS

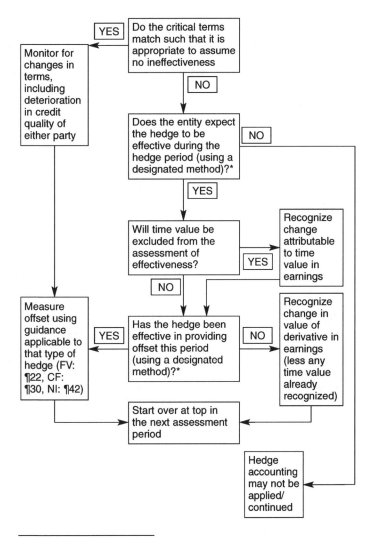

---

* These two methods do not need to be the same, but they must be applied consistently as long as the hedge remains designated and similar hedges must be assessed using the same methods.

Qualifications for Fair Value Hedge Accounting

In addition to the common hedging criteria discussed in the previous section, FAS-133 requires that additional criteria be met in a fair value hedge.

Types of Hedged Items

In a fair value hedge, the hedged item may be either a recognized asset or liability or a firm commitment that presents an exposure to changes in fair value attributable to the hedged risk that could affect reported earnings. (FAS-133, par. 21(b)) Generally, this means that the hedged item must have a fixed price and be a legally enforceable contract.

> ☛ **PRACTICE POINTER:** Internally generated intangible assets may not be designated as the hedged item in a fair value hedge because they are not *recognized*. (FAS-133, par. 437)

> ☛ **PRACTICE POINTER:** A company's own equity transactions do not qualify for hedge accounting because they do not affect reported earnings.

Hedges of Discrete Risks

FAS-133 permits hedges of the entire change in fair value of a qualifying hedged item or only discrete risks, as discussed below.

Financial instruments If the hedged item is a financial asset or liability (other than a held-to-maturity debt security), a recognized loan servicing right, or a nonfinancial firm commitment with financial components, the designated risk being hedged must be either (1) the risk of changes in the fair value of the entire hedged item or (2) the risk of changes in its fair value attributable to one or more of the following (from paragraph 21(f), unless otherwise noted):

- Changes in the designated benchmark interest rate (referred to as interest rate risk), including any prepayment option. The use of different benchmark interest rates for similar hedges should be rare and must be justified.
- Changes in the related foreign currency exchange rates (referred to as foreign exchange risk) (discussed later in this chapter).
- Both changes in the obligor's creditworthiness and changes in the spread over the benchmark interest rate with respect to the hedged item's credit sector at inception of the hedge (referred to as credit risk).

The effect of an embedded derivative of the same risk class must be considered in designating a hedge of an individual risk. For example, the effect of an embedded prepayment option must be considered in designating a hedge of interest rate risk.

Held-to-maturity securities If the hedged item is a debt security classified as held-to-maturity under FAS-115, the following risks may not be designated as being hedged:

- The risk of overall changes in fair value.
- The risk of changes in fair value attributable to interest rate risk.

However, credit risk, foreign currency risk, and the entire fair value of an option component that permits prepayment may be hedged. (FAS-133, par. 21(d))

> **OBSERVATION:** The FASB believes that certain types of hedges contradict an entity's stated intent to hold a security to maturity. Chapter 2, "Investments in Debt and Equity Securities," discusses the accounting for held-to-maturity securities.

Hedges of prepayment risk To hedge prepayment risk, an entity may either: (1) designate the embedded option component of a prepayable instrument as the portion being hedged (assessed on a fair value basis) or (2) designate the benchmark interest rate, including the prepayment option, as the specific risk being hedged. Prepayment options on mortgages are exercised for reasons other than changes in interest rates (e.g., borrowers move and prepay their mortgages). Those other factors should be considered in the effectiveness test. (FAS-133, par. 21(f))

Nonfinancial items If the hedged item is a nonfinancial asset or liability (other than a recognized loan servicing right or a nonfinancial firm commitment with financial components), the designated risk being hedged must be the risk of changes in the fair value of the *entire* hedged asset or liability (reflecting its actual location, if a physical asset). That is, the hedged risk of inventory may not be identified as the price risk of a major ingredient or a similar asset in a different location. (FAS-133, par. 21(e))

Hedging Groups of Assets or Liabilities

A group of similar assets or a group of similar liabilities may be aggregated and hedged as a portfolio only if the change in fair value attributable to the hedged risk for the individual items comprising the portfolio is expected to be within a very narrow range of the change in fair value of the aggregate portfolio attributable to the hedged risk. (FAS-133, par. 21(a)(1))

> ☞ **PRACTICE POINTER:** In aggregating loans to be hedged as a portfolio, the following factors might indicate that the loans are "similar": loan type, loan size, nature and location of collateral, interest rate type and the coupon interest rate (if fixed), scheduled maturity, prepayment history of the loans (if seasoned), and expected prepayment performance in varying interest rate scenarios. Entities should analyze which groupings provide them with the highest degree of offset, given the precise risks being hedged.

> ☞ **PRACTICE POINTER:** For hedges of mortgage (and other types of) servicing rights as a group, the grouping criteria of FAS-133 must be met. These conditions are considerably stricter than the grouping guidelines for impairment testing under FAS-140. In transition to FAS-133, entities were permitted to conform their FAS-140 grouping policies to comply with FAS-133 hedging requirements. However, entities are permitted to use different methods under the two different standards (presumably at a significant operational cost). (DIG F-1)

Hedging Parts of an Asset or Liability

The hedged item may be a specific portion of an asset or liability (or of a portfolio of similar assets or a portfolio of similar liabilities, as defined), if the hedged item falls into one of the following categories (FAS-133, par. 21(a)(2)):

- A single percentage of the entire asset or liability (or of the entire portfolio). (DIG F-8)
- One or more selected contractual cash flows (such as the portion of the asset or liability representing the present value of the interest payments in the first two years of a four-year debt instrument).
- An embedded put option, a call option, an interest rate cap, or an interest rate floor embedded in an existing asset or liability (or a price cap or floor on a firm commitment) that is not required to be accounted for separately under FAS-133 (DIG F-10)
- The residual value in a lessor's net investment in a direct financing or sales-type lease.

Mortgage servicing rights   Hedged items with *negative convexity,* such as mortgage servicing rights, pose significant challenges in terms of identifying derivatives that will meet the effectiveness tests under FAS-133. The proportion of a hedged item, such as a servicing right, may *not* be identified using the matrix method described in DIG Issue F-8 (i.e., on a "to be determined" basis, depending on actual changes in market conditions. For example, if prepayment speeds are X, then 80% of the servicing right is considered hedged, but if prepayment speeds are Y, 70% of the servicing right is considered hedged). However, a limited exception exists for certain collars used to hedge two different proportions of the same asset based on the upper and lower rate or price range of the asset referenced in those two options. Refer to the discussion of DIG Issue E-18 in the section on "Common Hedge Criteria."

> ☛ **PRACTICE POINTER:** DIG Issue F-8 discusses the complexities and challenges associated with hedging mortgage servicing rights. However, FAS-156, issued in March 2006, permits entities that use derivatives to manage risks inherent in servicing assets and servicing liabilities to elect to subsequently measure servicing assets and servicing liabilities at fair value with changes in value recognized in earnings. Fair value measurement of servicing assets and servicing liabilities obviates the need to qualify for special hedge accounting under FAS-133. Instead, entities can achieve natural income statement offset through the subsequent measurement at fair value of servicing assets and servicing liabilities and related derivatives, which are required to be measured at fair value under FAS-133. Refer to Chapter 4, "Servicing of Financial Assets," for a detailed discussion of the accounting guidance for servicing assets in servicing liabilities, including the implications of FAS-156.

Designating a portion of a pool of prepayable loans Pools of similar prepayable loans pose unique issues, because the entity does not know which specific loans will prepay, if any. DIG Issue F-9 contains tentative guidance on fair value hedges of portions of a pool of similar fixed-rate prepayable loans and generally prohibits an approach that would adjust the designated percentage retroactively so as to maintain a constant principal amount being hedged. Readers should monitor the FASB's progress on this issue, as it would seem to have repercussions for other types of hedges involving interest rate (prepayment) risk.

Partial-term hedges There are limitations on partial-term hedges in a fair value hedge. For example, an entity could not use a three-year swap to hedge the interest rate risk on a ten-year debt with the same notional/principal amounts, because the changes in fair value are not likely to offset (that is, the change in fair value of the debt incorporates changes attributable to the principal amount and the interest payments in years 4-10). To hedge *just* the interest payments during the first three years of a ten-year debt, the entity would have to find derivatives that provide offset for changes in the value of each interest payment (the interest payments take on the character of individual zero-coupon bonds). (DIG F-2)

Ongoing Expectation of Effectiveness

Both at inception of the hedge and on an ongoing basis, the derivative must be expected to be highly effective in providing gains and losses that offset changes in the fair value of the hedged item, which are attributable to the risk being hedged during the period that the hedge is designated. (FAS-133, par. 20(b))

Options   If the derivative is an option that provides only one-sided offset of the hedged risk, the increases (or decreases) in the fair value of the option must be expected to be highly effective in offsetting the decreases (or increases) in the fair value of the hedged item.

    For example, assume an entity decides to hedge declines in the fair value of an equity security with a purchased put option (assume the notional amounts and underlyings match). The entity documents that it will assess effectiveness based solely on changes in the intrinsic value of the option. The option will only have intrinsic value when the price of the security is below the strike price. The entity would assess effectiveness and recognize an earnings effect as follows:

Option	Security	Earnings Effect
In the money	Recognize decline in value in earnings	IV of option and change in value of security net to zero; recognize change in time value of option in earnings
At or Out of the money	Do not recognize change in value (the change would be recorded in OCI, under FAS-115)	Recognize change in time value of option in earnings

Methods of Assessing Effectiveness

The entity must have a reasonable basis for assessing the effectiveness of a hedging relationship and that method must be consistent with the risk management strategy documented for that particular transaction.

    An entity may evaluate the effect of possible changes in the value of the hedging derivative and the hedged item in a fair value hedge over shorter periods than the derivative's remaining life, provided that

that approach is documented and consistent with the entity's risk management strategy. For example, if an entity uses a five-year swap to hedge a five-year debt, the entity may document a method of assessing effectiveness (retrospectively and prospectively) at three-month intervals, rather than to declare up front that the swap is expected be highly effective for its entire five-year term. (DIG F-5)

Hedging a portfolio of prepayable fixed-rate loans   DIG Issue F-11 describes the use of an index-amortizing swap to hedge a portfolio of similar prepayable fixed-rate mortgages that the lender believes will respond in a proportionate way to changes in LIBOR. The notional amount of the swap amortizes based on a schedule that is expected to approximate the principal repayments of the loans (excluding prepayments). The FASB staff concluded that:

- An effectiveness method that would review actual effectiveness over the most recent three-month period and assess effectiveness prospectively over the upcoming three-month period is acceptable. Any difference between the change in fair value of the swap and the change in fair value of the existing mortgages attributable to interest rate risk (including prepayments) should be recognized currently.
- The percentage of the notional amount of the swap that is designated as the hedging instrument may need adjustment (by de-designating or redesignating part of the notional amount) over time as prepayments occur in the loan portfolio in order for the relationship to continue to be highly effective in the future. (DIG F-11)

Accounting for a Fair Value Hedge

Gains and losses on a qualifying fair value hedge should be accounted for as follows:

- The gain or loss on the derivative should be recognized currently in earnings.
- The change in fair value of the hedged item attributable to the risk being hedged should be recorded as an adjustment to the carrying amount of the hedged item with the offset recognized currently in earnings. (FAS-133, par. 22)

> ☞ **PRACTICE POINTER:** Companies may either include the gains and losses from derivatives used as hedges in the income statement line item associated with the hedged item or in a separate line item. An entity's policy for classifying hedge gains and losses in the income statement should be applied consistently for similar types of hedges.

When a hedge is perfectly effective, and no amount has been excluded from the assessment of effectiveness (such as the time value of an option), the net effect on earnings in the current period is zero. If effectiveness has been assessed using a method that excludes some or all of the time value of the derivative, the change in fair value attributable to that portion of time value would be recognized in earnings currently. Likewise, to the extent that any of the key terms of the derivative and hedged item do not match, an earnings effect from ineffectiveness would be expected to arise. Earnings will be affected whenever the entire gain or loss on the derivative is not offset by an equal adjustment of a hedged item's carrying amount, measured on a fair value basis (for the risk being hedged).

> **OBSERVATION:** It is crucial that companies understand that having a highly effective hedge can still result in an effect on earnings. Companies that use methods of assessing effectiveness that exclude parts of the change in fair value (such as time value) must understand that those excluded amounts fall directly to the bottom line—*on a fair value basis.* Options used in static hedging strategies are most likely to generate this issue. Entities are strongly encouraged to run a sensitivity analysis of the combined position prior to putting on a hedge to see the possible earnings volatility that could result. Note that if the hedged item has an offsetting embedded option, the effect on earnings would be reduced.

Hedges of Interest Rate Risk (the Benchmark)

In calculating the change in the hedged item's fair value attributable to changes in the benchmark interest rate, the estimated cash flows used in calculating fair value must be based on all of the contractual cash flows of the entire hedged item. (However, recall that the "hedged item" may be expressed as just coupons or just principal.) Excluding some of the hedged item's contractual cash flows (for example, the portion of the interest coupon in excess of the benchmark interest rate) from the calculation is not permitted for the purpose of assessing or measuring ineffectiveness. (FAS-133, par. 21(f))

Two methods that would comply with this limitation are:

1. Designating the entire debt instrument as the hedged item, and then discounting the contractual cash flows using the fixed rate on the hedged item (which includes the credit spread), adjusted for changes in the benchmark rate (Method 1).

2. Designating the entire debt instrument as the hedged item, and then discounting the contractual cash flows using the current benchmark rate (Method 2).

Both of these methods could result in an earnings effect from ineffectiveness because under Method 1, the cash flows of the debt instrument and the derivative will be measured using potentially different rates and, under Method 2, the contractual cash flows of the debt include the credit spread, which will likely be absent from the contractual cash flows of the swap and they are discounted using the same rate.

> **OBSERVATION:** An entity cannot "strip out" the credit spread and only assess changes in the "benchmark component" for purposes of measuring effectiveness. Therefore, unless the contractual coupon on the debt happens to reflect the same negligible level of credit risk inherent in the benchmark, an interest rate hedge will generate ineffectiveness.
>
> For a simple example, assume the fixed rate on a loan is 6 percent at a time when LIBOR is 5 percent. (The lender has built in a 100 b.p. credit spread.) The entity hedges the loan with a pay-fixed, receive-LIBOR interest rate swap. The hedger documents that it will measure effectiveness by discounting the contractual cash flows of the loan using the current LIBOR rate. Using that method, changes in the present value of the credit spread built into the coupon will fall through as ineffectiveness. This limitation makes the interest rate swap "shortcut" described later in this section that much more appealing because it allows the credit spread to be ignored. For hedges of portfolios of fixed-rate loans, the coupons would essentially have to be the same; otherwise, the change in the fair value of individual loans with different credit spreads could vary widely, which would disqualify them from hedging as a group.

> ☞ **PRACTICE POINTER:** Lenders and issuers that are significant hedgers of interest rate risk may want to increase the use of collateral and guarantees to minimize the credit spread built into their fixed-rate loans. That is, if the contractual coupons reflect the same level of credit risk inherent in the benchmark (say, AA or AAA), this issue is essentially resolved.

Sources of Earnings Volatility in a Fair Value Hedge

- Mismatches in underlyings, notional amounts, maturities, payment dates, optionality
- Option premiums
- Methods of effectiveness based on changes in spot prices of the underlying (because the derivative must be measured using forward rates)
- Interest rate hedges: Differences in credit quality between the benchmark rate and the contractual coupon (credit spread)

Accounting for Adjustments to the Hedged Item

The adjustment of the carrying amount of a hedged asset or liability should be accounted for in the same manner as other components of the carrying amount of that type of asset or liability. For example:

- An adjustment of the carrying amount of inventory would be included in its cost basis for the purpose of applying lower-of-cost-or-market accounting. Ignoring the complications of specific inventory methods, when the inventory is sold, the adjusted carrying amount would be recognized as the cost of the item sold in determining earnings.

- An adjustment of the carrying amount of an equity security would remain part of the carrying amount of the security until it is sold, at which point the carrying amount would be compared with the proceeds to determine the gain or loss on sale.

- An adjustment of the carrying amount of a hedged interest-bearing financial instrument would be amortized to interest income or expense. Amortization must begin no later than when the hedged item ceases to be adjusted for changes in its fair value attributable to the risk being hedged. (FAS-133, par. 24)

- The gain or loss recognized on a firm commitment to purchase inventory would be recorded as an adjustment of the basis of the item acquired. (FAS-133, par. 126) (For a firm commitment such as an operating lease, the company must document upfront how it will recognize changes in value of the lease in earnings.)

☞ **PRACTICE POINTER:** Impairment of the hedged item could modify the normal procedures, as discussed later in this section.

Hedges of available-for-sale securities Available-for-sale securities are carried at fair value with changes in fair value recognized in other comprehensive income under FAS-115. If the hedged item is an available-for-sale security or an instrument with significant prepayment risk that is accounted for like an available-for-sale security (FAS-140, par. 14), the adjustment of the hedged item's carrying amount should be recognized in earnings rather than in other comprehensive income in order to offset the gain or loss on the hedging instrument. (FAS-133, par. 23) Note that this provision of FAS-133 overrides EITF Issue 96-15 when the risk being hedged is foreign currency risk.

For insurance companies, hedges of nonmarketable equity securities that are carried at fair value with changes reported in other comprehensive income should be accounted for in the same manner as hedges of available-for-sale securities. (FAS-60, par. 46, as amended)

☞ **PRACTICE POINTER:**   To the extent that an entity hedges a discrete risk(s) on an available-for-sale security, the entity will report the change in value attributable to the risk(s) being hedged in earnings, and the remaining change in value attributable to *unhedged* risks in other comprehensive income.

The Shortcut Method for Fair Value Hedges

Recognizing that hedging the interest rate risk of debt instruments with interest rate swaps is one of the most common uses of derivatives, the FASB established a list of conditions that, if met, significantly simplifies the accounting for that specific transaction. If all of the conditions for the shortcut method are met, the transaction is accounted for as follows:

- The derivative is reported at fair value on the balance sheet.
- Changes in the fair value of the derivative are recorded as a basis adjustment of the hedged item.
- Interest is recognized using the variable-rate on the swap plus any difference between the fixed rate on the swap and debt instrument (adjusted by amortization of any premium or discount on the underlying debt instrument). (FAS-133, par. 114)

☞ **PRACTICE POINTER:**   Essentially, earnings are "plugged" for the amount necessary to create the desired floating rate.

To qualify for the shortcut method of fair value hedge accounting, all of the following conditions must be met (FAS-133, par. 68, as amended, unless noted):

- The hedged item must be a recognized interest-bearing asset or liability. (Operating leases do not qualify.)
- The notional amount and maturity of the swap match the principal amount (or a proportion thereof) and maturity, respectively, of the interest-bearing asset or liability (or group of similar assets or liabilities) being hedged. (DIG E-10)
- The fair value of the swap is zero at the inception of the hedging relationship (except, if the swap is a compound instrument that contains a mirror-image option as described in 8 below: (a) if the implicit option premium is "paid" up front as an original issue premium or discount, the fair value of the mirror option and embedded option must be equivalent, or (b) if the implicit option premium is "paid" over time as an adjustment of the interest rate, the fair value of the mirror and embedded options must both be zero).

- The fixed rate on the swap is the same throughout the term (but it need not be the same as the fixed rate on the debt).

- The variable rate is based on the same index throughout the term and includes the same spread (if any) throughout the term, and is not capped or floored. A stub rate for trades in between repricing dates does not violate this condition. (DIG E-12)

- The variable leg of the swap is based on the index that matches the benchmark interest rate designated as the interest rate risk being hedged.

- The interval between repricings of the variable interest rate in the swap is frequent enough to justify an assumption that the variable payment or receipt is at a market rate (generally three to six months or less).

- The interest-bearing asset or liability is not prepayable, unless the debt is prepayable solely due to an embedded call option and the hedging interest rate swap contains an embedded *mirror-image call option*. (For an interest-bearing asset or liability with an embedded put option, the hedging interest rate swap must contain an embedded mirror-image *put* option.)

- Any other terms in the interest-bearing financial instruments or interest rate swaps are typical of those instruments and do not invalidate the assumption of no ineffectiveness.

> **OBSERVATION:** The beauty of the shortcut method is multifaceted: (1) This narrow transaction is pre-cleared and removes any ambiguity about whether it will be highly effective. (2) The mechanics are vastly simpler. The change in fair value of the hedged item attributable to the risk being hedged does not need to be separately calculated. The basis adjustment of the hedged item does not need to be amortized. (3) There is no breakage to recognize in earnings. Of course, this simplicity comes at a cost—qualifying transactions must meet all of the necessary conditions, which severely limits an entity's flexibility in choosing investments and financing strategies and the types of derivatives used to hedge them.

> ☛ **PRACTICE POINTER:** The shortcut method may not be applied by analogy to other hedging relationships involving other types of derivatives or other hedged risks, regardless of how similar they might seem. Other hedge transactions must be accounted for under the regular hedge accounting model. (DIG E-4)

> **SEC REGISTRANT ALERT:** At the December 2005 AICPA National Conference on SEC and PCAOB developments, the SEC staff provided the following views regarding certain aspects of the shortcut method because of certain instances of its misapplication:

- Each individual criterion must be met to qualify for the short-cut method. The SEC staff believes there is no "principle" that can be used to justify application of the shortcut method without strictly complying with the stated criteria.

- All of the terms of a transaction must be considered in evaluating whether a swap has a fair value of zero at inception. A company may not conclude that because no cash was paid or received upon entering into the swap that the fair value of a swap is zero at inception. For example, in situations where a financing element is built into an interest rate swap as an adjustment to the pay or receive leg in lieu of exchanging funds for a broker fee or some other component of the transaction, the SEC staff has asserted that the fair value of the swap cannot be zero because the transaction involves multiple components.

- If the shortcut method has been inappropriately applied, the error must be quantified based on the hedging relationship being disqualified for the applicable periods (rather than quantifying the error for those periods using other "nonshortcut" methods for assessing fair value or cash flow hedge effectiveness).

At the December 2006 National Conference on Current SEC and PCAOB Developments, the SEC staff provided the following examples of situations where application of the shortcut method is not appropriate:

- *Hedges of trust preferred securities with an interest deferral feature with an interest rate swap with a "mirror" interest deferral option*: The SEC staff believes that the ability to defer the payment of interest is not typical of the simple debt instruments that the FASB had in mind when the criteria for the shortcut method were developed, and such a feature would invalidate the assumption of no ineffectiveness in the hedge relationship.

- *A debtor's cash flow hedge of variable-rate debt in which the debtor holds an option to call the debt at par at the interest reset date*: In this hedging relationship, companies generally want to avoid having a mirror image call option in the swap, because they are hedging forecasted cash flows that are they are asserting are probable of occurring, as opposed to the value of the embedded call option. The SEC staff disagrees with the argument that the debt instrument would not be considered prepayable because the debt instrument is essentially callable at fair value. The SEC believes the call price for the debt at the reset date is not adjusted for changes in credit sector spreads and changes in the debtors' creditworthiness, the call price would not be fair value, and the debt would in fact be considered prepayable.

The SEC staff noted that in both of these situations, it is quite possible that the hedging relationships will be highly effective with a small amount of ineffectiveness under a full effectiveness assessment, but application of the shortcut method is not appropriate. Furthermore, in instances where a company has inappropriately applied the shortcut method or assumed there is no ineffectiveness in a relationship, the SEC staff has objected to quantifying the amount of the error as the ineffectiveness that would have been recognized had a full assessment of hedge effectiveness been completed. Rather, an erroneous assumption that there is no ineffectiveness in a hedging relationship precludes hedge accounting for the applicable hedge period. (Speech by Mark Northan, Professional Accounting Fellow, Office of the Chief Accountant of the SEC at the 2005 AIPCA National Conference on SEC and PCAOB Developments, and speech by Timothy S. Kviz, Professional Accounting Fellow, Office of the Chief Accountant of the SEC at the 2006 AICPA National Conference on SEC and PCAOB Developments)

In addition, similar views on the application of the shortcut method are expressed in the SEC's Current Accounting and Disclosure Issues in the Division of Corporation Finance (November 30, 2006). It discusses that in some instances registrants assumed that they did not need to assess or measure ineffectiveness because they had met the "spirit" of the shortcut method. Consistent with the guidance in DIG Issue E4, the SEC staff does not believe that the shortcut criteria have a "spirit" or a principle that can be met without strictly complying with the stated requirements.

Reasons That A Transaction Might Not Qualify for the Shortcut

- The swap was previously designated as a hedge of an asset or liability that was sold, extinguished or prepaid, and the remaining swap does not precisely match any of the entity's assets or liabilities

- The swap is not based on a benchmark rate

- The swap does not have a fair value of zero, perhaps because it is being redesignated, or perhaps because it was acquired in a business combination

- It is not feasible to obtain a swap with precisely matching prepayment terms (such as to offset a prepayable mortgage)

Meaning of the term *prepayable*   In the context of FAS-133, par. 68(d), a debt instrument is considered prepayable when one party to the contract has the right to cause the payment of principal prior to the scheduled payment dates at an amount that is an economic advantage related to changes in the benchmark interest rate. For example, a fixed-rate debt instrument with a call option that permits the debt instrument to be called for a fixed amount (for example, at par or at a stated premium above par) would be considered prepayable.

The following types of contractual provisions do not render a debt "prepayable" for the purpose of applying the shortcut method:

- A right to cause a contract to be prepaid at its then fair value.
- A right to cause prepayment of the debt only upon the occurrence of an event related to the deterioration of the debtor's credit, violation of a debt covenant, or a debt restructuring.
- A right to cause prepayment of the debt contingent upon the occurrence of a specific event that is unrelated to changes in interest rates or any other market variable is beyond the control of the debtor or creditor, and is not probable of occurring at the time of debt issuance. (DIG E-6)

Hedging portfolios of similar assets or liabilities Portfolios of similar assets or similar liabilities may qualify for the shortcut method only if:

- The assets or liabilities are considered similar under paragraph 21(a);
- The aggregate principal (or proportion thereof) of the portfolio matches the notional amount of the swap; *and*
- All of the other conditions for the shortcut are met for every asset or liability comprising the portfolio.

A portfolio cannot qualify for the shortcut if it contains an asset or liability that would not qualify for the shortcut in its own right. (DIG E-10)

Continuing the shortcut method for swaps acquired in a business combination DIG Issue E-15 precludes the use of the shortcut method for swaps acquired in a business combination, except in the unlikely circumstance that the swap had a fair value of zero upon acquisition (paragraph 68(b)).

Required or Voluntary Termination of a Fair Value Hedge

An entity is required to discontinue hedge accounting prospectively in any of the following circumstances:

- The hedging relationship no longer meets one or more of the qualifying criteria for fair value hedge accounting, for example, the hedge is no longer expected to be highly effective.
- The entity elects to remove the designation of the fair value hedge.
- The derivative expires or is sold, terminated, or exercised.

In those circumstances, the entity may elect to designate prospectively a new qualifying derivative to hedge the same item or, in the first two circumstances, the entity may redesignate the existing derivative as a hedge of a different hedged item (in a fair value hedge or a cash flow hedge), provided that all of the qualifying conditions are met. (FAS-133, par. 25)

If, in the current period, the hedging relationship is not considered highly effective in accordance with paragraph 20(b), the entity should recognize the adjustment of the carrying amount of the hedged item through the earlier of:

- The last date on which compliance with the effectiveness criterion was established or
- The date on which an identifiable event or change in circumstances caused the hedging relationship to fail the effectiveness criterion.

If a fair value hedge of a firm commitment is discontinued because the hedged item no longer meets the definition of a firm commitment, the entity should derecognize any asset or liability previously recognized through fair value hedge accounting and recognize a corresponding loss or gain currently in earnings. (FAS-133, par. 26)

Assessing Hedged Items for Impairment

When an asset or liability has been designated as the hedged item in a fair value hedge, any applicable GAAP that requires an assessment of impairment for that type of asset or for recognizing an increased obligation for that type of liability continues to apply. However, those impairment requirements should be applied *after* the carrying amount of the hedged asset or liability has been adjusted for changes attributable to the risk being hedged, according to FAS-133.

For example, if a debt instrument had been designated as the hedged item in a fair value hedge in prior periods, and that debt instrument undergoes a troubled debt restructuring involving a transfer of assets as a full settlement, the debtor would measure the gain on restructuring as the difference between the fair value of the assets transferred to the creditor and the carrying amount of the payable *including* any adjustments from fair value hedge accounting. Chapter 11, "Extinguishments of Debt," discusses the debtor's accounting for a troubled debt restructuring in more detail.

A derivative is an asset or liability in its own right, and should not be considered in assessing or measuring impairment of the hedged item. (FAS-133, par. 27)

☛ **PRACTICE POINTER:** When the recorded investment of a loan has been adjusted under fair value hedge accounting, the effective rate is the discount rate that equates the present value of the loan's future cash flows with that adjusted recorded investment. Therefore, impaired loans that are measured using the present value of expected future cash flows under FAS-114 should be discounted using the *new* effective rate (based on the adjusted recorded investment) rather than the original effective rate. (DIG F-4)

Illustrations 14-1 through 14-5 provide examples of the accounting for common fair value hedges.

CASH FLOW HEDGES

An entity may designate a derivative as hedging the exposure to variability in expected future cash flows in a transaction, subject to the limitations discussed below.

Common Cash Flow Hedging Strategies

- Hedge of interest rate risk on a variable-rate debt instrument (asset or liability)
- Hedge of interest rate risk on the anticipated rollover of commercial paper or certificates of deposit
- Hedge of foreign currency risk and interest rate risk on a debt instrument
- Locking in the interest rate of a forecasted issuance of debt
- Locking in the price on a forecasted sale or purchase of goods (including currency risk)
- Locking in the price on a forecasted sale or purchase of an investment (including currency risk)

☞ **PRACTICE POINTER:** For purposes of this chapter, the term "hedged item" in a cash flow hedge includes both (1) the variable component of a contract or recognized asset or liability and (2) a forecasted transaction whose terms have not yet been agreed upon.

Documentation

To qualify for cash flow hedge accounting, an entity must document all of the following information at the inception of the hedging relationship (FAS-133, par. 28(a)(2) unless noted):

- All of the documentation requirements mentioned in the "Common Hedge Criteria" section, including: identification of the hedging instrument, the hedged transaction, the risk being hedged, and the method to be used to assess and measure effectiveness (and ineffectiveness).

- The date on or period within which the forecasted transaction is expected to occur. The period may be specified as a range of time, such as the first issuance of fixed-rate debt that occurs in the next year, or payments within the five-year contract on Project X, as long as the designation is specific enough so that when a transaction occurs, it is clear whether that transaction is the hedged transaction. (DIG G-16)

- For hedges of foreign currency exchange risk, the exact amount of foreign currency being hedged.

- For hedges of other risks, the quantity of the forecasted transaction (i.e., the number of items or units of measure) encompassed by the hedged forecasted transaction. If a forecasted sale or purchase is being hedged for price risk, the hedged transaction cannot be specified solely in terms of expected currency amounts (e.g., $100 worth of gold), nor can it be specified as a percentage of sales or purchases during a period.

- The method that will be used to reclassify amounts out of other comprehensive income (OCI) into earnings (as discussed later in this section).

☛ **PRACTICE POINTER:** The description of the hedged item should be sufficiently detailed so that when a transaction occurs, it is clear whether that transaction is the *hedged* transaction. For example, a hedged transaction could be identified as the sale of either the first 15,000 units of a Product Z sold during a specified three-month period or the first 5,000 units of Product Z sold in each of three specific months, but it could not be identified as the sale of the last 15,000 units of Product Z sold during a three-month period (because the last 15,000 units cannot be identified as they occur, but only after the period has ended). (FAS-133, par. 28(a))

☛ **PRACTICE POINTER:** Because some types of forecasted transactions represent transactions that a company plans to enter into, not necessarily binding agreements, the documentation requirements are strict. These requirements are not busy work for the back office—if an entity does not comply with all of these requirements at the inception of the transaction, hedge accounting is not allowed.

It is critical that the people buying and selling derivatives understand these requirements and have the support to comply with them. To the extent possible, the documentation requirements should be incorporated into a company's transaction processing systems to minimize unintended financial reporting consequences.

Qualifications for Cash Flow Hedge Accounting

In addition to the common hedging criteria discussed in the first section, FAS-133 requires that additional criteria be met in a cash flow hedge.

Types of Hedged Items

In a cash flow hedge, the hedged item may be an enforceable contract, a recognized asset or liability, or a forecasted (noncontractual) transaction that presents an exposure to changes in cash flow attributable to the hedged risk that could affect reported earnings. (FAS-133, par. 29(c)) Generally, this means that the hedged item must have a variable rate or price, either because the terms of the contract are explicitly variable or because the price has not yet been agreed upon.

In addition, the hedged item must have the following characteristics:

- The hedged item involves an unrelated party (except for certain foreign currency transactions, which are discussed later in this chapter) (FAS-133, par. 29(c))
- The forecasted transaction must be *probable* of occurring. (FAS-133, par. 29(b))

☛ **PRACTICE POINTER:** The transaction must be probable of occurring without regard to the type of derivative being used to hedge the transaction. For example, if an entity designates an option as a hedge of a forecasted purchase of an item, the forecasted purchase must be probable of occurring even if the option expires worthless. Said another way, the forecasted transaction cannot be contingent upon an event or circumstance unless it is probable that that event will occur or circumstance will exist. (DIG G-14)

☛ **PRACTICE POINTER:** For a cash flow hedge involving an existing asset or liability, such as a variable-rate loan, the forecasted transaction is the payment of interest and the *amount* is subject to change. The entity must conclude that the payment of interest is probable. The entity does *not* need to conclude that it is probable that the amount of interest *will change*. However, the entity must select a derivative that will be highly effective in offsetting those changes if and when they occur. (DIG G-4)

Risks Being Hedged

FAS-133 permits hedges of the entire change in cash flow of a qualifying hedged item or of only discrete risks, as discussed below.

Financial instruments If the hedged transaction is the forecasted purchase or sale of a financial asset or liability other than a held-to-maturity security (or the interest payments on that financial asset or liability) or the variable cash flows of an existing financial asset or liability, the designated risk being hedged must be either:

- The risk of overall changes in the cash flows related to the asset or liability, such as those relating to all changes in the purchase price or sales price *or*
- The risk of changes in its cash flows attributable to one or more of the following (from par. 29(h), unless otherwise noted):
  — The risk of changes in its cash flows attributable to changes in the designated benchmark interest rate (referred to as interest rate risk). Prepayment risk is a component of interest rate risk and may not be separately hedged in a cash flow hedge. The use of different benchmark interest rates for similar hedges should be rare and must be justified.
  — The risk of changes in the functional-currency-equivalent cash flows attributable to changes in the related foreign currency exchange rates (referred to as foreign exchange risk) (discussed later in this chapter).
  — The risk of changes in cash flows attributable to default, changes in the obligor's creditworthiness, and changes in the spread over the benchmark interest rate with respect to the hedged item's credit sector at inception of the hedge (referred to as credit risk).

Variable interest rates If the designated risk being hedged is interest rate risk (the benchmark interest rate), the cash flows of the hedged transaction must be explicitly based on the benchmark rate. However, an asset or liability indexed to a nonbenchmark rate, such as prime, may qualify for hedge accounting if the designated risk is the risk of overall changes in the hedged cash flows, provided that the other criteria for a cash flow hedge have been met. Ordinarily, that would mean that the derivative is also indexed to that nonbenchmark rate. (FAS-133, par. 29(h))

☛ **PRACTICE POINTER:** Interest cash flows that are not explicitly based on any index (e.g., auction rate notes that have an interest rate that is determined through a Dutch auction process) are not based on a benchmark rate. Therefore, the designated risk being hedged in an auction rate note cannot be interest rate risk. However, the designated risk may be the risk of overall changes in cash flows. (DIG G-26)

Held-to-maturity debt securities If the hedged item is a variable-rate debt security classified as held-to-maturity under FAS-115, the risk being hedged *may not* be the risk of changes in cash flow attributable to interest rate risk. However, credit risk, foreign currency risk or both may be hedged. (FAS-133, par. 29(e))

Hedging stock compensation liabilities Generally, stock compensation transactions do not qualify for hedge accounting because they are recorded in the issuing company's balance sheet as a component of equity. (FAS-133, pars. 21(c) and 29(f)) However, certain types of stock compensation are recorded as liabilities rather than equity, including stock appreciation rights (SARs). An SAR is an award entitling employees to receive cash, stock, or a combination of cash and stock for any amount in excess of the market value of a stated number of shares of the employer's stock over a stated price. An SAR generally has vesting provisions, for example, *pro-rata* vesting over a specified service period. Under FAS-123(R), for public companies, a cash-settled SAR is classified as a liability and reported at fair value at each reporting period through the date of settlement. Compensation cost is recognized over the service period for the portion of the SAR that is not yet vested based on changes in fair value during the period. Accordingly, compensation cost will vary depending upon the change in the fair value of the SAR.

To the extent that vesting is probable, an SAR may be designated as the hedged item in a cash flow hedge of changes in the future obligations associated with unrecognized, nonvested SARs. Such an award could be hedged with cash-settled purchased call options on the company's stock. Presumably, hedge effectiveness would be assessed based on changes in the entire value of the purchased call option designated as the hedging instrument. Changes in fair value of the hedging instrument would be recorded in OCI and would be reclassified in earnings concurrent with the recognition in earnings of compensation cost on the SAR related to changes in the fair value occurring during the hedge period. (DIG G-1)

> ☞ **PRACTICE POINTER:** For nonpublic companies, FAS-123(R) provides a choice for measuring cash-settled SARs at either fair value or based on changes in the issuing company's stock price (intrinsic value). However, DIG Issue G-1 does *not* permit recognizing changes in the intrinsic value of the purchased call option designated as the hedging instrument in OCI. Therefore, nonpublic companies should carefully consider the impact of the SAR's time value in designating and assessing the effectiveness of a cash flow hedge as described in DIG Issue G-1 if a cash-settled SAR designated as the hedged item will continue to be measured based on intrinsic value.

Nonfinancial assets If the hedged transaction is the forecasted purchase or sale of a nonfinancial asset, the designated risk being hedged may be either:

- The risk of changes in the functional-currency-equivalent cash flows attributable to changes in the related foreign currency exchange rates *or*

- The risk of changes in the cash flows relating to all changes in the purchase price or sales price of the asset reflecting its actual location if a physical asset (regardless of whether the price and cash flows are stated in a foreign currency). The designated risk may *not* be the risk of changes in the cash flows of a major ingredient or a similar asset in a different location. (FAS-133, par. 29(g))

> ☛ **PRACTICE POINTER:** For example, if an entity wanted to hedge the exposure to changes in the cash flows relating to the purchase of its bronze bar inventory with a copper derivative, it would have to be able to conclude that the copper derivative was highly effective in offsetting *all* of the changes in the purchase price of the bronze.

Hedging Groups of Forecasted Transactions

A group of individual transactions may be designated as the hedged item in a cash flow hedge if those individual transactions share the same risk exposure for which they are designated as being hedged. A forecasted purchase and a forecasted sale cannot be included in the same group of individual transactions, even if they have the same underlying. (FAS-133, par. 29(a))

> ☛ **PRACTICE POINTER:** Complex derivatives, such as an oil-linked interest rate cap, cannot be designated as a hedge of the difference between an interest rate exposure and sales of oil because those two transactions do not share the same risk exposure. Likewise, an entity could not define its hedged risk as the risk of changes in cash flows attributable to one variable (such as interest rate risk) for only those periods when a variable based on a different risk (e.g., the price of oil) is above or below a specified level. (DIG G-22)

Hedge of a portfolio of variable-rate loans   Changes in the components of a pool of loans (for example, from prepayment, sale, or default) make the variable cash flows on the departing loan no longer probable of occurring. Therefore, to achieve cash flow hedge accounting for a pool of loans, without constantly having to rejigger the components of the hedge, it is critical that the hedging relationship be documented in a way that is not dependent on the specific loans comprising the pool. (Rather, specific cash flows are designated.) Under the "first-payments-received" technique, changing the composition of the group of benchmark-floating-rate, interest-bearing financial assets due to repayment activity is permissible and does not automatically result in the discontinuation, in whole or part, of the original cash flow hedging relationship. For example, an entity could document its strategy as using a $100 million received-fixed, pay-LIBOR interest rate swap to hedge the first LIBOR-based interest payments received during each four-week period that begins one week before each quarterly due date for the next three years that, in the aggregate for each quarter, are interest payments on $100 million principal of its then existing LIBOR-indexed floating-rate loans.

If, instead, a company were to designate the same swap as a hedge of $100 million principal of specific LIBOR-indexed floating-rate loans, the mechanics are much more laborious if and when changes in the pool occur. For example, every time a member loan was removed, the deferred hedging gain or loss relating to that loan would have to be dealt with according to paragraph 33, the swap would have to be dedesignated and designated anew to the new group of loans (including a replacement loan), and so on. Patterns of changes in the underlying pool would also discredit the entity's ability to accurately forecast transactions and could affect the entity's ability to use cash flow hedge accounting for similar transactions in the future. (DIG G-13)

> **OBSERVATION:** The two methods have essentially the same effect. However, the first-payments-received method described above minimizes the bookkeeping requirements. Entities are not permitted to hedge a "generic" notional amount of loans to deal with dynamic portfolios—every hedged cash flow must relate to a *specific* transaction.

The "first-payments-received" technique also may be used for identifying the hedged forecasted transactions in a cash flow hedge of the variable prime-rate-based or other variable non-benchmark-rate-based interest receipts for a rolling portfolio of prepayable interest-bearing financial assets. Therefore, an entity that wishes to hedge the variability in interest cash flows related to a portfolio of prepayable prime-rate loans (or a portfolio of loans based on other variable rate indices that are not the benchmark interest rate as defined by FAS-133) should do so consistent with the methods described above for a hedge of a portfolio of LIBOR-based loans. Because of limitations in FAS-133, however, the shortcut method may not be applied to such hedges. All other conditions for cash flow hedge accounting must be satisfied. (DIG G-25)

> **OBSERVATION:** Cross-hedges may not qualify for the cash flow hedging technique described above if it cannot be asserted at the inception of the hedging relationship that the hedge is expected to be highly effective in offsetting the overall changes in designated cash flows. If it is determined that hedge accounting may be applied, then any difference between the changes in each

of the variable rates for the relevant hedge period would be recognized immediately in earnings to the extent the difference arose from an overhedge.

Hedges of commercial paper programs and certificates of deposit
Commercial paper and certificates of deposit typically are short-term instruments with explicit or implicit fixed rates. Entities issuing such instruments often plan to replace them with similar short-term borrowings as they mature, with fixed rates based on current market conditions (a "roll-over strategy"). When viewed as a longer-term financing program, the planned issuance of short-term borrowings at fixed rates based on then-current market conditions exposes an entity to cash flow risk, even though actual borrowings under the program may bear a fixed rate.

Provided that the entity meets all of the other cash flow hedging criteria, an entity may hedge the risk of *changes* in either (a) the fixed-rate coupon payments (or the interest element of the final cash flow if interest is paid only at maturity) or (b) the total proceeds attributable to changes in the benchmark interest rate related to the forecasted issuance of fixed-rate debt. The derivative used to hedge either of these risks must provide offsetting cash flows in order for the hedging relationship to be considered effective. (DIG G-19)

> ☞ **PRACTICE POINTER:**   Example 8 of FAS-133 (paragraphs 153–161) provides an example of a commercial paper program that is terminated midstream and replaced with long-term debt (in one scenario, fixed rate, and in another scenario, floating rate). The example also illustrates the use of offsetting swaps and the designation of two swaps together as a hedge of one debt instrument.

Hedging Instruments

There are a couple of interesting interpretations involving the use of derivatives in cash flow hedges.

Basis swaps   A basis swap is an exchange of cash flows based on a notional amount and two different variable rates. Basis swaps do not reduce the variability of cash flows; they simply change the nature of the variability. As such, a basis swap generally would not be highly effective in *offsetting* the variability in the cash flows of a single asset or liability. However, FAS-133 contains an exception that allows a basis swap to be designated as hedging both an existing asset (or group of similar assets) with variable cash flows and an existing liability (or group of similar liabilities) with variable cash flows if one leg of an interest rate swap has the *same* basis as the interest receipts for the designated asset and the other leg of the swap has the *same* basis as the interest payments for the designated liability. In this narrow situation, variable-rate assets and variable-rate liabilities may be included in the same "group" of hedged items. (FAS-133, par. 28(d))

> **OBSERVATION:** Paragraph 28(d) is a narrow exception to paragraphs 18 (which prohibits separating a derivative into parts), 28 (b), 29(a), and 29(h)(2) and it should not be applied by analogy to other situations. (All other cash flow hedge criteria must be met.)

Derivatives that involve physical settlements ("all-in-one hedges")
A cash flow hedge may involve the forecasted purchase or sale of a financial or nonfinancial asset—for example, the forecasted purchase of inventory. Derivatives are often used to "lock-in" the prices of such transactions. With a cash-settled derivative, the entity would typically (1) first close out the derivative for the net cash amount, then (2) buy (or sell) the item from (or to) a different party. However, some derivatives include provisions that require or permit delivery of the underlying asset, so that the entity may settle the derivative and the forecasted transaction in one step—by making (or taking) delivery of the underlying asset in exchange for the agreed upon amount of cash. Derivatives involving physical delivery of the underlying may be used in cash flow hedges, provided that all of the other conditions for cash flow hedge accounting have been met. (DIG G-2)

Ongoing Expectation of Effectiveness

Both at inception of the hedge and on an ongoing basis, the derivative must be expected to be highly effective in achieving offsetting cash flows attributable to the hedged risk during the term of the hedge (except for qualifying basis swaps, as discussed previously). All assessments of effectiveness should be consistent with the documented risk management strategy for that particular hedging relationship. (FAS-133, par. 28(b))

Assessing changes in creditworthiness in a cash flow hedge   In order to be highly effective in offsetting the variability of cash flows, the hedging entity must believe that the counterparty to the derivative is creditworthy and will make any contractually required payments required by the derivative instrument on time. In determining whether the risk of default has increased, the entity should also consider the effect of any available collateral or financial guarantees. When effectiveness is measured using a method that recognizes all changes in the fair value of a derivative, the effect of changes in creditworthiness would generally be recognized immediately (except perhaps in an underhedge). An entity must also assess the credit worthiness of the counterparty to the hedged forecasted transaction, if applicable, in determining whether the *forecasted transaction* is probable of occurring, particularly if the hedged transaction involves variable payments pursuant to a contractual obligation of the counterparty (for example, the debtor on a variable-rate loan). (DIG G-10)

Assuming no ineffectiveness when critical terms match   If at the inception of a cash flow hedging relationship, the critical terms of the derivative and the hedged forecasted transaction are the same, the entity can conclude that there is no ineffectiveness to be recorded. Subsequent assessments should be performed by verifying and documenting whether the critical terms of the hedging instrument and the forecasted transaction have changed during the period in review. Included in this assessment is whether the risk of default has increased with the counterparty to the derivative.

If there are no such changes in the critical terms, the entity may conclude that there is no ineffectiveness to be recorded. In that case, the entire change in fair value of the derivative would be deferred in OCI. However, if the critical terms of the derivative or the hedged forecasted transaction have changed (or if default risk has increased), the entity must measure the amount of ineffectiveness that must be recorded currently in earnings using an appropriate method (discussed later in this section). In addition, the entity must assess whether the hedging relationship is expected to continue to be highly effective using its established methodology. (DIG G-9)

FAS-133 states that an entity may assume that a hedge of a forecasted purchase of a commodity with a forward contract will be highly effective and that there will be no ineffectiveness to be recognized in earnings when all of the following conditions are met:

- The forward contract is for purchase of the same quantity of the same commodity at the same time and location as the hedged forecasted purchase.
- The fair value of the forward contract at inception is zero.
- The change in expected cash flows on the forecasted transaction is based on the forward price for the commodity. (FAS-133, par. 65)

> **SEC REGISTRANT ALERT:**   At the December 2006 National Conference on Current SEC and PCAOB Developments, the SEC staff discussed the "critical terms match" approach of assessing hedge effectiveness and indicated that it is inappropriate to simply assume there is no ineffectiveness in a hedging relationship while ignoring known sources of variability that are not perfectly matched. The SEC staff provided the following examples not addressed in paragraph 65 of FAS-133 which the critical terms match approach would likely not be appropriate:
>
> - A fair value hedge of an interest rate exposure using an interest rate swap, where the credit worthiness of the two counterparties might differ, thereby creating ineffectiveness.

- A relationship in which the settlement date of the forecasted transaction and the hedging instrument differed by several days. Even though the settlement dates differ by only a few days, the differences would create ineffectiveness that should be measured and recognized.

(Speech by Timothy S. Kviz, Professional Accounting Fellow, Office of the Chief Accountant, SEC at the December 2006 National Conference on Current SEC and PCAOB Developments)

At the March 14, 2007 EITF meeting, the SEC staff indicated that in instances where registrants have assumed no ineffectiveness in a hedging relationship (based on the "critical terms match" notion) when the terms of the hedging derivative and the hedged transaction do not exactly match, but the other provisions of paragraph 65 were satisfied, the SEC expects registrants to evaluate and support the reasonableness of the original conclusion that the terms of the hedge and the hedged item matched and perform a quantitative assessment to confirm that the relationship was highly effective and that any ineffectiveness was de minimis.

Continued application of hedge accounting may be acceptable if there was a reasonable basis to assert that (a) the terms matched, (b) the relationship was highly effective, and (c) any ineffectiveness was de minimis. However, if no ineffectiveness was assumed in a hedging relationship, but there was not a reasonable basis to assert (a) that the terms matched, (b) that the relationships were not highly effective, or (c) that the ineffectiveness was not de minimis, the SEC staff member indicated that registrants may want to discuss the matter with the SEC's Office of the Chief Accountant.

Assuming no ineffectiveness for certain options Late in the game, the FASB staff issued a favorable interpretation involving the use of certain options in static cash flow hedging strategies, including forecasted purchases and sales of financial instruments and nonfinancial assets and hedges of variable-rate instruments with one-sided risks, or risks within a specified range. DIG Issue E-19 provides that an entity may assess effectiveness by comparing the strike price of the option with the forward price of the hedged item, on an undiscounted basis. DIG Issue G-20 indicates that when a purchased option or a zero-cost collar is designated as hedging the variability of a price above a specific level or within a range and all of the following conditions exist, the hedge may be considered perfectly effective and the entire change in value of the option may be deferred in OCI until the hedged transaction occurs:

- The critical terms of the purchased option or collar (including the notional amount, underlying and maturity date) completely match the terms of the forecasted transaction.

- For a purchased option, the strike price matches the specified level above which the entity's exposure is being hedged. For a collar, the strike prices match the specified levels within which the entity's exposure is being hedged.
- The option or collar's cash flows at maturity completely offset the change in the hedged transaction's cash flows attributable to the risk being hedged. (This essentially means that the option should not be in the money at issuance.)
- The option can be exercised only on its contractual maturity (a European-style option). (If the option is terminated early or dedesignated, any gain deferred in OCI should be recognized in accordance with paragraphs 32–33 of FAS-133.)

☛ **PRACTICE POINTER:** This "shortcut" for options does *not* apply to written options and it does *not* apply to fair value hedges. In cash flow hedges that do not meet all of these conditions, effectiveness must be assessed in accordance with the "hypothetical perfect option method" described in Exhibit 14-5.

OBSERVATION: This interpretation generally avoids recognizing the change in time value of an option in earnings until the hedged transaction occurs. However, paragraph 31 of FAS-133 requires earlier recognition of deferred losses in certain situations (discussed later in this section). DIG Issue G-20 stipulates that entities must document compliance with every condition above, or hedge accounting is not permitted.

Assessing effectiveness when critical terms do not match   When the critical terms of a cash flow hedging relationship do not match, an entity must have the expectation, both at inception and ongoing, that the relationship will be highly effective at achieving offsetting cash flows. Entities must use methods and data that are reasonable under the circumstances to substantiate that expectation, including historical correlation, regression analysis, and other relevant information. Methods used to *measure* ineffectiveness are discussed in the next section.

Assessing effectiveness with options   When a combination of options (deemed to be a net purchased option) is used as the hedging instrument and the effectiveness of the hedge will be assessed based only on changes in intrinsic value, the entity may document that it will only assess changes in the underlying that could cause changes in the intrinsic value of the options (that it, it may exclude ranges of changes in the underlying for which there *is no change* in the hedging instrument's intrinsic value). An entity may not exclude changes in intrinsic value that actually occur. Changes in the fair value of the option attributable to time value (and any other source of ineffectiveness) would be recognized immediately in earnings. (DIG G-15 and DIG G-11)

Accounting for Cash Flow Hedges

Generally, the *effective* portion of the gain or loss on a derivative designated as a cash flow hedge is initially deferred and reported in other comprehensive income (OCI), a balance sheet account in the equity section. The ineffective portion (and any time value excluded from the effectiveness test) is reported currently in earnings. Deferred cash flow hedge gains and losses should be reclassified out of OCI into earnings in the same period(s) during which the hedged forecasted transaction affects earnings. (FAS-133, pars. 30 and 31)

The amount deferred in OCI cannot exceed the cumulative change in cash flows relating to the hedged item. The balance in OCI relating to each effective hedging relationship should be adjusted to reflect the lower of A or B, in absolute dollars:

A. The cumulative gain or loss on the **derivative** from inception of the hedge less (a) any excluded component and (b) any gains or losses already reclassified into earnings

B. The amount necessary to offset the cumulative change in the expected future cash flows on the **hedged item** less any derivative gains or losses already reclassified into earnings

Any necessary adjustment should be recorded in earnings. (FAS-133, par. 30(b)) If an entity uses the methods described in Exhibit 14-5 below, the amount in OCI will automatically comply with this limitation. Paragraphs 140–143 of FAS-133 illustrate the mechanics of this approach for other situations.

> ☞ **PRACTICE POINTER:** In summary, an overhedge results in an immediate earnings charge, but an underhedge does not.
>
> **OBSERVATION:** Gains and losses on derivatives are real—all of them should be recorded. But the gains and losses on forecasted transactions are simply estimates of probable transactions—the FASB allowed these "manufactured" gains and losses to be recognized only to the extent that they offset a derivative gain or loss, but not beyond that point.

Methods of Measuring Effectiveness

DIG Issue G-7 describes three methods of measuring the effectiveness of cash flow hedges involving variable-rate instruments and interest rate swaps. The guidance in DIG Issue G-7 applies to cash flow hedges of both existing assets and liabilities with variable cash flows, and to forecasted acquisitions or issuances of debt instruments with variable interest payments.

> **SEC REGISTRANT ALERT:** The SEC staff expressed the view that the assumption of no ineffectiveness under the change in variable cash flows method of in DIG Issue G7 would not be appropriate for a relationship involving variable-rate debt and an interest rate swap if the interest payment dates on the debt and the swap do not match. The difference in payment dates represents a basis difference that creates ineffectiveness, and a lack of basis differences is one of the criteria for assuming no ineffectiveness under the change in variable cash flows method. (Speech by Timothy S. Kviz, Professional Accounting Fellow, Office of the Chief Accountant of the SEC at the December 2006 AICPA National Conference on SEC and PCAOB Developments)

In addition, DIG Issue G-20 provides guidance on assessing and measuring effectiveness for purchased options used in cash flow hedges. Exhibit 14-5 summarizes the guidance applicable to situations that do not qualify for either the interest rate swap shortcut or the purchased option "shortcut" (DIG G-20).

EXHIBIT 14-5
METHODS OF MEASURING EFFECTIVENESS
FOR CASH FLOW HEDGES

Description of Method	Calculation	Earnings Effect	Balance in OCI*	Limitations	Simplifying Tips
Method 1: Comparing the Change in Variable Cash Flows (DIG G-7)					
Compare the floating-rate leg of the swap and the floating-rate on the hedged item	Compare the PV of the cumulative change in expected cash flows (PVECF) on (1) the swap and (2) the debt, both calculated using the swap rate.	Excess of PVECF on swap over PVECF on debt. (No amount is recognized in an underhedge.)	FV of swap less any amount recognized in earnings.	May only be used when the swap has a fair value at or near zero upon designation. Must consider risk of default by swap counter-party.	No ineffectiveness when:• Same index • Same reset dates • No basis differences (such as caps or floors) • Probable that obligor will not default.
Method 2A: Hypothetical Perfect Swap Method (DIG G-7)					
Construct a "hypothetical perfect swap" that would qualify for the	Compare the change in fair value of (1) the actual swap with	Excess of cumulative change in fair value of (1) the actual	The lesser of the cumulative change in the actual swap	Must consider risk of default by swap counterparty.	See list of conditions for the swap shortcut later

Description of Method	Calculation	Earnings Effect	Balance in OCI*	Limitations	Simplifying Tips
shortcut (except the rate could be non-benchmark)†	(2) the hypothetical swap.	swap over (2) the hypothetical swap. (No amount is recognized in an under-hedge.)	or the hypothetical swap.		in this section.

Method 2B: Hypothetical Perfect Option Method (DIG G-20)

Description of Method	Calculation	Earnings Effect	Balance in OCI*	Limitations	Simplifying Tips
Construct a "hypothetical perfect option" that would qualify for the option short-cut	Compare the change in fair value of (1) the actual option with (2) the hypothetical option.	Excess of cumulative change in fair value of (1) the actual option over (2) the hypothetical option. (No amount is recognized in an under-hedge.)	The lesser of the cumulative change in the actual option or the hypothetical option.	Must consider risk of default by option counterparty.	See list of conditions for option short-cut earlier in this section.

Method 3: Change in Fair Value Method (DIG G-7)

Description of Method	Calculation	Earnings Effect	Balance in OCI*	Limitations	Simplifying Tips
Compare change in fair value of actual derivative with change in expected cash flows	Compare the cumulative change in fair value of the swap with the cumulative change in expected cash flows on the hedged item, both calculated using the swap rate.	Excess of cumulative change in fair value of (1) the actual swap over (2) the change in PV on the debt. (No amount is recognized in an under-hedge.)	The lesser of the cumulative change in FV of the swap or the cumulative change in the PV of the cash flows on the debt.	Must consider risk of default by swap counterparty.	

---

† DIG Issue G-21 describes a fact pattern where a swap hedging a prepayable loan would not need to have an offsetting mirror "option."

* These methods automatically comply with paragraph 30, which imposes certain limitations on the amount of derivative gain or loss that may be deferred.

Reclassifying Amounts from OCI

Generally, amounts are reclassified out of OCI when the hedged transaction results in an earnings effect. The entity must document upfront how amounts will be reclassified into earnings (that is, what types of earnings events apply to that type of hedged item and when they will occur). Exhibit 14-6 highlights the typical methods of recognizing the income effects on some common cash flow hedge transactions.

EXHIBIT 14-6
METHODS OF RECLASSIFYING AMOUNTS OUT OF
OCI INTO EARNINGS

Nature of Qualifying Hedged Item	Typical Method of Reclassifying Amounts into Earnings*
Variable rate asset or liability	As interest is accrued on the asset or liability
Acquisition of a depreciable asset	Over the depreciable life of the acquired asset
Acquisition of an equity security (either nonmarketable or AFS)	When a gain or loss is recognized on the security, from sale or impairment
Acquisition of a debt security (not interest rate risk on a held-to-maturity security)	As interest is accrued on the security
Purchase of inventory	In the period that cost of goods sold is recognized
Forecasted issuance of debt	As interest expense is recognized
Sale of a loan or security	In the period that a gain or loss on sale is recognized
Sale of inventory	In the period that revenue is recognized

* Subject to the loss deferral measure discussed in paragraph 31 and impairment recognition of the hedged item.

Other Limitations on Amounts Deferred in OCI

If an entity expects at any time that continuing to defer a loss in OCI would lead to recognizing a net loss on the combination of the derivative and the hedged transaction (and related asset acquired or liability incurred) in one or more future periods, an amount should be reclassified immediately into earnings for the amount that is not expected to be recovered. For example, after a forecasted purchase of inventory occurs, if the sum of the cost basis of the inventory and a related deferred hedging loss in OCI exceeds the expected selling price of that inventory, an amount should be reversed out of OCI into earnings for the amount of the shortfall. (FAS-133, par. 31)

Interaction with impairment standards If, under other applicable GAAP, an impairment loss is recognized on an asset or an additional obligation is recognized on a liability to which a hedged forecasted transaction relates, any offsetting net gain related to that transaction in OCI should be reclassified immediately into earnings. Similarly, if a recovery is recognized on the asset or liability to which the forecasted transaction relates, any offsetting net loss that has been deferred in OCI should be reclassified immediately into earnings. (FAS-133, par. 35)

> **OBSERVATION:** Impairment losses and recoveries are considered an "earnings event" that triggers reclassification of any offsetting amounts out of OCI.

The Shortcut Method for Cash Flow Hedges

The FASB established a list of conditions that, if met, significantly simplify the accounting for interest rate swaps designated as hedging the interest rate risk of variable-rate debt instruments. If the conditions for the shortcut method are met, the transaction is accounted for as follows:

- The derivative is reported at fair value on the balance sheet.
- Changes in the fair value of the derivative are recorded in OCI.
- Interest is recognized using the fixed-rate on the swap plus any difference between the variable rate on the swap and debt instrument (adjusted for amortization of any premium or discount on the underlying debt instrument). (FAS-133, par. 132)

> **OBSERVATION:** Essentially, earnings are "plugged" with the amount necessary to create the desired fixed rate.

To qualify for the cash flow hedge accounting shortcut, the derivative and debt instrument must meet all of the following conditions:

> ☞ **PRACTICE POINTER:** Many of the conditions are the same as those required for the fair value shortcut, but there are also some significant differences. For ease of reference, all of the necessary conditions for the cash flow short cut are presented below; differences from the fair value requirements are highlighted in **bold.•**

The hedged item must be a recognized interest-bearing asset or liability.

- The notional amount of the swap matches the principal amount (or a proportion thereof) of the interest-bearing asset or liability or portfolio of similar assets or liabilities being hedged. (DIG E-10)

- During the term of the swap, all interest receipts or payments on the variable-rate asset or liability are designated as hedged, and no interest payments beyond the term of the swap are designated as hedged. (*Note:* The swap does not need to be for the entire term of the debt.)

- The repricing dates of the swap match those of the variable-rate asset or liability, including whether the variable rate will be applied prospectively or in arrears. (DIG E-16)

- The fair value of the swap is zero at the inception of the hedging relationship (except, if the swap is a compound instrument that contains a mirror-image option as described in 9 below: (a) if the implicit option premium is "paid" up front as an original issue premium or discount, the fair value of the mirror option and embedded option must be equivalent, or (b) if the implicit option premium is "paid" over time as an adjustment of the interest rate, the fair value of the mirror and embedded options must both be zero).

- The fixed rate on the swap is the same throughout the term of the hedge.

- The variable leg of the swap and the variable rate on the asset or liability are based on the same benchmark interest rate throughout the term and include the same spread, if any, throughout the term (for example, both rates are LIBOR-based, or both rates are Treasury-based, but one or both can be adjusted by a credit spread). Other nonbenchmark rates do not qualify, even if they match.

- The variable rate should not contain a cap or floor, unless the variable-rate asset or liability has a comparable cap or floor. (The cap (or floor) rates can differ by the amount of any spread.)

- The interest-bearing asset or liability is not prepayable (that is, able to be settled by either party prior to its scheduled maturity), unless the debt is prepayable solely due to an embedded call option and the hedging interest rate swap contains an embedded mirror-image call option. (For an interest-bearing asset or liability with an embedded put option, the hedging interest rate swap must contain an embedded mirror-image put option.)

- Any other terms in the interest-bearing financial instruments or interest rate swaps are typical of those instruments and do not invalidate the assumption of no ineffectiveness.

SEC REGISTRANT ALERT: The SEC staff has provided views regarding certain aspects of applying the shortcut method because of certain instances of misapplication of the method in practice. In addition, the FASB has under way a project to clarify existing guidance related to the application of the shortcut method. Refer to the SEC Registrant Alert in the section *The*

Shortcut Method for Fair Value Hedges earlier in this chapter for details.

☞ **PRACTICE POINTER:**   Operating (unrecognized) leases with variable cash flows and anticipated rollovers of short-term debt do not qualify for the shortcut method. They would have to be assessed for effectiveness using one of the methods specified under DIG Issue G-7. (DIG G-12)

Reasons That a Transaction Might Not Qualify for the Shortcut

- The variable interest rate on either the debt or the swap is not based on a benchmark rate

- The repricing dates on the swap do not match the repricing dates on the debt

- The swap was previously designated as a hedge of an asset or liability that was sold, extinguished or prepaid, and the remaining swap does not precisely match any of the entity's assets or liabilities

- The swap does not have a fair value of zero, perhaps because it is being redesignated, or perhaps because it was acquired in a business combination

- It is not feasible to obtain a swap with precisely matching prepayment terms (such as to offset a prepayable mortgage)

☞ **PRACTICE POINTER:**   The definition of "prepayable" discussed previously under the fair value interest rate swap shortcut also applies to the cash flow interest rate swap shortcut. Likewise, the concern expressed about swaps acquired in a business combination is equally applicable to the cash flow shortcut.

Hedging portfolios of similar variable-rate assets or liabilities Portfolios of similar variable-rate assets or similar liabilities may qualify for the shortcut method only if:

- The aggregate principal (or proportion thereof) of the portfolio matches the notional amount of the swap *and*

- All of the other conditions for the shortcut are met for every asset or liability comprising the portfolio.

For example, the repricing dates on the swap must be exactly the same as the repricing dates on the variable-rate assets or liabilities. (DIG E-10)

☞ **PRACTICE POINTER:**   For large institutions, it will be very difficult to amass large groups of loans and swaps that meet these precise requirements.

Required or Voluntary Termination of a Cash Flow Hedge

An entity is required to discontinue hedge accounting prospectively in any of the following circumstances:

- The hedging relationship no longer meets one or more of the qualifying criteria for cash flow hedge accounting, for example, the hedge is no longer expected to be highly effective.
- The entity elects to remove the designation of the cash flow hedge.
- The derivative expires or is sold, terminated, or exercised.

The entity may elect to designate prospectively a new qualifying derivative to hedge the same item or, in the first two circumstances, the entity may generally redesignate the existing derivative as a hedge of a different hedged item (in a cash flow hedge or a fair value hedge), provided that all of the qualifying conditions are met. (FAS-133, par. 32) However, if the counterparty to a derivative is experiencing financial difficulty, the derivative should no longer be designated in a hedging relationship.

When a cash flow hedge is discontinued, the net gain or loss should generally remain in OCI and be reclassified into earnings as specified in paragraph 31. However, the gain or loss should be recognized in earnings upon discontinuance when it is probable that the forecasted transaction will *not* occur:

- By the end of the originally specified time period (as documented at the inception of the hedging relationship) *or*
- Within an additional two-month period of time from that date.

In extenuating circumstances that are related to the nature of the forecasted transaction and are outside the control or influence of the reporting entity, the forecasted transaction may still be considered probable of occurring on a date that is beyond the additional two-month period of time. Such circumstances should be rare. (FAS-133, par. 33 and DIG G-3)

To summarize:

Probability of Transaction	*Treatment of Deferred Gain or Loss*
Probable will occur	Keep in OCI until transaction occurs
Possible will occur	Keep in OCI until transaction occurs
Probable will not occur	Reclassify into earnings

☛ **PRACTICE POINTER:** This is a one-way trip—once an amount has been released into earnings because it is probable that the forecasted transaction will not occur, an entity may *not* reassess the probabilities and reclassify amounts back into OCI. A pattern of reclassifying amounts into earnings because it is probable that the forecasted transaction will not occur will call into question an entity's ability to accurately forecast transactions and the propriety of applying hedge accounting to similar transactions in the future. (DIG G-3)

OBSERVATION: The provisions for discontinuing a cash flow hedge are designed to minimize the opportunities for "cherry-picking" gains and losses. Even if the entity changes its mind about hedging a transaction, the gain or loss must generally sit in OCI until the originally scheduled timeframe.

Changes in the terms of a forecasted transaction If a forecasted transaction becomes a firm commitment (other than through the derivative itself), there is no longer any variability in the cash flows. Accordingly, the derivative should be dedesignated, and any amount deferred in OCI should be recognized in earnings in accordance with paragraph 31. (The firm commitment could be hedged with a different derivative as a fair value hedge.)

When the terms of a forecasted transaction change (e.g., the amount of the purchase is smaller than anticipated, the timing of the transaction changes, or the term of a debt issuance is shorter than anticipated), entities should follow these steps:

- Step 1: Apply paragraph 30 of FAS-133 in the period that the change is made using the originally documented hedging strategy and the revised best estimate of cash flows.
- Step 2: Evaluate whether continuing hedge accounting is appro priate under paragraph 32 of FAS-133. Three scenarios are possible:
  - Scenario 1: If the forecasted transaction continues to be probable of occurring, cash flow hedge accounting remains appropriate. Going forward, the measurement of hedge effectiveness should be based on the revised cash flows.
  - Scenario 2: If the forecasted transaction is no longer probable of occurring, cash flow hedge accounting is no longer available (even if the forecasted transaction will occur within an additional two-month period of time after the originally specified date). Therefore, the entity must terminate the original hedging relationship. However, because it is still possible that the forecasted transaction will occur, the amounts deferred in OCI should be recognized in earnings in the period that the forecasted transaction affects earnings (that is, they should not be immediately reclassified into earnings).

— Scenario 3: If it is probable that the forecasted transaction will not occur, cash flow hedge accounting is no longer available and the entity must terminate the original hedging relationship. In addition, the entity should reclassify the amount of the net derivative gain or loss from OCI into earnings related to the specific non-occurring forecasted transaction(s). That amount should equal the portion of the present value of the derivative's cash flows intended to offset the changes in the original forecasted transaction(s) that the entity has determined will probably not occur by the date (or within the time period) originally specified or within an additional two-month period of time. (DIG G-16, G-17, and G-18)

☞ **PRACTICE POINTER:** Significant changes in the terms of forecasted transactions would call into question the entity's ability to accurately forecast transactions and could jeopardize the use of hedge accounting for similar transactions in the future. This is a hot button for the SEC and requires separate disclosure under FAS-133. Refer to Chapter 15, "Disclosures about Derivatives."

Replacing a roll-over strategy with long-term debt   If an entity is hedging the variable cash flows associated with the forecasted interest payments (or proceeds) on a series of short-term borrowings with a specified dollar amount and term, and the entity decides midstream to abandon that plan and instead issue long-term debt, the derivative no longer qualifies as a hedging instrument; however, the entity should not automatically reclassify any deferred amounts in OCI into earnings. Rather, the entity should evaluate whether interest payments are still probable of occurring over the original hedge timeframe, even if the amounts are fixed or different from the variable pattern that was originally expected. For example, if the roll-over strategy is replaced with the issuance of fixed-rate debt or variable-rate debt with a maturity at least as distant as the term of the original roll-over strategy, it is still probable that the entity will *make interest payments* over the originally scheduled hedge period. Therefore, the amounts should be reclassified into earnings over the period that interest payments on the debt affect earnings, through the term of the designated hedging relationship. (FAS-133, Example 8, pars. 153–161)

Illustrations 14-1 and 14-6 through 14-10 demonstrate the accounting for several common cash flow hedging strategies.

EXHIBIT 14-7
RECAP OF FAIR VALUE AND CASH FLOW HEDGING MODELS

Issue	Fair Value Hedge	Cash Flow Hedge
Eligible transactions*	Recognized assets and liabilities and firm commitments with fixed prices	Variable cash flows from recognized assets and liabilities, and forecasted transactions
Documentation requirements	For each hedging relationship, the risk management objective and strategy and: • The hedging instrument • The hedged item • The risk being hedged • How effectiveness will be assessed • How ineffectiveness will be measured • The method for determining changes in value of the hedged item for the risk being hedged • How recognized changes in a firm commitment will be recognized into earnings	For each hedging relationship, the risk management objective and strategy and: • The hedging instrument • The hedged item, including the currency or quantity, the date or period in which the transaction will occur, and the specific nature of the asset or liability involved • The risk being hedged • How effectiveness will be assessed • How ineffectiveness will be measured • How gains and losses will be reclassified out of OCI
Balance sheet presentation of derivative	Fair value	Fair value
Method of recording change in value of derivative	In earnings as they occur	Initially in OCI, if effective
Matching mechanism	Hedged item is adjusted for changes in fair value attributable to the hedged risk; offset in earnings, like derivative	Amounts deferred in OCI are reclassified into earnings to match timing of earnings effect on hedged transaction
Method of recording ineffectiveness in hedge	Flow to earnings currently as a result of the method (overhedges and underhedges)	Overhedges in earnings, underhedges not recognized

Issue	Fair Value Hedge	Cash Flow Hedge
Termination of hedge	All gains and losses on derivative have been recognized. Recognize basis adjustment on hedged item in a manner appropriate for that type of item (e.g., amortize or as part of gain or loss on sale)	Amounts deferred in OCI are still recognized in the period that the hedged transaction affects earnings, unless it is now probable that the hedged transaction will not occur (then, in earnings)
Shortcut for interest rate swaps	Mark swap to market and "plug" carrying amount of debt instrument for the same amount	Recognize the amount needed to create the desired fixed rate; defer the rest in OCI
Shortcut for options	N/A	Defer the entire change in fair value of the option in OCI until the hedged transaction occurs

* Exceptions are listed in the common hedge criteria and the sections for Fair Value Hedges and Cash Flow Hedges

Adapted from FASB Review Course on FAS-133, Instructor's Manual, Section 4.

FOREIGN CURRENCY HEDGES

Foreign currency hedges essentially fall into three categories:

1. A fair value hedge of a firm commitment or a recognized asset or liability.
2. A cash flow hedge of a forecasted transaction, a firm commitment, the functional-currency-equivalent cash flows associated with a recognized asset or liability, or a forecasted intercompany transaction.
3. A hedge of a net investment in a foreign operation.

Foreign currency hedges are complicated by the fact that most hedged items are accounted for under FAS-52. The FASB did not want to amend FAS-52 in any significant way, so hedge accounting "works around" the foreign currency translation model. Following is a summary of certain key aspects of FAS-52 that are relevant to hedge accounting under FAS-133.

Highlights of FAS-52

The key provisions of FAS-52 that are relevant to hedge accounting are:

- Foreign-currency-denominated assets and liabilities must be remeasured into the *functional currency* each period using the current spot rate, and the changes are recorded in earnings (FAS-52, pars. 15–16) (except the change for available-for-sale debt securities is recorded in OCI; see EITF Issue 96-15). Note that this process does not disqualify an item from hedge accounting because the item is not carried at fair value.

- Under FAS-52, gains and losses from remeasuring certain intercompany transactions survive in consolidation because of differences in functional currencies throughout an international organization.

- The books and records of foreign subsidiaries (net investments in foreign operations) must be translated into the reporting currency of the parent each period using the current spot rate (or an average rate). The resulting gains and losses are reported in a component of other comprehensive income called the "cumulative translation adjustment" (CTA). This account fluctuates over time as exchange rates change. The amount is not reversed into earnings unless the subsidiary is sold (then it becomes part of the gain or loss on sale). (FAS-52, pars. 12–14)

In addition, FAS-52 contained some specific hedging provisions that the FASB decided to carry forward. Those provisions differ from the general FAS-133 model in the following respects:

- The net investment in a foreign operation qualifies as a hedged item even though it represents the net position in dissimilar assets and liabilities. Generally under FAS-133, only similar assets *or* similar liabilities may be hedged as a group and *similar* is tightly defined.

- Foreign-currency-denominated cash instruments, such as loans and bonds, are permissible as hedging instruments in a hedge of (1) a net investment or (2) an unrecognized firm commitment in a fair value hedge. The general model under FAS-133 provides that only derivatives may be designated as hedging instruments.

The FASB rejected certain other provisions of FAS-52, including the general restriction against cross-currency hedges and limitations on the use of certain types of derivatives as hedges.

This information is provided as background, to help the reader understand why certain foreign currency hedging provisions are different from the general model under FAS-133. The precise requirements for foreign currency hedging are discussed in the next section.

Distinguishing between Foreign Currency Hedging Types

It is a bit challenging to characterize a foreign currency hedge, because even when a price is fixed in a foreign currency, the functional currency equivalent is subject to change. Exhibit 14-8 summarizes how several common foreign currency transactions would be characterized under FAS-133. Note that some transactions would qualify as either a cash flow hedge or a fair value hedge.

The unique aspects of foreign currency hedges are discussed in this section.

Common Foreign Currency Hedging Criteria

Regardless of the specific type of hedge, foreign currency hedges must meet all of the following criteria:

- In consolidated financial statements, either:
  - The operating unit that has the foreign currency exposure is a party to the hedging instrument or
  - Another member of the consolidated group that has the same functional currency as that operating unit is a party to the hedging instrument, and there is not an intervening subsidiary with a different functional currency. (See Exhibit 14-9)
- The hedged transaction is denominated in a currency other than the hedging unit's functional currency. (FAS-133, pars. 40(a) and (b))
- If members of a consolidated group enter into a foreign currency derivative with each other, the derivative may qualify as a hedging instrument in consolidation only if the risk has been transferred to an unrelated third party through an offsetting contract. (FAS-133, par. 36) (Additional requirements and restrictions apply to certain types of centralized hedging activities that are discussed later in this section.)

EXHIBIT 14-8
FOREIGN CURRENCY HEDGING TYPES

Hedged Item*	Hedging Instrument[†]	Objective	Type of Hedge[‡]
Fixed-rate foreign currency (FC) debt instrument (asset or liability)	Receive fixed FC, pay fixed US$ swap	Lock in US$ functional currency cash flows	Cash Flow
Floating-rate FC debt	Receive floating FC, pay fixed US$ swap	Lock in US$ functional currency cash flows	Cash Flow
Fixed-rate FC debt	Receive fixed FC, pay floating US$ swap	Reduce exposure to changes in interest rates and foreign currency	Fair value
Floating-rate FC debt	Receive floating FC, pay floating US$ swap	Reduce exposure to foreign currency (not interest rates)	Fair value
Fixed price FC firm commitment	Forward FC contract	Reduce exposure to foreign currency	Cash flow or Fair Value (DIG H-5)
Fixed price FC firm commitment	FC-denominated asset or liability	Reduce exposure to foreign currency	Fair value
Forecasted FC sale (including fixed price contracts that do not meet the definition of a firm commitment)	Forward FC contract	Reduce exposure to foreign currency	Cash flow (DIG H-5)
Forecasted intercompany FC transaction	Forward FC contract	Reduce exposure to foreign currency	Cash flow
Net investment in foreign operation	FC swap or FC-denominated asset or liability	Reduce exposure to foreign currency	Net investment hedge

[*] Assumes US$ is the functional currency.

[†] Nonderivatives (e.g., bonds or debt) may only be used to hedge the hedged items specifically mentioned. Nonderivatives may not be used in a cash flow hedge, or to hedge recognized assets and liabilities in a fair value hedge.

[‡] All qualifying criteria must be met.

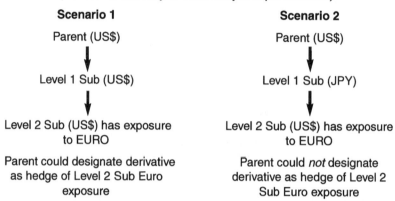

EXHIBIT 14-9
INTERVENING SUBSIDIARY RULE

(Functional currency of each entity is in parentheses)

Scenario 1	Scenario 2
Parent (US$)	Parent (US$)
↓	↓
Level 1 Sub (US$)	Level 1 Sub (JPY)
↓	↓
Level 2 Sub (US$) has exposure to EURO	Level 2 Sub (US$) has exposure to EURO
Parent could designate derivative as hedge of Level 2 Sub Euro exposure	Parent could *not* designate derivative as hedge of Level 2 Sub Euro exposure

Foreign Currency Fair Value Hedges

In addition to the common foreign currency criteria mentioned above, a foreign currency fair value hedge must meet *all* of the fair value hedge criteria discussed in the previous section (paragraphs 20–21 of FAS-133) and the hedged item must be either:

- A foreign-currency-denominated firm commitment or
- A recognized asset or liability that is denominated in a foreign currency.

If all of the relevant fair value hedge criteria are met, the hedge should be accounted for as described in the section on Fair Value Hedging (paragraphs 22–27 of FAS-133). However, there are some unique aspects of foreign currency fair value hedges that are discussed below.

Firm Commitments

A derivative or nonderivative instrument that may give rise to foreign currency transaction gains and losses may be designated as the hedging instrument in a hedge of changes in the fair value of a firm commitment attributable to changes in foreign exchange rates (or a proportion thereof). (FAS-133, par. 37)

☞ **PRACTICE POINTER:** A company may designate an *intercompany* loan as a nonderivative hedging instrument in a fair value hedge of a firm commitment and qualify for hedge accounting in consolidation if the counterparty to the intercompany loan enters into a third-party loan that offsets the foreign exchange exposure of that entity's intercompany loan. (DIG H-12)

The gain or loss on a nonderivative hedging instrument attributable to foreign currency risk is the foreign currency transaction gain or loss calculated under FAS-52 using spot rates. That foreign currency transaction gain or loss should be recognized currently in earnings along with the change in the fair value of the hedged firm commitment. (FAS-133, par. 39)

Recognized Assets and Liabilities

A derivative may be designated as hedging changes in the fair value of a recognized asset or liability that is denominated in a currency other than the entity's functional currency. (FAS-133, par. 37A) A nonderivative may *not* be designated as a hedge of a recognized asset or liability in a fair value hedge.

The hedged asset or liability remains subject to FAS-52, that is, the carrying amount should be remeasured using spot rates. Thus, if only foreign exchange risk is designated as the risk being hedged, there will be a mismatch between the measurement of the derivative (at fair value) and the hedged item (only changes in spot rates). In that case, the only advantage of actually designating the derivative in a hedging relationship is to characterize the derivative as a hedge for disclosure purposes and cash flow reporting purposes. (FAS-138 BFC, par. 27)

If *both* interest rate risk and currency risk are designated as being hedged, the entity would achieve better offset by first recording the adjustment of the carrying amount to reflect changes in fair value attributable to changes in interest rates; then that adjusted amount would be remeasured using spot rates.

☞ **PRACTICE POINTER:** In a dual-currency bond where fixed-rate interest payments are denominated in a foreign currency, a hedge of currency risk would have to be hedged under the cash flow hedging model. (Basically, the goal of that transaction is best described as locking in the functional currency cash flows, not reducing price risk.) (DIG H-4)

Interaction with the shortcut method for swaps If an entity wishes to hedge both the interest rate risk and currency risk of a recognized foreign-currency-denominated interest-bearing asset or liability, it may designate (1) an interest rate swap that qualifies for the interest rate swap shortcut method and (2) a separate currency swap to hedge the currency risk. Note that all of the requirements for the shortcut method must be met, including that the swap must be based on the benchmark rate appropriate in that market. The reason a company might want to hedge in two steps is that under the shortcut method, no ineffectiveness is recognized for changes attributable to the credit spread inherent in the fixed interest rate. Then, when the adjusted carrying amount is remeasured into the functional currency under FAS-52, the offset should be perfect (assuming that the terms of the currency swap match the terms of the debt instrument).

> ☛ **PRACTICE POINTER:** Entities may *not* apply the shortcut method to a combined (single) cross-currency interest rate swap.

Available-for-sale securities Available-for-sale debt securities are eligible for fair value foreign currency hedge accounting if they are denominated in a foreign currency. Available-for-sale *equity* securities may be hedged for changes in the fair value attributable to changes in foreign currency exchange rates only if the following two conditions are satisfied:

- The security is not traded on an exchange (or other established marketplace) on which trades are denominated in the investor's functional currency.
- Dividends or other cash flows to investors are all denominated in the same foreign currency as the currency expected to be received upon sale of the security. (FAS-133, par. 38)

As discussed previously, the portion of the change in fair value of hedged available-for-sale securities attributable to the risks being hedged (including foreign exchange risk) is reported in earnings, not in other comprehensive income. (FAS-133, par. 23)

Foreign Currency Cash Flow Hedges

In addition to the common foreign currency criteria mentioned above, a foreign currency cash flow hedge must meet *all* of the cash flow hedge criteria discussed in the previous section (paragraphs 28–29 of FAS-133) except for the condition that requires that the forecasted transaction be with an unrelated party (paragraph 29(c)). The hedged item in a foreign currency cash flow hedge may be any of the following:

- A forecasted transaction, such as foreign sales.
- A firm commitment denominated in a foreign currency.
- The forecasted functional-currency-equivalent cash flows associated with a recognized asset or liability, such as a fixed or variable interest payment denominated in a foreign currency.

- A forecasted intercompany transaction, such as a sale, purchase, or royalty payment, but not a dividend, because it does not affect earnings. (FAS-133, par. 40)

There are a few unique aspects of foreign currency cash flow hedge accounting.

Groups of Forecasted Transactions

Forecasted inflows of foreign currency (for example, from a forecasted sale) and forecasted outflows of foreign currency may *not* be included in the same group, except as specifically allowed by paragraph 40B. (FAS-133, par. 40(d))

Recognized Assets and Liabilities

In a hedge of a recognized foreign-currency-denominated asset or liability, all of the risks that contribute to the variability in the hedged item's functional-currency-equivalent cash flows must be encompassed in the hedging relationship. For example, in a hedge of a variable-rate foreign-currency-denominated asset or liability, the entity would have to hedge both foreign currency risk and interest rate risk because both risks contribute to the variability in the functional currency cash flows. (FAS-133, par. 40(e) and DIG H-16) However, an entity need not include all of the contractual cash flows of a recognized asset or liability in a cash flow hedge. That is, it is permissible to identify only specific cash flows as being hedged, including specific principal payments, interest payments or both as the hedged item in a foreign-currency cash flow hedge. (DIG Issue G-23)

In a cash flow hedge of the variability of the functional-currency-equivalent cash flows for a recognized foreign-currency-denominated asset or liability that is remeasured at spot exchange rates under paragraph 15 of FAS-52, the entity should reclassify an amount from OCI to earnings that will offset the related transaction gain or loss (to the extent that the derivative provided such offset) and adjust earnings for the cost to the purchaser (income to the seller) of the derivative. (FAS-133, par. 30(d))

DIG Issue G-23 states that a method similar to the Hypothetical Derivative Method (from DIG Issue G-7) should be used to measure the effectiveness of hedges of recognized foreign-currency-denominated assets and liabilities. That method is described in Exhibit 14-5 in the Cash Flow Hedging section. (Also see Illustration 14-8.)

Forecasted Purchases and Sales on Credit

When an entity forecasts a purchase or a sale, the ultimate payment of cash may not occur until a further point in the future if the purchase or sale is on credit. A forecasted purchase or sale involving foreign currency would have to be considered a cash flow hedge, but once the purchase or sale has occurred, the recognized payable or receivable could qualify as the hedged item in either a fair value hedge or a cash flow hedge, depending on which risks are being hedged. (For a short-term receivable or payable, presumably interest-rate risk is not significant.) An entity may hedge such transactions in either 1 step or 2 steps, as follows:

- Step one: A cash flow hedge of the foreign currency risk related to the ultimate payment or receipt of cash on the purchase or sale *or*
- Step one: A cash flow hedge of the foreign currency risk attributable to the purchase price or sale price (on credit) *and*
  Step two: Separately designate a fair value hedge of the resulting recognized foreign-currency-denominated receivable or payable. (FAS-133, par. 36A)

☛ **PRACTICE POINTER:** For short-term sales and purchase on credit, better offset in earnings is generally achieved using the one-step approach.

When the one-step method is used, the following steps should be used to initially defer and subsequently reclassify amounts out of OCI into earnings (DIG H-15):

1. Defer the effective portion of the change in value of the derivative in OCI during the period prior to the occurrence of the forecasted transaction.
2. Calculate the cost or income to ascribe to each period using the functional currency interest rate implicit in the hedging relationship. (For short-term hedges, a *pro rata* method may be used instead, based on the number of days or months in the hedging period.)
3. For forecasted sales on credit, reclassify the amount calculated above into earnings on the date of the sale. For forecasted purchases on credit, the amount calculated above is reclassified into earnings in the same periods that the asset acquired affects earnings (depending on its type).
4. As transaction gains and losses are recognized on the recognized receivable or payable, reclassify an offsetting amount from OCI into earnings.

Refer to Illustration 14-9 for an example involving a purchase of inventory on credit.

Forecasted Intercompany Transactions

In consolidation, the gain or loss deferred in OCI relating to a qualifying hedge of an intercompany foreign-currency-denominated sale should be reclassified into earnings in the period that revenue is recognized on the sale of the item or product to an unrelated third party. (In the separate company financial statements of the hedging entity, the gain or loss deferred in OCI should be reclassified into earnings when the sale to the related party occurs.) (DIG H-13)

Centralized hedging strategies Multinational companies frequently perform all of their hedging activities in one part of the firm, frequently called the *central treasury unit* (CTU). The exposures being hedged may reside in subsidiaries around the world. To reduce transaction costs, companies frequently determine their net exposure in each specific currency (which can be the sum of long and short positions held by numerous subsidiaries) and then enter into one derivative hedging transaction to hedge that net exposure. Exhibit 14-10 shows a very basic central treasury scenario. (I/C means *intercompany*.)

EXHIBIT 14-10
SIMPLE CENTRAL TREASURY HEDGE

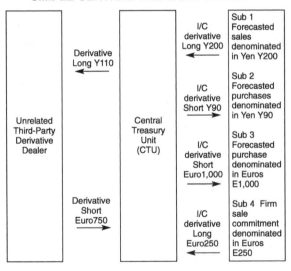

Centralized treasury activities conflict with the general FAS-133 model in a number of ways, including:

- Certain aspects of the transactions are of an intercompany nature.
- Netting long and short positions violates the basic requirement for one-on-one linkage of derivatives and hedged items.

However, the FASB granted an exception for transactions that meet all of the conditions described below. **Note that hedging net exposures is permitted only in a very narrow circumstance involving cash flow hedges of forecasted intercompany transactions—not for any recognized assets and liabilities.**

Use of intercompany derivatives   An intercompany derivative may be designated as the hedging instrument in the consolidated financial statements if the hedged risk is foreign currency risk, the hedging affiliate meets all of the criteria for the type of foreign currency hedge, and the following conditions are met:

- In a foreign currency fair value or cash flow hedge of an individual *recognized* asset or liability *or*
- In a net investment hedge:
  — The counterparty (i.e., the other member of the consolidated group) has entered into a contract with an unrelated third party that offsets the intercompany derivative completely, thereby hedging the exposure it acquired from issuing the intercompany derivative instrument to the hedging affiliate.
- In a foreign currency cash flow hedge of a *forecasted* borrowing, purchase or sale, or a firm commitment
  — The counterparty (CTU) has entered into a derivative contract with an unrelated third party to offset the exposure that results from that internal derivative *or*
  — If the conditions for netting currency exposures discussed below are met (paragraph 40B), the counterparty has entered into derivative contracts with unrelated third parties that would offset, on a *net basis for each foreign currency*, the foreign exchange risk arising from numerous internal derivative contracts. (FAS-133, pars. 36 and 40A, and DIG E-3 and H-1)

Criteria for offsetting net exposures   (FAS-133, par. 40B, unless noted) If a centralized treasury unit (an issuing affiliate) seeks to offset exposure arising from multiple internal derivative contracts on a net basis, the derivatives issued to hedging affiliates may qualify as cash flow hedges in the consolidated financial statements only if all of the following conditions are met:

- The derivative contract with the unrelated third party generates equal or closely approximating gains and losses when compared with the aggregate or net losses and gains generated by the derivative contracts issued to affiliates. That is, the CTU may not selectively keep any portion of that exposure.

- The internal derivatives are designated in qualifying cash flow hedges of forecasted transactions. That is, undesignated derivatives, derivatives designated in other types of hedges, and non-derivative (cash instruments) are *not* eligible for hedging on a net basis. Furthermore, once the forecasted transaction occurs (and becomes a recognized receivable or payable, as in a credit sale or purchase), it may no longer be hedged on a net basis. (FAS-133, par. 40C)

- The internal derivative transactions and the third-party derivative transactions must involve the same currency, mature within the same 31-day period, and be entered into within 3 days of designating the internal derivative as a hedging instrument. The currencies involved in the third-party derivative need not be the functional currency of the CTU, as long as the amount of the respective currencies are equivalent to each other based on forward exchange rates. (DIG H-14)

- The CTU must document the linkage between each internal derivative contract and the offsetting aggregate or net derivative contract with an unrelated third party.

- The CTU may not reposition the offsetting derivative unless the hedging affiliate initiates that action. Any change in the position (which should be rare) would preclude hedge accounting for the internal derivative on a prospective basis.

> **OBSERVATION:** These rules are very restrictive and significantly frustrate the efforts of a CTU. For example, entities that primarily purchase and sell on credit must switch from net hedging to gross hedging when the purchase or sale occurs and the payable/receivable is recorded.

> ☛ **PRACTICE POINTER:** The need for a thorough paper trail of these transactions cannot be overemphasized. Auditors and others will be looking to see that that risk is indeed being laid off with a third party, and that when the forecasted transaction occurs, the third party contract is terminated (or redesignated to another qualifying transaction). These transactions must also be constantly monitored for ongoing effectiveness. Failure to comply with any one of these requirements would disqualify an entity from hedge accounting for those transactions.

Refer to Illustration 14-11 for an example involving hedges of forecasted foreign currency cash flow hedges on a net, centralized basis.

Hedge of the Net Investment in a Foreign Operation

Net investment hedges have their own distinct model, which primarily was carried forward from FAS-52.

Qualifying Hedging Instruments

A foreign-currency-based derivative or a foreign-currency-denominated nonderivative financial instrument that is not measured at fair value may be designated as hedging the foreign currency exposure of a net investment in a foreign operation if the general foreign currency hedge criteria are met (paragraphs 40(a) and 40(b) of FAS-133). Both a derivative and a nonderivative may be designated as hedging different portions of the same net investment; however they must both be deemed effective in their own right. (DIG H-10)

> ☛ **PRACTICE POINTER:** A nonderivative financial instrument (such as foreign-currency-denominated debt) that is reported at fair value using the fair value option in FAS-159 cannot be designated as hedging the foreign currency exposure of a net investment in a foreign operation because it does not give rise to a foreign currency transaction gain or loss under FAS-52. (FAS-133, par. 42, as amended by FAS-159, par. C7)

> ☛ **PRACTICE POINTER:** FAS-133 does not limit the use of cross-currency hedges, as long as the hedging relationship is expected to be highly effective. However, there are limitations on the use of derivatives with multiple underlyings (including cross-currency interest rate swaps), as discussed below.

Limitations on derivatives with multiple underlyings Generally, derivatives must have foreign currency as their only underlying to qualify for designation as a hedge of a net investment in a foreign operation. However, the following two types of cross-currency *interest rate* swaps may be designated as a hedge of a net investment:

1. A receive-floating-rate, pay-floating-rate cross-currency interest rate swap in which the interest rates are based on the same currencies contained in the swap, and both legs of the swap have the same repricing intervals and dates.
2. A receive-fixed-rate, pay-fixed-rate cross-currency interest rate swap.

For these specific swaps, the FASB determined that foreign exchange risk is the predominant risk, not interest rate risk. Note that the underlying currency of the swap can differ from the currency relating to the hedged net investment (i.e., cross-currency hedges are permitted). Other types of cross-currency interest rate swaps, including swaps with one fixed-rate leg and one floating-rate leg, may *not* be designated as the hedging instrument in a net investment hedge. (DIG H-9)

☞ **PRACTICE POINTER:** FAS-133 does not permit a compound derivative that involves an underlying that is not based on foreign-currency risk (for example, the price of gold or the price of an S&P 500 contract) to be designated as the hedging instrument in a net investment hedge. (DIG H-9)

Accounting for the Net Investment

A hedged net investment should continue to be accounted for under FAS-52 (that is, translation gains and losses are reported as a cumulative translation adjustment in stockholders' equity (CTA). The change in fair value of a hedging derivative (or the foreign currency transaction gain or loss calculated under FAS-52 for a nonderivative hedging instrument) that is designated and effective as a hedge of the net investment in a foreign operation should likewise be reported as a component of the cumulative translation adjustment in stockholders' equity, *to the extent* it is effective as a hedge. Assessing effectiveness is discussed in the next section.

> **OBSERVATION:** Unlike a cash flow hedge, gains and losses on effective hedges of net investments are *not* reclassified out of CTA/OCI—the gains and losses are deferred indefinitely—until the subsidiary is sold.

Several DIG Issues (and FAS-52) establish guidance for assessing the effectiveness in a net investment hedge and measuring the earnings effect, if any.

Designating the amount of the net investment being hedged An entity must designate a specific amount as the hedged item in a net investment hedge (e.g., the beginning balance of xx,xxx foreign currency units). When the designated amount is expressed as the beginning balance, and the balance changes during the year, the entity must reassess the hedge designation whenever financial statements or earnings are reported, and at least every three months. (DIG H-7)

> ☞ **PRACTICE POINTER:** Primarily, DIG H-7 is concerned with a situation where the notional amount of the hedging instrument exceeds the net investment balance. However, in an "imperfect" hedge where ineffectiveness must be calculated, the exact amount of the net investment being hedged is a factor in the calculation.

Effectiveness of nonderivatives designated as hedges of net investments Nonderivatives that give rise to transaction gains and losses remain subject to FAS-52. No ineffectiveness may be assumed if:

- The nonderivative instrument is denominated in the functional currency of the hedged net investment.

- The notional amount of the nonderivative instrument matches the portion of the net investment designated as being hedged.

Hedge effectiveness may not be assumed if either:

- The notional amount of the nonderivative instrument does not match the portion of the net investment designated as being hedged *or*
- The nonderivative instrument is denominated in a currency other than the functional currency of the hedged net investment.

In that case, ineffectiveness must be assessed by comparing the foreign currency transaction gain or loss based on the spot rate change (after tax effects, if appropriate) of that nonderivative instrument to the transaction gain or loss based on the spot rate change (after tax effects, if appropriate) that would result from the appropriate hypothetical nonderivative instrument (of the same maturity as the actual derivative) that does not incorporate those differences. DIG Issue H-8 indicates that ineffectiveness must be recognized in earnings for both overhedges and underhedges.

Use of a nonderivative that is itself hedged for interest rate risk   A foreign-currency-denominated debt instrument that is designated as the hedged item in a fair value hedge of interest rate risk may be designated as the hedging instrument in a net investment hedge. For example, Parent A may designate its Euro-denominated debt instrument as the *hedging instrument* in a hedge of its net investment in a German subsidiary and also as the *hedged item* in a fair value hedge of interest rate risk.

As a result of applying fair value hedge accounting, the debt's carrying amount will be adjusted to reflect changes in its foreign-currency-denominated fair value attributable to interest rate risk. The notional amount of the debt that is designated as the hedging instrument in the net investment hedge will change over time such that it may not match the notional amount of the hedged net investment. Accordingly, ineffectiveness may need to be recognized as discussed later in this section. (DIG H-11)

Effectiveness of derivatives designated in a net investment hedge   Derivatives may be assessed for effectiveness in a net investment hedge using either spot rates or forward rates. However, an entity must consistently apply the same method to all net investment hedges. (DIG H-8)

Effectiveness based on forward rates No ineffectiveness may be assumed if the following conditions are met:

- The notional amount of the derivative designated as a hedge of a net investment in a foreign operation equals the portion of the net investment designated as being hedged, *and*
- Either
  - The derivative's underlying relates *solely* to the foreign exchange rate between the functional currency of the hedged net investment and the investor's functional currency *or*
  - The derivative is a cross-currency interest rate swap that meets the conditions of DIG Issue H-9 (discussed earlier in this section) *and* the swap involves an exchange of the functional currency of the hedged net investment for the investor's functional currency.

In such cases, the entire gain or loss on the derivative would be recorded as a component of CTA (i.e., including the time value of purchased options and the interest accrual/periodic cash settlement components of qualifying receive-floating-rate, pay-floating-rate and receive-fixed rate, pay-fixed-rate cross-currency interest rate swaps). (DIG H-8)

Ineffectiveness may not be assumed if either of these conditions is not met. Ineffectiveness would be calculated by comparing the change in fair value of the actual derivative to the change in fair value that would result from the appropriate hypothetical derivative instrument (of the same maturity, and for a cross-hedge of currencies, the same repricing and payment frequencies, as the actual derivative) that does not incorporate those differences. (DIG H-8)

Effectiveness based on spot rates If an entity elects (as a policy decision for all net investment hedges) to assess effectiveness based on changes in spot rates, it would always need to reflect the change in fair value of a derivative attributable to time value in earnings (that is, the difference between the change in spot and forward rates). GAAP does not permit amortizing these amounts ratably over the hedge period—they must be marked to market. (DIG H-6) In addition, any differences attributable to mismatches in notional amounts, currencies, or payment terms would need to be recognized in earnings. The effective portion of the change in value of the derivative would be reported in the CTA. (DIG H-8)

> **OBSERVATION:** Compared with the spot-rate method, the forward-rate method is simpler to document and implement and, when the critical terms of the derivative and net investment line up, it minimizes any earnings effect. Keep in mind that as the

balance of the net investment changes, the designation of the derivative may require adjustment.

Planned sale of a net investment   Under EITF Issue 01-5, when an entity has committed to a plan to sell a net investment in a foreign operation that will cause the CTA for that investment to be reclassified into earnings, and the investment is being evaluated for impairment, the carrying amount of the investment should include the CTA, and any deferred gains and losses from effective hedging transactions.

Illustrations 14-1 and 14-8 though 14-11 demonstrate the accounting for various types of foreign currency hedges.

After-Tax Hedging of Foreign Currency Risk

Foreign currency risk may be hedged on an after-tax basis, provided that the documentation of the hedge at its inception indicated that the assessment of effectiveness, including the calculation of ineffectiveness, will be on an after-tax basis (rather than on a pre-tax basis). If an entity has elected to hedge foreign currency risk on an after-tax basis, it must adjust the notional amount of its derivative appropriately to reflect the effect of tax rates. When ineffectiveness is required to be measured for such hedges, the hypothetical derivative contract used to measure ineffectiveness should have a notional amount that has been appropriately adjusted (pursuant to the documentation at inception) to reflect the effect of the after-tax approach.

The portion of the gain or loss on the hedging instrument that exceeds the loss or gain on the hedged item should be included as an offset to the related tax effects in the period in which those tax effects are recognized. (FAS-133, par. 71 and DIG H-8)

ENTITIES THAT DO NOT REPORT EARNINGS SEPARATELY

FAS-133 generally applies to not-for-profit organizations and other types of entities that do not report earnings as a separate caption in a statement of financial performance (including defined benefit pension plans). Such entities may apply fair value hedge accounting (including hedges of foreign currency risk) and foreign currency net investment hedge accounting if all of the applicable criteria are met. However, such entities are not permitted to use cash flow hedge accounting, because they do not report earnings separately. Nonprofit organizations should account for derivatives as follows:

- All derivatives should be reported at fair value in the statement of financial position.

- For derivatives not designated as hedges, changes in the fair value of a derivative should be recognized as a change in net assets.
- In a fair value hedge, the change in fair value of the derivative and the change in fair value of the hedged item attributable to the risk(s) being hedged should be recognized as a change in net assets.
- Changes in the fair value of derivative instruments and hedged items are generally classified as unrestricted unless their use is temporarily or permanently restricted by donors or by law. (AICPA Audit and Accounting Guide, Not-for-Profit Organizations, par. 8.29)
- For derivatives and nonderivatives designated as a hedge of the foreign currency exposure from a net investment in a foreign operation, changes in the fair value of the derivative and transaction gains and losses on the nonderivative should be recorded as an offset to the cumulative translation adjustment, to the extent they are effective. Ineffectiveness, if any, should be reported as a change in net assets. (FAS-133, par. 43)

> **OBSERVATION:** The restriction against cash flow hedge accounting exists for these entities because they do not report earnings separately.

Not-for-Profit Health Care Organizations

Not-for-profit health care organizations that report an "excess of revenues over expenses" are considered to report earnings separately for purposes of applying FAS-133. Such entities should apply FAS-133 in the same manner as for-profit organizations, including the disclosure requirements. If a transaction qualifies for cash flow hedge accounting, the effective portion of the derivative gain or loss should initially be deferred in other comprehensive income and the ineffective portion should be included in the performance measure. If hedge accounting is not applied, all derivative gains and losses should be included in the performance measure. (SOP 02-2)

REPORTING ELEMENTS OF HEDGE ACCOUNTING

Balance Sheet Reporting

Derivative assets and liabilities are reported separately in the balance sheet at fair value. They are assets and liabilities in their own right and should not be netted against (1) each other or (2) the item they are hedging, unless all of the conditions of FIN-39 for offsetting are met.

(Offsetting requirements are discussed in Chapter 17, "Offsetting Assets and Liabilities in the Balance Sheet.")

Classification of Derivatives

How derivative assets and liabilities are classified in the balance sheet will vary by reporting entity, depending on the materiality of derivatives to total assets and total liabilities. Entities with material amounts of derivatives will report them as separate line items. Entities with immaterial amounts of derivatives might include them with Other assets and Other liabilities. Companies that engage in trading activities will likely include their derivatives in Trading account assets and liabilities.

> ☛ **PRACTICE POINTER:**   GAAP does not specifically address how derivative assets and liabilities should be classified as current or noncurrent in the balance sheet.
>
> **SEC REGISTRANT ALERT:**   SEC Staff Accounting Bulletin 99, *Materiality*, provides guidance on assessing materiality, using both qualitative and quantitative factors.

Income Statement Reporting

FAS-133 does not provide guidance on how to classify gains and losses on derivatives used as fair value or cash flow hedges. Often, entities classify the effective portion of the gain or loss in the same income statement line item as the earnings effect from the hedged item. For example, the gain or loss on a swap used to hedge interest rate risk would typically be reported as an adjustment of interest income (or expense). Classification of gains and losses on derivatives is an accounting policy decision that should be applied consistently for similar types of hedges.

FAS-133 also does not provide guidance on the income statement classification of the ineffective portion of a derivative gain or loss, if any. However, FAS-133 requires disclosure of such amounts and where they have been classified in the income statement. (DIG K-4)

The classification of realized gains and losses on a gross or net basis for physically settled derivative contracts that are designated as hedging instruments (e.g., in an all-in-one cash flow hedge) is a matter of judgment that depends on the relevant facts and circumstances. An assessment of the facts and circumstances should involve (*a*) consideration of the context of the various activities of the entity (and not solely the terms of the contracts); (*b*) the economic substance of the transaction; (*c*) the guidance in APB-29 on nonmonetary exchanges; and (*d*) the gross versus net reporting indicators in EITF Issue 99-19. (EITF 03-11)

☛ **PRACTICE POINTER:** FAS-133 is clear that gains and losses on hedging instruments that are effective in hedging the net investment in a foreign operation must be classified in the cumulative translation adjustment account in other comprehensive income (a balance sheet account).

SEC REGISTRANT ALERT: The SEC staff believes that it is inappropriate to present unrealized gains and losses on a derivative instrument used as an economic hedge outside of the FAS-133 hedge accounting model in an income statement line (e.g., labeled "risk management activities") with reclassification of realized gains and losses arising from settlements associated with the derivatives into revenue and expense lines associated with the hedged exposure. Instead, the realized gains and losses should be reported in the same line item as the unrealized gains and losses on the derivative. (December 2003 speech by Gregory A. Faucette, Professional Accounting Fellow, Office of the Chief Accountant of the SEC, at the AICPA Conference on Current SEC Developments)

In the SEC's Current Accounting and Disclosure Issues in the Division of Corporation Finance (November 2006), the SEC staff provides specific guidance that it would not be appropriate for a financial institution to classify in the provision for loan losses all changes in credit derivatives used as economic hedges, given the importance of that line item to certain credit quality analyses.

Extinguishments of Debt That Was Hedged

If debt that had been the hedged item in a fair value hedge is extinguished, its basis would have been adjusted for hedge gains and losses. In that case, the extinguishment gain or loss would be calculated as the difference between the reacquisition price and the hedge-adjusted carrying amount of the debt. If the debt being extinguished had been the hedged item in a cash flow hedge, any deferred derivative gain or loss that is required to be reclassified from OCI to earnings should be excluded from the extinguishment gain or loss. (EITF Issue 00-9)

☛ **PRACTICE POINTER:** In April 2002, the FASB issued FAS-145, *Rescission of FASB Statements No. 4, 44, and 64, Amendment of FASB Statement No. 13, and Technical Corrections,* which requires that gains and losses on extinguishments of debt be classified as ordinary income unless the criteria of APB-30 (infrequent and unusual) are met. See Chapter 11, "Extinguishments of Debt" for additional information.

Capitalization of Interest Expense on Debt That Was Hedged

FAS-34 permits the capitalization of interest expense as part of the historical cost of acquiring certain assets. Generally, amounts recorded in an entity's income statement as interest costs should be reflected in the capitalization rate under FAS-34. Amortization of the adjustments of the carrying amount of the hedged liability in a fair value hedge would be eligible for capitalization, if the entity elects to begin amortization of hedge adjustments during the period in which interest is eligible for capitalization. However, even if the entity's policy is to classify hedge imperfections as interest expense, those amounts should not be reflected in the capitalization rate. If a variable-rate debt instrument is the hedged item in a cash flow hedge, and the interest on that debt instrument is eligible for capitalization, any amounts deferred in OCI should be reclassified into earnings over the depreciable life of the constructed asset, since that period coincides with the amortization period for the capitalized interest cost on the debt. (EITF 99-9)

Cash Flow Statement Presentation

Generally, cash flows from derivatives that are accounted for as fair value hedges or cash flow hedges may be (but are not required to be) classified in the same category as the cash flows from the items being hedged, provided that the entity discloses that accounting policy. (However, if the derivative contains more than an insignificant financing element at inception, all of the cash flows relating to the derivative must be classified by the debtor as cash flow from financing activities.) If, for any reason, hedge accounting for a derivative that hedges an asset, liability, firm commitment, or forecasted transaction is discontinued, then any cash flows subsequent to the date of discontinuance should be classified according to the nature of the instrument. (FAS-95, par. 14, fn. 4, as amended) FAS-95 illustrates that the purchase or sale of a futures contract is an investing activity. (FAS-95, par. 14, fn. 5)

> ☛ **PRACTICE POINTER:** Given that hedge accounting is elective (for the same derivative, at any point in its life), cash flow reporting of hedges in the same category as the hedged item is also elective, and the fact that the timing of cash flows from derivatives often will not match the recognition of gains and losses in income, it would be counterproductive for an investor to try to analyze a hedger's derivatives activity from a cash flow perspective (assuming the entity uses the indirect method of preparing the cash flow statement).

REGULATORY CONSIDERATIONS

On December 29, 1998, the federal banking agencies issued a joint statement that banking organizations must adopt FAS-133 for regulatory reporting purposes when they adopt it for other financial reporting purposes. However, for regulatory capital purposes, banks should exclude from Tier 1 capital any gains or losses on cash flow hedges that are deferred in other comprehensive income.

In addition, the Federal Reserve Board recently issued Supervisory Release No. 02-10, which imposes certain restrictions on the type of interest rate swap that may be used to hedge trust preferred stocks and still qualify as part of Tier 1 capital.

The National Association of Insurance Commissioners (NAIC) recently adopted SSAP 86, regarding reporting derivative and hedging transactions under statutory accounting principles. It requires the following key points:

- Derivatives not qualifying for hedge accounting would be carried at fair value (consistent with GAAP).
- Derivatives qualifying for hedge accounting would be measured in the same way as the hedged item, often *not* at fair value.
- The ineffective portion of hedge transactions would not be separately identified—a transaction is either effective (with all gains and losses deferred) or ineffective (with all gains and losses recognized in earnings).

Clearly, the statutory hedge accounting model differs significantly from current GAAP (but essentially maintains previous GAAP).

AUDIT CONSIDERATIONS

As discussed in Chapter 12, "Introduction to Derivatives," the primary audit guidance for derivatives and hedge accounting is provided in SAS-92, *Auditing Derivative Instruments, Hedging Activities, and Investments in Securities*. This guidance is expanded and analyzed in an AICPA Audit Guide, *Auditing Derivative Instruments, Hedging Activities, and Investments in Securities*. The AICPA Audit Guide contains numerous case studies that discuss accounting considerations and auditing considerations in detail. In addition, auditors should consider the applicability of SOP 01-3, *Performing Agreed-Upon Procedures Engagements That Address Internal Control Over Derivative Transactions as Required by the New York State Insurance Law*. The discussion below highlights certain aspects of hedge accounting that contribute to audit risk.

Hedge accounting has to be one of the most difficult areas of accounting to audit because the rules are highly complex, the designations are elective from period to period, the methods used to assess effectiveness are somewhat flexible, and the values of the contracts involved can fluctuate widely from period to period. For an entity that uses derivatives only as hedging instruments, appropriate designations must be made and documented as contracts are entered into by knowledgeable client personnel. Perhaps the most significant warning sign to an auditor would be a client that does not seem to understand FAS-133 or appreciate the importance of documenting designations and policy elections.

The key areas of audit risk relating to hedge accounting are summarized below. Chapter 12, "Introduction to Derivatives," includes a discussion of audit risk relating to derivatives in general, including valuation of derivatives.

- **Qualifications for hedge accounting** The qualifications for hedge accounting are detailed, multifaceted, and full of exceptions. Practitioners should gather evidence to ensure that only qualifying transactions receive special accounting.

- **Documentation** Unlike any accounting standard before it, FAS-133 contains certain documentation requirements that, if not fulfilled as designations are made, disqualify a company from hedge accounting. Company personnel must be thoroughly trained in the hedge accounting requirements—the penalty for failing to properly document transactions is mark-to-market accounting for all periods prior to an appropriate designation, which could result in a restatement of financial statements. Auditors should verify that formal documentation has been prepared contemporaneously with the inception of each hedging relationship, that is sufficiently specific to identify the transactions in question, and recalculate the assessment and measurement of effectiveness.

- **Hedge accounting is elective** If a transaction qualifies for hedge accounting, an entity can elect to apply hedge accounting or not, even for the same transaction within its life cycle. This adds to the complexity of an audit and increases the need for meticulous documentation of hedging strategies and designations. Lack of robust documentation should raise questions about the quality of earnings being reported.

- **Effectiveness may be assessed using "reasonable" methods, and different methods may be used for prospective and retrospective assessments** These tests are significant because they determine when hedge accounting can be applied. FAS-133 indicates that similar methods should be used for similar hedge transactions and that differences must be justified. Auditors should review an entity's documentation of its effectiveness methods, test that those methods are being followed, and be skeptical of changes in methods and differences in methods between similar types of hedges.

- **Measuring ineffectiveness** Auditors should test to ensure that the amount recognized in earnings each period reflects both (a) any amount that has been excluded from the assessment of hedge effectiveness (such as time value) and (b) any ineffectiveness that results from differences in the key terms of the hedge, keeping in mind that underhedges should not be recognized in earnings on a cash flow hedge. The shortcut (plug) methods can be applied only in the precise circumstances articulated in FAS-133. SEC Staff Accounting Bulletin 99, *Materiality*, and AU Section 312,

Audit Risk and Materiality in Conducting an Audit, discuss the impropriety of intentionally not recording required accounting adjustments on the basis of immateriality.

- **Probability assessments** In a cash flow hedge of a forecasted transaction, a derivative gain or loss is deferred in OCI on the basis of management's assessment of the probability of a transaction occurring. The auditor should evaluate management's assertion in light of observable facts and the attendant circumstances, including:

  — The frequency of similar transactions in the past.

  — The financial and operational ability of the entity to carry out the transaction.

  — The extent of loss or business disruption that could result if the transaction does not occur.

  — The likelihood that alternative transactions could be used to achieve the same business purpose. (FAS-133, par. 463)

  Other factors to consider include the length of time before a forecasted transaction is expected to occur (except when the transaction is a variable-rate enforceable contract) and the magnitude or volume of the transaction. For example, it may be more challenging to conclude that a transaction forecasted to occur in five years is probable than a transaction forecasted to occur in 6 months (or sales of 10 million units versus 1 million). (FAS-133, par. 465)

  A pattern of concluding that a transaction is no longer probable of occurring should call into question whether the entity may continue to apply cash flow hedge accounting for similar transactions in the future.

- **Reclassifications out of OCI into earnings** Auditors should test that the entity has documented a method for reclassifying amounts out of OCI into earnings in a pattern that reflects the earnings effect of the hedged item. Auditors should also confirm that FAS-133 has been properly applied with respect to termination of hedging relationships and that any early reclassifications into earnings are properly disclosed.

ILLUSTRATIONS

This section presents examples that illustrate the application of the hedge accounting provisions of FAS-133. The examples do not address all possible uses of derivatives as hedging instruments. For simplicity, commissions and most other transaction costs, initial margin, and income taxes are ignored. Some of the fair value amounts have been contrived, where the method is not central to the point of the example. Each illustration is based on the assumption that there are no changes in creditworthiness that would alter the effectiveness of any of the hedging relationships.

Illustration 14-1: Firm Commitment—Comparison of Possible Designations

Manufacturing Company orders a specialized machine from a foreign supplier. The price is 100 FC, which equals $100 on the transaction date. The machine will be completed and delivered in six months, at which time Manufacturing Co. will pay for the machine. The purchase order qualifies as a firm commitment. Manufacturing Co. seeks to lock in the price of the machine in dollars (and protect itself against a strengthening in the FC). It enters into a forward contract to buy 100 FC and sell $100 in six months. At the end of three months (period 1), the FC: $ exchange rate is 1.10:1. At the end of six months (period 2), the exchange rate is 1.03:1. On the first day of period 3, Manufacturing Co. buys the machine for 100 FC, which equals $103. Because the terms of the derivative and the hedged transaction match, Manufac turing Co. may assume that there will be no ineffectiveness in the hedging relationship.

The chart below summarizes the accounting for this transaction under three different scenarios:

> Scenario 1: Fair value hedge of the change in value of the firm commitment to buy the machine, attributable to foreign currency risk (assessed using forward rates).
>
> Scenario 2: Cash flow hedge of the variability of the contract to purchase the machine, attributable to changes in foreign currency rates (assessed using forward rates).
>
> Scenario 3: No hedge accounting designation.

Assume the following data:

End of	Gain (Loss) on Derivative	Change in Fair Value (Cash Flow) of Hedged Item for Currency Risk
Period 1	10	(10)
Period 2	(7)	7

	Scenario 1: Fair Value Hedge		Scenario 2: Cash Flow Hedge		Scenario 3: No Hedge Designated	
End of Period 1	DR Derivative		DR Derivative		DR Derivative	
Mark to market	Asset	10	Asset	10	Asset	10
derivative	CR Earnings	10	CR OCI	10	CR Earnings	10
	DR Earnings	10				
	CR Firm commitment	10				
	Hedged item is adjusted in a fair value hedge					

	Scenario 1: Fair Value Hedge		Scenario 2: Cash Flow Hedge		Scenario 3: No Hedge Designated	
End of Period 2	DR Earnings	7	DR OCI	7	DR Earnings	7
Mark to market	CR Derivative		CR Derivative		CR Derivative	
derivative	Asset	7	Asset	7	Asset	7
	DR Firm commitment	7				
	CR Earnings	7				
	(Net effect of zero on income)					

	Scenario 1: Fair Value Hedge		Scenario 2: Cash Flow Hedge		Scenario 3: No Hedge Designated	
Beginning Period 3	DR Cash CR Derivative	3	DR Cash CR Derivative	3	DR Cash CR Derivative	
Close out deriva- tive, take delivery of machine	Asset	3	Asset	3	Asset	3
	DR Machine	100	DR Machine	103	DR Machine	103
	DR Firm commitment	3	CR Cash	103	CR Cash	103
	CR Cash	103	Basis of machine is higher; deferred gain on derivative is amortized out of OCI to offset depreciation over the useful life of the machine.		Basis of machine is higher; depreciation is higher.	
	Basis of machine is lower; depreciation is lower.					
			DR OCI	3		
			CR Depreciation	3		
			(In total)			
Summary	Net gain on derivative deferred and recognized as a "basis adjust- ment" of the machine. There- fore, deprecia- tion will be lower (but the same as the cash flow hedge, net of the derivative).		Net gain on deriv- ative deferred and amortized out of OCI over the life of the machine as an offset to depreciation.		Gain recognized in Period 1, loss recog- nized in Period 2. Machine recognized at current dollar equivalent of $103.	

?: Fair Value Hedge of Interest Rate Risk in Fixed-Rate
bt

...˛ example is adapted from a similar example on the FASB website.

On April 3, 20X0, Global Tech issues at par a $100 million single-A-quality five-year fixed-rate noncallable debt instrument with an annual 8% interest coupon payable semiannually. On the same day, Global Tech enters into a five-year interest rate swap based on the LIBOR swap rate and designates it as the hedging instrument in a fair value hedge of the $100 million liability. Under the terms of the swap, Global Tech will receive a fixed interest rate at 8% and pay variable interest at LIBOR plus 78.5 basis points (current LIBOR 6.29%) on a notional amount of $101,970,000 (semiannual settlement and interest reset dates). A duration-weighted hedge ratio was used to calculate the notional amount of the swap necessary to offset the debt's fair value changes attributable to changes in the LIBOR swap rate.[2] PV01 represents the duration and expected price sensitivity of each item:

- PV01 debt = 4.14
- PV01 swap = 4.06
- Hedge ratio = PV01 debt / PV01 swap = 4.14/4.06 = 1.0197
- Swap notional = 1.0197 × $100 million = $101,970,000

The example assumes that the LIBOR swap rate increased 100 basis points to 9% on June 30, 20X0. The change in fair value of the swap for the period from April 3 to June 30, 20X0, is a loss of $4,016,000. The change in fair value of the debt attributable to changes in the benchmark interest rate for the period April 3 to June 30, 20X0, is calculated as follows:

Period	Principal Balance	Coupon Rate	Cash Flow— Interest	Cash Flow— Principal	Present Value
0.5	$100,000,000	0.08	2,000,000		1,956,464
1.5	$100,000,000	0.08	4,000,000		3,744,429
2.5	$100,000,000	0.08	4,000,000		3,583,185
3.5	$100,000,000	0.08	4,000,000		3,428,885
4.5	$100,000,000	0.08	4,000,000		3,281,230
5.5	$100,000,000	0.08	4,000,000		3,139,933
6.5	$100,000,000	0.08	4,000,000		3,004,721
7.5	$100,000,000	0.08	4,000,000		2,875,331
8.5	$100,000,000	0.08	4,000,000		2,751,513
9.5	$100,000,000	0.08	4,000,000	100,000,000	68,458,689
Present Value					96,224,380

---

[2] For additional information about calculating hedge ratios, refer to *Risk Management Approaches for Fixed Income Markets* by Bennett W. Golub and Leo M. Tilman (New York: John Wiley & Sons, Inc., 2000)

As of June 30, 20X0, 9.5 periods remain and the contractual cash flows are discounted at 9% (the initial 8% yield plus 100 b.p.), the current LIBOR swap rate. (The accrual for the first quarter interest was excluded.) The following journal entries illustrate the swap and debt fair value changes, attributable to changes in the LIBOR swap rate, excluding accruals:

Debt	3,775,620	
Earnings		3,775,620
Earnings	4,016,000	
Swap liability		4,016,000

The net earnings impact of the hedge was ($240,380) due to some imprecision in the calculated hedge ratio.

These calculations would be repeated for each period that the hedge remains designated and effective, using the current LIBOR swap rate to discount the remaining cash flows.

Illustration 14-3: Fair Value Hedge of Interest Rate Risk Using the Shortcut Method

(The basic facts in this Example are the same as those in Example 2 of FAS133, pars. 111–120)

On July 1, 20X1, Anthem Company borrows $1,000,000 to be repaid on June 30, 20X3. On that same date, Anthem also enters into a two-year receive-fixed, pay-variable interest rate swap. Anthem designates the interest rate swap as a hedge of the changes in the fair value of the fixed-rate debt attributable to changes in the designated benchmark interest rate. Anthem designates changes in LIBOR swap rates as the benchmark interest rate being hedged. The terms of the interest rate swap and the debt are as follows:

	Interest Rate Swap	Fixed-Rate Debt
Trade date and borrowing date[*]	July 1, 20x1	July 1, 20x1
Termination date and maturity date	June 30, 20x3	June 30, 20x3
Notional amount and principal amount	$1,000,000	$1,000,000
Fixed interest rate*	6.41%	6.41%
Variable interest rate	3-month US$ LIBOR	Not applicable
Settlement dates and interest payment dates*	End of each calendar quarter	End of each calendar quarter
Reset dates	End of each calendar quarter through March 31, 20x3	Not applicable

* These terms need not match to qualify for the shortcut method in a fair value hedge.

Accordingly, Anthem concludes that it qualifies for the shortcut method of fair value hedge accounting.

The US$ LIBOR rates that are in effect at inception of the hedging relationship and at each of the quarterly reset dates are assumed to be as follows:

Reset Date	3-Month LIBOR Rate
7/1/X1	6.41%
9/30/X1	6.48%
12/31/X1	6.41%
3/31/X2	6.32%
6/30/X2	7.60%
9/30/X2	7.71%
12/31/X2	7.82%
3/31/X3	7.42%

For simplicity, assume that the yield curve is flat. An upward-sloping yield curve would make the following computations more complex. Different interest rates would be used for each quarterly repricing date, and the present value of each future payment would be computed using a different rate. However, the basic principles are the same.

The following table illustrates the computation of interest expense using the shortcut method, based on paragraph 114 of FAS-133.

	(a)	(b)	(c)	(d)	(e)
Quarter Ended	Difference between Fixed Rates	Variable Rate on Swap	Sum (a) + (b)	Debt's Principal Amount	Interest Expense ((c) x (d))/4
9/30/20X1	0.00%	6.41%	6.41%	$1,000,000	$16,025
12/31/20X1	0.00%	6.48%	6.48%	1,000,000	16,200
3/31/20X2	0.00%	6.41%	6.41%	1,000,000	16,025
6/30/20X2	0.00%	6.32%	6.32%	1,000,000	15,800
9/30/20X2	0.00%	7.60%	7.60%	1,000,000	19,000
12/31/20X2	0.00%	7.71%	7.71%	1,000,000	19,275
3/31/20X3	0.00%	7.82%	7.82%	1,000,000	19,550
6/30/20X3	0.00%	7.42%	7.42%	1,000,000	18,550

Anthem would report the swap at fair value and adjust the carrying amount of the debt to reflect changes in the fair value of the swap. Note that the yield on the debt perfectly reflects the LIBOR rate for the period, which was the purpose of the hedge. Anthem would record the following balances and amounts in earnings.

	Interest Rate Swap			Debt		
Qtr Ended	**Asset (Liability)**	**Change in Fair Value***	**Hedge Adjustment**	**Carrying** Amount**	**Interest Expense**	**Yield**
Inception	$0			$1,000,000		
9/30/20X1	(1,149)	(1,149)	1,149	1,001,149	$16,025	6.4026%
12/31/20X1	0	1,149	(1,149)	1,000,000	16,200	6.4800%
3/31/20X2	1,074	1,074	(1,074)	998,926	16,025	6.4169%
6/30/20X2	(11,355)	(12,429)	12,429	1,011,355	15,800	6.2490%
9/30/20X2	(9,385)	1,970	(1,970)	1,009,385	19,000	7.5293%
12/31/20X2	(6,848)	2,537	(2,537)	1,006,848	19,275	7.6576%
3/31/20X3	(2,479)	4,369	(4,369)	1,002,479	19,550	7.8007%
6/30/20X3	0	2,479	(2,479)	1,000,000	18,550	7.4200%

* Anthem does not separately accrue interest on the swap. To simplify the accounting, the accrual of interest is captured in the mark-to-market of the swap.

** Under the shortcut method, adjustments to the carrying amount of the debt do not require separate amortization; as adjustments are made to reflect changes in the value of the swap, the adjustment is implicitly being amortized.

Illustration 14-4: Fair Value Hedge of Equity Security Using a Net Written Option Collar

At 1/1/X1, Colwin Industries owns 2,000 shares of XYZ stock classified as available-for-sale. To hedge the change in price of XYZ stock, XYZ enters into a combination of options (a collar) made up of the following:

- A purchased put option with a notional amount equal to 2,000 shares of XYZ stock and a strike price of $40 per share that may be exercised in 90 days. The purchased put option provides Colwin with a return of $2,000 for each dollar that the price of XYZ stock falls below $40.

- A written call option with a notional amount equal to 2,000 shares of XYZ stock and a strike price of $60 per share that may be exercised in 90 days. The written call option obligates Colwin to pay $2,000 for each dollar that the price of XYZ stock increases above $60.

Colwin receives a net premium of $2,000. Accordingly, the combination is considered a net written option and the written option test (FAS-133, par. 20(c)) applies.

The Symmetrical Gain and Loss Test

Colwin performs the following test to determine whether the potential for gain and loss is symmetrical under a 50% increase or decrease in price.

	Inception	50% Increase	50% Decrease
Purchased put			
Intrinsic value	0	0	15
Time value	5	3	1
	5	3	16
Written call			
Intrinsic value	0	(15)	0
Time value	(6)	(4)	(2)
	(6)	(19)	(2)
Equity security	50	75	25
Combined fair value	49	59	39
Change in fair value of combination		10	(10)
Percentage change		20%	-20%

Colwin demonstrates that the potential for gain and loss of the combined position is symmetrical. Accordingly, Colwin designates the collar as a hedge of 100% of the change in fair value of 2,000 shares of XYZ stock resulting from price changes below $40 per share and price changes above $60 per share. Effectiveness will be assessed by comparing the change in intrinsic value of the collar to the change in fair value of the 2,000 shares of stock.

Assume that the fair value of XYZ stock is $62, $58, and $35 at the end of Periods 1, 2, and 3, respectively, and the time value of the options changes as indicated below.

	Inception	Period 1	Period 2	Period 3
Collar				
Intrinsic value	0	(2)	0	5
Time value	(1)	(1)	(1)	0
	(1)	(3)	(1)	5
Fair value	$(2,000)	$(6,000)	$(2,000)	$10,000
Equity security	$100,000	$124,000	$116,000	$70,000

Colwin would record the following journal entries:

Inception

Cash		2,000
Net collar liability	2,000	

To record the net collar liability.

Period 1

Earnings		4,000
Collar liability	4,000	

To reflect the change in fair value of the collar. (Note: in this example, there was no net change in time value. If there were, it would flow through as part of this entry.)

Equity security	24,000	
Earnings		4,000
OCI		20,000

To record the change in fair value of the securities attributable to the hedged risk in earnings, limited to the change in intrinsic value of the collar (FAS-133, par. 23). The remainder is recorded in OCI in accordance with FAS-115.

Period 2

Net collar liability	4,000	
Earnings		4,000

To reflect the change in fair value of the collar. (Note: in this example, there was no net change in time value. If there were, it would flow through as part of this entry.)

Earnings	4,000	
OCI	4,000	
Equity security		8,000

To reflect the change in fair value of the security, through earnings to the extent of the change in intrinsic value on the collar.

Period 3

Net collar asset	10,000	
Net collar liability	2,000	
Earnings		12,000

To record the change in fair value of the collar.

Earnings	10,000	
OCI	36,000	
Security		46,000

To record the change in fair value of the security. The amount recorded in earnings is limited to the change in intrinsic value of the collar. The remainder is recorded in OCI in accordance with FAS-115.

Balances at the end of hedge (the balances as if no hedge accounting were applied are shown for comparative purposes only):

	Hedge	No Hedge
Securities, at fair value	$70,000	70,000
Net asset collar	10,000	10,000
OCI	(20,000)	(30,000)
Cumulative earnings effect	2,000*	12,000

* Represents the premium received on the collar. The $10,000 gain has been deferred as a component of OCI and remains there until the security is sold (or other-than-temporary impairment is recognized).

Illustration 14-5: Fair Value Hedge of Interest Rate Risk and Currency Risk on a Fixed-Rate Foreign-Currency-Denominated Loan (Fixed to Variable Scenario)

This example is adapted from a similar example on the FASB website.

Mullen Inc.'s functional currency is the U.S. dollar. On January 3, 200X, Mullen borrows 100 million fixed-rate Euro (EUR) at a yield to maturity of 5.68%. The loan has a term of five years and pays an annual coupon of 5.68%. This yield at inception is equivalent to Euribor plus 0.52% or (on a swapped basis) to US$ LIBOR plus 0.536%.

Also on January 3, 200X, Mullen enters into a five-year cross-currency swap in which it will receive fixed EUR at a rate of 5.68% on EUR100 million and pay floating US$ at US$ LIBOR plus 0.536% on US$102 million. There will be a final exchange of principal on maturity of the contract. Both the debt and the swap will pay annual coupons on December 31. The company designates the cross-currency swap as a fair value hedge of the changes in the fair value of the debt due to both interest and exchange rates.

The spot FX rates for EUR/US$, LIBOR flat EUR swap rates, EUR/US$ basis swap spreads and 1 year US$ LIBOR on December 31 each year over the life of the hedge were as follows:

Years	0	1	2	3	4	5
Spot FX	1.0200	1.0723	1.0723	1.1273	1.1851	1.2458
EUR Swap Rate	5.160%	5.151%	5.040%	4.854%	4.480%	N/A
Basis Swap Spread	(0.02)%	(0.02)%	(0.02)%	(0.02)%	(0.02)%	N/A
1 year US$ LIBOR	6.00%	5.50%	6.00%	6.50%	7.00%	N/A

The changes in fair value of the debt attributable to changes in both Euro interest rates and spot FX rates, and the values and changes in value (in US$)

of the receive-fixed Euro, pay-floating US$ swap, are shown in the following table:

(in US$ 000s, except for rates)

		1	2	3	4	5
A. Spot FX rate	1.0200	1.0723	1.0723	1.1273	1.1851	1.2458
B. Fair Value of Debt for Changes in IR (in EUR)	(100,000)	(100,032)	(100,322)	(100,567)	(100,647)	0
C. Debt at Spot (in US$) (A*B) per FAS-52	(102,000)	(107,265)	(107,575)	(113,366)	(119,274)	-
D. Cum. change on debt		(5,265)	(5,575)	(11,366)	(17,274)	-
E. Change in Period		(5,265)	(310)	(5,791)	(5,908)	17,274
F. EUR fixed-to-US$ Floating Swap		5,333	5,642	11,472	17,357	-
G. Change in Period		5,333	310	5,830	5,885	(17,357)

As a fair value hedge, changes in the value of the debt and the swap are recognized immediately in earnings. The income statement effect, including interest expense, is set forth below.

Years	**1**	**2**	**3**	**4**	**5**
Interest Expense*	($6,667)	($6,157)	($6,667)	($7,177)	($7,687)
Change in Value of Debt (E)	(5,265)	(310)	(5,791)	(5,908)	17,274
Hedge Gain/Loss (G)	5,333	310	5,830	5,885	(17,357)
Net Earnings Effect	(6,599)	(6,157)	(6,628)	(7,200)	(7,770)

* The fixed Euro interest expanse (calculated in Euros and remeasured into the US$ functional currency) is adjusted by the net cash payment on the cross currency swap (which reflects the variable U.S. Interest rate (LIBOR + .536%) inherent in the currency swap).

Illustration 14-6: Cash Flow Hedge of Interest Rate Risk Using the Interest Rate Swap Shortcut

The example is adapted from Example 5 in FAS-133, paragraphs 131–139.

On July 1, 20X1, Sherwood Enterprises invests $10,000,000 in variable-rate corporate bonds that pay interest quarterly at a rate equal to the three-month US$ LIBOR rate plus 225 basis points. The bonds were purchased at par. The $10,000,000 principal will be repaid on June 30, 20X3.

Also on July 1, 20X1, Sherwood enters into a two-year receive-fixed, pay-variable interest rate swap and designates it as a cash flow hedge of the variable-rate interest receipts on the corporate bonds. The risk designated as being hedged is the risk of changes in cash flows attributable to changes in the designated benchmark interest rate. Sherwood designates changes in LIBOR swap rates as the benchmark interest rate in hedging interest rate risk. The terms of the interest rate swap and the corporate bonds are shown below.

	Interest Rate Swap	Corporate Bond
Trade date and bor-rowing date*	July 1, 20X1	July 1, 20X1
Termination date and maturity date	June 30, 20X3	June 30, 20X3
Notional amount and principal amount	$10,000,000	$10,000,000
Fixed interest rate	6.65%	Not applicable
Variable interest rate†	3-month US$ LIBOR	3-month US$ LIBOR + 2.25%
Settlement dates and interest payment dates*	End of each calendar quarter	End of each calendar quarter
Reset dates	End of each calendar quarter through March 31, 20X3	End of each calendar quarter through March 31, 20X3

* These terms need not match to qualify for the shortcut method in a cash flow hedge.

† Only the benchmark interest rate must match. The credit spread does not disqualify the transaction from the shortcut method.

Accordingly, Sherwood concludes that it qualifies for the shortcut method of cash flow hedge accounting.

The three-month US$ LIBOR rates in effect at the inception of the hedging relationship and at each of the quarterly reset dates are assumed to be as follows:

Reset Date	Three-Month LIBOR Rate
7/1/X1	5.56%
9/30/X1	5.63%
12/31/X1	5.56%

Reset Date	Three-Month LIBOR Rate
3/31/X2	5.47%
6/30/X2	6.75%
9/30/X2	6.86%
12/31/X2	6.97%
3/31/X3	6.57%

Sherwood would report the swap at its fair value. Using the cash flow shortcut method described in paragraph 132 of FAS-133, the same amount would be reported in OCI. Because there is no difference between the variable rate on the bond and swap and the bond was purchased at par, interest income could be calculated as the variable rate on the bond plus the difference between the fixed rate and variable rate on the swap. Note that the yield equals the desired fixed rate (the fixed rate of 6.65% plus the credit spread of 2.25% divided by four quarters).

Qtr Ended	Fair Value of Swap*	Balance in OCI**	Variable Coupon	(Receipt) Payment on Swap	Interest Income
Inception	$0				
9/30/20X1	24,850	($24,850)	($195,250)	($27,250)	($222,500)
12/31/20X1	73,800	(73,800)	(197,000)	(25,500)	(222,500)
3/31/20X2	85,910	(85,910)	(195,250)	(27,250)	(222,500)
6/30/20X2	(42,820)	42,820	(193,000)	(29,500)	(222,500)
9/30/20X2	(33,160)	33,160	(225,000)	2,500	(222,500)
12/31/20X2	(21,850)	21,850	(227,750)	5,250	(222,500)
3/31/20X3	1,960	(1,960)	(230,500)	8,000	(222,500)
6/30/20X3	0	0	(220,500)	(2,000)	(222,500)

* Fair value after the current receipt or payment on the swap. For example, the change in fair value for the quarter ending 9/30/20X1 was a gain of $52,100. Receipt of the amount due on the swap ($27,250) brought the fair value attributable to remaining cash flows down to $24,850.

** A journal entry to "reclassify" an amount out of OCI is not required. Theoretically, it the same amount as the current payment or receipt on the swap. The balance in OCI is shown net of that "reclassification."

Termination of swap

Assume that Sherwood decides to terminate the swap on 3/31/X2 when its fair value is $85,910. If it is still probable that Sherwood will receive interest income on the bond, the swap gain should remain in OCI and be amortized into interest income as interest is recognized on the bond. If, however, Sherwood Corp. decides to sell the bond, the gain on the swap would be recognized in earnings in the period that the bond is sold, because it would be probable that interest will no longer be received on the bonds. The amount of the gain and the circumstances would require separate disclosure in the footnotes.

Illustration 14-7: Cash Flow Hedge of Forecasted Issuance of Fixed-Rate Debt (Rate Lock)

On January 15, 20X0, Saugatuck Corporation determines that it is probable that it will issue fixed-rate debt on or about February 15, 20X0 at the then current rate. The debt will be a five-year noncallable debt instrument with a par value of $100 million and will be rated single-A quality. Saugatuck wants to lock in a fixed rate for the debt based on today's Treasury yield curve plus a 90 b.p. credit spread above Treasuries (the fixed rate would be 7.611%). Saugatuck enters into a 30-day forward contract to sell a $100 million Treasury note with a maturity of November 15, 2004, and a current yield of 6.711% at a forward price of $105,759,298. Because the Treasury note has a remaining maturity of 4.5 years, while the maturity of the debt will be five years, Saugatuck determines the appropriate notional amount for the swap using a duration-weighted hedge ratio:

- PV01 corporate = .04095
- PV01 Treasury = .03872
- Hedge ratio = PV01 corporate / PV01 Treasury = 1.05759298
- Swap notional = 1.05759298 × $100 million = $105,759,298

Saugatuck documents the effect of a 50 b.p. shift in Treasury rates in either direction and concludes that the forward contract will be highly effective in offsetting changes in the amount of proceeds on the debt issuance if it is issued with a fixed rate of 7.611% (6.711 + .90). (This is a form of the dollar-offset method of assessing effectiveness.) Saugatuck designates the forward contract as a hedge of the variability of the proceeds it will receive in 30 days, attributable to changes in Treasury rates.

Assume that on February 15, rates have increased by 10 b.p. and the fair value of the forward contract is $408,500. Saugatuck issues the debt on February 16 with a fixed rate of 7.611% for proceeds of $99,591,522 (a discount of $408,478). Saugatuck would record the following journal entries.

February 15, 20X0

Forward contract	$408,500	
Earnings		22
OCI		$408,478

To record the forward contract at fair value and defer the effective portion of the gain in OCI. Ineffectiveness (for the excess of the effect of the rate change on the forward contract and the debt) is recognized currently. Had this been an underhedge, the difference would not have been recognized in earnings.

Cash	$408,500	
Forward contract		$408,500

To settle the forward contract.

February 16, 20X0

Cash	$99,591,522	
Debt discount	408,478	
Debt		$100,000,000

To record the issuance of debt at a discount. The discount would be amortized to interest expense as a yield adjustment over the life of the debt using the interest method.

Future periods

As interest expense is recognized on the debt, an amount would be reclassified out of OCI into earnings using the effective yield method (resulting in net interest expense at a rate of 7.166%).

OCI	$408,478	
Interest expense		$408,478

To amortize the deferred gain into earnings as interest expense is recognized on the debt.

Illustration 14-8: Cash Flow Hedge of Currency Risk in a Fixed-Rate Foreign-Currency-Denominated Loan

This example is adapted from a similar example on the FASB website.

On July 1, 20X0, Company DEF, a US$ functional currency entity, issues a zero-coupon debt instrument with a notional amount of FC154,766.79 for FC96,098.00. The interest rate implicit in the debt is 10%. The debt will mature on June 30, 20X5. DEF enters into a forward contract to buy FC154,766.79 in five years at the forward rate of 1.090148194 (US$ cost $168,718.74) and designates the forward contract as a hedge of the variability of the US$ functional currency equivalent cash flows on the debt. DEF will use the "Hypothetical Derivative" method to assess effectiveness (DIG Issue G-7). Because the currency, notional amount, and maturity of the debt and the forward contract match, the entity concludes that the forward contract is the perfect derivative and no ineffectiveness will result. The US$ interest rate implicit in the forward contract is 11.028%. The market data, period end balances, and journal entries from cash flow hedge accounting are shown below.

Period	Spot Rate US$/FC	Forward Rate US$/FC	Forward Rate Difference	FC Present Value	US$ Spot Amounts	US$ Debt (@11.028%)	Fair Value Forward US$
5	1.040604383	1.090148194	0	96,098.00	100,000.00	100,000.00	0.00
4	1.100000000	1.184985966	0.094837771	105,707.80	116,278.58	111,028.04	9,327.97
3	1.100000000	1.163142906	0.072994712	116,278.58	127,906.44	123,272.25	8,041.09
2	1.100000000	1.141702484	0.051554290	127,906.44	140,697.08	136,866.76	6,360.72
1	1.100000000	1.120657277	0.030509083	140,697.08	154,766.79	151,960.48	4,215.89
0	1.100000000	1.100000000	0.009851806	154,766.79	170,243.47	168,718.74	1,524.73

		Cash	Forward	Debt	OCI	Interest Expense	Trans. Loss
7/1/X0	Borrow Money	$100,000		($100,000)			
6/30/X1	Accrue Interest on Debt			(10,571)		$10,571	
6/30/X1	Mark Debt to Spot			(5,708)		($5,708)	
6/30/X1	Mark Forward to FV		$9,328		($4,077)	457	(5,708)
6/30/X1	Balances	100,000	9,328	(116,279)	(4,077)	11,028	0
6/30/X2	Accrue Interest on Debt			(11,628)		11,628	
6/30/X2	Mark Forward to FV		(1,287)		671	616	
6/30/X2	Balances	100,000	8,041	(127,907)	(3,406)	23,272	0
6/30/X3	Accrue Interest on Debt			(12,791)		12,791	
6/30/X3	Mark Forward to FV		(1,680)		877	803	
6/30/X3	Balances	100,000	6,361	(140,698)	(2,529)	36,866	0
6/30/X4	Accrue Interest on Debt			(14,070)		14,070	
6/30/X4	Mark Forward to FV		(2,145)		1,121	1,024	
6/30/X4	Balances	100,000	4,216	(154,768)	(1,408)	51,960	0
6/30/X5	Accrue Interest on Debt			(15,477)		15,477	
6/30/X5	Mark Forward to FV		(2,691)		1,409	1,282	
6/30/X5	Balances	$100,000	$1,525	($170,245)	$1*	$68,719	$0

* Difference due to rounding.

Journal Entries at Inception of the Loan and at the End of the First Year

7/1/X0

Cash	100,000	
FC Debt (at spot rate)		100,000

To record FC borrowing in US$.

6/30/X1

Interest Expense	10,571	
Debt		10,571

To accrue interest. Period end spot rate used for simplicity.

FC Transaction Loss	5,708	
Debt		5,708

To record a transaction loss on the debt under FAS-52.

Derivative Asset	9,328	
OCI		9,328

To record a derivative at fair value and record effective portion in OCI.

OCI	5,251	
Interest Expense		457
FC Transaction Loss		5,708

To reclassify an amount out of OCI (1) to increase interest expense to the US$ yield of 11.028% and (2) to offset the transaction loss on the debt.

Journal entries for the remaining four years are not displayed.

The above example would also be relevant for a noninterest-bearing foreign-currency-denominated receivable or payable. An amount based on the rate implicit in the forward contract would be reported in earnings each period as interest. Given the short maturities of many receivables and payables, the interest element could be small.

Illustration 14-9: Foreign Currency Hedge of a Forecasted Purchase on Credit

This example is adapted from DIG Issue H-15.

Intrepid Industries forecasts the purchase of inventory on credit for FC100,000. The purchase is projected to occur July 15 on credit. The payable will settle on August 29. Intrepid enters into a forward contract to purchase FC100,000 at .6614 US$ = 1 FC. Intrepid designates the forward as a hedge of the variability of the cash payment in the equivalent number of U.S. dollars (FC100,000 × .6614 = $66,140).

Intrepid will assess effectiveness based on forward rates. Exchange rates are as follows:

Period	Spot	8/29 Forward	7/15 Forward
1/14	0.6575	0.6614	0.6605
3/31	0.6757	0.6793	
6/30	0.6689	0.6734	
7/15	0.6761	0.6767	
8/29	0.6798	0.6798	

Intrepid would record the following journal entries at each date indicated.

	Cash	Inventory	Forward Contract	Accounts Payable	Earnings	OCI
Inception 1/14	—	—	—	—	—	—
3/31 (76 days) Mark forward to FV			$1,703			$(1,703)
6/30 (91 days) Mark forward to FV			(526)			526
7/15 (15 days) Purchase inventory		$67,610		$(67,610)		
8/29 entries (45 days): Mark forward to FV			663			(663)
FC transaction				(370)	370	
Reclass (par. 30d)					(370)	370
Interest element					78	(78)
Settlement of payable	$(67,980)			67,980		
Settlement of forward	1,840		(1,840)			
	$(66,140)	$67,610	$0	$0	$78	$(1,548)

Upon sale of the inventory, Intrepid would record cost of goods sold of $67,610 and reclassify $1,548 from OCI to earnings to achieve net cost of goods sold of $66,062. After the effect of the hedge, the net cost of the inventory was $66,140.

Explanation of the par. 30(d) reclassifications   After the foreign-currency-denominated payable is recognized, two amounts are reclassified out of OCI at the end of each period it remains outstanding: (1) an amount to offset the translation gain or loss and (2) the portion of the interest element that is attributable to each period (said another way, the amount necessary to result in an implied fixed US$ interest rate).

In this example, the daily interest implicit in the hedging relationship as a result of the forward contract is: $65,750PV, $66,140 FV, 227n, I=0.0026053%

Period		Periodic interest element
1/14	$65,750	
3/31	65,880	$130
6/30	66,036	156
7/15	66,062	26
8/29	**$66,140**	**78**

Only the amount for the last period is reclassified out of OCI, because the payable was not recorded prior to that point. These amounts may also be calculated using a *pro rata* method or a method that uses two foreign currency exchange rates, as described in DIG Issue H-15, footnote 1 and the Illustration of Step #2.

<hr>

Illustration 14-10: Hedge of Forecasted Sale with a Purchased Put Option

On July 1, 20X1, Bonami Engine Company forecasts that it will sell 100 engines to a foreign airline in 6 months for FC5,000,000. The current exchange rate is 2FC:1US$. Firm purchase orders do not yet exist for these sales, but Bonami concludes that it is probable that the sales will occur. To hedge against declines in the value of the US$, Bonami purchases 6 month FC put options with a notional amount of FC5,000,000 that are exercisable only at their maturity, December 31, 20X1. The contract rate (that is, the strike rate) is 2FC:1US$; accordingly, the options are at the money upon issuance. Bonami pays a premium of $8,000 for the options. Bonami designates the options as a hedge of potential declines in the US$ equivalent of the selling price (cash inflow) of the 100 engines to the foreign airline on or about December 31, 20X1. Bonami will assess effectiveness based on total changes in the option's cash flows upon exercise at its maturity date, using the hypothetical option method described in DIG Issue G-20. Because the purchased option meets all four of the conditions for a "perfect" hypothetical derivative, Bonami may defer the entire change in value of the derivative in OCI until the forecasted transaction occurs.

Assume the following data:

	Exchange Rate	Fair Value of Put Options	Change in Fair Value
July 1	2.0FC:$1	$8,000	—
September 30	2.2FC:$1	$231,273	$223,273
December 31	2.3FC:$1	$326,087	$94,814

On December 31, 20X1, the engine sales occur as planned. Bonami would record the following journal entries.

7/1/X1

FC Put Option	8,000	
Cash		8,000

To record the purchased FC put options.

9/30/X1

FC Put Option	223,273	
OCI		223,273

To defer the change in value of the FC put options in OCI.

12/31/X1

FC Put Option	94,814	

OCI		94,814

To defer the change in value of the FC put options in OCI.

Cash	326,087	
FC Put Option		326,087

To record the settlement of the put option.

Cash	2,173,913	
Sales revenue		2,173,913

To recognize sales of 100 engines for FC5,000,000 at the current exchange rate of FC2.3:1US$.

OCI	326,087	
Sales revenue	326,087	

To reclassify amounts out of OCI into earnings in the same period as the forecasted sales of engines. Note that the net effect of the sale and the hedge gain equals $2,500,000, the locked-in US$ equivalent selling price, less the cost of the option.

Illustration 14-11: Central Treasury Hedge of Foreign Currency Forecasted Transactions

This Illustration is adapted from a similar example on the FASB website.

The purpose of this example is to illustrate the application of paragraphs 40A and 40B of FAS-133. Specifically, this example illustrates the mechanism for offsetting risks assumed by a centralized treasury unit (CTU) using internal derivative contracts on a net basis with third-party contracts.

Dominion Corp. is a U.S. company with the U.S. dollar as both its functional currency and its reporting currency. Dominion has three subsidiaries: Subsidiary A is located in Germany and has the Euro as its functional currency, Subsidiary B is located in Japan and has the Japanese yen (JPY) as its functional currency, and Subsidiary C is located in the United Kingdom and has the British pound (BP) as its functional currency. Dominion utilizes a centralized treasury unit (CTU) to manage foreign exchange risk on a centralized basis. Foreign exchange risk assumed by Subsidiaries A, B, and C through transactions with external third parties is transferred to the CTU via internal contracts. The CTU then offsets that exposure to foreign currency risk via third-party contracts. To the extent possible, the CTU offsets exposure to each individual currency on a net basis with third-party contracts.

On January 1, Subsidiaries A, B, and C decide that various foreign-currency-denominated forecasted transactions with external third parties for purchases and sales of various goods are probable. Also on January 1, Subsidiaries A, B, and C enter into internal foreign currency forward contracts with the CTU to hedge the foreign exchange risk of those transactions with respect to their individual functional currencies. The CTU has the same functional currency as the parent company (U.S. dollar).

Subsidiaries A, B, and C have the following foreign currency exposures and enter into the following internal contracts with the CTU:

Subsidiary	Functional Currency	Forecasted Exposures		Date	Internal Contracts with CTU			
					Currency Received		Currency Paid	
A (German)	Euro	JPY payable	12,000	June 1	JPY	12,000	Euro	115*
		BP receivable	50	June 1	Euro	80*	BP	50
B (Japanese) 10,160*	JPY	US$ payable	100	June 15	US$	100	JPY	
		Euro receivable	100	June 15	JPY	10,432⁻ *	Euro	100
C (U.K.)	BP	US$ receivable	330	June 30	BP	201*	US$	330

* Computed based on forward exchange rates as of January 1.

The Subsidiaries document their designations, the dates and other relevant terms, and conclude that the requirements of paragraph 40A for foreign currency cash flow hedge accounting are satisfied. Accordingly, Subsidiaries A, B, and C designate the internal contracts with the CTU as cash flow hedges of their foreign currency forecasted purchases and sales (and those designations will survive in the consolidated financial statements).

The CTU determines that it will offset the exposure arising from the internal derivative contracts with Subsidiaries A, B, and C on a net basis with third-party contracts. In order to determine the net currency exposure arising from the internal contracts with Subsidiaries A, B, and C, the CTU performs the following analysis:

Subsidiary Perspective—Internal Contracts with the CTU

Subsidiary	Contract with CTU	Currency Received/ (Currency Paid)			
		Euro	JPY	BP	US$
A (German)	Internal Contract 1	(115)	12,000		
	Internal Contract 2	80		(50)	
B (Japanese)	Internal Contract 3		(10,160)		100
	Internal Contract 4	(100)	10,432		
C (U.K.)	Internal Contract 5			201	(330)
Net Exposure		**(135)**	**12,272**	**151**	**(230)**

CTU Perspective—Internal Contracts with the Subsidiaries

Subsidiary	Contract with CTU	Currency Received/ (Currency Paid)			
		Euro	JPY	BP	US$
A (German)	Internal Contract 1	115	(12,000)		
	Internal Contract 2	(80)		50	
B (Japanese)	Internal Contract 3		10,160		(100)
	Internal Contract 4	100	(10,432)		
C (U.K.)	Internal Contract 5			(201)	330
Net Exposure		**135**	**(12,272)**	**(151)**	**230**

The CTU determines that it will enter into the following three third-party foreign currency forward contracts. The CTU enters into the contracts on January 1. The contracts mature on June 30.

CTU's Contracts with Unrelated Third Parties

	Currency Bought/ (Currency Sold)			
	Euro	JPY	BP	US$
Third-Party Contract 1	(135)			138*
Third-Party Contract 2		12,272		(121)*
Third-Party Contract 3			151	(247)*
Net Exposure	**(135)**	**12,272**	**151**	**(230)**

_____

* Computed based on forward exchange rates as of January 1.

The CTU has documented its compliance with all of the remaining criteria of paragraph 40B, including specific linkage of internal and external contracts and its intent to maintain those positions unless an action is initiated by a hedging subsidiary.

At the end of the quarter, each subsidiary determines the functional currency gains and losses for each contract with the CTU:

Subsidiary	Contract with CTU	Beginning of Period Functional Currency Amount Receive/ (Pay)*	End of Period Functional Currency Amount Receive/ (Pay)*	Functional Currency Gain/ (Loss)**	US$ Gain/ (Loss)***
A (German)	Internal Contract 1	(115)	(115)	0	0
	Internal Contract 2	80	83	(3)	(3)
B (Japanese)	Internal Contract 3	(10,160)	(10,738)	578	5
	Internal Contract 4	10,432	10,421	11	0
C (U.K.)	Internal Contract 5	201	204	(3)	(5)
	Net US$ Gain / (Loss)				**(3)**

* Computed based on forward exchange rates as of January 1 and March 31.

** For simplicity, functional currency gains or losses are not discounted in this example.

*** Functional currency gains and losses converted to U.S. dollars based on current spot rates.

At the end of the quarter, the CTU determines its gains or losses on third-party contracts:

Contracts with Third Parties	Beginning of Period US$ Amount Receive/ (Pay)*	End of Period US$ Amount Receive/ (Pay)*	US$ Gain/ (Loss)**
Third-Party Contract 1	138	131	7
Third-Party Contract 2	(121)	(114)	(7)
Third-Party Contract 3	(247)	(244)	(3)
Net US$ Gain / (Loss)			**(3)**

* Computed based on forward exchange rates as of January 1 and March 31.

** For simplicity, gains or losses are not discounted in this example.

Journal Entries at March 31

Note: All journal entries are in U.S. dollars.

Subsidiaries' Journal Entries

German Subsidiary A

There is no entry for Contract 1 because the U.S. dollar gain or loss is zero.

OCI	3	
Derivative Liability: I/C		3

To record the loss on Internal Contract 2.

Japanese Subsidiary B

Derivative Asset: I/C	5	
OCI		5

To record the gain on Contract 3.

There is no entry for Internal Contract 4 because the U.S. dollar gain or loss is zero.

U.K. Subsidiary C

OCI	5	
Derivative Liability: I/C		5

To record the loss on Internal Contract 5.

CTU's Journal Entries

Journal Entries for Internal Contracts with Subsidiaries

There is no entry for Internal Contract 1 because the U.S. dollar gain or loss is zero.

Derivative Asset: I/C	3	
Earnings		3

To record the gain on Internal Contract 2 with German Subsidiary A.

Earnings	5	
Derivative Liability: I/C		5

To record the loss on Internal Contract 3 with Japanese Subsidiary B.

There is no entry for Internal Contract 4 because the U.S. dollar gain or loss is zero.

Derivative Asset: I/C	5	
Earnings		5

To record the gain on Internal Contract 5 with U.K. Subsidiary C.

Journal Entries for Third-Party Contracts

Derivative Asset	7	
Earnings		7

To record the gain on Third-Party Contract 1.

Earnings	7	
Derivative Liability		7

To record the loss on Third-Party Contract 1.
To record the loss on Third-Party Contract 2.

Earnings	3	
Derivative Liability		3

To record the loss on Third-Party Contract 3.

Results in Consolidation

Derivative Asset	7	
OCI	3	
Derivative Liability		10

In consolidation, the amounts in Subsidiary A, B, and C's balance sheets reflecting intercompany derivative assets and liabilities acquired from the CTU eliminate against the CTU's intercompany derivative liabilities and assets. The amount reflected in consolidated OCI reflects the net entry to OCI of Subsidiaries A, B, and C. The CTU's gross derivative asset and gross derivative liability arising from third-party contracts are also reflected in the consolidated balance sheet. Based on the assumptions in this illustration, the CTU's net loss on third-party derivatives*equals* the net gain on internal contracts issued to Subsidiaries A, B, and C. However, if the CTU's net gain or loss on third-party contracts does not equal the net loss or gain on internal derivatives designated as hedging instruments by affiliates, the difference must be recognized as ineffectiveness in consolidated earnings.

The reclassification of amounts out of consolidated OCI is based on the timing and amounts of the individual subsidiaries' forecasted transactions. In this illustration, at June 30, the forecasted transactions at Subsidiaries A, B, and C have been consummated and the net debit in consolidated OCI of $3 has been reversed.

CHAPTER 15
DISCLOSURES ABOUT DERIVATIVES

CONTENTS

Overview	15.02
Important Notice: FASB Project on Derivative Disclosures	15.02
Background	15.03
Disclosure about Derivatives	15.03
Scope	15.03
Qualitative Disclosures	15.04
Exhibit 15-1: Qualitative Disclosures about Derivatives and Hedging Activities	15.05
Disclosures about Certain Hybrid Instruments Measured at Fair Value	15.05
Quantitative Disclosures	15.06
Exhibit 15-2: Quantitative Disclosures about Hedging Relationships	15.07
Implementation Issues Relating to Quantitative Disclosures	15.09
Disclosure in Interim Periods	15.10
Accounting Policy Elections	15.10
Reporting Other Comprehensive Income (OCI)	15.11
Overlap with Other Standards	15.12
Fair Value Disclosures	15.12
Carrying Amounts of Securities and Loans	15.12
Derivative Loan Commitments	15.13
Guarantees	15.13
Foreign Currency Translation	15.13
Unconditional Purchase Obligations	15.13
Energy Trading Contracts	15.14
SEC Market Risk Disclosures	15.14
Audit Considerations	15.15
Illustrations	15.15
Illustration 15-1: Disclosure of Strategy and Accounting Policies Relating to Hedging Activities	15.15

Illustration 15-2: Narrative Discussion of Derivative Strategy   15.18

Illustration 15-3: Quantitative Disclosures about Hedging
Activities   15.19

Illustration 15-4: Reporting Cash Flow Hedges in Other
Comprehensive Income   15.21

OVERVIEW

Entities must disclose information about their objectives and strategies for holding or issuing derivatives. Entities that use derivatives as hedging instruments (and nonderivatives, in certain foreign currency hedges) must disclose the amount of ineffectiveness reported in earnings (including any change in time value that has been excluded from the analysis) and where it is classified in the income statement. Changes in other comprehensive income attributable to deferred gains and losses on cash flow hedges must be disclosed. Entities must disclose the earnings effect of unwound hedges of forecasted transactions and firm commitments that do not materialize. Public companies must disclose significantly more detailed information about derivatives in accordance with SEC regulations.

IMPORTANT NOTICE
FASB PROJECT ON DERIVATIVE DISCLOSURES

In December 2006, the FASB issued an Exposure Draft, *Disclosures about Derivative Instruments and Hedging Activities*. The proposed Statement will amend the disclosure requirements of FAS-133 to provide users of financial statements with an enhanced understanding of how and why an entity uses derivative instruments, how derivative instruments and related hedged items are accounted for under FAS-133, and how derivative instruments affect an entity's financial position, results of operations, and cash flows.

To achieve those objectives, the proposed Statement would modify FAS-133 to require the following disclosures:

- A discussion of objectives and strategies for using derivative instruments by the instrument's primary underlying risk that the reporting entity is intending to modify (e.g., interest rate, credit, foreign exchange rate, or overall price risk)
- Notional amounts and fair value of derivative instruments, the location and fair values of derivative instruments and related gains and losses reported in the balance sheet and income statement, and the location and amount of gains and losses reported in the income statement on hedged items designated and qualifying in hedging relationships (in a tabular format)

- Derivative instruments contain leverage factors
- Contingent features in derivative instruments, including the aggregate fair value amount of derivatives that contain those features and amounts required to be posted as collateral or transferred if the features were triggered
- Counterparty credit risk in derivative instruments.

The FASB projects issuance of a final Statement amending the disclosure requirements in FAS-133 as early as the third quarter of 2007. Readers should monitor developments on this project.

BACKGROUND

FAS-133 is the primary source of guidance on disclosures about derivatives and hedging activities. A few DIG Issues provide supplemental guidance. FIN-45 requires disclosure of incremental information about guarantees that meet the definition of a derivative.

> ☞ **PRACTICE POINTER:** The disclosures required by FAS-133 apply to all contracts that meet the definition of a derivative (and are required to be accounted for as such), rather than just the "classic" derivatives types. Other related disclosures, including disclosures about fair values of financial instruments and concentrations of credit risk, are covered in Chapter 18, "Fair Value Measurements, Fair Value Disclosures, and Other Financial Instrument Disclosures."

DISCLOSURES ABOUT DERIVATIVES

Scope

The disclosure requirements of FAS-133 apply to:

- Freestanding derivatives, as defined.
- Derivatives that have been bifurcated from a host contract and are being accounted for separately in accordance with paragraphs 12-16 of FAS-133.
- Nonderivative instruments that are used to hedge firm commitments in a foreign currency fair value hedge or to hedge a net investment in a foreign operation.

> ☞ **PRACTICE POINTER:** Entities that mark to market substantially all of their positions (including derivatives) must provide the qualitative disclosures about derivatives discussed below, but they would provide quantitative disclosures only if some of their deri-

vatives are designated as hedges of positions that are not marked to market (such as long-term debt).

Qualitative Disclosures

FAS-133 requires that an entity that holds or issues derivatives, as defined, provide a narrative description of the following information (paragraph 44):

- Its reasons for holding or issuing derivatives.
- The context necessary to understand those objectives.
- Its strategies for achieving those objectives.

The narrative must be broken down into 4 categories, if applicable:

1. Fair value hedges
2. Cash flow hedges
3. Hedges of net investments
4. All other

The narrative should include a description of the entity's risk management strategy, including a description of any qualifying hedged items. Within each category of hedge accounting, entities may experiment with the best manner in which to provide the information, for example, by risk type. Entities that hold or issue derivatives not designated as hedging instruments should clearly describe the purpose of the derivative activity.

FAS-133 encourages, but does not require, the entity to discuss its derivative strategies in relation to the entity's overall risk management approach.

> **OBSERVATION:**   A narrative discussion about derivatives has been required under GAAP for several years. Sometimes, companies provide robust disclosure, and the reader has an excellent understanding of the level and nature of derivative activity. However, in other cases, only the bare minimum information is provided—and it is rather general and "boilerplate." Recent calls for more transparent disclosure about the uses of and accounting policies applied to derivatives should improve the quality of disclosure in annual reports.

Exhibit 15-1 summarizes the qualitative disclosure requirements about derivatives (FAS-133, par. 44).

EXHIBIT 15-1
QUALITATIVE DISCLOSURES ABOUT DERIVATIVES AND
HEDGING ACTIVITIES

Narrative Disclosure	Fair Value Hedges	Cash Flow Hedges	Hedges of Net Investments	All Other
Reason for holding derivatives, context, and strategies for achieving objectives	✓	✓	✓	✓
Risk management strategy for hedge type	✓	✓	✓	N/A
Item(s) being hedged	✓	✓	✓	N/A
Classification of any hedge ineffectiveness	✓	✓	N/A	N/A
Types of events that will cause amounts deferred in OCI to be reversed into earnings	N/A	✓	N/A	N/A

N/A means not applicable.

Disclosures about Certain Hybrid Instruments Measured at Fair Value

Entities must disclose information to convey an understanding of the effect of changes in fair value on earnings (or, alternatively, for entities that do not report earnings, the effect on other performance indicators) for hybrid financial instruments measured at fair value under the FAS-133 election and for hybrid instruments measured at fair value under the FAS-133 practicability exception, which is applicable when an embedded derivative cannot be readily identified and measured. (FAS-133, par. 44B)

> **SEC REGISTRANT ALERT:** In December 2003, the SEC issued FR-72, *Interpretation: Commission Guidance Regarding Management's Discussion and Analysis of Financial Condition and Results of Operations,* to elicit more meaningful disclosures in several areas. FR-72 reminds registrants of the required discussion of critical accounting estimates and assumptions that supplements the description of accounting policies in the notes to the financial statements in the MD&A.
> Registrants are encouraged to provide disclosures that clearly distinguish accounting hedges from economic hedges when both

types of hedges are used and to provide a discussion of reasons for entering into derivatives for economic hedging purposes in the MD&A. Registrants are reminded to provide specific disclosure regarding the registrants' policy of how and where the impact of hedge effectiveness is recorded in the income statement, as well as where ineffectiveness is recorded, within the notes to the financial statements.

(December 2003 speech by Gregory A. Faucette, then a Professional Accounting Fellow, Office of the Chief Accountant of the SEC, at the AICPA Conference on Current SEC Developments)

The SEC's Current Accounting and Disclosure Issues (December 2005) encourages registrants to provide transparent, "plain English" disclosures related to derivatives, including a description of reasons for their use of derivatives, their hedging strategies, and methods and assumptions used for estimating fair value of derivatives. When hedge accounting has a material impact, registrants should have specific disclosures for each type of fair value and cash flow hedge that clearly describe the specific type of asset or liability being hedged and the derivative used. Registrants are encouraged to clearly describe the methodology used to test hedge effectiveness for each type of hedge and how often the tests are performed. In addition, registrants should consider providing disclosure regarding their use of FAS-133 accounting policy elections. (Refer to the section "Accounting Policy Elections" in this chapter for a list of accounting policy elections provided by FAS-133.)

Quantitative Disclosures

FAS-133 requires numerous quantitative disclosures about derivatives used in qualifying hedging relationships (and, for foreign currency fair value hedges of firm commitments and net investment hedges, disclosures about nonderivatives). In every reporting period for which a complete set of financial statements is presented, entities that elect hedge accounting for qualifying transactions must report information about:

- Hedge effectiveness
- Changes in the status of unexecuted transactions
- Activity in other comprehensive income (for cash flow hedges)

No quantitative information is required to be disclosed about derivatives not designated in a hedging relationship. (They are marked to market through earnings every period.)

There is some overlap in the quantitative disclosure requirements for the various types of hedges, but most of the requirements are designed to help the reader "back out" hedge accounting for that specific type of hedge, should they choose to do so. Within each category of hedge accounting, entities may experiment with the best manner in which to provide the data, for example, by risk type.

FAS-133 encourages, but does not require, the presentation of these quantitative disclosures about derivative and nonderivative hedging instruments in the context of other financial instruments or nonfinancial assets and liabilities used in the same business activity.

> **OBSERVATION:** The required quantitative disclosures will be very difficult for many companies to compile, even annually, unless their computer systems are programmed to capture this data and sort by specific hedge type. For fair value hedges, the piece that requires disclosure is only the amount of the overhedge or underhedge. Because this amount is generally not a discrete journal entry (it is the difference between two sets of journal entries), it would be very difficult to compile this information after the fact.

Exhibit 15-2 summarizes the quantitative disclosures required about qualifying hedging relationships (FAS-133, par. 45).

EXHIBIT 15-2
QUANTITATIVE DISCLOSURES ABOUT HEDGING RELATIONSHIPS

Disclosure Requirement	Fair Value Hedges	Cash Flow Hedges	Hedges of Net Investments
Disclosure Designed to Highlight Imperfect Hedges			
Net gain or loss in earnings from hedge ineffectiveness and any time value excluded from the effectiveness analysis	✓	✓	**N/A** (this is a bit of a loophole)
Identification of income statement line item where such amounts are reported	✓	✓	**N/A** (this is a bit of a loophole)
Disclosures Designed to Highlight Misjudgments or "Discretionary" Reversals			
Amount of net gain or loss reversed into earnings from firm commitment going "soft"	✓ (Penalty box to highlight misjudgments about whether a commitment is "firm" and/or discretionary changes)	N/A	N/A

Disclosure Requirement	Fair Value Hedges	Cash Flow Hedges	Hedges of Net Investments
Amount of net gain or loss reversed into earnings from forecasted transactions that are now probable of NOT occurring	N/A	✓ (Penalty box to highlight poor predictions of the probability of a forecasted transaction and/or discretionary changes)	N/A

Disclosures Involving Other Comprehensive Income

Disclosure Requirement	Fair Value Hedges	Cash Flow Hedges	Hedges of Net Investments
Estimated amount of net gain or loss deferred in OCI that will be reversed into earnings within the next 12 months	N/A	✓	N/A
The most distant point in time that a forecasted transaction is expected to occur (excluding variable-rate instruments)	N/A	✓	N/A
The net amount of effective gains or losses from derivatives (or non-derivatives) recorded as adjustments to CTA in OCI	N/A	N/A	3

☞ **PRACTICE POINTER:**   FAS-133 does not require disclosure of certain "volume-oriented" disclosures, including the types of derivatives that are held or issued (e.g., options, swaps, and futures) and their notional amounts. Having all derivatives on the balance sheet at fair value obviates the need for that kind of "raw data" if the reader's focus is on the rights and obligations associated with derivative contracts. Volume-related data may be obtained in certain filings with the SEC or other regulators.

SEC REGISTRANT ALERT: The quantitative disclosures required by FAS-133 focus on derivatives designated as hedges.

The SEC staff encourages disclosure of the amount of the change in fair value of derivatives that are not designated as hedges under FAS-133 as well as the income statement classification of such derivatives. The SEC staff also encourages greater clarity in disclosures when entities use derivatives as qualifying hedges under FAS-133 and as economic hedges. (December 2003 speech by Gregory A. Faucette, then a Professional Accounting Fellow, Office of the Chief Accountant of the SEC, at the AICPA Conference on Current SEC Developments)

OBSERVATION: These quantitative disclosures are a public "score card" of the effectiveness of a company's derivative activity for the period. However, unlike a real score card, they only report on what *didn't* work in management's hedging strategy. Other than the smoothing effect on the bottom line, there is no requirement to disclose the quantitative effect of *effective* hedges (with the exception of amounts deferred in CTA for net investment hedges). Entities may voluntarily disclose the amount of effective hedge gains and losses netted against various line items in the income statement.

Implementation Issues Relating to Quantitative Disclosures

Measuring amounts to be reclassified out of OCI   When a single derivative is designated as a cash flow hedge of multiple cash flows, such as a swap used to hedge the cash flows on a variable-rate debt, the amount deferred in OCI could be the sum of both positive and negative amounts relating to the forecasted cash settlements on the derivative over its term. For example, if the fixed rate on the swap is higher than some points on the yield curve, but lower than others, both cash payments and receipts could be expected over the term of the hedge. In such cases, the 12-month projection of reclassifications out of OCI into earnings should be calculated as follows:

- Allocate the total amount reported in OCI (as determined in accordance with paragraph 30(b)) for the hedging relationship to each of the related forecasted transactions. The allocation method used must be applied consistently and must consider any cumulative gain or loss on the derivative that has been recognized in earnings as hedge ineffectiveness.
- Add together those estimated amounts to be reclassified into earnings in the coming 12 months.

The amount required to be disclosed could end up being greater than or less than the net amount reported in OCI. (DIG I-2)

Transition adjustments involving cash flow hedges   Upon transition to FAS-133, entities were required to record a "cumulative-effect-type adjustment" to establish a separate component of OCI for any outstanding hedging relationships that were similar to cash flow hedges. Those adjustments are required to be reclassified into earnings in a manner consistent with paragraph 31 (i.e., in the same period that the forecasted transaction affects earnings). In the year of initial application of FAS-133, entities are required to disclose the amount of gains and losses relating to the transition adjustment that are scheduled to be reclassified into earnings during the ensuing 12 months. (FAS-133, par. 53)

Disclosure in Interim Periods

Disclosures about derivatives and hedging activities must be provided as part of a complete set of financial statements, for example, in annual reports and in conjunction with a securities registration statement (FAS-133, par. 45). Summarized financial information, including condensed quarterly reports, need not include the disclosures. However, entities should consider updating the qualitative disclosures whenever an entity significantly changes its objectives for holding or issuing derivative instruments, strategies for achieving their objectives, or both. Similarly, disclosure of the effect of cash flow hedges on other comprehensive income should be provided periodically if material events occur. (SEC Division of Corporate Finance, Current Accounting and Disclosure Issues, Topic II.D)

> ☞ **PRACTICE POINTER:** APB-28 provides guidance on what represents a complete set of financial statements.

Accounting Policy Elections

FAS-133 contains a number of accounting policy elections, including the following:

1. Whether the normal purchase and sale exception has been applied to qualifying transactions.
2. Whether hedge accounting has been applied for all qualifying transactions.
3. The methods of assessing and measuring hedge effectiveness (including whether time value is excluded).
4. The income statement classification of effective hedge gains and losses.
5. The income statement classification of ineffective hedge gains and losses (and how the entity will recognize any change in value of a hedged firm commitment in a fair value hedge).
6. Income statement classification of gains and losses on derivatives not designated as hedges.

7. The balance sheet classification of derivative assets and liabilities and any asset or liability recognized for hedged firm commitments in a fair value hedge.

8. The method of classifying cash flows from derivatives used as hedging instruments (i.e., net with the cash flows from the hedged item or according to their nature).

FAS-133 only explicitly requires disclosure of (5) and (8) above (the latter through an amendment of FAS-95). However, if any of the items above are material to the financial statements, the entity's policy should be disclosed as a significant accounting policy in accordance with APB-22. An entity's derivatives activities would be much more transparent if entities voluntarily disclosed this information in their footnotes.

For example, "Interest rate swaps are used to hedge the interest rate risk associated with certain debt instruments issued by the company. Gains and losses that were effective in offsetting changes in fair value (or cash flow) on the hedged item are reported as an adjustment of interest expense. Hedge imperfections of $x,xxx are reported in Other income (expense)."

With the exception of item (2) (whether hedge accounting is elected), entities should apply each of the accounting policy elections discussed in items (3) through (8) consistently for similar hedging transactions from period to period.

> **SEC REGISTRANT ALERT:** Rule 4-08 of Regulation S-X, as amended, requires expansive disclosures about the accounting policies followed for derivatives. Highlights of the requirements include: (1) a description of each accounting method used to account for derivatives and the types of derivatives subject to each method; (2) the criteria to be met for each accounting method; (3) the accounting for terminations of hedging relationships; and (4) the classification of derivatives, and their related gains and losses, in the statements of financial position, cash flows, and results of operations. Registrants should carefully review the requirements of this regulation to ensure full compliance.

Reporting Other Comprehensive Income (OCI)

An entity should display as a separate classification within other comprehensive income the net gain or loss on derivative instruments designated and qualifying as cash flow hedging instruments that are reported in comprehensive income. (FAS-133, par. 46)

FAS-130 requires separate disclosure of the beginning and ending accumulated derivative gain or loss, the related net change associated with current period hedging transactions, and the net amount of any reclassifications into earnings. Reclassification adjustments must be clearly presented so that the reader does not double count the same gain or loss (that is, first when it is deferred in OCI, and then again when it is reclassified into earnings). (FAS-133, par. 47)

Overlap with Other Standards

As a general rule, any disclosures required by other GAAP for a derivative or a hedged item should be provided in addition to the requirements of FAS-133. A few specific situations are discussed below.

Fair Value Disclosures

Derivatives that are financial instruments are also subject to the requirements of FAS-107. In addition, FAS-157 applies to both derivatives that are financial instruments and derivatives that are not financial instruments. Chapter 18, "Fair Value Measurement, Fair Value Disclosure, and Other Financial Instrument Disclosures," discusses the requirements of FAS-107 and FAS-157 in detail. In years after the adoption of FAS-133, there will be no difference between the carrying amount and fair value of derivatives, as defined. If derivative assets and liabilities are not reported as separate line items on the balance sheet, the fair value footnote disclosure would ideally specify the line items in which the derivative assets and liabilities have been classified (rather than lumping them in a line(s) called, "Financial Assets (Liabilities) Carried at Fair Value").

FAS-107 requires disclosure of the assumptions used to estimate the fair value of financial instruments. That disclosure is particularly important for derivatives that are not actively traded. (FAS-107, par. 10, as amended)

> ☛ **PRACTICE POINTER:** Some derivatives do not meet the technical definition of a financial instrument, for example, a commodity contract that requires delivery of a nonfinancial asset. Entities are permitted to voluntarily include those contracts in their fair value disclosures to present a more complete picture of their operations and strategies.

Carrying Amounts of Securities and Loans

FAS-115 requires certain disclosures about the net carrying amount of debt securities classified as held-to-maturity and available-for-sale. For securities that have been appropriately designated as the hedged item in a fair value hedge, the net carrying amount should include any adjustment resulting from fair value hedge accounting. (FAS-133, par. 534)

Similarly, when a loan has been designated as the hedged item in a fair value hedge, the *adjusted* recorded investment should be disclosed in accordance with FAS-118, if the loan is considered impaired. (DIG F-4)

Derivative Loan Commitments

The disclosures required in FAS-133 apply to loan commitments included in its scope; specifically, loan commitments that relate to the origination of mortgage loans that will be held for sale, as discussed in paragraph 21 of FAS-65 (as amended). Those loan commitments must be accounted for as derivatives only by the issuer of the loan commitment (the potential lender under the arrangement).

> ☞ **PRACTICE POINTER:** The AICPA practice aid, "Illustrative Disclosures on Derivative Loan Commitments," provides illustrative disclosures for derivative loan commitments required by SEC regulations, APB-22, FAS-133, and FAS-107.
>
> **SEC REGISTRANT ALERT:** SEC SAB-105 indicates that registrants should disclose their accounting policy for derivative loan commitments in accordance with APB-22.

Guarantees

FIN-45 requires numerous disclosures about written guarantees, including those that are accounted for as derivatives under FAS-133. Refer to Chapter 8, "Debt Financing," for additional information.

Foreign Currency Translation

FAS-52 requires certain disclosures about the aggregate transaction gains and losses reported in income during the period. Gains and losses on derivatives that represent foreign currency transactions should be disclosed in accordance with FAS-133. (FAS-52, par. 30)

FAS-52 requires disclosure of the activity in the cumulative translation adjustment account (CTA) for the period, including (at a minimum): beginning and ending balances, the aggregate adjustment from translation adjustments, gains and losses from hedges and certain intercompany transactions, the amount of income tax allocated to translation adjustments, and the amount of any reversal of CTA into earnings upon sale or liquidation of a foreign operation. (FAS-52, par. 31) FAS-133 disclosure about the amount of hedging gains and losses deferred as a component of CTA must be presented separately, if included as part of this analysis.

Unconditional Purchase Obligations

If an unconditional purchase obligation such as a take-or-pay contract or a throughput contract is subject to the requirements of both FAS-47 and FAS-133 (because it meets the definition of a derivative), the entity should provide all of the disclosures required by FAS-133 and the requirements of paragraph 7 of FAS-47, including the fixed and determinable amount of the gross obligation in the aggregate and over the next five-year period, and other information about the significance of such obligations. (DIG I-1)

Energy Trading Contracts

In addition to the requirements of FAS-133, SEC registrants engaged in material energy trading activities should consider providing supplemental information in MD&A about energy trading contracts, including derivatives, that are valued using estimation techniques (as opposed to market quotations). Management should consider including information about the trading activities, contracts, modeling methodologies, assumptions, variables and inputs, and a discussion of the effect of different circumstances or measurement methods. (Securities and Exchange Commission Statement about Management's Discussion and Analysis of Financial Condition and Results of Operations, January 22, 2002)

> ☛ **PRACTICE POINTER:** Under previous GAAP (primarily EITF Issue 98-10), contracts held in connection with energy trading activities were marked to market, even if they did not meet the definition of a derivative. In October 2002, the EITF decided to withdraw that guidance, and only permit mark-to-market accounting for *derivatives* held in connection with energy trading activities. Refer to EITF Issue 02-3 for additional information.

SEC Market Risk Disclosures

Rule 3-05 of Regulation S-K, "Market Risk Disclosures," requires certain disclosures about market risks inherent in derivatives and other financial instruments. In general, the rule requires disclosure of quantitative and qualitative market risk measures of financial instruments held and issued by large public companies, including a discussion of the entity's risk management policy, current exposure to market variables, and the results of risk management activities.

> ☛ **PRACTICE POINTER:** These disclosures apply to registrants that have material market risk arising from sources other than derivatives. For example, entities should discuss the effect of a reasonably possible change in rates on foreign currency exposures or interest-bearing instruments, if the effect would be material.

Companies may choose between providing tables of fair value and other data for individual financial instruments, sensitivity analyses, and value at risk-type information. Generally, the information must be grouped by the type of risk involved (e.g., interest rate risk and foreign currency risk). These disclosures should be presented outside the basic financial statements.

Certain aspects of the rule overlap with GAAP disclosures. The SEC intends to revisit these disclosure requirements and to eliminate any redundancies. (FASB Special Report: "GAAP-SEC Disclosure Requirements," March 6, 2001) Until that time, however, SEC registrants must comply with the SEC market risk disclosures (if applicable), FAS-133, FAS-107, and any other relevant disclosures.

AUDIT CONSIDERATIONS

The nature of the required disclosures about derivatives and hedging activities is largely driven by their classifications as hedges (and the specific type of hedge) or nonhedges. Audit risk relating to disclosures about derivatives and hedging activities is twofold: (1) if the transactions have been improperly classified or accounted for under FAS-133, the wrong disclosures could be provided, and (2) the level of disclosure could be inadequate. Previous chapters discuss how to reduce audit risk relating to accounting for derivatives and hedging activities. To reduce the risk of inadequate disclosure, auditors should compare the presentation and disclosure of derivatives with the requirements of FAS-133 (and, for public companies, SEC regulations, which are significantly more detailed). SAS-32, *Adequacy of Disclosures in Financial Statements* (AU 431), provides useful guidance in assessing the adequacy of disclosure that is not specifically required by GAAP.

ILLUSTRATIONS

Illustration 15-1:   Disclosure of Strategy and Accounting Policies Relating to Hedging Activities

The following is an excerpt from the Pfizer Inc. 2001 Annual Report, footnote 6D, Derivative Financial Instruments and Hedging Activities. Certain reported transactions have been omitted for brevity.

PURPOSE

A significant portion of revenues, earnings and net investments in foreign affiliates are exposed to changes in foreign exchange rates. We seek to manage our foreign exchange risk in part through operational means, including managing expected local currency revenues in relation to local currency costs and local currency assets in relation to local currency liabilities. Foreign exchange risk is also managed through the use of derivative financial instruments and foreign currency denominated debt. These financial instruments serve to protect net income against the impact of the translation into U.S. dollars of certain foreign exchange denominated transactions. At December 31, 2001, and 2000, the financial instruments are as follows:

- $3,627 million in 2001 and $3,827 million in 2000 notional amount of foreign currency forward-exchange contracts are used to offset the potential earnings effects from short-term foreign currency assets and liabilities in mostly intercompany cross-border transactions that arise from operations. We have entered into such contracts primarily to sell euro, U.K. pound and Japanese yen in exchange for U.S. dollars.

- $1,155 million of short-term and $457 million of long-term Japanese yen debt in 2001 and $1,262 million of short-term debt in 2000 is designated as a net investment hedge of our yen net investments in operations in order to limit the risk of adverse changes in the value of such investments related to foreign exchange.

- $160 million in 2001 and $36 million in 2000 notional amount of foreign currency swaps are designated as fair value hedges of euro debt investments maturing through mid-2003.

> **OBSERVATION:** Pfizer voluntarily provided the context about other assets and liabilities used in the same risk management activity.

Interest Rate Risk

Our interest-bearing investments, loans and borrowings are subject to interest rate risk. We invest and borrow primarily on a short-term or variable-rate basis. Significant interest rate risk is also managed through the use of derivative financial instruments as follows:

- $924 million in 2001 and $1,056 million in 2000 notional amount of yen interest rate swaps maturing in 2003 are designated as cash flow hedges of the yen "LIBOR" interest rate related to forecasted issuances of short-term debt. These swaps serve to reduce the variability of the yen interest rate by effectively fixing the rates on short-term debt at 1.2%.

- $600 million notional amount of interest rate swaps maturing in late 2004, $750 million notional amount of U.S. dollar interest rate swaps maturing in 2006, and $250 million interest rate swaps maturing in early 2008 are designated as fair value hedges of the changes in the fair value of fixed-rate debt. These swaps serve to reduce our exposure to long-term U.S. dollar interest rates by effectively converting the fixed rates associated with the majority of our long-term debt obligations to floating rates.

- $95 million notional amount of U.S. dollar interest rate swaps maturing in late 2004 are designated as cash flow hedges of "LIBOR" interest rates related to forecasted purchases of short-term fixed rate debt investments to be classified as available-for-sale securities. These swaps serve to reduce the variability of "LIBOR" interest rates by effectively fixing the rates on short-term debt securities at 3.5%.

ACCOUNTING POLICIES

In 2001, all derivative contracts are reported at fair value, with changes in fair value reported in earnings or deferred, depending on the nature and effectiveness of the offset or hedging relationship, as follows:

Foreign Exchange Risk

- We recognize the earnings impact of foreign currency forward-exchange contracts during the terms of the contracts, along with the earnings impact of the items they generally offset.
- We recognize the earnings impact of foreign currency swaps designated as cash flow or fair value hedges upon the recognition of the foreign exchange gain or loss on the translation to U.S. dollars of the hedged item.

Interest Rate Risk

- We recognize the earnings impact of interest rate swaps designated as cash flow hedges upon the recognition of the interest related to the hedged short-term debt and available-for-sale debt securities.
- We recognize the earnings impact of interest rate swaps designated as fair value hedges upon the recognition of the change in fair value for interest rate risk related to the hedged long-term debt.

Any ineffectiveness in a hedging relationship is recognized immediately into earnings. There was no significant ineffectiveness in 2001 and 2000.

In 2000, most derivative contracts were reported at contractual receipt or payable value. (*Editorial note*: In accordance with previous GAAP.)

The financial statements include the following items related to the derivatives and other financial instruments serving as hedges or offsets: (*Editorial note*: Information about 2000 classifications has been omitted, and the format has been changed for brevity.)

- *Other current liabilities* includes the fair value of foreign currency forward contracts and foreign currency swaps.
- *Other noncurrent liabilities* includes the fair value of interest rate swaps designated as cash flow hedges and fair value of foreign currency swaps designated as cash flow hedges.
- *Long-term debt* includes changes in the fair value of fixed rate debt hedged by interest rate swaps designated as fair value hedges.

- *Accumulated other comprehensive expense* includes changes in the fair value of interest rate swaps designated as cash flow hedges and changes in the foreign exchange translation of yen debt and foreign currency options.

- *Other income—net* includes changes in the fair value of foreign currency forward contracts, changes in the fair value of foreign currency swap contracts that hedge foreign exchange, changes in the fair value of interest rate swap contracts that hedge interest expense.

> **OBSERVATION:**   Pfizer has elected to report hedge gains and losses in one line item, rather than in the income statement category related to the item being hedged.

Illustration 15-2:   Narrative Discussion of Derivatives Strategy

The following is an excerpt from the 2001 Annual Report of CNA Financial Corp., footnote A, Summary of Significant Accounting Policies, Derivative Financial Instruments, that discusses the company's strategies in using derivatives (primarily *not* subject to hedge accounting).

CNA uses investment derivatives in the normal course of business, primarily to reduce its exposure to market risk (principally interest rate risk, equity stock price risk and foreign currency risk) stemming from various assets and liabilities. The Company's principal objective under such market risk strategies is to achieve the desired reduction in economic risk, even if the position will not receive hedge accounting treatment. The Company also uses derivatives for purposes of income enhancement, primarily via the sale of covered call options.

The Company's use of derivatives is limited by statutes and regulations promulgated by the various regulatory bodies to which it is subject, and by its own derivative policy. The derivative policy limits the authorization to initiate derivative transactions to certain personnel. The policy generally prohibits the use of derivatives with a maturity greater than 18 months, unless the derivative is matched with assets or liabilities having a longer maturity. The policy prohibits the use of derivatives containing greater than one-to-one leverage with respect to changes in the underlying price, rate or index. The policy also prohibits the use of borrowed funds, including funds obtained through repurchase transactions, to engage in derivative transactions.

Credit exposure associated with nonperformance by the counterparties to derivative instruments is generally limited to the gross fair value of the asset related to the instruments recognized in the Consolidated Balance Sheets. The Company mitigates the risk of nonperformance by using multiple counterparties and by monitoring their creditworthiness. The Company generally requires collateral from its derivative investment counterparties depending on the amount of the exposure and the credit rating of the counterparty.

The Company has exposure to economic losses due to interest rate risk arising from changes in the level of, or volatility of, interest rates. The Company attempts to mitigate its exposure to interest rate risk through active portfolio management, which includes rebalancing its existing portfolios of assets and liabilities, as well as changing the characteristics of investments to be purchased or sold in the future. In addition, various derivative financial instruments are used to modify the interest rate risk exposures of certain assets and liabilities. These strategies include the use of interest rate swaps, interest rate caps and floors, options, futures, forwards and commitments to purchase securities. These instruments are generally used to lock interest rates or unrealized gains, to shorten or lengthen durations of fixed maturity securities or investment contracts, or to hedge (on an economic basis) interest rate risks associated with investments, variable rate debt and life insurance liabilities. The Company has used these types of instruments as designated hedges against specific assets or liabilities on an infrequent basis.

The Company is exposed to equity price risk as a result of its investment in equity securities and equity derivatives. Equity price risk results from changes in the level or volatility of equity prices, which affect the value of equity securities, or instruments that derive their value from such securities. CNA attempts to mitigate its exposure to such risks by limiting its investment in any one security or index. The Company may also manage this risk by utilizing instruments such as options, swaps, futures and collars to protect appreciation in securities held. CNA uses derivatives in one of its separate accounts to mitigate equity price risk associated with its indexed group annuity contracts by purchasing Standard & Poor's 500® (S&P 500®) index futures contracts in a notional amount equal to the contract holder liability, which is calculated using the S&P 500® rate of return.

Foreign exchange rate risk arises from the possibility that changes in foreign currency exchange rates will impact the fair value of financial instruments denominated in a foreign currency. The Company's foreign transactions are primarily denominated in Canadian dollars, British pounds and euros. The Company manages this risk via asset/liability matching and through the use of foreign currency futures and/or forwards. The Company has infrequently designated these types of instruments as hedges against specific assets or liabilities.

> **OBSERVATION:** CNA voluntarily provides quantitative data about its derivatives in note C, including the notional/contractual amounts of major derivative types and recognized gains and losses.

Illustration 15-3: Quantitative Disclosures about Hedging Activities

The following is an excerpt from the 2001 Annual Report of Citigroup Inc., footnote 23, Derivatives and Other Hedging Activities.

The following table summarizes certain information related to the Company's hedging activities for the year ended December 31, 2001:

Fair Value Hedges:

Hedge ineffectiveness recognized in earnings	$168
Net gain excluded from assessment of effectiveness	85*

Cash Flow Hedges:

Hedge ineffectiveness recognized in earnings	20
Amount excluded from assessment of effectiveness	—

Net Investment Hedges:

Net gain included in foreign currency translation adjustment within accumulated other changes in equity from nonowner sources	432

Editorial Notes:

*This amount is recognized in earnings.

**Citigroup is not required to separately disclose the amount of *in* effectiveness in this type of hedge that has been recognized in earnings, if any.

Additionally, $313 million of net gains is expected to be reclassified from accumulated other changes in equity from nonowner sources within twelve months from December 31, 2001.

The accumulated other changes in equity from nonowner sources from cash flow hedges for 2001 can be summarized as follows (net of taxes):

(in millions of dollars)	2001
Beginning balance (1)	$ (3)
Net gains from cash flow hedges	315
Net amounts reclassified to earnings	(144)
Ending balance	$168

(1) Results from the cumulative effect of accounting change for cash flow hedges.

Illustration 15-4:   Reporting Cash Flow Hedges in Other Comprehensive Income

(This Illustration is adapted from Example 11 in FAS-133 (paragraphs 173-175).)

Grainworks Corporation's cash flow hedge transactions for the years 20X2 through 20X4 were as follows:

a. Throughout the period, corn futures contracts are purchased to hedge anticipated purchases of corn inventory.

b. In 20X2, Grainworks entered into a Euro exchange contract to hedge the foreign currency risk associated with the expected purchase of a grain processing machine with a five-year useful life that it bought from a vendor in Germany at the end of 20X2.

c. In 20X2, Grainworks entered into a 10-year interest rate swap to hedge the variable interest payments on the concurrent issuance of ten-year debt.

d. In January 20X4, Grainworks entered into a two-year Swiss franc forward exchange contract to hedge a forecasted export sale (denominated in Swiss francs, expected to occur in December 20X5) of grain to a large customer in Switzerland. In June 20X4, it closed the forward contract, but the forecasted transaction is still expected to occur.

Grainworks' accounting policy is to reflect the effective portion of gains and losses on hedging transactions in the same income statement line item as the item being hedged. The following table reconciles the beginning and ending OCI balances for 20X4. Assume that there are no other amounts in OCI.

Other Comprehensive Income—Debit (Credit)

	OCI at 1/1/X4	Changes in FV Recognized in 20X4	Reciases Adjustments	Note	OCI at 12/31/X4
Derivatives designated as hedges of:					
Inventory purchases	$230	$85	$(270)	1	$45
Equipment purchase	120	—	(30)	2	90

Other Comprehensive Income—Debit (Credit)

	OCI at 1/1/X4	Changes in FV Recognized in 20X4	Reclases Adjustments	Note	OCI at 12/31/X4
Variable interest rate payments	(40)	10	5	3	(25)
Export sale	0	(50)	0	4	(50)
Before-tax totals	$310	$45	$(295)		$60
After-tax totals*	$217	$32	$(207)		$42

*The after-tax amounts assume a 30 percent effective tax rate.

Notes:

1. The $85 represents the effective portion of the hedge gains deferred during the period. The $(270) reclass adjustment represents the amount released out of OCI and into cost of goods sold when the grain was sold to customers during the period.

2. No amounts were added to OCI because the derivative was closed out in a prior period. The $(30) reclass adjustment represents the amount released out of OCI into depreciation expense this year as the machine is depreciated over its five-year useful life. [$150 original deferred gain/5 years = 30 per year. $90 balance reflects two years' reclassifications]

3. The $10 represents the effective portion of the hedge gain deferred during the period. The $5 reclass adjustment is the amount released out of OCI into interest expense to create the desired fixed rate of interest.

4. The $(50) represents the effective portion of the hedge loss deferred during the period. There is no reclass adjustment because the forecasted sale has not yet occurred.

Effect of Selected Items on Shareholders' Equity
Year Ended December 31, 20X4 Debit (Credit)

Accumulated other comprehensive income:

Balance on December 31, 20X3	$ 217
Net change during the year related to cash flow hedges	(175)
Balance on December 31, 20X4	$ 42

PART IV:
EQUITY INSTRUMENTS

CHAPTER 16
ISSUER'S ACCOUNTING FOR EQUITY INSTRUMENTS AND RELATED CONTRACTS

CONTENTS

Overview	16.03
Background	16.04
Scope	16.04
Applicable Literature	16.06
Distinguishing between Liabilities and Equity	16.06
Important Notice: Financial Instruments with Characteristics of Liabilities, Equity, or Both	16.06
Definitions	16.07
Liabilities	16.07
Equity	16.07
Instruments with Characteristics of Both Liabilities and Equity	16.08
Temporary Equity	16.08
Accounting for Equity Transactions	16.09
Overview	16.09
Stock Issued for Cash	16.09
Costs Incurred in a Shelf Registration	16.09
Promises or Notes Received for Capital Stock	16.10
Dividends (General)	16.10
Cash Dividends	16.10
Dividends-in-Kind	16.11
Stock Dividends	16.11
Stock Splits	16.12
Treasury Stock (Equity Buy-Backs or Repurchases)	16.12
Purchase of Treasury Shares at Above-Market Price	16.14
Subsequent Sale of Treasury Stock	16.14
Subsidiary (or Joint Venture) Investment in Stock of Parent or Joint Venture Partner	16.14

Minority Interest 16.15

Sale of Subsidiary Shares 16.15

Equity Instruments That May Not Be Reported in Stockholders' Equity 16.16

Certain Redeemable Financial Instruments 16.16

Exhibit 16-1: Navigating the Literature on Equity-Linked Contracts 16.17

Trust-Preferred Securities 16.19

Exhibit 16-2: Summary of FSP FAS 150-3 Effective Date Deferrals for Certain Mandatorily Redeemable Instruments 16.20

Imputing Dividends on Preferred Stock 16.24

Extinguishment by a Parent of a Subsidiary's Mandatorily Redeemable Preferred Stock 16.25

Obligations to Issue a Variable Number of Shares 16.25

Surplus Notes Issued by Insurance Companies (AICPA PB-15) 16.26

Credit Union Member Shares/Deposits 16.26

Accounting for Derivatives with Characteristics of Debt and Equity 16.27

Contracts Indexed to and Potentially Settled in a Company's Own Stock 16.27

Applicability of FAS-150 versus EITF Issues 00-6 and 00-19 16.29

Initial and Subsequent Balance Sheet Classification and Measurement 16.30

Exhibit 16-3: Accounting for Contracts Indexed to a Company's Own Stock under EITF 00-19 16.34

Exhibit 16-4: Ongoing Accounting for Freestanding Indexed Contracts under EITF 00-19 16.37

Contract Reclassification 16.38

Interaction with FAS-133 16.39

Accounting by a Parent Company for Contracts Indexed to the Stock of a Consolidated Subsidiary (EITF 00-6) 16.40

Combinations of Contracts and Other Transactions 16.41

Accelerated Share Repurchases (EITF 99-7) 16.42

Equity Instruments Subject to Registration Payment Arrangements 16.42

Disclosures 16.45

Information about Capital Structure 16.45

Information about Securities 16.45

Liquidation Preference of Preferred Stock 16.46

Redeemable Stock 16.47

Equity Instruments Representing Obligations   16.47

Contracts Indexed to a Company's Own Stock   16.48

Registration Payment Arrangements   16.48

Earnings per Share   16.49

    Equity Instruments Excluded from EPS   16.50

    Participating Securities (EITF 03-6)   16.50

    Preferred Stock   16.52

    Contracts Indexed to and Potentially Settled
       in a Company's Own Shares   16.52

    Exhibit 16-5: *EPS Treatment of Contracts Indexed
       to a Company's Own Stock*   16.54

    Accelerated Share Repurchase Programs   16.55

    Fair Value   16.55

Regulatory Considerations   16.55

    Disclosures about Capital Adequacy   16.57

Audit Considerations   16.57

Illustrations   16.58

    Illustration 16-1: *Treasury Stock Buy-Back*   16.58

    Illustration 16-2: *Accounting for a Purchased Put
       Option Indexed to and Potentially Settled in a
       Company's Own Stock*   16.59

    Illustration 16-3: *Accounting for a Written Put
       Option Indexed to and Potentially Settled in a
       Company's Own Stock*   16.61

    Illustration 16-4: *Accounting for a Forward
       Purchase Contract*   16.62

OVERVIEW

Accounting for debt finance and equity finance is fundamentally different. Debt is recognized as a liability on the balance sheet and the cost of funds is recognized as interest expense in the income statement. Gains and losses are recognized in income when debt is extinguished. Equity instruments represent shareholders' ownership interests in the net assets of a company. Transactions involving a company's equity instruments generally do not affect net income, including dividends and other distributions to shareholders, and purchases and sales of the company's own stock. Repurchases of a company's outstanding stock (treasury stock) are reported as a deduction from stockholders' equity, not as assets.

Instruments issued in the form of equity that represent obligations of the issuer, such as mandatorily redeemable preferred stock, and obligations to issue a variable number of shares (representing a fixed monetary amount) should be reported as liabilities, not equity.

Certain instruments common in the marketplace have characteristics of both debt and equity instruments. Currently, separate guidelines exist to identify debt and equity instruments, or components of instruments, for (1) compound cash instruments such as convertible debt and (2) freestanding derivative contracts such as detachable stock purchase warrants and forward contracts to buy and sell stock. Chapter 10, "Convertible Debt and Similar Instruments," addresses the first category. The accounting model for freestanding derivative contracts is based primarily on whether the contract can be settled for stock, cash, or a choice between the two. Contracts that may require net cash settlement by the issuer are classified as assets or liabilities—*not* as permanent equity—and marked to market through income. To be classified as an equity instrument, the issuer must be contractually required or entitled to settle the contract in shares, and settlement in shares must be feasible. However, forward purchase contracts and written put options involving a company's own stock must be accounted for as liabilities (or as assets, if the fair value is positive), even when the contract must be settled in shares. If a contract is considered an equity instrument of the issuer, changes in fair value are not recognized.

Disclosures are required of a company's capital structure and about specific types of instruments. Earnings per share are computed using certain assumptions about settlement of contracts that differ in some cases from the assumptions used for accounting purposes. Certain adjustments are made to EPS for transactions involving a company's own stock that are required to be accounted for as liabilities.

BACKGROUND

Scope

Debt instruments and equity instruments are both financial instruments. However, an entity's own equity instruments are not accounted for as "financial instruments" *per se*. Accounting for equity instruments reflects their residual nature—they do not of themselves result in gains or losses to the enterprise. Accordingly, issues such as subsequent measurement, impairment, and interest income/expense do not arise for transactions that are properly categorized as the issuer's own equity.

This chapter provides an overview of accounting for a company's own equity, so that the reader understands the differences in accounting for debt versus equity finance. Additional information on equity instruments and other components of stockholders' equity is provided in Chapter 44, "Stockholders' Equity," and Chapter 13, "Earnings per Share," of CCH's *GAAP Guide Level A*.

Many types of financial instruments have attributes of both debt and equity instruments. This chapter addresses financial instruments that are issued in the form of shares but actually embody obligations that must be settled by a transfer of assets. Examples of those instruments are mandatorily redeemable preferred stock and certain forms of trust-preferred securities. This chapter addresses how to distinguish between debt and equity instruments for accounting purposes and how to account for freestanding contracts indexed to and potentially settled in a company's own stock.

Accounting for equity instruments and hybrids is complex because several accounting standards (and their interpretations) overlap. The following table summarizes where the issuer's accounting for various types of instruments is addressed in this book—for ease of reference, the chapters have been organized primarily by instrument type.

Issuer's accounting for . . .	*Addressed in . . .*
• Convertible debt	Chapter 10, "Convertible Debt and Similar Instruments"
• Equity instruments: — Common stock — Preferred stock — Redeemable stock	Chapter 16, "Issuer's Accounting for Equity Instruments and Related Contracts"
• Warrants, options, and forward contracts involving the issuer's own stock	Chapter 16, "Issuer's Accounting for Equity Instruments and Related Contracts" (some will be derivatives)
• Equity instruments with embedded put or call options	Chapter 13, "Embedded Derivatives"

A company issues its own stock for a variety of reasons other than to finance its own operations, including:

- To compensate employees.
- As payment for goods and services from nonemployees.
- In connection with business combinations and other strategic alliances.

Stock compensation (involving employees and nonemployees) has its own specialized accounting model that is addressed in FAS-123(R) and several interpretations by the APB, FASB and EITF. (Refer to Chapter 43, "Stock-Based Payments," of CCH's *GAAP Guide Level A* and Chapter 38, "Stock Compensation," of CCH's *GAAP Guide Levels B, C, and D* for additional information.) Likewise, accounting for business combinations is a specialized area of accounting addressed by FAS-141 and numerous interpretations. (Refer to Chapter 4, "Business Combinations," of CCH's *GAAP Guide Level A* and Chapter 6, "Business Combinations," of CCH's *GAAP Levels B, C, and D* for additional information.)

Applicable Literature

CON-6 sets forth the basic definitions of liabilities and equity instruments. APB-9 establishes the general principle that capital transactions should generally not affect net income. Accounting for basic equity instruments is primarily addressed by ARB-43, Chapters 1B and 7B, including treasury stock transactions, stock dividends, and stock splits. FAS-150 addresses accounting for and disclosure of certain instruments issued in the form of equity that represent obligations of the issuer, including forward purchase contracts and written put options. FAS-150 does not address hybrid contracts that have embedded debt and equity components, such as convertible debt (Chapter 10, "Convertible Debt and Similar Instruments," and Chapter 13, "Embedded Derivatives," provide additional information).

APB-14 addresses accounting for "traditional" detachable stock purchase warrants that require settlement in shares of the company's stock, if exercised. EITF Issue 00-19 addresses accounting for most "newer" forms of warrants and equity derivative contracts that could require net cash settlement, settlement in shares, or a choice between the methods at the time of settlement. FAS-133 applies to such contracts that are not considered equity instruments of the issuer and that meet the definition of a derivative. PB-15 addresses accounting for surplus notes issued by insurance companies.

FAS-129 requires disclosure of information about an entity's capital structure. SOP 01-6 requires certain disclosures for financial institutions about capital adequacy. There are numerous EITF issues that address unusual dividends on preferred stock, contracts involving the stock of a subsidiary, and how to reflect certain forms of settlement in earnings-per-share computations.

There are a variety of income tax issues associated with capital stock transactions, including accounting for the tax effects of transactions among or with shareholders and tax benefits and credits relating to dividend distributions. FAS-109 and several EITF Issues address those issues.

DISTINGUISHING BETWEEN LIABILITIES AND EQUITY

IMPORTANT NOTICE
FINANCIAL INSTRUMENTS WITH CHARACTERISTICS OF LIABILITIES, EQUITY, OR BOTH

After the issuance of FAS-150, the FASB began deliberations on "phase two" of the Liabilities and Equity project. The objective of this phase of the project is to develop comprehensive guidance for accounting and reporting for financial instruments with characteristics of liabilities, equity, or both. The FASB is considering three approaches for the classification and measurement of such instruments and expects to publish a Preliminary Views document in the third quarter of 2007. At a later stage, the FASB will develop a proposed Statement jointly with the International Accounting Standards Board (IASB). In January 2007, the FASB committed to an aggressive timeline for this project. Readers should be alert to developments on this important project.

Definitions

Liabilities

CON-6 provides definitions of liabilities and equity for accounting purposes. CON-6 defines liabilities as follows:

> Liabilities are probable future sacrifices of economic benefits arising from present obligations of a particular entity to transfer assets or provide services to other entities in the future as a result of past transactions or events. [Paragraph 35, footnote references omitted.]
>
> A liability has three essential characteristics: (a) it embodies a present duty or responsibility to one or more other entities that entails settlement by probable future transfer or use of assets at a specified or determinable date, on occurrence of a specified event, or on demand, (b) the duty or responsibility obligates a particular entity, leaving it little or no discretion to avoid the future sacrifice, and (c) the transaction or other event obligating the entity has already happened. [Paragraph 36]

Accounting for liabilities (debt) is addressed in Chapter 8, "Debt Financing," Chapter 9, "Securities Lending Arrangements, and Other Pledges of Collateral," Chapter 10, "Convertible Debt and Similar Instruments," and Chapter 11, "Extinguishments of Debt."

Equity

CON-6 defines equity as the residual interest in the assets of an entity that remain after deducting its liabilities (paragraph 49). Paragraph 60 discusses equity in more detail:

> In a business enterprise, the equity is the ownership interest. It stems from ownership rights (or the equivalent) and involves a relation between an enterprise and its owners *as owners* rather than as employees, suppliers, customers, lenders, or in some other nonowner role. [Paragraph 60, footnote references omitted.]
>
> Owners invest in a business enterprise with the expectation of obtaining a return on their investment as a result of the enterprise's providing goods or services to customers at a

profit. Owners benefit if the enterprise is profitable but bear the risk that it may be unprofitable. [Paragraph 61, certain references omitted.]

"Plain-vanilla" common stock and preferred stock are examples of equity instruments of issuers.

> **OBSERVATION:** A specific form of financing may be characterized by the Internal Revenue Service, a regulator, or another interested party as debt or equity. Those characterizations are based on different principles and objectives and are *not* determinative for accounting purposes.

Instruments with Characteristics of Both Liabilities and Equity

Notwithstanding these basic definitions, certain instruments have characteristics of both liabilities and equity, such as convertible debt, trust-preferred securities, and certain options and forward contracts involving the company's own stock that involve various settlement alternatives. Accounting for those instruments has been addressed by FAS-150, EITF Issues, and guidance published by the SEC.

FAS-150 primarily addresses accounting for instruments issued in the form of equity that must be reported as liabilities by the issuer. Examples include mandatorily redeemable preferred stock, forward purchase contracts and written put options on a company's own stock, and certain contracts that require (or permit at the issuer's choice) settlement with the issuer's own stock but that do not establish an ownership relationship. Depending on the terms, some of those contracts must be accounted for as debt obligations with the accrual of interest cost, and others must be accounted for like derivatives at fair value (contracts that met the definition of a derivative are subject to FAS-133).

> ☛ **PRACTICE POINTER:** FAS-150 was generally effective for instruments issued or modified after May 31, 2003, and for existing contracts at the beginning of the first interim period beginning after June 15, 2003. FSP FAS 150-3, "Effective Date, Disclosures, and Transition for Mandatorily Redeemable Financial Instruments of Certain Nonpublic Entities and Certain Mandatorily Redeemable Noncontrolling Interests under FASB Statement No. 150, *Accounting for Certain Instruments with Characteristics of both Liabilities and Equity*," defers the effective date for certain mandatorily redeemable instruments. Certain of those deferrals are indefinite, pending further FASB action. Details of those deferrals are discussed in the section below titled "Certain Redeemable Financial Instruments."

Temporary Equity

The SEC requires that public companies report certain instruments "outside of equity" if they do not have the essential elements of equity. Companies report such items either as debt, or in a separate category between debt and equity (sometimes called the "mezzanine").

> ☛ **PRACTICE POINTER:** Under current practice, *outside of permanent equity* generally means separate presentation on the balance sheet between debt and equity. Temporary equity is a regulatory notion—the FASB Concepts Statements do not acknowledge temporary equity as a financial statement element.
>
> FAS-150 does not permit presentation between liabilities and equity within a category if the stock is mandatorily redeemable. However, the SEC guidance related to mezzanine presentation continues to apply for certain types of mandatorily redeemable financial instruments that are not subject to FAS-150. Refer to the section *Certain Redeemable Financial Instruments* later in this chapter for further discussion.

ACCOUNTING FOR EQUITY TRANSACTIONS

Overview

Common stock and preferred stock are recorded in stockholders' equity at an amount equal to the par or stated value of the stock. Any amount received in excess of the par or stated value is recorded in additional paid-in capital. Warrants and other derivatives that are properly classified as equity instruments are recorded as additional paid-in capital until shares are actually issued. Transactions involving the company's own stock generally do not affect earnings (except certain arrangements that represent obligations). When shares are reacquired, treasury stock is reported as a reduction of stockholders' equity, not as an asset. Cash flows relating to issuances and repurchases of a company's own shares, and payments of dividends, are considered cash flows from financing activities.

Stock Issued for Cash

When stock is issued for cash, the stock is recorded at its par value and any excess over the par value is recorded in a separate category called "additional paid-in capital" or something similar. Any direct costs of issuing stock should be deducted from the related proceeds and the net amount should be recorded as capital stock or contributed capital. Indirect costs, such as officer's salaries, should be charged to expense as incurred. (AICPA TPA 4110.01)

Costs Incurred in a Shelf Registration

Legal and other fees incurred by a public company in connection with an SEC filing for an equity security it plans to offer under a shelf registration should be capitalized as a prepaid expense. When securities are taken off the shelf and sold, a portion of the costs attributable to the securities sold should be charged against paid-in capital. Any subsequent costs incurred to keep the filing active should be charged to expense as incurred. If the filing is withdrawn, any remaining capitalized costs should be charged to expense. (AICPA TPA, 4110.10)

Promises or Notes Received for Capital Stock

In a stock subscription, potential shareholders agree to purchase shares for a specified price at some time in the future. In other cases, investors pay for stock (or contribute capital) with a promissory note. Such promises or notes should be reported as a deduction from stockholder's equity except in rare circumstances. (That is, the amount receivable is netted against the shares to be issued or the capital contribution until the receivable is collected.) Reporting a receivable for stock (or a capital contribution) as an asset might be appropriate if (1) the note is collected in cash prior to the issuance of the financial statements or (2) if it is secured by an irrevocable letter of credit from a creditworthy institution or liquid collateral and it includes a stated maturity in a reasonably short period of time. (EITF 85-1)

> **OBSERVATION:** It is generally inappropriate to report notes receivable in a stock transaction as an asset because that would have the effect of immediately increasing equity. Notes receivable in an equity transaction are held to a higher standard, given the significance of the entry.

> **SEC REGISTRANT ALERT:** The SEC staff believes that only notes or receivables that are received in exchange for the issuance of fully vested, nonforfeitable equity instruments to a party unrelated to the issuer, and that are fully secured by specific assets other than the equity instruments granted can be classified in the issuer's balance sheet as assets. All other notes or receivables should be classified as a deduction from stockholders' equity. (June 10, 2002, letter from Robert K. Herdman, then Chief Accountant of the SEC to G. Michael Crooch, FASB, with respect to EITF Issue 02-1, which was subsequently withdrawn from the EITF's agenda)

Dividends (General)

Cash Dividends

Cash dividends are the most common type of dividend distribution. Preferred stock usually pays a fixed dividend, expressed in dollars or as a percentage.

Cash dividends are recorded on the books of the issuing corporation as a liability (dividends payable) on the date the board of directors formally declares a dividend to stockholders (declaration date). An equal amount is deducted from retained earnings. Dividends are paid only on authorized, issued, and outstanding shares. Cash dividends paid on instruments that are reported as equity are considered a cash flow from financing activities. (FAS-95, par. 20)

> **OBSERVATION:** Note that dividends paid on equity instruments are considered a financing cash flow, but interest paid on a debt instrument is considered an operating cash flow.

Dividends-in-Kind

A dividend-in-kind (a company's property other than its own stock) should be recorded at the fair value of the asset transferred, and a gain or loss should be recognized by the enterprise on the disposition of the asset. (APB-29, par. 18)

> **OBSERVATION:** A gain or loss recognized on a dividend-in-kind, if any, is attributable to the difference between the carrying amount and fair value of the asset being transferred. The gain or loss does not stem from a "transaction involving the company's own stock," and therefore does not violate the general principle that capital transactions should not affect net income.

Distribution of loans to shareholders EITF Issue 01-2, Issue 11, addresses a scenario where a company forms a subsidiary and transfers depreciated loans into it (i.e., their book value exceeds their fair value). The parent then distributes stock in the subsidiary to the parent's shareholders. Such transfers should be considered dividends-in-kind, and accounted for by the company and the recipient at fair value.

> ☞ **PRACTICE POINTER:** The transaction is not considered a spin-off (reorganization) because the subsidiary is not an operating company. APB-29, paragraph 23, and EITF Issue 01-2, Issue 12 address spin-offs, split-ups, and other reorganizations involving operating companies.

Stock Dividends

Stock dividends are distributions of a company's own capital stock to its existing stockholders in lieu of cash. Stock dividends are accounted for by transferring an amount equal to the fair market value of the stock from retained earnings to paid-in capital. The dividend is recorded at the date of declaration by reducing retained earnings and establishing a temporary account, such as "Stock Dividend to Be Distributed."

Because no asset distribution is required for a stock dividend, that account is part of stockholders' equity, in contrast to a cash dividend payable account, which is a liability. When the stock is distributed, the stock dividend account is eliminated and permanent capital accounts (e.g., common stock and additional paid-in capital) are increased. (ARB-43, Ch. 7B, par. 10)

Stock Splits

When a stock distribution is more than say 20 percent to 25 percent of the outstanding shares immediately before the distribution, it is generally considered a stock split. (ARB-43, Ch. 7B, par. 13) A stock split increases the number of shares of capital stock outstanding, and a reverse stock split decreases the number of shares of capital stock outstanding. The par or stated value per share of capital stock decreases or increases proportionately, but the total dollar amount of stockholders' equity does not change.

A stock split is used by a corporation to reduce the market price of its capital stock and make it more attractive to buyers. (ARB-43, Ch. 7B, par. 2) Thus, in a 4-for-1 straight stock split, the new shares would probably sell for about one-fourth of the previous market price of the old shares. Reverse stock splits are unusual and are used to increase the market price of a corporation's stock. For example, a reverse stock split of 1-for-4 of stock selling for $3 would probably increase the market price of the new shares to about $12 per share.

To record a stock split, only a memorandum entry in the capital stock account is required to indicate the new par or stated value of the stock and the number of new shares outstanding. Stock splits should *not* be referred to as dividends. (ARB-43, Ch. 7B, par. 15)

> **OBSERVATION:** Stock dividends and stock splits are similar in that they result in increased numbers of outstanding shares of stock for which stockholders make no payment. They differ, however, in size, in their effect on the stock's market price, and, most importantly, in managerial intent. In the case of a stock dividend, management's intent usually is to make a distribution to owners while preserving present cash; in the case of a stock split, management's intent is to affect (reduce) market price.

Treasury Stock (Equity Buy-Backs or Repurchases)

Shares that have been issued and then repurchased by a company are considered "held in treasury." Companies buy back their shares for a variety of reasons including:

- To satisfy share requirements on employee stock options.
- To deliver if an investor exercises convertible debt.

- To utilize excess cash, especially when management believes the company's stock price is low.
- To enhance earnings per share (by reducing the number of shares outstanding) and other ratios.

Sometimes share repurchases are effected with equity derivatives, such as forward purchase contracts and options. Those instruments are discussed later in this chapter.

Treasury shares are reported separately as a reduction of stockholders' equity. Shares in treasury are not considered outstanding (for earnings-per-share and other purposes). Dividends are not paid on treasury stock.

> ☛ **PRACTICE POINTER:** It is not in accordance with GAAP to report treasury shares as an asset of the company under any circumstances. Accordingly, it is never appropriate to recognize dividends on treasury stock as a credit to income.

Treasury share purchases are recorded at the amount paid (unless the price is significantly in excess of market value). When treasury shares are *retired*, an excess of purchase price over par or stated value may be accounted for in one of three ways:

1. Allocated between additional paid-in capital (limited to previous additions to paid-in capital and certain other items on the same issue) and retained earnings;
2. Reflected entirely as a deduction from additional paid-in capital (ARB-43, Ch. 1B, par. 7); or
3. Charged entirely to retained earnings in recognition of the fact that an enterprise can always capitalize or allocate retained earnings for such purposes. (APB-6, par. 12(a))

An excess of par or stated value over purchase price should be credited to additional paid-in capital. (APB-6, par. 12(a))

If an enterprise's stock is acquired for purposes *other than* retirement, or if ultimate disposition has not yet been decided, the cost of acquired stock may be shown:

- Separately as a deduction from the total of capital stock, additional paid-in capital, and retained earnings, or
- One of the methods for retired stock may be used. (APB-6, par. 12(b))

> ☛ **PRACTICE POINTER:** Reporting of treasury stock purchases is an accounting policy decision that should be applied consistently from period to period.

Purchase of Treasury Shares at Above-Market Price

A purchase of shares at a price significantly in excess of the current market price creates a presumption that the purchase price includes amounts attributable to items other than the shares purchased. Treasury shares should be reported at their fair value at the date the major terms of the agreement to purchase the shares are reached. The price paid in excess of the fair value of the shares purchased should be attributed to the other elements of the transaction and accounted for according to their substance. If no stated or unstated consideration in addition to the capital stock can be identified, the entire purchase price should be accounted for as the cost of treasury shares. The allocation of amounts paid and the accounting treatment for such amounts should be disclosed. (FTB 85-6)

> ☞ **PRACTICE POINTER:** The amount in excess of the fair value of the stock may represent "greenmail" or compensation for a stand-still agreement, which precludes the shareholder (or former shareholder) from purchasing additional shares for a period of time. Such fees should be expensed as incurred. (FTB 85-6)

Subsequent Sale of Treasury Stock

"Gains" on the reissuance or sale of treasury stock are recorded in additional paid-in capital. "Losses" may be charged to additional paid-in capital to the extent of any previous net "gains" from sales or retirements of the same class of stock; any excess loss should be recorded in retained earnings. (APB-6, par. 12(b))

> **OBSERVATION:** A subsequent sale of treasury stock at a price different from its historical purchase price does *not* affect net income.

Subsidiary (or Joint Venture) Investment in Stock of Parent or Joint Venture Partner

EITF Issue 98-2 sought to address accounting for (1) a subsidiary's investment in the stock of its parent and (2) a joint venture's investment in the stock of a venture partner in the separate company financial statements of the subsidiary or joint venture. (ARB-51, paragraph 13, requires that the investment be eliminated in consolidation and the shares not be considered outstanding.) The EITF did not reach a consensus on whether the investment should be reported by the subsidiary as an asset or as a deduction from stockholders' equity. However, if the only significant asset of the parent is its investment in the subsidiary, the investment should be reported in the subsidiary's separate financial statements in a manner similar to treasury stock—that is, as a deduction from stockholders' equity.

Minority Interest

A minority interest exists when a parent company controls (and therefore consolidates) another company, but does not own 100% of the stock. Typically, control is obtained through majority ownership of the stock of a subsidiary; therefore, the amount held by outsiders is usually a "minority interest."

When a parent consolidates a subsidiary it controls, it includes 100% of the assets, liabilities, revenues, and expenses of the subsidiary in its own consolidated financial statements, even if it owns less than 100%. The minority interest's claim on the net assets of the subsidiary is typically shown as a separate category between liabilities and equity. The minority interest's share of net income is typically shown as an adjustment of consolidated net income.

> ☛ **PRACTICE POINTER:** If losses applicable to the minority interest in a subsidiary exceed the recorded amount for minority interest, the excess and any further losses applicable to the minority interest should be charged against the majority interest, because the minority interest has no obligation to make good on such losses. If earnings resume in the future, however, the majority interest should be credited to the extent of any losses previously absorbed. (ARB-51, par. 15)

Sale of Subsidiary Shares

A sale of shares in a subsidiary that is consolidated is *not* considered a transfer of financial assets under FAS-140 if the subsidiary holds nonfinancial assets (such as real estate). (FAS-140 Q&A, par. 10)

> **SEC REGISTRANT ALERT:** SEC Topic 5H, "Accounting For Sales of Stock by a Subsidiary" (SAB Nos. 51 and 84) provides guidance for public companies when a subsidiary issues shares of its own stock. If the offering price is greater than the parent's carrying amount for the shares, the SEC will permit recognition of a gain, provided that the sale of such shares is not a part of a broader corporate reorganization contemplated or planned by the registrant. A company that elects to recognize gains on such transactions must consistently apply that policy to all similar transactions. Recognized gains (or losses) arising from issuances by a subsidiary of its own stock should be presented as a separate line item in the consolidated income statement without regard to materiality and be clearly designated as nonoperating income.

> ☛ **PRACTICE POINTER:** The FASB project on business combinations would significantly change the accounting for minority interests and the sale of subsidiary shares. Readers should monitor developments in this area.

Equity Instruments That May Not Be Reported in Stockholders' Equity

Certain types of instruments that are issued in the form of equity represent obligations of the issuer to transfer assets, and must be accounted for as liabilities. Any nonsubstantive or minimal features should be disregarded in assessing the instruments discussed below. Judgment is necessary to evaluate the substance and magnitude of features in the context of all of the terms of an instrument and other relevant facts and circumstances. (FAS-150, par. 8)

> ☛ **PRACTICE POINTER:**   Instruments that are required to be presented as liabilities may *not* be presented between liabilities and equity in the balance sheet as "mezzanine" or "temporary" equity.

Exhibit 16-1 provides a flowchart to help navigate the accounting literature governing this area.

Certain Redeemable Financial Instruments

FAS-150 defines a *mandatorily redeemable financial instrument* as an instrument issued in the form of equity that requires the issuer to redeem the instrument by transferring assets at a specified or determinable date (or dates) or upon an event that is certain to occur (other than the liquidation or termination of the reporting entity). (FAS-150, par. 9) Mandatorily redeemable financial instruments must be classified as liabilities in the balance sheet, and initially measured at fair value. Subsequently, such instruments should be accounted for as debt. (Refer to Chapter 8, "Debt Financing," for additional information about recognition of interest expense and classification of cash flows.)

Liability classification is required for freestanding warrants (and other similar instruments) for shares that are either puttable or mandatorily redeemable *regardless* of the timing of the redemption feature or redemption price. In addition, such warrants are classified as liabilities even if the share repurchase feature of the arrangement is conditional based on a defined contingency. (FSP FAS 150-5)

Financial instruments that are conditionally redeemable upon an event that is *not* certain to occur at issuance should be reported as equity (specifically, temporary equity). However, if the redemption event subsequently occurs or becomes certain to occur, the instrument has become mandatorily redeemable and should be reclassified as a liability. The liability should be recorded at its fair value and equity should be reduced by the same amount. No gain or loss should be recognized. If the fair value of the shares is different from the carrying value at the time of reclassification, the difference is an adjustment of net earnings available to common shareholders in the EPS calculation. (FAS-150, par. 23 and EITF Topic D-98)

EXHIBIT 16-1
NAVIGATING THE LITERATURE ON EQUITY-LINKED CONTRACTS

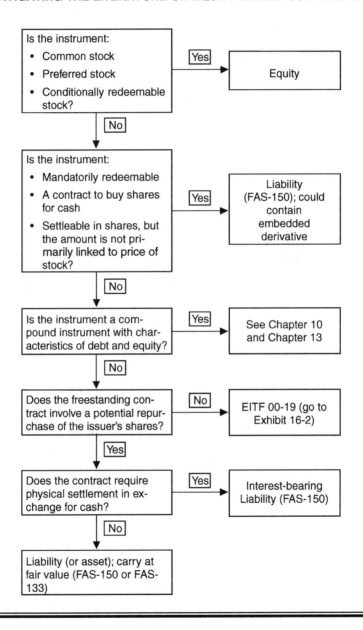

To summarize:

Type of Redeemable Stock	Balance Sheet Classification	Treatment of "Dividends"
Mandatorily	Debt	Interest expense
Conditionally	Equity	Retained earnings

FAS-150 was generally effective for instruments issued or modified after May 31, 2003, and for existing contracts at the beginning of the first interim period beginning after June 15, 2003. FSP FAS 150-3, issued in November 2003, deferred the effective date for certain mandatorily redeemable instruments as depicted in the Exhibit 16-2 below.

> **SEC REGISTRANT ALERT:** SEC Regulation S-X Rule 5-02.28 and EITF Topic D-98 still apply to mandatorily redeemable securities that are subject to the deferral under FSP FAS 150-3. The classification and measurement guidance in EITF Topic D-98 applies if both the classification and measurement guidance in FAS-150 has been deferred for an instrument. However, if the measurement guidance in FAS-150 has been deferred for an instrument, only the measurement guidance in EITF Topic D-98 would apply.
>
> EITF Topic D-98 provides the following classification and measurement guidance for instruments within its scope:
>
> • Securities with provisions that allow the holders to be paid upon the occurrence of events that are not solely within the issuer's control should be classified outside of permanent equity. Examples of such provisions are failure to comply with debt covenants or a reduction in the isser's credit rating.
>
> • Securities with provisions triggering redemption upon an event solely within the control of the issuer should be classified as part of permanent equity.
>
> • The initial carrying amount of redeemable preferred stock should be its fair value at the date of issue.
>
> • A security that is currently redeemable should be adjusted to its redemption amount at each balance sheet date. If it is probable that a security that is not currently redeemable will become redeemable, either of the following measurement methods is acceptable:
>
> — Accrete changes in the redemption value over the period from the date of issuance (or from the date that it becomes probable that the security will become redeemable, if later) to the earliest redemption date of the security using an appropriate methodology (usually the interest method).

— Recognize changes in the redemption value immediately as they occur and adjust the carrying value of the security to equal the redemption value at the end of each reportion period.

If it is not probable that the security will become redeemable, subsequent adjustment should not be made until it is probable that the security will become redeemable. However, disclosure of why it is not probable that the security will become redeemable must be made to the SEC.

Certain securities include multiple mutually exclusive options exercisable by the holder (for example, both a conversion option and a redemption feature) in which the redemption feature is exercisable following the passage of a specified time period. The probability assessment required by EITF Topic D-98 with respect to the redemption feature would not factor in the possible exercise of another option first. Because the security will become redeemable following only the passage of time, the instrument would be considered to be probable or become currently redeemable regardless of the likelihood of earlier conversion. Therefore, the changes in redemption values would be recognized over the period from the date of issuance to the earliest possible redemption date using either of the two methods in EITF D-98.

(Speech by Mark Northan, Professional Accounting Fellow, Office of the Chief Accountant of the SEC, at the December 2005 AICPA National Conference on SEC and PCAOB Developments)

Trust-Preferred Securities

Trust-preferred securities may be issued in many forms, including those called MIPS (Monthly Income Preferred Stock), QUIPS (Quarterly Income Preferred Stock), and TOPRS (Trust Originated Preferred Redeemable Stock).

Trust-preferred securities often have the following characteristics:

- A sponsoring entity establishes a special-purpose entity (SPE) or trust and purchases and holds all of the common equity of the SPE.
- The SPE issues preferred securities to investors and uses the proceeds to make a term loan to the sponsoring entity.
- The trust-preferred securities require redemption upon maturity of the underlying loan.

Under the provisions of FIN-46(R), *Consolidation of Variable Interest Entities* (revised December 2003), an entity that sponsors the type of structure described above generally should not consolidate the SPE.

EXHIBIT 16-2

SUMMARY OF FSP FAS 150-3 EFFECTIVE DATE DEFERRALS FOR CERTAIN MANDATORILY REDEEMABLE INSTRUMENTS

Instrument	Type of Issuer	Nature of Deferral of FAS-150 Provisions		
		Classification	Measurement	Disclosure*
Mandatorily Redeemable Financial Instruments Issued by Non-SEC Registrants (Not Issued by Subsidiaries)				
Mandatorily redeemable financial instruments with a fixed redemption date for an amount that is fixed or based on an external index	Nonpublic companies that are not SEC registrants	Deferred to fiscal periods beginning after December 15, 2004	Deferred to fiscal periods beginning after December 15, 2004	Deferred to fiscal periods beginning after December 15, 2004
All other mandatorily redeemable financial instruments	Nonpublic companies that are not SEC registrants	Deferred indefinitely	Deferred indefinitely	Deferred indefinitely
Certain Mandatorily Redeemable Noncontrolling Interests				
Mandatorily redeemable noncontrolling interests (MRNI) *not* classified as liabilities by the subsidiary** but classified as liabilities by the parent in consolidated financial statements	Public companies and nonpublic SEC registrants	Deferred indefinitely	Deferred indefinitely	No deferral. Apply FAS-150 disclosure requirements according to the effective date in that Statement

Instrument	Type of Issuer	Nature of Deferral of FAS-150 Provisions		
		Classification	Measurement	Disclosure*
	Nonpublic companies that are not SEC registrants	Deferred indefinitely	Deferred indefinitely	Deferred to fiscal periods beginning after December 15, 2004, for MRNI with a fixed redemption date for an amount that is fixed or based on an external index Deferred indefinitely for all other MRNI
Other MRNI issued *before* November 5, 2003	Public companies and nonpublic SEC registrants	No deferral. Apply FAS-150 effective date for classification	Deferred indefinitely	No deferral. Apply FAS-150 disclosure requirements according to the effective date in that Statement
	Nonpublic companies that are not SEC registrants	Deferred to fiscal periods beginning after December 15, 2004 for MRNI with a fixed redemption date for an amount that is fixed or based on an external index	Deferred indefinitely	Deferred to fiscal periods beginning after December 15, 2004, for MRNI with a fixed redemption date for an amount that is fixed or based on an external index

Nature of Deferral of FAS-150 Provisions

Instrument	Type of Issuer	Classification	Measurement	Disclosure*
Other MRNI issued on or *after* November 5, 2003		Deferred indefinitely for all other MRNI		Deferred indefinitely for all other MRNI
	Public companies and nonpublic SEC registrants	No deferral. Apply FAS-150 effective date for classification	No deferral. Apply FAS-150 effective date for measurement	No deferral. Apply FAS-150 disclosure requirements according to the effective date in that Statement
	Nonpublic companies that are not SEC registrants	Deferred to fiscal periods beginning after December 15, 2004, for MRNI with a fixed redemption date for an amount that is fixed or based on an external index	Deferred to fiscal periods beginning after December 15, 2004, for MRNI with a fixed redemption date for an amount that is fixed or based on an external index	Deferred to fiscal periods beginning after December 15, 2004 for MRNI with a fixed redemption date for an amount that is fixed or based on an external index
		Deferred indefinitely for all other MRNI	Deferred indefinitely for all other MRNI	Deferred indefinitely for all other MRNI

* FAS-129 disclosure requirements continue to apply as appropriate for situations in which FAS-150's disclosure requirements are deferred.

** Based on the exception in paragraph 9 of FAS-150 for interests that are mandatorily redeemable only upon liquidation or termination of the reporting entity.

The SPE is a variable interest entity (VIE) under FIN-46(R) because the equity investment in the SPE was financed through a term loan from the SPE to the sponsoring entity and therefore is not considered an equity investment at risk. For existing trust-preferred arrangements of the type described in this section, the sponsor should deconsolidate the SPE upon adoption of FIN-46(R). The sponsor is not the primary beneficiary of the SPE because it does not hold a variable interest in the SPE that absorbs the majority of the expected losses of the SPE. A call option embedded in the debt (a feature common in trust-preferred structures) is not considered a variable interest in the SPE. The sponsor should report its term loan from the SPE (a liability) and an equity-method investment in the common stock of the SPE. An investor in trust-preferred securities (the variable interests in the SPE) should evaluate whether the SPE is a VIE and, if so, whether the position held causes the investor to be considered the primary beneficiary of the SPE under FIN-46(R), in which case consolidation of the SPE would be required. (FIN-46(R), pars. B7 and B16)

> **OBSERVATION:** Prior to FIN-46(R), an entity that sponsored a trust-preferred arrangement as described in this section generally consolidated the SPE and reported the mandatorily redeemable preferred stock issued as either debt or minority interest in its consolidated financial statements. Some believed that FIN-46 was unclear regarding whether the sponsor should consolidate an SPE used in a trust-preferred arrangement. FIN-46(R) clarifies that issue and puts into place a new model for assessing which entity should consolidate an SPE. The focus of that assessment is on which entity would absorb the majority of the expected losses/ returns. In some trust-preferred structures, third-party investors absorb the majority of the expected losses/returns. The outcome is that the sponsor is *not* the primary beneficiary of the SPE used in some trust-preferred structures (such as the typical structure described in this section) and therefore would not consolidate the SPE. This is a major shift from prior practice, but it is based on the rationale that if the sponsor's equity is not at risk, it should not consolidate the SPE.

> **SEC REGISTRANT ALERT:** The deconsolidation of certain subsidiary trusts that issue preferred stock has led to the question of whether issuers of trust preferred securities may continue to provide the modified financial information permitted by Rule 3-10 of Regulation S-X, which presumes that consolidation is the basis for the 100%-owned requirement in that rule. The SEC staff believes that the guidance in FIN-46(R) leading to deconsolidation does not impede finance subsidiaries issuing trust preferred securities to avail themselves of Rule 3-10 if the requisite conditions are met and the following footnote disclosures are provided:
>
> • An explanation of the transaction between the parent and the subsidiary that resulted in debt appearing on the books of the subsidiary

- A statement of whether the finance subsidiary is consolidated (if the finance subsidiary is not consolidated, an explanation of why)

- If a deconsolidated finance subsidiary was previously consolidated and an explanation of the effect that deconsolidation had on the financial statements.

(Current Accounting and Disclosure Issues in the Division of Corporate Finance of the SEC, March 4, 2005)

Entities with only mandatorily redeemable shares   Some privately held companies issue shares that must be sold back to the company, for example, upon the holder's termination of employment or death. Such shares are considered liabilities because they are mandatorily redeemable upon the occurrence of an event that is certain to occur. If all of an entity's shares are mandatorily redeemable, the entity should describe the shares as *shares subject to mandatory redemption* in the balance sheet and distinguish those instruments from other liabilities. Payments to holders of such instruments and related accruals should be reported separately from interest and other payments due to creditors in the statements of cash flows and income. (FAS-150, par. 19)

For an entity with only mandatorily redeemable shares, if the shares issued can be redeemed at an amount greater than their book value, the entity must recognize a liability for the redemption price of the shares. If the redemption price is less than the book value of the shares, the difference should be reported as equity. (FSP FAS 150-2)

Imputing Dividends on Preferred Stock

Preferred stocks are sometimes issued with dividend rates that do not reflect current market conditions or that increase contractually over a stated period, causing the preferred stock to be issued at a discount. The EITF did not reach a consensus on the accounting for such instruments in EITF Issue 86-45. However, the SEC provided guidance for registrants that issue redeemable and nonredeemable preferred stock at a discount. Public companies should account for the discount as follows:

- If mandatorily redeemable, the carrying amount should be increased by periodic accretions, using the interest method, so that the carrying amount equals the mandatory redemption amount at the mandatory redemption date. The imputed dividend cost would be charged against retained earnings and increase the carrying amount of the preferred stock by a corresponding amount. (SEC Topic 3C, based on SAB-64)

- If nonredeemable, that is, the preferred stock is not redeemable or is redeemable only at the option of the issuer, the discount should be amortized over the period(s) before commencement of the perpetual dividend, using the interest method. (SEC Topic 5Q, based on SAB-68)

☛ **PRACTICE POINTER:** The guidance in SEC Topic 3C is expected to be revised to conform with FAS-150 (that is, under FAS-150, the imputed "dividend" on a mandatorily redeemable preferred stock should be reported as interest expense, not retained earnings). Registrants should monitor developments on this issue.

Extinguishment by a Parent of a Subsidiary's Mandatorily Redeemable Preferred Stock

If a company acquires the mandatorily redeemable preferred stock of its wholly owned subsidiary, the transaction should be accounted for as an extinguishment of debt. If the preferred stock is redeemable, but not *mandatorily* redeemable (that is, it is redeemable upon an event that is *not* certain to occur), the acquisition should be accounted for as a capital transaction and no gain or loss should be recognized. (EITF 86-32, as affected by FAS-150)

Obligations to Issue a Variable Number of Shares

A financial instrument that represents an unconditional obligation or a conditional obligation that the issuer must or may settle by issuing a variable number of its own shares should be classified as a liability (or as an asset, if the fair value is positive), if at inception, the monetary value is based solely or predominantly on any one of the following (FAS-150, par. 12):

- A fixed monetary amount (for example, a variable number of shares worth $10,000,000).
- A variable other than the fair value of the issuer's shares (for example, a note indexed to the FTSE, but settleable with a variable number of the issuer's shares).
- Changes inversely related to the price of the issuer's shares (for example, a net share settled written put option).

In such instruments, the issuer's stock is being used as "currency" and does not convey an ownership interest in the entity (unless and until it is delivered). Obligations to issue a variable number of shares should be measured initially at fair value and classified as liabilities in the balance sheet (or as assets, if the fair value is positive). Subsequently, the liability should be measured at fair value unless another measurement attribute is specified by FAS-133, FAS-150, or other accounting guidance. (FAS-150, par. 24)

> ☛ **PRACTICE POINTER:** An outstanding share of stock should not be considered a "conditional" obligation.

Surplus Notes Issued by Insurance Companies (AICPA PB-15)

Surplus notes (also known as certificates of contribution, surplus debentures, or capital notes) are financial instruments issued by insurance enterprises that are includable in surplus for statutory accounting purposes as allowed by state laws and regulations.

Typically, surplus notes have the following characteristics:

- Approval by the state insurance commissioner of issuance, as well as payment of principal and interest.
- Stated maturity date in most but not all cases and scheduled interest payments.
- Subordinate to all claims except those of shareholders for stock companies and policyholder residuals for mutual companies (after policyholder liabilities are settled).
- No or limited acceleration rights other than for rehabilitation, liquidation, or reorganization of the insurer by a governmental agency.
- Proceeds from issuance are in the form of cash, cash equivalent, or some other asset with a readily determinable fair value.

Surplus notes should be accounted for as debt instruments and presented as liabilities in the financial statements of the issuer. Interest should be accrued over the life of the surplus note, irrespective of the approval of interest and principal payments by the insurance commissioner, and recognized as an expense in the same manner as other debt. Chapter 8, "Debt Financing," provides additional information. Issuers of surplus notes should comply with existing disclosure requirements for debt instruments. In addition, disclosure is required regarding the commissioner's role and ability to approve or disapprove any interest and principal payments. Chapter 8, "Debt Financing," outlines the general disclosure requirements for debt. FAS-140 applies to determine whether a surplus note has been extinguished. Chapter 11, "Extinguishments of Debt," addresses those requirements in detail.

Credit Union Member Shares/Deposits

Member deposit accounts of credit unions, including member shares, should be reported clearly as liabilities in the balance sheet. Interest paid or accrued on these accounts should be reported as interest expense in the income statement, even if the payments are referred to as *dividends*. (SOP 01-6, par. 11(d))

> ☞ **PRACTICE POINTER:** It is not in accordance with GAAP to present all liabilities and equity together under one subheading, with savings accounts presented as the last item before retained earnings.

ACCOUNTING FOR DERIVATIVES WITH CHARACTERISTICS OF DEBT AND EQUITY

Contracts Indexed to and Potentially Settled in a Company's Own Stock

Companies enter into contracts that are indexed to and potentially settled in their own stock for various reasons, but primarily to buy or sell shares or to economically hedge the following types of transactions involving the company's stock:

- Share dilution caused by existing written call options,
- Planned future purchases of treasury stock,
- Planned future issuance of shares, *or*
- The cost of a business combination accounted for as a purchase.

The key accounting question is whether contracts indexed to and potentially settled in a company's own stock should be considered equity instruments or assets and liabilities (and possibly derivatives). This section applies only to the company *issuing* the contracts in its own stock (the issuer), not the counterparty to the contract (the holder).

The following are examples of such contracts:

- *Written call option (or a stock purchase warrant)*—a contract sold by a company giving the holder the right, but not the obligation, to purchase a specific number of the company's shares of common stock at a stated price on a future date.
- *Forward sale contract*—a contract requiring a company to sell a specific number of its shares of stock at a stated price on a future date.
- *Forward purchase contract*—a contract requiring a company to purchase a specific number of shares of its stock at a stated price on a future date.

- *Purchased put option*—a contract giving a company the right but not the obligation to sell a specific number of its shares of stock at a stated price on a future date.

- *Purchased call option*—a contract giving a company the right but not the obligation to buy a specific number of its shares of stock at a stated price on a future date.

- *Written put option*—a contract sold by a company giving the holder the right but not the obligation to sell to the company a specific number of the company's shares of stock at a stated price on a future date.

☛ **PRACTICE POINTER:** After the cost of a business combination has been established, subsequent accounting for contingent consideration that is indexed to and potentially settled in a company's own stock should be in accordance with FAS-150, FAS-133, or EITF 00-19, as applicable. (EITF 97-8)

Such contracts may have contractual terms that permit or require the following methods of settlement:

- *Physical share settlement*—the seller delivers the full stated number of shares and the buyer delivers the full stated amount of cash.

- *Net share settlement*—the party incurring a loss delivers to the party realizing a gain the number of shares equal to the amount of the gain. No cash is exchanged.

- *Net cash settlement*—the party incurring a loss pays cash to the party realizing a gain in an amount equal to the gain; no shares are exchanged.

The contracts may be freestanding, or they may be embedded in or attached to another contract. A freestanding instrument is entered into separately from any of the entity's other financial instruments or equity transactions or it is part of another transaction, but the components are legally detachable and separately exercisable. A freestanding instrument can be made up of more than one option or forward contract. For example, an instrument that is made up of a written put option on the issuer's stock and a purchased call option on the issuer's stock would be considered a freestanding contract (a net written option, a net purchased option, or a forward contract, depending on the circumstances). (FAS-150, pars. 13, A15, and A16 and DIG Issue K-3)

This section addresses only freestanding contracts. Chapter 10, "Convertible Debt and Similar Instruments," and Chapter 13, "Embedded Derivatives," address compound instruments with embedded features that are not legally detachable and separately exercisable.

☞ **PRACTICE POINTER:** APB-14 provides guidance on accounting for detachable stock purchase warrants that *require* settlement in the company's stock. EITF Issue 00-19 addresses stock purchase warrants that permit or require settlement in shares, net cash, or net shares. Note that a stock purchase warrant could be considered a liability under EITF Issue 00-19 if it requires net cash settlement or allows the counterparty to choose net cash settlement.

Applicability of FAS-150 versus EITF Issues 00-6 and 00-19

FAS-150 applies to freestanding contracts that represent obligations to repurchase the issuer's shares by transferring assets. Forward purchase contracts and written put options are examples of such obligations, regardless of whether they are to be physically settled or net cash settled. (Note that a forward purchase contract would be considered an asset, not an obligation, if it had a positive fair value.) Under FAS-150, the "issuer's shares" includes the stock of a wholly owned subsidiary.

EITF Issues 00-6 and 00-19 apply to other freestanding derivatives indexed to a company's own stock. Examples include forward sale contracts, purchased and written call options, and purchased put options.

FAS-150	EITF 00-6/00-19
Forward purchase contracts	Forward sale contracts
Written put options	Purchased put options
Put warrants	Written and purchased call options

Freestanding contracts that are within the scope of EITF Issues 00-19 and 00-6 are considered *indexed to a company's own stock* provided that:

- The contracts are indexed solely to shares in the reporting entity's own stock—
    - The stock of a consolidated subsidiary is *not* the company's own stock. (EITF Issue 00-6)
    - Contracts indexed to the company's own stock *and* another market variable, such as foreign currency, may *not* be considered equity. (DIG Issue C-8)
- Any contingency provisions that affect settlement are based on the company's own performance or actions, such as the occurrence of an IPO, the company's stock price reaching a specified level, or achieving a certain level of sales *and* once the contingent

events have occurred, the settlement amount is based solely on the issuer's stock.

☞ **PRACTICE POINTER:** A contingency that is based on an observable market variable or index that is broader than the company's sole performance (such as the S&P 500 reaching a certain level) *disqualifies* a contract from equity treatment. "Lock-up options" should not be evaluated under EITF Issue 00-19 unless and until the options become exercisable. (EITF 01-6)

☞ **PRACTICE POINTER:** A change-in-control provision that specifies that the contract will become indexed to the purchaser's stock in a business combination in which all stockholders receive the acquiring company's stock would not affect the classification of the contract.

Initial and Subsequent Balance Sheet Classification and Measurement

Forward purchase contracts that require physical settlement Under FAS-150, forward contracts that require physical settlement by a fixed number of the issuer's shares in exchange for cash should be reported as liabilities, and measured initially at the fair value of the shares at inception, adjusted for any consideration or unstated rights or privileges. Equity should be reduced by an amount equal to the fair value of the shares at inception. (FAS-150, par. 21) Subsequently, the liability should be measured as follows:

- If both the amount to be paid and the settlement date are fixed, the liability should be carried at the present value of the settlement amount, and interest expense should be accrued using the rate implicit at inception.

- If either the amount to be paid or the settlement date varies based on specified conditions, the instrument should be carried at the amount of cash that would be paid under the conditions specified in the contract if settlement occurred at the reporting date; the change from the previous reporting period should be reported as interest expense.

- Any amounts paid to holders of those contracts in excess of the initial measurement amount should be reported as interest expense. (FAS-150, par. 22)

☞ **PRACTICE POINTER:** Under FAS-150, the "issuer's shares" includes the stock of a wholly owned subsidiary. Thus, commitments to purchase shares of a subsidiary's stock are accounted for as described above. (FAS-150 nullified the section of EITF Issue 00-6 that governed *purchases* of subsidiary shares.)

Cash-settleable forward purchase contracts, written put options, and some put warrants Such instruments should be measured initially at fair value (which could be zero for a forward contract) and recognized as liabilities (or as assets if the fair value is positive). Subsequently, contracts that meet the definition of a derivative should be accounted for in accordance with FAS-133. Contracts that do not meet the definition of a derivative should be marked to market through earnings unless they are subject to other GAAP. Instruments that are not accounted for as derivatives under FAS-133 are not eligible for hedge accounting. (FAS-150, pars. 23 and 24)

Freestanding instruments composed of multiple option or forward contracts Freestanding instruments composed of multiple option or forward contracts must be evaluated under FAS-150 in their entirety. A freestanding financial instrument that is composed of more than one option or forward contract that involves an obligation to repurchase shares of the issuer and may require a transfer of assets must be classified as a liability even if the share repurchase is conditional. For example, the following instruments may require a transfer of assets and therefore must be classified by the issuer as a liability:

- A put warrant that permits the holder to elect to (1) exercise the warrant feature to acquire common stock of the issuer at a specified price or (2) exercise the put option feature to put the instrument back to the issuer for cash
- A put warrant that permits the holder to (1) exercise the warrant feature to acquire common stock of the issuer at a specified price and (2) exercise the put option feature to put the stock back to the issuer for cash immediately after exercise of the warrant

☛ **PRACTICE POINTER:** EITF Issue 88-9 has been nullified for both public and private companies.

For a freestanding instrument that comprises more that one option or a forward contract that involves an obligation to issue a variable number of shares, liability classification would be required if (1) any of the component obligations (if freestanding) were a liability and (2) the monetary value of such an obligation (if freestanding) were predominant relative to the monetary value of other component obligations. FSP FAS 150-1 provides examples for applying this guidance. (FSP FAS 150-1)

☛ **PRACTICE POINTER:** EITF Issue 00-19 applies to share-settled put warrants that are not liabilities under FAS-150.

Forward sale contracts, purchased put and call options, and written call options   Under EITF Issue 00-19, freestanding contracts that are indexed to and potentially settled in a company's own stock but do not embody obligations to repurchase shares are classified in the balance sheet based on the following broad principles:

- Contracts that must be settled in shares or may be settled in shares at the discretion of the *issuer* are equity instruments.

- Contracts that must be settled net for cash or that may be settled net for cash at the discretion of the *holder* are assets or liabilities.

- If the contract includes multiple settlement options (e.g., the issuer may choose the settlement method when he owes on a contract in a loss position, but the holder may choose the settlement method when the contract is in a gain position), the principles above apply to the circumstance where the *issuer* might have to pay under the contract.

- The likelihood that a particular method will be selected is not relevant, nor is a company's historical pattern of settlement, if any.

- If the settlement alternatives do not have the same economic value or if one of the settlement alternatives is fixed or has caps or floors, the economic substance of the itransaction determines the appropriate accounting (unless the reason is a limit on the number of shares allowed in a net-share settlement).

Exhibit 16-3 provides an overview of the framework for classifying contracts indexed to a company's own stock under EITF Issue 00-19.

Supplemental criteria for equity classification   To be classified as an equity instrument, *all* of the following additional conditions must be met:

- The contract specifically limits the number of shares to be delivered in a share settlement, even if the contract terminates when the stock price is at a stated trigger price. This requirement ensures that the maximum number of shares under the contract is calculable.

- The company has enough authorized but unissued shares available to settle the contract, after considering all of its other commitments that may require issuing stock during the period the contract could remain outstanding.

  ☛ **PRACTICE POINTER:**   If a contract limits the number of shares delivered at the contract's expiration in a net-share settlement, the company would compare the maximum number of shares needed with the available authorized but unissued shares.

☛ **PRACTICE POINTER:** When evaluating whether there are sufficient authorized and unissued shares available to settle such a contract, the maximum number of shares that could be required to be delivered under a registration payment arrangement must be considered as an existing share commitment, regardless of whether the instrument being evaluated is subject to that registration payment arrangement. (FSP EITF 00-19-2, fn 3)

- The company is permitted to settle the contract in unregistered shares (unless sufficient shares are registered at the inception of the contract and there are no outstanding filing requirements).

☛ **PRACTICE POINTER:** If the company had a failed registration during the previous six months, there should be a legal determination as to whether the company can deliver unregistered shares in a settlement in shares or in net shares.

☛ **PRACTICE POINTER:** The EITF is currently addressing in EITF 05-4 the effect of a liquidating damages provision in a registration rights agreement on the classification of an instrument within the scope of EITF 00-19. The issue specifically addresses transactions involving (1) a stock purchase warrant that may be physically settled or net-cash settled (at the investor's election), under which the company may deliver to the investor either registered or unregistered shares and (2) a separate registration rights agreement. That agreement requires the company to file a registration statement for resale of the shares underlying the warrant and have it declared effective within a specific time period or pay damages to the investor (based on a specified formula). The EITF expects to address how the existence of the separate registration rights agreement impacts the analysis of the instrument under EITF 00-19. Readers should monitor developments on this issue.

- The contract requires net cash settlement only in circumstances where shareholders would also receive cash for their shares.

☛ **PRACTICE POINTER:** A contract provision requiring net cash settlement in the event of bankruptcy would not preclude equity classification if it can be demonstrated that the counterparty's claims could be net-share settled or would rank no higher than the claims of the company's stockholders. The status of a claim in bankruptcy is a legal determination.

- The issuer is not required to pay cash to the counterparty if the counterparty has sold the shares initially delivered to it and the proceeds are less than a stated amount (i.e., "top off" or "make whole" provisions).
- The company is not required to make cash payments to the counterparty if the company fails to make timely filings with the SEC.

EXHIBIT 16-3
ACCOUNTING FOR CONTRACTS INDEXED TO A COMPANY'S
OWN STOCK UNDER EITF 00-19

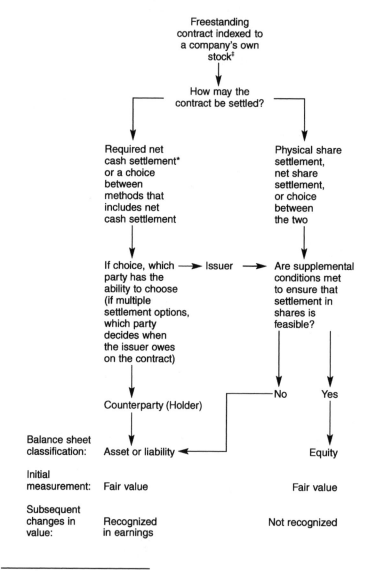

[‡] Contracts to potentially repurchase stock are subject to FAS-150, not EITF 00-19. See Exhibit 16-1.

[*] Contracts that require net settlement in cash should be reported as assets and liabilities, not equity.

- The counterparty's rights under a contract do not rank higher than those of the underlying stock's shareholders. A contract cannot give the counterparty any of the rights of a creditor. The contract does not require the company to post collateral for any reason.

☛ **PRACTICE POINTER:** Placing the equity securities to be delivered in trust does not affect the classification of the contract.

OBSERVATION: The gist of these extra requirements is that the company must actually be able to settle the transaction in shares either by (a) having an adequate number of shares already registered or (b) having the ability to deliver unregistered shares. The steps necessary to register shares are deemed outside the company's control—having the ability to deliver unregistered shares resolves that issue. These provisions were included to ensure that settlement alternatives involving stock are substantive, within the company's control, and feasible. If the company lacks the ability to settle in already registered shares or unregistered shares, the contract is deemed to have an in-substance cash settlement feature. Generally, if an event that is not within the company's control could require net-cash settlement, then the contract must be classified as an asset or a liability.

SEC REGISTRANT ALERT: In December 2005, the SEC discussed certain guidance on the classification and measurement of freestanding stock purchase warrants in response to practice issues in this area. Stock purchase warrants that are not derivatives under FAS-133 must be evaluated under paragraphs 12–32 of EITF 00-19 to determine whether the instrument should be accounted for as a liability or an equity instrument. The SEC staff noted two common reasons that warrants should be accounted for as liabilities:

1. Registrants could be required to settle in cash if certain events occurred (i.e., delisting from the primary stock exchange)

2. Registration rights exist where significant liquidated damages could be required to be paid to the holder if the issuer fails to register the shares under a preset time frame or where the registration statement fails to remain effective for a preset time frame

The SEC staff notes that the warrant must be classified as a liability if it is *possible*, but not probable, that cash settlement under EITF 00-19 may occur.

In addition, the SEC staff has reiterated the requirements in FR-67, which requires disclosure of all material off-balance-sheet transactions, arrangements, and obligations (including certain contingent obligations) in a separate caption of MD&A in all quarterly and annual reports filed with the SEC. Among other things, these disclosure requirements apply to derivative instruments that are classified as equity in accordance with other GAAP, including EITF Issue 00-19. Registrants should consider application of these disclosure requirements to equity linked contracts. Refer to Chapter 18, "Fair Value Measurements, Fair Value Disclosure, and Other Financial Instrument Disclosures," for a more detailed discussion of these disclosure requirements.

(December 2005 Current Accounting and Disclosure Issues in the Division of Corporation Finance, SEC and December 2005 Presentation, *Current Developments in the Division of Corporation Finance*, at the National Conference on Current SEC and PCAOB Developments)

Initial measurement All contracts are measured initially at fair value, regardless of whether they are equity or assets and liabilities.

> **AUTHOR'S NOTE:** In September 2006, the FASB issued FASB Statement No. 157, *Fair Value Measurements*. FAS-157 provides a single definition of the term *fair value*, establishes a framework for measuring fair value where permitted or required by existing GAAP, and expands disclosures about fair value measurements. The definition of fair value focuses on assets and liabilities, because they are a primary subject of accounting measurement. However, the definition of fair value also should be applied to instruments measured at fair value that are classified in stockholders' equity. Chapter 18, "Fair Value Measurements, Fair Value Disclosures, and Other Financial Instruments Disclosures," provides the detailed provisions of FAS-157 and specific fair value measurement guidance applicable to all financial instruments required to be measured at fair value under GAAP. The 2008 edition of CCH's *Financial Instruments* has been updated to incorporate the provisions of FAS-157. FAS-157 is effective for calendar-year-end companies as of January 1, 2008. Unless a company chooses to early adopt, prior GAAP is applicable for financial statements issued for 2007.
>
> As this book went to press, the FASB was addressing a possible delay of FAS-157's effective date. The FASB agreed to consider delaying the effective date for nonfinancial instruments and for certain types of entities, including private companies and "smaller" public companies (not yet defined). Readers should monitor the FASB's further deliberations regarding the nature of any delay of FAS-157's effective date. Also, readers should refer to the 2007 edition for GAAP related to the fair value measurement of financial instruments applicable before the effective date of FAS-157.

Subsequent measurement At each balance-sheet date before settlement, subsequent measurement is based on the current classification of the contract. Changes in value are recognized in earnings and disclosed for contracts that are considered assets and liabilities. Changes in value are not recognized on contracts that are considered equity instruments. Exhibit 16-4 summarizes the ongoing accounting for contracts indexed to a company's own stock under EITF Issue 00-19.

EXHIBIT 16-4
ONGOING ACCOUNTING FOR FREESTANDING INDEXED
CONTRACTS UNDER EITF 00-19

Settlement Requirements or Alternatives	Balance Sheet Classification	Subsequent Changes in Fair Value	Treatment If Settlement Differs from Expectation
Contracts that require settlement in:			
Physical shares	*Equity*	*Not recognized*	*Not applicable*
Net shares	*Equity*	*Not recognized*	*Not applicable*
Net cash*	*Assets or liabilities*	*Changes in fair value recognized in earnings and disclosed*	*Not applicable*
Contracts that allow the <u>company</u> to choose settlement in:			
Physical or net shares	*Equity*	*Not recognized*	*Amounts paid or received for contracts physically settled are included in contributed capital*
Net shares or net cash	*Equity*	*Not recognized*	*Amounts paid or received for contracts settled in cash are included in contributed capital*
Net cash or physical shares	*Equity*	*Not recognized*	*Amounts paid or received for contracts settled in cash are included in contributed capital*
Contracts that allow the <u>counterparty</u> to choose settlement in:			
Net shares or physical shares	*Equity*	*Not recognized*	*Not applicable*
Net cash or in shares (physical or net)*	*Assets or liabilities*	*Changes in fair value recognized in earnings and disclosed*	*Gains or losses are not reversed out of income even if the contract is ultimately settled in shares*

---

* Such contracts would almost certainly meet the definition of a derivative under FAS-133, because they are not considered equity instruments of the issuer and they have an explicit net cash settlement provision.

Contract Reclassification

A contract's classification should be reassessed at each balance-sheet date, not just at the inception of the contract. If necessary, a contract should be reclassified as of the date on which an event causing a change in classification has occurred. Contracts may be reclassified an unlimited number of times.

> **OBSERVATION:** A change could occur, for example, if other contracts involving the company's stock are retired (or additional contracts are issued), so there are no longer (now) sufficient shares to satisfy the requirements of the derivative contract in question.

A contract's change in classification should be accounted for as follows:

- *From equity to asset or liability*   Any (unrecognized) change in the fair value should be accounted for as an adjustment to stockholders' equity for the period between the date of the contract's last classification as equity to the date of reclassification to an asset or a liability. Subsequent changes in the contract's fair value should be recognized in income.
- *From asset or liability to equity*   Gains or losses should not be reversed. Subsequent changes in the contract's fair value should not be recognized.
- *Partial reclass of contracts*   If the total notional amount of a contract that can be partially settled in net shares can no longer be classified in permanent equity, the portion that could be settled in net shares as of the balance-sheet date would continue to be classified in permanent equity while the other portion would be reclassified in temporary equity, or as an asset or liability, as appropriate.

  If more than one of a company's derivative contracts may be partially settled, different methods can be used to determine which contracts, or portions thereof, should be reclassified. Acceptable methods include reclassifying:

  — All contracts proportionately
  — Contracts with the *earliest inception* date first
  — Contracts with the *earliest maturity* date first
  — Contracts with the *latest inception* date first
  — Contracts with the *latest maturity* date first

The reclassification method should be systematic, rational, and consistently applied.

Interaction with FAS-133

Some contracts that would meet the definition of a derivative are considered equity under EITF Issue 00-19, and therefore qualify for the scope exception in FAS-133, paragraph 11(a). Under FAS-133, a contract that has both of the following characteristics should *not* be accounted for as a derivative by the issuer:

- It is indexed solely to the company's own stock *and*
- It is classified in stockholders' equity in its statement of financial position. (FAS-133, par. 11(a))

To determine whether the issuer should classify a contract in stockholders' equity, the guidance in EITF Issue 00-19 should be applied *first*. If the contract should not be classified in stockholders' equity under that guidance, then the contract should be evaluated under FAS-133 to determine whether it meets the definition of a derivative.

If the contract meets the definition of a derivative, the accounting for changes in fair value depends on whether the contract has been designated and qualifies as part of a hedging relationship. There are limits on the types of transactions that qualify as hedged items. The following items are prohibited from being designated as the hedged item in a hedging transaction:

- A company's own equity instruments that are classified in stockholders' equity.
- A firm commitment to enter into a business combination or to buy or sell a subsidiary, minority interest, or equity method investee.
- The denominator in an EPS calculation (because equity shares do not give rise to an earnings effect).

However, a derivative could qualify as a hedge of a transaction that will give rise to income consequences, such as a nonvested (unrecognized) SAR obligation. (Refer to DIG Issue G-1.) Chapter 14, "Hedge Accounting," provides additional information.

> ☞ **PRACTICE POINTER:** Even if a contract is considered an equity instrument by the *issuer* of a contract, the holder must always evaluate the contract under FAS-133 to determine whether it must be accounted for as a derivative.

> **OBSERVATION:** At the risk of making this issue more complicated, the criteria used to define assets and liabilities (i.e., derivatives) are different under FAS-133 and EITF Issue 00-19. The definition of "net settlement" under FAS-133 is much broader than EITF Issue 00-19: in addition to an explicit contractual provision that permits cash settlement, net settlement is also deemed possible under FAS-133 if: (1) the contract can be settled net for shares, (2) the contract can be closed out through an exchange or other market mechanism, or (3) the underlying shares are publicly

traded (among other things). Accordingly, many contracts that are considered *equity* by the issuer (under EITF Issue 00-19) would nonetheless be considered derivatives by the counterparty (under FAS-133). Likewise, contracts that permit or require share settlement by the issuer, but fail to satisfy all of the supplemental equity criteria of EITF Issue 00-19, could well be considered derivatives under FAS-133. Chapter 12, "Introduction to Derivatives," discusses the definition of a derivative in more detail.

Temporary equity Previously, for public companies, EITF Issue 00-19 required that freestanding written puts and forward purchase contracts that require or permit physical settlement in shares be classified in temporary equity in accordance with Accounting Series Release (ASR) No. 268 (Presentation in Financial Statements of "Redeemable Preferred Stocks"). That guidance is nullified by FAS-150, which requires that those freestanding contracts be reported as liabilities. However, in analyzing a compound instrument under FAS-133 for embedded derivatives, the *original* guidance in EITF Issue 00-19 should be applied (presumably including the guidance on temporary equity). (FAS-150, par. 15) DIG Issue C-2 indicates that items reported in temporary equity qualify for the scope exception for equity instruments of the issuer in paragraph 11(a) of FAS-133. Therefore, embedded written puts and embedded forward purchase agreements on a company's own stock that require or permit settlement in shares would not require separate accounting under FAS-133.

Accounting by a Parent Company for Contracts Indexed to the Stock of a Consolidated Subsidiary (EITF 00-6)

A contract indexed to, and potentially settled, by transferring the stock of a consolidated subsidiary is *not* treated as an equity instrument by the parent company (reporting entity). Consequently, those contracts do not qualify for the scope exception in paragraph 11(a) of FAS-133 and, if they meet the definition of a derivative, they should be accounted for under FAS-133. [This section excludes obligations to repurchase subsidiary stock, which are subject to FAS-150.]

Some contracts involving a subsidiary's stock would not be accounted for under the guidance in FAS-133, including contracts that require physical settlement in shares of a subsidiary and (1) those shares are not readily convertible into cash and (2) the contract may not be net settled by means outside the contract, such as an exchange.

☛ **PRACTICE POINTER:** The term "net settlement" has been heavily interpreted. Refer to Chapter 12, "Introduction to Derivatives," for a detailed discussion.

Contracts involving a subsidiary's stock that are *not* considered derivatives should be accounted for by the parent. Commitments to sell shares of a subsidiary:

- Recognize the disposition of shares when the contract has settled and the shares have been transferred to the buyer.
- During the period of the contract, continue to recognize the subsidiary's income or loss in consolidation as if the forward contract were not outstanding.
- If the contract price and premium indicate that the investment is impaired, either at inception or subsequently as income is recognized, recognize a loss, by analogy to paragraph 19(h) of APB-18.

Purchased options to buy or sell shares of a subsidiary recognize the purchase or disposition of shares if and when the contract is exercised.

> **OBSERVATION:** The treatment of freestanding contracts involving a transfer of a subsidiary's stock is inconsistent with the treatment of debt convertible into a subsidiary's stock where settlement must be in stock or may be in stock at the issuer's election. EITF Issue 99-1 treats such instruments in the same manner as traditional convertible debt even though—on a stand-alone basis—the conversion feature would not be considered an equity instrument of the parent. Chapter 10, "Convertible Debt and Similar Instruments," discusses this issue in more detail.

Combinations of Contracts and Other Transactions

Generally, equity instruments that embody obligations should not be combined with other instruments in applying FAS-150. For example, a forward purchase contract should not be combined with an outstanding share of stock for accounting purposes—the forward purchase contract should be accounted for as a liability under paragraph 11 of FAS-150 and the stock should be accounted for as an outstanding equity instrument. (FAS-150, par. 14) However, if the conditions of DIG Issues K-1 (contracts designed to circumvent FAS-133) or K-3 (combinations of options) are met, the contracts should be combined for accounting purposes. See Chapter 12, "Introduction to Derivatives Accounting," for additional information.

> ☛ **PRACTICE POINTER:** FAS-150 nullifies some EITF Issues that required combined accounting, including Issue 98-12 on forward equity sale transactions, and Issue 00-4 on transactions involving the minority interest holder.

Accelerated Share Repurchases (EITF 99-7)

An accelerated share repurchase program is a combination of transactions involving an immediate purchase of a company's own shares (treasury stock) and a forward contract that usually involves averaging the price of the company's stock over the term of the contract. The program is designed to simulate the market impact and pricing benefits of a disciplined daily open market stock repurchase program, but with an immediate retirement of shares.

For example, an Investment Banker sells 1,000,000 shares of Company A common stock to Company A at the current market price of $50 per share. The shares are held in treasury. Company A simultaneously enters into a forward contract with the Investment Banker on 1,000,000 shares of its own common stock. On the settlement date, if the volume-weighted-average daily market price of Company A's common stock during the contract period exceeds the $50 initial purchase price, Company A will deliver to Investment Banker cash or shares of common stock (at Company A's option) equal to the price difference multiplied by 1,000,000. If the volume-weighted-average daily market price of Company A's common stock during the contract period is less than the $50 initial purchase price, the Investment Banker will deliver to Company A cash equal to the price difference multiplied by 1,000,000.

The issuer should account for accelerated share repurchase programs as two separate transactions—a treasury stock purchase and a forward contract indexed to and potentially settled in the company's own stock. The forward contract would be accounted for under EITF Issue 00-19 (discussed previously in this chapter). In the example above, the forward contract would be considered an equity instrument, because the company has the choice to settle in stock or cash when the contract is in a loss position (assuming the supplemental equity criteria are met).

Equity Instruments Subject to Registration Payment Arrangements

Registration rights are sometimes provided to investors as part of the issuance of a financial instrument, such as a warrant, preferred stock, or a debt instrument. Those rights can be conveyed either as part of the agreement or as a separate contract. For example, the issuer may enter into a registration payment arrangement that requires it to use its best efforts to file a registration statement with the SEC for resale of the instrument and to ensure that the registration is declared effective within a specific timeframe. If the registration statement is not declared effective or its effectiveness is not maintained by the issuer, investors are entitled to liquidated damages. Payments made under a registration payment arrangement may be in a lump sum or periodic.

The consideration may be in the form of cash, equity instruments, or adjustments to the terms of the financial instrument that are subject to the registration payment arrangement (e.g., an increased interest rate on a debt instrument).

The guidance in this section applies to a registration payment arrangement that has both of the following characteristics:

- The arrangement specifies that the issuer will endeavor to do either or both of the following:
  - File a registration statement for the resale of specified financial instruments and/or for the resale of equity shares that are issuable upon exercise or conversion of specified financial instruments and for that registration statement to be declared effective by the SEC or other applicable securities regulator within a specified grace period,
  - Maintain the effectiveness of the registration statement for a specified period of time or in perpetuity.
- The arrangement requires the issuer to transfer consideration to the counterparty if the registration statement for the resale of the financial instrument(s) subject to the arrangement is not declared effective or if effectiveness of the registration statement is not maintained.

An arrangement that requires the issuer to obtain and/or maintain a listing on a stock exchange instead of or in addition to obtaining an effective registration statement is within the scope of this guidance if the remaining characteristics above are also met.

> ☞ **PRACTICE POINTER:** The following types of arrangements are not covered by the scope of this guidance:
>
> - Arrangements that require registration or listing of convertible debt instruments or convertible preferred stock if the form of consideration that would be transferred to the counterparty is an adjustment to the conversion ratio
> - Arrangements in which the amount of consideration transferred is determined by reference to an observable market (other than the market for the issuer's stock) or an observable index
> - Arrangements in which the financial instrument(s) subject to the arrangement are settled when consideration is transferred.
>
> The guidance in FSP 00-19-2 may not be applied by analogy to other types of contracts. (FSP EITF 00-19-2)

Issuers must account for registration payment arrangements as follows:

- The contingent obligation to make future payments or otherwise transfer consideration under a registration payment arrangement must be recognized and measured separately in accordance with FASB Statement No. 5, *Accounting for Contingencies*, and FASB Interpretation No. 14, *Reasonable Estimation of the Amount of a Loss*. If an entity would be required to deliver shares under a registration payment arrangement, the transfer of that consideration is probable, and the number of shares to be delivered can be reasonably estimated, the issuer's share price at the reporting date must be used to measure the contingent liability under FAS-5.

- The financial instrument(s) subject to the registration payment arrangement must be recognized and measured in accordance with other applicable GAAP (e.g., EITF 00-19), without regard to the contingent obligation to transfer consideration pursuant to the registration payment arrangement.

> **SEC REGISTRANT ALERT:** Consistent with FSP EITF 00-19-2, the guidance in EITF Topic D-98 should be applied to a financial instrument subject to a registration payment arrangement without regard to the contingent obligation to transfer consideration pursuant to the registration payment arrangement (that is, the registration payment arrangement is considered to be a separate unit of account that does not impact the classification of the related financial instrument under EITF Topic D-98). (EITF Topic D-98)

- If the transfer of consideration under a registration payment arrangement is probable and can be reasonably estimated at inception, the contingent liability under the registration payment arrangement must be included in the allocation of proceeds from the related financing transaction using the measurement guidance in FAS-5. The remaining proceeds shall be allocated to the financial instrument(s) issued in conjunction with the registration payment arrangement based on the provisions of other applicable GAAP.

- If, subsequent to the inception of the registration payment arrangement, the transfer of consideration under a registration payment arrangement becomes probable and can be reasonably estimated, the contingent liability must be initially recognized in earnings.

- If the measurement of a previously recognized contingent liability increases or decreases in a subsequent period, the change must be recognized in earnings. (FSP EITF 00-19-2, pars. 7–11)

> ☞ **PRACTICE POINTER:** The guidance outlined is the comprehensive model for registration payment arrangements. Such arrangements are explicitly excluded from the scope of FAS-133, FAS-150, and FIN-45. However, additional disclosure requirements outlined later in this Chapter are incremental to other existing disclosure requirements for financial instruments subject to registration payment arrangements.

An issuer of financial instruments subject to a registration payment arrangement must account for those instruments without regard to the existence of the registration payment arrangement. For an issuance of warrants, the existence of a contingent obligation to make payments under the registration payment arrangement does not affect the company's analysis of whether the warrants are classified as liabilities or equity instruments under EITF 00-19.

If a company concurrently issues two financial instruments with a registration payment arrangement (such as shares of common stock and freestanding warrants or a debt instrument and freestanding warrants) and determines at inception it is probable that it will be required to make payments to investors under the registration payment arrangement (and the amount of the payment is reasonably estimable), the contingent liability under the registration payment arrangement must be deducted from the total proceeds from the offering. The remaining proceeds must be allocated between the financial instruments based on applicable GAAP. For example, if a debt instrument and warrants were issued concurrently, the remaining proceeds would be allocated on a relative fair value basis under APB-14.

> **AUTHOR'S NOTE:** The specific aspects of FSP 00-19-2 that relate to convertible instruments are addressed in Chapter 10, "Convertible Debt and Similar Instruments."

DISCLOSURES

Information about Capital Structure

FAS-129 requires information about a company's capital structure to be disclosed in three broad categories: Information about securities, liquidation preference of preferred stock, and redeemable stock.

Information about Securities

An entity must provide a summary explanation in its financial statements of the pertinent rights and privileges of its outstanding securities. Examples of the type of information that should be disclosed are:

- Dividend and liquidation preferences
- Participation rights
- Call prices and dates
- Conversion or exercise prices or rates and pertinent dates
- Sinking-fund requirements
- Unusual voting rights
- Significant terms of contracts to issue additional shares (FAS-129, par. 4)
- Any obligation to restrict dividend payments (FAS-5, par. 18)

In addition, the number of shares issued upon conversion, exercise, or satisfaction of required conditions during the most recent annual fiscal period and any subsequent interim period should be disclosed. (FAS-129, par. 5)

> ☛ **PRACTICE POINTER:** Disclosure of this information satisfies the requirements of APB-12, paragraph 10 (changes in the number of shares during the period).

> **SEC REGISTRANT ALERT:** The SEC recommends an approach to disclosure about "targeted" or "tracking" stock, which is stock that is referenced to a specific business unit, activity or assets of the registrant. The thrust of the SEC's recommendation is to avoid creating the impression that the investor has a direct or exclusive interest in that business unit because, in liquidation, those assets would typically be available to all of the registrant's creditors (and sometimes other shareholders). Refer to SEC Division of Corporation Finance: Frequently Requested Accounting and Financial Reporting Interpretations and Guidance, Section II.D, for a complete discussion of this issue.

Liquidation Preference of Preferred Stock

Entities that issue preferred stock (or other senior stock) that has a preference in involuntary liquidation that is significantly in excess of the par or stated value of the shares must disclose the relationship between the preference in liquidation and the par or stated value of the shares. (FAS-129, par. 6) That disclosure should be:

- Presented in the aggregate.
- In the equity section of the balance sheet, *either*
  — Parenthetically or
  — "In short"—that is, included in the body of the financial statements, but not added in the total of shareholders' equity.

> ☛ **PRACTICE POINTER:** Information about liquidation preferences may *not* be disclosed in the footnotes or presented on a per-share basis.

In addition, all entities should disclose either on the face of the balance sheet or in the footnotes:

- The aggregate *or* per-share amounts at which preferred stock may be called or is subject to redemption through sinking-fund operations or otherwise; *and*

- The aggregate *and* per-share amounts of cumulative preferred dividends in arrears. (FAS-129, par. 7)

Redeemable Stock

An entity that issues redeemable stock should disclose the amount of redemption requirements for all issues of capital stock that are redeemable at fixed or determinable prices on fixed or determinable dates for each of the five years following the date of the latest statement of financial position presented. The information may be provided separately by issue or in the aggregate. (FAS-129, par. 8)

Equity Instruments Representing Obligations

Issuers of equity instruments that must be reported as liabilities (or assets, if the fair value is positive) must disclose the following information (FAS-150, pars. 26–28):

- The nature and terms of the instruments and the rights and obligations embodied in those instruments, including information about settlement alternatives, if any, and who controls the settlement alternatives.
- For all outstanding instruments and for each settlement alternative:
  - The amount that would be paid, or the number of shares that would be issued and their fair value, determined under the conditions specified in the contract if the settlement were to occur at the reporting date.
  - How changes in the fair value of the issuer's equity shares would affect those settlement amounts.
  - If applicable, the maximum amount that the issuer could be required to pay to redeem the instrument by physical settlement, the maximum number of shares that could be required to be issued, or an acknowledgement that the contract does not limit those amounts.
  - For a forward contract or an option indexed to the issuer's equity shares, the forward price or option strike price, the number of issuer's shares to which the contract is indexed, and the settlement date or dates of the contract, as applicable.
- For entities that only have shares subject to mandatory redemption, the components of the liability that would otherwise be related to shareholders' interest and other comprehensive income (if any) subject to the redemption feature (for example, par value and other paid-in amounts of mandatorily redeemable instruments should be disclosed separately from the amount of retained earnings or accumulated deficit).

Contracts Indexed to a Company's Own Stock

EITF Issue 00-19, as amended, requires disclosure of the following information about all freestanding contracts within its scope that are indexed to and potentially settled in a company's own stock:

- The key terms of all contracts, including the issuer's accounting method(s) for each contract type (that is, as an asset, liability, or equity).
- If applicable, a description of the settlement alternatives, including who controls the settlement alternatives and the number of shares that could be required to be issued to net share settle a contract (including an acknowledgment, if applicable, that the number could be infinite).
- A contract's current fair value for each settlement alternative (denominated in monetary amounts or quantities of shares) and how changes in the price of the issuer's equity instruments would affect those settlement amounts.
- The amount of gains and losses on contracts that are classified as assets and liabilities.
- If contracts are reclassified between equity and assets/liabilities (including partial reclassifications)—the reason for the reclassification, the accounting method used for partial reclassifications, and the impact on the issuer's financial statements.

> ☞ **PRACTICE POINTER:** For contracts that are considered assets and liabilities under EITF Issue 00-19, these disclosures must be provided *in addition to* any disclosures required by FAS-133. Refer to Chapter 15, "Disclosures about Derivatives," for additional information. Practitioners should review the fine print of the requirements of EITF Issue 00-19 when such contracts are encountered in practice.

Registration Payment Arrangements

Specific disclosures are required for issuers of registration payment arrangements in connection with offerings of financial instruments, such as common stock, warrants, and debt instruments. The following disclosures are required for each registration payment arrangement or each group of similar arrangements:

- The nature of the arrangement, including the following:
  - The approximate term
  - The financial instruments covered

— The events or circumstances that would require a transfer of consideration

- Any settlement alternatives in the arrangement and which party controls the settlement alternatives

- The maximum potential consideration (undiscounted) that the issuer could be required to transfer, and any limit to the maximum potential consideration (this includes the maximum number of shares that may be required to be issued, if applicable under the arrangement). If the terms of the arrangement provide for no limitation to the maximum potential consideration (including shares) to be transferred, that fact must be disclosed.

- The current carrying amount of the liability representing the issuer's obligations under the registration payment arrangement and income statement classification of any gains or losses related to changes in that liability. (FSP EITF 00-19-2)

> **OBSERVATION:** These disclosures are required even if the likelihood of the issuer having to make any payments under the registration payment arrangement is remote.

Earnings per Share

Determining whether a financial instrument is debt or equity clearly has implications for earnings per share (EPS) computations and other important debt- and equity-based ratios. FAS-128 provides guidance on how to calculate basic and diluted EPS. Chapter 13 of CCH's *GAAP Guide Level A* and Chapter 14 of CCH's *GAAP Levels B, C, and D*, both called, "Earnings per Share," include a comprehensive discussion of the guidelines for presenting EPS. The guidance in this section is limited to unique EPS issues involving the instruments discussed in this chapter.

> ☛ **PRACTICE POINTER:** As part of the project to eliminate differences between U.S. GAAP and International Financial Reporting Standards (IFRS), the FASB and IASB are currently working on a project to converge guidance related to the computation of EPS. This project is expected to result in an amendment of FAS-128. A joint Exposure Draft is expected to be issued as early as the third quarter of 2007 (this is the third Exposure Draft to be issued by the FASB related to this project). A detailed summary of decisions on this project can be found on the FASB's website at http://www.fasb.org/project/short-term_intl_convergence.shtml.

In general, basic EPS is computed by dividing income available to common stockholders by the weighted-average number of common shares outstanding for the period.

- Preferred stock dividends should be deducted from net income (or added to the amount of a net loss) in computing income available to common stockholders.

- Treasury stock repurchased is not included in shares outstanding.

Diluted EPS reflects the potential dilution that could occur if securities or other contracts to issue common stock were exercised or converted into common stock, or resulted in the issuance of common stock that then shared in the earnings of the entity. The computation of diluted EPS should not assume conversion, exercise, or contingent issuance of securities that would have an *antidilutive* effect on earnings per share.

Periodic increases or decreases in the carrying amount of redeemable securities other than common stock and the carrying amount of redeemable common stock shall be treated in the same manner as dividends on nonredeemable stock and must be reflected as a charge against retained earnings (or, in the absence of retained earnings, paid-in-capital). If a class of common shares is redeemable at an amount that is other than the fair value of the shares, increases or decreases in the carrying amount of the redeemable shares should be reflected in EPS using a method akin to the two-class method in FAS-128 to reflect that one class of shareholders has, in substance, received a preferential distribution. (EITF D-98)

Equity Instruments Excluded from EPS

Entities that have issued mandatorily redeemable shares of common stock or entered into forward contracts that require physical settlement by repurchase of a fixed number of the issuer's equity shares of common stock in exchange for cash should exclude the common shares that are to be redeemed or repurchased in calculating basic and diluted earnings per share. Any amounts that have not already been recognized as interest costs, including contractual (accumulated) dividends and participation rights in undistributed earnings, attributable to shares that are to be redeemed or repurchased should be deducted in computing income available to common shareholders, in a manner consistent with the "two-class" method described in paragraph 61 of FAS-128. (FAS-150, par. 25)

Participating Securities (EITF 03-6)

FAS-128 discusses participating securities and the two-class method of computing basic EPS in paragraphs 60 and 61. EITF Issue 03-6 clarifies the definition of a participating security and the application of the two-class method to participating securities. The general provisions of EITF Issue 03-6 are included in this section. Guidance specific to convertible securities is presented in Chapter 10, "Convertible Debt."

A *participating security* is a security that may participate in undistributed earnings with common stock regardless of (1) whether the participation is preconditioned upon the occurrence of a specified event and (2) the form of the participation in undistributed earnings (that is, the participation right does not have to be a dividend).

The two-class method is required for all participating securities—including those that are convertible, non-convertible, or potential common stock securities (e.g., options, warrants, and forwards to issue common stock)—if, in their current form, they are entitled to receive dividends when declared on common stock.

> ☛ **PRACTICE POINTER:** A feature tied to the declaration of dividends that adjusts the exercise price of an instrument to issue an entity's common stock or, for a convertible security, reduces the security's conversion price (or increases the conversion ratio) does not represent a participation right. However, such a feature should be evaluated under EITF Issues 98-5 and 00-27 to determine whether it is a beneficial conversion feature.

> ☛ **PRACTICE POINTER:** Stock options and restricted shares issued as compensation that contain a right to receive dividends declared on the common stock of the issuer are not subject to the guidance in EITF Issue 03-6 until the options or shares are fully vested. Stock-based compensation is outside the scope of this book.

Undistributed earnings for the period must be allocated to a participating security based on contractual participation rights to share in those earnings on a pro forma basis *as if* all of the earnings for the period had been distributed. Undistributed earnings are allocated only if the terms of the participating security specify objectively determinable, nondiscretionary participation rights. In periods of net loss, an entity must allocate losses for purposes of computing basic EPS to participating securities if the securities had both the contractual right to participate in the earnings and the contractual obligation to share in the losses of the issuer.

> ☛ **PRACTICE POINTER:** Undistributed earnings are not required to be allocated to participating securities for which the participation rights are contingent or discretionary; however, such rights must be disclosed under FAS-129.

Presentation of basic and diluted EPS is not required for participating securities other than common stock; however, such a presentation is not precluded.

The FASB staff has drafted a proposed FSP (FSP FAS-128-a) to provide computational guidance addressing the application of the two-class method in computing diluted EPS when an entity has common stock, participating securities, and potential common stock. The proposed FSP sets forth three steps for computing diluted EPS under the two-class method and provides illustrations. It is expected that this guidance will be incorporated into FAS-128 through the joint project of the FASB and IASB to converge guidance related to the computation of EPS rather than through issuance of a final FSP.

Preferred Stock

Dividends on preferred stocks are deducted from net income (or added to the amount of a net loss) to arrive at net earnings available to common shareholders. An adjustment to net income or loss for preferred stock dividends is required for all preferred stock dividends, regardless of the form of payment (for example, company stock or cash). (EITF D-82) In addition, periodic increases in the carrying amount of conditionally redeemable preferred stock should be treated in the same manner as dividends on nonredeemable preferred stock, that is, reduce or increase income applicable to common shareholders. If charges or credits are material to income, separate disclosure of income applicable to common stockholders on the face of the income statement should be provided. (EITF D-98)

EITF Topics D-42 and D-53 provide guidance on the earnings per share implications for the redemption or induced conversion of preferred stock that is not mandatorily redeemable. Briefly, the SEC staff believes that the excess of (1) fair value of the consideration transferred to the holders of the preferred stock over (2) the carrying amount of the preferred stock in the registrant's balance sheet (reduced by the issuance costs of the preferred stock) should be subtracted from net earnings to arrive at net earnings available to common shareholders in the calculation of earnings per share. (Likewise, an excess of the carrying amount of preferred stock (reduced by the issuance costs of the preferred stock) over the fair value of the consideration transferred to the holders of the preferred stock would be added to net earnings to arrive at net earnings available to common shareholders.)

> ☞ **PRACTICE POINTER:** EITF Topic D-98 continues to apply to mandatorily redeemable securities issued by SEC registrants that are subject to the deferral under FSP FAS 150-3.

Contracts Indexed to and Potentially Settled in a Company's Own Shares

EITF Issue 00-19, EITF 03-6, and EITF Topic D-72 provide specific guidance on how to reflect contracts that are indexed to and potentially settled in a company's own stock in EPS calculations (other than physically settled forward purchase contracts that are reported as liabilities under FAS-150).

In computing basic EPS, EITF Issue 03-6 requires the use of the two-class method for forward contracts to issue an entity's own shares because such contracts are participating securities under that guidance. The participation right in a forward contract to issue an entity's own shares may be either in the form of a dividend declared on common stock or in the form of a provision that reduces the contract price per share when dividends are declared on the issuing entity's common stock.

In computing diluted EPS, FAS-128 requires use of the reverse treasury stock method to account for the dilutive effect of written put options and similar contracts that are "in the money" during the reporting period. Under that method, the incremental number of shares is computed as:

- The number of shares that would need to be issued for cash at the average market price during the period to obtain cash to satisfy the put obligation less
- The number of shares received from satisfying the put.

Purchased options should *not* be reflected in the computation of diluted EPS because to do so would be antidilutive.

For those contracts that provide the company (issuer) with a choice of settlement methods, the company should assume that the contract would be settled in shares for EPS purposes. That presumption may be overcome if past experience or a stated policy provides a reasonable basis to believe that it is probable that the contract will be paid partially or wholly in cash. For contracts in which the counterparty controls the means of settlement, past experience or a stated policy is not determinative. In those situations, the more dilutive of cash or share settlement should be used.

> **SEC REGISTRANT ALERT:**   For contracts that provide the issuer a choice of settlement method, the SEC staff cautions against nonsubstantive assertions regarding a stated policy or past practice of cash settlement to overcome the share settlement presumption of FAS-128. The SEC staff reminds registrants that a stated policy must have substance and cites the following factors for evaluating the policy:
>
> - The extent to which the flexibility to share settle is a factor in senior management's decision to approve the issuance of the instrument
> - Whether the issuer has the positive intent and ability to cash settle the instrument upon conversion (evidenced by a management attestation)
> - Whether disclosures acknowledge and support adherence to the stated policy
> - Whether previous contracts with a choice of settlement alternatives have been share settled
>
> (December 2003 speech by Robert J. Comerford, then a Professional Accounting Fellow, Office of the Chief Accountant of the SEC, at the AICPA Conference on Current SEC Developments)
>
> **OBSERVATION:**   The FASB is expected to eliminate the current ability to overcome the share-settlement presumption of FAS-128 as a result of its decision in the short-term convergence project addressing EPS.

A contract that is reported as an asset or liability for accounting purposes may require an adjustment to the numerator for any changes in income or loss that would result if the contract had been reported as an equity instrument for accounting purposes during the period. Likewise, a contract that is reported as an equity instrument for accounting purposes may require an adjustment to the numerator for any changes in income or loss that would result if the contract had been reported as an asset or liability for accounting purposes during the period.

> **OBSERVATION:** The balance sheet classification model in EITF Issue 00-19 does *not* consider a company's past experience in settling similar contracts or a stated policy as to how the company plans to settle whereas EITF Topic D-72 does. Thus, for a contract that provides the company with a choice of settlement methods, the entity could presume settlement of shares for balance sheet classification (book) purposes and settlement in cash for EPS purposes (or vice versa) depending on the circumstances. Such differences may require "pro forma" adjustments to the numerator, the denominator, or both, as described below.

Exhibit 16-5 summarizes the guidance contained in EITF Topic D-72, which explains the interaction of FAS-128 and Issue 00-19.

EXHIBIT 16-5
EPS TREATMENT OF CONTRACTS INDEXED TO A COMPANY'S OWN STOCK

Assumed Settlement for EPS Purposes*	Accounting for Book Purposes (per Issue 00-19)‡	Adjustment Required to Earnings (Numerator) for Purposes of Computing Diluted EPS?	Adjustment Required to Number of Shares Included in Denominator?
Shares	Asset/Liability	Yes (FAS-128, par. 29)	Yes
Shares	Equity	No	Yes
Cash	Asset/Liability	No	No
Cash	Equity	Yes (Topic D-72)	No

* Note that for purposes of computing EPS, delivery of the full stated amount of cash in exchange for delivery of the full stated number of shares (physical settlement) should be considered share settlement.
‡ This Exhibit does not apply to physically settled forward purchase contracts that are accounted for as liabilities under FAS-150.

Source: EITF Topic D-72.

Accelerated Share Repurchase Programs

In calculating basic and diluted EPS, the number of shares used to calculate the weighted-average common shares outstanding would be reduced by the shares repurchased as treasury stock. The guidance in FAS-128, as interpreted in Topic D-72, should be used to measure the effect of the forward contract on EPS. (EITF 99-7)

Fair Value

Fair value disclosure is *not* required for:

- Minority interests in consolidated subsidiaries.
- Equity investments in consolidated subsidiaries.
- Equity instruments issued by the entity and classified in stockholders' equity in the balance sheet. (FAS-107, par. 8 (h)-(j))

Fair value disclosure must be provided for any financial instrument that is properly classified as an asset or liability under the guidance in this chapter. Chapter 18, "Fair Value Measurements, Fair Value Disclosures, and Other Financial Instruments," provides additional information, including an exception for smaller, nonpublic companies.

> ☞ **PRACTICE POINTER:** FAS-107 generally does not apply to equity instruments of the issuer. However, paragraph 9 of FAS-107 states that it does not supersede or modify other GAAP that applies to specific financial instruments. As discussed previously, EITF Issue 00-19, as amended, requires disclosure of the fair value of each of the settlement alternatives (as well as a sensitivity analysis) for contracts indexed to a company's own stock that involve settlement alternatives. That disclosure is required even if the issuer classifies the contract as equity. FAS-150 requires similar disclosures about the fair value of various settlement alternatives and the effect of a change in fair value on those settlement amounts.

REGULATORY CONSIDERATIONS

Entities in regulated industries often are intensely interested in whether certain types of instruments qualify as capital or surplus (equity) for regulatory capital purposes, and for equity-based ratios.

In many instances, the treatment of a specific instrument differs for financial reporting purposes and for regulatory capital purposes. For example:

- Federal Reserve Board regulations allow certain trust-preferred securities (such as MIPS and TROPS) with long-term deferrals of distributions to qualify as Tier 1 capital for bank holding companies, with limitations on the amount. (Further guidance on capital treatment of trust preferred securities is provided below.)
- Qualifying surplus notes issued by insurance companies may be included in surplus.
- Certain forms of subordinated debt qualify as supplementary capital for banks and other financial institutions.

In March 2005, the Federal Reserve Board (FRB) issued a final rule on the risk-based capital treatment of trust preferred securities. The final rule updates interim guidance issued in 2003 and establishes new guidance for certain core capital elements. The final rule establishes the following:

- Trust preferred securities may continue to be included in Tier 1 capital. However, there is a limit on the aggregate amount of cumulative perpetual preferred stock, trust preferred securities, and minority interests in the equity accounts of most consolidated subsidiaries (collectively referred to as "restricted core elements") that may be included in Tier 1 capital to 25% of core capital elements, net of goodwill less any associated deferred tax liability. The netting of goodwill tightens the 25% of Tier 1 limit, which was determined under previous capital rules on a basis that did not deduct goodwill. "Internationally active bank holding companies," as defined by the rule, would be subject to a 15% Tier 1 limit.
- Amounts of restricted core capital elements in excess of the Tier 1 limit generally may be included in Tier 2 capital.
- Trust preferred securities must meet specific criteria in order to be eligible for inclusion in Tier 1 capital, including specific standards for the junior subordinated debt underlying trust preferred securities.
- The reaffirmation of the longstanding policy that voting common stock should be the dominant form of Tier 1 capital. However, excessive nonvoting elements generally will be reallocated to Tier 2 capital. In addition, the FRB will heighten its supervisory scrutiny when the predominance of voting common equity in Tier 1 capital begins to erode.

The final rule is required to be applied for capital computations of bank holding companies beginning on March 31, 2009. Full text of the final rule can be found at the Federal Reserve Board website at http://www.federalreserve.gov/boarddocs/press/bcreg/2005/20050301/attachment.pdf.

Regardless of the treatment for regulatory purposes, all financial instruments issued by an enterprise must be evaluated for financial reporting purposes under the applicable generally accepted accounting principles. Earnings per share calculations, if required, should be based on the classifications for GAAP, not regulatory or capital purposes.

> ☛ **PRACTICE POINTER:** At press time, the NAIC had not indicated how the issuance of FAS-150 would affect regulatory reporting. Readers should monitor developments in this area.

Disclosures about Capital Adequacy

SOP 01-6, in combination with several AICPA Audit and Accounting Guides, requires disclosure of applicable capital requirements for financial institutions, whether the requirements are met, and certain other information. These disclosures must be presented in the footnotes to the financial statements.

AUDIT CONSIDERATIONS

The primary audit risk in accounting for equity instruments is that they will be improperly classified in the balance sheet (which has a "trickle down" effect on the way payments and gains and losses are reported in the income statement and the statement of cash flows). The auditor should look beyond the creative labels attached to various instruments, and ensure that instruments are reported according to the applicable GAAP requirements. Similarly, auditors should be aware that certain regulated industries allow certain instruments to be counted as capital that are not classified in stockholders' equity for financial reporting purposes.

Stock or other equity instruments that are issued in connection with compensation of employees, in exchange for goods and services, or as part of a business combination are accounted for under specialized accounting models. Auditors should ensure that the applicable GAAP standards are being followed for those transactions.

Additional risks include:

- Failure to consider the effect of changes in the share requirements of other instruments issued by the entity (and other factors) on the current classification of contracts indexed to a company's own stock. Classification of contracts subject to EITF Issue 00-19 is *not* a one-time affair.
- Failure to adequately disclose the terms of equity or equity-linked securities, in accordance with FAS-150, FAS-129, and EITF Issue 00-19, if applicable.

- Failure to identify embedded derivatives in debt and equity instruments and account for them separately. (See Chapter 13, "Embedded Derivatives")

- Estimating the fair value of contracts indexed to a company's own stock, particularly when contingencies are involved.

- For instruments with legally detachable equity components, such as debt with detachable stock warrants, ensuring that the allocation based on relative fair value is proper. (See Chapter 10, "Convertible Debt and Similar Instruments.")

ILLUSTRATIONS

Illustration 16-1: Treasury Stock Buy-Back

French Mill Supply, Inc., reports the following stockholders' equity at December 31, 20X1:

Common stock, par value $1, authorized	
100,000 shares, issued 50,000 shares	$50,000
Contributed capital in excess of par	$150,000
Retained earnings	$75,000
Total stockholders' equity	$275,000

Management concludes that its stock is undervalued in the marketplace and decides to use $60,000 to buy back as much stock as possible. The stock is currently trading for $5 per share. Management buys back 12,000 shares on January 15, 20X2. Management does not currently plan to retire the shares. The following entry is recorded:

Treasury stock	$60,000	
Cash		$60,000

To record the purchase of treasury shares using the cost method.

On August 10, 20X2, management sells 7,000 shares out of treasury at $6 per share (greater than the cost of purchasing those shares).

Cash	$42,000	
Treasury stock (7,000 shares, at cost of $5)		$35,000
Contributed capital (from treasury stock transactions)		$7,000

To record the sale of treasury stock at a price greater than its cost.

On December 18, 20X2, the price of the stock has fallen, and management sells 4,000 shares out of treasury at $2 per share (less than the cost of purchasing the shares).

Cash	$8,000	
Contributed capital (from treasury stock transactions)	$7,000	
Retained earnings	$5,000	
Treasury stock (4,000 shares, at cost of $5)		$20,000

To record the sale of treasury stock at a price less than its cost. The debit to contributed capital is limited to the amount added by previous transactions in the same class of stock. Any remaining difference must be charged to retained earnings.

At December 31, 20X2, the stockholders' equity section for French Mill Supply, Inc. would reflect the activity in treasury stock for the year as follows (assume for simplicity that no other transactions affected contributed capital or retained earnings):

Common stock, par $1, authorized 100,000 shares, issued 50,000 shares	$50,000
Contributed capital in excess of par	$150,000
Retained earnings	$70,000
Treasury stock at cost	($5,000)
Total stockholders' equity	$265,000

> **OBSERVATION:** Treasury stock transactions do not affect net income.

Illustration 16-2: Accounting for a Purchased Put Option Indexed to and Potentially Settled in a Company's Own Stock

On July 15, 20X5, Benton Company, a public company, purchases a put option to sell 100 shares of its own common stock at $25 per share, when the fair value of the stock is $25 per share. The option expires on 10/13/X5. The option premium is $150. Assume that the price of each common share and the fair value of the option are $23 and $225 respectively, on 9/30/X5 and $20 and $500, respectively, on 10/13/X5, the settlement date. Two scenarios are presented to illustrate the significance of the contractual settlement terms of the contracts under EITF 00-19.

Scenario 1: The company can choose to settle in net shares or net cash

At inception of the contract—7/15/X5

Because the company can choose the method of settlement, the indexed option is an equity transaction under EITF Issue 00-19, provided that all of the supplemental conditions for equity treatment are met.

Additional paid-in capital	$150	
Cash		$150

At interim dates—9/30/X5

Subsequent changes in the fair value of contracts recorded as equity transactions are not recognized. Note that the contract is excluded from FAS-133 under paragraph 11(a).

At settlement—10/13/X5

The company chooses to receive settlement in net cash. Because the price per share is $20 on the settlement date, the option is worth $500 [($25 − $20) × 100]. The counterparty pays the company $500 to settle the contract.

Cash	$500	
Additional paid-in capital		$500

Scenario 2: The counterparty can choose to settle in net cash or in net shares

At inception of the contract—7/15/X5

Because the counterparty can elect settlement in net cash, the indexed option is recognized as an asset.

Purchased indexed option	$150	
Cash		$150

Note that the option could meet the definition of a derivative; if so, it is subject to all of the disclosure requirements of FAS-133 and EITF Issue 00-19.

At interim dates—9/30/X5

The per share price has increased to $23. The company increases the carrying amount of the option to its fair value of $225 and recognizes a gain of $75 ($225 − $150).

Purchased indexed option	$75	
Gain on indexed option		$75

At settlement—10/13/X5

The counterparty chooses to settle in net shares. Because the price per share is $20 on the settlement date—$5 less than the reference price of $25—the option is worth $500. The company, therefore, had a total gain of $350 on the contract ($500 less the $150 premium paid for the option). The counterparty settles the contract by delivering 25 of the company's shares (25 x $20), which are reported as treasury shares. The gain recognized on settlement is $275 ($500 less the $225 recorded amount of the option).

Treasury stock	$500	
Purchased indexed option		$225
Gain on indexed option		275

Illustration 16-3: Accounting for a Written Put Option Indexed to and Potentially Settled in a Company's Own Stock

On December 15, 20X5, Benton Company sells a put option on 100 shares of its own common stock at a price of $25 per share when the fair value of the stock is $25 per share. The option expires on 3/14/X6. The option premium is $150.

Assume that the price of each common share and the fair value of the option are $22 and $330, respectively, on 12/31/X5 and $20 and $500, respectively, on 3/14/X6, the settlement date.

Regardless of the settlement alternatives, the written put option would be considered a liability under FAS-150, paragraph 11. If Benton Co. is a public company, the option will most likely meet the definition of a derivative, even if the option requires or permits physical settlement.

At inception of the contract—12/15/X5

Cash	$150	
Written indexed option		$150

At year-end—12/31/X5 (interim date)

The per share price of $22 is $3 less than the $25 per share price on settlement. The company adjusts the liability to the option's fair value of $330 and recognizes a loss of $180.

Loss on indexed option contract	$180	
Written indexed option		$180

At settlement—3/14/X6

Assume that the counterparty chooses to receive settlement in net shares. Because the price per share is $20 on the settlement date—$5 less than the reference price of $25—the option is worth $500. The company, therefore, has a total loss of $350 on the contract ($500 less $150 premium). The company settles the contract by delivering 25 shares ($500/$20) to the counterparty to settle the contract. The loss recognized on settlement is $170 ($500 less the $330 recorded liability).

Loss on indexed option contract	$170	
Written indexed option	330	
Common stock		$500

Illustration 16-4: Accounting for a Forward Purchase Contract

On July 16, 20X1, Benton Company enters into a contract to purchase 100 shares of its own common stock at $25 per share when the fair value of the stock is $23 per share. The contract must be settled in one year by physical delivery of 100 shares in exchange for cash. The contract is considered a liability under paragraph 11 of FAS-150.

At inception of the contract—7/16/X1

Common stock	$2,300	
Debt		$2,300

To record an obligation to repurchase 100 shares in one year for $2,500 at its present value. The implicit rate in the contract is 9%.

At interim dates

Interest would be accrued over the year, using the rate implicit in the contract. The implicit rate would reflect any dividends expected to be paid during the one-year period. The entry below shows the accretion of the debt discount in total (for simplicity).

Interest expense	$200	
Debt		$200

At settlement—7/15/X2

Debt	$2,500	
Cash		$2,500

To record the settlement of the transaction (the shares have already been recorded).

PART V:
PERVASIVE ISSUES

CHAPTER 17
OFFSETTING ASSETS AND LIABILITIES IN THE BALANCE SHEET

CONTENTS

Overview	17.02
Background	17.02
Display versus Derecognition	17.02
Motivation for Netting	17.03
Accounting Guidance	17.04
General Principle	17.04
Demonstrating the Right of Setoff	17.04
Exceptions to the General Rule	17.06
Offsetting Derivative Assets and Liabilities	17.06
Offsetting Receivables and Payables from Repurchase Agreements	17.08
Effect on Interest Income and Expense	17.10
Exhibit 17-1: Criteria for Offsetting Assets and Liabilities	17.11
Other Authoritative Literature Addressing Offsetting	17.12
Trade Date Receivables and Payables	17.12
Offsetting Government Securities and Tax Liabilities	17.12
Life Insurance Policy Loans	17.13
Offsetting Liabilities and Insurance Recoveries	17.13
Derivatives Used as Hedges	17.13
Nonrecourse Debt	17.13
Foreclosed Assets	17.14
Wrap-Around Mortgages	17.14
Reacquisitions of Debt by an Intermediary	17.14
Offsetting Credit Receivables and Insurance Payables in Consolidation	17.15
Disclosures	17.15
Audit Considerations	17.17
Illustrations	17.17
Illustration 17-1: Application of FIN-39	17.17

Illustration 17-2: Disclosure of Compliance with FIN-39   17.18

Illustration 17-3: Derivative Used as a Hedge   17.18

Illustration 17-4: Offsetting Reverse Repurchase Agreements and Repurchase Agreements   17.18

Illustration 17-5: Offsetting Credit Receivables and Insurance Payables in Consolidation   17.19

OVERVIEW

Generally, assets and liabilities should only be offset (netted against each other) in the balance sheet when a right of setoff exists and the entity intends to exercise that right. Exceptions to the general rule exist for certain types of financial instruments, including derivatives and repurchase agreements, and certain industry practices. Offsetting relates only to the display of recognized assets and liabilities in the financial statements. It differs from derecognition (removal) in that no gain or loss is recognized.

BACKGROUND

APB-10 establishes the general principle that assets and liabilities should not be offset unless a *right of setoff* exists. FIN-39 provides the definition of the right of setoff and provides an exception to the general criteria for derivatives that are subject to a master netting agreement between two parties. FIN-41 provides a different exception for receivables and payables arising from *repurchase agreements* and *reverse repurchase agreements* that meet several conditions. Various AICPA Audit Guides, EITF Issues, and SEC staff guidance also provide guidance about offsetting of assets and liabilities in specific situations.

Display versus Derecognition

When a recognized asset and recognized liability are offset against each other, they are presented in the financial statements as a single net asset or liability (depending on which item is greater). Although the net effect on the balance sheet may be similar, offsetting is different from derecognizing an asset and extinguishing a liability in the following respects:

- No gain or loss is recognized.
- Unlike a transfer of assets where the entity surrenders control (a sale), the reporting entity continues to control the asset it owns.

- Unlike an extinguishment of debt, where the debtor is legally released, the debtor remains obligated to repay the debt.

Offsetting is simply a method of displaying outstanding claims to cash and debts that the entity *intends* to offset. Offsetting is generally an accounting *election* when certain conditions are met, rather than an accounting requirement.

Motivation for Netting

From a financial reporting perspective, netting in the balance sheet affects footings of total assets and liabilities (and subtotals, such as current assets and current liabilities) and related financial ratios. Depending on the specific assets and liabilities involved, offsetting could affect the following key ratios (among others):

- Current ratio
- Return on assets
- Leverage ratio
- Debt to equity

For example, assume a company had the following current assets and liabilities at a reporting period, including both a receivable from Company A and a payable to Company A for which it had the right of setoff. Note the differences in total current assets and liabilities and certain financial ratios that arise from netting the two amounts in the balance sheet.

	Receivable and Payable Reported Separately	Net
Current Assets:		
Cash	$150	$150
Receivable from Company A	**250**	**150**
Other current assets	400	400
	$800	$700
Current liabilities:		
Payable to Company A	**$100**	—
Other current liabilities	300	300
	$400	300

	Receivable and Payable Reported	
	Separately	Net
Net income	$15	$15
Working capital	400 (800 – 400)	400 (700 – 300)
Current ratio	2.0:1 (800 ÷ 400)	2.33:1 (700 ÷300)
Return on assets ratio	.019 (15 ÷ 800)	.021 (15 ÷ 700)

Although working capital is not affected by the change in presentation, the company's current ratio and return on assets ratio improve when the receivable from and payable to Company A are netted. Therefore, offsetting of current assets and current liabilities can affect a company's perceived liquidity and profitability.

From a business standpoint, entities in capital-intensive industries often must hold capital against recognized asset balances, according to prescribed formulas. Accordingly, netting assets and liabilities helps companies reduce their capital requirements (as permitted by applicable regulation).

In addition, entering into contracts with the legal right of setoff helps companies manage their credit risk and settlement risk with counterparties.

☞ **PRACTICE POINTER:** Regulatory accounting principles for financial institutions and statutory accounting principles for insurance companies generally follow GAAP with respect to offsetting in the balance sheet.

ACCOUNTING GUIDANCE

General Principle

Recognized assets and liabilities should only be offset against each other in the balance sheet if the right of setoff exists. (APB-10, par. 1) A debtor having a valid right of setoff may offset the related asset and liability and report the net amount. (FIN-39, par. 5) The right of setoff is precisely defined in FIN-39.

Demonstrating the Right of Setoff

A right of setoff is a debtor's legal right to satisfy all or a portion of a debt owed to another party with funds owed to the debtor by that same party. Paragraph 5 of FIN-39 identifies four conditions that must all be met for the right of setoff to exist:

• Each of *two* parties owes the other determinable amounts.

- The reporting entity has the right to set off the amount payable with the amount receivable from the other party.
- The reporting entity intends to set off.
- The right of setoff is enforceable at law.

Note that even though the right of setoff is a "legal" term, for accounting purposes, the right of setoff does not exist unless the reporting entity intends to set off the two amounts. Essentially, this makes offsetting in the balance sheet a choice of the reporting entity (but only if the other conditions are met). Two exceptions to the intent condition are discussed later in this chapter.

Specific implementation guidelines for right of setoff criteria are discussed below.

Two parties owe each other determinable amounts   Cash on deposit at a financial institution is considered by the depositor as *cash* rather than a receivable from the financial institution. (FIN-39, fn. 2) Accordingly, cash collateral placed with a bank may not be offset against a loan from that same bank. However, financial institutions that accept deposits may have balances due to and from the same depository institution (referred to as *reciprocal balances*). Reciprocal balances should be offset if they will be offset in the process of payment or collection. (SOP 01-06, par. 14b)

> ☞ **PRACTICE POINTER:**   The offsetting guidance for reciprocal balances applies only to financial institutions and should not be applied by analogy in other situations. (SOP 01-6, par. A.47)

The amounts owed between the parties need not be in the same currency or bear the same interest rate if the other criteria are met. (FIN-39, par. 44)

The reporting entity intends to net settle   FIN-39 requires that in addition to the legal right of setoff, the reporting entity must intend to set off the asset and liability in question. This condition is necessary to faithfully represent the entity's expected sources and uses of cash. An entity can demonstrate its intent to net settle by documenting its intent and, if applicable, by a history of execution of setoff in similar situations. (FIN-39, par. 45)

An arrangement that provides for the legal right of offset only in the event of the default of one of the parties to the contract does not meet the accounting definition of the right of setoff because the parties do not intend to net settle the contract in the normal course of business. (FIN-39, par. 49)

If the maturities of the receivable and payable differ, only the party with the nearer maturity may offset, because the party with the longer term maturity must settle in the manner that the other party selects at the earlier maturity date. (FIN-39, par. 44)

If a receivable or payable does not have an explicit settlement date, the entity cannot assert that it intends to net settle the transaction. (AICPA Audit Guide, *Brokers and Dealers in Securities*, pars. 4.34 and 7.33)

The right of setoff is enforceable at law   Various laws and regulations around the world may provide restrictions or prohibitions against the right of setoff in certain circumstances, which may contradict the rights otherwise provided by contract or as a matter of common law. Therefore, it is important that legal constraints be considered to determine whether the right of setoff is enforceable. (FIN-39, par. 6)

> **OBSERVATION:**   Various trade organizations, such as the Bond Market Association and the International Swaps and Derivatives Association have sought to establish standard netting agreements that would be upheld in jurisdictions around the world to reduce this legal risk.

"Enforceable at law" encompasses the notion that the right of setoff should be upheld in bankruptcy. The nature of support required for an assertion in financial statements that a right of setoff is enforceable at law is subject to a cost-benefit constraint and depends on the facts and circumstances. All of the information that is available, either supporting or questioning enforceability, should be considered. Offsetting is appropriate only if the available evidence, both positive and negative, indicates that there is reasonable assurance that the right of setoff would be upheld in bankruptcy. (EITF Topic D-43)

> ☛ **PRACTICE POINTER:**   A right of setoff can be *enforceable at law* even if it is not specifically included in the contractual agreements if regulatory procedures or normal business practices would offset the contracts. (FIN-39, par. 47)

Exceptions to the General Rule

The FASB granted two exceptions to the general criteria for offsetting for transactions entered into under specific contractual arrangements.

Offsetting Derivative Assets and Liabilities

Generally, the fair value of a derivative asset (including any amounts recognized as accrued receivables) should not be offset against the fair value of a derivative liability (including any amounts recognized as accrued payables) unless all four of the criteria for offsetting are met. However, when derivatives are entered into with the same counterparty under a *master netting agreement,* even if the reporting entity does *not* have the intent to net settle, the reporting entity may offset the fair value amount recognized for derivative instruments (i.e., a net derivative position) against the fair value amounts (or approximate fair value amount) recognized for the right to reclaim cash collateral (a receivable) or the obligation to return cash collateral (a payable). (FIN-39, par. 10, as amended by FSP FIN-39-1)

☞ **PRACTICE POINTER:** The balance sheet asset or liability associated with cash collateral is recognized under FAS-140 as a separate receivable for return of cash collateral posted or a separate payable for an obligation to return cash collateral received.

Under a master netting arrangement, individual contracts are effectively consolidated into a single agreement between the two counterparties. Cross-product master netting arrangements consolidate a variety of types of derivative products with a single counterparty. If one party fails to make a payment under a master netting arrangement, the other party is entitled to terminate the entire arrangement and demand the net settlement of all contracts. (FIN-39, pars. 21 and 30)

☞ **PRACTICE POINTER:** When derivatives are entered into subject to a master netting agreement, they do not automatically qualify for netting. The legal enforceability of the contract must be evaluated.

To simplify application of this guidance, companies are permitted to offset a net derivative position against an amount recognized for the related cash collateral if a receivable or payable representing the collateral is a fair value amount or an amount that approximates fair value. However, the guidance related to use of an approximate fair value amount is specific to this situation and may not be applied by analogy in other situations. (FSP FIN-39-1, par. A3)

This guidance is applicable to contracts that meet the definition of a derivative in FAS-133 and that are measured at fair value, regardless of whether they qualify for a scope exception to FAS-133. However, if a master netting arrangement covers multiple instruments, some of which do not meet the definition of a derivative in FAS-133 or are not recognized at fair value, a reporting entity is still permitted to offset fair value amounts related to other derivative instruments under that master netting agreement that do qualify for offsetting. In that case, the reporting entity must develop a supportable methodology for determining the amount of cash collateral receivable or payable that can be offset against the net derivative position. (FSP FIN-39-1, pars. A7–A8)

☞ **PRACTICE POINTER:**   The fair value recognized for some contracts may include an accrual component for the periodic receivables and payables that result from the contract; those accruals may also be offset for contracts executed with the same counterparty under a master netting arrangement.

A reporting entity must make an accounting policy decision to offset net derivative payables or receivables against cash collateral receivable or payable executed with the same counterparty under a master netting agreement and must apply that choice consistently. If elected, the reporting entity may offset fair value amounts related to derivative instruments only if those amounts are offset against the fair value amounts (or approximate fair value amounts) related to cash collateral. However, if the amount recognized for the right to reclaim cash collateral or the obligation to return cash collateral is deemed not to be a fair value amount (or an amount that approximates fair value), the reporting entity may offset fair value amounts related to the derivative instruments only. (FIN-39, par. 10A, as amended by FSP FIN-39-1)

OBSERVATION: If elected as an accounting policy, net presentation of fair value amounts recognized for receivables or payables related to cash collateral and fair value amounts recognized for related derivative contracts executed with the same counterparty under a master netting arrangement is *required* (subject to the exception above), because it is a true representation of the amount of credit risk exposure under the entire arrangement.

Although this is technically an accounting election, most financial institutions consistently elect to offset their derivative contracts with the same counterparty in the balance sheet.

Offsetting Receivables and Payables from Repurchase Agreements

In a *repurchase agreement* (a "repo"), one party agrees to sell securities to another for cash, with a simultaneous agreement to repurchase the same or equivalent securities at a specific price at a later date. The payable recognized for a repo that is accounted for as a secured borrowing represents the amount of the seller/borrower's obligation for the future repurchase of the securities from the buyer/lender. (FIN-41, fn. 1)

A *reverse repurchase agreement* ("reverse repo") is the purchase of a security for cash, with a simultaneous agreement to resell the same or equivalent securities at a later date for a specified price. The receivable recognized for a reverse repo that is accounted for as a collateralized loan represents the amount due from the seller/borrower for the future repurchase of the securities from the buyer/lender. (FIN-41, fn. 2)

☞ **PRACTICE POINTER:**   Investment companies (for example, mutual funds) use the same terminology to refer to the opposite transactions.

☞ **PRACTICE POINTER:**   Not all repurchase agreements are accounted for as secured borrowings. This discussion on netting only applies to (reverse) repurchase agreements that have been properly accounted for as secured borrowings under FAS-140. The accounting for repos and reverse repos is addressed in Chapter 9, "Securities Lending Arrangements, and Other Pledges of Collateral."

☞ **PRACTICE POINTER:**   Even though certain aspects of repurchase agreement transactions are similar to securities lending transactions, FIN-41 *only* applies to repurchase agreements and may not be applied by analogy to other transactions that might be similar economically. (AICPA Audit and Accounting Guides, *Depository and Lending Institutions: Banks and Savings Institutions, Credit Unions, Finance Companies and Mortgage Companies,* par. 14.30, *Brokers and Dealers in Securities,* par. 7.33)

Banks, broker dealers, and other financial institutions often operate as both borrowers and lenders in the repo market on the same day. FIN-41, paragraphs 3 and 4, provides that amounts recognized as payables under repurchase agreements may be offset against amounts recognized as receivables under reverse repurchase agreements provided that all of the following conditions are met:

- The receivables and payables involve the same counterparty.
- The receivables and payables have the same explicit settlement date, set forth at the inception of the agreement.

  OBSERVATION: Agreements that have open-ended maturities would not meet this criterion. (FIN-41, par. 16)

- The repurchase and reverse repurchase agreements are executed in accordance with a master netting arrangement (as described in FIN-39).
- The securities underlying the agreements exist in "book entry" form and can be transferred only by means of entries in the records of the transfer system operator or securities custodian.
- The agreements will be settled on a securities transfer system that enables the counterparties to instruct the securities custodian to deliver securities in settlement of its obligations (thereby reducing the necessary cash flow).
- The company has banking arrangements that require it to maintain cash on deposit for any *net* amounts that are due at the end of the business day and it must be probable that the account will

provide sufficient *daylight overdraft or other intraday credit* at the settlement date for each of the parties.

- The company intends to use the same account at the clearing bank or other financial institution at the settlement date in settling the reverse repo and the offsetting repo.

Footnotes 4–8 of FIN-41 elaborate on certain aspects of qualifying securities transfer systems and associated banking arrangements.

> ☛ **PRACTICE POINTER:** These requirements are largely based on the characteristics of the Fedwire Securities Transfer System in the U.S. However, transactions occurring on other securities transfer systems that meet all of these conditions would also qualify.
>
> **OBSERVATION:** This exception permits netting regardless of whether the entity *intends* to net settle. The FASB decided that in this narrow set of circumstances, the settlement mechanism in place is the "functional equivalent" of net settlement. Repos and reverse repos that do not meet all of the conditions in FIN-41 may only be presented net if all of the conditions of FIN-39 are met, including intent to net settle.

Entities that meet these conditions are permitted, but not required to net receivables and payables involving the same counterparty. The company must consistently apply its decision to offset or not. (FIN-41, par. 3)

> ☛ **PRACTICE POINTER:** Net receivables/payables from one counterparty should not be offset against net payables/receivables from another counterparty. (FIN-41, par. 3)

Effect on Interest Income and Expense

There is no specific accounting literature that addresses whether interest income and expense on assets and liabilities that have been offset in the balance sheet in accordance with FIN-39 or FIN-41 should also be offset in the income statement. However, the Instructions to the Call Report for banks and other financial institutions state that if receivables from reverse repurchase agreements have been offset against payables from repurchase agreements in accordance with FIN-41, the income and expense from those agreements may be presented net in Schedule RI (the income statement). (FFIEC 031 and 041, Item 2.b)

EXHIBIT 17-1
CRITERIA FOR OFFSETTING ASSETS AND LIABILITIES
(References to FIN-39 unless otherwise noted)

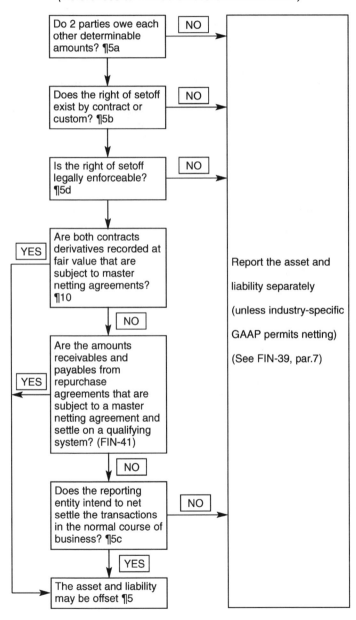

> ☛ **PRACTICE POINTER:**   Broker-dealers may also offset income
> and expense from matched-book and certain other trading stra-
> tegies, with disclosure of the gross amounts. (AICPA Audit Guide,
> *Brokers and Dealers in Securities*, par. 7.58)

Other Authoritative Literature Addressing Offsetting

The provisions of FIN-39 are not intended to supersede or modify the
accounting provided by other GAAP that specifies accounting treat-
ments that result in the offsetting of assets and liabilities or in a
balance sheet presentation that is similar to the effect of offsetting.
FIN-39 specifically mentions the following literature that does not
relate to financial instruments covered in this book (FIN-39, par. 7,
as amended):

- FAS-13 (leveraged leases, paragraphs 42–47)
- FAS-87 (accounting for pension plan assets and liabilities)
- FAS-106 (accounting for plan assets and liabilities)
- FAS-109 (net tax asset or liability amounts reported)

Several other pieces of literature provide specific guidance involving financial instruments, as described below.

Trade Date Receivables and Payables

Broker-dealers in securities may report payables and receivables arising from unsettled regular-way transactions net in an account titled
"Net receivable (or payable) for unsettled regular-way trades." This
exception for broker-dealers applies even if the counterparties are not
the same. (AICPA Audit Guide, *Brokers and Dealers in Securities*, par.
7.20) Refer to Chapter 2, "Investments in Debt and Equity Securities,"
for additional information about trade date accounting.

> **OBSERVATION:**   The AICPA granted an exception for unsettled
> securities trades of broker-dealers because special attributes of
> their transactions make the risk of nonperformance minimal.

Offsetting Government Securities and Tax Liabilities

APB-10 generally prohibits offsetting cash or other assets (including
most securities issued by governments) against income tax liabilities.
However, when a purchase of government securities that are specifically designated as being acceptable for the payment of taxes of that

government is in substance an advance payment of taxes that will be payable in the near future, paragraph 7 of APB-10 permits offsetting the amount of securities held against the taxes payable.

Life Insurance Policy Loans

A company may take out a loan from its insurance company against a life insurance policy that it owns. If the policyholder has the right to offset the loan against the proceeds received on maturity or cancellation of the policy, and intends to do so, the amount of the loan may be offset against the cash surrender value, with disclosure of the amount so offset, provided that the right of setoff is enforceable at law. (AICPA TPA 2240.01)

Offsetting Liabilities and Insurance Recoveries

EITF Topic D-79 addresses the purchase of retroactive insurance by companies other than insurance companies to cover a liability that has been appropriately accrued under FAS-5. (The issue does not apply to situations where the policy extinguishes the entity's liability.) A liability incurred as a result of a past insurable event and amounts receivable under an insurance contract that indemnifies the company against that loss do not meet the criteria for offsetting under FIN-39. EITF Topic D-79 provides additional information about how to account for the purchased retroactive insurance.

Derivatives Used as Hedges

As discussed in Chapter 12, "Introduction to Derivatives," all derivatives should be reported in the balance sheet at fair value. The fair value of a derivative used in a qualifying fair value hedging relationship may not be netted against the hedged item in the balance sheet or in the fair value disclosures required by FAS-107 unless all of the criteria of FIN-39 are met. (FAS-107, par. 10, as amended)

Nonrecourse Debt

A *nonrecourse loan* gives the lender recourse only to specific property of the borrower, not to the borrower's general credit or other assets. Offsetting the assets pledged as collateral with nonrecourse debt is appropriate only in those circumstances in which a legal right of offset exists. (FTB 86-2, par. 21) (Note: FAS-13 provides certain exceptions for leveraged leases.)

> **OBSERVATION:** For the entity to have the legal right of setoff as defined in FIN-39, the borrower and the lender would need to *owe each other* determinable amounts. That is, the asset pledged by the borrower as collateral in the nonrecourse financing would need to be a receivable *from the lender*. In addition, the borrower would have to intend to net settle in the normal course of business, not just in the case of default.

Foreclosed Assets

A lender may at times foreclose on assets supporting a loan that are subject to senior debt. In such cases, the amount of that debt should be reported as a liability at the time of foreclosure and not be netted against the carrying value of the foreclosed assets. Interest that accrues after foreclosure should be recognized as interest expense. (SOP 92-3, par. 13)

> **OBSERVATION:** SOP 92-3 was effectively superseded by FAS-144. However, this guidance remains appropriate under FIN-39.

Wrap-Around Mortgages

If a company sells real estate subject to a mortgage and takes from the purchaser a wrap-around mortgage whereby the purchaser will make mortgage payments to the company but the company will continue to make payments on the original mortgage, the balance of the original mortgage should not be offset against the receivable from the purchaser (the wrap-around mortgage) since the payable and receivable involve different counterparties. (SAB Topic 11-D)

Reacquisitions of Debt by an Intermediary

In EITF Issue 86-18 (which was carried forward as part of Issue 96-19), the EITF addressed the following fact pattern:

- A borrower, instead of reacquiring its own debt securities directly, loans funds to a third party, who in turn acquires the borrower's outstanding debt securities.
- The borrower and the third party agree that they may settle their respective receivables and obligations by right of setoff as payments became due, contingent upon the third party's continued retention of the borrower's original debt.

The EITF concluded that the borrower should not account for the original debt securities as extinguished. In addition, the original debt securities (now held by the third party) should not be offset against the receivable from the third party in the borrower's financial statements. Refer to Chapter 11, "Extinguishments of Debt," for additional guidance relating to exchanges and modifications of debt instruments involving intermediaries.

> **OBSERVATION:** Interestingly, EITF members did not agree on the rationale supporting this conclusion. Some asserted that the parties lacked the intent to net settle the receivable and payable (perhaps because the lender was not obligated to keep the debt securities).

Offsetting Credit Receivables and Insurance Payables in Consolidation

In accordance with SOP 01-06, unearned premiums and unpaid claims on certain *credit life* and credit accident and health insurance policies issued to finance customers of a subsidiary should be deducted from or netted against finance receivables in the consolidated balance sheet.

> **OBSERVATION:** The rationale behind this practice is that the unearned premiums and unpaid claim balances represent intercompany items because they are added to the customers' finance receivables, and most or all of the proceeds on claims are applied to reduce the related finance receivables.

However, the following items should not be offset in the consolidated balance sheet:

- Unearned premiums and unpaid claims for credit life and accident health coverage should be reported as liabilities in the consolidated balance sheet when the related receivables are assets of unrelated companies. (SOP 01-06, par. 14(j))
- Unpaid claims for property insurance and level term life insurance should not be offset against related finance receivables in the consolidated balance sheet because finance companies generally do not receive substantially all of the proceeds of those claims. (SOP 01-06, par. 14(k))

DISCLOSURES

The following are required disclosures related to offsetting of fair value amounts related to derivative instruments against fair value amounts related to the right to reclaim cash collateral (a receivable) or the obligation to return cash collateral (a payable):

- A reporting entity's accounting policy to offset or not offset

- If the reporting entity has made an accounting policy decision to offset fair value amounts, separate disclosure of the following is required:
  - Amounts recognized for the right to reclaim cash collateral or the obligation to return cash collateral that have been offset against net derivative positions
  - Amounts recognized for the right to reclaim cash collateral or the obligation to return cash collateral under master netting arrangements that have not been offset against net derivative positions (because they are not fair value amounts or arise from instruments that are not eligible to be offset)
- If a reporting entity has made an accounting policy decision to *not* offset fair value amounts, it must separately disclose amounts recognized for the right to reclaim cash collateral or the obligation to return cash collateral under master netting arrangements. (FIN-39, par. 10B, as amended by FSP FIN-39-1)

> **OBSERVATION:** The objective of these disclosures is to provide information about the extent to which cash collateral affects a company's credit exposure related to derivative instruments.

FAS-107, as amended, requires disclosure of information about master netting agreements and their effect on credit risk. Refer to Chapter 18, "Fair Value Measurements, Fair Value Disclosures, and Other Financial Instrument Disclosures" for additional information.

> **OBSERVATION:** If material amounts of assets and liabilities are offset in the balance sheet, that practice should be disclosed as a significant accounting policy.

When financial assets and liabilities have been offset in the balance sheet, disclosure of the net fair value of the assets and liabilities complies with the requirements of FAS-107. (FIN-41, par. 19)

Paragraph 14(j) of SOP 01-06 requires that if unearned premiums or unpaid claims on certain credit life and credit accident and health insurance are netted against credit receivables of a subsidiary in the consolidated balance sheet, the notes to the financial statements should adequately disclose the amounts of unearned premiums and unpaid claims netted against those receivables and the allowance for losses.

AUDIT CONSIDERATIONS

There is no specific audit guidance on offsetting amounts in the balance sheet. Because offsetting is a display issue and not a recognition issue, the amounts recorded for the related receivables and payables should be audited in accordance with the literature applicable to those types of transactions. Thereafter, the primary audit risk is that amounts are offset in circumstances other than those specifically allowed by FIN-39, FIN-41, and other specific authoritative literature that provides guidance on offsetting.

Evaluating whether a legal right of offset exists and whether the right is enforceable at law is primarily a legal determination. Use of a legal specialist may be necessary to conclude that those conditions of offsetting are met. Refer to AU 336 for specific audit guidelines regarding the use of specialists. Certain aspects of AU 9336, *The Use of Legal Interpretations as Evidential Matter to Support Management's Assertion that a Transfer of Financial Assets Has Met the Isolation Criterion in Paragraph 9(a) of Financial Accounting Standards Board Statement No. 140*, may be helpful in assessing whether a right of setoff would be upheld in bankruptcy. For derivative transactions and repurchase agreements, using standardized master netting agreements developed by industry trade associations can reduce legal risk.

One of the conditions required for offsetting under FIN-39 is that the reporting entity intends to net settle (except for derivatives subject to master netting agreements). Auditors should review the terms of the agreements (including the reasonableness of the dates), documentation of management's intent, and management's previous actions in similar situations, if applicable, to corroborate management's representation.

ILLUSTRATIONS

Illustration 17-1: Application of FIN-39

Traditional Industries Corporation took out a $12,000,000 loan from Soundview Bank. To obtain a favorable rate, Traditional is required to maintain deposits of at least $2,000,000 in a money market account with Soundview. In its balance sheet, Traditional may not net the $12,000,000 loan against the $2,000,000 deposit because the deposit is considered cash, not a receivable. If instead, Traditional purchased a $2,000,000 debt security of Soundview Bank, it still would only be allowed to offset the debt security with the loan if it had the legal right of setoff and Traditional intends to net settle the principal and interest payments on the loan and debt security in the normal course of business (*not* only in the event of default).

Illustration 17-2: Disclosure of Compliance with FIN-39

The following disclosure is excerpted from the December 31, 2001 annual report of Fibermark, Inc.:

Note 2, Significant Accounting Policies (Commitments and Contingencies)

Liabilities for loss contingencies, including environmental remediation costs, arising from claims, assessments, litigation, fines and penalties, and other sources are recorded when it is probable that a liability has been incurred and the amount of the assessment and/or remediation can be reasonably estimated. Recoveries from third parties that are probable of realization are separately recorded, and are not offset against the related environmental liability, in accordance with FIN-39.

Illustration 17-3: Derivative Used as a Hedge

Fortress Company issued a $1,000,000 fixed-rate bond to numerous investors and contemporaneously entered into a pay floating, receive fixed interest rate swap with Majesty Bank. The swap was used to hedge the interest rate risk on the fixed rate debt. Fortress, having met all of the appropriate hedge criteria, applied fair value hedge accounting. In the subsequent quarter, Fortress recorded a $40,000 derivative asset, representing the change in fair value of the interest rate swap, and a gain in earnings. In addition, assuming no hedge ineffectiveness, Fortress recorded a basis adjustment of ($40,000) to reflect the change in the fair value of the debt attributable to interest rate risk (the basis adjustment represents a loss—the carrying amount of the debt is increased). Fortress would report separately the $40,000 derivative asset and a debt obligation of $1,040,000. If Fortress had several other derivative transactions with Majesty Bank, and they were entered into subject to a legally enforceable master netting agreement, the swap asset could be netted against any liabilities arising from other derivatives entered into with Majesty Bank. Refer to Chapter 14, "Hedge Accounting," for additional information about fair value hedge accounting.

Illustration 17-4: Offsetting Reverse Repurchase Agreements and Repurchase Agreements

High Finance Co. is a major player in the repo market involving Treasury securities. All of its repos have explicit settlement dates, are executed under master netting agreements, and settle over the Fedwire system. All of its repos and reverse repos are appropriately recognized as secured borrowings under FAS-140. At year-end, High Finance has the following transactions outstanding with its three major counterparties.

	Reverse Repurchase Agreements	Repurchase Agreements
Counterparty A	$5,000,000	($2,000,000)
Counterparty B	$7,000,000	($3,000,000)
Counterparty C	$1,000,000	($9,000,000)

High Finance meets all of the conditions for offsetting under FIN-41 and elects to offset in the balance sheet. At year-end, High Finance would report the following net assets and liabilities in its balance sheet.

Net reverse repos	$7,000,000 (sum of net exposure to Counterparty A and B)
Net repos	$8,000,000 (net position with Counterparty C)

The net reverse repo receivables and net repo payables could not be netted against each other.

Illustration 17-5:   Offsetting Credit Receivables and Insurance Payables in Consolidation

Assume that a consumer obtained a personal loan from Omega Company's finance subsidiary. The consumer also obtained credit life insurance from Omega Company's insurance subsidiary that provides for repayment of the loan if the consumer dies before the loan is fully paid. Because Omega's finance subsidiary would be the recipient of any claims paid on the insurance policy through Omega's insurance subsidiary, Omega may offset the un-earned insurance premiums against the loan in its consolidated balance sheet in accordance with SOP 01-06.

CHAPTER 18
FAIR VALUE MEASUREMENTS, FAIR VALUE DISCLOSURES, AND OTHER FINANCIAL INSTRUMENT DISCLOSURES

CONTENTS

Overview	18.03
Background	18.03
Important Notice: New FASB Statement on Fair Value Measurement	18.04
Fair Value Measurement	18.05
Scope	18.05
Exhibit 18-1: Practicability Exceptions to Fair Value Measurement	18.05
Definition of Fair Value	18.07
Key Concepts Underlying the Fair Value Measurement Model	18.08
Objective of Fair Value Measurement	18.08
The Specific Asset or Liability	18.08
Unit of Account	18.08
The Exchange Occurs in an Orderly Transaction	18.09
The Principal (or Most Advantageous) Market	18.09
Market Participants	18.10
Transaction Costs and Transportation Costs	18.10
The Fair Value Premise for Assets and Liabilities	18.10
Application of the Fair Value Premise to Assets	18.10
Exhibit 18-2: "In-Use" and "In-Exchange" Valuation Premise	18.11
Application of the Fair Value Premise to Liabilities	18.11
Measurement of Fair Value	18.12
Specific Considerations for Initial Measurement	18.12
Valuation Techniques	18.13
Exhibit 18-3: Characteristics of Approaches for Measuring Fair Value	18.13

Inputs to Valuation Techniques   18.16
Exhibit 18-4: *Types of Markets for Financial Instruments*   18.17
The Fair Value Hierarchy   18.17
Disclosures about Financial Instruments   18.21
Interaction of GAAP Related to Financial Instruments
Disclosures   18.21
Disclosures about Fair Value of Financial Instruments (FAS-107)   18.21
Scope   18.21
Exhibit 18-5: Scope of FAS-107   18.22
*Exhibit 18-6: Applicability of Nonpublic Company
Exception in Prior Periods*   18.24
Fair Value Disclosures   18.24
Disclosures for Assets and Liabilities Measured at Fair
Value (FAS-157)   18.27
Exhibit 18-7: FAS-157 Disclosure Requirements   18.28
Disclosures about Concentrations of Credit Risk of
Financial Instruments   18.29
Encouraged Disclosure about Market Risk of All
Financial Instruments   18.31
Disclosures of Certain Significant Risks and Uncertainties   18.32
Certain Public Company Disclosures in Management's
Discussion and Analysis (MD&A)   18.33
Public Company Disclosures about Off-Balance-Sheet
Arrangements   18.34
Audit Considerations   18.35
Illustrations   18.37
*Illustration 18-1: Integrated Disclosures about Fair
Value Measurements and Changes in Fair Values
Included in Current-Period Earnings*   18.37
*Illustration 18-2: Assets Measured at Fair Value on a
Recurring Basis*   18.38
*Illustration 18-3: FAS-157 Disclosures About Assets Measured
at Fair Value on a Nonrecurring Basis*   18.40
*Illustration 18-4: Fair Value Disclosures by a Financial
Entity*   18.40
*Illustration 18-5: Disclosure of Significant Concentrations
of Credit Risk*   18.42
*Illustration 18-6: Use of Estimates in Preparation of
Financial Statements*   18.42

OVERVIEW

Fair value is defined as the price that would be received to sell an asset or paid to transfer a liability in an orderly transaction between market participants at the measurement date. (FAS-157, par. 5) For entities and transactions that are subject to accounting pronouncements that require or permit fair value measurement, GAAP provide a framework for determining fair value consistently across all such pronouncements. The framework includes a fair value hierarchy for prioritizing inputs when valuation techniques are used for estimating fair value. The definition of fair value and the framework for measuring fair value is required to be applied uniformly (with the exception of situations in which a specific scope or practicability exception is provided).

Generally accepted accounting principles (GAAP) require most entities to disclose the fair value of their financial instruments; however, certain disclosures are optional for small, nonpublic companies that do not hold derivatives. Certain types of financial instruments are also exempt from the disclosure requirements.

All entities are required to disclose information about significant concentrations of credit risk from an individual counterparty or groups of counterparties arising from financial instruments.

Entities are encouraged, but not required, to disclose quantitative information about the market risks of financial instruments in a manner that reflects the way the entity manages or adjusts those risks.

Entities are required to disclose certain risks and uncertainties involved in the preparation of their financial statements, including the use of estimates that are susceptible to change and vulnerability from significant concentrations inherent in their business activities.

BACKGROUND

FAS-157 establishes a single definition and framework for determining fair value and is applicable for existing accounting pronouncements that require or permit fair value measurements (with several specific scope exceptions). It does not expand fair value measurement requirements beyond those already required by existing GAAP. FAS-157 also requires significant disclosures about fair value measurements.

FAS-107, as amended by FAS-126, FAS-133, FAS-140, FAS-157, and other standards (hereafter referred to as FAS-107), requires disclosure of the fair value of financial instruments whether the instruments are recognized or unrecognized in the balance sheet, with certain exceptions. FAS-107 does not change any existing requirements for recognition, measurement, or classification of financial instruments in financial statements. FAS-107 also requires disclosure of significant concentrations of credit risk by all entities.

SOP 94-6 requires certain disclosures about risks and uncertainties involved in the preparation of financial statements. The requirements apply to the use of estimates in determining the carrying amounts of assets, liabilities, and contingencies, including financial instruments. SOP 94-6 also requires disclosure of vulnerability from significant concentrations in business activities. Those requirements do not apply to financial instruments, *per se*, but predominantly financial entities could be subject to these disclosure requirements if their business activities involve concentrations.

Quantitative disclosures about off-balance-sheet credit risk relating to certain contracts written by financial institutions are discussed in Chapter 3, "Loans and the Allowance for Credit Losses," along with the accounting for such arrangements.

IMPORTANT NOTICE
NEW FASB STATEMENT ON FAIR VALUE MEASUREMENT

In September 2006, the FASB issued FAS-157, *Fair Value Measurements*. This Statement defines fair value, establishes a framework for measuring fair value under GAAP, and expands disclosures about fair value measurements. It applies under existing accounting pronouncements that require or permit fair value measurements, with several specific scope exceptions. FAS-157 does not expand fair value measurement requirements beyond those already required by existing GAAP.

FAS-157 is definitional in nature. It establishes a measurement framework, including a fair value hierarchy that prioritizes the market inputs when valuation techniques are used for estimating fair value. For some entities, the application of the definition of fair value and the measurement framework will change the measurements used in current practice.

FAS-157 is effective for calendar-year-end companies as of January 1, 2008. Generally, the Statement is prospective, except for several specific situations in which retrospective application is required. Earlier application encouraged for companies that have not yet issued annual or interim financial statements. Readers should refer to the effective date and transition provisions of FAS-157 for further detail on those requirements, including disclosure requirements upon initial adoption.

In an additional development, in February 2007, the FASB issued FAS-159, *The Fair Value Option for Financial Assets and Financial Liabilities*, which provides an option to report selected financial assets and liabilities at fair value. FAS-159 is addressed in Chapter 19. Companies are given the option of implementing FAS-159 to coincide with the adoption of FAS-157.

> **AUTHOR'S NOTE:** The 2008 edition of CCH *Financial Instruments* has been updated to incorporate the provisions of FAS-157. FAS-157 is effective for calendar-year-end companies as of January 1, 2008. Unless a company chooses to early adopt, prior GAAP is applicable for financial statements issued for 2007.
>
> As this book went to press, the FASB was addressing a possible delay of FAS-157's effective date. The FASB agreed to consider delaying the effective date for nonfinancial instruments and for certain types of entities, including private companies and "smaller" public companies (not yet defined). Readers should monitor

the FASB's further deliberations regarding the nature of any delay of FAS-157's effective date. Also, readers should refer to the 2007 edition for GAAP related to the fair value measurement of financial instruments applicable before the effective date of FAS-157.

FAIR VALUE MEASUREMENT

Scope

The fair value measurement guidance in FAS-157 as outlined in this Chapter applies under other accounting pronouncements that require or permit fair value measurements, except for share-based payment transactions. FAS-157 also provides a number of practicability exceptions to its fair value measurement requirement, as outlined in Exhibit 18-1.

FAS-157 applies to positions in financial instruments (including blocks) held by all entities. Among many other types of transactions, FAS-157 is applicable to derivatives and other financial instruments that are measured at fair value under FAS-133. This includes hybrid financial instruments permitted to be measured at fair value as discussed in Chapter 13.

> **OBSERVATION:** FAS-157 prohibits the use of blockage factors in valuing positions by all entities, including broker-dealers and investment companies that were specifically permitted to use that approach based on previous guidance in the AICPA Audit and Accounting Guides for those industries.

FAS-157 does not eliminate the practicability exceptions to fair value measurement in a number of existing pronouncements, including the following listed in Exhibit 18-1.

EXHIBIT 18-1
PRACTICABILITY EXCEPTIONS TO FAIR VALUE MEASUREMENT

Pronouncement	Nature of the Practicability Exception	Commentary
APB-29 and FAS-153 (Nonmonetary Assets)	Fair value measurement for nonmonetary assets is not required if fair value is not determinable.	
FAS-107 (Fair Value Disclosure)	If it is not practicable for an entity to estimate fair value of a financial instrument or a class of financial instrument, FAS-107 disclosures about fair value are not required.	Practicability exception is based on whether cost of determining fair value is excessive. Specific disclosures are required if the practicability exception is invoked.

Pronouncement	Nature of the Practicability Exception	Commentary
FAS-87/FAS-106 (Pensions/Other Postretirement Benefits)	Fair value measurement for participation rights is not required if fair value is not determinable.	
FAS-116 (Contributions Received and Made) and AICPA Audit and Accounting Guide, *Not-for-Profit Organizations*	Fair value measurement is not required if fair value cannot be measured with sufficient reliability.	
FAS-140 (Transfers and Servicing)	• Fair value measurement of financial assets obtained and liabilities incurred upon completion of a transfer accounted for as a sale if it is not practicable to do so. • In addition, FAS-140 requires use of the transaction price to measure the fair value of financial assets and liabilities upon completion of a transfer.	Practicability exception is based on whether a reliable estimate can be made. The transaction price (an entry price) may not equal the exit price for the asset or liability. FAS-157 requires use of an exit price to measure fair value.
FAS-141 (Business Combinations)	Measurement methods other than fair value may be used to measure certain components of a business combination.	
FAS-143 (Asset Retirement Obligations)	Fair value measurement for asset retirement obligations is not required if fair value is not determinable	
FAS-146 (Exit and Disposal Activities)	Fair value measurement for restructuring obligations is not required if fair value is not determinable	
FIN-45 (Guarantees)	Transaction price is to be used to measure the fair value of guarantees at initial recognition.	A transaction price is an entry price. FAS-157 requires use of an exit price to measure fair value. In certain circumstances, entry price and exit price may not be equal.
FIN-47 (Conditional Asset Retirement Obligations)	Fair value measurement for conditional asset retirement obligations is not required if fair value is not determinable	

Pronouncement	Nature of the Practicability Exception	Commentary
EITF-85-40 (Sales of Marketable Securities With Put Arrangements)	Fair value measurement of financial assets obtained and financial liabilities incurred in sales of marketable securities with put options if it is not practicable to do so.	
EITF 99-17, (Advertising Barter Transactions)	Fair value measurement for nonmonetary assets is not required if fair value is not determinable	

> **OBSERVATION:** The nature of the practicability exceptions referenced above can be different. For example, practicable in FAS-107 means the estimate can be made without incurring excessive cost. Practicable in FAS-140 means a sufficiently *reliable* estimate can be made.

Definition of Fair Value

Fair value is the price that would be received to sell an asset or paid to transfer a liability in an orderly transaction between market participants at the measurement date. (FAS-157, par. 5)

> **OBSERVATION:** FAS-157 provides a single definition of fair value and a single measurement framework that must be applied to all fair value measurements, regardless of the accounting pronouncement that requires or permits that measurement. Under previous practice, there were multiple definitions of the term *fair value* in GAAP. The measurement of affected instruments under a single definition and framework will likely change measurements determined under current practice in some cases.

> ☞ **PRACTICE POINTER:** The definition of fair value in FAS-157 is based on the concept of an exit price, which is the price at which a company would sell or otherwise dispose of its assets or pay to settle a liability, rather than the concept of an entry price, which is the price a company would pay to acquire the asset or receive to assume the liability. Conceptually, entry prices and exit prices are different, because companies may not sell assets at the prices paid to acquire them and may not transfer liabilities at the prices received to assume them. However, in practice, in many cases, the entry price and the exit price are the same.

Key Concepts Underlying the Fair Value Measurement Model

The following paragraphs discuss the key concepts underlying the fair value measurement model in FAS-157.

Objective of Fair Value Measurement

The objective of a fair value measurement under FAS-157 is to determine the price that would be received to sell the asset or paid to transfer the liability at the measurement date (an exit price). To reach this objective, the fair value measurement model in FAS-157 requires that the measure of fair value reflect the perspective of market participants using assumptions that market participants would use, rather than an entity-specific estimate. The exit price objective requires that all of the following be determined in developing the fair value measurement of an asset or liability:

- The particular asset or liability that is the subject of the measurement (consistent with its unit of account)
- For an asset, the valuation premise appropriate for the measurement (consistent with its highest and best use)
- The principal (or most advantageous) market for the asset or liability (for an asset, consistent with its highest and best use)
- The valuation technique appropriate for the measurement.

The paragraphs below elaborate on each of those elements of the fair value measurement of an asset or liability.

The Specific Asset or Liability

Because a fair value measurement is for a particular asset or liability, the measurement should consider attributes specific to the asset or liability (e.g., the condition and/or location of the asset or liability and restrictions, if any, on the sale or use of the asset at the measurement date). (FAS-157, par. 6)

Unit of Account

The fair value measurement of an asset or liability as a standalone asset or liability (e.g., a single financial instrument) or as a group depends on its unit of account, or level of aggregation. The unit of account is determined based on the provisions of other accounting pronouncements. However, there is one exception to this rule. If a company holds a position in a single financial instrument (including a block) that is traded in an active market, the fair value of the position must be measured using the quoted price for the individual instrument multiplied by the quantity held. That is, FAS-157 prohibits the quoted price to be adjusted for a blockage factor. (FAS-157, pars. 6 and 27)

The Exchange Occurs in an Orderly Transaction

A premise in FAS-157 is that the asset or liability is exchanged in an orderly transaction between market participants to sell the asset or transfer the liability at the measurement date. An orderly transaction assumes market activity that is usual and customary for transactions involving the particular asset or liability being exchanged in the transaction; it is not a forced liquidation or distress sale. (FAS-157, par. 7)

The Principal (or Most Advantageous) Market

FAS-157 introduces the concept of the principal market and the most advantageous market in its fair value measurement model. Under FAS-157, fair value measurement assumes that the transaction to sell the asset or transfer the liability occurs as follows:

- If there is a *principal market*, assume the transaction occurs in the *principal market*—the market in which the company would sell the asset or transfer the liability with the greatest volume and level of activity for the asset or liability.
- If no principal market exists, assume the transaction occurs in the *most advantageous market* for the asset or liability—the market in which the company would sell the asset or transfer the liability with the price that maximizes the amount that would be received for the asset or minimizes the amount that would be paid to transfer the liability, after considering transaction costs.

☛ **PRACTICE POINTER:**   The principal or most advantageous market is considered from the perspective of the reporting entity. Therefore, differences in determining the principal or most advantageous market may arise between companies with different activities.

If there is a principal market for the asset or liability, the price in that market must be used to determine the fair value measurement, even if the price in a different market is potentially more advantageous at the measurement date. The price in the principal market may be directly observable or determined using a valuation technique. (FAS-157, pars. 8-9)

Market Participants

Market participants are buyers and sellers in the principal or most advantageous market for the asset or liability that have the following specific characteristics. They are:

- Independent of the reporting entity.
- Knowledgeable about the asset or liability and the transaction based on all available information, including information obtained through due diligence efforts that are usual and customary.
- Able to transact for the asset or liability.
- Willing to transact (i.e., they are not forced to enter into the transaction). (FAS-157, par. 10)

The fair value of the asset or liability must be determined based on the assumptions that market participants would use in pricing the asset or liability. For example, the effect on the fair value measurement of a restriction on the sale or use of an asset will depend on whether the restriction would be considered by market participants in pricing the asset. (FAS-157, par. 11) Chapter 2, "Investments in Debt and Equity Securities," provides specific guidance related to the fair value measurement of restricted securities.

Transaction Costs and Transportation Costs

The price in the principal (or most advantageous) market used to measure the fair value of the asset or liability must not be adjusted for transaction costs. Such costs must instead be accounted for in accordance with other relevant accounting pronouncements. However, transportation costs must be taken into account in determining the measurement of fair value if location is an attribute of the asset or liability (e.g., in the case of a commodity). In that case, the price in the principal (or most advantageous) market used to measure the fair value of the asset or liability must be adjusted for the cost of transporting the asset or liability to (or from) its principal (or most advantageous) market. (FAS-157, par. 9 and fn. 5)

The Fair Value Premise for Assets and Liabilities

Application of the Fair Value Premise to Assets

Fair value measurement of an asset under FAS-157 assumes the highest and best use of that asset by market participants. The highest and best use is the use of the asset by market participants that maximizes the value of the asset. Because this use is determined from the perspective of market participants, and not by the reporting entity, the fair value measurement must consider the assumptions that market participants would use in pricing the asset. This is the case *even if* the intended use of the asset by the reporting entity is different from the use that would be assumed by market participants. (FAS-157, pars. 12 and 14)

Measuring the fair value of an asset using the concept of the highest and best use encompasses two alternatives—fair value "in-use" and fair value "in-exchange," as outlined in Exhibit 18-2 below.

EXHIBIT 18-2
"IN-USE" AND "IN-EXCHANGE" VALUATION PREMISE

	"In-use" Valuation Premise	"In-exchange" Valuation Premise
When to use the premise for fair value measurement of the asset	if the highest and best use of the asset is in-use—if the asset would provide maximum value to market participants principally through its use in combination with other assets as a group (as installed or otherwise configured for use).	if the highest and best use of the asset is in-exchange—if the asset would provide maximum value to market participants principally on a standalone basis.
How to determine fair value of the asset under the premise	Fair value is determined based on the price that would be received in a current transaction to sell the asset assuming that the asset would be used with other assets as a group and that those assets would be available to market participants.	Fair value of the asset is determined based on the price that would be received in a current transaction to sell the asset on a standalone basis.
Example	Certain non-financial assets	Financial assets

Source: FAS-157, par. 13

Application of the Fair Value Premise to Liabilities

Fair value measurement of liabilities under FAS-157 assumes the following:

- The liability is transferred to a market participant at the measurement date (the liability to the counterparty continues; it is not settled)
- The nonperformance risk relating to that liability (i.e., the risk that the obligation will not be fulfilled) is the same before and after the transfer.

A key concept for the fair value measurement of liabilities under FAS-157 is that the reporting entity must consider the effect of its credit risk on the fair value of the liability in all periods in which the liability is measured at fair value. That effect depends on the nature of the liability and the terms of any credit enhancements related to the liability. (FAS-157, par. 15)

Measurement of Fair Value

The fair value measurement model in FAS-157 applies for both initial measurement and subsequent measurement of assets and liabilities required to be measured at fair value.

Specific Considerations for Initial Measurement

In many cases, the transaction price will equal the exit price and therefore will represent the fair value of the asset or liability at initial recognition. If a transaction occurs in an entity's principal market, the transaction price represents fair value to that entity at initial recognition. If a pricing model will be used to measure the fair value in subsequent periods, the model should be calibrated so that the value at initial recognition equals the transaction price. (FAS-157, fn. 18)

However, a transaction price might not represent the fair value of an asset or liability at initial recognition if one of the following conditions exists:

- The transaction is between related parties.
- The transaction occurs under duress or seller is forced to accept the price in the transaction, for example, if the seller is experiencing financial difficulty.
- The unit of account represented by the transaction price is different from the unit of account for the asset or liability measured at fair value (e.g., if the transaction includes unstated elements that should be separately measured or the transaction price includes transaction costs).
- The market in which the transaction occurs is not the principal or most advantageous market. This may be the case if the reporting entity is a securities dealer and the counterparty is a retail customer. (FAS-157, par. 17)

If the transaction price (entry price) does not equal an exit price, the transaction price may not be used to measure the asset or liability at initial recognition and, instead, the reporting entity must determine the fair value based on an exit price.

☞ **PRACTICE POINTER:** FAS-157 nullifies the guidance in foot-note 3 of EITF Issue 02-3, which precluded immediate recognition in earnings of an unrealized gain or loss (the difference between the transaction price and the fair value of the instrument at initial recognition) if the fair value of the instrument was determined using significant unobservable inputs. Instead, FAS-157 requires application of the objective of fair value measurement based on an exit price, with appropriate adjustment for risk, at initial recognition of a transaction under FAS-133. FAS-157 requires specific disclosures about fair value measurements using significant unobservable inputs and the effects of such measurements on earnings.

SEC REGISTRANT ALERT: The SEC staff has cautioned that there are many instances in which recognizing gains upon inception of certain derivatives are inappropriate. The SEC staff reminds registrants of the guidance in FAS-157 that use of a pricing model in instances when a transaction occurs in an entity's principal market would not give rise to a day-one gain because the model value must be calibrated to match the transaction price. (Speech by Joseph D. McGrath, Professional Accounting Fellow, Office of the Chief Accountant, SEC at the December 2006 AICPA National Conference on Current SEC and PCAOB Developments)

Valuation Techniques

There are three approaches to measuring fair value under FAS-157. Characteristics of those approaches are depicted in Exhibit 18-3.

EXHIBIT 18-3
CHARACTERISTICS OF APPROACHES FOR MEASURING FAIR VALUE

	Market Approach	Income Approach	Cost Approach
Method	Uses of prices and other relevant information generated by market transactions involving identical or comparable assets or liabilities (including a business).	Uses of valuation techniques to convert future amounts (for example, cash flows or earnings) to a single present amount (discounted).	Uses the current replacement cost of an asset.
Application of Method	Such valuation techniques often use market multiples derived from a set of comparables. Multiples might lie in ranges	The measurement is based on the value indicated by current market expectations about those future amounts.	From the perspective of a market participant (seller), the price that would be received is determined based on the cost to a buyer

	Market Approach	Income Approach	Cost Approach
	with a different multiple for each comparable. The selection of where within the range the appropriate multiple falls requires judgment, considering factors specific to the measurement.		to acquire or construct a substitute asset of comparable utility, adjusted for obsolescence. Obsolescence encompasses physical deterioration, functional (technological) obsolescence, and economic (external) obsolescence.
Examples	• Matrix pricing, principally used to value debt securities by relying on the securities' relationship to other benchmark quoted securities.	• Present value techniques • Option-pricing models, such as the Black-Scholes-Merton formula and a binomial model • Multiperiod excess earnings method, used to measure the fair value of certain intangible assets.	—

Source: FAS-157, par. 18

Companies are required to use valuation techniques that are appropriate in the circumstances and for which sufficient data are available. In some cases, a single valuation technique will be appropriate (e.g., when valuing an asset or liability using quoted prices in an active market for identical assets or liabilities), while in other cases, use of multiple valuation techniques would be appropriate. If multiple valuation techniques are used to measure fair value, the results must be evaluated and weighted. The fair value measurement is the point within that range that is most representative of fair value in the circumstances.

Valuation techniques are required to be consistently applied. However, a change in a valuation technique or its application is appropriate if the change results in a measurement that is equally or more representative of fair value in the circumstances, such as:

- New markets develop.
- New information becomes available.
- Information previously used is no longer available.
- Valuation techniques improve. (FAS-157, pars. 19-20)

> **OBSERVATION:** FAS-157 does not specify the valuation technique that should be used in any particular circumstance, and judgment must be used in determining the most appropriate valuation technique to be used.

> ☛ **PRACTICE POINTER:** Once selected, if a valuation technique or its application is changed, revisions resulting from the change must be accounted for as a change in accounting estimate (FAS-154, par. 19). However, the disclosure provisions of FAS-154 for a change in accounting estimate are *not* required for such revisions.

Use of present value techniques FAS-157 incorporates guidance from CON-7 regarding use of present value techniques consistent with the income approach. This guidance is applicable to all fair value measurements determined based on present value techniques. The guidance establishes key principles governing the application of present value techniques and requires that the following elements (from the perspective of market participants as of the measurement date) be incorporated in the measure:

- Estimated future cash flows for the asset or liability being measured
- Expectations about possible variations in the amount and timing of the cash flows reflecting uncertainty inherent in the cash flows
- The time value of money (represented by the rate on risk-free monetary assets that have maturity dates or durations that coincide with the period covered by the cash flows)
- A risk premium for bearing the uncertainty inherent in the cash flows
- Other case-specific factors that would be considered by market participants
- In the case of a liability, the nonperformance risk relating to that liability, including the reporting entity's (obligor's) own credit risk. (FAS-157, par. B2)

The following are two types of present value techniques:

- *Discount rate adjustment technique*—This technique uses a risk-adjusted discount rate and contractual, promised, or most likely cash flows. The cash flows are conditional upon the occurrence of specified events and are discounted at a rate that corresponds to an observed market rate associated with such conditional cash flows (market rate of return). (FAS-157, par. B7)

- *Expected present value technique*—This technique uses probability-weighted (expected) cash flows and adjusts for systemic risk (i.e., general market risk) using one of the following methods:
  - Adjust expected cash flows for systemic risk by subtracting a risk premium and discount adjusted cash flows using a risk-free interest rate (Method 1)
  - Adjust the risk-free interest rate for systemic risk by adding a risk premium and discount *unadjusted* expected cash flows using the risk-adjusted discount rate (Method 2). (FAS-157, pars. B12-B15)

☛ **PRACTICE POINTER:**   As clarified in FAS-157, when using an expected present value technique, the adjustment for systemic risk may be reflected in *either* the expected cash flows or in the discount rate.

Inputs to Valuation Techniques

Inputs to valuation techniques are the assumptions that market participants would use in pricing the asset or liability; inputs may be observable or unobservable, as follows:

- *Observable inputs*—Inputs that reflect the assumptions market participants would use in pricing the asset or liability developed based on market data obtained from sources independent of the reporting entity.
- *Unobservable inputs*—Inputs that reflect the reporting entity's own assumptions about the assumptions market participants would use in pricing the asset or liability based on the best information available in the circumstances.

Valuation techniques used to measure fair value should maximize the use of observable inputs and minimize the use of unobservable inputs. (FAS-157, par. 21)

Exhibit 18-4 provides examples of markets in which inputs might be observable for some assets and liabilities (for example, financial instruments).

EXHIBIT 18-4
TYPES OF MARKETS FOR FINANCIAL INSTRUMENTS

Type of Market	Description of Activity	Availability of Price Information	Example
Exchange market	Formal organizations where member firms buy and sell financial instruments	Closing prices are both readily available and generally representative of fair value	The New York Stock Exchange
Dealer market	Dealers stand ready to buy and sell for their own account, thereby providing liquidity	Bid and asked prices are more readily available than closing prices	Over-the-counter (OTC) markets
Brokered market	Brokers attempt to match buyers with sellers but do not stand ready to trade for their own account	Prices of completed transactions are sometimes available, but each party is unaware of another party's price requirements	Electronic communication networks, in which buy and sell orders are matched, commercial and residential real estate markets
Principal-to-principal market	Principal-to-principal transactions, both originations and resales are negotiated independently, with no intermediary	Little, if any, information is released publicly	

Source: FAS-157, par. A20 and FAS-107, par. 19

The Fair Value Hierarchy

The fair value hierarchy prioritizes the *inputs* to valuation techniques used to measure fair value into three broad levels, as follows:

Level 1   Quoted prices (unadjusted) in active markets for identical assets or liabilities that the reporting entity has the ability to access at the measurement date.

Level 2   Inputs other than quoted prices included within Level 1 that are observable for the asset or liability, either directly or indirectly

Level 3   Unobservable inputs for the asset or liability

Companies must select inputs to valuation techniques based on the availability and reliability of those inputs. If the inputs used to measure the fair value of an asset or liability fall into different levels of the hierarchy, the level in the hierarchy within which fair value measurement in its entirety falls is determined based on the lowest level input that is significant to the fair value measurement in its entirety. Assessing the significance of a particular input to the fair value measurement in its entirety requires judgment, considering factors specific to the asset or liability.

> **OBSERVATION:** The level of the fair value hierarchy within which the entire fair value measurement falls affects the nature of the disclosures required for that particular asset or liability.

Level 1 inputs   Level 1 inputs include quoted prices (unadjusted) for identical assets or liabilities in active markets (where transactions for the asset or liability occur with sufficient frequency and volume to provide pricing information on an ongoing basis) that the reporting entity has the ability to access at the measurement date. Generally, a quoted price for an identical asset in an active market should be used whenever available.

The fair value of a position in a single financial instrument (including a block) traded in an active market is computed as the product of the quoted price for the individual instrument times the quantity held. An adjustment of the quoted price using a blockage factor is prohibited, even if the daily trading volume in a market is not sufficient to absorb the quantity held in a single transaction. That prohibition applies for positions in financial instruments held by all entities, including broker-dealers and investment companies within the scope of the AICPA Audit and Accounting Guides for those industries.

The emphasis within Level 1 is on determining whether the reporting entity has the ability to access the price in the principal or most advantageous market for the asset or liability at the measurement date. If that price is not readily accessible (for example, for a block of securities), an alternative method that does not rely exclusively on quoted prices (e.g., matrix pricing) should be used as a practical expedient. In that case, the resulting measurement would fall into a lower level in the fair value hierarchy.

In some situations, a quoted price in an active market might not represent fair value at the measurement date, for example, significant events (principal-to-principal transactions, brokered trades, or announcements) occur after the close of a market but before the measurement date. The reporting entity should establish and consistently apply a policy for identifying those events that might affect fair value measurements. However, if the quoted price is adjusted for new information, the adjustment renders the fair value measurement a lower level measurement. (FAS-157, pars. 24-26)

Level 2 inputs Level 2 inputs are inputs other than quoted prices included in Level 1 that are observable for the asset or liability, either directly or indirectly, including the following:

- Quoted prices for similar assets or liabilities in active markets.
- Quoted prices for identical or similar assets or liabilities in markets that are not active (as in some brokered markets or principal-to-principal market).
- Inputs other than quoted prices that are observable for the asset or liability (e.g., interest rates and yield curves observable at commonly quoted intervals, volatilities, prepayment speeds, loss severities, credit risks, and default rates).
- Inputs that are derived principally from or corroborated by observable market data by correlation or other methods. (FAS-157, par. 28)

If the asset or liability has a specified contractual term, a Level 2 input must be observable for substantially the full term of the asset or liability. Adjustments to Level 2 inputs will vary, depending on factors specific to the asset or liability, such as the condition or location of the asset or liability, the extent to which the inputs relate to items that are comparable to the asset or liability, and the volume and level of activity in the markets within which the inputs are observed.

FAS-157 includes the following examples of Level 2 inputs:

- For an interest-rate swap based on the LIBOR swap rate, the LIBOR swap rate if that rate is observable at commonly quoted intervals for the full term of the swap
- For a foreign currency swap based on a foreign-currency-denominated yield curve, the swap rate based on a foreign-denominated yield curve that is observable at commonly quoted intervals for substantially the full term of the swap (for example, if the swap is 10 years and that rate is observable at commonly quoted intervals for 9 years)
- For a swap based on a bank's own prime rate, the bank's prime rate derived through extrapolation if the extrapolated values are corroborated by observable market data
- For a three-year option on exchange-traded shares, the implied volatility for the shares derived through extrapolation to year 3 if prices for one- and two-year options on the shares are observable and the extrapolated implied volatility of a three-year option is corroborated by observable market data for substantially the full term of the option (FAS-157, par. A24(a)-(d))

Level 3 inputs Level 3 inputs are *unobservable* inputs for the asset or liability. Unobservable inputs reflect the reporting entity's own assumptions about the assumptions that market participants would use in pricing the asset or liability and must be developed based on the best information available in the circumstances. The reporting entity must use information about market participant assumptions that is reasonably available without undue cost and effort. Also, the reporting entity must adjust its own data used to develop unobservable inputs if information is reasonably available without undue cost and effort that indicates that market participants would use different assumptions. For example, a measurement (for example, a "mark-to-model" measurement) that does not include an adjustment for risk would not represent a fair value measurement if market participants would include such an adjustment in pricing the asset or liability. (FAS-157, par. 30)

FAS-157 includes the following examples of Level 3 inputs:

- For a long-dated currency swap, the interest rates in a specified currency that are not observable and cannot be corroborated by observable market data at commonly quoted intervals or otherwise for substantially the full term of the currency swap
- For a three-year option on exchange-traded shares, the historical volatility (i.e., the volatility for the shares derived from the shares' historical prices)
- For an interest rate swap, an adjustment to a mid-market consensus price for the swap developed using data that are not directly observable and that cannot otherwise be corroborated by observable market data (FAS-157, par. A25(a)-(c))

Use of bid and ask prices   If an input used to measure the fair value of an asset or liability is based on bid and ask prices, the price within the bid-ask spread that is most representative of fair value in the circumstances should be used to measure fair value within all levels of the fair value hierarchy, provided that the price is consistently determined. (FAS-157, pars. 31 and C91)

> ☛ **PRACTICE POINTER:** Companies are permitted to use judgment in this area. FAS-157 does not preclude the use of mid-market pricing or other pricing conventions as a practical expedient for fair value measurements within a bid-ask spread.

> **SEC REGISTRANT ALERT:**   SEC Accounting Series Release No. 118 (ASR-118) provides investment companies and broker-dealers flexibility in selecting the bid-ask pricing method used to measure fair value. FAS-157 permits bid-ask spread pricing methods appropriate under ASR-118 to continue to be employed. Therefore, the use of bid prices for assets and ask prices for short positions liabilities is permitted but not required.

DISCLOSURES ABOUT FINANCIAL INSTRUMENTS

Interaction of GAAP Related to Financial Instruments Disclosures

FAS-107 establishes disclosure requirements for all financial instruments, except for those specifically excluded from its scope. Those disclosure requirements encompass:

- Fair value disclosures.
- Disclosures about concentrations of credit risk.
- Market risk of all financial instruments.

For financial instruments recognized at fair value in the statement of financial position, the fair value disclosure requirements of FAS-157 also apply. Those disclosures are incremental to the existing FAS-107 disclosures and disclosures required by other applicable pronouncements (e.g., FAS-115 related to investments in debt and equity securities or FAS-140 related to securitization transactions).

FAS-157 establishes a definition of fair value and framework for measuring fair value for all pronouncements that require fair value measurement, including FAS-107. Previous fair value measurement guidance included in FAS-107 has been superseded.

FAS-157 encourages presentation of integrated disclosures, to the extent practicable, of fair value information under FAS-157 and other pronouncements (e.g., FAS-107) as well as other similar measurements (e.g., inventories measured at market value under ARB-43, Chapter 4) in the periods in which those disclosures are required. In addition, in instances where the fair value option is elected under FAS-159 for eligible financial instruments, companies are encouraged (but not required) to present the disclosures required by FAS-159 in combination with related fair value information required to be disclosed required to be disclosed under FAS-107 and FAS-157. See Chapter 19, *The Fair Value Option for Financial Instruments*, for the detailed requirements of FAS-159.

Disclosures about Fair Value of Financial Instruments (FAS-107)

Scope

FAS-107 applies to all financial instruments, except those specifically excluded from its scope. FAS-107 applies to recognized financial assets and liabilities (such as loans, securities and derivatives) as well as contingent or unexecuted contracts that represent financial instruments such as financial guarantees, standby letters of credit, commitments to extend credit, and commitments to buy and sell securities. Such contracts are sometimes called "unrecognized," even though fees or premiums might have been recorded. Exhibit 18-5 summarizes the scope exclusions for disclosures about fair value and about credit risk concentrations (and highlights a few items that are in the scope, even though seemingly similar contracts are not).

EXHIBIT 18-5
SCOPE OF FAS-107

Instrument Type	Fair Value Disclosures (par. 8)	Credit Risk Concentrations (par. 15B)
Employee benefits, including pensions, health care and life insurance, postemployment, stock awards, and other forms of deferred compensation in the *employer's* financial statements	Excluded	Excluded
Financial instruments of a pension plan in the *Plan's* financial statements	Included	Included
Substantively extinguished debt whose accounting was grandfathered by FAS-140	Excluded	Not applicable
Insurance contracts, other than financial guarantees and investment contracts	Excluded	Excluded
Reinsurance receivables and prepaid reinsurance contracts	Excluded*	Included[†]
Lease contracts	Excluded	Included
Warranty obligations and rights	Excluded	Excluded
Unconditional purchase obligations	Excluded	Excluded
Investments accounted for under the equity method	Excluded	Excluded
Equity investments and minority interests in consolidated subsidiaries	Excluded	Not applicable

Instrument Type	Fair Value Disclosures (par. 8)	Credit Risk Concentrations (par. 15B)
An entity's own equity instruments	Excluded	Not applicable

---

* Based on the FASB Current Text Section F25, "Financial Instruments: Disclosure," which excludes contracts within the scope of Section In6, "Insurance Industry," including reinsurance. Literally, FAS-107, paragraph 8(c) only excludes contracts within the scope of FAS-60 and FAS-97, which were subsequently amended by FAS-113 to *exclude* reinsurance.

† FAS-113, paragraph 28, as amended.

☞ **PRACTICE POINTER:** The fair value and credit risk disclosure requirements in FAS-107 are in *addition* to other information required to be disclosed by GAAP for a specific instrument type. Instrument- or transaction-specific disclosure requirements have been addressed in this book in the chapters relating to those items.

☞ **PRACTICE POINTER:** If an embedded derivative is split out and accounted for separately, the fair value of the remaining "host contract" that is a financial statement must be disclosed under FAS-107 (or other applicable literature, such as FAS-115).

Exception for certain nonpublic entities   Disclosures about the fair value of financial instruments are not required for an entity that meets all of the following criteria:

- The entity is *nonpublic*.
- The entity's total assets are less than $100 million on the date of the financial statements.
- The entity has no instrument that, in whole or in part, is accounted for as a derivative under FAS-133 (other than commitments related to the origination of mortgage loans to be held for sale) during the reporting period. (FAS-126, par. 2, as amended by FAS-149)

For purposes of applying FAS-126, a nonpublic entity is any entity other than the following:

- An entity whose debt or equity securities trade in a public market either on a stock exchange or in an over-the-counter market (including securities quoted only locally or regionally).
- An entity that is a conduit bond obligor for conduit debt securities that are traded in a public market (a domestic or foreign stock exchange or an over-the-counter market, including local or regional markets).

- An entity that makes a filing with a regulatory agency in preparation for the sale of any class of debt or equity securities in a public market.
- An entity that is controlled by one of the entities above. (FAS-126, par. 3, as amended by FSP FAS-126-1).

The criteria should be applied to the most recent year presented in comparative financial statements to determine whether fair value disclosures must be provided. Exhibit 18-6 summarizes the requirements for fair value disclosures when prior periods are presented in comparative financial statements. (FAS-126, par. 25)

> ☛ **PRACTICE POINTER:** The nonpublic company exception only applies to fair value disclosures. It does *not* apply to the concentration-of-credit risk disclosure.

EXHIBIT 18-6
APPLICABILITY OF NONPUBLIC COMPANY EXCEPTION IN PRIOR PERIODS

If Disclosures for the Current Period Are:	And Disclosures for Prior Periods Were:	Then Disclosures for Prior Period Presented in Comparative Statements Are:
Optional	Optional	Optional
Optional	Required	Optional
Required	Optional	Optional
Required	Required	Required

Source: FAS-126, par. 25

> **OBSERVATION:** If an entity qualifies for the exception and is not required to provide fair value disclosures under FAS-107, it still must provide any fair value disclosures or measurements required under other GAAP, such as FAS-115 (securities) or FAS-140 (e.g., fair value of collateral) and EITF Issue 00-19 (contracts indexed to a company's own stock). (FAS-126, par. 4)

Fair Value Disclosures

FAS-107 requires disclosure of the following information for financial instruments within its scope, either in the body of the financial statements or in the accompanying notes:

- An entity must disclose the fair value of financial instruments for which it is practicable to do so. When fair value information is presented in the notes:

  — Fair value information must be presented together with the related carrying amount in a form that makes it clear whether the instruments are assets or liabilities and how the carrying amounts relate to what is reported in the statement of financial position.

  — If disclosed in more than one note, for example, by instrument type, the footnotes must include a summary table that contains the fair values, related carrying amounts, and cross-references to the location(s) of other FAS-107 disclosures. (FAS-107, par. 10, as amended by FAS-133)

☛ **PRACTICE POINTER:** The "carrying amount" of an unrecognized financial instrument could be zero, or could represent accruals for fees paid (or received).

- The method(s) and significant assumptions used to estimate the fair value of financial instruments. (FAS-107, par. 10)

- If it is not *practicable* for an entity to estimate the fair value of a financial instrument or a class of financial instruments, the entity must disclose the following:

  a. Information pertinent to estimating the fair value of that financial instrument or class of financial instruments, such as, for a debt instrument, the carrying amount, effective interest rate, and maturity.

  b. The reasons why it is not practicable to estimate fair value. (FAS-107, par. 14)

FAS-107 defines *practicable* as the ability to estimate fair value without incurring excessive costs. The following factors should be considered:

- The cost of developing or obtaining the estimate should be considered in relation to the materiality of the instruments to the entity.

- If it is practicable to determine the fair value for a class of financial instruments in a portfolio or on a portfolio basis, the fair value of the portfolio should be disclosed.

- If it is practicable for an entity to estimate the fair value of only a subset of a class of financial instruments, the fair value of that subset should be disclosed. (FAS-107, par. 15)

☞ **PRACTICE POINTER:** It is uncommon for an entity to invoke the practicability exception in practice.

- An entity may not net the fair value of separate financial instruments—even if those financial instruments are considered to be related, for example, by a hedging relationship—except to the extent that the offsetting of carrying amounts in the statement of financial position is permitted under FIN-39 or FIN-41, as appropriate. (FAS-107, par. 13, as amended by FAS-133) Refer to Chapter 17, "Offsetting Assets and Liabilities in the Balance Sheet," for additional information.
- Fair value disclosures must be provided for each year for which a statement of position is presented for comparative purposes. (FAS-107, par. 17)

  SEC REGISTRANT ALERT: Generally, FAS-107 disclosures are not required to be included in interim financial statements filed with the SEC. However, material changes in fair values, resulting from events such as changes in market conditions, generally warrant a discussion in MD&A included in interim reports. (Regulation S-X, 10-01(a))

FAS-107 provides the following specific disclosure guidance:

- *Trade receivables and payables* Trade receivables and payables, for which the carrying amount in the financial statements approximates fair value (because of the relatively short period of time between the origination of the instruments and their expected realization), fair value disclosure is not required. (FAS-107, par. 13)

  SEC REGISTRANT ALERT: The SEC staff believes that a registrant must have documented evidence to support an assertion that the fair value of an asset or liability approximates its carrying amount to avoid making the disclosure of fair value.

- *Deposit liabilities* In estimating the fair value of deposit liabilities, a financial institution should *not* take into account the value of its long-term relationships with depositors, commonly known as core deposit intangibles, which are separate intangible assets, not financial instruments. For deposit liabilities with no defined maturities, fair value should be considered the amount payable on demand at the reporting date. (FAS-107, par. 12)

> **OBSERVATION:** An entity may voluntarily disclose the estimated fair value of any of its nonfinancial intangible or tangible assets and nonfinancial liabilities to provide a more complete picture of its current financial position. (FAS-107, par. 12)

Disclosures for Assets and Liabilities Measured at Fair Value (FAS-157)

For assets and liabilities that are measured at fair value on a recurring basis, the reporting entity must disclose information that enables users of its financial statements to assess both of the following:

- For assets and liabilities that are measured at fair value on a recurring basis in periods subsequent to initial recognition (e.g., trading securities), the inputs used to develop those measurements

- For recurring fair value measurements using significant unobservable inputs (Level 3), the effect of the measurements on earnings (or changes in net assets) for the period.

For assets and liabilities that are measured at fair value on a nonrecurring basis in periods subsequent to initial recognition (for example, impaired assets), the reporting entity must disclose information that enables users of its financial statements to assess the inputs used to develop those measurements. (FAS-157, pars. 32 and 33)

Exhibit 18-7 outlines the detailed disclosure requirements for assets and liabilities measured at fair value on a recurring basis and on a nonrecurring basis.

EXHIBIT 18-7
FAS-157 DISCLOSURE REQUIREMENTS

Disclosure Requirement	Items Measured on a Recurring Basis	Items Measured on a Non-recurring Basis
The fair value measurements at the reporting date	✓	
The fair value measurements recorded during the period and the reasons for the measurements		✓
The level within the fair value hierarchy in which the fair value measurements in their entirety fall, segregating fair value measurements as follows:	✓	✓

- Level 1—quoted prices in active markets for identical assets or liabilities
- Level 2—significant other observable inputs
- Level 3—significant unobservable inputs

For fair value measurements using significant unobservable inputs (Level 3), a reconciliation of the beginning and ending balances, separately presenting changes during the period attributable to the following:	✓	

- Total gains or losses for the period (realized and unrealized), segregating those gains or losses included in earnings (or changes in net assets), and a description of where those gains or losses included in earnings (or changes in net assets) are reported in the statement of income (or activities). In addition:
  - The amount of attributable to the change in unrealized gains or losses relating to those assets and liabilities still held at the reporting date
  - A description of where those unrealized gains or losses are reported in the statement of income (or activities)
- Purchases, sales, issuances, and settlements (net)
- Transfers in and/or out of Level 3 (for example, transfers due to changes in the observability of significant inputs)

This reconciliation may be presented net for derivative assets and liabilities.

Disclosure Requirement	Items Measured on a Recurring Basis	Items Measured on a Non-recurring Basis
For fair value measurements using significant unobservable inputs (Level 3), a description of the inputs and the information used to develop the inputs		✓
In annual periods only, the valuation technique(s) used to measure fair value and a discussion of changes in valuation techniques, if any, during the period.	✓	✓
In annual periods only, the valuation technique(s) used to measure fair value and a discussion of changes in valuation techniques, if any, during the period.		✓

Note: The disclosures outlined in this Exhibit are required for each interim and annual period (except as otherwise specified) separately for each major category of assets and liabilities. Quantitative disclosures required must be presented using a tabular format.

> **OBSERVATION:** A key objective of the required disclosures, especially those required for recurring measurements, is to provide information to users of financial statements on fair value measurements developed using Level 3 inputs, including information to understand the earnings impact of such measurements by segregating unrealized gains and losses related to items measured using Level 3 inputs.

Companies are encouraged, but not required, to provide the following, if practicable:

- Combined fair value information disclosed under FAS-157 and under other accounting pronouncements (e.g., FAS-107) in the periods in which those disclosures are required.
- Information about other similar measurements (e.g., inventories measured at market value under ARB-43, Chapter 4), if practicable. (FAS-157, par. 35)

Disclosures about Concentrations of Credit Risk of Financial Instruments

FAS-107, paragraphs 15A and 15B ("relocated" from FAS-105 by FAS-133), require disclosure of all significant concentrations of credit risk arising from financial instruments, whether from an individual counterparty or groups of counterparties. Group concentrations of credit risk exist if a number of counterparties are engaged in similar activities and have similar economic characteristics that would cause their ability to meet contractual obligations to be similarly affected by changes in economic or other conditions.

In addition, the terms of certain loan products may increase an entity's exposure to and result in a concentration of credit risk. Possible shared characteristics in which significant concentrations may be determined include:

- Borrowers subject to significant payment increases (for example, related to loans that bear an initial interest rate that is below the market interest rate for the initial period of the loan term that may increase significantly when that period ends)
- Loans with terms that permit negative amortization
- Loans with high loan-to-value ratios (including multiple loans on the same collateral that when combined result in a high loan-to-value ratio)

Judgment is required to determine whether loan products have terms that give rise to a concentration of credit risk. (FSP SOP 94-6-1)

> ☞ **PRACTICE POINTER:**   Credit risk represents the possibility that a loss may occur from failure of another party to perform according to the terms of a contract. Debt instruments have credit risk for the holder, but not the issuer. Commitments to extend credit have credit risk for the writer, because the holder could draw down the loan and then default. Most equity securities do not bear credit risk, because the investor is not contractually owed money (other than a dividend that has been declared).

The following information must be disclosed about each significant concentration of credit risk:

- Information about the activity, region, or economic characteristic that identifies the concentration.
- The maximum amount of loss due to credit risk that, based on the gross fair value of the financial instrument, the entity would incur if parties to the financial instruments that make up the concentration failed completely to perform according to the terms of the contracts and the collateral or other security, if any, for the amount due proved to be of no value to the entity.
- The entity's policy of requiring collateral or other security for financial instruments subject to credit risk, information about the nature and accessibility of the collateral held.
- The entity's policy of entering into master netting arrangements to mitigate the credit risk of financial instruments, information

about the terms of such arrangements, and a description of the extent to which they would reduce the entity's maximum amount of loss due to credit risk.

☞ **PRACTICE POINTER:** Many of these disclosures previously were required by FAS-105, which was superseded. FAS-133 modified the disclosures about credit risk somewhat and moved them into FAS-107.

☞ **PRACTICE POINTER:** SOP 01-6 requires additional disclosures about credit risk relating to "off-balance-sheet" financial instruments, such as loan commitments and financial guarantees, for certain financial institutions. Refer to Chapter 3, "Loans and the Allowance for Credit Losses," for additional information. Also, refer to Chapter 6, "Securitizations," for a discussion of SEC FR-67, related to disclosure of "off-balance-sheet" arrangements.

Encouraged Disclosure about Market Risk of All Financial Instruments

An entity is encouraged, but not required, to disclose quantitative information about the market risks of financial instruments in a manner that is consistent with the way it manages or adjusts those risks. (FAS-107, par. 15C, added by FAS-133)

☞ **PRACTICE POINTER:** Market risk is the possibility that future changes in market prices may make a financial instrument less valuable or more onerous.

Depending on the type of entity and the entity's approach to managing market risk, the following quantitative information about market risk could be disclosed:

- More details about current positions and activity during the period,
- A sensitivity analysis showing the hypothetical effects on comprehensive income (or net assets) or income, of several possible changes in market prices,
- A *gap analysis* of interest rate repricing or maturity dates,
- The *duration* of the financial instruments, *or*
- The entity's *value at risk* from derivatives and from other positions at the end of the reporting period and the average value at risk during the year.

Entities are encouraged to develop other ways of reporting quantitative information. (FAS-107, par. 15D, added by FAS-133)

> **SEC REGISTRANT ALERT:** Rule 3-05 of Regulation S-K, "Market Risk Disclosures," requires certain disclosures about market risk inherent in derivatives and other financial instruments outside the financial statements. Chapter 15, "Disclosures about Derivatives," discusses the requirements in more detail. While the market risk disclosure requirements are often discussed in the context of derivatives, it should be stressed that the requirements also apply to other types of financial instruments that give risk to material market risk.

Disclosures of Certain Significant Risks and Uncertainties

SOP 94-6 requires disclosure of estimates used in determining the carrying amounts of assets and liabilities and in disclosure of gain or loss contingencies when information available prior to issuance of the financial statements indicates that both of the following criteria are met:

- It is at least reasonably possible that the estimate of the effect on the financial statements of a condition, situation, or set of circumstances that existed at the date of the financial statements will change in the near term due to one or more future confirming events.
- The effect of the change would be material to the financial statements.

Paragraph 14 of SOP 94-6 requires that the disclosure describe the nature of the uncertainty and include an indication that it is at least reasonably possible that a change in the estimate will occur in the near term. If the estimate involves a loss contingency covered by FAS-5, the disclosure should also include an estimate of the possible loss or range of loss, or state that such an estimate cannot be made.

Disclosures about the use of estimates in the preparation of financial statements may be required for some financial instruments, including:

- The allowance for loan losses.
- Credit-related commitments, such as guarantees.
- Estimates of the fair value of financial instruments for accounting and disclosure purposes.
- The carrying amounts of instruments affected by prepayment assumptions, such as mortgage servicing rights, and premiums and discounts related to mortgage-related securities.

SOP 94-6 requires certain disclosures about vulnerability due to certain concentrations that meet all of the following criteria:

- The concentration exists at the balance sheet date,
- Makes the enterprise vulnerable to a near-term severe impact, and
- It is at least reasonably possible that the events that could cause the severe impact will occur in the near term. (SOP 94-6, par. 21)

Those disclosures do not apply to financial instruments *per se* (note that FAS-107, as amended, requires disclosures about concentrations of credit risk). However, predominantly financial institutions may need to provide information about the following types of concentrations:

- The volume of business transacted with a particular customer, supplier, lender, grantor, or contributor.
- Revenue from particular products or services.
- Available sources of supply of assets used in the entity's operations.
- The market or geographic area in which an entity conducts its operations.

  ☞ **PRACTICE POINTER:** Certain loan products have contractual terms that expose entities to certain risks and uncertainties. Entities involved with such loan products (for example, in capacities such as originator, holder, or guarantor) should consider whether disclosure of concentrations in revenue from such products, or other concentrations arising from involvement with such products, is warranted. (FSP SOP 94-6-1)

  ☞ **PRACTICE POINTER:** The AICPA Audit and Accounting Guide, "Depository and Lending Institutions: Banks and Savings Institutions, Credit Unions, Finance Companies and Mortgage Companies," discusses the application of SOP 94-6 in paragraphs 5.118–15.132.

Certain Public Company Disclosures in Management's Discussion and Analysis (MD&A)

In May 2002, the SEC issued a proposed rule that would significantly expand the required disclosures about critical accounting estimates (and the initial adoption of accounting policies) in the MD&A section of annual reports and other filings. At the AICPA–SEC Conference held in December 2003, the SEC staff encouraged registrants to follow the proposed guidance. That proposed rule remains under consideration.

In December 2003, the SEC issued FR-72, *Interpretation: Commission Guidance Regarding Management's Discussion and Analysis of Financial Condition and Results of Operations.* The Interpretation does not establish new requirements; however, it reminds registrants of existing disclosure requirements related to the MD&A in order to elicit more meaningful disclosures in several areas. In particular, the Interpretation focuses on known trends, demands, commitments, events and uncertainties, liquidity, capital resources, and critical accounting estimates. In brief, the guidance indicates that companies must identify and disclose known trends, events, demands, commitments, and uncertainties that are reasonably likely to have a material effect on financial condition or operating performance. Companies should disclose sources and needs for capital, the ability to meet cash requirements over the short and long term, and certain material covenants. Companies should consider enhanced discussion and analysis of critical accounting estimates and assumptions that (1) supplements the description of accounting policies in the notes to the financial statements and (2) provides insight into the quality and variability of information regarding financial condition and operating performance. The interpretation was immediately applicable upon issuance (that is, no transition was provided). The entire reporting release is available on the SEC's website at http://www.sec.gov/rules/interp/33-8350.htm.

Public Company Disclosures about Off-Balance-Sheet Arrangements

In January 2003, the SEC issued Financial Reporting Release No. 67 (FR-67), "Disclosure in Management's Discussion and Analysis About Off-Balance-Sheet Arrangements and Aggregate Contractual Obligations," which requires disclosure of all material off-balance-sheet transactions, arrangements and obligations (including certain contingent obligations) in a separate caption of MD&A in all quarterly and annual reports that are filed with the SEC. The rule was issued in accordance with the Sarbanes-Oxley Act of 2002.

FR-67 requires disclosure of off-balance-sheet arrangements that either have, or are reasonably likely to have, a current or future effect on a registrant's financial condition, changes in financial condition, revenues or expenses, results of operations, liquidity, capital expenditures or capital resources that is material to investors. The following types of arrangements are subject to this requirement:

- Certain guarantee contracts, as defined in FIN-45,
- Retained or contingent interests in assets transferred to an unconsolidated entity that serve as credit, liquidity, or market risk support to the entity for those assets,
- Derivative instruments that are classified as equity in accordance with other GAAP, including EITF Issue 00-19, *and*

- All material variable interests in unconsolidated entities regardless of whether those entities are deemed VIEs under FIN-46(R).

The following information should be presented to the extent necessary to provide an understanding of off-balance-sheet arrangements:

- The nature and business purpose of the registrant's off-balance-sheet arrangements,
- Their importance to the registrant for liquidity, capital resources, market risk or credit risk support, or other benefits,
- The financial effect of the arrangements on the registrant's revenues, expenses, cash flows, and securities issued,
- The registrant's exposure to risk as a result of the arrangements (for example, from retained interests or contingent obligations),
- Known events, demands, commitments, trends, or uncertainties that affect the registrant's ability to benefit from its off-balance-sheet arrangements, *and*
- Any other information that is necessary for an understanding of the registrant's off-balance-sheet arrangements and their specified material effects.

In addition, registrants (other than small business issuers) must provide a table that summarizes amounts owed by the registrant under specified contractual obligations for specified time periods. The entire reporting release is available on the SEC's website: http://www.sec.gov/rules/final/33-8182.htm.

> ☞ **PRACTICE POINTER:** Registrants should provide these disclosures in addition to any information required to be provided in the audited footnotes by other GAAP. Cross-referencing is permitted with certain limitations.

AUDIT CONSIDERATIONS

In the absence of observed market prices, estimating the fair value of a financial instrument requires a significant amount of judgment. Management must project or model future cash flows, sometimes over long periods of time, using subjective assumptions about default rates, prepayment rates, and volatilities. Reasonable people might disagree about the selection of those assumptions, methods, or both. The auditor should obtain evidence supporting management's assertions about the fair value of financial instruments measured or disclosed at fair value and ensure that the valuation techniques are appropriately documented and applied consistently in similar situations.

The following guidelines should help to reduce the audit risk relating to fair value disclosures:

- Similar financial instruments should be valued using similar methods and assumptions. It would be inappropriate to use significantly different values or assumptions for similar financial instruments.
- The assumptions used should be consistent with current market conditions and all relevant factors should be considered.
- The methods of estimation and significant assumptions should be documented and properly disclosed.
- Assertions that it is not practicable to determine fair value should be met with a healthy amount of skepticism.
- The appropriate GAAP method must be used to determine the fair value of the entity's derivatives, securities, retained interests, and certain other financial instruments.
- Assertions that the carrying amount of certain receivables and payables approximates fair value should be adequately documented, not automatically assumed. For example, changes in credit risk could affect the value of a short-term receivable.

The following literature is relevant to audits involving fair value disclosures:

- AU 328 on auditing fair value estimates (SAS-101).
- AU 342 on obtaining and evaluating sufficient competent evidential matter to support significant accounting estimates. AU 342 specifically addresses audit issues relating to required and voluntary fair value disclosures.
- AICPA Audit Guide, *Auditing Derivative Instruments, Hedging Activities, and Investments in Securities,* as well as SAS-92, "Auditing Derivative Instruments, Hedging Activities, and Investments in Securities."
- AU 336 on the use of the work of a specialist in performing substantive procedures.
- Independence Standards Board Interpretation 99-1, "FAS-133 Assistance," which, among other things, describes the level of involvement that an auditor may have in assisting a client with valuation issues without compromising his or her independence.

ILLUSTRATIONS

Illustration 18-1: Integrated Disclosures about Fair Value Measurements and Changes in Fair Values Included in Current-Period Earnings

This illustration integrates selected disclosures required annually by FAS-107 (fair value disclosures), FAS-157 (incremental disclosures for assets and liabilities measured at fair value on a recurring basis), and FAS-159 (changes in fair values of assets and liabilities for which the fair value option has been elected). The illustration also provides voluntary disclosures about where in the income statement changes in fair values of assets and liabilities reported at fair value are included in earnings.

In addition to the table presented below, a company might provide either of the following additional disclosures to comply with the requirements of FAS-159, paragraphs 18(a) and 18(b):

- Management's reasons for electing a fair value option for each eligible item or group of similar eligible items
- If the fair value option is elected for some but not all eligible items within a group of similar eligible items, both of the following:
  —A description of those similar items and the reasons for partial election
  —Information to enable users to understand how the group of similar items relates to individual line items on the statement of financial position.

See Chapter 19, *The Fair Value Option for Financial Instruments*, Exhibit 19-2, for a summary of disclosure requirements under FAS-159.

($ in millions)

Description	Total Carrying Amount in Statement of Financial Position 12/31/XX	FAS-107 Fair Value Estimate 12/31/XX	Assets/ Liabilities Measured at Fair Value 12/31/XX	Fair Value Measurements at December 31, 20XX, Using Quoted Prices in Active Markets for Identical Assets (Level 1)	Signifi-cant Other Observ-able Inputs (Level 2)	Signifi-cant Un-observ-able Inputs (Level 3)
Trading securities	$115	$115	$115	$105	$10	—
Available-for-sale securities	75	75	75	75	—	—
Loans, net*	400	412	150	0	100	$50
Derivatives	60	60	60	25	15	20
Private equity investments	125	138	75**	0	25	50
Long-term debt	(200)	(206)	(60)	(30)	(10)	(20)

($ in millions)	Changes in Fair Values for the 12-Month Period Ended December 31, 20XX, for Items Measured at Fair Value Pursuant to Election of the Fair Value Option				
Description	Trading Gains and Losses	Other Gains and Losses	Interest Income on Loans	Interest Expense on Long-Term Debt	Total Changes in Fair Values Included in Current-Period Earnings
Trading securities	$10	—	—	—	$10
Available-for-sale securities	—	—	—	—	—
Loans, net*	—	$(3)	$10	—	7
Derivatives	5	—	—	—	5
Private equity investments	—	(18)	—	—	(18)
Long-term debt	—	13	—	$(4)	9

* Loans are included in loans and lease receivables. As of December 31, 20XX, approximately $160,000 of lease receivables are included in loans and lease receivables in the statement of financial position and are not eligible for the fair value option.

** Represents investments that would otherwise be accounted for under the equity method of accounting.

Source: Adapted from FAS-159, pars. B5-B6

In the illustration above, the column entitled "Total Carrying Amount in Statement of Financial Position" discloses carrying amount information required annually by FAS-107 only for major categories of assets and liabilities that include items measured at fair value. The column entitled "FAS-107 Fair Value Estimate" discloses fair value estimates required annually by FAS-107 only for major categories of assets and liabilities that include items measured at fair value. The disclosure of amounts shown in the column entitled "Trading Gains and Losses" is permitted but not required; the amount is shown for completeness.

Illustration 18-2: Assets Measured at Fair Value on a Recurring Basis

This example illustrates one presentation for quantitative disclosures required by FAS-157 for assets measured at fair value on a recurring basis, including measurements using significant unobservable inputs (Level 3). A similar table would be preserved for liabilities.

($ in millions)		Fair Value Measurements at the Reporting Date Using		
Description	**12/31/XX**	**Quoted Prices in Active Markets for Identical Assets (Level 1)**	**Significant Other Observable Inputs (Level 2)**	**Significant Unobservable Inputs (Level 3)**
Trading securities	$115	$105	$10	
Available-for-sale securities	75	75		
Derivatives	60	25	15	$20
Venture capital investments	10			10
Total	$260	$205	$25	$30

Source: FAS-157, par. A34

The following illustrates a reconciliation of the beginning and ending balances for the major asset categories (derivatives and venture capital investments) that are measured by the example entity using Level 3 inputs. (Note that a similar table would be presented for major categories of liabilities measured using Level 3 inputs.)

($ in millions)	Fair Value Measurements Using Significant Unobservable Inputs (Level 3)		
	Derivatives[*]	**Venture Capital Investments**	**Total**
Beginning balance	$14	$11	$25
Total gains or losses (realized/ unrealized)			
Included in earnings (or changes in net assets)	11	(3)	8
Included in other comprehensive income	4		4
Purchases, issuances, and settlements	(7)	2	(5)
Transfers in and/or out of Level 3	(2)	0	(2)
Ending balance	$20	$10	$30
The amount of total gains or losses for the period included in earnings (or changes in net assets) attributable to the change in unrealized gains or losses relating to assets still held at the reporting date	$7	$2	$9

[*] The reconciliation for derivative assets and liabilities may be presented net.
Source: FAS-157, par. A35

Illustration 18-3: FAS-157 Disclosures About Assets Measured at Fair Value on a Nonrecurring Basis

Assets Measured at Fair Value on a Nonrecurring Basis

This example illustrates one presentation about fair value measurements for each major category of assets measured at fair value on a nonrecurring basis during the period.

($ in millions)		Fair Value Measurements Using			
Description	**Year Ended 12/31/XX**	**Quoted Prices in Active Markets for Identical Assets (Level 1)**	**Significant Other Observable Inputs (Level 2)**	**Significant Unobserv-able Inputs (Level 3)**	**Total Gains (Losses)**
Long-lived assets held and used	$75*	—	$75	—	$(25)
Goodwill	30*	—	—	$30	(35)
Long-lived assets held for sale	26*	—	26	—	(15)
					$(75)

* Reflects effect of writing down the assets to fair value (implied fair value for goodwill) under applicable pronouncements, resulting in the impairment charges for each asset category reflected in the total gains/(losses) column, which is included in earnings for the period.

Source: Adapted from FAS-157, par. A36

Illustration 18-4: Fair Value Disclosures by a Financial Entity (FAS-107)

The following table discloses fair value information for on- and off-balance sheet financial instruments. The fair values of financial instruments are estimates based upon market conditions and perceived risks at December 31, 20X2, and 20X1.

December 31, (millions)	20X2		20X1	
	Carrying Value	**Fair Value**	**Carrying Value**	**Fair Value**
Financial Assets				
Assets for which carrying amounts approximate fair values	$73,940	$73,940	$71,735	$71,735
Investment in securities	$43,747	$43,910	$43,052	$42,963
Loans	$26,213	$26,118	$23,680	$23,594
Derivative instruments (assets)	$ 105	$ 105	$ 217	$ 217
Financial Liabilities				
Liabilities for which carrying amounts approximate fair values	$68,975	$68,975	$60,932	$60,932
Derivative instruments (liabilities)	$25	$25	$31	$31
Long-term debt	$ 4,711	$ 4,743	$ 5,995	$ 5,949
Credit-related commitments (liabilities)	$18	$21	$16	$20

The following methods and significant assumptions were used to estimate the fair values of financial assets and financial liabilities:

Assets for which carrying amounts approximate fair values include cash and cash equivalents, accounts receivable and accrued interest, and certain other assets that mature within 90 days.

For variable-rate loans that reprice within a year where there has been no significant change in counterparties' creditworthiness, fair values are based on carrying amounts.

The fair values of all other loans, except those with significant credit deterioration, are estimated using discounted cash flow analysis, using current interest rates for loans with similar terms to borrowers of similar credit quality. For loans with significant credit deterioration, fair values are based on estimates of future cash flows discounted at rates commensurate with the risk inherent in the revised cash flow projections, or for collateral dependent loans, on collateral values.

For commercial paper, other borrowed funds, and short-term accounts payable, fair value approximates carrying value due to the relatively short period of time between their origination and expected realization.

For investment securities for which it was practicable to determine fair value, fair value is based either on exchange-traded prices or broker dealer quotations for the same or similar securities.

It was not practicable to estimate the fair value of an investment representing 14% of the issued common stock of an untraded company. That investment is carried at its original cost of $475,000.

Illustration 18-5: Disclosure of Significant Concentrations of Credit Risk (FAS-107, as amended)

The following disclosure is an excerpt from the 2001 Annual Report of The Boeing Company (*dollars in millions*):

Note 25. Significant Group Concentrations of Credit Risk

Financial instruments involving potential credit risk are predominantly with commercial aircraft customers and the U.S. Government. As of December 31, 2001, off-balance-sheet financial instruments described in Note 24 predominantly related to commercial aircraft customers. Of the $15,554 in accounts receivable and customer financing included in the Consolidated Statements of Financial Position, $7,235 related to commercial aircraft customers ($366 of accounts receivable and $6,869 of customer financing) and $2,597 related to the U.S. Government. AMR Corporation and UAL Corporation were associated with 23% and 13% of all financial instruments related to customer financing. Financing for aircraft is collateralized by security in the related asset, and historically the Company has not experienced a problem in accessing such collateral. Of the $6,869 of aircraft customer financing, $6,440 related to customers the Company believes have less than investment-grade credit. Similarly, of the $7,508 of irrevocable financing commitments related to aircraft on order including options, $7,113 related to customers the Company believes have less than investment-grade credit.

Illustration 18-6: Use of Estimates in Preparation of Financial Statements (SOP 94-6)

Note 1. Significant Accounting Policies

The preparation of financial statements in conformity with generally accepted accounting principles requires management to make estimates and assumptions that affect the reported amounts of assets and liabilities, disclosure of contingent assets and liabilities at the date of the financial statements, and the reported amounts of revenue and expenses during the reporting period. While actual results could differ from these estimates, management believes that the estimates are reasonable.

Significant estimates underlying the accompanying consolidated financial statements [that relate to financial instruments] include the allowance for doubtful accounts, accruals for guarantees written and other credit-related commitments, the valuation of retained interests in securitization transactions, the amortization periods for servicing rights, the fair value of financial instruments when quoted market prices are not available, and the amortization periods for costs and premiums and discounts relating to certain large groups of homogeneous, prepayable loans.

CHAPTER 19
THE FAIR VALUE OPTION FOR
FINANCIAL INSTRUMENTS

CONTENTS

Overview   19.01
Important Notice: New FASB Statement on the Fair Value Option for Financial Instruments   19.02
Applying the Fair Value Option   19.03
  Scope   19.03
  Exhibit 19-1: Scope of the Fair Value Option   19.04
  Election Dates   19.05
  Fair Value Option Election in Consolidated versus Separate Company Financial Statements   19.06
  Application on an Instrument-by-Instrument Basis   19.06
   Instruments Issued or Acquired in a Single Transaction   19.07
   Subsequent Measurement   19.07
   Fees and Costs   19.08
   Dividend Income, Interest Income, and Interest Expense   19.08
Financial Statement Presentation   19.08
Disclosure Requirements   19.09
  Exhibit 19-2: Summary of FAS-159's Disclosure Requirements   19.10
Audit Considerations   19.15
Illustrations   19.15
  Illustration 19-1: Fair Value Measurements and Changes in Fair Values Included in Current-Period Earnings   19.15

OVERVIEW

For many years, the FASB has held the view that fair value is the relevant measurement attribute for financial instruments. Over time, the FASB has implemented fair value measurement requirements for certain types of financial instruments on a piecemeal basis. In FASB Statement No. 159, *The Fair Value Option for Financial Assets and Financial Liabilities,* the FASB now permits companies to measure certain financial assets and liabilities at fair value. The election is available on an instrument-by-instrument basis, is irrevocable for the term of the item, can be made only at initial recognition or in response to certain specified events and can be applied only to entire instruments (not to portions of instruments). The fair value option election triggers significant new disclosure requirements for affected items and does not eliminate other incremental disclosure requirements.

IMPORTANT NOTICE
NEW FASB STATEMENT ON THE FAIR VALUE OPTION FOR FINANCIAL INSTRUMENTS

Since the last edition of CCH *Financial Instruments,* the FASB has issued two new and important Statements related to fair value.

In February 2007, the FASB issued FAS-159, *The Fair Value Option for Financial Assets and Financial Liabilities,* which is covered in this Chapter. The new Statement provides companies with an option to report certain financial assets and liabilities at fair value with the objectives of reducing (1) the complexity of accounting for financial instruments, (2) the volatility in earnings created by measuring related assets and liabilities differently, and (3) the need for companies to apply detailed hedge accounting rules to avoid mismatches in reported earnings.

At the effective date of FAS-159, a company may elect the fair value option for eligible items that exist at that date. The difference between the carrying amount and the fair value of eligible items for which the fair value option is elected at the effective date must be removed from the statement of financial position and included in the cumulative-effect adjustment. Those differences may relate to the following:

- Unamortized deferred costs, fees, premiums, and discounts
- Valuation allowances (e.g., allowances for loan losses)
- Accrued interest, which would be reported as part of the fair value of the eligible item.

FAS-159 is effective for calendar-year-end companies as of January 1, 2008. Early adoption is permitted as of the beginning of a fiscal year that begins on or before November 15, 2007, provided the entity also elects to apply the provisions of FAS-157, *Fair Value Measurements.* (FAS-157, issued in September 2006, defines fair value, establishes a framework for measuring fair value under GAAP, and expands disclosures about fair value measurements. Readers should refer to Chapter 18, "Fair Value Measurements, Fair Value Disclosures, and Other Financial Instrument Disclosure," for the detailed provisions of FAS-157.)

AUTHOR'S NOTE: The 2008 edition of CCH's *Financial Instruments* has been updated to incorporate the provisions of FAS-159. FAS-159 is effective for calendar-year-end companies as of January 1, 2008. Unless a company chooses to early adopt the provisions of FAS-159, the fair value option is not available for financial statements issued for 2007. (However, the fair value election for certain hybrid financial instruments, as discussed in Chapter 13, "Embedded Derivatives," would be applicable.) Readers should refer to the 2007 edition for relevant GAAP for financial instruments prior to the effective date of FAS-159.

APPLYING THE FAIR VALUE OPTION

FAS-159 permits companies to choose, at specified election dates, to measure eligible financial instruments at fair value, with unrealized gains and losses reported in earnings (or another performance indicator if the company does not report earnings) at each subsequent reporting date. The accounting guidance in FAS-159 does not affect any existing guidance that requires certain assets and liabilities to be measured at fair value.

The fair value option election may be made for an eligible item subject to certain guidelines. That is, the election:

- Must be applied on an instrument-by-instrument basis, except in certain specific cases involving multiple advances, equity method investments, and insurance contracts with riders
- Is irrevocable (unless a new election date occurs)
- Must be applied only to an entire instrument and not to only specified risks, specific cash flows, or a portion of an asset or liability. (FAS-159, par. 5)

A company may decide to:

- Elect the fair value option for each eligible item on its election date
- Elect the fair value option according to a preexisting policy for specified types of eligible items.

Scope

FAS-159 is applicable to all types of entities, including not-for-profit organizations. Note that FAS-159 may also by applied to nonpublic companies that have elected the exception in FASB Statement No. 126, *Exemption from Certain Required Disclosures about Financial Instruments for Certain Nonpublic Entities,* from having to disclose fair values under FAS-107. (See Chapter 18, "Fair Value Measurements, Fair

Value Disclosures, and Other Financial Instrument Disclosure," for further discussion of the disclosure requirements under FAS-107 and the exception in FAS-126.)

Exhibit 19-1 outlines the financial assets and liabilities that are eligible and ineligible for the fair value option.

EXHIBIT 19-1
SCOPE OF THE FAIR VALUE OPTION

Eligible Items	Ineligible Items
A recognized financial asset and financial liability (except if the asset or liability is included in the column listing ineligible items) (FAS-159, par. 7(a))	An investment in a subsidiary that the entity is required to consolidate (FAS-159, par. 8(a))
A firm commitment that would otherwise not be recognized at inception and that involves only financial instruments (e.g., a forward purchase contract for a loan that is not readily convertible to cash that would not be recognized because it is not a derivative under FAS- 133) (FAS-159, par. 7(b))	An interest in a variable interest entity (VIE) that the entity is required to consolidate (FAS-159, par. 8(b))
A written loan commitment that is not accounted for as a derivative under FAS-133 (FAS-159, par. 7(c))	Employers' and plans' obligations (or assets representing net over-funded positions) for pension benefits, other postretirement, postemployment benefits, employee stock option and stock purchase plans, and other forms of deferred compensation arrangements (FAS-159, par. 8(c))
The rights and obligations under an insurance contract that is not a financial instrument (because it requires or permits the insurer to provide goods or services rather than a cash settlement) but whose terms permit the insurer to settle by paying a third party to provide those goods or services (FAS-159, par. 7(d))	Financial assets and financial liabilities recognized under leases as defined in FAS-13, *Accounting for Leases* (However, this exception does not apply to a guarantee of a third-party lease obligation or a contingent obligation arising from a cancelled lease.) (FAS-159, par. 8(d))
The rights and obligations under a warranty that is not a financial instrument (because it requires or permits the warrantor to provide goods or services rather than a cash settlement) but whose terms permit the warrantor to settle by paying a third party to provide those goods or services (FAS-159, par. 7(e))	Deposit liabilities, withdrawable on demand, of banks, savings and loan associations, credit unions, and other similar depository institutions (FAS-159, par. 8(e))

Eligible Items	Ineligible Items
A host financial instrument resulting from bifurcation of an embedded nonfinancial derivative instrument from a nonfinancial hybrid instrument (except if the instrument is included in the column to the right) (An example of such a nonfinancial hybrid instrument is an instrument in which the value of the bifurcated embedded derivative is payable in cash, services, or merchandise but the debt host is payable only in cash.) (FAS-159, par. 7(f))	Financial instruments that are, in whole or in part, classified by the issuer as a component of shareholder's equity including temporary equity. An example is a convertible debt security with a noncontingent beneficial conversion feature. (FAS-159, par. 8(f))
	Deferred income tax assets and liabilities, because those assets and liabilities are not contractual. (FAS-159, par. A10)

☛ **PRACTICE POINTER:** In late 2007, the FASB is scheduled to begin Phase 2 of the Fair Value Option project, which will consider permitting a fair value option for certain nonfinancial assets and liabilities and the deposit liabilities of depository institutions, which were excluded from the scope of FAS-159. Readers should monitor developments on this project.

Election Dates

A company may choose to elect the fair value option for an eligible item only on the date that one of the following occurs:

- The company first recognizes the eligible financial asset or financial liability.
- The company enters into an eligible firm commitment.
- Financial assets that have been reported at fair value with unrealized gains and losses included in earnings because of specialized accounting principles no longer qualify for that specialized accounting.
- The accounting treatment for an investment in another entity changes because one of the following circumstances arises:

  (1) The investment becomes subject to the equity method of accounting.
  (2) The investor ceases to consolidate a subsidiary or variable interest entity (VIE) but retains an interest.

- An event that requires an eligible financial asset or financial liability to be measured at fair value at the time of the event but does not require fair value measurement at each reporting date after that, *excluding* the recognition of impairment under lower-of-cost-or-market accounting or other-than-temporary impairment. Such an event may occur because of the following:

(1)   A business combination
(2)   The consolidation or deconsolidation of a subsidiary or VIE
(3)   Significant modifications of debt. (FAS-159, par. 9)

When a contract is modified after initial recognition, a company may elect the fair value option only if the modification is accounted for as the termination of the original contract and the origination of a new contract, in which case the fair value option could be elected at the date of the new contract's initial recognition. If the modification is accounted for as a continuation of the existing contract, then the fair value option election is available only at the date of initial recognition of that contract, not at the date of modification. (FAS-159, par. A15)

An entity may elect the fair value option according to a preexisting policy for specified types of eligible items.

☞ **PRACTICE POINTER:**   The FASB specifically decided against permitting the fair value option election in response to changes in (a) the legal form and substance of the item and (b) a company's risk management strategy with respect to the item. (FAS-159, par. A13)

☞ **PRACTICE POINTER:**   If an entity is required to recognize a contract on the trade date under applicable GAAP, the fair value option would also need to be elected on the trade date and not on the settlement date. (FAS-159, par. A17)

Fair Value Option Election in Consolidated versus Separate Company Financial Statements

There are special considerations related to the fair value option in consolidated financial statements and separate company financial statements. Specifically, an acquirer, parent, or primary beneficiary in a (VIE) decides whether to apply the fair value option to eligible items of an acquiree, subsidiary, or consolidated VIE, but that decision applies only in the consolidated financial statements. A fair value option election made by an acquired entity, subsidiary, or VIE continues to apply in separate financial statements of those entities if they issue separate financial statements. (FAS-159, par. 11)

Application on an Instrument-by-Instrument Basis

The fair value option may be elected for a single eligible financial asset or financial liability without electing it for other identical items. However, there are four restrictions:

1. *Multiple advances under a single contract*: If multiple advances are made to a borrower pursuant to a single contract (e.g., a line of credit or a construction loan) and the individual advances lose their identity and become part of a larger loan balance, the fair value option must be applied only to the larger balance and not to each advance individually.

2. *Equity method investments*: If the fair value option is applied to an investment that would otherwise be accounted for under the equity method, it must be applied to all of the investor's financial interests in the same entity (equity and debt, including guarantees) that are eligible items.

3. *Insurance and reinsurance contracts*: If the fair value option is applied to an eligible insurance or reinsurance contract, it must be applied to all claims and obligations under the contract.

4. *Insurance contracts with riders*: If the fair value option is elected for an insurance contract having integrated or nonintegrated contract features or coverages (riders) that are issued either concurrently or subsequently, the fair value option also must be applied to those features. (FAS-159, par. 12)

A financial instrument that is legally a single contract may not be separated into parts for purposes of applying the fair value option. (FAS-159, par. 13)

Instruments Issued or Acquired in a Single Transaction

The fair value option is *not* required to be applied to all instruments issued or acquired in a single transaction, except in the situations described below. For example:

- Investors in shares of stock and registered bonds are permitted to apply the fair value option to only some of the shares or bonds issued or acquired in a single transaction.

- Each loan made under a loan syndication arrangement is a separate instrument, and the fair value option may be elected for some of those loans but not others.

An investor in an equity security may elect the fair value option for its entire investment in that equity security, including any fractional shares issued by the investee (e.g., fractional shares that are acquired in a dividend reinvestment program). (FAS-159, par. 13)

Subsequent Measurement

A business entity shall report unrealized gains and losses on items for which the fair value option has been elected in earnings (or another performance indicator if the business entity does not report earnings) at each subsequent reporting date.

Not-for-profit entities must apply the provisions of FAS-159's subsections of this subtopic with the following modifications:

- References to an income statement shall be replaced with references to a statement of activities, statement of changes in net assets, or statement of operations.

- References to earnings should be replaced with references to changes in net assets, except for health care organizations subject to the AICPA Audit and Accounting Guide, *Health Care Organizations*, which must report unrealized gains and losses on items for which the fair value option has been elected within the performance indicator or as a part of discontinued operations, as appropriate. Under FAS-117, *Financial Statements of Not-for-Profit Organizations*, such organizations may present gains and losses either within or outside of other intermediate measures of operations unless such gains and losses are part of discontinued operations.

Fees and Costs

Upfront costs and fees related to items for which the fair value option is elected shall be recognized in earnings as incurred and not deferred.

Dividend Income, Interest Income, and Interest Expense

FAS-159 does not specify a method to be used for recognizing and measuring the amount of dividend income, interest income, and interest expense for items for which the fair value option has been elected.

FINANCIAL STATEMENT PRESENTATION

Companies are required to report assets and liabilities that are measured at fair value pursuant to the fair value option in a manner that separates those reported fair values from the carrying amounts of similar assets and liabilities measured using another measurement attribute. Companies may either:

- Present the aggregate of fair value and non-fair-value amounts in the same line item in the statement of financial position and parenthetically disclose the amount measured at fair value included in the aggregate amount
- Present two separate line items to display the fair value and non-fair-value carrying amounts. (FAS-159, par. 15)

☛ **PRACTICE POINTER:** The FASB believes that presentation in a tabular format will be more easily understood, but did not require such presentation. (FAS-159, par. A30)

Cash flow statement presentation Companies must classify cash receipts and cash payments related to items measured at fair value according to their nature and purpose as required by FAS-95. (FAS-159, par. 16)

DISCLOSURE REQUIREMENTS

There are numerous disclosure requirements related to the fair value option. The objectives of the disclosure requirements are to enable users of financial statements to make comparisons (a) between companies that elect the fair value option and companies that do not elect the fair value option for similar assets and liabilities and (b) between assets and liabilities in the financial statements of a single company that elects the fair value option for some assets and liabilities and not other identical assets and liabilities.

> **OBSERVATION:** The elective nature of FAS-159, which creates challenges for financial statement users when comparing financial statements issued by similar companies, and the lack of eligibility requirements to qualify for the fair value option election led to the thorough disclosure requirements in FAS-159. The disclosure requirements are designed to provide information to financial statement users to enhance the understanding of the financial position of companies that elect the fair value option for selected financial assets and liabilities and those that do not.

The following general principles apply to the disclosure requirements in FAS-159:

- The disclosures are required for items measured at fair value under the option in FAS-159 and the option for reporting certain hybrid financial instruments at fair value in paragraph 16 of FAS-133 (as amended by FAS-155). (Chapter 13, "Embedded Derivatives," discusses this option in further detail.)
- The disclosures are not required for the following:
  - Securities classified as trading securities under FAS-115 (see Chapter 2, "Investments in Debt and Equity Securities");
  - Servicing rights measured at fair value pursuant to FAS-140 as amended by FAS-156, *Accounting for Servicing of Financial Assets* (see Chapter 4, "Servicing of Financial Assets"); and
  - Life settlement contracts measured at fair value under FASB Staff Position FTB 85-4-1, "Accounting for Life Settlement Contracts by Third-Party Investors."

- The disclosures are required in both interim and annual financial statements.

- The disclosure requirements do not eliminate other disclosure requirements under other pronouncements, including disclosure requirements relating to fair value measurement as required by FAS-107 and FAS-157. (Additional disclosure requirements for financial instruments are discussed in Chapter 18, "Fair Value Measurements, Fair Value Disclosures, and Other Financial Instrument Disclosures".) (FAS-159, par. 20).

- Companies are encouraged (but not required) to present the disclosures required by FAS-159 in combination with related fair value information required to be disclosed under FAS-107 and FAS-157, where meaningful. (See Chapter 18, "Fair Value Measurements, Fair Value Disclosures, and Other Financial Instrument Disclosures," for those disclosure requirements.)

EXHIBIT 19-2
SUMMARY OF FAS-159'S DISCLOSURE REQUIREMENTS

Disclosures Required as of Each Date a Statement of Financial Position Is Presented (FAS-159, par. 18)

Disclosure Requirement	Frequency	Comments
Management's reasons for electing a fair value option for each eligible item or group of similar eligible items (FAS-159, par. 18(a))	As of each date an interim or annual statement of financial position is presented	
If the fair value option is elected for some but not all eligible items within a group of similar eligible items: (1) A description of those similar items and the reasons for partial election (2) Information to enable users to understand how the group of similar items relates to individual line items on the statement of financial position (FAS-159, par. 18(b))	As of each date an interim or annual statement of financial position is presented	

Disclosure Requirement	Frequency	Comments
For each line item in the statement of financial position that includes item(s) for which the fair value option has been elected: (1) Information to enable users to understand how each line item in the statement of financial position relates to major categories of assets and liabilities presented in accordance with FAS-157's fair value disclosure requirements (2) The aggregate carrying amount of items included in each line item in the statement of financial position that are not eligible for the fair value option, if any (FAS-159, par. 18(c))	As of each date an interim or annual statement of financial position is presented	With respect to Item (1), FAS-107, par. 10 also requires companies to relate carrying amounts to amounts reported in the balance sheet.
The difference between the aggregate fair value and the aggregate unpaid principal balance of: (1) Loans and long-term receivables (other than securities subject to FAS-115) that have contractual principal amounts and for which the fair value option has been elected (2) Long-term debt instruments that have contractual principal amounts and for which the fair value option has been elected (FAS-159, par. 18(d))	As of each date an interim or annual statement of financial position is presented	
For loans held as assets for which the fair value option has been elected: (1) The aggregate fair value of loans that are 90 days or more past due	As of each date an interim or annual statement of financial position is presented	

Disclosure Requirement	Frequency	Comments
(2) If the entity's policy is to recognize interest income separately from other changes in fair value, the aggregate fair value of loans in nonaccrual status (3) The difference between the aggregate fair value and the aggregate unpaid principal balance for loans that are 90 days or more past due, in nonaccrual status, or both (FAS-159, par. 18(e))		
For investments that would have been accounted for under the equity method if the entity had not chosen to apply the fair value option, the information required by APB 18, par. 20 (excluding paragraphs 20(a)(3), 20(b), and 20(e)) (FAS-159, par. 18(f))	As of each date an interim or annual statement of financial position is presented	This applies to investments in common stock, investments in in-substance common stock, and other investments that would otherwise be required to be accounted for under the equity method and would be required to satisfy the disclosure requirements of APB 18, par. 20.

Disclosures Required as of Each Date an Income Statement Is Presented (FAS-159, par. 19)[*]

Disclosure Requirement	Frequency	Comments
For each line item in the statement of financial position that relates to an item for which the fair value option has been elected, the amounts of gains and losses from fair value changes included in earnings during the period and in which line in the income statement those gains and losses are reported (FAS-159, par. 19(a)	For each period in which an interim or annual income statement is presented	An entity may meet this requirement by disclosing amounts of gains and losses that include amounts of gains and losses for other items measured at fair value.

Disclosure Requirement	Frequency	Comments
For items for which the fair value option has been elected, a description of how interest and dividends are measured and where they are reported in the income statement (FAS-159, par. 19(b)	For each period in which an interim or annual income statement is presented	FAS-159 does not address the methods used for recognizing and measuring the amount of dividend income, interest income, and interest expense for items for which the fair value option has been elected.
For loans and other receivables held as assets for which the fair value option has been elected: (1) The estimated amount of gains or losses included in earnings during the period attributable to changes in instrument-specific credit risk (2) How the gains or losses attributable to changes in instrument-specific credit risk were determined (FAS-159, par. 19(c)	For each period in which an interim or annual income statement is presented	FAS-159 provides no computational guidance for determining the amount of the loans' change in fair value change attributable to the change in instrument-specific credit risk.
For liabilities for which the fair value option has been elected with fair values that have been significantly affected during the reporting period by changes in the instrument-specific credit risk: (1) The estimated amount of gains and losses from fair value changes included in earnings that are attributable to changes in the instrument-specific credit risk (2) Qualitative information about the reasons for those changes	For each period in which an interim or annual income statement is presented	FAS-159 provides no guidance about (a) whether a change in instrument-specific credit risk is considered significant or (b) how to determine the amount of the liabilities' fair value change attributable to the change in instrument-specific credit risk.

Disclosure Requirement	Frequency	Comments
(3) How the gains and losses attributable to changes in instrument-specific credit risk were determined. (FAS-159, par. 19(d)		

Other Required Disclosures (FAS-159, par. 21-22)

Disclosure Requirement	Frequency	Comments
The methods and significant assumptions used to estimate the fair value of items for which the fair value option has been elected. (FAS-159, par. 21)	Annual periods only	Because FAS 107 already requires this, this applies to instruments outside the scope of FAS-107 (for example, certain insurance contracts) for which the fair value option has been elected.
If an entity elects the fair value option at the time one of the events in FAS-159, par. 9(d) and 9(e) occurs, the entity shall disclose the following in the financial statements: (1) Qualitative information about the nature of the event (2) Quantitative information by line item in the statement of financial position indicating which line items in the income statement include the effect on earnings of initially electing the fair value option for an item. (FAS-159, par. 22)	The period of the election	FAS-159, par. 9(d) and 9(e) provide that an entity may elect the fair value option on the date that the accounting treatment for an investment in another entity changes (par. 9(d)) or when an event occurs that requires an eligible item to be measured at fair value at the time of the event, but not ongoing (par. 9(e)).

---

* For not-for-profit operations, these disclosures apply not only with respect to the effect on performance indicators or other intermediate measures of operations, if presented, but also with respect to the effect on the change in each of the net asset classes (unrestricted, temporarily restricted, and permanently restricted), as applicable.

☞ **PRACTICE POINTER:** For loans and other receivable measured at fair value under the election of the fair value option, the FASB provided no computational guidance for determining the amount of the fair value change attributable to the change in borrower-specific credit risk. Similarly, for liabilities, the FASB provided no guidance about when a change in instrument-specific credit risk is considered significant and no computational guidance for determining the amount of the fair value change attributable to the change in instrument-specific credit risk. However, in both cases, FAS-159 requires companies to disclose the effect of changes in instrument-specific credit risk on fair value and how the gains and losses attributable to such risk are computed.

AUDIT CONSIDERATIONS

FAS-159 permits an entity to establish a policy to elect the fair value option for specified classes of financial assets and financial liabilities. Auditors should consider whether an established accounting policy for applying the fair value option to particular classes of financial assets and financial liabilities designated as being covered by the policy is adhered to on an ongoing basis. In addition, entities making the election must comply with the required timing for such elections. Auditors should consider whether the fair value option is made for an eligible item only on a date or in response to an event as permitted by FAS-159. FAS-159 does not establish any specific documentation requirements related to the fair value option. However, as a matter of internal control, such evidence should be created and maintained by companies electing the fair value option.

On April 17, 2007, the Center for Audit Quality issued an alert that addresses early adoption of FAS-159. It asserts that if an entity plans to adopt the fair value option to achieve an accounting result that is inconsistent with the objectives of FAS-159, the auditor should conclude that the entity's proposed accounting departs from GAAP. For example, if an entity proposes to adopt FAS-159 record unrealized losses on available-for-sale and held-to-maturity securities directly in retained earnings without the intent to continue to apply fair value as the measurement attribute to those securities, that approach should be viewed as inconsistent with the principles and objectives of FAS-159. The full text of the alert can be found on the Center for Audit Quality website (www.thecaq.org).

ILLUSTRATIONS

Illustration 19-1: Fair Value Measurements and Changes in Fair Values Included in Current-Period Earnings

This illustration is reproduced with permission from the illustrative disclosure in FAS-159, paragraphs B8–B9. This disclosure illustrates selected disclosure requirements for items reported at fair value based on the fair value option election in FAS-159. The disclosure represents the fair value hierarchy table set forth in FAS-157, supplemented to provide information about where in the income statement changes in fair values of financial assets and financial liabilities for which the fair value option has been elected are included in earnings.

The following specific disclosure requirements are illustrated below:

- For each line item in the statement of financial position, the amounts of gains and losses from fair value changes included in earnings during the period and in which line in the income statement those gains and losses are reported. This disclosure relates to each period for which an interim or annual income statement is presented, for items for which the fair value option has been elected. (FAS-159, par. 19(a)).

- As of each date for which interim or annual statement of financial position is presented, and for each line item in the statement of financial position that includes an item for which the fair value option has been elected, the following should be disclosed:

  (1) Information to enable users to understand how each line item in the statement of financial position relates to major categories of assets and liabilities presented in accordance with FAS-157's fair value disclosure requirements

  (2) The aggregate carrying amount of items included in each line item in the statement of financial position that are not eligible for the fair value option, if any. (FAS-159, par. 18(c)).

($ in millions) Description	Fair Value Measure- ments 12/31/XX	**Fair Value Measurements at December 31, 20XX, Using**		
		Quoted Prices in Active Markets for Identical Assets (Level 1)	Significant Other Observable Inputs (Level 2)	Significant Unobserv- able Inputs (Level 3)
Trading securities	$115	$105	$10	
Available-for-sale securities	75	75		
Loans	150	0	100	$50
Derivatives	60	25	15	20
Private equity investments*	75	0	25	50
Long-term debt	(60)	(30)	(10)	(20)

Changes in Fair Values for the 12-Month Period Ended December 31, 20XX, for Items Measured at Fair Value Pursuant to Election of the Fair Value Option

Description	Other Gains and Losses	Interest Income on Loans	Interest Expense on Long-Term Debt	Total Changes in Fair Values Included in Current Period Earnings
Trading securities				
Available-for-sale securities				
Loans	$(3)	$10		$ 7
Derivatives				
Private equity investments*	(18)			(18)
Long-term debt	13		$(4)	9

* Represents investments that would otherwise be accounted for under the equity method of accounting.
Source: Adapted from FAS-159, par. B8.

OBSERVATION: This is only one possible presentation of required disclosure information. FAS-159 does not preclude companies from complying with FAS-159, paragraph 19(a) by disclosing amounts of gains and losses that include amounts of gains and losses for other items measured at fair value, such as items required to be measured at fair value.

A company might provide additional disclosures required by FAS-159, paragraphs 18(a) and 18(b) to accompany the table presented.

See Illustration 18-1 in Chapter 18, "Fair Value Measurements, Fair Value Disclosures, and Other Financial Instrument Disclosures," for a version of this disclosure that also integrates disclosures required annually by FAS-107 as well as additional voluntary disclosures.

Glossary

Accelerated Share Repurchase   A combination of transactions that permits an entity to purchase a targeted number of shares immediately with the final purchase price of those shares determined as the average market price over a fixed period of time. (EITF 99-7) [*See* Chapter 16.]

Accounting Arbitrage   The ability to select between different accounting models, based on differences in form or for other reasons. For example, loans and debt securities are accounted for under different accounting standards. [*See* Chapter 2.]

Adequate Compensation   The amount of benefits of servicing that would fairly compensate a substitute servicer should one be required, which includes the profit that would be demanded in the marketplace. (FAS-140, par. 364) Used to estimate fair value and to identify servicing assets and liabilities. [*See* Chapter 4.]

Affiliate   A party that, directly or indirectly through one or more intermediaries, controls, is controlled by, or is under common control with an enterprise. (FAS-57, par. 24(a)) [*See* Chapter 3, Chapter 5, Chapter 6, and Chapter 10.] *Also see* **Related Party**.

AFS   Available-for-sale security. AFS securities are carried at fair value; unrealized gains and losses are recorded in other comprehensive income (a component of equity in the balance sheet). [*See* Chapter 2.]

Annuity Contract   A contract that provides fixed or variable periodic payments from a stated or contingent date and continuing for a specified period, such as for a number of years or for life. (FAS-60, par. 66) [*See* Chapter 13.] *Also see* **Variable Annuity Contract.**

Antidilutive   An increase in earnings per share amounts or a decrease in loss per share amounts. (FAS-128, par. 171) [*See* Chapter 10 and Chapter 16.]

Attached Call   A call option held by the transferor of a financial asset that becomes part of and is traded with the underlying instrument. Rather than being an obligation of the transferee, an attached call is traded with and diminishes the value of the underlying instrument transferred subject to that call. (FAS-140, par. 364) [*See* Chapter 5 and Chapter 6.]

Attached Derivative   An attached derivative is transferable and separately exercisable from its host contract. The counterparties to an attached derivative and its host contract may be different. An attached derivative should be evaluated as a freestanding derivative under FAS-133. [*See* Chapters 12–15.]

Benchmark Interest Rate   A widely recognized and quoted rate in an active financial market that is broadly indicative of the overall level of interest rates attributable to high-credit-quality obligors in that market. It is a rate that is widely used in a given financial market as an underlying basis for determining the interest rates of individual financial instruments and commonly referenced in interest-rate-related transactions.

In the United States, currently only the interest rates on direct Treasury obligations of the U.S. government and, for practical reasons, the LIBOR swap rate are considered to be benchmark interest rates. In other markets, government borrowing rates or an interbank offered rate may serve as a benchmark, depending on the facts and circumstances. In each financial market, only the one or two most widely used and quoted rates that meet the above criteria may be considered benchmark interest rates. (FAS-133, par. 540) [*See* Chapter 14.]

Beneficial Interests   Rights to receive all or portions of specified cash inflows to a trust or other entity, including senior and subordinated shares of interest, principal, or other cash inflows to be "passed-through" or "paid-through," premiums due to guarantors, commercial paper obligations, and residual interests, whether in the form of debt or equity. (FAS-140, par. 364) [*See* Chapter 2, Chapter 5, and Chapter 6.]

Benefits of Servicing   Revenues from contractually specified servicing fees, late charges, and other ancillary sources, including "float." (FAS-140, par. 364) Used to estimate fair value and to identify servicing assets and liabilities. [*See* Chapter 4.]

Best Efforts Remarketing Agreement   An agreement in which an agent (usually an investment banker) agrees to buy only those securities that it is able to sell to others. If the agent is unable to remarket the debt, the issuer remains obligated to pay off the debt. [*See* Chapter 8 and Chapter 11.]

BIH   Beneficial interest holders. [*See* Chapter 6.]

Book-Entry Securities   Securities that exist only as items in the accounting records maintained by a securities transfer system. (FIN-41, fn. 4) [*See* Chapter 17.]

Borrowing Capacity   The product of the remaining term and the maximum available credit of a line-of-credit or revolving debt arrangement. Changes in borrowing capacity are used to determine the accounting for deferred fees and costs when changes are made to credit arrangements. [*See* Chapter 8.]

Bullet Provision   In a revolving-period securitization, cash proceeds from the underlying assets are reinvested in short-term investments other than the underlying revolving-period receivables during the period prior to liquidating distributions to investors. Those investments mature or are sold to make a single "bullet" payment to certain classes of investors. [*See* Chapter 6.]

Callable Obligation   An obligation that the creditor has the right at that date to demand, or to give notice of its intention to demand, repayment of obligations owed to it by the debtor. (FAS-78, fn. 1) [*See* Chapter 8.]

Cap   A form of option contract in which the cap writer (seller) agrees to limit, or cap, the holder's (purchaser's) risk associated with an increase in a referenced rate or index, in exchange for a premium. For example, with an interest rate cap, if rates rise above a specified interest rate level (the strike rate), the cap holder will receive an amount equal to the excess of the current rate over the strike rate multiplied by the notional amount of the contract. [*See* Chapters 12–15.]

Carrying Amount (of Debt)   The face amount increased or decreased by applicable accrued interest, unamortized premium, discount, finance charges, or issue costs. Implicitly, this would include deferred gains and losses from fair value hedge accounting. (FAS-15, par. 13) [*See* Chapter 11.] *Also see* **Net Carrying Amount**.

Cash Equivalent Cash equivalents are short-term, highly liquid investments that are both (a) readily convertible to known amounts of cash and (b) so near their maturity that they present insignificant risk of changes in value because of changes in interest rates. (FAS-95, par. 8) Cash equivalents may be reported net in the statement of cash flows. [*See* Chapter 1.]

Catch-up Method of Changing Cash Flow Estimates A method of reflecting changes in cash flow estimates whereby the revised estimate of remaining cash flows are discounted using the *original* effective rate. The carrying amount of the investment is adjusted to that new discounted amount. (This approach is used to reflect impairment of loans within the scope of FAS-114.) [*See* Chapter 3 and Chapter 7.]

Clean-up Call An option held by the servicer or its affiliate, which may be the transferor, to purchase the remaining transferred financial assets, or the remaining beneficial interests held by third parties, if the amount of outstanding assets or beneficial interests falls to a level at which the cost of servicing those assets or beneficial interests becomes burdensome in relation to the benefits of servicing. (FAS-140, par. 364) [*See* Chapter 5 and Chapter 6.]

Collar A combination of options in which the holder has bought a cap at one level and, to reduce some or all of its cost, has sold a floor at a lower level. [*See* Chapters 12–15.] *Also see* **Cap** and **Floor**.

Collateral Personal or real property in which a security interest has been given. (FAS-140, par. 364) Market participants call certain transfers of financial assets (such as cash) "collateral," that are considered "proceeds" for accounting purposes. [*See* Chapter 9.]

Commitment Date (for Debt with a Beneficial Conversion Feature) The date on which a binding agreement is reached with an unrelated party. The agreement must have both of the attributes of a **firm commitment**. Statutory rights under which the nondefaulting party can pursue damages suffered represent a sufficiently large disincentive for nonperformance. An agreement that contains subjective cancellation clauses does not meet this definition. [*See* Chapter 10.]

Commitment Fees Fees charged for entering into an agreement that obligates the enterprise to make or acquire a loan or to satisfy an obligation of the other party under a specified condition. (FAS-91, par. 80) Fees for letters of credit and obligations to purchase loans are considered commitment fees. [*See* Chapter 7.]

Compensating Balances Amounts that a company must keep on deposit with a bank according to an informal or formal agreement to support outstanding borrowings and possibly the assurance of future credit availability. From the lender's perspective, compensating balances can provide some security, enhance the yield on a loan, and provide indirect compensation for bank services that are provided at no explicit charge. [*See* Chapter 1 and Chapter 8.]

Contractually Specified Servicing Fees All amounts that are due to the servicer (contractually) in exchange for servicing a financial asset and would no longer be received by a servicer if the beneficial owners of the serviced assets (or their trustees or agents) were to exercise their actual or potential authority under the contract to shift the servicing to another servicer. Depending on the servicing contract, those fees may include some or all of the difference between the interest rate collectible on the asset being serviced and the rate to be paid to the beneficial owners of those assets. (FAS-140, par. 364) Used to distinguish interest-only (I/O) strips from servicing assets and liabilities. [*See* Chapter 4.]

Conversion An exchange of a convertible debt instrument into equity securities or a combination of equity securities and other consideration. [*See* Chapter 10.]

Correlation A measure of the degree to which two variables or underlyings are related. A correlation coefficient is a number between -1 and $+1$ that indicates the strength and direction of the relationship between two variables. For example, a correlation coefficient of -1 indicates that the two variables are perfectly negatively correlated (that is, offsetting). A correlation coefficient of zero means that the two variables are not correlated at all, and a correlation coefficient of $+1$ means that they are perfectly correlated. [*See* Chapter 14.]

Cost Recovery Method A method of recognizing interest income on loans with credit concerns whereby any cash flows received are recorded as a reduction of the cost basis of the investment until it is reduced to zero; thereafter, any amounts received are reported as income. [*See* Chapter 3 and Chapter 7.]

Covered Call Strategy The sale of call options against an asset that is held by the entity. The option writer foregoes any upside potential above the strike price in exchange for the option premium. The written call option generally does not qualify for hedge accounting under FAS-133. (FAS-133, par. 20(c)) [*See* Chapter 14.]

Credit Life Insurance Credit life contracts provide benefits to the lender if the borrower dies before the debt is repaid or expires at the end of the term. [*See* Chapter 17.]

Cross-Hedge The use of a hedging instrument with a different underlying basis than the item being hedged. For example, the use of a Treasury-based derivative to hedge a prime-based loan is a cross-hedge. Another example is the use of a derivative based on Canadian dollars to hedge a Euro exposure. [*See* Chapter 14.]

Current Assets Cash or other assets that are reasonably expected to be realized in cash or sold or consumed during the normal operating cycle of the business. (ARB-43, Ch. 3A, par. 4) [*See* Chapter 1 and Chapter 8.]

Current Liabilities Obligations whose liquidation is reasonably expected to require the use of existing resources properly classifiable as current assets or the creation of other current liabilities. (ARB-43, Ch. 3A, par. 7) [*See* Chapter 1 and Chapter 8.]

Daylight Overdraft or Other Intraday Credit An accommodation in banking arrangements that allows transactions to be completed even if there is insufficient cash on deposit during the day provided that there is sufficient cash to cover the net cash requirement at the end of the day. That accommodation may be through a credit facility or from a deposit of collateral. (FIN-41, fn. 6) [*See* Chapter 17.]

***De Facto* Agent** Parties that are presumed to act on behalf of the reporting entity, including: a party that relies on the reporting entity for financial support; a party that received its interest as a contribution from the reporting entity; an officer, employee, or board member of the reporting entity; a party that must obtain permission to transfer its interests in the entity; and a party that has a close business relationship with the reporting entity. Interests held by *de facto* agents should be considered interests of the reporting entity for the purpose of identifying the Primary Beneficiary. [*See* Chapter 6.]

Deferred Annuity Contract An annuity contract for which payments have not yet commenced. During the accumulation phase, payments received by the insurance company are accumulated and earn either a fixed or variable return; the cash surrender value may be withdrawn. During the payout phase, annuity income payments are made to the annuitant. Some contracts allow withdrawal of some or all of the present value of the contractual annuity within a specified period during the payout phase. [*See* Chapter 13.]

Delta-Neutral Hedging Strategy   A hedging strategy in which the hedger monitors the option's "delta"—the ratio of changes in the option's price to changes in the price of the underlying asset—and constantly repositions the options to neutralize any changes in the fair value of the underlying asset. The delta ratio also changes as the price of the asset changes, the exercise period decreases, as interest rates change, and as expected volatility changes. Such hedging strategies must be assessed for effectiveness on a fair value basis (not on an intrinsic value basis). (FAS-133, par. 85) [*See* Chapter 14.]

Deposit Float   Checks that have been deposited by customers and that are in the process of collection—they are not currently available for withdrawal. [*See* Chapter 1.]

Derecognize   To remove previously recognized assets or liabilities from the balance sheet. (FAS-140, par. 364) [*See* Chapter 5, Chapter 6, and Chapter 11.]

Derivative Instrument   For accounting purposes, a contract whose value is derived by reference to a market variable and the level of investment required is less than the notional amount (quantity) specified in the contract. A key characteristic of a derivative is that the contract can be settled for only the net change in value (or the contract requires delivery of a highly liquid asset, leaving the counterparties in essentially same position as net settlement). The precise definition, and numerous exceptions, is contained in FAS-133, paragraphs 6–11 and 57–59. [*See* Chapters 12–15.]

Direct Method   A method of presenting cash flows from operating activities in the cash flow statement using gross cash receipts and gross cash payments by major category. Very few companies use this "encouraged" method of reporting. [*See* Chapter 1.] *Also see* **Indirect Method.**

Dollar Offset Method   A method of assessing and measuring hedge effectiveness whereby the change in fair value (or intrinsic value, as permitted) of the derivative is compared with the change in fair value or cash flow attributable to the risk being hedged on the hedged item. The method can be applied period by period or on a cumulative basis from the inception of the hedge through the present. [*See* Chapter 14.]

Dollar Rolls   Repurchase and reverse repurchase agreements that involve similar, but not the same, securities. Dollar rolls typically involve mortgage-backed securities. [*See* Chapter 9.]

Duration   Duration is the result of a calculation based on the timing of future cash flows and can be thought of as the life (in years) of a hypothetical zero-coupon bond whose fair value would change by the same amount as the real bond or portfolio in response to a change in market interest rates. (FAS-119, par. 69) Duration is an indicator of the price-sensitivity of a fixed-rate instrument to changes in interest rates. [*See* Chapter 18.]

Effective Yield Method   *See* **Interest Method**. [*See* Chapter 7 and Chapter 8.]

Embedded Derivative   A derivative is *embedded* when provisions that meet the definition of a derivative are incorporated into a single contract by the issuer, and the derivative is not transferable independent of the "host" instrument. Embedded derivatives must be accounted for separate from their host contracts under FAS-133. [*See* Chapters 12–15.] *Also see* **Attached Derivative**.

Equity Restructuring   A nonreciprocal transaction between an entity and its shareholders that causes the per-share fair value of the shares underlying an option or similar award to change, such as a stock dividend, stock split, spinoff, rights offering, or recapitalization through a large, nonrecurring cash dividend. (FAS 123(R)) [*See* Chapter 10.]

Expected Present Value Technique   The sum of probability-weighted present values in a range of estimated cash flows, all discounted using the same interest rate convention. (CON-7, Introduction) [*See* Chapter 5 and Chapter 8.]

Factoring Arrangements   Factoring arrangements are a means of discounting accounts receivable on a nonrecourse, notification basis. Accounts receivable are sold outright, usually to a transferee (the factor) that assumes the full risk of collection, without recourse to the transferor in the event of a loss. Debtors are directed to send payments to the transferee. (FAS-140, par. 112) Factoring arrangements are a form of transfer of financial assets. [*See* Chapter 5.]

Fair Value   The price that would be received to sell an asset or paid to transfer a liability in an orderly transaction between market participants at the measurement date.

Federal Funds (Fed funds)   Funds that commercial banks deposit at Federal Reserve Banks. A borrowing bank records a liability (federal funds purchased) and a selling bank records an asset (federal funds sold). Banks may operate on both sides of the fed funds market on the same day. [*See* Chapter 1 and Chapter 9.]

Financial Asset   Cash, evidence of an ownership interest in an entity, or a contract that conveys to one entity a right (1) to receive cash or another financial instrument from a second entity or (2) to exchange other financial instruments on potentially favorable terms with the second entity.

Financial Liability   A contract that imposes on one entity an obligation (1) to deliver cash or another financial instrument to a second entity or (2) to exchange other financial instruments on potentially unfavorable terms with the second entity.

Firm Commitment   An agreement with an unrelated party, binding on both parties and usually legally enforceable, with both of the following characteristics:

- All significant terms are specified, including the quantity, the fixed price, and the timing of the transaction. The fixed price may be expressed as functional currency or foreign currency amount or as a specified interest rate or yield.
- Performance is probable, because the agreement includes a sufficiently large disincentive for nonperformance. (FAS-133, par. 540)

Enforceable statutory rights to pursue remedies for default equivalent to the damages suffered by the nondefaulting party represent a sufficiently large disincentive for nonperformance to make performance probable for purposes of identifying firm commitment. (DIG F-3) [*See* Chapter 14.]

Floor   A form of option contract in which the writer (seller) agrees to limit the risk associated with a decrease in a referenced rate or index, in exchange for a premium. For example, in an interest rate floor, if rates fall below the specified level (the strike rate), the holder (purchaser) will receive an amount equal to the difference between the current rate and the strike rate multiplied by the notional amount of the contract. [*See* Chapters 12–15.]

Forecasted Transaction A transaction that is expected to occur for which there is no firm commitment (as defined). Because no transaction has yet occurred and the transaction when it occurs will be at the prevailing market price, a forecasted transaction does not give an entity any present rights to future benefits or a present obligation for future sacrifices. (FAS-133, par. 540) [*See* Chapter 14].

Forward Contract An agreement that commits one party to purchase and the other to sell a specific quantity of an asset at a specified future date for a fixed or determinable price. Both parties to a forward contract have the potential for gains and losses, that is, the contracts have upside and downside potential. See **futures contract** for an exchange-traded forward contract. [*See* Chapters 12–15.]

Functional Currency An entity's functional currency is the currency of the primary economic environment in which the entity operates; normally, that is the currency of the environment in which an entity primarily generates and expends cash. (FAS-52, par. 39) [*See* Chapter 1 and Chapter 14.]

Futures Contract A standardized forward contract traded on an organized exchange. The terms of each type of futures contract are standardized, including the quantity and quality of the underlying, the time and place of delivery, and the method of payment. Futures contracts are entered into directly with the exchange clearinghouse. Contracts are generally settled by purchasing an equal but opposite position that leaves the clearinghouse with a net position of zero. Futures contracts are available for a wide range of underlying instruments, including commodities, precious metals, Eurodollars, Treasuries, stock indexes, and foreign currencies. [*See* Chapters 12–15.]

GAAP Generally accepted accounting principles.

Gap Analysis An approach to the measurement of interest rate risk whereby the carrying amounts of rate-sensitive assets and liabilities, and the notional principal amounts of swaps and other derivatives, are grouped by expected repricing or maturity date. The results are summed to show a cumulative interest sensitivity "gap" between assets and liabilities. (FAS-119, par. 69) [*See* Chapter 18.]

Grace Period The time allowed to cure a default or violation of any provision of a debt agreement. [*See* Chapter 8.]

Guarantee   An agreement that obligates a company (guarantor) to reimburse the guaranteed party for a loss incurred because a specified debtor fails to pay when due. [*See* Chapter 3, Chapter 6, Chapter 7, Chapter 8, and Chapter 12.]

Guaranteed Mortgage Securitization   A securitization of mortgage loans that is within the scope of FAS-65, as amended (mortgage banking activities), and includes a substantive guarantee by a third party. (FAS-140, par. 364) [*See* Chapter 4 and Chapter 6.]

HTM   Held-to-maturity debt security. HTM debt securities are carried at amortized cost if they meet numerous qualifying criteria. [*See* Chapter 2.]

Indirect Guarantee of Indebtedness   An agreement that obligates a company (guarantor) to transfer funds to a debtor upon the occurrence of specified events, under conditions whereby (a) the funds are legally available to creditors of the debtor and (b) those creditors may enforce the debtor's claims against the first entity under the agreement. (FIN-45, par. 17) [*See* Chapter 5, Chapter 6, and Chapter 8.]

Indirect Method   A method of presenting cash flows from operating activities in the cash flow statement whereby the company starts with net income and backs out noncash revenues and gains and noncash expenses and losses. Some common adjustments involving financial instruments include: the allowance for loan losses, amortization of premiums, discounts, and deferred fees and costs, mark-to-market (or the lower-of-cost-or-market) accounting, and the reversal of gains and losses on (1) sales of assets that give rise to investing cash flows, such as available-for-sale securities and (2) gains and losses on liabilities that give rise to financing cash flows. Certain amounts must be disclosed separately (e.g., interest and taxes paid). Most companies use this "allowed alternative." [*See* Chapter 1.]

If-Converted Method   A method of computing the dilutive effect of convertible securities on diluted earnings per share. The method assumes conversion at the beginning of the reporting period (or at time of issuance, if later) and that number of shares is added to the denominator, along with certain "pro forma" adjustments of the numerator (earnings). [*See* Chapter 10 and Chapter 16.]

In-substance Defeasance   A transaction intended to retire debt, whereby the debtor irrevocably places cash or other assets in a trust to be used solely for satisfying scheduled payments of both interest and principal of a specific obligation and the possibility that the debtor will be required to make future payments with respect to that debt is remote. Debt is *not* considered extinguished for accounting purposes if the transaction occurred after December 31, 1996. [*See* Chapter 11.]

Interest Method   A method of recognizing interest income and expense that results in a level effective rate on the sum of (1) the face amount of the debt instrument and (2) any unamortized premium or discount (and other adjustments to the cost basis of a debt instrument) at the beginning of each period. The amount of reported interest income or expense would equal the sum of the amount of periodic amortization and the nominal interest (coupon interest) for the period. [*See* Chapter 7 and Chapter 8.]

I-O (Interest-Only) Strip   A contractual right to receive some or all of the interest due on an interest-bearing debt instrument. [*See* Chapter 2, Chapter 4, and Chapter 12.]

Internal Reserve Method   A method of making payments to investors for collections of principal and interest on mortgage loans by issuers of GNMA securities. (FAS-65, par. 34) [*See* Chapter 4.]

Issue Costs   Amounts paid to third parties in connection with the issuance of debt or equity securities. For convertible securities, issuance costs include incremental and direct costs incurred with parties *other than the investor* in the convertible instrument. [*See* Chapter 8 and Chapter 10.]

Liabilities   Probable future sacrifices of economic benefits arising from present obligations of a particular entity to transfer assets or provide services to other entities in the future as a result of past transactions or events. (CON-6, par. 35) [*See* Chapter 8 and Chapter 16.]

LIBOR (London Interbank Offered Rate)   A benchmark interest rate in international capital markets. It represents the average rate at which several of the most creditworthy financial institutions would lend to each other, usually in Eurodollars, for various points in time on the yield curve. Interest rates are often quoted at a spread above or below LIBOR, depending on the creditworthiness of a particular borrower (for example, LIBOR + 100 basis points). A LIBOR-based loan is considered a variable-rate loan under FAS-91. [*See* Chapter 7 and Chapter 14.]

Loan Participations Groups of banks or other entities may jointly fund large borrowings through loan participations in which a single lender makes a large loan to a borrower and subsequently transfers undivided interests in the loan to other entities. (FAS-140, par. 104) Loan participations are considered transfers of financial assets. Whether they are accounted for as sales or borrowings depends on the facts and circumstances. [*See* Chapter 5.]

Loan Syndications When a company seeks to borrow a large amount of money, lenders sometimes share the risk by forming a syndicate. One lender (the syndicator) typically manages the transaction with the borrower, but each member of the syndicate funds its respective portion of the loan. Loan syndications are not transfers of assets. [*See* Chapter 5.]

Lock-box Arrangement Contractual provisions of a loan arrangement that, in the normal course of business and without another event occurring, require the debtor to use its cash receipts (working capital) to repay the amounts outstanding on a borrowing. [*See* Chapter 8.]

LOCOM The lower of cost or market value. Loans held for sale are measured at LOCOM. [*See* Chapter 3.]

Long-Term Obligations Obligations that are scheduled to mature beyond one year (or the operating cycle, if longer) from the date of a company's balance sheet. [*See* Chapter 8.]

Mandatorily Redeemable A financial instrument issued in the form of shares that represents an unconditional obligation to redeem the instrument by transferring cash or other assets at a specified or determinable date or upon an event that is certain to occur, including death. Under FAS-150, the issuer must account for mandatorily redeemable stock as a liability. Under FAS-115, an investor would consider any equity security that is (a) mandatorily redeemable or (b) redeemable at the option of the investor a debt security. [*See* Chapter 2 and Chapter 16.]

Mark-to-Market Accounting An accounting method whereby some financial instruments are carried in the balance sheet at their fair values; changes in fair value are reported in earnings as they occur. Trading securities, short sale obligations and derivatives (that are not properly accounted for as cash flow hedges) are examples of items that are marked to market. [*See* Chapter 2 and Chapter 12.]

Master Netting Arrangement A contract between two parties that provides for the net settlement of all outstanding contracts (involving similar or different products) through a single payment in a single currency in the event of default or termination of any one contract. [*See* Chapter 17.]

Matrix Pricing Model A mathematical technique used to value normal institutional-size trading units of debt securities without relying exclusively on quoted prices of the specific security. Factors such as the issue's coupon or stated interest rate, maturity, and rating and quoted prices of similar issues are considered in developing the issue's current market yield. (AICPA Audit Guide, Brokers and Dealers in Securities, Glossary) [*See* Chapter 18.]

Mirror-Image Options In determining whether a hedging relationship qualifies for the "shortcut method," one of the conditions requires that (1) the terms of the hedging call option and embedded call option match (including matching maturities, strike price (meaning the amount for which the debt could be called), related notional amounts, timing and frequency of payments, and dates on which the instruments may be called) and (2) the entity is the writer of one call option and the holder (or purchaser) of the other call option. The same requirements apply for put options. (FAS-133, par. 68(d) and DIG E-20) [*See* Chapter 14.]

Negative Convexity The tendency for the price of an interest-sensitive instrument to fall faster for a given increase in interest rates than it rises for a decrease in interest rates of the same magnitude. Mortgage-related instruments have negative convexity, due to their embedded options. [*See* Chapter 14.]

Net Carrying Amount of Debt The amount due at maturity, adjusted for unamortized premium, discount, debt issuance costs, and deferred gains or losses on fair value hedges. Used to calculate the gain or loss on extinguishment of debt. [*See* Chapter 11.] *Also see* **Carrying Amount (of Debt)**.

Nonadmitted Assets A term used for statutory reporting purposes by insurance companies to identify assets that are reported as charges to surplus because they cannot be used to fulfill policyholder obligations (either because of their illiquid nature or because they are encumbered in some way). [*See* Chapter 4.]

Nonpublic Entity   A nonpublic entity is any entity other than one—

- Whose debt or equity securities trade in a public market either on a stock exchange or in the over-the-counter market
- That makes a filing with a regulatory agency in preparation for the sale of any class of debt or equity securities in a public market, or
- That is controlled by an entity that meets either of these conditions. [*See* Chapter 18.]

Nonrecourse Debt   A loan in which the lender (creditor) agrees, as part of the original loan negotiations, to accept only the assets being financed as security for the debt and cannot look to any other assets of the debtor to satisfy the debt. [*See* Chapter 11 and Chapter 17.]

Notional Amount   A number of currency units, shares, bushels, pounds, or other units stated in a derivative instrument that is used to calculate the settlement amount. [*See* Chapters 12–15.]

OCI   Other comprehensive income. A separate component of stockholders' equity in the balance sheet, used to report (separately) unrealized gains and losses on available-for-sale securities, derivatives designated in qualifying cash flow hedges, and foreign currency translation adjustments. [*See* Chapter 2 and Chapter 14.]

Off-Balance-Sheet Financing   A term used to describe the accounting for transfers of financial assets that are accounted for as sales rather than borrowings. That is, the "credit" is recorded as a reduction of the assets transferred rather than as debt that is collateralized by those assets. If the assets are sold to a special-purpose entity, the transaction would only be considered "off-balance-sheet financing" if the transferor is not required to consolidate the entity. [*See* Chapter 5 and Chapter 6.]

Offsetting   The display of a recognized asset and a recognized liability as one net amount (a net asset or a net liability) in the balance sheet. [*See* Chapter 17.]

Operating Cycle   The average amount of time between the acquisition of materials or services for cash and the realization of cash from the sale of those items as finished goods or services. [*See* Chapter 8.]

Options   Contracts that give the holder (purchaser) the right, but not the obligation, to buy or sell an item at a price (the strike price), during a period or on a specific date. A call option allows the holder to buy the item, and a put option allows the holder to sell the item. The holder benefits from favorable movements in price, but cannot lose more than the premium paid. The writer (seller) has virtually unlimited downside risk but his gain is limited to the amount of premium received. Options are traded on exchanges and over the counter. [*See* Chapters 12–15.]

Origination Fees   Fees charged to the borrower in connection with the process of originating, refinancing, or restructuring a loan. This term includes, but is not limited to, points, management, arrangement, placement, application, underwriting, and other fees pursuant to a lending or leasing transaction and also includes syndication and participation fees to the extent they are associated with the portion of the loan retained by the lender. (FAS-91, par. 80) [*See* Chapter 7.]

Passive Financial Instrument (as used in FAS-140)   A financial asset or derivative financial instrument that does not require its holder to make decisions, such as to exercise options or voting rights (other than the decisions inherent in servicing). [*See* Chapter 6.]

P-O (Principal-Only) Strip   A contractual right to receive some or all of the principal due on a debt instrument [*See* Chapter 2.]

Primary Beneficiary   Under FIN-46, the entity that holds the majority of the expected losses, expected residual returns, or both, of a variable interest entity. The Primary Beneficiary, if any, must consolidate the assets and liabilities of a variable interest entity. [*See* Chapter 6.]

Prime Rate   The interest rate charged by major commercial banks to their most creditworthy customers. Prime rate is often used as a baseline in determining the interest rate on a loan (a credit spread is then added or subtracted, depending on the creditworthiness of that particular borrower). Note that prime rate is *not* considered a benchmark interest rate for the purpose of applying FAS-133. [*See* Chapter 7 and Chapter 14.]

Probable   A condition where a future event is "likely to occur." Probable is a higher level of likelihood than "more likely than not" but it does not mean "virtually certain." [*See* Chapter 3 and Chapter 8.]

Proceeds Cash, derivatives, or other assets that are obtained in a transfer of financial assets. Proceeds less any liabilities incurred is called "net proceeds." To be considered proceeds, the recipient must be permitted by contract or custom to sell or repledge the assets received. (FAS-140, fn. 22) A beneficial interest in the transferred assets is considered an interest that continues to be held by a transferor, *not* proceeds. [*See* Chapter 5, Chapter 6, and Chapter 9.]

Prospective Method of Changing Cash Flow Estimates A method of reflecting changes in cash flow estimates whereby interest is recognized using the new effective rate that relates the carrying amount and the revised cash flows. The carrying amount of the investment is *not* adjusted. [*See* Chapter 7.]

QSPE (Qualifying Special-Purpose Entity) A trust or other legal entity that is used to transform financial assets from one form to another. QPSEs are often used in securitizations, which simply means that the beneficial interests issued by the entity are in the form of securities. A QSPE is significant for accounting purposes because the transferor (seller) of assets into a QSPE never needs to consolidate the assets and liabilities of the SPE into its own balance sheet. To qualify, an SPE must meet all of the requirements and limitations of FAS-140. [*See* Chapter 6.]

Reacquisition Price of Debt The amount paid on extinguishment, including a call premium and miscellaneous costs of reacquisition. (APB-26, par. 3) [*See* Chapter 11.]

Reciprocal Balances Balances due to and from the same depository institution. [*See* Chapter 17.]

Recorded Investment in a Loan The face amount of a loan increased or decreased by applicable accrued interest and unamortized premium, discount, and deferred net acquisition fees and costs. The recorded investment may reflect a previous direct write-down of the loan but does not include an allowance for estimated uncollectible amounts or other valuation account, if any. [*See* Chapter 3].

Redeemable Preferred Stock Securities with redemption features that are not solely within the control of the issuer. [*See* Chapter 16.]

Registration Payment Arrangement An arrangement with both of the following characteristics:

- The arrangement specifies that the issuer will endeavor (1) to file a registration statement for the resale of specified financial instruments and/or for the resale of equity shares that are issuable upon exercise or conversion of specified financial instruments and for that registration statement to be declared effective by the SEC (or other applicable securities regulator if the registration statement will be filed in a foreign jurisdiction) within a specified grace period, and/or (2) to maintain the effectiveness of the registration statement for a specified period of time (or in perpetuity).

- The arrangement requires the issuer to transfer consideration to the counterparty if the registration statement for the resale of the financial instrument or instruments subject to the arrangement is not declared effective or if effectiveness of the registration statement is not maintained. That consideration may be payable in a lump sum or it may be payable periodically, and the form of the consideration may vary. For example, the consideration may be in the form of cash, equity instruments, or adjustments to the terms of the financial instrument or instruments that are subject to the registration payment arrangement (such as an increased interest rate on a debt instrument).

Regression Analysis   A mathematical technique that uses historical data to calculate the expected effect of a change in one variable on one or more other variable(s). The ability to explain the relationship is measured by the coefficient of determination, or R-square. An R-square of .90 means that 90% of the change in one variable can be explained by a change in the other(s). In a hedging relationship, regression analysis can be used to assess whether a derivative is expected to be highly effective in offsetting changes in the value or cash flow of a hedged item. [*See* Chapter 14.]

Related Party   Affiliates of the enterprise; entities for which investments are accounted for by the equity method by the enterprise; trusts for the benefit of employees, such as pension and profit-sharing trusts that are managed by or under the trusteeship of management; principal owners of the enterprise; its management; members of the immediate families of principal owners of the enterprise and its management; and other parties with which the enterprise may deal if one party controls or can significantly influence the management or operating policies of the other to an extent that one of the transacting parties might be prevented from fully pursuing its own separate interests. (FAS-57, par. 24(f)) [*See* Chapter 3 and Chapter 6.]

Remote The chance of the future event or events occurring is slight. (FAS-5, par. 3) [*See* Chapter 12.]

Repurchase Agreement ("Repo") An agreement whereby one party agrees to sell securities to another for cash, with a simultaneous agreement to repurchase the same or equivalent securities at a specific price at a later date. [*See* Chapter 9 and Chapter 17.] *Also see* **Reverse Repurchase Agreement**. Note that certain industries, including investment companies, use the same terminology to refer to the opposite transactions.

Retrospective Method of Changing Cash Flow Estimates A method of reflecting changes in cash flow estimates whereby a new effective rate is computed, based on the original carrying amount, actual cash flows to date, and remaining estimated cash flows. The carrying amount of the investment is adjusted to reflect what the balance would have been if the revised cash flow information had been known at inception, with the offset to interest income. Interest is recognized in subsequent periods using the new effective rate. (This approach is required by FAS-91 and EITF Issue 96-12.) [*See* Chapter 7.]

Reverse Repurchase Agreement ("Reverse Repo" or "Resale") An agreement whereby one party agrees to buy securities from another for cash, with a simultaneous agreement to resell the same or equivalent securities at a specific price at a later date. [*See* Chapter 9 and Chapter 17.] *Also see* **Repurchase Agreement**.

Revolving-period Securitization A securitization in which short-term receivables are used to back long-term beneficial interests. Collections from transferred receivables are used to purchase additional receivables during a defined period called the revolving period. Thereafter, the collections are used to redeem beneficial interests in due course. (FAS-140, par. 192) [*See* Chapter 6.]

Right of Setoff A debtor's legal right, by contract or otherwise, to discharge all or a portion of the debt owed to another party by applying against the debt an amount that the other party owes to the debtor. (FIN-39, par. 5) [*See* Chapter 17.]

Securities Lending Agreement The loan of specific securities to a party who agrees to return a like quantity of the same security. The lender typically receives collateral, including cash, other securities, or a bank letter of credit, to secure the return of their securities. The lender receives a fee, often called a rebate. [*See* Chapter 9.]

Securitization The process of transforming assets such as loans and receivables into securities. The cash flows from the original assets are the primary source of cash flow for the securities that are issued, although derivatives and credit enhancements are often included in the pool of assets being securitized. [*See* Chapter 6.]

Security A share, participation, or other interest in property or in an enterprise of the issuer or an obligation of the issuer that (a) either is represented by an instrument issued in bearer or registered form or, if not represented by an instrument, is registered in books maintained to record transfers by or on behalf of the issuer, (b) is of a type commonly dealt in on securities exchanges or markets or, when represented by an instrument, is commonly recognized in any area in which it is issued or dealt in as a medium for investment, and (c) either is one of a class or series or by its terms is divisible into a class or series of shares, participations, interests, or obligations. (FAS-115, par. 137) [*See* Chapter 2.]

Sell-Buybacks (also called "buy-sells") Two transactions entered into at the same time whereby (1) a security is sold and (2) the same security is purchased for settlement at a future date. The forward price is derived using an interest rate such as the repo rate. [*See* Chapter 9.]

Short-Term Obligations Obligations that are scheduled to mature within one year (or, the operating cycle, if longer) from the date of a company's balance sheet. [*See* Chapter 8.]

Silo A term used in securitizations to describe aggregations of assets and liabilities within a larger variable interest entity, where specified assets are the only source of payment for specified liabilities. [*See* Chapter 6.]

Special-Purpose Entity (SPE) A legal entity, such as a trust, partnership, or corporation, that is established by a seller of assets or sponsor to carry out a specific business purpose. A common use of SPE's is to issue beneficial interests in the assets held by the entity, often with modified interest rate and credit characteristics (asset-backed securities). [*See* Chapter 6.] *Also see* **QSPE**.

Split-Interest Agreement An arrangement involving donations to a not-for-profit organization whereby benefits held in trust (or in other structures) are shared with other beneficiaries. The "lead interest" is the right to the benefits of the transferred assets during the term of the agreement, which generally terminates either (1) after a specified number of years (period-certain) or (2) upon the occurrence of a certain event, usually death (life-contingent). The "remainder interest" is the right to receive all or a portion of the assets remaining at the end of the agreement's term. Chapter 6 of the AICPA Audit and Accounting Guide, *Not-for-Profit Organizations,* provides additional information. [*See* Chapter 13.]

Subjective Acceleration Clause A provision in a debt agreement that allows the creditor to accelerate the scheduled maturities of the obligations under conditions that are not objectively determinable (for example, a "material adverse change" clause or a "failure to maintain satisfactory operations" clause). [*See* Chapter 8.]

Substantially the Same Two assets that have the same primary obligor, identical form, type and contractual interest rates, the same maturity, similar assets as collateral, and the same aggregate unpaid principal amount or principal amounts within accepted "good delivery" standards for the type of security involved. This definition is critical in determining whether a repurchase agreement or a "dollar-roll" is accounted for as a sale or a secured borrowing. [*See* Chapter 5 and Chapter 9.]

Swap A contract to exchange cash flows at specified dates based on the performance of two different underlying instruments, typically without exchanging the instruments themselves. For example, in an interest rate swap, the holder could receive changes in 3-month LIBOR multiplied by the notional amount of the contract and pay a fixed rate times the notional amount of the contract. Generally, only the difference between the amount owed and the amount due is exchanged at each payment date. Swaps generally are negotiated between a dealer and a counterparty (that is, they are traded over the counter). Swaps can involve interest rates, foreign currency, commodities and equity instruments. [*See* Chapters 12–15.]

Taint The consequence of selling or transferring held-to-maturity (HTM) debt securities for unacceptable reasons. A "tainted" entity may be required to reclassify any remaining HTM securities to available for sale and may be prohibited from using the HTM classification for a period of time. [*See* Chapter 2.]

Temporary Equity (also called Mezzanine) For SEC reporting purposes, certain instruments may not be reported as part of permanent equity, but rather, must be displayed in a separate category between liabilities and equity. The caption is intended to indicate that an instrument could represent an obligation to the enterprise, despite the fact that the instrument is issued in the form of equity, including conditionally redeemable preferred stock. [*See* Chapter 16.]

Total Return Swap A contract whereby one party agrees to pay the other the "total return" of a specified asset (or portfolio), including gains, losses, and dividends or interest as applicable, usually in return for a floating rate of interest based on the notional amount of the contract. Typically, the underlying asset (or notional amount) is not exchanged in a total return swap. [*See* Chapter 16.]

Treasury Stock Method A method of computing the dilutive effect of in-the-money options and warrants on diluted earnings per share. The method assumes that any proceeds from the hypothetical exercise would be used to purchase common stock at the average market price during the period. The incremental shares assumed issued are added to the denominator. [*See* Chapter 10 and Chapter 16.]

Troubled Debt Restructuring A restructuring of debt under which the creditor, for reasons related to the debtor's financial difficulties, grants a concession to the debtor that it would not otherwise consider. The concession could be negotiated between the debtor and the creditor or be imposed by a court of law. [*See* Chapter 3 and Chapter 11.]

Trust-Preferred Securities Trust-preferred securities are issued under several names. Generally, a parent entity establishes a special-purpose entity (SPE) or trust that it controls; the SPE then issues preferred securities to investors and uses the proceeds to make a term loan back to the parent entity. Most trust-preferred securities require redemption upon maturity or redemption of the underlying loan. [*See* Chapter 16.]

Turbo Provision In a securitization, a disproportionate distribution of cash flows to various classes of investors during the amortization period. For example, a turbo provision might require the first $10 million of cash received during the amortization period to be paid to one class of investors before any cash is paid to other investors. [*See* Chapter 6.]

Underlying In a derivative, a specified interest rate, security price, commodity price, foreign exchange rate, index of prices or rates, or other variable (including the occurrence or nonoccurrence of a specified event). (FAS-133, par. 540) For example, the "underlying" in an oil futures contract is the price of a barrel of oil. [*See* Chapter 12.]

Unilateral Ability A capacity for action not dependent on the actions (or failure to act) of any other party. (FAS-140, par. 364) [*See* Chapter 5 and Chapter 6.]

Value at Risk Value at risk is the expected loss from an adverse market movement with a specified probability over a period of time. For example, based on a simulation of a large number of possible scenarios, an entity can determine with 97.5 percent probability (corresponding to calculations using about 2 standard deviations) that any adverse change in the portfolio value over 1 day will not exceed a calculated amount, the value at risk. (FAS-119, par. 69) [*See* Chapter 18.]

Variable Annuity Contract An annuity in which the amount of payments to be made are specified in units rather than in dollars. When payment is due, the amount is determined based on the value of the investments in the annuity fund. (FAS-60, par. 66) [*See* Chapter 13.]

Variable Interest A contractual arrangement that varies with changes in the net asset value of a variable interest entity. Examples include stock, subordinated beneficial interests, and guarantees. [*See* Chapter 6.]

Variable Interest Entity An entity that lacks adequate capitalization (generally, the equity capital does not exceed the expected losses of the entity) or whose equity capital does not convey meaningful rights that are proportionate to the holders' shares of the expected losses and rewards of the entity. FIN-46(R) governs whether a reporting entity must consolidate a variable interest entity with which it has significant involvement. [*See* Chapter 6.]

Violation of a Provision The failure to meet a condition in a debt agreement or a breach of a provision in the agreement for which compliance is objectively determinable, such as failure to make a payment or default, whether or not a grace period is allowed or the creditor is required to give notice of its intention to demand repayment. (FAS-78, fn. 2) [*See* Chapter 8.]

Warrants Instruments that give the holder the right to purchase the underlying security at a specified price and time. Warrants are issued as separate instruments and they are sometimes attached to other securities, including debt. Accounting for warrants depends on the settlement terms of the contract, whether the reporting entity is the issuer, and the marketability of the underlying stock. [*See* Chapter 10, Chapter 12, and Chapter 16.]

Working Capital The excess of current assets over current liabilities; identifies the relatively liquid portion of total enterprise capital which constitutes a margin or buffer for meeting obligations within the ordinary operating cycle of the business. (Chapter 3A of ARB-43, par. 3) [*See* Chapter 1 and Chapter 8.]

Cross-Reference

ORIGINAL PRONOUNCEMENTS TO
2008 *FINANCIAL INSTRUMENTS*

This locator provides instant cross-reference between an original pronouncement and the chapter(s) in this publication in which a pronouncement is covered. Original pronouncements are listed chronologically on the left and the chapter(s) in which they appear in the 2008 Edition of *Financial Instruments* on the right. When an original pronouncement has been superseded in recent years, cross-reference has been made to the new pronouncement.

ACCOUNTING RESEARCH BULLETINS (ARBs)

(Accounting Research Bulletins 1–42 were revised, restated, or withdrawn at the time ARB No. 43 was issued.)

ORIGINAL PRONOUNCEMENT	2008 *FINANCIAL INSTRUMENTS* REFERENCE[1]
ARB No. 43 Restatement and Revision of Accounting Research Bulletins	Portions amended or superseded by APB-5, 6, 9, 10, 20, 21, 25, 26, FAS-5, 6, 52, 78, 94, 109, 111, 115, 123, 133, 135, and 151. Cash and Cash Equivalents, ch. **1** Investments in Debt and Equity Securities, ch. **2** Debt Financing, ch. **8** Securities Lending Arrangements, and Other Pledges of Collateral, ch. **9** Extinguishments of Debt, ch. **11** Issuer's Accounting for Equity Instruments and Related Contracts, ch. **16**
ARB No. 51 Consolidated Financial Statements	Portions amended or superseded by APB-10, 11, 16, 18, 23, FAS-58, 71, 94, 109, 111, 131, and 144. Also see FIN-46. Investments in Debt and Equity Securities, ch. **2** Securitizations, ch. **6** Debt Financing, ch. **8** Issuer's Accounting for Equity Instruments and Related Contracts, ch. **16**

---

[1] In cases where there has been a series of amended standards on the same topic, such as income taxes, or transfers of financial assets, only the most recent amendment is cited in the status information below.

ACCOUNTING PRINCIPLES BOARD OPINIONS (APBs)

ORIGINAL PRONOUNCEMENT | 2008 *FINANCIAL INSTRUMENTS* REFERENCE

APB Opinion No. 6
Status of Accounting Research Bulletins

Portions amended or superseded by APB-11, 16, 17, 26, 28, FAS-8, 52, 71, 109, 111, and 135.
Issuer's Accounting for Equity Instruments and Related Contracts, ch. **16**

APB Opinion No. 9
Reporting the Results of Operations

Portions amended or superseded by APB-13, 20, 30, FAS-16, and 111.
Issuer's Accounting for Equity Instruments and Related Contracts, ch. **16**

APB Opinion No. 10
Omnibus Opinion—1966

Portions amended or superseded by APB-12, 14, 16, 18, and FAS-111 and 129. Also see FIN-39.
Offsetting Assets and Liabilities in the Balance Sheet, ch. **17**

APB Opinion No. 12
Omnibus Opinion—1967

Portions amended or superseded by APB-14, and FAS-87, 106, and 111.
Calculating Yields on Debt Investments, ch. **7**
Issuer's Accounting for Equity Instruments and Related Contracts, ch. **16**

APB Opinion No. 14
Accounting for Convertible Debt and Debt Issued with Stock Purchase Warrants

Convertible Debt and Similar Instruments, ch. **10**

APB Opinion No. 18
The Equity Method of Accounting for Investments in Common Stock

Portions amended or superseded by APB-23, 30, FAS-13, 58, 94, 115, 128, 142, and 144.
Investments in Debt and Equity Securities, ch. **2**
Securitizations, ch. **6**
Issuer's Accounting for Equity Instruments and Related Contracts, ch. **16**

APB Opinion No. 20
Accounting Changes

Replaced by FAS-154.

APB Opinion No. 21
Interest on Receivables and Payables

Portions amended or superseded by FAS-34 and 109.
Calculating Yields on Debt Investments, ch. **7**
Debt Financing, ch. **8**

APB Opinion No. 22
Disclosure of Accounting Policies

Portions amended by FAS-2, 52, 95, and 111.
Debt Financing, ch. 8
Issuer's Accounting for Equity Instruments and Related Contracts, ch. **16**

APB Opinion No. 26
Early Extinguishment of Debt

Portions amended or superseded by APB-30, FAS-4, 15, 71, 84, and 140.
Convertible Debt and Similar Instruments, ch. **10**
Extinguishments of Debt, ch. **11**

APB Opinion No. 29

Accounting for Nonmonetary Transactions

Portions amended or superseded by FAS-71, 109, 123, 141, 144, and 153.
Investments in Debt and Equity Securities, ch. **2**
Transfers of Financial Assets, ch. **5**
Issuer's Accounting for Equity Instruments and Related Contracts, ch. **16**

APB Opinion No. 30

Reporting the Results of Operations—
Discontinued Events and Extraordinary Items

Portions amended or superseded by FAS-4, 16, 60, 83, 97, 101, 109, 128, 141, 144, and 145.
Extinguishments of Debt, ch. **11**

AMERICAN INSTITUTE OF CERTIFIED PUBLIC ACCOUNTS (AICPA) INTERPRETATIONS (AIN-APBs)

ORIGINAL PRONOUNCEMENT	2008 *FINANCIAL INSTRUMENTS* REFERENCE

AIN-APB 18

The Equity Method of Accounting for Investments in Common Stock

Portions amended or superseded by FAS-109 and 111.
Investments in Debt and Equity Securities, ch. **2**

AIN-APB 26

Early Extinguishment of Debt

Portions amended by FAS-111.
Convertible Debt and Similar Instruments, ch. **10**
Extinguishments of Debt, ch. **11**

AICPA STATEMENTS OF POSITION (SOPs)

ORIGINAL PRONOUNCEMENT	2008 *FINANCIAL INSTRUMENTS* REFERENCE

SOP 78-9

Accounting for Investments in Real Estate Ventures

Investments in Debt and Equity Securities, ch. **2**
Loans and the Allowance for Credit Losses, ch. **3**

SOP 90-3

Definition of the Term "Substantially the Same" for Holders of Debt Instruments, as Used in Certain Audit Guides and a Statement of Position

Portions effectively amended by FAS-140.
Securities Lending Arrangements, and Other Pledges of Collateral, ch. **9**

SOP 90-7

Financial Reporting by Entities in Reorganization under the Bankruptcy Code

Extinguishments of Debt, ch. **11**

SOP 92-3

Accounting for Foreclosed Assets

Effectively superseded by FAS-144.
Offsetting Assets and Liabilities in the Balance Sheet, ch. **17**

SOP 94-6

Disclosure of Certain Significant Risks and Uncertainties

Fair Value and Other Disclosures about Financial Instruments, ch. **18**

SOP 97-1

Accounting by Participating Mortgage Loan Borrowers

Portions superseded by FAS-145.
Debt Financing, ch. **8**
Convertible Debt and Similar Instruments, ch. **10**
Extinguishments of Debt, ch. **11**

SOP 01-6

Accounting by Certain Entities (Including
Entities with Trade Receivables) That Lend to 1
or Finance the Activities of Others

Portions affected by FAS-149, FAS-150, and
FAS-156.
Generally effective for fiscal years beginning
after December 31, 2001.
Cash and Cash Equivalents, ch. **1**
Investments in Debt and Equity Securities, ch. **2**
Loans and the Allowance for Credit Losses,
ch. **3**
Servicing of Financial Assets, ch. **4**
Transfers of Financial Assets, ch. **5**
Securitizations, ch. **6**
Calculating Yields on Debt Investments, ch. **7**
Debt Financing, ch. **8**
Securities Lending Arrangements, and Other
Pledges of Collateral, ch. **9**
Issuer's Accounting for Equity Contracts and
Related Contracts, ch. **16**
Offsetting Assets and Liabilities in the Balance
Sheet, ch. **17**
Fair Value and Other Disclosures about
Financial Instruments, ch. **18**

SOP 02-2

Accounting for Derivative Instruments and
Hedging Activities by Not-for-Profit
Health Care Organizations, and Clarification of
the Performance Indicator

Hedge Accounting, ch. **14**

SOP 03-3

Accounting for Certain Loans or Debt
Securities Acquired in a Transfer

Loans and the Allowance for Credit Losses,
ch. **3**
Calculating Yields on Debt Instruments, ch. **7**

AICPA AUDIT AND ACCOUNTING GUIDES

ORIGINAL PRONOUNCEMENT

2008 *FINANCIAL INSTRUMENTS* REFERENCE

Depository and Lending Institutions:
Banks and Savings Institutions, Credit Unions,
Finance Companies, and Mortgage Companies

Portions revised by FAS-156.

Cash and Cash Equivalents, ch. **1**
Loans and the Allowance for Credit Losses,
ch. **3**
Servicing of Financial Assets, ch. **4**
Debt Financing, ch. **8**
Securities Lending Arrangements, and Other
Pledges of Collateral, ch. **9**
Convertible Debt and Similar Instruments,
ch. **10**
Issuer's Accounting for Equity Instruments
and Related Contracts, ch. **16**
Offsetting Assets and Liabilities in the Balance
Sheet, ch. **17**

Brokers and Dealers in Securities

Securities Lending Arrangements, and Other
Pledges of Collateral, ch. **9**
Offsetting Assets and Liabilities in the Balance
Sheet, ch. **17**

Auditing Derivative Instruments, Hedging
Activities, and Investments in Securities

Portions amended by FAS-138 and 149 and
interpreted by subsequent DIG Issues.
Investments in Debt and Equity Securities, ch. **2**
Convertible Debt and Similar Instruments,
ch. **10**
Introduction to Derivatives, ch. **12**
Embedded Derivatives, ch. **13**
Hedge Accounting, ch. **14**

Disclosures about Derivatives, ch. **15**
Issuer's Accounting for Equity Instruments
and Related Contracts, ch. **16**
Fair Value and Other Disclosures about
Financial Instruments, ch. **18**

Audits of Investment Companies   Investments in Debt and Equity Securities, ch. **2**
Securitizations, ch. **6**

Not-for-Profit Organizations   Loans and the Allowance for Credit Losses,
ch. **3**
Embedded Derivatives, ch. **13**
Hedge Accounting, ch. **14**

AICPA PRACTICE BULLETINS (PBs)

ORIGINAL PRONOUNCEMENT   2008 *FINANCIAL
INSTRUMENTS* REFERENCE

Practice Bulletin 1
Purpose and Scope of AcSEC Practice Bulletins
and Procedures for Their Issuance (Exhibit I)   Loans and the Allowance for Credit Losses,
ch. **3**
Calculating Yields on Debt Investments, ch. **7**

Practice Bulletin 4
Accounting for Foreign Debt/Equity Swaps   Loans and the Allowance for Credit Losses,
ch. **3**

Practice Bulletin 5
Income Recognition on Loans to Financially
Troubled Countries   Loans and the Allowance for Credit Losses,
ch. **3**

Practice Bulletin 6
Amortization of Discounts on Certain
Acquired Loans   Amended by AICPA SOP 03-3
Portions effectively superseded by FAS-114
and FAS-115.
Loans and the Allowance for Credit Losses,
ch. **3**
Calculating Yields on Debt Investments, ch. **7**

Practice Bulletin 15
Accounting by the Issuer of Surplus Notes   Issuer's Accounting for Equity Instruments
and Related Contracts, ch. **16**

AICPA TECHNICAL PRACTICE AIDS

ORIGINAL PRONOUNCEMENT   2008 *FINANCIAL
INSTRUMENTS* REFERENCE

Practice Alert 00-1
Accounting for Certain Equity Transactions   Extinguishments of Debt, ch. **11**

Practice Alert 05-1
Auditing Procedures with Respect to Variable
Interest Entities   Securitizations, ch. **6**

Practice Aid
Auditing Estimates and Other Soft Accounting
Information   Loans and the Allowance for Credit Losses,
ch. **3**

Section 1400.29
Consolidated Versus Combined Financial
Statements under FASB Interpretation No. 46(R)   Securitizations, ch. **6**

Section 2110.06
Disclosure of Cash Balances in Excess of
Federally Insured Amounts

Cash and Cash Equivalents, ch. 1

Section 2130.11
Determining Evidence of Significant Delays
and Shortfalls Relative to SOP 03-3

Calculating Yields on Debt Investments, ch. 7

Section 2130.12
Determining Evidence of Deterioration of
Credit Quality and Probability of Contractual
Payment Deficiency in Accordance with
SOP 03-3

Calculating Yields on Debt Investments, ch. 7

Section 2130.13
Nonaccrual Loans Part I: Nonaccrual Loans
under SOP 03-3

Calculating Yields on Debt Investments, ch. 7

Section 2130.14
Nonaccrual Loans Part II: Consumer Loans on
Nonaccrual Status under SOP 03-3

Calculating Yields on Debt Investments, ch. 7

Section 2130.16
Treatment of Commercial Revolving Loans
under SOP 03-3

Calculating Yields on Debt Investments, ch. 7

Section 2130.18
Loans Reacquired Under Recourse under
SOP 03-3

Calculating Yields on Debt Investments, ch. 7

Section 2130.19
Acquired Loans Where Purchase Price Is
Greater Than Fair Value under SOP 03-3

Calculating Yields on Debt Investments, ch. 7

Section 2130.20
Acquired Loans Where Purchase Price Is Less
Than Fair Value under SOP 03-3

Calculating Yields on Debt Investments, ch. 7

Section 2130.27
Income Recognition for Nonaccrual Loans
Acquired under SOP 03-3

Calculating Yields on Debt Investments, ch. 7

Section 2130.28
Estimating Cash Flows under SOP 03-3

Calculating Yields on Debt Investments, ch. 7

Section 2130.32-33
Pool Accounting under SOP 03-3

Calculating Yields on Debt Investments, ch. 7

Section 2130.34
Application to Fees Expected to Be Collected
under SOP 03-3

Calculating Yields on Debt Investments, ch. 7

Section 2130.35
Application to Cash Flows from Collateral and
Other Sources under SOP 03-3

Calculating Yields on Debt Investments, ch. 7

Section 2240.01
Balance Sheet Classification of Life Insurance
Policy Loan

Offsetting Assets and Liabilities in the Balance
Sheet, ch. 17

Section 4110.10
Costs Incurred in Shelf Registration

Issuer's Accounting for Equity Instruments
and Related Contracts, ch. 16

Section 4130.03
Warrants Reacquired

Convertible Debt and Similar Instruments,
ch. 10

AICPA STATEMENTS OF AUDITING STANDARDS (SAS)

ORIGINAL PRONOUNCEMENT	2008 *FINANCIAL INSTRUMENTS* REFERENCE
AU Section 324	
Service Organizations	Introduction to Derivatives, ch. **12**
	Embedded Derivatives, ch. **13**
AU Section 328 (a.k.a. SAS 101)	
Auditing Fair Value Measurements and Disclosures	Investments in Debt and Equity Securities, ch. **2**
	Transfers of Financial Assets, ch. **5**
	Introduction to Derivatives, ch. **12**
	Fair Value and Other Disclosures about Financial Instruments, ch. **18**
AU Section 332 (a.k.a. SAS 92)	
Auditing Derivative Instruments, Hedging Activities, and Investments in Securities	Investments in Debt and Equity Securities, ch. **2**
	Loans and the Allowance for Credit Losses, ch. **3**
	Servicing of Financial Assets, ch. **4**
	Transfers of Financial Assets, ch. **5**
	Securitizations, ch. **6**
	Securities Lending Arrangements, and Other Pledges of Collateral, ch. **9**
	Introduction to Derivatives, ch. **12**
	Embedded Derivatives, ch. **13**
	Hedge Accounting, ch. **14**
AU Section 332, Interpretation 1	
Auditing Investments in Securities Where a Readily Determinable Fair Value Does Not Exist	Investments in Debt and Equity Securities, ch. **2**
AU Section 334	
Related Parties	Securitizations, ch. **6**
	Introduction to Derivatives, ch. **12**
AU Section 336 (and 9336)	
Using the Work of a Specialist	Loans and the Allowance for Credit Losses, ch. **3**
	Servicing of Financial Assets, ch. **4**
	Transfers of Financial Assets, ch. **5**
	Securitizations, ch. **6**
	Securities Lending Arrangements, and Other Pledges of Collateral, ch. **9**
AU Section 342	
Auditing Accounting Estimates	Loans and the Allowance for Credit Losses, ch. **3**
	Servicing of Financial Assets, ch. **4**
	Transfers of Financial Assets, ch. **5**
	Securitizations, ch. **6**
	Securities Lending Arrangements, and Other Pledges of Collateral, ch. **9**
	Introduction to Derivatives, ch. **12**
	Embedded Derivatives, ch. **13**
AU Section 380 (a.k.a. SAS 61)	
Communication with Audit Committees	Loans and the Allowance for Credit Losses, ch. **3**

AU Section 560

Subsequent Events

Loans and the Allowance for Credit Losses, ch. **3**

FINANCIAL ACCOUNTING STANDARDS BOARD STATEMENTS (FASs)

ORIGINAL PRONOUNCEMENT	2008 *FINANCIAL INSTRUMENTS* REFERENCE

FASB Statement No. 4

Reporting Gains and Losses from
Extinguishment of Debt

Superseded by FAS-145.

FASB Statement No. 5

Accounting for Contingencies

Portions amended or superseded by FAS-11, 60, 71, 87, 111, 112, 113, 114, and 123.

Cash and Cash Equivalents, ch. **1**

Loans and the Allowance for Credit Losses, ch. **3**

Servicing of Financial Assets, ch. **4**

Transfers of Financial Assets, ch. **5**

Securitizations, ch. **6**

Debt Financing, ch. **8**

Extinguishments of Debt, ch. **11**

Issuer's Accounting for Equity Instruments and Related Contracts, ch. **16**

Fair Value and Other Disclosures about Financial Instruments, ch. **18**

FASB Statement No. 6

Classification of Short-Term Obligations
Expected to Be Refinanced

Debt Financing, ch. **8**

FASB Statement No. 15

Accounting by Debtors and Creditors for
Troubled Debt Restructurings

Portions amended or superseded by FAS-71, 111, 114, 135, 141, 144, 145, and 149.

Loans and the Allowance for Credit Losses, ch. **3**

Calculating Yields on Debt Investments, ch. **7**

Securities Lending Arrangements, and Other Pledges of Collateral, ch. **9**

Extinguishments of Debt, ch. **11**

Fair Value and Other Disclosures about Financial Instruments, ch. **18**

FASB Statement No. 19

Financial Accounting and Reporting by Oil and
Gas Producing Companies

Portions amended or superseded by FAS-25, 69, 71, 109, 143, 144, and 145.

Embedded Derivatives, ch. **13**

FASB Statement No. 34

Capitalization of Interest Cost

Portions amended or superseded by FAS-42, 58, 62, 71, and 144.

Debt Financing, ch. **8**

Hedge Accounting, ch. **14**

FASB Statement No. 47

Disclosure of Long-Term Obligations

Portions superseded by FAS-129.

Debt Financing, ch. **8**

Disclosures about Derivatives, ch. **15**

FASB Statement No. 52

Foreign Currency Translation

Portions amended and superseded by FAS-109, 130, 133, 135, and 142.

Cash and Cash Equivalents, ch. **1**

Debt Financing, ch. **8**

Embedded Derivatives, ch. **13**

Hedge Accounting, ch. **14**

Disclosures about Derivatives, ch. **15**

FASB Statement No. 57

Related Party Disclosures

Portions amended by FAS-95 and 109.

Loans and the Allowance for Credit Losses, ch. **3**

FASB Statement No. 58

Capitalization of Interest Cost in Financial Statements That Include Investments Accounted for by the Equity Method

See FAS-34.

FASB Statement No. 60

Accounting and Reporting by Insurance Enterprises

Portions amended or superseded by FAS-91, 97, 109, 113, 114, 115, 120, 124, 133, 135, 144, 145, and 149.

Investments in Debt and Equity Securities, ch. **2**

Introduction to Derivatives, ch. **12**

Hedge Accounting, ch. **14**

FASB Statement No. 64

Extinguishments of Debt Made to Satisfy Sinking-Fund Requirements

Superseded by FAS-145.

FASB Statement No. 65

Accounting for Certain Mortgage Banking Activities

Portions amended or superseded by FAS-91, 115, 124, 133, 134, 135, 140, and 149.

Investments in Debt and Equity Securities, ch. **2**

Loans and the Allowance for Credit Losses, ch. **3**

Servicing of Financial Assets, ch. **4**

Transfers of Financial Assets, ch. **5**

Securitizations, ch. **6**

Calculating Yields on Debt Investments, ch. **7**

Introduction to Derivatives, ch. **12**

FASB Statement No. 71

Accounting for the Effects of Certain Types of Regulation

Portions amended or superseded by FAS-90, 92, 109, 135, 142, and 144.

Extinguishments of Debt, ch. **11**

FASB Statement No. 76

Extinguishment of Debt

Superseded by FAS-140.

FASB Statement No. 77

Reporting by Transferors for Transfers of Receivables with Recourse

Superseded by FAS-140.

FASB Statement No. 78

Classification of Obligations That Are Callable by the Creditor

Debt Financing, ch. **8**

FASB Statement No. 80

Accounting for Futures Contracts

Superseded by FAS-133.

FASB Statement No. 84

Classification of Obligations That Are Callable
by the Creditor

Convertible Debt and Similar Instruments,
ch. **10**

Extinguishments of Debt, ch. **11**

FASB Statement No. 91

Accounting for Nonrefundable Fees and Costs
Associated with Originating or Acquiring
Loans and Initial Direct Costs of Leases

Portions amended or superseded by FAS-98,
114, 115, 124, and 149.

Investments in Debt and Equity Securities, ch. **2**

Loans and the Allowance for Credit Losses,
ch. **3**

Servicing of Financial Assets, ch. **4**

Securitizations, ch. **6**

Calculating Yields on Debt Investments, ch. **7**

Introduction to Derivatives, ch. **12**

FASB Statement No. 94

Consolidation of all Majority-Owned
Subsidiaries

Portions amended or superseded by FAS 131
and 144. Also see FIN-46.

Investments in Debt and Equity Securities, ch. **2**

Securitizations, ch. **6**

FASB Statement No. 95

Statement of Cash Flows

Portions amended by FAS-102, 104, 117, 133,
141, 145, and 149.

Cash and Cash Equivalents, ch. **1**

Investments in Debt and Equity Securities, ch. **2**

Loans and the Allowance for Credit Losses, ch. **3**

Servicing of Financial Assets, ch. **4**

Transfers of Financial Assets, ch. **5**

Securitizations, ch. **6**

Calculating Yields on Debt Investments, ch. **7**

Debt Financing, ch. **8**

Securities Lending Arrangements, and
Other Pledges of Collateral, ch. **9**

Convertible Debt and Similar Instruments, ch. **10**

Extinguishments of Debt, ch. **11**

Introduction to Derivatives, ch. **12**

Hedge Accounting, ch. **14**

Disclosures about Derivatives, ch. **15**

Issuer's Accounting for Equity Instruments and
Related Contracts, ch. **16**

FASB Statement No. 97

Accounting by Insurance Companies for
Certain Long-Duration Contracts and Realized
Gains & Losses on Investment Sales

Portions amended or superseded by FAS-113,
115, and 120.

Introduction to Derivatives, ch. **12**

FASB Statement No. 102

Statement of Cash Flows—Exemption of
Certain Enterprises and Classification of Cash
Flows from Certain Securities Acquired for
Resale

Portions amended by FAS-115, 135, and 145.

Cash and Cash Equivalents, ch. **1**

Transfers of Financial Assets, ch. **5**

Securitizations, ch. **6**

FASB Statement No. 104

Statement of Cash Flows—Net Reporting of Certain Cash Receipts and Cash Payments and Cash Payments and Classification of Cash Flows from Hedging Transactions

Debt Financing, ch. **8**
Cash and Cash Equivalents, ch. **1**

FASB Statement No. 105

Disclosure of Information about Financial Instruments with Off-Balance-Sheet Risk and Financial Instruments with Concentrations of Credit Risk

Superseded by FAS-133.

FASB Statement No. 107

Disclosures about the Fair Value of Financial Instruments

Portions amended or superseded by FAS-112, 123, 126, 133, and 140.

Debt Financing, ch. **8**

Introduction to Derivatives, ch. **12**

Embedded Derivatives, ch. **13**

Disclosures about Derivatives, ch. **15**

Offsetting Assets and Liabilities in the Balance Sheet, ch. **17**

Fair Value and Other Disclosures about Financial Instruments, ch. **18**

FASB Statement No. 109

Accounting for Income Taxes

Portions amended or superseded by FAS-115, 123, 130, 135, and 141.

Investments in Debt and Equity Securities, ch. **2**

Loans and the Allowance for Credit Losses, ch. **3**

Transfers of Financial Assets, ch. **5**

Securities Lending Arrangements, and Other Pledges of Collateral, ch. **9**

Convertible Debt and Similar Instruments, ch. **10**

Introduction to Derivatives, ch. **12**

Issuer's Accounting for Equity Instruments and Related Contracts, ch. **16**

FASB Statement No. 113

Accounting and Reporting for Reinsurance of Short-Duration and Long-Duration Contracts

Portions amended by FAS-120 and 133.
Introduction to Derivatives, ch. **12**

Fair Value and Other Disclosures about Financial Instruments, ch. **18**

FASB Statement No. 114

Accounting by Creditors for Impairment of a Loan

Portions amended or superseded by FAS-118.

Loans and the Allowance for Credit Losses, ch. **3**

Transfers of Financial Assets, ch. **5**

Calculating Yields on Debt Investments, ch. **7**

Securities Lending Arrangements, and Other Pledges of Collateral, ch. **9**

Disclosures about Derivatives, ch. **15**

Fair Value and Other Disclosures about Financial Instruments, ch. **18**

FASB Statement No. 115

Accounting for Certain Investments in
Debt and Equity Securities

Portions amended or superseded by FAS-124, 130, 133, 134, 135, 140, 144, and 145.

Cash and Cash Equivalents, ch. **1**

Investments in Debt and Equity Securities, ch. **2**

Loans and the Allowance for Credit Losses, ch. **3**

Servicing of Financial Assets, ch. **4**

Transfers of Financial Assets, ch. **5**

Securitizations, ch. **6**

Calculating Yields on Debt Investments, ch. **7**

Securities Lending Arrangements, and Other Pledges of Collateral, ch. **9**

Embedded Derivatives, ch. **13**

Hedge Accounting, ch. **14**

Fair Value and Other Disclosures about Financial Instruments, ch. **18**

FASB Statement No. 117

Financial Statements of Not-for-Profit
Organizations

Portions amended or superseded by FAS-124, 144, and 149.

Cash and Cash Equivalents, ch. **1**

Calculating Yields on Debt Investments, ch. **7**

FASB Statement No. 118

Accounting by Creditors for Impairment of a
Loan—Income Recognition and Disclosures

Loans and the Allowance for Credit Losses, ch. **3**

Calculating Yields on Debt Investments, ch. **7**

Disclosures about Derivatives, ch. **15**

FASB Statement No. 119

Disclosure about Derivative Financial
Instruments and Fair Value of Financial
Instruments

Superseded by FAS-133.

FASB Statement No. 123(R)

Share-Based Payment

Hedge Accounting ch. **14**

FASB Statement No. 124

Accounting for Certain Investments Held by
Not-for-Profit Organizations

Portions amended by FAS-133.

Investments in Debt and Equity Securities, ch. **2**

Fair Value and Other Disclosures about Financial Instruments, ch. **18**

FASB Statement No. 125

Accounting for Transfers and Servicing of
Financial Assets and Extinguishments of
Liabilities

Superseded by FAS-140.

FASB Statement No. 126

Exemption from Certain Required Disclosures
about Financial Instruments for Certain Nonpublic Entities

Portions amended by FAS-133 and 149.

Fair Value and Other Disclosures about Financial Instruments, ch. **18**

FASB Statement No. 127

Deferral of the Effective Date of Certain
Provisions of FASB Statement No. 125

Superseded by FAS-140.

FASB Statement No. 128
Earnings per Share

Portions amended by FAS-135, 141, 145, and 150.

Convertible Debt and Similar Instruments, ch. **10**

Issuer's Accounting for Equity Instruments and Related Contracts, ch. **16**

FASB Statement No. 129
Disclosure of Information about Capital Structure

Convertible Debt and Similar Instruments, ch. **10**

Issuer's Accounting for Equity Instruments and Related Contracts, ch. **16**

FASB Statement No. 130
Reporting Comprehensive Income

Portions amended by FAS-135.

Investments in Debt and Equity Securities, ch. **2**

Disclosures about Derivatives, ch. **15**

FASB Statement No. 133
Accounting for Derivative Instruments and Hedging Activities

Portions amended by FAS-123(R), 137, 138, 140, 141, 149, 150, and 155.

Cash and Cash Equivalents, ch. **1**

Investments in Debt and Equity Securities, ch. **2**

Loans and the Allowance for Credit Losses, ch. **3**

Servicing of Financial Assets, ch. **4**

Transfers of Financial Assets, ch. **5**

Securitizations, ch. **6**

Calculating Yields on Debt Investments, ch. **7**

Debt Financing, ch. **8**

Securities Lending Arrangements, and Other Pledges of Collateral, ch. **9**

Convertible Debt and Similar Instruments, ch. **10**

Introduction to Derivatives, ch. **12**

Embedded Derivatives, ch. **13**

Hedge Accounting, ch. **14**

Disclosures about Derivatives, ch. **15**

Issuer's Accounting for Equity Instruments and Related Contracts, ch. **16**

Offsetting Assets and Liabilities in the Balance Sheet, ch. **17**

Fair Value and Other Disclosures about Financial Instruments, ch. **18**

FASB Statement No. 134
Accounting for Mortgage-Backed Securities Retained after the Securitization of Mortgage Loans Held for Sale by a Mortgage Banking Enterprise

Investments in Debt and Equity Securities, ch. **2**

Loans and the Allowance for Credit Losses, ch. **3**

Securitizations, ch. **6**

FASB Statement No. 137
Accounting for Derivative Instruments and Hedging Activities—Deferral of the Effective Date of FASB Statement No. 133 (an Amendment of FASB Statement No. 133)

See FAS-133.

FASB Statement No. 138

Accounting for Certain Derivative Instruments
and Certain Hedging Activities (an
Amendment of FASB Statement No. 133)   See FAS-133.

FASB Statement No. 140

Accounting for Transfers and Servicing of
Financial Assets and Extinguishments of Debt   Portions amended or superseded by FTB 01-1
and FAS-155 and 156.

Cash and Cash Equivalents, ch. **1**

Investments in Debt and Equity Securities, ch. **2**

Loans and the Allowance for Credit Losses,
ch. **3**

Servicing of Financial Assets, ch. **4**

Transfers of Financial Assets, ch. **5**

Securitizations, ch. **6**

Calculating Yields on Debt Investments, ch. **7**

Debt Financing, ch. **8**

Securities Lending Arrangements, and Other
Assets Pledged as Collateral, ch. **9**

Extinguishments of Debt, ch. **11**

Introduction to Derivatives, ch. **12**

Embedded Derivatives, ch. **13**

Issuer's Accounting for Equity Instruments
and Related Contracts, ch. **16**

Offsetting Assets and Liabilities in the Balance
Sheet, ch. **17**

Fair Value and Other Disclosures about
Financial Instruments, ch. **18**

FASB Statement No. 141

Business Combinations   Portions amended by FAS-144, 145, and 147.

Securitizations, ch. **6**

FASB Statement No. 142

Goodwill and Other Intangible Assets   Calculating Yields on Debt Investments, ch. **7**

FASB Statement No. 144

Accounting for the Impairment or Disposal of
Long-Lived Assets   Extinguishments of Debt, ch. **11**

FASB Statement No. 145

Rescission of FASB Statements No. 4, 44, and
64, Amendment of FASB Statement No. 13, and   Extinguishments of Debt, ch. **11**
Technical Corrections

FASB Statement No. 149

Amendment of Statement 133 on Derivative
Instruments and Hedging Activities   See FAS-133.

FASB Statement No. 150

Accounting for Certain Financial Instruments
with Characteristics of Both Liabilities and
Equity   Securitizations, ch. **6**

Convertible Debt and Similar Instruments,
ch. **10**

Introduction to Derivatives, ch. **12**

Embedded Derivatives, ch. **13**

Issuer's Accounting for Equity Instruments
and Related Contracts, ch. **16**

FASB Statement No. 153
Exchanges of Nonmonetary Assets, an
Amendment of APB Opinion No. 29   Investments in Debt and Equity Securities, ch. **2**

FASB Statement No. 154
Accounting Changes and Error Corrections—
A Replacement of APB Opinion No. 20 and
FASB Statement No. 3   Servicing of Financial Assets, ch. **4**

FASB Statement No. 155
Accounting for Certain Hybrid Financial
Instruments—An Amendment of FASB
Statements No. 133 and 140   Embedded Derivatives, ch. **13**
                                                   Transfers of Financial Assets, ch. **5**

FASB Statement No. 156
Accounting for Servicing of Financial
Assets—An Amendment of FASB Statement
No. 140   Servicing of Financial Assets, ch. **4**
                                                   Transfers of Financial Assets, ch. **5**
                                                   Securitizations, ch. **6**

FASB Statement No. 157
Fair Value Measurements   Investments in Debt and Equity Securities, ch. **2**
                                                   Loans and the Allowance for Credit Losses, ch. **3**
                                                   Servicing of Financial Assets, ch. **4**
                                                   Transfers of Financial Assets, ch. **5**
                                                   Securitizations, ch. **6**
                                                   Calculating Yields on Debt Investments, ch. **7**
                                                   Debt Financing, ch. **8**
                                                   Convertible Debt, ch. **10**
                                                   Introduction to Derivatives, ch. **12**
                                                   Embedded Derivatives, ch. **13**
                                                   Equity Instruments and Related Contracts, ch. **16**
                                                   Fair Value Measurements, Fair Value
                                                       Disclosures, and Other Financial Instrument
                                                       Disclosures, ch. **18**

FASB Statement No. 159
The Fair Value Option for Financial Assets
and Financial Liabilities   Cash and Cash Equivalents, ch. **1**
                                                   Investments in Debt and Equity Securities, ch. **2**
                                                   Loans and the Allowance for Credit Losses, ch. **3**
                                                   Servicing of Financial Assets, ch. **4**
                                                   Transfers of Financial Assets, ch. **5**
                                                   Securitizations, ch. **6**
                                                   Calculating Yields on Debt Investments, ch. **7**
                                                   Debt Financing, ch. **8**
                                                   Convertible Debt, ch. **10**
                                                   Introduction to Derivatives, ch. **12**
                                                   Embedded Derivatives, ch. **13**
                                                   Hedge Accounting, ch. **14**
                                                   Equity Instruments and Related Contracts, ch. **16**
                                                   Fair Value Measurements, Fair Value
                                                       Disclosures, and Other Financial Instrument
                                                       Disclosures, ch. **18**
                                                   The Fair Value Option for Financial
                                                       Instruments, ch. **19**

FINANCIAL ACCOUNTING STANDARDS
BOARD INTERPRETATIONS (FINs)

ORIGINAL PRONOUNCEMENT	2008 *FINANCIAL INSTRUMENTS* REFERENCE
FASB Interpretation No. 8	
Classification of a Short-Term Obligation Repaid Prior to Being Replaced by a Long-Term Security	Debt Financing, ch. **8**
FASB Interpretation No. 14	
Reasonable Estimation of the Amount of a Loss	Loans and the Allowance for Credit Losses, ch. **3**
FASB Interpretation No. 28	
Accounting for Stock Appreciation Rights and Other Variable Stock Option or Award Plans	Superseded by FAS-123(R)
FASB Interpretation No. 34	
Disclosure of Indirect Guarantees of Indebtedness of Others	Superseded by FIN-45.
FASB Interpretation No. 35	
Criteria for Applying the Equity Method of Accounting for Investments in Common Stock	Investments in Debt and Equity Securities, ch. **2**
FASB Interpretation No. 39	
Offsetting of Amounts Related to Certain Contracts	Portions amended by FAS-113, 135, and 144.
	Cash and Cash Equivalents, ch. **1**
	Transfers of Financial Assets, ch. **5**
	Securitizations, ch. **6**
	Securities Lending Arrangements, and Other Assets Pledged as Collateral, ch. **9**
	Introduction to Derivatives, ch. **12**
	Hedge Accounting, ch. **14**
	Offsetting Assets and Liabilities in the Balance Sheet, ch. **17**
	Fair Value and Other Disclosures about Financial Instruments, ch. **18**
FASB Interpretation No. 41	
Offsetting of Amounts Related to Certain Repurchase and Reverse Repurchase Agreements	Securities Lending Arrangements, and Other Assets Pledged as Collateral, ch. **9**
	Offsetting Assets and Liabilities in the Balance Sheet, ch. **17**
	Fair Value and Other Disclosures about Financial Instruments, ch. **18**
FASB Interpretation No. 45	
Guarantor's Accounting and Disclosure Requirements for Guarantees, Including Indirect Guarantees of Indebtedness of Others	Loans and the Allowance for Credit Losses, ch. **3**
	Transfers of Financial Assets, ch. **5**
	Securitizations, ch.**6**
	Debt Financing, ch. **8**
	Extinguishments of Debt, ch. **11**

FASB Interpretation No. 46(R)
Consolidation of Variable Interest Entities

Portions amended by FAS-123(R).
Investments in Debt and Equity Securities, ch. 2
Securitizations, ch. 6

FASB TECHNICAL BULLETINS (FTBs)

ORIGINAL PRONOUNCEMENT

2008 *FINANCIAL INSTRUMENTS REFERENCE*

FASB Technical Bulletin No. 79-3
Subjective Acceleration Clauses in Long-Term
Debt Agreements

Debt Financing, ch. 8

FASB Technical Bulletin No. 80-1
Early Extinguishment of Debt through
Exchange for Common or Preferred Stock

Portions amended by FAS-111 and 145.
Convertible Debt and Similar Instruments, ch. 10
Extinguishments of Debt, ch. 11

FASB Technical Bulletin No. 80-2
Classification of Debt Restructurings by
Debtors and Creditors

Extinguishments of Debt, ch. 11

FASB Technical Bulletin No. 81-6
Applicability of Statement 15 to Debtors in
Bankruptcy Situations

Loans and the Allowance for Credit Losses, ch. 3
Extinguishments of Debt, ch. 11

FASB Technical Bulletin No. 85-4
Accounting for Purchases of Life Insurance

Introduction to Derivatives, ch. 12

FASB Technical Bulletin No. 85-6
Accounting for a Purchase of Treasury Shares
and Costs Incurred in Defending against a
Takeover Attempt

Issuer's Accounting for Equity Instruments
and Related Contracts, ch. 16

FASB Technical Bulletin No. 86-2
Accounting for an Interest in the Residual
Value of a Leased Asset

Portions superseded by FAS-140.
Offsetting Assets and Liabilities in the Balance
Sheet, ch. 17

FASB Technical Bulletin No. 87-3
Accounting for Mortgage Servicing Fees
and Rights

Portions superseded by FAS-140.
Servicing of Financial Assets, ch. 4

FASB Technical Bulletin No. 94-1
Application of Statement 115 to Debt Securities
Restructured in a Troubled Debt Restructuring

Investments in Debt and Equity Securities, ch. 2
Securitizations, ch. 6

FASB Technical Bulletin No. 01-1
Effective Date for Certain Financial Institutions
of Certain Provisions of Statement 140 Related
to the Isolation of Transferred Financial Assets

Securitizations, ch. 6

FASB STAFF POSITIONS (FSPs)

ORIGINAL PRONOUNCEMENT	2008 *FINANCIAL INSTRUMENTS REFERENCE*
FSP FAS 115-1 and FAS 124-1 The Meaning of Other-than-Temporary Impairment and Its Application to Certain Investments	Investments in Debt and Equity Securities, ch. **2**
FSP FAS 123(R)-1 Classification and Measurement of Freestanding Financial Instruments Originally Issued in Exchange for Employee Services under FASB Statement No. 123(R)	Introduction to Derivatives, ch. **12**
FSP FAS 126-1 Applicability of Certain Disclosure and Interim Reporting Requirements for Obligors of Conduit Debt Securities	Fair Value Measurements, Fair Value Disclosures, and Other Financial Instrument Disclosures, ch. **18**
FSP FAS 129-1 Disclosure Requirements under FASB Statement No. 129, *Disclosure of Information about Capital Structure*, Relating to Contingently Convertible Financial Instruments	Convertible Debt and Similar Instruments, ch. **10**
FSP FAS 140-1 Accounting for Accrued Interest Receivable Related to Securitized and Sold Receivables under Statement 140	Transfers of Financial Assets, ch. **5** Securitizations, ch. **6**
FSP FAS 140-2 Clarification of the Application of Paragraphs 40(b) and 40(c) of FASB Statement No. 140	Securitizations, ch. **6**
FSP FAS 144-1 Determination of Cost Basis for Foreclosed Assets under FASB Statement No. 15, *Accounting by Debtors and Creditors for Troubled Debt Restructurings*, and the Measurement of Cumulative Losses Previously Recognized under Paragraph 37 of FASB Statement No. 144, *Accounting for the Impairment or Disposal of Long-Lived Assets*	Loans and the Allowance for Credit Losses, ch. **3**
FSP FAS 150-1 Issuer's Accounting for Freestanding Financial Instruments Composed of More Than One Option or Forward Contract Embodying Obligations under FASB Statement No. 150, *Accounting for Certain Financial Instruments with Characteristics of Both Liabilities and Equity*	Issuer's Accounting for Equity Instruments and Related Contracts, ch. **16**

FSP FAS 150-2

Accounting for Mandatorily Redeemable Shares Requiring Redemption by Payment of an Amount that Differs from the Book Value of Those Shares, under FASB Statement No. 150, *Accounting for Certain Financial Instruments with Characteristics of Both Liabilities and Equity*

Issuer's Accounting for Equity Instruments and Related Contracts, ch. **16**

FSP FAS 150-3

Effective Date, Disclosures, and Transition for Mandatorily Redeemable Financial Instruments of Certain Nonpublic Entities and Certain Mandatorily Redeemable Noncontrolling Interests under FASB Statement No. 150, *Accounting for Certain Financial Instruments with Characteristics of Both Liabilities and Equity*

Issuer's Accounting for Equity Instruments and Related Contracts, ch. **16**

FSP FAS 150-5

Issuer's Accounting under FASB Statement No. 150 for Freestanding Warrants and Other Similar Instruments on Shares That Are Redeemable

Issuer's Accounting for Equity Instruments and Related Contracts, ch. **16**

FSP FTB 85-4-1

Accounting for Life Settlement Contracts by Third Party Investors

Introduction to Derivatives Accounting, ch. **12**

FSP FIN 39-1

Amendment of FASB Interpretation No. 39

Offsetting Assets and Liabilities, ch. **17**

FSP FIN 45-1

Accounting for Intellectual Property Infringement Indemnifications under FASB Interpretation No. 45, *Guarantor's Accounting and Disclosure Requirements for Guarantees, Including Indirect Guarantees of Indebtedness of Others*

Debt Financing, ch. **8**

FSP FIN 45-2

Whether FASB Interpretation No. 45, *Guarantor's Accounting and Disclosure Requirements for Guarantees, Including Indirect Guarantees of Indebtedness of Others*, Provides Support for Subsequently Accounting for a Guarantor's Liability at Fair Value

Debt Financing, ch. **8**

FSP FIN 45-3

Application of FIN-45 to Minimum Revenue Guarantees Granted to a Business or Its Owners

Debt Financing, ch. **8**

FSP FIN 46(R)-1

Reporting Variable Interests in Specified Assets of Variable Interest Entities under Paragraph 13 of FASB Interpretation No. 46 (revised December 2003), *Consolidation of Variable Interest Entities*

Securitizations, ch. **6**

FSP FIN 46(R)-2

Calculation of Expected Losses under FASB Interpretation No. 46 (revised December 2003), *Consolidation of Variable Interest Entities*

Securitizations, ch. **6**

FSP FIN 46(R)-3

Evaluating Whether as a Group the Holders of
the Equity Investment at Risk Lack the Direct or
Indirect Ability to Make Decisions about an
Entity's Activities through Voting Rights or
Similar Rights under FASB Interpretation No.
46, *Consolidation of Variable Interest Entities*   Securitizations, ch. **6**

FSP FIN 46(R)-4

Technical Correction of FASB Interpretation
No. 46 (revised December 2003), Consolidation
of Variable Interest Entities, Relating to Its
Effects on Question 12 of EITF Issue 96-21,
"Implementation Issues in Accounting for
Leasing Transactions Involving Special-
Purpose Entities."   Securitizations, ch. **6**

FSP FIN 46(R)-5

Implicit Variable Interests under FASB Inter-
pretation No. 46 (revised December 2003)   Securitizations, ch. **6**

FSP FIN 46(R)-6

Determining the Variability to Be Considered
in Applying FASB Interpretation No. 46(R)   Securitizations, ch. **6**

FSP FIN 46(R)-7

Application of FASB Interpretation No. 46(R)
to Investment Companies   Securitizations, ch. **6**

FSP EITF 00-19-1

Application of EITF Issue No. 00-19-1 to
Freestanding Financial Instruments Originally
Issued as Employee Compensation   Issuer's Accounting for Equity Instruments
and Related Contracts, ch. **16**

FSP EITF 00-19-2

Accounting for Registration Payment
Arrangements   Debt Financing, ch. **8**
      Convertible Debt, ch. **10**
      Introduction to Derivatives, ch. **12**
      Equity Instruments and Related Contracts, ch. **16**

FSP EITF 03-1-1

Effective Date of Paragraphs 10-20 of EITF 03-1,
"The Meaning of Other-Than-Temporary
Impairment and Its Application to Certain   Superseded by FSP FAS 115-1 and FAS 124-1.
Investments"

FSP SOP 94-6-1

Terms of Loan Products That May Give Rise to
a Concentration of Credit Risk   Cash and Cash Equivalents, ch. **1**
      Servicing of Financial Assets, ch. **4**
      Fair Value and Other Disclosures, ch. **18**

FSP AAG INV-1 and SOP 94-4-1

Reporting of Fully Benefit-Responsive
Investment Contracts Held by Certain
Investment Companies Subject to the AICPA
Investment Company Guide and
Defined-Contribution Health and Welfare
and Pension Plans   Introduction to Derivatives Accounting, ch. **12**

INTERPRETATIONS OF THE INDEPENDENCE
STANDARDS BOARD

ORIGINAL PRONOUNCEMENT | 2008 *FINANCIAL INSTRUMENTS* REFERENCE

Interpretation 99-1
FAS-133 Assistance

Transfers of Financial Assets, ch. **5**

Securitizations, ch. **6**

Introduction to Derivatives, ch. **12**
Embedded Derivatives, ch. **13**
Fair Value and Other Disclosures about
  Financial Instruments, ch. **18**

CONSENSUS POSITIONS OF THE EMERGING
ISSUES TASK FORCE (EITFS)[2]

ORIGINAL PRONOUNCEMENT | 2008 *FINANCIAL INSTRUMENTS* REFERENCE

EITF Issue 84-19
Mortgage Loan Payment Modifications

Loans and the Allowance for Credit Losses,
  ch. **3**

EITF Issue 84-20
GNMA Dollar Rolls

Partially resolved by FAS-140 and affected by
  FAS-133.
Securities Lending Arrangements, and Other
  Pledges of Collateral, ch. **9**

EITF Issue 85-1
Classifying Notes Received for Capital Stock

Issuer's Accounting for Equity Instruments
  and Related Contracts, ch. **16**

EITF Issue 85-9
Revenue Recognition on Options to Purchase
Stock of Another Entity

Affected by FAS-133 and FAS-155.
Convertible Debt and Similar Instruments,
  ch. **10**

EITF Issue 85-13
Sale of Mortgage Service Rights on Mortgages
Owned by Others

Servicing of Financial Assets, ch. **4**

EITF Issue 85-17
Accrued Interest upon Conversion of
Convertible Debt

Convertible Debt and Similar Instruments,
  ch. **10**
Extinguishments of Debt, ch. **11**

EITF Issue 85-20
Recognition of Fees for Guaranteeing a Loan

Affected by FAS-133 and FIN-45.
Debt Financing, ch. **8**
Extinguishments of Debt, ch. **11**

---

[2]   This cross-reference does not include some older EITF Issues that have been completely nullifled or resolved by subsequent literature. Note that transactions that were "grandfathered" in transition to a new standard could still be subject to previous GAAP. Such circumstances are discussed in the relevant chapters.

EITF Issue 85-29
Convertible Bonds with a "Premium Put"

Partially nullified by FAS-133. Affected by FAS-155.
Convertible Debt and Similar Instruments, ch. **10**

EITF Issue 85-40
Sales of Marketable Securities with Put Arrangements

Partially nullified by FAS-140.
Transfers of Financial Assets, ch. **5**

EITF Issue 85-44
Differences between Loan Loss Allowances for GAAP and RAP

Loans and the Allowance for Credit Losses, ch. **3**

EITF Issue 86-5
Classifying Demand Notes with Repayment Terms

Debt Financing, ch. **8**

EITF Issue 86-8
Sale of Bad Debt Recovery Rights

Loans and the Allowance for Credit Losses, ch. **3**

EITF Issue 86-15
Increasing-Rate Debt

Partially nullified by FAS-133. Affected by FAS-155.
Debt Financing, ch. **8**

EITF Issue 86-18
Debtor's Accounting for a Modification of Debt Terms

Carried forward as part of EITF 96-19.
Extinguishments of Debt, ch. **11**
Offsetting Assets and Liabilities in the Balance Sheet, ch. **17**

EITF Issue 86-28
Accounting Implications of Indexed Debt Instruments

Partially nullified by FAS-133. Affected by FAS-155.
Debt Financing, ch. **8**
Convertible Debt and Similar Instruments, ch. **10**
Embedded Derivatives, ch. **13**

EITF Issue 86-30
Classification of Obligations When a Violation Is Waived by the Creditor

Debt Financing, ch. **8**

EITF Issue 86-32
Early Extinguishment of a Subsidiary's Mandatorily Redeemable Preferred Stock

Affected by SOP 01-6 and FAS-150.
Issuer's Accounting for Equity Instruments and Related Contracts, ch. **16**

EITF Issue 86-35
Debentures with Detachable Stock Purchase Warrants

See EITF Issue 96-13.

EITF Issue 86-36
Invasion of a Defeasance Trust

Extinguishments of Debt, ch. **11**

EITF Issue 86-40
Investments in Open-End Mutual Funds That Invest in U.S. Government Securities

Partially nullified by FAS-115.
Investments in Debt and Equity Securities, ch. **2**

EITF Issue 86-45

Imputation of Dividends on Preferred Stock Redeemable at the Issuer's Option with Initial Below-Market Dividend Rate

Affected by FAS-150.

Issuer's Accounting for Equity Instruments and Related Contracts, ch. **16**

EITF Issue 87-18

Use of Zero Coupon Bonds in a Troubled Debt Restructuring

Partially nullified by FAS-114 and 144; affected by FAS-140.

Loans and the Allowance for Credit Losses, ch. **3**

EITF Issue 87-19

Substituted Debtors in a Troubled Debt Restructuring

Loans and the Allowance for Credit Losses, ch. **3**

EITF Issue 87-34

Sale of Mortgage Servicing Rights with a Sub-servicing Agreement

Servicing of Financial Assets, ch. **4**

EITF Issue 88-9

Put Warrants

Nullified by FAS-150.

EITF Issue 88-15

Classification of Subsidiary's Loan Payable in Consolidated Balance Sheet When Subsidiary's and Parent's Fiscal Years Differ

Debt Financing, ch. **8**

EITF Issue 88-18

Sales of Future Revenues

Transfers of Financial Assets, ch. **5**

Debt Financing, ch. **8**

EITF Issue 88-20

Difference between Initial Investment and Principal Amount of Loans in a Purchased Credit Card Portfolio

Affected by FAS-140 and 142.

Calculating Yields on Debt Investments, ch. **7**

EITF Issue 88-22

Securitization of Credit Card and Other Portfolios

Portions nullified by FAS-140.

Securitizations, ch. **6**

EITF Issue 89-14

Valuation of Repossessed Real Estate

Loans and the Allowance for Credit Losses, ch. **3**

EITF Issue 90-15

Impact of Nonsubstantive Lessors, Residual Value Guarantees, and Other Provisions in Leasing Transactions

Nullified by FIN-45.

EITF Issue 90-19

Convertible Bonds with Issuer Option to Settle for Cash upon Conversion

Partially nullified by FAS-128 and 133. Affected by FAS-155.

Convertible Debt and Similar Instruments, ch. **10**

Embedded Derivatives, ch. **13**

EITF Issue 90-21
Balance Sheet Treatment of a Sale of Mortgage
Servicing Rights with a Subservicing
Agreement

Servicing of Financial Assets, ch. 4

EITF Issue 91-2
Debtor's Accounting for Forfeiture of Real
Estate Subject to a Nonrecourse Mortgage

Extinguishments of Debt, ch. **11**

EITF Issue 91-5
Nonmonetary Exchange of Cost-Method
Investments

Partially amended and nullified by FAS-115
and 141.

Investments in Debt and Equity Securities,
ch. **2**

EITF Issue 92-2
Measuring Loss Accruals by Transferors for
Transfers of Receivables with Recourse

Partially nullified by FAS-140. Affected by
FAS-133.

Transfers of Financial Assets, ch. **5**

EITF Issue 92-5
Amortization Period for Net Deferred Credit
Card Origination Costs

Calculating Yields on Debt Investments, ch. **7**

EITF Issue 93-1
Accounting for Individual Credit Card
Acquisitions

Calculating Yields on Debt Investments, ch. **7**

EITF Issue 94-8
Accounting for Conversion of a Loan into a
Debt Security in a Debt Restructuring

Investments in Debt and Equity Securities, ch. **2**

Loans and the Allowance for Credit Losses,
ch. **3**

EITF Issue 95-5
Determination of What Risks and Rewards, If
Any, Can Be Retained and Whether Any
Unresolved Contingencies May Exist in a Sale
of Mortgage Loan Servicing Rights

Servicing of Financial Assets, ch. **4**

Transfers of Financial Assets, ch. **5**

EITF Issue 95-6
Accounting by a Real Estate Investment Trust
for an Investment in a Service Corporation

Partially nullified by FIN-46.

Investments in Debt and Equity Securities, ch. **2**

EITF Issue 95-13
Classification of Debt Issue Costs in the
Statement of Cash Flows

Cash and Cash Equivalents, ch. **1**

Debt Financing, ch. **8**

EITF Issue 95-22
Balance Sheet Classification of Borrowings
Outstanding under Revolving Credit
Agreements That Include Both a Subjective
Acceleration Clause and a Lock-Box
Arrangement

Debt Financing, ch. **8**

EITF Issue 96-10
Impact of Certain Transactions on the Held-
to-Maturity Classification under FASB
Statement No. 115

Partially nullified by FAS-140.

Investments in Debt and Equity Securities,
ch. **2**

Transfers of Financial Assets, ch. **5**

EITF Issue 96-11

Accounting for Forward Contracts and
Purchased Options to Acquire Securities
Covered by FASB Statement No. 115

Partially nullified by FAS-133 and 149.

Investments in Debt and Equity Securities, ch. **2**

Securities Lending Arrangements, and Other
Pledges of Collateral, ch. **9**

EITF Issue 96-12

Recognition of Interest Income and Balance
Sheet Classification of Structured Notes

Partially nullified by FAS-133. Affected by
FAS-155.

Investments in Debt and Equity Securities, ch. **2**

Calculating Yields on Debt Investments, ch. **7**

EITF Issue 96-13

Accounting for Derivative Financial
Instruments Indexed to, and Potentially Settled
in, a Company's Own Stock

See EITF Issue 00-19.

EITF Issue 96-15

Accounting for the Effects of Changes in
Foreign Currency Exchange Rates on
Foreign-Currency-Denominated
Available-for-Sale Debt Securities

Partially nullified by FAS-133.

Investments in Debt and Equity Securities, ch. **2**

Embedded Derivatives, ch. **13**

Hedge Accounting, ch. **14**

EITF Issue 96-16

Investor's Accounting for an Investee When the
Investor Has a Majority of the Voting Interest
but the Minority Shareholder or Shareholders
Have Certain Approval or Veto Rights

Securitizations, ch. **6**

EITF Issue 96-19

Debtor's Accounting for a Modification or
Exchange of Debt Instruments

Affected by FAS-145.

Calculating Yields on Debt Investments, ch. **7**

Debt Financing, ch. **8**

Extinguishments of Debt, ch. **11**

Offsetting Assets and Liabilities in the Balance
Sheet, ch. **17**

EITF Issue 96-21

Implementation Issues in Accounting for
Leasing Transactions involving Special-
Purpose Entities

Largely nullified by FIN-46.

EITF Issue 96-22

Applicability of the Disclosures Required by
FASB Statement No. 114 When a Loan Is
Restructured in a Troubled Debt Restructuring
into Two (or More) Loans

Loans and the Allowance for Credit Losses,
ch. **3**

EITF Issue 97-1

Implementation Issues in Accounting for Lease
Transactions, including Those involving
Special-Purpose Entities

Nullified by FIN-46.

EITF Issue 97-2

Application of FASB Statement No. 94 and
APB Opinion No. 16 to Physician Practice
Management Entities and Certain Other
Entities with Contractual Management
Arrangements

Partially nullified by FAS-141. Affected by
FIN-46.

Securitizations, ch. **6**

EITF Issue 97-3

Accounting for Fees and Costs Associated with
Loan Syndications and Loan Participations
after the Issuance of FASB Statement No. 125

Calculating Yields on Debt Investments, ch. **7**

EITF Issue 97-8

Accounting for Contingent Consideration
Issue in a Purchase Business Combination

Affected by FAS-133.

Issuer's Accounting for Equity Instruments and
Related Contracts, ch. **16**

EITF Issue 97-14

Accounting for Deferred Compensation
Arrangements Where Amounts Earned Are
Held in a Rabbi Trust and Invested

Investments in Debt and Equity Securities, ch. **2**

EITF Issue 98-1

Valuation of Debt Assumed in a Purchase
Business Combination

Debt Financing, ch. **8**

EITF Issue 98-2

Accounting by a Subsidiary or Joint Venture
for an Investment in the Stock of Its Parent
Company or Joint Venture Partner

Issuer's Accounting for Equity Instruments
and Related Contracts, ch. **16**

EITF Issue 98-5

Accounting for Convertible Securities
with Beneficial Conversion Features or
Contingently Adjustable Conversion Ratios

Affected by FAS-133 and FAS-155.

Convertible Debt and Similar Instruments,
ch. **10**

EITF Issue 98-6

Investor's Accounting for an Investment in a
Limited Partnership When the Investor Is the
Sole General Partner and the Limited Partners
Have Certain Approval or Veto Rights

Securitizations, ch. **6**

EITF Issue 98-7

Accounting for Exchanges of Similar Equity
Method Investments

See EITF Issue 01-2.

EITF Issue 98-8

Accounting for Transfers of Investments That
Are in Substance Real Estate

Transfers of Financial Assets, ch. **5**

EITF Issue 98-10

Accounting for Contracts Involved in Energy
Trading and Risk Management Activities

Superseded by EITF Issue 02-3.

EITF Issue 98-12

Application of Issue No. 00-19 to Forward
Equity Sales Transactions

Nullified by FAS-150.

EITF Issue 98-13

Accounting by an Equity Method Investor for Investee Losses When the Investor Has Loans to and Investments in Other Securities of the Investee

Investments in Debt and Equity Securities, ch. 2

Loans and the Allowance for Credit Losses, ch. 3

EITF Issue 98-14

Debtor's Accounting for Changes in Line-of-Credit or Revolving-Debt Arrangements

Debt Financing, ch. 8

EITF Issue 98-15

Structured Notes Acquired for a Specified Investment Strategy

Investments in Debt and Equity Securities, ch. 2

EITF Issue 99-1

Accounting for Debt Convertible into the Stock of a Consolidated Subsidiary

Convertible Debt and Similar Instruments, ch. 10

Issuer's Accounting for Equity Instruments and Related Contracts, ch. 16

EITF Issue 99-2

Accounting for Weather Derivatives

Introduction to Derivatives, ch. 12

EITF Issue 99-3

Application of Issue No. 96-13 to Derivative Instruments with Multiple Settlement Alternatives

See EITF Issue 00-19.

EITF Issue 99-4

Accounting for Stock Received from the Demutualization of a Mutual Insurance Company

Investments in Debt and Equity Securities, ch. 2

EITF Issue 99-7

Accounting for an Accelerated Share Repurchase Program

Issuer's Accounting for Equity Instruments and Related Contracts, ch. 16

EITF Issue 99-8

Accounting for Transfers of Assets That Are Derivative Instruments but That Are Not Financial Assets

Introduction to Derivatives, ch. 12

EITF Issue 99-9

Effect of Derivative Gains and Losses on the Capitalization of Interest

Debt Financing, ch. 8

Hedge Accounting, ch. 14

EITF Issue 99-10

Percentage Used to Determine the Amount of Equity Method Losses

Investments in Debt and Equity Securities, ch. 2

Loans and the Allowance for Credit Losses, ch. 3

EITF Issue 99-11

Subsequent Events Caused by Year 2000

Consensus withdrawn.

EITF Issue 99-20

Recognition of Interest Income and Impairment on Purchased and Retained

Beneficial Interests in Securitized Financial Assets	Affected by FAS-155.
	Investments in Debt and Equity Securities, ch. **2**
	Loans and the Allowance for Credit Losses, ch. **3**
	Servicing of Financial Assets, ch. **4**
	Transfers of Financial Assets, ch. **5**
	Calculating Yields on Debt Investments, ch. **7**
	Embedded Derivatives, ch. **13**

EITF Issue 00-4

Majority Owner's Accounting for a Transaction in the Shares of a Consolidated Subsidiary and a Derivative Indexed to the Minority Interest in That Subsidiary	Nullified by FAS-150.

EITF Issue 00-5

Determining Whether a Nonmonetary Transaction Is an Exchange of Similar Productive Assets	Transfers of Financial Assets, ch. **5**

EITF Issue 00-6

Accounting for Freestanding Derivative Financial Instruments Indexed to, and Potentially Settled in, the Stock of a Consolidated Subsidiary	Affected by FAS-150.
	Convertible Debt and Similar Instruments, ch. **10**
	Embedded Derivatives, ch. **13**
	Issuer's Accounting for Equity Instruments and Related Contracts, ch. **16**

EITF Issue 00-7

Application of Issue No. 96-13 to Equity Derivative Transactions That Contain Certain Provisions That Require Net Cash Settlement If Certain Events Outside the Control of the Issuer Occur	See EITF Issue 00-19.

EITF Issue 00-8

Accounting by a Grantee for an Equity Instrument to Be Received in Conjunction with Providing Goods or Services	Investments in Debt and Equity Securities, ch. **2**

EITF Issue 00-9

Classification of a Gain or Loss from a Hedge of Debt That Is Extinguished	Affected by FAS-145.
	Extinguishments of Debt, ch. **11**
	Hedge Accounting, ch. **14**

EITF Issue 00-15

Classification in the Statement of Cash Flows of the Income Tax Benefit Received by a Company upon Exercise of Nonqualified Employee Stock Options	Cash and Cash Equivalents, ch. **1**

EITF Issue 00-17

Measuring the Fair Value of Energy-Related Contracts in Applying Issue No. 98-10	Superseded by EITF Issue 02-3.

EITF Issue 00-18

Accounting Recognition for Certain Transactions involving Equity Instruments Granted to Other Than Employees	Investments in Debt and Equity Securities, ch. **2**

EITF Issue 00-19

Accounting for Derivative Instruments
Indexed to, and Potentially Settled in, a
Company's Own Stock

Affected by FAS-133, FAS-150, and FAS-155.

Securitizations, ch. **6**
Introduction to Derivatives, ch. **12**
Embedded Derivatives, ch. **13**
Issuer's Accounting for Equity Instruments
and Related Contracts, ch. **16**

EITF Issue 00-27

Application of Issue No. 98-5 to Certain
Convertible Instruments

Affected by FAS-150.
Convertible Debt and Similar Instruments, ch. **10**

EITF Issue 01-2

Interpretations of APB Opinion No. 29

Affected by FAS-141.
Investments in Debt and Equity Securities, ch. **2**
Transfers of Financial Assets, ch. **5**

EITF Issue 01-5

Application of FASB Statement No. 52 to an
Investment Being Evaluated for Impairment
That Will Be Disposed Of

Hedge Accounting, ch. **14**

EITF Issue 01-6

The Meaning of "Indexed to a Company's Own
Stock"

Issuer's Accounting for Equity Instruments
and Related Contracts, ch. **16**

EITF Issue 01-7

Creditor's Accounting for a Modification or
Exchange of Debt Instruments

Extinguishments of Debt, ch. **11**

EITF Issue 01-12

The Impact of the Requirements of FASB
Statement No. 133 on Residual Value
Guarantees in Connection with a Lease

Introduction to Derivatives, ch. **12**

EITF Issue 02-1

Balance Sheet Classification of Assets Received
in Exchange for Equity Instruments

Issue resolved by SEC.

EITF Issue 02-3

Accounting for Contracts Involved in Energy
Trading and Risk Management Activities

Introduction to Derivatives, ch. **12**
Disclosures about Derivatives, ch. **15**

EITF Issue 02-4

Determining Whether a Debtor's Modification
or Exchange of Debt Instruments Is within the
Scope of FASB Statement No. 15

Extinguishments of Debt, ch. **11**

EITF Issue 02-9

Accounting for Changes That Result in a
Transferor Regaining Control of Financial
Assets Sold

Affected by FAS-156.
Transfers of Financial Assets, ch. **5**
Securitizations, ch. **6**

EITF Issue 02-15

Determining Whether Certain Conversions of
Convertible Debt to Equity Securities Are
within the Scope of FASB Statement No. 84

Convertible Debt and Similar Instruments,
ch. **10**

EITF Issue 02-18

Accounting for Subsequent Investments in an Investee after Suspension of Equity Method Loss Recognition

Investments in Debt and Equity Securities, ch. **2**

Loans and the Allowance for Credit Losses, ch. **3**

EITF Issue 03-1

The Meaning of Other-Than-Temporary Impairment and Its Application to Certain Investments

Superseded by FSP FAS 115-1 and FAS 124-1.

Calculating Yields on Debt Investments, ch. **7**

EITF Issue 03-6

Participating Securities and the Two-Class Method under FASB Statement No. 128

Convertible Debt and Similar Instruments, ch. **10**

Issuer's Accounting for Equity Instruments and Related Contracts, ch. **16**

EITF Issue 03-7

Accounting for the Settlement of the Equity-Settled Portion of a Convertible Debt Instrument That Permits or Requires the Conversion Spread to Be Settled in Stock (Instrument C of Issue No. 90-19)

Affected by FAS-155.
Convertible Debt and Similar Instruments, ch. **10**

EITF Issue 03-11

Reporting Realized Gains and Losses on Derivative Instruments That Are Subject to FASB Statement No. 133 and Not "Held for Trading Purposes" as Defined in Issue No. 02-3

Introduction to Derivatives, ch. **12**

EITF Issue 04-7

Determining Whether an Interest Is a Variable Interest in a Potential Variable Interest Entity

Securitizations, ch. **6**

EITF Issue 04-8

The Effect of Contingently Convertible Debt on Diluted Earnings per Share

Convertible Debt and Similar Instruments, ch. **10**

EITF Issue 05-1

Accounting for the Conversion of an Instrument That Becomes Convertible upon the Issuer's Exercise of a Call Option

Convertible Debt and Similar Instruments, ch. **10**

EITF Issue 05-2

The Meaning of "Conventional Convertible Debt Instrument" in Issue No. 00-19

Convertible Debt and Similar Instruments, ch. **10**

EITF Issue 05-7

Accounting for Modifications to Conversion Options Embedded in Debt Securities and Related Issues

Convertible Debt and Similar Instruments, ch. **10**

EITF Issue 06-6

Debtor's Accounting for a Modification (or Exchange) of Convertible Debt Instruments

Convertible Debt, ch. **10**

EITF Issue 06-7

Issuer's Accounting for a Previously Bifurcated Conversion Option in a Convertible Debt Instrument When the Conversion Option No Longer Meets the Bifurcation Criteria in FASB Statement No. 133

Convertible Debt, ch. **10**

SEC AND FASB STAFF ANNOUNCEMENTS
(EITF Topic Ds)

ORIGINAL PRONOUNCEMENT	2008 *FINANCIAL INSTRUMENTS* REFERENCE
EITF Topic D-2	
Applicability of FASB Statement No. 65 to Savings and Loan Associations	Loans and the Allowance for Credit Losses, ch. 3
EITF Topic D-4	
Argentine Government Guarantee of U.S. Dollar-Denominated Loans to the Argentine Private Sector	Loans and the Allowance for Credit Losses, ch. 3
EITF Topic D-8	
Accruing Bad Debt Expense at Inception of a Lease	Calculating Yields on Debt Investments, ch. **7**
EITF Topic D-10	
Required Use of Interest Method in Recognizing Interest Income	Calculating Yields on Debt Investments, ch. **7**
EITF Topic D-11	
Impact of Stock Market Decline	Investments in Debt and Equity Securities, ch. **2**
EITF Topic D-14	
Transactions involving Special-Purpose Entities	Nullified by FIN-46.
EITF Topic D-23	
Subjective Acceleration Clauses and Debt Classification	Debt Financing, ch. **8**
EITF Topic D-39	
Questions Related to the Implementation of FASB Statement No. 115	Partially resolved by FTB 94-1. Investments in Debt and Equity Securities, ch. **2**
EITF Topic D-41	
Adjustments in Assets and Liabilities for Holding Gains and Losses as Related to the Implementation of FASB Statement No. 115	Affected by FAS-120. Investments in Debt and Equity Securities, ch. **2**
EITF Topic D-42	
The Effect on the Calculation of Earnings per Share for the Redemption or Induced Conversion of Preferred Stock	Affected by FAS-150. Convertible Debt and Similar Instruments, ch. **10** Issuer's Accounting for Equity Instruments and Related Contracts, ch. **16**
EITF Topic D-43	
Assurance That a Right of Setoff Is Enforceable in a Bankruptcy under FASB Interpretation No. 39	Offsetting Assets and Liabilities in the Balance Sheet, ch. **17**
EITF Topic D-44	
Recognition of Other-Than-Temporary Impairment upon the Planned Sale of a Security Whose Cost Exceeds Fair Value	Superseded by FSP FAS 115-1 and FAS 124-1.

EITF Topic D-46
Accounting for Limited Partnership
Investments

Investments in Debt and Equity Securities, ch. **2**

EITF Topic D-49
Classifying Net Appreciation on Investments
of a Donor-Restricted Endowment Fund

Investments in Debt and Equity Securities, ch. **2**

EITF Topic D-50
Classification of Gains and Losses from the
Termination of an Interest Rate Swap
Designated to Commercial Paper

Affected by FAS-133.
Hedge Accounting, ch. **14**

EITF Topic D-51
The Applicability of FASB Statement No. 115 to
Desecuritizations of Financial Assets

Affected by FAS-133.

Investments in Debt and Equity Securities, ch. **2**
Loans and the Allowance for Credit Losses, ch. **3**
Securitizations, ch. **6**

EITF Topic D-53
Computation of Earnings per Share for a Period
That Includes a Redemption or an Induced
Conversion of a Portion of a Class of Preferred
Stock

Convertible Debt and Similar Instruments,
ch. **10**
Issuer's Accounting for Equity Instruments
and Related Contracts, ch. **16**

EITF Topic D-61
Classification by the Issuer of Redeemable
Instruments That Are Subject to Remarketing
Agreements

Debt Financing, ch. **8**

EITF Topic D-65
Maintaining Collateral in Repurchase
Agreements and Similar Transactions under
FASB Statement No. 125

Reaffirmed in FAS-140. Affected by FAS-133.

Transfers of Financial Assets, ch. **5**
Securities Lending Arrangements, and Other
Pledges of Collateral, ch. **9**

EITF Topic D-69
Gain Recognition on Transfers of Financial
Assets under FASB Statement No. 125

Reaffirmed, but modified by FAS-140. Affected
by FAS-156.

Securitizations, ch. **6**
Fair Value and Other Disclosures about
Financial Instruments, ch. **18**

EITF Topic D-72
Effect of Contracts That May Be Settled in
Stock or Cash on the Computation of Diluted
Earnings per Share

Affected by FAS-150.

Convertible Debt and Similar Instruments,
ch. **10**

Issuer's Accounting for Equity Instruments
and Related Contracts, ch. **16**

EITF Topic D-74
Issues Concerning the Scope of the AICPA
Guide on Investment Companies

Affected by FIN-46.
Investments in Debt and Equity Securities, ch. **2**

EITF Topic D-77
Accounting for Legal Costs Expected to Be
Incurred in Connection with a Loss
Contingency

Loans and the Allowance for Credit Losses,
ch. **3**

EITF Topic D-79
Accounting for Retroactive Insurance
Contracts Purchased by Entities Other Than
Insurance Enterprises

Offsetting Assets and Liabilities in the Balance
Sheet, ch. **17**

EITF Topic D-80
Application of FASB Statements No. 5 and No.
114 to a Loan Portfolio

Loans and the Allowance for Credit Losses,
ch. **3**

EITF Topic D-82
Effect of Preferred Stock Dividends Payable in
Common Shares on Computation of Income
Available to Common Stockholders

Issuer's Accounting for Equity Instruments
and Related Contracts, ch. **16**

EITF Topic D-86
Issuance of Financial Statements

Loans and the Allowance for Credit Losses, ch. **3**
Debt Financing, ch. **8**

EITF Topic D-94
Questions and Answers Related to the
Implementation of FASB Statement No. 140

Superseded by FTB 01-1.

EITF Topic D-95
Effect of Participating Convertible Securities on
the Computation of Basic Earnings per Share

Nullified by EITF Issue 03-6

EITF Topic D-98
Classification and Measurement of
Redeemable Securities

Partially nullified by FAS-150.
Issuer's Accounting for Equity Instruments
and Related Contracts, ch. **16**

EITF Topic D-99
Questions and Answers Related to Servicing
Activities in a Qualifying Special-Purpose
Entity under FASB Statement No. 140

Incorporated into FAS-140 Q&A

EITF Topic D-102
Documentation of the Method Used to
Measure Hedge Ineffectiveness under FASB
Statement No. 133

Hedge Accounting, ch. **14**

EITF Topic D-105
Accounting in Consolidation for Energy
Trading Contracts between Affiliated Entities
When the Activities of One but Not Both
Affiliates Are within the Scope of Issue
No. 98-10

Superseded by EITF Issue 02-3.

EITF D-109
Determining the Nature of a Host Contract
Related to a Hybrid Financial Instrument Is-
sued in the Form of a Share under FASB
Statement No. 133

Embedded Derivatives, ch. **13**

FASB DERIVATIVES IMPLEMENTATION GROUP
INTERPRETATIONS (DIG Issues)

ORIGINAL PRONOUNCEMENT	2008 *FINANCIAL INSTRUMENTS* REFERENCE
Section A, Definition of a Derivative	Introduction to Derivatives, ch. **12** Embedded Derivatives, ch. **13**
Section B, Embedded Derivatives	Transfers of Financial Assets, ch. **5** Securitizations, ch. **6** Embedded Derivatives, ch. **13**
Section C, Scope Exceptions	Transfers of Financial Assets, ch. **5** Securitizations, ch. **6** Calculating Yields on Debt Investments, ch. **7** Securities Lending Arrangements, and Other Pledges of Collateral, ch. **9** Introduction to Derivatives, ch. **12** Embedded Derivatives, ch. **13**
Section D, Recognition and Measurement Of Derivatives	Investments in Debt and Equity Securities, ch. **2** Transfers of Financial Assets, ch. **5** Securitizations, ch. **6** Introduction to Derivatives, ch. **12** Embedded Derivatives, ch. **13**
Section E: Hedging—General	Hedge Accounting, ch. **14** Securitization, ch. **6**
Section F: Fair Value Hedges	Loans and the Allowance for Credit Losses, ch. **3** Servicing of Financial Assets, ch. **4** Calculating Yields on Debt Investments, ch. **7** Hedge Accounting, ch. **14**
Section G: Cash Flow Hedges	Securities Lending Arrangements, and Other Pledges of Collateral, ch. **9** Hedge Accounting, ch. **14**
Section H: Foreign Currency Hedges	Hedge Accounting, ch. **14**
Section I: Disclosures	Disclosures about Derivatives, ch. **15**
Section J: Transition	[Not included]
Section K: Miscellaneous	Introduction to Derivatives, ch. **12** Embedded Derivatives, ch. **13** Hedge Accounting, ch. **14**

FASB CONCEPTS STATEMENTS (CONs)

ORIGINAL PRONOUNCEMENT	2008 *FINANCIAL INSTRUMENTS* REFERENCE
FASB Concepts Statement No. 6	
Elements of Financial Statements	Debt Financing, ch. **8** Securities Lending Arrangements, and Other Pledges of Collateral, ch. **9** Issuer's Accounting for Equity Instruments and Related Contracts, ch. **16**
FASB Concepts Statement No. 7 Using Cash Flow Information and Present Value in Accounting Measurements	Loans and the Allowance for Credit Losses, ch. **3** Servicing of Financial Assets, ch. **4** Calculating Yields on Debt Investments, ch. **7** Introduction to Derivatives, ch. **12** Fair Value and Other Disclosures about Financial Instruments, ch. **18**

FASB IMPLEMENTATION GUIDES (Q&As)

ORIGINAL PRONOUNCEMENT	2008 *FINANCIAL INSTRUMENTS* REFERENCE

FAS-91 Q&A

A Guide to Implementation of Statement 91 on Accounting for Nonrefundable Fees and Costs Associated with Originating or Acquiring Loans and Initial Direct Costs of Leases

Portions revised to conform with subsequent standards.

Calculating Yields on Debt Investments, ch. 7

FAS-115 Q&A

A Guide to Implementation of Statement 115 on Accounting for Certain Investments in Debt and Equity Securities

Portions revised to conform with subsequent standards.

Cash and Cash Equivalents, ch. 1

Investments in Debt and Equity Securities, ch. 2

Loans and the Allowance for Credit Losses, ch. 3

Debt Financing, ch. 8

Securities Lending Arrangements, and Other Pledges of Collateral, ch. 9

Embedded Derivatives, ch. 13

FAS-140 Q&A

A Guide to Implementation of Statement 140 on Accounting for Transfers and Servicing of Financial Assets and Extinguishments of Liabilities.

Portions revised to conform with subsequent standards.

Cash and Cash Equivalents, ch. 1

Investments in Debt and Equity Securities, ch. 2

Loans and the Allowance for Credit Losses, ch. 3

Servicing of Financial Assets, ch. 4

Transfers of Financial Assets, ch. 5

Securitizations, ch. 6

Debt Financing, ch. 8

Securities Lending Arrangements, and Other Pledges of Collateral, ch. 9

Extinguishments of Debt, ch. 11

Introduction to Derivatives, ch. 12

SECURITIES AND EXCHANGE COMMISSION STAFF ACCOUNTING BULLETINS (SABs) AND FINANCIAL REPORTING RELEASES (FRs)

ORIGINAL PRONOUNCEMENT	2008 *FINANCIAL INSTRUMENTS* REFERENCE

SAB Nos. 51 and 84 (Topic 5H)

Accounting for Sales of Stock by a Subsidiary

Issuer's Accounting for Equity Instruments and Related Contracts, ch. 16

SAB No. 59 (Topic 5M)

Accounting for Noncurrent Marketable Equity Securities

Investments in Debt and Equity Securities, ch. 2

SAB 64 (Topic 3C)
Redeemable Preferred Stock

Issuer's Accounting for Equity Instruments
and Related Contracts, ch. **16**

SAB 68 (Topic 5Q)
Increasing Rate Preferred Stock

Issuer's Accounting for Equity Instruments
and Related Contracts, ch. **16**

SAB No. 99 (Topic 1M)
Materiality

Hedge Accounting, ch. **14**

SAB No. 101 (Topic 13)
Revenue Recognition in Financial Statements

Calculating Yields on Debt Investments, ch. **7**
Debt Financing, ch. **8**

SAB No. 102 (Topic 6L)
Selected Loan Loss Allowance Methodology
and Documentation Issues

Loans and the Allowance for Credit Losses,
ch. **3**

SAB No. 103
Update of Codification of Staff Accounting
Bulletins

Investments in Debt and Equity Securities, ch. **2**

SAB No. 105
Application of Accounting Principles to Loan
Commitments

Introduction to Derivatives, ch. **12**

SAB No. 107 (Topic 14)
Share-Based Payment

Investments in Debt and Equity Securities, ch. **2**

FR-67
Disclosure in Management's Discussion
and Analysis about Off-Balance Sheet
Arrangements and Aggregate Contractual
Obligations

Fair Value and Other Disclosures, ch. **18**
Debt Financing, ch. **8**

FR-72
Interpretation: Commission Guidance
Regarding Management's Discussion and
Analysis of Financial Condition and Results of
Operations

Introduction to Derivatives, ch. **12**

Index

References are to page numbers.

A

Accounting
  cash and cash equivalents, for,
    1.04–1.14
  collateral pledges, 9.06–9.10
  convertible debt and similar
    instruments, 10.06–10.29
  debt extinguishments, 11.03–11.21
  derivatives, 12.32–12.37
    scope exceptions, contracts
     meeting, 12.28
  embedded derivatives, 13.26–13.32
  equity instruments
    derivatives with characteristics
     of both debt and equity,
     16.27–16.45
    EITF Issue 00-6, 16.40–16.41
    equity transactions, 16.09–16.27
    FAS 150-3, 16.20–16.24
  hedge accounting. *See* Hedge
    accounting
  loans, 3.06–3.40
  offsetting assets and liabilities in
    balance sheet, 17.04–17.15
  securities
    for-profit enterprises, by,
     2.11–2.35
    not-for-profit enterprises, for,
     2.37–2.38
    securities portfolio, for, 2.54–2.57
  securities lending arrangements,
    9.10–9.21
  securitization, 6.07–6.28
  servicing financial assets, 4.04–4.21
  transfers of financial assets,
    5.08–5.31
  troubled debt restructuring, 11.20
ADC loans, 3.05–3.06
Annuity contracts, embedded
  derivatives, 13.21–13.25
APB-30, 11.21
ARB-43, 11.15
Asset-backed security transactions,
  disclosures, 6.50–6.51
Asset transfers. *See* Transfers of
  financial assets
Assignment of derivatives, 12.13
Auditing considerations
  cash and cash equivalents, 1.15

convertible debt and similar
  instruments, 10.36
debt extinguishments, 11.22–11.23
debt financing, 8.40–8.41
debt investment yields, 7.53
derivative disclosures, 15.15
derivatives, 12.37–12.39
embedded derivatives, 13.35
equity instruments, 16.57–16.58
fair value, 18.35–18.36
fair value option, 19.16–19.18
hedge accounting, 14.85–14.87
loans, 3.51–3.53
offsetting assets and liabilities in
  balance sheet, 17.17
securities, 2.52–2.53
securities lending arrangements,
  9.22–9.23
securitization, 6.54–6.56
servicing financial assets, 4.23–4.25
transfers of financial assets,
  5.32–5.34
  achieving isolation, 5.32–5.33
  fair value estimates, 5.33–5.34

B

Balance sheet presentations
  cash and cash equivalents, 1.06–1.07
    current and noncurrent assets,
     1.06–1.07
    reciprocal balances, 1.07
  current and noncurrent assets,
    1.06–1.07
  derivatives, 12.32–12.34
  embedded derivatives, 13.32
  equity instruments, contracts indexed
    to and potentially settled in
    company's own stock, 16.30–16.37
  hedge accounting, 14.81–14.82
  hybrid financial instruments,
    13.34–13.35
  interest method, 7.32
  mortgage banking model, 3.40
  offsetting assets and liabilities in. *See*
    Offsetting assets and liabilities in
    balance sheet
  reciprocal balances, 1.07
  servicing financial assets, 4.19

Beneficial interests, embedded derivatives, 13.12–13.15
Benefit plan contracts, FAS-133 scope exceptions, 12.24
Bonds, mortgage-backed, 5.31
Business combination
    exchange of cost method investments, 2.47
    FAS-133 scope exceptions, 12.19–12.32

C

Calls, 13.13, 16.32
Capital adequacy, 16.57
Capitalization of interest expense on debt, 14.83–14.84
Capital structure information, 16.45–16.47
Cash and cash equivalents, Ch. 1
    accounting for, 1.04–1.14
    auditing considerations, 1.15
    background, 1.02–1.04
    balance sheet presentations, 1.06–1.07
        current and noncurrent assets, 1.06–1.07
        reciprocal balances, 1.07
    cash flow hedges. *See* Hedge accounting
    cash flow statements. *See* Cash flow statements
    cash reserve accounts, 1.04
    cash settlement, convertible debt, 10.16–10.17, 10.20, 10.34–10.35
    collateral, cash received as, 1.05
    components of cash, 1.03–1.04
    defined, 1.03–1.04
    disclosures, 1.14–1.15
        cash equivalents, 1.14, 1.16
        compensating balances, 1.17
        deposits in excess of insured limits, 1.14
        restricted cash, 1.14–1.15
        securities, 1.16
    foreign currency, 1.05
    measuring cash and cash equivalents, 1.05–1.06
    overview, 1.02
    recognizing cash, 1.04–1.05
    securities, as, 1.05–1.06, 1.16
Cash flow hedges. *See* Hedge accounting
Cash flow statements, 1.07–1.14
    cash equivalents, 1.08
    cash receipts and payments, classification of, 1.09–1.12
    common classifications, 1.13–1.14

convertible debt and similar instruments, 10.26
debt extinguishments, cash flow reporting, 11.21
derivatives, 1.12, 12.36
fair value option elected, when, 1.11
financing, classifying as, 1.09–1.10
foreign currency cash flows, 1.13
gross and net cash flows, 1.08–1.10
hedge accounting, 14.84
interest method, 7.32
investing, classifying as, 1.09
loans, 3.36–3.37
operating, classifying as, 1.10–1.11
securities lending arrangements, 9.20–9.21
    sales and purchases, 9.20
    secured borrowings, 9.21
servicing financial assets, 4.20
significant prepayment risk, 1.12
trading activities, cash flows from, 1.11
Cash reserve accounts, 1.04, 6.24–6.25
Centralized treasury hedge of foreign currency forecasted transactions, 14.106–14.111
Certificates of deposit, cash flow hedges, 14.48
Charge-offs of loans, 3.31–3.34
Coinsurance arrangements, embedded derivatives, 13.25–13.26
Collars, 14.12
Collateral. *See* Securities
Collateralized loans, 3.49
Collateral pledges
    accounting, 9.06–9.10
    cash collateral, 9.07–9.08
    collateral versus secured borrowing proceeds, 9.07
    disclosure, 9.21–9.22
    FAS-115, 9.10
    illustrations, 9.27
    loans, 3.09
    noncash collateral, 9.08–9.09
    regulatory considerations, 9.22
    safekeeping and custody, 9.10
    sales of collateral received, 9.10
    short sales, 9.10
    sufficient, 9.14–9.15
Combinations. *See* Business combination
Commercial paper, cash flow hedges, 14.48
Commitment fees, 7.21
Company stock, indexed contracts. *See* Equity instruments
Consolidation of securitization entities. *See* Securitization

Contracts
  indexed to company stock. *See* Equity
    instruments
  types, summary analysis,
    12.30–12.32
Control, transfers of financial assets,
  5.13–5.14
Convertible debt and similar
  instruments, Ch. 10
  accounting, 10.06–10.29
  auditing considerations, 10.36
  background, 10.03–10.05
  beneficial conversion features, 10.30,
    10.39
  cash flows, 10.26
  cash settlement options, 10.16–10.17,
    10.20
  components of, 10.08
  contingent features, 10.29–10.30
  contingently convertible instruments,
    10.33–10.34
  conversions, 10.24
  debt extinguishments, 11.07–11.08
  debt with beneficial conversion
    features, 10.05, 10.21–10.26
  debt with detachable warrants, 10.05,
    10.15–10.16
  descriptions of securities,
    10.04–10.05
  disclosures, 10.29–10.36
  earnings per share, 10.30–10.36
    basic EPC, 10.32–10.33
    basic EPS, 10.40
    diluted EPC, 10.33–10.36
  EITF Issue 00-27, 10.21–10.22
  EITF Issue 98-5, 10.21–10.22
  embedded conversion options no
    longer requiring bifurcation,
    10.18, 10.30
  extinguishments, 10.13, 10.24
  fair value option, 10.28–10.29
  FAS-133, 10.21
  financial instruments with liabilities
    and equity, 10.05
  illustrations, 10.36–10.40
  inception, accounting at, 10.08–10.10,
    10.15–10.16, 10.22–10.23
  income tax considerations,
    10.26–10.27
  induced conversions, 10.11–10.13,
    10.35–10.36, 10.38–10.39
  modification or exchange,
    accounting for, 10.14–10.15
  mortgages, 10.10
  navigating literature, 10.06–10.08
  nondetachable BCFS, 10.25–10.26
  nontraditional, 10.16–10.21,
    10.35
  ongoing accounting, 10.23–10.26
    original terms, conversion according
      to, 10.10–10.11
    overview, 10.02–10.03
    preferred stock, 10.18–10.19
    registration payment arrangements,
      subject to, 10.27
    revised terms, conversion according
      to, 10.11–10.13
    SEC registrant alert, 10.22, 10.35
    securities, information about,
      10.29–10.30
    subsidiaries, 10.09–10.10
    traditional, 10.04–10.05, 10.08–10.13,
      10.37–10.38
    variable prices and contingencies,
      10.23
    warrants, 10.16, 10.36–10.37
Credit, receivables and insurance
  payables offsets, 17.15, 17.19
Credit cards
  fees and costs, 7.22–7.23
  purchases and originations,
    disclosures, 7.50
Credit risk concentrations, fair value
  disclosures, 18.29–18.31, 18.42
Credit union member shares/deposits,
  16.26–16.27
Custody arrangements, collateral, 9.10

D

Debt
  convertible debt and similar
    instruments. *See* Convertible debt
    and similar instruments
  extinguishments. *See* Debt
    extinguishments
  financing. *See* Debt financing
  investment yields. *See* Debt
    investment yields
  troubled debt restructurings. *See*
    Troubled debt restructurings
Debt and equity securities. *See* Securities
Debt-equity hybrids, accounting, 10.06
Debt extinguishments, Ch. 11
  accounting, 11.03–11.21
  after balance sheet date, 11.07
  auditing considerations, 11.22–11.23
  background, 11.03
  binding contract to reacquire debt,
    11.14
  cash flow estimates, 11.18–11.19
  convertible debt, 11.07–11.08
  criteria for derecognition,
    11.03–11.04
  debt financing, 8.26
  debtholders, transactions among,
    11.12

Debt extinguishments, Ch. 11, *cont.*
deferred hedge gains and losses,
11.05–11.06
disclosures, 11.21–11.22
EITF Issue 96-19, 11.09
gain or loss, classification of, 11.05
grandfathered defeasance trust,
invasion of, 11.08–11.09
guarantees, 11.21
hedge accounting and, 14.83
identifying agents and principals,
11.12
illustrations, 11.23–11.26
induced conversions, 11.07–11.08
in-substance defeasance, 11.08–11.09,
11.22
liens, sale of assets subject to, 11.07
loan participation and syndication,
11.14–11.15
loss on, 11.23–11.24
modifications and exchanges of
convertible debt, 11.08
nontroubled exchanges and
modification of instruments,
11.09–11.15, 11.24–11.25
overview, 11.02–11.03
participating mortgage loans, 11.05
recognition of extinguishments,
11.04–11.05
reporting cash flows, 11.21
secondary liability, 11.06–11.07
SEC registrant alert, 11.13–11.14
significant exchanges and
modifications, 11.11–11.15
substantially different, defined, 11.10
third-party intermediaries,
11.12–11.14
troubled debt restructurings. *See*
Troubled debt restructurings
Debt financing, Ch. 8
accounting, 8.07–8.34
auditing considerations, 8.40–8.41
current liabilities, 8.11–8.13
debt extinguishments, 8.26
disclosures
available sources of credit, 8.37
deposit liabilities, 8.36
financial institutions, applicable
to, 8.35–8.37
guarantees, 8.37–8.38
interest costs, 8.37
interest elements of debt, 8.46
long-term debt, 8.34–8.35, 8.42,
8.45–8.46
maturities, 8.34
noncash financing activities,
8.35
participating mortgages, 8.35
public company disclosures in
MD&A, 8.39–8.40
related topics, 8.40
restrictive covenants, 8.35
secured borrowings, 8.37
short-term debt, 8.34
terms of debt, 8.36
EITF Issue 96-19, 8.26–8.27
EITF Issue 98-14, 8.27–8.28
fair value option, 8.08–8.09
FIN-45, 8.30
guarantees
disclosures, 8.37–8.38
fair value, estimating, 8.33
FAS-140, 8.33–8.34
initial recognition, 8.31–8.32
recording of, 8.46–8.47
subsequent measurement,
8.32–8.33
income statement recognition
capitalization of interest costs,
8.22
debt issue costs, 8.23
increasing-rate debt, 8.23–8.24
indexed rate instruments,
8.24–8.25
participating mortgages,
8.25–8.26
special application of interest
method, 8.23–8.26
line-of-credit arrangements, changes
in, 8.27–8.28
long-term debt, 8.19–8.21
classification of, 8.20–8.21
lock-box arrangements, 8.20–8.21,
8.46
remarketing agreement, with,
8.21
subjective acceleration clauses,
8.19–8.20
modification or exchange of debt
instruments with different terms,
8.26–8.27
new loan test, 8.26–8.27
ratios of current liabilities, 8.12–8.13
registration payment arrangements,
8.07–8.08
revolving credit arrangement,
modification of, 8.44–8.45
revolving debt arrangements,
changes in, 8.27–8.28
SEC registrant alert, 8.15, 8.22–8.23,
8.34, 8.38, 8.40
short-term debt, 8.13–8.19
amount excluded from current
liabilities, 8.15
classification of, 8.16–8.17,
8.43–8.44

intent to seek new financing,
8.15–8.17
repaid prior to being replaced,
8.18–8.19
rollovers of short-term
obligations, 8.17–8.18
subsequent measurement, 8.09–8.10
subsidiary debt in consolidated
balance sheet, 8.21–8.22
Debt investment yields, Ch. 7
amortization
contractual payment terms, based
on, 7.54–7.55
estimated prepayment patterns,
based on, 7.55–7.56
auditing considerations, 7.53
background, 7.04–7.06
credit card fees and costs, 7.22–7.23
delinquency fees, 7.24
disclosures, 7.49–7.52
anticipating prepayments, 7.50
credit card purchases and
originations, 7.50
entities engaged in lending
activities, 7.49–7.50
FAS-115-1, 7.52
FAS-124-1, 7.52
investments in beneficial interests
in securitized assets with
unrealized losses, 7.52, 7.59–7.62
loans and securities purchased at
credit-related discount,
7.50–7.52
SOP 03-3, 7.50–7.52
factoring commissions, 7.25
FAS-91, 7.25–7.32
FASB Concepts Statement No. 7,
7.04–7.05
fees and costs from lending and
investing, 7.12–7.25
group, loans purchased as, 7.18
illustrations, 7.53–7.68
imputing interest on receivables and
payables, 7.07–7.12
amortizing premiums and
discounts, 7.09–7.10
bundled rights and privileges,
notes with, 7.10
discount rate, selecting, 7.08
embedded derivatives, notes with,
7.11
fair value option, 7.11–7.12
FAS-133, 7.11
goods or services, notes
exchanged for, 7.10–7.11
premiums and discounts, 7.09
increasing rate provisions,
7.56–7.58

interest method
aggregation of loans, 7.25–7.26
anticipating prepayments in
effective yield calculation,
7.28–7.30
balance sheet presentation, 7.32
beneficial interests in
securitization trust, 7.36–7.40
cash flow statement presentation,
7.32
certain investments, 7.33–7.49
construction loans and permanent
financing, 7.30
decreasing-rate loans, 7.27
demand loans, 7.30
effective interest rate, 7.26–7.27
EITF Issue 96-12, 7.33–7.36
EITF Issue 99-20, 7.36–7.40
estimated cash flows, changes in,
7.29–7.30
FAS-91, 7.25–7.32
grouping loans to anticipate
prepayment, 7.29
income statement presentation,
7.32
increasing-rate loans, 7.27
instruments purchased at
discount due to credit quality,
7.41–7.46, 7.62–7.68
mortgage banking activities, 7.49
nonaccrual loans, 7.32
not-for-profit organizations,
investment income for,
7.46–7.48
revolving lines of credit,
7.30–7.31
SOP 03-3, 7.41–7.46, 7.62–7.68
structured notes, 7.33–7.36
subsequent sale of aggregated
loan, 7.26
sum-of-the-years'-digits, 7.28
uncertain payment terms, loans
with, 7.30–7.31
variable interest rates, 7.27–7.28
variable-rate loans, 7.28
loan commitments, 7.20–7.23
loan origination fees and costs,
7.14–7.18
calculating internal costs, 7.17
enhancement of loan's yield,
deferred and recognized as, 7.14
external loan origination costs,
7.15–7.16
internal loan origination costs,
7.16–7.17
pending loans, costs on, 7.18
reduction of loan's yield, deferred
and recognized as, 7.15

Debt investment yields, Ch. 7, *cont.*
    standard costing methods,
        7.17–7.18
    loan syndication fees, 7.24
    overview, 7.03
    prepayment fees, 7.24
    purchased loans, fees and costs on,
        7.18
    rebates, 7.24–7.25
    refinancings and restructurings, fees
        and costs on, 7.19–7.20
        blended-rate loans, 7.20
        minor, defined, 7.19–7.20
        tests for new loan, 7.19
    SEC registrant alert, 7.37, 7.50
    standby commitments to purchase
        loans, 7.23–7.24
    terminology to describe cost basis,
        7.05–7.06
    troubled debt restructurings, fees and
        costs in, 7.20
    variable-rate provisions based on
        factor at inception, 7.58–7.59
Deep-in-the-money puts, 5.30
Defeasance, in-substance, 11.08–11.09,
    11.22
Deferrals for mandatorily redeemable
    instruments, 16.20–16.22
Deferred tax consequences
    loans, 3.34
    transfers of financial assets, 5.31
Delinquency fees, 7.24
Deposits exceeding insured limits,
    disclosures, 1.14
Derivative disclosures, Ch. 15
    accounting policies, 15.15–15.18
        elections, 15.10–15.11
    auditing considerations, 15.15
    background, 15.03
    cash flow hedges
        other comprehensive income,
            15.21–15.22
        transition adjustments involving,
            15.09–15.10
    energy trading contracts and,
        15.14
    fair value and, 15.05–15.06, 15.12
    foreign currency translation and,
        15.13
    foreign exchange risk, 15.17
    guarantees and, 15.13
    hedging, 15.06, 15.09–15.10,
        15.19–15.22
    hybrid instruments, 15.05–15.06
    illustrations, 15.15–15.22
    interim periods, 15.10
    narrative discussion of strategy,
        15.18–15.19

other comprehensive income
    cash flow hedges, 15.21–15.22
    measuring amounts to be
        reclassified out of, 15.09
    quantitative disclosures, 15.08
    reporting, 15.11–15.12
overlap with other standards,
    15.12–15.14
overview, 15.02
qualitative, 15.04–15.06, 15.19–15.20
quantitative, 15.06–15.10
scope, 15.03–15.04
SEC market risk, 15.13, 15.14–15.15
SEC registrant alert, 15.05–15.06,
    15.08–15.09, 15.11
securities and loans and, 15.12
unconditional purchase obligations
    and, 15.13–15.14
Derivatives, Ch. 12
    accounting, 12.32–12.37
    assessment timing, 12.15–12.18
    assignment, 12.13
    auditing considerations, 12.37–12.39
    background, 12.03
    balance sheet recognition, 12.32–12.34
    benefit plans, contracts held by,
        12.24
    business combinations, contracts
        issued in, 12.20
    cash flows from, 1.12
    cash flow statement presentation,
        12.36
    characteristics of, 12.03–12.18
    characteristics of both debt and
        equity, with, 16.27–16.45
    contract becoming, 12.15–12.16
    contract ceasing to be, 12.15
    defined, 12.03–12.18
    disclosures. *See* Derivative
        disclosures
    embedded. *See* Embedded derivatives
    entities not reporting earnings, 12.35–
        12.36
    equity contracts, 12.19–12.20
    evaluation of common contracts,
        12.16–12.18
    evolving nature of, 12.38
    fair value determination, 12.33–12.34
    FAS-133, 12.14–12.15, 12.25–12.29,
        12.38
    financing element, with, 12.36
    guarantee contracts, 12.21–12.22
    identifying, 12.29–12.30, 12.37–12.38
    illustrations, 12.40–12.42
    impediments to sale accounting,
        12.22
    income statement classification,
        12.35–12.36

income tax considerations, 12.36–12.37
initial investment, 12.06–12.08
insurance contracts, 12.20–12.21
interest-only strips, 12.23–12.24
interest rate swap accounting, 12.40–12.41
life insurance, investments in, 12.25
loan commitments, 12.22–12.23, 15.13
market mechanism, 12.11–12.13
net settlement, 12.08–12.14
nonfinancial asset exception, 12.28
normal purchases and sales, 12.26–12.27
notional amount, 12.05–12.06
offsetting assets and liabilities in balance sheet
  assets and liabilities, 17.06–17.08
  hedges, used as, 17.13, 17.18
option accounting, 12.41–12.42
overview, 12.02–12.03
payment provisions, 12.06
penalty clauses, 12.10–12.11
physical and other variables, contracts involving, 12.27–12.28
principal-only strips, 12.23–12.24
properly identifying, 12.39
recognizing changes in value, 12.34–12.36
registration payment arrangements, 12.25
regulatory considerations, 12.39
residual value guarantees, 12.24
scope exceptions, 12.19–12.32
security trades, 12.25
small initial investment, 12.06–12.08
stock compensation, 12.20
summary analysis of contract types, 12.30–12.32
transfers and extinguishment, 12.34
underlying, reference to, 12.04–12.05
valuation, 12.38–12.39
Disclosures
  cash equivalents, 1.14, 1.16
  collateral pledges, 9.21–9.22
  compensating balances, 1.17
  convertible debt and similar instruments, 10.29–10.36
  debt extinguishments, 11.21–11.22
  debt financing. *See* Debt financing
  debt investment yields. *See* Debt investment yields
  derivatives. *See* Derivative disclosures
  equity instruments, 16.45–16.55
  fair value disclosures. *See* Fair value disclosures
  fair value option, 19.10–19.15

loans, 3.41–3.49
  EITF Issue 84-19, 3.48
  FAS-118, 3.56–3.57
offsetting assets and liabilities in balance sheet, 17.15–17.16
restrictive covenants, 8.35
secured borrowings, 8.37
securities, 1.16, 2.31–2.35, 2.43–2.45, 2.58–2.59, 15.12
securities lending arrangements, 9.21–9.22
securitization, 6.46–6.51
servicing financial assets, 4.21–4.23, 4.27
transfers of financial assets, 5.31–5.32
troubled debt restructurings, 11.22, 11.26
Discount rate adjustment technique, 18.15–18.16
Distributions to shareholders, 6.13
Dividends, 16.10–16.12
  cash dividends, 16.10–16.11
  dividends-in-kind, 16.11
  fair value option, dividend income, 19.08
  for-profit enterprise accounting, 2.29
  stock dividends, 16.11–16.12
  stock splits, 16.12
Dollar rolls, 9.04, 9.13–9.14

E

Earnings per share
  convertible debt and similar instruments, 10.30–10.36, 10.40
    basic EPS, 10.32–10.33
    diluted EPS, 10.33–10.36
  equity instruments. *See* Equity instruments
EITF Issue 00-6
  accounting, 16.40–16.41
  contracts indexed to and potentially settled in company's own stock, 16.29–16.30
EITF Issue 00-19, 16.29–16.30
EITF Issue 00-27, 10.21–10.22
EITF Issue 02-4, 11.16
EITF Issue 03-6, 16.50–16.52
EITF Issue 84-19, 3.48
EITF Issue 96-12, 7.33–7.36
EITF Issue 96-19
  debt extinguishments, 11.09
  debt financing, 8.26–8.27
  troubled debt restructurings, 11.19
EITF Issue 98-5, 10.21–10.22
EITF Issue 98-14, 8.27–8.28
EITF Issue 99-7, 16.42

EITF Issue 99-20, 7.36–7.40
Embedded derivatives, Ch. 13
  accounting, 13.26–13.32
  assessment timing, 13.07
  auditing considerations, 13.35
  background, 13.03–13.04
  balance sheet presentation, 13.32
  beneficial interests, 13.12–13.15
  bifurcation, 13.26–13.32
  calls, 13.13
  clearly and closely related, 13.07,
    13.10–13.12
  coinsurance arrangements,
    13.25–13.26
  debt financing, 8.06
  debt instruments, 13.09–13.12
  defined, 13.03–13.04
  equity-indexed annuities,
    13.23–13.25
  equity-indexed life insurance,
    13.20–13.21
  equity instruments, 13.08–13.09
  equity-line note, bifurcating,
    13.35–13.38
  FAS-155, 13.32–13.33
  FAS-159, 13.33–13.34
  foreign currency, 13.15–13.18,
    13.38–13.39
  host contracts, 13.07–13.26,
    13.30–13.31
  hybrid debt instruments, 13.17–13.18
  identifying, 13.04–13.26
  illustrations, 13.35–13.39
  imputing interest on receivables and
    payables, 7.11
  insurance products, 13.18–13.26
  interest rates, 13.09–13.12
  leases, 13.15
  leveraged yield test, 13.10
  loans with, 3.10
  market-value annuities, 13.25
  negative yield test, 13.09–13.10, 13.38
  options
    bifurcating option-based
      derivatives, 13.29
    combinations of option contracts,
      13.29–13.30
  overview, 13.02–13.03
  prepayment risk, 13.14–13.15
  property and casualty insurance,
    13.21
  puts, 13.13
  regulatory considerations, 13.35
  SEC registrant alert, 13.05, 13.27
  separate accounting, 13.04–13.07
  split accounting, 13.06
  split-interest agreement, not-for-
    profit organization, 13.26

variable annuity contracts,
  13.21–13.24
Energy trading contracts, derivative
  disclosures, 15.14
Equitable right of redemption, 6.16
Equity
  contracts, 12.19–12.20
  embedded derivatives, 13.08–13.09
  equity-indexed annuities, 13.23–13.25
  equity-indexed life insurance,
    embedded derivatives, 13.20–13.21
  equity-linked note, bifurcating,
    13.35–13.38
  grant of equity interest in full
    settlement, 11.17
Equity instruments, Ch. 16
  accelerated share repurchases, 16.42
  accounting
    derivatives with characteristics of
      both debt and equity,
      16.27–16.45
    EITF Issue 00-6, 16.40–16.41
    equity transactions, 16.09–16.27
    FAS 150-3, 16.20–16.24
  auditing considerations, 16.57–16.58
  background, 16.04–16.06
  capital adequacy, 16.57
  capital stock, promises or notes
    received for, 16.10
  capital structure information,
    16.45–16.47
  combinations of contracts and other
    transactions, 16.41–16.42
  contracts indexed to and potentially
    settled in company's own stock,
    16.27–16.38
    balance sheet presentation,
      16.30–16.37
    disclosures, 16.48
    EITF Issue 00-6, 16.29–16.30
    EITF Issue 00-19, 16.29–16.30
    FAS-150, 16.29–16.30
    forward purchase contracts,
      16.30–16.31
    forward sale contracts, 16.32
    freestanding instruments, 16.31
    initial measurement, 16.36
    purchased call options, 16.32
    purchased put options, 16.32,
      16.59–16.60
    put warrants, 16.31
    reclassification, 16.38
    subsequent measurement,
      16.36–16.37
    supplemental criteria, 16.32–16.36
    written call options, 16.32
    written put options, 16.31, 16.61
  disclosures, 16.45–16.55

dividends, 16.10–16.12
  cash dividends, 16.10–16.11
  dividends-in-kind, 16.11
  stock dividends, 16.11–16.12
  stock splits, 16.12
earnings per share, 16.49–16.55
  accelerated share repurchase
    programs, 16.55
  contracts indexed to and
    potentially settled in company's
    own stock, 16.52–16.54
  EITF Issue 03-6, 16.50–16.52
  instruments excluded from, 16.50
  participating securities,
    16.50–16.51
  preferred stock, 16.52
EITF Issue 99-7, 16.42
embedded derivatives, 13.08–13.09
fair value disclosures, 16.55
FAS-133, 16.39–16.40
forward purchase contract,
  accounting, 16.62
goods, received for, 2.50–2.51
illustrations, 16.58–16.62
liabilities distinguished from equity,
  16.06–16.09
  equity, defined, 16.07–16.08
  financial instruments with
    characteristics of both debt and
    equity, 16.06–16.08
  liabilities, defined, 16.07
literature, 16.06, 16.17
minority interest, 16.15
not reported in stockholder's equity,
  16.16–16.27
  credit union member shares/
    deposits, 16.26–16.27
  extinguishment by parent of
    subsidiary's mandatorily
    redeemable preferred stock,
    16.25
  imputing dividends on preferred
    stock, 16.24–16.25
  insurance companies, surplus
    notes issued by, 16.26
  redeemable financial instruments,
    16.16–16.22, 16.24
  trust-preferred securities,
    16.19–16.24
  variable number of shares,
    obligation to issue, 16.25–16.26
obligations, representing, 16.47
overview, 16.03–16.04
preferred stock, liquidation
  preference, 16.46–16.47
redeemable stock, 16.47
registration payment arrangements
  disclosures, 16.48–16.49
  subject to, 16.42–16.45

regulatory considerations,
  16.55–16.57
scope, 16.04–16.05
SEC registrant alert, 16.18,
  16.22–16.23, 16.35–16.36, 16.44,
  16.46, 16.53
securities, disclosures, 16.45–16.46
services, received for, 2.50–2.51
shelf registration, costs incurred in,
  16.09–16.10
stock issued for cash, 16.09–16.10
subsidiary shares
  contracts indexed to, 16.40–16.41
  sale of, 16.15
temporary equity, 16.08–16.09, 16.40
treasury stock, 16.12–16.14
  buy-backs, 16.58–16.59
  purchase at above-market price,
    16.14
  subsequent sale, 16.14
  subsidiary investment in stock of
    parent, 16.14
trust-preferred securities, 16.19–16.24
Expected present value technique,
  18.16
Extinguishment of debt. *See* Debt
extinguishments

F

Factoring commissions, 7.25
Fair value, Ch. 18
  auditing considerations,
    18.35–18.36
  background, 18.03–18.05
  defined, 18.07
  derivative disclosures and,
    15.05–15.06, 15.12
  derivatives, determinations,
    12.33–12.34
  disclosures. *See* Fair value disclosures
  election, 2.13
  hedges. *See* Hedge accounting
  hybrid financial instruments, election
    for, 13.32–13.34
  measurements. *See* Fair value
    measurements
  overview, 18.03
  securities, 2.25–2.27
  servicing financial assets, fair value
    not practicable to determine,
    4.28–4.29
  transfers of financial assets
    auditing considerations, fair value
      estimates, 5.33–5.34
    measurement, 5.27–5.29
    not practicable to estimate fair
      value, 5.28–5.29, 5.31

Fair value disclosures, 18.21–18.35
  assets and liabilities measured at fair
    value, 18.27–18.29
  credit risk concentrations,
    18.29–18.31, 18.42
  equity instruments, 16.55
  estimates, use of, 18.42
  FAS-107, 18.22–18.25
  FAS-157, 18.28–18.29, 18.38–18.40
  financial entity, by, 18.40–18.41
  financial instruments, 18.21–18.27
    nonpublic entity exception,
      18.23–18.24
    requirements, 18.24–18.27
    scope, 18.21–18.24
  GAAP, interaction with, 18.21–18.35
  illustrations, 18.37–18.42
  integrated disclosures, 18.37–18.38
  market risk, 18.31–18.32
  nonrecurring basis, assets measured
    at fair value on, 18.40
  public company disclosures
    MD&A, in, 18.33–18.34
    off-balance-sheet arrangements,
      about, 18.34–18.35
  recurring basis, assets measured at
    fair value on, 18.38–18.39
  SEC registrant alert, 18.26, 18.32
  significant risks and uncertainties,
    18.32–18.33
Fair value measurements, 18.05–18.20
  bid and ask prices, use of, 18.20
  discount rate adjustment technique,
    18.15–18.16
  expected present value technique,
    18.16
  fair value hierarchy, 18.17–18.20
  fair value option and, 19.16–19.17
  fair value premise, 18.10–18.12
    assets, application to, 18.10–18.11
    in-exchange premise, 18.11
    in-use premise, 18.11
    liabilities, application to,
      18.11–18.12
  initial measurements, 18.12–18.13
  inputs to present value techniques,
    18.16–18.17
  key underlying concepts, 18.08–18.10
  Level 1 inputs, 18.18
  Level 2 inputs, 18.19
  Level 3 inputs, 18.19–18.20
  loans, 3.06–3.07, 3.10
  market participants, 18.10
  measurement model, 18.12–18.20
  most advantageous market, 18.09
  objective of, 18.08
  orderly transaction, exchange
    occurring in, 18.09

  practicability exceptions,
    18.05–18.07
  present value techniques,
    18.15–18.16
  principal market, 18.09
  scope, 18.05–18.07
  SEC registrant alert, 18.13, 18.20
  specific asset or liability, 18.08
  transaction costs, 18.10
  transportation costs, 18.10
  types of markets, 18.17
  unit of account, 18.08–18.09
  valuation techniques, 18.13–18.16
Fair value of collateral method,
  3.21–3.22
Fair value option, Ch. 19
  application of, 19.03–19.08
  auditing considerations, 19.16–19.18
  cash flow statements when elected,
    1.11
  contract-by-contract basis,
    19.06–19.08
  convertible debt, 10.28–10.29
  debt financing, 8.08–8.09
  disclosures, 19.09–19.15
  dividend income, 19.08
  election dates, 19.05–19.06
  fair value changes and, 19.16–19.17
  fair value measurements and,
    19.16–19.17
  FAS-159, 19.10–19.15
  fees and costs, 19.08
  financial statement presentation,
    19.08–19.09
    consolidated versus separate
      company, 19.06
  imputing interest on receivables and
    payables, 7.11–7.12
  interest income and expense, 19.08
  loans, 3.06–3.07, 3.10
  overview, 19.01–19.03
  scope of, 19.03–19.05
  securities, 2.22–2.23
  single transaction, instruments issued
    or acquired in, 19.07
  subsequent measurement,
    19.07–19.08
FAS-5
  impairment of loans, 3.13–3.16,
    3.22–3.24, 3.55–3.56
  loans, 3.24–3.25
FAS-15, 11.15
FAS-52, 14.65–14.66
FAS-65, 3.37–3.40
FAS-91
  debt investment yields, 7.25–7.32
  interest method, 7.25–7.32
FAS-107, 18.22–18.25

FAS-114
  impairment of loans, 3.13–3.19,
    3.53–3.55
  troubled debt restructurings, 11.19
FAS-115
  collateral pledges, 9.10
  securities, 2.06–2.08, 2.13–2.27,
    2.46–2.47
  securities lending arrangements, 9.10,
    9.20
FAS-115-1
  disclosures, 7.52
  securities, 2.43–2.45
FAS-118, 3.56–3.57
FAS-124-1
  disclosures, 7.52
  securities, 2.43–2.45
FAS-133
  avoiding, 12.14–12.15
  background, 12.03
  benefit plan contracts, 12.24
  business combination, 12.19–12.32
  convertible debt, 10.17–10.21
  derivative disclosures, 15.02–15.15,
    15.21
  derivatives, 12.03, 12.14–12.15,
    12.20–12.21, 12.25–12.29, 12.38
  discretion, 12.40
  equity instruments, 16.39–16.40
  guarantee contracts, 12.21–12.22
  identifying derivatives under,
    12.29–12.30
  imputing interest on receivables and
    payables, 7.11
  interpretations, 12.40
  life insurance, 12.25
  residual value, 12.24
  scope exceptions, 12.19–12.32
  security trades, 12.25
  servicing financial assets, 4.10–4.12
  stock compensation, 12.20
FAS-140
  categories of financial asset transfers,
    5.06–5.07
  excluded transactions, 5.05–5.06
  FASB project to amend, 5.09
  guarantees, 8.33–8.34
  securities lending arrangements,
    9.10–9.21
  transfers of financial assets, 5.03,
    5.05–5.06, 5.09
FAS-144, 11.17
FAS-145, 11.21
FAS-150, 16.29–16.30
FAS-155, 13.32–13.33
FAS-157, 18.28–18.29, 18.38–18.40
FAS-159
  embedded derivatives, 13.33–13.34
  fair value option, 19.10–19.15

FASB projects
  derivative disclosures, 15.02–15.03
  loan disclosures, 3.41
FDIC receivership, 5.16
Federal funds purchased and sold, 9.05
FIN-39, 17.17–17.18
FIN-45, 8.30
FIN-46(R), 6.34, 6.42–6.44, 6.49
Financial institutions, reciprocal
  balances, 1.07
Financial statement presentation
  available-for-sale securities, 2.31
  fair value option, 19.08–19.09
    consolidated versus separate
      company, 19.06
  securities, 2.30–2.31
  securitization, 6.23
  trading securities, 2.31
  transfers of financial assets,
    classification of, 5.11, 5.13
Financing, classifying cash receipts and
  payments, 1.09–1.10
Fixed-rate foreign-currency-
  denominated loans, cash flow hedges,
  14.101–14.103
Foreclosed assets, offsetting in balance
  sheet, 17.14
Foreign currency
  cash and cash equivalents, 1.05
  cash flows, 1.13
  contracts, embedded derivatives,
    13.15–13.18
  derivative disclosures, 15.13
  embedded derivatives, 13.38–13.39
  hedges. *See* Hedge accounting
  securities, 2.21
Foreign debt-equity swaps, 3.47
Foreign exchange risk, derivative
  disclosures, 15.17
Foreign loans, government guarantee
  of, 3.48
Foreign operation, hedge of net
  investment in, 14.75–14.80
For-profit enterprises, accounting for
  securities. *See* Securities
Forward contracts, 16.30–16.32, 16.62
FR-72, 15.05
Freestanding instruments, 16.31

G

Generally accepted accounting principles
  fair value disclosures, interaction
    with, 18.21–18.35
  loans and, 3.53
  transfers of financial assets, 5.03
Goods, equity instruments received for,
  2.50–2.51

Government National Mortgage
Association (GNMA) securities,
4.20–4.21
Government securities, offsetting assets
and liabilities in balance sheet,
17.12–17.13
Gross and net cash flows, 1.08–1.10
Guarantee contracts
derivatives, 12.21–12.22
FAS-133 scope exceptions,
12.21–12.22
Guarantees
debt extinguishments, 11.21
debt financing. *See* Debt financing
derivative disclosures, 15.13
residual value, FAS-133 scope
exceptions, 12.24
securitization, 6.48

H

Health care organizations, hedge
accounting, 14.81
Hedge accounting, Ch. 14
assessing effectiveness, methods of,
14.19–14.24
auditing considerations, 14.85–14.87
background, 14.04–14.24
balance sheet reporting, 14.81–14.82
capitalization of interest expense on
debt, 14.83–14.84
cash flow hedges, 14.41–14.64
all-in-one hedges, 14.49
assuming no ineffectiveness,
14.50–14.52
basis swaps, 14.48–14.49
certificates of deposit, 14.48
changes in creditworthiness,
assessing, 14.49–14.50
changes in terms of forecasted
transactions, 14.61–14.62
commercial paper, 14.48
common strategies, 14.41
derivative disclosures,
15.09–15.10, 15.21–15.22
documentation, 14.41–14.42
financial instruments, 14.44
fixed-rate foreign-currency-
denominated loans,
14.101–14.103
forecasted issuance of fixed-rate
debt, 14.100–14.101
groups of forecasted transactions,
14.46–14.48
hedging instruments, 14.48–14.49
held-to-maturity securities,
14.44–14.45

interest rate swap shortcut,
14.98–14.99
limitations on amounts deferred
in OCI, 14.56–14.57
methods of measuring
effectiveness, 14.53–14.55
nonfinancial assets, 14.45–14.46
ongoing expectation of
effectiveness, 14.49–14.52
options, 14.52
portfolio of variable-rate loans,
14.46–14.48
portfolios of similar variable-rate
assets or liabilities, 14.59
qualifications, 14.43–14.52
reclassifying amounts from OCI,
14.55–14.56
replacing rollover strategy with
long-term debt, 14.62
risks being hedged, 14.43–14.46
shortcut method, 14.57–14.59
stock compensation liabilities,
14.45
termination, 14.60–14.64
types of items, 14.43
variable interest rates, 14.44
cash flow statement presentation,
14.84
centralized treasury hedge of foreign
currency forecasted transactions,
14.106–14.111
changes in methods, 14.22
collars, 14.12
combining derivatives, 14.17
common hedge criteria, 14.08–14.17
consistency of methods, 14.22
data to include in assessment,
14.21–14.22
debt extinguishments and,
11.05–11.06, 14.83
derivative disclosures, 15.06,
15.09–15.10, 15.19–15.22
derivatives, classification of, 14.82
description, 14.05
designating part of derivative, 14.17
disqualified hedged items,
14.14–14.17
entities not reporting earnings
separately, 14.80–14.81
fair value hedge accounting,
14.24–14.41
adjustments to hedged items,
14.34–14.35
available-for-sale securities,
14.34–14.35
common strategies, 14.24
discrete risks, 14.26–14.27
documentation, 14.24–14.25

effectiveness, methods of
assessing, 14.30–14.31
equity security using net written
option collar, 14.93–14.96
financial instruments, 14.26–14.27
fixed-rate foreign-currency-
denominated loans, 14.96–14.97
fixed-rate noncallable debt,
interest rate risk in, 14.90–14.91
foreign currency hedges,
14.68–14.70
groups of assets or liabilities,
14.27–14.28
held-to-maturity securities, 14.27
impairment, assessing hedged
items for, 14.40–14.41
interest rate risk, 14.32–14.33
mortgage servicing rights,
14.28–14.29
nonfinancial items, 14.27
ongoing expectation of
effectiveness, 14.30
options, 14.30
partial-term hedges, 14.29–14.30
parts of assets or liabilities,
14.28–14.30
portion of pool of prepayable
loans, designating, 14.29
prepayable, defined, 14.38–14.39
prepayable fixed-rate loans,
portfolios of, 14.31
prepayment risk, 14.27
qualifications, 14.26–14.31
shortcut method, 14.35–14.39,
14.91–14.93
similar assets or liabilities,
portfolios of, 14.39
swaps acquired in business
combinations, 14.39
termination, 14.39–14.40
types of hedged items, 14.26
firm commitment, 14.88–14.89
forecasted sale with purchased put
option, 14.105–14.106
foreign currency hedges, 14.64–14.80
accounting for net investment,
14.77–14.80
after-tax hedging of foreign
currency risk, 14.80
available-for-sale securities, 14.70
cash flow hedges, 14.70–14.75
centralized hedging strategies,
14.73–14.74
common criteria, 14.66–14.68
derivatives designated as hedges,
effectiveness of, 14.78–14.80
designating amount of net
investment being hedged, 14.77

distinguishing between types,
14.66
fair value hedges, 14.68–14.70
FAS-52, 14.65–14.66
firm commitments, 14.68–14.69
forecasted intercompany
transactions, 14.72–14.75
forecasted purchases and sales on
credit, 14.71–14.72,
14.103–14.105
groups of forecasted transactions,
14.71
hedge of net investment in foreign
operation, 14.75–14.80
interaction with shortcut method
for swaps, 14.69–14.70
intercompany derivatives,
14.74–14.75
limitations on derivatives with
multiple underlyings,
14.76–14.77
nonderivatives designated as
hedges, effectiveness of,
14.77–14.78
nonderivatives hedged for interest
rate risk, 14.78
planned sale of net investment,
14.80
qualifying hedging instruments,
14.76–14.77
recognized assets and liabilities,
14.69–14.70, 14.71
groups of assets and liabilities, 14.18
hedged items, 14.13–14.14
hedging instruments, 14.10–14.13
hedging relationship, documentation
of, 14.09–14.10
highly effective, defined, 14.22–14.23
illustrations, 14.87–14.111
income statement reporting,
14.82–14.84
intercompany derivatives, limitations
on, 14.12–14.13
interest rate risk, 14.14
offsetting effects, expectation of,
14.18–14.19
overview, 14.04
qualifying versus measuring
effectiveness, 14.23–14.24
regulatory considerations,
14.84–14.85
reporting elements, 14.81–14.84
SEC registrant alert, 14.20,
14.36–14.38, 14.50–14.51, 14.54,
14.58–14.59, 14.82–14.83
types of hedges, 14.05–14.08
unit of measure issues, 14.17–14.18
written options, 14.11

Held-to-maturity securities, 2.14–2.19
    desecuritization, 3.11
    reasons to sell or transfer, 2.15–2.17
    restrictions against classification,
        2.17–2.18
    sales, 2.27–2.28
    servicing financial assets, 4.05–4.06
    unacceptable sales or transfers,
        2.18–2.19
Host contracts, embedded derivatives,
    13.07–13.26
Hybrid financial instruments
    accounting, 13.03
    balance sheet presentations,
        13.34–13.35
    derivative disclosures, 15.05–15.06
    embedded derivatives, 13.17–13.18
    fair value election, 13.32–13.34
    loans with embedded derivatives,
        3.10
    securities
        accounting for, 2.18
        fair value election, 2.13

I

Impairment
    hedged items, assessing for,
        14.40–14.41
    investments, 2.39–2.45
        determining, 2.39–2.40
        other-than-temporary, 2.43
        other than temporary, evaluating,
            2.40–2.42
        recognizing loss, 2.43
    loans. *See* Loans
Imputed interest, 7.49
Income statements
    servicing financial assets, 4.19–4.20
    troubled debt restructurings,
        classification, 11.21
Income tax considerations
    convertible debt, 10.26–10.27
    derivatives, 12.36–12.37
Indexed instruments, 13.20–13.21
Induced conversions, 10.11–10.13,
    10.35–10.36, 10.38–10.39, 11.07–11.08
In-substance defeasance, 11.08–11.09,
    11.22
Insurance
    coinsurance arrangements,
        embedded derivatives, 13.25–13.26
    derivatives, FAS-133 scope
        exceptions, 12.20–12.21
    insurance companies
        nonmarketable equity securities at
            fair value, 2.08
    surplus notes issued by,
        16.26
    offsetting assets and liabilities in
        balance sheet, 17.13
    products, embedded derivatives,
        13.18–13.26
Integrated disclosures, 18.37–18.38
Interest
    debt financing disclosures
        interest costs, 8.37
        interest elements of debt, 8.46
    derivative disclosures, interest rate
        risk, 15.16–15.18
    fair value option, interest income and
        expense, 19.08
    for-profit enterprise accounting,
        interest income, 2.30
    imputed interest, 7.49
    interest-only strips, 4.07, 4.12–4.14,
        12.23–12.24
    loans, ceasing recognition of interest
        income, 3.52
    offsetting assets and liabilities in
        balance sheet, effect on interest
        income and expense, 17.10–17.12
    rates, embedded derivatives,
        13.09–13.12
    rate swap accounting, 12.40–12.41
    troubled debt restructurings, variable
        interest rates, 11.18–11.19
Interest method. *See* Debt investment
    yields
Intermediaries
    debt extinguishments, third-party
        intermediaries, 11.12–11.14
    offsetting assets and liabilities in
        balance sheet, reacquisition of debt
        by intermediary, 17.14–17.15
Investments
    classifying cash receipts and
        payments, 1.09
    debt and equity securities. *See*
        Securities
    debt investment yields. *See* Debt
        investment yields
    equity method, 2.46–2.50
    impairment, 2.39–2.45
        determining, 2.39–2.40
        other-than-temporary, 2.43
        other than temporary, evaluating,
            2.40–2.42
        recognizing loss, 2.43
    investment company accounting,
        securities, 2.45–2.46
    life insurance, FAS-133 scope
        exceptions, 12.25
    structured notes, 2.50
Isolation, 5.15–5.16, 6.15–6.16

L

Leases, embedded derivatives,
13.15
Lending arrangements. *See* Securities
lending arrangements
Liabilities distinguished from equity,
16.06–16.09
equity, defined, 16.07–16.08
financial instruments with
characteristics of both debt and
equity, 16.06–16.08
liabilities, defined, 16.07
Liens, sale of assets subject to, 11.07
Life insurance
derivatives, FAS-133 scope
exceptions, 12.25
equity-indexed, embedded
derivatives, 13.20–13.21
policy loans, offsetting assets and
liabilities in balance sheet, 17.13
Line-of-credit arrangements, changes in,
8.27–8.28
Liquidation preference of preferred
stock, 16.46–16.47
Loan commitments, 7.20–7.22
derivatives, accounted as, 7.23
Loan origination fees and costs,
7.14–7.18
calculating internal costs, 7.17
enhancement of loan's yield, deferred
and recognized as, 7.14
external loan origination costs,
7.15–7.16
internal loan origination costs,
7.16–7.17
pending loans, costs on, 7.18
reduction of loan's yield, deferred
and recognized as, 7.15
standard costing methods, 7.17–7.18
Loans, Ch. 3. *See also* Securities
accounting, 3.06–3.40
policies and disclosures, 3.41–3.43
accrual, 3.24–3.25
ADC loans, 3.05–3.06
allocation of carrying amount of loans
sold, 4.27–4.28
auditing considerations, 3.51–3.53
background, 3.04–3.06
cash flow statement presentation,
3.36–3.37
categories, presentation of, 3.12
charge-offs, 3.31–3.34
classification of, 3.10–3.12, 3.51–3.52
collateralized loans, 3.49
commitments, 12.22–12.23
conversion into debt security, 2.47
costs to sell, 3.19

credit losses on off-balance-sheet
commitments, 3.30–3.31
debt extinguishments, loan
participation and syndication,
11.14–11.15
deferred tax consequences, 3.34
defined, 3.05–3.06
derivative disclosures, 15.12
derivatives, loan commitments,
12.22–12.23, 15.13
disclosures, 3.41–3.49
EITF Issue 84-19, 3.48
FAS-118, 3.56–3.57
embedded derivatives, with, 3.10
equity method and other
investments, 3.48
expected future cash flows,
recognizing changes in, 3.19–3.20
fair value measurement, 3.06–3.07,
3.10
fair value of collateral method,
3.21–3.22
fair value option, 3.06–3.07, 3.10
FAS-5, 3.24–3.25
FASB project on loan disclosures, 3.41
foreign debt-equity swaps, 3.47
foreign loans, government guarantee
of, 3.48
GAAP accounting and, 3.53
grouping loans, 3.19, 3.23
guidance, 3.19–3.29
held for investment, 3.11
held-to-maturity securities,
desecuritization of, 3.11
hybrid financial instruments, 3.10
illustrations, 3.53–3.57
impairment, 3.12–3.18
determining, 3.17–3.18
FAS-5, 3.13–3.16, 3.22–3.24,
3.55–3.56
FAS-114, 3.13–3.19, 3.53–3.55
identifying loans for evaluation,
3.15–3.17
income recognition after, 3.34
literature, 3.14–3.15
measuring, 3.18, 3.23–3.24,
3.52–3.53
quantitative disclosures,
3.43–3.47
recognition, 3.52
recording, 3.19
initial measurement, 3.06–3.10
interest income, ceasing recognition
of, 3.52
LDC loans, 3.48
lending fees and costs, 3.08–3.09
life insurance policy, offsetting, 17.13
loan splitting, 3.45–3.46

Loans, Ch. 3, *cont.*
  mortgage banking model, 3.37–3.40
    affiliates, transactions with, 3.39
    balance sheet classification, 3.40
    categories, transfers between,
      3.39–3.40
    cost basis components, 3.38
    fair value determinations,
      3.38–3.39
    FAS-65, 3.37–3.40
    securitization of mortgages held
      for sale, 3.40
  mortgage loan payment
    modifications, 3.48
  nonaccrual loans, 3.34, 3.46
  nonmortgage loans held for sale,
    3.11
  nonrecourse loans, 11.17
  observable market price method, 3.21
  off-balance-sheet credit risk, 3.47
  originated loans, 3.07–3.08
  overview, 3.03–3.04
  past due loans, 3.46
  pledges of collateral, 3.09
  portfolios, 3.16, 3.55–3.56
  present value method, 3.20–3.21
  purchased loans, 3.08
  recorded investment, 3.43–3.44
  refinancing, purchased servicing
    right, 4.21
  regulatory considerations, 3.49–3.51
  sales and other transfers, 3.34–3.36
    bad-debt recovery rights, 3.36
    loans held for investment, 3.35
    mortgage loans held for sale,
      3.38–3.40
  SEC registrant alert, 3.22, 3.31,
    3.35–3.37, 3.40, 3.42–3.43, 3.45
  securities
    accounted like, 3.09–3.10
    terminology differences, 3.12
  servicing rights, 3.09
  subsequent measurement, 3.10–3.12
  transfers, loans acquired in, 3.46
  transfers of financial assets, 5.12,
    5.29–5.31, 5.36–5.38
  troubled debt restructurings. *See*
    Troubled debt restructurings
Loan syndication fees, 7.24
Lock-box arrangements, 8.20–8.21, 8.46
Long-term debt financing. *See* Debt
  financing

M

Management's discussion and analysis
  (MD&A), 8.39–8.40, 18.33–18.34

Market risk, fair value disclosures,
  18.31–18.32
Market-value annuities, 13.25
Minority interest, 16.15
Modification of debt. *See* Debt
  extinguishments
Mortgages
  convertible debt, 10.10
  debt extinguishments, participating
    mortgage loans, 11.05
  debt financing disclosures,
    participating mortgages, 8.35
  GNMA, servicing, 4.20–4.21
  loans, mortgage banking model. *See*
    Loans
  mortgage loan payment
    modifications, 3.48
  securities, mortgage-backed,
    2.26–2.27
  transfers of financial assets,
    mortgage-backed bonds, 5.31
  wrap-around, 17.14
Multiple option contracts, 16.31

N

Net settlement of derivatives,
  12.08–12.14
New loan test, 8.26–8.27
Nonaccrual loans, 3.34, 3.36
Nonmarketable equity securities,
  accounting for investments, 2.35–2.36
Nonpublic entities, fair value
  disclosures, 18.23–18.24
Nonrecourse debt, offsetting assets and
  liabilities in balance sheet, 17.13–17.14
Nonrecourse loans, 11.17
Notes
  equity linked, bifurcating,
    13.35–13.38
  received for capital stock, 16.10
Not-for-profit enterprises
  accounting for securities investments,
    2.37–2.38
  hedge accounting, 14.81
  investment income for, 7.46–7.48
  split-interest agreement, 13.26
Notional amount, 12.05–12.06

O

Observable market price method, 3.21
Off-balance-sheet arrangements
  loans
    credit losses, 3.30–3.31
    credit risk, 3.47

public company disclosure,
18.34–18.35
Offsetting assets and liabilities in balance
sheet, Ch. 17
accounting guidance, 17.04–17.15
auditing considerations, 17.17
authoritative literature, 17.12–17.15
background, 17.02–17.04
credit receivables and insurance
payables, 17.15, 17.19
criteria, 17.11
derivatives
assets and liabilities, 17.06–17.08
hedges, used as, 17.13, 17.18
determinable amounts owed, 17.05
disclosures, 17.15–17.16
display versus derecognition,
17.02–17.03
exceptions, 17.06–17.12
FIN-39, 17.17–17.18
foreclosed assets, 17.14
general principle, 17.04–17.06
government securities, 17.12–17.13
insurance recoveries, 17.13
interest income and expense, effect
on, 17.10–17.12
intermediary, reacquisition of debt
by, 17.14–17.15
life insurance policy loans, 17.13
netting, motivation for, 17.03–17.04
nonrecourse debt, 17.13–17.14
overview, 17.02
reporting party intending to settle,
17.05–17.06
repurchase agreements
receivables and payables from,
17.08–17.10, 17.18–17.19
reverse repurchase agreements,
17.18–17.19
right of setoff
demonstrating, 17.04–17.06
enforceability, 17.06
tax liabilities, 17.12–17.13
trade date receivables and payables,
17.12
wrap-around mortgages, 17.14
Operating, classifying cash receipts and
payments, 1.10–1.11
Option accounting, 12.41–12.42
Options
calls, 13.13, 16.32
derivatives, option accounting, 12.41–
12.42
embedded derivatives
bifurcating option-based
derivatives, 13.29
combinations of option contracts,
13.29–13.30

forward-based derivatives,
bifurcating, 13.28–13.29
multiple option contracts, 16.31
puts, 13.13, 16.31–16.32, 16.59–16.61
Originated loans, 3.07–3.08
Other comprehensive income, derivative
disclosures
cash flow hedges, 15.21–15.22
measuring amounts to be reclassified
out of, 15.09
quantitative disclosures, 15.08
reporting, 15.11–15.12

P

Parent companies. *See* Subsidiaries
Placement fees, 7.49
Pledges of collateral. *See* Collateral
pledges
Preferred stock
conversion, 10.35–10.36
convertible debt, 10.18–10.19
extinguishment by parent of
subsidiary's mandatorily
redeemable preferred stock, 16.25
liquidation preference, 16.46–16.47
Prepayment fees, 7.24
Prepayment risk
accounting for, 2.19
cash and cash equivalents, 1.12
Present value method, 3.20–3.21
Present value techniques, fair value
measurements, 18.15–18.16
Principal-only strips, 12.23–12.24
Promises received for capital stock, 16.10
Public company disclosures
MD&A, in, 8.39–8.40, 18.33–18.34
off-balance-sheet arrangements,
about, 18.34–18.35
securitization, 6.50–6.51
Purchased loans, 3.08
Puts, 13.13, 16.31–16.32, 16.59–16.61

Q

Qualifying special-purpose entities
(QSPE)
applying sale criteria in transfers
involving, 6.14–6.20
attributes, 6.07–6.14
change in status, 6.28
commingled, identifying new
interests in, 6.25
conditions constraining transferee,
6.17

consideration other than beneficial interests in transferred assets, 6.15
consolidation, 6.29–6.30, 6.55–6.56
demonstrably distinct from transferor, 6.07–6.08
desecuritization of financial assets, 6.15
equitable right of redemption, 6.16
identification, 6.55
illustrations, 6.56–6.59
isolation, 6.15–6.16
limited and automatic sales, 6.12–6.13
limits on holdings, 6.09–6.12
maintaining effective control, 6.17–6.19
prescribed and limited activities, 6.08–6.09
removal of accounts provisions, 6.18–6.19
right to reacquire assets, 6.19–6.20
significance of, 6.06
transfers of financial assets, 5.07, 6.23–6.28

R

Rebates, 7.24–7.25
Receivable and payables
imputing interest on receivables and payables. *See* Debt investment yields
offsetting in balance sheet. *See* Offsetting assets and liabilities in balance sheet
Receivership
FDIC, 5.16
other entities, 5.16
Reciprocal balances, 1.07
Redeemable financial instruments
not reported in stockholder's equity, 16.16–16.22, 16.24
stock, disclosure, 16.47
Refinancings and restructurings, fees and costs on, 7.19–7.20
blended-rate loans, 7.20
minor, defined, 7.19–7.20
tests for new loan, 7.19
Registration payment arrangements, 8.07–8.08, 10.27, 12.25
equity instruments
disclosures, 16.48–16.49
subject to, 16.42–16.45
Related parties
debt extinguishments, 11.06
sales between, 5.16

Removal of accounts provisions (ROAP)
analysis of, 6.19
QPSEs
limited and automatic sales, 6.12
securitization and, 6.18–6.19
rights to reacquire assets, 6.19–6.20
transfers of financial assets, 5.21
Repurchase agreements
defined, 9.04
offsetting assets and liabilities in balance sheet
receivables and payables from, 17.08–17.10, 17.18–17.19
reverse repurchase agreements, 17.18–17.19
Residual value guarantees, 12.24
Restricted cash, 1.14–1.15
Restricted stock, 2.07
Restrictive covenants, 8.35
Restructuring fees. *See* Refinancings and restructurings, fees and costs on
Reverse repurchase agreements, 17.18–17.19
Revolving credit arrangement, modification of, 8.44–8.45
Revolving debt arrangements, changes in, 8.27–8.28
Revolving-period securitizations, 6.26–6.28
Rollovers of short-term obligations, 8.17–8.18

S

Sale accounting impediments, 12.22
Sale-buyback
accounting as sale, 9.23
securities lending arrangements, 9.05, 9.23–9.25
SEC market risk, 15.14–15.15
SEC registrant alerts
convertible debt and similar instruments, 10.22, 10.35
debt extinguishments, 11.13–11.14
debt financing, 8.15, 8.22–8.23, 8.34, 8.38, 8.40
debt investment yields, 7.37, 7.50
derivative disclosures, 15.05–15.06, 15.08–15.09, 15.11
embedded derivatives, 13.05, 13.27
equity instruments, 16.18, 16.22–16.23, 16.35–16.36, 16.44, 16.46, 16.53
fair value disclosures, 18.26, 18.32
fair value measurements, 18.13, 18.20
hedge accounting, 14.20, 14.36–14.38, 14.50–14.51, 14.54, 14.58–14.59, 14.82–14.83

loans, 3.22, 3.31, 3.35–3.37, 3.40, 3.42–3.43, 3.45
securities, 2.24, 2.34–2.35, 2.41–2.42, 2.51
securitization, 6.24, 6.50
transfers of financial assets, 5.14
variable interest entities, 6.33–6.35, 6.38, 6.41
Secured borrowings
disclosures, 8.37
transfers of financial assets accounted as, 5.12–5.13, 5.29–5.31, 5.36–5.38
Securities, Ch. 2. *See also* Convertible debt and similar instruments
accounting
for-profit enterprises, by, 2.11–2.35
not-for-profit enterprises, for, 2.37–2.38
securities portfolio, for, 2.54–2.57
auditing considerations, 2.52–2.53
available-for-sale securities, 2.20–2.22
deferred tax and, 2.21–2.22
financial statement presentation, 2.31
foreign currency, 2.21
sales, 2.28
background, 2.03–2.11
cash equivalents as, 1.05–1.06, 1.16
cash flow reporting, 2.30–2.31
changes in marketability, influence, or form, 2.46–2.48
classification and measurement, 2.13–2.27
consideration for goods and services, 2.50–2.51
contracts to purchase non-derivatives, 2.48
current and noncurrent assets, 2.30
debt securities
accounting, 2.37–2.38
defined, 2.05–2.06
defined, 2.04–2.11
derivative disclosures, 15.12
disclosures, 1.16, 2.31–2.35, 2.43–2.45, 2.58–2.59, 15.12
dividends, 2.29
equity instruments, disclosures, 16.45–16.46
equity method investment, 2.46–2.50
equity securities, defined, 2.06–2.08
fair value, 2.25–2.27
mortgage-backed securities, 2.26–2.27
restricted securities, 2.26
fair value option, 2.22–2.23
FAS-115, 2.06–2.08, 2.13–2.27, 2.46–2.47

FAS-115-1, 2.43–2.45
FAS-124-1, 2.43–2.45
financial statement presentation, 2.30–2.31
for-profit enterprises, accounting for, 2.11–2.35
Government National Mortgage Association (GNMA) securities, costs of issuing, 4.20–4.21
held-to-maturity securities, 2.14–2.19
reasons to sell or transfer, 2.15–2.17
restrictions against classification, 2.17–2.18
sales, 2.27–2.28
servicing financial assets, 4.05–4.06
unacceptable sales or transfers, 2.18–2.19
hybrid financial instruments
accounting for, 2.18
fair value election for, 2.13
illustrations, 2.54–2.59
impairment of investment securities, 2.39–2.45
determining, 2.39–2.40
other than temporary, 2.40–2.43
recognizing loss, 2.43
initial measurement, 2.13
instruments accounted for like securities, 2.10–2.11
insurance company exception, 2.08
interest income, 2.30
investment company accounting, 2.45–2.46
lending arrangements. *See* Securities lending arrangements
literature, 2.08–2.10
loans
accounted like, 3.09–3.10
terminology differences, 3.12
marketable equity securities, accounting, 2.37–2.38
mortgage-backed securities, 2.26–2.27
nonmarketable equity securities, accounting, 2.35–2.36
not-for-profit enterprises, accounting for, 2.37–2.38
other financial investments, accounting, 2.38
overview, 2.03
prepayable loan accounted as security, reclassification of, 2.24–2.25
regulatory considerations, 2.51
restricted stock, 2.07
revolving-period securitization, 4.06

Securities, Ch. 2, *cont.*
  sales and other transfers, 2.27–2.29
  SEC registrant alert, 2.24, 2.27,
    2.34–2.35, 2.41–2.42, 2.51
  short sales, 2.29
  stock receipt in demutualization,
    2.47–2.48
  trade date accounting, 2.11–2.13
  trades, FAS-133 scope exceptions,
    12.25
  trading securities, 2.19–2.20, 2.28
    elective use of category, 2.20
    financial statement presentation,
      2.31
    hedges, 2.20
    required classification, 2.19
    sales, 2.28
  transfers, 2.27–2.29
    between categories, 2.23–2.25
Securities lending arrangements, Ch. 9.
  See also Collateral pledges
  accounting, 9.10–9.21
  audit considerations, 9.22–9.23
  background, 9.03–9.06
  borrow-versus-pledge transactions,
    9.16–9.17
  cash flow statement, 9.20–9.21
    sales and purchases, 9.20
    secured borrowings, 9.21
  deferred tax, 9.20
  defined, 9.05
  disclosures, 9.21–9.22
  dollar rolls, 9.04, 9.13–9.14
  FAS-115, 9.10, 9.20
  FAS-140, 9.10–9.21
  federal funds purchased and sold,
    9.05
  gains and losses, classification of,
    9.17–9.18
  illustrations, 9.23–9.27
  overview, 9.02–9.03
  proceeds other than beneficial
    interests in transferred assets,
    9.16–9.17
  receivables and payables
    classification of, 9.19
    measurement of, 9.18–9.19
    offsetting, 9.19
  regulatory considerations, 9.22
  repurchase agreements, 9.04
  repurchase or redemption of
    transferred assets, 9.11–9.16
    call options, repurchase
      agreements evaluated as,
      9.15–9.16
    dollar rolls, 9.13–9.14
    maturity, repurchase before, 9.15
    substantially the same, 9.13–9.14
    sufficient collateral, 9.14–9.15

  restricted-use or no collateral,
    9.19–9.20
  sales, 9.17–9.18
  secured borrowings, 9.18–9.19,
    9.25–9.26
  security-for-security transactions,
    9.16–9.17
  sell-buybacks, 9.05, 9.23–9.25
  terminology, 9.04–9.06
  transaction elements, 9.05–9.06
  transferee's right to pledge or
    exchanges, 9.11
Securitization, Ch. 6
  accounting, 6.07–6.28
  accrued interest receivable, 6.25
  asset-backed security transactions,
    disclosures, 6.50–6.51
  auditing considerations, 6.54–6.56
  background, 6.03–6.06
  calculating gain or loss on sale,
    6.23–6.24
  cash reserve accounts, valuing,
    6.24–6.25
  common features, 6.04–6.06
  consolidation of securitization
    entities, 6.28–6.46
    adequately capitalized entities
      issuing voting equity, 6.30–6.31
    variable interest entities, 6.31–6.46
  diagrams, 6.06
  disclosures, 6.46–6.51
  existing securities, 6.26
  financial assets, 6.47–6.48
  illustrations, 6.56–6.59
  overview, 6.03
  public company disclosures,
    6.50–6.51
  qualifying special-purpose entities
    (QSPE). *See* Qualifying special-
    purpose entities
  regulatory considerations, 6.52–6.54
  removal of accounts provisions
    (ROAP)
    analysis of, 6.19
    rights to reacquire assets,
      6.19–6.20
  revolving-period securitizations,
    6.26–6.28
  sale not occurring, 6.25–6.26
  SEC registrant alert, 6.24, 6.50
  securitization trust, 12.24
  special-purpose entities (SPEs)
    consolidation, 6.55–6.56
    identification, 6.55
    qualifying special-purpose entities
      (QSPE). *See* Qualifying special-
      purpose entities
    sales by, 6.13–6.14
    terms disqualifying, 6.14

subordinated assets, assumptions involved in valuing, 6.24

transfers of financial assets, 6.21–6.28
  financial statement classification, 6.23
  subsequent measurement of beneficial interests, 6.22–6.23
  variable interest entities. *See* Variable interest entities
  written guarantees, 6.48

Services, equity instruments received for, 2.50–2.51

Servicing financial assets, Ch. 4
  accounting, 4.04–4.21
  adequate compensation, 4.06
  allocation of carrying amount of loans sold, 4.27–4.28
  auditing considerations, 4.23–4.25
  background, 4.03–4.04
  balance sheet presentation, 4.19
  cash flow statements, 4.20
  costs of issuing GNMA securities, 4.22
  disclosures, 4.21–4.23
  fair value not practicable to determine, 4.28–4.29
  income statement presentation, 4.19–4.20
  initial measurement, 4.06–4.07
    I-O strips, 4.07
  overview, 4.02–4.03
  purchased servicing right on refinanced loan, 4.21
  recognition of assets and liabilities, 4.04–4.06
  recording and amortizing, 4.25–4.26
  regulatory considerations, 4.23
  revolving-period securitization, 4.06
  sale of receivables with servicing obtained, 4.26–4.29
  sales and other transfers of servicing rights, 4.16–4.19
    for participation in income stream, 4.17
    subcontracting of servicing obligation, 4.18–4.19
    with subservicing agreement, 4.17–4.18
  servicing, defined, 4.03–4.04
  subsequent measurement, 4.07–4.16
    adequate compensation, 4.15
    amortization method, 4.08–4.10
    assets and liabilities, 4.07
    benefits of servicing, 4.15
    fair value of servicing rights, 4.14–4.16
    FAS-133, 4.10–4.12
    hedging, 4.10–4.12

identifying classes for purposes of, 4.07–4.08
  impairment evaluation, 4.08–4.10
  I-O strips, 4.12–4.14
  SEC registrant alert, 4.09
  transfers between classes, 4.08
  transferring servicing assets for no cash, 4.21

Servicing rights, 3.09

Setoff. *See* Offsetting assets and liabilities in balance sheet

Shareholders
  distributions to, 6.13
  equity instruments not reported. *See* Equity instruments

Shelf registration, costs incurred in, 16.09–16.10

Short sales, 9.10

Short-term debt financing. *See* Debt financing

SOP 03-3
  disclosures, 7.50–7.52
  interest method, 7.41–7.46, 7.62–7.68

SOP 90-7, 11.15–11.22

Special-purpose entities (SPEs)
  consolidation, 6.55–6.56
  identification, 6.55
  qualifying special-purpose entities (QSPE). *See* Qualifying special-purpose entities
  sales by, 6.13–6.14
  terms disqualifying, 6.14

Special-purpose entity. *See* Securitization

Split-interest agreement, not-for-profit organization, 13.26

Stock
  derivatives, FAS-133 scope exceptions, 12.20
  preferred stock. *See* Preferred stock
  receipt in demutualization, 2.47–2.48
  redeemable financial instruments. *See* Redeemable financial instruments
  stock purchase warrants, convertible debt, 10.15–10.16, 10.36–10.37
  treasury stock. *See* Treasury stock

Stockholders
  distributions to, 6.13
  equity instruments not reported. *See* Equity instruments

Subsidiaries
  contracts indexed to shares, 16.40–16.41
  convertible debt, 10.09–10.10
  debt in consolidated balance sheet, 8.21–8.22
  extinguishment by parent of subsidiary's mandatorily redeemable preferred stock, 16.25

Subsidiaries, *cont.*
  sale of shares, 16.15
Substantially different, defined, 11.10
Sum-of-the-years'-digits, 7.28
Syndication fees, 7.24

T

Tax liabilities, offsetting in balance sheet, 17.12–17.13
TDRs. *See* Troubled debt restructurings
Temporary equity, 16.08–16.09, 16.40
Trade date accounting, 2.11–2.13
Trades, security, 12.25
Transfers of financial assets, Ch. 5
  accounting, 5.08–5.31
  allocating previous carrying amount, 5.22
  auditing considerations, 5.32–5.34
    achieving isolation, 5.32–5.33
    fair value estimates, 5.33–5.34
  background, 5.03–5.06
  categories, 5.06–5.07
  changes in control, 5.13–5.14
  commitments to repurchase or redeem assets, 5.19–5.20
  credit enhancements and recourse, 5.24–5.27
  deep-in-the-money puts, 5.30
  deferred tax consequences, 5.31
  disclosures, 5.31–5.32
  excluded transactions, 5.05–5.06
  fair value measurement, 5.27–5.29
  FAS-140, 5.05–5.06, 5.09
  FDIC receivership, 5.16
  financial statements, classification in, 5.11, 5.13
  GAAP, 5.03
  illustrations, 5.34–5.38
  implementation guidance, 5.14–5.31
  interests held by transferor, 5.22–5.27
  isolation, 5.15–5.16
  loss of control, changes causing, 5.14
  magnified risks, interests held with, 5.24
  mortgage-backed bonds, 5.31
  new and retained interests, 5.11–5.12, 5.22–5.27
  no effective control by transferor, 5.18–5.22
  note receivable from investor as proceeds, 5.22
  not practicable to estimate fair value, 5.28–5.29, 5.31
  overview, 5.02–5.03
  partial sales, 5.20
  pledge or exchange, 5.17–5.18

qualifying special-purpose entities (QSPE), 5.07, 6.23–6.28
  recording, 5.09
  regulatory considerations, 5.32
  related party sales, 5.16
  removal of accounts provisions, 5.21
  return of assets, 5.20–5.22
  rights to reacquire transferred assets, 5.22–5.23
  sales, accounted as, 5.12, 5.34–5.36
  SEC registrant alert, 5.14
  secured borrowings, accounted as, 5.12–5.13, 5.29–5.31, 5.36–5.38
  steps upon completion, 5.10
  terminology, 5.03
  transferor's accounting, 5.09–5.12
  troubled debt restructurings, 11.16–11.17, 11.26
Treasury stock, 16.12–16.14
  buy-backs, 16.58–16.59
  purchase at above-market price, 16.14
  subsequent sale, 16.14
  subsidiary investment in stock of parent, 16.14
Troubled debt restructurings, 11.15–11.21
  accounting, 11.20
  APB-30, 11.21
  ARB-43, 11.15
  cash flow estimates, 11.18–11.19
  combination of types, 11.19–11.20, 11.26
  contingent payments, 11.18, 11.21
  direct costs, 11.21
  disclosures, 11.22, 11.26
  EITF Issue 02-4, 11.16
  EITF Issue 96-19, 11.19
  FAS-15, 11.15
  FAS-114, 11.19
  FAS-144, 11.17
  FAS-145, 11.21
  fees and costs in, 7.20
  forfeiture of real estate subject to nonrecourse loan, 11.17
  grant of equity interest in full settlement, 11.17
  implementation issues, 3.29–3.34, 11.20–11.21
  income statement classification, 11.21
  measurement date, 11.20–11.21
  modification of terms, 11.18–11.19, 11.25
  overview, 3.25–3.29
  SOP 90-7, 11.15–11.22
  transfers of financial assets, 11.16–11.17, 11.26
  variable interest rates, 11.18–11.19

Trusts
  securitization trusts, 12.24
  trust-preferred securities, equity
    instruments, 16.19–16.24

U

Unconditional purchase obligations,
  15.13–15.14

V

Variable annuity contracts, 13.21–13.24
Variable interest entities
  assessment timing, 6.44–6.45
  consolidation of securitization
    entities, 6.31–6.46
  deconsolidation, 6.46
  de minimis involvement exception,
    6.35
  disclosures, 6.48–6.50

  examples, 6.39–6.40
  expected losses, assessing, 6.40–6.42
  FIN-46(R), 6.34, 6.42–6.44, 6.49
  general principle, 6.40
  identifying, 6.35–6.39
  residual returns, assessing,
    6.40–6.42
  SEC registrant alert, 6.33–6.35, 6.38,
    6.41

W

Warrants
  convertible debt, 10.16, 10.36–10.37
  detachable, 10.05, 10.34
Wrap-around mortgages, 17.14

Y

Yields on debt investments. *See* Debt
  investment yields